W9-CCR-933

The GALE ENCYCLOPEDIA of CHILDREN'S HEALTH

INFANCY THROUGH ADOLESCENCE

The GALE
ENCYCLOPEDIA *of*
CHILDREN'S
HEALTH

INFANCY THROUGH ADOLESCENCE

VOLUME

3

L-R

KRISTINE KRAPP AND JEFFREY WILSON, EDITORS

THOMSON
━━━━✦━━━━ ™
GALE

Detroit • New York • San Francisco • San Diego • New Haven, Conn. • Waterville, Maine • London • Munich

The Gale Encyclopedia of Children's Health: Infancy through Adolescence

Product Manager
Kate Millson

Project Editors
Kristine M. Krapp, Jeffrey J. Wilson

Editorial
Donna Batten, Shirelle Phelps, Erin Watts

Editorial Support Services
Luann Brennan, Andrea Lopeman, Mark Springer

Rights Acquisition Management
Margaret Abendroth, Ann Taylor

Imaging
Randy Bassett, Lezlie Light, Dan Newell, Christine O'Bryan, Robyn Young

Product Design
Michelle DiMercurio, Tracey Rowens

Composition and Electronic Prepress
Evi Seoud, Mary Beth Trimper

Manufacturing
Wendy Blurton, Dorothy Maki

Indexing
Synapse Corp. of Colorado

LIBRARY OF CONGRESS CATALOGING-IN-PUBLICATION DATA

The Gale encyclopedia of children's health : infancy through adolescence / Kristine Krapp and Jeffrey Wilson, editors.
    p. cm.
        Includes bibliographical references and index.
        ISBN 0-7876-9241-7 (set hardcover : alk. paper) –
        ISBN 0-7876-9427-4 (v. 1) – ISBN 0-7876-9428-2 (v. 2) –
        ISBN 0-7876-9429-0 (v. 3) – ISBN 0-7876-9430-4 (v. 4)
        1. Children–Health and hygiene–Encyclopedias.
        2. Children–Diseases–Encyclopedias. 3. Pediatrics–
        Encyclopedias. [DNLM: 1. Pediatrics–Encyclopedias–
        English. 2. Pediatrics–Popular Works. 3. Child
        Welfare–Encyclopedias–English. 4. Child Welfare–
        Popular Works. 5. Infant Welfare–Encyclopedias–English.
        6. Infant Welfare–Popular Works. WS 13 G1515 2005]
        I. Title: Encyclopedia of children's health. II. Krapp,
        Kristine M. III. Wilson, Jeffrey, 1971- IV. Gale Group.

RJ26.G35 2005
618.92'0003–dc22   2005003478

This title is also available as an e-book
ISBN 0-7876-9425-8 (set)
Contact your Gale sales representative for ordering information.
ISBN 0-7876-9241-7 (set)
0-7876-9427-4 (Vol. 1)
0-7876-9428-2 (Vol. 2)
0-7876-9429-0 (Vol. 3)
0-7876-9430-4 (Vol. 4)
Printed in Canada
10 9 8 7 6 5 4 3 2 1

CONTENTS

LIST OF ENTRIES

A

Abandonment
Abdominal wall defects
Acetaminophen
Acne
Acromegaly and gigantism
Acting out
Adaptive behavior scales for infants and early childhood
Addiction
Adenoid hyperplasia
Adenovirus infections
Adjustment disorders
Adolescence
Adoption
Aggressive behavior
Albinism
Alcoholism
Allergic purpura
Allergic rhinitis
Allergies
Allergy shots
Allergy tests
Allowance and money management
Alopecia
Alpha-fetoprotein test
Alternative school
Amblyopia
Amenorrhea
Amniocentesis
Anabolic steroids
Analgesics
Anaphylaxis
Anatomical age
Anemias

Angelman's syndrome
Animal bite infections
Anorexia nervosa
Antenatal testing
Antepartum testing
Antiacne drugs
Antiasthmatic drugs
Antibiotics
Antibiotics, topical
Antidepressants
Antiepileptics
Antihistamines
Antisocial behavior
Antisocial personality disorder
Antiviral drugs
Anxiety
Apgar testing
Apnea of infancy
Appendicitis
Arteriovenous fistula
Asphyxia neonatorum
Assessment
Asthma
Ataxia telangiectasia/chromosome breakage disorders
Atopic dermatitis
Atrial septal defect
Attachment between infant and caregiver
Attention-deficit/Hyperactivity disorder (AD/HD)
Audiometry
Auditory discrimination test
Autism

B

Babysitters
Battered child syndrome
Bayley Scales of Infant Development
Bed-wetting
Beery-Buktenica test
Bejel
Bell's palsy
Biliary atresia
Bilingualism/Bilingual education
Bilirubin test
Binge eating disorder
Bipolar disorder
Birth order
Birthmarks
Bites and stings
Blood sugar tests
Bonding
Botulism
Brachial plexopathy, obstetric
Breast development
Breath holding spells
Breech birth
Bronchiolitis
Bronchitis
Bruises
Bruton's agammaglobulinemia
Bulimia nervosa
Bullies
Burns

Fear
Febrile seizures
Fetal alcohol syndrome
Fetal hemoglobin test
Fever
Fever of unknown origin
Fifth disease
Fine motor skills
Fingertip injuries
Flu vaccine
Fluoridation
Folic acid
Food allergies and sensitivities
Food poisoning
Foreign objects
Foster care
Fractures
Fragile X syndrome
Friedreich's ataxia
Frostbite and frostnip

G

Galactosemia
Gangs
Gastroenteritis
Gastroesophageal reflux disease
Gender constancy
Gender identity
Gross motor skills
Growth hormone tests

H

Handedness
Hand-eye coordination
Hand-foot-mouth disease
Head injury
Head Start programs
Headache
Hearing impairment
Heart murmurs
Heat disorders
Heavy metal poisoning
Heimlich maneuver

Hemophilia
Hemophilus infections
Hepatitis A
Hepatitis B
Hepatitis B vaccine
Hereditary fructose intolerance
Hereditary hemorrhagic
    telangiectasia
Hernia
Herpes simplex
Hib vaccine
High-risk pregnancy
Hirschsprung's disease
Histiocytosis X
HIV infection and AIDS
Hives
Home schooling
Homosexuality and bisexuality
Hospitalization
Human bite infections
Hydrocephalus
Hyperglycemia
Hyperhidrosis
Hyper-IgM syndrome
Hypertension
Hyperthyroidism
Hypoglycemia
Hypogonadism
Hypospadias
Hypothyroidism
Hypotonia

Idiopathic thrombocytopenic
    purpura
Ileus
Immobilization
Immune system development
Immunodeficiency
Immunoglobulin deficiency
    syndromes
Impetigo
Impulse control disorders
Inclusion conjunctivitis
Infant massage

Infant mortality
Infectious mononucleosis
Influenza
Insect sting allergy
Intelligence
Intermittent explosive disorder
Intersex states
Intestinal obstructions
Intrauterine growth retardation
Intravenous rehydration
Iron deficiency anemia
Irritable bowel syndrome
Itching

J

Jaundice
Juvenile arthritis

K

Kawasaki syndrome
Klinefelter syndrome

L

Labyrinthitis
Lactation
Lactose intolerance
Language delay
Language development
Language disorders
Laxatives
Lead poisoning
Learning disorders
Leukemias, acute
Leukemias, chronic
Lice infestation
Lipidoses
Lisping
Listeriosis
Lying
Lyme disease
Lymphadenitis

M

Macrocephaly
Magnetic resonance imaging
Malnutrition
Malocclusion
Marfan syndrome
Massage therapy
Mastoiditis
Masturbation
Maxillofacial trauma
Measles
Meningitis
Meningococcal meningitis
    vaccine
Meningococcemia
Menstruation
Mental retardation
Methylphenidate
Mineral deficiency
Mineral toxicity
Minerals
Minnesota Multiphasic Personality
    Inventory
Minority health
Mitochondrial disorders
MMR vaccine
Moles
Mood disorders
Moral development
Motion sickness
Movement disorders
Mucopolysaccharidoses
Multicultural education/curriculum
Multiple endocrine neoplasia
    syndromes
Multiple pregnancy
Mumps
Munchausen syndrome
Muscle spasms and cramps
Muscular dystrophy
Mutism
Myers-Briggs Type Indicator
Myopathies
Myopia
Myotonic dystrophy
Myringotomy and ear tubes

N

Nail-patella syndrome
Narcolepsy
Narcotic drugs
Nasal trauma
Nausea and vomiting
Near-drowning
Necrotizing enterocolitis
Neonatal jaundice
Neonatal reflexes
Neurofibromatosis
Neurologic exam
Night terrors
Nightmares
Nonsteroidal anti-inflammatory
    drugs
Nosebleed
Numbness and tingling
Nursemaid's elbow
Nutrition
Nystagmus

O

Obesity
Obsessive-compulsive disorder
Oligomenorrhea
Oppositional defiant disorder
Oral contraceptives
Oral hygiene
Orthodontics
Osteochondroses
Osteogenesis imperfecta
Osteopetroses
Otitis externa
Otitis media
Overhydration

P

Pacifier use
Pain
Pain management
Parent-child relationships

Patau syndrome
Patent ductus arteriosus
Peer acceptance
Peer pressure
Penicillins
Perforated eardrum
Perinatal infection
Periodontal disease
Peroxisomal disorders
Personality development
Personality disorders
Pervasive developmental disorders
Phenylketonuria
Phobias
Pica
Piercing and tattoos
Pinta
Pinworms
Pituitary dwarfism
Pityriasis rosea
Platelet count
Play
Pneumonia
Poison ivy, oak, and sumac
Poisoning
Polio
Polio vaccine
Polydactyly and syndactyly
Porphyrias
Post-concussion syndrome
Prader-Willi syndrome
Precocious puberty
Prematurity
Premenstrual syndrome
Prenatal development
Prenatal surgery
Preschool
Prickly heat
Protein-energy malnutrition
Psoriasis
Psychological tests
Psychosocial personality disorders
Puberty
Pulmonary function tests

R

Rabies
Rabies vaccine
Rape and sexual assault
Rashes
Rat-bite fever
Red blood cell indices
Reflex tests
Renal vein thrombosis
Respiratory distress syndrome
Respiratory syncytial virus infection
Retention in school
Retinoblastoma
Reye's syndrome
Rheumatic fever
Rhinitis
Ringworm
Rocky Mountain spotted fever
Roseola
Rotavirus infections
Rubella
Running away

S

Safety
Salmonella food poisoning
Sarcomas
Savant syndrome
Scabies
Scarlet fever
Schizophrenia
School phobia/school refusal
Scoliosis
Seborrheic dermatitis
Security objects
Seizure disorder
Self-esteem
Self-mutilation
Separation anxiety
Severe combined immunodeficiency
Sexually transmitted diseases

Shaken baby syndrome
Shigellosis
Shyness
Sibling rivalry
Sickle cell anemia
Single-parent families
Sinusitis
Skeletal development
Sleep
Sleep disorders
Smoke inhalation
Smoking
Social competence
Somnambulism
Sore throat
Spasticity
Special education
Specific language impairment
Speech disorders
Spina bifida
Spinal cord injury
Spinal muscular atrophy
Sports
Sports injuries
Sprains and strains
Stanford-Binet intelligence scales
Staphylococcal infections
Stealing
Stepfamilies
Stimulant drugs
Stomatitis
Strabismus
Stranger anxiety
Strep throat
Streptococcal infections
Stridor
Stroke
Sturge-Weber syndrome
Stuttering
Styes and chalazia
Subdural hematoma
Substance abuse and dependence
Sudden infant death syndrome
Suicide and suicidal behavior
Sulfonamides

Sunburn
Sunscreens
Sweat test

T

Tantrums
Tay-Sachs disease
Television habits
Temperament
Testicular torsion
Tetanus
Tetracyclines
Tetralogy of Fallot
Thalassemia
Thematic Apperception Test
Therapeutic baths
Throat culture
Thumb sucking
Tics
Time-out procedure
Toilet training
Tonsillitis
Tooth decay
Toothache
TORCH test
Tourette syndrome
Toxic shock syndrome
Toxoplasmosis
Toys
Tracheoesophageal fistula
Trachoma
Transposition of the great arteries
Traumatic amputations
Trichotillomania
Truancy
Tuberculosis
Tuberous sclerosis
Turner syndrome
Twins

U

Undescended testes

PLEASE READ—IMPORTANT INFORMATION

The Gale Encyclopedia of Children's Health is a medical reference product designed to inform and educate readers about a wide variety of health issues related to children, ranging from prenatal to adolescence. Thomson Gale believes the product to be comprehensive, but not necessarily definitive. It is intended to supplement, not replace, consultation with a physician or other healthcare practitioner. While Thomson Gale has made substantial efforts to provide information that is accurate, comprehensive, and up-to-date, Thomson Gale makes no representations or warranties of any kind, including without limitation, warranties of merchantability or fitness for a particular purpose, nor does it guarantee the accuracy, comprehensiveness, or timeliness of the information contained in this product. Readers should be aware that the universe of medical knowledge is constantly growing and changing, and that differences of medical opinion exist among authorities. They are also advised to seek professional diagnosis and treatment for any medical condition, and to discuss information obtained from this book with their healthcare provider.

INTRODUCTION

The Gale Encyclopedia of Children's Health: Infancy Through Adolescence (GECH) is a one-stop source for medical information that covers common and rare diseases and medical conditions, immunizations and drugs, procedures, and developmental issues. It particularly addresses parents' concerns about their children's health from before birth through age 18. The book avoids medical jargon, making it easier for the layperson to use. *The Gale Encyclopedia of Children's Health* presents authoritative, balanced information and is more comprehensive than single-volume family medical guides.

SCOPE

Approximately 600 full-length articles are included in *The Gale Encyclopedia of Children's Health*. Articles follow a standardized format that provides information at a glance. Rubrics include:

Diseases/Disorders
- Definition
- Description
- Demographics
- Causes and symptoms
- Diagnosis
- Treatment
- Prognosis
- Prevention
- Parental concerns
- Resources
- Key terms

Procedures
- Definition
- Purpose
- Description
- Risks
- Normal results

- Parental concerns
- Resources
- Key terms

Immunizations/Drugs
- Definition
- Description
- General use
- Precautions
- Side effects
- Interactions
- Parental concerns
- Resources
- Key terms

Development
- Definition
- Description
- Common problems
- Parental concerns
- Resources
- Key terms

A preliminary list of diseases, conditions, procedures, drugs, and developmental issues was compiled from a wide variety of sources, including professional medical guides and textbooks, as well as consumer guides and encyclopedias. The advisory board, composed of seven doctors with specialties in pediatric medicine, evaluated the topics and made suggestions for inclusion. Final selection of topics to include was made by the medical advisors in conjunction with Thomson Gale editors.

INCLUSION CRITERIA

A preliminary list of diseases, conditions, procedures, drugs, and developmental issues was compiled from a wide variety of sources, including professional medical guides and textbooks, as well as consumer guides and encyclopedias. The advisory board, composed of seven doctors with specialties in pediatric medicine, evaluated the topics and made suggestions for inclusion. Final selection of topics to include was made by the medical advisors in conjunction with Thomson Gale editors.

ABOUT THE CONTRIBUTORS

The essays were compiled by experienced medical writers, including healthcare practitioners and educators, pharmacists, nurses, and other healthcare professionals. *GECH* medical advisors reviewed all of the completed essays to insure that they are appropriate, up-to-date, and medically accurate.

HOW TO USE THIS BOOK

The Gale Encyclopedia of Children's Health has been designed with ready reference in mind:

- Straight **alphabetical arrangement** allows users to locate information quickly.

- Bold faced terms function as *print hyperlinks* that point the reader to related entries in the encyclopedia.

- A list of **key terms** is provided where appropriate to define unfamiliar words or concepts used within the context of the essay. Additional terms may be found in the **glossary**.

- **Cross-references** placed throughout the encyclopedia direct readers to where information on subjects without their own entries can be found. Synonyms are also cross-referenced.

- A **Resources section** directs users to sources of further medical information.

- An appendix of updated **growth charts** from the U.S. Centers for Disease Control for children from birth through age 20 is included.

- An appendix of **common childhood medications** is arranged alphabetically and includes descriptions of each drug and important information about their uses.

- A comprehensive **general index** allows users to easily target detailed aspects of any topic, including Latin names.

GRAPHICS

The Gale Encyclopedia of Children's Health is enhanced with approximately 300 full-color images, including photos, tables, and customized line drawings.

ADVISORY BOARD

An advisory board made up of prominent individuals from the medical community provided invaluable assistance in the formulation of this encyclopedia. They defined the scope of coverage and reviewed individual entries for accuracy and accessibility. The editors would therefore like to express our appreciation to them.

CONTRIBUTORS

Margaret Alic, PhD
Medical Writer
Eastsound, WA

Kim Saltel Allan, R.D., BHEcol
Clinical Dietitian
Winnipeg, Manitoba, Canada

Linda K. Bennington, MSN, CNS, RNC
Lecturer, School of Nursing
Old Dominion University
Norfolk, VA

Mark A. Best, MD, MBA, MPH
Pathologist
Eastview, KY

Rosalyn Carson-Dewitt, M.D.
Medical Writer
Durham, NC

Angela Costello
Medical Editor
Cleveland, OH

L. Lee Culvert
Medical Writer
Alna, ME

Tish Davidson, MA
Medical Writer
Fremont, CA

L. Fleming Fallon, Jr., MD, DrPH
Professor of Public Health
Bowling Green University
Bowling Green, OH

Paula Ford-Martin, MA
Medical Writer
Warwick, RI

Janie Franz
Medical Writer
Grand Forks, ND

Rebecca J. Frey, PhD
Medical Writer
New Haven, CT

Clare Hanrahan
Medical Writer
Asheville, NC

Crystal H. Kaczkowski, MSc.
Medical Writer
Chicago, IL

Christine Kuehn Kelly
Medical Writer
Havertown, PA

Monique Laberge, Ph.D.
Medical Writer
Philadelphia, PA

Aliene S. Linwood, BSN, DPA, FACHE
Medical and Science Writer
Athens, Ohio

Mark Mitchell, M.D.
Medical Writer
Seattle, WA

Deborah L. Nurmi, M.S.
Medical Writer, Public Health Researcher
Atlanta, GA

Martha Reilly, OD
Clinical Optometrist
Madison, WI

Joan M. Schonbeck, RN
Medical Writer
Marlborough, MA

Stephanie Dionne Sherk
Medical Writer
Ann Arbor, MI

Judith Sims, MS
Science Writer
Logan, UT

Jennifer E. Sisk, M.A.
Medical Writer
Philadelphia, PA

Genevieve Slomski, Ph.D.
Medical Writer
New Britain, CT

Deanna M. Swartout-Corbeil, RN
Medical Writer
Thompsons Station, TN

Samuel Uretsky, PharmD
Medical Writer
Wantagh, NY

Ken R. Wells
Freelance Writer
Laguna Hills, CA

Labor and delivery *see* **Childbirth**

Labyrinthitis

Definition

Labyrinthitis is an inflammation of the inner ear that is often a complication of infection of the middle ear (**otitis media**). It is usually caused by the spread of bacterial or viral infections from the head or respiratory tract into the inner ear.

Description

The labyrinth is a group of interconnected canals chambers located in the inner ear. It is made up of the cochlea and the semicircular canals. The cochlea is involved in transmitting sounds to the brain. The semicircular canals send information to the brain about the head's position and how it is moving. The brain uses this information to maintain balance. Labyrinthitis is caused by the inflammation of the labyrinth. Its most frequent symptom is vertigo (**dizziness**), because the information that the semicircular canals send to the brain about the position of the head is affected.

Demographics

Labyrinthitis is rare and is more likely to occur after middle ear infections, **meningitis**, or upper respiratory infection. It may also occur after trauma, because of a tumor, or after the ingesting of toxic substances. It is thought to be more common in females than in males.

Causes and symptoms

When a disease agent causes labyrinthitis, the disease agent usually reaches the inner ear by one of three routes:

- Bacteria may be carried from the middle ear or the membranes that cover the brain.
- Viruses, such as those that cause **mumps**, **measles**, **influenza**, and colds may reach the inner ear following an upper respiratory infection.
- The **rubella** virus can cause labyrinthitis in infants prior to birth.

Labyrinthitis can also be caused by toxins, by a tumor in the ear, by trauma to the ear, and sometimes high doses of medications or **allergies**.

The primary symptoms of labyrinthitis are vertigo and hearing loss, along with a sensation of ringing in the ears called tinnitus. Vertigo occurs because the inner ear controls the sense of balance, as well as hearing. Some individuals also experience **nausea and vomiting** and spontaneous eye movements in the direction of the unaffected ear. Bacterial labyrinthitis may produce a discharge from the infected ear.

When to call the doctor

If a child has vertigo, especially along with **nausea**, **vomiting**, or hearing loss, the doctor should be called.

Diagnosis

Diagnosis of labyrinthitis is based on a combination of the individual's symptoms and history, especially a history of a recent upper respiratory infection. The doctor will test the child's hearing and order a laboratory culture to identify the organism if the patient has a discharge.

If there is no history of a recent infection, the doctor will order tests such as a commuted topography (CT) scan or a **magnetic resonance imaging** (MRI) scan to help rule out other possible causes of vertigo, such as tumors. If it is believed a bacterium is causing the labyrinthitis, blood tests may be done, or any fluid draining from the ear may be analyzed to help determine what type of bacteria is present.

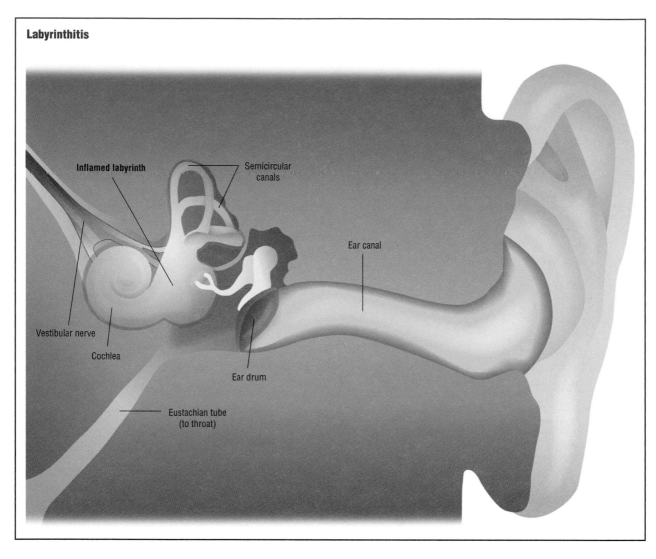

Labyrinthitis

Inflamed labyrinth

Semicircular canals

Ear canal

Vestibular nerve

Cochlea

Ear drum

Eustachian tube (to throat)

Labyrinthitis, or inner ear infection, causes the labyrinth area of the ear to become inflamed. *(Illustration by GGS Information Services.)*

Treatment

If a bacterial agent is found to be the cause, the individual is given **antibiotics** to clear up the infection. Antibiotics cannot cure viral infections. Some patients may require surgery to drain the inner and middle ear. If an underlying condition such as a tumor is found to be the cause of the labyrinthitis, treatment will depend on the underlying condition.

Because most labyrinthitis resolves on its own, most treatment is focused on controlling the symptoms. Medications may be prescribed to help reduce vertigo and nausea. If vomiting cannot be controlled, so that fluids cannot be kept down, fluids may be administered intravenously to prevent **dehydration**.

Individuals with labyrinthitis should rest in bed until the acute dizziness subsides. Some experts believe that recovery is aided by moving around once the most acute symptoms are no longer present. This can be difficult, however, because moving often makes symptoms worse.

Prognosis

Most people who have labyrinthitis recover completely, although it often takes five to six weeks for the vertigo to disappear entirely and the individual's hearing to return to normal. In a few cases, the hearing loss may be permanent. Permanent hearing loss is more common in cases of labyrinthitis that are caused by bacteria. For

KEY TERMS

Labyrinth—The bony cavity of the inner ear.

Otitis media—Inflammation or infection of the middle ear space behind the eardrum. It commonly occurs in early childhood and is characterized by ear pain, fever, and hearing problems.

Vertigo—A feeling of dizziness together with a sensation of movement and a feeling of rotating in space.

some individuals, episodes of dizziness may still occur months after the main episode is over.

Prevention

The most effective preventive strategy includes prompt treatment of middle ear infections, as well as monitoring of patients with mumps, measles, influenza, or colds for signs of dizziness or hearing problems.

Parental concerns

Labyrinthitis generally resolves by itself; however, in some cases permanent hearing loss can result. Labyrinthitis may cause repeated episodes of vertigo even after the main symptoms have gone away. If the episodes occur when the head is moved suddenly, this can make it difficult for a child to engage in some physical activities or **sports**.

Resources

BOOKS

Goebel, Joel A., ed. *Practical Management of the Dizzy Patient.* Philadelphia: Lippincott Williams & Wilkins, 2001.

Labyrinthitis: A Medical Dictionary, Bibliography, and Annotated Research Guide to Internet References. San Diego, CA: Icon Group International, 2004.

Poe, Dennis. *The Consumer Handbook on Dizziness and Vertigo.* Sedona, AZ: Auricle Ink Publishers, 2005.

PERIODICALS

Aferzon, Mark, and Carl L. Reams. "Labyrinthitis ossificans." *Ear, Nose, and Throat Journal* 80 (October 2001): 700.

Hartnick, Christopher J., et al. "Preventing Labyrinthitis Ossificans: The Role of Steroids." *Archives of Otolaryngology—Head & Neck Surgery* 127 (February 2001): 180.

Sandhaus, Sonia. "Stop the Spinning: Diagnosing and Managing Vertigo." *The Nurse Practitioner* 27 (August 2002): 11–20.

ORGANIZATIONS

American Academy of Pediatrics. 141 Northwest Point Boulevard, Elk Grove Village, IL 60007–1098. Web site: <www.aap.org>.

Helen Davidson

Lactation

Definition

Lactation refers to the formation of milk in the breasts during the period following **childbirth**. Breastfeeding is the process of the infant obtaining milk by suckling at the breast.

Description

Although **breast development** begins around **puberty**, development of mammary function is only completed in pregnancy. During the first half of pregnancy the mammary ducts proliferate and group together to form large lobules. During the second half of pregnancy, secretory activity increases and the alveoli become distended by accumulating colostrum. After 16 weeks of pregnancy, lactation occurs even if the pregnancy does not progress.

The ability of the mammary gland to secrete milk during later pregnancy is called lactogenesis, stage 1. During this time, breast size increases and fat droplets accumulate in the secretory cells. The onset of copious milk secretions after birth is lactogenesis, stage 2, and usually occurs from day two or three to eight days postpartum. During this time, the milk goes through a maturation process to match the infant's needs. Without the hormone prolactin, lactation would not occur. During pregnancy prolactin helps to increase breast mass but does not cause lactation because it is inhibited by the hormone progesterone, which is made by the placenta. The inhibiting influence of progesterone is so strong that lactation is delayed if any of the placenta is retained after birth. Prolactin levels rise and fall in direct proportion to the frequency, intensity, and duration of nipple stimulation from the infant's suckling. During the first week after birth, prolactin levels in breastfeeding women fall about 50 percent. If a mother does not breastfeed, prolactin levels usually reach the levels of the nonpregnant state by seven days postpartum. After milk "comes in" or rapidly increases in volume, lactation is no longer driven by the hormone prolactin. It shifts control to a milk removal driven process, i.e., sucking stimulus. Thus, the initiation of lactation is not driven by breastfeeding, but breastfeeding is necessary for the continuation of lactation.

The breast is not a passive container of milk. It is an organ that actively produces milk due to the stimulus of the infant's sucking; the removal of milk from the breasts causes continued milk production. It is a supply and demand response that regulates the production of milk to match the intake of the infant. The composition of breast milk changes to meet the specific needs of the growing infant. In response to suckling, the hormone oxytocin causes the milk ejection reflex or "let-down" reflex to occur. Milk ejection is the forceful expulsion of milk from the alveoli openings. Oxytocin secretion is also nature's way of causing a woman's uterus to contract after birth to control postpartum bleeding and assist in uterine involution. These contractions can continue for up to 20 minutes after feeding and may be painful during the first few days. The benefit of this, however, is that uterine discharge diminishes faster and the uterine involution occurs more quickly.

Colostrum is thick and creamy yellow as compared with mature milk, which is thin and bluish-white. Compared with mature milk, colostrum is richer in protein and **minerals** and lower in carbohydrates, fat, and some **vitamins**. The high concentration of total protein and minerals in colostrum gradually changes to meet the infant's needs over the first two to three weeks until lactation is established. The key component in colostrum and breast milk is immunoglobulins or antibodies that serve to protect the infant against infections or viruses. Breast milk also facilitates the development of the infant's own immune system to mature faster. As a result, breast-fed babies have fewer ear infections, **diarrhea**, **rashes**, **allergies**, and other medical problems than bottle-fed babies. Human milk is rich in proteins, lipids, carbohydrates, vitamins, minerals, hormones, enzymes, growth factors, and many types of protective agents. It contains about 10 percent solids for energy and growth and the rest is water, which is essential to maintain hydration. This is also why a breastfed baby does not need additional water. Infants can digest breast milk much more rapidly than formula and, therefore, do not get constipated. On average, it takes about 30 minutes longer to digest formula as opposed to breast milk. Breastfed babies have better cheekbone development and better jaw alignment.

Besides the benefits of the contracting uterus, the process of producing milk burns calories, which helps the mother to lose excess weight gained during pregnancy. After all, that is why pregnant women put on extra fat during pregnancy—energy storage for milk production. Breastfeeding is also related to a lower risk of breast **cancer** and ovarian cancer. For every year of life spent breastfeeding, a woman's risk of developing breast cancer drops by 4.3 percent and this is on top of the 7 percent reduction she enjoys for every baby to whom she gives birth.

Additionally, there is the convenience. Breast milk is always with the mother. Mothers do not have to store it. It is always at the right temperature. It is free. It does not require sterilization. In fact, it prevents diseases and has protective factors resulting in healthier babies and decreased healthcare costs. It saves money as there is no need to buy formula, bottles, and nipples.

Procedure

It is best to begin breastfeeding immediately after birth as it is an infant's natural instinct to nurse then. Regardless of the baby's initial suckling behavior, this interaction stimulates uterine contractions, promotes colonization of harmless bacteria on the nipple, and helps to protect the infant from pathogenic bacteria. It is an important time to nuzzle. Women breastfeed for a longer duration if feedings are started early. The first several feedings have an imprinting effect. It is recommended to continue feeding about every two to three hours. It is important to remember that all babies are different; some need to nurse almost constantly at first, while others can go much longer between feedings. There are babies and mothers who have no trouble breastfeeding, while others may need some assistance. Once the baby begins to suck, the mother makes sure that the entire dark area around the nipple (areola) is in the baby's mouth. This helps stimulate milk flow and allows the baby to get enough milk. Nipple soreness can be a result of the infant not getting a good grasp of the entire areola. A newborn needs to be fed at least eight to 12 times in 24 hours. Since breast milk is so easily digested, a baby may be hungry again as soon as one and one-half hours after the last feeding.

Mothers need to be comfortable when nursing; therefore, loose, front-opening clothes and a good nursing bra are essential. They need to explore different positions for breastfeeding to determine what is best for them. The cradle hold works well in bed or sitting in a comfortable chair. The football hold is excellent if the woman had a **cesarean section**. The mother can use pillows to support the baby and a footstool to flatten her

Lactation

Signs of good breastfeeding progress	Warning signs
Eight to 12 feeding per 24 hours	Fewer than eight feedings in 24 hours; baby sleeps four to six hours at time
Baby nurses every 1.5 to three hours	Baby nurses every hour or more, but never seems satisfied
Six to eight wet diapers every 24 hours after the third day	Fewer than six wet diapers after the third day
Soft yellow stools, about 1 tablespoon or larger	Dark black, green, or brown stools after the third day
After the third day, four to 10 stools per day	Fewer than three or four stools per day after the third day
Average daily weight gain of 15 to 30 g once milk comes in	Baby does not regain birth weight by 10 days of age
Milk comes in; breasts are full and warm and may leak milk	Milk does not seem to come in by the fifth day
Intermittent periods of rhythmic sucking and audible swallows	Milk comes in, but sucking or swallowing is not audible
Breasts are tender and may be slightly painful or sore	Sore and painful nipples throughout most feedings; scabbed or cracked nipples
Breasts soften after a feed	Severe engorgement; breast remain very hard after a feed

(Table by GGS Information Services.)

lap. The mother can position the baby's head by snuggling it in one arm and supporting her breast with the other hand by keeping her thumb well above the areola and the rest of the fingers below and under the breast (sometimes called the C-hold). In this position, the mother can lift her breast and guide her nipple in any direction as she helps the baby to take in more of the areola.

For early feedings, the infant should be offered both breasts at each feeding as this stimulates the need-supply response. The length of the feeding is up to the mother. The general rule is to watch the baby, not the clock. If, however, it is a first time mother, 20 to 30 minutes on the first side can be suggested. If the baby falls asleep at the breast, the next feeding should begin with the breast that was not nursed. Mothers can tell if the baby is getting enough milk by checking diapers; a baby who is wetting between four to six disposable diapers (six to eight cloth) and who has three or four bowel movements in 24 hours is getting enough milk.

Common problems

New mothers may experience nursing problems, including the following:

Lactation

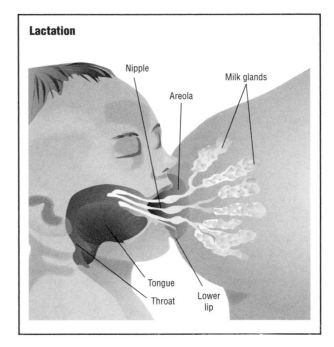

When an infant is properly latched onto the breast, the baby's nose touches (or nearly touches) the breast. He or she takes the entire areola into the mouth, facilitating the intake of milk far back into the throat. *(Illustration by GGS Information Services.)*

- Engorgement: Breasts that are too full can prevent the baby from suckling because they cannot be grasped. Expressing milk manually or with a breast pump can alleviate this problem.

- Sore nipples: Transient soreness can occur during the first week postpartum and is usually temporary. Air drying the nipples and rubbing colostrum or breast milk into them provides relief. Prolonged, abnormal soreness lasts longer than a week postpartum. Discontinuing use of soap on breasts while bathing and applying purified lanolin to nipples and air drying them helps.

- Infection: Soreness and inflammation on the breast surface or a fever in the mother may be an indication of breast infection (mastitis). If it is just starting, the mother should drink lots of water and nurse frequently on the affected breast. **Antibiotics** may be necessary if the infection persists.

Lactation consultants work at almost every hospital where babies are delivered. First-time mothers can request the lactation consultant to visit her. The mother should make a note of the lactation consultant's phone number should problems be encountered after mother and infant go home.

There are no rules about when to stop breastfeeding. A baby needs breast milk for at least the first year of life and it is preferred that no solid food be given for at least

KEY TERMS

Alveoli—The tiny air sacs clustered at the ends of the bronchioles in the lungs in which oxygen-carbon dioxide exchange takes place.

Bromocriptine—Also known as Parlodel, it is a dopamine receptor agonist used to treat galactorrhea by reducing levels of the hormone prolactin and is also used to treat Parkinson's disease.

Colostrum—Milk secreted for a few days after birth and characterized by high protein and antibody content.

Ergotamine—A drug used to prevent or treat migraine headaches. It can cause vomiting, diarrhea, and convulsions in infants and should not be taken by women who are nursing.

Involution—The return of a large organ to normal size.

Lactogenesis—The initiation of milk secretion.

Lithium—A medication prescribed to treat the manic (excited) phases of bipolar disorder.

Mammary—Relating to the breast.

Methotrexate—A drug that interferes with cell growth and is used to treat rheumatoid arthritis as well as various types of cancer. Side-effects may include mouth sores, digestive upsets, skin rashes, and hair loss. Since this drug can supress an infant's immune system, it should not be taken by nursing mothers.

Placenta—The organ that provides oxygen and nutrition from the mother to the unborn baby during pregnancy. The placenta is attached to the wall of the uterus and leads to the unborn baby via the umbilical cord.

Postpartum—After childbirth.

Progesterone—The hormone produced by the ovary after ovulation that prepares the uterine lining for a fertilized egg.

Prolactin—A hormone that helps the breast prepare for milk production during pregnancy.

the first six months to prevent allergies. As long as a baby eats age-appropriate solid food, the mother may nurse for several years.

Parental concerns

The majority of illnesses are not transmitted via breast milk; in fact, breast milk prevents many illnesses.

However, some viruses, including HIV (the virus that causes **AIDS** can be passed in breast milk; for this reason, women who are HIV-positive should not breastfeed unless they are living in a country that does not have clean water to make formula. A lack of clean water to make formula could result in an infant dying from diarrhea.

Many medications have not been tested in nursing women, so it is not certain what drugs can affect a breastfed child. A nursing woman should always check with her doctor or lactation consultant before taking any medications, including over-the-counter drugs. The mother can usually take antibiotics without discontinuing breastfeeding.

The following drugs are not safe for a mother to take while she is nursing:

- radioactive drugs for some diagnostic tests
- chemotherapy drugs for cancer
- bromocriptine
- ergotamine
- lithium
- methotrexate
- street drugs (including marijuana, heroin, amphetamines)
- tobacco

Resources

BOOKS

Behrmann, Barbara L. *The Breastfeeding Café: Mothers Share the Joys, Challenges, and Secrets of Nursing*. Ann Arbor, MI: University of Michigan Press, 2005.

Hanson, Lars A. *Immunobiology of Human Milk: How Breastfeeding Protects Babies*. Armillo, TX: Pharmasoft Publishing, 2004.

La Leche League International Staff. *The Womanly Art of Breastfeeding*. East Rutherford, NJ: Penguin Group, 2004.

Lim, Robin. *Eating for Two: Recipes for Pregnant and Breastfeeding Women*. Berkeley, CA: Celestial Arts Publishing, 2004.

Olds, Sally, et al. *Maternal-Newborn Nursing & Women's Health Care*, 7th ed. Saddle River, NJ: Prentice Hall, 2004.

Riordan, Jan. *Breastfeeding and Human Lactation*, 3rd ed. Boston, MA: Jones and Bartlett Publishers, 2004.

ORGANIZATIONS

International Lactation Consultants Association. 1500 Sunday Drive, Suite 102; Raleigh, NC 27607. Web site: <www.ilca.org/>.

La Leche League International. 1400 North Meacham Rd., Schaumburg, IL 60173. Web site: <www.lalecheleague.org/>.

National Alliance for Breastfeeding Advocacy. 9684 Oak Hill Drive; Ellicott City, MD 21042. Web site: <www.healthfinder.gov/orgs/HR2952.htm>.

Linda K. Bennington

Lactose intolerance

Definition

Lactose intolerance refers to the inability of the body to digest lactose.

Description

Lactose is the predominant form of sugar present in milk. The enzyme lactase, which is normally produced by cells lining the small intestine, breaks down lactose into substances that can be absorbed into the bloodstream. When dairy products are ingested, the lactose reaches the digestive system and is broken down by lactase into the simpler sugars glucose and galactose, which can then be absorbed into the bloodstream. Lactose intolerance occurs when, due to a deficiency of lactase, lactose is not completely broken down and consequently blood sugar levels do not rise. While not usually a dangerous condition, lactose intolerance can cause severe discomfort.

Lactose intolerance is also referred to as lactase deficiency, milk intolerance, dairy product intolerance, or disaccharidase deficiency.

Demographics

From 30 to 50 million Americans suffer from the symptoms of lactose intolerance by the age of 20. People from cultures in which adult consumption of milk and milk products occurred earliest are less likely to be lactose intolerant than people from areas where dairy farming began more recently. The prevalence of deficiency in production of the lactase enzyme, therefore, varies among different ethnic groups. Among Asian populations it is almost 100 percent, with symptoms occurring around the age of five; among Native Americans it is 80 percent; among blacks it is 70 percent, with symptoms appearing by the age of 10; and among American Cauca-

sians, the prevalence of lactose intolerance is only 20 percent. However, individuals who are mildly or moderately deficient in the production of the lactase enzyme may not exhibit symptoms of lactose intolerance.

Causes and symptoms

Lactose intolerance can be caused by some diseases of the digestive system (for example, celiac sprue and **gastroenteritis**) and by injuries to the small intestine that result in a decreased production of lactase. While rare, some children are also born unable to produce the enzyme. For most people, however, lactase deficiency develops naturally because, after about two years of age, the body produces less lactase. Before humans became dairy farmers, they usually did not continue to drink milk, so their bodies did not produce lactase after early childhood.

Symptoms of lactose intolerance include **nausea**, cramps, **diarrhea**, floating and foul-smelling stools, bloating, and intestinal gas. The symptoms usually occur between 30 minutes to two hours after eating or drinking lactose-containing foods. A child may also exhibit weight loss, slow growth, and **malnutrition**.

When to call the doctor

If a child develops symptoms of lactose intolerance, the doctor should be consulted concerning dietary substitutions.

Diagnosis

To diagnosis lactose intolerance, usually healthcare professionals measure the absorption of lactose in the digestive system by using the lactose tolerance test, the hydrogen breath test, or the stool acidity test. Each of these can be performed as an outpatient in a hospital, clinic, or doctor's office.

Children who are to take the lactose tolerance test must fast before being tested. They then drink a lactose-containing liquid for the test; medical personnel take blood samples during the next two hours to measure the children's blood glucose level. The blood glucose level, or blood sugar level, indicates how well the body is digesting the lactose. A diagnosis of lactose intolerance is confirmed when blood glucose level does not rise. This test is not administered to infants and very young children because of the risk of **dehydration** from drinking the lactose-containing liquid, which can cause diarrhea in those who are lactose intolerant, resulting in dehydration.

Hydrogen is usually detected only in small amounts in the breath. However, when undigested lactose found in the colon is fermented by bacteria, hydrogen in the breath is produced in greater quantities. The hydrogen is exhaled after being absorbed from the intestines and carried through the bloodstream to the lungs. The hydrogen breath test involves having the child drink a lactose-containing beverage. Healthcare professionals monitor the breath at regular intervals to see if the hydrogen levels rise, which indicates improper lactose digestion. Children taking the test who have had certain foods, medications, or cigarettes before the test may get inaccurate results. While the test is useful for children and adults, infants and young children should not take it because of the risk of dehydration from diarrhea in those who are lactose intolerant.

The stool acidity test measures the amount of acid in the stool. This is a safe test for newborns and young children. The test detects lactic acid and other short-chain fatty acids from undigested lactose fermented by bacteria in the colon. Glucose may also be found in the stool sample, resulting from unabsorbed lactose in the colon.

Some parents may try to self-diagnose lactose intolerance in their child by using an **elimination diet**, a diet that eliminates obvious milk and milk products. However, because there are so many food products that may contain hidden sources of milk, such a diet should be supervised by a dietician or developed by following a guide to a lactose-eliminating diet. A simpler way to self-diagnose lactose intolerance is by a milk challenge. The child fasts overnight, drinks a glass of milk in the morning, and then fasts for the next three to five hours. If the child is lactose intolerant, the child should experience symptoms within several hours. If symptoms do occur, the child should be evaluated by a healthcare professional to rule out the possibility of a milk allergy. However, milk **allergies** are rare and usually only occurs in infants and young children.

Treatment

Since there is no treatment that can improve the body's ability to produce lactase, treatment for lactose deficiency is focused on controlling the diet.

Most children affected by lactose intolerance do well if they limit their intake of lactose-containing food and drinks. Individuals differ in the amounts they can handle before experiencing symptoms. Many children may only need to eliminate major milk-containing products from their diet, while others who are intolerant to even small amounts of lactose may be required to follow severe dietary restrictions.

Foods that contain lactose include milk, low-fat milk, skim milk, chocolate milk, buttermilk, sweetened condensed milk, dried whole milk, instant nonfat dry milk, low-fat yogurts, frozen yogurt, ice cream, ice milk, sherbet, cheese, cottage cheese, low-fat cottage cheese, cream, and butter. Other foods that may contain hidden lactose are: nondairy creamers, powdered artificial sweeteners, foods containing milk power or nonfat milk solids, bread, cake, margarine, creamed soups, pancakes, waffles, processed breakfast cereals, salad dressings, lunch meats, puddings, custards, confections, and some meat products. Lactose is also used as the base for more than 20 percent of prescription drugs and 6 percent of over-the-counter drugs.

For infants younger than two years of age, soy formulas are adequate substitutes for milk. Toddlers may drink rice or soymilk, while older children who are sensitive to lactose can take lactase enzymes, which are available without a prescription. Using the liquid form of lactase enzymes, children can add a few drops in their milk, put the milk in the refrigerator and drink it after 24 hours, when the lactase enzymes have reduced the lactose content by 70 percent. If the milk is heated first and double the amount of lactase liquid enzymes is added, the milk will be 90 percent lactose-free. Supermarkets also carry lactose-reduced milk and other products, which contain nutrients found in the regular products but without the lactose.

In the early 2000s, researchers have developed a chewable lactase enzyme tablet. Taking three to six tablets just before eating helps some children digest lactose-containing solid foods.

Nutritional concerns

Eliminating milk from the diet can result in deficiencies of calcium, vitamin D, riboflavin, and protein. Milk substitutes for children are a necessity, as other sources of calcium are required. Fermented milk products such as yogurt are often tolerated. Buttermilk and cheeses have less lactose than milk. Goat's milk can sometimes be tolerated but should be consumed with meals.

Prognosis

Lactose intolerance is easy to manage and is not considered dangerous. People of all ages, but especially children, have to replace the calcium that is lost by cutting back on milk products; this can be accomplished by taking supplements and eating calcium-rich foods, such as broccoli, kale, canned salmon with bones, calcium-fortified foods, and tofu. They may also add lactase enzymes to dairy products to reduce lactose content as

KEY TERMS

Galactose—One of the two simple sugars (glucose is the other one) that makes up the protein, lactose, found in milk. Galactose can be toxic in high levels.

Glucose—A simple sugar that serves as the body's main source of energy.

Lactase—The enzyme produced by cells that line the small intestine that allows the body to break down lactose.

Lactose—A sugar found in milk and milk products.

well as use lactose-reduced dairy products. Many children who suffer with lactose intolerance are able to continue eating some milk products.

Prevention

Often lactose intolerance is a natural occurrence that cannot be avoided. However, people can prevent symptoms by managing the condition with diet and lactase supplements.

Parental concerns

Parents must guard the health of a child who is lactose intolerant by carefully managing the child's diet to avoid foods that will result in symptoms while providing foods that contain necessary nutrients for the child's health and growth.

Resources

BOOKS

Dobler, Merri Lou. *Lactose Intolerance Nutrition Guide.* Chicago, IL: American Dietetic Association, 2004.

The Official Patient's Sourcebook on Lactose Intolerance: A Revised and Updated Directory for the Internet Age. San Diego, CA: Icon Health Publications, 2002.

ORGANIZATIONS

American Dietetic Association. 120 South Riverside Plaza, Suite 2000 Chicago, IL 60606–6995. Web site: <www.eatright.org/Public/>.

Judith Sims
Lisette Hilton

Langerhans cell histiocytosis *see*
  Histiocytosis X

Language delay

Definition

A language delay is **language development** that is significantly below the norm for a child of a specified age.

Description

Language delay is a communication disorder, a category that includes a wide variety of speech, language, and hearing impairments. The milestones of language development, including the onset of babbling and a child's first words and sentences, normally occur within approximate age ranges. However, individual children vary enormously regarding the exact age at which each milestone is reached. There also are different styles of language development. Most children have acquired good verbal communication by the age of three. But one child may be wordless until the age of two and a half and then immediately start talking in three-word sentences. Another child might have several words at ten months but add very few additional words over the following year. Other children start talking at about 12 months and progress steadily.

Language delay usually becomes apparent during infancy or early childhood. Any delay in general development usually causes language delay. Children with language delay may acquire language skills in the usual progression but at a much slower rate, so that their language development may be equivalent to a normally developing child of a much younger chronological age. Maturation delay, also called developmental language delay, is one of the most common types of language delay. Children with a maturation delay may be referred to as "late talkers" or "late bloomers." Maturation delays frequently run in families.

Demographics

Speech/language delay is the most common developmental disorder in children aged three to 16 years, affecting approximately 3 to 10 percent of children. It is three to four times more common in boys than in girls.

Causes and symptoms

Environmental causes

Common nonphysical causes of language delay include circumstances in which the following are the case:

- The child is concentrating on some other skill, such as walking perfectly, rather than on language.

- The child has a twin or sibling very close in age and thus may not receive as much individual attention.

- The child has older siblings who interpret so well that the child has no need to speak or whose talk is so continuous that the child lacks the opportunity to speak.

- The child is in a daycare situation with too few adults to provide individual attention.

- The child is under the care of a non-English speaker.

- The child is bilingual or multilingual, learning two or more languages simultaneously but at a slower speed; the child's combined comprehension of the languages is normal for that age.

- The child suffers from psychosocial deprivation such as poverty, **malnutrition**, poor housing, neglect, inadequate linguistic stimulation, emotional stress.

- The child is abused; abusive parents are more likely to neglect their children and less likely to communicate with them verbally.

Physical causes

Language delay may result from a variety of underlying disorders, including the following:

- **mental retardation**

- maturation delay (This delay in the maturation of the central neurological processes required to produce speech is often the cause of late talking.)

- **hearing impairment**

- **dyslexia**, a specific reading disorder which may cause language delay in preschoolers

- a learning disability

- cerebral palsy, in which numerous factors may contribute to language delay

- autism, a developmental disorder in which, among other things, children do not use language or use it abnormally

- congenital blindness, even in the absence of other neurological impairment

- brain damage

- Klinefelter syndrome, a disorder in which males are born with an extra X chromosome

- receptive aphasia or receptive language disorder, a deficit in spoken language comprehension or in the ability to respond to spoken language, resulting from brain damage

- expressive aphasia, an inability to speak or write, although comprehension is normal; caused by malnutrition, brain damage, or hereditary factors

- childhood apraxia of speech, a nervous system disorder

Mental retardation accounts for more than 50 percent of language delays. Language delay is usually more severe than other developmental delays in retarded children, and it is often the first noticeable symptom of mental retardation. Mental retardation causes global language delay, including delayed auditory comprehension and use of gestures.

Impaired hearing is one of the most common causes of language delay. Any child who does not hear speech in a clear and consistent manner will have language delay. Even a minor hearing impairment can significantly affect language development. In general the more severe the impairment, the more serious the language delay. Children with congenital (present at birth) hearing impairment or hearing loss that occurs within the first two years of life (known as prelingual hearing loss) experience serious language delay, even when the impairment is diagnosed and treated at an early age. However, deaf children born to parents who use sign language develop infant babble and a fully expressive sign language at the same rate as hearing children.

Symptoms of language delay

Symptoms of language delay include the following:

- failure to meet the developmental milestones for language development

- language development that lags behind other children of the same age by at least one year

- inability to follow directions

- slow or incomprehensible speech after three years of age

- serious difficulties with syntax (placing words in a sentence in the correct order)

- serious difficulties with articulation, including the substitution, omission, or distortion of certain sounds

Language delays resulting from underlying conditions may have symptoms specific to the condition. Nonetheless, specific symptoms of language delay may include the following:

- not babbling by 12 to 15 months of age

- not understanding simple commands by 18 months of age

- not talking by two years of age

- not using sentences by three years of age

- not being able to tell a simple story by four or five years of age

Symptoms of language delay with mental retardation

Mentally impaired children usually babble during their first year and may speak their first words within the normal age range. However, they often cannot do the following:

- put words together
- speak in complete sentences
- acquire a larger, more varied vocabulary
- develop grammatically

Mentally impaired children in conversation may be repetitive and routine, exhibiting little **creativity**. Nevertheless vocabulary and grammatical development appear to proceed by very similar processes in mentally retarded and developmentally normal children.

In general the severity of language delay depends on the severity of the mental retardation. Levels of retardation and language skill are ranked as follows:

- mild retardation (**intelligence** quotient [IQ] range of 52–68): usually eventually develop language skills
- moderate retardation (IQ range of 36–51): usually learn to talk and communicate
- severe retardation (IQ range of 20–35): have limited language but can speak a few words

Language delays among mentally retarded children vary greatly. Some severely mentally impaired children who also have **hydrocephalus** or **Williams syndrome** may acquire exceptional conversational language skills, sometimes called the "chatterbox syndrome." Some children (called savants) test as mentally retarded but learn their native language, as well as foreign languages, very easily. With **Down syndrome** and some other disorders, language delay is more severe than other mental impairments. This factor may be due to the characteristic facial abnormalities and relatively large tongues of Down-syndrome children. Children with Down syndrome also are at higher risk for hearing impairment and ear infections that cause hearing loss.

Symptoms of language delay with other disorders

Symptoms of language delay in a hearing-impaired child include the following:

- babbling at an older-than-normal age
- babbling that is less varied and less sustained

- first words at age two or older
- only two-word sentences by age four or five in a profoundly deaf child

Dyslexic children have difficulty separating parts of words and single words within a group of words. Symptoms of dyslexia may include:

- poor articulation
- difficulties identifying sounds within words, blending sounds, or rhyming
- difficulty putting sounds in the correct order
- hesitation in choosing words

A learning-disabled child usually exhibits an uneven pattern of language development. In addition, about 50 percent of autistic children never learn to speak. Those who do speak often have severe language delay and may use words in unusual ways. They rarely participate in interactive dialogue and often speak with an unusual rhythm or pitch. The speech of some autistic children has an atonic or sing-song quality.

Children with congenital blindness average about an eight-month delay in speaking words. Although blind children develop language in much the same way as sighted children, they may rely more on conversational formulas.

The speech of children with receptive aphasia is both delayed and sparse, ungrammatical, and poorly articulated. Children with expressive aphasia fail to speak at the usual age although they have normal speech comprehension and articulation. Children with defined lesions in language areas on either side of the brain have initial but quite variable language delays. Usually their language catches up by the age of two or three without noticeable deficits.

Apraxia affects the ability to sequence and vocalize sounds, syllables, and words. Children with apraxia know what they want to say, but their brains do not send the correct signals to the lips, jaw, and tongue to form the words. In addition to language delay, apraxia often causes other expressive **language disorders**.

When to call the doctor

Children who are not talking at all by the age of two should have a complete developmental **assessment**. Children who are not progressing in word-learning skills by the end of the first grade should be tested for dyslexia.

Diagnosis

Diagnosis of language delay requires a complete physical examination and a thorough developmental history, with special attention to language milestones. In young children it may be very difficult to distinguish between a late talker and a developmental expressive disorder. The diagnosis often is made by a speech/language pathologist. Language performance of bilingual children must be compared to that of other bilingual children of a similar cultural and linguistic background. Generalized delay in all developmental milestones suggests mental retardation.

Numerous tests are used to screen for language delay and assess language development. Some of these are described below:

- The Denver Developmental Screening Test is the most popular test in clinical use for children from birth to six years of age. Since language delay is the most common early symptom of global intellectual impairment, the test provides a comprehensive developmental assessment.

- The Early Language Milestone Scale is a simple tool for assessing language development in children under the age of three. It relies on parents' reports and a very short test focusing on visual, receptive, and expressive language.

- The Mullen Scales of Early Learning is a comprehensive assessment of language, motor, and perceptual abilities in children from birth to five years eight months of age.

- The Peabody Picture Vocabulary Test, for children aged two-and-a-half to 18 years, is a useful screening instrument for word comprehension.

- The Receptive One-Word Picture Vocabulary Test provides information about a child's ability to understand language.

Other tests for language delay include:

- Early Speech Perception Test
- Assessing Prelinguistic and Early Linguistic Behaviors in Developmentally Young Children
- Joliet 3-Minute **Preschool** Speech and Language Screen
- Fluharty Preschool Speech and Language Screening Test
- Assessment of Fluency in School-Age Children
- Children's Articulation Test
- Clinical Evaluation of Language Fundamentals

- Phonological Assessment of Child Speech (Initial assessment may indicate the need for additional testing to identify underlying physical conditions.)

Treatment

About 60 percent of language delays in children under age three resolve spontaneously. Early detection and intervention for language delay can help prevent social, cognitive, and emotional problems. Treatment of language delay is individualized for each child with the primary goal of teaching the child strategies for comprehending spoken language and producing appropriate linguistic or communicative behavior. Depending on the type and cause of the delay, the healthcare team may include a physician, a speech/language pathologist, an audiologist, a psychologist, an occupational therapist, and a social worker. Psychotherapy may be recommended if the language delay is accompanied by **anxiety** or depression. Speech therapy is used to help mentally impaired children develop intelligible language. Behavior therapy may help autistic children progress in speech acquisition.

Hearing-impaired children who are identified and receive early intervention before six months of age develop significantly better language skills than children identified after six months of age. Early, consistent, and conscious use of visual communication modes such as sign language, finger spelling, and cued speech, and/or hearing amplification and oral training can reduce the language delay. Since only about 10 percent of deaf children are born to deaf parents, hearing parents can promote their deaf child's language development by learning and using sign language. Many types of hearing aids are available for children as young as three months. **Cochlear implants** may be used for profoundly deaf children aged two to six. These children usually develop better language skills than those with hearing aids or other devices.

Prognosis

With appropriate intervention language-delayed children usually catch up with their peers. Children with maturation delay usually have normal language development by the time they enter school. Although a bilingual home environment can cause a temporary language delay, most children become proficient in both languages before the age of five. Nevertheless, early language delays may cause problems with behavior and social interactions. A language delay can lead to elective **mutism**, a condition in which children choose not to speak.

KEY TERMS

Apraxia—Impairment of the ability to make purposeful movements, but not paralysis or loss of sensation.

Expressive aphasia—A developmental disorder in which a child has lower-than-normal proficiency in vocabulary, production of complex sentences, and word recall, although language comprehension is normal.

Maturation delay—Developmental language delay; a language delay caused by the slow maturation of speech centers in the brain; often causes late talking.

Receptive aphasia—A developmental disorder in which a child has difficulty comprehending spoken and written language.

Such children typically speak when they are on their own, with their friends, and sometimes with their parents; however, they will not speak in school, in public situations, or with strangers.

Most mentally retarded children eventually develop at least some degree of language. But frustration and anger at their inability to communicate effectively can lead to numerous social and behavioral problems. An adolescent with Down syndrome and an IQ of about 50 may speak at the grammatical level of an unaffected three-year-old, with short, repetitive, simple sentences. Nevertheless, Down-syndrome children often are very sociable and interested in conversational language.

Children who receive early intervention for hearing impairments can develop at nearly the same rate as other children. However, depending on the severity of their hearing loss, they may continue to have difficulties with articulation and speech quality as well as with written language. Children who lose their hearing after the first few years of life have far fewer language delays than children who are deaf from birth or who lose their hearing within the first year.

Most children with receptive aphasia gradually acquire a language of their own, understood only by those close to them. Children with expressive aphasia will not develop normal language skills without intervention and are at risk for language-based learning disabilities.

Prevention

There are no known preventions for most language delays. Prenatal care and good **nutrition** during pregnancy and early childhood may help prevent some expressive language delays. Hearing-impaired children who use sign language within their families usually have no signed-language delay.

Parental concerns

A speech/language pathologist can teach parents methods for encouraging and enhancing their child's language development. Special programs also are available for helping language-delayed children and their parents. Parents, caregivers, and teachers of children with language delay should take the following steps:

- adjust their speech to the child's level
- use consistent language
- use meaningful language
- repeat words, phrases, sentences, and stories
- use small-group instruction

Resources

BOOKS

Agin, Marilyn C., et al. *The Late Talker: What to Do If Your Child Isn't Talking Yet.* New York: St. Martin's Press, 2003.

PERIODICALS

Kripke, Clarissa. "Therapy for Speech and Language Delay." *American Family Physician* 69, no. 12 (June 15, 2004): 282–34.

Toppelberg C. O., and T. Shapiro. "Language Disorders: A 10-Year Research Update Review." *Journal of the American Academy of Child and Adolescent Psychiatry* 39 (2000): 143–52.

ORGANIZATIONS

American Speech-Language-Hearing Association. 10801 Rockville Pike, Rockville, MD 20852. Web site: <http://asha.org>.

Help for Kid's Speech. 631 6th Ave. South, Second Floor, St. Petersburg, FL 33701. Web site: <www.helpforkidspeech.org>.

WEB SITES

Busari, Jamiu O., and Nielske M. Weggelaar. "How to Investigate and Manage the Child Who Is Slow to Speak." *bmj.com*, December 8, 2003. Available online at <http://bmj.bmjjournals.com/cgi/content/full/328/7434/272?etoc> (accessed December 29, 2004).

"Late Blooming or Language Problem?" *American Speech-Language-Hearing Association*, 2004. Available online at <www.asha.org/public/speech/disorders/Late-Blooming-or-Language-Problem.htm> (accessed December 29, 2004).

"NICHCY-Info About Speech & Language Disorders." *KidSource Online*, 2000. Available online at <www.kidsource.com/NICHCY/speech.html> (accessed December 29, 2004).

"Speech and Language Delay: What Does This Mean for My Child?" *familydoctor.org*, August 2002. Available online at <http://familydoctor.org/442.xml> (accessed December 29, 2004).

"Warning Signs of a Language/Communication Developmental Delay." *BabyCenter*, 2004. Available online at <www.babycenter.com/general/12293.html?CP_bid=> (accessed December 29, 2004).

Margaret Alic, PhD

Language development

Definition

Language development is the process by which children come to understand and communicate language during early childhood.

Description

From birth up to the age of five, children develop language at a very rapid pace. The stages of language development are universal among humans. However, the age and the pace at which a child reaches each milestone of language development vary greatly among children. Thus, language development in an individual child must be compared with norms rather than with other individual children. In general girls develop language at a faster rate than boys. More than any other aspect of development, language development reflects the growth and maturation of the brain. After the age of five it becomes much more difficult for most children to learn language.

Receptive language development (the ability to comprehend language) usually develops faster than expressive language (the ability to communicate). Two different styles of language development are recognized. In referential language development, children first speak single words and then join words together, first into two-word sentences and then into three-word sentences. In expressive language development, children first speak in long unintelligible babbles that mimic the cadence and rhythm of adult speech. Most children use a combination these styles.

Infancy

Language development begins before birth. Towards the end of pregnancy, a fetus begins to hear sounds and speech coming from outside the mother's body. Infants are acutely attuned to the human voice and prefer it to other sounds. In particular they prefer the higher pitch characteristic of female voices. They also are very attentive to the human face, especially when the face is talking. Although crying is a child's primary means of communication at birth, language immediately begins to develop via repetition and imitation.

Between birth and three months of age, most infants acquire the following abilities:

- seem to recognize their mother's voice
- quiet down or smile when spoken to
- turn toward familiar voices and sounds
- make sounds indicating pleasure
- cry differently to express different needs
- grunt, chuckle, whimper, and gurgle
- begin to coo (repeating the same sounds frequently) in response to voices
- make vowel-like sounds such as "ooh" and "ah"

Between three and six months, most infants can do the following:

- turn their head toward a speaker
- watch a speaker's mouth movements
- respond to changes in a tone of voice
- make louder sounds including screeches
- vocalize excitement, pleasure, and displeasure
- cry differently out of **pain** or hunger
- laugh, squeal, and sigh
- sputter loudly and blow bubbles
- shape their mouths to change sounds
- vocalize different sounds for different needs
- communicate desires with gestures
- babble for attention
- mimic sounds, inflections, and gestures
- make many new sounds, including "p," "b," and "m," that may sound almost speech-like

The sounds and babblings of this stage of language development are identical in babies throughout the world, even among those who are profoundly deaf. Thus all babies are born with the capacity to learn any language. Social interaction determines which language they eventually learn.

Six to 12 months is a crucial age for receptive language development. Between six and nine months babies begin to do the following:

• search for sources of sound

• listen intently to speech and other sounds

• take an active interest in conversation even if it is not directed at them

• recognize "dada," "mama," "bye-bye"

• consistently respond to their names

• respond appropriately to friendly and angry tones

• express their moods by sound and body language

• **play** with sounds

• make long, more varied sounds

• babble random combinations of consonants and vowels

• babble in singsong with as many as 12 different sounds

• experiment with pitch, intonation, and volume

• use their tongues to change sounds

• repeat syllables

• imitate intonation and speech sounds

Between nine and 12 months babies may begin to do the following:

• listen when spoken to

• recognize words for common objects and names of **family** members

• respond to simple requests

• understand "no"

• understand gestures

• associate voices and names with people

• know their own names

• babble both short and long groups of sounds and two-to-three-syllable repeated sounds (The babble begins to have characteristic sounds of their native language.)

• use sounds other than crying to get attention

• use "mama" and "dada" for any person

• shout and scream

• repeat sounds

• use most consonant and vowel sounds

• practice inflections

• engage in much vocal play

Toddlerhood

During the second year of life language development proceeds at very different rates in different children. By the age of 12 months, most children use "mama/dada" appropriately. They add new words each month and temporarily lose words. Between 12 and 15 months children begin to do the following:

• recognize names

• understand and follow one-step directions

• laugh appropriately

• use four to six intelligible words, usually those starting with "b," "c," "d," and "g," although less than 20 percent of their language is comprehensible to outsiders

• use partial words

• gesture and speak "no"

• ask for help with gestures and sounds

At 15 to 18 months of age children usually do the following:

• understand "up," "down," "hot," "off"

• use 10 to 20 intelligible words, mostly nouns

• use complete words

• put two short words together to form sentences

• chatter and imitate, use some echolalia (repetitions of words and phrases)

• have 20 to 25 percent of their speech understood by outsiders

At 18 to 24 months of age toddlers come to understand that there are words for everything and their language development gains momentum. About 50 of a child's first words are universal: names of foods, animals, family members, **toys**, vehicles, and clothing. Usually children first learn general nouns, such as "flower" instead of "dandelion," and they may overgeneralize words, such as calling all toys "balls." Some children learn words for social situations, greetings, and expressions of love more readily than others. At this age children usually have 20 to 50 intelligible words and can do the following:

• follow two-step directions

• point to parts of the body

• attempt multi-syllable words

• speak three-word sentences

- ask two-word questions
- enjoy challenge words such as "helicopter"
- hum and sing
- express pain verbally
- have 50 to 70 percent of their speech understood by outsiders

After several months of slower development, children often have a "word spurt" (an explosion of new words). Between the ages of two and 18 years, it is estimated that children add nine new words per day. Between two and three years of age children acquire:

- a 400-word vocabulary including names
- a word for most everything
- the use of pronouns
- three to five-word sentences
- the ability to describe what they just saw or experienced
- the use of the past tense and plurals
- names for body parts, colors, toys, people, and objects
- the ability to repeat rhymes, songs, and stories
- the ability to answer "what" questions

Children constantly produce sentences that they have not heard before, creating rather than imitating. This **creativity** is based on the general principles and rules of language that they have mastered. By the time a child is three years of age, most of a child's speech can be understood. However, like adults, children vary greatly in how much they choose to talk.

Preschool

Three to four-year-olds usually can do the following:

- understand most of what they hear
- converse
- have 900 to 1,000-word vocabularies, with verbs starting to predominate
- usually talk without repeating syllables or words
- use pronouns correctly
- use three to six-word sentences
- ask questions
- relate experiences and activities
- tell stories (Occasional **stuttering** and stammering is normal in preschoolers.)

Language skills usually blossom between four and five years of age. Children of this age can do the following:

- verbalize extensively
- communicate easily with other children and adults
- articulate most English sounds correctly
- know 1,500 to 2,500 words
- use detailed six to eight-word sentences
- can repeat four-syllable words
- use at least four prepositions
- tell stories that stay on topic
- can answer questions about stories

School age

At age five most children can do the following:

- follow three consecutive commands
- talk constantly
- ask innumerable questions
- use descriptive words and compound and complex sentences
- know all the vowels and consonants
- use generally correct grammar

Six-year-olds usually can correct their own grammar and mispronunciations. Most children double their vocabularies between six and eight years of age and begin reading at about age seven. A major leap in reading comprehension occurs at about nine. Ten-year-olds begin to understand figurative word meanings.

Adolescents generally speak in an adult manner, gaining language maturity throughout high school.

Common problems

Language delay is the most common **developmental delay** in children. There are many causes for language delay, both environmental and physical. About 60 percent of language delays in children under age three resolve spontaneously. Early intervention often helps other children to catch up to their age group.

Common circumstances that can result in language delay include:

- concentration on developing skills other than language
- siblings who are very close in age or older siblings who interpret for the younger child

- inadequate language stimulation and one-on-one attention
- bilingualism, in which a child's combined comprehension of two languages usually is equivalent to other children's comprehension of one language
- psychosocial deprivation

Language delay can result from a variety of physical disorders, including the following:

- mental retardation
- maturation delay (the slower-than-usual development of the speech centers of the brain), a common cause of late talking
- a hearing impairment
- a learning disability
- cerebral palsy
- autism (a developmental disorder in which, among other things, children do not use language or use it abnormally)
- congenital blindness, even in the absence of other neurological impairment
- Klinefelter syndrome, a disorder in which males are born with an extra X chromosome

Brain damage or disorders of the central nervous system can cause the following:

- receptive aphasia or receptive language disorder, a deficit in spoken language comprehension or in the ability to respond to spoken language
- expressive aphasia, an inability to speak or write despite normal language comprehension
- childhood apraxia of speech, in which a sound is substituted for the desired syllable or word

Parental concerns

Language development is enriched by verbal interactions with other children and adults. Parents and caregivers can have a significant impact on early language development. Studies have shown that children of talkative parents have twice the vocabulary as those of quiet parents. A study from the National Institute of Child Health and Human Development (NICHD) found that children in high-quality childcare environments have larger vocabularies and more complex language skills than children in lower-quality situations. In addition language-based interactions appear to increase a child's capacity to learn. Recommendations for encouraging language development in infants include:

- talking to them as much as possible and giving them opportunities to respond, perhaps with a smile; short periods of silence help teach the give-and-take of conversation
- talking to infants in a singsong, high-pitched speech, called "parentese" or "motherese" (This is a universal method for enhancing language development.)
- using one- or two-syllable words and two to three-word sentences
- using proper words rather than baby words
- speaking slowly, drawing-out vowels, and exaggerating main syllables
- avoiding pronouns and articles
- using animated gestures along with words
- addressing the baby by name
- talking about on-going activities
- asking questions
- singing songs
- commenting on sounds in the environment
- encouraging the baby to make vowel-like and consonant-vowel sounds such as "ma," "da," and "ba"
- repeating recognizable syllables and repeating words that contain the syllable

When babies reach six to 12 months-of-age, parents should play word games with them, label objects with words, and allow the baby to listen and participate in conversations. Parents of toddlers should do the following:

- talk to the child in simple sentences and ask questions
- expand on the toddler's single words
- use gestures that reinforce words
- put words to the child's gestures
- name colors
- count items
- gently repeat correctly any words that the child has mispronounced, rather than criticizing the child

Parents of two to three-year-olds should do the following:

- talk about what the child and parent are doing each day
- encourage the child to use new words
- repeat and expand on what the child says
- ask the child yes-or-no questions and questions that require a simple choice

Language development

Age	Activity
Two months	Cries, coos, and grunts.
Four months	Begins babbling. Makes most vowel sounds and about half of consonant sounds.
Six months	Vocalizes with intonation. Responds to own name.
Eight months	Combines syllables when babbling, such "Ba-ba."
Eleven months	Says one word (or fragment of a word) with meaning.
Twelve months	Says two or three words with meaning. Practices inflection, such as raising pitch of voice at the end of a question.
Eighteen months	Has a vocabulary between five and 20 words, mostly nouns. Repeats word or phrase over and over. May start to join two words together.
Two years	Has a vocabulary of 150–300 words. Uses I, me, and you. Uses at least two prepositions (in, on, under). Combines words in short sentences. About two-thirds of what is spoken is understandable.
Three years	Has a vocabulary of 900–1000 words. Uses more verbs, some past tenses, and some plural nouns. Easily handles three-word sentences. Can give own name, sex, and age. About 90% of speech is understandable.
Four years	Can use at least four prepositions. Can usually repeat words of four syllables. Knows some colors and numbers. Has most vowels and diphthongs and consonants p, b, m, w, and n established. Talks a lot and repeats often.
Five years	Can count to ten. Speech is completely understandable, although articulation might not be perfect. Should have all vowels and consonants m, p, b, h, w, k, g, t, d, n, ng, y. Can repeat sentences as long as nine words. Speech is mostly grammatically correct.
Six years	Should have all vowels and consonants listed above, has added, f, v, sh, zh, th, l. Should be able to tell a connected story about a picture.
Seven years	Should have consonants s–z, r, voiceless th, ch, wh, and soft g. Should be able to do simple reading and print many words.
Eight years	All speech sounds established. Carries on conversation at a more adult level. Can tell complicated stories of past events. Easily uses complex and compound sentences. Reads simple stories with ease and can write simple compositions.

SOURCE: Child Development Institute. 2004. http://www.childdevelopmentinfo.com.

(Table by GGS Information Services.)

- encourage the child to ask questions
- read books about familiar things, with pictures, rhymes, repetitive lines, and few words

- read favorite books repeatedly, allowing the child to join in with familiar words
- encourage the child to pretend to read
- not interrupt children when they are speaking

Parents of four to six-year-olds should:

- not speak until the child is fully attentive
- pause after speaking to give the child a chance to respond
- acknowledge, encourage, and praise speech
- introduce new words
- talk about spatial relationships and opposites
- introduce limericks, songs, and poems
- talk about the television programs that they watch
- encourage the child to give directions
- give their full attention when the child initiates a conversation

Parents of six to 12-year-olds should talk to the children, not at them, encourage conversation by asking questions that require more than a yes-or-no answer, and listen attentively as the child recounts the day's activities.

Additional recommendations for parents and caregivers, by the American Academy of Pediatrics and others, include:

- talking at eye level with a child and supplementing words with body language, gestures, and facial expressions to enhance language comprehension
- talking in ways that catch a child's attention
- using language to comfort a child
- using correct pronunciations
- using expressive language to discuss objects, actions, and emotions
- playing with sounds and words
- labeling objects and actions with words
- providing objects and experiences to talk about
- choosing activities that promote language
- listening carefully to children and responding in ways that let them know that they have been understood, as well as encouraging further communication
- using complete sentences and adding detail to expand on what a child has said
- knowing when to remain silent
- reading to a child by six months of age at the latest

KEY TERMS

Apraxia—Impairment of the ability to make purposeful movements, but not paralysis or loss of sensation.

Expressive aphasia—A developmental disorder in which a child has lower-than-normal proficiency in vocabulary, production of complex sentences, and word recall, although language comprehension is normal.

Expressive language—Communicating with language.

Expressive language development—A style of language development in which a child's babble mimics the cadence and rhythm of adult speech.

Receptive aphasia—A developmental disorder in which a child has difficulty comprehending spoken and written language.

Receptive language—The comprehension of language.

Referential language development—A style of language development in which a child first speaks single words and then joins words together into two- and three-word sentences.

- encouraging children to ask questions and seek new information

- encouraging children to listen to and ask questions of each other

Television viewing does not promote language development.

When to call the doctor

Parents should call the pediatrician immediately if they suspect that their child may have a language delay or a hearing problem. Warning signs of language delay in toddlers include:

- avoiding eye contact

- neither understanding nor speaking words by 18 months of age

- difficulty learning nursery rhymes or simple songs

- not recognizing or labeling common objects

- inability to pay attention to a book or movie

- poor articulation, such that a parent cannot understand the child more than 50 percent of the time

Resources

BOOKS

Bochner, Sandra, and Jane Jones. *Child Language Development: Learning to Talk.* London: Whurr Publishers, 2003.

Buckley, Belinda. *Children's Communications Skills: From Birth to Five Years.* New York: Routledge, 2003.

Oates, John, and Andrew Grayson. *Cognitive and Language Development in Children.* Malden, MA: Blackwell, 2004.

PERIODICALS

Howard, Melanie. "How Babies Learn to Talk." *Baby Talk* 69, no. 3 (April 2004): 69–72.

Tsao, Feng-Ming, et al. "Speech Perception in Infancy Predicts Language Development in the Second Year of Life: A Longitudinal Study." *Child Development* 75, no. 4 (July/August 2004): 1067–84.

Van Hulle, Carol A., et al. "Genetic, Environmental, and Gender Effects on Individual Differences in Toddler Expressive Language." *Journal of Speech, Language, and Hearing Research* 47, no. 4 (August 2004): 904–12.

ORGANIZATIONS

American Academy of Pediatrics. 141 Northwest Point Blvd., Elk Grove Village, IL 60007. Web site: <www.aap.org>.

American Speech-Language-Hearing Association. 10801 Rockville Pike, Rockville, MD 20852. Web site: <http://asha.org>.

Child Development Institute. 3528 E. Ridgeway Road, Orange, CA 92867. Web site: <www.cdipage.com/index.htm>.

WEB SITES

"Activities to Encourage Speech and Language Development." *American Speech-Language-Hearing Association.* Available online at <www.asha.org/public/speech/development/Parent-Stim-Activities.htm> (accessed December 29, 2004).

Dougherty, Dorthy P. "Developing Your Baby's Language Skills." *KidsGrowth.* Available online at <www.kidsgrowth.com/resources/articledetail.cfm?id=714> (accessed December 29, 2004).

Genishi, Celia. "Young Children's Oral Language Development." *Child Development Institute.* Available online at <www.childdevelopmentinfo.com/development/oral_language_development.shtml> (accessed December 29, 2004).

"How Does Your Child Hear and Talk?" *American Speech-Language-Hearing Association.* Available online at <www.asha.org/public/speech/development/child_hear_talk.htm> (accessed December 29, 2004).

"Language Development in Children." *Child Development Institute.* Available online at

<www.childdevelopmentinfo.com/development/
language_development.shtml> (accessed December 29,
2004).

Lorenz, Joan Monchak. "Common Concerns about Speech
Development: Part I." *KidsGrowth*. Available online at
<www.kidsgrowth.com/resources/
articledetail.cfm?id=965< (accessed December 29, 2004).

Rafanello, Donna. "Facilitating Language Development."
Healthy Child Care America, Summer 2000. Available
online at <www.healthychildcare.org/pdf/LangDev.pdf>
(accessed December 29, 2004).

Margaret Alic, PhD

Language disorders

Definition

A language disorder is a deficit or problem with any function of language and communication.

Description

Speech and language disorders are extremely common. They can range from slow acquisition of language to sound substitution or **stuttering** to the inability to understand or produce and language at all. The federal Agency for Healthcare Research and Quality estimated in 2002 that communication disorders cost the United States between $30 and $154 billion annually in lost productivity and money spent on medical care, **special education**, and remediation.

Language disorders and the brain

Speech and language pathologists and neurologists (doctors who specialize in the brain and nervous system) have known for about 100 years that certain areas in the left hemisphere of the brain—Broca's area in the posterior frontal lobe and Wernicke's area in the temporal lobe—are centrally involved in language functions. Damage to Broca's area results in problems with language fluency: shortened sentences, impaired flow of speech, poor control of rhythm and intonation, and a telegraphic style with missing inflections. Damage to Wernicke's area produces speech that is fluent and often rapid, but with relatively senseless content, many invented words, and word substitutions.

With the invention of new technologies, including **computed tomography** (CT) scans and **magnetic resonance imaging** (MRI), several studies have looked at the **language development** in very young children with lesions in the traditional language areas of the brain. There is surprising agreement among the studies in their results: all find initial delays in language development followed by remarkably similar progress after about age two to three years. Lasting deficits have not been noticed in these children. Surprisingly, there are also no dramatic effects of laterality; lesions to either side of the brain seem to produce virtually the same effects. However, most of the data comes from conversational analysis or relatively unstructured testing, and these children have not been followed until school age. Nevertheless, the findings suggest remarkable plasticity and robustness of language in spite of brain lesions that would devastate an adult's language abilities.

Language disorders and hearing loss

Children with a hearing loss, either from birth or acquired during the first year or two of life, generally have a serious delay in spoken language development. The hearing loss occurs despite very early diagnosis and fitting with appropriate hearing aids. However, in the unusual case that sign language is the medium of communication in the **family** rather than speech, the child shows no delay in learning to use that language. Hearing development is always one of the first things checked if a pediatrician or parent suspects a **language delay**. The deaf child exposed only to speech will usually begin to babble ("baba, gaga") at a slightly later point than the hearing child. Recent work suggests that the babbling is neither as varied nor as sustained as in hearing children. However, there is often a long delay until the first words are spoken, sometimes not until age two years or older.

Depending on the severity of the hearing loss, the stages of early language development are also quite delayed. It is not unusual for the profoundly deaf child at age four or five years to only have two-word spoken sentences. It is only on entering specialized training programs for oral language development that the profoundly deaf child begins to acquire more spoken language. Often, such children do not make the usual **preschool** language gains until they reach grade school. Many deaf children learning English have pronounced difficulties in articulation and speech quality, especially if they are profoundly deaf, since they get no feedback in how they sound. A child who has hearing for the first few years of life has an enormous advantage in speech quality and oral language learning over a child who is deaf from birth or within his or her first year.

Apart from speech difficulties, deaf children learning English often show considerable difficulty with the inflection and syntax of the language, which marks their writing as well as their speech. The ramifications of this delayed language are also significant for learning to read, and reading proficiently. The average deaf high school student often only reads at fourth grade level.

Language disorders and mental retardation

Mental retardation can also affect the age at which children learn to talk. A mentally retarded child is defined as one who falls in the lower end of the range of **intelligence**, usually with an IQ (intelligence quotient) below 80 on some standardized IQ tests. There are many causes of mental retardation, including identified genetic syndromes such as **Down syndrome**, **Williams syndrome**, or **fragile X syndrome**.

Retardation can also be caused by damage to the fetus during pregnancy due to alcohol, drug abuse or toxicity, and disorders of the developing nervous system such as **hydrocephalus**. Finally, there are environmental causes following birth such as **lead poisoning**, anoxia, or **meningitis**.

Any of these situations is likely to slow down the child's rate of development in general, and thus to have effects on language development. However, most children with very low IQs develop some language, suggesting it is a relatively "buffered" system that can survive a good deal of insult to the developing brain. In cases of hydrocephalus, for example, it has been noted that children who are otherwise quite impaired intellectually can have impressive conversational language skills. Sometimes called the "chatterbox syndrome," this linguistic sophistication belies their poor ability to deal with the world. In an extreme case, a young man with a tested IQ in the retarded range has an apparent gift for acquiring foreign languages, and could learn a new one with very little exposure. For example, he could do fair translations at a rapid pace from written languages as diverse as Danish, Dutch, Hindi, Polish, French, Spanish, and Greek. He is, in fact, a savant in the area of language, and delights in comparing linguistic systems, although he does not have the mental capacity to live independently.

Adults should not consider retarded children to be a uniform class; different patterns can arise with different syndromes. For example, in hydrocephalic children and Williams syndrome, language skills may be preserved to a degree greater than their general intellectual level. In other groups, including Down syndrome, there may be more delay in language than in other mental abilities.

Most retarded children babble during the first year and develop their first words within a normal time span, but are then slow to develop sentences or a varied vocabulary. Vocabulary size is one of the primary components of standardized tests of verbal intelligence, and it grows slowly in retarded children. Nevertheless, the process of vocabulary development seems quite similar: retarded children also learn words from context and by incidental learning, not just by direct instruction.

Grammatical development, though slow, comes in the same way, and in the same order, as it does for normal IQ children. The child's conversation, however, may contain more repetition. The Down syndrome adolescent with an IQ of around 50 points does not seem to progress beyond the grammatical level of the normally intelligent child at three years, with short sentences that are restricted in variety and complexity. Children with Down syndrome are also particularly delayed in speech development. This is due in part to the facial abnormalities that characterize this syndrome, including a relatively large tongue. It is also linked to the higher risk they appear to suffer from ear infections and hearing loss.

Specific language impairment

Specific language impairment describes a condition of markedly delayed language development in the absence of any apparent handicapping conditions such as deafness, **autism**, or mental retardation. Specific language impairment (SLI) is also sometimes called childhood dysphasia, or developmental language disorder.

Children with SLI usually begin to talk at approximately the same age as normal children, but are markedly slower in their progress. They seem to have particular problems with inflection and word forms, such as leaving off endings when forming verb tenses (for example, the -ed ending when forming the past tense). This problem can persist much longer than early childhood, often into grade school and beyond, where these children encounter difficulties in reading and writing. The child with SLI often has difficulties learning language "incidentally," (picking up the meaning of a new word from context or generalizing a new syntactic form). This is in contrast to the normal child's development, where incidental learning and generalization are the hallmarks of language acquisition. Children with SLI are not cognitively impaired and are not withdrawn or socially aloof like the autistic child.

Very little is known about the cause or origin of specific language impairment, although evidence is growing that the underlying condition may be a form of brain abnormality. However, any such brain abnormality is not readily apparent with existing diagnostic technologies. When compared to other children, SLI children do not

Speech therapists help children overcome their speech and language disorders. *(© Bob Rowan; Progressive Image/Corbis.)*

have clear brain lesions or marked anatomical differences in either brain hemisphere.

Demographics

About one in six people, or 42 million individuals in the United States, have some type of communication disorder. About 28 million have speech, voice, or language problems associated with hearing loss, and about 14 million have similar problems not associated with impaired hearing. More than one million children in special education classes are categorized as having a speech or language disability.

Causes and symptoms

Language disorders can arise at many points in the language production process such as:

• from damage to the part of the brain that produces language

• from damage to the part of the brain that understands language

• from hearing loss

• from damage to the muscles and tissues of the mouth and throat needed for speech (e.g. **cleft palate**)

• from neurological disorders that interrupt the transmission of information necessary to receive and produce language

• from unknown (idiopathic) causes

Symptoms of language disorders vary widely, but include:

• slow acquisition of speech and language

• inability to make the physical sounds associated with language production (mutism)

• failure to make sense of spoken or written words

• inability to speak under certain social circumstances (selective mutism)

- transformations of words or sounds when speaking
- inability to recall known words

When to call the doctor

Parents should talk to their pediatrician immediately if their child appears to have **hearing impairment**. They should also consult with their doctor if the child does not babble or begin to use single words within the normal time frame. Parents of older children may need a referral to a speech and language specialist if their child stutters, lisps, has difficulty forming words or producing coherent speech, or exhibits certain learning disabilities.

Diagnosis

Speech and language disorders are usually diagnosed by a speech and language pathologist, often with the help of a pediatrician, audiologist (hearing specialist), and neurologist. Many **assessment** tests are designed specifically for use in children, including the Clinical Evaluation of Language Fundamentals (also available in Spanish); the Preschool Language Scale (also available in Spanish); the Test of Language Development, Primary; and the Test of Language, Intermediate. There are assessments designed to evaluate speech production, such as the Goldman-Fristoe test of Articulation.

Treatment

Treatment varies, depending on the type and cause of the language disorder. However, in all language disorders and delays, early intervention is key to improvement. Many educators of the deaf now urge early compensatory programs in signed languages, because the deaf child shows no handicap in learning a visually based language. Deaf children born to signing parents begin to "babble" in sign at the same point in infancy that hearing infants babble speech, and proceed from there to learn a fully expressive language. However, only 10 percent of deaf children are born to deaf parents, so hearing parents must show a commitment and willingness to learn sign language. Furthermore, command of at least written English is still a necessity for such children to be able to function in the larger community.

Speech therapy can be a considerable aid to many children with language disorders For example, it can help to make a Down syndrome child's speech more intelligible. Despite the delay, children with Down syndrome are often quite sociable and interested in language for conversation.

Surgery, followed by speech therapy, can correct physical deformities, such as cleft palate, that interfere with speech production.

Psychotherapy can help older children whose language disorders are psychologically based.

Prognosis

Prognosis varies on an individual basis, depending on the cause, type, and severity of the language disorder. Those children who receive early intervention therapies are more likely to have a better outcome than those for whom services are delayed.

Prevention

Many language disorders are not preventable. However, those that arise from damage to the fetus due to the mother's use of drugs or alcohol during pregnancy can be prevented by avoiding these substances.

Parental concerns

Language is such a critical part of our society that parents are justly concerned when their child has a language disorder. The parents' approach to the disorder can greatly influence the child's self-image, **self-esteem**, and ultimately his or her success in reaching the fullest language potential.

Resources

BOOKS

Bahr, Diane Chapman. *Oral Motor Assessment and Treatment: Ages and Stages.* Boston: Allyn and Bacon, 2001.

Freed, Donald B. *Motor Speech Disorders: Diagnosis & Treatment.* San Diego: Singular Pub. Group, 2000.

PERIODICALS

Conti-Ramsden, Gina. "Processing and Linguistic Markers in Young Children with Specific Language Impairment." *Journal of Speech, Language, and Hearing Research* 46, no. 5 (October 2003): 1029–38.

Fujiki, Martin, et al. "The Relationship of Language and Emotion Regulation Skills to Reticence in Children with Specific Language Impairment." *Journal of Speech,*

Language, and Hearing Research 47, no. 3 (June 2004): 637–47.

Nation, Kate, et al. "Hidden Language Impairments in Children: Parallels Between Poor Reading Comprehension and Specific Language Impairment?" *Journal of Speech, Language, and Hearing Research.* 47, no. 1 (February 2004): 199–212.

ORGANIZATIONS

American Speech-Language-Hearing Association. 10801 Rockville Pike, Rockville, MD 20852. (800) 638 8255. Web site: <www.asha.org>.

Tish Davidson, A.M.
Jill De Villiers, Ph.D.

Laxatives

Definition

Laxatives are products that promote bowel movements.

Description

Laxatives may be grouped by mechanism of action.

Saline cathartics include dibasic sodium phosphate (Phospo-Soda), magnesium citrate, magnesium hydroxide (milk of magnesia), magnesium sulfate (Epsom salts), sodium biphosphate, and others. They act by attracting and holding water in the intestinal lumen, and may produce a watery stool. Magnesium sulfate is the most potent of the laxatives in this group.

Stimulant and irritant laxatives increase the peristaltic movement of the intestine. Examples include cascara and bisadocyl (Dulcolax). Castor oil works in a similar fashion.

Bulk producing laxatives increase the volume of the stool, and will both soften the stool and stimulate intestinal motility. Psyillium (Metamucil, Konsil) and methylcellulose (Citrucel) are examples of this type. The overall effect is similar to that of eating high-fiber foods, and this class of laxative is most suitable for regular use.

Docusate (Colace) is the only representative example of the stool softener class. It holds water within the fecal mass, providing a larger, softer stool. Docusate has no effect on acute **constipation**, since it must be present before the fecal mass forms to have any effect, but may

be useful for prevention of constipation in patients with recurrent problems, or those who are about to take a constipating drug, such as narcotic **analgesics**.

Mineral oil is an emollient laxative. It acts by retarding intestinal absorption of fecal water, thereby softening the stool.

The hyperosmotic laxatives are glycerin and lactulose (Chronulac, Duphalac), both of which act by holding water within the intestine. Lactulose may also increase peristaltic action of the intestine.

General use

Laxatives are used to treat constipation—the passage of small amounts of hard, dry stools, usually fewer than three times a week. Constipation may be caused by several conditions, some of which are potentially serious, and require medical attention:

- Neurologic—caused by failure of nerves to stimulate movement of the muscles of the intestines.
- Obstructive—failure of the muscles in the intestine to open, or presence of a mass that's blocking passage of the feces through the intestine.
- Endocrine/metabolic—caused by some diseases including hypothyroidism.
- Medicinal—caused by some drugs, including narcotic analgesics, iron, and some drugs used in **cancer** treatment.

Chronic constipation occurs in 1–4% of children between the ages of four and 10. If constipation continues, it should be treated by a physician.

A reasonable first step is to assure that there is enough fiber in the diet. This may be done by switching to a high fiber breakfast cereal. If this doesn't lead to improvement, then medical attention is necessary.

Precautions

Short term use of laxatives is generally safe except in **appendicitis**, fecal impaction, or intestinal obstruction. Lactulose is composed of two sugar molecules; galactose and fructose, and should not be administered to patients who require a low galactose diet.

Chronic use of laxatives may result in fluid and electrolyte imbalances, steatorrhea, osteomalacia, **diarrhea**, cathartic colon, and liver disease. Excessive intake of mineral oil may cause impaired absorption of oil soluble

KEY TERMS

Carbohydrates—Compounds, such as cellulose, sugar, and starch, that contain only carbon, hydrogen, and oxygen, and are a major part of the diets of people and other animals.

Cathartic colon—A poorly functioning colon, resulting from the chronic abuse of stimulant cathartics.

Colon—The part of the large intestine that extends from the cecum to the rectum. The sigmoid colon is the area of the intestine just above the rectum; linking the descending colon with the rectum. It is shaped like the letter S.

Diverticulitis—Inflammation of the diverticula (small outpouchings) along the wall of the colon, the large intestine.

Fiber—Carbohydrate material in food that cannot be digested.

Hyperosmotic—Hypertonic, containing a higher concentration of salts or other dissolved materials than normal tissues.

Osteomalacia—A bone disease that occurs in adults due to a prolonged period of vitamin D deficiency. It is characterized by softening of the bone and is sometimes referred to as adult rickets.

Steatorrhea—An excessive amount of fat in the feces due to poor fat absorption in the gastrointestinal tract.

Stool—The solid waste that is left after food is digested. Stool forms in the intestines and passes out of the body through the anus.

vitamins, particularly A and D. Excessive use of magnesium salts may cause hypermanesemia.

Side effects

Excessive use of laxatives may result in dependency on these products. This may cause a condition known as cathartic colon.

Excessive use of laxatives that contain sodium or magnesium may result in dangerously high blood levels of these elements.

Interactions

Mineral oil and docusate should not be used in combination. Docusate is an emulsifying agent which will increase the absorption of mineral oil.

Bisacodyl tablets are enteric coated, and so should not be used in combination with antacids. The antacids will cause premature rupture of the enteric coating.

Preventing side effects

Used properly, laxatives are very safe. Do not overuse or give in doses larger than those labeled. If constipation persists, obtain medical help.

Parental concerns

Laxatives should not be used too frequently. Bulk laxatives such as psyllium should be the normal first choice.

Mineral oil should not be given to infants or other children while laying down. This may result in the oil going into the lungs.

Resources

BOOKS

Beers, Mark H. and Robert Berkow, eds. *The Merck Manual of Diagnosis and Therapy, 17th ed.* Whitehouse Station, NJ: Merck and Company, Inc., 1999.

McAvoy, G., Miller J., Litvak K. *AHFS Drug Information 2004.* Amer. Soc Healthsys. Pharm, Bethesda 2004.

Siberry G.K., Iannone R. *The Harriet Lane Handbook 15th ed.* Mosby Publishing, Philadelphia, 2000.

PERIODICALS

Bell, EA, Wall, GC. "Pediatric constipation therapy using guidelines and polyethylene glycol 3350." *Ann Pharmacother.* 2004 Apr;38(4):686-93.

"Constipation, Laxatives and Dietary Fiber." *HealthTips* (April 1993): 9.

Griffin, GC, Roberts, SD, Graham, G. "How to resolve stool retention in a child. Underwear soiling is not a behavior problem." *Postgrad Med* 1999 Jan;105(1):159-61, 165-6, 172-3.

"Overuse Hazardous: Laxatives Rarely Needed." (Includes related article on types of laxatives.) *FDA Consumer* (April 1991): 33.

Patel, H, Law, A, Gouin, S. "Predictive factors for short-term symptom persistence in children after emergency department evaluation for constipation." *Arch Pediatr Adolesc Med.* 2000 Dec;154(12):1204-8.

ORGANIZATIONS

American Academy of Family Physicians 11400 Tomahawk Creek Parkway Leawood, KS 66211-2672.

WEB SITES

Constipation in Infants and Children: Evaluation and Treatment. American Academy of Pediatrics. <http://www.aap.org/policy/constipation.htm> (accessed February 15, 2005).

Section on Gastroenterology and Nutrition (SOGN). American Academy of Pediatrics. <http://www.aap.org/sections/gstrnut.htm> (accessed February 15, 2005).

Samuel Uretsky, PharmD

Lazy eye *see* **Amblyopia**

Lead poisoning

Definition

Lead **poisoning** occurs when a person swallows, absorbs, or inhales lead in any form. The result can be damaging to the brain, nerves, and many other parts of the body. Acute lead poisoning, which is somewhat rare, occurs when a relatively large amount of lead is taken into the body over a short period of time. Chronic lead poisoning is a common problem in children that occurs when small amounts of lead are ingested over a longer period. The Centers for Disease Control and Prevention (CDC) defines childhood lead poisoning as a whole-blood lead concentration equal to or greater than 10 micrograms/dL.

Description

Lead can damage almost every system in the human body, and it can also cause high blood pressure (**hypertension**). It is particularly harmful to the developing brain of fetuses and young children. The higher the level of lead in a child's blood and the longer this elevated level lasts, the greater the chance of ill effects. Over the long term, lead poisoning in a child can lead to learning disabilities, behavioral problems, and even **mental retardation**. At very high levels, lead poisoning can cause seizures, coma, and even death.

Many children with elevated blood levels are exposed to lead through peeling paint in older homes. Others are exposed through dust or soil that has been contaminated by old paint or past emissions of leaded gasoline. Since children between the ages of 12 and 36 months are apt to put things in their mouths, they are more likely than older children to take in lead. Pregnant women who come into contact with lead can pass it along to the fetus.

Over 80 percent of American homes built before 1978 have lead-based paint in them, according to the Centers for Disease Control and Prevention (CDC). The older the home, the more likely it is to contain lead paint, and the higher the concentration of lead in the paint is apt to be. Some homes also have lead in the water pipes or plumbing. Without knowing it, people may have lead in the paint, dust, or soil around their homes or in their drinking water, since lead cannot be seen, smelled, or tasted. Because lead does not break down naturally, it can continue to cause problems until it is removed.

Demographics

According to the Agency for Toxic Substances and Disease Registry, approximately one out of every six children in the United States has a high level of lead in the blood. According to the National Center for Environmental Health, there were about 200 deaths from lead poisoning in the United States between 1979 and 1998. Most of the deaths were among males (74%), African Americans (67%), adults over the age of 45 (76%), and Southerners (70%).

Causes and symptoms

Before scientists knew how harmful it could be, lead was widely used in paint, gasoline, water pipes, and many other products. In the early 2000s house paint is almost lead-free, gasoline is unleaded, and household plumbing is no longer made with lead materials. Still, remnants of the old hazards remain. Following are some sources of lead exposure:

- Lead-based paint: This is the most common source of exposure to large amounts of lead among preschoolers. Children may eat paint chips from older homes that have fallen into disrepair. They may also chew on painted surfaces such as windowsills. In addition, paint may be disturbed during remodeling.

- Dust and soil: These can be contaminated with lead from old paint or past emissions of leaded gasoline. In addition, pollution from operating or abandoned industrial sites and smelters can find its way into the soil, resulting in soil contamination.

- Drinking water: Exposure may come from lead water pipes, found in many homes built before 1930. Even newer copper pipes may have lead solder. Also, some new homes have brass faucets and fittings that can leach lead.

- Jobs and hobbies: A number of activities can expose participants to lead. These include making pottery or stained glass, refinishing furniture, doing home repairs,

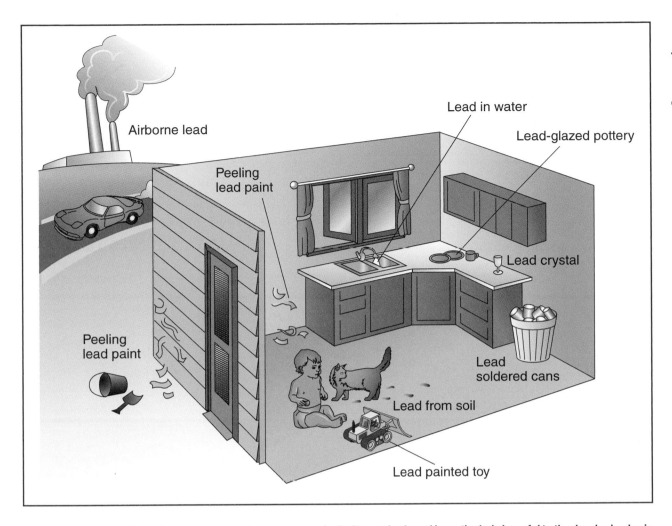

Airborne lead

Lead in water

Lead-glazed pottery

Peeling lead paint

Lead crystal

Peeling lead paint

Lead soldered cans

Lead from soil

Lead painted toy

Continuous exposure to lead can damage nearly every system in the human body and is particularly harmful to the developing brain of fetuses and young children. Common sources of lead exposure include lead-based paint, dust and soil, drinking water, food from cans, and eating utensils, such as plates and drinking glasses, that are lead-based. *(Illustration by Electronic Illustrators Group.)*

and using indoor firing ranges. When adults take part in such activities, they may inadvertently expose children to lead residue that is on their clothing or on scrap materials.

• Food: Imported food cans often have lead solder. Lead may also be found in leaded crystal glassware and some imported ceramic or old ceramic dishes (e.g., ceramic dishes from Mexico). A 2003 study of cases of lead poisoning in pregnant women found that 70 percent of affected people were Hispanics, most of whom had absorbed the lead from their pottery. In addition, food may be contaminated by lead in the water or soil.

• Folk medicines: Certain folk medicines (for example, alarcon, alkohl, azarcon, bali goli, coral, ghasard, greta, liga, pay-loo-ah, and rueda) and traditional cosmetics (kohl, for example) contain high concentrations of lead.

• Moonshine whiskey: Lead poisoning from drinking illegally distilled liquor is still a cause of death among adults in the southern United States.

• Gunshot **wounds**: Toxic amounts of lead can be absorbed from bullets or bullet fragments that remain in the body after emergency surgery.

Evidence as of 2004 suggested that lead may be harmful to children even at low levels that were once thought to be safe, and the risk of damage rises as blood levels of lead increase. The symptoms of chronic lead poisoning take time to develop, however. Children can appear healthy despite having high levels of lead in their blood. Over time, though, problems such as the following may arise:

• learning disabilities

• hyperactivity

- mental retardation
- slowed growth
- hearing loss
- headaches

It is also known that certain genetic factors increase the harmful effects of lead poisoning in susceptible children; however, these factors are not completely understood.

Lead poisoning is also harmful to adults, in whom it can cause high blood pressure, digestive problems, nerve disorders, memory loss, and muscle and joint **pain**. In addition, it can lead to difficulties during pregnancy, as well as cause reproductive problems in both men and women.

In the early 2000s, chronic exposure to lead in the environment has been found to speed up the progression of kidney disorders in people without diabetes.

Acute lead poisoning

Acute lead poisoning, while less common, shows up more quickly and can be fatal. Symptoms such as the following may occur:

- severe abdominal pain
- diarrhea
- nausea and vomiting
- weakness of the limbs
- seizures
- coma

When to call the doctor

The CDC recommends testing all children at 12 months of age and, if possible, again at 24 months. Testing should start at six months for children at risk for lead poisoning.

Diagnosis

A high level of lead in the blood can be detected with a simple blood test. In fact, testing is the only way to know for sure if children without symptoms have been exposed to lead, since they can appear healthy even as long-term damage occurs. Based on test results and a child's risk factors, the doctor will then decide whether further testing is needed and how often. In some states, more frequent testing is required by law.

Children at risk

Children with an increased risk of lead poisoning include those for whom the following is true:

- They live in or regularly visit a house built before 1978 in which chipped or peeling paint is present.
- They live in or regularly visit a house that was built before 1978 where remodeling is planned or underway.
- They have a brother or sister, housemate, or playmate who has been diagnosed with lead poisoning.
- They have the habit of eating dirt or have been diagnosed with pica.
- They live with an adult whose job or hobby involves exposure to lead.
- They live near an active lead smelter, battery-recycling plant, or other industry that can create lead pollution.

Adults at risk

Testing is also important for adults whose job or hobby puts them at risk for lead poisoning. This need applies to people who take part in the following activities:

- glazed pottery or stained glass production
- furniture refinishing
- home renovation
- target shooting at indoor firing ranges
- battery reclamation
- precious metal refining
- radiator repair
- art restoration

Treatment

The first step in treating lead poisoning is to avoid further contact with lead. For adults, this usually means making changes at work or in hobbies. For children, it means that parents and guardians need to find and remove sources of lead in the home. In most states, the public health department can help assess the home and identify lead sources.

If the problem is lead paint, a professional with special training should remove it. Removal of lead paint is not a do-it-yourself project. Scraping or sanding lead paint creates large amounts of dust that can poison people in the home. This dust can stay around long after the work is completed. In addition, heating lead paint can release lead into the air. For these reasons, lead paint should only be removed by someone who knows how to do the job safely

KEY TERMS

Chelation therapy—A treatment using chelating agents, compounds that surround and bind to target substances allowing them to be excreted from the body.

Dimercaprol—A chemical agent used to remove excess lead from the body.

Edetate calcium disodium—A chemical chelating agent used to remove excess lead from the body.

Penicillamine (Cuprimine, Depen)—A drug used to treat medical problems (such as excess copper in the body and rheumatoid arthritis) and to prevent kidney stones. It is also sometimes prescribed to remove excess lead from the body.

Pica—A desire that sometimes arises in pregnancy to eat nonfood substances, such as dirt or clay.

Succimer—A chelating agent that is used to remove excess lead from the body. Sold under the trade name Chemet.

and has the equipment to clean up thoroughly. Occupants, especially children and pregnant women, should leave the home until the cleanup is finished.

Medical professionals should take all necessary steps to remove bullets or bullet fragments from people with gunshot injuries.

If blood levels of lead are high enough, the doctor may also prescribe chelation therapy. This refers to treatment with chemicals that bind to the lead and help the body pass it in urine at a faster rate. There are four chemical agents that may be used for this purpose, either alone or in combination. Edetate calcium disodium (EDTA calcium) and dimercaprol (BAL) are given through an intravenous line or in shots, while succimer (Chemet) and penicillamine (Cuprimine, Depen) are taken by mouth. (Although many doctors prescribe penicillamine for lead poisoning, this use of the drug has not been approved by the Food and Drug Administration.)

Changes in diet are no substitute for medical treatment. However, getting enough calcium, zinc, and protein may help reduce the amount of lead the body absorbs. Iron is also important, since people who are deficient in this nutrient absorb more lead. Garlic and thiamine, a B-complex vitamin, have been used to treat lead poisoning in animals. However, their usefulness in humans for this purpose has not as of 2004 been demonstrated. Nutritional, botanical, and homeopathic medicines can be administered once the source is removed to help correct any imbalances brought on by lead toxicity.

Prognosis

If acute lead poisoning reaches the stage of seizures and coma, there is a high risk of death. Even if the person survives, there is a good chance of permanent brain damage. The long-term effects of lower levels of lead can also be permanent and severe. However, if chronic lead poisoning is caught early, these negative effects can be limited by reducing future exposure to lead and getting proper medical treatment.

Prevention

Many cases of lead poisoning can be prevented. The following steps can help:

- Keep the areas where children **play** as clean and dust-free as possible.

- Wash pacifiers and bottles when they fall to the floor and wash stuffed animals and **toys** often.

- Make sure children wash their hands before meals and at bedtime.

- Mop floors and wipe windowsills and other chewable surfaces, such as cribs, twice a week with a solution of powdered dishwasher detergent in warm water.

- Plant bushes next to an older home with painted exterior walls to keep children at a distance.

- Plant grass or another ground cover in soil that is likely to be contaminated, such as soil around a home built before 1960 or located near a major highway.

- Have household tap water tested to find out if it contains lead.

- Use only water from the cold-water tap for drinking, cooking, and making baby formula, since hot water is likely to contain higher levels of lead.

- If the cold water has not been used for six hours or more, run it for several seconds, until it becomes as cold as it will get, before using it for drinking or cooking. The more time water has been sitting in the pipes, the more lead it may contain.

- Do not store food in open cans, especially imported cans.

- Do not store or serve food in pottery meant for decorative use.

- People who work with lead in a job or hobby should change their clothes before they go home.

Nutritional concerns

Avoid preparing or serving food in containers that have lead in their glazing. Do not consume homemade liquor that has been distilled.

Parental concerns

Lead tastes sweet. Parents living in homes built prior to 1978 should be vigilant regarding removing all flaking or peeling paint. Simply re-painting such surfaces will not resolve the problem. Parents must monitor the environments in which their children play and the objects that go into their children's mouths. Cleanliness is a must if old paint is in a child's environment. Removal (stripping paint to bare metal or bare wood) of lead is the best way to prevent lead exposure in children.

Resources

BOOKS

Goto, Collin S. "Heavy Metal Intoxication." In *Nelson Textbook of Pediatrics*, 17th ed. Edited by Richard E. Behrman, et al. Philadelphia: Saunders, 2003, pp. 2355–7.

Gupta, S. K., et al. *Emergency Toxicology: Management of Common Poisons*. Boca Raton, FL: CRC Press, 2003.

Klaasen, Curtis D., and John Doull. *Casarett and Doull's Toxicology: The Basic Science of Poisons*, 6th ed. New York: McGraw Hill, 2001.

Markowitz, Morrie. "Lead Poisoning." In *Nelson Textbook of Pediatrics*, 17th ed. Edited by Richard E. Behrman, et al. Philadelphia: Saunders, 2003, pp. 2358–61.

PERIODICALS

Clark, S., et al. "The influence of exterior dust and soil lead on interior dust lead levels in housing that had undergone lead-based paint hazard control." *Journal of Occupational and Environmental Hygiene* 1, no. 5 (2004): 273–82.

Dietert, R. R., et al. "Developmental immunotoxicology of lead." *Toxicology and Applied Pharmacology* 198, no. 2 (2004): 86–94.

Dorea, J. G. "Mercury and lead during breast-feeding." *British Journal of Nutrition* 92, no. 1 (2004): 21–40.

Kwong W. T., et al. "Interactions between iron deficiency and lead poisoning: epidemiology and pathogenesis." *Science of the Total Environment* 330, no. 1–3 (2004): 21–37.

Sandel, M., et al. "The effects of housing interventions on child health." *Pediatric Annals* 33, no. 7 (2004): 474–81.

Stretesky, P. B., and M. J. Lynch. "The relationship between lead and crime." *Journal of Health and Social Behavior* 45, no. 2 (2004): 214–29.

ORGANIZATIONS

American Academy of Clinical Toxicology. 777 East Park Drive, PO Box 8820, Harrisburg, PA 17105–8820. Web site: <www.clintox.org/index.html>.

American Academy of Family Physicians. 11400 Tomahawk Creek Parkway, Leawood, KS 66211–2672. Web site: <www.aafp.org/>.

American Academy of Pediatrics. 141 Northwest Point Boulevard, Elk Grove Village, IL 60007–1098. Web site: <www.aap.org/default.htm>.

American Association of Poison Control Centers. 3201 New Mexico Avenue NW, Washington, DC 20016. Web site: <www.aapcc.org/>.

American College of Occupational and Environmental Medicine. 55 West Seegers Road, Arlington Heights, IL 60005. Web site: <www.acoem.org/>.

WEB SITES

"CDC Childhood Lead Poisoning Prevention Program: Spotlight on Lead." *Centers for Disease Control and Prevention.* Available online at <www.cdc.gov/nceh/lead/lead.htm> and <www.cdc.gov/nceh/lead/factsheets/leadfcts.htm> (accessed November 11, 2004).

"Lead-based Paint Hazard Control Grant Program." *U.S. Department of Housing and Urban Development.* Available online at <www.hud.gov/offices/lead/> (accessed November 11, 2004).

"Lead in Paint, Dust, and Soil." *U.S. Environmental Protection Agency.* Available online at <www.epa.gov/lead/> (accessed November 11, 2004).

"Lead Poisoning." *National Library of Medicine.* Available online at <www.nlm.nih.gov/medlineplus/leadpoisoning.html> (accessed November 11, 2004).

"Occupational Lead Poisoning." *American Academy of Family Physicians.* Available online at <www.aafp.org/afp/980215ap/stauding.html> (accessed November 11, 2004).

L. Fleming Fallon, Jr., MD, DrPH

Learning disorders

Definition

Learning disorders are academic difficulties experienced by children and adults of average to above-average **intelligence**. People with learning disorders have difficulty with reading, writing, mathematics, or a combination of the three. These difficulties significantly interfere with academic achievement or daily living.

Description

Children with learning disorders, or disabilities, have specific impairments in acquiring, retaining, and processing information. Standardized tests place them well below their IQ range in their area of difficulty. The five main types of learning disorders are reading disorders, mathematics disorders, disorders of written expression, disorders of **fine motor skills**, and information processing disorders.

Reading disorders

Reading disorders are the most common type of learning disorder. Children with reading disorders have difficulty recognizing and interpreting letters and words (**dyslexia**). They are unable to recognize and decode the sounds and syllables (phonetic structure) behind written words and language in general. This condition lowers accuracy and comprehension in reading.

Mathematics disorders

Children with mathematics disorders (dyscalculia) have problems recognizing and counting numbers correctly. They have difficulty using numbers in everyday settings. Mathematics disorders are typically diagnosed in the first few years of elementary school when formal teaching of numbers and basic math concepts begins. Children with mathematics disorders usually have a co-existing reading disorder, a disorder of written expression, or both.

Disorders of written expression

Disorders of written expression typically occur in combination with reading disorders or mathematics disorders or both. The condition is characterized by difficulty with written compositions (dysgraphia). Children with this type of learning disorder have problems with spelling, punctuation, grammar, and organizing their thoughts in writing.

Disorders of fine motor skills

Children with motor skill disorders (dyspraxia) have coordination problems and may have difficulty with handwriting tasks and speech patterns. Dyspraxia tends to affect boys more than girls.

Information processing disorders

Information processing disorders often occur along with other types of learning disorders. Children with this problem have difficulty processing the sensory input they receive, specifically sight and sound information. They can see and hear adequately, but they have difficulty distinguishing between different visual cues and auditory signals, and may have problems understanding spatial relationships and sequencing the sights and sounds they observe.

Demographics

Learning disorders affect approximately two million children between the ages of six and 17 (5 percent of public school children), although some experts think the figure may be as high as 15 percent. The male to female ratio for learning disorders is about five to one.

Causes and symptoms

Learning disorders are thought to be caused by neurological abnormalities or differences that trigger impairments in the regions of the brain that control visual and language processing and attention and planning. These traits may be genetically linked. Children from families with a history of learning disorders are more likely to develop disorders themselves. In 2003, a team of Finnish researchers reported finding a candidate gene for developmental dyslexia on human chromosome 15q21.

Learning difficulties may also be caused by such medical conditions as a traumatic brain injury or brain infections such as **encephalitis** or **meningitis**.

The defining symptom of a learning disorder is academic performance that is markedly below a child's age and grade capabilities and measured IQ. Children with a reading disorder may confuse or transpose words or letters and omit or add syllables to words. The written homework of children with disorders of written expression is filled with grammatical, spelling, punctuation, and organizational errors. The child's handwriting is often extremely poor. Children with mathematical disorders are often unable to count in the correct sequence, to name numbers, and to understand numerical concepts.

When to call the doctor

A child thought to have a learning disorder should undergo a complete medical examination to rule out an organic cause of the problem. This may include an eye exam by an ophthalmologist, a psychological exam by a psychologist, and an exam by an otolaryngologist (an ear, nose, and throat doctor, or ENT).

Diagnosis

Problems with vision or hearing, mental disorders (depression, **attention-deficit/hyperactivity disorder**), **mental retardation**, cultural and language differences, and inadequate teaching may be mistaken for learning disorders or may complicate a diagnosis. A comprehensive medical, psychological, and educational **assessment** is critical to making a correct diagnosis.

A psychoeducational assessment should be performed by a psychologist, psychiatrist, neurologist, neuropsychologist, or learning specialist. A complete medical, **family**, social, and educational history is compiled from existing medical and school records and from interviews with the child and the child's parents and teachers. A series of written and verbal tests are then given to the child to evaluate his or her cognitive and intellectual functioning. Commonly used tests include the Wechsler Intelligence Scale for Children (WISC-III), the Woodcock-Johnson Psychoeducational Battery, the Peabody Individual Achievement Test-Revised (PIAT-R) and the California Verbal Learning Test (CVLT). Federal legislation mandates that this testing is free of charge within the public school system.

Treatment

Once a learning disorder has been diagnosed, an individual education plan (IEP) is developed for the child in question. IEPs are based on psychoeducational test findings. They provide for annual retesting to measure a child's progress. Learning-disordered students may receive special instruction within a regular general education class or they may be taught in a **special education** or learning center for a portion of the day.

Common strategies for the treatment of reading disorders focus first on improving a child's recognition of the sounds of letters and language through phonics training. Later strategies focus on comprehension, retention, and study skills. Students with disorders of written expression are often encouraged to keep journals and to write with a computer keyboard instead of a pencil. Instruction for students with mathematical disorders emphasizes real-world uses of arithmetic, such as balancing a checkbook or comparing prices.

Prognosis

The high school dropout rate for children with learning disabilities is almost 40 percent. Children with learning disabilities that go undiagnosed or are improperly treated may never achieve functional literacy. They often develop serious behavior problems as a result of

Common strategies for the treatment of reading disorders focus first on improving a child's recognition of the sounds of letters and language through phonics training. (© Robert Maass/Corbis.)

their frustration with school. In addition, their learning problems are often stressful for other family members and may strain family relationships. The key to helping these students reach their fullest potential is early detection and the implementation of an appropriate individualized education plan (IEP). The prognosis is good for a large percentage of children with reading disorders that are identified and treated early. Learning disorders typically persist into adulthood, but with proper educational and vocational training, an individual can complete college and pursue a challenging career. Studies of the occupational choices of adults with dyslexia indicate that they do particularly well in people-oriented professions and occupations, such as nursing or sales.

Prevention

Some studies have indicated that one-on-one tutoring of children at risk for developing learning disorders

KEY TERMS

Dyslexia—A type of reading disorder often characterized by reversal of letters or words.

IEP—Individualized Education Plan. Under federal law governing special education, every child in public schools who is determined through assessment to have special mental disability needs has an IEP. An IEP is typically developed by a team of professionals that may include special education teachers, physical, occupational and speech therapists, psychologists, parents or guardians, and others who may be called on to provide expertise. The team meets at least once a year to set goals for the next school year and to assess progress on already established goals. Parents who are not satisfied with school-based assessments have the right to ask for independent assessments that must be paid for by the school system.

IQ—Intelligence quotient, a measure of intellectual functioning determined by performance on standardized intelligence tests. It is usually calculated by dividing an individual's mental age (determined by testing) by his/her chronological age and multiplying that result by 100.

Phonics—A system to teach reading by teaching the speech sounds associated with single letters, letter combinations, and syllables.

may be effective in preventing later reading and writing problems.

Parental concerns

Parents of children with learning disorders should stay in close contact with educators and school administrators to ensure that their child's IEP undergoes a regular review and continues to provide the maximum educational benefit for their child.

Resources

BOOKS

American Psychiatric Association. *Diagnostic and Statistical Manual of Mental Disorders.* 4th edition, text revision (DSM-IV-TR). Washington, DC: American Psychiatric Press, Inc., 2000.

Marshall, Abagail. *The Everything Parent's Guide To Children With Dyslexia: All You Need To Ensure Your Child's Success.* Adams Media, 2004.

PERIODICALS

Gillberg, C., and H. Soderstrom. "Learning Disability." *Lancet* 362 (September 6, 2003): 811–821.

Taipale, M., N. Kaminen, J. Nopola-Hemmi, et al. "A Candidate Gene for Developmental Dyslexia Encodes a Nuclear Tetratricopeptide Repeat Domain Protein Dynamically Regulated in Brain." *Proceedings of the National Academy of Sciences in the USA* 100 (September 30, 2003): 11553–11558.

Witt, W. P., A. W. Riley, and M. J. Coiro. "Childhood Functional Status, Family Stressors, and Psychosocial Adjustment Among School-Aged Children with Disabilities in the United States." *Archives of Pediatric and Adolescent Medicine* 157 (July 2003): 687–695.

ORGANIZATIONS

Learning Disabilities Association of America. 4156 Library Road, Pittsburg, PA 15234. (412) 341–1515. Web site: <www.ldanatl.org>.

National Center for Learning Disabilities (NCLD). 381 Park Avenue South, Suite 1401, New York, NY 10016. (410) 296–0232. Web site: <www.ncld.org>.

WEB SITES

The Interactive Guide to Learning Disabilities for Parents, Teachers, and Children. Available online at: <www.ldonline.org>.

LD Online Page. Available online at: <www.ldonline.org>.

Paula Ford-Martin
Rebecca J. Frey, PhD

Left-handedness *see* **Handedness**

Legg-Calé-Perthes disease *see* **Osteochondroses**

Lesbian issues *see* **Homosexuality and bisexuality**

Leukemias, acute

Definition

Leukemia is a **cancer** that starts in the organs that make blood, namely the bone marrow and the lymph system. Depending on their characteristics, leukemias can be divided into two broad types. Acute leukemias are the rapidly progressing leukemias, while the **chronic leukemias** progress more slowly. The vast majority of the childhood leukemias are of the acute form.

Description

The cells that make up blood are produced in the bone marrow and the lymph system. The bone marrow is the spongy tissue found in the large bones of the body. The lymph system includes the spleen (an organ in the upper abdomen), the thymus (a small organ beneath the breastbone), and the tonsils (an organ in the throat). In addition, the lymph vessels (tiny tubes that branch like blood vessels into all parts of the body) and lymph nodes (pea-shaped organs that are found along the network of lymph vessels) are also part of the lymph system. Lymph is a milky fluid that contains cells. Clusters of lymph nodes are found in the neck, underarm, pelvis, abdomen, and chest.

Blood is made up of red blood cells (RBCs), which carry oxygen and other materials to all tissues of the body; white blood cells (WBCs), which fight infection; and platelets, which play a part in the clotting of the blood. The white blood cells can be further subdivided into three main types: granulocytes, monocytes, and lymphocytes.

The granulocytes, as their name suggests, contain particles (granules). These granules contain special proteins (enzymes) and several other substances that can break down chemicals and destroy microorganisms, such as bacteria. Monocytes are the second type of white blood cell. They are also important in defending the body against pathogens.

The lymphocytes form the third type of white blood cell. There are two main types of lymphocytes: T lymphocytes and B lymphocytes. They have different functions within the immune system. The B cells protect the body by making antibodies, which are proteins that can attach to the surfaces of bacteria and viruses. This attachment sends signals to many other cell types to come and destroy the antibody-coated organism. The T cells protect the body against viruses. When a virus enters a cell, it produces certain proteins that are projected onto the surface of the infected cell. The T cells recognize these proteins and make certain chemicals that are capable of destroying the virus-infected cells. In addition, the T cells can destroy some types of cancer cells.

The bone marrow makes stem cells, which are the precursors of the different blood cells. These stem cells mature through stages into RBCs, WBCs, or platelets. In acute leukemias, the maturation process of the white blood cells is interrupted. The immature cells (blasts) proliferate rapidly and begin to accumulate in various organs and tissues, thereby affecting their normal function. This uncontrolled proliferation of the immature cells in the bone marrow affects the production of the normal red blood cells and platelets as well.

Acute leukemias are of two types: acute lymphocytic leukemia and acute myelogenous leukemia. Different types of white blood cells are involved in the two leukemias. In acute lymphocytic leukemia (ALL), it is the T or the B lymphocytes that become cancerous. The B cell leukemias are more common than T cell leukemias. Acute myelogenous leukemia, also known as acute non-lymphocytic leukemia (ANLL), is a cancer of the monocytes and/or granulocytes.

Demographics

Leukemias account for 2 percent of all cancers. Because leukemia is the most common form of childhood cancer, it is often regarded as a disease of childhood. However, leukemias affect nine times as many adults as children. Half of the cases occur in people who are 60 years of age or older. The incidence of acute and chronic leukemias is about the same.

Leukemia strikes both sexes and all ages. The human T-cell leukemia virus (HTLV-I) is believed to be the causative agent for some kinds of leukemias. However, as of 2004, the cause of most leukemias is not known. Acute lymphoid leukemia (ALL) is more common among Caucasians than among African-Americans, while acute myeloid leukemia (AML) affects both races equally. The incidence of acute leukemia is slightly higher among men than women. People with Jewish ancestry have a higher likelihood of getting leukemia. A higher incidence of leukemia has also been observed among persons with **Down syndrome** and some other genetic abnormalities.

Causes and symptoms

Exposure to ionizing radiation and to certain organic chemicals, such as benzene, is believed to increase the risk of developing leukemia. Having a history of diseases that damage the bone marrow, such as aplastic anemia, or a history of cancers of the lymphatic system puts people at a high risk for developing acute leukemias. Similarly, the use of anticancer medications, immunosuppressants, and the antibiotic chloramphenicol are also considered risk factors for developing acute leukemias.

The symptoms of leukemia are generally vague and non-specific. A patient may experience all or some of the following symptoms:

• weakness or chronic fatigue

• fever of unknown origin

- weight loss that is not due to dieting or exercise
- frequent bacterial or viral infections
- headaches
- skin rash
- non-specific bone pain
- easy bruising
- bleeding from gums or nose
- blood in urine or stools
- enlarged lymph nodes and/or spleen
- abdominal fullness

Diagnosis

Like all cancers, acute leukemias are most successfully treated when found early. There were as of 2004 no screening tests available.

If the doctor has reason to suspect leukemia, he or she will conduct a very thorough physical examination to look for enlarged lymph nodes in the neck, underarm, and pelvic region. Swollen gums, enlarged liver or spleen, **bruises**, or pinpoint red **rashes** all over the body are some of the signs of leukemia. Urine and blood tests may be ordered to check for microscopic amounts of blood in the urine and to obtain a complete differential blood count. This count gives the numbers and percentages of the different cells found in the blood. An abnormal blood test might suggest leukemia; however, the diagnosis has to be confirmed by more specific tests.

The doctor may perform a bone marrow biopsy to confirm the diagnosis of leukemia. During the biopsy, a cylindrical piece of bone and marrow is removed. The tissue is generally taken out of the hipbone. These samples are sent to the laboratory for examination. In addition to diagnosis, the biopsy is also repeated during the treatment phase of the disease to see if the leukemia is responding to therapy.

A spinal tap (lumbar puncture) is another procedure that the doctor may order to diagnose leukemia. In this procedure, a small needle is inserted into the spinal cavity in the lower back to withdraw some cerebrospinal fluid and to look for leukemic cells.

Standard imaging tests, such as x rays, **computed tomography** scans (CT scans), and **magnetic resonance imaging** (MRI) may be used to check whether the leukemic cells have invaded other areas of the body, such as the bones, chest, kidneys, abdomen, or brain. A gallium scan or bone scan is a test in which a radioactive chemical is injected into the body. This

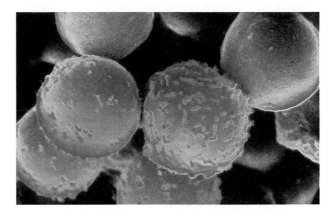

An enhanced transmission electron microscopy (TEM) image of white blood cells from a patient with acute myelogenous leukemia cells. (© Professor Aaron Polliack, Science Source/Photo Researchers, Inc.)

chemical accumulates in the areas of cancer or infection, allowing them to be viewed with a special camera.

Treatment

There are two phases of treatment for leukemia. The first phase is called induction therapy. As the name suggests, during this phase, the main aim of the treatment is to reduce the number of leukemic cells as far as possible and induce a remission in the patient. Once the patient shows no obvious signs of leukemia (no leukemic cells are detected in blood tests and bone marrow biopsies), the patient is said to be in remission. The second phase of treatment is then initiated. This is called continuation or maintenance therapy, and the aim in this case is to kill any remaining cells and to maintain the remission for as long as possible.

Chemotherapy is the use of drugs to kill cancer cells. It is usually the treatment of choice and is used to relieve symptoms and achieve long-term remission of the disease. Generally, combination chemotherapy, in which multiple drugs are used, is more efficient than using a single drug for the treatment. Some drugs may be administered intravenously (through a vein) in the arm; others may be given by mouth in the form of pills. If the cancer cells have invaded the brain, then chemotherapeutic drugs may be put into the fluid that surrounds the brain through a needle in the brain or back. This is known as intrathecal chemotherapy.

Because leukemia cells can spread to all the organs via the blood stream and the lymph vessels, surgery is not considered an option for treating leukemias.

KEY TERMS

Antibody—A special protein made by the body's immune system as a defense against foreign material (bacteria, viruses, etc.) that enters the body. It is uniquely designed to attack and neutralize the specific antigen that triggered the immune response.

Biopsy—The surgical removal and microscopic examination of living tissue for diagnostic purposes or to follow the course of a disease. Most commonly the term refers to the collection and analysis of tissue from a suspected tumor to establish malignancy.

Chemotherapy—Any treatment of an illness with chemical agents. The term is usually used to describe the treatment of cancer with drugs that inhibit cancer growth or destroy cancer cells.

Computed tomography (CT)—An imaging technique in which cross-sectional x rays of the body are compiled to create a three-dimensional image of the body's internal structures; also called computed axial tomography.

Cytokines— Chemicals made by the cells that act on other cells to stimulate or inhibit their function. They are important controllers of immune functions.

Immunotherapy—A mode of cancer treatment in which the immune system is stimulated to fight the cancer.

Lumbar puncture—A procedure in which the doctor inserts a small needle into the spinal cavity in the lower back to withdraw spinal fluid for testing. Also known as a spinal tap.

Magnetic resonance imaging (MRI)—An imaging technique that uses a large circular magnet and radio waves to generate signals from atoms in the body. These signals are used to construct detailed images of internal body structures and organs, including the brain.

Maturation—The process by which stem cells transform from immature cells without a specific function into a particular type of blood cell with defined functions.

Radiation therapy—A cancer treatment that uses high-energy rays or particles to kill or weaken cancer cells. Radiation may be delivered externally or internally via surgically implanted pellets. Also called radiotherapy.

Remission—A disappearance of a disease and its symptoms. Complete remission means that all disease is gone. Partial remission means that the disease is significantly improved, but residual traces of the disease are still present. A remission may be due to treatment or may be spontaneous.

Radiation therapy, which involves the use of x-rays or other high-energy rays to kill cancer cells and shrink tumors, may be used in some cases. For acute leukemias, the source of radiation is usually outside the body (external radiation therapy). If the leukemic cells have spread to the brain, radiation therapy can be given to the brain.

Bone marrow transplantation is a process in which the patient's diseased bone marrow is replaced with healthy marrow. There are two ways of doing a bone marrow transplant. In an allogeneic bone marrow transplant, healthy marrow is taken from a donor whose tissue is either the same as or very closely resembles the patient's tissues. The donor may be a twin, a sibling, or a person who is not related at all. First, the patient's bone marrow is destroyed with very high doses of chemotherapy and radiation therapy. Healthy marrow from the donor is then given to the patient through a needle in a vein to replace the destroyed marrow.

In the second type of bone marrow transplant, called an autologous bone marrow transplant, some of the patient's own marrow is taken out and treated with a combination of anticancer drugs to kill all the abnormal cells. This marrow is then frozen and saved. The marrow remaining in the patient's body is destroyed with high-dose chemotherapy and radiation therapy. The marrow that was frozen is then thawed and given back to the patient through a needle in a vein. This mode of bone marrow transplant is in the early 2000s being investigated in clinical trials.

Biological therapy or immunotherapy is a mode of treatment in which the body's own immune system is harnessed to fight the cancer. Substances that are routinely made by the immune system (such as growth factors, hormones, and disease-fighting proteins) are either synthetically made in a laboratory or their effectiveness is boosted and they are then put back into the patient's body. This treatment mode is also being investigated in the early 2000s in clinical trials all over the United States at major cancer centers.

Prognosis

Like all cancers, the prognosis for leukemia depends on the patient's age and general health. According to statistics, more than 60 percent of the patients with leukemia survive for at least a year after diagnosis. Acute myelocytic leukemia (AML) has a poorer prognosis rate than acute lymphocytic leukemias (ALL) and the chronic leukemias. Between 1985 and 2004, the five-year survival rate for patients with ALL increased from 38 to 57 percent.

Interestingly enough, since most childhood leukemias are of the ALL type, chemotherapy has been highly successful in their treatment. This is because chemotherapeutic drugs are most effective against actively growing cells. Due to the new combinations of anticancer drugs being used, the survival rates among children with ALL have improved dramatically. Eighty percent of the children diagnosed with ALL as of 2004 survive for five years or more, as compared to 50 percent in the late 1970s.

Prevention

Most cancers can be prevented by changes in lifestyle or diet, which will reduce the risk factors. However, in leukemias, there are as of 2004 no such known risk factors. Therefore, as of 2004, no way is known to prevent leukemias from developing. People who are at an increased risk for developing leukemia because of proven exposure to ionizing radiation or exposure to the toxic liquid benzene, and people with Down syndrome, should undergo periodic medical checkups.

Parental concerns

Parents of a child with leukemia must balance their own fears for their child's health with the child's fears and worries. Also, given the large financial burden leukemia treatment entails, parents will want to make sure they are aware of what and what is not covered by their insurance. Parents can find a variety of sources, written and online, that will help them deal with the new circumstances of themselves and their **family**.

Resources

Campana, Dario, and Ching-Hon Pui. "Childhood Leukemia." In *Clinical Oncology.* Edited by Martin D. Abeloff. London: Churchill Livingstone, 2000.

Thompson, George H. "The Neck." In *Nelson Textbook of Pediatrics.* Edited by Richard E. Behrman et al. Philadelphia: Saunders, 2004.

Tubergen, David G., and Archie Bleyer. "The Leukemias." In *Nelson Textbook of Pediatrics.* Edited by Richard E. Behrman et al. Philadelphia: Saunders, 2004.

ORGANIZATIONS

American Cancer Society. 1599 Clifton Rd., NE, Atlanta, GA 30329–4251. Web site: <www.cancer.org>.

Cancer Research Institute. 681 Fifth Ave., New York, NY 10022. Web site: <www.cancerresearch.org>.

Leukemia Society of America Inc. 600 Third Ave., New York, NY 10016. Web site: <www.leukemia.org>.

National Cancer Institute. Building 31, Room 10A31, 31 Center Drive, MSC 2580, Bethesda, MD 20892–2580. <www.nci.nih.gov>.

Lata Cherath, PhD
Rosalyn Carson-DeWitt, MD

Leukemias, chronic

Definition

Chronic leukemia is a disease in which abnormal, cancerous white blood cells are made in the bone marrow. Depending on the type of white blood cell that is involved, chronic leukemia can be classified as chronic lymphocytic leukemia or chronic myeloid leukemia.

Description

Chronic leukemia is a **cancer** that starts in the blood cells made in the bone marrow. The bone marrow is the spongy tissue found in the large bones of the body. The bone marrow makes precursor cells called blasts or stem cells, which mature into different types of blood cells. Unlike **acute leukemias**, in which the process of maturation of the blast cells is interrupted, in chronic leukemias, the cells do mature and only a few remain as immature cells. However, even though the cells appear normal, they do not function as normal cells.

Bone marrow produces different types of cells: red blood cells (RBCs), which carry oxygen and other materials to all tissues of the body; white blood cells (WBCs), which fight infection; and platelets, which play a part in the clotting of the blood. The white blood cells can be further subdivided into three main types: the granulocytes, monocytes, and the lymphocytes.

The granulocytes, as their name suggests, contain granules (particles). These granules contain special proteins (enzymes) and several other substances that can break down chemicals and destroy microorganisms such as bacteria.

Monocytes are the second type of white blood cell. They are also important in defending the body against pathogens.

The lymphocytes form the third type of white blood cell. There are two main types of lymphocytes: T lymphocytes and B lymphocytes. They have different functions within the immune system. The B cells protect the body by making antibodies, which are proteins that can attach to the surfaces of bacteria and viruses. This attachment sends signals to many other cell types to come and destroy the antibody-coated organism. The T cell protects the body against viruses. When a virus enters a cell, it produces certain proteins that are projected onto the surface of the infected cell. The T cells can recognize these proteins and produce certain chemicals (cytokines) that are capable of destroying the virus-infected cells. In addition, the T cells can destroy some types of cancer cells.

Chronic leukemias develop very gradually. The abnormal lymphocytes multiply slowly, but in a poorly regulated manner. They live much longer and thus their numbers build up in the body. The two types of chronic leukemias can be easily distinguished under the microscope. Chronic lymphocytic leukemia (CLL) involves the T or B lymphocytes. B cell abnormalities are more common than T cell abnormalities. T cells are affected in only 5 percent of the patients. The T and B lymphocytes can be differentiated from the other types of white blood cells based on their size and by the absence of granules inside them. In chronic myelogenous leukemia (CML), the cells that are affected are the granulocytes.

Chronic lymphocytic leukemia (CLL) often has no symptoms at first and may remain undetected for a long time. Chronic myelogenous leukemia (CML), by contrast, may progress to a more acute form.

Demographics

Chronic leukemias account for 1.2 percent of all cancers. Because leukemia is the most common form of childhood cancer, it is often regarded as a disease of childhood. However, leukemias affect nine times as many adults as children. In chronic lymphoid leukemia, 90 percent of the cases are seen in people who are 50 years or older, with the average age at diagnosis being 65. The incidence of the disease increases with age. It is almost never seen in children. Chronic myeloid leukemias are generally seen in people in their mid-40s. In addition, it accounts for about 4 percent of childhood leukemia cases.

Causes and symptoms

Leukemia strikes both sexes and all ages. Although the cause is unknown, chronic leukemia is linked to genetic abnormalities and environmental factors. For example, exposure to ionizing radiation and to certain organic chemicals, such as benzene, is believed to increase the risks for getting leukemia. Chronic leukemia occurs in some people who are infected with two human retroviruses (HTLV-I and HTLV-II). An abnormal chromosome known as the Philadelphia chromosome is seen in 90 percent of those with CML. The incidence of chronic leukemia is slightly higher among men than women.

The symptoms of chronic leukemia are generally vague and non-specific. In chronic lymphoid leukemia (CLL), a patient may experience all or some of the following symptoms:

- swollen lymph nodes
- an enlarged spleen, which could make the patient complain of abdominal fullness
- chronic fatigue
- a general feeling of ill-health
- fever of unknown origin
- night sweats
- weight loss that is not due to dieting or exercise
- frequent bacterial or viral infections

In the early stages of chronic myeloid leukemia (CML), the symptoms are more or less similar to CLL. In the later stages of the disease, the patient may experience the following symptoms:

- non-specific bone **pain**
- bleeding problems
- mucus membrane irritation
- frequent infections
- a pale color due to a low red blood cell count (anemia)
- swollen lymph glands
- fever
- night sweats

Diagnosis

There are no screening tests available for chronic leukemias. The detection of these diseases may occur by chance during a routine physical examination.

If the doctor has reason to suspect leukemia, he or she will conduct a very thorough physical examination to look for enlarged lymph nodes in the neck, underarm, and pelvic region. Swollen gums, an enlarged liver or spleen, **bruises**, or pinpoint red **rashes** all over the body are some of the signs of leukemia. Urine and blood tests may be ordered to check for microscopic amounts of blood in the urine and to obtain a complete differential blood count. This count will give the numbers and percentages of the different cells found in the blood. An abnormal blood test might suggest leukemia; however, the diagnosis has to be confirmed by more specific tests.

The doctor may perform a bone marrow biopsy to confirm the diagnosis of leukemia. During the bone marrow biopsy, a cylindrical piece of bone and marrow is removed. The tissue is generally taken out of the hipbone. These samples are sent to the laboratory for examination. In addition to diagnosis, bone marrow biopsy is also done during the treatment phase of the disease to see if the leukemia is responding to therapy.

Standard imaging tests such as x-rays, **computed tomography** scans (CT scans), and **magnetic resonance imaging** (MRI) may be used to check whether the leukemic cells have invaded other organs of the body, such as the bones, chest, kidneys, abdomen, or brain.

Treatment

The treatment depends on the specific type of chronic leukemia and its stage. In general, **chemotherapy** is the standard approach to both CLL and CML. Radiation therapy is occasionally used. Because leukemia cells can spread to all the organs via the blood stream and the lymph vessels, surgery is not considered an option for treating leukemias.

Bone marrow transplantation (BMT) is in the early 2000s becoming the treatment of choice for CML because it has the possibility of curing the illness. BMT is generally not considered an option in treating CLL because CLL primarily affects older people, who are not considered to be good candidates for the procedure.

In BMT, the patient's diseased bone marrow is replaced with healthy marrow. There are two ways of doing a bone marrow transplant. In an allogeneic bone marrow transplant, healthy marrow is taken from another person (donor) whose tissue is either the same or very closely resembles the patient's tissues. The donor may be a twin, a sibling, or a person who is not related at all. First, the patient's bone marrow is destroyed with very high doses of chemotherapy and radiation therapy. To replace the destroyed marrow, healthy marrow from the donor is given to the patient through a needle in the vein.

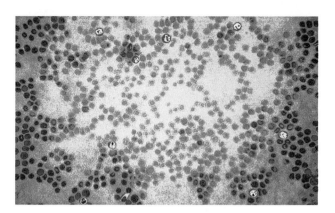

Chronic lyphocytic leukemia cells, colorized and magnified 400 times. (© 1999 Custom Medical Stock Photo, Inc.)

In the second type of bone marrow transplant, called an autologous bone marrow transplant, some of the patient's own marrow is taken out and treated with a combination of anticancer drugs to kill all the abnormal cells. This marrow is then frozen to save it. The marrow remaining in the patient's body is then destroyed with high dose chemotherapy and radiation therapy. Following that, the patient's own marrow that was frozen is thawed and given back to the patient through a needle in the vein. This mode of bone marrow transplant is as of the early 2000s being investigated in clinical trials.

In chronic lymphoid leukemia (CLL), chemotherapy is generally the treatment of choice. Depending on the stage of the disease, single or multiple drugs may be given. Drugs commonly prescribed are steroids, chlorambucil, fludarabine, and cladribine. Low dose radiation therapy may be given to the whole body, or it may be used to alleviate the symptoms and discomfort due to an enlarged spleen and lymph nodes. The spleen may be removed in a procedure called a splenectomy.

In chronic myeloid leukemia (CML), the treatment of choice is bone marrow transplantation. During the slow progress (chronic phase) of the disease, chemotherapy may be given to try to improve the cell counts. Radiation therapy, which involves the use of x rays or other high-energy rays to kill cancer cells and shrink tumors, may be used in some cases to reduce the discomfort and pain due to an enlarged spleen. For chronic leukemias, the source of radiation is usually outside the body (external radiation therapy). If the leukemic cells have spread to the brain, radiation therapy can be directed at the brain. As the disease progresses, the spleen may be removed in an attempt to try to control the pain and to improve the blood counts.

KEY TERMS

Antibody—A special protein made by the body's immune system as a defense against foreign material (bacteria, viruses, etc.) that enters the body. It is uniquely designed to attack and neutralize the specific antigen that triggered the immune response.

Biopsy—The surgical removal and microscopic examination of living tissue for diagnostic purposes or to follow the course of a disease. Most commonly the term refers to the collection and analysis of tissue from a suspected tumor to establish malignancy.

Chemotherapy—Any treatment of an illness with chemical agents. The term is usually used to describe the treatment of cancer with drugs that inhibit cancer growth or destroy cancer cells.

Computed tomography (CT)—An imaging technique in which cross-sectional x rays of the body are compiled to create a three-dimensional image of the body's internal structures; also called computed axial tomography.

Cytokines—Chemicals made by the cells that act on other cells to stimulate or inhibit their function. They are important controllers of immune functions.

Immunotherapy—A mode of cancer treatment in which the immune system is stimulated to fight the cancer.

Lumbar puncture—A procedure in which the doctor inserts a small needle into the spinal cavity in the lower back to withdraw spinal fluid for testing. Also known as a spinal tap.

Magnetic resonance imaging (MRI)—An imaging technique that uses a large circular magnet and radio waves to generate signals from atoms in the body. These signals are used to construct detailed images of internal body structures and organs, including the brain.

Maturation—The process by which stem cells transform from immature cells without a specific function into a particular type of blood cell with defined functions.

Radiation therapy—A cancer treatment that uses high-energy rays or particles to kill or weaken cancer cells. Radiation may be delivered externally or internally via surgically implanted pellets. Also called radiotherapy.

Remission—A disappearance of a disease and its symptoms. Complete remission means that all disease is gone. Partial remission means that the disease is significantly improved, but residual traces of the disease are still present. A remission may be due to treatment or may be spontaneous.

In the acute phase of CML, aggressive chemotherapy is given. Combination chemotherapy, in which multiple drugs are used, is more efficient than using a single drug for the treatment. The drugs may either be administered intravenously (through a vein) in the arm or by mouth in the form of pills. If the cancer cells have invaded the central nervous system (CNS), chemotherapeutic drugs may be put into the fluid that surrounds the brain through a needle in the brain or back. This is known as intrathecal chemotherapy.

Biological therapy or immunotherapy is a mode of treatment in which the body's own immune system is harnessed to fight the cancer. Substances that are routinely made by the immune system (such as growth factors, hormones, and disease-fighting proteins) are either synthetically made in a laboratory, or their effectiveness is boosted and they are then put back into the patient's body. This treatment mode in the early 2000s is also being investigated in clinical trials all over the United States at major cancer centers.

Prognosis

The prognosis for leukemia depends on the patient's age and general health. According to statistics, in chronic lymphoid leukemia, the overall survival for all stages of the disease is nine years. Most of the deaths in people with CLL are due to infections or other illnesses that occur as a result of the leukemia.

In CML, if bone marrow transplantation is performed within one to three years of diagnosis, 50 to 60 percent of the patients survive three years or more. If the disease progresses to the acute phase, the prognosis is poor. Less than 20 percent of these patients go into remission.

Prevention

Most cancers can be prevented by changes in lifestyle or diet, which will reduce the risk factors. However, in leukemias, there were as of 2004 no known risk factors. Therefore, as of 2004, there was no way known to prevent the leukemias from developing. People who are at an increased risk for developing leukemia because of proven exposure to ionizing radiation, the organic liquid benzene, or people who have a history of other cancers of the lymphoid system (Hodgkin's lymphoma) should undergo periodic medical checkups.

Parental concerns

Parents of a child with leukemia must balance their own fears for their child's health with the child's fears and worries. Also, given the large financial burden leukemia treatment entails, parents will want to make sure they are aware of what and what is not covered by their insurance. Parents can find a variety of sources, written and online, that will help them deal with the new circumstances of themselves and their **family**.

Resources

BOOKS

Cheson, Bruce D. "Chronic Lymphoid Leukemias." In *Clinical Oncology.* Edited by Martin D. Abeloff. London: Churchill Livingstone, 2000.

———. "Chronic Myeloid Leukemias." In *Clinical Oncology.* Edited by Martin D. Abeloff. London: Churchill Livingstone, 2000.

Tubergen, David G., and Archie Bleyer. "The Leukemias." In *Nelson Textbook of Pediatrics.* Edited by Richard E. Behrman et al. Philadelphia: Saunders, 2004.

ORGANIZATIONS

American Cancer Society. 1599 Clifton Rd., NE, Atlanta, GA 30329–4251. Web site: <www.cancer.org>.

Cancer Research Institute. 681 Fifth Ave., New York, NY 10022. Web site: <www.cancerresearch.org>.

Leukemia Society of America Inc. 600 Third Ave., New York, NY 10016. Web site: <www.leukemia.org>.

National Cancer Institute. Building 31, Room 10A31, 31 Center Drive, MSC 2580, Bethesda, MD 20892–2580. Web site: <www.nci.nih.gov>.

Lata Cherath, PhD
Rosalyn Carson-DeWitt, MD

Lice infestation

Definition

A lice infestation, or pediculosis, is caused by parasites living on human skin. Lice are tiny, wingless insects with sucking mouthparts that feed on human blood and lay eggs on body hair or in clothing. Lice **bites** can cause intense **itching**.

Description

There are three related species of human lice:

- head lice, *Pediculus humanus capitis*
- body lice, *Pediculosis humanus corpus*
- pubic lice, *Phthirus pubis*, commonly called crab lice

Pediculosis capitis is an infestation of head lice. A body lice infestation is called pediculosis corporis. Pediculosis palpebrarum or phthiriasis palpebrarum, caused by crab lice, is an infestation of the pubic hair.

Head lice live and crawl on the scalp, sucking blood every three to six hours. Their claws are adapted for clinging to hair or clothing. Adult head lice can be silvery-white to reddish-brown. They are about the size of a sesame seed. Female lice lay their eggs in sacs called nits that are about 0.04 in (1 mm) long and are glued to shafts of hair close to the scalp. During her one-month lifespan a female louse may lay more than 100 eggs. The nymphs hatch in three to 14 days and must feed on blood within one day. Nymphs are smaller and lighter in color than adults and become sexually mature after nine to 12 days.

Body lice lay their nits in clothing or bedding. Occasionally the nits are attached to body hair. Body lice nits are oval and yellow to white in color. They may not hatch for up to 30 days. Nymphs mature in about seven days.

Pubic lice have large front legs and look like tiny crabs. Females are larger than males. Nits hatch in about one week and the nymphs mature in about seven days.

Transmission

Lice are endemic in human populations, spreading through personal contact or contact with infested clothing or other personal items. They can be transmitted when unaffected clothing is stored with infested items. Among children head lice are commonly transmitted by the sharing of hats, combs, brushes, hair accessories, headphones, pillows, and stuffed **toys**. Pubic lice are sexually transmitted, although occasionally they can be transmitted through infested bedding, towels, or clothing.

Lice do not jump, hop, or fly and they do not live on pets. Head lice cannot survive without a human host for more than a few days at most. Body lice can live without human contact for up to 10 days. Pubic lice can survive for one to two weeks without human contact.

Demographics

Head lice infestations are extremely common among children in schools, childcare facilities, camps, and playgrounds. They are the second most common communicable health problem in children, after the **common cold**, and appear to be on the increase. Some 6 to 12 million American children get head lice every year. In developing countries more than 50 percent of the general population may be infested. Although anyone can get head lice, children aged three to ten and their families are most affected. Girls and women are more susceptible than boys and men. Although American black children are much less likely to have head lice than white or Hispanic children, the incidence is increasing, particularly in black children with thick hair, hair extensions, or wraps. In Africa head lice have adapted their claws to the curly, elliptical hair shafts of blacks. Neither frequent brushing or shampooing nor hair length affects the likelihood of a head lice infestation.

In general body lice infestations occur in crowded, unsanitary facilities, such as prisons and military or refugee camps. They usually are associated with poor personal hygiene, as may occur during war or natural disasters or in cold climates. They are common among the homeless.

Causes and symptoms

Lice infestations are characterized by intense itching caused by an allergic reaction to a toxin in lice saliva. The itching can interfere with **sleep** and concentration. Repeated bites can lead to generalized skin eruptions or inflammation. Swelling or inflammation of the neck glands are common complications of head lice.

Body lice bites first appear as small red pimples or puncture marks and may cause a generalized skin rash. Intense itching can result in deep scratches around the shoulders, flanks, or neck. If the infestation is not treated, complications may develop, including **headache**, **fever**, and skin infection with scarring.

When to call the doctor

A doctor may need to distinguish between body lice and **scabies** (a disease caused by skin mites) and between pubic lice and eczema (a skin condition). A doctor should be consulted if complications develop from a lice infestation or if a child contracts a bacterial infection from scratching the bites.

Diagnosis

Lice usually are diagnosed by the itching; however, itching may not occur until several weeks after infestation, if at all. The tickling caused by moving lice may be noticeable. Definite diagnosis requires identification of lice or their nits.

Head lice may cause irritability in children and scalp irritations or sores may be present. Head lice in children are usually confined to the scalp. An adult louse may be visible as movement on the scalp, especially around the ears, nape of the neck, and centerline of the crown, the warmest parts of the head. Since less than 20 mature lice may be present at a given time during infestation, the nits often are easier to spot. Nits vary in color from grayish-white to yellow, brown, or black. They are visible at the base or on the shaft of individual hairs. Applying about 10 oz (280 gm) of isopropyl (rubbing) alcohol to the hair and rubbing with a white towel for about 30 seconds releases lice onto the towel for identification.

Body lice appear similar to head lice; however, they burrow into the skin and are rarely seen except on clothing where they lay their nits in seams. Over time body lice infestations can lead to a thickening and discoloring of the skin around the waist, groin, and upper thighs.

Pubic lice usually appear first on genital hair, although they may spread to other body hair. In young children pubic lice usually are seen on the eyebrows or eyelashes. Pubic lice appear as brown or gray moving dots on the skin. There are usually only a few live lice present and they move very quickly away from light. Their white nits can be seen on hair shafts close to the skin. Although pubic lice sometimes produce small, bluish spots called maculae ceruleae on the trunk or thighs, usually it is easier to spot scratching marks. Small, dark-brown specks of lice excretion may be visible on underwear.

Since pediculicides (medications for treating lice) are usually strong insecticides with potential side effects, it is important to rule out other causes of scratching and skin inflammation. Oval-shaped head lice nits can be distinguished from dandruff because they are glued at an angle to the hair shaft, whereas flat, irregularly shaped flakes of dandruff shake off easily.

Treatment

Most authorities believe that head lice should be treated immediately upon discovery. Before beginning any treatment, parents should test a small scalp section for allergic reactions to the medication, use a vinegar rinse to help loosen nits, and wash hair with regular shampoo.

Infested eyebrows should be treated with petroleum jelly for several days and the nits should be plucked off with tweezers or fingernails. Infested eyelashes are treated with a thick coating of prescription petroleum ointment, applied twice daily for ten days.

The treatment for body lice is a thorough washing of the entire body and replacement of infected clothing. Clothing and bedding should be washed at 140°F (60°C) and dried at high temperature or dry-cleaned.

Pediculicides

Head and pubic lice infestations usually are treated with insecticidal lotions, shampoos, or cream rinses. These pediculicides should not be used on children under two; near broken skin, eyes, or mucous membranes; in the bathtub or shower; by those with **allergies**, **asthma**, epilepsy, or certain other medical conditions. Itching may not subside for several days following treatment.

All U.S. Food and Drug Administration (FDA)-approved non-prescription pediculicides contain relatively safe and effective pyrethroids. Insecticidal pyrethrins (0.33%) (RID, A-200) are extracts from chrysanthemum flowers. Permethrin (1%)(Nix) is a more stable synthetic pyrethrin. Pyrethroid pediculicides also usually contain 4 percent piperonyl butoxide.

Pyrethroids are applied for a specified length of time (usually ten minutes) and then thoroughly rinsed out. The hair should not be washed for one or two days after treatment. Cream rinse, conditioner, hair spray, mousse, gel, mayonnaise, or vinegar should not be used before treatment or within one week after treatment since these products can reduce pediculicide effectiveness.

Prescription insecticides are used when other lice treatments fail or cannot be used. The following are prescription insecticides, which carry certain risks:

• Malathion (0.5% in Ovide), a neurotoxic organophosphate, was withdrawn from the U.S. market due to an increase in malathion-resistant lice. It was reintroduced in 1999. It is foul-smelling and flammable. Sometimes infested clothing is treated with a 1 percent malathion powder.

• Lindane (1% or higher) (Kwell), an organochloride neurotoxin, can induce seizures and death in susceptible people, even when used according to the directions. In 2003 the FDA required new labeling and a reduction in bottle size.

• Ivermectin (Stromectol), an oral treatment for intestinal parasites, is effective against head lice but as of 2004 had not been approved for that use by the FDA.

Experts disagree about the effectiveness and/or safety of pediculicides. Pediculicides do not kill nits, so nit removal and a second application in seven to 10 days are required. During the 1990s, as schools began requiring children to be lice- and nit-free, the use of pyrethroids rose significantly and the FDA began receiving reports of their ineffectiveness. Pediculicides can be poisonous if used improperly or too frequently and overuse can lead to the proliferation of chemically resistant lice. Pediculicide residue may remain on the hair for several weeks and can cause skin or eye irritations.

Alternative treatment

Olive oil or petroleum ointment may be used to smother head lice. After applying to the hair and scalp, the child's head is covered with a shower cap for four to six hours. The treatment is repeated daily for three or four days. Cutting the hair or shaving the head also may be effective. Other treatments for head lice include:

• olive oil (three parts) and essential oil of lavender (one part)

• herbal shampoos or pomades

• RID Pure Alternative, a nontoxic, hypoallergenic, dye- and fragrance-free product

• a spray containing phenethyl propionate, cedar oil, peppermint oil, and sodium lauryl sulfate (LiceFree)

• cocamide DEA (a lathering agent), triethanolamine (a local irritant), and disodium EDTA (a chelator) (SafeTek) are both a nontoxic pediculicide and a conditioner for combing out lice and nits.

A common herbal treatment for pubic lice consists of pennyroyal oil (25%), garlic oil (25%), distilled water (50%). The mixture is applied to the pubic hair once a day for three days.

Nit removal

Treatment does not kill all lice nits. Hair and pubic lice nits must be removed manually to prevent re-infestation as the eggs hatch. Manual removal alone may treat a lice infestation effectively.

Before removing head lice nits, one of the following procedures may be used:

• a 50 percent vinegar rinse to loosen the nits

• wiping individual locks of hair from base to tip with a cloth soaked in vinegar

• catching live lice with a comb, tweezers, fingernails, or by sticking them with double-sided tape

• an enzymatic lice-egg remover

In addition, hair should be clean, damp, and untangled; clothing should be removed and a towel placed between the hair and shoulders; the hair should be divided into square-inch sections with the use of clips or elastics to divide long hair.

Head lice nits are removed by combing through each hair section from scalp to tip. Between each passing, the comb should be dipped in water and wiped with a paper towel to remove lice and nits. The comb should be held up to the light to be sure it is clean. If necessary the comb may be cleaned with a toothbrush, fingernail brush, or dental floss. Good light and possibly a magnifying glass are required. Long, thick hair may take an hour to comb out thoroughly. Towels and clothing should be washed after combing. The process should be repeated at least twice a week for at least two weeks.

Nits also can be manually removed with any fine-toothed comb, including pet flea combs, a specialized nit comb (LiceMeister, LiceOut), a battery-powered vibrating or anti-static comb, tweezers, baby safety scissors, and fingernails.

Re-infestation

Re-infestation occurs often with all types of lice due to the following:

• ineffective or incomplete treatment

• chemical-resistant lice

• failure to remove live nits

• failure to treat all infected household members and playmates

• failure to remove nits from clothing, bedding, towels, or other items

• re-infestation from another source

Head lice re-infestation can be prevented by the following:

• repeating lice checks and nit removal daily until no more are found

• notifying school, camp, or daycare, and parents of playmates

• checking and treating household members, playmates, schoolmates, school or daycare staff, and others in close contact with the child

• treating combs and brushes with rubbing alcohol, Lysol, or soapy water above 130°F (54°C)

A close-up view of a body louse. *(Custom Medical Stock Photo Inc.)*

• washing all bedding, clothing, headgear, scarves, and coats with soapy water at 130°F (54°C) and drying with high heat for at least 20 minutes

• washing or vacuuming stuffed animals and other toys

• vacuuming all helmets, carpets, rugs, mattresses, pillows, upholstery, and car seats (Permethrin sprays for treating mattresses, furniture, and other items are not recommended.)

• removing the vacuum-cleaner bag after use, sealing in a plastic bag, and placing in the outside garbage

• dry-cleaning non-washable items or sealing them in a plastic bag for up to four weeks

• repeating treatment if necessary

Re-infestation with body or pubic lice can be prevented by washing underclothes, sleepwear, bedding, and towels in hot, soapy water and drying with high heat for at least 20 minutes. Clothing infected with body lice should be ironed under high heat.

Prognosis

Lice infestations are not usually dangerous. Despite the presence of chemically-resistant lice and the thoroughness required to prevent re-infestation, all lice infestations are eradicated eventually.

Prevention

Prevention of lice infestation depends on adequate personal hygiene and consistently not sharing combs, brushes, hair accessories, hats, towels, or bedding. Hair should be checked weekly for lice and nits.

KEY TERMS

Crabs—An informal or slang term for pubic lice.

Endemic—Natural to or characteristic of a particular place, population, or climate.

Insecticide—Any substance used to kill insects.

Lindane—A benzene compound that is used to kill body and pubic lice. Lindane is absorbed into the louse's central nervous system, causing seizures and death.

Malathion—An insecticide that can be used in 1% powdered form to disinfect the clothes of patients with body lice.

Neurotoxin—A poison that acts directly on the central nervous system.

Nits—The eggs produced by head or pubic lice, usually grayish white in color and visible at the base of hair shafts.

Pediculicide—Any substance that kills lice.

Pediculosis—A lice infestation.

Permethrin—A medication used to rid the scalp of head lice. Permethrin works by paralyzing the lice, so that they cannot feed within the 24 hours after hatching required for survival.

Petroleum jelly or ointment—Petrolatum, a gelatinous substance obtained from oil that is used as a protective dressing.

Piperonyl butoxide—A liquid organic compound that enhances the activity of insecticides.

Pyrethrin, pyrethroid—A naturally occurring insecticide extracted from chrysanthemum flowers. It paralyzes lice so that they cannot feed.

Regular lice checks in schools and "no nit" reentry policies have not been shown to be effective. The American Academy of Pediatrics, the Harvard School of Public Health, and the National Association of School Nurses recommend their elimination, although many healthcare professionals disagree.

Parental concerns

Usually children are not allowed to return to daycare or school until they are lice- and nit-free. The discovery of head lice may cause distress for children and their families. Parents should stay calm and explain to the child:

• what head lice are and how they are transmitted

• that lice are very common and that many—if not most—children have them at some point

• that it is nothing to be embarrassed or ashamed about

• that the infestation is not the child's fault

Scratching or scraping at lice bites may cause **hives** or abrasions that can lead to bacterial skin infections. In developing countries head lice infestations are a significant cause of contagious bacterial infections. Body lice can carry and transmit disease-causing organisms. Although pubic lice do not carry diseases, they often are found in association with other **sexually transmitted diseases**. Crab lice in children may be an indication of sexual activity or abuse.

Resources

BOOKS

Derkazarian, Susan. *You Have Head Lice!* Danbury, CT: Scholastic Library Publishing, 2005.

Grossman, Leigh B. *Infection Control in the Child Care Center and Preschool.* Philadelphia: Lippincott Williams & Wilson, 2003.

Official Patient's Sourcebook on Head Lice Infestation. San Diego, CA: Icon Group International, 2002.

PERIODICALS

Blenkinsopp, Alison. "Head Lice." *Primary Health Care* 13 (October 2003): 33–4.

Burgess, I. F. "Human Lice and Their Control." *Annual Review of Entomology* 49 (2004): 457.

Elston, D. M. "Drug-Resistant Lice." *Archives of Dermatology* 139 (2003): 1061–4.

Evans, Jeff. "Pediatric Dermatology: Simple Methods Often Best: Lice, Mosquitoes, Warts." *Family Practice News* 34 (January 15, 2004): 56.

Flinders, David C., and Peter De Schweinitz. "Pediculosis and Scabies." *American Family Physician* 69 (January 15, 2004): 341–52.

Heukelbach, Jorg, and Hermann Feldmeier. "Ectoparasites— The Underestimated Realm." *Lancet* 363 (March 13, 2004): 889–91.

Kittler, R., et al. "Molecular Evolution of *Pediculus humanus* and the Origin of Clothing." *Current Biology* 13 (August 19, 2003): 1414–17.

"Recommendations Provided for Back-to-School Head Lice Problem." *Health & Medicine Week* (October 6, 2003): 329.

Yoon, K. S., et al. "Permethrin-Resistant Human Head Lice *Pediculus capitis*, and Their Treatment." *Archives of Dermatology* 139 (August 2003): 994–1000.

Zepf, Bill. "Treatment of Head Lice: Therapeutic Options." *American Family Physician* 69 (February 1, 2004): 655.

ORGANIZATIONS

American Academy of Dermatology (AAD). PO Box 4014, Schaumburg, IL 60168-4014. Web site: <www.aad.org>.

American Academy of Pediatrics (AAP). 141 Northwest Point Boulevard, Elk Grove Village, IL 60007-1098. Web site: <www.aap.org>.

Centers for Disease Control and Prevention. National Center for Infectious Diseases, Division of Parasitic Diseases. 1600 Clifton Road, Atlanta, GA 30333. Web site: <www.cdc.gov/ncidod/dpd/parasites/lice/default.htm>.

National Pediculosis Association (NPA), Inc. 50 Kearney Road, Needham, MA 02494. Web site: <www.headlice.org>.

WEB SITES

"Lice." *MayoClinic.com*, August 5, 2002 Available online at <www.mayoclinic.com/invoke.cfm?id=DS00368> (accessed December 29, 2004).

"Lindane Shampoo and Lindane Lotion Questions and Answers." *Center for Drug Evaluation and Research, U.S. Food and Drug Administration*, April 15, 2003. Available online at <www.fda.gov/cder/drug/infopage/lindane/lindaneQA.htm> (accessed December 29, 2004).

Rebecca J. Frey, PhD
Margaret Alic, PhD

Lipidoses

Definition

Lipidoses are genetic disorders, passed from parents to their children, characterized by defects of the digestive system that impair the way the body uses dietary fat. When the body is unable to properly digest fats, lipids accumulate in body tissues in abnormal amounts.

Description

The digestion, storage, and use of fats (lipids) from foods are complex processes that involve hundreds of chemical reactions in the body. In most people, the body is already programmed by its genetic code to produce all of the enzymes and chemicals necessary to carry out these functions. These genetic instructions are passed from parents to their offspring.

People with lipidoses are born without the genetic codes needed to tell their bodies how to complete a particular part of the fat digestion and utilization process. In most of these disorders, the body does not produce a certain enzyme, or specialized chemical. Over 30 different disorders of fat metabolism are related to genetic defects. Some people can carry the gene for these defects, but be free of symptoms; although the defects are passed from parents to children, the parents often do not have the disorders themselves.

There is great variance in the symptoms, available treatments, and long-term consequences of these conditions. Some of the conditions become apparent shortly after the infant is born. In other lipid disorders, symptoms may not develop until adulthood. For most of the lipidoses, diagnosis is suspected based on symptoms and **family** history. Tests of blood, urine, and tissue can be used to confirm the diagnosis. Genetic testing can be used, in some cases, to identify the defective gene. Some of these disorders can be controlled with changes in the diet, medications, or enzyme supplements. However, for many of these diseases, no treatment is available. Some may cause death in childhood or contribute to a shortened life expectancy. This section focuses on some of the most common or most serious lipidoses.

Demographics

Lipidoses are very rare. The number of people affected depends on the disease, but for many diseases incidence is as little as one in 40,000 people. Some diseases have a higher prevalence in specific populations.

Fabry's disease

Causes and symptoms

Approximately one in every 40,000 males is born with Fabry's disease. This condition has an X-linked, recessive pattern of inheritance, meaning that the defective gene is carried on the X chromosome. A female who carries a defective recessive gene on one of her two X chromosomes will not have the disease because she also has one good X chromosome. However, she has a 50 percent chance of passing the defective gene to her sons. The sons inheriting one defective gene will develop the disorder because a male has only one X chromosome, which he receives from his mother and one Y chromosome from his father. The mother also has a 50 percent chance of passing the defective recessive gene to her daughters who will be carriers of the disorder (like their mother), but will not show symptoms of the disease. Some female carriers of Fabry's disease show mild signs of the disorder, especially cloudiness of the cornea.

The gene that is defective in Fabry's disease causes a deficiency of the enzyme alpha-galactosidase A. Without this enzyme, fatty compounds start to line the blood vessels. The collection of fatty deposits eventually affects blood vessels in the skin, heart, kidneys, and nervous system. The first symptoms in childhood are **pain** and discomfort in the hands and feet brought on by **exercise**, **fever**, stress, or changes in the weather. A raised rash of dark red-purple spots is common, especially on skin between the waist and the knees. Other symptoms include a decreased ability to sweat and changes in the cornea or outer layer of the eye. Although the disease begins in childhood, it progresses very slowly. Kidney and heart problems develop in adulthood.

Diagnosis

A diagnosis of Fabry's disease can be confirmed by a blood test to measure for alpha-galactosidase A. Women who are carriers of the defective gene can also be identified by a blood test.

Treatment

Treatment focuses on prevention of symptoms and long-term complications. Daily doses of diphenylhydantoin (Dilantin) or carbamazapine (Tegretol) can prevent or reduce the severity of pain in the hands and feet associated with this condition. A diet low in sodium and protein may be beneficial to those individuals who have some kidney complications. If kidney problems progress, kidney dialysis or kidney transplantation may be required. Enzyme replacement therapy is being explored.

Prognosis

Although patients with Fabry's disease usually survive to adulthood, they are at increased risk for **stroke**, heart attack, and kidney damage.

Gaucher disease

Causes and symptoms

Gaucher (pronounced go-shay) disease is the most common of the lipid storage disorders. It is found in populations all over the world (20,000–40,000 people have a type of the disease), and it occurs with equal frequency in males and females. Gaucher disease has a recessive pattern of inheritance, meaning that a person must inherit a copy of the defective gene from both parents in order to have symptoms of the disease. The genetic defect causes a deficiency of the enzyme glucocerebrosidase that is responsible for breaking down a certain type of fat and releasing it from fat cells. These

fat cells begin to crowd out healthy cells in the liver, spleen, bones, and nervous system. Symptoms of Gaucher disease can start in infancy, childhood, or adulthood.

Three types of Gaucher disease have been identified, but there are many variations in how symptoms develop. Type 1 is the most common and affects both children and adults. It occurs much more often in people of Eastern European and Russian Jewish (Ashkenazi) ancestry, affecting one out of every 450 live births in this population. The first signs of the disease include an enlarged liver and spleen, causing the abdomen to swell. Children with this condition may be shorter than normal. Other symptoms include tiredness, pain, bone deterioration, broken bones, anemia, and increased bruising. Type 2 Gaucher disease is more serious, beginning within the first few months after birth. Symptoms, which are similar to those in type 1, progress rapidly, but also include nervous system damage. Symptoms of type 3 Gaucher disease begin during early childhood with symptoms like type 1. Unlike type 2, the progress of the disease is slower, although it also includes nervous system damage.

Diagnosis

Gaucher disease may be suspected, based on symptoms, and is confirmed with a blood test for levels of the deficient enzyme. Samples of tissue from an affected area may also confirm a diagnosis.

Treatment

The symptoms of Gaucher disease can be stopped and even reversed by treatment with enzyme replacement injections. Two enzyme drugs available are alglucerase (Ceredase) and imiglucerase (Cerezyme). Other treatments address specific symptoms such as anemia, broken bones, or pain.

Prognosis

The pain and deformities associated with symptoms can make coping with this illness very challenging for individuals and families. With treatment and control of symptoms, people with type 1 Gaucher disease may lead fairly long and normal lives. Most infants with type 2 die before age two. Children with type 3 Gaucher disease may survive to **adolescence** and early adulthood.

Krabbe's disease

Causes and symptoms

Krabbe's disease is caused by a deficiency of the enzyme galactoside beta- galactosidase. It has a recessive pattern of inheritance and is believed to occur in one out of 40,000 births in the United States. This condition, which is also called globoid cell leukodystrophy or Krabbe leukodystrophy, is characterized by acute nervous system degeneration. It develops in early infancy with initial symptoms of irritability, **vomiting**, and episodes of partial unconsciousness. Symptoms progress rapidly to seizures, difficulty swallowing, blindness, deafness, **mental retardation**, and paralysis.

Treatment

No treatment is available.

Prognosis

Children born with Krabbe's disease die in infancy.

Niemann-pick disease

Causes and symptoms

At least five different forms of Niemann-Pick disease (NPD) have been identified. The different types seem to be related to the activity level of the enzyme sphingomyelinase. In patients with types A and B NPD, there is a build-up of sphingomyelin in cells of the brain, liver, spleen, kidney, and lung. Type A is the most common form of NPD and the most serious, with death usually occurring by the age of 18 months. Symptoms develop within the first few months of life and include poor appetite, failure to grow, enlarged liver and spleen, and the appearance of cherry red spots in the retina of the eye. Type B develops in infancy or childhood with symptoms of mild liver or spleen enlargement and lung problems. Types C and D NPD are related to cholesterol transfer out of cells. Children with types C or D grow normally in early childhood, but eventually develop difficulty in walking and loss of muscle coordination. Ultimately, the nervous system becomes severely damaged and these patients die. Type C occurs in any population, while type D has been identified only in individuals from Nova Scotia, Canada.

Diagnosis

Diagnosis is confirmed by analyzing a sample of tissue. Prenatal diagnosis of types A and B NPD can be done with **amniocentesis** or chorionic villi sampling.

Treatment

Treatment consists of supportive care to deal with symptoms and the development of complications. Bone marrow transplantation is being investigated as a possible treatment. Low-cholesterol diets may be helpful for patients with types C and D.

Prognosis

Patients with type A NPD usually die within the first 18 months of life. Type B patients generally live to adulthood but suffer from significant liver and lung problems. With types C and D NPD, there is significant nervous system damage leading to severe **muscle spasms**, seizures, and eventually coma and death. Some patients with types C and D die in childhood, while less severely affected individuals may survive to adulthood.

Refsum's disease

Causes and symptoms

Refsum's disease has a recessive pattern of inheritance and affects populations from Northern Europe, particularly Scandinavians. It is due to a deficiency of phytanic acid hydroxylase, an enzyme that breaks down a fatty acid called phytanic acid. This condition affects the nervous system, eyes, bones, and skin. Symptoms, which usually appear by age 20, include vision problems (retinitis pigmentosa and rhythmic eye movements, or **nystagmus**), loss of muscle coordination, loss of sense of smell (anosmia), pain, **numbness**, and elevated protein in the cerebrospinal fluid.

Treatment

A diet free of phytanic acid (found in dairy products, tuna, cod, haddock, lamb, stewed beef, white bread, white rice, boiled potatoes, and egg yolk) can reduce some of the symptoms. Plasmapheresis—a process where whole blood is removed from the body, processed through a filtering system, and then returned to the body—may be used to filter phytanic acid from the blood.

Tay-Sachs disease

Causes and symptoms

Tay-Sachs disease (TSD) is a fatal condition caused by a deficiency of the enzyme hexosaminidase A (Hex-A). The defective gene that causes this disorder is found in roughly one in 250 people in the general population. However, certain populations have significantly higher rates of TSD. French-Canadians living near the St. Lawrence River and in the Cajun regions of Louisiana are at higher risk of having a child with TSD. The highest risk seems to be in people of Eastern European and Russian Jewish (Ashkenazi) descent. Tay-Sachs disease has a recessive pattern of inheritance, and approximately one in every 27 people of Jewish ancestry in the United States carries the TSD gene. Symptoms develop in infancy and are due to the accumulation of a fatty acid compound in the nervous system. Early symptoms include loss of vision and physical coordination, seizures, and mental retardation. Eventually, the child develops problems with breathing and swallowing. Blindness, paralysis, and death follow.

Diagnosis

Carriers of the Tay-Sachs related gene can be identified with a blood test. Amniocentesis or chorionic villi sampling can be used to determine if the fetus has Tay-Sachs disease.

Treatment

There is no treatment for Tay-Sachs disease. Parents who are identified as carriers may want to seek genetic counseling. If a fetus is identified as having TSD, parents can then consider their options.

Prognosis

Children born with Tay-Sachs disease become increasingly debilitated; most die by about age four.

Wolman's disease

Causes and symptoms

Wolman's disease is caused by a genetic defect with a recessive pattern of inheritance that results in a deficiency of an enzyme that breaks down cholesterol. This causes large amounts of fat to accumulate in body tissues. Symptoms begin in the first few weeks of life and include an enlarged liver and spleen, adrenal calcification (hardening of adrenal tissue due to deposits of calcium salts), and fatty stools.

Treatment

No treatment is available.

Prognosis

Death generally occurs before six months of age.

Prevention

There is no known way to prevent lipidoses. Couples who have family histories of genetic defects can undergo genetic testing and counseling to see if they are at risk for having a child with one of the lipidoses disorders. During pregnancy, cell samples can be collected from the fetus using amniocentesis or chorionic villi sampling. The results of these tests can indicate if the developing fetus has a lipidosis disorder.

Parental concerns

Lipidoses have a variety of different symptoms and progressions. There are treatments for some—but not all—lipidoses. Treating the symptoms is always an integral part of lessening the impact of the disease. If parents have one child with a lipidoses disorder and are consider-

Lisping

ing having other children, genetic counseling or in utero testing of the fetus may be beneficial.

Resources

BOOKS

Desnick, Robert J., and Michael M. Kaback, eds. *Tay-Sachs Disease*. San Diego, CA: Academic, 2001.

Vinken, Pierre J., and George W. Bruyn, eds. *Neurodystrophies and Neurolipidoses*. New York: Elsevier, 1996.

PERIODICALS

Enderlin, Carol, et al. "Gaucher Disease." *American Journal of Nursing* 103, no. 12 (December 2003): 50–62.

Futerman, Anthony H. et al. "New Directions in the Treatment of Gaucher Disease." *Trends in Pharmacological Sciences* 25, no. 3 (March 2004): 147–52.

Wilcox, William R., et al. "Long-term Safety and Efficacy of Enzyme Replacement Therapy for Fabry Disease." *American Journal of Human Genetics* 75, no. 1 (July 2004): 65–75.

ORGANIZATIONS

National Organization for Rare Diseases. 55 Kenosia Avenue, PO Box 1968, Danbury, CT 06813-1968. (203) 744-0100 or 1-800- 999-6673. Fax: (203) 798-2291. Web site: <www.rarediseases.org>.

Tish Davidson, A.M.
Altha Roberts Edgren

Lisping

Definition

A lisp is a functional speech disorder that involves the inability to correctly pronounce one or more sibilant consonant sounds, usually *s* or *z*.

Description

Lisping is a speech disorder characterized by the inability to correctly pronounce the sounds of *s* or *z*, known as the sibilant consonants. Usually *th* sounds are substituted for the sibilants. The word "lisp," for example, would be pronounced "lithp" by someone with this speech disorder.

Many children lisp at certain stages of speech development, especially when they lose their front primary teeth. Lisping is, therefore, sometimes called a develop-

mental phonetic disorder. Frontal or interdental lisp is produced when the tongue protrudes through the front teeth when teeth are missing and is the most familiar type of lisp. Sibilant production may be interfered with in a number of other ways as well. These are all classified as lisping and include excessive pressure by the tongue against the teeth, the tongue held too far back along the midline of the palate, and a "substitute hiss" produced in the throat or larynx.

Sometimes children with functional **speech disorders** have problems making other sounds, such as *sh*, *l*, *r*, and *ch*. When a child cannot produce these sounds correctly, the condition is usually not considered a true lisp, but is a functional speech disorder.

Children can have a functional speech disorder as well as a developmental phonological disorder. The latter is not a matter of being able to physically make a specific sound but is a language disorder. These children have trouble organizing the sounds of speech in common patterns and may consistently replace one sound with another. For example, a child may say "wun" instead of "sun" or "doe" instead of "so."

There are four main types of lisps.

• Interdental lisp—occurs when the tongue protrudes between the front teeth and the *s* or *z* is pronounced like *th*.

• Dentalized lisp or dentalized production—occurs when the tongue pushes against the front teeth.

• Lateral lisp—sounds wet because the air flows around the tongue, which is in the normal position to produce the *l* sound.

• Palatal lisp—the middle of the tongue touches the soft palate, or roof of the mouth, when trying to produce the *s* sound.

Demographics

According to the National Institute on Deafness and Other Communication Disorders, about one in six people in the United States (42 million adults and children) has a communication disorder. Of them, 14 million have a speech, voice, or language disorder that is not linked to hearing loss. Functional speech disorders with no known cause, such as lisping, affect 10 percent of the population; 8–9 percent serious enough to require treatment. Nearly 5 percent of first graders have functional speech disorders, and 50–70 percent of all children with functional speech disorders struggle academically throughout elementary school and high school.

Causes and symptoms

As a functional speech disorder, lisping has no clear known cause. It is often referred to as a speech delay of unknown origin. Structural irregularities of the tongue, palate, or teeth (including abnormalities in the number or position of the teeth) may be implicated in lisping, but they generally are not the main causes. Mild hearing loss involving high frequencies may also impair a child's ability to hear language correctly and be able to repeat phonetic sounds. In some cases, a child with no physical abnormality will develop a lisp. It has been thought that some of these children may be imitating another child or an adult who lisps.

Lisping is also associated with immature development. Some children will adopt a lisp as a means of gaining attention. Other children will begin to lisp after they have experienced unusual stress or trauma. This behavior is part of a regression into a more secure period and can include other types of regressive behaviors such as bed wetting or wanting to **sleep** with the light on in the bedroom.

One theory of the cause of lisping is the result of tongue thrusting, a physiological behavior that causes the tongue to flatten and thrust forward during swallowing and speaking. It is suggested that **thumb sucking**, overuse of pacifiers, bottle feeding, and recurrent upper respiratory illnesses cause tongue thrusting. Thumbs (or fingers), artificial nipples, and pacifiers keep the tongue flat and do not allow the muscles of the tongue to develop in a normal fashion. When the child speaks, the tongue shoots forward, creating a lisp.

Frequent upper respiratory illnesses often stuff the nose, forcing these children to breathe through their mouths. The sounds that they make when they speak may be thick and garbled, and may encourage lisping. Closing the mouth and teeth to make s or z sounds cuts off the breath, so children compensate by trying to speak without closing their mouths completely. Thus, a lisp develops.

When to call the doctor

The interdental lisp and the dentalized lisp are common in normal speech development. However, if they persist well past four-and-one-half years and garble the speech so that the child is not understood, he or she should be evaluated. The evaluation will determine if there is a physiological basis for the lisp and identify the type of lisp. In some cases, the child will be evaluated and observed for several months or longer to see if the condition can be outgrown. Lateral and palatal lisps are not found in typical speech development and should be evaluated by a speech-language pathologist. If untreated, lisping can persist into adulthood.

For some children, everything they say seems to be interdental. In these cases, there may be an obstruction of the nose because of infection, allergy, enlarged adenoids, or other facial problems. Excessive interdental speech can also be related to mouth breathing and sucking habits. These children should be seen by a physician to treat the health problems and then referred to a speech-language pathologist to correct the lisp.

Diagnosis

A physician can determine whether there are structural irregularities within the mouth or problems with the child's hearing, and can treat related **allergies** and nasal problems. However, true assessment of a child's ability to make speech sounds must be done by a speech-language pathologist. The child's medical history will be taken and the speech-language pathologist will examine the anatomy of the child's mouth and the movements it can make. Next, the child's speech and reading aloud is often recorded for later analysis. This speech sample will also yield information about the quality of the child's voice, how fluent speech occurs, and the child's semantic and physical sound- making skill.

Treatment

Typical treatment is called articulation therapy. The speech-language pathologist finds out whether the child can hear proper speech sounds, and proceeds to read a list of words with specific sounds that the child is having trouble articulating. Lists of contrast words are also read so that the child can hear the subtle differences in word sounds. Therapy then moves to working on the position in the word where the sound occurs; that is, at the beginning, in the middle, or at the end. Specific word exercises follow, beginning with single sounds, then syllables, and moving on to words, phrases, and sentences. Finally, the child participates in controlled conversations such as talking casually during a meal.

Prognosis

Most lisps are developmental and resolve themselves in children by the time they are about five to eight years old. If they last longer or are of a specific type, speech therapy is recommended. The outcome of speech therapy is usually quite good. Depending on the specifics of the therapy and the nature of the lisp, treatment can be relatively short term, lasting only a few months. Some cases may take a year or more.

Prevention

Parents can reduce the risk of a lisp developing because of tongue thrusting by restricting **pacifier use** or choosing to breastfeed their babies. They can also speak clearly in complete sentences around their children and not use baby talk. They should treat allergies and respiratory illnesses immediately to keep the nose open and breathing free. The child's hearing and teeth should be checked periodically to make sure he or she can hear speech clearly and form words correctly. Parents can also encourage the musculature of the mouth by showing children how to drink from straws and how to blow bubbles. In addition, playing word and naming games encourages good speech development and stimulates learning.

Parental concerns

In many families, a child's lisp goes unnoticed, especially if it does not interfere with understanding what the child is saying. These children may grow up content to keep a lisp, feeling that it is a specific part of what makes them who they are, just as some people keep a gap between their front teeth and see it as distinct characteristic. (Lauren Hutton kept the gap between her teeth even as she became a top model, and Boris Karloff had one of the most famous lisps in the world.)

Outside of the home, some children may be teased by other children or feel embarrassed to speak up in the classroom. They may have trouble spelling or even reading because they cannot make some of the sounds necessary to read and write well. These children may have serious **self-esteem** issues related to their lisps. In these cases, seeing a speech-language pathologist early in their lives and correcting their lisps could bolster self-confidence and ability to learn.

Still other families may think that a child's lisp is endearing and cute. They may even encourage the child to continue lisping because he or she receives positive regard whenever the lisping sounds are made. Sometimes, these same families suddenly decide that lisping is no longer cute and want their children to drop their lisps and grow up. These children still can benefit from speech therapy, but they may become resistant to treatment because they are confused about the abrupt change in the family's behavior. In this case, counseling is recommended in addition to sessions with a speech-language pathologist.

A lisp can be a source of distress for adolescent boys and young men who may be told that they are gay because they lisp. A functional speech disorder has no connection with a person's sexual orientation. Many young men, although they **fear** it may be too late, seek out speech-language pathologists as adults to correct their lisps because of this teasing.

> ## KEY TERMS
>
> **Palate**—The roof of the mouth.
>
> **Tongue thrusting**—A physiological behavior that causes the tongue to flatten and thrust forward during swallowing and speaking.

Resources

BOOKS

Bernthal, J. E., and N. W. Bankson. *Articulation and Phonological Disorders*, 4th ed. Boston: Allyn and Bacon, 1998.

Cantwell, Dennis P. *Developmental Speech and Language Disorders*. New York: Guilford Press, 1987.

Hamaguchi, Patricia McAleer. *Childhood Speech, Language and Listening Problems: What Every Parent Should Know*. New York: John Wiley and Sons, 1995.

Lass, N. J., et al. *Handbook on Speech-Language Pathology and Audiology*. Philadelphia: B. C. Decker, 1988.

PERIODICALS

Catts, H. et al. "Estimating the Risk of future Reading Difficulties in Kindergarten Children: A Research-based Model and its Clinical Implementation." *Language Speech and Hearing Services in Schools* 32 (2001): 38–50.

Catts, H. et al. "The Relationship between Speech-language Impairments and Reading Disabilities." *Journal of Speech and Hearing Research*. 36, no. 5 (1993):948–58

ORGANIZATIONS

American Speech-Language-Hearing Association 10801 Rockville Pike Rockville, MD 20785. (301) 897-5700. Web site: <wwww.asha.org>.

Council for Exceptional Children. Division for Children with Communication Disorders. 1920 Association Drive Reston, VA 22091. (703) 620-3660.

National Institute on Deafness and Other Communication Disorders National Institutes of Health. 31 Center Drive, MSC 2320 Bethesda, MD 20892-2320.

Janie Franz

Listeriosis

Definition

Listeriosis is an illness caused by the bacterium *Listeria monocytogenes* that is acquired by eating contaminated food. The organism can spread to the blood stream and central nervous system. In women who contract listeriosis while pregnant, the disease often causes miscarriage or stillbirth.

Description

Listeriosis is caused by an infection with the bacterium *Listeria monocytogenes*. These bacteria can be carried by many animals and birds, and they have been found in soil, water, sewage, and animal feed. Five out of every 100 people carry *Listeria monocytogenes* in their intestines. Listeriosis is considered a food-borne illness because most people are probably infected after eating food contaminated with *Listeria monocytogenes*. However, a woman can pass the bacteria to her baby during pregnancy. In addition, there have been a few cases where workers have developed *Listeria* skin infections by touching infected calves or poultry.

In the 1980s, the United States government began taking measures to decrease the occurrence of listeriosis. Subsequently, processed meats and dairy products were tested for the presence of *Listeria monocytogenes*. The Food and Drug Administration (FDA) and the Food Safety and Inspection Service (FSIS) can legally prevent food from being shipped, or order food recalls, if they detect any *Listeria* bacteria. These inspections, in combination with the public education regarding the proper handling of uncooked foods, appear to be helping. Nonetheless, as of 2004, about 2,500 individuals become seriously ill from *Listeria* annually, with about 500 deaths.

Demographics

Persons at particular risk for listeriosis include the elderly, pregnant women, newborns, and those with a weakened immune system (called immunocompromised). Risk is increased when a person suffers from diseases such as **AIDS, cancer,** kidney disease, **diabetes mellitus,** or by the use of certain medications. Infection is most common in babies younger than one month old and adults over 60 years of age. Pregnant women account for 27 percent of the cases, and immunocompromised persons account for almost 70 percent. Persons with AIDS are 280 times more likely to get listeriosis than others.

Causes and symptoms

As noted, persons become infected with *Listeria monocytogenes* by eating contaminated food. *Listeria* has been found on raw vegetables, fish, poultry, raw (unpasteurized) milk, fresh meat, processed meat (such as deli meat, hot dogs, and canned meat), and certain soft cheeses. Listeriosis outbreaks in the United States since the 1980s have been linked to cole slaw, milk, Mexican-style cheese, undercooked hot dogs, undercooked chicken, and delicatessen foods. Unlike most other bacteria, *Listeria monocytogenes* does not stop growing when food is in the refrigerator; its growth is merely slowed. Fortunately, typical cooking temperatures and the pasteurization process do kill this bacteria.

Listeria bacteria can pass through the wall of the intestines, and from there they can get into the blood stream. Once in the blood stream, they can be transported anywhere in the body but are commonly found the central nervous system (brain and spinal cord); and in pregnant women they are often found in the placenta (the organ which connects the baby's umbilical cord to the uterus). *Listeria monocytogenes* live inside specific white blood cells called macrophages. Inside macrophages, the bacteria can hide from immune responses and become inaccessible to certain **antibiotics.** *Listeria* bacteria are capable of multiplying within macrophages and then may spread to other macrophages.

After people consume food contaminated with this bacteria, they may see symptoms of infection 11 to 70 days later. Most people do not get any noticeable symptoms. Scientists suspect that *Listeria monocytogenes* can cause upset stomach and intestinal problems just like other food-borne illnesses. Persons with listeriosis may develop flu-like symptoms such as **fever, headache, nausea and vomiting,** tiredness, and **diarrhea.**

Pregnant women experience a mild, flu-like illness with fever, muscle aches, upset stomach, and intestinal problems. They recover, but the infection can cause miscarriage, premature labor, early rupture of the birth sac, and stillbirth. Half of the newborns infected with *Listeria* die from the illness.

There are two types of listeriosis in the newborn baby: early-onset disease and late-onset disease. Early-onset disease refers to a serious illness that is present at birth and usually causes the baby to be born prematurely. Babies infected during the pregnancy usually have a blood infection (sepsis) and may have a serious, whole body infection called granulomatosis infantisepticum. When a full-term baby becomes infected with *Listeria* during **childbirth,** that situation is called late-onset disease. Commonly, symptoms of late-onset listeriosis appear about two weeks after birth. Babies with late-term disease typically have **meningitis** (inflammation of the brain and spinal tissues); yet they have a better chance of surviving than those with early-onset disease.

Immunocompromised adults are at risk for a serious infection of the blood stream and central nervous system (brain and spinal cord). Meningitis occurs in about half of the cases of adult listeriosis. Symptoms of listerial meningitis occur about four days after the flu-like symptoms and include fever, personality change, uncoordinated muscle movement, tremors, muscle contractions, seizures, and slipping in and out of consciousness.

Listeria monocytogenes causes endocarditis in about 7.5 percent of the cases. Endocarditis is an inflammation of heart tissue due to the bacterial infection. Listerial endocarditis causes death in about half of the patients. Diseases which have been caused by *Listeria monocytogenes* include brain abscess, eye infection, hepatitis (liver disease), peritonitis (abdominal infection), lung infection, joint infection, arthritis, heart disease, bone infection, and gallbladder infection.

Diagnosis

Listeriosis may be diagnosed and treated by infectious disease specialists and internal medicine specialists. The diagnosis and treatment of this infection should be covered by most insurance providers.

The only way to diagnose listeriosis is to isolate *Listeria monocytogenes* from blood, cerebrospinal fluid, or stool. A sample of cerebrospinal fluid is removed from the spinal cord using a needle and syringe. This procedure is commonly called a spinal tap. The amniotic fluid (the fluid which bathes the unborn baby) may be tested in pregnant women with listeriosis. This sample is obtained by inserting a needle through the abdomen into the uterus and withdrawing fluid. *Listeria* grows well in laboratory media, and test results can be available within a few days.

Treatment

Listeriosis is treated with the antibiotics ampicillin (Omnipen) or sulfamethoxazole-trimethoprim (Bactrim, Septra). Because the bacteria live within macrophage cells, treatment may be difficult, and the treatment periods may vary. Usually, pregnant women are treated for two weeks; newborns, two to three weeks; adults with mild disease, two to four weeks; persons with meningitis, three weeks; persons with brain abscesses, six weeks; and persons with endocarditis, four to six weeks.

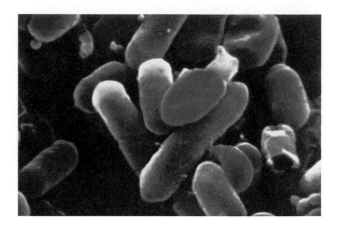

Scanning electron micrograph (SEM) scan of lysteria monocytogenes. *(© CNRI/Phototake.)*

Patients are often hospitalized for treatment and monitoring. Other drugs may be provided to relieve **pain** and fever and to treat other reactions to the infection.

Prognosis

The overall death rate for listeriosis is 26 percent. This high death rate is due to the serious illness suffered by newborns, the elderly, and immunocompromised persons. Healthy adults and older children have a low death rate. Complications of *Listeria* infection include: meningitis, sepsis, miscarriage, stillbirth, **pneumonia**, shock endocarditis, abscess (localized infection) formation, and eye inflammation.

Prevention

As of the early 2000s the United States government has done much to prevent listeriosis. Persons at extremely high risk (pregnant women, immunocompromised persons, etc.) must use extra caution. High risk persons should avoid soft cheeses, such as Mexican cheese, feta, Brie, Camembert, and blue cheese (cottage cheese is safe); thoroughly cook leftovers and ready-to-eat foods (such as hot-dogs); and avoid foods from the deli.

For all people, the risk of listeriosis can be reduced by taking these precautions:

- Completely cook all meats and eggs.
- Carefully wash raw vegetables before eating.
- Keep raw meat away from raw vegetables and prepared foods. After cutting raw meat, wash the cutting board with detergent before using it for vegetables.

KEY TERMS

Abscess—A localized collection of pus in the skin or other body tissue caused by infection.

Immunocompromised—A state in which the immune system is suppressed or not functioning properly.

Macrophage—A large white blood cell that engulfs and digests foreign invaders, such as bacteria and viruses, in an attempt to stop them from causing disease within the body.

Meningitis—An infection or inflammation of the membranes that cover the brain and spinal cord. It is usually caused by bacteria or a virus.

Sepsis—A severe systemic infection in which bacteria have entered the bloodstream or body tissues.

- Avoid drinking unpasteurized milk or foods made from such milk.
- Wash hands thoroughly after handling raw meat.
- Follow the instructions on food labels. Observe food expiration dates and storage conditions.

Resources

BOOKS

Baltimore, Robert S. "*Listeria monocytogenes.*" In *Nelson Textbook of Pediatrics.* Edited by Richard E. Behrman et al. Philadelphia: Saunders, 2004.

Lorber, Bennet. "*Listeria monocytogenes.*" In *Principles and Practice of Pediatric Infectious Diseases*, 2nd ed. Edited by Sarah S. Long et al. St. Louis, MO: Elsevier, 2003.

PERIODICALS

Goldenberg, R. L. "The infectious origins of stillbirth." *American Journal of Obstetrics and Gynecology* 189 September 2003): 861–873.

Ressel, G. W. "CDC Issues recommendations for diagnosing, managing, and reporting foodborne illnesses." *American Family Physician* 86 (September 2004): 981–985.

WEB SITES

"Listeriosis." *Centers for Disease Control.* Available online at <www.cdc.gov/ncidod/dbmd/diseaseinfo/ listeriosis_g.htm#greatrisk> (accessed January 7, 2005).

Belinda Rowland, PhD
Rosalyn Carson-DeWitt, MD

Liver function test *see* **Bilirubin test**

Lockjaw *see* **Tetanus**

Louis-Bar syndrome *see* **Ataxia telangiectasia/chromosome breakage disorders**

Low blood sugar *see* **Hypoglycemia**

Lumbar puncture *see* **Cerebrospinal fluid (CSF) analysis**

Lung function test *see* **Pulmonary function test**

Lying

Definition

A lie is any deliberate deviation from the truth; it is a falsehood communicated with the intention to mislead or deceive.

Description

Lies differ in type, incidence, magnitude and consequence, with many gradations of severity, from harmless exaggeration and embellishment of stories, to intentional and habitual deceit. Behavioral scientist Wendy Gamble identified four basic types of lies for a University of Arizona study in 2000:

- Prosocial: Lying to protect someone, to benefit or help others.
- Self-enhancement: Lying to save face, to avoid embarrassment, disapproval or punishment.
- Selfish: Lying to protect the self at the expense of another, and/or to conceal a misdeed.
- Antisocial: Lying to hurt someone else intentionally.

Lying is considered by most child development specialists to be a natural developmental occurrence in childhood. Though there is no empirical data about how children learn to lie, parental honesty is recognized as a primary influence on the development of truthfulness in children.

Preschool

Making up stories is part of a normal fantasy life for young children. It is a positive sign of developing **intelligence** and of an active and healthy imagination. Preschool children who are beginning to express themselves through language are not yet able to make a clear distinction between reality and make-believe. Storytelling at this age is seldom an intentional effort to deceive. When preschool children do engage in intentional deceit, it is usually to avoid reprimand. They are concerned with pleasing the parent, and may **fear** the punishment for admitting a mistake or misdeed.

Many children are socialized by their parents at a very early age to tell "white"; lies to avoid hurting another's feelings. "White lies" or "fibs" are commonplace in many households and social settings and are observed and imitated by children. The incidence of prosocial or "white lies," tends to increase in children as they grow older.

Dr. Kang Lee of the Department of Psychology at Queens University in Kingston, Ontario, Canada, observed young children telling so-called "white lies" to avoid disappointing the researcher. Such prosocial lying behavior occurred in children as young as age three. Dr. Lee's research found that over 60 percent of the 400 boys and girls he studied would pretend to be pleased when asked how they liked a used bar of soap, given as a prize after playing a game with researchers. When parents instructed the children to "be polite" when the researcher asked if they liked the soap, as many as 80 percent of these children, ages three to 11 years of age were dishonest.

Dr. Michael Lewis of Robert Wood Johnson Medical School, has found that as many as 65 percent of the children he studied had learned to lie by age two and one half. This research also reveals a correlation between higher IQ and the incidence of lying in children.

School-age children

Children from age five or six have learned the difference between lies and truth. The motives for lying in this age group are more complex. Prosocial lying may increase, particularly among peers, to avoid hurting another's feelings. In addition, if a parent's expectations for the child's performance are too high, the child may engage in self-enhancing lies out of fear of censure. School-age children also experiment with selfish lies to avoid punishment, or to gain advantage. They are testing the limits as they try to understand how the rules work and what the consequences may be for stepping out of bounds.

By age seven children have developed the ability to convincingly sustain a lie. This capacity has serious implications with regard to children's competency to testify in a court of law. The veracity of child witnesses and their understanding of the concept of an oath are important research issues. Children at this age recognize the difference between what they are thinking and how they can manipulate the thinking of another to serve their own ends.

The type and frequency of lies and the reasons why a child may be dishonest are also related to their stage of **moral development**.

Children progress sequentially through several stages of moral development, according to psychologist Lawrence Kohlberg:

- avoiding punishment
- doing right for self-serving reasons
- fitting in with and pleasing others
- doing one's duty
- following agreed upon rules
- acting on principles

Adolescents are developmentally involved in becoming independent persons. They are working hard to establish their own identity, one that is separate from that of their parents. Peer approval is more important than parental approval during **adolescence**. Conflicts during these years between parental control versus personal autonomy may lead to increased lying to preserve a sense of separation and power from parents, teachers, and other authority figures. Adolescents may also lie to cover up serious behavior problems. A discerning parent will attempt to discover the motive behind the lie.

Common problems

Childhood lying has many causes, including the need to maintain parental approval, to gain attention, to avoid disappointing others, to evade the consequences of misbehavior, or to avoid responsibility. Older children may lie as a means of breaking away from parental control. Issues of **self-esteem**, fear of consequences, the desire to have one's own way, the need to gain attention, or to protect oneself from harm, are also a factor. Difficult circumstances in the home and social environment of the child may increase the likelihood of problem lying.

Early intervention in the case of compulsive lying may reduce the risk of the child developing a life-time habit of deceit. Children who are chronic liars are often found to engage in other antisocial behaviors. If a child's lying is accompanied by fighting, cheating, **stealing**, cruelty, and other impulse control problems, appropriate intervention is required. Lying that is consistently self-serving with no prosocial motive is a serious issue. Lying with malice and without any sign of remorse may indicate that the child has not yet developed a moral conscience, and may need help to move toward a higher stage of moral development, one that includes a concern for the impact of one's actions upon others.

Children become more adept liars with practice. As they grow older it may become increasingly difficult for a parent, teacher or caregiver to detect dishonesty. Close observation and familiarity with the child, as well as an understanding of their developmental stage, are critical to the diagnosis of problem lying.

Most children with the benefit of a loving **family** environment, one where honesty is valued and modeled and dishonesty is appropriately challenged, will more often than not come to recognize that lying is not an acceptable behavior. Early and appropriate intervention when problem lying persists will increase the possibility that the child will choose honesty in subsequent interactions.

Children may observe much routine dishonesty in the home, school and surrounding culture. Parental examples of honesty in interpersonal relationships are critical if a child is to develop an ethic of truthfulness. Children commonly experiment with lying in the natural course of development. They need help recognizing and understanding the distinction between prosocial and anti-social lying.

Exaggeration and embellishment when relating incidents or telling stories, and the so-called "white lies," told to avoid disappointing or hurting others feelings, do not have the negative, antisocial consequences of serious lying. Parents should intervene when the lying is of a serious nature and explain the impact of dishonesty on another's feelings. This will help the child to develop a moral sense of right and wrong and to value honesty in interpersonal relationships.

Parental concerns

Repetitive lying can develop into a serious habit leading to adjustment problems later in life. Lying that persists and worsens year after year is cause for concern. Chronic lying is often accompanied by other antisocial behaviors. Adolescents may lie to cover up illicit drug or alcohol abuse. Early parental intervention in situations of serious lying may interrupt the formation of a habit of lying in young children. Parents who model truth telling and praise honesty will encourage trust in the parent-child relationship.

When to call the doctor

Serious and repetitive lying may require the professional intervention of a school psychologist or a commu-

---

KEY TERMS

Antisocial personality disorder—A disorder characterized by a behavior pattern that disregards for the rights of others. People with this disorder often deceive and manipulate, or their behavior might include aggression to people or animals or property destruction, for example. This disorder has also been called sociopathy or psychopathy.

Conduct disorder—A behavioral and emotional disorder of childhood and adolescence. Children with a conduct disorder act inappropriately, infringe on the rights of others, and violate societal norms.

Prosocial behaviors—Social behavior characterized by positive, cooperative, and reciprocal social exchanges.

---

nity mental health agency. Counseling may help to uncover any underlying conditions such as attention-deficit/hyperactivity disorder (AD/HD), **bipolar disorder**, or learning disabilities. Pathological lying often accompanies serious psychiatric problems such as **conduct disorder** or **antisocial personality disorder**, which normally have their onset during adolescence. Children who use lying as a primary means of avoiding personal responsibility, particularly in adolescence, may be attempting to cover up more serious problems with substance abuse.

Resources

BOOKS

Brazelton, T. Berry, M.D. and Joshua D. Sparrow, M.D. *Touchpoints Three to Six.* Cambridge: Perseus Publishing, 2001.

Rincover, Arnold, Ph.D. *The Parenting Challenge, Your Child's Behavior from 6 to 12.* New York: Pocket Books, Simon & Schuster, Inc., 1991.

Walker, Hill M., et. al. *Antisocial Behavior In School.* Second Edition. Belmont, Ca: Wadsworth/Thomson Learning, 2004.

PERIODICALS

Leutwyler, Kristin. "Why Kids Lie." *Scientific American.com* November 21, 2000. [cited August 23, 2004]. <www.sciam.com/ print_version.cfm?articleID=000A6FF-1457-1C68-B882809EC5>.

Stouthamer-Loeber, Magda. "Lying as a problem behavior in children: A review." *Clinical Psychology Review* 6, no. 4

(1986): 267-289. [cited August 26, 2004]. </www.0-www.sciencedirect.com.wncln.wncln.org>.

Atkins, Andrea, "Truth & Consequences." *Parenting*. 13, no. 9 (1999).

WEB SITES

Baker, Megan. "Lies in Everyday Life." *Capital News 9 Story*. 2004. [cited August 17, 2004].

"Children and Lying." *American Academy of Child & Adolescent Psychiatry*. no. 44 (November 1995). [cited August 17, 2004]. Available online at <www.aacap.org/publications/factsfam/lying.htm>.

Godber, Yvonne. "Lying, A Handout for Parents and Teachers." *National Mental Health and Education Center*.National Association of School Psychologists, 1998. [cited August 17, 2004]. Available online at <www.naspcenter.org/lying_ho.html>.

"Growth and Development, Lying and Stealing." *Lucile Packard Children's Hospital at Stanford*. [cited August 17, 2004] Available online at <www.lpch.org/DiseaseHealthInfo/HealthLibrary/growth>.

Houle, Dr. Thomas. "Lying in children and what to do about it." *Ask Dr. Houle,* The Houle Psychology Clinic, 2003. [cited August 26, 2004].

"Lying." *American Academy of Pediatrics, Medical Library*. Excerpt from "Caring for your school-age child: Ages 5-12." Bantam, 1999. [cited August 17, 2004]. Available online at <www.medem.com/MedLB/article>.

McArthur, Greg. "Do Kids Lie? Yes—and they're good at it." *The Kingston Whig-Standard*. March 8, 2003. [cited August 17, 2004]. Available online at <qsilver.queensu.ca/law/witness/dokidslie.htm>.

McGinley, Susan. "Children and Lying." *The University of Arizona College of Agriculture and Life Sciences*. May 25, 2001. [cited August 26, 2004]. Available online at <cals.arizona.edu/media/archives/4.3.html>.

"Queen's researchers launch unprecedented study of children testifying in court." *Queen's News Centre, Queen's University* June 12, 1999. [cited August 17, 2004]. Available online at <qnc.queensu.ca/story_loader.php?id=3d4d476d5289>.

Samson, Jeri and Beth Keen, Ph.D. "Lying And Dishonesty." *not MYkid.org*. [cited August 17, 2004]. Available online at <www.notmykid.org/parentArticles/Lying/>.

Walbridge, Jean. "On Lying in Adolescence." *Mental-health-matters.com*. [cited August 17, 2004]. Available online at <www.mental-health-maters.com/articles/print.pht?artID=142>.

Wood, Derek, RN, BC, MS. "What is Antisocial Personality Disorder?" *Mental Health Matters*. [cited August 17, 2004]. Available online at <www.mental-health-matters.com/articles/print.php?artID=51>.

"When does a child know he's lying?" *Erikson Institute*. [cited August 17, 2004]. Available online at <www.erikson.edu/print.asp?file=qa=2>.

Clare Hanrahan

Lyme disease

Definition

Lyme disease is an inflammatory disease transmitted through the bite of a deer tick carrying the spiral-shaped bacterium *Borrelia burgdorferi*. Symptoms can include skin rash, joint inflammation, **fever**, **headache**, fatigue, and muscle **pain**. Lyme disease is also called Lyme borreliosis.

Description

Lyme disease is an inflammatory, systemic disease, meaning that it affects multiple body systems. Although clinical signs of Lyme disease have been reported for more than 100 years, the disease was not recognized as a distinct illness until 1975, when a cluster of unusual arthritis cases in Lyme, Connecticut, led physicians to discover that town residents living near heavily wooded areas were most affected by arthritis and other symptoms. Tick **bites** were then linked to the cause of the arthritis cases. *Borrelia burgdorferi*, the spiral-shaped bacterium called a spirochete, that causes Lyme disease, was not discovered until 1981 by Willy Burgdorfer.

Although Lyme disease is easily treated, it is not easily diagnosed, since symptoms are often attributed to other conditions. If not treated early and properly with **antibiotics**, Lyme disease can have long-term and disabling effects. In its early stages, Lyme disease affects the skin and produces flu-like symptoms; the disease spreads to the joints and nervous system in its later stages.

Transmission

Lyme disease is a vector-borne disease, meaning that it is transmitted from one host to another by a carrier—called a vector—that transmits but does not become infected with the disease. In the United States, the deer tick in the genus *Ixodes* is the vector for *Borrelia burgdorferi* and Lyme disease transmission. Lyme disease is transmitted when a tick carrying the *Borrelia burgdorferi* bacterium bites a human to feed on blood. The bacterium is transferred from the intestines of the tick through the mouthparts and into the bloodstream while the tick is feeding. Ticks are most likely to transmit *Borrelia burgdorferi* after remaining attached and feeding for two or more days. In most areas, ticks are most active from April to October, but in milder climates, ticks may bite year-round.

During their two-year life cycle and three life stages (larva, nymph, and adult), deer ticks feed on a number of mammals that may carry the *Borrelia burgdorferi* bacterium in their blood, but the white-footed mouse is the most common source of infection. In the summer, the larval ticks hatch from eggs laid in the ground and feed by attaching themselves to small animals and birds. At this stage, they are not a problem for humans. It is the next stage—the nymph—that causes most cases of Lyme disease. Nymphs are very active from spring through early summer, at the height of outdoor activity for most people. Because they are still quite small (less than 2 mm), they are difficult to spot, giving them ample opportunity to transmit *Borrelia burgdorferi* while feeding. Although far more adult ticks than nymphs carry *Borrelia burgdorferi*, the adult ticks are much larger, more easily noticed, and more likely to be removed before they have fed long enough to transmit *Borrelia burgdorferi*. Neither *Borrelia burgdorferi* nor Lyme disease can be transmitted directly from one person to another or from pets to humans.

Demographics

Lyme disease is the most common vector-borne disease in the United States. In 2002 alone, 23,763 cases were reported to the Centers for Disease Control and Prevention (CDC), a 40-percent increase over the number reported in 2001. According to the CDC, the actual number of Lyme cases may exceed 200,000 due to underreporting and limitations in disease surveillance methods. CDC statistics indicate that the largest proportion of Lyme disease cases occurs in children aged five to 14 years, and more than 50 percent of Lyme disease cases involve children under age 12. Although cases of Lyme disease have been reported in 49 of the 50 states, more than 95 percent of reported cases occur in just twelve states: Connecticut, Rhode Island, New York, Pennsylvania, Delaware, New Jersey, Maryland, Maine, New Hampshire, Minnesota, Massachusetts, and Wisconsin. In the United States, the Great Lakes region and the Pacific Northwest also have a higher incidence of Lyme disease. The disease is also found in Scandinavia, continental Europe, the countries of the former Soviet Union, Japan, China, and Australia.

Causes and symptoms

Lyme disease is caused by the *Borrelia burgdorferi* bacterium. Once *Borrelia burgdorferi* gains entry to the body through a tick bite, it can move through the bloodstream quickly. Only 12 hours after entering the bloodstream, *Borrelia burgdorferi* can be found in cerebrospinal fluid (which means it can affect the nervous system). Treating Lyme disease early and thoroughly is important because Lyme disease can hide for long periods within the body in a clinically latent state. That ability explains why symptoms can recur in cycles and can flare up after months, years, or decades.

Lyme disease is usually described in terms of length of infection (time since the person was bitten by a tick infected with Lyme disease) and whether *Borrelia burgdorferi* is localized or disseminated (spread through the body by fluids and cells carrying *Borrelia burgdorferi*). Furthermore, when and how symptoms of Lyme disease appear can vary widely from patient to patient. People who experience recurrent bouts of symptoms over time are said to have chronic Lyme disease.

Early localized Lyme disease

The most recognizable indicator of Lyme disease is a rash around the site of the tick bite. Often, the tick exposure has not been recognized. The eruption might be warm or itch. The rash—erythema migrans (EM)—generally develops within three to 30 days and usually begins as a round, red patch that expands outward from the tick bite. About 80 percent of patients with Lyme disease develop EM. Clearing may take place from the center out, leaving a bull's-eye effect; in some cases, the center gets redder instead of clearing. On children with dark skin, the rash may look like a bruise. Of those who develop Lyme disease, about 50 percent notice flu-like symptoms, including fatigue, headache, chills and fever, muscle and joint pain, and lymph node swelling. Many children with Lyme disease can develop neurologic symptoms within a few weeks following a tick bite. Neurologic symptoms in children with early Lyme disease include **dizziness**, stiff neck, unilateral or bilateral facial palsy, inflammation of brain membranes (a form of **meningitis**), knee and/or wrist arthralgia, tingling/numbness, **sleep** disturbance, and difficulties with memory, concentration, and learning.

Late disseminated disease and chronic Lyme disease

Weeks, months, or even years after an untreated tick bite, symptoms can appear in several forms, including the following:

- fatigue, forgetfulness, confusion, mood swings, irritability, numbness

- neurologic problems, such as pain (unexplained and not triggered by an injury), **Bell's palsy** (facial paralysis, usually one-sided but possibly on both sides), a mimicking of the inflammation of brain membranes known as meningitis fever, and severe headache

- arthritis (short episodes of pain and swelling in joints) and other musculoskeletal complaints (Arthritis eventually develops in about 60 percent of patients with untreated Lyme disease.)

In adults, less common effects of Lyme disease are heart abnormalities (such as irregular rhythm or cardiac block) and eye abnormalities (such as swelling of the cornea, tissue, or eye muscles and nerves). However, children with Lyme disease frequently complain of chest pain and have papilledema (swelling of the optic nerve). In addition, children with late-stage Lyme disease are more likely than adults to have fever and joint swelling and pain.

When to call the doctor

A child should see a doctor if an attached tick is found that is engorged with blood (usually indicating attachment for more than six hours). Parents should remove the tick gently with tweezers. Medical laboratories can test the tick for *Borrelia burgdorferi* if the tick is alive; parents should place the tick in a tightly sealed plastic bag or small bottle with a moistened cotton ball and take it to the doctor. Most doctors will not prescribe antibiotics immediately following a tick bite but will ask parents to monitor their child for symptoms of early Lyme disease.

Less than 50 percent of children realize that they have been bitten by a tick. And, according to pediatricians specializing in Lyme disease, many children already have chronic Lyme disease when they are first diagnosed because children have difficulties effectively verbalizing their symptoms and their symptoms may be misdiagnosed. Any child that develops a round, bull's-eye skin rash, joint pain, flu-like symptoms, and/or neurologic symptoms as described above should see a doctor. Because many children do not develop a rash or the rash may not be readily visible (e.g., on the scalp under hair), children living in or visiting areas with a high incidence of Lyme disease and those participating

in frequent outdoor activities during active tick months who develop joint pain and neurologic symptoms should see a doctor.

Diagnosis

In children, symptoms of Lyme disease can mimic those of other common childhood conditions, and children may not realize they have been bitten by a tick; therefore, diagnosis of Lyme disease in children can be difficult. Therefore, diagnosis of Lyme disease relies on information the patient and parents provide and the doctor's clinical judgment, particularly through elimination of other possible causes of the symptoms. Differential diagnosis (distinguishing Lyme disease from other diseases) is based on clinical evaluation with laboratory tests used for clarification when necessary. A two-test approach is common to confirm the results. Because of the potential for misleading results (false-positive and false-negative), laboratory tests alone cannot establish the diagnosis.

In February 1999 the Food and Drug Administration (FDA) approved a new blood test for Lyme disease called PreVue. The test, which searches for antigens (substances that stimulate the production of antibodies) produced by *Borrelia burgdorferi*, gives results within one hour in the doctor's office. A positive result from the PreVue test is confirmed by a second blood test known as the Western blot, which must be done in a laboratory.

Doctors generally know which disease-causing organisms are common in their geographic area. The most helpful piece of information is whether a tick bite or rash was noticed and whether it happened locally or while traveling. Doctors may not consider Lyme disease if it is rare locally but will take it into account if a patient mentions vacationing in an area where the disease is commonly found.

Treatment

The treatment for Lyme disease is antibiotic therapy. If a child has strong indications of Lyme disease (symptoms and medical history), the doctor will probably begin treatment on the presumption of this disease. The American College of Physicians recommends treatment for a patient with a rash resembling EM or who has arthritis, a history of an EM-type rash, and a previous tick bite.

The benefits of early treatment must be weighed against the risks of overtreatment. The longer a patient is ill with Lyme disease before treatment, the longer the course of therapy must be, and the more aggressive the

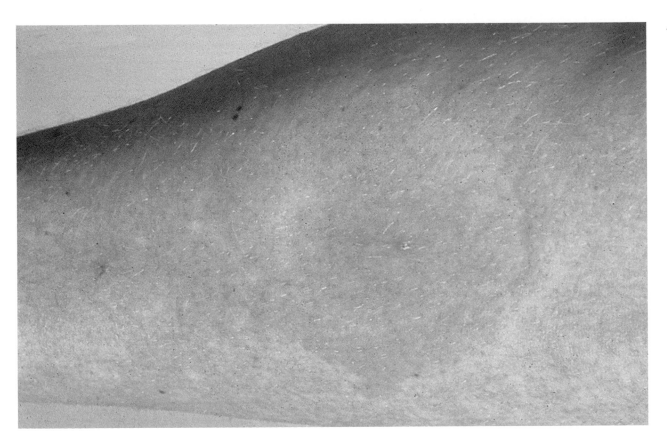

The first sign of lyme disease is usually an itchy bull's-eye rash around the site of the tick bite. *(© 1993 Science Photo Library. Custom Medical Stock Photo, Inc.)*

treatment. The development of opportunistic organisms may produce other symptoms. For example, after long-term antibiotic therapy, patients can become more susceptible to yeast infections. Treatment may also be associated with adverse drug reactions.

For most children, oral antibiotics (amoxicillin) are prescribed for 21 days. When symptoms indicate nervous system involvement or a severe episode of Lyme disease, an intravenous antibiotic (ceftriaxone, cefotaxime, ampicillin) may be given for four to six weeks or longer. Some physicians consider intravenous ceftriaxone the best therapy for any late manifestation of disease, but treatments for late Lyme disease are still controversial as of 2004. Corticosteroids (oral) may be prescribed if eye abnormalities occur, but they should not be used without first consulting an eye doctor. Nonsteroidal anti-inflammatory medications (ibuprofen) may be prescribed for joint pain and inflammation.

The doctor may have to adjust the treatment regimen or change medications based on the patient's response. Treatment can be difficult because *Borrelia burgdorferi* comes in several strains (some may react to different antibiotics than others) and may even have the ability to switch forms during the course of infection. Also, *Borrelia burgdorferi* can shut itself up in cell niches, allowing it to hide from antibiotics. Finally, antibiotics can kill *Borrelia burgdorferi* only while it is active rather than dormant.

Alternative treatment

Supportive therapies may minimize symptoms of Lyme disease or improve the immune response. These include vitamin and nutritional supplements, mostly for chronic fatigue and increased susceptibility to infection. For example, yogurt and *Lactobacillus acidophilus* preparations help fight yeast infections, which are common in patients on long-term antibiotic therapy. In addition, botanical medicine and homeopathy can be considered to help bring the body's systems back to a state of health and well-being. A Western herb, spilanthes (*Spilanthes* spp.), may be effective in treating diseases such as Lyme disease that are caused by spirochetes (spiral-shaped bacteria). Therapy using a low-current electrical field or magnetic pulses is also as of 2004 under research to treat bacterial infections. It is important to note that no alternative treatments have been proven to cure Lyme disease.

Prognosis

If aggressive antibiotic therapy is given early and the patient cooperates fully and sticks to the medication schedule, recovery should be complete. Only a small percentage of Lyme disease patients fail to respond or relapse (have recurring episodes). Most long-term effects of the disease result when diagnosis and treatment is delayed or missed. Co-infection with other infectious organisms spread by ticks in the same areas as *Borrelia burgdorferi* (babesiosis and ehrlichiosis, for instance) may be responsible for treatment failures or more severe symptoms. Most fatalities reported with Lyme disease involved patients coinfected with babesiosis.

Prevention

Lyme disease can be prevented by taking the following measures to reduce exposure to tick bites:

- Avoid areas likely to be infested with ticks, especially during spring and summer, when tick nymphs are most likely to feed. Areas most likely to be infested with ticks include moist and shady areas, wooded and brushy areas, overgrown grassy areas, and areas with a high rodent and deer population.

- When outdoors, wear light-colored clothing, long-sleeved shirts, and long pants tucked into socks or boots.

- Use insect repellents according to **safety** guidelines for children.

- Perform a full-body "tick check" after outdoor activities and use tweezers to gently remove and dispose of ticks.

- Do not try to remove the tick by using petroleum jelly, alcohol, or a lit match.

- Place the tick in a closed container (for species identification later, should symptoms develop) or dispose of it by flushing or by placing the tick between scotch tape.

- Check pets frequently for ticks, since ticks can migrate to children from pets.

Update on vaccination

A vaccine for Lyme disease known as LYMErix was available from 1998 to 2002, when it was removed from the United States market. The decision was influenced by reports that LYMErix may be responsible for neurologic complications in vaccinated patients. As of late 2004, the

---

KEY TERMS

Babesiosis—A infection transmitted by the bite of a tick and characterized by fever, headache, nausea, and muscle pain.

Bell's palsy—Facial paralysis or weakness with a sudden onset, caused by swelling or inflammation of the seventh cranial nerve, which controls the facial muscles. Disseminated Lyme disease sometimes causes Bell's palsy.

Blood-brain barrier—An arrangement of cells within the blood vessels of the brain that prevents the passage of toxic substances, including infectious agents, from the blood and into the brain. It also makes it difficult for certain medications to pass into brain tissue.

Cerebrospinal fluid—The clear, normally colorless fluid that fills the brain cavities (ventricles), the subarachnoid space around the brain, and the spinal cord and acts as a shock absorber.

Disseminated—Spread to other tissues.

Erythema migrans—A red skin rash that is one of the first signs of Lyme disease in about 75% of patients.

Lyme borreliosis—Another name for Lyme disease.

Spirochete—A type of bacterium with a long, slender, coiled shape. Syphilis and Lyme disease are caused by spirochetes.

Vector—A carrier organism (such as a fly or mosquito) which serves to deliver a virus (or other agent of infection) to a host. Also refers to a retrovirus that had been modified and is used to introduce specific genes into the genome of an organism.

---

best prevention strategy was minimizing risk of exposure to ticks and using personal protection precautions.

Parental concerns

Because most children do not realize they have been in tick-infested areas or been bitten by a tick and because deer ticks can be the size of a poppy seed or smaller, parents should be diligent about checking children for ticks, especially if the **family** lives in or visits an area with a high incidence of Lyme disease or an area near tick habitats. Also, because Lyme disease is difficult to diagnose in children, parents who suspect Lyme disease in their children should inform their doctor about the possibility of the disease and be proactive in requesting further medical evaluation and treatment.

Resources

BOOKS

"Bacterial Diseases Caused by Spirochetes: Lyme Disease (Lyme Borreliosis)." Section 13, Chapter 157 in *The Merck Manual of Diagnosis and Therapy*. Edited by Mark H. Beers and Robert Berkow. Whitehouse Station, NJ: Merck Research Laboratories, 2002.

Stewart, Gail B. *Lyme Disease*. Indianapolis, IN: Lucent Books, 2003.

PERIODICALS

Bryant, K. A., and Marshall G. S. "Clinical Manifestations of Tick-Borne Infections in Children." *Clinical and Diagnostic Laboratory Immunology* 7 (July 2000): 523–27.

Krupp, et al. "Study and Treatment of Post Lyme Disease (STOP-LD): A Randomized Double Masked Clinical Trial." *Neurology* 60 (June 24, 2003): 1923–30.

Nachman, S. A., and L. Pontrelli. "Central Nervous System Lyme Disease." *Seminars in Pediatric Infectious Diseases* 14 (April 2003): 123–30.

Pavia, C. S. "Current and Novel Therapies for Lyme Disease." *Expert Opinion on Investigational Drugs* 12 (June 2003): 1003–16.

Wormser, G. P., et al. "Duration of Antibiotic Therapy for Early Lyme Disease: A Randomized, Double-Blind, Placebo-Controlled Trial." *Annals of Internal Medicine* 138 (May 6, 2003): 697–704.

ORGANIZATIONS

Centers for Disease Control and Prevention. 1600 Clifton Rd., NE, Atlanta, GA 30333. Web site: <www.cdc.gov>.

Lyme Disease Foundation. One Financial Plaza, Hartford, CT 06103. Web site: <www.lyme.org>.

Lyme Disease Network of New Jersey Inc. 43 Winton Road, East Brunswick, NJ 08816. Web site: <www.lymenet.org>.

National Institute of Allergy and Infectious Diseases (NIAID). 31 Center Drive, Room 7A50 MSC 2520, Bethesda, MD 20892. Web site: <www.niaid.nih.gov>.

WEB SITES

"CDC Lyme Disease Home Page." *Centers for Disease Control and Prevention, Division of Vector-Borne Infectious Diseases.* Available online at <www.cdc.gov/ncidod/dvbid/lyme> (accessed November 21, 2004).

"Children's Corner." *Lyme Disease Foundation.* Available online at <www.lyme.org/children.html>(accessed November 21, 2004).

Edlow, Jonathan A. "Tick-Borne Diseases, Lyme." *eMedicine*, December 13, 2002. Available online at <www.emedicine.com/emerg/topic588.htm> (accessed November 21, 2004).

"Neurological Manifestations of Lyme Disease in Children." *LymeNet*. Available online at <http://library.lymenet.org> (accessed November 21, 2004).

Jennifer E. Sisk, MA

Lymphadenitis

Definition

Lymphadenitis is the inflammation of lymph nodes. It is often a complication of bacterial infections, although it can also be caused by viruses or other disease agents. Lymphadenitis may be either generalized, involving a number of lymph nodes, or limited to a few nodes in the area of a localized infection. Lymphadenitis is sometimes accompanied by lymphangitis, which is the inflammation of the lymphatic vessels that connect the lymph nodes.

Description

The lymphatic system is a network of vessels (channels), nodes (glands), and organs. It is part of the immune system, which protects against and fights infections, inflammation, and cancers. The lymphatic system also participates in the transport of fluids, fats, proteins, and other substances throughout the body. The lymph nodes are small structures that filter the lymph fluid and contain many white blood cells to fight infections. Lymphadenitis is marked by swollen lymph nodes that develop when the glands are overwhelmed by bacteria, virus, fungi, or other organisms. The nodes may be tender and hard or soft and "rubbery" if an abscess has formed. The skin over an inflamed node may be red and hot. The location of the affected nodes is usually associated with the site of an underlying infection, inflammation, or tumor. In most cases, the infectious organisms are *Streptococci* or *Staphylococci*. If the lymphatic vessels are also infected, in a condition referred to as lymphangitis, there will be red streaks extending from the wound in the direction of the lymph nodes, throbbing **pain**, and high **fever** and/or chills. The child will generally feel ill, with loss of appetite, **headache**, and muscle aches.

The extensive network of lymphatic vessels throughout the body and their relation to the lymph nodes helps to explain why bacterial infection of the nodes can spread rapidly to or from other parts of the body. Lymphadenitis in children often occurs in the neck area because these lymph nodes are close to the ears and throat, which are frequent locations of bacterial infections in children.

Lymphadenitis is also referred to as lymph node infection, lymph gland infection, or localized lymphadenopathy.

Demographics

Lymphadenitis and lymphangitis are common complications of bacterial infections.

Causes and symptoms

Streptococcal and staphylococcal bacteria are the most common causes of lymphadenitis, although viruses, protozoa, rickettsiae, fungi, and the **tuberculosis** bacillus can also infect the lymph nodes. Diseases or disorders that involve lymph nodes in specific areas of the body include rabbit fever (tularemia), **cat-scratch disease**, lymphogranuloma venereum, chancroid, genital herpes, infected **acne**, dental abscesses, and bubonic plague. Lymphadenitis can also occur in conjunction with cellulitis, which is a deep, widespread tissue infection that develops from a cut or sore. In children, **tonsillitis** or bacterial sore throats are the most common causes of lymphadenitis in the neck area. Diseases that involve lymph nodes throughout the body include mononucleosis, **cytomegalovirus infection**, **toxoplasmosis**, and brucellosis.

The early symptoms of lymphadenitis are swelling of the nodes caused by a build-up of tissue fluid and an increased number of white blood cells resulting from the body's response to the infection. Further developments include fever with chills, loss of appetite, heavy perspiration, a rapid pulse, and general weakness.

Diagnosis

Physical examination

The diagnosis of lymphadenitis is usually based on a combination of the child's medical history, external symptoms, and laboratory cultures. The doctor will press (palpate) the affected lymph nodes to see if they are sore or tender, and search for an entry point for the infection, like a scratch or bite. Swollen nodes without soreness are sometimes caused by cat-scratch disease, which is an uncommon illness. In children, if the lymphadenitis is severe or persistent, the doctor may need to rule out

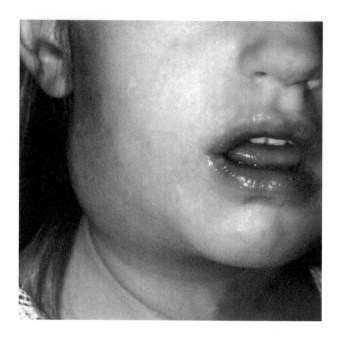

Swollen lymph node glands in a young girl's neck. *(Custom Medical Stock Photo Inc.)*

mumps, HIV, tumors in the neck region, and congenital cysts that resemble swollen lymph nodes.

Although lymphadenitis is usually diagnosed in lymph nodes in the neck, arms, or legs, it can also occur in lymph nodes in the chest or abdomen. If the child has acutely swollen lymph nodes in the groin, the doctor will need to rule out a **hernia** in the groin that has failed to reduce (incarcerated inguinal hernia). Hernias occur in 1 percent of the general population; 85 percent of children with hernias are male.

Laboratory tests

The most significant tests are a white blood cell count (WBC) and a blood culture to identify the organism. A high proportion of immature white blood cells indicates a bacterial infection. Blood cultures may be positive, most often for a species of staphylococcus or streptococcus. In some cases, the doctor may order a biopsy of the lymph node to look for unusual infection or lymphoma.

When to call the doctor

If a child develops symptoms of lymphadenitis, he or she should be taken to the doctor or emergency room.

KEY TERMS

Hernia—A rupture in the wall of a body cavity, through which an organ may protrude.

Lymph nodes—Small, bean-shaped collections of tissue located throughout the lymphatic system. They produce cells and proteins that fight infection and filter lymph. Nodes are sometimes called lymph glands.

Lymphangitis—Inflammation of the lymphatic vessels. It often occurs together with lymphadenitis (inflammation of the lymph nodes).

Septicemia—A systemic infection due to the presence of bacteria and their toxins in the bloodstream. Septicemia is sometimes called blood poisoning.

Streptococcus—Plural, *streptococci*. Any of several species of spherical bacteria that form pairs or chains. They cause a wide variety of infections including scarlet fever, tonsillitis, and pneumonia.

Treatment

Medications

The medications given for lymphadenitis vary according to the bacterium or virus that causes it. For bacterial infections, the child will be treated with **antibiotics**, usually a penicillin, clindamycin, a cephalosporin, or erythromycin.

Supportive care

Supportive care of lymphadenitis includes resting the affected area and applying hot moist compresses to reduce inflammation and pain.

Surgery

Cellulitis associated with lymphadenitis should not be treated surgically because of the risk of spreading the infection. Pus is drained only if there is an abscess and usually after the child has begun antibiotic treatment. In some cases, biopsy of an inflamed lymph node is necessary if no diagnosis has been made and no response to treatment has occurred.

Inflammation of lymph nodes due to other diseases requires treatment of the underlying causes.

Prognosis

The prognosis for recovery is good if the child is treated promptly with antibiotics. In most cases, the infection can be brought under control in three or four days. However, in some cases it may take weeks or months for swelling to disappear; the length of recovery depends on the underlying cause of the infection. Children with untreated lymphadenitis may develop abscesses, cellulitis, or blood poisoning (septicemia), which is sometimes fatal.

Prevention

Prevention of lymphadenitis depends on prompt treatment of bacterial and viral infections.

Parental concerns

Parents may be concerned that enlarged lymph nodes in their child are malignant. They should seek immediate medical attention for the child so concerns can be addressed in a timely manner.

Resources

BOOKS

Mandal, B., et al. *Lecture Notes on Infectious Disease.* Oxford, UK: Blackwell Publishing, 2004.

WEB SITES

Lymphadenitis. Available online at: <www.emedicine.com/ped/topic32/htm>.

Judith Sims
Rebecca J. Frey, Ph.D.

Macrocephaly

Definition

Macrocephaly is a condition in which the head is larger than normal.

Description

Also called macrocephalia and megalocephaly, macrocephaly is diagnosed when the circumference of the head is more than two standard deviations above average for the child's age, sex, race, and period of gestation. The fontanelle (soft spot) of the newborn is wide, but facial features are usually normal. Macrocephaly is distinguished from **hydrocephalus** in that there is no increase in pressure within the head; however, hydrocephalus can result in macrocephaly in some children. The disorder can result from a defect in formation during the embryonic stage, as a result of certain degenerative diseases, as a part of various genetic syndromes, or as an inherited **family** trait. Mental deficiency, seizures, and **movement disorders** are common in macrocephalic children.

Demographics

Because of the many conditions that cause macrocephaly, a true assessment of its incidence is difficult. It is a relatively rare condition that does not appear to affect children of any particular race, gender, or nationality with more frequency.

Causes and symptoms

Macrocephaly may be caused by many conditions. The most common causes for an enlarged head are megalencephaly, or an enlarged brain, and hydrocephalus, or excessive cerebrospinal fluid (**CSF**) in the brain.

When macrocephaly is a result of megalencephaly, it is often impossible to determine the cause. However, megalencephaly is often associated with metabolic diseases such as Canavan's disease or Alexander's disease or with syndromes such as **gigantism**, achondroplasia (**dwarfism** or small stature), **osteogenesis imperfecta**, **neurofibromatosis**, and some chromosomal anomalies. In each of these disorders, there is an enlargement of brain tissues.

In hydrocephalus, excess CSF collects in the large sections of the brain called the ventricles. This may occur for many reasons, including **Chiari malformation**, abnormal cysts within the brain, and infections such as **meningitis**.

In some cases, a child may have benign macrocephaly. In these children, the only abnormality is an enlarged head. Usually there are other family members with large heads, and the condition is considered a family trait. These children do not have an underlying condition and usually do not have any additional complications.

The major symptom of macrocephaly is an enlarged head circumference. Other symptoms can include, delay in reaching developmental milestones, **mental retardation**, rapid head growth, and slowed growth of the rest of the body.

Diagnosis

Macrocephaly is usually diagnosed by the pediatrician during a physical examination. In some cases this may be the only diagnosis necessary. Some children will require additional diagnostic imaging procedures, such as **computed tomography** scan (CAT scan), x ray, and **magnetic resonance imaging** (MRI), to determine the cause of the macrocephaly and the appropriate treatment.

KEY TERMS

Achondroplasia—A congenital disturbance of growth plate development in long bones that results in a person having shortened limbs and a normal trunk.

Alexander's disease—A progressive, degenerative disorder of the central nervous system.

Canavan disease—A serious genetic disease more common in the Eastern European Jewish population that causes mental retardation and early death. Canavan disease is caused by the lack of an enzyme called aspartoacylase.

Chiari II anomaly—A structural abnormality of the lower portion of the brain (cerebellum and brainstem) associated with spina bifida. The lower structures of the brain are crowded and may be forced into the foramen magnum, the opening through which the brain and spinal cord are connected.

Computed tomography (CT)—An imaging technique in which cross-sectional x rays of the body are compiled to create a three-dimensional image of the body's internal structures; also called computed axial tomography.

Fontanelle—One of several "soft spots" on the skull where the developing bones of the skull have yet to fuse.

Gigantism—Excessive growth, especially in height, resulting from overproduction of growth hormone during childhood or adolescence by a pituitary tumor. Untreated, the tumor eventually destroys the pituitary gland, resulting in death during early adulthood. If the tumor develops after growth has stopped, the result is acromegaly, not gigantism.

Magnetic resonance imaging (MRI)—An imaging technique that uses a large circular magnet and radio waves to generate signals from atoms in the body. These signals are used to construct detailed images of internal body structures and organs, including the brain.

Megalencephaly—A condition in which the brain is abnormally large.

Megalocephaly—An abnormally large head.

Neurofibromatosis—A progressive genetic condition often including multiple café-au-lait spots, multiple raised nodules on the skin (neurofibromas), developmental delays, slifhtly larger head size, and freckles in the armpits, groin, and iris. Also known as von Recklinghausen's disease.

Osteogensis imperfecta—An inherited disorder of the connective tissue which involves multiple symptoms, including weakened bones that break easily.

Standard deviation—A measure of the distribution of scores around the average (mean). In a normal distribution, two standard deviations above and below the mean includes about 95% of all samples.

Treatment

There is no specific treatment for macrocephaly. Medical care for children with macrocephaly focuses on management of specific symptoms such as developmental delays and mental retardation and treatment of the primary diagnosis responsible for the macrocephaly.

Prognosis

For children with benign familial macrocephaly, the prognosis is excellent. These children usually do not have any complications and have normal **intelligence**. For other children with macrocephaly, the prognosis is dependent upon the cause. In children with hydrocephalus, the prognosis can be excellent depending on what type of hydrocephalus they have. Unfortunately, many children with macrocephaly experience delayed development, slow growth, seizure disorders, and limited intelligence. All of these are related to the underlying condition that caused the macrocephaly.

Prevention

Macrocephaly is often present at birth or is a result of conditions that are present at birth. As of 2004 there was no known prevention.

Parental concerns

When mental deficiency and the attendant diseases or disorders are severe, the child may require a life-support system. When the mental deficiency is less severe, the child may be diagnosed with minimal brain dysfunction or as neurologically handicapped. Minimal brain dysfunction can include any or all of the following: memory and language problems, neuromotor functioning problems, and behavior and social problems. The degree of dysfunction is a key factor in parents' deciding whether the child can continue to live at home and what type of schooling is appropriate. Parents and teachers need to be cognizant of the nature of the child's dysfunction. What was once seen as laziness and lack of motivation on the child's part has begun in the early 2000s to be recognized as a medical condition that can be corrected or modified through psychotherapy. Sometimes, though, a child may suffer several years of frustrating failure and abnormal development or behavior before the problem is recognized and he or she is properly diagnosed.

Resources

BOOKS

Key, Doneen. *Do You Want to Take Her Home?: Trials and Tribulations of Living Life as a Handicapped Person Due to Multiple Birth Defects.* Lancaster, CA: Empire Publishing, 2001.

Moore, Keith L., et al. *Before We Are Born: Essentials of Embryology and Birth Defects.* Kent, UK: Elsevier— Health Sciences Division, 2002.

ORGANIZATIONS

Abiding Hearts. PO Box 5245 Bozeman, MT 59717. Web site: <www.abidinghearts.com>.

American Association on Mental Retardation 1719 Kalorama Road, NW Washington, DC 20009–2683. Web site: <www.aamr.org>.

March of Dimes Birth Defects Foundation. 1275 Mamaroneck Avenue, White Plains, NY 10605. Web site: <www.modimes.org>.

"National and Regional Learning and Developmental Disabilities Organizations." *Greater Boston Physicians for Social Responsibility.* Available online at <http://psr.icg.org/ihw-natl-reg-ldd-orgs.htm> (accessed October 19, 2004).

WEB SITES

"Birth Defects." *National Center on Birth Defects and Developmental Disabilities.* Available online at <www.cdc.gov/nebddd/bd/> (accessed October 19, 2004).

Deborah L. Nurmi, MS

Magnetic resonance imaging

Definition

Magnetic resonance imaging (MRI) is a diagnostic imaging procedure that uses radio waves, a magnetic field, and a computer to generate images of the anatomy.

Purpose

MRI is used to visualize the body to assist doctors in their efforts to diagnose certain diseases or conditions and to evaluate injuries. For pediatric imaging, MRI is used for a variety of purposes, including the following:

- diagnosing diseases of the central nervous system, including the brain and spine
- detecting musculoskeletal disorders and injuries
- identifying complications of infectious diseases, such as those associated with **Lyme disease** or acquired **immunodeficiency** syndrome (AIDS)
- imaging the cardiovascular system
- detecting congenital heart defects in neonates
- determining the stage of certain types of **cancer**
- evaluating bone marrow disease
- assessing blood vessels in the brain for **stroke** and other abnormalities
- assisting in the planning of surgery and cancer treatment
- evaluating the urinary tract

MRI provides images with excellent contrast that allow clinicians to clearly see details of soft tissue, bone, joints, and ligaments. MRI angiography is an imaging technique used to evaluate the blood vessels, for example, to detect aneurysms or cardiovascular problems. Because MRI does not use ionizing radiation to produce images, like x ray and CT, it is often the examination of choice for pediatric imaging and for imaging the male and female reproductive systems, pelvis and hips, and urinary tract and bladder.

MRI can also be used to evaluate brain function for assessing language, senses, neurologic disorders, and **pain**. This technique, called functional MRI, involves rapid imaging to display changes in the brain's blood flow in response to tasks or visual and auditory stimuli. Functional MRI is being researched to image neurologic disorders, such as attention deficit hyperactivity disorder (ADHD), delayed **cognitive development**, and epilepsy.

MRI spectroscopy is another emerging imaging technique for evaluating pediatric brain disorders. In MRI spectroscopy, chemicals in the brain are measured and brain tissue is imaged. This technique is being investigated to evaluate traumatic brain injury, speech delay, creatine deficiency syndromes, and **mood disorders** in young children.

Interventional and intraoperative MRI is another developing field that involves performing interventional procedures, primarily brain surgeries, using a specially designed MRI unit in an operating room.

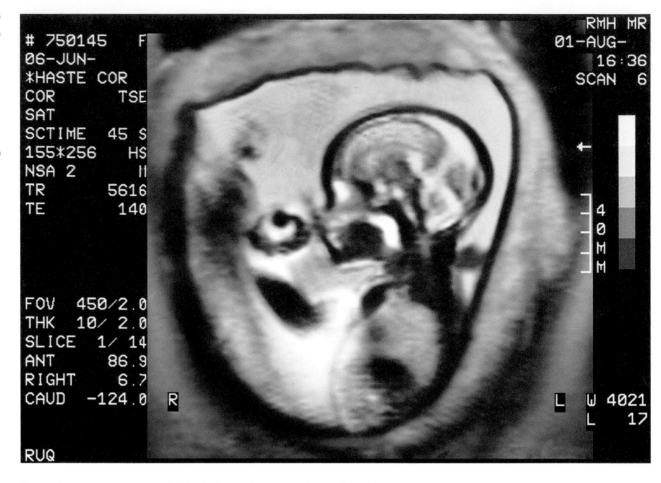

```
# 750145       F
06-JUN-
*HASTE COR
COR        TSE
SAT
SCTIME   45 S
155*256    HS
NSA 2      II
TR       5616
TE        140




FOV   450/2.0
THK   10/ 2.0
SLICE  1/ 14
ANT      86.9
RIGHT     6.7
CAUD  -124.0   R

RUQ
```

```
RMH MR
01-AUG-
16:36
SCAN  6
```

```
4
0
M
M
```

```
L  W 4021
L      17
```

Magnetic resonance imaging (MRI) of a fetus. (*© Lester Lefkowitz/Corbis.*)

Description

MRI is performed using a specialized scanner, a patient table, systems that generate radio waves and magnetic fields, and a computer workstation. The scanner, which is usually shaped like a large rectangle with a hole in the center, contains the systems that generate the magnetic field. A motorized and computer-controlled patient table moves into the scanner's center hole during the scan. A technologist operates the MRI scanner from an adjacent control room that contains a computer system and an intercom system for communicating with the patient during the scan.

In most MRI scanners, the patient opening is like a long tube, and some patients may become claustrophobic. To be more patient-friendly, different types of MRI scanners have been developed. Newer MRI scanners have shorter patient openings that allows the patient's head to remain outside the machine during body scans. Open MRI scanners are available with columns and open sides to alleviate claustrophobia.

Depending on the body area being scanned, special body coils may be used to enhance the images. These coils are foam and plastic braces or wraparound pads that are placed on the body part being imaged. For head imaging, the coil may be shaped like a head or neck rest.

Children undergoing an MRI scan are appropriately positioned on the patient table by the technologist. For some scans, an injected contrast material may be used and is administered using an intravenous catheter. Once the patient is positioned, the technologist goes to an adjacent control room to operate the scanner. The technologist uses an intercom system to instruct the child to hold their breath or remain still at certain times during the scan. Scans range from 30 minutes to 90 minutes, depending on the type of scan. When the MRI machine is scanning, the child hears loud clanging and whirring noises. To alleviate **fear** or stress related to hearing this noise and being in the small scanning tube, the child may be offered earplugs or specially designed head phones for listening to music. Centers that specialize in pediatric imaging often also have special video goggles so that the child can watch a cartoon or movie during the scan. For infants, neonatal noise guards—special padded ear shields—are available.

MRI scans are performed in a hospital radiology department for inpatients and emergency cases. For scans requested by a physician, the MRI examination can be performed in the hospital radiology department on an outpatient basis or in an imaging center. Hospitals that do not have their own MRI systems may schedule MRI scans by contracting with a company that brings an MRI scanner in a specially designed mobile trailer. Mobile MRI services are frequently used in rural areas. For some conditions, such as orthopedic disorders or injuries, an MRI may be performed in a physician's office using a small MRI unit called an extremity MRI scanner. These scanners are designed to image only the joints or the head. During this type of scan, only the body part to be scanned is placed in the smaller scanner while the patient lies on a couch or sits in a chair.

The images from an MRI examination are called slices, because they are acquired in very small (milli-meter-size) sections of the body. The image slices are displayed on a computer monitor for viewing or printed as a film. A specialist called a radiologist interprets the images produced during the MRI examination. For emergency scans, images are interpreted immediately so that the child can be treated quickly. For non-urgent outpatient MRI scans, the radiologist interprets the images and sends a report to the referring physician within a few days.

Precautions

MRI is a safe procedure that does not involve radiation. However, the magnetic field generated during an MRI examination is so strong that metal objects or objects with metal in them, such as jewelry, **eyeglasses**, oxygen canisters, and even wheelchairs, will be pulled toward the machine. Therefore, MRI staff must take special precautions to ensure that no metallic objects enter the MRI suite. MRI technologists inspect patient clothing and accessories to make sure there are no metals on them during the scan.

Preparation

Prior to any MRI scan, patients are required to remove all metal objects and remove any clothing with metal on them (zippers, snaps). In most cases, parents have to complete a survey regarding their child's past surgical procedures and medical history to indicate whether the child has any metallic implants. Metallic implants include artificial joints, pacemakers, aneurysm clips, metal plates, pins or screws, and surgical staples. Children with metallic implants are likely to undergo a **computed tomography** (CT) examination instead of an MRI.

Unlike CT, no fasting or **laxatives** are required prior to an MRI scan. Only one type of MRI scan, called a

KEY TERMS

Anaphylaxis—Also called anaphylactic shock; a severe allergic reaction characterized by airway constriction, tissue swelling, and lowered blood pressure.

Cholangiopancreatography—An examination of the bile ducts and pancreas.

Claustrophobia—Fear of small, enclosed spaces.

Computed tomography (CT)—An imaging technique in which cross-sectional x rays of the body are compiled to create a three-dimensional image of the body's internal structures; also called computed axial tomography.

Intravenous—Into a vein; a needle is inserted into a vein in the back of the hand, inside the elbow, or some other location on the body. Fluids, nutrients, and drugs can be injected. Commonly called IV.

Radiography—Examination of any part of the body through the use of x rays. The process produces an image of shadows and contrasts on film.

Radiologist—A medical doctor specially trained in radiology, the branch of medicine concerned with radioactive substances and their use for the diagnosis and treatment of disease.

magnetic resonance cholangiopancreatography (MRCP), which scans the bile ducts, requires that the child not eat or drink anything for two to three hours prior to the scan.

During the examination, the child must lie still. The MRI scanner does make loud noises throughout the examination, which can be frightening for some children. Before the examination, the procedure should be explained to the child, and it should be emphasized that the examination is painless. Most facilities have specially designed music systems so that patients can wear headsets and listen to music during the scan; some facilities even have special video goggles so children can watch a cartoon or movie during the scan.

Aftercare

No special aftercare is required following MRI scans, unless sedation or general anesthesia was used during the scan. Then children are required to remain in a supervised recovery area for an hour or more following the procedure to monitor for reactions to anesthesia. If injected contrast material is used, some minor first aid (small bandage, pain relief) for the injection site may be necessary.

Risks

MRIs present no radiation exposure. Magnetic fields used in MRI have no side effects for the patient. The contrast material used in MRI contains a material called gadolinium, that is much less likely to cause severe anaphylactic (allergic) reactions than the iodinated material used for CT scans.

Because the MRI examination is long and the patient opening in the machine is small, some children and adolescents may feel claustrophobic. Light sedation or relaxants may be administered, or an MRI scanner with a more open design may be used. For younger infants and children that require sedation or anesthesia to complete the examination, reactions to the anesthesia are possible, including headaches and **vomiting**.

Parental concerns

Younger children may be frightened of the MRI scanner, and a parent or other **family** member may be required to be present in the scanning room. To help alleviate fear, taking the child into the MRI room to see the equipment prior to the procedure may be helpful. Anyone remaining in the scanning room during the MRI examination must remove any metal objects, including jewelry and eyeglasses.

Resources

BOOKS

Medical Tests: A Practical Guide to Common Tests. Boston, MA: Harvard Health Publications, 2004.

PERIODICALS

Harvey, D. "Evaluating Pediatric Trauma: Imaging vs. Lab Tests." *Radiology Today* 5 (August 2, 2004): 14–16.

Panigrahy, A., et al. "Advances in Magnetic Resonance Imaging of Pediatric Congenital Heart Disease." *Applied Radiology*. Supplement (June 2002): 103–11.

Surface, D. "MRI Spectroscopy and Pediatric Brain Disorders." *Radiology Today* 4 (August 4, 2003): 6–8.

ORGANIZATIONS

American College of Radiology. 1891 Preston White Dr., Reston, VA 20190. Web site: <www.acr.org>.

Radiological Society of North America. 820 Jorie Blvd., Oak Brook, IL 60523–2251. Web site: <www.rsna.org>.

WEB SITES

"Magnetic Resonance Imaging (MRI)." *eMedicine Consumer Health*, July 13, 2004. Available online at <www.emedicinehealth.com/Articles/6622-1.asp> (accessed November 29, 2004).

"MR Imaging (MRI)—Body." *Radiology Info: The Radiology Information Source for Patients*, August 2004. Available online at <www.radiologyinfo.com/content/mr%5Fof%5Fthe%5Fbody.htm> (accessed November 29, 2004).

Jennifer Sisk, MA

Malnutrition

Definition

Malnutrition is a condition that develops when the body does not get the proper amount of protein, energy (calories), **vitamins**, and other nutrients it needs to maintain healthy tissues and organ function.

Description

Poor eating habits or lack of available food may lead to malnutrition. Malnutrition occurs in children who are either undernourished or overnourished. Children who are overnourished may become overweight or obese, which may lead to long-term health problems and social stress.

Undernutrition

Undernutrition is a consequence of consuming little energy and other essential nutrients, or using or excreting them more rapidly than they can be replaced. This state of malnutrition is often characterized by infections and disease. Malnutrition intensifies the effect of every disease. Severe malnutrition is most often found in developing countries. Rarely in the United States do children suffer from severe malnutrition that is not related to severe chronic illness. Deficiency in one nutrient occurs less often than deficiency in several nutrients. A child suffering from malnutrition is usually deficient in a variety of nutrients.

The leading cause of death in children in developing countries is **protein-energy malnutrition**. This type of malnutrition is the result of inadequate intake of protein and energy. Children who are already undernourished can suffer from protein-energy malnutrition when rapid growth, infection, or disease increases the need for protein and essential nutrients.

Overnutrition

In the United States, nutritional deficiencies have generally been replaced by dietary imbalances or excesses associated with many of the leading causes of death and disability. Overnutrition results from eating too much, eating too many of the wrong foods, not exercising enough, or taking too many vitamins or other dietary replacements.

Risk of overnutrition is also increased by being more than 20 percent overweight, consuming a diet high in fat and salt, and taking high doses of:

- nicotinic acid (niacin) to lower elevated cholesterol levels
- vitamin B_6 to relieve premenstrual syndrome
- vitamin A to clear up skin problems
- iron or other trace **minerals** not prescribed by a doctor

Nutritional disorders can affect any system in the body and the senses of sight, taste, and smell. Malnutrition begins with changes in nutrient levels in blood and tissues. Alterations in enzyme levels, tissue abnormalities, and organ malfunction may be followed by illness and death.

Complications

Poorly nourished children often have weakened immune systems, thus increasing their chances of illness. Underweight, malnourished teenagers (such as those with an eating disorder) have an increased risk of osteoporosis and may not have menstrual periods. They may have heart and other organ problems with severe malnutrition. Malnutrition, if left untreated, can lead to physical or mental disability, or even death.

Children who are overweight have an increased risk for long-term conditions and diseases, including cardiovascular disease, **high cholesterol**, high blood pressure, type 2 diabetes, **asthma**, **sleep** apnea, and certain cancers. Health consequences range from a higher risk of premature death to chronic conditions that reduce a person's quality of life.

Demographics

Malnutrition is a major cause of illness and death throughout the world. Throughout the developing world, malnutrition affects almost 800 million people, or 20 percent of the population. Approximately half of the 10.4 million children who die each year are malnourished. It often causes disease and disability in the children who survive. Diarrheal diseases are also a major world health problem, and may be a cause of malnutrition. Nearly all of these deaths occur in impoverished parts of Africa and Asia, where they often result from contamination of the water supply by animal and human feces.

Worldwide, the most common form of malnutrition is iron deficiency, affecting up to 80 percent of the population, as many as four or five billion people.

In contrast, children in many parts of the world are becoming increasingly overweight. What was thought of as a problem for industrialized nations only until recently, is now affecting children in developing countries. Approximately 25–30 percent of school-age children in the United States are overweight.

Causes and symptoms

Worldwide, poverty and lack of food are the primary reasons why malnutrition occurs. Families of low-income households do not always have enough healthy food to eat. When there is a household food shortage, children are the most vulnerable to malnutrition because of their high energy needs.

There is an increased risk of malnutrition associated with chronic diseases, especially disease of the intestinal tract, kidneys, and liver. Children with chronic diseases like **cancer**, **cystic fibrosis**, **AIDS**, **celiac disease**, and intestinal disorders may lose weight rapidly and become susceptible to malnutrition because they cannot absorb valuable vitamins, iron, and other necessary nutrients. Children who are lactose intolerant have difficulty digesting milk and milk products, and may be at risk for malnutrition, particularly a calcium deficiency.

Symptoms of malnutrition vary, depending on what nutrients are deficient in the body. Unintentionally losing weight may be a sign of malnutrition. Children who are malnourished may be skinny or bloated and may be short for their age (stunted). Their skin is pale, thick, dry, and easily bruised. **Rashes** and changes in pigmentation are common.

Hair is thin, tightly curled, and easily pulled out. Joints ache and bones are soft and tender. The gums bleed. The tongue may be swollen, or shriveled and cracked. Visual disturbances include night blindness and increased sensitivity to light and glare.

Other symptoms of malnutrition include:

- fatigue
- dizziness
- anemia
- **diarrhea**
- disorientation
- goiter (enlarged thyroid gland)
- loss of reflexes and lack of coordination
- muscle twitches
- decreased immune response
- scaling and cracking of the lips and mouth

Children who are overnourished are visibly overweight or obese, and consume more food than their bodies need (or expend too little energy through physical activity).

When to call the doctor

Parents who worry about malnutrition can discuss their concerns with a doctor, registered dietitian, or other health care provider. Though not an exhaustive list, treatment should be sought for a child if:

- there is a change in bodily functions (impairment)
- the child is not growing
- the child faints
- the child rapidly loses hair
- a girl at **puberty** stops menstruating or is underweight and fails to start menstruating

Diagnosis

Overall appearance, behavior, body-fat distribution, and organ function can alert a **family** physician, internist, or **nutrition** specialist to the presence of malnutrition. Parents may be asked to record what a child eats during a specific period. **X rays** or a CT scan can determine bone density and reveal gastrointestinal disturbances, as well as heart and lung damage.

Blood and urine tests are used to measure levels of vitamins, minerals, and waste products. Nutritional status can also be determined by:

- comparing a child's weight to standardized charts
- calculating body mass index (BMI) according to a formula that divides height into weight
- measuring skin-fold thickness or the circumference of the upper arm

Treatment

Normalizing nutritional status starts with a nutritional **assessment**. This process enables a registered dietitian or nutritionist to confirm the presence of malnutrition, assess the effects of the disorder, and formulate a diet that will restore adequate nutrition. For children suffering malnutrition due to an illness or underlying disorder, the condition should be treated concurrently.

Nutritional concerns

Children who cannot or will not eat, or who are unable to absorb nutrients taken by mouth, may be fed

Child suffering from the severe effects of malnutrition. *(Photograph by Bruce Brander. National Audubon Society Collection/Photo Researchers, Inc.)*

intravenously (parenteral nutrition) or through a tube inserted into the gastrointestinal tract (enteral nutrition).

Tube feeding is often used to provide nutrients to children who have **burns**, inflammatory bowel disease, or other long-term conditions that cause chronic malnutrition or malabsorption (e.g. cystic fibrosis or AIDS), and interfere with the ability to take in enough calories. This procedure involves inserting a thin tube through the nose and carefully guiding it along the throat until it reaches the stomach or small intestine. If long-term tube feeding is necessary, the tube may be placed directly into the stomach or small intestine through an incision in the abdomen.

Tube feeding cannot always deliver adequate nutrients to children who:

- are severely malnourished
- require surgery
- are undergoing **chemotherapy** or radiation treatments
- have been seriously burned
- have persistent diarrhea or vomiting
- have a gastrointestinal tract that is not functional

Intravenous feeding can also supply some or all of the nutrients these children need.

Doctors or registered dietitians can help parents can monitor overweight or obese children. These professionals may suggest a weight loss program if the child is more than 40 percent overweight. Keeping weight gain under control can be accomplished by changing eating habits, lowering fat intake, and increasing physical activity.

Prognosis

Some children with protein-energy malnutrition recover completely. Others have many health problems throughout life, including mental disabilities and the inability to absorb nutrients through the intestinal tract. Prognosis is dependent on age and the length and severity of the malnutrition, with young children having the highest rate of long-term complications and death. Death usually results from heart failure, electrolyte imbalance, or low body temperature. Children with semiconsciousness, persistent diarrhea, **jaundice**, or low blood sodium levels have a poorer prognosis.

A good prognosis exists for overweight children who make lifestyle changes and adhere to a diet and **exercise** program.

Prevention

Every child admitted to the hospital for poor weight gain or malnutrition should be screened for the presence of illnesses and conditions that could lead to protein-energy malnutrition. Children with higher-than-average risk for malnutrition should be more closely assessed, and evaluated often.

Nutritional concerns

Proper nutrition is required to ensure optimal health. Consumption of a wide variety of foods, with adequate vitamin and mineral intake, is the basis of a healthy diet. Researchers state that no single nutrient is the key to good health, but that optimum nutrition is derived from eating a diverse diet, including a variety of fruits and vegetables. Because foods such as fruits and vegetables provide many more nutrients than vitamin supplements, food is the best source for acquiring needed vitamins and minerals.

Breastfeeding a baby for at least six months is considered the best way to prevent early-childhood malnutrition. The United States Department of Agriculture and Health and Human Services recommends that all Americans over the age of two:

• consume plenty of fruits, grains, and vegetables

KEY TERMS

Anemia— A condition in which there is an abnormally low number of red blood cells in the bloodstream. It may be due to loss of blood, an increase in red blood cell destruction, or a decrease in red blood cell production. Major symptoms are paleness, shortness of breath, unusually fast or strong heart beats, and tiredness.

Electrolytes—Salts and minerals that produce electrically charged particles (ions) in body fluids. Common human electrolytes are sodium chloride, potassium, calcium, and sodium bicarbonate. Electrolytes control the fluid balance of the body and are important in muscle contraction, energy generation, and almost all major biochemical reactions in the body.

Minerals—Inorganic chemical elements that are found in plants and animals and are essential for life. There are two types of minerals: major minerals, which the body requires in large amounts, and trace elements, which the body needs only in minute amounts.

Nutrient—Substances in food that supply the body with the elements needed for metabolism. Examples of nutrients are vitamins, minerals, carbohydrates, fats, and proteins.

Vitamins—Small compounds required for metabolism that must be supplied by diet, microorganisms in the gut (vitamin K) or sunlight (UV light converts pre-vitamin D to vitamin D).

• eat a variety of foods that are low in fats and cholesterol, and contain only moderate amounts of salt, sugars, and sodium

• engage in moderate physical activity for at least 30 minutes, at least several times a week

• achieve or maintain their ideal weight

• use alcohol sparingly or avoid it altogether

Iron deficiency can be prevented by consuming red meat, egg yolks, and fortified breads, flour, and cereals.

Parental concerns

Infants, young children, and teenagers need additional nutrients to provide for growth requirements. This is also true for women who are pregnant or breastfeeding; a mother's nutritional status affects her baby. Nutrient loss can be accelerated by diarrhea, excessive sweating, heavy bleeding (hemorrhage), or kidney failure. Nutrient intake can be restricted by age-related illnesses and conditions, excessive dieting, severe injury, serious illness, a lengthy **hospitalization**, or substance abuse.

Children usually eat as much or as little as they need in order to feel satisfied. Children should be allowed to select what they want to eat among healthy food choices; they should be allowed to stop eating when they feel full. An underweight, overweight, or normal weight child should be allowed to decide how much to eat or whether to eat at all, within reason.

Parents must proactively prevent childhood **obesity** by recognizing weight imbalances when they begin. They can help an overweight child to lose weight (if medically necessary) by being supportive, rather than scolding. Parents should offer their children nutritious food choices and encourage physical activity. With proper intervention, an overweight child is not destined to become an overweight adult, but weight loss goals should be realistic.

Resources

BOOKS

Kleinman, Ronald E., and the American Academy of Pediatrics Committee on Nutrition. *Pediatric Nutrition Handbook,* 5th ed. Elk Grove Village, IL: American Academy of Pediatrics, 2003.

Physicians Committee for Responsible Medicine. *Healthy Eating for Life for Children.* Hoboken, NJ: Wiley, 2002.

Willett, Walter C., and P.J. Skerrett. *Eat, Drink, and Be Healthy: The Harvard Medical School Guide to Healthy Eating.* New York: Simon & Schuster Source, 2002.

ORGANIZATIONS

American Academy of Pediatrics. 141 Northwest Point Blvd., Elk Grove Village, IL 60007-1098. (847) 434-4000.

American College of Emergency Physicians. 1125 Executive Circle, Irving, TX 75038-2522. (800) 798-1822.

American College of Nutrition. 300 S. Duncan Ave. Ste. 225, Clearwater, FL 33755. (727) 446-6086.

American Dietetic Association. 120 South Riverside Plaza, Suite 2000, Chicago, IL 60606-6995. (800) 877-1600.

Food and Nutrition Information Center. Agricultural Research Service, USDA, National Agricultural Library, Room 105, 10301 Baltimore Boulevard, Beltsville, MD 20705-2351. Web site: <www.nal.usda.gov/fnic/fniccomments.html>.

Mary K. Fyke
Crystal Heather Kaczkowski, MSc.

Malocclusion

Definition

Malocclusion is the misalignment of the upper and lower teeth when biting or chewing.

Description

The word malocclusion literally means "bad bite." The condition may also be referred to as an irregular bite, crossbite, or overbite. Malocclusion may be seen as crooked, crowded, or protruding teeth. It may affect a child's appearance, speech, and/or ability to eat.

Demographics

Most children have some degree of malocclusion. Malocclusion usually does not require treatment except for cosmetic reasons. It is more likely to occur if the parents have malocclusion, the child sucks his or her thumb or a pacifier, or if a tooth is lost prematurely.

Causes and symptoms

Malocclusions are most often inherited, but may be acquired. Inherited conditions include too many or too few teeth, too much or too little space between teeth, irregular mouth and jaw size and shape, and atypical formations of the jaws and face, such as a **cleft palate**. Malocclusions may be acquired from habits like finger or **thumb sucking**, tongue thrusting, premature loss of teeth from an accident or dental disease, and possibly from medical conditions such as enlarged tonsils and adenoids that lead to mouth breathing.

Malocclusions may cause no symptoms, or they may produce **pain** from the increased stress on oral structures. Teeth may show abnormal signs of wear on the chewing surfaces or decay in areas of tight overlap. Chewing may be difficult.

When to call the doctor

A dentist or orthodontist should be consulted if a child's teeth seem to be particularly misaligned or if a child complains of dental or jaw pain.

Diagnosis

Malocclusion is most often found during a routine dental examination. A dentist will check a patient's occlusion by watching how the teeth make contact when the child bites down normally. The dentist may ask the

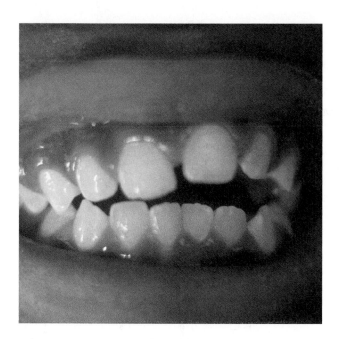

This patient's teeth are misarranged because of excessive thumb sucking. *(Photograph by K.L. Boyd. Custom Medical Stock Photo, Inc.)*

child to bite down with a piece of coated paper between the upper and lower teeth. This paper will leave colored marks at the points of contact. When malocclusion is suspected, photographs and **x rays** of the face and mouth may be taken for further study. To confirm the presence and extent of malocclusion, the dentist makes plaster or plastic models of the patient's teeth from impressions. These models duplicate the fit of the teeth and are very useful in planning treatment.

Treatment

Malocclusion may be remedied by orthodontic treatment. **Orthodontics** is a specialty of dentistry that manages the growth and correction of dental and facial structures. Braces are the most commonly used orthodontic appliances in the treatment of malocclusion. At any given time, approximately four million people in the United States are wearing braces, most of whom are children and teenagers.

Braces apply constant gentle force to slowly change the position of the teeth, straightening and properly aligning them with the opposing teeth. Braces consist of brackets cemented to the surface of each tooth and wires of stainless steel or nickel titanium alloy. When the wires are threaded through the brackets, they exert pressure against the teeth, causing them to gradually move.

Braces are not removable for daily tooth brushing. To prevent **tooth decay**, the child must be especially diligent about keeping the mouth clean and removing food particles that become easily trapped. Crunchy foods should be avoided to minimize the risk of breaking the appliance. Hard fruits, vegetables, and breads must be cut into bite-sized pieces before eating. Foods that are sticky, including chewing gum, should be avoided because they may pull off the brackets or weaken the cement. Carbonated beverages may also weaken the cement, as well as contribute to tooth decay. Teeth should be brushed immediately after eating. Special floss threaders are available to make flossing easier.

If overcrowding is creating malocclusion, one or more teeth may be extracted (surgically removed), giving the others room to move. If a tooth has not yet erupted or is prematurely lost, the orthodontist may insert an appliance, called a space maintainer, to keep the other teeth from moving out of their natural position. In severe cases of malocclusion, surgery may be necessary and the patient is referred to another specialist, an oral or maxillofacial surgeon.

Once the teeth have been moved into their new position, the braces are removed, and a retainer is worn until the teeth stabilize in that position. Retainers do not move teeth, they only hold them in place. Often a retainer is initially worn all the time; its use is gradually tapered until it is only worn at night, and eventually not at all.

Orthodontic treatment is the only effective treatment for malocclusion not requiring surgery. However, depending on the cause and severity of the condition, an orthodontist may be able to suggest other appliances as alternatives to braces. If the malocclusion is thought to be caused by the child sucking on fingers or a pacifier and the child is stopped early enough, the malocclusion may resolve spontaneously without treatment.

Alternative treatment

There are some techniques of craniosacral therapy that can alter structure. This therapy may allow correction of some cases of malocclusion. If surgery is required, pre- and post-surgical care with homeopathic remedies, as well as vitamin and mineral supplements, can enhance recovery. Night guards are sometimes recommended to ease the strain on the jaw and to limit teeth grinding.

Prognosis

Depending on the cause and severity of the malocclusion and the appliance used in treatment, a patient may expect correction of the condition to take two or more years. Patients typically wear braces 18–24 months, and a retainer for another year. Treatment is faster and more successful in children and teens whose teeth and bones are still developing. The time needed for treatment is also affected by how well the patient follows orthodontic instructions.

Prevention

In general, malocclusion is not preventable. It may be minimized by controlling habits such as thumb sucking. An initial consultation with an orthodontist before a child is seven years of age may lead to appropriate management of the growth and development of the child's dental and facial structures, circumventing many of the factors contributing to malocclusion.

Parental concerns

Most of the time, malocclusion is treated for cosmetic reasons. Children, however, may not want treatment because they will have to wear braces. It is usually possible to schedule the beginning of treatment for a time that is convenient for the child and the parent. Talking with children or teenagers and obtaining their input about treatment may be beneficial in increasing compliance. Full compliance with the orthodontist's instructions helps to ensure that the treatment is successful.

Resources

BOOKS

Bishara, Samir E., ed. *Textbook of Orthodontics*. Philadelphia: Saunders, 2001.

Subtelny, Daniel J. *Early Orthodontic Treatment*. Chicago: Quintessence Publishing Company, 2000.

PERIODICALS

"Duration of Pacifier Use, Thumb Sucking May Affect Dental Arches." *Journal of the American Dental Association* 133, no. 2 (December 2002): 1610–12.

Kluemper, G. Thomas, et al. "Early Orthodontic Treatment: What are the Imperatives?" *Journal of the American Dental Association* 131, no. 5 (May 2000): 613–21.

ORGANIZATIONS

American Association of Orthodontists. 401 North Lindberg Boulevard, St. Louis, MO 63141-7816. (800) STRAIGHT Fax: (3314)-997-1745. Web site: </www.braces.org>.

American Dental Association. 211 East Chicago Avenue, Chicago IL, 60611-2678. (312) 440-2500. Web site: <http://www.ada.org>.

Tish Davidson, A.M.
Bethany Thivierge

Manic depression *see* **Bipolar disorder**

Marfan syndrome

Definition

Marfan syndrome is an inherited disorder of the connective tissue that causes abnormalities of a child's eyes, cardiovascular system, and musculoskeletal system. It is named for the French pediatrician, Antoine Marfan (1858-1942), who first described it in 1896.

Description

Marfan syndrome affects three major organ systems of the body: the heart and circulatory system, the bones and muscles, and the eyes. The genetic mutation responsible for Marfan was discovered in 1991. It affects the body's production of fibrillin, which is a protein that is an important part of connective tissue. Fibrillin is the primary component of the microfibrils that allow tissues to stretch repeatedly without weakening. Because the child's fibrillin is abnormal, his or her connective tissues are looser than usual, which weakens or damages the support structures of the entire body.

The most common external signs associated with Marfan syndrome include excessively long arms and legs, with the child's arm span being greater than his or her height. The fingers and toes may be long and slender, with loose joints that can be bent beyond their normal limits. This unusual flexibility is called hypermobility. The child's face may also be long and narrow, and he or she may have a noticeable curvature of the spine. It is important to note, however, that children with Marfan vary widely in the external signs of their disorder and in their severity; even two children from the same **family** may look quite different. Most of the external features of Marfan syndrome become more pronounced as the child gets older, so that diagnosis of the disorder is often easier in adults than in children. In many cases, the child may have few or very minor outward signs of the disorder, and the diagnosis may be missed until the child develops vision problems or cardiac symptoms.

Marfan syndrome by itself does not affect a child's **intelligence** or ability to learn. There is, however, some clinical evidence that children with Marfan have a slightly higher rate of hyperactivity and attention-deficit disorder (ADD) than the general population. In addition, a child with undiagnosed nearsightedness related to Marfan may have difficulty seeing the blackboard or reading printed materials, and thus do poorly in school.

Marfan syndrome affects males and females equally, and appears to be distributed equally among all races and ethnic groups. The rate of mutation of the fibrillin gene, however, appears to be related to the age of the child's father; older fathers are more likely to have new mutations appear in chromosome 15.

Marfan syndrome is sometimes called arachnodactyly, which means "spider-like fingers" in Greek, since one of the characteristic signs of the disease is disproportionately long fingers and toes.

Demographics

It is estimated that one person in every 3000-5000 has Marfan syndrome, or about 50,000 people in the United States. Marfan syndrome is one of the more common inheritable disorders.

Causes and symptoms

Marfan syndrome is caused by a single gene for fibrillin on chromosome 15, which is inherited in most cases from an affected parent. Between 15 and 25 percent of cases result from spontaneous mutations. Mutations of the fibrillin gene (FBNI) are unique to each family affected by Marfan, which makes rapid genetic diagnosis impossible, given present technology. The syndrome is an autosomal dominant disorder, which means that someone who has it has a 50 percent chance of passing it on to any offspring.

Another important genetic characteristic of Marfan syndrome is variable expression. This term means that the mutated fibrillin gene can produce a variety of symptoms of very different degrees of severity, even in members of the same family.

Cardiac and circulatory abnormalities

The most important complications of Marfan are those affecting the heart and major blood vessels; some are potentially life-threatening. About 90 percent of children with Marfan will develop cardiac complications, including:

• Aortic enlargement. This is the most serious potential complication of Marfan syndrome. Because of the abnormalities of the child's fibrillin, the walls of the aorta (the large blood vessel that carries blood away from the heart) are weaker than normal and tend to stretch and bulge out of shape. This stretching increases the likelihood of an aortic dissection, which is a tear or separation between the layers of tissue that make up the aorta. An aortic dissection usually causes severe **pain** in the abdomen, back, or chest, depending on the section of the aorta that is affected. Rupture of the aorta is a medical emergency requiring immediate surgery and medication.

• Aortic regurgitation. A weakened and enlarged aorta may allow some blood to leak back into the heart during each heartbeat; this condition is called aortic regurgitation. Aortic regurgitation occasionally causes shortness of breath during normal activity. In serious cases, it causes the left ventricle of the heart to enlarge and may eventually lead to heart failure.

• Mitral valve prolapse. Between 75 and 85% of children with Marfan have loose or "floppy" mitral valves, which are the valves that separate the chambers of the heart. When these valves do not cover the opening between the chambers completely, the condition is called mitral valve prolapse. Complications of mitral valve prolapse include **heart murmurs** and arrhythmias. In rare cases, mitral valve prolapse can cause sudden death.

• Infective endocarditis. Infective endocarditis is an infection of the endothelium, the tissue that lines the heart. In children with Marfan, it is the abnormal mitral valve that is most likely to become infected.

• Other complications. Some children with Marfan develop cystic disease of the lungs or recurrent spontaneous pneumothorax, which is a condition in which air accumulates in the space around the lungs. Many will also eventually develop emphysema.

Musculoskeletal abnormalities

Marfan syndrome causes an increase in the length of the child's bones, with decreased support from the ligaments that hold the bones together. As a result, the child may develop various deformities of the skeleton or disorders related to the relative looseness of the ligaments.

Disorders of the spine

Children with Marfan syndrome also can experience spinal disorders, including:

- **Scoliosis**. Scoliosis, or curvature of the spine, is a disorder in which the vertebrae that make up the spine twist out of line from side to side into an S-shape or a spiral. It is caused by a combination of the rapid growth of children with Marfan, and the looseness of the ligaments that help the spine to keep its shape.

- Kyphosis. Kyphosis is an abnormal outward curvature of the spine at the back, sometimes called hunch back when it occurs in the upper back. Children with Marfan may develop kyphosis either in the upper (thoracic) spine or the lower (lumbar) spine.

- Spondylolisthesis. Spondylolisthesis is the medical term for a forward slippage of one vertebra on the one below it. It produces an ache or stiffness in the lower back.

- Dural ectasia. The dura is the tough, fibrous outermost membrane covering the brain and the spinal cord. The weak dura in a child with Marfan swells or bulges under the pressure of the spinal fluid. This swelling is called ectasia. In most cases, dural ectasia occurs in the lower spine, producing low back ache, a burning feeling, or **numbness** or weakness in the legs.

Disorders of the chest and lower body

Disorders of the chest and lower body of children with Marfan include:

- Pectus excavatum. Pectus excavatum is a malformation of the chest in which the child's breastbone, or sternum, is sunken inward. It can cause difficulties in breathing, especially if the heart, spine, and lung have been affected by Marfan. It also usually causes concerns about appearance.

- Pectus carinatum. In other children with Marfan, the sternum is pushed outward and narrowed. Although pectus carinatum does not cause breathing difficulties, it can cause embarrassment about appearance. A few children with Marfan may have a pectus excavatum on one side of their chest and a pectus carinatum on the other.

- Foot disorders. Children with Marfan are more likely to develop pes planus (flat feet) or so-called "claw" or "hammer" toes than people in the general population. They are also more likely to suffer from chronic pain in their feet.

- Protrusio acetabulae. The acetabulum is the socket of the hip joint. In a child with Marfan, the acetabulum

becomes deeper than normal during growth, for reasons that are not yet understood. Although protrusio acetabulae does not cause problems during childhood and **adolescence**, it can lead to a painful form of arthritis in adult life.

Disorders of the eyes and face

Although the visual problems that are related to Marfan syndrome are rarely life-threatening, they are important in that they may be the child's first indication of the disorder. Eye disorders related to the syndrome include the following:

- Myopia (nearsightedness). Most children with Marfan develop nearsightedness, usually in childhood.

- Ectopia lentis. Ectopia lentis is the medical term for dislocation of the lens of the eye. Between 65 and 75 percent of children with Marfan have dislocated lenses. This condition is an important indication for diagnosis of the syndrome because there are relatively few other disorders that produce it.

- Glaucoma. This condition is much more prevalent in children with Marfan syndrome than in the general population.

- Cataracts. Children with Marfan are more likely to develop cataracts, and to develop them much earlier in life, sometimes as early as 40 years of age.

- Retinal detachment. Children with Marfan are more vulnerable to this disorder because of the weakness of their connective tissues. Untreated retinal detachment can cause blindness. The danger of retinal detachment is an important reason for children to avoid contact **sports** or other activities that could cause a blow on the head or being knocked to the ground.

- Other facial problems. Children with Marfan sometimes develop dental problems related to crowding of the teeth caused by a high-arched palate and a narrow jaw.

Other disorders

Other disorders associated with Marfan syndrome include:

- Striae. Striae are stretch marks in the skin caused by rapid weight gain or growth; they frequently occur in pregnant women, for example. Children with Marfan often develop striae over the shoulders, hips, and lower back at an early age because of rapid bone growth. Although the child may be self-conscious about the striae, they are not a danger to health.

- Obstructive **sleep** apnea. Obstructive sleep apnea refers to partial obstruction of the airway during sleep, causing irregular breathing and sometimes snoring. In children with Marfan, obstructive sleep apnea is caused by the unusual flexibility of the tissues lining the child's airway. This disturbed breathing pattern increases the risk of aortic dissection.

When to call the doctor

Prospective parents with a family history of Marfan syndrome should check with their doctor concerning genetic counseling. Also a doctor should be called if a child has symptoms suggestive of Marfan syndrome.

Diagnosis

Presently, there is no objective diagnostic test for Marfan syndrome, in part because the disorder does not produce any measurable biochemical changes in the child's blood or body fluids, or cellular changes that can be detected from a tissue sample. Although researchers in molecular biology are currently investigating the FBNI gene through a process called mutational analysis, it is presently not useful as a diagnostic test because there is evidence that there can be mutations in the fibrillin gene that do not produce Marfan. Similarly, there is no reliable prenatal test, although some physicians have used ultrasound to try to determine the length of fetal limbs in at-risk pregnancies.

The diagnosis is made by taking a family history and a thorough examination of the child's eyes, heart, and bone structure. The examination should include an echocardiogram taken by a cardiologist, a slit-lamp eye examination by an ophthalmologist, and a work-up of the child's spinal column by an orthopedic specialist. In terms of the cardiac examination, a standard electrocardiogram (EKG) is not sufficient for diagnosis; only the echocardiogram can detect possible enlargement of the aorta. The importance of the slit-lamp examination is that it allows the doctor to detect a dislocated lens, which is a significant indication of the syndrome.

The symptoms of Marfan syndrome in some children resemble the symptoms of homocystinuria, which is an inherited disorder marked by extremely high levels of homocystine in the child's blood and urine. This possibility can be excluded by a urine test.

In other cases, the diagnosis remains uncertain because of the mildness of the child's symptoms, the absence of a family history of the syndrome, and other variables. These borderline conditions are sometimes referred to as marfanoid syndromes.

Treatment

The treatment and management of Marfan is tailored to the specific symptoms of each child. Some children find that the syndrome has little impact on their overall lifestyle; others have found their lives centered on the disorder.

Cardiovascular system

After a child has been diagnosed with Marfan, he or she should be monitored with an echocardiogram every six months until it is clear that the aorta is not growing larger. After that, he or she should have an echocardiogram once a year. If the echocardiogram does not allow the physician to visualize all portions of the aorta, CT (**computed tomography**) or MRI (**magnetic resonance imaging**) may be used. In cases involving a possible aortic dissection, the child may be given a TEE (transesophageal echocardiogram).

Medications. A child with Marfan may be given drugs called beta-blockers to slow down the rate of aortic enlargement and decrease the risk of dissection by lowering the blood pressure and decreasing the forcefulness of the heartbeat. The most commonly used beta-blockers in chidren with Marfan are propranolol (Inderal) and atenolol (Tenormin). Children who are allergic to beta-blockers may be given a calcium blocker such as verapamil.

Because children with Marfan are at increased risk for infective endocarditis, they must take a prophylactic dose of an antibiotic before having dental work or minor surgery, as these procedures may allow bacteria to enter the bloodstream. Penicillin and amoxicillin are the **antibiotics** most often used.

Surgical treatment. Surgery may be necessary if the width of the child's aorta increases rapidly or reaches a critical size (about 2 inches [5 cm]). The most common surgical treatment involves replacing the child's aortic valve and several inches of the aorta itself with a composite graft, which is a prosthetic heart valve sewn into one end of a Dacron tube. This surgery has been performed widely since about 1985; most children who have had a composite graft have not needed additional surgery. Children who have had a valve replaced must take an anticoagulant medication, usually warfarin (Coumadin), in order to minimize the possibility of a clot forming on the prosthetic valve.

Musculoskeletal system

Children diagnosed with Marfan should be checked for scoliosis by their pediatricians at each annual physical examination. The doctor simply asks the child to bend forward while the back is examined for changes in the curvature. In addition, the child's spine should be x rayed in order to measure the extent of scoliosis or kyphosis. The curve is measured in degrees by the angle between the vertebrae as seen on the x ray. Curves of 20 degrees or less are not likely to become worse. Curves between 20 and 40

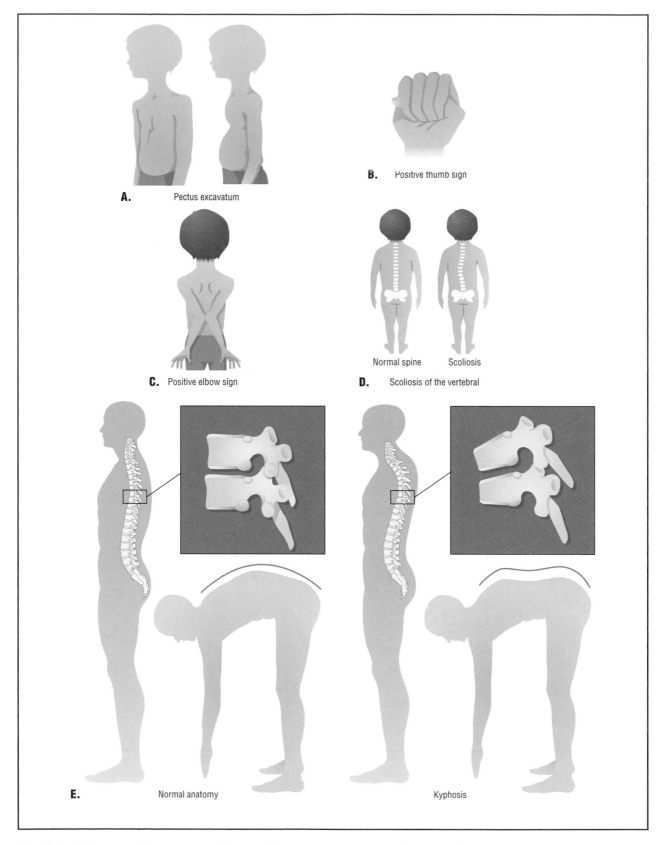

A. Pectus excavatum

B. Positive thumb sign

C. Positive elbow sign

Normal spine   Scoliosis

D. Scoliosis of the vertebral

E. Normal anatomy   Kyphosis

Five clinical signs of Marfan syndrome: (left to right) pectus excavatum, positive thumb sign, positive elbow sign, normal spine compared with scoliosis, normal anatomy compared with kyphosis. *(Illustration by Argosy, Inc.)*

degrees are likely to increase in children or adolescents. Curves of 40 degrees or more are highly likely to worsen, even in an adult, because the spine is so badly imbalanced that the force of gravity will increase the curvature.

Scoliosis between 20 and 40 degrees in children is usually treated with a back brace. The child must wear this appliance about 23 hours a day until growth is complete. If the spinal curvature increases to 40 or 50 degrees, the child may require surgery in order to prevent lung problems, back pain, and further deformity. Surgical treatment of scoliosis involves straightening the spine with metal rods and fusing the vertebrae in the straightened position.

Spondylolisthesis is treated with a brace in mild cases. If the slippage is more than 30 degrees, the slipped vertebra may require surgical realignment.

Dural ectasia can be distinguished from other causes of back pain on an MRI. Mild cases are usually not treated. Medication or spinal shunting to remove some of the spinal fluid are used to treat severe cases.

Pectus excavatum and pectus carinatum can be treated by surgery. In pectus excavatum, the deformed breastbone and ribs are raised and straightened by a metal bar. After four to six months, the bar is removed in an outpatient procedure.

Protrusio acetabulae may require artificial hip joint surgery in adult life, if the arthritic pains are severe.

Pain in the feet or limbs is usually treated with a mild analgesic such as **acetaminophen**. Children with Marfan should consider wearing shoes with low heels, special cushions, or orthotic inserts. Foot surgery is rarely necessary.

Visual and dental concerns

Children with Marfan should have a thorough eye examination, including a slit-lamp examination, to test for dislocation of the lens as well as nearsightedness. Dislocation can be treated by a combination of special glasses and daily use of one percent atropine sulfate ophthalmic drops, or by surgery.

Because children with Marfan are at increased risk of glaucoma, they should have the fluid pressure inside the eye measured every year as part of an eye examination. Glaucoma can be treated with medications or with surgery.

Cataracts are treated with increasing success by implant surgery. It is important, however, to seek treatment at medical centers with eye surgeons familiar with the possible complications of cataract surgery in children with Marfan syndrome.

All children with Marfan should be taught to recognize the signs of retinal detachment (sudden blurring of

---

KEY TERMS

Arachnodactyly—A condition characterized by abnormally long and slender fingers and toes.

Ectopia lentis—Dislocation of the lens of the eye. It is one of the most important single indicators in diagnosing Marfan syndrome.

Fibrillin—A protein that is an important part of the structure of the body's connective tissue. In Marfan's syndrome, the gene responsible for fibrillin has mutated, causing the body to produce a defective protein.

Hypermobility—Unusual flexibility of the joints, allowing them to be bent or moved beyond their normal range of motion.

Kyphosis—An extreme, abnormal outward curvature of the spine, with a hump at the upper back.

Pectus carinatum—An abnormality of the chest in which the sternum (breastbone) is pushed outward. It is sometimes called "pigeon breast."

Pectus excavatum—An abnormality of the chest in which the sternum (breastbone) sinks inward; sometimes called "funnel chest."

Scoliosis—An abnormal, side-to-side curvature of the spine.

---

vision in one eye becoming progressively worse without pain or redness) and ask their parents to seek professional help immediately.

Children with Marfan should be evaluated by their dentist at each checkup for crowding of the teeth and possible misalignment and referred to an orthodontist if necessary.

Athletic activities and occupational choice

Children with Marfan should avoid sports or occupations that require heavy weight lifting, rough physical contact, or rapid changes in atmospheric pressure (e.g., scuba diving). Weight lifting increases blood pressure, which in turn may enlarge the aorta. Rough physical contact may cause retinal detachment. Sudden changes in air pressure may produce pneumothorax. Regular noncompetitive physical **exercise**, however, is beneficial for children with Marfan. Good choices include brisk walking, shooting baskets, and slow-paced tennis.

Social and lifestyle issues

Smoking is particularly harmful for children and adolescents with Marfan because it increases their risk of emphysema.

Children and adolescents with Marfan may benefit from supportive counseling regarding appearance, particularly if their symptoms are severe enough to cause them to withdraw from social activities.

Prognosis

The prognosis for children with Marfan has improved markedly in recent years. By 1995, the life expectancy of people with the syndrome increased to 72 years, up from 48 years in 1972. This dramatic improvement is attributed to new surgical techniques, improved diagnosis, and new techniques of medical treatment.

The most important single factor in improving the child's prognosis is early diagnosis. The earlier that a child can benefit from the new techniques and lifestyle modifications, the more likely he or she is to have a longer life expectancy.

Prevention

Marfan syndrome that occurs because of spontaneous new mutations (15% to 25% of the cases) cannot be prevented. However, for prospective parents with a family history of Marfan syndrome, genetic counseling is recommended. Also, older fathers are more likely to have new mutations appear in chromosome 15.

Parental concerns

Families may wish to seek counseling regarding the effects of the syndrome on relationships within the family. Many people respond with guilt, **fear**, or blame when a genetic disorder is diagnosed in the family, or they may overprotect the affected member. Support groups are often good sources of information about Marfan; they can offer helpful suggestions about living with it as well as emotional support.

Resources

BOOKS

Marfan Syndrome: A Medical Dictionary, Bibliography, and Annotated Research Guide to Internet References. San Diego, CA: Icon Health Publications, 2004.

The Official Patient's Sourcebook on Klinefelter Syndrome. San Diego, CA: Icon Health Publications, 2002.

PM Medical Health News. *21st Century Complete Medical Guide to Marfan Syndrome: Authoritative Government Documents, Clinical References, and Practical Information for Patients and Physicians.* CD-ROM.Washington, DC: Progressive Management, 2004.

Pyeritz, Reed E., and Cheryll Gasner. *The Marfan Syndrome.* New York: National Marfan Syndrome, 1999.

Robinson, Peter. *Marfan Syndrome.* New York: Kluwer Academic Publishers, 2004.

ORGANIZATIONS

Alliance of Genetic Support Groups, 4301 Connecticut Avenue, Washington, DC, 20008. (202) 652-5553. <http:www.geneticalliance.org>.

National Marfan Foundation, 22 Manhasset Avenue, Port Washington, NY, 11050-2023. (516) 883-8712, (800). 862-7326. <http:www.marfan.org>.

WEB SITES

Marfan Syndrome, National Institutes of Health. <http://www.nlm.nih.gov/medlineplus/marfansyndrome.html>.

Judith Sims, MS
Rebecca J. Frey, PhD

Martin-Bell syndrome *see* **Fragile X syndrome**

Massage therapy

Definition

Massage therapy is the scientific manipulation of the soft tissues of the body, consisting primarily of manual (hands-on) techniques such as applying fixed or movable pressure, holding, and moving muscles and body tissues.

Purpose

Generally, massage is delivered to improve the flow of blood and lymph (fluid in lymph glands, part of immune system), to reduce muscular tension or flaccidity, to affect the nervous system through stimulation or sedation, and to enhance tissue healing. Therapeutic massage may be recommended for children and adults to deliver benefits such as the following:

• reducing muscle tension and stiffness

• relieving muscle spasms

• increasing joint and limb flexibility and range of motion

• increasing ease and efficiency of movement

• relieving points of tension and overall stress; inducing relaxation

• promoting deeper and easier breathing

- improving blood circulation and movement of lymph
- relieving tension-related headaches and eyestrain
- promoting faster healing of soft tissue injuries, such as pulled muscles and sprained ligaments
- reducing **pain** and swelling related to injuries
- reducing the formation of scar tissue following soft tissue injuries
- enhancing health and nourishment of skin
- improving posture by changing tension patterns that affect posture
- reducing emotional or physical stress and reducing **anxiety**
- promoting feelings of well-being
- increasing awareness of the mind-body connection and improving mental awareness and alertness generally

Massage therapy may also be recommended for its documented clinical benefits such as improving pulmonary function in young **asthma** patients, reducing psychoemotional distress in individuals who suffer from chronic inflammatory bowel disease, helping with weight gain, improving motor development in premature infants, and enhancing immune system functioning.

Description

Massage therapy is one of the oldest healthcare practices known. References to massage are found in ancient Chinese medical texts written more than 4,000 years ago. Massage has been advocated in Western healthcare practices since the time of Hippocrates, the "father of medicine."

Massage therapy is the scientific manipulation of the soft tissues of the body for the purpose of normalizing those tissues and consists of a group of manual techniques that include applying fixed or movable pressure, holding, and/or causing movement to parts of the body. While massage therapy is applied primarily with the hands, sometimes the forearms or elbows are used. These techniques affect the muscular, skeletal, circulatory, lymphatic, nervous, and other systems of the body. The basic philosophy of massage therapy embraces the concept of *vis Medicatrix naturae*, which means "aiding the ability of the body to heal itself."

Touch is the fundamental medium of massage therapy. While massage can be described in terms of the type of techniques performed, touch is not used solely in a mechanistic way in massage therapy. Because massage usually involves applying touch with some degree of pressure and movement, the massage therapist must use touch with sensitivity in order to determine the optimal amount of pressure to use for each person. For example, using too much pressure may cause the body to tense up, while using too little may not have enough effect. Touch used with sensitivity also allows the massage therapist to receive useful information via his or her hands about the individual's body, such as locating areas of muscle tension and other soft tissue problems. Because touch is also a form of communication, sensitive touch can convey a sense of caring to the person receiving massage, enhancing the individual's sense of self and well being.

In practice, many massage therapists use more than one technique or method in their work and sometimes combine several. Effective massage therapists ascertain each person's needs and then use the techniques that will best meet those needs.

Swedish massage is the most commonly used form of massage. It uses a system of long gliding strokes, kneading, and friction techniques on the more superficial layers of muscles, generally in the direction of blood flow toward the heart, and sometimes combined with active and passive movements of the joints. It is used to promote general relaxation, improve circulation and range of motion, and relieve muscle tension.

Deep tissue massage is used to release chronic patterns of muscular tension using slow strokes, direct pressure, or friction directed across the grain of the muscles. It is applied with greater pressure and to deeper layers of muscle than Swedish, which is why it is called deep tissue and is effective for chronic muscular tension.

Sports massage uses techniques that are similar to Swedish and deep tissue but are specially adapted to deal with the effects of athletic performance on the body and the needs of athletes regarding training, performing, and recovery from injury.

Neuromuscular massage is a form of deep massage that is applied to individual muscles. It is used primarily to release trigger points (intense knots of muscle tension that refer pain to other parts of the body) and also to increase blood flow. It is often used to reduce pain. Trigger point massage and myotherapy are similar forms.

Acupressure applies finger or thumb pressure to specific points located on the energy pathways or "meridians" in order to release blocked energy along these meridians that may be causing physical discomfort. The rebalance of energy flow releases tension and restores function of organs and muscles in the body. Shiatsu is a Japanese form of acupressure that applies these principles.

Massage therapy sessions can be at home or in a professional office. Most sessions are one hour. Frequency of massage sessions can vary widely as needed based on

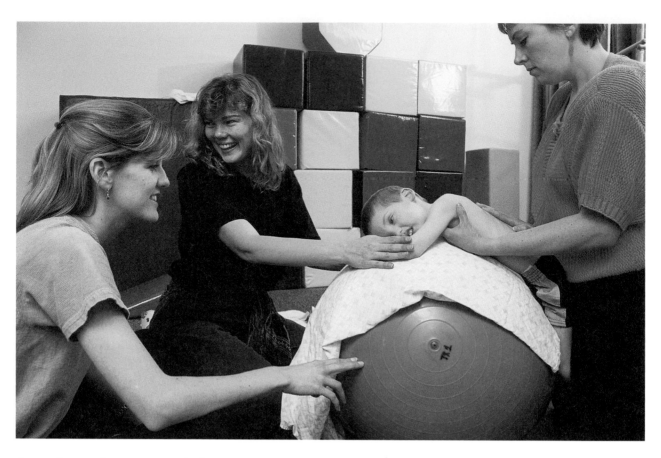

A young boy receives a massage. *(© Owen Franken/Corbis.)*

the condition being treated. The cost of massage therapy varies according to geographic location, experience of the massage therapist, and length of the massage. In the United States, as of 2004, the average range is from $35 to $60 for a one-hour session.

The first appointment generally begins with information gathering, such as the reason for getting massage therapy, physical condition and medical history, and other areas. The client is asked to remove clothing to one's level of comfort. Undressing takes place in private, and a sheet or towel is provided for draping. The massage therapist will undrape only the part of the body being massaged. The individual's modesty is respected at all times. The massage therapist may use an oil or cream, which is quickly absorbed into the skin.

Insurance coverage for massage therapy varies widely. There tends to be greater coverage in states that license massage therapy. In most cases, a physician's prescription for massage therapy is needed. Once massage therapy is prescribed, authorization from the insurer may be needed if coverage is not clearly spelled out in one's policy or plan.

Massage therapy may be recommended for children to help relieve conditions such as **allergies**, anxiety and stress, arthritis, asthma and **bronchitis**, joint or limb injuries, post-surgical muscle rehabilitation, chronic and temporary pain, circulatory problems, depression, digestive disorders, tension headaches, **sleep** problems or insomnia, myofascial pain, **sports injuries**, and eating problems associated with temporomandibular joint dysfunction.

Precautions

Massage is comparatively safe; however, it should not be used if the child has one of the following conditions.

- advanced heart disease
- hypertension (high blood pressure)
- phlebitis
- thrombosis
- embolism
- kidney failure

If the child has **cancer**, massage is not advisable if the cancer is the kind that can spread to other organs (metastatic cancer) or if it involves tissue damage due to chemotherapy or other treatment. Massage may also not be advisable if the child has any of the following conditions.

- a cold
- an infectious disease
- a contagious skin conditions
- an acute inflammation
- an infected injuries
- an unhealed fractures
- dislocations
- is postoperative with a condition in which pain and muscular splinting are increased
- has frostbite
- has large hernias
- has torn ligaments
- has any condition prone to hemorrhage
- has a psychosis
- has any other psychological state that may impair communication or perception

Massage should not be used locally on affected areas (i.e., avoid using massage on the specific areas of the body that are affected by the condition) for the following conditions: eczema, goiter (thyroid dysfunction), and open skin lesions. Massage may be used on the areas of the body that are not affected by these conditions. The decision to use massage must be based on whether it may cause harm. A physician's recommendation is appropriate before a child with any health condition receives massage therapy.

Preparation

Going for a massage requires little in the way of preparation. Generally, one should be clean and should not eat just before a massage. Massage therapists generally work by appointment and usually provide information about how to prepare for an appointment. To receive the most benefit from a massage, parents should give the therapist accurate health information about the child and report discomfort of any kind (whether it is from the massage itself or due to the room temperature or any other distractions). The child can be encouraged to be as receptive to the process as possible.

Aftercare

There are no special recommendations for after a massage. A period of quiet activity or rest following the massage helps maintain full benefits from the procedure.

KEY TERMS

Lymph—Clear, slightly yellow fluid carried by a network of thin tubes to every part of the body. Cells that fight infection are carried in the lymph.

Manipulation—Moving muscles or connective tissue to enhance function, ease tension, and reduce pain in those tissues as well as other beneficial effects.

Mind-body connection—Rather than relying on an understanding of the term "psychosomatic," mind-body medicine acknowledges the influence of thinking and the cognitive process on the behavior of chemicals in the body, involving the mind in both creating the conditions for disease and helping to heal the effects of disease.

Psychoses—Mental illness that interferes with an individual's ability to manage life's challenges and everyday activities. The impairment of cognitive ability that distorts reality.

Risks

Massage therapy does not have notable side effects. Rather than feeling too relaxed or too mentally unfocused after a massage, a child may be both more relaxed and more alert.

Parental concerns

Parents who may not have experienced therapeutic massage themselves or who have doubts about its effectiveness may be interested in the results of research studies, particularly those conducted on groups of children. Well designed studies have documented the benefits of massage therapy for the treatment of acute and chronic pain, acute and chronic inflammation, chronic lymphedema, **nausea**, muscle spasm, various soft tissue dysfunctions, anxiety, depression, insomnia, and psychoemotional stress, which may aggravate mental illness.

Premature infants treated with daily massage therapy gain more weight and have shorter hospital stays than infants who are not massaged. A study of 40 low-birth-weight babies found that the 20 massaged babies had a 47 percent greater weight gain per day and stayed in the hospital an average of six fewer days than 20 infants who did not receive massage, resulting in a cost savings of approximately $3,000 per infant. Cocaine-exposed, preterm infants given massage three times daily for a 10-day period showed significant improvement. Results indicated that massaged infants had fewer postnatal complications and exhibited fewer stress behaviors during the 10-day period, had a 28 percent greater daily weight gain, and demonstrated more mature motor behaviors.

A study comparing 52 hospitalized depressed and adjustment disorder children and adolescents with a control group that viewed relaxation videotapes, found massage therapy subjects were less depressed and anxious and had lower saliva cortisol levels (an indicator of less depression).

Resources

BOOKS

Braun, Mary Beth, et al. *Introduction to Massage Therapy.* Baltimore, MD: Lippincott Williams & Wilkins, 2004.

Greene, Elliot, et al. *The Psychology of the Body.* Baltimore, MD: Lippincott Williams & Wilkins, 2003.

Hendrickson, Thomas G. *Treating Soft Tissue Conditions with Orthopedic Massage.* Baltimore, MD: Lippincott Williams & Wilkins, 2002.

Sinclair, Marybetts. *Pediatric Massage Therapy.* Baltimore, MD: Lippincott Williams & Wilkins, 2004.

ORGANIZATIONS

American Massage Therapy Association. 820 Davis Street, Suite 100, Evanston, IL 60201. Web site: <www.amtamassage.org>.

WEB SITES

National Certification Board for Therapeutic Massage and Bodywork. Available online at <www.ncbtmb.com> (accessed October 20, 2004).

L. Lee Culvert
Elliot Greene

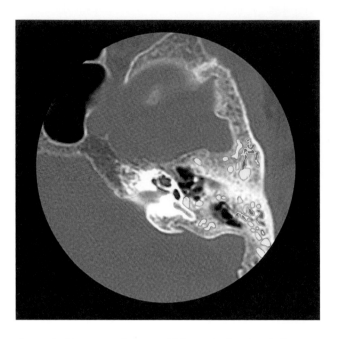

Computed tomography scan (CT scan) showing inflammation and fluid within the air spaces (represented in yellow) of the mastoid. (© Neil Borden/Photo Researchers, Inc.)

Mastoiditis

Definition

Mastoiditis is a bacterial infection of the air cells in the mastoid bone of the skull. Mastoiditis most commonly affects children. Before the use of **antibiotics**, mastoiditis was one of the leading causes of death in children. As of the early 2000s, it is a relatively uncommon and much less dangerous disorder.

Description

Mastoiditis is usually a consequence of a middle ear infection called acute **otitis media** (AOM). The infection may spread from the ear to the mastoid bone of the skull, which is the bony bump off the base of the skull, located just behind the ears slightly above the level of the earlobe. The mastoid bone is composed of air cells that are in communication with the middle ear. If the air cells fill with infected materials, the mastoid honeycomb-like structure may deteriorate. Mastoiditis has been classified into two types, acute and subacute. Acute or classic mastoiditis refers to acute disease following AOM and involves the development of an abscess behind the ear. Subacute mastoiditis refers to a more chronic disease, often following partial treatment of AOM with antibiotics.

Demographics

In the United States and first world countries, the incidence of mastoiditis is 0.004 percent. Developing countries have a higher incidence of mastoiditis, presumably resulting from untreated otitis media. The highest incidence occurs in infants aged six to 13 months. As of 2004 reports indicated that acute mastoiditis is on the increase.

Causes and symptoms

The bacteria that cause mastoiditis are those most commonly associated with AOM. They include the following:

KEY TERMS

Abscess—A localized collection of pus in the skin or other body tissue caused by infection.

Audiogram—A chart or graph of the results of a hearing test conducted with audiographic equipment. The chart reflects the softest (lowest volume) sounds that can be heard at various frequencies or pitches.

Computed tomography (CT)—An imaging technique in which cross-sectional x rays of the body are compiled to create a three-dimensional image of the body's internal structures; also called computed axial tomography.

Gram-negative—Refers tof bacteria that have a cell wall composed of a thin layer of peptidoglycan surrounded by an outer membrane made of polysaccharides and proteins. They take on the red color of the counterstain used in the Gram stain procedure.

Mastoid bone—The prominent bone behind the ear that projects from the temporal bone of the skull.

Mastoiditis—An inflammation of the bone behind the ear (the mastoid bone) caused by an infection spreading from the middle ear to the cavity in the mastoid bone.

Myringotomy—A surgical procedure in which an incision is made in the ear drum to allow fluid or pus to escape from the middle ear.

Otitis—Inflammation of the ear, which may be marked by pain, fever, abnormalities of hearing, hearing loss, noise in the ears, and dizzy spells.

Otoscope—A hand-held instrument with a tiny light and a funnel-shaped attachment called an ear speculum, which is used to examine the ear canal and eardrum.

- *Streptococcus pneumoniae*
- *Haemophilus influenzae*
- *Moraxella catarrhalis*
- *Staphylococcus aureus*
- *Pseuodomonas aeruginosa*
- *Klebsiella*
- *Escherichia coli*
- *Proteus*
- *Prevotella*
- *Fusobacterium*
- *Porphyromonas*
- *Bacteroides*

Gram-negative organisms are found more frequently in chronic mastoiditis, and in young infants, which may be due to prolonged antibiotic therapy.

The main symptoms of mastoiditis are increasing earache, **fever**, and the development of redness and swelling behind the ear. The eardrum is inflamed with swelling of the ear canal wall. Mastoiditis typically develops over the few days following an ear infection. This interval is sometimes more prolonged particularly if the initial infection was treated with antibiotics but not completely eliminated (subacute mastoiditis).

When to call the doctor

Children will usually complain of severe **pain** in the affected ear, which may become swollen. Parents should contact their healthcare provider if a child's symptoms indicate mastoiditis. Appointments with the healthcare provider should also be made if a known ear infection does not respond to treatment or is followed by new symptoms.

Diagnosis

In addition to a complete medical history and physical examination, the physician inspects using an otoscope the outer ears and eardrums of the child. Diagnosis is established by clinical tests showing bacterial growth in cultures of ear drainage. Pus taken from the ear or sucked out of the abscess with a needle is sent to a laboratory so that the infecting bacteria can be identified. Imaging studies are used to confirm diagnosis. X rays are considered unreliable but can show clouding of the mastoid air cells. A head CT scan or CT of the ear may show a fluid-filled middle ear and an abnormality in the mastoid bone. Audiograms can also be performed to assess hearing loss.

Treatment

Antibiotics are typically the first course of action in treating mastoiditis. If these do not work, a tube can be inserted to drain off pus or fluid. An incision can be made with the same end purpose. Surgery may also be a recourse, to remove the affected portion of the mastoid bone, to remove a cyst should one be present, and do any further repair required.

Prognosis

Mastoiditis is curable with treatment but may be hard to treat and may recur. Acute mastoiditis usually recovers completely after treatment with no long term damage to hearing and no increased risk of further ear trouble later in life if complications have not occurred.

Prevention

Rapid and complete treatment of ear infections significantly lowers the risk of developing mastoiditis.

Parental concerns

Ear pain is a common complaint from children, but parents should suspect serious ear infection if the ear area is red and swollen. Mastoiditis often causes the ear to be sticking out at an angle. Parents should be aware that ear infections are very common in children, especially those younger than two years of age.

Resources

BOOKS

Block, Mary A. *No More Antibiotics: Preventing and Treating Ear and Respiratory Infections the Natural Way.* New York: Kensington Publishing, 2000.

Friedman, Ellen M., et al. *My Ear Hurts: A Complete Guide to Understanding and Treating Your Child's Ear Infection.* Collingdale, PA: DIANE Publishing Co., 2004.

Schmidt, Michael. *A Parent's Guide to Childhood Ear Infections.* Berkeley, CA: North Atlantic Books, 2004.

PERIODICALS

Khan, I., and F. Shahzad. "Mastoiditis in Children." *Journal of Laryngology Otology* 117, no. 3 (March 2003): 177–81.

Nussinovitch, M., et al. "Acute mastoiditis in children: epidemiologic, clinical, microbiologic, and therapeutic aspects over past years." *Clinical Pediatrics (Philadelphia)* 43, no. 3 (April 2004): 261–67.

Robinson, R. F., et al. "Increased frequency of acute mastoiditis in children." *American Journal of Health-System Pharmacy* 61, no. 3 (February 2004): 304–06.

Taylor, M. F., and R. G. Berkowitz. "Indications for mastoidectomy in acute mastoiditis in children." *Annals of Otology, Rhinology, Laryngology* 113, no. 1 (January 2004): 69–72.

ORGANIZATIONS

American Academy of Otolaryngology—Head and Neck Surgery Inc. One Prince St., Alexandria VA 22314–3357. Web site: <www.entnet.org>.

American Hearing Research Foundation. 55 E. Washington St., Suite 2022, Chicago, IL 60602. Web site: <www.american-hearing.org>.

Better Hearing Institute. 515 King Street, Suite 420, Alexandria, VA 22314. Web site: <www.betterhearing.org>.

WEB SITES

"Mastoiditis." Available online at <www.healthscout.com/ency/43/483/main.html> (accessed October 20, 2004).

Monique Laberge, Ph.D.

Masturbation

Definition

Masturbation is the erotic stimulation of one's own genitals for pleasure.

Description

Masturbation is the self-stimulation of the sex organs, most often to the point of orgasm. Sixty to ninety percent of adolescent boys and 40 percent of girls masturbate. Although people's attitudes about masturbation differ widely, there is no evidence that masturbation is in any way physically, psychologically, or emotionally harmful. For many young people, masturbation is an opportunity for private sexual exploration before deciding to engage is sexual activity with another person. It is also considered the safest form of sex in the prevention of **sexually transmitted diseases**, including human **immunodeficiency** virus (HIV).

Masturbation allows a healthy way to express and explore one's sexuality and to release sexual tension without the associated risks of sexual intercourse, according to many healthcare providers. They also agree that masturbation is a natural, normal, and healthy way of self-exploration and sexual expression.

It is increasingly recognized among mental health professionals that masturbation can relieve depression and lead to a higher sense of self worth. Masturbation can also be particularly useful in relationships in which one partner wants more sexual activity than the other, in which case masturbation provides a balancing effect.

Many conservative religious groups teach that masturbation is a sinful practice. The Catechism of the Catholic Church, paragraph 2352, lists masturbation as one of the "Offenses against Chastity" and calls it "an intrinsically and gravely disordered action" because "use of the sexual faculty, for whatever reason, outside of marriage is essentially contrary to its purpose." It goes on to caution that extenuating factors could exist, such as immaturity, habitual, or psychological problems.

The discussion of masturbation has been controversial for hundreds of years and still is to some extent in the early 2000s, more so in the United States than Europe and other Western nations. Children caught by their parents masturbating are often punished and told it is a sin. In fact, there is no mention of the word "masturbation" or "self-pleasure" in the Bible. Children are also often told it is wrong or unhealthy, myths that are not supported by medical research.

In the early 2000s, masturbation has become more accepted for both males and females yet there is still a stigma about discussing it openly. College courses on human sexuality include materials and discussion of masturbation, and many parenting manuals deal with ways to affirm a child's self-pleasing habits rather than degrading or punishing the child. Many sex therapists believe that to have better sexual experiences with a partner, an individual needs to learn to masturbate first since it is the best way to learn what one likes and does not like in his or her sex acts.

Most people think of masturbation as a very personal and private act involving using only the hands to manipulate the genitals. Ways of masturbating common to both males and females include pressing or rubbing the genital area against an object, inserting a finger or other object into the anus, and stimulating the penis or clitoris with electric vibrators, which can also be inserted into the anus or vagina. Some males and females enjoy touching, rubbing, or pinching their nipples while masturbating, and both sexes also sometimes use lubricants, such as hand lotion, to improve the sensation.

Masturbation in males

The most common form of masturbation, especially in circumcised males, is to wrap one or both hands or several fingers and thumb around the erect penis and stroke it up and down until ejaculation. This action results in no direct stimulation of the head of the penis and ejaculation is achieved almost entirely from stimulation of the penis shaft and its contact against the underside of the head of the penis only. In uncircumcised males, it is most common to grip the skin of the penis and move it up and down, resulting in repeated sliding of the foreskin back and forth over the head of the penis until orgasm is reached.

Another common method is to rub the erect penis against a smooth surface, such as a mattress or pillow until ejaculation is reached. Less common masturbation techniques include use of an artificial vagina or other "sex toy."

In 2003, an Australian research team led by Graham Giles of the **Cancer** Council published a medical study that concluded frequent masturbation by males may help prevent the development of prostate cancer and that it would be more helpful than ejaculation through sexual intercourse because intercourse can transmit diseases which can increase the risk of cancer instead.

Masturbation in females

Females most commonly masturbate by stroking or rubbing the vulva, especially the clitoris, with hands and fingers until orgasm is reached. Females also may use running water to stimulate the vulva or insert fingers or a hard object into the vagina. Many women are only able to achieve orgasm through masturbation. Some women can experience sexual stimulation simply by crossing their legs tightly.

One enduring myth is that female masturbation can lead to decreased sensitivity of the clitoris resulting in a decrease in the frequency and intensity of female orgasm. However, the evidence points the other way and suggests that women who have engaged in masturbation have a better understanding of their own genital anatomy and can guide their sexual partners in appreciating the specific sexual acts that contribute to female orgasm.

Infancy and toddlerhood

Some and probably all children are capable of what appear to be sexual responses even in earliest years. Most infants probably explore and fondle their own genitals, but not in a goal directed way. Masturbation by infants is also referred to as gratification disorder or infantile masturbation. It is sometimes mistakenly identified by physicians for epilepsy. A study published in the March 2004 issue of *Archives of Disease in Childhood* reported the median age at first symptoms was ten and one-half months, with an age range of three months to five years and five months. The median frequency was seven times a week and the median length was two and one-half minutes. Masturbation in infants is difficult to recognize because it often does not involve manual stimulation of the genitals at all, the study reported.

Preschool

Occasional masturbation is a normal behavior in preschool-age children and most commonly occurs "when a child is sleepy, bored, watching television, or under stress," according to a 2002 advisory in the annual journal *Clinical Reference Systems*. The advisory states that up to one third of preschool-age children discover masturbation while exploring their bodies. They often continue to masturbate simply because it feels good. Some children masturbate frequently because they are unhappy or under stress or are reacting to punishment or pressure to stop masturbation completely. Once a child discovers masturbation, he or she seldom stops doing it completely, according to the advisory. It is not abnormal or excessive unless it is deliberately done in public places after age five or six, when most children learn discretion and masturbate only in private.

"It is impossible to eliminate masturbation in a child. Accept the fact you're your child has learned about it and enjoys it," the advisory states. "The only thing you can control is where he or she does it. A reasonable goal is to permit it in the bedroom and bathroom only. ... If you completely ignore the masturbation, no matter where it's done, your child will think he or she can do it freely in any setting."

School age

As a child grows, masturbation to orgasm becomes more and more likely. Researchers and experts disagree on how many children masturbate before **adolescence**. Most children seem to have the biological capacity to derive pleasure from self-stimulation. Masturbation becomes almost universal at **puberty** in response to normal surges in sex hormones and sexual drive. Most studies suggest that approximately 94 percent of teenage males and about 70 percent of teenage girls admit they masturbate. The actual number of youngsters who masturbate is believed to be higher, since the use of the word "admit" in surveys can imply wrong-doing.

Most males learn to masturbate during adolescence; fewer females do. Some sex therapists believe that girls who do not masturbate miss an important step in their sexual development, since masturbation provides an opportunity to learn how one's body responds to erotic stimulation. Because boys usually masturbate and girls often do not, boys are more likely to learn a sexuality that is genitally focused. Boys learn their sexuality in a context with other boys who bestow a sense of esteem on them. Boys often masturbate with another boy or group of boys. This in itself does not imply **homosexuality** or **bisexuality**. Girls who masturbate almost always discover it alone. Girls generally talk among themselves about masturbation but do not perform with other girls or in front of others. There is no peer support for sexual exploration or reward for teaching orgasm. Boys emerge from adolescence both sexually advantaged and disadvantaged. They are practiced at having orgasms and comfortable with the physical aspects of sex. They are less adept at handling emotional relationships with girls.

Common problems

There is no credible scientific or medical evidence that manual masturbation is damaging to either one's physical or mental health. The exception to this includes some cases of Peyronie's disease in which aggressive manipulation, such as inversion during adolescence, and bending or twisting of the penis, results in a localized benign tumor, distorting the erectile appearance.

Contrary to popular myth, masturbation does not make the palms hairy or cause blindness or genital shrinkage. It has also been alleged that masturbation can reduce sensitivity in the male penis. This statement is also false. The only side-effects recorded are that repeated masturbation may result in tiredness or soreness, which tend to make repeated masturbation self-limiting in any case and that the volume of ejaculate is temporarily reduced in men after multiple ejaculations until normal semen volume is regained in a day or so. Also, people from a socially conservative or religious background may experience feelings of guilt during or after masturbation.

Parental concerns

Studies show that kids who feel they can talk with their parents about masturbation and other sexual issues—because their moms and dads speak openly and listen carefully to them—are less likely to engage in high-risk behavior as teens than kids who do not feel they can talk with their parents about the subject. Parents should explore their own feelings about sex and masturbation. Parents who are uncomfortable with the subject should read books or articles on masturbation and discuss their feelings with a trusted friend, relative, physician, or clergy member. The more parents examine the subject, the more confident they will feel discussing it. If a child has not started asking questions about masturbation, parents should look for a good opportunity to mention it.

While children need to know the biological facts about masturbation, they also need to understand that sexual relationships involve caring, concern, and responsibility. If parents discuss with their children the emotional aspect of a sexual relationships, the children will be better informed to make decisions later on and to resist **peer pressure**.

KEY TERMS

Circumcision—A surgical procedure, usually with religious or cultural significance, where the prepuce or skin covering the tip of the penis on a boy, or the clitoris on a girl, is cut away.

Clitoris—The most sensitive area of the external genitals. Stimulation of the clitoris causes most women to reach orgasm.

Ejaculation—The process by which semen (made up in part of prostatic fluid) is ejected by the erect penis.

Genital—Refers to the sexual or reproductive organs that are visible outside the body.

Infantile masturbation—The masturbation by infants, also called gratification disorder.

Orgasm—Another word for sexual climax. In the male, orgasm is usually accompanied by ejaculation but may be experienced as distinct from ejaculation.

Peyronie's disease—A disease of unknown origin which causes a hardening of the corpora cavernosa, the erectile tissue of the penis. The penis may become misshapen and/or curved as a result and erections are painful.

Vulva—The external genital organs of a woman, including the outer and inner lips, clitoris, and opening of the vagina.

When to call the doctor

In the vast majority of cases masturbation is considered to be a normal activity but the following scenarios may suggest that a problem exists:

- If a child masturbates frequently and appears to be relating to adults in a sexually precocious manner.

- If masturbation becomes a compulsive activity and the person is driven to do it at certain times each day and it almost becomes a ritualistic activity, at the exclusion of almost all else.

- If masturbation takes place in a public place.

Resources

BOOKS

Bockting, Walter O., and Eli Coleman. *Masturbation as a Means of Achieving Sexual Health.* New York: Haworth Press, 2003.

Cornog, Martha. *BIG Book of Masturbation.* Burlingame, CA: Down There Press, 2003.

Richardsom, Justin, and Mark A Schuster. *Everything You Never Wanted Your Kids to Know about Sex, but Were Afraid They'd Ask: The Secrets to Surviving Your Child's Sexual Development from Birth to the Teens.* New York: Crown Publishers, 2003.

Scott, Elijah. *Masturbation: It's Time to Talk.* New York: Light Publishing, 2000.

PERIODICALS

Howard, Barbara J. "Sexuality in Young Children." *Pediatric News* (January 2003): 27.

Nechay, A., et al. "Gratification Disorder (Infantile Masturbation): A Review." *Archives of Disease in Childhood* (March 2004): 225–26.

Nolan, Peter. "Solitary Sex: A Cultural History of Masturbation." *Mental Health Practice* (March 2004): 24–25.

Schmitt, B. D. "Masturbation in Preschoolers. (Behavioral Health Advisor 2002.1)" *Clinical Reference Systems* (Annual 2002): 2020.

"Strong-arm Tactics: Masturbation is Good for Prostate Health.)" *Men's Health* (October 2003): 64.

ORGANIZATIONS

American Academy of Pediatrics. 141 Northwest Point Blvd., Elk Grove Village, IL 60007. Web site: <www.aao.org>.

WEB SITES

"Sexual Experience: Masturbation." *Palo Alto Medical Group*, October 2003. Available online at <www.pamf.org/teen/sex/masturbation/> (accessed October 25, 2004).

Ken R. Wells

Maxillofacial trauma

Definition

Maxillofacial trauma refers to any injury to the face or jaw caused by physical force, the presence of **foreign objects**, animal or human **bites**, or **burns**.

Description

Maxillofacial trauma includes injuries to any of the bony or fleshy structures of the face. Any part of the face may be affected. Teeth may be knocked out or loosened.

The eyes and their muscles, nerves, and blood vessels may be injured as well as the eye socket (orbit), which can be fractured by a forceful blow. The lower jaw (mandible) may be dislocated by force. Although anchored by strong muscles for chewing, the jaw is unstable in comparison with other bones and is easily dislocated from the temporomandibular joints that attach it to the skull. A fractured nose or jaw may affect the ability to breathe or eat. Any maxillofacial injury may also prevent the passage of air or be severe enough to cause a **concussion** or more serious brain damage.

Athletes are particularly at risk of maxillofacial injuries; one researcher estimates that 10.4 percent of all **fractures** of the facial bones are related to **sports**. Boxers suffer repeated blows to the face and occasional knockouts (traumatic brain injury). Football, basketball, hockey, and soccer players, and many other athletes are at risk for milder forms of brain injury called concussions. Burns to the face are also categorized as maxillofacial trauma.

Demographics

About 3 million injuries to the face and jaw occur in the United States each year. Falls account for 78 percent of facial injuries in preschoolers and 47 percent of such injuries in children between the ages of six and 15. In older adolescents and adults, violent crime or other personal assaults account for almost 50 percent of facial injuries, with automobile accidents accounting for 29 percent and sports-related accidents for another 11 percent. One researcher estimates that about 2 percent of all children or adolescents who participate in sports eventually suffer a facial injury severe enough to require medical attention. Patients between the ages of 17 and 30 are more likely to suffer facial injuries from gunshot **wounds**, while older adults are more likely to be injured by attacks with blunt objects. About 10 percent of facial injuries in young children are caused by parental abuse.

Children who grow up on farms are at significant risk for injury by animals. Of one group of 96 children who required inpatient treatment for head or facial injuries, 39 had been kicked or bitten by horses or other farm animals. Another 37 children had been injured by farm machinery, most commonly a tractor.

Causes and symptoms

Causes

Automobile accidents are a major cause of maxillofacial trauma, as well as participation in sports, fights, and other violent acts. Athletes may sustain facial injuries from colliding with other players (as in football or rugby), from direct contact with equipment (baseball bats, hockey sticks, goal posts, parallel bars, etc.), or from contact with other objects related to the sport (baseballs, hockey pucks, lacrosse balls, skis, etc.) People most at risk are athletes, anyone who drives a vehicle or rides in one, and those who live on farms, do dangerous work, or engage in aggressive types of behavior.

Animals are a common cause of maxillofacial trauma. Horses and other large farm animals can cause severe injury to the face and jaw from kicks or bites. In addition, some large pet dogs can bite hard enough to fracture a small child's facial bones.

Domestic violence and abuse is also a common cause of facial injuries in children and adolescents.

Symptoms

The major symptoms of most facial injuries are **pain**, swelling, bleeding, and bruising, although a fractured jaw also prevents the person from working his jaw properly. Symptoms of a fractured nose include black eyes and possible blockage of the airway due to swelling and bleeding.

Symptoms of eye injury or orbital fracture can include blurred or double vision, decreased mobility of the eye, and **numbness** in the area of the eye. In severe injuries there can be temporary or permanent loss of vision.

Burn symptoms include pain, redness, and possibly blisters, **fever**, and **headache**. Extensive burns can cause the victim to go into shock. In that situation, the person will have low blood pressure and a rapid pulse.

Symptoms of traumatic brain injury include problems with thinking, memory, and judgment as well as mood swings and difficulty with coordination and balance. These symptoms may linger for weeks or months and in severe cases can be permanent. Double vision for months after the injury is not uncommon.

When to call the doctor

Parents should call 911 or take their child to an emergency room at once in the event of a facial injury. The following describe emergency situations that require immediate medical care:

- The child or adolescent is bleeding profusely.
- The patient is having difficulty breathing normally.
- The child or adolescent has lost consciousness or is comatose.
- The patient is nauseated and **vomiting**.

- There are penetrating injuries of the skin, ear, or eye.
- The injury involves a gun, blunt instrument, or animal or human bites.
- The child is seeing double, has other visual disturbances, or staggers when trying to walk.
- Blood or watery fluid is leaking from the child's nose or ears.

Diagnosis

Maxillofacial trauma is often diagnosed and treated by specialists in emergency medicine. About 50 percent of patients with facial injuries have suffered trauma to other organ systems or other parts of the body, however, and may need care from specialists in ophthalmology, plastic surgery, otolaryngology, trauma surgery, oral surgery, and psychiatry as well as from doctors with specialized training in emergency medicine. Injuries to the face and jaw area require special attention because they involve the senses of sight, hearing, taste, and smell as well as such vital functions as breathing. From a psychological perspective, maxillofacial trauma can be additionally upsetting if the patient's appearance is permanently affected.

The doctor will begin by taking a history, either from the patient if he is able to talk or from the parents or other witnesses. In the case of a known accident, sports injury, or assault, the doctor begin with the ABCs, which means that he or she will check the child or adolescent's *airway*, *breathing*, and *circulation*. The doctor will usually have the patient sit upright or lie on one side and will remove blood clots, broken teeth, vomitus, or other foreign bodies from the nose or throat. He or she will then carry out a systematic examination of the patient's face and head. The most common pattern of examination moves from the inside of the nose and mouth to the outside of the face, and from the bottom of the face to the top.

The doctor looks for signs of bruising and tissue swelling as well as bleeding and gently palpates, or touches, the various facial bones for movement and stability. If the doctor suspects that the nose is fractured, he or she will listen for crepitus (a crackling sound) when the nose is gently moved and will look for evidence of a dislocated septum or a septal hematoma, which appears as a bluish bulging mass within the nasal septum. The child's teeth will be examined for looseness, and the muscles and nerves of the face will be evaluated. If there is a discharge from the nose, the doctor will look at it to see whether it contains cerebrospinal fluid, which would indicate damage to the bones of the skull as well as the nasal bones. Lastly, the doctor examines the patient's eyes to make sure that the pupils are responding normally to light and that the patient is not seeing double or having other visual problems that might indicate nerve damage or damage to the eye itself.

In cases involving animal kicks, bites, or other tearing or crushing injuries to the skin and external tissues of the face and jaw, the doctor carefully cleanses the broken skin with soap and water or benzalkonium chloride and checks for fractured facial bones.

Emergency room doctors are required by law to report to local law enforcement authorities cases of suspected **family** abuse.

Treatment

Treatment of maxillofacial trauma varies according to the type and extent of the injury.

Jaw

Dislocation of the jaw can be treated by a primary care physician by exerting pressure in the proper manner. If muscle spasm prevents the jaw from moving back into alignment, a sedative is administered intravenously (IV) to relax the muscles. Afterward, the child must avoid opening the jaw wide to minimize the risk of another dislocation.

A jaw fracture may be minor enough to heal with simple limitation of movement and time. More serious fractures require complicated multistep treatment. The jaw must be surgically immobilized by a qualified oral or maxillofacial surgeon or an otolaryngologist. The jaw is properly aligned and secured with metal pins and wires. Proper alignment is necessary to ensure that the bite is correct. If the bite is off, the patient may develop a painful disorder called temporomandibular joint syndrome.

During the weeks of healing the patient is limited to a liquid diet sipped through a straw and must be careful not to choke or vomit since he cannot open his mouth to expel the vomitus. The surgeon will prescribe pain relievers and perhaps muscle relaxants. The recovery time varies according to the patient's overall health but takes at least several weeks.

Nose

Another common maxillofacial fracture is a broken nose. The bones that form the bridge of the nose may be fractured, but cartilage may also be damaged, particularly the nasal septum that separates the two nostrils. If the child's nose is hit from the side, the bones and cartilage are displaced to the side, but if hit from the front, they are splayed out. Severe swelling can inhibit diagnosis and treatment. Mild trauma to the nose can sometimes heal without the person being aware of the fracture unless there is an obvious deformity. The nose will be tender for at least three weeks.

Either before the swelling begins or after it subsides, some ten days after the injury, the doctor can assess the extent of the damage. Physical examination of the inside using a speculum and the outside, in addition to a detailed history of how the injury occurred, determines appropriate treatment. The doctor should be informed of any previous nasal fractures, nasal surgery, or such chronic diseases as diabetes or bleeding disorders. Sometimes an x-ray is useful for diagnosis, but it is not always required.

A primary care physician may treat a nasal fracture himself, but if there is extensive damage or the air passage is blocked, he will refer the patient to an otolaryngologist or a plastic surgeon for treatment. Initially the nose may be packed to control bleeding and hold the shape. It is reset under anesthesia. A protective shield or bandage may be placed over it while the fracture heals.

Eyes

In the case of orbital fractures, there is great danger of permanent damage to vision. Double vision and decreased mobility of the eye are common complications of facial trauma. Surgical reconstruction may be required if the fracture changes the position of the eye or there is other facial deformity. Proper treatment of these injuries requires a maxillofacial surgeon.

When the eyes have been exposed to chemicals, they must be washed out for 15 minutes with clear water. **Contact lenses** may be removed only after rinsing the eyes. The eyes should then be kept covered until the person can be evaluated by a primary care physician or ophthalmologist.

When a foreign object is lodged in the eye, the person should not rub the eye or put pressure on it which would further injure the eyeball. The eye should be covered to protect it until medical attention can be obtained.

Mouth and teeth

Several kinds of traumatic injuries can occur to the mouth. A person can suffer a laceration (cut) to the lips or tongue or loosening of teeth or have teeth knocked out. Such injuries often accompany a jaw fracture or other facial injury. Wounds to the soft tissues of the mouth bleed freely, but the plentiful blood supply that leads to this heavy bleeding also helps healing. It is important to clean mouth wounds thoroughly with salt water or a hydrogen peroxide rinse to prevent infection. Large cuts may require sutures and should be done by a maxillofacial surgeon for a good cosmetic result, particularly when the laceration is on the edge of the lip line (vermilion). The doctor will prescribe an antibiotic because there is normally a large amount of bacteria present in the mouth.

Any injury to the teeth should be evaluated by a dentist for treatment and prevention of infection. Implantation of a tooth is sometimes possible if it has been handled carefully and protected. The tooth should be held by the crown, not the root, and kept in milk, saline, or contact lens fluid. The child's dentist can refer him to a specialist in this field.

Facial burns

For first-degree burns, the child's parent can put a cold-water compress on the area or run cold water on it and cover it with a clean bandage for protection. Second- and third-degree burn victims must be taken to the hospital for treatment.

In the hospital, the child will be given replacement fluids through an IV. This treatment is vital since a patient in shock will die unless those lost fluids are replaced quickly. **Antibiotics** are given to combat infection since the burns make the body vulnerable to infection.

Head injuries

Treatment for a **head injury** requires examination by a primary care physician unless the child's symptoms point to a more serious injury. In that case, the victim must seek emergency care. A concussion is treated with rest and avoidance of contact sports. Very often athletes who have suffered a concussion are allowed to **play** again too soon, perhaps in the mistaken impression that the injury is not so bad if the player did not lose consciousness. Anyone who has had one concussion is at increased risk of another one.

Danger signs that a head injury is more serious include worsening headaches, vomiting, weakness, numbness, unsteadiness, change in the appearance of the eyes, seizures, slurred speech, confusion, agitation, or a change in mental status. These signs require immediate transport to the hospital. A neurologist will evaluate the situation, usually with a CT scan. A stay in a rehabilitation facility may be necessary.

In the case of animal bites on the face or head, the child may be given passive or active immunization against **rabies** if there is a chance that the animal is rabid. This precaution is particularly important, as the incubation period of the rabies virus is much shorter for bites on the head and neck than for bites elsewhere on the body.

Alternative treatment

Fractures, burns, and deep lacerations require treatment by a doctor but alternative treatments can help the body withstand injury and assist the healing process. Calcium, **minerals**, **vitamins**, all part of a balanced and nutrient-rich diet, as well as regular **exercise**, build strong bones that can withstand force well. After an injury, craniosacral therapy may help healing and ease the headaches that follow a concussion or other head trauma. A physical therapist can offer ultrasound treatment, which raises skin temperature to ease pain, or biofeedback, a technique in which the patient learns how to tense and relax muscles to relieve pain. Hydrotherapy may ease the emotional stress of recovering from trauma. Traditional Chinese medicine seeks to reconnect the chi (energy flow) along the body's meridians and thus aid healing. Homeopathic physicians may prescribe such remedies as *Arnica* or *Symphytum* to enhance healing.

Prognosis

When appropriate treatment is obtained quickly after a facial injury, the prognosis can be excellent. If the child or adolescent has a weakened immune system or a debilitating chronic disease, healing is more problematic. Healing also depends upon the extent of the injury. An automobile accident or a gunshot wound, for example, can cause severe facial trauma that may require multiple surgical procedures and a considerable amount of time to heal. Burns and lacerations cause scarring that might be improved by plastic surgery.

Prevention

Safety equipment is vital for preventing maxillofacial trauma from automobile accidents and sports. Here is a partial list of equipment people should always use:

- seatbelts
- automobile air bags
- approved child safety seats
- helmets for riding motorcycles or bicycles, skateboarding, snowboarding, and other sports
- safety glasses for yard work and sports
- such other approved safety equipment for sports as mouthguards, masks, and goggles

---

KEY TERMS

Corneal abrasion—A scratch on the surface of the cornea.

Crepitus—A crackling sound.

Hematoma—A localized collection of blood, often clotted, in body tissue or an organ, usually due to a break or tear in the wall of blood vessel.

Mandible—The lower jaw, a U-shaped bone attached to the skull at the temporomandibular joints.

Maxilla—The bone of the upper jaw which serves as a foundation of the face and supports the orbits.

Nasal septum—The partition that separates the nostrils.

Orbit—The eye socket which contains the eyeball, muscles, nerves, and blood vessels that serve the eye.

Otolaryngologist—A doctor who is trained to treat injuries, defects, diseases, or conditions of the ear, nose, and throat. Also sometimes known as an otorhinolaryngologist.

Shock—A medical emergency in which the organs and tissues of the body are not receiving an adequate flow of blood. This deprives the organs and tissues of oxygen and allows the build-up of waste products. Shock can be caused by certain diseases, serious injury, or blood loss.

Temporomandibular joint disorder—Inflammation, irritation, and pain of the jaw caused by improper opening and closing of the temporomandibular joint. Other symptoms include clicking of the jaw and a limited range of motion. Also called temporomandibular joint syndrome.

Temporomandibular joint (TMJ)—One of a pair of joints that attaches the mandible of the jaw to the temporal bone of the skull. It is a combination of a hinge and a gliding joint.

Vermilion border—The line between the lip and the skin.

Parental concerns

Parental concerns regarding maxillofacial trauma depend on the cause and severity of the injury. Minor **bruises** and uncomplicated fractures caused by accidents generally heal without problems and are quickly absorbed into the family's routine. Complex fractures or other injuries requiring a second operation may require explanation or discussion with the child. Facial injuries, particularly repeated injuries related to the neighborhood or farm setting, lifestyle choices, or family violence, however, suggest the importance of professional counseling and changes in the family's structure, geographical location, or level of functioning. Children or adolescents who are severely disfigured by facial injuries may require extra reassurance from family members as well as professional counseling in order to cope with their changed appearance.

Resources

BOOKS

"Fractures of the Nose." Section 7, Chapter 86 in *The Merck Manual of Diagnosis and Therapy*, edited by Mark H. Beers and Robert Berkow. Whitehouse Station, NJ: Merck Research Laboratories, 2002.

PERIODICALS

Alvi, A., T. Doherty, and G. Lewen. "Facial Fractures and Concomitant Injuries in Trauma Patients." *Laryngoscope* 113 (January 2003): 102–6.

Delilbasi, C., et al. "Maxillofacial Fractures Sustained During Sports Played with a Ball." *Oral Surgery, Oral Medicine, Oral Pathology, Oral Radiology, and Endodontics* 97 (January 2004): 23–7.

Gordy, F. M., N. P. Eklund, and S. DeBall. "Oral Trauma in an Urban Emergency Department." *Journal of Dentistry for Children (Chicago)* 71 (January–April 2004): 14–6.

Haug, R. H., L. L. Cunningham, and M. T. Brandt. "Plates, Screws, and Children: Their Relationship in Craniomaxillofacial Trauma." *Journal of Long-Term Effects of Medical Implants* 13 (2003): 271–87.

King, R. E., J. M. Scianna, and G. J. Petruzzelli. "Mandible Fracture Patterns: A Suburban Trauma Center Experience." *American Journal of Otolaryngology* 25 (September–October 2004): 301–7.

Smith, G. A., et al. "Pediatric Farm-Related Injuries: A Series of 96 Hospitalized Patients." *Clinical Pediatrics* 43 (May 2004): 335–42.

Tu, A. H., et al. "Facial Fractures from Dog Bite Injuries." *Plastic and Reconstructive Surgery* 109 (April 1, 2002): 1259–65.

ORGANIZATIONS

American Academy of Family Physicians (AAFP). 11400 Tomahawk Creek Parkway, Leawood, KS 66211–2672. Web site: <www.aafp.org>.

American Academy of Otolaryngology—Head and Neck Surgery. One Prince Street, Alexandria, VA 22314–3357. Web site: <www.entnet.org>.

American Association of Oral & Maxillofacial Surgeons. 9700 W. Bryn Mawr Ave., Rosemont, IL 60018. Web site: <www.acoms.org>.

American College of Sports Medicine (ACSM). 401 West Michigan Street, Indianapolis, IN 46202–3233. Web site: <www.acsm.org>.

Brain Injury Association Inc. 105 N. Alfred St., Alexandria, VA 22314. Web site: <www.biausa.org>.

WEB SITES

Parsa, Tatiana, et al. "Initial Evaluation and Management of Maxillofacial Injuries." *eMedicine*, August 17, 2004. Available online at <www.emedicine.com/med/topic3222.htm> (accessed November 11, 2004).

Ross, Adam T., and Daniel G. Becker. "Fractures, Nasal and Septal." *eMedicine*, July 13, 2004. Available online at <www.emedicine.com/ent/topic159.htm> (accessed November 11, 2004).

Rupp, Timothy J., Marian Bednar, and Stephen Karageanes. "Facial Fractures." *eMedicine*, August 29, 2004. Available online at <www.emedicine.com/sports/topic33.htm> (accessed November 11, 2004).

Barbara J. Mitchell

▌Measles

Definition

Measles is an infection caused by a virus, which causes an illness displaying a characteristic skin rash known as an exanthem. Measles is also sometimes called rubeola, five-day measles, or hard measles.

Description

Measles is a very contagious disease primarily characterized by **cough**, runny nose, red eyes (**conjunctivitis**), and a characteristic rash on the skin and inside of the cheeks. The most common complications are ear infection and **diarrhea**, although more serious complications can include **pneumonia**, **meningitis**, or **encephalitis**. Measles is fatal (due to complications) in about two out of every 1,000 cases.

Demographics

Measles infections appear all over the world. Prior the effective immunization program used in the early

2000s, large-scale measles outbreaks occurred on a two to three-year cycle, usually in the winter and spring. Smaller outbreaks occurred during the off years. Babies up to about eight months of age are usually protected from contracting measles, due to immune cells they receive from their mothers in the uterus. Once someone has had measles infection, he or she can never get it again.

Causes and symptoms

Measles is caused by a type of virus called a paramyxovirus. It is an extremely contagious infection, spread through the tiny droplets that may spray into the air when an individual carrying the virus sneezes or coughs. About 85 percent of those people exposed to the virus will become infected with it. About 95 percent of those people infected with the virus will develop the illness called measles. Once someone is infected with the virus, it takes about seven to 18 days before he or she actually becomes ill. The most contagious time period is the three to five days before symptoms begin through about four days after the characteristic measles rash has begun to appear.

The first signs of measles infection are **fever**; extremely runny nose; red, runny eyes; and a cough. A few days later, a rash appears in the mouth, particularly on the mucous membrane that lines the cheeks. This rash consists of tiny white dots (like grains of salt or sand) on a reddish bump. These are called Koplik's spots and are unique to measles infection. The throat becomes red, swollen, and sore.

A couple of days after the appearance of the Koplik's spots, the measles rash begins. It appears in a characteristic progression, from the head, face, and neck, to the trunk, then abdomen, and next out along the arms and legs. The rash starts out as flat, red patches but eventually develops some bumps. The rash may be somewhat itchy. When the rash begins to appear, the fever usually climbs higher, sometimes reaching as high as 105°F (40.5°C). There may be **nausea**, **vomiting**, diarrhea, and multiple swollen lymph nodes. The cough is usually more problematic at this point, and the patient feels awful. The rash usually lasts about five days. As it fades, it turns a brownish color and eventually the affected skin becomes dry and flaky.

Many patients (about 5–15%) develop other complications. Bacterial infections, such as ear infections, sinus infections, and pneumonia are common, especially in children. Other viral infections may also strike the patient, including **croup**, **bronchitis**, laryngitis, or viral pneumonia. Inflammation of the liver, appendix, intes-

tine, or lymph nodes within the abdomen may cause other complications. Rarely, inflammations of the heart or kidneys, a drop in **platelet count** (causing episodes of difficult-to-control bleeding), or reactivation of an old **tuberculosis** infection can occur.

An extremely serious complication of measles infection is swelling of the brain. Called encephalitis, this condition can occur up to several weeks after the basic measles symptoms have resolved. About one out of every thousand patients develops this complication, and about 10 to 15 percent of these patients die. Symptoms include fever, **headache**, sleepiness, seizures, and coma. Long-term problems following recovery from measles encephalitis may include seizures and **mental retardation**.

A very rare complication of measles can occur up to ten years following the initial infection. Called subacute sclerosing panencephalitis, this is a slowly progressing, smoldering swelling and destruction of the entire brain. It is most common among people who had measles infection prior to the age of two years. Symptoms include changes in personality, decreased **intelligence** with accompanying school problems, decreased coordination, involuntary jerks and movements of the body. The disease progresses so that the individual becomes increasingly dependent, ultimately becoming bedridden and unaware of his or her surroundings. Blindness may develop, and the temperature may spike (rise rapidly) and fall unpredictably as the brain structures responsible for temperature regulation are affected. Death is inevitable.

Measles during pregnancy is a serious disease, leading to increased risk of a miscarriage or stillbirth. In addition, the mother's illness may progress to pneumonia.

Diagnosis

Measles infection is almost always diagnosed based on its characteristic symptoms, including Koplik's spots, and a rash which spreads from central body structures out towards the arms and legs. If there is any doubt as to the diagnosis, then a specimen of body fluids (mucus, urine) can be collected and combined with fluorescent-tagged measles virus antibodies. Antibodies are produced by the body's immune cells that can recognize and bind to markers (antigens) on the outside of specific organisms, in this case the measles virus. Once the fluorescent antibodies have attached themselves to the measles antigens in the specimen, the specimen can be viewed under a special microscope to verify the presence of measles virus.

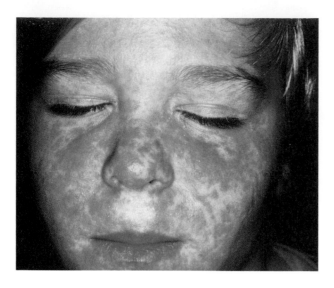

Measles rash on a child's face. *(© CNRI/Photo Researchers, Inc.)*

Treatment

As of 2004 there are no treatments available to stop measles infection. Treatment is primarily aimed at helping the patient to be as comfortable as possible and watching carefully so that **antibiotics** can be started promptly if a bacterial infection develops. Fever and discomfort can be treated with **acetaminophen**. Children with measles should never be given aspirin, as aspirin is correlated with the fatal disease **Reye's syndrome**. A cool-mist vaporizer may help decrease the cough. Patients should be given a lot of liquids to drink, in order to avoid **dehydration** from the fever.

Some studies have shown that children with measles encephalitis benefit from relatively large doses of vitamin A.

Prognosis

The prognosis for an otherwise healthy, well-nourished child who contracts measles is usually quite good. In developing countries, however, death rates may reach 15 to 25 percent. Adolescents and adults usually have a more difficult course. Women who contract the disease while pregnant may give birth to a baby with **hearing impairment**. Although only one in 1,000 patients with measles will develop encephalitis, 10 to 15 percent of those who do will die, and about another 25 percent will be left with permanent brain damage.

Prevention

Measles is a highly preventable infection. A very effective vaccine exists, made of live measles viruses that have been treated so that they cannot cause actual infection. The important markers on the viruses are intact, however, which causes an individual's immune system to react. Immune cells called antibodies are produced, which in the event of a future infection with measles virus quickly recognize the organism and kill it off. Measles vaccines are usually given to children at about 15 months of age; prior to that age, the baby's immune system is not mature enough to initiate a reaction strong enough to insure long-term protection from the virus. A repeat injection should be given at about ten or 11 years of age. Outbreaks on college campuses have occurred among students who were not immunized or who were incorrectly immunized.

Measles vaccine should not be given to pregnant women, however, in spite of the seriousness of gestational measles. The reason for not giving this particular vaccine during pregnancy is the risk of transmitting measles to the unborn child.

Parental concerns

New cases of measles began being reported in some countries—including Great Britain—in 2001 because of parents' fears about vaccine safety. The combined vaccine for measles, **mumps**, and **rubella** (MMR) was claimed to cause **autism** or bowel disorders in some children. However, the World Health Organization (WHO) position is there is no scientific merit to these claims. The United Nations expressed concern that unwarranted **fear** of the vaccine would begin spreading the disease in developing countries and ultimately in developed countries as well. Parents in Britain began demanding the measles vaccine as a separate dose, and scientists were exploring that option as an alternative to the combined **MMR vaccine**. Unfortunately, several children died during an outbreak of measles in Dublin because they had not received the vaccine. Child mortality due to measles is considered largely preventable, and making the MMR vaccine widely available in developing countries is part of WHO strategy to reduce child mortality by two-thirds by the year 2015.

Resources

BOOKS

Katz, Samuel L. "Measles (Rubeola)." In *Principles and Practice of Pediatric Infectious Diseases*, 2nd ed. Edited by Sarah S. Long et al. St. Louis, MO: Elsevier, 2003.

Maldonado, Yvonne. "Measles." In *Nelson Textbook of Pediatrics*. Edited by Richard E. Behrman et al. Philadelphia: Saunders, 2004.

PERIODICALS

Kerr, C. "Good response rate for MMRV vaccine." *Lancet Infectious Disease* 3 (December 2003): 748.

Stalkup, J. R. "A review of measles virus." *Dermatology Clinics* 20 (April 2002): 209–215.

ORGANIZATIONS

American Academy of Pediatrics (AAP). 141 Northwest Point Blvd., Elk Grove Village, IL 60007. Web site: <www.aap.org>.

Centers for Disease Control and Prevention. 1600 Clifton Rd., NE, Atlanta, GA 30333. Web site: <www.cdc.gov>.

Rosalyn Carson-DeWitt, MD
Rebecca J. Frey, PhD

Measles, mumps, rubella vaccine *see* MMR vaccine

Meditation *see* Yoga

Mediterranean fever *see* Familial Mediterranean fever

Meningitis

Definition

Meningitis is a serious inflammation of the meninges, the membranes (lining) that surround the brain and spinal cord. It can be of bacterial, viral, or fungal origin.

Description

Meningitis is usually the result of a viral or bacterial infection. Viral meningitis, also called aseptic meningitis, is generally less severe and often disappears without specific treatment, while bacterial meningitis can be quite serious and may result in brain damage, hearing loss, or learning disabilities in children. The infection may even cause death.

Bacterial meningitis is either monococcal or pneumococcal, depending on the type of bacteria responsible for the infection. Meningitis caused by *Haemophilus influenzae* and related strains (A, B C, Y, and W135) is also called meningococcal meningitis. Similarly, meningitis due to *Streptococcus pneumoniae* is also called pneumococcal meningitis.

Transmission

Most types of meningitis are contagious. A person may be exposed to meningitis bacteria when someone with meningitis coughs or sneezes. The bacteria can also spread through kissing or sharing eating utensils or a toothbrush.

Demographics

According to the National Institute of Neurological Disorders and Stroke (NINDS), some 6,000 cases of pneumococcal meningitis are reported in the United States each year. Meningococcal meningitis is common in minors ages two to 18. Each year about 2,600 people get this highly contagious disease. High-risk groups include infants under the age of one year, people with suppressed immune systems, travelers to foreign countries where the disease is endemic, and college students and Army recruits who reside in dormitories and other close quarters. Between 10 and 15 percent of cases are fatal, with another 10 to 15 percent involving brain damage and other serious side effects.

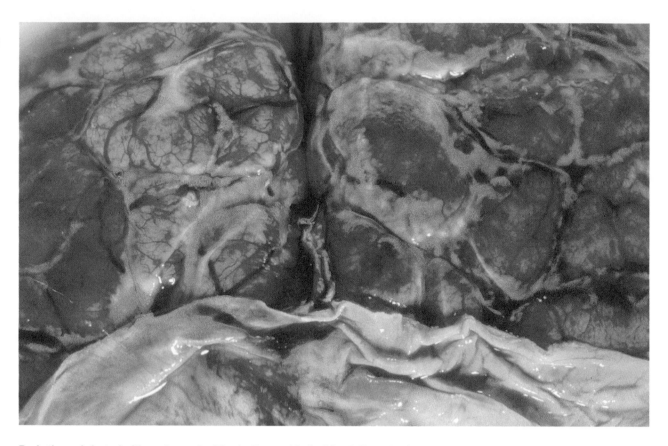

Brain tissue infected with acute meningitis. *(© Custom Medical Stock Photo, Inc.)*

Causes and symptoms

The bacteria which cause bacterial meningitis live in the back of the nose and throat region and are carried by 10 to 25 percent of the population. They cause meningitis when they get into the bloodstream and travel to the meninges.

At least 50 kinds of bacteria can cause bacterial meningitis. According to the Centers for Disease Control (CDC), before the 1990s, *Haemophilus influenzae* type b (Hib) was the leading cause of bacterial meningitis, but subsequent vaccines given to all children as part of their routine immunizations have reduced the occurrence of the disease due to *H. influenzae*. As of 2004, *Streptococcus pneumoniae* and *Neisseria meningitidis* were the leading causes of bacterial meningitis.

In newborns, the most common agents of meningitis are those that are contracted from the newborn's mother, including Group B streptococci (becoming an increasingly common infecting organism in the newborn period), *Escherichia coli*, and *Listeria monocytogenes*. The highest incidence of meningitis occurs in babies less than a month old, with an increased risk of meningitis continuing through about two years of age.

Older children are more frequently infected by the bacteria *Haemophilus influenzae*, *Neisseria meningitidis*, and *Streptococci pneumoniae*.

Most cases of viral meningitis are caused by enteroviruses (viruses that typically cause stomach flu). However, many other types of viruses, such as the **herpes simplex** virus, the **mumps** and **measles** viruses (against which most children are protected due to mass immunization programs), the virus that causes **chickenpox**, the **rabies** virus, and a number of viruses that are acquired through the **bites** of infected mosquitoes.

Meningitis symptoms include high **fever**, **headache**, and stiff neck in children over the age of two years. These symptoms can develop over several hours, or they may take one to two days. Other symptoms may include **nausea**, **vomiting**, discomfort looking into bright lights, confusion, and sleepiness. In some cases, a rash may be present. In newborns and small infants, these symptoms may be absent or difficult to detect, and the infant may only appear slow or inactive, or be irritable, have vomiting, or be feeding poorly. As the disease progresses, patients of any age may also have seizures.

When to call the doctor

Parents should call a doctor if a child has a temperature above 101°F (38.5°C). If any meningitis symptoms occur, the child should see a doctor immediately, as early diagnosis and treatment are very important for a successful outcome.

Diagnosis

Viral meningitis often remains undiagnosed because its symptoms are similar to those of the common flu. As for bacterial meningitis, the diagnosis is established by growing bacteria from a sample of spinal fluid. The spinal fluid is obtained by performing a lumbar puncture (also called a spinal tap), in which a needle is inserted into an area in the lower back where fluid in the spinal canal is readily accessible.

Treatment

Bacterial meningitis treatment usually involves intravenous administered **antibiotics**, for a minimum of four days. The type of meningitis contracted will determine the specific antibiotic used. It is imperative that treatment start as early as possible, in order to avoid brain damage and death.

Viral meningitis cases usually resolve without complications, but typically, antibiotics are ineffective in treating it, so none are prescribed. The child will be told to get as much rest as he or she can. If the child has **pain** related to the disease such as headaches or other body pains, medication can be used to treat it.

Prognosis

The long-term outlook for children who develop bacterial meningitis varies significantly. The outcome depends on the child's age, the bacteria causing the infection, complications, and the treatment the child receives. The complications of bacterial meningitis can be severe and include neurological problems such as hearing loss, visual impairment, seizures, and learning disabilities. The heart, kidneys, and adrenal glands may also be affected. Although some children develop long-lasting problems, most children who receive prompt diagnosis and treatment recover fully.

The majority of cases of viral meningitis resolve with no complications.

KEY TERMS

Analgesics—A class of pain-relieving medicines, including aspirin and Tylenol.

Antibody—A special protein made by the body's immune system as a defense against foreign material (bacteria, viruses, etc.) that enters the body. It is uniquely designed to attack and neutralize the specific antigen that triggered the immune response.

Antigen—A substance (usually a protein) identified as foreign by the body's immune system, triggering the release of antibodies as part of the body's immune response.

Bacterial meningitis—Meningitis caused by bacteria. Depending on the type of bacteria responsible for the infection, bacterial meningitis is either classified as monococcal or pneumococcal.

Immunization—A process or procedure that protects the body against an infectious disease by stimulating the production of antibodies. A vaccination is a type of immunization.

Meninges—The three-layer membranous covering of the brain and spinal cord, composed of the dura mater, arachnoid, and pia mater. It provides protection for the brain and spinal cord, as well as housing many blood vessels and participating in the appropriate flow of cerebrospinal fluid.

Viral meningitis—Meningitis caused by a virus. Also called aseptic meningitis.

Prevention

Many children as of 2004 routinely receive vaccines against meningitis, starting at about two months of age. Immunizations are recommended by the American Academy of Pediatrics and many other organizations. If a child has not been vaccinated, parents should talk to their doctor about the Hib and pneumococcal (Prevnar 7) vaccines.

Vaccines are available for both meningococcal and pneumococcal meningitis. Specifically, there are vaccines against Hib and against some strains of *N. meningitidis* and many types of *Streptococcus pneumoniae*. The vaccines against Hib are very safe and highly effective. There is a vaccine that protects against four strains of *N. meningitidis*, but it is not routinely used in the United States. There are also vaccines to prevent meningitis due to *S. pneumoniae*, which can also prevent other forms of infection due to *S. pneumoniae*.

Parents should teach children to wash their hands often, especially before they eat and after using the bathroom, or after petting animals. They should be taught how to wash their hands vigorously, covering both the front and back of each hand with soap and rinsing thoroughly under running water.

Parental concerns

Some forms of bacterial meningitis are contagious. The bacteria are spread through coughing, kissing, and sneezing. Fortunately, the bacteria that cause meningitis are not as contagious as the **common cold** or the flu, and they are not spread by casual contact or by simply breathing the air where a person with meningitis has been. However, people in the same household or daycare center, or anyone with direct contact with a patient's oral secretions is considered at increased risk of acquiring the infection.

Awareness of the symptoms and signs of meningitis, especially the rash which may accompany meningococcal meningitis is very important.

Resources

BOOKS

Leigh, Jenny. *A Dr. Spot Casebook: George Has Meningitis.* London: Haldane & Mason, 2003.

Routh, Kristina. *Meningitis (Just the Facts).* Chicago: Heineman Library, 2004.

Tunkel, Allan R. *Bacterial Meningitis.* Philadelphia: Lippincott Williams & Wilkins, 2001.

PERIODICALS

Anderson, V., et al. "Cognitive and executive function 12 years after childhood bacterial meningitis: effect of acute neurologic complications and age of onset." *Journal of Pediatrics & Psychology* 29, no. 2 (March 2004): 67–81.

Gupta, S., and A. B. Tuladhar. "Does early administration of dexamethasone improve neurological outcome in children with meningococcal meningitis?" *Archives of Disease in Childhood* 89, no. 1 (January 2004): 82–83.

Hvidd, A., and M. Melhye. "Impact of routine vaccination with a conjugate Haemophilus influenzae type b vaccine." *Vaccine* 22, no. 3–4 (January 2004): 378–82.

Posfay-Barbe, K. M., and E. R. Wald. "Pneumococcal vaccines: do they prevent infection and how?" *Current Opinions in Infectious Diseases* 17, no. 3 (June 2004): 177–84.

Spach, D. H. "New issues in bacterial meningitis in adults. Antibiotic resistance has complicated treatment." *Postgraduate Medicine* 114, no. 5 (November 2004): 43–50.

ORGANIZATIONS

Meningitis Foundation of America. 6610 North Shadeland Avenue, Suite 200, Indianapolis, IN 46220–4393. Web site: <www.musa.org>.

National Institute of Allergy and Infectious Diseases (NIAID). National Institutes of Health, 6610 Rockledge Drive, MSC 6612, Bethesda, MD 20892–6612. Web site: <www.meningitis.org>.

National Meningitis Foundation. 22910 Chestnut Road, Lexington Park, MD 20653. Web site: <www.nmaus.org>.

Meningitis Research Foundation. Midland Way, Thornbury, Bristol BS35 2BS, UK. Web site: <www.meningitis.org>.

WEB SITES

"Meningococcal Disease Homepage." *Centers for Disease Control and Prevention.* Available online at <www.cdc.gov/ncidod/dbmd/diseaseinfo/ meningococcal_g.htm> (accessed October 25, 2004).

Monique Laberge, Ph.D.

Meningocele *see* **Spina bifida**

Meningococcal meningitis vaccine

Definition

The meningococcal **meningitis** vaccine is given by injection (shots) to provide immunization against meningococcal disease and meningitis caused by the bacterium *Neisseria meningitides*.

Description

Meningococcal disease, or **meningococcemia**, is a leading cause of meningitis in children, and then disease can also lead to infections of the blood. People who acquire the disease can become very ill, especially the young children. Meningococcal disease is treated with **antibiotics**, and the vaccine is not routinely recommended for most people in the United States. Particularly, it is not for children under age two, except under special circumstances.

Meningococcal meningitis is different from the meningitis in infants for which **vaccination** is routinely given. Before the 1990s, *Haemophilus influenzae* type b (Hib) was the leading cause of bacterial meningitis. However, vaccines given to all children as part of their routine immunization have reduced the frequency of the invasive diseases caused by *H. influenzae* and *Streptococcus pneumonia*, leaving neisseria meningitis as one of the leading causes of bacterial meningitis.

The meningococcal vaccine contains inactivated bacteria and cannot cause the disease. It is effective against four of the five subtypes of meningococcal meningitis. It is a one-time injection (except for the very young), and the effects last for four to five years. Adverse reactions are uncommon with this vaccine. Localized redness at the injection site lasting one or two days may occur. Less likely is an allergic reaction to the vaccine.

General use

Meningococcal vaccine is recommended for children and young adults as follows:

- children two years old and older in a population where an outbreak has occurred
- college students who live in close quarters (dormitories), who consume alcohol, smoke, or are regularly around smokers
- those with certain chronic conditions, including those with spleen damage or immune disease
- anyone traveling to or living in a part of the world where meningococcal disease is common, such as West Africa
- household or institutional members who have contact with anyone with meningococcal disease (The same individuals should also receive prophylaxis antibiotic therapy.)
- medical and laboratory personnel at risk of exposure to meningococcal disease

Precautions

Children who are mildly ill at the time the shot is due can still get meningococcal vaccine. Children with moderately severe illnesses should wait until they recover. Children two years old and over receive one dose, while children three months to two years old need two doses, three months apart. Immunizations should be deferred during any acute illness. Pregnant women should not receive the vaccine because it may affect the fetus.

Side effects

Children who get the meningitis vaccine may have mild side effects, such as tenderness, redness, or a painful lump on the skin at the injection site; symptoms usually last one to two days. A small percentage of the patients who receive the vaccine develop a slight **fever**. The meningitis vaccine, like any other injection, may in rare cases lead to a serious allergic reaction. Symptoms of allergic reaction include swelling in the mouth or throat, trouble breathing, weakness, hoarseness or wheezing, a fast heart beat, **hives**, **dizziness**, paleness, and a high fever. If a serious allergic reaction occurs the symptoms will start within a few minutes to a few hours after the shot. The child should be seen immediately by a doctor. The doctor will need to know the date of the vaccination and when exactly the symptoms started. A health-care provider should file a report using the vaccine adverse events reporting system (VAERS) form.

Interactions

If the vaccine is given to children receiving immunosuppressive therapy, as in **chemotherapy** for **cancer** or HIV/AIDs, the immune response may not take place. Moreover, the meningitis vaccine should not be given to individuals known to be sensitive to thimerosal (mercury derivative) or other ingredients of the vaccine.

Parental concerns

Meningitis passes from person to person, mainly by coughing and sneezing. The risk of contracting the disease increases if the child spends time in close contact with the local population at schools, crowded markets, or public buildings. In addition, young adults living in close quarters on college campuses are at risk for contracting the disease. Vaccines are available at student health services on campuses.

Resources

BOOKS

Shmaefsky, Brian, et al. *Meningitis*. Langhorne, PA: Chelsea House Publishers, 2005.

Tunkel, Alan R. *Bacterial Meningitis*. London: Lippincott Williams & Wilkins, 2001.

Viral Meningitis: A Medical Dictionary, Bibliography, and Annotated Research Guide to Internet References. San Diego, CA: Icon Group International, 2004.

ORGANIZATIONS

Meningitis Foundation of America. 6610 North Shadeland Ave., Suite 200, Indianapolis, IN 46220–4393. Web site: <www.musa.org/>.

WEB SITES

"Meningitis." *MedlinePlus*, January 6, 2004. Available online at <www.nlm.nih.gov/medlineplus/ency/article/000680.htm> (accessed December 18, 2004).

Aliene Linwood, RN, DPA, FACHE

Meningococcemia

Definition

Meningococcemia is the presence of meningococcus in the bloodstream. Meningococcus, a bacteria formally called *Neisseria meningitidis*, can be one of the most dramatic and rapidly fatal of all infectious diseases.

Causes and symptoms

Meningococcemia, a relatively uncommon infection, occurs most commonly in children and young adults. In susceptible people, it may cause a very severe

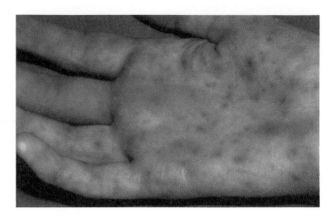

A close-up image of a person's hand with meningococcemia, caused by *Neisseria meningitidis*. The organism can cause multiple illnesses and can damage small blood vessels. *(Custom Medical Stock Photo Inc.)*

illness that can produce death within hours. The bacteria, which can spread from person to person, usually first causes a colonization in the upper airway, but without symptoms. From there, it can penetrate into the bloodstream to the central nervous system and cause **meningitis** or develop into a full-blown bloodstream infection (meningococcemia). Fortunately in most colonized people, this does not happen, and the result of this colonization is long-lasting immunity against the particular strain.

After colonization is established, symptoms can develop within one day to one to two weeks. After a short period of time (one hour up to one to two days) when the patient complains of **fever** and muscle aches, more severe symptoms can develop. Unfortunately during this early stage, a doctor cannot tell this illness from any other illness, such as a viral infection like **influenza**. Unless the case is occurring in a person known to have been exposed to or in the midst of an epidemic of meningococcal disease, there may be no specific symptoms or signs found that help the doctor diagnose the problem. Rarely, a low-grade bloodstream infection called chronic meningococcemia can occur.

After this initial period, the patient will often complain of continued fever, shaking chills, overwhelming weakness, and even a feeling of impending doom. The organism is multiplying in the bloodstream, unchecked by the immune system. The severity of the illness and its dire complications are caused by the damage the organism does to the small blood vessel walls. This damage is called a vasculitis, an inflammation of a blood vessel. Damage to the small vessels causes them to become leaky. The first signs of the infection's severity are small bleeding spots seen on the skin (petechiae). A doctor should always suspect meningococcemia when he or she finds an acutely ill patient with fever, chills, and petechiae.

Quickly (within hours), the blood vessel damage increases, and large bleeding areas on the skin (purpura) are seen. The same changes are taking place in the affected person's internal organs. The blood pressure is often low, and there may be signs of bleeding from other organs (like coughing up blood, nose bleeds, blood in the urine). The organism not only damages the blood vessels by causing them to leak, but also causes clotting inside the vessels. If this clotting occurs in the larger arteries, it results in major tissue damage. Essentially, large areas of skin, muscle, and internal organs die from lack of blood and oxygen. Even if the disease is quickly diagnosed and treated, the patient has a high risk of dying.

Diagnosis

The diagnosis of meningococcemia can be made by the growth of the organism from blood cultures. Treatment should begin when the diagnosis is suspected and should not be delayed by the doctor's waiting for positive cultures. Obtaining fluid from a petechial spot and staining it in the laboratory can assist in quickly seeing the organism.

Treatment

Immediate treatment of a suspected case of meningococcemia begins with **antibiotics** that work against the organism. Possible choices include penicillin G, ceftriaxone (Rocephin), cefotaxime (Claforan), or trimethoprim/sulfamethoxazole (Bactrim, Septra). If the patient is diagnosed in a doctor's office, antibiotics should be given immediately if possible, even before transfer to the hospital and even if cultures cannot be obtained before treatment. It is most likely that the speed of initial treatment will affect the ultimate outcome.

Prognosis

As many as 15 to 20 percent of patients with meningococcemia will die as a result of the acute infection. A significant percentage of the survivors have tissue damage that requires surgical treatment. This treatment may consist of skin grafts, or even partial or full amputations of an arm or leg. Certain people with immune system defects (particularly those with defects in the complement system) may have recurrent episodes of meningococcemia. These patients, however, seem to have a less serious outcome.

KEY TERMS

Blood culture—A procedure where blood is collected from a vein and is placed in a small bottle that contains a special liquid; the liquid will make any organisms that are present in the blood sample grow. These organisms can then be grown and identified in the laboratory so that the proper antibiotic can be given to the patient.

Colonization—The presence of bacteria on a body surface (like on the skin, mouth, intestines or airway) without causing disease in the person.

Complement—One of several proteins in the blood that acts with other proteins to assist in killing bacteria.

Meningitis—An infection or inflammation of the membranes that cover the brain and spinal cord. It is usually caused by bacteria or a virus.

Prevention

Although a vaccine is available for meningococcus, it is still difficult as of 2004 to produce a vaccine for the type B organism, the most common one in the United States. Because of this and the short time that the vaccine seems to offer protection, the product has not been routinely used in the United States. It can be used for travelers going to areas where meningococcal disease is more common or is epidemic. In the early 2000s, the vaccine has been suggested for use in incoming college freshmen, particularly those living in dormitories. These students appear to have a somewhat higher risk of meningococcal infections.

It is, however, recommended that all people take certain antibiotics if they have had contact (like at home or in a daycare) with a person who has meningococcal infection. The most common antibiotics given are rifampin (Rifadin) or ciprofloxacin (Cipro). These medicines are usually taken by mouth twice a day for two days. This treatment will decrease the risk of infection in these people who have been exposed. However, the overall risk to people who have been exposed, even without antibiotic use, is probably no more than 1 to 2 percent.

Resources

BOOKS

Swanberg, Margaret M., et al "Speech and Language." In *Textbook of Clinical Neurology.* Edited by Christopher G. Goetz. Philadelphia: Saunders, 2003.

Woods, Charles R. "Neisseria meningitidis (Meningococcus)." In *Nelson Textbook of Pediatrics.* Edited by Richard E. Behrman et al. Philadelphia: Saunders, 2004.

PERIODICALS

Lepow, M. L. "Meningococcal immunology." *Immunology and Allergy Clinics of North America* 23 (November 2003): 768–86.

Weir E. "Meningococcal disease." *Canadian Medical Association Journal* 166 (April 2002): 1064–6.

Larry I. Lutwick, MD
Rosalyn Carson-DeWitt, MD

Meningomyelocele *see* **Spina bifida**

Menstruation

Definition

Menstruation is the vaginal bleeding that occurs in adolescent girls and women as a result of hormonal changes. It normally happens in a predictable pattern, once a month.

Description

Menstruation is part of the menstrual cycle, which helps a woman's body prepare for the possibility of pregnancy each month. The parts of the body involved in the menstrual cycle include the uterus and cervix, the ovaries, fallopian tubes, the brain and pituitary gland, and the vagina. Certain body chemicals known as hormones rise and fall during the month, causing the menstrual cycle to occur.

In the first half of the menstrual cycle, estrogen levels rise, causing the lining of the uterus to grow and thicken. This lining is called the endometrium. The two small, grape-shaped organs inside the abdomen on either side of the uterus, known as the ovaries, are filled with hundreds of thousands of eggs and are the organs that allow pregnancy to occur. When a girl reaches **puberty**, the ovaries respond to a rise in follicle-stimulating hormone and cause one of the eggs to mature. About half way through the menstrual cycle, a surge of luteinizing hormone takes place, and the egg is released. This mature egg is called an ovum, and its release is called ovulation. When the egg is released it travels through one of the two fallopian tubes and down towards the uterus. If the ovum is fertilized by a sperm at this time,

pregnancy occurs. However, if a sperm does not fertilize the egg, the body no longer needs the uterine lining to support the fertilized egg. Estrogen and progesterone levels then drop, triggering the uterine lining to gently fall away from the wall of the uterus, and to be shed through the vagina. The discharge of this lining is the menstrual flow. The entire process is called menstruation.

A "normal" menstrual period usually occurs every 28 days, from the first day of a period to the first day of the next. However, this can vary from 22 to 36 days. Each period usually lasts from three to seven days, with the average being five. It may take several years from the start of menstruation for periods to settle into a pattern. Irregular periods are common in early **adolescence**. Even after adolescence, many factors can throw off the timing of menstruation. These include weight changes, starting a new job or school, and relationship problems.

Menstrual hygiene products

Once a girl begins menstruating, she needs to choose from the various menstrual hygiene products which are available. Menstrual hygiene products can be divided into two basic categories: sanitary pads and tampons. Absorbency and a comfortable fit are the main features girls need to look for when purchasing menstrual products. Because a girl's menstrual flow may vary from day to day during the cycle, she may want to use different types of products during her period.

Sanitary pads are worn inside the underwear where they collect the menstrual flow. They come in different sizes, thicknesses, and styles. Some pads have flaps or "wings" that wrap around and attach to the underside of underwear. Others have deodorant and contain perfume. Some girls find that the perfume irritates their skin.

Tampons are the another option for absorbing menstrual flow. Tampons come in various absorbency categories and should be chosen based on the amount of flow experienced. The absorbency of a tampon can be determined by how often it needs to be changed. Girls should use the tampon with the least absorbency necessary to absorb the flow. Tampons should be changed every four to six hours. Tampons also come with a variety of applicators, including plastic and cardboard. Tampons are comfortable to wear and may be a good choice for active girls. They should be inserted carefully to avoid any irritation. A rare, but serious, condition called **toxic shock syndrome** (TSS) can be connected to tampon use. The higher the absorbency of tampons used, the higher the risk for TSS. To decrease the risk of TSS, girls should choose the lowest absorbency necessary.

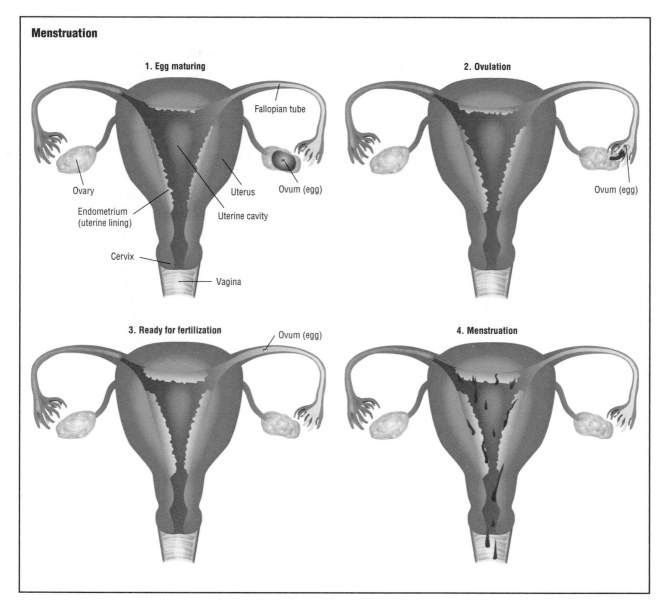

Menstruation

1. Egg maturing

Fallopian tube

Ovary

Endometrium
(uterine lining)

Uterus

Ovum (egg)

Uterine cavity

Cervix

Vagina

2. Ovulation

Ovum (egg)

3. Ready for fertilization

Ovum (egg)

4. Menstruation

In this illustration, the menstrual cycle is divided into four stages. First, an egg matures inside the ovary (1), which then releases the egg (2), allowing it to travel through the fallopian tube, where it rests awaiting fertilization (3). If the egg is not fertilized, it is flushed out with the menstrual flow (4). *(Illustration by GGS Information Services.)*

Problems with menstruation

DYSMENORRHEA Dysmenorrhea is the medical term for menstrual cramps, the dull or throbbing **pain** in the lower abdomen that many women experience just before and during their menstrual periods. It can be primary or secondary. Primary dysmenorrhea involves no abnormality. Secondary dysmenorrhea involves an underlying physical cause, such as uterine fibroids, pelvic inflammatory disease, or endometriosis. Signs and symptoms of dysmenorrhea, whether it is primary or secondary, may include the following:

- dull, throbbing pain in the lower abdomen

- radiating pain to the lower back and thighs

- nausea, loose stools, sweating, and **dizziness** (though these are much less common)

If menstrual cramps become severe enough to keep a girl from going about her day-to-day routine, she should see a doctor. The doctor will perform a medical history and physical examination, including a pelvic exam, where he or she will look for any abnormalities, signs of infection, and possible causes of secondary dysmenorrheal. In addition, the doctor may request a variety of diagnostic tests, such as imaging tests, laparoscopy, and hysteroscopy.

Complications can arise from secondary dysmenorrhea. If pelvic inflammatory disease is present, the fallopian tubes may become scarred and possibly cause later infertility or other reproductive problems. Endometriosis can also lead to fertility problems as well.

Many experts believe that prostaglandins, hormone-like substances involved in pain and inflammation and which trigger uterine muscle contractions, are responsible for causing menstrual cramping. Whether the dysmenorrhea is primary or secondary, there are effective ways to treat menstrual pain. **Nonsteroidal anti-inflammatory drugs** (NSAIDS), such as ibuprofen or naproxen, may block the production of prostaglandins and can be very effective in the treatment of menstrual cramps. In the case of severe cramping, doctors may recommend a low-dose oral contraceptive to prevent ovulation, which may reduce the release of prostaglandins and the severity of the cramps.

DYSFUNCTIONAL UTERINE BLEEDING Dysfunctional uterine bleeding (DUB) is prolonged or heavy bleeding that often occurs in a menstrual cycle where ovulation did not occur. Heavy bleeding is defined as more than 15 soaked pads or tampons per period, and prolonged bleeding is that which lasts for more than 8 to 10 days. Although DUB is quite common in the first few years after menstruation starts, it can be frightening and should always be reported to a physician. DUB that is accompanied by dizziness and a low blood pressure should be considered a medical emergency. DUB is usually caused by hormonal imbalances. Other causes of bleeding are sexually transmitted disease, an ectopic pregnancy, ovarian cysts, and uterine fibroids or polyps. Young women within the first menstrual period are not usually treated unless symptoms are exceptionally severe or if anemia develops.

Demographics

Girls may start their menstrual period as early as nine years of age and as late as 16 years old. The average age a girl begins menstruating is 12. Girls who are very active in **sports** or who are quite thin may not develop until a later age. Losing weight while experiencing a growth spurt may also delay menstruation.

In the early 2000s, some people have voiced concern about girls starting their periods at younger and younger ages. However, a study reported in 2003 found that overall, girls in the United States are not beginning menstruation earlier than in the past. Less than 10 percent of girls start their periods before 11 years of age, and 90 percent of all U.S. girls are menstruating by age 14. This age is not significantly different than that reported for girls in 1973. African-American girls on average begin menstruating before Caucasian- and Hispanic-American girls.

Causes and symptoms

The menstrual cycle takes place each month in response to the hormonal changes which occur when pregnancy does not take place. A number of symptoms can occur just before and during a girl's period which may cause discomfort. These include:

- having pelvic area cramps
- feeling bloated or puffy
- breast tenderness or swelling
- headaches and backaches
- acne breakouts
- mild nausea

These symptoms usually stop or lessen a day or two after the period begins.

Diagnosis

There are several reasons why a girl should see her healthcare provider regarding her menstrual cycle. These include:

- if menstruation has not started by the age of 16
- if a menstrual period lasts for more than seven days
- if periods suddenly stop
- if she is experiencing excessive bleeding
- if she feels suddenly ill while using tampons
- if she bleeds more than a few drops between periods
- if she experiences excessive pain during her period

Treatment

No specific medical treatment is necessary for an uncomplicated menstrual cycle, as it is a normal, healthy process in girls and women.

Alternative treatment

Some girls may find relief from menstrual discomfort through meditation, **yoga**, or massage. These stress-relieving activities are unlikely to cause any harm.

Menstruation, painful *see* **Dysmenorrhea**

Mental development *see* **Cognitive development**

KEY TERMS

Dysmenorrhea—Painful menstruation.

Menarche—The first menstrual cycle in a girl's life.

Parental concerns

Though menstruation is no longer the taboo subject it once was, many parents still find that discussing the issue with their daughters can be uncomfortable. This is especially common in families in which the mother is not present. Still, it is important to discuss menstruation with girls when they are preteens, so that they do not experience the potential embarrassment or trauma if they start their first period without knowledge about what is happening to their bodies. Taking the time to prepare may help to make this discussion less awkward.

Resources

BOOKS

Loulan, JoAnn, and Bonnie Worthen. *Period: A Girl's Guide to Menstruation.* Minnetonka, MN: Book Peddlers, 2001.

PERIODICALS

Chumlea, William Cameron, et al. "Age at Menarche and Racial Comparisons in U.S. Girls." *Pediatrics* 111 (January 2003): 110–14.

ORGANIZATIONS

American College of Obstetricians and Gynecologists. 409 12th Street, SW, PO Box 96920, Washington, DC 20090–6290. Web site: <www.acog.org>.

The Center for Young Women's Health. 300 Longwood Avenue, Box 310, Boston, MA 02115. Web site: <www.youngwomenshealth.org>.

WEB SITES

"Frequently Asked Questions about Menstruation and the Menstrual Cycle." *4woman.gov-The National Women's Health Information Center*, November 2002. Available online at <www.4woman.gov/faq/menstru.htm> (accessed October 25, 2004).

"Period Talk: Preparing Your Preteen for Menstruation." Available online at <www.mayoclinic.com/invoke.cfm?id=FL00040> (accessed October 25, 2004).

Deanna M. Swartout-Corbeil, RN

Menstruation, infrequent *see*
Oligomenorrhea

Menstruation, painful *see* **Dysmenorrhea**

Mental development *see* **Cognitive development**

Mental retardation

Definition

Mental retardation is a developmental disability that first appears in children under the age of 18. It is defined as an intellectual functioning level (as measured by standard tests for **intelligence** quotient) that is well below average and significant limitations in daily living skills (adaptive functioning).

Description

According to statistics made available by the Centers for Disease Control and Prevention in the 1990s, mental retardation occurs in 2.5 to 3 percent of the general population. About 6 to 7.5 million mentally retarded individuals live in the United States alone. Mental retardation begins in childhood or **adolescence** before the age of 18. In most cases, it persists throughout adulthood. A diagnosis of mental retardation is made if an individual has an intellectual functioning level well below average and significant limitations in two or more adaptive skill areas. Intellectual functioning level is defined by standardized tests that measure the ability to reason in terms of mental age (intelligence quotient or IQ). Mental retardation is defined as IQ score below 70 to 75. Adaptive skills are the skills needed for daily life. Such skills include the ability to produce and understand language (communication); home-living skills; use of community resources; health, **safety**, leisure, self-care, and social skills; self-direction; functional academic skills (reading, writing, and arithmetic); and work skills.

In general, mentally retarded children reach developmental milestones such as walking and talking much later than the general population. Symptoms of mental retardation may appear at birth or later in childhood. Time of onset depends on the suspected cause of the disability. Some cases of mild mental retardation are not diagnosed before the child enters **preschool**. These children typically have difficulties with social, communication, and functional academic skills. Children who have a neurological disorder or illness such as **encephalitis** or **meningitis** may suddenly show signs of cognitive impairment and adaptive difficulties.

Mental retardation varies in severity. There are four different degrees of mental retardation: mild, moderate, severe, and profound. These categories are based on the functioning level of the individual.

Mild mental retardation

Approximately 85 percent of the mentally retarded population is in the mildly retarded category. Their IQ score ranges from 50 to 75, and they can often acquire academic skills up to the sixth grade level. They can become fairly self-sufficient and in some cases live independently, with community and social support.

Moderate mental retardation

About 10 percent of the mentally retarded population is considered moderately retarded. Moderately retarded individuals have IQ scores ranging from 35 to 55. They can carry out work and self-care tasks with moderate supervision. They typically acquire **communication skills** in childhood and are able to live and function successfully within the community in a supervised environment such as a group home.

Severe mental retardation

About 3 to 4 percent of the mentally retarded population is severely retarded. Severely retarded individuals have IQ scores of 20 to 40. They may master very basic self-care skills and some communication skills. Many severely retarded individuals are able to live in a group home.

Profound mental retardation

Only 1 to 2 percent of the mentally retarded population is classified as profoundly retarded. Profoundly retarded individuals have IQ scores under 20 to 25. They may be able to develop basic self-care and communication skills with appropriate support and training. Their retardation is often caused by an accompanying neurological disorder. The profoundly retarded need a high level of structure and supervision.

The American Association on Mental Retardation (AAMR) has developed another widely accepted diagnostic classification system for mental retardation. The AAMR classification system focuses on the capabilities of the retarded individual rather than on the limitations. The categories describe the level of support required. They are: intermittent support, limited support, extensive support, and pervasive support. Intermittent support, for example, is support needed only occasionally, perhaps during times of stress or crisis. It is the type of support typically required for most mildly retarded individuals.

At the other end of the spectrum, pervasive support, or life-long, daily support for most adaptive areas, would be required for profoundly retarded individuals.

Demographics

For children, the mental retardation rate is 11.4 per 1,000 and varies approximately nine fold, ranging from 3.2 in New Jersey to 31.4 in Alabama. For adults, the rate is 6.6 and varies approximately six fold, ranging from 2.5 in Alaska to 15.7 in West Virginia. In 42 states, the rate for children is higher than that for adults; in seven states, the rate for adults is higher, and in two states, both rates are similar. The correlation between state-specific rates for children and for adults is 0.66. Overall, 69 percent of the state-specific variation in prevalence rates for adults is accounted for by median household income, the percentage of total births to teenaged mothers, and the percentage of the population with less than a ninth-grade education. Low educational attainment was the most important correlate of mental retardation rates among adults.

Causes and symptoms

Low IQ scores and limitations in adaptive skills are the hallmarks of mental retardation. Aggression, self-injury, and **mood disorders** are sometimes associated with the disability. The severity of the symptoms and the age at which they first appear depend on the cause. Children who are mentally retarded reach developmental milestones significantly later than expected, if at all. If retardation is caused by chromosomal or other genetic disorders, it is often apparent from infancy. If retardation is caused by childhood illnesses or injuries, learning and adaptive skills that were once easy may suddenly become difficult or impossible to master. In about 35 percent of cases, the cause of mental retardation cannot be found. Biological and environmental factors that can cause mental retardation include genetics, prenatal illnesses and issues, childhood illnesses and injuries, and environmental factors.

Genetics

About 5 percent of mental retardation is caused by hereditary factors. Mental retardation may be caused by an inherited abnormality of the genes, such as **fragile X syndrome**. Fragile X, a defect in the chromosome that determines sex, is the most common inherited cause of mental retardation. Single gene defects such as **phenylketonuria** (PKU) and other inborn errors of metabolism may also cause mental retardation if they are not found and treated early. An accident or mutation in genetic development may also cause retardation. Examples of such accidents are development of an extra chromosome 18 (trisomy 18) and **Down syndrome**. Down syndrome is caused by an abnormality in the development of chromosome 21. It is the most common genetic cause of mental retardation.

Prenatal illnesses and issues

Fetal alcohol syndrome affects one in 600 children in the United States. It is caused by excessive alcohol intake in the first twelve weeks (trimester) of pregnancy. Some studies have shown that even moderate alcohol use during pregnancy may cause learning disabilities in children. Drug abuse and cigarette **smoking** during pregnancy have also been linked to mental retardation.

Maternal infections and illnesses such as glandular disorders, **rubella**, **toxoplasmosis**, and **cytomegalovirus infection** may cause mental retardation. When the mother has high blood pressure (**hypertension**) or blood poisoning (toxemia), the flow of oxygen to the fetus may be reduced, causing brain damage and mental retardation.

Birth defects that cause physical deformities of the head, brain, and central nervous system frequently cause mental retardation. Neural tube defect, for example, is a birth defect in which the neural tube that forms the spinal cord does not close completely. This defect may cause children to develop an accumulation of cerebrospinal fluid on the brain (**hydrocephalus**). By putting pressure on the brain hydrocephalus can cause learning impairment.

Childhood illnesses and injuries

Hyperthyroidism, **whooping cough**, **chickenpox**, **measles**, and Hib disease (a bacterial infection) may cause mental retardation if they are not treated adequately. An infection of the membrane covering the brain (meningitis) or an inflammation of the brain itself (encephalitis) cause swelling that in turn may cause brain damage and mental retardation. Traumatic brain injury caused by a blow or a violent shake to the head may also cause brain damage and mental retardation in children.

Environmental factors

Ignored or neglected infants who are not provided the mental and physical stimulation required for normal development may suffer irreversible learning impairments. Children who live in poverty and suffer from **malnutrition**, unhealthy living conditions, and improper or inadequate medical care are at a higher risk. Exposure to lead can also cause mental retardation. Many children develop **lead poisoning** by eating the flaking lead-based paint often found in older buildings.

When to call the doctor

If mental retardation is suspected, a comprehensive physical examination and medical history should be done immediately to discover any organic cause of symptoms. Conditions such as hyperthyroidism and PKU are treatable. If these conditions are discovered early, the progression of retardation can be stopped and, in some cases, partially reversed. If a neurological cause such as brain injury is suspected, the child may be referred to a neurologist or neuropsychologist for testing.

The symptoms of mental retardation are usually evident by a child's first or second year. In the case of Down syndrome, which involves distinctive physical characteristics, a diagnosis can usually be made shortly after birth. Mentally retarded children lag behind their peers in developmental milestones such as smiling, sitting up, walking, and talking. They often demonstrate lower than normal levels of interest in their environment and responsiveness to others, and they are slower than other children in reacting to visual or auditory stimulation. By the time a child reaches the age of two or three, retardation can be determined using physical and **psychological tests**. Testing is important at this age if a child shows signs of possible retardation because alternate causes, such as impaired hearing, may be found and treated.

Diagnosis

A complete medical, **family**, social, and educational history is compiled from existing medical and school records (if applicable) and from interviews with parents. Children are given intelligence tests to measure their learning abilities and intellectual functioning. Such tests include the Stanford-Binet Intelligence Scale, the Wechsler Intelligence Scales, the Wechsler Preschool and Primary Scale of Intelligence, and the Kaufmann Assessment Battery for Children. For infants, the **Bayley Scales of Infant Development** may be used to assess motor, language, and problem-solving skills. Interviews with parents or other caregivers are used to assess the child's daily living, muscle control, communication, and social skills. The Woodcock-Johnson Scales of Independent Behavior and the Vineland Adaptive Behavior Scale (VABS) are frequently used to test these skills.

Treatment

Federal legislation entitles mentally retarded children to free testing and appropriate, individualized education and skills training within the school system from ages three to 21. For children under the age of three, many states have established early intervention programs that assess, recommend, and begin treatment programs. Many day schools are available to help train retarded children in basic skills such as bathing and feeding themselves. **Extracurricular activities** and social programs are also important in helping retarded children and adolescents gain **self-esteem**.

Training in independent living and job skills is often begun in early adulthood. The level of training depends on the degree of retardation. Mildly retarded individuals can often acquire the skills needed to live independently and hold an outside job. Moderate to profoundly retarded individuals usually require supervised community living. **Family therapy** can help relatives of the mentally retarded develop coping skills. It can also help parents deal with feelings of guilt or anger. A supportive, warm home environment is essential to help the mentally retarded reach their full potential. However, as of 2004, there is no cure for mental retardation.

A promising but controversial treatment for mental retardation involves stem cell research. In the early 2000s scientists are exploring the potential of adult stem cells in treating mental retardation. They have transplanted bone marrow cells into living embryos in the uteri of animals to approach congenital diseases, birth defects, and mental retardation. Stem cells are primitive cells that are capable of forming diverse types of tissue. Because of this remarkable quality, human stem cells hold huge promise for the development of therapies to regenerate damaged organs and heal people who are suffering from terrible diseases. Embryonic stem cells are derived from human embryos. Their use is controversial because such stem cells cannot be used in research without destroying the living embryo. Other sources of stem cells are available, however, and can be harvested from umbilical cord blood as well as from fat, bone marrow, and other adult tissue without harm to the donor. An enormous amount of research involving adult stem cells is going on as of 2004 in laboratories in the United States.

Prognosis

Individuals with mild to moderate mental retardation are frequently able to achieve some self-sufficiency and to lead happy and fulfilling lives. To reach these goals, they need appropriate and consistent educational, community, social, family, and vocational supports. The outlook is less promising for those with severe to profound retardation. Studies have shown that these individuals have a shortened life expectancy. The diseases that are usually associated with severe retardation may cause the shorter life span. People with Down syndrome develop in later life the brain changes that characterize Alzheimer's disease and may develop the clinical symptoms of this disease as well.

Prevention

Immunization against diseases such as measles and Hib prevents many of the illnesses that can cause mental retardation. In addition, all children should undergo routine developmental screening as part of their pediatric care. Screening is particularly critical for those children who may be neglected or undernourished or may live in disease-producing conditions. Newborn screening and immediate treatment for PKU and hyperthyroidism can usually catch these disorders early enough to prevent retardation. Good prenatal care can also help prevent retardation. Pregnant women should be educated about the risks of drinking and the need to maintain good **nutrition** during pregnancy. Tests such as **amniocentesis** and ultrasonography can determine whether a fetus is developing normally in the womb.

Parental concerns

All states are required by law to offer early intervention programs for mentally retarded children from the time they are born. The sooner the diagnosis of mental retardation is made, the more the child can be helped. With mentally retarded infants, the treatment emphasis is on sensorimotor development, which can be stimulated by exercises and special types of **play**. It is required that **special education** programs be available for retarded children starting at three years of age. These programs concentrate on essential self-care, such as feeding, dressing, and **toilet training**. There is also specialized help available for language and communication difficulties and physical disabilities. As children grow older, training in daily living skills, as well as academic subjects, is offered.

Counseling and therapy are another important type of treatment for the mentally retarded. Retarded children are prone to behavioral problems caused by short attention span, low tolerance for frustration, and poor impulse control. Behavior therapy with a mental health professional can help combat negative behavior patterns and replace them with more functional ones. A counselor or therapist can also help retarded children cope with the

KEY TERMS

Amniocentesis—A procedure performed at 16–18 weeks of pregnancy in which a needle is inserted through a woman's abdomen into her uterus to draw out a small sample of the amniotic fluid from around the baby for analysis. Either the fluid itself or cells from the fluid can be used for a variety of tests to obtain information about genetic disorders and other medical conditions in the fetus.

Developmental delay—The failure of a child to meet certain developmental milestones, such as sitting, walking, and talking, at the average age. Developmental delay may indicate a problem in development of the central nervous system.

Down syndrome—A chromosomal disorder caused by an extra copy or a rearrangement of chromosome 21. Children with Down syndrome have varying degrees of mental retardation and may have heart defects.

Hib disease—An infection caused by *Haemophilus influenza* type b (Hib). This disease mainly affects children under the age of five. In that age group, it is the leading cause of bacterial meningitis, pneumonia, joint and bone infections, and throat inflammations.

Inborn error of metabolism—One of a group of rare conditions characterized by an inherited defect in an enzyme or other protein. Inborn errors of metabolism can cause brain damage and mental retardation if left untreated. Phenylketonuria, Tay-Sachs disease, and galactosemia are inborn errors of metabolism.

Phenylketonuria (PKU)—A rare, inherited, metabolic disorder in which the enzyme necessary to break down and use phenylalanine, an amino acid necessary for normal growth and development, is lacking. As a result, phenylalanine builds up in the body causing mental retardation and other neurological problems.

Trisomy—An abnormal condition where three copies of one chromosome are present in the cells of an individual's body instead of two, the normal number.

Ultrasonography—A medical test in which sound waves are directed against internal structures in the body. As sound waves bounce off the internal structure, they create an image on a video screen. Ultrasonography is often used to diagnose fetal abnormalities, gallstones, heart defects, and tumors. Also called ultrasound imaging.

low self-esteem that often results from the realization that they are different from other children, including siblings. Counseling can also be valuable for the family of a retarded child to help parents cope with painful feelings about the child's condition and with the extra time and patience needed for the care and education of a special-needs child. Siblings may need to talk about the pressures they face, such as accepting the extra time and attention their parents must devote to a retarded brother or sister. Sometimes parents have trouble **bonding** with an infant who is retarded and need professional help and reassurance to establish a close and loving relationship.

Current social and healthcare policies encourage keeping mentally retarded persons in their own homes or in informal group home settings rather than institutions. The variety of social and mental health services available to the mentally retarded, including pre-vocational and vocational training, are geared toward making this possible.

Resources

BOOKS

Ainsworth, Patricia, and Pamela Baker. *Understanding Mental Retardation.* Jackson, MS: University Press of Mississippi, 2004.

Libal, Autumn. *My Name Is Not Slow: Youth with Mental Retardation.* Broomall, PA: Mason Crest Publishers, 2004.

Wehmeyer, Michael L., et al. *Teaching Students with Mental Retardation: Providing Access to the General Curriculum.* Baltimore: Brookes Publishing Co., 2001.

PERIODICALS

Cinamon, Rachel Gali, and Limor Gifsh. "Conceptions of Work among Adolescents and Young Adults with Mental Retardation." *Career Development Quarterly* 52 (March 2004): 212–24.

Howard, Barbara J. "Mental Retardation Challenges." *Pediatric News* 38 (September 2004): 20–1.

Kerker, Bonnie D., et al. "Mental Health Disorders among Individuals with Mental Retardation: Challenges to Accurate Prevalence Estimates." *Public Health Reports* 119 (August 2004): 409–17.

Ly, Tran M., and Robert M. Hodapp. "Maternal Attribution of Child Noncompliance in Children with Mental Retardation: Down Syndrome versus Other Causes." *Journal of Developmental & Behavioral Pediatrics* 23 (October 2002): 322–29.

ORGANIZATIONS

American Association on Mental Retardation. 444 North Capitol Street NW, Suite 846, Washington, DC 20001–1512. Web site: <www.aamr.org>.

National Academy of Child & Adolescent Psychiatry. 3615 Wisconsin Ave. NW, Washington, DC 20016. Web site: <www.aacap.org>.

WEB SITES

"Introduction to Mental Retardation." *The Arc*, 2004. Available online at <www.thearc.org/faqs/mrqa.html> (accessed November 11, 2004).

"Mental Retardation." *National Dissemination Center for Children with Disabilities*, January 2004. Available online at <www.nichcy.org/pubs/factshe/fs8txt.htm> (accessed November 11, 2004).

"Morbidity and Mortality Weekly Report." *Centers for Disease Control and Prevention*, January 26, 1996. Available online at <www.cdc/mmwr/preview/mmwrhtml/00040023.htm> (accessed November 11, 2004).

Paula Anne Ford-Martin
Ken R. Wells

Methamphetamine *see* **Stimulant drugs**

Methylphenidate

Definition

The generic name for the drug Ritalin, the most commonly prescribed medication for treating children with attention-deficit hyperactivity disorder (ADHD).

Description

Methylphenidate is one of a group of drugs called central nervous system (CNS) stimulants. It is used to treat attention-deficit hyperactivity disorder, **narcolepsy** (uncontrollable desire for **sleep** or sudden attacks of deep sleep), and other conditions as determined by a physician or other healthcare provider.

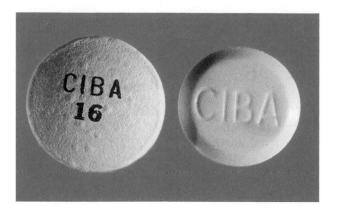

Psychostimulants such as methylphenidate (Ritalin) are commonly prescribed to treat attention-deficit/hyperactivity disorder (AD/HD). *(Photo Researchers, Inc.)*

Methylphenidate contributes to the treatment of ADHD by increasing attention and decreasing restlessness in children and adults who are overactive, cannot concentrate for very long, or are easily distracted, and are impulsive. Methylphenidate is intended to be used as part of a total treatment program that also includes social, educational, and psychological treatment.

A central nervous system stimulant, methylphenidate is also used to control narcolepsy, a condition characterized by an overpowering desire to sleep. Methylphenidate comes in short- and long-acting tablets. The latter should be swallowed whole, never broken into smaller pieces or chewed.

General use

Initially methylphenidate is prescribed in two daily doses of 2.5 mg each, taken at breakfast and lunch time. The dosage is gradually increased until the daily amount reaches 10.0 mg. The dosages should be strictly followed, and since anorexia is an important side effect, the dosages should always be accompanied by a meal or snack. The primary side effect of methylphenidate is growth suppression. Others include irritability, restlessness, agitation, **nausea**, and headaches. Occasionally it causes sleeplessness, in which case the last dosage of the day should be a short-action tablet. Physicians often recommend regular drug-free periods to combat these side effects. In many cases, a child only takes methylphenidate during the school year.

Precautions

Methylphenidate can be addictive and dosage should be tapered off gradually. Signs of physical depen-

KEY TERMS

Attention deficit hyperactivity disorder (ADHD)— A condition in which a person (usually a child) has an unusually high activity level and a short attention span. People with the disorder may act impulsively and may have learning and behavioral problems.

Narcolepsy—A life-long sleep disorder marked by four symptoms: sudden brief sleep attacks, cataplexy (a sudden loss of muscle tone usually lasting up to 30 minutes), temporary paralysis, and hallucinations. The hallucinations are associated with falling asleep or the transition from sleeping to waking.

dency include the need to increase the dosage in order to achieve results, mental depression, unusual behavior, and unusual tiredness or weakness. Some medical professionals believe that methylphenidate is prescribed too often. They call for better diagnostic procedures conducted by trained personnel rather than relying primarily on subjective observations by parents and teachers.

The dosage of methylphenidate is different for different people. It is important to follow the prescribing physician's orders or the instructions that appear on the label of the container. Do not change dosages unless a physician approves such an alteration.

Side effects

Any serious reaction to the drug, such as shortness of breath, irregular heartbeat, or allergic reaction, should be reported to one's doctor. Less severe, more common side effects include blurred vision, insomnia, drowsiness, gastrointestinal distress (nausea or **vomiting**), **dizziness**, headaches, and possible **addiction**.

Interactions

Persons taking methylphenidate should be aware of the possible adverse interactions with the following drugs: amphetamines, appetite suppressants, **caffeine**, chlophedianol, cocaine, **asthma** medication, cold, sinus and hay fever medications, nabilone, pemoline, monoamine oxidase inhibitors, and pimozide. Methylphenidate is also affected by epilepsy, Tourette's syndrome, glaucoma, high blood pressure, psychosis, severe **anxiety**, and **tics**.

Parental concerns

The use of methyphenidate has been subject to controversy over the last several years. Parents concerned about whether the drug is being properly prescribed for their children should seek out the opinion of the most suitable physician for the type of problems their child is having. If a parent is uncomfortable with a physician's response, they should not hesitate to get a second opinion.

Resources

BOOKS

Castro, E. A., and R. W. Hill. *Getting Rid of Ritalin: How Neurofeedback Can Successfully Treat Attention Deficit Disorder without Drugs.* Charlottesville, VA: Hampton Roads Publishing Company, 2002.

DeGrandpre, Richard J. *Ritalin Nation: Rapid-Fire Culture and the Transformation of Human Consciousness.* New York: Norton, 2000.

Ferreiro, Carmen. *Ritalin and Other Methylphenidate-Containing Drugs.* Langhorne, PA: Chelsea House Publishers, 2004.

Greenhill, Laurence L., and Bette B. Osman. *Ritalin: Theory and Practice.* Larchmont, NY: Mary Ann Liebert Incorporated, 2000.

PERIODICALS

Golan, N., et al. "Sleep disorders and daytime sleepiness in children with attention-deficit/hyperactive disorder." *Sleep* 27, no. 2 (2004): 261–6.

Mott, T. F., and L. Leach. "Is methylphenidate useful for treating adolescents with ADHD?" *Journal of Family Practice* 53, no. 8 (2004): 659–61.

ORGANIZATIONS

American Academy of Family Physicians. 11400 Tomahawk Creek Parkway, Leawood, KS 66211–2672. Web site: <www.aafp.org/>.

American Academy of Pediatrics. 141 Northwest Point Boulevard, Elk Grove Village, IL 60007–1098. Web site: <www.aap.org/>.

American College of Physicians. 190 N. Independence Mall West, Philadelphia, PA 19106–1572. Web site:

American Medical Association. 515 N. State Street, Chicago, IL 60610. Web site: .

American Osteopathic Association. 142 East Ontario Street, Chicago, IL 60611. Web site: .

American Psychiatric Association. 1400 K Street NW, Washington, DC 20005. Web site: .

National Institute of Mental Health. 6001 Executive Boulevard, Rm. 8184, MSC 9663, Bethesda, MD 20892–9663. Web site: <www.nimh.nih.gov/home.cfm>.

OTHER

"ADHD Medicines." *Kid's Health.* Available online at <http://kidshealth.org/kid/feel_better/things/ritalin.html> (accessed November 11, 2004).

"Methylphenidate (Ritalin)." *National Institute of Drug Abuse.* Available online at <www.nida.nih.gov/Infofax/ritalin.html> (accessed November 11, 2004).

"Methylphenidate." *Internet Mental Health.* Available online at <www.mentalhealth.com/drug/p30-r03.html> (accessed November 11, 2004).

"Ritalin: Miracle Drug or Cop-Out?" *Public Broadcasting System.* Available online at <www.pbs.org/wgbh/pages/frontline/shows/medicating/readings/publicinterest.html> (accessed November 11, 2004).

L. Fleming Fallon, Jr., MD, DrPH

Midget *see* **Dwarfism**

Mineral deficiency

Definition

Mineral deficiency is a reduced level of any of the **minerals** essential to human health. An abnormally low mineral concentration is usually defined as a level that may impair a function dependent on that mineral.

Description

Minerals are essential nutrients for every living cell in the human body. Defined in the study of human **nutrition** as all the inorganic elements or molecules required for life, minerals assist in body functions such as producing energy, growing, and healing. Minerals are required for fluid balance, blood and bone development, maintaining a healthy nervous system, and regulating muscles, including heart muscles. Minerals, like **vitamins**, function as coenzymes. They participate in all enzyme reactions in the body and help in the assimilation and use of vitamins and other nutrients.

Minerals occur either as bulk minerals (macrominerals) or trace minerals (microminerals). The body needs more bulk minerals than it does trace minerals, although both are essential for health. Minerals are consumed in food from plants and plant-eating animals. These sources of minerals develop in a sequence that takes millions of years, beginning with rock formation, the breakdown of rocks into mineral salts, and the assimilation of these salts into soil that nourishes edible plants.

Recommended daily allowances exist for a number of minerals, such as calcium. However, minimum daily requirements for some minerals such as boron, chromium, and molybdenum, do not exist. The essential bulk minerals include:

- Calcium—essential for strong bones and teeth, healthy gums, and bone growth and mineral density in children. Calcium helps regulate the heart rate and nerve impulses, lower cholesterol, prevent atherosclerosis, develop muscles, and prevent muscle cramping. Calcium is an important component of blood clotting. Calcium and phosphorus are closely related minerals that should be balanced. About 99 percent of calcium and 85 percent of phosphate occur in the skeleton as crystals of calcium phosphate. Both nutrients occur in a variety of foods such as milk, eggs, and green, leafy vegetables. Calcium deficiency due to lack of dietary calcium occurs only rarely and is often due to **vitamin D deficiency**, because vitamin D is required for efficient absorption of dietary calcium. Significant depletion of calcium stores can lead to osteoporosis.

- Magnesium—assists in the utilization of calcium and potassium, and functions in enzyme reactions to produce energy. Magnesium protects the lining of arteries and helps form bones. It helps prevent cardiovascular disease, osteoporosis, and some cancers. By acting with vitamin B_6, magnesium can help prevent or dissolve calcium oxalate kidney stones, the most common kind of stones. Dietary magnesium deficiency is uncommon, but may occur in chronic alcoholics, persons taking diuretic drugs, and as a result of severe, prolonged **diarrhea**.

- Sodium—sodium deficiency (hyponatremia) is a serious deficiency, arising most often after excessive losses of body fluid (**dehydration**) during prolonged and severe diarrhea or **vomiting**. Sodium and potassium are electrolytes that must be balanced in the body. Since most people get more than enough salt in the diet, potassium may be needed to balance it. Together, these minerals control fluid balance through a mechanism called "the sodium/potassium pump." Prolonged imbalances in sodium and potassium can contribute to heart disease.

- Potassium—important for a healthy nervous system and a steady heart rate, helps to prevent **stroke**, and, with sodium, is critical in maintaining fluid balance. Potassium, an electrolyte, must be balanced with sodium. Potassium deficiency is usually associated with sodium deficiency and both are associated with dehydration stemming from excessive losses of body fluid.

- Phosphorus—helps form bones and teeth, supports cell growth, and regulates heart muscle contraction and kidney function. Phosphorus converts food to energy and supports the utilization of vitamins. Deficiency is rare because phosphate is plentiful in plant and animal foods and is efficiently absorbed from the diet. Phosphorus is closely related to calcium and the two minerals should be in balance with each other and with magnesium. Deficiency in one will affect all and will ultimately have an unwanted effect on body function. Calcium and phosphorus are stored in the bones as crystals of calcium phosphate. Milk, eggs, and green, leafy vegetables are rich in calcium and phosphate.

Trace minerals essential for human health include:

- Boron—required for healthy bones, brain function, alertness, and the metabolism of bulk minerals such as calcium, phosphorus, and magnesium. Deficiencies are rare except in aging, when supplementation may help absorb calcium. A deficiency in boron is associated with vitamin D deficiency. Boron supplements can improve calcium levels as well as vitamin D levels, and can help prevent osteoporosis in postmenopausal women by promoting calcium absorption.

- Chromium—required for maintaining energy levels. Chromium helps metabolize glucose and stabilize glucose levels. It helps the body manufacture and use cholesterol and protein.

- Copper—helps form healthy bones, joints, and nerves as well as hemoglobin and red blood cells. Copper contributes to healing, energy production, taste, and hair and skin color. It is essential in forming collagen for healthy bones and connective tissue, and helps prevent osteoporosis. Except in osteoporosis, copper deficiency is rare, although dramatic changes in copper metabolism occur in two serious genetic diseases, Wilson disease and Menkes' disease.

- Germanium—helps improve the delivery of oxygen to tissues and remove toxins and poisons from the body. Germanium gives garlic its natural antibiotic properties.

- Iodine—helps promote healthy physical and mental development in children. Iodine is required for thyroid gland function and metabolizing fats. Iodine deficiency is a public health problem in parts of the world that have iodine-deficient soils. Iodine is needed to make thyroid hormone, which has a variety of roles in human embryo development. A deficiency during pregnancy can cause serious birth defects. Deficiency in adults can result in an enlarged thyroid gland (goiter) in the neck.

- Iron—critical in the production of hemoglobin, the oxygen-carrying protein in red blood cells, and myoglobin found in muscle tissue. Iron is essential for important enzyme reactions, growth, and maintaining a healthy immune system. In the blood, iron is found in larger amounts than any other mineral. Iron deficiency causes anemia (low hemoglobin and reduced numbers of red blood cells), which results in tiredness and shortness of breath because of poor oxygen delivery.

- Manganese—essential for metabolizing fat and protein, regulating blood glucose, and supporting immune system and nervous system function. Manganese is necessary for normal bone growth and cartilage development. It is involved in reproductive functions and helps produce mother's milk. Along with B vitamins, manganese produces feelings of well-being. Deficiency can lead to convulsions, vision and hearing problems, muscle contractions, tooth-grinding and other problems in children; and atherosclerosis, heart disease, and **hypertension** in older adults.

- Molybdenum—found in bones, kidneys, and liver. Only extremely small amounts are needed to metabolize nitrogen and promote proper cell function. Molybdenum is present in beans, peas, legumes, whole grains, and green leafy vegetables. A diet low in these foods can lead to mouth and gum problems and cancer.

- Selenium—an important antioxidant that works with vitamin E to protect the immune system, heart, and liver, and may help prevent tumor formation. Selenium deficiency occurs in regions of the world where soils are selenium-poor and low-selenium foods are produced. Premature infants are naturally low in selenium with no known serious effects.

- Silicon—helps form bones and connective tissue, nails, skin, and hair. Silicon is important in preventing cardiovascular disease.

- Sulfur—disinfects the blood and helps to rid the body of harmful bacteria and toxic substances.

- Vanadium—vital to cell metabolism, and helps reduce cholesterol and form healthy bones and teeth. Vanadium functions in reproduction. Deficiencies may be associated with heart and kidney disease and reproductive disorders. Vanadium deficiency may be associated with infant mortality.

- Zinc—important in the growth of reproductive organs and regulation of oil glands. Zinc is required for protein synthesis, immune system function, protection of the liver, collagen formation, and wound healing. A component of insulin and major body enzymes, zinc helps vitamin absorption, particularly vitamins A and E. Deficiency is rare.

Trace and bulk minerals are stored in muscles and bones and delivered to tissue cells through blood circulation. They work together synergistically and must be chemically balanced in the body; if one is deficient or out of balance, it can affect all the others, often resulting in illness. If zinc, for example, is present at high levels, calcium levels will be reduced because the two minerals compete for absorption. Similarly, too much calcium will deplete magnesium, and so on. Deficiency in one nutrient occurs less often than deficiency in several nutrients. A child suffering from **malnutrition** will likely be deficient in a variety of nutrients. Deficiencies in one nutrient do occur, however, such as in populations living in iodine-poor regions, and in iron deficient persons who lose excess iron by abnormal bleeding. All uncorrected mineral deficiencies can affect body functions, produce symptoms, and result in illness.

Demographics

Statistics are not available for most individual mineral deficiencies, most likely because such deficiencies are rare in the United States. Surveys of lower-income families in the United States reveal that about 6 percent of infants are anemic, indicating a possible deficiency of iron in the diet (all **anemias** are not iron-deficiency related).

Diarrheal diseases and related sodium and potassium deficiencies are responsible for about two million infant deaths each year worldwide. Few of these deaths occur in the United States.

Causes and symptoms

Calcium and phosphorus deficiencies

Calcium and phosphorus are plentiful in foods, and dietary deficiencies are rare. Vitamin D deficiency impairs the absorption of dietary calcium and can provoke calcium deficiency (hypocalcemia) even when adequate calcium is consumed. Vitamin D deficiency can be found among young infants and the elderly who may be shielded from sunshine for prolonged periods. As women age, reductions in the hormone estrogen can affect the rate of calcium loss. Significant depletion of calcium stores can lead to osteoporosis. Deficiency of calcium or imbalances with phosphorus and magnesium can produce muscle cramping and digestive problems. Symptoms of calcium deficiency include joint **pain**, brittle nails, eczema, **high cholesterol**, insomnia, high blood pressure, nervousness, and **tooth decay**. Calcium

deficiency can also contribute to cognitive problems (confusion, inattention, learning, and memory), convulsions, depression, and hyperactivity. Phosphorus deficiency can produce **anxiety**.

Sodium and potassium deficiencies

Deficiency or imbalance in sodium and potassium does not usually result from a lack of these minerals in the diet, but from imbalances in body fluids. This can be caused by excessive losses of body fluid (dehydration) from severe diarrhea or vomiting; laxative abuse; or during treatment of heart disease or high blood pressure (hypertension) with diuretic drugs, which are used to reduce fluid overload. Sodium and potassium imbalances can cause cardiac arrhythmias and shock (a reduced flow of blood and oxygen to tissues throughout the body). Although diarrheal fluids deplete a number of electrolytes (sodium, potassium, chloride, calcium, phosphorus, and magnesium), the main concern in avoiding shock is replacing sodium and water. Potassium deficiency alone can also affect nerve function.

Magnesium deficiency

Dietary magnesium deficiency is rare because the mineral is found in nearly all foods, but it can occur through poor diet or in malnutrition, or result from excessive losses due to severe diarrhea or vomiting. Symptoms of magnesium deficiency include faulty transmission of nerve and muscle impulses, irritability, nervousness, and **tantrums**. Confusion, poor digestion, rapid or irregular heartbeat (arrhythmia), and seizures can also result. Magnesium deficiency is associated with cardiac arrest, **asthma**, chronic fatigue syndrome, chronic pain, depression, insomnia, **irritable bowel syndrome**, and lung conditions.

Boron deficiency

Boron deficiency is rare, although reduced levels do occur with aging and with reduced levels of vitamin D. Because boron is involved in the absorption of calcium, the only symptom may be reduced levels of calcium or the inability to absorb supplemental calcium.

Chromium deficiency

Many Americans are deficient in dietary chromium, which can be associated with poor regulation of insulin and related imbalances in glucose (either diabetes or **hypoglycemia**). Symptoms include fatigue, anxiety, poor protein metabolism, and glucose intolerance (as in diabetes). In adults, chromium deficiency can be a sign of coronary artery disease.

Copper deficiency

Copper is obtained through a balanced diet and deficiency is rare. Signs of copper deficiency may include anemia, diarrhea, weakness, poor respiratory function, baldness, skin sores, and increased lipid (fat) levels in the blood. Severe alterations in copper metabolism are seen in two rare genetic diseases: Wilson disease and Menkes' disease, which occur in about one in 100,000 births. Both diseases involve mutations in copper transport proteins, special channels that allow copper ions to pass through cell membranes. Menkes' disease, called the "kinky hair disease," results in tangled, grayish, steely, or kinky hair and chubby, rosy cheeks. Untreated Menkes' disease is associated with **mental retardation** and death before three years of age. Wilson disease involves decreases in copper in blood cells, the liver and brain; and increases in copper (copper toxicosis) in the cells of the intestines and kidneys. It results in degenerative changes in the brain, liver disease, and hemolytic anemia. Children older than five years who have any form of liver disease are often evaluated for serum and cellular copper levels to determine if Wilson disease is present.

Germanium deficiency

Germanium deficiency is rare; in fact, there is no established deficiency level.

Iodine deficiency

Iodine deficiency occurs when soil is iodine-poor and foods grown in the soil are correspondingly low in iodine. An iodine intake of 0.10–0.15 mg/day is considered to be nutritionally adequate. Iodine deficiency occurs when intake is below 0.05 mg/day. Goiter, an enlargement of the thyroid gland in the neck, results from iodine deficiency. Although goiter continues to be a problem in other parts of the world, it no longer occurs in the United States because of the fortification of foods with iodine. Iodine deficiency during pregnancy can result in cretinism in newborns, involving mental retardation and a large tongue.

Iron deficiency

Iron deficiency occurs most often because of poor iron intake and poor absorption. In children, iron deficiency is due to periods of dietary deficiency and heavy demands for iron during rapid growth. Human milk and cow's milk both contain low levels of iron; however, the iron in human milk is in a highly absorbable form. Infants are at risk for acquiring iron deficiency because their rapid rate of growth needs a corresponding increased supply of dietary iron, for use in making blood and muscles. Cow's milk formula is fortified with iron. Human milk is a better source of iron than cow's milk, since about half of the iron in human breast milk is absorbed by the infant's digestive tract. In contrast, only 10 percent of the iron in cow's milk is absorbed by the infant. Toddlers who drink excessive whole cow's milk are at risk for iron deficiency. Iron deficiency can also be caused by excess phosphorus in the diet, chronic intestinal bleeding, poor digestion and absorption, prolonged illness, ulcers, and the use of antacids. In women and teenage girls, blood loss through **menstruation** can result in iron deficiency. Symptoms of iron deficiency include anemia and resulting fatigue and weakness, especially during physical exertion. Fragile bones, brittle hair and nails, hair loss, spoon-shaped fingernails or ridges from the base of the nails to the ends, difficulty swallowing, nervousness, paleness, and lagging mental responses are also possible iron deficiency symptoms.

Manganese deficiency

Deficiency of manganese is very rare. Experimental studies of individuals fed a manganese deficient diet have revealed that the deficiency produces a scaly, red rash on the skin of the upper torso.

Selenium deficiency

Selenium deficiency may occur in premature infants who naturally tend to have about one-third the selenium levels of full-term infants. It is not known if these lower levels result in adverse consequences. Selenium deficiency occurs in regions of the world containing low-selenium soils, including parts of China, New Zealand, and Finland. In Keshan Province, China, a condition (Keshan disease) occurs that results in deterioration of regions of the heart and the development of fibers in these areas. Keshan disease, which may be fatal, is thought to result from a combination of selenium deficiency and a virus.

Zinc deficiency

Zinc deficiency can be caused by diarrhea, liver and kidney disease, **alcoholism**, diabetes, malabsorption, and overconsumption of fiber. Symptoms of zinc deficiency include **acne**, recurrent colds and flu, loss of senses of taste and smell, poor night vision, slow growth, lack of sexual maturation, lack of pubic hair, and small stature. Studies have shown that signs of zinc deficiency are detectable after two to five weeks of consuming a zinc-free diet. Signs include a rash on the face, groin, hands and feet, and diarrhea. Administering zinc will correct these symptoms.

When to call the doctor

Mineral deficiencies present with a wide variety of symptoms. Parents should observe children closely and report any unusual symptoms to the pediatrician, such as tiredness, weakness, depression or anxiety, irritability, nervousness, skin irritations, dehydration from vomiting or diarrhea, and slow growth or development of skills. Other than providing regular vitamin supplements and a balanced diet to prevent deficiencies, parents should not attempt to diagnose and treat deficiencies on their own.

Diagnosis

Individual minerals can be measured in blood serum, red blood cells, tissue cells, or urine, to estimate available levels and determine normal or abnormal status. Since each mineral performs strikingly different functions, tests to confirm deficiency are markedly different from each other. Testing can range from simple to extensive. Physicians will consider the possible consequences of each type of deficiency and evaluate the function of organ systems affected by the particular mineral.

In addition to determining serum calcium, phosphorus, and vitamin D levels, the diagnosis of calcium and phosphorus deficiency may involve taking **x rays** of the skeleton.

Diagnosing iron deficiency will require measuring iron levels and investigating anemia by performing blood tests such as a complete blood count (CBC) to determine the number of red blood cells, hemoglobin level, red cell volume, and cell maturity (morphology). A stair-stepping test may be used to evaluate stamina, but a blood test is required to diagnose iron deficiency.

Diagnosing low levels or imbalances of the electrolytes sodium, potassium, calcium, magnesium, or phosphate involves measuring the serum levels of each. Measurement determines the circulating blood level at the time blood was drawn. Laboratory values of sodium and potassium, which are present within cells and in the fluid between cells, can change rapidly depending on the individual's overall condition. They may be measured repeatedly to determine a trend and to monitor correction of the deficiency or imbalance after diagnosis.

Normal serum magnesium levels are 1.2–2.0 mE/l, while levels in deficiency (hypomagnesemia) are below 0.8 mE/l. Because calcium and magnesium must remain balanced, magnesium levels below 0.5 mE/l can provoke a decline in serum calcium levels. Hypomagnesemia can also result in low serum potassium. Symptoms of hypomagnesemia, such as twitching and convulsions, may actually result from the hypocalcemia. Other symptoms, such as cardiac arrhythmias, actually occur because of low potassium. All three minerals will be measured.

Iodine deficiency is diagnosed by measuring the concentration of iodine in urine. A urinary level greater than 0.05 mg iodine per gram of creatinine (another metabolite excreted in urine) indicates adequate iodine status. Levels under 0.025 mg iodine/gram creatinine indicate serious risk. The doctor may also examine the neck with the eyes and hands to see if a goiter is present.

Urinary zinc levels will differ between normal dietary intake (16 mg per day) and low-zinc diets (0.3 mg per day); normal urinary zinc is about 0.45 mg per day while low-zinc urinary levels are about 0.150 mg per day. Plasma zinc levels tend to be maintained during a dietary deficiency in zinc. Plasma and urinary zinc levels can be influenced by a variety of factors, and for this reason cannot provide a clear picture of zinc status.

Selenium can be measured in plasma or red blood cells and compared to normal values. The activity of an enzyme (glutathione peroxidase) in platelets (small blood cells essential in blood clotting) may be evaluated to assess selenium status.

Treatment

Most mineral deficiencies can be successfully treated through diet or supplementation, except when caused by disease, which requires treatment of the disease.

Treating fluid imbalances and related deficiencies in sodium, potassium, calcium, and phosphate usually requires intravenous (IV) infusion of the deficient mineral in fluid over a period of time. Sudden changes in sodium and potassium levels can be just as dangerous as low levels; caution is used to restore balance gradually. Children may be given oral pediatric preparations to gradually restore fluids and minerals.

Iron deficiency requires oral supplementation or injectable iron. Vitamin C helps to assimilate iron.

Iodine deficiency is easily treated and prevented by consuming foods fortified with iodine, such as table salt. Goiter is reversible with treatment but cretinism is not.

A magnesium-rich diet will correct magnesium deficiency. If deficiency is due to prolonged depletion, treatment may include injections of magnesium sulfate; if severe enough to provoke convulsions, intravenous infusions may be given.

Selenium deficiency can be treated by supplementation. Children can be given supplements containing 1.0 mg sodium selenite.

Zinc and copper deficiencies are rare and can be treated with supplementation.

Prognosis

The prognosis for mineral deficiencies depends on the extent of deficiency at diagnosis, the degree of effects or symptoms, and the overall health of the individual. Correction through diet or supplements usually produces good results. Symptoms may sometimes be relieved promptly with supplementation. Some deficiencies produce permanent effects of varying severity.

In iodine deficiency, the prognosis for treating goiter is excellent. Sodium and potassium deficiencies or imbalances can be corrected if diagnosed and treated promptly, but can be life-threatening if untreated. Anemia and other effects of iron deficiency are not usually life-threatening and can be corrected with supplementation. "Silent" or undiagnosed calcium loss may result in osteoporosis, which may produce disability or complications by the time it is diagnosed.

Alternative treatment

Sea vegetables (sea weeds such as dulse, kelp, wakambe, and hijiki) are an excellent source of minerals obtained from the ocean. They can be used to make soup stock, added to stews and casseroles, or served with vegetables. Herbs are a valuable source of minerals as well. For example, calcium is found in alfalfa, burdock root, chamomile, dandelion, flaxseed, paprika, raspberry leaves, rose hips, and other herbs. Iron is found in the same herbs as calcium, and in the Chinese herb *dong quai* (angelica), as well as other herbs.

Prevention

Ensuring an adequate intake of essential nutrients through a balanced diet and supplements is the best way to prevent mineral deficiencies. The Required Dietary Allowances (RDA) guidelines can help ensure that minerals are being obtained. Safe amounts of certain minerals are often included in multivitamins. Because excess mineral levels can also cause health problems, taking excessive amounts of any mineral supplement is not advised unless a deficiency is diagnosed. When mineral deficiency is the result of disease, medical attention, other than preventive measures, is required.

Nutritional concerns

A balanced diet includes fresh vegetables and fruits, legumes, whole grains (cereal, bread, rice, pasta, and other grains), eggs, dairy products, fish, fowl, and lean

---

KEY TERMS

Electrolytes—Salts and minerals that produce electrically charged particles (ions) in body fluids. Common human electrolytes are sodium chloride, potassium, calcium, and sodium bicarbonate. Electrolytes control the fluid balance of the body and are important in muscle contraction, energy generation, and almost all major biochemical reactions in the body.

Nutrient—Substances in food that supply the body with the elements needed for metabolism. Examples of nutrients are vitamins, minerals, carbohydrates, fats, and proteins.

Osteoporosis—Literally meaning "porous bones," this condition occurs when bones lose an excessive amount of their protein and mineral content, particularly calcium. Over time, bone mass and strength are reduced leading to increased risk of fractures.

Recommended Dietary Allowance (RDA)—The Recommended Dietary Allowances (RDAs) are quantities of nutrients in the diet that are required to maintain good health in people. RDAs are established by the Food and Nutrition Board of the National Academy of Sciences, and may be revised every few years. A separate RDA value exists for each nutrient. The RDA values refer to the amount of nutrient expected to maintain good health in people. The actual amounts of each nutrient required to maintain good health in specific individuals differ from person to person.

---

meat as preferred. A diet high in refined foods, prepared foods, sugars, and fats will not provide sufficient quantities of essential minerals. Water delivers nutrients throughout the body; it is essential to drink enough clean water daily to maintain fluid balance and distribute nutrients.

Essential mineral nutrients are found in a variety of sources, as in these examples:

• Boron is abundant in apples, pears, grapes, leafy greens, carrots, whole grains, and nuts.

• Primary calcium sources are dairy foods, eggs, fish, and green leafy vegetables. Other calcium-rich foods are figs, broccoli, cabbage, oats, almonds and filberts, yogurt, and blackstrap molasses. Spinach and Swiss chard bind calcium in the digestive tract and are not a ready source.

- Chromium is found in brown rice and other whole grains, cheeses, meats, dried beans, corn, eggs, mushrooms, and potatoes.

- Copper is found in nuts, mushrooms, broccoli, garlic, lentils, salmon, and green vegetables. It is also found in plumbing and cooking pots, which may leach into food and water.

- Germanium occurs primarily in garlic, shiitake mushrooms, and onions.

- Iron can be provided by eating green leafy vegetables, raisins, meat, eggs, liver, fish and fowl, nuts, and whole grains. It can also be obtained by cooking in iron skillets.

- Magnesium is found in most foods, primarily animal and fish sources.

- Potassium food sources include dairy foods, fish, fresh and dried fruits, beans and peas, meats, fish and fowl, and whole grains.

- Zinc sources include brewer's yeast, eggs, fish, meats, beans, mushrooms, nuts and seeds, and whole grains.

Parental concerns

Good nutrition is a concern of all parents. In the United States, it is relatively easy to provide a balanced diet with essential nutrients if a wide variety of whole foods are prepared for **family** meals and snacks, while avoiding refined and prepared foods high in fats and sugars. RDA guidelines and public health resources can help assure parents that they can prevent dietary deficiencies in their young children and teens.

Resources

BOOKS

Balch, James, and Phyllis Balch. *Prescription for Nutritional Healing,* 3rd ed. New York: Avery Publishing Group, 2002.

Brody, Tom. *Nutritional Biochemistry.* San Diego: Academic Press, 1998.

ORGANIZATIONS

American Society for Nutritional Sciences (ASNS). 9650 Rockville Pike, Suite 4500, Bethesda, MD 20814. (301) 634-7050. Web site: <www.nutrition.org>.

WEB SITES

Food and Nutrition Information (FNIC). [cited October 9, 2004]. Available online at: <www.nal.usda.gov/fnic/>.

L. Lee Culvert
Tom Brody, Ph.D.

Mineral toxicity

Definition

The term mineral toxicity refers to a condition in which the concentration in the body of any one of the **minerals** necessary for life is abnormally high, and which has an adverse effect on health.

Description

The mineral nutrients are defined as all the inorganic elements or inorganic molecules that are required for life. As far as human **nutrition** is concerned, the inorganic nutrients include water, sodium, potassium, chloride, calcium, phosphate, sulfate, magnesium, iron, fluorine, copper, zinc, chromium, manganese, iodine, selenium, and molybdenum. The last nine elements in this list are sometimes called trace minerals or micronutrients because humans need only small amounts of them in the diet. In high doses all nine trace minerals can be toxic in humans.

In general, mineral toxicity results when a person accidentally consumes too much of any mineral, as with drinking ocean water (sodium toxicity), or is overexposed to industrial pollutants, household chemicals, or certain drugs. Iron toxicity in children, for example, frequently results from accidental swallowing of dietary supplement tablets.

Mineral toxicity may also refer to toxic conditions resulting from certain diseases or injuries. For example, a disorder known as hemochromatosis leads to iron toxicity, while Wilson's disease results in copper toxicity. Severe trauma can lead to hyperkalemia or potassium toxicity.

Demographics

Iron **poisoning** is the most common form of mineral toxicity in children in the United States and is one of the leading causes of fatal poisoning in children younger than six years of age. About 20,000 children are reported as accidentally swallowing iron tablets each year in the United States, although not all of these cases end in death. In one Indian study of 21 children treated for iron poisoning, four of the patients died.

With regard to diseases leading to mineral toxicity, about one person in ten in the United States has the genetic mutation that can lead to hemochromatosis; however, not everyone with this mutation necessarily develops the disease. It is thought that there are about 1 million persons in the United States with hemachromatosis as of the early 2000s. About one person in 30,000 has the genetic defect that causes Wilson's disease, while about 1.1 percent of the general population are carriers of the mutant gene. The incidence of Menkes disease, which primarily affects boys, is variously estimated at one in 50,000 to one in 250,000 persons. Wilson's disease and Menkes disease occur at the same rate in all races and ethnic groups.

Causes and symptoms

The causes and symptoms of mineral toxicity depend on the specific mineral in question:

- Sodium: An increase in sodium concentration in the bloodstream can be toxic. The normal concentration of sodium in human blood plasma is 136–145 mM, while levels over 152 mM can result in seizures and death. Increased plasma sodium, which is called hypernatremia, causes the cells in various body tissues, including those of the brain, to shrink. Shrinkage of the brain cells results in confusion, coma, paralysis of the lung muscles, and death. Death has occurred when table salt (sodium chloride) was accidentally used to feed infants instead of sugar. Death due to sodium toxicity has also resulted when baking soda (sodium bicarbonate) was used to treat excessive **diarrhea** or **vomiting**. Although a variety of processed foods contain high levels of sodium chloride, the levels in these items are not enough to result in sodium toxicity.

- Potassium: The normal level of potassium in the bloodstream is in the range of 3.5–5.0 mM, while levels of 6.3–8.0 mM (severe hyperkalemia) result in cardiac arrhythmias or even death due to cardiac arrest. Potassium is potentially quite toxic; however, potassium poisoning is usually prevented because of the vomiting reflex. The consumption of food results in mild increases in the concentration of potassium in the bloodstream, but these levels of potassium do not become toxic because of the uptake of potassium by various cells of the body as well as by the action of the kidneys transferring the potassium ions from the blood to the urine. The body's regulatory mechanisms can easily be overwhelmed, however, when potassium chloride is injected intravenously, as high doses of injected potassium can easily result in death.

- Iodine: Iodine toxicity can result from an intake of 2.0 mg of iodide per day. Toxic levels of iodine inhibit the secretion of thyroid hormone, resulting in lower levels of thyroid hormone in the bloodstream. As a result, the thyroid gland becomes enlarged. This condition is known as goiter or **hyperthyroidism**. Goiter is usually caused by iodine deficiency. In addition to goiter, iodine toxicity produces a brassy taste in the mouth,

excessive production of saliva, and ulcers on the skin. This skin condition has been called kelp **acne** because of its association with eating kelp, an ocean plant that contains high levels of iodine. Iodine toxicity occurs fairly frequently in Japan, where people consume large amounts of seaweed.

- Iron: Iron toxicity is not unusual in small children due to the wide distribution of dietary supplements containing iron. A lethal dose of iron is in the range of 200—250 mg iron/kg body weight, meaning that a child who accidentally eats 20 or more iron tablets may die as a result of iron poisoning. Children are unfortunately likely to take large amounts of these pills because they look like candy. Within six hours of ingestion, iron toxicity can result in vomiting, diarrhea, abdominal **pain**, seizures, and possibly coma. In the second period of iron poisoning, the patient's symptoms appear to improve; however, this phase is followed by a terminal phase in which shock, low blood sugar levels, liver damage, convulsions, and death occur 12 to 48 hours after the fatal dose.

- Nitrite: Nitrite poisoning should be considered along with iron toxicity, since nitrite produces its toxic effect by reacting with the iron atom in hemoglobin. Hemoglobin is an iron-containing protein that resides within the red blood cells. This protein is responsible for transporting nearly all of the oxygen acquired from the lungs to various tissues and organs of the body. Hemoglobin accounts for the red color of red blood cells. A very small fraction of hemoglobin spontaneously oxidizes per day, producing a protein of a slightly different structure called methemoglobin. Normally, the amount of methemoglobin constitutes less than 1 percent of the total hemoglobin. Methemoglobin can accumulate in the blood as a result of nitrite poisoning. Infants are especially susceptible to poisoning by nitrite.

- Nitrate: Nitrate is naturally present in green leafy vegetables and in the water supply. It is rapidly converted to nitrite by the bacteria that live in the mouth as well as in the intestines and then absorbed into the bloodstream. The amount of nitrate that is supplied by leafy vegetables and drinking water is generally about 100 to 170 mg/day. The amount of nitrite supplied by a typical diet is much lower, about 0.1 mg nitrite per day. Poisoning by nitrite (or nitrate after its conversion to nitrite) results in the inability of hemoglobin to carry oxygen throughout the body. This condition can be seen by the blue color of the skin. Adverse symptoms occur when over 30 percent of the hemoglobin has been converted to methemoglobin. These symptoms include cardiac arrhythmias, **headache**, **nausea and vomiting**, and in severe cases, seizures.

- Calcium and phosphate: Calcium and phosphate are closely related nutrients. Calcium toxicity is rare, but overconsumption of calcium supplements may lead to deposits of calcium phosphate in the soft tissues of the body. Phosphate toxicity can result from the overuse of **laxatives** or enemas that contain phosphate. Severe phosphate toxicity can result in hypocalcemia and in various symptoms resulting from low plasma calcium levels. Moderate phosphate toxicity occurring over a period of months may result in the deposit of calcium phosphate crystals in various tissues of the body.

- Zinc: Zinc toxicity is rare but is more likely to occur in adults than in children. It is usually related to occupational hazards and has been reported to occur in metal workers exposed to fumes containing zinc. A few instances of zinc toxicity have been reported in people who consumed acidic food or beverages that had been stored in galvanized zinc containers. Taking excessive supplemental zinc can result in **nausea**, vomiting, and diarrhea. The chronic intake of excessive zinc supplements can result in copper deficiency, as zinc inhibits the absorption of copper.

- Copper: Copper toxicity in humans is usually the result of disease. Severe alterations in copper metabolism occur in two genetic diseases, Wilson's disease and Menkes disease. These diseases are rare. They involve mutations in the proteins that transport copper, that is, in special channels that allow the passage of copper ions through cell membranes. Wilson's disease, which is caused by a mutation of the ATP7B gene on chromosome 13, first produces symptoms in teenagers and young adults. Copper accumulates in the liver, kidney, and brain, resulting in damage to the liver and nervous system. In Menkes disease, which is usually first noticed in infancy, impaired transport of copper from the digestive tract results in low levels of copper in the blood, while copper accumulates in the kidney, pancreas, and skeletal muscle. Children with Menkes disease have characteristic kinky hair, seizures, developmental failures, and progressive degeneration of the brain.

- Selenium: Selenium toxicity occurs in a few regions of the world, most notably some parts of China where soils contain high levels of the mineral. A daily intake of 0.75 to 5.0 mg selenium may occur in these regions due to the presence of selenium in foods and water. Early signs of selenium toxicity include nausea, weakness, and diarrhea. Continued intake of selenium results in changes in the fingernails, hair loss, and damage to the nervous system. The person's breath may acquire a characteristic garlic odor as a result of the increased production of dimethylselenide in the body and its release via the lungs.

- Manganese: Manganese toxicity is most likely to affect adults rather than children. It occurs most commonly in workers in manganese mines who must breathe air containing high levels of manganese dust (in a concentration of 5–250 mg/cubic meter). Manganese toxicity in miners has been documented in Chile, India, Japan, Mexico, and elsewhere. Symptoms of manganese poisoning typically occur within several months or years of exposure. These symptoms include a mental disorder resembling **schizophrenia** as well as hyperirritability, violent acts, hallucinations, and difficulty in walking.

When to call the doctor

The most common form of mineral toxicity for children and adolescents in the United States is accidental poisoning from iron supplements. Parents should take a child who is known to have swallowed iron tablets to the doctor or a hospital emergency room for treatment as soon as possible, as an iron overdose is potentially fatal.

Children born into families with a history of Wilson's disease should have a blood test for the disease at some point in their second year of life, before symptoms of the disease develop.

Diagnosis

An initial diagnosis of mineral toxicity requires taking a careful history. The doctor asks the parents of a small child questions intended to identify any unusual aspects of the family's diet or intake of drugs and chemicals. An older teenager in the workforce may be asked about possible occupational exposure. The mineral content of the body may be measured by testing samples of body fluids, most commonly blood plasma, red blood cells from whole blood, and urine. Diagnosis of mineral toxicities also involves measuring the concentration of various metals in the plasma or urine. Concentrations that are above the normal range can confirm the initial suspected diagnosis.

Menkes disease may be diagnosed by the unusual appearance of the hair, skin, and facial features in male infants with the disorder as well as by their developmental problems.

In addition to a deficiency in blood plasma of a protein known as ceruloplasmin, Wilson's disease is characterized by gold or greenish-gold discolorations of the cornea of the eye known as Kayser-Fleischer rings. These rings may be detected by an ophthalmologist during a slit-lamp examination. The doctor may also suspect

Wilson's disease in a child above the age of five with unexplained episodes of hepatitis or such symptoms of copper toxicity in the brain as drooling, loss of coordination, tremor, sudden drop in academic performance, or frank psychotic episodes. The clinical symptoms of Wilson's disease do not appear in young children; however, measurements of serum ceruloplasmin can be taken in children over 12 months of age if a **family** history of Wilson's disease is a risk factor.

Treatment

Iron toxicity is treated by efforts to remove the remaining iron from the stomach by administering a solution of 5 percent sodium bicarbonate. Where plasma iron levels have risen above 0.35 mg/dL, the patient is treated with deferoxamine. Treatment of manganese toxicity involves removal of the patient from the high manganese environment as well as giving him or her lifelong doses of the drug L-dopa. The treatment is only partially successful. Treatment of nitrite or nitrate toxicity involves inhalation of 100 percent oxygen for several hours. If oxygen treatment is not effective, then a solution of 1.0 percent methylene blue may be injected in a dose of 1.0 mg methylene blue/kg body weight.

With regard to disorders of copper metabolism, Wilson's disease can be successfully controlled by lifelong treatment with d-penicillamine, trientine, and zinc acetate. Treatment also involves avoiding foods that are high in copper, such as liver, nuts, chocolate, and mollusks. After an initial period of treatment with penicillamine, Wilson's disease may be treated with zinc (150 mg oral Zn/day). The zinc inhibits the absorption of dietary copper. Patients with this disease must, however, comply with treatment for the rest of their lives, as untreated Wilson's disease is invariably fatal. Patients who develop liver failure as a result of the disease may be candidates for a liver transplant.

Children with Menkes disease are sometimes helped temporarily by intravenous injections of copper supplements. There is, however, no cure for the disease as of the early 2000s, and most children with the disorder live only a few years.

Nutritional concerns

Families consuming a well-balanced diet without overuse of dietary supplements are unlikely to have problems with mineral toxicity. Children or adolescents diagnosed with Wilson's disease must observe the dietary limitations described earlier.

Prognosis

The prognosis for mineral toxicity due to sodium, potassium, calcium, and phosphate is usually excellent. Toxicity due to the deposit of calcium phosphate crystals is not usually reversible. The prognosis for treating iodine toxicity is excellent. For any mineral overdose that causes coma or seizures, the prognosis for recovery is often poor, and death results in a small fraction of patients. For any mineral toxicity that causes nerve damage, the prognosis is often fair to poor. Wilson's disease is fatal, usually before age 30, unless the patient complies with continual lifelong treatment to prevent brain or liver disease. Children diagnosed with Menkes disease rarely live past their third birthday.

Prevention

When mineral toxicity results from the excessive consumption of mineral supplements, toxicity can be prevented by minimizing the use of dietary supplements and keeping iron tablets in particular out of the reach of children. Zinc toxicity may be prevented by not storing food or beverages in zinc containers. In the case of iodine, toxicity can be prevented by avoiding overconsumption of seaweed or kelp. In the case of selenium toxicity resulting from high-selenium soils, toxicity can be prevented by relying on food and water acquired from a low-selenium region.

Such genetic diseases as Wilson's disease and Menkes disease cannot be prevented as of the early 2000s.

Parental concerns

Parental concerns about mineral toxicity in most children should be directed toward preventing accidental consumption of iron and other mineral supplements in young children and in monitoring the adoption of fad diets in teenagers.

In the case of children with hemachromatosis or Wilson's disease, parents will need to make sure that the affected child complies with all aspects of necessary treatment. In the case of a child with Menkes disease, parents should seek genetic counseling, as the grim prognosis of this illness places a heavy emotional as well as economic burden on a family.

See also Heavy metal poisoning; Poisoning.

KEY TERMS

Arrhythmia—Any deviation from a normal heart beat.

Goiter—Chronic enlargement of the thyroid gland.

Hemochromatosis—An inherited blood disorder that causes the body to retain excessive amounts of iron. This iron overload can lead to serious health consequences, including painful joints, diabetes, and liver damage, if the iron concentration is not lowered.

Hyperkalemia—An abnormally high level of potassium in the blood.

Hypernatremia—An abnormally high level of sodium in the blood.

Hypocalcemia—A condition characterized by an abnormally low level of calcium in the blood.

Menkes disease—A genetic disease caused by a mutation on the X chromosome and resulting in impaired transport of copper from the digestive tract. It was first identified in 1962.

Methemoglobin—A compound formed from hemoglobin by oxidation of its iron component. Methemoglobin cannot carry oxygen.

Micronutrient—An organic compound such as vitamins or minerals essential in small amounts and necessary to the growth and health of humans and animals.

Trace element—An element that is required in only minute quantities for the maintenance of good health. Trace elements are also called micronutrients.

Wilson's disease—A rare inherited disease in which excessive amounts of copper accumulate in the liver or brain. It is fatal unless the patient complies with lifelong treatment with penicillamine and zinc oxidase. Wilson's disease is also known as inherited copper toxicosis.

Resources

BOOKS

"Mineral Deficiency and Toxicity." Section 1, Chapter 4 in *The Merck Manual of Diagnosis and Therapy*, edited by Mark H. Beers and Robert Berkow. Whitehouse Station, NJ: Merck Research Laboratories, 2002.

PERIODICALS

Dunn, A. M., C. Burns, and B. Sattler. "Environmental Health of Children." *Journal of Pediatric Health Care* 17 (September-October 2003): 223–31.

Singhi, S. C., and A. K. Baranwal. "Acute Iron Poisoning: Clinical Picture, Intensive Care Needs, and Outcome." *Indian Pediatrics* 40 (December 2003): 1177–82.

U.S. Preventive Services Task Force. "Screening for Presence of Deficiency, Toxicity, and Disease." *Nutrition in Clinical Care* 6 (October-December 2003): 120–22.

ORGANIZATIONS

American Academy of Emergency Medicine (AAEM). 555 East Wells Street, Suite 1100, Milwaukee, WI 53202. Web site: <www.aaem.org>.

American Academy of Family Physicians (AAFP). 11400 Tomahawk Creek Parkway, Leawood, KS 66211–2672. Web site: <www.aafp.org>.

National Institute of Child Health and Human Development (NICHD). 31 Center Drive, Room 2A32, Bethesda, MD 20892–2425. <www.nichd.nih.gov>.

National Organization for Rare Disorders Inc. (NORD). 55 Kenosia Avenue, Danbury, CT 06813–1968. Web site: <www.rarediseases.org>.

Wilson's Disease Association International (WDA). 1802 Brookside Drive, Wooster, OH 44691. Web site: <www.wilsonsdisease.org>.

WEB SITES

Chang, Celia H. "Menkes Disease." *eMedicine*, February 8, 2002. Available online at <www.emedicine.com/neuro/topic569.htm> (accessed November 29, 2004).

Spanierman, Clifford. "Toxicity, Iron." *eMedicine*, April 12, 2004. Available online at <www.emedicine.com/emerg/topic285.htm> (accessed November 29, 2004).

Tom Brody, PhD

Minerals

Definition

Minerals are inorganic nutrients. That is, they are materials found in foods that are essential for growth and health and do not contain the element carbon. The minerals that are relevant to human **nutrition** are water, sodium, potassium, chloride, calcium, phosphate, sulfate, magnesium, iron, copper, zinc, manganese, iodine, selenium, and molybdenum. Cobalt is a required mineral for human health, but it is supplied by vitamin B_{12}. There is some evidence that chromium, boron, and other inorganic elements play some part in human nutrition, but their role has not been proven.

Description

Minerals should be provided by a normal, healthy diet. In special cases, additional mineral supplements may be called for. Preterm (low birth weight) infants have special needs for calcium, phosphorus, and sodium, as well as extra needs for vitamin D. Iron supplements may also be recommended.

The amount of each mineral that is needed to support growth during infancy and childhood, to maintain body weight and health, and to facilitate pregnancy and **lactation**, are listed in a table called the Recommended Dietary Allowances (RDA). This table was compiled by the Food and Nutrition Board, a committee that serves the United States government. The values listed in the RDA indicate the daily amounts that are expected to maintain health throughout most of the general population. The actual levels of each inorganic nutrient required by any given individual is likely to be less than that stated by the RDA. The RDAs are all based on studies that provided the exact, minimal requirement of each mineral needed to maintain health. However, the RDA values are actually greater than the minimal requirement, as determined by studies on small groups of healthy human subjects, in order to accommodate the variability expected among the general population.

Because of differences in individual diets and individual needs, the decision regarding any child's need for supplements should be made by the parents after discussion with the pediatrician and, where appropriate, a nutritionist. Children on a well-balanced diet do not require supplements, while those who are picky eaters or who routinely eat a poor diet may benefit from supplementation.

Girls should get their calcium from foods, particularly dairy products, rather than supplements. Dairy products were associated with higher bone mineral density in the spine, while calcium supplements had no such benefit.

General use

The following discussion describes the role of the major minerals in human nutrition.

Iron is essential for the formation of hemoglobin, the chemical in the blood that carries oxygen to the cells. Low levels of iron cause anemia. In severe cases, the children become flabby, and they fail to grow normally. Milder cases of iron deficiency may not produce any physical symptoms, but children may learn at a slower pace than children with a proper amount of iron in their diet. The combination of rice, beans, and meat consumed with fresh citrus fruit provides an excellent source of absorbable iron. Iron supplements are suggested for children who cannot or will not follow a proper diet through the first two years of life.

Calcium is required for proper development of bones and teeth. It is also needed for proper muscle activity and blood clotting. Lack of calcium can cause rickets, a condition in which the bones are soft and develop in abnormal shapes. Calcium must be accompanied by vitamin D in order to have the proper effects. Foods rich in calcium include almonds, swiss cheese, collards, sardines and salmon with bones, spinach, ice cream, kale, beet greens, cheddar cheese, molasses, oysters, milk, and broccoli.

Zinc deficiency has been associated with reduced growth and **mental retardation**. The best foods for zinc are lamb, beef, leafy grains, root vegetables such as potatoes and carrots, shellfish, and organ meats such as liver or kidneys. While a high fiber diet is important for health, too much fiber can reduce the absorption of zinc and lead to a zinc deficiency.

Iodine is needed in the diet for proper thyroid function. The best source of iodine is fish, but table salt normally has iodine added to it, and even modest amounts of salt will meet the daily iodine requirements.

Fluoride is needed for strong teeth. In many areas, drinking water contains fluoride that meets all normal needs, but for children who do not drink water or drink filtered or bottled water, fluoride supplements may be useful. Fluoride supplements may be useful for infants and then may be discontinued as the child gets older and starts drinking water.

Magnesium is found in so many parts of the body that it is almost impossible to describe the effects of low magnesium levels. The most common problems are twitching, and, because of the need for magnesium in the parathyroid gland, soft bones even when calcium and vitamin D are adequate. Because magnesium is found in most foods, deficiency is usually associated with absorption problems and requires medical attention.

Copper is required for blood and nerve fiber development. It is found in liver, nuts, and seafood.

Phosporus is needed for energy production, metabolism, and healthy bone development. The best sources are milk, cheese, meats, whole grains, eggs, peas, and beans.

Potassium is needed for muscle contractions and nerve function. Good sources of potassium are orange juice, milk, cheese, whole grains, and vegetables.

Selenium is needed for proper thyroid function. It has also been associated with prevention of some types of **cancer** in adults. Selenium supplements are not normally required except in children with **phenylketonuria** receiving a low-protein diet, although it may sometimes be associated with thyroid problems. In these cases, medical care is required.

Precautions

Although the greatest nutritional concern is with inadequate levels of minerals, it is possible to take too much, particularly when people already eating a normally healthy diet take supplements. The daily intake of minerals should be reviewed to prevent adverse effects.

Excess calcium may lead to **constipation** and kidney problems. Too much zinc may lead to **diarrhea**, **vomiting**, and kidney and heart problems. Excess iron may cause problems of the stomach and digestive tract, liver problems, an increased risk of diabetes, and male sexual problems.

Side effects

When minerals are taken properly, they have no side effects.

Interactions

Minerals can interact with drugs and in excess with each other. Iron and calcium are known to bind to drugs of the tetracycline family and inactivate the antibiotic. The compound of calcium and tetracycline may also be absorbed into a child's teeth, causing discoloration.

Too much calcium in the diet may inhibit absorption of iron, magnesium, phosphorus, and zinc. Excess iron may reduce the absorption of zinc.

Parental concerns

Following a proper balanced diet is the best prevention of both **mineral deficiency** and mineral overdose. Since many children and adolescents cannot or will not eat a balanced diet, the possible need for supplements should be discussed with an appropriate professional.

Many children fail to follow a proper diet. This may be because of excess intake of fast foods and snack foods of low nutritional value. It is important for parents to

---

KEY TERMS

Inorganic—Pertaining to chemical compounds that are not hydrocarbons or their derivatives.

Parathyroid gland—A pair of glands adjacent to the thyroid gland that primarily regulate blood calcium levels.

Phenylketonuria (PKU)—A rare, inherited, metabolic disorder in which the enzyme necessary to break down and use phenylalanine, an amino acid necessary for normal growth and development, is lacking. As a result, phenylalanine builds up in the body causing mental retardation and other neurological problems.

Rickets—A condition caused by the dietary deficiency of vitamin D, calcium, and usually phosphorus, seen primarily in infancy and childhood, and characterized by abnormal bone formation.

---

teach children the benefits of proper nutrition and the importance of maintaining a healthful diet.

At the same time, adolescents, particularly those who engage in **sports**, may feel that they will do better with increased levels of nutrients. Because of the risk of toxic reactions to minerals and some **vitamins**, children should be discouraged from taking vitamin supplements unless there is clear evidence of increased need.

Resources

BOOKS

Siberry, George K., and Robert Iannone, eds. *The Harriett Lane Handbook*, 15th ed. St. Louis, MO: Mosby, 2000.

PERIODICALS

Chanoine, J. P. "Selenium and thyroid function in infants, children, and adolescents." *Biofactors* 19 (2003): 137–43.

Matkovic, V., et al. "Nutrition influences skeletal development from childhood to adulthood: a study of hip, spine, and forearm in adolescent females." *Journal of Nutrition* 134 (March 2004): 701S–5S.

ORGANIZATIONS

American Dietetic Association. 120 South Riverside Plaza, Suite 2000, Chicago, IL 60606–6995. Web site: <www.eatright.org>.

Tom Brody, PhD
Samuel Uretsky, PharmD

Minnesota Multiphasic Personality Inventory

Definition

The Minnesota Multiphasic Personality Inventory (MMPI-2; MMPI-A) is a written psychological **assessment**, or test, used to diagnose mental disorders.

Purpose

The MMPI is used to screen for personality and psychosocial disorders in adults (i.e., over age 18) and adolescents age 14 to 18. It is also frequently administered as part of a neuropsychological test battery to evaluate cognitive functioning.

Description

The original MMPI was developed at the University of Minnesota and introduced in 1942. The current standardized version for adults 18 and over, the MMPI-2, was released in 1989, with a subsequent revision of certain test elements in early 2001. The MMPI-A, a version of the inventory developed specifically for adolescents age 14 to 18, was published in 1992.

The adolescent inventory is shorter than the standard adult version, was developed at a sixth-grade reading level, and is geared towards adolescent issues and personality "norms." The MMPI-A has 478 true/false items, or questions, (compared to 567 items on the MMPI-2) and takes 45 minutes to an hour to complete (compared to 60 to 90 minutes for the MMPI-2). There is also a short form of the test that is comprised of the first 350 items from the long-form MMPI-A.

The questions asked on the MMPI-A are designed to evaluate the thoughts, emotions, attitudes, and behavioral traits that comprise personality. The results of the test reflect an adolescent's personality strengths and weaknesses, and may identify certain disturbances of personality (psychopathologies) or mental deficits caused by neurological problems.

There are eight validity scales and ten basic clinical or personality scales scored in the MMPI-A, and a number of supplementary scales and subscales that may be used with the test. The validity scales are used to determine whether the test results are actually valid (i.e., if the test taker was truthful, answered cooperatively and not randomly) and to assess the test taker's response style (i.e., cooperative, defensive). Each clinical scale uses a set or subset of MMPI-A questions to evaluate a specific personality trait. Some were designed to assess potential problems that are associated with **adolescence**, such as eating disorders, social problems, **family** conflicts, and alcohol or chemical dependency.

Precautions

The MMPI should be administered, scored, and interpreted by a qualified clinical professional trained in its use, preferably a psychologist or psychiatrist. The MMPI is only one element of psychological assessment, and should never be used as the sole basis for a diagnosis. A detailed history of the test subject and a review of psychological, medical, educational, or other relevant records are required to lay the groundwork for interpreting the results of any psychological measurement.

Cultural and language differences in the test subject may affect test performance and may result in inaccurate MMPI results. The test administrator should be informed before psychological testing begins if the test taker is not fluent in English and/or has a unique cultural background.

Preparation

The administrator should provide the test subject with information on the nature of the test and its intended use, and complete standardized instructions for taking the MMPI (including any time limits, and information on the confidentiality of the results).

The MMPI should be scored and interpreted by a trained professional. When interpreting test results for test subjects, the test administrator will review what the test evaluates, its precision in evaluation and any margins of error involved in scoring, and what the individual scores mean in the context of overall norms for the test and the background of the test subject.

Risks

There are no risks involved in taking the MMPI. However, parents should try to make sure the test is properly administered, and the results evaluated appropriately, to avoid an unnecessary negative label on their child.

Parental concerns

Test anxiety can have an impact on a child's performance, so parents should attempt to take the stress off their child by making sure they understand that the MMPI is not an achievement test and the child's honest answers are all that is required. Parents can also ensure

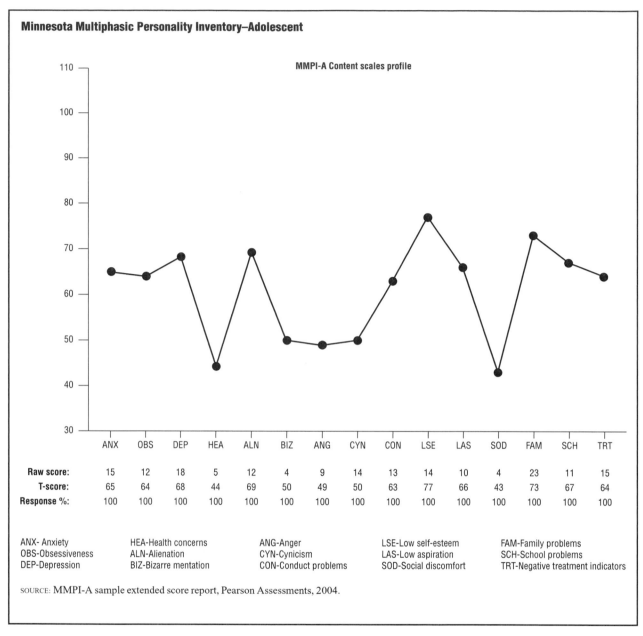

Minnesota Multiphasic Personality Inventory–Adolescent

MMPI-A Content scales profile

	ANX	OBS	DEP	HEA	ALN	BIZ	ANG	CYN	CON	LSE	LAS	SOD	FAM	SCH	TRT
Raw score:	15	12	18	5	12	4	9	14	13	14	10	4	23	11	15
T-score:	65	64	68	44	69	50	49	50	63	77	66	43	73	67	64
Response %:	100	100	100	100	100	100	100	100	100	100	100	100	100	100	100

ANX- Anxiety
OBS-Obsessiveness
DEP-Depression

HEA-Health concerns
ALN-Alienation
BIZ-Bizarre mentation

ANG-Anger
CYN-Cynicism
CON-Conduct problems

LSE-Low self-esteem
LAS-Low aspiration
SOD-Social discomfort

FAM-Family problems
SCH-School problems
TRT-Negative treatment indicators

SOURCE: MMPI-A sample extended score report, Pearson Assessments, 2004.

Sample profile from the Content scales profile of the MMPI-Adolescent. Although the data is interpreted by trained professionals, this adolescent's score shows a low self-esteem and probable family problems. *(Illustration by GGS Information Services.)*

that their children are well-rested on the testing day and have a nutritious meal beforehand.

When interpreting test results for parents, the test administrator will review what the test evaluates, its precision in evaluation and any margins of error involved in scoring, and what the individual scores mean in the context of overall norms for the test and the background of the adolescent.

See also Psychological tests.

Resources

BOOKS

Braaten, Ellen and Gretchen Felopulos. *Straight Talk About Psychological Testing for Kids.* New York: Guilford Press, 2003.

ORGANIZATIONS

American Psychological Association. Testing and Assessment Office of the Science Directorate. 750 First St., N.E., Washington, DC 20002–4242. (202)336–6000. Web site: <www.apa.org/science/testing.html>.

Neuropsychological testing—Tests used to evaluate patients who have experienced a traumatic brain injury, brain damage, or organic neurological problems (e.g., dementia). It may also be used to evaluate the progress of a patient who has undergone treatment or rehabilitation for a neurological injury or illness.

Norms—A fixed or ideal standard; a normative or mean score for a particular age group.

Psychopathology—The study of mental disorders or illnesses, such as schizophrenia, personality disorder, or major depressive disorder.

Standardization—The process of determining established norms and procedures for a test to act as a standard reference point for future test results.

WEB SITES

Pearson Assessments. *The MMPI-A*. Available online at: <www.pearsonassessments.com/tests/mmpia.htm> (accessed September 10, 2004).

Paula Ford-Martin

Minority health

Definition

Minority health addresses the special medical and health needs associated with specific ethnic and other minority groups.

Description

The United States, along with many other countries, experiences cultural diversity. This fact poses health issues that are specific to ethnic and other minority groups. Additionally, the propensity for certain diseases or illnesses is of concern in certain minority groups. These specific health issues include **infant mortality** rates, **cancer**, cardiovascular disease, diabetes, **HIV infection**, and immunizations. The primary minority groups in the United States are Hispanics, African Americans, Native Americans and Native Alaskans, Native

Hawaiians and other Pacific Islanders, and gays and lesbians.

One of the major health problems in the United States is overweight and **obesity**, which lead to increased risks for a wide variety of conditions, including cardiovascular disease, diabetes, **hypertension**, and cancer. A 2003 study by the Agency for Healthcare Research and Quality shows that African-American and Hispanic children face much higher odds of being overweight than non-Hispanic white or Asian-American and Pacific Islander children. African-American children ages six to 11 are more than twice as likely as non-Hispanic white children to be overweight, and Hispanic children are roughly twice as likely. The odds change dramatically when children become teenagers. For example, as children, Asian Americans and Pacific Islanders have the lowest prevalence of being overweight, but once they reach **adolescence**, the reverse is true. As teens, they have the highest prevalence of being overweight—more than four times that of non-Hispanic white teenagers. African American children have the highest rate of being overweight, but once they reach their teen years, they are no more likely than white children to be overweight. Hispanic teens are one-and-a-half times more likely than white or African American teens to be overweight.

Researchers and policymakers have attributed the poorer health of minority Americans in part to their reduced access to medical care and the lower quality of primary care they receive. Indeed, when asked about the primary care they receive, minority patients—particularly Asian Americans—give the primary care they receive lower marks than white patients do, according to a 2001 report by the Agency for Healthcare Research and Quality. After adjustment for socioeconomic and other factors, Asian Americans gave their primary care significantly lower scores (out of 100 total) than whites for communication (69 versus 79) and comprehensive knowledge of patients (48 versus 56), as well as all other areas of primary care except continuity of care and integration of care. African American and Hispanics reported significantly less financial access to care than whites (60 and 56, respectively, versus 65), and African Americans reported significantly less continuity of care than whites (74 versus 78), but their assessments of other aspects of primary care did not differ significantly from whites. This study agrees with others which show that Asian Americans tend to be the least satisfied with quality of care. However, this study was limited by the small number of Asian and Hispanic patients surveyed, as well as the lack of patient's country of origin and physician's ethnicity, factors that may affect patient evaluations of primary care.

Infant mortality rates

Infant mortality rates (IMRs) in the United States and in all countries worldwide are an accurate indicator of health status. They provide information concerning programs about pregnancy education and counseling, technological advances, and procedures and aftercare. IMRs vary among racial groups. Infant mortality among African Americans in 2000 occurred at a rate of 14.1 deaths per 1,000 live births. This is more than twice the national average of 6.9 deaths per 1,000 live births. The leading causes of infant death include congenital abnormalities, pre-term/low birth weight, **sudden infant death syndrome** (SIDS), problems related to complications of pregnancy, and **respiratory distress syndrome**. SIDS deaths among Native American and Alaska Natives is 2.3 times the rate for non-Hispanic white mothers.

Cancer

Cancer is a serious national, worldwide, and minority health concern. It is the second cause of death in the United States, claiming over 500,000 lives each year. Approximately 50 percent of persons who develop cancer die of the disease. There is great disparity among the cancer rates in minority groups. Across genders, cancer death rates for African Americans are 35 percent higher when compared to statistics for Caucasians. The death rates for prostate cancer (two times more) and lung cancer (27 times more) are disproportionately higher when compared to Caucasians. There are also gender differences among ethnic groups and specific cancers. Lung cancers in African American and Hawaiian men are evaluated compared with Caucasian males. Vietnamese females who live in the United States have five times more new cases of cervical cancer when compared to Caucasian women. Hispanic females also have a greater incidence of cervical cancer than Caucasian females. Additionally, Alaskan native men and women have a greater propensity for cancers in the rectum and colon than do Caucasians.

Cardiovascular disease

Cardiovascular disease is the leading cause of disability and death, about equal to the rate of death from all other diseases combined. Cardiovascular disease can affect the patient's lifestyle and function in addition to having an impact on **family** members. The financial costs are very high. Among ethnic and racial groups cardiovascular disease is the leading cause of death. **Stroke** is the leading cause of cardiovascular-related death, which occurs in higher numbers for Asian-American males when compared to Caucasian men. Mexican-American men and women and African-American males have a higher incidence of hypertension. African American women have higher rates of being overweight, which is a major risk factor of cardiovascular disease. African Americans are 13 percent less likely to undergo coronary angioplasty and one-third less likely to undergo bypass surgery than are Caucasians.

Diabetes

Diabetes, a serious health problem among Americans and ethnic groups, is the seventh leading cause of death in the United States. The prevalence of diabetes in African Americans is about 70 percent higher than Caucasians. The burden of diabetes is much greater for minority populations than the white population. For example, 10.8 percent of non-Hispanic blacks, 10.6 percent of Hispanics, and 9 percent of Native Americans and Native Alaskans have diabetes, compared with 6.2 percent of whites. Certain minorities also have much higher rates of diabetes-related complications and death, in some instances by as much as 50 percent more than the total population. Diabetes-related mortality rates for African Americans, Hispanic Americans, and Native Americans and Native Alaskans are higher than those for white people. Asians and Pacific Islanders have the lowest diabetes-related mortality of any racial/ethnic group in the United States.

HIV and AIDS

HIV infection/AIDS is the most common cause of death for all persons age 25 to 44 years old. Ethnic groups account for 25 percent of the U.S. population and 54 percent of all **AIDS** cases. In addition to sexual transmission there is an increase in HIV among ethnic groups related to intravenous drug usage. African Americans with HIV infection are less likely to be on antiretroviral therapy, less likely to receive prophylaxis for Pneumocystis **pneumonia**, and less likely to be receiving protease inhibitors than other persons with HIV. An HIV infection data coordinating center, under development in 2004, will allow researchers to compare contemporary data on HIV care to determine whether disparities in care among groups are being addressed and to identify any new patterns in treatment that arise. Among children, the disparities are dramatic, with African-American and Hispanic children representing more than 80 percent of pediatric AIDS cases in 2000. Approximately 78 percent of HIV-infected women are minorities and most become infected through heterosexual transmission.

In 2002, African Americans accounted for 50 percent of all new AIDS cases, while Hispanics accounted for 20 percent, according to the Centers for Disease

Control and Prevention (CDC). Although the virus is still most likely to be passed on by gay and bisexual males, as of 2004 more than 25 percent of AIDS cases are women, most of whom are African American or Hispanic. According to the National Center for Health Statistics, black females age 15 and older are 15.5 times more likely to die of AIDS than whites—a figure even more dramatic than the one presented in the vice presidential debates, according to an article in the October 16, 2004 *Los Angeles Times*.

Immunizations

Data show that in 2000 children living below the poverty level have lower immunization coverage rates. Although significant progress has been made in improving childhood immunization rates, some disparities in overall immunization coverage rates among racial and ethnic groups continue. This disparity is of great concern in large urban areas with underserved populations because of the potential for outbreaks of vaccine-preventable diseases.

Demographics

The overall health of the U.S. population improved during the last decades of the twentieth century, but all Americans have not shared equally in these improvements. Among nonelderly adults, for example, 17 percent of Hispanic and 16 percent of black Americans report they are in minimally fair or poor health, compared with 10 percent of white Americans.

Causes and symptoms

Most IMRs are correlated with prenatal care. Women who receive adequate prenatal care tend to have better pregnancy outcomes when compared to those who receive little or no care. Women who receive inadequate prenatal care tend to have increased chances of delivering a very low birth weight (VLBW) infant, which is linked to risk of early death.

Cancer is related to several preventable lifestyle choices. Diet and tobacco and sun exposure can be shaped by lifestyle modifications. Additionally many cancers can occur due to lack of interest in and/or lack of availability for screening and educational programs.

Cardiovascular diseases are higher among persons with high blood cholesterol and high blood pressure. Certain lifestyle choices that may increase the chance for heart disease include lack of **exercise**, overweight, and cigarette use. Cardiovascular disease is responsible for over 50 percent of the deaths in persons with diabetes.

HIV occurs at a higher frequency among gay males (the number of African-American males who have AIDS through sex with men has as of 2004 increased). Additionally unprotected sexual intercourse and sharing used needles for IV drug injection are strongly correlated with infection.

Vaccinations are an effective method of preventing certain disease such as **polio**, **tetanus**, pertussis, **diphtheria**, **influenza**, **hepatitis b**, and pneumococcal infections. Approximately 90 percent of influenza-related mortality is associated with persons aged 65 and older. This is mostly due to neglect of vaccinations. About 45,000 adults each year die of diseases related to hepatitis B, pneumococcal and influenza infections.

When to call the doctor

Parents of minority children should contact their family physician or other healthcare provider when they have any concern about their child's health.

Diagnosis

The diagnosis of VLBW occurs when newborns are weighed. Infants who weigh 52.5 ounces (1,500 grams) are at high risk for death. For cancer, the diagnosis can be made through screening procedures such as mammography (for breast cancer), PAP smear (for cervical cancer). Lifestyle modifications such as avoidance of sun, cessation of cigarette **smoking**, maintaining a balanced diet, and adequate **nutrition**, all positively affect one's health. Other specific screening tests (PSA, prostate surface antigen) are helpful for diagnosing prostate cancer. Cardiovascular diseases can be detected by medical check-up. Blood pressure and cholesterol levels can be measured. Obesity can be diagnosed by assessing a person's weight compared to the person's height. Diabetes and its complications can be detected by blood tests, in-depth eye examinations, and studies that assess the flow of blood through blood vessels in the legs. HIV can be detected through a careful history and physical examination and analysis of blood using a special test called a western blot. Infections caused by lack of immunizations can either be detected by conducting physical examination and culturing the specific microorganism in the laboratory.

Treatment

Treatment should be directed toward the primary causes(s) that minorities have increased chances of developing disease(s). Cancer may require treatment using surgery, radiotherapy, or **chemotherapy**. Cardiovascular diseases may require surgical procedures for establishing a diagnosis and initiating treatment. Depending on the extent of disease, cardiovascular management can become complicated requiring medications and daily lifestyle modifications. Treatment usually includes medications, dietary modifications, and—if complications arise—specific interventions tailored to alleviating the problem. HIV can be treated with specific medications and more often than not with symptomatic treatment as complications arise. Diseases caused by lack of immunizations are treated based on the primary disease. The best method of treatment is through prevention and generating public awareness through widespread education on the topic.

Alternative treatment

Alternative therapies do exist, but as of 2004 more research is needed to substantiate available data. Most physicians say the diseases that relate to minority health are best treated with nationally accepted standards of care.

Prognosis

Generally the prognosis is related to the diagnosis, patients' state of health, age, and the presence of another disease or complication in addition to the presenting problem. The course for IMRs is related to educational programs and prenatal care, which includes medical and psychological treatments. The prognosis for chronic diseases such as cardiovascular problems, high blood pressure, cancer, and diabetes is variable. As of 2004, these diseases are not cured, and control is achieved by standardized treatment options. Eventually complications, despite treatment, can occur. For HIV the clinical course as of 2004 is death, even though this process may take years. Educational programs with an emphasis on disease prevention can potentially improve outcomes concerning pediatric and geriatric diseases.

Prevention

Prevention is accomplished best through educational programs specific to target populations. IMRs can be prevented by increasing awareness, interest, and accessibility for prenatal care that offers a comprehensive approach for the needs of each patient. Regular physicals and special screening tests can potentially prevent certain cancers in high-risk groups. Educational programs concerning lifestyle modifications, diet, exercise, and testing may prevent the development of cardiovascular disease and diabetes. Educational programs for illicit IV drug abusers and persons who engage in unprotected sexual intercourse may decrease the incidence of HIV infection.

Parental concerns

All children should have regular well-child check ups according to the schedule recommended by their physician or pediatrician. The American Academy of Pediatrics (AAP) advises that children be seen for well-baby check ups at two weeks, two months, four months, six months, nine months, 12 months, 15 months, and 18 months of age. Well-child visits are recommended at ages two, three, four, five, six, eight, ten, and annually thereafter through age 21. Parents can take some precautions to ensure the health of their children. **Childproofing** the home, following a recommended immunization schedule, educating kids on **safety**, learning **cardiopulmonary resuscitation** (CPR), and taking kids for regular well-child check-ups all help to protect against physical harm. In addition, encouraging open communication with children can help them grow both emotionally and socially. Providing a loving and supportive home environment can help to nurture an emotionally healthy child who is independent, self-confident, socially skilled, insightful, and empathetic towards others.

Resources

BOOKS

LaVeist, Thomas. *Race, Ethnicity, and Health: A Public Health Reader.* Hoboken, NJ: Jossey-Bass, 2002.

Shannon, Joyce Brennfleck. *Ethnic Diseases Sourcebook: Basic Consumer Health Information for Ethnic and Racial Minority Groups in the United States.* Detroit, MI: Omnigraphics, 2001.

PERIODICALS

El-Mohandes, Ayman A. E., et al. "The Effect of a Parenting Education Program on the Use of Preventive Pediatric Health Care Services among Low-Income, Minority Mothers: A Randomized, Controlled Study." *Pediatrics* 111 (June 2003): 1324–32.

Harrison, Patricia A., et al. "The Adolescent Health Review: A Test of a Computerized Screening Tool in School-Based Clinics." *Journal of School Health* 73 (January 2003): 15–20.

Walsh, Catherine, and Lainie F. Ross. "Are Minority Children Under- or Over-represented in Pediatric Research?" *Pediatrics* 112 (October 2003): 890–95.

Wechsler, Jill. "Health Plans Examine Minority Healthcare Gap: Research Examines Racial and Ethnic Disparities in

KEY TERMS

Angioplasty—A medical procedure in which a catheter, or thin tube, is threaded through blood vessels. The catheter is used to place a balloon or stent (a small metal rod) at a narrowed or blocked area and expand it mechanically.

Cardiopulmonary resuscitation (CPR)—An emergency procedure designed to stimulate breathing and blood flow through a combination of chest compressions and rescue breathing. It is used to restore circulation and prevent brain death to a person who has collapsed, is unconscious, is not breathing, and has no pulse.

Cardiovascular—Relating to the heart and blood vessels.

Congenital—Present at birth.

Hypertension—Abnormally high arterial blood pressure, which if left untreated can lead to heart disease and stroke.

Healthcare." *Managed Healthcare Executive* 13 (November 2003): 8.

ORGANIZATIONS

National Center on Minority Health and Health Disparities. National Institutes of Health. 6707 Democracy Blvd., Suite 800, MSC-5465, Bethesda, MD 20892–5465. Web site: <http://ncmhd.nih.gov>.

Office of Minority Health Resource Center. PO Box 37337, Washington, DC 20013–7337. Web site: <www.omhrc.gov/omhrc>.

WEB SITES

"Eliminating Minority Health Disparities." *U.S. Department of Health and Human Services*, July 12, 2004. Available online at <http://raceandhealth.hhs.gov> (accessed November 11, 2004).

"Minority Children's Health Gets Poor Report Card." *Texas Health Resources*. 2004. Available online at <www.minoritynurse.com/vitalsigns/jan03-3.html> (accessed November 11, 2004).

Laith Farid Gulli, M.D.
Nicole Mallory, M.S.
Ken R. Wells

Mitochondrial disorders

Definition

Mitochondrial disorders, also called mitochondrial cytopathies, are a diverse group of diseases caused by damage to small structures found in human cells that are essential in converting food to energy. The result is decreased energy production and associated symptoms.

Description

Cells are the building blocks of the human body, microscopic structures that are bound by a membrane and contain numerous components called organelles that are responsible for functions such as cell reproduction, transportation of materials, and protein synthesis. Cellular respiration, a process by which food molecules are converted into high-energy molecules used as a source of energy, takes place in structures called mitochondria. The energy produced by mitochondria is essential for cell functions.

Before the mid-twentieth century, little was known about mitochondrial disorders. The first diagnosis of a mitochondrial disorder occurred in 1959, and the genetic material of microchondria, called mtDNA, was discovered in 1963. In the 1970s and 1980s, as more was learned about the mitochondria and more mitochondrial disorders were discovered, the term "mitochondrial myopathies" (myopathy meaning a disease of muscle tissue) was coined to describe the group of diseases. Further research in the 1990s led to classification of mitochondrial disorders. As it became evident that tissues other than muscle could be affected by mitochondrial defects, the term "mitochondrial cytopathies" (cytopathy meaning cell disorder) was adopted.

Disorders in which skeletal muscle is the primary target of the mitochondrial dysfunction are called mitochondrial **myopathies**. Mitochondrial encephalomyopathies are disorders in which muscle and brain tissue is involved.

Common mitochondrial disorders

As of 2004 there were more than 40 distinct mitochondrial cytopathies. Some of the more common disorders include:

- Kearns-Sayre syndrome (KSS). Onset of KSS usually occurs before the age of 20. Symptoms include progressively constrained eye movements, droopy eye lids, muscle weakness, short stature, hearing loss, loss of coordination, heart problems, cognitive delays, and diabetes.

- Myoclonus epilepsy with ragged-red fibers (MERRF). MERFF is a mitochondrial encephalomyopathy in which a mitochondrial defect as well as a tissue abnormality called "ragged-red fibers" (an accumulation of diseased mitochondria) is found microscopically. The resulting symptoms include seizures, loss of coordination, short stature, build-up of lactic acid in the blood, difficulty speaking, dementia, and muscle weakness.

- Mitochondrial encephalomyopathy with lactic acidosis and stroke-like episodes (MELAS). MELAS is a progressive mitochondrial disease that involves multiple organ systems including the central nervous system, cardiac muscle, skeletal muscle, and gastrointestinal system. Symptoms include muscle weakness, stroke-like events, eye muscle paralysis, and cognitive impairment.

- Leber hereditary optic neuropathy (LHON). LHON causes progressive loss of vision resulting in various degrees of blindness and primarily affects men over the age of 20. Heart abnormalities may also occur.

- Leigh syndrome. This degenerative brain disorder is usually diagnosed at a young age (e.g. before age two). Deterioration is often rapid with symptoms such as seizures, dementia, feeding and speech difficulties, respiratory dysfunction, heart problems, and muscle weakness. Prognosis is poor with death typically occurring within a few years of diagnosis.

- Myoneurogenic gastrointestinal encephalopathy (MNGIE). Key features include symptoms that mimic gastrointestinal obstruction and nervous system abnormalities. Other symptoms may include eye muscle paralysis, muscle weakness, loss of coordination, and brain abnormalities.

- Pearson syndrome. With symptoms usually first appearing in childhood, the characteristics of this rare syndrome include pancreatic dysfunction and anemia (low red blood cells). Difficulty gaining weight, **diarrhea**, and enlarged liver are other signs of Pearson syndrome.

- Neuropathy, ataxia, and retinitis pigmentosa (NARP). The symptoms implied by this disorder's name include nervous system abnormalities, loss of coordination, and progressive loss of vision. Developmental delays, dementia, and muscle weakness may also result. Onset usually occurs in childhood.

Demographics

Approximately 1,000 to 4,000 children are born with mitochondrial disease in the United States each year. Typically, by the age of ten, approximately one in 4,000 American children is diagnosed with mitochondrial disease.

Causes and symptoms

Although mitochondrial disorders may be caused by distinctly different damage to the mitochondrial genetic material, and thus affect any of the hundreds of chemical reactions required to convert food and oxygen into energy, they all share a common feature: the ability of mitochondria to generate energy is damaged. Byproducts of the numerous reactions can begin to accumulate in the cells and interfere with other chemical reactions and over time damage the mitochondria further.

Inheritance of mitochondrial disorders

In many cases, a mitochondrial disorder is passed genetically from parent to child (inheritance). It can often be helpful for the type of inheritance to be determined, as parents can then make an educated decision about the risks of passing the condition on to another child or the risks of another **family** member developing the disease. Genetic defects may be passed through nuclear DNA (nDNA), the genetic material found in each cell that determines the majority of hereditary characteristics, or through mtDNA. Some types of mitochondrial disorder inheritance include:

- Autosomal recessive inheritance. Each individual has two sets of genes, one inherited from each parent. In some genetic diseases, a person needs to have two copies of a defective gene in order to show symptoms of the disease; if only one of the two genes is defective, the person is considered a carrier. In autosomal recessive inheritance, the affected individual has inherited a defective gene from each parent.

- Maternal inheritance. mtDNA is only passed from mother to child because the mitochondria of a sperm is located in the sperm's tail, which is not involved in conception. Some mitochondrial disorders are, therefore, only passed from mother to child.

- X-linked recessive inheritance. The sex of a child is determined through the inheritance of strands of DNA called chromosomes. A female child inherits two X chromosomes, while a male child inherits an X chromosome from one parent and a Y chromosome from the other. If a defective gene encoding for a disease is found on the X chromosome, then a male child cannot have a healthy copy of the gene (since he only has one X chromosome); therefore, he will develop the disorder. Female children are at less risk because they have to have two copies of the defective gene (one on each X chromosome) in order to develop the disease.

- Autosomal dominant inheritance. As opposed to autosomal recessive inheritance, only one defective copy of a gene needs to be inherited in order for an individual to develop the disease. Each successive child, therefore, has a 50 percent chance of developing the disorder.

In some cases, no other family members are affected by the disease and there appears to be no genetic link. These cases are called random or sporadic occurrences and may be caused by a number of environmental factors including certain drugs (e.g. medications used to treat human **immunodeficiency** virus [HIV] have been linked to mitochondrial damage), **anorexia nervosa** (a disease characterized by self-starvation), exposure to certain toxins, prolonged periods of insufficient oxygen, or older parental age (mtDNA mutations may accumulate over time).

Symptoms

Because more than 90 percent of the energy needed by the human body to function is generated by mitochondria, the effects of mitochondrial disorders can be far-reaching. Research has shown that cells of the brain, nerves, skeletal muscles, liver, heart, kidneys, ears, eyes, and pancreas seem to be particularly affected because of their high energy requirements. Some of the more common symptoms of mitochondrial diseases by organ system include the following:

- brain: confusion, memory loss, headaches, seizures, developmental delays, and stroke-like episodes
- nerves: **pain** caused by nerve abnormalities (neuropathic pain), gastrointestinal problems linked to nerve abnormalities, abnormal sweating, and fainting
- skeletal muscles: muscle weakness, muscle cramping, muscle pain, loss of coordination, **exercise** intolerance, and poor growth
- liver: liver failure not due to excessive alcohol use and low blood sugar (hypoglycemia)
- heart: heart muscle weakness and disturbed electrical signals in the heart (called heart block)
- kidneys: abnormalities that cause difficulty with absorbing nutrients and electrolytes back into the body (called Fanconi syndrome)
- ears: hearing loss
- eyes: eye muscle paralysis, progressive loss of vision
- pancreas: diabetes (a group of conditions characterized by excessive urine excretion and persistent thirst) and pancreatic failure

Other symptoms include **failure to thrive** in infants, poor growth, short stature, fatigue, respiratory disorders, swallowing difficulties, and increased risk of infection.

When to call the doctor

The array of symptoms that are displayed by children suffering from mitochondrial disorders are common to many other diseases, and the age of onset can range from early infancy to adulthood. Often, the hallmark sign of a mitochondrial disorder that distinguishes it from other diseases with similar symptoms is additional features (such as the above symptoms) that do not normally appear with the non-mitochondrial disease. Parents should notify their healthcare provider if their child develops symptoms atypical for their previously diagnosed condition or if those symptoms get worse or recur with infection.

Diagnosis

Because of the complex nature of mitochondrial disorders, physicians take a multi-faceted approach to diagnosing such diseases. The process usually starts with a comprehensive physical exam and evaluation of the patient's medical and family history. Often a neurological exam is performed to determine if there are any brain abnormalities. To diagnose a mitochondrial disorder and rule out other diseases, more extensive tests may need to be performed. Some examples are as follows:

- Initial evaluation. The first line of testing usually involves the least invasive methods, such as sending a sample of blood for evaluation. In some cases a diagnosis can be made based on blood tests; in others, blood tests may indicate that further testing is necessary.
- Secondary evaluation. These tests may be more intensive, more invasive, and/or carry more risks. Examples include lumbar puncture (spinal tap), urine collection, **magnetic resonance imaging** (MRI), additional blood tests, or electrocardiogram (ECG).
- Tertiary evaluation. Complex and/or invasive procedures such as skin or muscle biopsy (taking a small sample of tissue for microscopic evaluation) are considered tertiary tests. In some cases such tests are necessary to make a definitive diagnosis.

In some cases, a physician may not be able to diagnose the patient with a specific mitochondrial disorder even after extensive evaluation. Parents should, therefore, be advised that despite the complexity of testing for mitochondrial disorders, diagnosis is not always possible.

Treatment

As of 2004, there are no cures for mitochondrial disorders. Treatment plans focus on delaying progression of the disease or reducing a patient's symptoms. The method of treatment depends on many factors, including the patient's disease, age, affected organs, and health status. Not all patients benefit from treatment; those with less severe disease generally respond better. Treatment may consist of **vitamins**, supplements, physical or occupational therapy, or traditional medications. Examples of these include:

- vitamins, such as B vitamins (thiamine, riboflavin, niacin, folate, biotin, and pantothenic acid), vitamin E, and vitamin C

- coenzyme Q10 (CoQ10), which is involved in cellular respiration in normal mitochondria

- levocarnitine (Carnitor), taken orally or intravenously, to replace a cofactor necessary in cellular respiration

- antioxidant therapy, a treatment under investigation that may help to keep mitochondrial damage under control

- physical or occupational therapy for myopathies

Alternative treatment

For some patients, avoiding physiological stressors such as extreme cold, extreme heat, poor **nutrition**, fasting, and lack of **sleep** may improve their condition. Alcohol, cigarette smoke, and monosodium glutamate (MSG, added to many Asian foods) may also exacerbate a mitochondrial disorder.

Nutritional concerns

In some cases, a properly devised diet is necessary to avoid worsening symptoms. Parents of a child affected with a mitochondrial disorder may be referred to a dietician to help formulate a diet specific to his or her disease. The plan is individualized to the child and may include suggestions such as avoiding long periods of time without eating, eating small but frequent meals, increasing or decreasing the amount of fat consumed, and avoiding or supplementing with certain vitamins or **minerals**.

Prognosis

The prognosis of mitochondrial disease depends on many factors, including the specific disorder, the mode of inheritance, the age of onset, and what organs are affected. Two children suffering from the same mitochondrial disorder may have two distinctly different courses. In some cases, patients may be able to control their symptoms to a great degree with various treatments, or progression of the disease is slow. In other cases, the disease progresses rapidly and inevitably leads to death.

Prevention

Prevention of inherited mitochondrial disorders is not possible unless parents decide against having more children. In the case of mitochondrial cytopathies that are caused by environmental factors such as certain drugs or toxins, avoidance of these substances may minimize the risk of developing mitochondrial disease.

Parental concerns

Because of the potential of passing on inherited mitochondrial disorders to other children, parents may be interested in genetic counseling. Genetic counselors are health professionals who are trained to help families determine the risk or probability of developing or passing on a genetic disorder. Genetic testing, however, cannot determine with certainty if or when a child will develop a mitochondrial disease or what the severity will be.

Resources

BOOKS

Desnuelle, Claude, et al. *Mitochondrial Disorders: From Pathophysiology to Acquired Defects.* New York: Springer France Editions, 2002.

Schapira, Anthony, H. V., et al. *Mitochondrial Disorders in Neurology.* Kent, UK: Elsevier Science & Technology Books, 2002.

PERIODICALS

Cohen, Bruce H. and Deborah R. Gold. "Mitochondrial Cytopathy in Adults: What We Know So Far." *Cleveland Clinic Journal of Medicine* 68, no. 7 (July 2001): 625–42.

ORGANIZATIONS

United Mitochondrial Disease Foundation. 8085 Saltsburg Rd., Suite 201, Pittsburgh, PA 15239. Web site: <www.umdf.org>.

WEB SITES

"Mitochondrial Disorders." Available online at <www.epilepsy.com/epilepsy/epilepsy_mitochondrial.html> (accessed October 26, 2004).

"NINDS Mitochondrial Myopathies Information Page." *National Institute of Neurological Disorders and Stroke.* Available online at <www.ninds.nih.gov/health_and_medical/disorders/mitochon_doc.htm> (accessed October 26, 2004).

KEY TERMS

Cellular respiration—The process by which food molecules are converted into high-energy molecules used as a source of energy.

Electrocardiagram (ECG, EKG)—A record of the electrical activity of the heart, with each wave being labeled as P, Q, R, S, and T waves. It is often used in the diagnosis of cases of abnormal cardiac rhythm and myocardial damage.

Mitochondrial inheritance—Inheritance associated with the mitochondrial genome which is inherited exclusively from the mother.

Ragged-red fibers—A microscopic accumulation of diseased mitochondria.

Scaglia, Fernando. "MELAS Syndrome." *eMedicine*, July 2, 2002. Available online at <www.emedicine.com/ped/topic1406.htm> (accessed October 26, 2004).

Stephanie Dionne Sherk

MMPI *see* **Minnesota Multiphasic Personality Inventory**

▌ MMR vaccine

Definition

MMR vaccine is a combined vaccine to protect children against **measles**, **mumps**, and **rubella**, which are dangerous and potentially deadly diseases. Alternative names are rubella **vaccination**, mumps vaccination, vaccine-MMR.

Description

The MMR, which does not contain mercury, consists of live viruses that have been weakened (attenuated) so that the vaccine is still capable of inducing a productive immune response but does not cause the disease that the original or "wild-type" viruses can. The MMR vaccine is a mix of three vaccines: attenuvax (measles), mumpsvax (mumps), and meruvax II (rubella).

The three-in-one MMR vaccine protects against measles, mumps, and rubella. Although single antigen (individual) vaccines are available for each part of the MMR, they are only used in specific situations, in which one of the three diseases occurs and public health officials decide to immunize infants six to 15 months of age for that particular disease. (Single antigen vaccines pose less risk to children younger than the recommended age of 15 months for the MMR.)

Measles (rubeola)

Before vaccination, epidemics of measles peaked in the spring every two to four years. Measles is an endemic disease in many undeveloped countries and in countries where measles immunization levels are low. Because the risk of contracting measles in other countries is greater than in the United States, infants and children should be as well protected as possible before traveling.

Measles is caused by a virus that grows in the nose, mouth, throat, and the eyes, and in their secretions. It is highly communicable and may not be recognized early because the symptoms often resemble cold symptoms. The incubation period is 10 to 11 days. Measles begins with slight temperature rise and a runny nose and eyes. About the second or third day, blush-white pinpoint spots with a red rim, known as Koplick's spots, appear in the mouth. Small dark red pimples appear on the head and spread gradually over the body. These pimples grow larger and in groups, giving a blotchy appearance, which is an important difference between measles and **scarlet fever**. In scarlet fever, the skin appears red all over.

The respiratory symptoms grow worse. The child sneezes often, the eyes are sore, and nasal secretion becomes purulent. Light hurts the eyes (photophobia). The child's throat is sore. The rash is greatest about the fourth day, and it may last up to ten days. During the second week, the skin begins to flake off, and it continues to do so for five to ten days.

Treatment is limited to combating the symptoms of measles because **antiviral drugs** as of 2004 are ineffective. The disease has serious possible complications. For example, encephalomyelitis (inflammation of the brain and spinal cord) occurs in one to two cases out of 1000 patients; the disease is fatal at that same rate. Immune globulin injections help prevent or reduce measles infection if given within six days of exposure. Complications can be brought on by measles. **Encephalitis** occurs in one out of 6000 cases; 20 percent of these infections are fatal. Thrombocytopenic purpura (skin hemorrhages because of decreased **platelet count**) occur in one out of 3000 cases.

Mumps (epidemic parotitis)

Mumps, another viral disease, affects the salivary glands, especially the parotid gland. Children under the age of two years old seldom have mumps; adults rarely have this disease. A closer contact is necessary to transmit mumps than other contagious diseases. The incubation period lasts from two to three weeks, averaging about 18 days.

In most cases, the first sign of mumps is a swelling in the parotid glands; occasionally, mumps may begin with a slight fever, **headache**, and malaise before the swelling appears. Sometimes only one of the parotid glands is affected, but both may be inflamed at the same time or one after the other. The glands become swollen and tender and are painful. It hurts for the child to suck while nursing or in older children to open his mouth and eat, but otherwise he may not feel sick at all. After two or three days, the swelling begins to go down, and usually disappears by the tenth day. As a rule, keeping children isolated or out of school for two weeks is long enough to prevent communicating the infection to others. Treatment is entirely palliative; as of 2004, there was no effective antiviral treatment.

Mumps can cause certain complications. The nervous system is affected in 65 percent of patients; 10 percent display symptoms of this, and 2 percent of these cases are fatal. Testicular complications occur in 14 to 35 percent of post-pubertal boys, and complications regarding the ovaries in 7 percent of post-pubertal females. These complications are rare in prepubescent children, however. Deafness in one or both ears occurs in one out of 15,000 cases. More than half of the deaths from mumps occur in those over 19 years of age. Mumps infection during the first trimester of pregnancy increases the risk of spontaneous abortion.

Rubella (German measles)

Rubella is also caused by a virus, but the disease is mild and last only a short time. The symptoms are like measles but are not nearly as severe, and spots never appear on the mucous membranes of the mouth. Sometimes the rash that appears on the face is the first noticeable sign of a rubella infection. The rash spreads quickly and disappears just as rapidly; sometimes it is gone from the face and the neck by the time it reaches the arms and the legs. The rash usually lasts two to four days.

Isolation from other children is brief or not carried out at all; since the infectious stage is so brief, there is little danger of passing on the infection after the rash appears. The greatest risk of German measles is fetal malformations which occur when a mother is infected in the early months of pregnancy.

Children and adults may can have rubella more than once; 3 to 10 percent of those who have had rubella and 14 to 18 percent of those immunized become infected on exposure to the virus. Some reinfections are subclinical (i.e., have no visible symptoms). In fact, some 25 to 50 percent of rubella infections are asymptomatic.

General use

Recommended MMR vaccination schedule

Because the risk of serious disease from infection with either mumps or rubella in infants is low, mumps and rubella vaccines should not be given to infants younger than 12 months old. When the measles vaccine is needed a single-antigen measles vaccine is given. However, parents of an infant less than 12 months of age should be immune to mumps and rubella so they will not expose the infant or become infected if the infant becomes ill.

The first dose of the vaccine is given to children 12 to 15 months old. The second dose of the MMR vaccine should be given at four to six years of age. All children are to be fully immunized before starting school in the United States. Children who have not the second dose as recommended should complete the immunization by 11 or 12 years of age.

MMR traveling recommendations

Before infants and children of 12 months of age or older leave the United States, they should receive two doses of MMR vaccine separated by at least 28 days, with the first dose given on their birthday. Infants under 12 months of age should receive a dose of monovalent (single antigen) measles vaccine before departure. If monovalent vaccine is not available, no specific contraindication exists to giving MMR to infants six to eleven months of age. The risk for serious disease from either mumps or rubella infection among infants is low.

Infants who receive the monovalent measles vaccine or MMR before their first birthday are vulnerable to all three diseases and should be revaccinated with two doses of MMR. The first should be given when the infant is 12 to 15 months of age (12 months if the infant remains in an area where disease risk is high) and the second at least 28 days later.

Parents or adults who travel or live abroad with infants less than 12 months old should have evidence of immunity to rubella and mumps, as well as measles, to avoid becoming infected if the infants are exposed to the diseases.

An infant less than six months of age is usually protected against measles, mumps, and rubella by maternal antibodies. As a rule, the infant does not need added protection unless the mother is diagnosed with measles.

Maternal immunity to MMR

Most fetuses receive some natural immunity to measles from their mothers in utero. This passive immunity fades over time and is less effective in children of immunized mothers than in children of mothers who had the measles.

The duration of protection is dependent to a great extent on the maternal antibody titer and the antibodies received by the infant during pregnancy. Women who have had the disease have higher measles antibody titers than women who have not had measles but have been vaccinated. Women who have not had measles nor vaccination have no measles antibodies.

Precautions

There are few reasons not to be vaccinated. Some of these are as follows:

- being allergic to gelatin or neomycin or having had an allergic reaction to a previous MMR vaccination
- being moderately or severely ill
- being pregnant
- in males, mumps can cause inflammation of the testes; in female, the ovaries, external genitals, or breasts may be affected

Side effects

Most of the time inactivated vaccines are given intramuscularly (IM), and live virus vaccines are given subcutaneously (SC). Vaccines that are used intramuscularly may cause local reactions (such as irritation, skin discoloration, inflammation, and granuloma formation) if injected into subcutaneous tissue. The vaccine may also be less effective if it is not given by the proper route.

Interactions

There is varying incidence of vaccine reactions. Some of these are as follows:

- fever (one out of six)
- mild rash (one out of 20)

KEY TERMS

Acellular—Without whole cells. An acellular vaccine contains on parts of the cells which can produce immunity in a person receiving the vaccine.

Active immunity—Produced by the body when the immune system is triggered to produce antibodies, either by immunization or a disease.

Adverse effect—A negative side effect of a vaccine.

Anaphylaxis—Also called anaphylactic shock; a severe allergic reaction characterized by airway constriction, tissue swelling, and lowered blood pressure.

Encephalitis—Inflammation of the brain, usually caused by a virus. The inflammation may interfere with normal brain function and may cause seizures, sleepiness, confusion, personality changes, weakness in one or more parts of the body, and even coma.

Incubation period—The time period between exposure to an infectious agent, such as a virus or bacteria, and the appearance of symptoms of illness. Also called the latent period.

Inflammation—Pain, redness, swelling, and heat that develop in response to tissue irritation or injury. It usually is caused by the immune system's response to the body's contact with a foreign substance, such as an allergen or pathogen.

Passive immunity—The body reception of proteins that act as antibodies instead of making the antibodies itself. Immunoglobulins may produce this immunity. All babies have antibodies from their mothers, which give them short-term protection.

- swollen glands (rare)
- seizure (one out of 3,000)
- **pain** and joint stiffness (one out of 20)
- low platelet count (one out of 30,000)
- serious allergic reaction (less than one out of 1,000,000)

Parental concerns

Parents often express concern about combining three vaccines in one injection. As of 2004 there is no published evidence showing a benefit to separating the combination MMR vaccine into three individual shots. The CDC continues to recommend two doses of the combined MMR vaccine for all children.

Because signs of **autism** may appear around the time children receive the MMR vaccine, some parents worry that the vaccine causes autism. Research has not found a relationship between MMR vaccine and autism.

It is sometimes difficult for parents to adhere to the recommended vaccine schedule, including the spacing between doses. If the intervals between doses is longer than usual, there is no need to restart the series of any vaccine.

MMR vaccinations are appropriate for children with chronic diseases such as diabetes and cardiovascular condition as advised by the pediatrician.

Symptoms of low-grade fever, irritability, and soreness at the injection site following the MMR immunization can be relieved with an analgesic such as acetaminophen as recommended by the pediatrician. Cool compresses to the injection site are also comforting.

Resources

BOOKS

Behrman, Richard E., et al., eds. *Nelson Textbook of Pediatrics*, 16th ed. Philadelphia: Saunders, 2000.

Horton, Richard. *A Jab in the Dark: Anxiety and Rationality in the MMR Controversy*. New York: New York Review of Books, 2005.

WEB SITES

"Childhood Immunization Support Program." *American Academy of Pediatrics*. Available online at <www.cispimmunize.org/> (accessed December 18, 2004).

Aliene Linwood, R.N., DPA, FACHE

Moles

Definition

A mole (nevus) is a pigmented (colored) spot on the outer layer of the skin (epidermis).

Description

Moles can be round, oval, flat, or raised. They can occur singly or in clusters on any part of the body. Most moles are brown, but colors can range from pinkish flesh tones to yellow, dark blue, or black.

A mole usually lasts about 50 years before beginning to fade. Some moles disappear completely, and some never lighten at all. Some moles develop stalks that raise them above the skin's surface; these moles eventually drop off.

Types of moles

Moles that are present at birth are called congenital nevi.

Other types of moles include:

- junctional moles, which are usually brown and may be flat or slightly raised
- compound moles, which are slightly raised, range in color from tan to dark brown, and involve pigment-producing cells (melanocytes) in both the upper and lower layers of the skin (epidermis and dermis)
- dermal moles, which range from flesh-color to brown, are elevated, most common on the upper body, and may contain hairs
- sebaceous moles, which are produced by over-active oil glands and are yellow and rough-textured
- blue moles, which are slightly raised, colored by pigment deep within the skin, and most common on the head, neck, and arms of women

Most moles are benign (not cancerous), but atypical moles (dysplastic nevi) may develop into malignant melanoma, a potentially fatal form of skin **cancer**. Atypical moles are usually hereditary. Most are bigger than a pencil eraser, and the shape and pigmentation are irregular.

Congenital nevi are more apt to become cancerous than moles that develop after birth, especially if they are more than eight inches in diameter. Lentigo maligna (melanotic freckle of Hutchinson), most common on the face and after the age of 50, first appears as a flat spot containing two or more shades of tan. It gradually becomes larger and darker. One in three of these moles develop into a form of skin cancer known as lentigo maligna melanoma.

Demographics

Nearly everyone has at least a few moles. They generally appear by the time a person is 20 and at first resemble freckles. A mole's color and shape do not usually change; however, changes in hormone levels that occur during **puberty** and pregnancy can make moles larger and darker. New moles may also appear during this period. About 1 to 3 percent of all babies have one or more moles when they are born. Only about one in 1 million moles is cancerous.

Causes and symptoms

The cause of moles is unknown, although atypical moles seem to run in families and result from exposure to sunlight. During the early 2000s, researchers identified two genes known as CDKN2A and CDK4 that govern susceptibility to melanoma in humans. Other susceptibility genes are being sought. Most experts, however, think that these susceptibility genes are not sufficient by themselves to account for moles becoming cancerous but are influenced by a combination of other inherited traits and environmental factors.

When to call the doctor

Only a small percentage of moles require medical attention. A mole that has the following symptoms should be evaluated by a dermatologist (a physician specializing in skin diseases):

- bleeds
- itches
- looks unusual or changes in any way

Diagnosis

A doctor who suspects skin cancer will remove all or part of the mole for microscopic examination. This procedure, which is usually performed in a doctor's office, is simple, relatively painless, and does not take more than a few minutes. It does leave a scar.

The doctor may also use a dermatoscope to examine the mole before removal. The dermatoscope, which can be used to distinguish between benign moles and melanomas, is an instrument that resembles an ophthalmoscope used to look at the eye. An oil is first applied to the mole to make the outer layers of skin transparent.

A combination of high-frequency ultrasound and color Doppler studies has also been shown to have a high degree of accuracy in distinguishing between melanomas and benign moles.

Treatment

If laboratory analysis confirms that a mole is cancerous, the dermatologist will remove the rest of the mole. Patients should realize that slicing off a section of a malignant mole will not cause the cancer to spread.

Removing a mole for cosmetic reasons involves numbing the area and using scissors or a scalpel to remove the elevated portion. The patient is left with a flat mole the same color as the original growth. Cutting out parts of the mole above and beneath the surface of the skin can leave a scar more noticeable than the mole.

Scissors or a razor can be used to temporarily remove hair from a mole. Permanent hair removal, however, requires electrolysis or surgical removal of the mole.

Prognosis

Moles are rarely cancerous and, once removed, unlikely to recur. A dermatologist should be consulted if a mole reappears after being removed.

Prevention

Wearing a sunscreen and limiting sun exposure may prevent some moles. Anyone who has moles should examine them every month and see a dermatologist if changes in size, shape, color, or texture occur or if new moles appear.

A team of researchers at Duke University reported in 2003 that topical application of a combination of 15 percent vitamin C and 1 percent vitamin E over a four-day period offered significant protection against **sunburn**. The researchers suggest that this combination may protect skin against aging caused by sunlight as well.

Anyone with a **family** history of melanoma should see a dermatologist for an annual skin examination. Everyone should know the ABCDEs of melanoma:

- A: asymmetry, which occurs when the two halves of the mole are not identical
- B: borders that are irregular or indistinct
- C: color that varies in a single mole
- D: diameter, which should be no larger than a pencil eraser (about 6 mm)
- E: elevated above the surrounding tissue

A mole with any of these characteristics should be evaluated by a dermatologist.

Advances in photographic technique had as of 2004 made it easier to track the development of moles with the help of whole-body photographs. A growing number of hospitals are offering these photographs as part of outpatient mole-monitoring services.

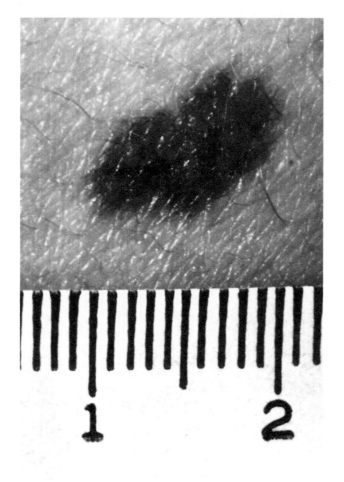

Close up of a mole. *(Custom Medical Stock Photo Inc.)*

Parental concerns

Very few moles are cancerous. Moles on the face or other frequently exposed areas of skin may be troubling for children. If a child is particularly troubled by a mole, a dermatologist can be consulted about its possible removal, although this often leaves a scar.

Resources

BOOKS

Crowson, Neil A., et al. *The Melanocytic Proliferations: A Comprehensive Textbook of Pigmented Lesions.* New York: Wiley-Liss, 2001.

Thompson, June. *Spots, Birthmarks, and Rashes: The Complete Guide to Caring for Your Child's Skin.* Westport, CT: Firefly Books, 2003.

PERIODICALS

"About Moles, Melanomas, and Lasers: The Dermatologist's Schizophrenic Attitude toward Pigmented Lesions." *Archives of Dermatology* 139 (November 2003): 1405–7.

Bates, Betsy. "Imaging Devices Assist in Skin Cancer Diagnosis." *Family Practice* 33 (January 1, 2003): 18.

Chamilin, Sarah L. "Shedding Light on Moles, Melanoma, and the Sun." *Contemporary Pediatrics* 19 (June, 2002): 102–10.

ORGANIZATIONS

American Academy of Dermatologists. PO Box 4014 Schaumburg, IL 60168–4014. Web site: <www.aad.org>.

Tish Davidson, A.M.
Maureen Haggerty
Rebecca J. Frey, PhD

Money *see* **Allowance and money management**

Mongolism *see* **Down syndrome**

Mononucleosis *see* **Infectious mononucleosis**

Monosomy X *see* **Turner syndrome**

Mood disorders

Definition

Mood disorders are mental disorders characterized by periods of depression, sometimes alternating with periods of elevated mood.

Description

While many people go through sad or elated moods from time to time, people with mood disorders suffer from severe or prolonged mood states that disrupt their daily functioning. Among the general mood disorders are major depressive disorder, **bipolar disorder**, and dysthymia. In classifying and diagnosing mood disorders, doctors determine if the mood disorder is unipolar or bipolar. When only one extreme in mood (the depressed state) is experienced, this condition is called unipolar. Major depression refers to a single severe period of depression, marked by negative or hopeless thoughts and physical symptoms like fatigue. In major depressive disorder, some patients have isolated episodes of depression. In between these episodes, the patient does not feel depressed or have other symptoms associated with depression. Other patients have more frequent episodes.

Bipolar depression or bipolar disorder (sometimes called manic depression) refers to a condition in which people experience two extremes in mood. They alternate between depression (the low mood) and mania or hypomania (the high mood). These patients go from depression to a frenzied, abnormal elevation in mood. Mania and hypomania are similar, but mania is usually more severe and debilitating to the patient. Dysthymia is a recurrent or lengthy depression that may last a lifetime. It is similar to major depressive disorder, but dysthymia is chronic, long-lasting, persistent, and mild. Patients may have symptoms that are not as severe as major depression, but the symptoms last for many years. It seems that a mild form of the depression is always present. In some cases, people may also experience a major depressive episode on top of their dysthymia, a condition sometimes referred to as double depression.

Psychologists have identified the teenage years as one of the most difficult phases of human life. Although they are often seen as a time for enjoying friendship and engaging in activities that adults would not usually do, the teenage period can be difficult. Many changes in the human mind take place during **puberty**. Apart from the onset of sexual maturity, teenagers must also make key decisions about their future, develop their identities, change schools and meet a new sets of friends, find out about their family's past, and cope with a wide range of other issues. Many young people have difficulty coping with these stresses.

Four out of five teenagers who commit **suicide** are male, but the average female teenager is prone to attempt suicide four more times during her teen years than the average male. White teenage males are more likely to commit suicide than any other ethnic group, but teenage suicide among blacks was as of 2004 increasing. Teenagers who have unsuccessfully tried to commit suicide in the past are more likely to attempt suicide in the future. The odds increase after each failed attempt. There are two groups of teens that are at the highest risk for committing suicide: Native Americans and teens who are gay, lesbian, bisexual, and transgendered.

Gay and bisexual male teens, which represent about 10 percent of the male teen population, are six to seven times more at risk for attempting suicide than their heterosexual peers. Several surveys show gay and lesbian youth account for 30 percent of all suicides among teens, according to the U.S. Department of Health and Human Services. Yet most studies of teen suicide have not been concerned with identifying sexual orientation.

Demographics

As many as 14 percent of children will experience at least one episode of major depression by age 15. Girls are significantly more likely to experience depression than boys after the age of 16. Out of 100,000 adolescents, two to three thousand will have mood disorders out of which 8 to 10 will commit suicide. In the early 2000s, suicide, attempted suicide, and thoughts of committing suicide are growing problems among adolescents in the United States and much of the world. It is the third leading cause of death among 15 to 19 year olds in the United States and the sixth leading cause of death among 10 to 14 year olds. About 2 percent of adolescent girls and 1 percent of adolescent boys attempt suicide each year in the United States. Another 5 to 10 percent of children and teens each year come up with a plan to commit suicide.

Causes and symptoms

Mood disorders tend to run in families. These disorders are associated with imbalances in certain chemicals that carry signals between brain cells (neurotransmitters). These chemicals include serotonin, norepinephrine, and dopamine. Women are more vulnerable to unipolar depression than are men. In adults, major life stressors (like **divorce**, serious financial problems, death of a **family** member, etc.) will often provoke the symptoms of depression in susceptible people. Children's versions of these stressors contribute to their vulnerability to depression.

Major depression is more serious than just feeling sad or "blue." The symptoms of major depression may include the following:

• loss of appetite

• change in the **sleep** pattern, like not sleeping (insomnia) or sleeping too much

Light therapy is a treatment for mood disorders. *(Photograph by Najlah Feanny. © Stock Boston, Inc.)*

- feelings of worthlessness, hopelessness, or inappropriate guilt
- fatigue
- difficulty in concentrating or making decisions
- overwhelming and intense feelings of sadness or grief
- disturbed thinking
- certain physical symptoms such as stomachaches or headaches

Bipolar disorder includes mania or hypomania. Mania is an abnormal elevation in mood. These individuals may be excessively cheerful, have grandiose ideas, and may sleep less. They may talk nonstop for hours, have unending enthusiasm, and demonstrate poor judgment. Sometimes the elevation in mood is marked by irritability and hostility rather than cheerfulness. While the person may at first seem normal with an increase in energy, others who know the person well see a marked difference in behavior. The patient may seem to be in a frenzy and will often make poor, bizarre, or dangerous choices in his or her personal and professional lives. Hypomania is not as severe as mania and does not cause

the level of impairment in work and social activities that mania can.

When to call the doctor

There are many methods for helping teenagers deal with mood disorders, both medical and psychological. Most teenagers who have mood disorders believe their problems are too hard or embarrassing to talk about, so it is important for a helper to show they can be trusted and talked to. Seeing a psychologist is widely recommended as well. Psychologists can improve a teenager's vision of life by listening to them and making them feel it will work out for the best.

If a child or teen is so depressed that he or she is talking about suicide, doctors recommend that parents or other helpers do not ask the adolescent what reason they have to think of such a thing to do; rather, one should listen and wait for the child to gain trust enough so that he or she finally can feel comfortable in talking about the problem. Helpers should, however, show understanding of the teenager's situation. Doctors also recommend that helpers do not mention any "reasons to live" to the teenager, as that might send the teenager back into depressing thoughts, e.g. "What reason do I have to live?" Many doctors recommend that teenagers be taken to a hospital immediately after they express the desire to commit suicide.

Diagnosis

Doctors diagnose mood disorders based on the patient's description of the symptoms as well as the patient's family history. The length of time the patient has had symptoms is also important. Generally patients are diagnosed with dysthymia if they feel depressed more days than not for at least two years. The depression is mild but long lasting. In major depressive disorder, the patient is depressed almost all day nearly every day of the week for at least two weeks. The depression is severe. Sometimes laboratory tests are performed to rule out other causes for the symptoms (like thyroid disease). The diagnosis may be confirmed when a patient responds well to medication.

Treatment

The most effective treatment for mood disorders is a combination of medication and psychotherapy. The four different classes of drugs used in mood disorders are as follows:

- heterocyclic **antidepressants** (HCAs), such as amitriptyline (Elavil)
- selective serotonin reuptake inhibitors (SSRI inhibitors), such as fluoxetine (Prozac), paroxetine (Paxil), and sertraline (Zoloft)
- monoamine oxidase inhibitors (MAOI inhibitors), such as phenelzine sulfate (Nardil) and tranylcypromine sulfate (Parnate)
- mood stabilizers, such as lithium carbonate (Eskalith) and valproate, often used in people with bipolar mood disorders

A number of psychotherapy approaches are useful as well. Interpersonal psychotherapy helps the patient recognize the interaction between the mood disorder and interpersonal relationships. Cognitive-behavioral therapy explores how the patient's view of the world may be affecting his or her mood and outlook.

When depression fails to respond to treatment or when there is a high risk of suicide, electroconvulsive therapy (ECT) is sometimes used. ECT is believed to affect neurotransmitters like the medications do. Patients are anesthetized and given muscle relaxants to minimize discomfort. Then low-level electric current is passed through the brain to cause a brief convulsion. The most common side effect of ECT is mild, short-term memory loss.

Alternative treatment

There are many alternative therapies that may help in the treatment of mood disorders, including acupuncture, botanical medicine, homeopathy, aromatherapy, constitutional hydrotherapy, and light therapy. The therapy used is an individual choice. Short-term clinical studies have shown that the herb St. John's wort (*Hypericum perforatum*) can effectively treat some types of depression. Though it appears very safe, the herb may have some side effects and its long-term effectiveness has not been proven. It has not been tested in patients with bipolar disorder. St. John's wort and antidepressant drugs should not be taken simultaneously, so patients should tell their doctor if they are taking St. John's wort.

Prognosis

Most cases of mood disorders can be successfully managed if properly diagnosed and treated.

Prevention

People can take steps to improve mild depression and keep it from becoming worse. They can learn stress management (like relaxation training or breathing exercises), **exercise** regularly, and avoid drugs or alcohol.

Parental concerns

Parents who are concerned that their child may have a mood disorder should seek help, such as from a psychiatrist, psychologist, or counselor. Make an appointment with a therapist or counselor who can talk to the child about his or her problems and ways to cope. There are a number of ways parents can help children and teens deal with loneliness, depression, and suicidal feelings. First, parents should let the child do the talking, and they should listen very carefully. They should let the child know they take his or her feelings and thoughts seriously. They should try to find out what is the root of the problem. They may also ask direct questions of the child, such as "Are you thinking of committing suicide?" or "Are you thinking of ending your life?" Third, they should stay with the child. They should not leave the child alone if they say they want to commit suicide. By staying with the child, the parent may be saving the child's life.

See also Depressive disorders.

Resources

BOOKS

Empfield, Maureen, and Nicholas Bakalar. *Understanding Teenage Depression: A Guide to Diagnosis, Treatment, and Management.* New York: Owl Books, 2001.

Frank, Kim. *The Handbook for Helping Kids with Anxiety and Stress.* Chapin, SC: Youthlight Inc., 2003.

Ghaemi, S. Nassir. *Mood Disorders: A Practical Guide.* New York: Lippincott Williams & Wilkins, 2003.

Nutt, David, et al. *Mood and Anxiety Disorders in Children and Adolescents.* Florence, KY: Martin Dunitz, Ltd., 2001.

PERIODICALS

Cassano, Giovanni B., et al. "The Mood Spectrum in Unipolar and Bipolar Disorder: Arguments for a Unitary Approach." *American Journal of Psychiatry* 161 (July 2004): 1264–69.

Coyle, Joseph T., et al. "Depression and Bipolar Support Alliance Consensus Statement on the Unmet Needs in Diagnosis and Treatment of Mood Disorders in Children and Adolescents." *Journal of the American Academy of Child and Adolescent Psychiatry* 42 (December 2003): 1494–1503.

Koplewicz, Harold S. "More than Moody: Recognizing and Treating Adolescent Depression." *The Brown University Child and Adolescent Behavior Letter* 18 (December 2002): 1–3.

Youngstrom, Eric A., et al. "Comparing the Diagnostic Accuracy of Six Potential Screening Instruments for Bipolar Disorder in Youths Aged 5 to 17 Years." *Journal of the American Academy of Child and Adolescent Psychiatry* 43 (July 2004): 847–58.

ORGANIZATIONS

Child & Adolescent Bipolar Foundation. 1000 Skokie Blvd., Suite 425, Wilmette, IL 60091. Web site: <www.bpkids.org>.

National Academy of Child & Adolescent Psychiatry. 3615 Wisconsin Ave. NW, Washington, DC 20016. Web site: <www.aacap.org>.

WEB SITES

"Child and Adolescent Mental Health: Overview of Mood Disorders." *Medical University of South Carolina*, 2004. Available online at <www.musckids.com/health_library/mentalhealth/overview.htm> (accessed November 11, 2004).

"Mood Disorders." *National Youth Network*, 2004. Available online at <www.nationalyouth.com/mooddisorders.html> (accessed November 11, 2004).

Robert Scott Dinsmoor
Ken R. Wells

Moral development

Definition

Moral development is the process throught which children develop proper attitudes and behaviors toward other people in society, based on social and cultural norms, rules, and laws.

Description

Moral development is a concern for every parent. Teaching a child to distinguish right from wrong and to behave accordingly is a goal of parenting.

Moral development is a complex issue that—since the beginning of human civilization—has been a topic of discussion among some of the world's most distinguished psychologists, theologians, and culture theorists. It was not studied scientifically until the late 1950s.

Piaget's theory of moral reasoning

Jean Piaget, a Swiss psychologist, explored how children developed moral reasoning. He rejected the idea that children learn and internalize the rules and morals of society by being given the rules and forced to adhere to them. Through his research on how children formed their judgments about moral behavior, he recognized that children learn morality best by having to deal with others in groups. He reasoned that there was a process by which children conform to society's norms of what is right and wrong, and that the process was active rather than passive.

Piaget found two main differences in how children thought about moral behavior. Very young children's thinking is based on how actions affected them or what the results of an action were. For example, young children will say that when trying to reach a forbidden cookie jar, breaking 10 cups is worse than breaking one. They also recognize the sanctity of rules. For example, they understand that they cannot make up new rules to a game; they have to play by what the rule book says or what is commonly known to be the rules. Piaget called this "moral realism with objective responsibility." It explains why young children are concerned with outcomes rather than intentions.

Older children look at motives behind actions rather than consequences of actions. They are also able to examine rules, determining whether they are fair or not, and apply these rules and their modifications to situations requiring negotiation, assuring that everyone affected by the rules is treated fairly. Piaget felt that the best moral learning came from these cooperative decision-making and problem-solving events. He also believed that children developed moral reasoning quickly and at an early age.

Kohlberg's theory of moral development

Lawrence Kohlberg, an American psychologist, extended Piaget's work in cognitive reasoning into **adolescence** and adulthood. He felt that moral development was a slow process and evolved over time. Still, his six stages of moral development, drafted in 1958, mirrors Piaget's early model. Kohlberg believed that individuals made progress by mastering each stage, one at a time. A person could not skip stages. He also felt that the only way to encourage growth through these stages was by discussion of moral dilemmas and by participation in consensus democracy within small groups. Consensus democracy was rule by agreement of the group, not majority rule. This would stimulate and broaden the thinking of children and adults, allowing them to progress from one stage to another.

PRECONVENTIONAL LEVEL The child at the first and most basic level, the preconventional level, is concerned with avoiding punishment and getting needs met. This level has two stages and applies to children up to 10 years of age.

Stage one is the Punishment-Obedience stage. Children obey rules because they are told to do so by an authority figure (parent or teacher), and they **fear** punishment if they do not follow rules. Children at this stage are not able to see someone else's side.

Stage two is the Individual, Instrumentation, and Exchange stage. Here, the behavior is governed by moral reciprocity. The child will follow rules if there is a known benefit to him or her. Children at this stage also mete out justice in an eye-for-an-eye manner or according to Golden Rule logic. In other words, if one child hits another, the injured child will hit back. This is considered equitable justice. Children in this stage are very concerned with what is fair.

Children will also make deals with each other and even adults. They will agree to behave in a certain way for a payoff. "I'll do this, if you will do that." Sometimes, the payoff is in the knowledge that behaving correctly is in the child's own best interest. They receive approval from authority figures or admiration from peers, avoid blame, or behave in accordance with their concept of self. They are just beginning to understand that others have their own needs and drives.

CONVENTIONAL LEVEL This level broadens the scope of human wants and needs. Children in this level are concerned about being accepted by others and living up to their expectations. This stage begins around age 10 but lasts well into adulthood, and is the stage most adults remain at throughout their lives.

Stage three, Interpersonal Conformity, is often called the "good boy/good girl" stage. Here, children do the right thing because it is good for the **family**, peer group, team, school, or church. They understand the concepts of trust, loyalty, and gratitude. They abide by the Golden Rule as it applies to people around them every day. Morality is acting in accordance to what the social group says is right and moral.

Stage four is the Law and Order, or Social System and Conscience stage. Children and adults at this stage abide by the rules of the society in which they live. These laws and rules become the backbone for all right and wrong actions. Children and adults feel compelled to do their duty and show respect for authority. This is still moral behavior based on authority, but reflects a shift from the social group to society at large.

POST-CONVENTIONAL LEVEL Some teenagers and adults move beyond conventional morality and enter morality based on reason, examining the relative values and opinions of the groups with which they interact. Few adults reach this stage.

Correct behavior is governed by the sixth stage, the Social Contract and Individual Rights stage. Individuals in this stage understand that codes of conduct are relative to their social group. This varies from culture to culture and subgroup to subgroup. With that in mind, the individual enters into a contract with fellow human beings to treat them fairly and kindly and to respect authority when it is equally moral and deserved. They also agree to obey laws and social rules of conduct that promote respect for individuals and value the few universal moral values that they recognize. Moral behavior and moral decisions are based on the greatest good for the greatest number.

Stage six is the Principled Conscience or the Universal/Ethical Principles stage. Here, individuals examine the validity of society's laws and govern themselves by what they consider to be universal moral principles, usually involving equal rights and respect. They obey laws and social rules that fall in line with these universal principles, but not others they deem as aberrant. Adults here are motivated by individual conscience that transcends cultural, religious, or social convention rules. Kohlberg recognized this last stage but found so few people who lived by this concept of moral behavior that he could not study it in detail.

Carol Gilligan and the morality of care

Kohlberg's and Piaget's theories have come under fire. Kohlberg's six stages of moral development, for example, have been criticized for elevating Western, urban, intellectual (upper class) understandings of morality, while discrediting rural, tribal, working class, or Eastern moral understandings. Feminists have pointed out potential sexist elements in moral development theories devised by male researchers using male subjects only (such as Kohlberg's early work). Because women's experiences in the world differ from men's in every culture, it would stand to reason that women's moral development might differ from men's, perhaps in significant ways.

Carol Gilligan deemed Kohlberg's research biased because he only used male subjects to reach his findings. Because of this, his model is based on a concept of morality based on equity and justice, which places most men in stage five or six. Gilligan found that women, who value social interaction more than men, base their moral decisions on a culture of caring for other human beings. This would place them at stage three, making women appear to be inferior morally to men. Men determine immorality based on treating others unfairly, and women base it on turning away someone in need.

Gilligan's work, however, doesn't solve the gender question, because newer research has found that both males and females often base their moral judgments and behaviors on both justice and care. Nevertheless, the morality of care theory opened up explorations of moral reasoning in many groups and cultures.

Bronfenbrenner

Urie Bronfenbrenner studied children and schools in different cultures since many ethnic, religious, and social groups often have their own rules for moral behavior. His research found five moral orientations, regardless of culture, social group, or developmental stage. Movement from the first stage to any of the others was dependent on participation in the family and other social institutions within each culture. Movement to the last stage involved exposure to a different moral system that might be in conflict with one's own. This moral pluralism forces individuals to examine their own moral reasoning and beliefs. This often occurs when people work in other countries or cultures and come face to face with different sets of moral conventions.

Bronfenbrenner also noted that individuals could slide back into a previous moral orientation when they experienced the breakdown of their familiar social order as in war, regime changes, genocide, famine, or large scale natural disasters that destroy social infrastructures. People narrow their attention to their own pressing needs and ignore the welfare of the larger society.

Self-oriented morality coincided with Kohlberg's pre-conventional morality. Behavior is based on self-interest and motivated by who can help children get what they want or who is hindering that process. This stage was found in all children and some adults in all cultures.

Authority-oriented morality again is similar to Kohlberg's Law and Order stage. This applies not only to parents' rules but to teachers, religious leaders, and government officials. This moral orientation was culturally defined. It was very evident in Middle Eastern cultures where religious authority is the law.

Peer-authority morality is moral conformity based on the conventions and rules of a social group. This is evident among teenagers in Western cultures and even among some adults.

Collective-oriented morality is an extension of the peer-authority stage. Here a larger group's rule supercedes individual rights and interests. Duty is the law. This moral orientation was found in Asian cultures.

Objectively-oriented morality is akin to Kohlberg's universal principles stage. Here, however, these rules transcend individual moral perspectives and become entities in themselves. Like Kohlberg's last stage, this moral orientation was found in relatively few people in any culture.

Other theories

There are several other approaches to the study of moral development, which are categorized in a variety of ways. Briefly, the social learning theory approach claims that humans develop morality by learning the rules of acceptable behavior from their external environment, an essentially behaviorist approach. Psychoanalytic theory proposes instead that morality develops through humans' conflict between their instinctual drives and the demands of society. **Cognitive development** theories view morality as an outgrowth of cognition, or reasoning, whereas personality theories are holistic in their approach, taking into account all the factors that contribute to human development.

The differences between these approaches rest on two questions: How moral are infants at birth? and How is moral maturity defined? The contrasting philosophies at the heart of the answers to these questions determine the essential perspective of each moral development theory. Those who believe infants are born with no moral sense tend toward social learning or behaviorist theories, because all morality must therefore be learned from the external environment. Others who believe humans are innately aggressive and completely self-oriented are more likely to accept psychoanalytic theories where morality is the learned management of socially destructive internal drives. Those who believe it is the reasoning abilities that separate humans from the rest of creation will find cognitive development theories the most attractive. And those who view humans as holistic beings born with a full range of potentialities will most likely be drawn to personality theories.

What constitutes mature morality is a subject of great controversy. Each society develops its own set of norms and standards for acceptable behavior, leading many to say that morality is entirely culturally conditioned. There is debate over whether or not this means that there are no universal truths, and no cross-cultural standards for human behavior. This debate fuels the critiques of many moral development theories.

Definitions of what is or is not moral are in a state of upheaval within individual societies. Controversies rage over the morality of warfare (especially nuclear), ecological conservation, genetic research and manipulation, alternative fertility and childbearing methods, abortion, sexuality, pornography, drug use, euthanasia, racism, sexism, and human rights issues, among others. Deter-

mining the limits of moral behavior becomes increasingly difficult as human capabilities, choices, and responsibilities proliferate with advances in technology and scientific knowledge. For example, prenatal testing techniques that determine birth defects in the womb force parents to make new moral choices about whether to give birth to a child.

The rise in crime, drug and alcohol abuse, gang violence, teen parenthood, and **suicide** in Western society has also caused a rise in concern over morality and moral development. Parents and teachers want to know how to raise moral children, and they turn to moral development theorists to find answers. Freudian personality theories became more widely known to the Western public in the 1960s and were understood to imply that repression of a child's natural drives would lead to neuroses. Many parents and teachers were therefore afraid to **discipline** their children, and permissiveness became the rule. Cognitive development theories did little to change things, as they focus on reasoning and disregard behavior. Behaviorist theories, with their complete denial of free will in moral decision-making, are unattractive to many and require precise, dedicated, behavior modification techniques.

Schools are returning to character education programs, popular in the 1920s and 1930s, where certain virtues such as honesty, fairness, and loyalty, are taught to students along with the regular academic subjects. Unfortunately, there is little or no agreement as to which virtues are important and what exactly each virtue entails.

Another approach to moral education that became popular in the 1960s and 1970s is known as values clarification or values modification. The purpose of these programs is to guide students to establish or discern their own system of values on which to base their moral decisions. Students are also taught that others may have different values systems, and that they must be tolerant of those differences. The advantages of this approach are that it promotes self-investigation and awareness and the development of internal moral motivations, which are more reliable than external motivations, and prevents fanaticism, authoritarianism, and moral coercion. The disadvantage is that it encourages moral relativism, the belief that "anything goes." Values clarification is generally seen as a valuable component of moral education, but incomplete on its own.

Lawrence Kohlberg devised a moral education program in the 1960s based on his cognitive development theory. Called the Just Community program, it utilizes age-appropriate or stage-appropriate discussions of moral dilemmas, democratic consensus rule-making, and the creation of a community context where students and teachers could act on their moral decisions. Just Community programs have been established in schools, prisons, and other institutions with a fair amount of success. Exposure to moral questions and the opportunity to practice moral behavior in a supportive community appear to foster deeper moral reasoning and more constructive behavior.

Overall, democratic family and school systems are much more likely to promote the development of internal self-controls and moral growth than are authoritarian or permissive systems. Permissive systems fail to instill any controls, while authoritarian systems instill only fear of punishment, which is not an effective deterrent unless there is a real chance of being caught or punishment becomes a reward because it brings attention to the offender. True moral behavior involves a number of internal processes that are best developed through warm, caring parenting with clear and consistent expectations, emphasis on the reinforcement of positive behaviors rather than the punishment of negative ones, modeling of moral behavior by adults, and creation of opportunities for the child to practice moral reasoning and actions.

According to personal (social) goal theory, moral behavior is motivated by the desire to satisfy a variety of personal and social goals, some of which are self-oriented (selfish), and some of which are other-oriented (altruistic). The four major internal motivations for moral behavior as presented by personal (social) goal theorists are: 1) empathy; 2) the belief that people are valuable in and of themselves and therefore should be helped; 3) the desire to fulfill moral rules; and 4) self-interest.

In social domain theory, moral reasoning is said to develop within particular social domains: 1) moral (e.g., welfare, justice, rights); 2) social-conventional (social rules for the orderly function of society); and 3) personal (pure self-interest, exempt from social or moral rules).

Most people have more than one moral voice and shift among them depending on the situation. In one context, a person may respond out of empathy and place care for an individual over concern for social rules. In a different context, that same person might instead insist on following social rules for the good of society, even though someone may suffer because of it. People also show a lack of consistent morality by sometimes choosing to act in a way that they know is not moral, while continuing to consider themselves moral people. This discrepancy between moral judgment (perceiving an act as morally right or wrong) and moral choice (deciding whether to act in the morally right way) can be explained

in a number of ways, any one of which may be true in a given situation:

- weakness of will (the person is overwhelmed by desire)
- weakness of conscience (guilt feelings are not strong enough to overcome temptation)
- limited/flexible morality (some latitude allowed in moral behavior while still maintaining a "moral" identity)

The Moral Balance model proposes that most humans operate out of a limited or flexible morality. Rather than expecting moral perfection from ourselves or others, people set certain limits beyond which they cannot go. Within those limits, however, there is some flexibility in moral decision-making. Actions such as taking coins left in the change-box of a public telephone may be deemed acceptable (though not perfectly moral), while **stealing** money from an open, unattended cash register is not. Many factors are involved in the determination of moral acceptability from situation to situation, and the limits on moral behavior are often slippery. If given proper encouragement and the opportunity to practice a coherent inner sense of morality, however, most people will develop a balanced morality to guide their day-to-day interactions with their world.

Common problems

Religious development often goes hand in hand with moral development. Children's concepts of divinity, right and wrong, and who is ultimately responsible for the world's woes are shaped by the family and by the religious social group to which each child belongs. Their concepts also mirror cognitive and moral developmental stages.

In general, in the earliest stage (up to age two years), the child knows that religious objects and books are to be respected. The concept of a divine being is vague, but the child enjoys the regularity of the religious rituals such as prayer.

In the next stage (from two to 10 years), children begin to orient religion concepts to themselves as in the catechism litany, "Who made you? God made me." The concept of a divine being is usually described in anthropomorphic ways for children around six years old. In other words, children perceive God to look like a human being only bigger or living in the sky. At this stage, God is physically powerful and often is portrayed as a superhero. God may also be the wish-granter and can fix anything. Children embrace religious holidays and rituals during this stage.

KEY TERMS

Altruistic—Thinking of others.

Anthropomorphic—Taking on human characteristics or looking like humans.

Cognition—The act or process of knowing or perceiving.

Flat affect—Showing no emotion.

Moral choice—Deciding whether to act in the morally right way.

Moral judgment—Perceiving an act as morally right or wrong.

In the Intermediate Stage during pre-adolescence, children are considered to be in the pre-religious stage. The anthropomorphized divinity is pictured as being very old and wise. God is also thought of as doing supernatural things: having a halo, floating over the world, or performing miracles. Children in this stage understand the panoply of religious or divine beings within the religious belief system. For example, Christian children will distinguish between God and Jesus and the disciples or saints.

The last stage in adolescence focuses on personalizing religious rituals and drawing closer to a divine being. Teenagers begin to think of God in abstract terms and look at the mystical side of the religious experience. They may also rebel against organized religion as they begin to question the world and the rules around them.

Some adults who are considered highly religious consider God to be an anthropomorphized divine being or may reject the supernatural or mystical religious experience. This does not mean that these adults have somehow been arrested in their religious development. This just means that the variation among these stages is great and is determined by the particular religious community in which the individual is involved.

Parental concerns

When to call the doctor

Every child misbehaves and will sometimes act selfishly and hurtfully. It is when these acts increase, impulses cannot be controlled, or authority defiance becomes troublesome, that parents may need to seek professional help. Lack of impulse control and authority defiance can be symptoms of medical conditions and psychological disorders. Self-centered behavior, coupled with lack of acceptance of wrongdoing that continues

into older childhood and adolescence, may be a problem that requires family or individual counseling.

Risky behaviors such as speeding, drinking, **smoking**, doing drugs, or engaging in sexual behavior may be related to **peer pressure** and wanting to conform to the group or may be a way to defy authority. These behaviors, though deemed morally wrong by most societies, may also be symptoms of deeper psychological troubles.

Of extreme concern is the rare child who acts with no remorse, and appears to have to conscience. This is usually signaled by early violent outbursts, destructive behavior, or by acts of cruelty to pets or other children. After each incident, the child has a flat affect (no emotion) or fails to admit that there was anything wrong with the his or her actions. These children need intervention immediately. Behaviors such as these may be indicators of sociopathic disorders.

Resources

BOOKS

Child Psychology and Childhood Education: A Cognitive-Developmental View. New York: Longman, 1987.

Coles, Robert. *The Moral Intelligence of Children: How to Raise a Moral Child.* New York: Random House, 1997.

Crittenden, Paul. *Learning to be Moral: Philosophical Thoughts About Moral Development.* Atlantic Highlands, NJ: Humanities Press International, 1990.

Essays on Moral Development, II: The Psychology of Moral Development. San Francisco: Harper & Row, 1984.

Gilligan, Carol. *In a Different Voice: Psychological Theory and Women's Development.* Cambridge: Harvard University Press, 1982.

Huxley, Ronald. *Love and Limits: Achieving a Balance in Parenting.* San Diego: Singular Publishing Group, Inc., 1998.

Kohlberg, Lawrence. *Essays on Moral Development, I: The Philosophy of Moral Development: Moral Stages and the Idea of Justice.* San Francisco: Harper & Row, 1981.

Kurtines, William M., and Jacob L. Gewirtz, eds. *Moral Development: An Introduction.* Boston: Allyn and Bacon, 1995.

Piaget, J. *The Moral Judgment of the Child.* New York: The Free Press, 1965.

Power, F. C., et al. *Lawrence Kohlberg's Approach to Moral Education: A Study of Three Democratic High Schools.* New York: Columbia University Press, 1989.

Schulman, Michael, and Eva Mekler. *Bringing Up a Moral Child: A New Approach for Teaching Your Child to Be*

Kind, Just, and Responsible. rev. ed. New York: Main Street Books/Doubleday, 1994.

PERIODICALS

Bersoff, David M. and Joan G. Miller. "Culture, Context, and the Development of Moral Accountability Judgments." *Developmental Psychology* 29, no. 4 (July 1993): 664–77.

ORGANIZATIONS

Association for Moral Education Dr. James M. Dubois Center for Health Care Ethics. Saint Louis University, Salus Center 3545 Lafayette Ave. St. Louis, MO 63104.

Developmental Studies Center 2000 Embarcadero, Suite 305 Oakland, CA 94606-5300. (510) 533-0213 or (800) 666-7270.

Center for the Advancement of Ethics and Character. Boston University School of Education. 605 Commonwealth Ave., Room 356 Boston, MA 02215. (617) 353-3262. Fax: (617) 353-3924.

Educators for Social Responsibility (ESR). 23 Garden St. Cambridge, MA 02138. (800) 370-2515.

The Heartwood Institute. 425 N. Craig St., Suite 302 Pittsburgh, PA 15213. (800) 432-7810.

Janie Franz
Dianne K. Daeg de Mott

Morphine *see* **Narcotic drugs**

Mother-child relationships *see* **Parent-child relationships**

Motion sickness

Definition

Motion sickness is uncomfortable **dizziness, nausea**, and **vomiting** that people experience when their sense of balance and equilibrium is disturbed because their brain cannot make sense of conflicting information about their body's location in space and motion in their environment.

Description

Motion sickness is connected to the role of the sensory organs. The sensory organs control a body's sense of balance by telling the brain what direction the body is pointing, the direction it is moving, and if it is standing still or turning. These messages are relayed by the inner ear (or labyrinth); the eyes; the skin pressure receptors (such as in those in the feet), the muscle and joint sensory receptors, which track what body parts are moving to the central nervous system (the brain and spinal cord). The brain then is responsible for processing all incoming information and making sense out of it. Riding in a car, being on a ship, or taking an amusement park ride can cause conflicting stimulation of the different sense organs. The result is motion sickness.

For example, when reading a book in the back seat of a moving car, the inner ears and skin receptors sense the motion, but the eyes register only the stationary pages of the book. This conflicting information may cause the usual motion sickness symptoms of dizziness, nausea, and vomiting. While motion sickness can be bothersome, it is not a serious illness, and it can be prevented.

Demographics

Although nearly 80 percent of the general population experiences motion sickness at one time in their lives, children between the ages of four and ten are most vulnerable. Children often out grow motion sickness. Toddlers under age two are rarely motion sick. Adults who frequently get migraine headaches are more likely than others to have recurrent episodes of motion sickness.

Researchers at the Naval Medical Center in San Diego, California, reported in 2003 that 70 percent of research subjects with severe motion sickness had abnormalities of the vestibular system. Research also suggests that some people inherit a predisposition to motion sickness. This predisposition is more marked in some ethnic groups than in others. One study published in 2002 found that persons of Chinese or Japanese ancestry are significantly more vulnerable to motion sickness than persons of British ancestry.

Causes and symptoms

While all of the body's sensory organs contribute to motion sickness, excess stimulation to the vestibular system within the inner ear (the body's balance center) has been shown to be one of the primary reasons for this condition. Balance problems (vertigo) are often caused by a conflict between what is seen and how the inner ear perceives it, leading to confusion in the brain. This confusion may result in higher heart rates, rapid breathing, nausea and sweating, along with dizziness and vomiting.

Additional factors that may contribute to the occurrence or severity of motion sickness include the following:

- poor ventilation

- anxiety or **fear** (Both have been found to lower a person's threshold for experiencing motion sickness symptoms.)

- food (A heavy meal of spicy and greasy foods before traveling is thought to increase motion sickness symptoms.)

- alcohol consumption

- genetic factors

- pregnancy (Susceptibility in women to vomiting during pregnancy appears to be related to motion sickness, although the precise connections are not well understood as of 2004.)

Often viewed as a minor annoyance, some travelers are temporarily immobilized by motion sickness, and a few continue to feel its effects for hours and even days after a trip.

When to call the doctor

Most cases of motion sickness are mild and self-limiting. Parents should call the doctor before giving young children over-the-counter medications for motion sickness. Some remedies are recommended only for older children.

Diagnosis

Most cases of motion sickness are self-diagnosed. If symptoms such as dizziness become chronic, a doctor may be able to help alleviate the discomfort by looking further into a patient's general health. Questions regarding medications, head injuries, recent infections, and other questions about the ear and neurological system will be asked. An examination of the ears, nose, and throat, as well as tests of nerve and balance function, may also be performed.

Severe cases of motion sickness or those that become progressively worse may require additional, specific tests. Diagnosis in these situations deserves the attention and care of a doctor with specialized skills in diseases of the ear, nose, throat, equilibrium, and neurological system.

Treatment

Medications to help ease the symptoms of motion sickness are available without a prescription (over-the-counter or OTC). Normally these are taken 30 to 60 minutes before traveling to prevent motion sickness symptoms, as well as during extended trips.

Over-the-counter drugs

The following OTC drugs contain ingredients that are considered by the United States Food and Drug Administration (FDA) to be safe and effective for the treatment of motion sickness:

- Marezine (and others) includes the active ingredient cyclizine and is not for use in children under six years of age.

- Benadryl (and others) includes the active ingredient diphenhydramine and is not for use in children under age two without a doctor's permission.

- Dramamine (and others) includes the active ingredient dimenhydrinate and is not for use in children under two years of age.

- Bonine (and others) includes the active ingredient meclizine and is not for use in children under age 12.

The FDA recommends that people with emphysema, chronic **bronchitis**, glaucoma, or difficulty urinating due to an enlarged prostate do not use OTC drugs for motion sickness unless directed by their doctor. Children should not be given OTC motion sickness medication without first checking with a healthcare professional.

Prescription drugs

Longer trips may require a prescription medication called scopolamine available in the form of a skin patch or gel that is rubbed on the skin. Another prescription drug that is sometimes given for motion sickness is ondansetron (Zofran), which was originally developed to treat nausea associated with **cancer chemotherapy**. It appears to be safe for use in children under the age of six. In March 2003, the FDA approved a new anti-emetic (anti-nausea) drug. Known as aprepitant, it is sold under the brand name Emend.

Alternative treatment

Ginger (*Zingiber officinale*) in its various forms is often used to calm the stomach, and the oils it contains (gingerols and shogaols) appear to relax the intestinal tract in addition to mildly depressing the central nervous system. Some of the most effective forms of ginger are the powdered, encapsulated form; ginger tea prepared from sliced ginger root; and candied pieces. All forms of ginger should be taken on an empty stomach.

Placing manual pressure on the Neiguan or Pericardium-6 acupuncture point (located about three finger-widths above the wrist on the inner arm), either by acupuncture, acupressure, or a mild, electrical pulse, has shown to be effective against the symptoms of motion sickness. Elastic wristbands sold at most drugstores are

Motion sickness

also used as a source of relief due to the pressure they place in this area. Pressing the small intestine 17 (just below the earlobes in the indentations behind the jawbone) may also help in the functioning of the ear's balancing mechanism.

There are several homeopathic remedies that work specifically for motion sickness. They include *Cocculus*, *Petroleum*, and *Tabacum*.

Prognosis

Motion sickness is not a serious disorder and almost always resolves once the conflicting motion messages have stopped.

Prevention

Because motion sickness is easier to prevent than treat once it has begun, the best treatment is prevention. The following steps may help deter the unpleasant symptoms of motion sickness before they occur:

- Avoid reading while traveling.
- Ride in a location that allows the eyes to see the same motion that the body and inner ears feel. Safe positions include the front seat of the car (for older children) while looking at distant scenery; the deck of a ship where the horizon can be seen; and sitting by the window of an airplane. The least motion on an airplane is in a seat over the wings.
- Maintain a fairly straight-ahead view.
- Eat a light meal before traveling, or if already nauseated, avoid food altogether.
- Avoid watching or talking to another traveler who is having motion sickness.
- Take motion sickness medicine at least 30 to 60 minutes before travel begins or as recommended by a physician.

Even those who frequently endure motion sickness can learn to travel by anticipating the conditions of their next trip. Research also suggests that increased exposure to the stimulation that causes motion sickness may help decrease symptoms on future trips.

Parental concerns

Parental concerns center primarily on making the child comfortable and anticipating the logistics of traveling with a child who is motion sick. Rarely do children vomit to the point of becoming dehydrated. Prevention and practical steps such as taking something for the child

to vomit into and carrying a change of clothes can ease parents' worries about motion sickness.

Resources

BOOKS

ABBE Research Division Staff. *Air, Sea, and Car Motion Sickness: Index and Analysis of New Knowledge.* Washington, DC: A B B E Publishers Association, 2004.

Motion Sickness: A Medical Dictionary, Bibliography, and An Annotated Research Guide to Internet References. San Diego, CA: Icon Group International, 2004.

Pelletier, Kenneth R. *The Best Alternative Medicine.* New York: Simon and Schuster, 2002.

PERIODICALS

Black, F. O. "Maternal Susceptibility to Nausea and Vomiting of Pregnancy: Is the Vestibular System Involved?" *American Journal of Obstetrics and Gynecology* 185 (May 2002)(Supplement 5): S204–9.

Hoffer, M. E., et al. "Vestibular Testing Abnormalities in Individuals with Motion Sickness." *Otology and Neurotology* 24 (July 2003): 633–6.

O'Brien, C. M., et al. "A Comparison of Cyclizine, Ondansetron, and Placebo as Prophylaxis against Postoperative Nausea and Vomiting in Children." *Anaesthesia* 58 (July 2003): 707–11.

ORGANIZATIONS

Vestibular Disorders Association. PO Box 4467, Portland, OR 97208–4467. Web site: <www.teleport.com/~veda>.

WEB SITES

Hamid, Mohamed, and Nicholas Lorenzo. "Dizziness, Vertigo, and Imbalance." *eMedicine*, October 28, 2004. Available online at <www.emedicine.com/neuro/topic693.htm> (accessed January 12, 2005).

Keim, Samuel, and Michael Kent. "Vomiting and Nausea." *eMedicine*, July 13, 2004. Available online at <www.emedicine.com/aaem/topic476.htm> (accessed January 12, 2005).

Tish Davidson, A.M.
Beth Kapes
Rebecca Frey, PhD

Motor skills, fine *see* **Fine motor skills**

Motor skills, gross *see* **Gross motor skills**

Mouth sores *see* **Stomatitis**

Movement disorders

Definition

Movement disorders are a group of diseases and syndromes affecting the ability to produce and control bodily movements.

Description

It seems simple and effortless, but normal movement requires an astonishingly complex system of control. Disruption of any portion of this system can cause a person to produce movements that are too weak, too forceful, too uncoordinated, or too poorly controlled for the task at hand. Unwanted movements may occur at rest. Intentional movement may become impossible. Such conditions are called movement disorders.

Abnormal movements are symptoms of underlying disorders. In some cases, the abnormal movements are the only symptoms. Childhood disorders or conditions that may cause abnormal movements include:

- **cerebral palsy**
- choreoasthetosis
- encephalopathies
- essential tremor

- inherited ataxias (**Friedreich's ataxia**, Machado-Joseph disease, and spinocerebellar ataxias)
- multiple sclerosis
- parkinsonism and juvenile Parkinson's disease
- **poisoning** by carbon monoxide, cyanide, methanol, or manganese
- psychogenic disorders
- restless legs syndrome
- **spasticity**
- **stroke**
- **Tourette syndrome** and other tic disorders
- Wilson disease

Demographics

The incidence rates and demographics vary for different types of movement disorders. Restless legs syndrome (RLS) affects approximately 12 million people in the United States. The disorder can affect males and females and can begin at any age, although it may become worse as a person gets older. The most common ataxia is Friedreich's ataxia; in the United States, it affects one in 50,000 people, both male and female.

Causes and symptoms

Causes

Movement is produced and coordinated by several interacting brain centers, including the motor cortex, the cerebellum, and a group of structures in the inner portions of the brain called the basal ganglia. Sensory information provides critical input on the current position and velocity of body parts, and spinal nerve cells (neurons) help prevent opposing muscle groups from contracting at the same time.

To understand how movement disorders occur, it is helpful to consider a normal voluntary movement, such as reaching to touch a nearby object with the right index finger. To accomplish the desired movement, the arm must be lifted and extended. The hand must be held out to align with the forearm, and the forefinger must be extended while the other fingers remain flexed.

THE MOTOR CORTEX Voluntary motor commands begin in the motor cortex, located on the outer wrinkled surface of the brain. Movement of the right arm is begun by the left motor cortex, which generates a large volley of signals to the involved muscles. These electrical signals pass along upper motor neurons through the midbrain to the spinal cord. Within the spinal cord, they connect to lower motor neurons, which convey the signals out of the spinal cord to the surface of the muscles involved. Electrical stimulation of the muscles causes contraction, and the force of contraction pulling on the skeleton causes movement of the arm, hand, and fingers.

Damage to or death of any of the neurons along this path causes weakness or paralysis of the affected muscles.

ANTAGONISTIC MUSCLE PAIRS The previous description of movement is too simple, however. One important refinement to it comes from considering the role of opposing, or antagonistic, muscle pairs. Contraction of the biceps muscle, located on the top of the upper arm, pulls on the forearm to flex the elbow and bend the arm. Contraction of the triceps, located on the opposite side, extends the elbow and straightens the arm. Within the spine, these muscles are normally wired so that willed (voluntary) contraction of one is automatically accompanied by blocking of the other. In other words, the command to contract the biceps provokes another command within the spine to prevent contraction of the triceps. In this way, these antagonist muscles are kept from resisting one another. Spinal cord or brain injury can damage this control system and cause involuntary simultaneous contraction and spasticity, an increase in resistance to movement during motion.

THE CEREBELLUM Once the movement of the arm is initiated, sensory information is needed to guide the finger to its precise destination. In addition to sight, the most important source of information comes from the "position sense" provided by the many sensory neurons located within the limbs (proprioception). Proprioception is what allows a person to touch a finger to his or her nose, even with eyes closed. The balance organs in the ears provide important information about posture. Both postural and proprioceptive information are processed by a structure at the rear of the brain called the cerebellum. The cerebellum sends out electrical signals to modify movements as they progress, "sculpting" the barrage of voluntary commands into a tightly controlled, constantly evolving pattern. Cerebellar disorders cause inability to control the force, fine positioning, and speed of movements (ataxia). Disorders of the cerebellum may also impair the ability to judge distance so that a person under- or over-reaches the target (dysmetria). Tremor during voluntary movements can also result from cerebellar damage.

THE BASAL GANGLIA Both the cerebellum and the motor cortex send information to a set of structures deep within the brain that help control involuntary components of movement (basal ganglia). The basal ganglia send output messages to the motor cortex, helping to initiate movements, regulate repetitive or patterned movements, and control muscle tone.

Circuits within the basal ganglia are complex. Within this structure, some groups of cells begin the action of other basal ganglia components and some groups of cells block the action. These complicated feedback circuits are not entirely understood. Disruptions of these circuits are known to cause several distinct movement disorders. A portion of the basal ganglia called the substantia nigra sends electrical signals that block output from another structure called the subthalamic nucleus. The subthalamic nucleus sends signals to the globus pallidus, which in turn blocks the thalamic nuclei. Finally, the thalamic nuclei send signals to the motor cortex. The substantia nigra, then, begins movement and the globus pallidus blocks it. This complicated circuit can be disrupted at several points.

Disruptions in other portions of the basal ganglia are thought to cause **tics**, tremors, dystonia, and a variety of other movement disorders, although the exact mechanisms are not well understood.

Some movement disorders, including Huntington's disease and inherited ataxias, are caused by inherited genetic defects. Some diseases that cause sustained muscle contraction limited to a particular muscle group (focal dystonia) are inherited, but others are caused by trauma. The cause of most cases of Parkinson's disease is unknown, although genes have been found for some familial forms.

Symptoms

Abnormal movements are broadly classified as either hyperkinetic (too much movement) and hypokinetic (too little movement). Hyperkinetic movements include:

- Dystonia—sustained muscle contractions, often causing twisting or repetitive movements and abnormal postures. Dystonia may be limited to one area (focal) or may affect the whole body (general). Focal dystonias may affect the neck (cervical dystonia or torticollis); the face (one-sided or hemifacial spasm, contraction of the eyelid or blepharospasm, contraction of the mouth and jaw or oromandibular dystonia, simultaneous spasm of the chin and eyelid or Meige syndrome); the vocal cords (laryngeal dystonia); or the arms and legs (writer's cramp or occupational cramps). Dystonia may be painful as well as incapacitating.

- Tremor—uncontrollable (involuntary) shaking of a body part. Tremor may occur only when muscles are relaxed or only during an action or while holding an active posture.

- Tics—involuntary, rapid, non-rhythmic movement or sound. Tics can be controlled briefly.
- Myoclonus—a sudden, brief, jerky, shock-like involuntary muscle contraction. Myoclonic jerks may occur singly or repetitively. Unlike tics, myoclonus cannot be controlled even briefly.
- Spasticity—an abnormal increase in muscle tone. It may be associated with involuntary **muscle spasms**, sustained muscle contractions, and exaggerated deep tendon reflexes that make movement difficult or uncontrollable.
- Chorea—rapid, non-rhythmic, uncontrolled jerky movements, most often in the arms and legs. Chorea also may affect the hands, feet, trunk, neck, and face. Choreoathetosis is a syndrome of continuous random movements that usually occur at rest and may appear to be fidgety, dancing, or writhing.
- Ballism—like chorea, but the movements are much larger, more explosive and involve more of the arm or leg. This condition, also called ballismus, can occur on both sides of the body or on one side only (hemiballismus).
- Akathisia—restlessness and a desire to move to relieve uncomfortable sensations. Sensations may include a feeling of crawling, **itching**, stretching, or creeping, usually in the legs.
- Athetosis—slow, writhing, continuous, uncontrollable movement of the arms and legs.

Hypokinetic movements include:

- Bradykinesia—extreme slowness and stiffness of movement.
- Freezing—inability to begin a movement or involuntary stopping of a movement before it is completed.
- Rigidity—an increase in muscle tension when an arm or leg is moved by an outside force.
- Postural instability—loss of the ability to maintain upright posture caused by slow or absent righting reflexes.

Diagnosis

Diagnosis of movement disorders requires a careful medical history and a thorough physical and neurological examination.

The medical history helps the physician evaluate the presence of other conditions or disorders that might contribute to or cause the disorder. Records of previous diagnoses, surgeries, and treatments are reviewed. The child's **family** medical history is evaluated to determine if there is a history of muscular or neurological disorders. Genetic testing is available for some forms of movement disorders.

The physical and neurological exams may include an evaluation of the child's motor reflexes, including muscle tone, mobility, strength, balance, and endurance; heart and lung function; cranial nerve function; and an examination of the child's abdomen, spine, throat, and ears. The child's height, weight, and blood pressure also are checked and recorded. Routine blood and urine analyses are performed.

Brain imaging studies are usually performed. Imaging techniques include **computed tomography** scan (CT scan), positron emission tomography (PET), or **magnetic resonance imaging** (MRI) scans. A lumbar puncture (spinal tap) may be necessary. Video recording of the abnormal movement is often used to analyze movement patterns and track progress of the disorder and its treatment.

Other tests may include **x rays** of the spine and hips or diagnostic blocks with local anesthetics to provide information on the effectiveness of potential treatments.

To aid diagnosis, a multi-disciplinary team may be consulted so the proper treatment can be planned. Occupational and physical therapy evaluations may be helpful to determine upper and lower extremity movement patterns and passive range of motion.

In some cases, nerve conduction studies with electromyography of the affected muscles may be performed to evaluate the child's muscular activity and provide a comprehensive **assessment** of nerve and muscle function.

In both tests, the examiner uses a computer, monitor, amplifier, loudspeaker, stimulator, and high-tech filters to see and hear how the muscles and nerves are responding during the test. In the nerve conduction study, small electrodes are placed on the skin over the muscles to be examined. A stimulator delivers a very small electrical current (that does not cause damage to the body) through the electrodes, causing the nerves to fire. In the electromyogram, a very thin, sterilized needle is inserted into various muscles. The needle is attached by wires to a recording machine. The patient is asked to relax and contract the muscles being examined. The electrical signals produced by the nerves and muscles during these tests are measured and recorded by a computer and displayed as electrical waves on the monitor. The test results are interpreted by a specially trained physician.

An EEG (**electroencephalogram**) may be performed to detect seizures, analyze general brain functioning, and measure brain activity associated with movement or sensation. This test measures the electrical signals from the brain. Surface electrodes attached to the scalp measure voltages in the brain. The electrical activity can be measured while the child is resting or, in some cases, when the child is moving. An evoked potentials study may be part of the EEG test. Evoked potentials record the response of the brain to a sensory, visual, or auditory stimulus.

Treatment

Treatment of a movement disorder begins with a proper diagnostic evaluation. Treatment options include physical and occupational therapies, medications, surgery, or a combination of these treatments.

The goals of treatment are to increase the child's comfort, decrease **pain**, ease mobility, help with activities of daily living such as hygiene, ease rehabilitation procedures, and prevent or decrease the risk of developing a joint contracture. The type of treatment recommended will depend upon the severity of the disorder; the child's overall health; the potential benefits, limitations, and side effects of the treatment; and the impact of the treatment on the child's quality of life.

Clinicians should work with the child and parents or caregivers to develop an individual treatment plan. Specific treatment goals will vary from one person to the next. Treatment should be provided by a movement disorders specialist or specially trained pediatric neurologist and a multi-disciplinary team of specialists that may include a physiatrist, physical therapist, occupational therapist, gait and movement specialists, social worker, and surgical specialists as applicable, such as a pediatric orthopedic surgeon or pediatric neurosurgeon.

In some cases, treatment is not recommended or desired, because it would actually interfere with the patient's current mobility and it would not improve function. For example, some people with multiple sclerosis who experience significant leg weakness find that spasticity makes their legs more rigid, helping them to stand, transfer to a chair or bed, or walk.

Physical and occupational therapies

Physical therapy includes stretching exercises, muscle group strengthening exercises, and range of motion exercises to prevent muscles from shortening (contracture), preserve flexibility and range of motion, and reduce the severity of symptoms. Exercises should be practiced daily, as recommended by the physical therapist. Prolonged stretching can lengthen muscles, and strengthening exercises can restore the proper strength to affected muscles. Aquatic therapy also may be recommended, since there is less stress on the body when in the water.

A physical therapist can instruct the patient on proper posture guidelines. Proper posture is critical, especially while sitting and sleeping, to maintain proper alignment of the hips and back. Balancing rest and **exercise** is also important.

Occupational therapy may include splints, casts, or braces on the affected arm or leg to enable proper limb positioning, and maintain flexibility and range of motion. The therapy may include training for proper limb positioning while seated in a wheelchair or lying in bed.

Physical and occupational therapists can provide guidelines on how to adapt the child's environment to ensure **safety** and comfort.

Medications

Medications can help compensate for some imbalances of the basal ganglionic circuit. Drugs to treat movement disorders include oral medications, injected medications, and continuous delivery medications. These medications work by preventing nerves from signaling the muscles to contract, thereby preventing muscle contractions.

If treatment with a single medicine fails to effectively treat the disorder, a different medicine may be tried or an additional medicine may be prescribed. The most important medication guidelines are to ensure that the child takes the medication exactly as prescribed, and to never discontinue any medication without first talking to the child's doctor, even if the medication does not seem to be working or is causing unwanted side effects.

ORAL MEDICATIONS Baclofen (Lioresal) is a muscle relaxant that works on nerves in the spinal cord to reduce spasticity. The benefits of baclofen include decreased stretch reflexes, improved passive range of motion, and reduced muscle spasms, pain, and tightness. Side effects include drowsiness and sedation, as well as weakness, decreased muscle tone, confusion, fatigue, **nausea**, and **dizziness**. Baclofen should not be taken with central nervous system depressants or alcohol.

Levodopa (L-dopa) is a medication that is converted to dopamine in the brain. Dopamine is a chemical that aids in the transmission of nerve signals. Sinemet is a combination medication containing levodopa and carbidopa. Carbidopa enables L-dopa to be converted to dopamine after the L-dopa enters the brain, thereby lowering the oral dose and decreasing side effects. Side effects include nausea, **diarrhea**, and low blood pressure.

Anticholinergics, including trihexyphenidyl (Artane) and benztropine (Benztrop MES, Cogentin), block acetylcholine receptors in the brain. Acetylcholine receptors are integral proteins that respond to the neurotransmitter acetylcholine by opening a pathway in the membrane for ion diffusion across the cell membrane. Side effects include dry mouth, blurred vision, **constipation**, urinary retention, and rapid heart rate. These side effects are usually much less frequent in children than adults; therefore, much higher doses are usually prescribed in children.

Benzodiazepines, such as diazepam (Valium), clonazepam (Klonopin, Rivotril), and lorazepam (Ativan) act on the central nervous system to improve passive range of motion, reduce muscle overactivity and painful spasms, and provide overall relaxation. These medications are often taken at night because they cause drowsiness, but they also can relieve muscle spasms that interrupt **sleep**. Side effects include unsteadiness, loss of strength, low blood pressure, gastrointestinal symptoms, memory problems, confusion, and behavioral problems.

Dantrolene sodium (Dantrium) acts on the muscles to directly interfere with the chemistry of the muscle contraction. It is generally used when other medications are not effective. Benefits may include improved passive movement, decreased muscle tone, and reduced muscle spasms, tightness, and pain. Side effects include generalized weakness—including weakness of the respiratory muscles—as well as drowsiness, fatigue, diarrhea, and sensitivity to the sun. Liver problems may occur with this medication, and frequent lab tests are performed to evaluate liver function.

Tizanidine (Zanaflex) acts on the central nervous system. It does not usually cause reduced muscle strength. The most common side effect is sedation, and other side effects include low blood pressure, dry mouth, dizziness, and hallucinations. Liver problems may occur with this medication, and frequent lab tests are performed to evaluate liver function.

A variety of other medications may be used to treat movement disorders, including antiepileptic drugs that stimulate GABA receptors in the brain's basal ganglia; neuroleptics that block dopamine D2-like receptors; Clonidine (Catapres) and selective serotonin reuptake inhibitors (SSRIs, such as fluoxetine, commonly known as Prozac) for the treatment of tics; and channel modulators that affect the behavior of channels that transport small molecules such as potassium, sodium, or calcium across cell membranes.

INJECTED MEDICATIONS Botulinum-toxin type A (Botox, Dysport) or type B (Myobloc) is injected locally into the affected muscle group to relax the muscles in dystonia or spasticity. It works by preventing nerves from sending signals to the muscles that cause them to contract. Although the treatment takes one to two weeks to reach its full effectiveness, the beneficial effects last three to four months. Botulinum-toxin allows more normal limb positioning and improved mobility. In some patients, the injections also decrease pain. Injections may be used to make casting easier, ease the adjustment of a new brace, or delay surgery.

Botulinum-toxin is made by the bacteria that cause **botulism**. However, the amount of botulinum-toxin injected to treat spasticity is such a small amount that it would not cause botulism poisoning. This treatment is very safe, and the injections can be given in a doctor's office without the use of sedation or anesthesia. Injections can be repeated, but should be spaced from three to six months apart to avoid exceeding the recommended dose. Botulinum-toxin injections may be used in combination with other treatments.

Botulinum-toxin injections are typically expensive and may not be covered by insurance. A Reimbursement Hotline established by Allergan, the manufacturer of Botox, is a resource for reimbursement questions: (800) 530-6680 or online at <www.botox.com>. Elan, the manufacturer of Myobloc, also has resources available to answer questions about reimbursement. Interested persons may call (888) 461-2255 or go online at <www.elan.com>.

Alcohol and phenol are injected in combination, but are less common treatments. The medications are injected directly onto nerves that supply spastic muscles to destroy them. The injections cut off the signals to those muscles, allowing them to relax. This treatment may be used to treat spasticity in larger muscle groups closer to the trunk, such as the thigh muscles. Although this treatment is generally less expensive than botulinum-toxin injections, there are more serious side effects.

Short-term medications such as lidocaine, a local anesthetic, can be used to assess the potential benefit of botulinum-toxin or alcohol and phenol injections.

CONTINUOUS DELIVERY MEDICATIONS Baclofen usually is taken as an oral medication but also can be delivered directly into the spinal fluid when the oral medication does not effectively control symptoms. An intrathecal baclofen delivery system, surgically placed by a neurosurgeon, continuously releases prescribed amounts of baclofen in small doses directly into the spinal fluid via a small catheter and pump. This type of delivery system causes fewer and less severe side effects than the oral baclofen.

Pump refills and medication adjustments are generally made once every two to three months after the initial dosage is established. The pump system lasts from three to five years, at which time it needs to be replaced.

Surgery

Surgery is only recommended when all other treatments have been tried and have not effectively controlled the child's symptoms.

Selective dorsal rhizotomy surgery, also called selective posterior rhizotomy, involves a surgical resection of part of the spinal nerve. By cutting the sensory nerve rootlets that cause the spasticity, muscle stiffness is decreased while other functions are maintained. Potential benefits of this surgical procedure include pain relief, reduced spasticity to improve walking or aid sitting in a wheelchair, increased ability to bend at the waist, and improved use of the hands. Sometimes rhizotomy results in improved breathing and better control of the arms, legs, and head.

Thalamotomy is a surgical procedure used to destroy part of the thalamus, which is thought to produce abnormal brain activity that causes tremor. Pallidotomy is a surgical procedure used to destroy part of the globus pallidus, which is thought to become overactive with certain disorders, such as Parkinson's disease. Although effective, these surgeries have significant risks, including paralysis, loss of vision, or loss of speech if the precise location of the brain is not targeted during surgery. With the advent of a less invasive approach called deep brain stimulation, these surgeries have become less common.

Deep brain stimulation (DBS) is a way to inactivate the parts of the brain thought to cause overactivity or tremor in certain muscles, without destroying a part of the brain. It is currently a treatment option for adult patients with Parkinson's disease, but research is underway to determine if the procedure can benefit children with movement disorders.

During the DBS procedure, an electrode placed in a precise area of the brain delivers small, electrical shocks to interrupt the abnormal brain activity that leads to symptoms. The electrode has four metal contacts that can be used in different combinations. A few patients may have stimulators implanted on both sides of the brain, but this increases the risk for complications. The electrode is connected by a wire to a pacemaker-like device implanted under the skin in the chest. This device generates the electrical shocks. The electrical stimulation can be adjusted as the patient's condition progresses over time, and the stimulator can be turned off in the event that other beneficial therapies, such as brain cell transplantation, are performed.

Orthopedic surgery may be performed to correct a contracture. During contracture release surgery, the tendon of a contractured muscle is cut, the joint repositioned to a more normal angle, and a cast is applied. Regrowth of the tendon to this new length occurs over several weeks following surgery. After the cast is removed, physical therapy can help strengthen the muscles and improve range of motion. This procedure is most commonly performed on the Achilles tendon but may also be performed on the knees, hips, shoulders, elbows, and wrists. Tendon transfer surgery is another technique to treat contractures. During this procedure, the tendon attached to a spastic muscle is cut and transferred to a different site, preventing the muscle from being pulled into an abnormal position. The disadvantages of these orthopedic procedures are that they are irreversible and they may need to be repeated.

Other orthopedic surgeries that may accompany contracture release surgery include osteotomy, in which a small wedge is removed from a bone to allow repositioning. A cast is applied while the bone heals in a more natural position. Osteotomy is more commonly performed on the bones in the hips or feet. Arthrodesis is a fusing of bones that normally move independently, to limit the ability of a spastic muscle to pull the joint into an abnormal position. Arthrodesis is more commonly performed on the bones in the ankle.

Other treatments

Transplantation of fetal cells into the basal ganglia has produced mixed results in Parkinson's disease and is being researched for application in other movement disorders.

Brief application (about 10 minutes) of cold packs to spastic muscles may help ease pain and improve function for a short period of time.

Electrical stimulation may be used to stimulate a weak muscle to counteract the action of a stronger, spastic muscle.

Alternative treatment

Alternative and complementary therapies include approaches that are considered to be outside the mainstream of traditional health care. Among the therapies that may be helpful are acupuncture, homeopathy, touch therapies, postural alignment therapies, and biofeedback.

The progress made will depend on the individual and his or her condition.

Biofeedback training may be used to teach the patient how to consciously reduce muscle tension. Biofeedback uses an electrical signal that indicates when a spastic muscle relaxes. The patient may be able to use biofeedback to learn how to consciously reduce muscle tension and possibly reduce symptoms.

Coenzyme Q10 supplements may be beneficial, as some people with movement disorders may have low levels of this substance. Coenzyme Q10 is a natural substance produced by the body that transports electrons during cellular respiration, or the process in which cells get their energy from oxygen.

Initial trials of cannabinoids, the active ingredient in marijuana, have shown promise in the treatment of muscle stiffness and limb straightening associated with multiple sclerosis. Further research is needed to determine the beneficial effects of marijuana-derived substances on neuromuscular symptoms associated with movement disorders. Researchers caution that smoking marijuana is dangerous, especially since there may be other harmful substances mixed in with the illegal drug.

Before learning or practicing any particular technique, it is important for the parent or caregiver and child to learn about the therapy, its safety and effectiveness, potential side effects, and the expertise and qualifications of the practitioner. Although some practices are beneficial, others may be harmful to certain patients. Alternative therapies should not be used as a substitute for medical therapies prescribed by a doctor. Parents should discuss these alternative treatments with the child's doctor to determine the techniques and remedies that may be beneficial for the child.

Nutritional concerns

Dietary guidelines are individualized, based on the child's age, diagnosis, overall health, severity of disability, and level of functioning. Specific nutritional problems, such as swallowing or feeding difficulties, may be a concern in some patients and should be managed by a team of specialists, including a speech therapist. Early identification, treatment, and correction of specific feeding problems will improve the health and nutritional status of the patient.

A well-balanced and carefully planned diet will help maintain general good health for people with movement disorders. Specialists recommend that people with multiple sclerosis and other movement disorders adhere to the same low-fat, high fiber diet that is recommended for the general population. A diet rich in fresh fruits and vegeta-

bles will ensure adequate intake of antioxidants, substances that help protect against free radical damage.

Children with movement disorders may have different energy needs, depending on their condition. One study indicated that ambulatory and non-ambulatory adolescents with cerebral palsy had decreased energy needs compared with a control group of normal adolescents. Therefore, a child's specific calorie needs should be evaluated by a registered dietitian who can work with the parents to develop an individualized meal plan. The child's weight should be obtained once a week or at least once a month to determine if caloric intake is adequate.

A child's self-feeding skills can impact his or her health outcome. One study indicated that 90 percent of children with good to fair motor and feeding skills reached adulthood. In contrast, a lack of self-feeding skills was associated with a six-fold increase in mortality (rate of death).

Maintaining a healthy weight is important to prevent the development of chronic diseases such as diabetes, high blood pressure (**hypertension**), and heart disease.

Tube feedings may be required in some patients with **failure to thrive**, aspiration **pneumonia**, difficulty swallowing, or an inability to ingest adequate calories orally to maintain nutritional status or promote growth.

Prognosis

The prognosis for a patient with a movement disorder depends on the specific disorder. There is no cure for movement disorders. However, they can be well-managed with the proper combination of physical and occupational therapies, medication, and surgery. The long-term outlook depends on the severity of the disorder.

Prevention

Prevention depends on the specific disorder.

Parental concerns

Parents should work closely with the child's therapists and doctors to create an effective treatment plan. It is important for parents to communicate their treatment goals with the health care team. Parents should take an active role in the child's exercise program and help the child practice the exercises, as prescribed, every day.

There are many tips to make the home and school environments safer for a child with a movement disorder. An occupational therapist can work with parents to assess the home environment and provide resources for

KEY TERMS

Active motion—Spontaneous; produced by active efforts. Active range of motion exercises are those that are performed by the patient without assistance.

Activities of daily living (ADL)—The activities performed during the course of a normal day, for example, eating, bathing, dressing, toileting, etc.

Acupuncture—Based on the same traditional Chinese medical foundation as acupressure, acupuncture uses sterile needles inserted at specific points to treat certain conditions or relieve pain.

Anoxia—Lack of oxygen.

Ataxia—A condition marked by impaired muscular coordination, most frequently resulting from disorders in the brain or spinal cord.

Autonomic nervous system—The part of the nervous system that controls so-called involuntary functions, such as heart rate, salivary gland secretion, respiratory function, and pupil dilation.

Biofeedback—A training technique that enables an individual to gain some element of control over involuntary or automatic body functions.

Botulinum toxin—A potent bacterial toxin or poison made by *Clostridium botulinum*; causes paralysis in high doses, but is used medically in small, localized doses to treat disorders associated with involuntary muscle contraction and spasms, in addition to strabismus. Commonly known as Botox.

Bradykinesia—Extremely slow movement.

Central nervous system—Part of the nervous system consisting of the brain, cranial nerves, and spinal cord. The brain is the center of higher processes, such as thought and emotion and is responsible for the coordination and control of bodily activities and the interpretation of information from the senses. The cranial nerves and spinal cord link the brain to the peripheral nervous system, that is the nerves present in the rest of body.

Cerebral palsy—A nonprogressive movement disability caused by abnormal development of or damage to motor control centers of the brain.

Chorea—Involuntary movements in which the arms or legs may jerk or flail uncontrollably.

Choreoathetosis—Involuntary rapid, irregular, jerky movements or slow, writhing movements that flow into one another.

Clonic—Referring to clonus, a series of muscle contractions and partial relaxations that alternate in some nervous diseases in the form of convulsive spasms.

Computed tomography (CT)—An imaging technique in which cross-sectional x rays of the body are compiled to create a three-dimensional image of the body's internal structures; also called computed axial tomography.

Contraction—A tightening of the uterus during pregnancy. Contractions may or may not be painful and may or may not indicate labor.

Contracture—A tightening or shortening of muscles that prevents normal movement of the associated limb or other body part.

Encephalopathy—Any abnormality in the structure or function of brain tissues.

Essential tremor—An uncontrollable (involuntary) shaking of the hands, head, and face. Also called familial tremor because it is sometimes inherited, it can begin in the teens or in middle age. The exact cause is not known.

Fasciculations—Small involuntary muscle contractions visible under the skin.

Fetal tissue transplantation—A method of treating Parkinson's and other neurological diseases by grafting brain cells from human fetuses onto the basal ganglia. Human adults cannot grow new brain cells but developing fetuses can. Grafting fetal tissue stimulates the growth of new brain cells in affected adult brains.

General anesthesia—Deep sleep induced by a combination of medicines that allows surgery to be performed.

Hereditary ataxia—One of a group of hereditary degenerative diseases of the spinal cord or cerebellum. These diseases cause tremor, spasm, and wasting of muscle.

Homeopathy—A holistic system of treatment developed in the eighteenth century. It is based on the idea that substances that produce symptoms of sickness in healthy people will have a curative effect when given in very dilute quantities to sick people who exhibit those same symptoms. Homeopathic remedies are believed to stimulate the body's own healing processes.

Huntington's disease—A rare hereditary disease that causes progressive chorea (jerky muscle movements) and mental deterioration that ends in dementia. Huntington's symptoms usually appear in patients in their 40s. Also called Huntington's chorea.

Hyperactive reflexes—Reflexes that persist too long and may be too strong. For example, a hyperactive grasp reflex may cause the hand to stay clenched in a tight fist.

Hypermobility—Unusual flexibility of the joints, allowing them to be bent or moved beyond their normal range of motion.

Hypertonia—Having excessive muscular tone or strength.

Levodopa (L-dopa)—A substance used in the treatment of Parkinson's disease. Levodopa can cross the blood-brain barrier that protects the brain. Once in the brain, it is converted to dopamine and thus can replace the dopamine lost in Parkinson's disease.

Local anesthesia—Pain-relieving medication used to numb an area while the patient remains awake. Also see general anesthesia.

Magnetic resonance imaging (MRI)—An imaging technique that uses a large circular magnet and radio waves to generate signals from atoms in the body. These signals are used to construct detailed images of internal body structures and organs, including the brain.

Mask—An expressionless look, caused by reduced movements of the face.

Motor neuron—A nerve cell that specifically controls and stimulates voluntary muscles.

Multiple sclerosis—A progressive, autoimmune disease of the central nervous system characterized by damage to the myelin sheath that covers nerves. The disease, which causes progressive paralysis, is marked by periods of exacerbation and remission.

Muscle spasm—Localized muscle contraction that occurs when the brain signals the muscle to contract.

Myoclonus—Involuntary contractions of a muscle or an interrelated group of muscles. Also known as myoclonic seizures.

Neurologist—A doctor who specializes in disorders of the nervous system, including the brain, spinal cord, and nerves.

Neurosurgeon—Physician who performs surgery on the nervous system.

Nocturnal leg cramps—Cramps that may be related to exertion and awaken a person during sleep.

Occupational therapist—A healthcare provider who specializes in adapting the physical environment to meet a patient's needs. An occupational therapist also assists patients and caregivers with activities of daily living and provide instructions on wheelchair use or other adaptive equipment.

Orthopedist—A doctor specializing in treatment of the musculoskeletal system.

Parkinsonism—A set of symptoms originally associated with Parkinson disease that can occur as side effects of neuroleptic medications. The symptoms include trembling of the fingers or hands, a shuffling gait, and tight or rigid muscles.

Parkinson's disease—A slowly progressive disease that destroys nerve cells in the basal ganglia and thus causes loss of dopamine, a chemical that aids in transmission of nerve signals (neurotransmitter). Parkinson's is characterized by shaking in resting muscles, a stooping posture, slurred speech, muscular stiffness, and weakness.

Passive movement—Movement that occurs under the power of an outside source such as a clinician. There is no voluntary muscular contraction by the individual who is being passively moved.

Periodic limb movement disorder—A disorder characterized by involuntary flexion of leg muscles, causing twitching and leg extension or kicking during sleep.

Peripheral nerves—Nerves outside the brain and spinal cord that provide the link between the body and the central nervous system.

Physiatrist—A physician who specializes in physical medicine and rehabilitation.

Physical therapist—A healthcare provider who teaches patients how to perform therapeutic exercises to maintain maximum mobility and range of motion.

Positron emission tomography (PET)—A computerized diagnostic technique that uses radioactive substances to examine structures of the body. When used to assess the brain, it produces a three-dimensional image that shows anatomy and function, including such information as blood flow, oxygen consumption, glucose metabolism, and concentrations of various molecules in brain tissue.

Progressive supranuclear palsy—A rare disease that gradually destroys nerve cells in the parts of the brain that control eye movements, breathing, and muscle coordination. The loss of nerve cells causes palsy, or paralysis, that slowly gets worse as the disease progresses. The palsy affects ability to move the eyes, relax the muscles, and control balance. Also called Steele-Richardson-Olszewski syndrome.

KEY TERMS (contd.)

Psychogenic disorders—A variety of unusual, involuntary movements that occur in children with psychiatric disorders or in response to anxiety, stress, depression, anger, or grief. Psychogenic movements are thought to represent the physical expression of an intolerable mental conflict.

Range of motion (ROM)—The range of motion of a joint from full extension to full flexion (bending) measured in degrees like a circle.

Restless legs syndrome (RLS)—A disorder in which the patient experiences crawling, aching, or other disagreeable sensations in the calves that can be relieved by movement. RLS is a frequent cause of difficulty falling asleep at night.

Rigidity—A constant resistance to passive motion.

Scissoring—Involuntary crossing of the legs.

Spinal cord injury—Injury to the spinal cord, via blunt or penetrating trauma.

Stroke—Interruption of blood flow to a part of the brain with consequent brain damage. A stroke may be caused by a blood clot or by hemorrhage due to a burst blood vessel. Also known as a cerebrovascular accident.

Tourette syndrome—A neurological disorder characterized by multiple involuntary movements and uncontrollable vocalizations called tics that come and go over years, usually beginning in childhood and becoming chronic. Sometimes the tics include inappropriate or obscene language (coprolalia).

Wilson disease—A rare, inherited disorder that causes excess copper to accumulate in the body. Steadily increasing amounts of copper circulating in the blood are deposited primarily in the brain, liver, kidneys, and the cornea of the eyes. It can cause psychiatric symptoms resembling schizophrenia.

adaptive equipment that may be helpful. Some of these tips include:

- All throw rugs should be removed unless they are firmly attached to the floor.

- There must be proper lighting. Nightlights should be placed along key pathways of the home.

- The top and bottom of stairs should be highlighted with a contrasting color or texture to distinguish them.

- The floor should be free of clutter, to prevent tripping or falling.

- Handrails should be installed, especially along stairways and in the bathroom.

- All electrical cords and other cords should be kept out of the way.

Raising a child with a movement disorder can be challenging. Support groups are available to provide information and assistance.

See also Tics; Tourette syndrome.

Resources

BOOKS

Jankovic, Joseph J., and Eduardo Tolosa. "A Guide to Movement Disorders." In *Parkinson's Disease and Movement Disorders.* 4th ed. Philadelphia: Lippincott, Williams, and Wilkins, 2002: 704.

Martini, Frederic. *Fundamentals of Anatomy and Physiology.* Englewood Cliffs, NJ: Prentice Hall, 1989.

Watts, Ray L., and William C. Koller, eds. *Movement Disorders: Neurologic Principles and Practice.* New York: McGraw-Hill, 1997.

PERIODICALS

"Position of the American Dietetic Association: Providing Nutrition Services for Infants, Children and Adults with Developmental Disabilities and Special Health Care Needs." *Journal of the American Dietetic Association* 104, no. 1 (2004): 97–107.

"Task Force on Childhood Motor Disorders Consensus Report of a Meeting at the National Institutes of Health." (2001): April 22–24. <www.ninds.nih.gov>

ORGANIZATIONS

Brain Injury Association of America. 8201 Greensboro Dr., Ste. 611, McLean, VA 22102. (800) 444-6443 or (703) 761-0750. Web site: &;lt;http://www.biausa.org>.

Movement Disorders Society. 555 East Wells St., Suite 1100, Milwaukee, WI 53202-3823. (414) 276-2145. Web site: <www.movementdisorders.org>.

National Center on Birth Defects and Developmental Disabilities. Centers for Disease Control. 4770 Buford Highway., NE, Ste. F-35, Atlanta, GA 30341. (770) 488-7080. Web site: <http://cdc.gov/ncbddd/dh>.

National Institute on Disability and Rehabilitation Research. Office of Special Education and Rehabilitative Services. U.S. Department of Education, 400 Maryland Ave., SW,

Washington, DC 20202-7100. (202) 245-7640. Web site: <www.ed.gov/about/offices/list/osers/nidrr>.

National Institute of Neurological Disorders and Stroke (NINDS). National Institutes of Health. P.O. Box 5801, Bethesda, MD 20824. (800) 352-9424 or (301) 496-5751. Web site: <www.ninds.nih.gov/about_ninds/>.

National Rehabilitation Information Center (NARIC). 4200 Forbes Blvd., Ste. 202, Lanham, MD 20700. (800) 346-2742 or (301) 459-5900. Web site: <www.naric.com>.

National Spinal Cord Injury Association. 6701 Democracy Blvd., #300-9, Bethesda, MD 20817. (800) 962-9629 or (301) 214-4006. info@spinalcord.org. Web site: <www.spinalcord.org>.

WE MOVE (Worldwide Education and Awareness for Movement Disorders). 204 W. 84th St. New York, NY 10024. (800) 437-MOVE. Web site: <www.wemove.org>.

WEB SITES

Spinal Cord Injury Information Network. Available online at: <www.spinalcord.uab.edu>.

Richard Robinson
Angela M. Costello

MRI *see* **Magnetic resonance imaging**

Mucopolysaccharidoses

Definition

Mucopolysaccharidosis (MPS) is a general term for many different related inherited disorders that are caused by the accumulation of mucopolysaccharides in body tissues. This accumulation interferes with the individual's development.

Description

Mucopolysaccharides are long chains of sugar molecules that are essential for building the bones, cartilage, skin, tendons, and other tissues in the body. Another name for mucopolysaccharides is glycosaminoglycans (GAGs). Normally, the human body continuously breaks down and rebuilds cells that contain GAGs. There are many different types of GAGs, and different GAGs are unable to be broken down in each of the MPS conditions. Several enzymes are involved in breaking down each GAG, and a deficiency or absence of any of the essential enzymes can cause the GAG not to be broken down completely. This condition results in the accumulation of GAGs in the tis-

sues and organs in the body. The accumulating GAGs are stored in cellular structures called lysosomes, and these disorders are known as lysosomal storage diseases. When too many GAGs accumulate, organs and tissues become damaged or do not function properly.

Before specific deficient enzymes were identified, MPS disorders were diagnosed by the signs and symptoms seen in an individual. The discovery of individual enzyme deficits resulted in a reclassification of some of the MPS disorders. Types of MPS disorders are MPS I, MPS II, MPS III, MPS IV, MPS VI, MPS VII, and MPS IX. However, these conditions are also referred to by their original names, which are Hurler, Hurler-Scheie, Scheie (all MPS I), Hunter (MPS II), Sanfilippo (all MPS III), Morquio (all MPS IV), Maroteaux-Lamy (MPS VI), Sly (MPS VII), and Hyaluronidase deficiency (MPS IX).

Demographics

MPS disorders are rare, and the frequency with which they occur varies depending on the type of the disorder. For all MPS types combined, the disorder occurs in only about one of every 25,000 people. Except for MPS II, individuals of both genders are affected equally. Because of its inheritance pattern, MPS II is found only in males. All MPS disorders are present at birth, although symptoms appear at different times, depending on the type of disorder. There appears to be no race or ethnic component in the distribution of MPS disorders.

Causes and symptoms

All MPS disorder except MPS II are inherited in an autosomal recessive manner. An individual with an autosomal recessive disorder inherits one non-working genes from each parent. The parents are called carriers of the disorder. If the parent has one good copy of the gene and one defective copy, the parent will not have MPS and may be unaware that he or she has a defective gene. MPS only occurs when both of an individual's genes that produce the same enzyme contain a mutation or defect, causing them not to function properly. As a result, either no enzyme is produced, or the amount produced is inadequate. When two people are carriers for an autosomal recessive disorder, they have a 25 percent chance with each pregnancy to have a child with the disorder. Some individuals who have MPS are able to have children. Children of MPS parents are all carriers of the disorder, because they inherit one bad copy of the gene from the affected parent. However, these children are not at risk to develop the disorder unless the other parent is a carrier or affected with the same autosomal recessive condition.

Unlike the other MPS conditions, MPS II is inherited in an X-linked recessive manner, which means that the gene causing the condition is located on the X chromosome, one of the two sex chromosomes. A male child inherits an X chromosome from his mother and a Y chromosome from his father. He will have the disorder if the X chromosome inherited from his mother carries the defective gene, since he has only one (nonfunctioning) copy of the gene. Females inherit one X chromosome from their mother and a second X chromosome from their father. Because they have two X chromosomes, they are carriers of the disorder if one of their X chromosomes has the gene that causes the condition, while the other X chromosome does not.

Although MPS are all inherited disorders, each type is caused by a deficiency of one particular enzyme involved in breaking down GAGs. The accumulation of the GAGs in the tissues and organs in the body causes the symptoms characteristic of the MPS disorders. Symptoms and their time of onset vary widely depending on which form of the disorder the individual inherits.

MPS I

MPS I is caused by a deficiency of the enzyme alpha-L-iduronidase. Three conditions, Hurler, Hurler-Scheie, and Scheie syndromes, are caused by a deficiency of this enzyme. Initially, these three conditions were believed to be separate, because each was associated with different physical symptoms and prognoses. However, once the underlying cause of these conditions was identified, it was realized that these three conditions are variants of the same disorder.

MPS I H (Hurler syndrome)

About one child in 100,000 is born with Hurler syndrome. This tends to be the most severe form of MPS I. Symptoms of Hurler syndrome are often evident within the first year or two after birth. Often these infants initially grow faster than expected, but then reach a point where they begin to lose the skills that they have learned. Their growth slows and typically stops by age three.

Facial features begin to coarsen. These children develop a short nose, flatter face, thicker skin, and a protruding tongue. Their heads become larger, and they develop more hair on their bodies, with the hair becoming coarser. Their bones are also affected, and they usually develop joint contractures (stiff joints), kyphosis (a specific type of curve to the spine), and broad hands with short fingers. Many of these children have breathing difficulties, and respiratory infections are common. Other common problems include heart valve dysfunction, thickening of the heart muscle (cardiomyopathy),

enlarged spleen and liver, clouding of the cornea, hearing loss, and carpal tunnel syndrome. These children typically do not live past age 12.

MPS I H/S (Hurler-Scheie syndrome)

Hurler-Scheie syndrome an intermediate form of MPS I, meaning that the symptoms are not as severe as those in individuals who have MPS I H but not as mild as those in MPS I S. Approximately one baby in 115,000 is born with Hurler-Scheie syndrome. These individuals tend to be shorter than expected. They can have normal **intelligence**; however, some individuals with MPS I H/S experience learning difficulties. These individuals may develop some of the same physical features as those with Hurler syndrome, but usually they are not as severe. The prognosis for children with MPS I H/S is variable with some individuals dying during childhood, while others live to adulthood.

MPS I S (Scheie syndrome)

Scheie syndrome is the mild form of MPS I. About one baby in 500,000 is born with Scheie syndrome. Individuals with MPS I S usually have normal intelligence, although there have been some reports of individuals with MPS I S developing psychiatric problems. Common physical problems include corneal clouding, heart abnormalities, and orthopedic difficulties involving their hands and back. Individuals with MPS I S do not develop the facial features seen with MPS I H and usually these individuals have a normal life span.

MPS II (Hunter syndrome)

Hunter syndrome is caused by a deficiency of the enzyme iduronate-2-sulphatase. All individuals with Hunter syndrome are male, because the gene that causes the condition is located on their single X chromosome. Like many MPS conditions, Hunter syndrome is divided into two forms, mild and severe. About one in 110,000 males are born with Hunter syndrome, with the severe form being three times more common than the mild form.

The severe form of MPS II is associated with progressive **mental retardation** and physical disability, with most individuals dying before age 15. In the milder form, most of these individuals live to adulthood and have normal intelligence or only mild mental impairments. Males with the mild form of Hunter syndrome develop physical differences similar to the males with the severe form, but not as quickly. Males with mild Hunter syndrome can have a normal life span and some have had children. Most males with Hunter syndrome develop joint stiffness, chronic **diarrhea**, enlarged liver and spleen, heart valve problems, hearing loss, and kyphosis. They also tend to be shorter than expected. These symptoms progress at different rates depending on whether the individual has the mild or severe form of MPS II.

MPS III (Sanfilippo syndrome)

MPS III, like the other MPS conditions, was initially diagnosed by the individual having certain physical signs and symptoms. It was later discovered that the physical symptoms associated with Sanfilippo syndrome could be caused by a deficiency in one of four enzymes. MPS III is in the early 2000s subdivided into four groups, labeled A through D, based on the specific enzyme that is deficient. All four of these enzymes are involved in breaking down the same GAG, heparan sulfate. Heparan sulfate is mainly found in the central nervous system and accumulates in the brain when it cannot be broken down because one of those four enzymes is deficient or missing.

MPS III is a variable condition, with symptoms beginning to appear between two and six years of age. Because of the accumulation of heparan sulfate in the central nervous system (CNS), the CNS is severely affected. In MPS III, signs that the CNS is degenerating usually become evident between six and ten years of age. Many children with MPS III develop seizures, sleeplessness, thicker skin, joint contractures, enlarged tongues, cardiomyopathy, behavior problems, and mental retardation. The life expectancy in MPS III is also variable. On average, individuals with MPS III live until they are teenagers, with some living longer and others not that long.

MPS IIIA (Sanfilippo syndrome type A) is caused by a deficiency of the enzyme heparan N-sulfatase. Type IIIA is the most severe of the four types of MPS III. Symptoms appear and death occurs at an earlier age than in other subtypes. A study in British Columbia estimated that one in every 325,000 babies is born with MPS IIIA. MPS IIIA is the most common of the four types in Northwestern Europe. The gene that causes MPS IIIA is located on the long arm of chromosome 17.

MPS IIIB(Sanfilippo syndrome type B) is due to a deficiency in N-acetyl-alpha-D-glucosaminidase (NAG). This type of MPS III is not as severe as type IIIA, and the characteristic signs and symptoms vary. Type IIIB is the most common of the type III disorders in southeastern Europe. The gene associated with MPS IIIB is also located on the long arm of chromosome 17.

MPS IIIC (Sanfilippo syndrome type C) is caused by a deficiency in the enzyme acetyl-CoA-alpha-glucosaminide acetyltransferase. This is a rare form of MPS

III. The gene involved in MPS IIIC is believed to be located on chromosome 14.

MPS IIID (Sanfilippo syndrome type D) is caused by a deficiency in the enzyme N-acetylglucosamine-6-sulfatase. This form of MPS III is also rare. The gene involved in MPS IIID is located on the long arm of chromosome 12.

MPS IV A (Morquio syndrome type A)

MPS IV A is the severe form of the disorder and is caused by a deficiency in the enzyme galactosamine-6-sulphatase. The gene involved with MPS IV A is located on the long arm of chromosome 16. The major organs affected by MPS IV are the cornea and the cartilage, particularly the cartilage of the neck. Bowel and bladder function also can be impaired. Respiratory problems and **sleep** apnea are common. Individuals with MPS IV appear healthy at birth but show skeletal deformities and growth retardation by age three. Death often occurs early in individuals with the severe form of this disorder.

MPS IV B (Morquio syndrome type B) is the milder form of the disorder. The enzyme, beta-galactosidase, is deficient in MPS IV B. The gene that produces beta-galactosidase is located on the short arm of chromosome 3. Individuals with the MPS IV B can have normal lifespans (into their 70s).

MPS VI (Maroteaux-Lamy syndrome)

MPS VI, which is another rare form of MPS, is caused by a deficiency of the enzyme N-acetylglucosamine-4-sulphatase. This condition is also variable; individuals may have a mild or severe form of the disorder. Typically, the nervous system or intelligence of an individual with MPS VI is not affected. Individuals with a more severe form of MPS VI can have airway obstruction, develop **hydrocephalus** (accumulation of fluid in the brain), and exhibit bone changes. Individuals with a severe form of MPS VI are more likely to die while in their teens. With a milder form of the disorder, individuals tend to be shorter than expected for their age, develop corneal clouding, and live longer. The gene involved in MPS VI is believed to be located on the long arm of chromosome 5.

MPS VII (Sly syndrome)

MPS VII is an extremely rare form of MPS and is caused by a deficiency of the enzyme beta-glucuronidase. It is also highly variable, but symptoms are generally similar to those seen in individuals with Hurler syndrome. The gene that causes MPS VII is located on the long arm of chromosome 7.

Mucopolysaccharidoses

MPS IX (Hyaluronidase deficiency)

MPS IX, a condition first described in 1996, is caused by a deficiency of the enzyme hyaluronidase. In the few individuals described with this condition, the symptoms are variable. Some individuals develop soft tissue masses (growths) under the skin. Also, these individuals are shorter than expected for their age. The gene involved in MPS IX is believed to be located on the short arm of chromosome 3.

When to call the doctor

Parents should inform the doctor immediately if MPS runs in their **family**, so that early testing can be done on their children. In addition, any time they have questions about their child's growth and development, they should talk to their pediatrician.

Diagnosis

While a diagnosis for each type of MPS can be made based on the physical signs described above, several of the conditions have similar features. Therefore, enzyme analysis is used to determine the specific MPS disorder. Enzyme analysis often cannot accurately determine if an individual is a carrier for an MPS disorder, because the enzyme levels in individuals who are not carriers overlaps the enzyme levels seen in those individuals who are carrier for MPS. With many of the MPS conditions, several mutations have been found in each gene involved that can cause symptoms of each condition. If the specific mutation is known in a family, DNA analysis may be possible.

Once a couple has had a child with MPS, prenatal testing is available to them to help determine if another fetus is affected with the same MPS as their previous other child. This can be accomplished using procedures such as an **amniocentesis** or chorionic villus sampling (CVS), after which parents can explore their options relating to the pregnancy.

Treatment

As of 2004 there was no cure for MPS, although several types of experimental therapies are being investigated in the early 2000s. Typically, treatment involves trying to relieve the symptoms and improve quality of life. For MPS I and VI, bone marrow transplantation has been attempted as a treatment option. For those types of MPS, bone marrow transplantation has sometimes helped slow down the progression or reverse some of symptoms of the disorder in some children. The benefits of bone marrow transplantation are more likely to be noticed when performed on children less than two years of age. However, bone marrow transplantation is not thought to be helpful in other MPS disorders. Availability of donors is limited, and as a result, very few bone marrow transplantations are done for MPS. There are risks as well as benefits with this procedure, and mortality resulting from the procedure is high.

Another experimental treatment for MPS I involves extended treatment with recombinant human alpha-L-iduronidase. Some individuals treated with this technique show an improvement in some symptoms. Additionally, there is ongoing research involving gene replacement therapy (the insertion of normal copies of a gene into the cells of patients whose gene copies are defective), although this was as of 2004 still highly experimental.

Prognosis

The course of this disorder varies with the specific type of MPS the individual has. MPS I H is often fatal in childhood, with individuals rarely living past age 12. Individuals with MPS I H/S may die in childhood or live to adulthood. Individuals with MPS I H have health problems but usually have a normal lifespan. Individuals with mild MPS II live relatively normal lives, while individuals with the severe form of the disorder usually die in their teens. The life expectancy in MPS III and MPS IV is also variable, depending on the severity of the disorder. Individuals with MPS VI often have shorter than average life spans. As of 2004 MPS IX had been diagnosed so recently that little information is available.

Prevention

No specific measures can prevent the gene mutations that cause MPS. For some of the MPS diseases, biochemical tests may be able to identify healthy individuals who are carriers of the defective gene, allowing them to make informed reproductive decisions. Prenatal testing can also diagnose MPS in the fetus, but this testing is normally done only when there is some reason to expect to find the disorder (e.g. family history of the disease).

Parental concerns

Many individuals with an MPS condition have problems with airway constriction. This constriction may be so serious as to create significant difficulties in administering general anesthesia. Therefore, it is recommended that surgical procedures be performed under local anesthesia whenever possible.

KEY TERMS

Cardiomyopathy—A disease of the heart muscle.

Enzyme—A protein that catalyzes a biochemical reaction without changing its own structure or function.

Joint contractures—Stiffness of the joints that prevents full extension.

Kyphosis—An extreme, abnormal outward curvature of the spine, with a hump at the upper back.

Lysosome—A membrane-enclosed compartment in cells, containing many hydrolytic enzymes, where large molecules and cellular components are broken down.

Mucopolysaccharide—A complex molecule made of smaller sugar molecules strung together to form a chain. It is found in mucous secretions and intercellular spaces.

Recessive gene—A type of gene that is not expressed as a trait unless inherited by both parents.

X-linked gene—A gene carried on the X chromosome, one of the two sex chromosomes.

Resources

PERIODICALS

Kakkis, E. D., et al. "Enzyme-Replacement Therapy in Mucopolysaccharidosis I." *The New England Journal of Medicine* 344 (2001): 182–8.

ORGANIZATIONS

National MPS Society. PO Box 736, Bangor, ME 04402–0736. Web site: <www.mpsspciety.org>.

National Organization for Rare Disorders Inc. 55 Kenosia Ave, PO Box 1968, Danbury, CT 06813–1968. Web site: <www.rarediseases.org>.

WEB SITES

Braverman, Nancy, and Julie Hoover-Fong. "Mucopolysaccharidosis Type IV." *eMedicine.com*, March 28, 2003. Available online at <www.emedicine.com/ped/topic1477.htm> (accessed January 13, 2005).

McGovern, Margaret. "Mucopolysaccharidosis Type VI." *eMedicine.com* October 15, 2003. Available online at <www.emedicine.com/ped/topic1373.htm> (accessed January 13, 2005).

Nash, Donald, and Surendra Vama. "Mucopolysaccharidosis Type I H/S." *eMedicine.com*, June 19, 2003. Available online at <www.emedicine.com/ped/topic1032.htm> (accessed January 13, 2005).

"NINDS Mucopolysaccharidoses Information Page." *National Institute of Neurological Disorders and Stroke*, December 4, 2004. Available online at <www.ninds.nih.gov/health_and_medical/disorders/mucopolysaccharidoses.htm> (accessed January 13, 2005).

Tish Davidson, A.M.
Sharon A. Aufox, MS, CGC

Multicultural education/curriculum

Definition

Multicultural education describes a system of instruction that attempts to foster cultural pluralism and acknowledges the differences between races and cultures. It addresses the educational needs of a society that contains more than one set of traditions, that is a mixture of many cultures.

Description

The goal of multicultural education is to help students understand and appreciate cultural differences and similarities and to recognize the accomplishments of diverse ethnic, racial, and socioeconomic groups. It is a practice that hopes to transform the ways in which students are instructed by giving equal attention to the contributions of all the groups in a society. Special focus may be placed on minority groups that have been underrepresented in the past. A multicultural curriculum strives to present more than one perspective of a cultural phenomenon or an historical event. The old American melting pot metaphor is challenged as no longer being valid. Adherents of multicultural educational theory believe that the idea that students should be Americanized, in reality, assumed they should conform to a white, Eurocentric cultural model. In its place, multiculturalists believe school curricula should embrace a whole host of voices that exist in multicultural U.S. society. Their belief is that this transformation in the methods of learning is a start in addressing inequities in U.S. society. They believe this is increasingly important because of the changing population mix in the United States. For example, demographers estimate that by the year 2020, 46 percent of all public school students will be children of color.

The roots of multicultural education lie in the civil rights movements of various groups, including African Americans and women. In addition, the rise in ethnic consciousness and a more critical analysis of textbooks and other materials played a role. Community leaders, activists, and parents began to demand curricula that were more supportive and consistent with the cultural and racial diversity in the United States. In the late 1960s and 1970s, the concepts of multicultural education begin to emerge, and by the 1980s, an entire body of scholarship addressing multiculturalism existed.

One of the pioneers of multicultural education was James Banks, who believed all aspects of education needed to be transformed in order to create a multicultural school environment. These aspects include teaching methods, instructional materials, teacher attitudes, as well as the way the performance of students is assessed. Banks described five areas of multicultural education in which teachers and researchers are involved:

- Content integration: Concepts, values, and materials from a variety of cultures are included in teaching.

- Knowledge construction: This belief asserts that all knowledge is created in the minds of human beings and can, therefore, be challenged. A critical part of multicultural education, the idea that knowledge is a human construct challenges teachers to alter their own perceptions of the world before they can teach multiculturally.

- Equity pedagogy: Teachers must modify their methods of instruction by allowing for students' cultural differences before they can encourage academic achievement.

- Prejudice reduction: Teachers must work to shift students' prejudices regarding race and ethnicity. Prejudice reduction may also encompass teaching the tolerance of various religions, sexual preferences, and disabilities.

- Empowering school culture: Schools must identify those aspects of education that hinder learning and then empower families and students from all backgrounds, so that the full development of students is achieved.

Types of multicultural education programs

As of the early 2000s, there is no universally agreed upon multicultural curriculum. Teachers tend, however, to take one of two approaches. Some use what has been called the multicultural festival approach, in which students are invited to celebrate ethnic diversity by being exposed to foods, holidays, and festivals of other cultures. Many critics say that this conveys the notion that diversity is only important during celebratory moments. Other teachers apply a transformative approach, weaving different perspectives on cultures throughout the curriculum. Multicultural education can also be roughly divided into three different categories:

- Content-focused: These are the most common types of multicultural educational programs. Their overall objective is to include subject matter in the curriculum about various cultural groups in order to cultivate students' knowledge about these groups. Content may include holiday celebrations, recognizing heroes from different racial and ethnic groups, and focusing on the achievements of women and minorities. It may also include single-group studies, for example, black, ethnic, or women's studies programs.

- Student-focused: Many programs go beyond changes in the curriculum and specifically address the academic needs of defined groups of students, usually minorities. In this type of approach, the curriculum may not be changed significantly. Instead, the focus may be on aiding students in making the transition into the mainstream of education. Student-focused programs can take many forms, including efforts to draw on culturally-based learning styles and bilingual programs.

- Socially focused: These programs seek to reduce bias and increase cultural and racial tolerance. Included here might be desegregation programs, programs designed to increase contact among different races and cultures. Also, having teachers who are themselves members of minorities would be encouraged.

In spite of the fact that there are a variety of approaches to multicultural education, supporters point to several shared ideals among those who practice this kind of education. Shared ideals include:

- Each student must have equal opportunities to achieve his or her full potential.

- Every student must be able to participate in an increasingly multicultural society.

- Teachers must be able to facilitate learning for every student, no matter how similar or different each student is from the teacher.

- Schools must actively work towards ending oppression of all types, by ending it within their own walls.

- Education must include the voices and experiences of all students.

Common problems

There are many people who are either opposed to multicultural education or believe it has numerous problems. Some feel that the idea of multicultural education tends to divide cultures instead of building tolerance between them. They believe that American students should be taught to think of themselves as part of a whole rather than as people from different places who just happen to live in the same country.

Others believe multicultural education interferes with a child expressing his or her own individuality, by placing too much emphasis on ethnic or racial backgrounds. Even supporters recognize that someone's culture may be influenced as much by their sex or socioeconomic status as their race or ethnicity. Culture is itself complex and varies from community to community, **family** to family, or from person to person. The dynamic and variable nature of culture makes teaching about multiple cultural influences a daunting if not impossible task.

Critics also point out that educating students about the formation of U.S. democracy inevitably focuses on its European origins. If students are not informed that the dominant participants in the formation of the United States were white males, these critics say, students will not receive an accurate picture of U.S. history. In addition, there is the belief that if citizens are not willing to subordinate some parts of their heritage to the present set of dominant cultural values, then these citizens may find it even harder to integrate the mainstream.

Parental concerns

Parents should feel free to speak up about any concerns they have with the curriculum in their child's classroom. Multicultural education came about in part because parents expressed a need for the unique cultures of their children to be acknowledged and honored in school.

Resources

BOOKS

Grant, Carl A., et al. *Education Policy and Politics: Multicultural Education: Research, Theory, and Pedagogy.* Florence, KY: Routledge, 2005.

———. *The Student in the Classroom: Multicultural Education: Research, Theory, and Pedagogy.* Florence, KY: Routledge, 2005.

Peters-Davis, Norah, et al. *Challenges of Multicultural Education: Teaching and Taking Diversity Courses.* Taos, NM: Paradigm Publications, 2005.

Phillion, Jo Ann, et al. *Narrative and Experience in Multicultural Education.* Thousand Oakes, CA: Sage Publications, 2005.

Ramsey, Patricia G. *Teaching and Learning in a Diverse World: Multicultural Education for Young Children.* New York: Teachers College Press, 2004.

PERIODICALS

Aldridge, Jerry, Charles Calhoun, and Ricky Aman. "15 Misconceptions about Multicultural Education." *Focus on Elementary* 12 (Spring 2000): 3.

ORGANIZATIONS

Center for Multicultural Education. 110 Miller Hall, Box 353600, University of Washington, Seattle, WA 98195–3600. Web site: <http://depts.washington.edu/centerme/home.htm>.

National Association for Multicultural Education. 733 Fifteenth Street, NW, Suite 430, Washington, DC 20005. Web site: <www.nameorg.org>.

WEB SITES

Gorski, Paul. "Defining Multicultural Education." *Working Definition*, 2000. Available online at <www.edchange.org/multicultural/initial.html> (accessed January 13, 2005).

Hanley, Mary Stone. "The Scope of Multicultural Education." *New Horizons for Learning*, 2002. Available online at <www.newhorizons.org/strategies/multicultural/hanley.htm> (accessed January 13, 2005).

Deanna M. Swartout-Corbeil, RN

Multiple endocrine neoplasia syndromes

Definition

The multiple endocrine neoplasia (MEN) syndromes are three related inherited disorders affecting the thyroid and other hormone producing (endocrine) glands of the body. Before the early 2000s, MEN was called familial endocrine adenomatosis.

Description

There are three types of MEN: MEN 1 (Wermer's syndrome), MEN 2A (Sipple syndrome), and MEN 2B (previously known as MEN 3). All MEN types are the result of inherited genetic mutations that predispose the individual to excessive growth of cells (hyperplasia) and tumor formation in multiple endocrine glands. For all types of MEN, the children of an affected individual have a 50 percent chance of inheriting the defective gene that causes the disorder.

Demographics

MEN 1 is uncommon and occurs in only about one of every 30,000 individuals. The disorder runs in families, and males are twice as likely to develop the disorder as females. Individuals with MEN 1 can show symptoms of excessive parathyroid secretion by age five, and almost all individuals with MEN 1 show parathyroid symptoms by age 40.

MEN 2 affects about one in every 40,000 individuals. MEN 2A is ten to 20 times more common than MEN 2B.

Causes and symptoms

MEN 1 is caused by a mutation at the PYGM gene on chromosome 11. PYGM is one of a group of genes known as tumor suppressor genes that help to control cell division. An individual who inherits one defective copy of a tumor suppressor gene from either parent has a strong likelihood of developing MEN 1, because there is a high probability of another mutation developing in the other copy of the PYGM gene at some point during the thousands of cell divisions that occur with growth and development. When a second mutation occurs, the cell that contains the mutation no longer has any normal copy of the tumor suppressor gene. When both copies are defective, tumor suppression fails and tumors develop.

As a result, individuals with MEN 1 have uncontrolled cell growth and develop tumors in several endocrine glands, including the parathyroid glands (80–95% of patients), the pancreas (about 50% of patients) and the pituitary (around 25% of patients). The most frequent symptom of MEN 1 is hyperparathyroidism, which is excessive growth of the parathyroid gland and excessive secretion of parathyroid hormone. This condition leads to increased amounts of calcium in the blood, kidney stones, weakened bones, and nervous system depression. Children with MEN 1 can show signs of hyperparathyroidism as young as age five.

Tumors of the pancreas, known as gastrinomas, are also common in MEN 1. Excessive secretion of gastrin (a hormone secreted into the stomach to aid in digestion) by these tumors can cause upper gastrointestinal ulcers. The anterior pituitary gland and the adrenal glands can also be affected. Unlike MEN 2, the thyroid gland is rarely involved in MEN 1 symptoms. Children with MEN1 rarely develop tumors of the pancreas until they reach adulthood.

There are two types of MEN 2. Both MEN 2A and MEN 2B are caused by mutations in another gene, known as RET. A mutation in only one copy of the RET gene is sufficient to cause disease. A number of different mutations can lead to MEN 2A, but only one specific genetic alteration causes MEN 2B.

Patients with both MEN 2A and MEN 2B experience two main symptoms, medullary thyroid **cancer** (MTC) and a tumor of the adrenal gland medulla known as pheochromocytoma. MTC is a slow-growing cancer, but one that can be cured in less than 50 percent of cases. Pheochromocytoma is usually a benign (noncancerous) tumor that causes excessive secretion of adrenal hormones. This, in turn, can cause life-threatening high blood pressure (**hypertension**) and irregular heart beat (cardiac arrhythmia).

The two forms of MEN 2 are distinguished by other symptoms. Individuals with MEN 2A have a predisposition to develop tumors of the parathyroid gland. Although similar to MEN 1, less than 20 percent of MEN 2A patients show parathyroid involvement.

Individuals with MEN 2B show a variety of additional conditions: a characteristic facial appearance with swollen lips; tumors of the mucous membranes of the eye, mouth, tongue, and nasal cavity; enlarged colon; and skeletal abnormalities. Symptoms develop early in life (often before five years of age) in cases of MEN 2B and the medullary thyroid cancer is much more aggressive and may develop in patients who are one year old.

When to call the doctor

Since MEN is inherited and runs in families, the doctor should be informed of this history when the child is born, so that genetic testing can be done immediately.

Diagnosis

In the past, classical diagnosis of MEN was based on clinical features and on testing for elevated hormone levels. For MEN 1, the relevant hormone was parathyroid hormone. For both types of MEN 2, the greatest concern is development of medullary thyroid cancer. MTC can be detected by measuring levels of the thyroid hormone, calcitonin. Numerous other hormone levels can be measured to assess the involvement of the various other endocrine glands.

Diagnosis of MEN 2B can be made by physical examination alone. However, MEN 2A shows no distinct physical features and must be identified by measuring hormone levels or by finding endocrine tumors.

Since 1994, genetic screening using DNA technology has been available for both MEN 1 and MEN 2. This methodology allows diagnosis before the onset of symptoms. Before the development of genetic testing, there was no way to definitively identify which children had inherited the defective gene. As a result, all offspring of individuals with MEN had to be considered at risk. In the case of MEN 2A and MEN 2B, children would undergo frequent calcitonin testing. Molecular techniques as of the early 2000s allow a positive distinction to be made between children who are and are not carrying the defective genes that cause MEN.

Treatment

As of 2004 no comprehensive treatment is available for genetic conditions such as MEN. However, some of the consequences of MEN can be symptomatically treated. Pheochromocytoma in both types of MEN 2 can be cured by surgical removal of this slow growing tumor.

Treatment of MTC is by surgical removal of the thyroid. After thyroidectomy, the patient receives normal levels of thyroid hormone by mouth or by injection. Even when thyroid surgery is performed early, metastatic spread of the cancer may have already occurred. Since MTC is slow growing, metastasis may not be obvious. Metastasis is very serious in MTC because **chemotherapy** and radiation therapy are not effective in controlling its spread.

Prognosis

Diagnosed early through genetic testing, the prognosis for the MEN diseases is reasonably good, even for MEN 2B, the most dangerous of the three forms. Even in the absence of treatment, a few individuals with MEN 2A mutations never show any symptoms at all. Analysis of at-risk **family** members using molecular genetic techniques leads to earlier treatment and improved outcomes.

Prevention

As of 2004 there is no way to block the occurrence of genetic mutations that cause MEN. One of the most

---

KEY TERMS

Adrenal glands—A pair of endocrine glands (glands that secrete hormones directly into the bloodstream) that are located on top of the kidneys. The outer tissue of the glands (cortex) produces several steroid hormones, while the inner tissue (medulla) produces the hormones epinephrine (adrenaline) and norepinephrine.

Endocrine—Refers to glands that secrete hormones circulated in the bloodstream or lymphatic system.

Medullary thyroid cancer—A slow-growing tumor associated with multiple endocrine neoplasia syndromes.

Neoplasm—An abnormal formation of new tissue. A neoplasm may be malignant or benign.

Pancreas—A five-inch-long gland that lies behind the stomach and next to the duodenum. The pancreas releases glucagon, insulin, and some of the enzymes which aid digestion.

Parathyroid gland—A pair of glands adjacent to the thyroid gland that primarily regulate blood calcium levels.

Parathyroid hormone—A chemical substance produced by the parathyroid glands. This hormone plays a major role in regulating calcium concentration in the body.

Pheochromocytoma—A tumor that originates from the adrenal gland's chromaffin cells, causing overproduction of catecholamines, powerful hormones that induce high blood pressure and other symptoms.

Pituitary gland—The most important of the endocrine glands (glands that release hormones directly into the bloodstream), the pituitary is located at the base of the brain. Sometimes referred to as the "master gland," it regulates and controls the activities of other endocrine glands and many body processes including growth and reproductive function. Also called the hypophysis.

Thyroid gland—An endocrine gland in the neck overlying the windpipe (trachea) that regulates the speed of metabolic processes by producing a hormone, thyroxin.

---

serious consequences of MEN is MTC. Children who are identified as carriers of the RET gene can be offered total thyroidectomy as a preventative (prophylactic) measure to prevent the development of MTC.

Parental concerns

MEN is an inherited disorder. Individuals who have MEN in their families may wish to get genetic counseling before attempting a pregnancy.

Resources

BOOKS

Gagel, Robert F., and Stephen J. Marx. "Multiple Endocrine Neoplasia." In *Williams Textbook of Endocrinology*, 10th ed. Edited by P. Reed Larsen. Philadelphia: Saunders, 2003.

ORGANIZATIONS

Alliance of Genetic Support Groups. 4301 Connecticut Avenue NW, Suite 404, Washington, DC 20008–2304. Web site: <www.geneticalliance.org>.

Pituitary Network Association. 223 East Thousand Oaks Blvd. #320, Thousand Oaks, CA 91360. Web site: <www.pituitary.org>.

WEB SITES

Radebold, Klaus, and Christian A. Kock. "Multiple Endocrine Neoplasia." *eMedicine.com*, July 26, 2004. Available online at <www.emedicine.com/ped/topic1496.htm> (accessed January 13, 2005).

Tish Davidson, A.M.
Victor Leipzig, PhD

Multiple pregnancy

Definition

Multiple pregnancy, usually referred to as multiple gestation, is one in which more than one fetus develops simultaneously in the mother's womb.

Description

The frequency of multiple births in the United States has been steadily increasing with advances in reproductive technologies. It is estimated that pregnancies resulting from assisted technologies have a 25–30 percent incidence of **twins** and a 5 percent incidence of triplets. The frequency of naturally occurring twins is approximately one in 80 births; however the frequency of multiple births in the United States for 2002 was as follows:

- twins, one in 32
- triplets, one in 583
- quadruplets, one in 9,267
- quintuplets and up, one in 58,286

Twin birth is by far the most common multiple birth. There are two types of twin pregnancy: fraternal and identical. Fraternal twins develop from two separate ova released at the same time and fertilized by two separate sperm. Fraternal twins are referred to as dizygotic twins, meaning that two unions of two gametes or male/female sex cells occurred to produce two separate embryos. Characteristically, with fraternal twins, each has its own placenta and amniotic sac. They may be the same or different sex, occur twice as frequently as identical twins, and have a mortality rate of 11.5 percent. Identical twins represent the splitting of a single fertilized zygote (union of two gametes or male/female sex cells to produce a developing embryo) into two separate individuals. Identical twins will have the same DNA, genetic material (genotype), but it may be expressed differently (phenotype). There are three ways identical twins can exist in the uterus: dichorionic-diamniotic twins; monochorionic-diamniotic twins; monochorionic-monoamniotic twins. In the instance of dichorionic-diamniotic twins, division of the fertilized egg occurs within 72 hours past fertilization, before the inner cell mass has developed. About 30 percent of identical twins have this classification, and each twin has its own chorion, amnion, and placenta. The mortality rate for this type of twinning is 9 percent. With monochorionic-diamniotic twins, division occurs in the range of four to eight days after fertilization, and the inner cell mass divides in two. The placenta has one chorion and two amnions, so each twin has its own amniotic sac. Approximately 68 percent of identical twins are in this classification, and they have a mortality rate of 25 percent. Thirdly, monochorionic-monoamniotic twins are contained in the same amniotic sac. The division of the fertilized egg in this case occurs nine to 13 days past fertilization or near the time of implantation in the uterus. Since they share an amniotic sac, they have an increased risk of their umbilical cords becoming entangled or knotted. Only 2 percent of identical twins are in this classification, and they have a mortality rate of greater than 50 percent. If a complete separation does not take place during the division process, the result is Siamese (or conjoined) twins.

The human female typically releases only one egg every menstrual cycle. A hormone called progesterone, released by the first egg to be produced, prevents any other egg from maturing during that cycle. When this control fails, fertilization of more than one egg is possible. Fertility drugs inhibit these controls, allowing multiple gestation to occur. It seems as if, however, that more pregnancies start out naturally with twins than was originally believed. The development of improved technology, such as ultrasound, has made it possible to determine more accurately the early pregnancy loss rate of twins to include both complete pregnancy loss and spontaneous resorption of one twin, frequently referred to as the vanishing twin phenomenon. Recent research suggests that 75 percent of twin pregnancies are lost before the end of the first trimester. Moreover, only about 50 percent of pregnancies diagnosed in the first trimester with twins result in the birth of two live infants.

An old adage related to multiple gestation is the human female was not meant to have more than twins because she only had two breasts for feeding. Of course, pregnancies with more than two babies have occurred throughout history. However, once the number of babies reaches three, overexpansion of a woman's uterus begins to cause difficulties. The implantation of several embryos and placentas in the endometrium of the uterus results in a competition for space and inevitably some implant in an area without good circulation. During a pregnancy, it is essential that the uterus be well perfused to sustain the fetus with nutrients and oxygen. A lack of oxygen can cause central nervous system damage in the fetuses that implanted in a less than desirable area. Since the human female was not made to carry an indefinite number of fetuses, multiple gestations can have many of the following complications:

- increased rate of spontaneous abortion
- two to three times greater risk of developing severe **hypertension** or preeclampsia (increased blood pressure)
- maternal anemia due to increased fetal demands
- premature rupture of membranes (bag of water)
- incompetent cervix (cervix opens due to pressure)
- intrauterine growth restriction of one or more fetuses
- preterm labor due to overstretched uterus
- abnormal fetal presentations
- need for **cesarean section**
- rare complications with twins, such as twin-to-twin-transfusion syndrome (one fetus receives more nutrients than the other due to more blood vessels perfusing one baby)
- conjoined twins
- postpartum hemorrhage

Causes and symptoms

Twinning seems to run in some families, is mainly confined to fraternal (dizygotic twins) and seems to be entirely a property of the mother, not the father. The primary cause is an increased chance of multiple ovulation, when a woman releases two or more eggs. Another major factor is maternal age; a woman who gives birth at 37 is four times more likely to have fraternal twins than at age 18. The 37-year-old is also more likely to be unable to conceive, since many women's ovaries are already starting to fail at that age. The third major factor is race; West Africans are ten times more likely to have fraternal twins than Chinese or Japanese, with Caucasians intermediate. This increased chance is also seen in African Americans. In addition, the more pregnancies a woman has had, the greater her chances of having twins. In fact, by the fourth or fifth pregnancy, the likelihood of having twins is four times higher than it was for the first pregnancy.

The use of assisted reproduction techniques, particularly ovarian stimulation, has caused a dramatic increase in the number of twin and higher multiple births. The normal process of single ovulation is interrupted because fertility drugs permit more than one egg at a time to mature and be released. The first drug to be used for this was clomiphene (Clomid). This was followed by the development of two natural hormones, follicle-stimulating hormone and chorionic gonadotrophin (Pergonal) to produce multiple eggs ovulation. The chance of multiple gestation with in vitro fertilization (IVF) is about the same as with the use of fertility drugs, because several embryos are inserted into the womb to increase the odds of conception. Similarly, other fertility techniques such as gamete intrafallopian transfer (GIFT) and zygote intrafallopian transfer (ZIFT) are also more likely to result in multiple gestations. The use of intrauterine insemination or artificial insemination (the injection of sperm into a woman's uterus with a syringe) is the only fertility treatment that does not increase the chances of conceiving multiples—of course, the woman is usually taking fertility drugs with this procedure also.

Diagnosis

If a multiple pregnancy occurred spontaneously, the obstetrician would suspect a problem with the dates because the uterus would grow faster than usual. The gestational age of a pregnancy is determined from the first day of the last menstrual period (LMP). In a multiple gestation, the uterine measurements would be larger than dates, which normally correspond. If multiple gestation is suspected, an ultrasound may be performed to determine the gestational age of the fetus or to check for more than one fetus. With the use of assisted reproductive technology, an ultrasound is usually performed with ten days to see if any of the embryos were successful with implantation, and a multiple gestation would be revealed at that time. Following the birth of multiples, the placenta is carefully examined to determine if they are fraternal or identical. One placenta indicates identical twins.

A multiple pregnancy almost always means increased monitoring and surveillance for complications. This often means more frequent visits to the healthcare provider, serial ultrasounds to make sure that the babies are growing satisfactorily, **amniocentesis** to check for lung development, and close monitoring for preterm labor.

Treatment

Ultrasound examinations play an important role in the care and treatment of multiple gestations. It assists with dating the pregnancy, determining the number of fetuses, detecting fetal anomalies, following the growth and development of each fetus, and serves to monitor the length of the cervix in anticipation of preterm labor. Premature birth is the constant threat of multiple gestation, and the primary threat of **prematurity** is related to lung development. Premature infants lack a substance, called surfactant, that permits their lungs to expand and breathe normally. If it becomes apparent that a multiple gestation is going to have a preterm delivery, the mother will be given an injection of a steroid, beta-methasone, to help the lungs mature. It is more beneficial if the steroid can be given twice in a 48 hour period; however, if there is not time for this, surfactant has been developed that can be administered into the lungs of a premature infant to facilitate breathing. An additional problem with the premature infant involves the lack of body fat. In a normal pregnancy the fetus spends the last four to six weeks growing and gaining weight, primarily body fat. This fat helps a newborn maintain his or her body temperature. Since premature infants do not have this fat, they use energy they cannot afford to stay warm.

Although research has shown that bed rest is not effective, a woman is often placed on bed rest during a multiple pregnancy to try to prevent pre-term labor and delivery. If preterm labor is impossible to control at home, the mother may be hospitalized and medication used to attempt to control contractions and dilatation of the cervix. Multiple gestations greater than twins in number are almost always delivered via cesarean section.

Alternative treatment

There are no specific treatments to alleviate medical difficulties caused by multiple pregnancies; however, there are supportive measures that may help both mother and children recover from the birthing process. There are treatments to encourage breast milk production and to combat postpartum difficulties. Various homeopathic remedies and massage can be helpful to both mother and children during the early adjustment period after birth.

KEY TERMS

Amnion—Thin, tough, innermost layer of the amniotic sac.

Amniotic membrane—The thin tissue that creates the walls of the amniotic sac.

Chorion—The outer membrane of the amniotic sac. Chorionic villi develop from its outer surface early in pregnancy. The villi establish a physical connection with the wall of the uterus and eventually develop into the placenta.

Gene—A building block of inheritance, which contains the instructions for the production of a particular protein, and is made up of a molecular sequence found on a section of DNA. Each gene is found on a precise location on a chromosome.

Gestation—The period from conception to birth, during which the developing fetus is carried in the uterus.

Ova—The plural of ovum, it is the female reproductive cell.

Ovulate—To release a mature egg for fertilization.

Placenta—The organ that provides oxygen and nutrition from the mother to the unborn baby during pregnancy. The placenta is attached to the wall of the uterus and leads to the unborn baby via the umbilical cord.

Sequela—Plural, sequalae. An abnormal condition resulting from a previous disease or disorder.

Zygote—The result of the sperm successfully fertilizing the ovum. The zygote is a single cell that contains the genetic material of both the mother and the father.

Prognosis

Many multiple pregnancies reach fruition without difficulties; however, many do not. Despite medical advances, if the babies are born too early, they may survive but will have sequelae that limit the quality of life. If the babies are born prematurely, immediate medical care increases the chance of survival without any complications.

Parental concerns

Mothers with multiple pregnancy should be especially careful to get adequate prenatal care, including any necessary **vitamins** or recommended tests. Because of the extra stress on the mother's body, increased rate of complications, and threat of prematurity, the mother should be vigilant in making sure she gets enough rest, reduces stress, and maintains a healthy diet.

See also Antepartum testing; Cesarean section.

Resources

BOOKS

Bowers, Nancy, R.N., B.S.N. *The Multiple Pregnancy Source Book.* Lincolnwood, IL: Contemporary Books, 2001.

Olds, Sally et al. *Maternal-Newborn Nursing & Women's Health Care, 7th ed.* Saddle River, NJ: Prentice Hall, 2004.

PERIODICALS

Evans, M.I., et al., "Fetal Reduction from Twins to a Singleton." *Obstetrics and Gynecology* 104 (2004) 102–109.

Evans M.I., D. Ciorica, and D.W. Britt. "Do reduced multiples do better?" *Best Practice Research Clinical Obstetrics and Gynaecology.* 18, no. 4 (2004): 601–12.

Britt D.W., W.J. Evans, S.S. Mehta, and M.I. Evans. "Framing the decision: determinants of how women considering multifetal pregnancy reduction as a pregnancy-management strategy frame their moral dilemma." *Fetal Diagnostic Therapy* 19, no. 3 (2004): 232–40.

Evans, M.I., E.L. Krivchenia, S.E. Gelber, and R.J. Wapner. "Selective reduction." *Clinical Perinatology* 30, no. 1 (2003): 103–11.

ORGANIZATIONS

Association of Women's Health, Obstetric and Neonatal Nursing. 2000 L Street, N.W. Suite 740, Washington, DC 20036. Web site: <www.awhonn.org>.

American College of Obstetricians and Gynecologists. 409 12th Street, S.W., P. O. Box 96920, Washington, DC 20090.

WEB SITES

Questions about Multiple Pregnancy. [cited March 6, 2005]. Available online at: <http://www.marvelousmultiples.com/abtmultpreg.htm>.

Linda K. Bennington, MSN, CNS

Mumps

Definition

Mumps is a relatively mild short-term viral infection of the salivary glands that usually occurs during childhood.

Description

Typically, mumps is characterized by a painful swelling of both cheek areas, although the person could have swelling on one side or no perceivable swelling at all. The salivary glands are also called the parotid glands; therefore, mumps is sometimes referred to as an inflammation of the parotid glands (epidemic parotitis). The word mumps comes from an old English dialect, meaning lumps or bumps within the cheeks.

Demographics

Mumps is a very contagious infection that spreads easily in such highly populated environments as daycare centers and schools. Although not as contagious as **measles** or **chickenpox**, mumps was once quite common. Prior to the release of a mumps vaccine in the United States in 1967, approximately 92 percent of all children had been exposed to mumps by the age of 15. In the pre-vaccine years, most children contracted mumps between the ages of four and seven. Mumps epidemics came in two to five year cycles. The greatest mumps epidemic was in 1941 when approximately 250 cases were reported for every 100,000 people. In 1968, the year after the live mumps vaccine was released, only 76 cases were reported for every 100,000 people. By 1985, fewer than 3,000 cases of mumps were reported throughout the entire United States, the equivalent of about one case per 100,000 people. The reason for the decline in mumps was the increased usage of the mumps vaccine. However, 1987 noted a five-fold increase in the incidence of the disease because of the reluctance of some states to adopt comprehensive school immunization laws. After that, state-enforced school entry requirements achieved student immunization rates of nearly 100 percent in kindergarten and first grade. In 1996, the Centers for Disease Control and Prevention (CDC) reported only 751 cases of mumps nationwide, that is, about one case for every 5 million people.

Causes and symptoms

The paramyxovirus that causes mumps is harbored in the saliva and is spread by sneezing, coughing, and other direct contact with another person's infected saliva. Once the person is exposed to the virus, symptoms generally occur in 14 to 24 days. Initial symptoms include chills, **headache**, loss of appetite, and a lack of energy. However, an infected person may not experience these initial symptoms. Swelling of the salivary glands in the face (parotitis) generally occurs within 12 to 24 hours of the above symptoms. Accompanying the swollen glands is **pain** on chewing or swallowing, especially with acidic beverages, such as lemonade. A **fever** as high as 104°F (40°C) is also common. Swelling of the glands reaches a maximum on about the second day and usually disappears by the seventh day. Once individuals have contracted mumps, they become immune to the disease, despite how mild or severe their symptoms may have been.

While the majority of cases of mumps are uncomplicated and pass without incident, some complications can occur. Complications are, however, more noticeable in adults who get the infection. In 15 percent of cases, the covering of the brain and spinal cord becomes inflamed (**meningitis**). Symptoms of meningitis usually develop within four or five days after the first signs of mumps. These symptoms include a stiff neck, headache, **vomiting**, and a lack of energy. Mumps meningitis is usually resolved within seven days, and damage to the brain is exceedingly rare.

The mumps infection can spread into the brain causing inflammation of the brain (**encephalitis**). Symptoms of mumps encephalitis include the inability to feel pain, seizures, and high fever. Encephalitis can occur during the parotitis stage or one to two weeks later. Recovery from mumps encephalitis is usually complete, although complications, such as seizure disorders, have been noted. Only about one person in 100 with mumps encephalitis dies from the complication.

About one-fourth of all post-pubertal males who contract mumps can develop a swelling of the scrotum (orchitis) about seven days after the parotitis stage. Symptoms include marked swelling of one or both testicles, severe pain, fever, **nausea**, and headache. Pain and swelling usually subside after five to seven days, although the testicles can remain tender for weeks.

Girls occasionally suffer an inflammation of the ovaries (oophoritis) as a complication of mumps, but this condition is far less painful than orchitis in boys.

Diagnosis

When mumps reaches epidemic proportions, diagnosis is relatively easy on the basis of the physical symptoms. The doctor will take the child's temperature, gently palpate (touch) the skin over the parotid glands, and look inside the child's mouth. If the child has mumps, the openings to the ducts inside the mouth will be slightly inflamed and have a "pouty" appearance. With so many people vaccinated as of the early 2000s, a case of mumps must be properly diagnosed in the event the salivary glands are swollen for reasons other than viral infection. For example, in persons with poor **oral hygiene**, the salivary glands can be infected with

bacteria. In these cases, **antibiotics** are necessary. Also in rare cases, the salivary glands can become blocked, develop tumors, or swell due to the use of certain drugs, such as iodine. A test can be performed to determine whether the person with swelling of the salivary glands actually has the mumps virus.

In late 2002, researchers in London reported the development of a bioassay for measuring mumps-specific IgG. This test would allow a doctor to check whether an individual patient is immune to mumps and allow researchers to measure the susceptibility of a local population to mumps in areas with low rates of **vaccination**.

Treatment

When mumps does occurs, the illness is usually allowed to run its course. The symptoms, however, are treatable. Because of difficulty swallowing, the most important challenge is to keep the patient fed and hydrated. The individual should be provided a soft diet, consisting of cooked cereals, mashed potatoes, broth-based soups, prepared baby foods, or foods put through a home food processor. Aspirin (only for individuals over the age of 20), **acetaminophen**, or ibuprofen can relieve some of the pain due to swelling, headache, and fever. Patients should void fruit juices and other acidic foods or beverages that can irritate the salivary glands. They should also avoid dairy products that can be hard to digest. In the event of complications, a physician should be contacted at once. For example, if orchitis occurs, a physician should be called. Also, supporting the scrotum in a cotton bed on an adhesive-tape bridge between the thighs can minimize tension. Ice packs are also helpful.

Prognosis

When mumps is uncomplicated, prognosis is excellent. However, in rare cases, a relapse occurs after about two weeks. Complications can also delay complete recovery.

Prevention

A vaccine exists to protect against mumps. The vaccine preparation (MMR) is usually given as part of a combination injection that helps protect against measles, mumps, and **rubella**. MMR is a live vaccine administered in one dose between the ages of 12 and 15 months, between four and six years of age, or 11 and 12 years of age. Persons who are unsure of their mumps history and/or mumps vaccination history should be vaccinated. Susceptible healthcare workers, especially those who work in hospitals, should be vaccinated. Because mumps is

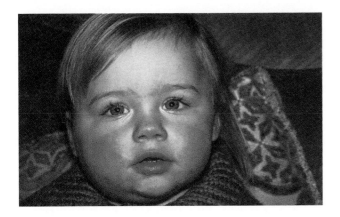

A young child with mumps. *(Photo Researchers, Inc.)*

still prevalent throughout the world, susceptible persons over the age of one year who are traveling abroad would benefit from receiving the mumps vaccine.

The mumps vaccine is extremely effective, and virtually everyone should be vaccinated against this disease. There are, however, a few reasons why people should not be vaccinated against mumps:

- Pregnant women who contract mumps during pregnancy have an increased rate of miscarriage but not birth defects. As a result, pregnant women should not receive the mumps vaccine because of the possibility of damage to the fetus. Women who have had the vaccine should postpone pregnancy for three months after being vaccinated.

- Unvaccinated persons who have been exposed to mumps should not get the vaccine, as it may not provide protection. The persons should, however, be vaccinated if no symptoms result from the exposure to mumps.

- Persons with minor fever-producing illnesses, such as an upper respiratory infection, should not get the vaccine until the illness has subsided.

- Because mumps vaccine is produced using eggs, individuals who develop **hives**, swelling of the mouth or throat, **dizziness**, or breathing difficulties after eating eggs should not receive the mumps vaccine.

- Persons with immune deficiency diseases and/or those whose immunity has been suppressed with anti-cancer drugs, corticosteroids, or radiation should not receive the vaccine. **Family** members of immunocompromised people, however, should get vaccinated to reduce the risk of mumps.

- The CDC recommends that all children infected with human **immunodeficiency** disease (HIV) who are

KEY TERMS

Asymptomatic—Persons who carry a disease and are usually capable of transmitting the disease but who do not exhibit symptoms of the disease are said to be asymptomatic.

Autism—A developmental disability that appears early in life, in which normal brain development is disrupted and social and communication skills are retarded, sometimes severely.

Encephalitis—Inflammation of the brain, usually caused by a virus. The inflammation may interfere with normal brain function and may cause seizures, sleepiness, confusion, personality changes, weakness in one or more parts of the body, and even coma.

Epidemic parotitis—The medical name for mumps.

Immunoglobulin G (IgG)—Immunoglobulin type gamma, the most common type found in the blood and tissue fluids.

Meningitis—An infection or inflammation of the membranes that cover the brain and spinal cord. It is usually caused by bacteria or a virus.

Orchitis—Inflammation of one or both testes, accompanied by swelling, pain, fever, and a sensation of heaviness in the affected area.

Paramyxovirus—A genus of viruses that includes the causative agent of mumps.

Parotitis—Inflammation and swelling of one or both of the parotid salivary glands.

asymptomatic should receive an the **MMR vaccine** at 15 months of age.

Parental concerns

The mumps vaccine has been controversial in the early 2000s because of concern that its use was linked to an increased rate of childhood **autism**. The negative publicity given to the vaccine in the mass media led some parents to refuse to immunize their children with the MMR vaccine. One result has been an increase in the number of mumps outbreaks in several European countries, including Italy and the United Kingdom.

In the fall of 2002, the *New England Journal of Medicine* published a major Danish study disproving the hypothesis of a connection between the MMR vaccine and autism. A second study in Finland showed that the vaccine is also not associated with aseptic meningitis or encephalitis. Since these studies were published, U.S. primary care physicians have once again reminded parents of the importance of immunizing their children against mumps and other childhood diseases.

Resources

BOOKS

Gutierrez, Kathleen A. "Mumps Virus." In *Principles and Practice of Pediatric Infectious Diseases*, 2nd ed. Edited by Sarah S. Long et al. St. Louis, MO: Elsevier, 2003.

Maldonado, Yvonne A. "Mumps." In *Nelson Textbook of Pediatrics*. Edited by Richard E. Behrman et al. Philadelphia: Saunders, 2004.

Ron Gasbarro, PharmD
Rebecca J. Frey, PhD
Rosalyn Carson DeWitt, MD

Munchausen syndrome

Definition

Munchausen syndrome is a psychiatric disorder that causes an individual to self-inflict injury or illness or to fabricate symptoms of physical or mental illness in order to receive medical care or **hospitalization**. In a variation of the disorder, Munchausen by proxy (MSBP), an individual, typically a mother, intentionally causes or fabricates illness in a child or other person under her care.

Description

Munchausen syndrome takes its name from Baron Karl Friederich von Munchausen, an eighteenth century German military man known for his tall tales. The disorder first appeared in psychiatric literature in the early 1950s when it was used to describe patients who sought hospitalization by inventing symptoms and complicated medical histories, and/or inducing illness and injury in themselves. Categorized as a factitious disorder (a disorder in which the physical or psychological symptoms are under voluntary control), Munchausen syndrome seems to be motivated by a need to assume the role of a patient. Unlike malingering, there does not seem to be any clear secondary gain (e.g., money) in Munchausen syndrome.

Individuals with Munchausen by proxy syndrome use their child (or another dependent person) to fulfill their need to step into the patient role. The disorder most commonly victimizes children from birth to eight years old. Parents or caregivers with MSBP may only exaggerate or fabricate their child's symptoms, or they may deliberately induce symptoms through various methods, including **poisoning**, suffocation, starvation, or introducing bacteria into open **wounds**. They often display an extraordinary depth of medical knowledge and may even be in the medical profession themselves.

Demographics

Both Munchausen syndrome and Munchausen syndrome by proxy are thought to be rare, but there are no solid statistics on the frequency of either diagnosis. Data on Munchausen syndrome in children and adolescents specifically are very limited. In 2000 one review found that among the 42 cases reported in the medical literature, 71 percent were female and the mean age was 14 years of age. Children age 14 and younger were more likely to admit to falsifying symptoms when confronted than those between the ages of 15 and 18.

Munchausen syndrome by proxy is also hard to quantify due to the number of undetected or undiagnosed cases. The incidence of the condition in the United States is not known, but a 1996 study of children in Ireland and the United Kingdom estimated that Munchausen syndrome by proxy occurred annually in 0.5 of every 100,000 children under age 16, and in 2.8 of every 100,000 children under the age of one.

Causes and symptoms

The exact cause of Munchausen syndrome is unknown. It has been theorized that Munchausen patients are motivated by a desire to be cared for, a need for attention, dependency, an ambivalence toward doctors, or a need to suffer. Factors that may predispose an individual to Munchausen include a serious illness in childhood or an existing personality disorder. Some research indicates that children and adolescents who develop Munchausen syndrome are more likely to have been previous victims of Munchausen syndrome by proxy.

The Munchausen and Munchausen by proxy patient can appear to have a wide array of physical or psychiatric symptoms, usually limited only by their (or their caregiver's) medical knowledge. Many Munchausen patients are very familiar with medical terminology and symptoms. Some common complaints include fevers, **rashes**, abscesses, bleeding, and **vomiting**. Common Munchausen by proxy symptoms include apnea (cessation of breathing), **fever**, vomiting, and **diarrhea**. In both Munchausen and MSBP syndromes, the suspected illness does not respond to a normal course of treatment, and diagnostic tests turn up nothing out of the ordinary. Patients or parents may push for invasive procedures and display an extraordinary depth of knowledge of medical therapies.

Diagnosis

Because Munchausen sufferers often go from doctor to doctor, gaining admission into many hospitals along the way, diagnosis can be difficult. They are typically detected rather than diagnosed. During a course of treatment, they may be discovered by a hospital employee who encountered them during a previous hospitalization. Their caregivers may also notice that symptoms such as high fever occur only when the patient is left unattended. Occasionally, medication used to induce symptoms is found with the patient's belongings. When the patient is confronted, they often react with outrage and check out of the hospital to seek treatment at another facility with a new caregiver.

A diagnosis of Munchausen syndrome may be even more difficult in children and adolescents. A physician may be able to recognize a pattern of symptoms (e.g., those that occur only when the child is alone or that begin only when the parent is present with the child) or the child may admit to fabricating or self-inflicting symptoms upon questioning. Surveillance video may record the child or the child's caregiver inducing symptoms.

Treatment

There is no clearly effective treatment for Munchausen syndrome. Extensive psychotherapy may be helpful with some Munchausen patients. If Munchausen syndrome coexists with other mental disorders, such as a personality disorder, the underlying disorder is typically treated first. Children who develop the syndrome may respond more favorably to therapy than adults, particularly if they are diagnosed at an early age.

Children who are victims of Munchausen syndrome by proxy are usually removed from the offending caregiver immediately and placed in protective custody. Therapy may also be beneficial to these children in recovering from the emotional trauma of MSBP.

Prognosis

The infections and injuries Munchausen patients self-inflict can cause serious illness. Patients often undergo countless unnecessary surgeries throughout their lifetimes. In addition, because of their frequent

hospitalizations, they have difficulty holding down a job. Further, their chronic health complaints may damage interpersonal relationships with **family** and friends.

Children victimized by sufferers of MSBP are at a real risk for serious injury and possible death. A UK study published in 1998 found that although the majority of children with MSBP studied (90 percent) were placed in child protection care at diagnosis, at two-year follow up the number had fallen to 32 percent. A reported 17 percent of children who were victims of MSBP and who were eventually returned to an abusive caregiver suffered further abuse. Those who survive physically unscathed may suffer developmental and emotional problems.

Prevention

Because the cause of Munchausen syndrome is unknown, formulating a prevention strategy is difficult. Some medical facilities and healthcare practitioners have attempted to limit hospital admissions for Munchausen patients by sharing medical records. While these attempts may curb the number of hospital admissions, they do not treat the underlying disorder and may endanger Munchausen sufferers that have made themselves critically ill and require treatment. Children who are found to be victims of persons with Munchausen by proxy syndrome should be immediately removed from the care of the abusing parent or guardian.

Parental concerns

Parents who suspect that their child may be deliberately hurting themselves or falsifying symptoms should contact their pediatrician immediately for assessment. Children who are thought to pose potentially life-threatening danger to themselves may require hospitalization, and a referral to a child psychologist or therapist will be necessary. It is important to remember that properly treating the condition requires addressing the motives and emotions behind the disorder, not simply punishing the behavior.

Resources

BOOKS

Diagnostic and Statistical Manual of Mental Disorders, 4th ed., text revision (DSM-IV-TR). Washington, DC: American Psychiatric Press Inc., 2000.

Feldman, Marc. *Playing Sick?: Untangling the Web of Munchausen Syndrome, Munchausen by Proxy, Malingering, and Factitious Disorder*. New York: Brunner-Routledge, 2004.

Mart, Eric G. *Munchausen's Syndrome by Proxy Reconsidered*. Manchester, NH: Bally Vaughn, 2002.

PERIODICALS

Libow, Judith. "Child and Adolescent Illness Falsification." *Pediatrics* 105, no. 2 (February 2000): 336.

Schreier, Herbert. "Munchausen by Proxy Defined." *Pediatrics* 110, no. 5 (November 2002): 985.

ORGANIZATIONS

American Psychiatric Association. 1000 Wilson Blvd., Suite 1825, Arlington, VA 22209. Web site: <www.psych.org>.

American Psychological Association (APA). 750 First St. NE, Washington, DC 20002–4242. Web site: <www.apa.org>.

National Alliance for the Mentally Ill (NAMI). Colonial Place Three, 2107 Wilson Blvd., Ste. 300, Arlington, VA 22201–3042. Web site: <www.nami.org>.

National Institute of Mental Health (NIMH). Office of Communications, 6001 Executive Boulevard, Room 8184, MSC 9663, Bethesda, MD 20892–9663. Web site: <www.nimh.nih.gov>.

Paula Ford-Martin

Muscle contractures *see* **Spasticity**

Muscle spasms and cramps

Definition

Muscle spasms and cramps are spontaneous, often painful muscle contractions.

Description

The rapid, uncontrolled muscle contraction, or spasm, happens unexpectedly, with either no stimulation or some trivially small one. The muscle contraction and **pain** last for several minutes and then slowly ease. Cramps may affect any muscle but are most common in the calves, feet, and hands. While painful, they are harmless and, in most cases, not related to any underlying disorder. Nonetheless, cramps and spasms can be manifestations of many neurological or muscular diseases.

The terms cramp and spasm can be somewhat vague, and they are sometimes used to include types of abnormal muscle activity other than sudden painful contraction. These include stiffness at rest, slow muscle relaxation, and spontaneous contractions of a muscle at rest (fasciculation). Fasciculation is a type of painless muscle spasm, marked by rapid, uncoordinated contraction of many small muscle fibers. A critical part of diagnosis is distinguishing these different meanings and allowing the patient to describe the problem as precisely as possible.

Demographics

The exact incidence of muscle cramps and spasms is not known. They are more likely to occur in older children and teenagers who are participating in organized, competitive **sports** and strenuous aerobic activities.

Causes and symptoms

Causes

Normal voluntary muscle contraction begins when electrical signals are sent from the brain through the spinal cord along nerve cells called motor neurons. These include both the upper motor neurons within the brain and the lower motor neurons within the spinal cord and leading out to the muscle. At the muscle, chemicals released by the motor neuron stimulate the internal release of calcium ions from stores within the muscle cell. These calcium ions then interact with muscle proteins within the cell, causing the proteins (actin and myosin) to slide past one another. This motion pulls their fixed ends closer, thereby shortening the cell and, ultimately, the muscle itself. Recapture of calcium and unlinking of actin and myosin allow the muscle fiber to relax.

Abnormal contraction may be caused by unusual activity at any stage in this process. Certain mechanisms within the brain and the rest of the central nervous system help regulate contraction. Interruption of these mechanisms can cause spasm. Motor neurons that are overly sensitive may fire below their normal thresholds. The muscle membrane itself may be overly sensitive, causing contraction without stimulation. Calcium ions may not be recaptured quickly enough, causing prolonged contraction.

Structural disorders such as flat feet, hyperextended knees (genu recurvatum), and hypermobility syndrome (joints that can move beyond the normal range of motion) may predispose a person to developing leg cramps. Prolonged sitting, inappropriate leg positioning during sedentary activity, or standing on concrete flooring for prolonged periods may be associated with an increased incidence of leg cramps.

Interruption of brain mechanisms and overly sensitive motor neurons may result from damage to the nerve pathways. Possible causes include **stroke**, multiple sclerosis, **cerebral palsy**, neurodegenerative diseases, trauma, **spinal cord injury**, and nervous system poisons such as strychnine, **tetanus**, and certain insecticides. Nerve damage may lead to a prolonged or permanent muscle shortening called contracture.

Changes in muscle responsiveness may be due to or associated with the following:

- Prolonged **exercise**: Curiously, relaxation of a muscle actually requires energy to be expended. The energy is used to recapture calcium and to unlink actin and myosin. Normally, sensations of pain and fatigue signal that it is time to rest. Ignoring or overriding those warning signals can lead to such severe energy depletion that the muscle cannot be relaxed, causing a cramp. The familiar advice about not swimming after a heavy meal, when blood flow is directed away from the muscles, is intended to avoid this type of cramp.

- Exercising or participating in activities in high or humid temperatures: Copious sweating during prolonged exercise can lead to heat cramps, a condition associated with brief, painful cramps, especially in the legs, sweating, and mild **fever**, usually less than 102°F. Heat cramps are more likely to occur when the child has not taken in enough fluids before, during, and after the activity. Exercising in high temperatures without adequate fluid intake may increase the risk of **dehydration**.

- Dehydration and salt depletion: This condition may be brought on by repeated bouts of **vomiting** or **diarrhea** or by copious sweating during prolonged exercise. Loss of fluids, salts, and minerals—especially sodium, potassium, magnesium, and calcium—can disrupt ion balances in both muscle and nerves. This imbalance can prevent the muscles and nerves from responding and recovering normally and can lead to cramping.

- Metabolic disorders that affect the energy supply in muscle: These are inherited diseases in which particular muscle enzymes are deficient. They include deficiencies of myophosphorylase (McArdle's disease), phosphorylase b kinase, phosphofructokinase, phosphoglycerate kinase, and lactate dehydrogenase.

- Myotonia: Myotonias include **myotonic dystrophy**, myotonia congenita, paramyotonia congenita, and neuromyotonia. These conditions cause stiffness due to delayed relaxation of the muscle but do not cause the spontaneous contraction usually associated with cramps. However, many patients with myotonia do experience cramping from exercise. Symptoms of myotonia are often worse in cold temperatures.

Fasciculation may be due to fatigue, cold, medications, metabolic disorders, nerve damage, or neurodegenerative disease, including amyotrophic lateral sclerosis (ALS, also known as Lou Gehrig's disease). Most people experience brief, mild fasciculation from time to time, usually in the calves.

Symptoms

The pain of a muscle cramp is intense, localized, and often debilitating. Coming on quickly, it may last for minutes and fade gradually. Contractures develop more slowly, over days or weeks, and may be permanent if untreated. Fasciculation may occur at rest or after muscle contraction and may last several minutes.

Exercising in high temperatures can lead to dehydration. Dehydration should be suspected if these symptoms are present: dry mouth or tongue, increased or excessive thirst, few or no tears when crying, decreased urination, dark yellow urine, irritability, low energy, lightheadedness or fainting, severe weakness, and sunken abdomen, eyes and cheeks.

When to call the doctor

Prompt medical attention is required if the child has any of the symptoms associated with dehydration, as listed above. Prompt medical attention also is required if the child has a high fever—temperature of 102°F or 38.9°C, or above. Parents also should call the child's pediatrician if the following symptoms are present:

- acute pain associated with the muscle cramp or spasm

- prolonged muscle contractions

- cramps or spasms that cause twisting and repetitive movement or abnormal posture

- apparent development of muscle contractures (prolonged joint flexion in an abnormal position)

Diagnosis

A usual bout of muscle cramps should not require a visit to the doctor. However, medical treatment is essential if the child has any symptoms of dehydration associated with the muscle cramps. In addition, any abnormal contractions or frequent muscle cramps or spasms that cause concern should be evaluated by a physician. Abnormal muscle contractions are diagnosed through a careful medical history, as well as a physical and neurological examination. In some cases when a structural abnormality is suspected, x rays may be performed.

The medical history helps the physician evaluate the presence of other conditions or disorders that might contribute to or cause the abnormal contractions. Records of previous diagnoses, surgeries, and treatments are reviewed. The child's **family** medical history is evaluated to determine if there is a history of muscular or neurological disorders.

Questions about the child's medical history may include:

- When were the symptoms first noticed?
- How long have the symptoms lasted?
- Are the symptoms always present?
- What muscles are affected?
- What makes the symptoms improve?
- What specific treatments or techniques have been tried?
- What makes the symptoms worse?
- Do certain activities, emotions, or events seem to aggravate the symptoms?
- Are other symptoms present?

The physical and neurological exams may include an evaluation of the child's motor reflexes including muscle tone, mobility, strength, balance, and endurance; heart and lung function; cranial nerve function; and an examination of the child's abdomen, spine, throat, and ears. The child's height and weight and blood pressure also are checked and recorded.

When a neurological cause is suspected, a multi-disciplinary team may be consulted to provide an accurate diagnosis, so the proper treatment can be planned. Occupational and physical therapy evaluations may be helpful to determine upper and lower extremity movement patterns and passive range of motion.

In some cases, nerve conduction studies with electromyography of the affected muscles may be performed to evaluate an underlying neuromuscular disorder. These tests are useful in evaluating a child's muscular activity and provide a comprehensive **assessment** of nerve and muscle function.

In both tests, the examiner uses a computer, monitor, amplifier, loudspeaker, stimulator, and high-tech filters to see and hear how the muscles and nerves are responding during the test. In the nerve conduction study, small electrodes are placed on the skin over the muscles to be examined. A stimulator delivers a very small electrical current (that does not cause damage to the body) through the electrodes, causing the nerves to fire. In the electromyogram, a very thin, sterilized needle is inserted into various muscles, usually those affected most by **spasticity** symptoms. The needle is attached by wires to a recording machine. The patient is asked to relax and contract the muscles being examined. The electrical signals produced by the nerves and muscles during these tests are measured and recorded by a computer and displayed as electrical waves on the monitor. The test results are interpreted by a specially trained physician.

Treatment

Most cases of simple cramps require no treatment other than patience and stretching. When heat cramps occur, the child should stop the activity, move to a cool or shady place, remove excess clothing, drink cool water or a sports drink with electrolytes, such as Gatorade, and rest. If the child appears nauseous or is feeling dizzy, he should lie down, with feet slightly elevated. Directing a fan on the child will help cool the child. Gently and gradually stretching and massaging the affected muscle may ease the pain and hasten recovery.

Briefly applying cold packs to cramped muscles, for about ten minutes, may help ease pain.

Acetaminophen (such as Tylenol) or ibuprofen (such as Advil or Motrin) should be used sparingly for relief of discomfort. Ask the child's doctor for specific guidelines. More prolonged or regular cramps may be treated with prescribed medications.

If the child has any signs of dehydration, generous amounts of fluids and an oral rehydrating solution containing glucose and electrolytes should be given. Oral rehydrating solutions, including brands such as Pedialyte, Infalyte, Ceralyte, and Oralyte, are available at most grocery stores and drug stores. They are essential for replacing fluids, **minerals**, and salts. Dehydration can upset the body's electrolyte balance, leading to potentially life-threatening problems such as heart beat abnormalities (arrhythmia). Prolonged, severe dehydration requires medical treatment with intravenous (IV) fluids and may require **hospitalization**.

Treatment of underlying metabolic or neurologic diseases, when possible, may help relieve symptoms.

KEY TERMS

Active motion—Spontaneous; produced by active efforts. Active range of motion exercises are those that are performed by the patient without assistance.

Acupuncture—Based on the same traditional Chinese medical foundation as acupressure, acupuncture uses sterile needles inserted at specific points to treat certain conditions or relieve pain.

Anoxia—Lack of oxygen.

Ataxia—A condition marked by impaired muscular coordination, most frequently resulting from disorders in the brain or spinal cord.

Biofeedback—A training technique that enables an individual to gain some element of control over involuntary or automatic body functions.

Central nervous system—Part of the nervous system consisting of the brain, cranial nerves, and spinal cord. The brain is the center of higher processes, such as thought and emotion and is responsible for the coordination and control of bodily activities and the interpretation of information from the senses. The cranial nerves and spinal cord link the brain to the peripheral nervous system, that is the nerves present in the rest of body.

Cerebral palsy—A nonprogressive movement disability caused by abnormal development of or damage to motor control centers of the brain.

Clonic—Referring to clonus, a series of muscle contractions and partial relaxations that alternate in some nervous diseases in the form of convulsive spasms.

Contraction—A tightening of the uterus during pregnancy. Contractions may or may not be painful and may or may not indicate labor.

Contracture—A tightening or shortening of muscles that prevents normal movement of the associated limb or other body part.

Dystonia—Painful involuntary muscle cramps or spasms.

Fasciculations—Small involuntary muscle contractions visible under the skin.

Genu recurvatum—Hyperextension of the knee.

Hyperactive reflexes—Reflexes that persist too long and may be too strong. For example, a hyperactive grasp reflex may cause the hand to stay clenched in a tight fist.

Hypermobility—Unusual flexibility of the joints, allowing them to be bent or moved beyond their normal range of motion.

Hypertonia—Having excessive muscular tone or strength.

Idiopathic—Refers to a disease or condition of unknown origin.

Motor neuron—A nerve cell that specifically controls and stimulates voluntary muscles.

Multiple sclerosis—A progressive, autoimmune disease of the central nervous system characterized by damage to the myelin sheath that covers nerves. The disease, which causes progressive paralysis, is marked by periods of exacerbation and remission.

Muscle spasm—Localized muscle contraction that occurs when the brain signals the muscle to contract.

Myoclonus—Involuntary contractions of a muscle or an interrelated group of muscles. Also known as myoclonic seizures.

Neurologist—A doctor who specializes in disorders of the nervous system, including the brain, spinal cord, and nerves.

Neurosurgeon—Physician who performs surgery on the nervous system.

Nocturnal leg cramps—Cramps that may be related to exertion and awaken a person during sleep.

Occupational therapist—A healthcare provider who specializes in adapting the physical environment to meet a patient's needs. An occupational therapist also assists patients and caregivers with activities of daily living and provide instructions on wheelchair use or other adaptive equipment.

Orthopedist—A doctor specializing in treatment of the musculoskeletal system.

Passive movement—Movement that occurs under the power of an outside source such as a clinician. There is no voluntary muscular contraction by the individual who is being passively moved.

Periodic limb movement disorder—A disorder characterized by involuntary flexion of leg muscles, causing twitching and leg extension or kicking during sleep.

Peripheral nerves—Nerves outside the brain and spinal cord that provide the link between the body and the central nervous system.

Physiatrist—A physician who specializes in physical medicine and rehabilitation.

Physical therapist—A healthcare provider who teaches patients how to perform therapeutic exercises to maintain maximum mobility and range of motion.

KEY TERMS (contd.)

Range of motion (ROM)—The range of motion of a joint from full extension to full flexion (bending) measured in degrees like a circle.

Restless legs syndrome (RLS)—A disorder in which the patient experiences crawling, aching, or other disagreeable sensations in the calves that can be relieved by movement. RLS is a frequent cause of difficulty falling asleep at night.

Rigidity—A constant resistance to passive motion.

Spinal cord injury—Injury to the spinal cord, via blunt or penetrating trauma.

Stroke—Interruption of blood flow to a part of the brain with consequent brain damage. A stroke may be caused by a blood clot or by hemorrhage due to a burst blood vessel. Also known as a cerebrovascular accident.

Alternative treatment

Alternative and complementary therapies include approaches that are considered to be outside the mainstream of traditional health care. In adults, alternative treatments for cramps include gingko (*Ginkgo biloba*) or Japanese quince (*Chaenomeles speciosa*). Supplements of vitamin E, niacin, calcium, and magnesium may also help to relieve the likelihood of night cramps, especially when taken at bedtime. Indications for these treatments in children have not been documented.

There are several alternative therapies that can be useful when treating **movement disorders**. Among the therapies that may be helpful are acupuncture, homeopathy, touch therapies, postural alignment therapies, and biofeedback. The progress made will depend on the individual and his/her condition.

Biofeedback training may be used to teach older children how to consciously reduce muscle tension. Biofeedback uses an electrical signal that indicates when a spastic muscle relaxes. The patient may be able to use biofeedback to learn how to consciously reduce muscle tension and possibly reduce symptoms.

Before learning or practicing any particular technique, it is important for the parent or caregiver and child to learn about the therapy, its safety and effectiveness, potential side effects, and the expertise and qualifications of the practitioner. Although some practices are beneficial, others may be harmful to certain patients. Alternative therapies should not be used as a substitute for medical therapies prescribed by a doctor. Parents should discuss these alternative treatments with the child's doctor to determine the techniques and remedies that may be beneficial for the child.

Prognosis

Occasional cramps are common and have no special medical significance.

Prevention

The likelihood of developing cramps may be reduced with regular exercise to build up energy reserves in the muscles. Avoiding exercising in extreme heat helps prevent heat cramps. Heat cramps can also be avoided by drinking plenty of water before and during exercise in extreme heat. Practicing proper body mechanics while sitting (sitting with both feet on the floor, back straight and legs uncrossed) can help prevent the development of leg cramps. Taking a warm bath before bedtime may increase circulation to the legs and reduce the incidence of nighttime leg cramps.

Nutritional concerns

The likelihood of developing cramps may be reduced by eating a well-balanced, healthy diet with appropriate levels of minerals. A registered dietitian can work with parents to identify a child's specific calorie needs and develop an individualized meal plan.

Fluids should be encouraged during all strenuous activities, especially in warm weather. People should aim for two to four eight-ounce glasses of fluid per hour of activity.

If an underlying neurological disorder has been identified, dietary guidelines are individualized, based on the child's age, diagnosis, overall health, caloric and energy needs, and level of functioning. Early identification, treatment, and correction of specific feeding problems will improve the health and nutritional status of the patient.

Parental concerns

Occasional muscle cramps are common. The most important concern is preventing dehydration, especially when the child is exercising in high or humid temperatures. Make sure the child drinks enough fluids before, during, and after sports and other activities. Pack a water bottle and/or sports drink for the child to have at sports practices, games, and other physical activities. Make sure the coach provides time out for water breaks. After the activity, encourage the child to continue drinking water to replace lost fluids.

If a movement disorder has been diagnosed, parents should work closely with the child's therapists and doctors to create an effective treatment plan. It is important for parents to communicate their treatment goals with the health care team. Parents should take an active role in the child's exercise program.

Raising a child with a movement disorder can be challenging. There are several support groups available to provide information and assistance.

Resources

BOOKS

Bradley, Walter G., et al. *Neurology in Clinical Practice*, 4th ed. Woburn, MA: Butterworth-Heinemann, 2003.

Martini, Frederic H. *Fundamentals of Anatomy and Physiology*, 6th ed. Englewood Cliffs, NJ: Prentice Hall, 2002.

ORGANIZATIONS

National Institute of Neurological Disorders and Stroke (NINDS). National Institutes of Health. PO Box 5801, Bethesda, MD 20824. Web site: <www.ninds.nih.gov/about_ninds>.

National Rehabilitation Information Center (NARIC). 4200 Forbes Blvd., Ste. 202, Lanham, MD 20700. Web site: <www.naric.com>.

Richard Robinson
Angela M. Costello

Muscular dystrophy

Definition

Muscular dystrophy is the name for a group of inherited disorders in which strength and muscle bulk gradually decline. Nine types of muscular dystrophies are generally recognized.

Description

The muscular dystrophies include:

• Duchenne muscular dystrophy (DMD), which affects young boys, causing progressive muscle weakness, usually beginning in the legs. It is the most severe form of muscular dystrophy.

• Becker muscular dystrophy (BMD), which affects older boys and young men, following a milder course than DMD

• Emery-Dreifuss muscular dystrophy (EDMD), which affects young boys, causing contractures and weakness in the calves, weakness in the shoulders and upper arms, and problems in the way electrical impulses travel through the heart to make it beat (heart conduction defects). Female carriers of EDMD are at risk for heart block.

• Limb-girdle muscular dystrophy (LGMD), which begins in late childhood to early adulthood and affects both men and women, causing weakness in the muscles around the hips and shoulders. It is the most variable of the muscular dystrophies, and there are as of 2004 several different forms of the disease recognized. Many people with suspected LGMD have probably been misdiagnosed in the past; therefore, the prevalence of the disease is difficult to estimate.

• Facioscapulohumeral muscular dystrophy (FSH), also known as Landouzy-Dejerine disease, which begins in late childhood to early adulthood and affects both men and women, causing weakness in the muscles of the face, shoulders, and upper arms. The hips and legs may also be affected.

• **Myotonic dystrophy**, also known as Steinert's disease, which affects both men and women, causing generalized weakness first seen in the face, feet, and hands. It is accompanied by the inability to relax the affected muscles (myotonia). Symptoms may begin any time from birth through adulthood.

• Oculopharyngeal muscular dystrophy (OPMD), which affects adults of both sexes, causing weakness in the eye muscles and throat

• Distal muscular dystrophy (DD), which begins in middle age or later, causing weakness in the muscles of the feet and hands

• Congenital muscular dystrophy (CMD), which is present from birth, results in generalized weakness, and usually progresses slowly. A subtype, called Fukuyama CMD, also involves **mental retardation**. Both are rare.

Demographics

DMD occurs in about one in 3,500 male births and affects approximately 8,000 boys and young men in the United States. A milder form occurs in very few female carriers.

BMD occurs in about one in 30,000 male births.

Fewer than 300 cases of EDMD have been identified.

The number of people affected with LGMD in the United States may be in the low thousands.

FSH occurs in about one out of every 20,000 people and affects approximately 13,000 people in the United States.

Myotonic dystrophy is the most common form of muscular dystrophy, affecting more than 30,000 people in the United States.

OPMD is most common among French Canadian families in Quebec and in Spanish-American families in the southwestern United States.

DD is most common in Sweden and rare in other parts of the world.

Fukuyama CMD is most common in Japan.

Causes and symptoms

Causes

Several of the muscular dystrophies, including DMD, BMD, CMD, and most forms of LGMD, are due to defects in the genes for a complex of muscle proteins. This complex spans the muscle cell membrane to unite a fibrous network on the interior of the cell with a fibrous network on the outside. As of 2004 the theory was that by linking these two networks, the complex acts as a "shock absorber," redistributing and evening out the forces generated by contraction of the muscle, thereby preventing rupture of the muscle membrane. Defects in the proteins of the complex lead to deterioration of the muscle. Symptoms of these diseases set in as the muscle gradually exhausts its ability to repair itself. Both DMD and BMD are caused by flaws in the gene for the protein called dystrophin. The flaw leading to DMD prevents the formation of any dystrophin, while that of BMD allows some protein to be made, accounting for the differences in severity and onset between the two diseases. Differences among the other diseases in the muscles involved and the ages of onset are less easily explained.

The causes of the other muscular dystrophies are not as well understood:

• One form of LGMD is caused by defects in the gene for a muscle enzyme, calpain. The relationship between this defect and the symptoms of the disease is unclear.

• EDMD is due to a defect in the gene for a protein called emerin, which is found in the membrane of a cell's nucleus, but whose exact function is unknown.

• Myotonic dystrophy is linked to gene defects for a protein that may control the flow of charged particles within muscle cells. This gene defect is called a triple repeat, meaning it contains extra triplets of DNA code. It is possible that this mutation affects nearby genes as well, and that the widespread symptoms of myotonic dystrophy are due to a range of genetic disruptions.

• The gene for OPMD appears to also be mutated with a triple repeat. The function of the affected protein may involve translation of genetic messages in a cell's nucleus.

• The cause of FSH is unknown. The genetic region responsible for it has been localized on its chromosome, however.

• The gene responsible for DD has not yet been found.

Genetics and patterns of inheritance

The muscular dystrophies are genetic diseases, meaning they are caused by defects in genes. Genes, which are linked together on chromosomes, have two functions. They code for the production of proteins, and they are the material of inheritance. Parents pass along genes to their children, providing them with a complete set of instructions for making their own proteins.

Because both parents contribute genetic material to their offspring, each child carries two copies of almost every gene, one from each parent. For some diseases to occur, both copies must be flawed. Such diseases are called autosomal recessive diseases. Some forms of LGMD and DD exhibit this pattern of inheritance, as does CMD. A person with only one flawed copy, called a carrier, will not have the disease but may pass the flawed gene on to children. When two carriers have children, the chances of having a child with the disease is one in four for each pregnancy.

Other diseases occur when only one flawed gene copy is present. Such diseases are called autosomal dominant diseases. Other forms of LGMD exhibit this pattern of inheritance, as do DM, FSH, OPMD, and some forms of DD. When a person affected by the disease has a child with someone not affected, the chances of having an affected child is one in two.

Because of chromosomal differences between the sexes, some genes are not present in two copies. The chromosomes that determine whether a person is male or female are called the X and Y chromosomes. A person with two X chromosomes is female, while a person with one X and one Y is male. While the X chromosome carries many genes, the Y chromosome carries almost none. Therefore, a male has only one copy of each gene on the X chromosome, and if it is flawed, he will have the disease that defect causes. Such diseases are said to be X-linked. X-linked diseases include DMD, BMD, and

EDMD. Women are not usually affected by X-linked diseases, since they will likely have one unaffected copy between the two chromosomes. Some female carriers of DMD suffer a mild form of the disease, probably because their one unaffected gene copy is shut down in some of their cells.

Women carriers of X-linked diseases have a one-in-two chance of passing the flawed gene on to each child born. Daughters who inherit the disease gene are carriers. A son born without the disease gene is free of the disease and cannot pass it on to his children. A son born with the defect has the disease. He will pass the flawed gene on to each of his daughters, who will then be carriers, but to none of his sons (because they inherit his Y chromosome).

Not all genetic flaws are inherited. As many as one-third of the cases of DMD are due to new mutations that arise during egg formation in the mother. New mutations are less common in other forms of muscular dystrophy.

Symptoms

All of the muscular dystrophies are marked by muscle weakness as the major symptom. The distribution of symptoms, age of onset, and progression differ significantly. **Pain** is sometimes a symptom of each, usually due to the effects of weakness on joint position.

DMD   A boy with Duchenne muscular dystrophy usually begins to show symptoms as a preschooler. The legs are affected first, making walking difficult and causing balance problems. Most affected persons walk three to six months later than expected and have difficulty running. Later on, the boy with DMD will push his hands against his knees to rise to a standing position, to compensate for leg weakness. About the same time, his calves will begin to swell, though with fibrous tissue rather than with muscle and feel firm and rubbery; this condition gives DMD one of its alternate names, pseudo-hypertrophic muscular dystrophy. The boy will widen his stance to maintain balance and walk with a waddling gait to advance his weakened legs. Contractures (permanent muscle tightening) usually begin by age five or six, most severely in the calf muscles. This pulls the foot down and back, forcing the boy to walk on tip-toes, called equinus, and further decreases balance. Frequent falls and broken bones are common beginning at this age. Climbing stairs and rising unaided may become impossible by age nine or ten, and most boys use a wheelchair for mobility by the age of 12. Weakening of the trunk muscles around this age often leads to **scoliosis** (a side-to-side spine curvature) and kyphosis (a front-to-back curvature).

The most serious weakness of DMD is weakness of the diaphragm, the sheet of muscles at the top of the abdomen that perform the main work of breathing and coughing. Diaphragm weakness leads to reduced energy and stamina and increased lung infection because of the inability to **cough** effectively. Young men with DMD often live into their twenties and beyond, provided they have mechanical ventilation assistance and good respiratory hygiene.

About one third of boys with DMD experience specific learning disabilities, including trouble learning by ear rather than by sight and trouble paying attention to long lists of instructions. Individualized educational programs usually compensate well for these disabilities.

BMD   The symptoms of BMD usually appear in late childhood to early adulthood. Though the progression of symptoms may parallel that of DMD, the symptoms are usually milder, and the course more variable. The same pattern of leg weakness, unsteadiness, and contractures occurs later for the young man with BMD, often allowing independent walking into the twenties or early thirties. Scoliosis may occur but is usually milder and progresses more slowly. Heart muscle disease (cardiomyopathy) occurs more commonly in BMD. Problems may include irregular heartbeats (arrhythmias) and congestive heart failure. Symptoms may include fatigue, shortness of breath, chest pain, and **dizziness**. Respiratory weakness also occurs and may lead to the need for mechanical ventilation.

EDMD   This type of muscular dystrophy usually begins in early childhood, often with contractures preceding muscle weakness. Weakness affects the shoulder and upper arm originally, along with the calf muscles, leading to foot-drop. Most men with EDMD survive into middle age, although a defect in the heart's rhythm (heart block) may be fatal if not treated with a pacemaker.

LGMD   While there are at least six genes that cause the various types of LGMD, two major clinical forms of LGMD are usually recognized. A severe childhood form is similar in appearance to DMD but is inherited as an autosomal recessive trait. Symptoms of adult-onset LGMD usually appear in a person's teens or twenties and are marked by progressive weakness and wasting of the muscles closest to the trunk. Contractures may occur, and the ability to walk is usually lost about 20 years after onset. Some people with LGMD develop respiratory weakness that requires use of a ventilator. Lifespan may be somewhat shortened. (Autosomal dominant forms usually occur later in life and progress relatively slowly.)

FSH FSH varies in its severity and age of onset, even among members of the same **family**. Symptoms most commonly begin in the teens or early twenties, though infant or childhood onset is possible. Symptoms tend to be more severe in those with earlier onset. The disease is named for the regions of the body most severely affected by the disease: muscles of the face (facio-), shoulders (scapulo-), and upper arms (humeral). Hips and legs may be affected as well. Children with FSH often develop partial or complete deafness.

The first symptom noticed is often difficulty lifting objects above the shoulders. The weakness may be greater on one side than the other. Shoulder weakness also causes the shoulder blades to jut backward, called scapular winging. Muscles in the upper arm often lose bulk sooner than those of the forearm, giving a "Popeye" appearance to the arms. Facial weakness may lead to loss of facial expression, difficulty closing the eyes completely, and inability to drink through a straw, blow up a balloon, or whistle. A person with FSH may not develop strong facial wrinkles. Contracture of the calf muscles may cause foot-drop, leading to frequent tripping over curbs or rough spots. People with earlier onset often require a wheelchair for mobility, while those with later onset rarely do.

MYOTONIC DYSTROPHY Symptoms of myotonic dystrophy include facial weakness and a slack jaw, drooping eyelids (ptosis), and muscle wasting in the forearms and calves. A person with this dystrophy has difficulty relaxing his grasp, especially if the object is cold. Myotonic dystrophy affects heart muscle, causing arrhythmias and heart block, and the muscles of the digestive system, leading to motility disorders and **constipation**. Other body systems are affected as well: myotonic dystrophy may cause cataracts, retinal degeneration, low IQ, frontal balding, skin disorders, testicular atrophy, **sleep** apnea, and insulin resistance. An increased need or desire for sleep is common, as is diminished motivation. Severe disability affects most people with this type of dystrophy within 20 years of onset, although most do not require a wheelchair even late in life.

OPMD OPMD usually begins in a person's thirties or forties, with weakness in the muscles controlling the eyes and throat. Symptoms include drooping eyelids, difficulty swallowing (dysphagia), and weakness progresses to other muscles of the face, neck, and occasionally the upper limbs. Swallowing difficulty may cause aspiration or the introduction of food or saliva into the airways. **Pneumonia** may follow.

DD DD usually begins in the twenties or thirties with weakness in the hands, forearms, and lower legs.

Difficulty with fine movements such as typing or fastening buttons may be the first symptoms. Symptoms progress slowly, and the disease usually does not affect life span.

CMD CMD is marked by severe muscle weakness from birth, with infants displaying "floppiness" and very little voluntary movement. Nonetheless, a child with CMD may learn to walk, either with or without some assistive device, and live into young adulthood or beyond. In contrast, children with Fukuyama CMD are rarely able to walk and have severe mental retardation. Most children with this type of CMD die in childhood.

When to call the doctor

A doctor should be consulted whenever muscle development is thought to be abnormal or slow.

Diagnosis

Diagnosis of muscular dystrophy involves a careful medical history and a thorough physical exam to determine the distribution of symptoms and to rule out other causes. Family history may give important clues, since all the muscular dystrophies are genetic conditions (though no family history will be evident in the event of new mutations).

Lab tests may include the following:

- Blood level of the muscle enzyme creatine kinase (CK). CK levels rise in the blood due to muscle damage and may be seen in some conditions even before symptoms appear.

- Muscle biopsy, in which a small piece of muscle tissue is removed for microscopic examination. Changes in the structure of muscle cells and presence of fibrous tissue or other aberrant structures are characteristic of different forms of muscular dystrophy. The muscle tissue can also be stained to detect the presence or absence of particular proteins, including dystrophin.

- Electromyogram (EMG). EMG is used to examine the response of the muscles to stimulation. Decreased response is seen in muscular dystrophy. Other characteristic changes are seen in DM.

- Genetic tests. Several of the muscular dystrophies can be positively identified by testing for the presence of the mutated gene involved. Accurate genetic tests are available for DMD, BMD, DM, several forms of LGMD, and EDMD.

- Other specific tests as necessary. For EDMD and BMD, for example, an electrocardiogram may be nee-

MD patient Sarah Schwegel with Jerry Lewis at the Muscular Dystrophy Telethon, which raises money for research for the cure and treatment of muscular dystrophy. *(Muscular Dystrophy Association.)*

ded to test heart function, and hearing tests are performed for children with FSH.

For most forms of muscular dystrophy, accurate diagnosis is not difficult when done by someone familiar with the range of diseases. There are exceptions, however. Even with a muscle biopsy, it may be difficult to distinguish between FSH and another muscle disease, polymyositis. Childhood-onset LGMD is often mistaken for the much more common DMD, especially when it occurs in boys. BMD with an early onset appears very similar to DMD, and a muscle biopsy may be needed to accurately distinguish them. The muscular dystrophies may be confused with diseases involving the motor neurons, such as **spinal muscular atrophy**; diseases of the neuromuscular junction, such as myasthenia gravis; and other muscle diseases, as all involve generalized weakening of varying distribution.

Treatment

Drugs

As of 2004 there were no cures for any of the muscular dystrophies. Prednisone, a corticosteroid, has been shown to delay the progression of DMD somewhat, for reasons that as of 2004 are still unclear. Prednisone is also prescribed for BMD.

Treatment of muscular dystrophy is mainly directed at preventing the complications of weakness, including decreased mobility and dexterity, contractures, scoliosis, heart defects, and respiratory insufficiency.

Physical therapy

Physical therapy, in particular regular stretching, is used to maintain the range of motion of affected muscles and to prevent or delay contractures. Braces are used as well, especially on the ankles and feet to prevent equinus. Full-leg braces may be used in DMD to prolong the period of independent walking. Strengthening other muscle groups to compensate for weakness may be possible if the affected muscles are few and isolated, as in the earlier stages of the milder muscular dystrophies. Regular, nonstrenuous **exercise** helps maintain general good health. Strenuous exercise is usually not recommended, since it may damage muscles further.

Surgery

When contractures become more pronounced, tenotomy surgery may be performed. In this operation, the tendon of the contractured muscle is cut, and the limb is braced in its normal resting position while the tendon regrows. In FSH, surgical fixation of the scapula can help compensate for shoulder weakness. For a person with OPMD, surgical lifting of the eyelids may help compensate for weakened muscular control. For a person with DM, sleep apnea may be treated surgically to maintain an open airway. Scoliosis surgery is often needed in DMD but much less often in other muscular dystrophies. Surgery is recommended at a much lower degree of curvature for DMD than for scoliosis due to other conditions, since the decline in respiratory function in DMD makes surgery at a later time dangerous. In this surgery, the vertebrae are fused together to maintain the spine in the upright position. Steel rods are inserted at the time of operation to keep the spine rigid while the bones grow together.

When any type of surgery is performed in people with muscular dystrophy, anesthesia must be carefully selected. People with MD are susceptible to a severe reaction, known as malignant hyperthermia, when given halothane anesthetic.

Occupational therapy

The occupational therapist suggests techniques and tools to compensate for the loss of strength and dexterity. Strategies may include modifications in the home, adaptive utensils and dressing aids, compensatory movements and positioning, wheelchair accessories, or communication aids.

Nutrition

Good **nutrition** helps to promote general health in all the muscular dystrophies. No special diet or supplement has as of 2004 been shown to be of use in any of

KEY TERMS

Autosomal dominant—A pattern of inheritance in which only one of the two copies of an autosomal gene must be abnormal for a genetic condition or disease to occur. An autosomal gene is a gene that is located on one of the autosomes or non-sex chromosomes. A person with an autosomal dominant disorder has a 50 percent chance of passing it to each of their offspring.

Autosomal recessive—A pattern of inheritance in which both copies of an autosomal gene must be abnormal for a genetic condition or disease to occur. An autosomal gene is a gene that is located on one of the autosomes or non-sex chromosomes. When both parents have one abnormal copy of the same gene, they have a 25 percent chance with each pregnancy that their offspring will have the disorder.

Becker muscular dystrophy (BMD)—A type of muscular dystrophy that affects older boys and men and usually follows a milder course than Duchenne muscular dystrophy.

Contracture—A tightening or shortening of muscles that prevents normal movement of the associated limb or other body part.

Distal muscular dystrophy (DD)—A form of muscular dystrophy that usually begins in middle age or later, causing weakness in the muscles of the feet and hands.

Duchenne muscular dystrophy (DMD)—The most severe form of muscular dystrophy, DMD usually affects young boys and causes progressive muscle weakness, usually beginning in the legs.

Dystrophin—A protein that helps muscle tissue repair itself. Both Duchenne muscular dystrophy and Becker muscular dystrophy are caused by flaws in the gene that tells the body how to make this protein.

Facioscapulohumeral muscular dystrophy (FSH)—This form of muscular dystrophy, also known as Landouzy-Dejerine disease, begins in late childhood to early adulthood and affects both men and women, causing weakness in the muscles of the face, shoulders, and upper arms.

Limb-girdle muscular dystrophy (LGMD)—A form of muscular dystrophy that begins in late childhood to early adulthood and affects both men and women. It causes weakness in the muscles around the hips and shoulders.

Myotonic dystrophy—A form of muscular dystrophy, also known as Steinert's disease, that affects both men and women. It is characterized by delay in the ability to relax muscles after forceful contraction (myotonia) and wasting of muscles, as well as other abnormalities.

Oculopharyngeal muscular dystrophy—A type of muscular dystrophy that affects adults of both sexes, causing weakness in the eye muscles and throat.

---

the conditions. The weakness in the throat muscles seen especially in OPMD and later DMD may necessitate the use of a gastrostomy tube, inserted in the stomach to provide nutrition directly.

Cardiac care

The arrhythmias of EDMD and BMD may be treatable with antiarrhythmia drugs such as mexiletine or nifedipine. A pacemaker may be implanted if these do not provide adequate control. Heart transplants are increasingly common for men with BMD.

Respiratory care

People who develop weakness of the diaphragm or other ventilatory muscles may require a mechanical ventilator to continue breathing deeply enough. Air may be administered through a nasal mask or mouthpiece or through a tracheostomy tube, which is inserted through a surgical incision through the neck and into the windpipe. Most people with muscular dystrophy do not need a tracheostomy, although some may prefer it to continual use of a mask or mouthpiece. Supplemental oxygen is not needed. Good hygiene of the lungs is critical for health and long-term survival of a person with weakened ventilatory muscles. Assisted cough techniques provide the strength needed to clear the airways of secretions; an assisted cough machine is also available and provides excellent results.

Experimental treatments

Two experimental procedures aiming to cure DMD have attracted a great deal of attention. In myoblast transfer, millions of immature muscle cells are injected into an affected muscle. The goal of the treatment is to promote the growth of the injected cells, replacing the defective host cells with healthy new ones. Despite continued claims to the contrary by a very few researchers, this procedure is widely judged a failure.

Gene therapy introduces good copies of the dystrophin gene into muscle cells. The goal is to allow the existing muscle cells to use the new gene to produce the dystrophin it cannot make with its flawed gene. Problems have included immune rejection of the virus used to introduce the gene, loss of gene function after several weeks, and an inability to get the gene to enough cells to make a functional difference in the affected muscle. Nonetheless, after a number of years of refining the techniques in mice, researchers began human trials in 1998. These trials are ongoing.

Prognosis

The expected life span for a male with DMD has increased significantly since the 1970s. Most young men live into their early or mid-twenties. Respiratory infections become an increasing problem as their breathing becomes weaker, and these infections are usually the cause of death.

The course of the other muscular dystrophies is more variable; expected life spans and degrees of disability are hard to predict but may be related to age of onset and initial symptoms. Prediction is made more difficult because, as new genes are discovered, it becomes clear that several of the dystrophies are not uniform disorders but rather symptom groups caused by different genes.

People with dystrophies with significant heart involvement (BMD, EDMD, Myotonic dystrophy) may nonetheless have almost normal life spans, provided that cardiac complications are monitored and treated aggressively. The respiratory involvement of BMD and LGMD similarly require careful and prompt treatment.

Prevention

As of 2004 there was no way to prevent any of the muscular dystrophies in a person who has the genes responsible for these disorders. Accurate genetic tests, including prenatal tests, are available for some of the muscular dystrophies. Results of these tests may be useful for purposes of family planning.

Nutritional concerns

There is no known link between nutrition and the onset of muscular dystrophy.

Parental concerns

Prospective parents with first-degree relatives (parents, siblings, or other children) who have been diagnosed with muscular dystrophy should consider including counseling in their family planning process.

Resources

BOOKS

Barohn, Richard J. "Muscle Diseases." In *Cecil Textbook of Medicine*, 22nd ed. Edited by Lee Goldman et al. Philadelphia: Saunders, 2003, pp. 2387–99.

Brown, Robert H., and Jerry R. Mendell. "Muscular Dystrophies and Other Muscle Diseases." In *Harrison's Principles of Internal Medicine*, 15th ed. Edited by Eugene Braunwald et al. New York: McGraw-Hill, 2001, pp. 2529–40.

Emery, Alan E. *Muscular Dystrophies.* Cary, NC: Oxford University Press, 2003.

Muscular Dystrophy: A Medical Dictionary, Bibliography, and Annotated Research Guide to Internet References. San Diego, CA: Icon Health Publications, 2003.

Sarnat, Harvey B. "Muscular Dystrophies." In *Nelson Textbook of Pediatrics*, 17th ed. Edited by Richard E. Behrman et al. Philadelphia: Saunders, 2003, pp. 2060–9.

PERIODICALS

Cossu, G., and M. Sampaolesi. "New therapies for muscular dystrophy: cautious optimism." *Trends in Molecular Medicine* 10, no. 10 (2004): 516–20.

Rando, T. A. "Artificial sweeteners—enhancing glycosylation to treat muscular dystrophies." *New England Journal of Medicine* 351, no. 12 (2004): 1254–6.

ORGANIZATIONS

American Academy of Physical Medicine and Rehabilitation. One IBM Plaza, Suite 2500, Chicago, IL 60611–3604. Web site: <www.aapmr.org/>.

Muscular Dystrophy Association. National Headquarters, 3300 E. Sunrise Drive, Tucson, AZ 85718. Web site: <www.mdausa.org/

WEB SITES

"Muscular Dystrophies." *Merck Manual.* Available online at <www.merck.com/mrkshared/mmanual/section14/chapter184/184a.jsp> (accessed January 7, 2005).

"Muscular Dystrophy." *Milton S. Hershey Medical Center School of Medicine.* Available online at <www.hmc.psu.edu/healthinfo/m/musculardystrophy.htm> (accessed January 7, 2005).

L. Fleming Fallon, Jr., MD, DrPH

Mutism

Definition

Mutism is a rare childhood condition characterized by a consistent failure to speak in situations where talking is expected.

Description

In mutism, the child has the ability to converse normally and does so, for example, in the home, but consistently fails to speak in specific situations such as at school or with strangers. The condition is also called selective mutism, to differentiate it from children who are physically unable to speak. Experts believe that this selective problem is associated with **anxiety** and **fear** in social situations such as in school or in the company of adults. It is, therefore, often considered a type of social phobia. This is not a communication disorder because the affected children can converse normally in some situations. It is not a developmental disorder because their ability to talk, when they choose to do so, is appropriate for their age level. This problem has been linked to anxiety, and one of the major ways in which both children and adults attempt to cope with anxiety is by avoiding whatever provokes the anxiety. Affected children are typically shy and are especially so in the presence of strangers and unfamiliar surroundings or situations. However, the behaviors of children with this condition go beyond **shyness**.

These children understand language and are able to talk normally in settings where they are comfortable, secure and relaxed. Over 90 percent of children with mutism also have social phobia or social anxiety, and some experts view mutism as a symptom of social anxiety. Others view it as a separate, but related, disorder. It is not yet understood why some individuals develop typical symptoms of social anxiety, like reluctance to speak in front of a group of people or feeling embarrassed easily, while others experience the inability to speak that characterizes mutism. What is clear is that children and adolescents with mutism have an actual fear of speaking and of social interactions where there is an expectation to talk. They may also be unable to communicate nonverbally, may be unable to make eye contact, and may stand motionless with fear as they are confronted with specific social settings. This can be quite heart wrenching to watch and is often very debilitating for the child as well as frustrating for parents and teachers.

A child meets the criteria for mutism if the following are true:

- The child does not speak in certain selected places such as school or at particular social events.
- The child speaks normally in at least one environment, usually in the home, but a small percentage of children with mutism are mute at home.
- The child's inability to speak interferes with his or her ability to function in school and/or social settings.
- The mutism has persisted for at least one month.
- The mutism is not caused by a communication disorder (such as **stuttering**) and does not occur as part of other mental disorders (such as **autism**).

Demographics

It is estimated that one in every 1,000 school-age children are affected by mutism.

Causes and symptoms

Mutism is believed to arise from anxiety experienced in social situations where the child may be called upon to speak. Refusing to speak or speaking in a whisper spares the child from the possible humiliation or embarrassment of saying the "wrong" thing. When asked a direct question by teachers, for example, the affected child may act as if they are unable to answer. Some children may communicate via gestures, nodding, or very brief utterances. Additional features may include excessive shyness, oppositional behavior, and impaired learning at school.

The majority of children with mutism have a genetic predisposition to anxiety. In other words, they have inherited the tendency to be anxious from **family** members and may be vulnerable to the development of an anxiety disorder. Very often, these children show signs of anxiety, such as difficulty separating from parents, moodiness, clinging behavior, inflexibility, **sleep** problems, frequent **tantrums** and crying, and extreme shyness starting in infancy. When they reach the age when they begin to interact socially outside the family environment, their persistent fear of speaking or communicating begins to manifest in symptoms like freezing, lack of response, stiff posture, blank facial expression, lack of smiling, and mutism. Studies have shown that some children are born with inhibited temperaments, which means that even as infants, they are more likely to be fearful and wary of new situations. There is reason to believe that many or most children with mutism were born with this inhibited personality type.

Research has also shown that these behaviorally inhibited children have a decreased threshold of excitability in the area of the brain called the amygdala. The normal function of the amygdala is to receive and process signals of potential danger and set off a series of reactions that will help individuals protect themselves, such as the fight-or-flight response. In anxious individuals, the amygdala seems to overreact and set off these responses even when the individual is not really in danger. In the case of selectively mute children, the anxiety responses are triggered by social interactions in settings such as school, the playground, or social gatherings. Over time, a child with selective mutism becomes mute because of an inability to cope with fearful feelings that occur when he or she is expected to speak. When the child does not respond, the pressure is usually removed and the child feels relief from fear.

Besides genetics and biological factors, researchers believe that other factors may contribute to the development of selective mutism. A significant number of children with mutism also have expressive **language disorders**, and a fairly large number come from a bilingual environment, which may add to a child's vulnerability to mutism. Anxiety is still the root cause of the mutism, and it is theorized that these language difficulties may make the child more self-conscious about his or her speaking skills and thus may increase the fear of being judged by others. These risk factors are probably additive; in other words, if a child has genetic risk of anxiety, plus a bilingual environment or a speech disorder, the likelihood of that child developing selective mutism becomes higher with each added factor.

When to call the doctor

If selective mutism persists for more than a month, parents should discuss this pattern with their child's teachers, family physician, or pediatrician. The doctor may refer the child to a speech therapist, psychiatrist or psychologist.

Diagnosis

The diagnosis of mutism is fairly easy to make because the signs and symptoms are clear-cut and easily observable. However, other social disorders effecting social speech, such as autism or **schizophrenia**, must be considered in the diagnosis. The average age of diagnosis is between three and eight years of age; however, in retrospect many parents will say that their child displayed signs of excessive shyness and inhibition since infancy. It is not until children enter school, where there is an expectation to perform, interact, and speak, that mutism becomes more apparent. Often a parent suspects during the **preschool** years that there is a problem, but lack of knowledge about selective mutism makes it diffi-

cult to find help. It is all too common for parents to question their child's pediatrician about the child's inability to speak in public and be told that the child is just shy and will outgrow the behavior. Once a child enters school, though, teachers often point out the severity of the problem to the parents. Some parents are also reluctant to have their child evaluated and treated.

Treatment

Since selective mutism is an anxiety disorder, successful treatment focuses on methods to lower anxiety, increase **self-esteem**, and increase confidence and communication in social settings. The emphasis should never be on "getting a child to talk," nor should the goal of treatment be for the child to speak to the therapist. Progress outside the clinic or doctor's office is much more important than whether the child speaks during the therapy session. Initially, all expectations for verbalization should be removed. As the child's anxiety is lowered and confidence increases, verbalization usually follows. If it does not occur spontaneously, techniques can later be added to help encourage progress. A professional should devise an individualized treatment plan for each child and allow the child, family, and school to have a great deal of input into the treatment process. Therapy usually involves some combination of behavioral therapy, cognitive behavioral therapy, **play therapy**, or psychoanalytic therapy, medication, and in some cases, **family therapy**.

Behavioral therapy

The primary types of behavioral therapy used for selective mutism are desensitization, fading, and positive reinforcement techniques. Desensitization means exposing a child to something that is feared in a gradual way, in order to help the child overcome the fear. Fading therapy is a type of desensitization that creates a series of events or exposures that starts with a situation that is comfortable for the child, such as being alone in the classroom with a parent and playing a board game. New variables that are progressively more difficult are gradually added. For example, having the teacher walk past the room and overhear the child speaking to the parent, and then having the teacher enter the room, and eventually have the child interacting with the teacher in the classroom. Positive reinforcement, or the use of rewards for changes in behavior, should only be introduced after anxiety is lowered and the child is ready to begin working on goals. It is also important to realize that there are many intermediate steps between being mute and being verbal. During the early stages of treatment, nonverbal communication such as pointing, nodding, and use of pictures to express needs, can be encouraged and rewarded. Though some may fear that allowing nonverbal communication will enable the mutism to continue, many therapists believe it is a necessary step for most children with mutism to overcome their communication anxiety in a step-by-step manner.

Cognitive behavioral therapy

Cognitive behavioral therapy (CBT) helps children change their thoughts (the cognitive part) and their actions (the behavioral part). CBT therapists recognize that anxious children tend to exaggerate the frightening aspects of certain situations, so they help the children gain a more realistic perspective in order to decrease anxiety. They also know that anxious children avoid situations they fear or (in the case of selectively mute children) avoid speech in anxiety-provoking situations. Avoidance makes anxiety worse. Therefore, CBT helps the child overcome avoidance by gradually facing what is feared with lots of praise and positive reinforcement for doing so. Parents, teachers, and other adults around the child can be very helpful in this process. Cognitive strategies for the selectively mute child aim to reduce the social anxiety that is often part of the disorder. Cognitive strategies help the child challenge negative expectations and replace them with more realistic ones. This process is combined with behavioral strategies that focus on helping the selectively mute child to talk in increasingly challenging situations. The therapist carefully collects information on where and with whom the child already speaks and then helps the child choose a goal to work on in a situation that is just slightly more challenging.

Play therapy

Play therapy is an adaptation of psychoanalytic therapy, which is a psychological treatment based on helping people understand their unconscious thoughts. This field of psychology includes Freudian theories but also many other modern theories about how our minds work. Play therapy refers to the use of play as communication; therapists who are trained in these techniques observe and participate in play activities with the child and interpret the child's actions as a form of subconscious communication. There is not a lot of evidence for play therapy being effective in the treatment of mutism; however, a well trained play therapist might be able to help a child with mutism better understand and express emotions and may be a part of an overall treatment plan. It may be especially useful when a stressful event or environment is a factor. For some children there may be contributing factors such as the death of a parent or other loved one, a **divorce**, or a move. Play therapists may be able to help a child to express and better understand the emotions that they are experiencing in these situations.

Family therapy

Since there is no evidence of family pathology being the cause of most cases of mutism, this type of therapy is not necessary in most cases. However, if there are unusual circumstances or a highly stressful family environment, then it may be advisable for families to participate in more intensive family therapy.

Prognosis

The prognosis for mutism is good. Sometimes it disappears suddenly on its own. The negative impact on learning and school activities may, however, persist into adult life.

Prevention

Mutism cannot be prevented because the cause is not known. However, family conflict or problems at school contribute to the seriousness of the symptoms.

Parental concerns

Parents should remove all pressure and expectations for the child to speak, conveying to their child that they understand he or she feels "scared" to speak or has difficulty speaking at times. Many parents report that simply removing the pressure and letting the child know that they understand can help to improvement the child's symptoms. Parents should also reassure their child that they will help him or her through this difficult time. The child's accomplishments and efforts should be praised, and support and understanding should be offered when the child has difficulties and frustrations. Parents should read as much information as they can to become well informed about selective mutism.

It is important for family members to be educated and informed about selective mutism and to be included in the child's treatment plan in order to provide a supportive environment for the child's recovery. The stress of dealing with the child's mutism may have created various imbalances in family dynamics, and parents may need help in coming to terms with their own emotions and becoming more consistent in their parenting styles. It is also common for parents to begin to recognize their own anxiety as they are learning to help their child. Many times they will seek help in overcoming social anxiety to improve their ability to advocate for their child's needs and to become a positive role model for their child.

KEY TERMS

Amygdala—An almond-shaped brain structure in the limbic system that is activated in stressful situations to trigger the emotion of fear. It is thought that the emotional overreactions in Alzheimer's patients are related to the destruction of neurons in the amygdala.

Autism—A developmental disability that appears early in life, in which normal brain development is disrupted and social and communication skills are retarded, sometimes severely.

Behavior modification—A form of therapy that uses rewards to reinforce desired behavior. An example would be to give a child a piece of chocolate for grooming appropriately.

Cognitive-behavioral therapy—A type of psychotherapy in which people learn to recognize and change negative and self-defeating patterns of thinking and behavior.

Family therapy—A type of therapy in which the entire immediate family participates.

Play therapy—A type of psychotherapy for young children involving the use of toys and games to build a therapeutic relationship and encourage the child's self-expression.

Resources

BOOKS

Baldwin, Sylvia, and Tony Cline. *Selective Mutism in Children.* London: Whurr Publishers Ltd., 2004.

Spencer, Elizabeth DuPont, et al. *The Anxiety Cure for Kids: A Guide for Parents.* Hoboken, NJ: Wiley, 2003.

PERIODICALS

Bergman, R. Lindsey, et al. "Prevalence and Description of Selective Mutism in a School-Based Sample." *Journal of the American Academy of Child and Adolescent Psychiatry* 41 (August 2002): 938–46.

Krysanski, Valerie L. "A Brief Review of Selective Mutism Literature." *The Journal of Psychology* 137 (January 2003): 29–40.

Schum, Robert L. "Selective Mutism: An Integrated Treatment Approach." *ASHA Leader* 7 (September 24, 2002): 4–6.

Yeganeh, Robin, et al. "Clinical Distinctions Between Selective Mutism and Social Phobia: An Investigation of Childhood Psychopathology." *Journal of the American Academy of Child and Adolescent Psychiatry* 42 (September 2003): 1069–1075.

ORGANIZATIONS

Anxiety Disorders Association of America. 8730 Georgia Avenue, Suite 600, Silver Spring, MD 20910. Web site: <www.adaa.org>.

National Academy of Child & Adolescent Psychiatry. 3615 Wisconsin Ave. NW, Washington, DC 20016. Web site: <www.aacap.org>.

WEB SITES

Gallagher, Richard. "About Selective Mutism—Profiles of Silence." *New York University Child Study Center*, 2004. Available online at <www.aboutourkids.org/aboutour/articles/about_mutism.html> (accessed November 12, 2004).

"Selective Mutism." *American Speech-Language-Hearing Association*, 2004. Available online at <www.asha.org/public/speech/disorders/Selective-Mutism.htm> (accessed November 12, 2004).

Donald Garner Barstow
Ken R. Wells

Myers-Briggs Type Indicator

Definition

The Myers-Briggs Type Indicator (MBTI) is a widely used personality inventory, or test, employed in vocational, educational, and psychotherapy settings to evaluate personality type in adolescents and adults age 14 and older.

Purpose

In an educational setting, the MBTI may be performed to assess student learning style. In a classroom setting, the MBTI may be used to help teens and young adults better understand their learning, communication, and social interaction styles. Guidance counselors also might use the test to help teens determine which occupational field or college major they might be best suited for.

Because the MBTI is also a tool for self-discovery, mental health professionals may administer the test in counseling sessions to provide their patients with insight into their behavior. Among adults, the MBTI is also used in organizational settings to assess management skills and facilitate teamwork and problem solving.

Description

In 2000, an estimated two million people took the MBTI, making it the most frequently used personality inventory available. First introduced in 1942, the test was the work of mother and daughter Katharine C. Myers Briggs and Isabel Briggs. There are now several different versions of the test available. Form M, which contains 93 items and is a self-scoring **assessment**, is the most commonly used. It can be used in a classroom or other group setting, and takes approximately 15 to 25 minutes to complete.

The Myers-Briggs inventory is based on Carl Jung's theory of types, outlined in his 1921 work *Psychological Types*. Jung's theory holds that human beings are either introverts or extraverts, and their behavior follows from these inborn psychological types. He also believed that people take in and process information in different ways, based on their personality traits.

The Myers-Briggs evaluates personality type and preference based on the four Jungian psychological types:

• extraversion (E) or introversion (I)

• sensing (S) or intuition (N)

• thinking (T) or feeling (F)

• judging (J) or perceiving (P)

A derivative version of the MBTI, developed by Elizabeth Murphy and Charles Meisgeier, is available for children age seven through 13 (grades two through eight). The assessment, called the Murphy-Meisgeier Type Indicator for Children (MMTIC) uses the same four psychological types as the MBTI, but is written for a second grade reading level.

Precautions

The MBTI should only be administered, scored, and interpreted by a professional trained in its use (except in the case of Form M, which can be self-scored but should still be administered and interpreted by a professional). Cultural and language differences in the test subject may affect performance and may result in inaccurate test results. The test administrator should be informed before testing begins if the test taker is not fluent in English and/or he or she has a unique cultural background.

Preparation

Prior to the administration of the MBTI, the test subject should be fully informed about the nature of the test and its intended use. He or she should also receive

---

KEY TERMS

Multi-tasking—Performing multiple duties or taking on multiple responsibilities and roles simultaneously.

Vocational—Relating to an occupation, career, or job.

---

standardized instructions for taking the test and any information on the confidentiality of the results.

Normal results

Myers-Briggs results are reported as a four-letter personality type (e.g., ESTP, ISFJ). Each letter corresponds to an individual's preference in each of the four pairs of personality indicators (i.e., E or I, S or N, T or F, and J or P). There are a total of sixteen possible combinations of personality types on the MBTI.

• Letter One: E or I: Extraverts focus more on people and things, introverts on ideas.

• Letter Two: S or N: Sensing-dominant personalities prefer to perceive things through sight, sound, taste, touch, and smell, while intuition-dominant types look to past experience and are more abstract in their thinking.

• Letter Three: T or F: The third subtype is a measure of how people use judgment. Thinking types use logic to judge the world, while feeling types tend to view things on the basis of what emotions they invoke.

• Letter Four: J or P: Everyone judges and perceives, but those who are judging dominant are said to be more methodical and results-oriented, while perceiving dominant personalities are good at multi-tasking and are flexible.

Risks

There are no risks involved with the Myers-Briggs Type Indicator test.

Parental concerns

When interpreting test results, the test administrator will review what the test evaluates, its precision in evaluation and any margins of error involved in scoring, and what the individual scores mean in the context of overall norms for the test and the background of the adolescent.

Resources

BOOKS

Keirsey, David. *Please Understand Me II*. Del Mar, CA: Prometheus Nemesis Book Co., 2002.

PERIODICALS

Folger, Wendy A. et al. "Analysis of MBTI type patterns in college scholars." *College Student Journal*. 37, no.4 (Dec 2003): 598(6).

Himmelberg, Michele. "Explore your skills, values and personality type to find best job." *The Orange County Register*. Knight Ridder/Tribune News Service (June 12, 2001): K4909.

Sak, Ugur. "A synthesis of research on psychological types of gifted adolescents." *Journal of Secondary Gifted Education*. 15, no. 2 (Winter 2004): 70(10).

ORGANIZATIONS

American Psychological Association. Testing and Assessment Office of the Science Directorate. 750 First St., N.E., Washington, DC 20002 (202)336–6000 Web site: <www.apa.org/science/testing.html.>.

WEB SITES

The Myers and Briggs Foundation. <www.myersbriggs.org> (accessed September 5, 2004).

Paula Ford-Martin

Myopathies

Definition

Myopathies are diseases of skeletal muscle that are not caused by nerve disorders. These diseases cause the skeletal or voluntary muscles to become weak or shrunken (atrophied).

Description

There are many different types of myopathies. Some are inherited, some inflammatory, and some caused by endocrine or metabolic problems. Myopathies usually are not fatal. Typically they cause muscle weakness and movement problems. The shoulders and thigh muscles are usually, but not always, affected earlier than the muscles of the hands and feet. Most myopathies are degenerative, meaning they become more pronounced over time. Some weaknesses are transitory. Only rarely do individuals become dependent on a wheelchair. However, **muscular dystrophy** (technically a myopathy) is far more severe. Some types of muscular dystrophy are fatal in early adulthood.

Causes and symptoms

There is great variety among myopathies, but what they all share are effects on the skeletal muscles. The main causes of myopathies are genetic, inflammatory (caused by infection), endocrine (hormonal), and metabolic (errors in how cells function). Often the cause of the myopathy is not known (idiopathic disease).

Genetic myopathies

Among their many functions, genes are responsible for overseeing the production of proteins important in maintaining healthy cells. Muscle cells produce thousands of proteins. With each of the inherited myopathies, a genetic defect is linked to a lack of, or defect in, one of the proteins needed for normal muscle cell function.

There are several different kinds of myopathy caused by defective genes:

- central core disease
- centronuclear (myotubular) myopathy
- myotonia congenita
- nemaline myopathy
- paramyotonia congenita
- periodic paralysis (hypokalemic and hyperkalemic forms)
- mitochondrial myopathies

Most, but not all, of these genetic myopathies are inherited through an autosomal dominant pattern of inheritance. In this pattern of inheritance, one copy of each gene comes from each parent. Only one of these two copies needs to have the mutation (change) or defect in order for the child to have the disease. The parent with the defective gene has the disease, and each of this parent's children has a 50 percent chance of inheriting the disease. This percentage is not changed by results of other pregnancies. With this pattern of inheritance, male and female children are equally at risk of developing the disease.

However, for a child to have one type of myotonia congenita and some forms of nemaline myopathy, two defective genes must be inherited—one from each parents. This is called an autosomal recessive pattern of inheritance. Neither parent may have symptoms of the disease, but each carries a recessive defective gene for it. Each child of such parents has a 25 percent chance of inheriting both genes and showing signs of the disease, and a 50 percent chance of inheriting one defective gene from only one parent. If the child has inherited just one defective gene, he or she will be a carrier of the disease and can pass the gene on to his or her offspring, while showing no signs of the disease himself.

A few forms of centronuclear myopathy develop primarily in males. Females who inherit the defective gene are usually carriers without symptoms, like their mothers, but they can pass on the disease to their sons. Mitochondrial myopathies are inherited only through the mother, since sperm do not contain mitochondria.

The major symptoms associated with the genetic myopathies are:

- Central core disease: mild weakness of voluntary muscles, especially in the hips and legs; hip displacement; delays in reaching developmental motor milestones; problems with running, jumping, and climbing stairs develop in childhood.

- Centronuclear myopathy: weakness of voluntary muscles, including those on the face, arms, legs, and trunk; drooping upper eyelids; facial weakness; foot drop; affected muscles almost always lack reflexes.

- Myotonia congenita: voluntary muscles of the arms, legs, and face stiff or slow to relax after contracting (myotonia); stiffness triggered by fatigue, stress, cold, or long rest periods, such as a night's **sleep**; stiffness can be relieved by repeated movement of the affected muscles.

- Nemaline myopathy: moderate weakness of voluntary muscles in the arms, legs, and trunk; mild weakness of facial muscles; delays in reaching developmental motor milestones; decreased or absent reflexes in affected muscles; long, narrow face; high-arched palate; jaw projects beyond upper part of the face.

- Paramyotonia congenita: stiffness of voluntary muscles in the face, hands, and forearms; attacks spontaneous or triggered by cold temperatures; stiffness made worse by repeated movement; episodes of stiffness last longer than those seen in myotonia congenita.

- Periodic paralysis: attacks of temporary muscle weakness (muscles work normally between attacks); in the hypokalemic (low potassium) form, attacks triggered by vigorous **exercise**, heavy meals high in carbohydrates, insulin, stress, alcohol, infection, pregnancy; in the hyperkalemic (high potassium) form, attacks triggered by vigorous exercise, stress, pregnancy, missing a meal, steroid drugs, high potassium intake.

- Mitochondrial myopathies: symptoms vary quite widely with the form of the disease and may include progressive weakness of the eye muscles (ocular myopathy), weakness of the arms and legs, or multi-

system problems primarily involving the brain and muscles.

Endocrine-related myopathies

In some cases, myopathies can be caused by a malfunctioning endocrine gland that produces either too much or too little of the chemical messengers called hormones. Hormones travel through the bloodstream. One of their many functions is to help regulate muscle activity. Problems in producing hormones can lead to muscle weakness

Hyperthyroid myopathy and hypothyroid myopathy affect different muscles in different ways. Hyperthyroid myopathy occurs when the thyroid gland produces too much of the hormone thyroxine, leading to muscle weakness, some muscle wasting in hips and shoulders, and, sometimes, problems with eye muscles. The hypothyroid type of myopathy occurs when too little hormone is produced, leading to stiffness, cramps, and weakness of arm and leg muscles.

Inflammatory myopathies

Some myopathies are caused by inflammation. Inflammation is a protective response of injured tissues characterized by redness, increased heat, swelling, and/or **pain** in the affected area. Examples of this type of myopathy include **dermatomyositis**, polymyositis, and myositis ossificans.

Dermatomyositis is a disease of the connective tissue that also involves weak, tender, inflamed muscles. Muscle tissue loss may be so severe that the individual may be unable to walk. Skin inflammation is also present. The cause of dermatomyositis is as of 2004 unknown, but viral infection and antibiotic use are associated with the condition. In some cases, dermatomyositis is associated with rheumatologic disease or **cancer**. Polymyositis involves inflammation of many muscles, usually accompanied by deformity, swelling, sleeplessness, pain, sweating, and tension. It, too, may be associated with cancer. Myositis ossificans is a rare inherited disease in which muscle tissue is replaced by bone, beginning in childhood.

Muscular dystrophies

While considered a separate group of diseases, the muscular dystrophies also involve muscle wasting and can be described as myopathies. Symptoms of muscular dystrophy (MD) diseases usually appear during childhood and **adolescence**. These are genetic disorders that result in defects in the production of specific proteins. The forms of muscular dystrophy differ according to the way they are inherited, the age at which symptoms begin, the muscles they affect, and how fast they progress.

Demographics

Myopathies are not common. About 14 percent of myopathies are inherited. Worldwide the rate of inflammatory myopathies is about five to ten individuals per 100,000. These myopathies are more often seen in women. MD is found in about 63 of every 1 million individuals, but the rates vary widely depending on the type of MD. The most common type is Duchenne MD, affecting one in every 3,300 boys. Other more common types of MD are Becker's, **myotonic dystrophy**, limb-girdle MD, and facioscapulohumeral MD. MD is more common in boys. The rate of metabolic and endocrine myopathies was, as of 2004, not known.

When to call the doctor

Parents should let the doctor know as soon as possible if there is a **family** history of muscle weakness or muscle wasting disease. Otherwise, they should contact their pediatrician if the child is showing any signs of delayed or abnormal growth or unexplained muscle weakness.

Diagnosis

Early diagnosis of myopathy is important in order to provide the best care possible. An experienced physician can diagnose a myopathy by evaluating a child's medical history and by performing a thorough physical examination. Diagnostic tests can help differentiate among the different types of myopathies, as well as between myopathy and other neuromuscular disorders. If the doctor suspects a genetic myopathy, a thorough family history will also be taken. Genetic tests are available for a few myopathies.

Diagnostic tests the doctor may order include: measurements of potassium, (K) creatine kinase,(CK) lactic dehydrogenase (LDH) and pyruvate kinase (PK) and certain antibodies in the blood; muscle tissue biopsy; and electromyogram (EMG).

Treatment

As of 2004, there was no cure for many myopathies. Treatment depends on the specific type of myopathy the person has and is aimed at controlling symptoms. Specific treatment approaches for specific forms of myopathies are as follows:

- periodic paralysis: medication and dietary changes

- hyperthyroid or hypothyroid myopathy: treatment of the underlying thyroid abnormality

- myositis ossificans: medication to help prevent abnormal bone formation, but there is no cure following onset

---

KEY TERMS

Electrooculography (EOG)—A diagnostic test that records the electrical activity of the muscles that control eye movement.

Hyperkalemia—An abnormally high level of potassium in the blood.

Hypokalemia—A condition characterized by a deficiency of potassium in the blood.

Inflammation—Pain, redness, swelling, and heat that develop in response to tissue irritation or injury. It usually is caused by the immune system's response to the body's contact with a foreign substance, such as an allergen or pathogen.

Mitochondria—Spherical or rod-shaped structures of the cell. Mitochondria contain genetic material (DNA and RNA) and are responsible for converting food to energy.

Voluntary muscles—Muscles that can be moved by conscious thought.

- central core disease: no treatment

- nemaline myopathy: no treatment

- centronuclear (myotubular) myopathy: no treatment

- paramyotonia congenita: treatment often unnecessary

- myotonia congenita: drug treatment (if necessary), but drugs do not affect the underlying disease, and attacks may still occur

General treatments aim at supporting the individual's functioning and independence. Physical therapy can help preserve or increase strength and flexibility in muscles. Ankle and wrist braces can support weakened limbs. Occupational therapy is used to develop tools and techniques to compensate for loss of strength and dexterity. A speech-language pathologist can provide retraining for weakness in the muscles controlling speech and swallowing.

Prognosis

The prognosis for patients with myopathy depends on the type and severity of the individual's disease. In most cases, the myopathy symptoms can be successfully treated, but in others, the disease can be fatal in childhood or adolescence.

Muscular dystrophy is generally a more serious disease than many other types of myopathies. Duchenne's

MD is usually fatal by the late teens; Becker's MD is less serious and may not be fatal until the 50s.

Prevention

As of 2004 there is no way to prevent the genetic mutations that cause myopathies, nor are there ways to prevent metabolic and endocrine failures that result in myopathies. Inflammatory myopathies often occur as a result of exposure to viruses or drugs, but it is almost impossible to predict their development.

Parental concerns

Individuals with known myopathies who wish to become parents may want to seek genetic counseling before attempting to have children.

See also Muscular dystrophy; Myotonic dystrophy.

Resources

BOOKS

Barnes, P. R. J., et al. *Myopathies in Clinical Practice*. Oxford, UK: Isis Medical Media, 2003.

The Official Patient's Sourcebook on Mitochondrial Myopathies. San Diego, CA: Icon Group International, 2002.

ORGANIZATIONS

Muscular Dystrophy Association. 3300 East Sunrise Dr., Tucson, AZ 85718. Web site: <ww.mdausa.org>.

National Organization for Rare Disorders Inc. 55 Kenosia Ave, PO Box 1968, Danbury, CT 06813–1968. Web site: <www.rarediseases.org>.

WEB SITES

"NINDS Myopathy Information Page." *National Institute of Neurological Disorders and Stroke*, January 6, 2005. Available online at <www.ninds.nih.gov/health_and_medical/disorders/myopathy.htm> (accessed January 13, 2005).

Tish Davidson, A.M.
Carol A. Turkington

Myopia

Definition

Myopia, or nearsightedness, is a condition in which objects in the distance are blurred either because the eye is too long or too strong. It is the result of both environmental and genetic factors.

Description

The degree to which one is myopic depends on the powers of the cornea and the lens of the eye and the length of the eyeball. In a normal eye the incoming visual images meet on the retina in the back of the eye. If these visual images converge in front of the retina instead of on the retina, then one is myopic.

There are several types of myopia, of which simple myopia is the most common. Individuals with simple myopia have eyes that are either too long or too powerful. Congenital myopia develops in infants. Individuals with high myopia, greater than six diopters, can develop pathological changes in the retina, called degenerative myopia. Nocturnal myopia, another type of myopia sometimes referred to as "night blindness," is blurred vision only in darkness. Myopia can also be induced by co-existing medical problems and drug exposure.

A child's refractive status or power of the eye when he or she begins school is a good indicator of whether the child will become nearsighted. Most children are hyperopic, or far-sighted, at birth and experience a decrease in far-sightedness throughout early childhood. Myopia is less likely to develop by age 13 if a child still has at least 0.75 diopters of hyperopia at age eight. But if a child has become at least 0.25 diopters myopic at this age then there is a 60 percent chance that the child will require spectacle correction for nearsightedness by age 13.

Myopia does decreases in later life. This appears not to be related to a decrease in close work as is often suggested but rather due to some factor intrinsically related to ageing. It has been hypothesized the power of the lens of the eye changes in later life.

High myopia has been associated with various syndromes: Ehlers-Danlos, Marfan, Down, and Stickler syndromes. Myopia is often observed in retinopathy of **prematurity** (ROP). ROP is seen in 68 percent of infants with low birth weights and over 80 percent of infants born with ROP will be myopic. The myopia associated with ROP increases through age five, after which it stabilizes.

Transmission

Although no gene for myopia has been isolated, heredity is believed to play a role in myopia. If both parents are myopic, then the odds that the child will be myopic are as high as 60 percent. This drops to at most 40 percent when only one parent is nearsighted, and for 15 percent of myopic children, neither parent has myopia. High myopia is especially likely to have a genetic component.

Demographics

Overall, 25 percent of those living in the United States are myopic. Myopia is slightly more prevalent among females than males, and among those with advanced academic training. Less than 5 percent of five year olds are myopic, but this percentage increases to 25 percent by late teens and to approximately 35 percent for young adults and to 42 percent of those middle-aged. These percentages decrease to 20 percent by age 65 and to less than 13 percent by age 80.

Myopia is more prevalent in Asian countries; as much as 70 percent of the Chinese population is nearsighted.

Causes and symptoms

Congenital myopia develops because of an obstruction along the visual pathway such as cataract. The eye becomes elongated in response to blur these causes, creating a myopic eye.

A first sign that a child might have myopia is difficulty in seeing things in the distance, such as the chalkboard. The child may not see things in the distance as well as a classmate or sibling.

For the 2 percent of the population who are extremely nearsighted, an inherently weak sclera, whose fibers are not held together tightly, causes the eye to stretch. This stretching can continue into adulthood, increasing myopia.

Other causes of increasing nearsightedness include difficulty with converging, the process through which the eyes move inwardly together when reading, and esophoria, the condition in which the eyes are more comfortable positioned close to the nose. Doing a lot of close work, such as playing **video games** and using the computer for extended periods, may increase myopia for these children.

Causes of induced myopia include cataracts and elevations of blood sugar in diagnosed or undiagnosed diabetics. Some drugs, such as corticosteroids, **antihistamines**, and some **antibiotics**, including **sulfonamides**, can induce myopia.

Another cause of increasing myopia is the over wearing of **contact lenses**. Swelling of the cornea can occur if the eye does not have sufficient oxygen causing a transient increase in myopia. Silicone contact lenses allow a marked increase in oxygen to reach the eye decreasing the probability of myopic increases.

For the child with diabetes, fluctuations in blood sugars can cause swelling of the cornea of the eye, leading to transient increases in myopia, which stabilize once the diabetes is controlled. But the child may independently become more myopic later in life.

In the early 2000s, it has been suggested that insulin resistance, which accompanies type 2 diabetes and pre-diabetes, may increase myopia in children and adolescents. The level of insulin-like growth factor binding protein 3 (IGFBP-3), a hormone that works with insulin to lower blood glucose levels, is low in individuals who are insulin resistant. This decreased level, in turn, decreases the sensitivity of ocular tissue to another compound called retinoic acid, which prevents increases in the length of the eye. Thus, if insulin levels are higher than normal, the risk of myopia may be increased.

Asthenopia or a feeling of eye strain is not common in myopia. If a child complains of eye strain, then usually there is another cause of the eye strain, including an astigmatism, a condition in which the eye is football shaped; anisometropia, a condition in which the eyes are of different powers; or difficulty with focusing.

When to call the doctor

There are many reasons why a child cannot see well in the distance. Myopia is the most common cause of distance blur, and since much of what a child learns comes from vision and visual cues, correction of myopia is important. Also, problems with vision may be a sign of a more serious ocular problem, such as cataracts, or of a medical problem, such as diabetes.

Diagnosis

Myopia is diagnosed by determining a child's unaided vision and is confirmed objectively by the eye care practitioner with various techniques, including retinoscopy and refraction.

The type and extent of myopia is determined by additional testing. These tests include an evaluation of the child's binocular vision, his eye movements, his ability to converge and focus on objects close-up, and his ocular health. Dilation of the eye allows the doctor to check for complications of ROP, diabetes, or degenerative myopia. Since children are capable of over focusing, dilation can help the eye care practitioner determine a child's true prescription because the drugs used to dilate also impair this tendency to over focus. Over focusing can cause a child to appear to be myopic when he or she is actually not.

Treatment

Myopia is most commonly treated with spectacles or glasses. Myopia in **preschool** children does not need to be corrected with glasses, unless either anisometropia, a condition in which there is a difference of more than 1.00 diopters between the two eyes, or **amblyopia**, a condition in which a child cannot be corrected to 20/20 with spectacles, is present. As the child enters school, distance vision becomes critical for learning, and children with prescriptions of at least 1.00 diopter of myopia or who have 20/40 vision or worse should be given glasses. Once a child is diagnosed with myopia, he or she should be examined every six months to a year, and each eye should be corrected to 20/20 at each visit. The glasses are then usually worn full time, except for children with difficulty with convergence (esophoria), who may remove their glasses for close work.

Some adolescents may want to wear contact lenses. Wearing contact lenses can improve appearance. Peripheral vision is improved with contact lenses, especially for those with high degrees of myopia or who have anisometropia.

Rigid gas permeable (RGPs) contact lenses are used to correct myopia. The rate at which myopia increases may be slowed by RGP lenses. RGPs are also employed in orthokeratology, a technique in which RGP lenses of gradually decreasing flatness are worn for specified amounts of time. These lenses, called ortho-K lenses, flatten the cornea, changing the power of the cornea over time and decreasing myopia. This effect of ortho-K lenses is not permanent and an ortho-K lens must be worn periodically or the original myopia reappears. For some individuals—for example, those with keratoconus, a disease of the cornea—RGPs may offer the only way to correct vision.

For some children the development of myopia may be slowed with reading glasses or bifocals. If bifocals are prescribed, then either progressive or no-lines, or a lined bifocal may be given. If a lined bifocal is prescribed, then the line is always placed higher for the child than for the adult. This is done to encourage use of the power of the bifocal.

Refractive surgery is also used to correct myopia, but only on fully grown individuals. A child's eyes change and the **safety** of these procedures have not been established in the growing eye.

The most common surgical procedure performed to correct myopia is laser in situ keratomileusis (LASIK). Other techniques to correct myopia include photorefractive keratectomy (PRK), radial keratomy (RK), laser epithelial keratomileusis (LASEK), intraocular lens

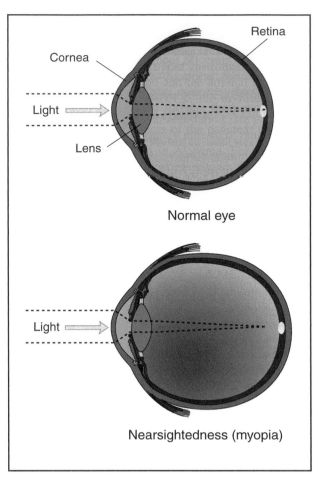

Myopia, or nearsightedness, is a condition of the eye in which objects are seen more clearly when close to the eye while distant objects appear blurred or fuzzy. *(Illustration by Electronic Illustrators Group.)*

implants and intrastromal corneal rings. Inflammation of the eye, increased dryness of the eye, and cataracts are some of the risks associated with refractive surgery.

Alternative treatment

Cycloplegic drugs, such as atropine, may decrease myopia, but they may hinder the child's ability to see up close. As of 2004 pirenzepine, which has shown to decrease the rate of myopia in children without sacrificing the ability of the child to do close work, is in clinical trial.

Prognosis

Most infants are born far-sighted and eventually reach emmetropia or normal vision, by age six. Over one third of children go on to become myopic as adults.

KEY TERMS

Accommodation—The ability of the lens to change its focus from distant to near objects and vice versa. It is achieved through the action of the ciliary muscles that change the shape of the lens.

Anisometropia—An eye condition in which there is an inequality of vision between the two eyes. There may be unequal amounts of nearsightedness, farsightedness, or astigmatism, so that one eye will be in focus while the other will not.

Astigmatism—An eye condition in which the cornea doesn't focus light properly on the retina, resulting in a blurred image.

Cataract—A condition in which the lens of the eye turns cloudy and interferes with vision.

Convergence—The natural movement of the eyes inward to view objects close-up.

Cornea—The clear, dome-shaped outer covering of the eye that lies in front of the iris and pupil. The cornea lets light into the eye.

Diopter (D)—A unit of measure for describing the refractive power of a lens.

Emmetropia—Normal vision.

Retina—The inner, light-sensitive layer of the eye containing rods and cones. The retina transforms the image it receives into electrical signals that are sent to the brain via the optic nerve.

Sclera—The tough, fibrous, white outer protective covering of the eyeball.

Patients with high myopia, greater than 6.00 diopters, have an increased risk of developing a retinal tear, hole, or detachment; a posterior staphyloma; a posterior vitreous detachment; or glaucoma. Rarely are these pathological changes of myopia seen in children or adolescents. Retinal detachments and tears are possible, however, in highly myopic children or adolescents who play contact **sports**. If a retinal problem is diagnosed or suspected, referral to a retinal specialist is necessary.

Prevention

For individuals who have difficulty with convergence or focusing or who are esophoric, close work may increase myopia. Children diagnosed with these problems would benefit from frequent breaks while doing close work. Increases in myopia for these children may

be slowed with bifocals and/or removal of glasses for reading and homework.

Nutritional concerns

Since elevated levels of insulin may be associated with increased myopia; a diet low in those foods that increase insulin secretion, such as refined carbohydrates, may help decrease myopia.

Parental concerns

Children rely on their vision in their learning processes; if they have difficulty seeing this handicap affects academic performance. Thus, any vision problem should be corrected promptly. Once myopia is diagnosed, it typically increases through childhood and vision correction is needed for classroom work and for sports. If a child is not corrected fully and continues to have blurred vision, the eye may elongate in response to blur, perpetuating the myopia.

Myopia cannot be diagnosed by school screenings or by simply reading eye chart at the pediatrician's office. A comprehensive eye exam as given by an ophthalmologist or an optometrist is needed, if myopia is suspected. Most cases of myopia result from changes within the eye, but the condition can be a manifestation of other more serious problems, such as cataract or diabetes.

See also Diabetes mellitus; Ehlers-Danlos syndrome; Marfan's syndrome.

Resources

BOOKS

Cordain, Loren. *The Paleo Diet*. Hoboken, NJ: John Wiley & Sons, 2002.

Murillo-Lopez, Fernando H. "Myopia." In *Current Ocular Therapy*. Philadelphia: Saunders, 2000.

Prett, Ronald C. "Pathologic Myopia." In *Principles and Practice of Ophthalmology*. Philadelphia: Saunders, 2000.

Steidl, Scott M., and Ronald C. Pruett. "Myopia and Systemic Disorders." In *Principles and Practice of Ophthalmology*. Philadelphia: Saunders, 2000.

PERIODICALS

Byrne, Jennifer. "Pirenzepine Showing Promise in Clinical Trials for Topical Myopia Treatment." *Primary Care Optometry News* 8, no. 10 (October 2003): 10–1.

Cordain, Loren, et al. "An Evolutionary Analysis of the Aetiology and Pathogenesis of Juvenile-Onset Myopia." *Acta Ophthalmologica Scandinavica* 80, no. 2 (April 2002): 125–35.

Karpecki, Paul M. "What's New in Refractive Surgery." *Review of Optometry* (May 15, 2001): 71–4.

Karpecki, Paul M., and Marc Bloomenstein. "Phakic IOLs: The LASIK Alternative." *Review of Optometry* (February 15, 2003): 91–2.

Mutti, Donald O., and Karla Zadnik. "Age-Related Decreases in the Prevalence of Myopia: Longitudinal Change of Cohort Effect?" *Investigative Ophthalmology & Visual Science* 41, no. 8 (July 2000): 2103–07.

WEB SITES

"Myopia (Nearsightedness)." *All About Vision*. Available online at <www.allaboutvision.com/conditions/myopia.htm> (accessed November 30, 2004).

Martha Reilly, OD

Myotonic dystrophy

Definition

Myotonic dystrophy is a progressive disease in which the muscles are weak and slow to relax after contraction.

Description

Myotonic dystrophy (DM), also called dystrophia myotonica, myotonia atrophica, or Steinert disease, is a common form of **muscular dystrophy**. DM is an inherited disease. It causes general weakness, usually beginning in the muscles of the hands, feet, neck, or face. It slowly progresses to involve other muscle groups, including the heart and a wide variety of other organ systems.

There are four types of DM as determined by when symptoms appear. These are:

• Congenital: Severe symptoms are apparent at birth.

• Juvenile: Symptoms appear between birth and adolescence.

• Adult: Symptoms appear in individuals ages 20–40.

• Late onset: Mild symptoms appear after age 40.

Transmission

DM is an inherited disease. It is passed from parent to child through an autosomal dominant pattern of inheritance. In the case of DM, one copy of each gene is inherited from each parent. In an autosomal dominant pattern of inheritance, only one of these two copies needs to have the mutation (change) or defect in order for the child to have DM. Therefore, there is a 50 percent chance that a parent who has DM will pass it onto each child. This percentage is not changed by results of other pregnancies. In each pregnancy, a parent with DM has a 50% chance of having a child with DM.

Demographics

Myotonic dystrophy is an uncommon disease occurring in about one out of every 8,000 individuals. It is found worldwide. The congenital form of DM is much rarer, occurring in only about one out of every 100,000 births. DM affects males and females approximately equally.

Causes and symptoms

The most common type of DM is called DM1, which is caused by a mutation in a gene called myotonic dystrophy protein kinase (DMPK). The DMPK gene is located on chromosome 19. The specific mutation that causes DM1 is called a trinucleotide repeat expansion. In people who have DM1, a particular unit of the gene is repeated too many times—more than the normal range of five to 38 times—and thus this section of the gene is too big and is unstable. The enlarged section of the gene is called a trinucleotide repeat expansion.

People who have repeat numbers in the normal range will not develop DM1 and cannot pass it to their children. Having more than 50 repeats causes DM1. People who have 38–49 repeats have what is called a premutation. They do not develop DM1, but can pass DM1 on to their children.

Myotonic dystrophy has an effect called "anticipation." This means that when a person with repeat numbers in the affected or premutation range (above 38) has children, the expansion grows larger, and the child has more of the repeated genetic unit (a higher repeat number). As a result, symptoms of the disease tend to appear at an earlier age in children than in their affected parent. Anticipation happens more often when a mother, rather than the father, passes DM1 to children. Occasionally, repeat sizes stay the same or even get smaller when they are passed to a person's children.

In general, the more repeats above 38 an individual has, the earlier the age of onset of symptoms and the more severe the symptoms. Having repeat numbers greater than 1,000 causes congenital myotonic dystrophy. However, this is a general rule. It is not possible to look at a person's repeat number and predict at what age he or she will begin to have symptoms or how the condition will progress.

Some families with symptoms of DM do not have a mutation in the DMPK gene. Instead, they have a mutation in a gene on chromosome 3 that causes four units within the gene to be repeated. This genetic defect is called DM2 or proximal myotonic myopathia (PROMM). Symptoms of DM2 are almost never apparent at birth. This defect has only been decoded since 2001; therefore, less is known about how it functions.

Symptoms of DM vary in severity, and not everyone will have all of the symptoms. In general, myotonic dystrophy causes weakness and delayed muscle relaxation called myotonia. Exactly how the repeat of genetic information causes myotonia, the inability to relax muscles, is not yet understood. The disease somehow blocks the flow of electrical impulses across the muscle cell membrane. Without proper flow of charged particles, the muscle cannot return to its relaxed state after it has contracted.

The most severe form of DM, congenital myotonic dystrophy, may appear in newborns of mothers who have DM1. Congenital myotonic dystrophy is marked by severe weakness, poor sucking and swallowing responses, respiratory difficulty, delayed motor development, and **mental retardation**. Death in infancy is common in babies with congenital DM.

Symptoms of juvenile and adult onset DM include facial weakness and a slack jaw, drooping eyelids called ptosis, and muscle wasting in the forearms and calves. A person with DM has difficulty relaxing his or her grasp, especially in the cold. DM affects the heart muscle, causing irregularities in the heartbeat. It also affects the muscles of the digestive system, causing **constipation** and other digestive problems. DM may cause cataracts in the eye, retinal degeneration, low IQ, early frontal balding, skin disorders, atrophy of the testicles, and diabetes. It can also cause **sleep** apnea, a condition in which normal breathing is interrupted during sleep. DM increases the need for sleep and decreases motivation. Often, severe disabilities do not set in until about 20 years after symptoms begin. Most people with myotonic dystrophy maintain the ability to walk, even late in life.

Some people who have a trinucleotide repeat expansion in their DMPK gene do not have DM symptoms or have very mild symptoms that go unnoticed. It is not unusual for a woman to be diagnosed with DM after she has an infant with congenital myotonic dystrophy.

When to call the doctor

Parents should let the doctor know as soon as possible if there is a **family** history of DM. Otherwise, they should contact their pediatrician if the child shows any signs of delayed or abnormal growth, or unexplained muscle weakness.

Diagnosis

Diagnosis of DM is not difficult once the disease is considered. However, the diagnosis may be masked because symptoms can begin at any age, can be mild or severe, and can occur with a wide variety of associated complaints. Diagnosis of DM begins with a careful medical history and a thorough physical examination to determine the distribution of symptoms and to rule out other causes. A family history of DM or unexplained weakness helps to establish the diagnosis.

Genetic testing, usually using a blood sample, establishes a definitive diagnosis of DM. The DNA in the blood cells is examined and the number of repeats in the affected gene is determined. Other tests may be done to help establish the diagnosis, but only rarely would other testing be needed. An electromyogram (EMG) is a test used to examine how muscles respond to stimulation. Characteristic changes revealed by this test, and seen in DM, help distinguish it from other muscle diseases. Removing a small piece of muscle tissue for microscopic examination is called a muscle biopsy. DM is marked by characteristic changes in the structure of muscle cells that can be seen on a muscle biopsy. An electrocardiogram could be performed to detect abnormalities in heart rhythm associated with DM. These symptoms often appear later in the course of the disease.

If genetic testing in a family has identified a DMPK mutation, it is possible to test a fetus during pregnancy. Testing can be done at 10–12 weeks gestation by a procedure called chorionic villus sampling (CVS) that involves removing a tiny piece of the placenta and analyzing DNA from its cells. It can also be done by **amniocentesis** after 14 weeks gestation by removing a small amount of the amniotic fluid surrounding the fetus and analyzing the cells in the fluid. Each of these procedures carries a small risk of miscarriage. Those who are interested in learning more should check with their doctor or genetic counselor.

Treatment

Myotonic dystrophy cannot be cured, and no treatment can delay its progression. However, many of its symptoms can be treated. Physical therapy can help

KEY TERMS

Electrocardiagram (ECG, EKG)—A record of the electrical activity of the heart, with each wave being labeled as P, Q, R, S, and T waves. It is often used in the diagnosis of cases of abnormal cardiac rhythm and myocardial damage.

Electromyography (EMG)—A diagnostic test that records the electrical activity of muscles. In the test, small electrodes are placed on or in the skin; the patterns of electrical activity are projected on a screen or over a loudspeaker. This procedure is used to test for muscle disorders, including muscular dystrophy.

Muscular dystrophy—A group of inherited diseases characterized by progressive wasting of the muscles.

Sleep apnea—A sleep disorder characterized by periods of breathing cessation lasting for 10 seconds or more.

Trinucleotide repeat expansion—A sequence of three nucleotides that is repeated too many times in a section of a gene.

preserve or increase strength and flexibility in muscles. Ankle and wrist braces can support weakened limbs. Occupational therapy is used to develop tools and techniques to compensate for loss of strength and dexterity. A speech-language pathologist can provide retraining for weakness in the muscles controlling speech and swallowing.

Irregularities in heartbeat may be treated with medication or a pacemaker. A yearly electrocardiogram is usually recommended. **Diabetes mellitus** in DM is treated in the same way that it is in the general population. A high-fiber diet can help prevent constipation. Sleep apnea may be treated with surgical procedures to open the airways or with nighttime ventilation. Treatment of sleep apnea may reduce drowsiness. Lens replacement surgery is available when cataracts develop.

Prognosis

The course of myotonic dystrophy varies. When symptoms appear earlier in life, disability tends to become more severe. Occasionally people with DM may require a wheelchair later in life. Children with congenital DM often die in infancy. If they survive, they usually require special educational programs and physical and occupational therapies. Respiratory infections pose a danger if weakness becomes severe.

Prevention

There is no way to prevent the genetic mutations that cause DM. However, it is possible to test someone who is at risk for developing DM1 before symptoms arise, to see whether he or she inherited an expanded trinucleotide repeat. This is called predictive testing. Predictive testing cannot determine the age at which someone will begin to have symptoms or the course of the disease.

Another procedure, called preimplantation diagnosis, allows a couple to have a child that does not have the genetic condition. This procedure is still experimental. Those interested in learning more about the procedure should check with their doctor or genetic counselor.

Parental concerns

Pregnant woman should be cared for by an obstetrician familiar with the particular problems of DM because complications can occur during pregnancy, labor, and delivery.

It is advisable for children or adults with DM to wear a medical alert bracelet. Some emergency medications may have dangerous effects on the heart rhythm in a person with DM. Adverse reactions to general anesthesia may also occur.

See also Muscular dystrophy.

Resources

PERIODICALS

The International Myotonic Dystrophy Consortium (IDMC). "New nomenclature and DNA testing guidelines for myotonic dystrophy type 1 (DM1)." *Neurology* 54 (2000): 1218–21.

Meola, Giovanni. "Myotonic Dystrophies." *Current Opinion in Neurology* 13 (2000): 519–25.

ORGANIZATIONS

International Myotonic Dystrophy Organization. P.O. Box 1121, Sunland, CA 91041-1121. (866) 679-7954 or (818)951-2311. Web site: <www.myotonicdystrophy.org>.

Muscular Dystrophy Association. 3300 East Sunrise Dr., Tucson, AZ 85718. (520) 529-2000 or (800) 572-1717. Web site: <www.mdausa.org>.

WEB SITES

Bird, Thomas D. "Myotonic Dystrophy Type 1." *Gene Reviews* [cited August 9, 2004]. Available online at: <www.genetests.org/profiles/myotonic_d/details.html>.

Smith, Corrine O'Sullivan. *Myotonic Dystrophy: Making an Informed Choice About Genetic Testing.* University of Washington. Available online at: <www.depts.washington.edu/neurogen/Myotonic.pdf>.

"What Is Myotonic Muscular Dystrophy?" *Muscular Dystrophy Association* [cited October 9, 2004]. Available online at: <www.mda.org/publications/fa-mmd-qa.html>.

Tish Davidson, A.M.
Karen M. Krajewski, M.S., C.G.C.

Myringotomy and ear tubes

Definition

Myringotomy is a surgical procedure in which a small incision is made in the eardrum (the tympanic membrane), usually in both ears. The word comes from *myringa*, modern Latin for drum membrane, and *tomē*, Greek for cutting. It is also called myringocentesis, tympanotomy, tympanostomy, or paracentesis of the tympanic membrane. The doctor can withdraw fluid from the middle ear through the incision.

Ear tubes, or tympanostomy tubes, are small tubes open at both ends that are inserted into the incisions in the eardrums during a myringotomy. The tubes come in various shapes and sizes and are made of plastic, metal, or both. They are left in place until they fall out by themselves or until they are removed by a doctor. Ear tubes are also sometimes called ventilation tubes.

Purpose

Myringotomy with the insertion of ear tubes is an optional treatment for inflammation of the middle ear with fluid collection (effusion), also called glue ear, that lasts more than three months (chronic **otitis media** with effusion) and does not respond to drug treatment. Myringotomy is the recommended treatment if the condition lasts four to six months. Effusion is the collection of fluid that escapes from blood vessels or the lymphatic system. In this case, the effusion collects in the child's middle ear.

Initially, acute inflammation of the middle ear with effusion is treated with one or two courses of antibiotic drugs. **Antihistamines** and **decongestants** have also been used to treat otitis media, but they have not been proven effective unless the child also has hay fever or some other allergic inflammation that contributes to the ear problem. Myringotomy with or without the insertion of ear tubes is *not* recommended as the initial treatment for otherwise healthy children with middle ear inflammation with effusion.

In about 10 percent of children, the ear effusion lasts for three months or longer; at that point the condition is considered chronic. Systemic steroids may help children with chronic ear infections, but the evidence that these drugs are beneficial is not clear, and there are risks associated with steroid use.

Myringotomy with insertion of ear tubes becomes an option when medical treatment does not stop the effusion after three months in a child who is one to three years old, is otherwise healthy, and has hearing loss in both ears. If the effusion lasts for four to six months, myringotomy with insertion of ear tubes may be recommended. Although doctors in the past sometimes removed the child's tonsils or adenoids to treat recurrent otitis media with effusion, this practice is not recommended as of the early 2000s.

Myringotomy may be performed to relieve the **pain** and other symptoms of otitis media; to restore the child's hearing; to take a sample of the fluid to examine in the laboratory in order to identify any microorganisms present; or to insert ventilation tubes.

Ear tubes can be inserted into the incision during a myringotomy and left there. The eardrum heals around them, securing them in place. They usually fall out on their own in six to 12 months or are removed by a doctor.

While in place, the tubes keep the incision from closing, forming an open channel between the middle ear and the outer ear. This channel allows fresh air to reach the middle ear, allows fluid to drain out, and prevents pressure from building up in the middle ear. The patient's hearing returns to normal immediately and the risk of recurrence diminishes.

Parents often report that children talk better, hear better, are less irritable, **sleep** better, and behave better after myringotomy with the insertion of ear tubes.

Description

The procedure is usually performed in an ambulatory surgical unit under general anesthesia, although some physicians do it in the office with sedation and local anesthesia, especially in older children. Most primary care physicians prefer to refer children who need a myringotomy and tube placement to an otolaryngologist.

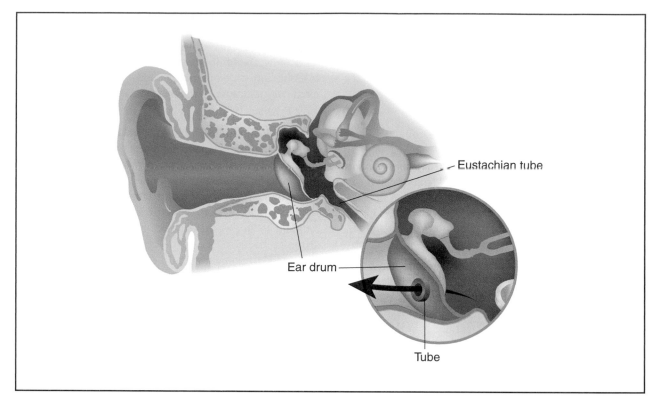

Eustachian tube

Ear drum

Tube

The insertion of ear tubes in the eardrum helps to alleviate chronic middle ear infections. *(Illustration by Argosy, Inc.)*

The ear is washed, a small incision made in the eardrum, the fluid sucked out, a tube inserted, and the ear packed with cotton to control bleeding.

Carbon dioxide lasers may also be used to perform the myringotomy. Laser-assisted myringotomy can be performed in a doctor's office with only a local anesthetic. It has several advantages over the older technique: it is less painful; less frightening to children; and minimizes the need for tube insertion because the hole in the eardrum produced by the laser remains open longer than an incision made with a scalpel. On the other hand, laser-assisted myringotomies have a higher rate of recurrence of infection.

Another technique to keep the incision in the eardrum open without the need for tube insertion is application of a medication called mitomycin C, which was originally developed to treat bladder **cancer**. The mitomycin prevents the incision from sealing over. As of the early 2000s, however, this technique is still in its experimental stages.

Some researchers have designed ear tubes that are easier to insert or to remove or that stay in place longer.

Precautions

As of 2004 clinical practice guidelines emphasized the importance of watchful waiting and medical treatment before performing a myringotomy and the importance of distinguishing between children at risk for speech or hearing problems from otitis media from others with chronic ear infections.

Preparation

A child scheduled for a myringotomy should not have food or water for four to six hours before being given anesthesia. **Antibiotics** are usually not needed before the procedure.

Aftercare

The use of antimicrobial drops after a myringotomy is controversial. Water should be kept out of the ear canal until the eardrum is intact. A doctor should be notified if the tubes fall out.

An additional element of postoperative care is the recommendation by many doctors that the child use ear plugs to keep water out of the ear during bathing or swimming to reduce the risk of infection and discharge.

KEY TERMS

Acute otitis media—Inflammation of the middle ear with signs of infection lasting less than three months.

Chronic otitis media—Inflammation of the middle ear with signs of infection lasting three months or longer.

Effusion—The escape of fluid from blood vessels or the lymphatic system and its collection in a cavity.

Middle ear—The cavity or space between the eardrum and the inner ear. It includes the eardrum, the three little bones (hammer, anvil, and stirrup) that transmit sound to the inner ear, and the eustachian tube, which connects the inner ear to the nasopharynx (the back of the nose).

Tympanic membrane—The eardrum, a thin disc of tissue that separates the outer ear from the middle ear. It can rupture if pressure in the ear is not equalized during airplane ascents and descents.

Tympanostomy tube—An ear tube. A tympanostomy tube is small tube made of metal or plastic that is inserted during myringotomy to ventilate the middle ear.

Risks

The risks of a myringotomy and ear tube placement include the following:

- cutting the outer ear
- formation of granular nodes due to inflammation at the site of the myringotomy
- formation of a cholesteatoma, which is a mass of skin cells and cholesterol in the middle ear that can grow and damage the surrounding bone
- permanent perforation of the eardrum
- hearing loss in late **adolescence** or early adulthood
- a 13 percent risk of persistent discharge from the ear (otorrhea)

If the procedure is repeated, structural changes in the eardrum can occur, such as loss of tone (flaccidity), shrinkage or retraction, or hardening of a spot on the eardrum (tympanosclerosis). The risk of hardening is 51 percent; its effects on hearing were not known as of 2004, but they are probably insignificant.

It is also possible that the incision will not heal properly, leaving a permanent hole in the eardrum, which can cause some hearing loss and increases the risk of infection.

It is also possible that the ear tube will move inward and get trapped in the middle ear rather than move out into the external ear, where it either falls out on its own or can be retrieved by a doctor. The exact incidence of tubes moving inward is not known, but this possibility could increase the risk of further episodes of middle-ear inflammation, inflammation of the eardrum or the part of the skull directly behind the ear, formation of a mass in the middle ear, or infection due to the presence of a foreign body.

The surgery may not be a permanent cure. As many as 30 percent of children undergoing myringotomy with insertion of ear tubes need to undergo another procedure within five years.

The other risks include the usual risks associated with sedatives or general anesthesia.

Parental concerns

Parental concerns with regard to a myringotomy and tube insertion are usually related to the risks associated with the procedure itself, such as the child's reaction to the anesthetic, the possibility that the procedure will have to be repeated at a later date, and the risk of eventual mild hearing loss. These potential complications against the risks of **language delay**, possible learning problems, or hearing loss resulting from chronic otitis media.

See also Ear exam with an otoscope; Hearing impairment; Otitis media.

Resources

BOOKS

"Acute Otitis Media." Section 7, Chapter 84 in *The Merck Manual of Diagnosis and Therapy.* Edited by Mark H. Beers, and Robert Berkow. Whitehouse Station, NJ: Merck Research Laboratories, 2002.

Lanternier, Matthew L. "Otolaryngology: Ear Pathology." Chapter 20 in *The University of Iowa Family Practice Handbook*, 4th ed. Edited Mark Graber and Matthew L. Lanternier. St. Louis, MO: Mosby, 2001.

PERIODICALS

Cotter, C. S., and J. R. Kosko. "Effectiveness of Laser-Assisted Myringotomy for Otitis Media in Children." *Laryngoscope* 114 (March 2004): 486–9.

de Beer, B. A., et al. "Hearing Loss in Young Adults who Had Ventilation Tube Insertion in Childhood." *Annals of Otology, Rhinology, and Laryngology* 113 (June 2004): 438–44.

d'Eredita, R. "Contact Diode Laser Myringotomy and Mitomycin C in Children." *Otolaryngology and Head and Neck Surgery* 130 (June 2004): 742–6.

Koopman, J. P., et al. "Laser Myringotomy versus Ventilation Tubes in Children with Otitis Media with Effusion: A Randomized Trial." *Laryngoscope* 114 (May 2004): 844–9.

Rosenfeld, R. M., et al. "Clinical Practice Guideline: Otitis Media with Effusion." *Otolaryngology and Head and Neck Surgery* 130, Supplement 5 (May 2004): S95–S118.

ORGANIZATIONS

American Academy of Family Physicians (AAFP). 11400 Tomahawk Creek Parkway, Leawood, KS 66211–2672. Web site: <www.aafp.org>.

American Academy of Otolaryngology, Head and Neck Surgery Inc. One Prince St., Alexandria, VA 22314–3357. Web site: <www.entnet.org>

American Academy of Pediatrics (AAP). 141 Northwest Point Boulevard, Elk Grove Village, IL 60007. Web site: <www.aap.org>.

WEB SITES

Jones, Michael, Leslie Wilson, and David Malis. "Otitis Media." *eMedicine*, September 21, 2004. Available online at <www.emedicine.com/ped/topic1689.htm> (accessed November 30, 2004).

Mary Zoll, PhD

Myxedema *see* **Hypothyroidism**

N

Nail-patella syndrome

Definition

Nail-patella syndrome is a genetic disease of the connective tissue that produces defects in the fingernails, bone joints, and kidneys.

Description

Patients who have nail-patella syndrome may show a variety of physical defects. The most common features of this syndrome are missing or poorly developed fingernails, toenails, and patellae (kneecaps). Other common abnormalities include elbow deformities, abnormally shaped pelvis bone (hip bone), and kidney (renal) disease.

Less common medical findings include defects of the upper lip, the roof of the mouth, and unusual skeletal abnormalities. Skeletal abnormalities may include poorly developed shoulder blades (scapulae), sideways bent fingers (clinodactyly), **clubfoot**, **scoliosis**, and unusual neck bones. There are also other effects, such as thickening of the basement membrane in the skin and tiny clusters of capillaries (glomeruli) in the kidney. Nail-patella syndrome is associated with open-angle glaucoma, which, if untreated, may lead to blindness. Patients may also have cataracts, drooping eyelids (ptosis), or corneal problems such as glaucoma. In addition, scientists have recognized an association between nail-patella syndrome and colon **cancer**.

People with nail-patella syndrome may display only a few or many of the recognized signs of this disease, with symptoms varying widely from person to person. Symptoms even vary within a single **family** with multiple affected members.

Nail-patella syndrome is also known as Fong disease, hereditary onycho-osteodysplasia (HOOD), Iliac Horn syndrome, and Turner-Kieser syndrome.

Demographics

Nail-patella syndrome is a rare genetic disease. The incidence of nail-patella syndrome is approximately one in 50,000 births. This disorder affects males and females equally. It is found throughout the world and occurs in all ethnic groups. The strongest risk factor for nail-patella syndrome is a family history of the disease.

Causes and symptoms

Nail-patella syndrome has been recognized as an inherited disorder for over a hundred years. It is caused by mutations in a gene known as LIM Homeobox Transcription Factor 1-Beta (LMX1B), located on the long arm of chromosome 9. The LMX1B gene codes for a protein that is important in organizing embryonic limb development. Mutations in this gene have been detected in many unrelated people with nail-patella syndrome. Scientists have also been able to interrupt this gene in mice to produce defects similar to those seen in human nail-patella syndrome.

Nail-patella syndrome is inherited in an autosomal dominant manner. This means that possession of only one copy of the defective gene is enough to cause disease. When a parent has nail-patella syndrome, each of the children has a 50 percent chance to inherit the disease-causing mutation.

A new mutation causing nail-patella syndrome can also occur, causing disease in a child with no family history of the syndrome. This is called a sporadic occurrence and accounts for approximately 20 percent of cases of nail-patella syndrome. The children of a person with sporadic nail-patella syndrome are also at a 50 percent risk of inheriting the disorder.

Medical signs of nail-patella syndrome vary widely between patients. Some patients with this disorder do not display symptoms. These patients are discovered to have the nail-patella syndrome only when genetic studies are conducted to trace their family history.

The most obvious sign associated with nail-patella syndrome is absent, poorly developed, or unusual fingernails. Fingernail abnormalities are found in about 98 percent of children with this disorder. Abnormalities may be found in one or more fingernails. Only rarely are all fingernails affected. This disease most commonly affects the fingernails of the thumbs and index fingers. The pinky fingernail is least likely to be affected. Fingernails may be small and concave with pitting, ridges, splits, and/or discoloration. Toenails are less often affected.

Kneecap abnormalities, present in about 92 percent of children with this disorder, are the second most common sign associated with this disorder. Either or both kneecaps may be missing or poorly formed. If present, kneecaps are likely to be dislocated. The knees of people with nail-patella syndrome may have a square appearance. Besides the kneecap, other support structures including bones, ligaments, and tendons may also be malformed. Since these support structures stabilize the knee, patients with some leg malformations may have difficulty in walking. There may also be some hip bone anomaly or other skeletal symptoms, for example, clubfoot.

Kidney disease is present in about 30 to 50 percent of people with nail-patella syndrome. Kidney disease has been reported in children with nail-patella syndrome, but renal involvement more commonly develops during adulthood, usually during the fourth decade of life.

Eye problems may be present and vary from person to person. Nail-patella syndrome is thought to be associated with open-angle glaucoma, a condition caused by blockage of the outflow of fluid (aqueous humor) from the front chamber of the eyes. Nail-patella syndrome has also been associated with abnormalities of the cornea, cataracts, and astigmatism. Additionally, the irises of the eye may be multicolored.

When to call the doctor

The doctor should be called if a parent detects the symptoms of nail-patella syndrome in a child previously not diagnosed with the syndrome.

Diagnosis

Genetic testing for nail-patella syndrome is usually available only at research institutions that are working to further characterize this disorder. However, genetic testing cannot predict which signs of the disease will develop nor predict the severity of disease symptoms.

Diagnosis of this disease is most often made on visual medical symptoms such as the characteristic

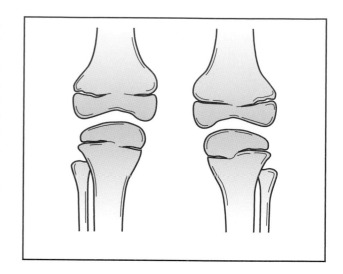

Illustration of bones around the knees showing absence of the patella in nail-patella syndrome. *(Illustration by Argosy, Inc.)*

abnormalities of the fingernails and kneecaps. Diagnosis is confirmed by x-ray images of the affected bones and, when indicated, kidney biopsy. The bony pelvic spurs found in children with nail-patella syndrome are not associated with any other disease.

Treatment

Treatment for children affected by nail-patella syndrome depends on the child's specific symptoms.

A wheelchair may be required if walking becomes painful due to bone, tendon, ligament, or muscle defects. Orthopedic surgery may be necessary for congenital clubfoot deformity. Manipulation or surgery may be required to correct hip dislocation. Cataracts are also surgically treated. Medical treatment at early signs of glaucoma prevents progression of the disease to blindness.

Controlling blood pressure may slow the rate of deterioration of kidney function. Severe kidney disease can be treated with dialysis or a kidney transplant. Children receiving kidney transplants do not develop nail-patella-type renal complications in their new kidney.

Because many possible manifestations of nail-patella syndrome exist, parents are advised to obtain extra medical care for their child with nail-patella syndrome, including regular urinalysis to monitor blood and protein levels to detect kidney disease as well as eye exams to detect glaucoma. Children with nail-patella syndrome should be periodically screened for scoliosis and lordosis.

KEY TERMS

Chorionic villus sampling—A procedure used for prenatal diagnosis at 10–12 weeks gestation. Under ultrasound guidance a needle is inserted either through the mother's vagina or abdominal wall and a sample of the chorionic membrane. These cells are then tested for chromosome abnormalities or other genetic diseases.

Glaucoma—A common eye disease characterized by increased fluid pressure in the eye that damages the optic nerve, which carries visual impulses to the brain. Glaucoma can be caused by another eye disorder, such as a tumor or congenital malformation, or can appear without obvious cause, but if untreated it generally leads to blindness.

Glomerulus—Plural, glomeruli; a network of capillaries located in the nephron of the kidney where wastes are filtered from the blood.

Hematuria—The presence of blood in the urine.

Hypnogogic hallucination—A vivid, dream-like hallucination, such as the sensation of falling, that occurs at the onset of sleep.

Patella—The kneecap.

Proteinuria—Abnormally large quantites of protein in the urine.

Prognosis

Symptoms vary from person to person and for one person through time. The long-term prognosis is extremely variable. One person may exhibit mild symptoms, while another person may become wheelchair-bound or require a kidney transplant.

Survival among patients with nail-patella syndrome is not decreased unless they exhibit renal complications. It is estimated that 8 percent of individuals with nail-patella syndrome who come to medical attention eventually die of kidney disease.

Prevention

Genetic counseling can be offered to persons who have the disease. Parents with this disease have a 50 percent chance of passing it to each of their children.

Parental concerns

Families may wish to seek counseling regarding the effects on relationships within the family after the birth of a child with nail-patella syndrome, for many people respond with guilt, **fear**, or blame when a genetic disorder is manifested within a family. Support groups are often good sources of information about nail-patella syndrome and can offer emotional and psychological support.

Resources

BOOKS

Nail Patella Syndrome: A Medical Dictionary, Bibliography, and Annotated Research Guide to Internet References. San Diego, CA: Icon Health Publications, 2004.

ORGANIZATIONS

Nail Patella Syndrome Networking/Support Group. 67 Woodlake Dr., Holland, PA 18966. Web site: <www.hometown.aol.com/pacali/npspage.html>.

National Organization for Rare Disorders Inc. 55 Kenosia Ave., PO Box 1968, Danbury, CT 06813–1968. Web site: <www.rarediseases.org>.

Judith L. Sims, MS
John T. Lohr, PhD
Judy C. Hawkins, MS

Narcolepsy

Definition

Narcolepsy is a disorder of the nervous system marked by excessive daytime sleepiness, uncontrollable **sleep** attacks, and cataplexy (a sudden loss of muscle tone, usually lasting up to half an hour). The American Psychiatric Association (APA) classifies narcolepsy as a sleep disorder in the fourth edition of the *Diagnostic and Statistical Manual of Mental Disorders*, or *DSM-IV*. The National Institute of Neurological Disorders and Stroke (NINDS) defines narcolepsy as a "disorder caused by the brain's inability to regulate sleep-wake cycles normally." The disorder is sometimes called Gélineau's syndrome because it was first identified in 1880 by the French neurologist Jean-Baptiste Gélineau. The word *narcolepsy* itself comes from two Greek words that together mean "seized by sleepiness."

Description

Narcolepsy is the second-leading cause of excessive daytime sleepiness (after obstructive sleep apnea). Persistent sleepiness and sleep attacks are the hallmarks of this condition. The sleepiness has been compared to the feeling of trying to stay awake after not sleeping for two or three days. It is not correct, however, to describe people with narcolepsy as sleeping longer or spending more time asleep in a 24-hour period than people without the disorder. Although patients with narcolepsy experience drowsiness and sleep attacks during the daytime, they also wake up frequently during the nighttime hours. For this reason, narcolepsy is more accurately described as a disorder of the normal boundaries between sleep and wakefulness.

People with narcolepsy fall asleep suddenly—anywhere, at any time, maybe even in the middle of a conversation. These sleep attacks can last from a few seconds to more than an hour. Depending on where they occur, they may be mildly inconvenient or even dangerous. Some people continue to function outwardly during the sleep episodes, such as talking or putting things away. But when they wake up, they have no memory of the event.

Narcolepsy is related to the deep, dreaming part of sleep known as rapid eye movement (REM) sleep. Normally when people fall asleep, they experience 80 to 100 minutes of non-REM sleep, which is then followed by about 20 minutes of REM sleep. People with narcolepsy, however, enter REM sleep immediately. In addition, REM sleep occurs inappropriately throughout the day in patients with narcolepsy.

Demographics

There has been considerable debate in the early 2000s over the incidence of narcolepsy. Some researchers think the disorder is underdiagnosed. According to NINDS, the disorder affects one American in every 2000, or about 135,000 people in the general United States population. However, the rates in other countries vary considerably, from one in 600 people in Japan to one in 500,000 in Israel. The reasons for these variations in different ethnic groups are not yet fully understood.

Males and females seem to experience this disorder at about the same rate.

Narcolepsy is a somewhat unusual disorder in terms of age distribution. Although the disorder has been identified in children as young as three years of age, most patients with narcolepsy are diagnosed either between the ages of ten and 25 or between the ages of 40 and 45. It is uncommon for a person to develop the signs of narcolepsy for the first time after age 55.

Causes and symptoms

Causes

In 1999 researchers identified the gene that causes narcolepsy on chromosome 12. The gene allows cells in the hypothalamus (the part of the brain that regulates sleep behavior) to receive messages from other cells. When this gene is abnormal, cells cannot communicate properly, and abnormal sleeping patterns develop. However, not everyone who has the gene develops narcolepsy; between 12 percent and 35 percent of the United States population is thought to carry the gene but only 0.02 percent develop the disorder. Narcolepsy sometimes clusters in families; first-degree relatives of a person diagnosed with the disorder have a 1 percent to 2 percent risk of developing narcolepsy themselves, or about 10 to 40 times the risk of a person in the general population.

In the late 1990s, three independent research groups discovered a neuropeptide system in the hypothalamus, the part of the brain that regulates body temperature and appetite. The newly discovered system, which has been called the hypocretinergic system, regulates sleep and wakefulness. The nerve cells, or neurons, in this part of the hypothalamus secrete substances known as hypocretins or orexins, which regulate the sleep/wake cycle in humans. There are two of these compounds, known as orexin-A and orexin-B, or as hypocretin-1 and hypocretin-2. As of the early 2000s, narcolepsy is thought to be an orexin deficiency syndrome; that is, it develops when a person's hypothalamus does not secrete enough orexins to keep the person from falling asleep at inappropriate times. Samples of cerebrospinal fluid taken from patients with narcolepsy contain little or no orexins. MRI scans of these patients indicate that there is some loss of brain tissue in the hypothalamus itself, suggesting that the neurons responsible for secreting orexins have died.

In a few cases, the first signs of narcolepsy are triggered by traumatic damage to the part of the brain that governs REM sleep or from a rapidly growing tumor that puts pressure on this region of the brain. It is also thought that the hormonal changes of **puberty** may affect this region of the brain in some people.

Symptoms

Narcolepsy is defined by four major symptoms:

• Excessive daytime sleepiness (EDS).
• Cataplexy, the most dramatic symptom of narcolepsy, affecting 75 percent of people with the disorder. During an attack of cataplexy, the person's knees buckle and the neck muscles go slack. In extreme cases, the person may become paralyzed and

fall to the floor. This loss of muscle tone is temporary, lasting from a few seconds to half an hour, but it is frightening to other **family** members or friends. Attacks of cataplexy can occur at any time but are often triggered by such strong emotions as anger, joy, or surprise.

- Hypnagogic hallucinations, intense and sometimes terrifying experiences that occur as the person is falling asleep. The hallucinations may be either visual or auditory. They are thought to represent an intrusion of REM sleep/dreaming into the wakeful state.

- Sleep paralysis, a frightening inability to move shortly after awakening or dozing off.

When to call the doctor

The symptoms of narcolepsy in children below the age of ten are somewhat different from the classical signs of the disorder in adolescents and adults. They may include the following (in addition to cataplexy and daytime sleepiness):

- unexplained falls or dropping of objects
- night terrors
- moodiness and abrupt episodes of irritability
- restlessness and hyperactivity
- difficulty waking up in the morning

Children between the ages of ten and 12 frequently report falling asleep in school or being unable to pay attention during class. In some cases a sudden drop in the child's academic performance is the first indication of narcolepsy.

Parents who suspect that their child may have narcolepsy should consult a specialist (usually a pediatric neurologist) and have the child tested in a sleep clinic. Children with narcolepsy have often been misdiagnosed as having attention-deficit hyperactivity disorder, while adolescents have sometimes been misdiagnosed as having substance abuse or **personality disorders**. The sooner narcolepsy is correctly identified, the better the child's chances of maintaining normal academic and social development.

Diagnosis

Narcolepsy is a complex disorder, and it is not always easy to identify. It takes ten years on average for an individual to be correctly diagnosed. The diagnosis of younger patients is additionally complicated by the fact that children with narcolepsy rarely have all four of the classical symptoms of the disorder as described in adults. Most often, the first symptom in children is an over-

whelming feeling of fatigue. After several months or years, cataplexy and the other classical symptoms of the disorder may appear.

The child's doctor will not be able to diagnose narcolepsy on the basis of a routine physical examination. If the child has experienced both excessive daytime sleepiness and cataplexy, a tentative diagnosis may be made on the basis of the patient's history. In addition, the doctor may give the child or adolescent a short self-administered list of eight questions known as the Epworth Sleepiness Scale (ESS). First published by an Australian doctor in 1991, the ESS asks the person to rate how likely they are to doze off or fall asleep in eight different situations from everyday life. A score above ten (maximum score is 24) generally indicates that the doctor should consider laboratory testing for narcolepsy.

Imaging studies are not helpful in diagnosing narcolepsy, although in some cases the doctor may order an MRI or CT scan to rule out a brain tumor or other abnormality in brain structure. Laboratory tests used to evaluate a person for narcolepsy include an overnight polysomnogram (a test in which sleep is monitored with electrocardiography, a video camera, and respiratory parameters). A multiple sleep latency test, which measures sleep latency (onset) and how quickly REM sleep occurs, may also be used. People who have narcolepsy usually fall asleep much more rapidly that people without the disorder, often in less than five minutes.

If the diagnosis is still questionable, a genetic blood test can reveal the existence of certain substances in people who have a tendency to develop narcolepsy. Positive test results suggest but do not prove that the person has narcolepsy. As of the early 2000s, the diagnosis of narcolepsy also can be confirmed by taking a sample of the patient's cerebrospinal fluid by a spinal tap and testing it for the presence of hypocretin-1. Patients with narcolepsy have no hypocretin-1 in their spinal fluid.

Treatment

There is no cure for narcolepsy. The disorder is neither progressive nor fatal, but it is chronic. The symptoms, however, can be managed with a combination of medications and lifestyle adjustments. Amphetamine-like **stimulant drugs** are often prescribed to control drowsiness and sleep attacks. Patients who do not like taking high doses of stimulants may choose to take smaller doses and make adjustments in their lifestyles, such as napping every couple of hours, to relieve daytime sleepiness. **Antidepressants** are also often effective in treating symptoms of abnormal REM sleep.

Newer nonamphetamine wake-promoting drugs are available to treat narcolepsy. These medications lack the unpleasant side effects of amphetamines, particularly jitteriness and **anxiety**. Modafinil (Provigil) is the most commonly prescribed of the newer psychostimulants. As of 2004, however, researchers do not know exactly how modafinil prevents the drowsiness associated with narcolepsy. Its most common side effect is **headache**. A study published in 2003 reported that modafinil appears to be safe for use in children.

With discovery of the gene that causes narcolepsy, researchers are hopeful that therapies can eventually be designed to relieve the symptoms of the disorder.

Alternative treatment

The botanical remedy yohimbe (*Pausinystalia yohimbe*) may be useful in promoting alertness. As with any herbal preparation or medication, however, individuals should check with their healthcare professional before taking the remedy to treat narcolepsy.

Nutritional concerns

Children with narcolepsy sometimes fall asleep while eating, but the disorder itself does not cause or lead to **malnutrition**. Adolescents should be advised to avoid tobacco, **caffeine**, and alcoholic beverages, as these substances can increase daytime sleepiness in patients with narcolepsy.

Prognosis

The symptoms of narcolepsy are more severe when they develop in children than when they emerge in adult life. Narcolepsy is not a degenerative disease, however, and patients do not develop other neurologic symptoms. In fact, older patients often report that their symptoms decrease in severity after age 60. Apart from falls or other accidents, narcolepsy does not affect a person's life expectancy. It can, however, severely interfere with a young person's ability to study, **play**, participate in **sports** and other social activities, and develop close relationships with others. The sooner it is diagnosed and treated, the better the child's outlook for a happy and productive adult life.

Prevention

There is no way to prevent narcolepsy as of the early 2000s.

KEY TERMS

Cataplexy—A symptom of narcolepsy in which there is a sudden episode of muscle weakness triggered by emotions. The muscle weakness may cause the person's knees to buckle, or the head to drop. In severe cases, the patient may become paralyzed for a few seconds to minutes.

Hypocretins—Chemicals secreted in the hypothalamus that regulate the sleep/wake cycle.

Hypothalamus—A part of the forebrain that controls heartbeat, body temperature, thirst, hunger, body temperature and pressure, blood sugar levels, and other functions.

Orexin—Another name for hypocretin, a chemical secreted in the hypothalmus that regulates the sleep/wake cycle. Narcolepsy is sometimes described as an orexin deficiency syndrome.

Sleep paralysis—An abnormal episode of sleep in which the patient cannot move for a few minutes, usually occurring on falling asleep or waking up. Often found in patients with narcolepsy.

Parental concerns

Narcolepsy can affect a family in a number of ways before it is diagnosed. Younger children are at risk of injuring themselves by falling, and adolescents with driving privileges are at high risk of automobile accidents. Poor performance in school and difficulty making friends as a result of irritability or embarrassment over sleep attacks can have a lasting impact on a child's chances of preparation for college or the choice of a challenging and satisfying line of work. In many cases the child is accused of being lazy or stupid, which can have devastating effects on his or her **self-esteem**. Misdiagnoses can lead to inappropriate treatment and psychological depression for the affected child. In addition, sleep attacks and cataplexy can be frightening to other family members who witness them.

Narcolepsy can be particularly stressful for a family when the affected child reaches **adolescence**, because of **peer pressure** to experiment with **smoking** and recreational drugs, and because of resentment about restrictions on learning to drive or use of the family car. Families with a child diagnosed with narcolepsy should consider joining a support group for people affected by the disorder.

Resources

BOOKS

American Psychiatric Association. *Diagnostic and Statistical Manual of Mental Disorders,* 4th ed., Text Revision. Washington, DC: American Psychiatric Association, 2000.

"Sleep Disorders: Narcolepsy." Section 14, Chapter 173 in *The Merck Manual of Diagnosis and Therapy.* Edited by Mark H. Beers, and Robert Berkow. Whitehouse Station, NJ: Merck Research Laboratories, 2002.

PERIODICALS

Beuckmann, C. T., and M. Yanagisawa. "Orexins: From Neuropeptides to Energy Homeostasis and Sleep/Wake Regulation." *Journal of Molecular Medicine* 80 (June 2002): 329–42.

Ivanenko, A., R. Tauman, and D. Gozal. "Modafinil in the Treatment of Excessive Daytime Sleepiness in Children." *Sleep Medicine* 4 (November 2003): 579–82.

Kotagal, S. "Sleep Disorders in Childhood." *Neurologic Clinics* 21 (November 2003): 961–81.

Ohayon, M. M., et al. "Prevalence of Narcolepsy Symptomatology and Diagnosis in the European General Population." *Neurology* 58 (June 25, 2002): 1826–33.

Silvestri, A. J., et al. "The Central Nucleus of the Amygdala and the Wake-Promoting Effects of Modafinil." *Brain Research* 941 (June 21, 2002): 43–52.

ORGANIZATIONS

American Sleep Disorders Association. 1610 14th St. NW, Suite 300, Rochester, MN 55901. Web site: <www.sleepapnea.org>.

Narcolepsy Network. PO Box 42460, Cincinnati, OH 45242. Web site: <www.narcolepsynetwork.org>.

National Center on Sleep Disorders Research. Two Rockledge Centre, 6701 Rockledge Dr., Bethesda, MD 20892. Web site: <www.nhlbi.nih.gov/health/public/sleep>.

National Institute of Neurological Disorders and Stroke (NINDS). National Institutes of Health. 9000 Rockville Pike, Bethesda, MD 20892. Web site: <http://www.ninds.nih.gov>.

National Sleep Foundation. 1522 K St., NW, Suite 500, Washington, DC 20005. Web site: <www.sleepfoundation.org>.

Stanford Center for Narcolepsy. 1201 Welch Rd-Rm P-112, Stanford, CA 94305. Web site: <http://blackdogstudieos.com/portfolio/Web/narcolepsy>.

University of Illinois Center for Narcolepsy Research. 845 S. Damen Ave., Chicago, IL 60612. Web site: <www.uic.edu/depts./cnr/>

WEB SITES

Baker, Matthew J., and Selim R. Benbadis. "Narcolepsy." *eMedicine,* October 4, 2004. Available online at <www.emedicine.com/neuro/topic522.htm> (accessed January 14, 2005).

OTHER

National Institute of Neurological Disorders and Stroke (NINDS). *Narcolepsy Fact Sheet.* Bethesda, MD: NINDS, 2003.

Michelle Lee Brandt

Narcotic drugs

Definition

Narcotics are addictive drugs that reduce the user's perception of **pain** and induce euphoria (a feeling of exaggerated and unrealistic well-being). The English word narcotic is derived from the Greek *narkotikos,* which means "numbing" or "deadening." Although the term can refer to any drug that deadens sensation or produces stupor, it is commonly applied to the opioids—that is, to all natural or synthetic drugs that act like morphine.

Description

Historical background

Narcotics are the oldest as well as the strongest **analgesics,** or pain-relieving drugs, known to humans. Ancient Sumerian and Egyptian medical texts dated as early as 4000 B.C. mention the opium poppy (*Papaver somniferum*) as the source of a milky fluid (opium latex) that could be given to relieve coughs and insomnia as well as ease pain. Traditional Chinese medicine recommended the opium poppy, known to Chinese physicians as *ying su ke,* for the treatment of **asthma,** severe **diarrhea,** and dysentery as well as chronic pain and insomnia. Opium latex contains between 10 and 20 percent morphine, which in its purified form is a white crystalline powder with a bitter taste.

Narcotics are central nervous system depressants that produce a stuporous state in the person who takes them. These drugs often induce a state of euphoria or feeling of extreme well-being, and they are powerfully addictive. The body quickly builds a tolerance to narcotics in as little as two to three days, so that greater doses are required to achieve the same effect. Because of the addictive qualities of these drugs, most countries in the twenty-first century have strict laws regarding the production and distribution of narcotics. These laws became necessary when opium **addiction** in the nineteenth century became a widespread social problem in the developed countries. Opium, which was the first of the opioids to be widely used, had been a common folk remedy for centuries that often led to addiction for the user; in fact, many popular Victorian patent medicines for "female complaints" actually contained opium. The invention of the hypodermic needle in the mid-nineteenth century, however, increased the number of addicts because it allowed opioids to be delivered directly into the bloodstream, thereby dramatically increasing their effect.

Classification of narcotics

As of the early 2000s, narcotics are commonly classified into three groups according to their origin:

• Natural derivatives of opium: Narcotics in this group include morphine itself and codeine.

• Partially synthetic drugs derived from morphine: These drugs include heroin, oxycodone (OxyContin), hydromorphone (Dilaudid), and oxymorphone (Numorphan).

• Synthetic compounds that resemble morphine in their chemical structure: Narcotics in this group include fentanyl (Duragesic), levorphanol (Levo-Dromoran), meperidine (Demerol), methadone, and propoxyphene (Darvon).

Narcotics are available in many different forms, ranging from oral, intramuscular, and intravenous preparations to patches that can be applied to the skin (fentanyl). Illegal street heroin can be taken by inhalation as well as by injection.

How narcotics work

The central nervous system in humans and other mammals contains five different types of opioid receptor proteins, located primarily in the brain, spinal cord, and digestive tract. When a person takes an opioid medication, the drug attaches to these opioid receptors in the brain and spinal cord and decreases the person's perception of pain. Narcotics do not, however, reduce or eliminate the cause of the pain.

Some of the opioid receptors (known as mu and sigma receptors) influence a person's perception of pleasure. When a narcotic medication stimulates these receptor proteins, the person typically experiences intense sensations of euphoria or well-being. The speed with which these drugs take effect depends on the method of administration; IV narcotics reach their peak effectiveness within ten minutes, while oral narcotics take about an hour and a half, and skin patches take between two and four hours.

Overdoses of narcotics can cause drowsiness, unconsciousness, and even death because these drugs suppress respiration.

General use

Narcotics have several legitimate uses:

• Analgesic: Doctors frequently prescribe oral codeine and propoxyphene (alone or in combination with aspirin) for pain control after oral surgery, for severe menstrual cramps, and for temporary pain relief after other outpatient surgical procedures. Intravenous narcotics may be given for several days after major surgery to relieve the patient's discomfort. Subsequent methods of administering opioids following surgery include a sustained-release injected form of morphine sulfate (DepoMorphine) and a patient-controlled transdermal system (E-TRANS) that releases doses of fentanyl when the patient pushes a button attached to the arm or upper chest. Intravenous narcotics may also be used for palliative care, to relieve the pain of patients diagnosed with terminal **cancer**.

• Antitussive: Antitussives are medications given to control coughing. Codeine is often effective in relieving severe coughs and is a common ingredient in prescription **cough** mixtures.

• Antidiarrheal: Paregoric, a liquid preparation containing powdered opium, anise oil, and glycerin, is sometimes prescribed for severe diarrhea. The opium in paregoric works to control diarrhea because it slows down the rhythmic contractions of the intestines that ordinarily move food through the digestive tract. Lomotil, another antidiarrheal medication, contains a synthetic opioid known as diphenoxylate; it is often recommended for treating cancer patients with diarrhea caused by radiation therapy.

Precautions

In the United States, opioids are as of 2004 classified as Schedule II drugs under the Controlled Substances Act of 1970. Drugs in this category are described by the government as having a high potential for abuse and a liability for dependence and yet an approved medical use in **pain management**. The corresponding Canadian legislation, the Controlled Drugs and Substances Act of 1997, classifies medications containing any narcotic under the heading (N) but specifies varying levels of regulation ranging from strict controls for highly addictive single-drug products to lesser controls on drugs combining a narcotic with non-narcotic substances. As both countries' legal controls indicate, narcotics should be used cautiously, for as short a period of time as possible, and only under a doctor's supervision. In particular, they should never be used together with certain other categories of prescription drugs or herbal preparations.

Side effects

In addition to the risk of dependency or addiction, narcotics have a number of physical side effects, including the following:

- **constipation**
- drowsiness
- withdrawal symptoms after extended use (tearing, sweating, diarrhea, **vomiting**, gooseflesh, muscle twitching, runny nose, loss of appetite, and hot or cold flashes)

Interactions

Narcotics can be dangerous because of their potential for deadly interactions with other medications as well as their potential for dependence and addiction. Narcotics should never be combined with other types of drugs that depress the central nervous system. These categories of drugs include the following:

- alcohol
- benzodiazepine tranquilizers, including such drugs as diazepam (Valium), alprazolam (Xanax), and chlordiazepoxide (Librium)
- barbiturates, used to treat insomnia and **anxiety**, including such medications as pentobarbital (Nembutal) and mephobarbital (Mebaral)
- antihistamines, even over-the-counter cold or allergy medications, which can interact with narcotics to intensify drowsiness and repress breathing

Narcotics can also interact with certain herbal preparations to cause central nervous system depression. Anyone taking narcotics for pain relief should avoid using herbal preparations containing kava kava (*Piper methysticum*), valerian (*Valeriana officinalis*), chamomile (*Matricaria recutita*), or lemon balm (*Melissa officinalis*), as these herbs intensify the tendency of opioids to cause drowsiness and slow down breathing. Ginseng (*Panax ginseng*) should also be avoided because it interferes with the pain-relieving qualities of opioid medications.

Prevention

Scientists have attempted to develop ways to use the pain-killing properties of narcotics while counteracting their addictive qualities. Substances known as narcotic or opioid antagonists are drugs that block the actions of narcotics and are used to reverse the side effects of narcotic abuse or an overdose. A class of drugs, a mixture of opioids and opioid antagonists, has been developed so that patients can be relieved of pain without the addictive or other unpleasant side effects associated with narcotics.

Parental concerns

One minor concern that parents may have if the doctor prescribes narcotic medications for their child is that such side effects as constipation or sleepiness are more common and more severe in children younger than 18 years of age.

Far more seriously, narcotic drugs are among those substances used illegally or abused by adolescents. Some researchers estimate that as many as 90 percent of adult drug addicts began a pattern of substance abuse during **adolescence**. Teenagers are particularly likely to begin experimenting with narcotics in the form of prescription cough syrup and such pain relievers as Darvon or Oxy-Contin and to combine narcotics with alcohol or other drugs of abuse. Moreover, although opioid medications account for fewer cases of drug abuse than cocaine, alcohol, or several other drugs, they still account for 4 to 5 percent of emergency room visits. In addition, the death rate of opioid abusers is proportionately significantly higher than the mortality of people who abuse PCP or cocaine.

The American Academy of Child and Adolescent Psychiatry (AACAP) lists opiates as common drugs of abuse among teenagers and notes that children as young as 12 may be using narcotics. In many cases, children can obtain these drugs at home in the form of medications prescribed for other **family** members. Children who are abusing opioid medications may show the following signs:

- euphoria or "feeling no pain"
- constipation
- slurred speech
- shallow breathing
- itching or flushing of the skin
- mental confusion and poor judgment
- bloodshot eyes with small pupils
- nausea and vomiting
- unusual drowsiness

KEY TERMS

Analgesics—A class of pain-relieving medicines, including aspirin and Tylenol.

Antitussive—A drug used to suppress coughing.

Euphoria—A feeling or state of well-being or elation.

Morphine—The principal alkaloid derived from the opium poppy for use as a pain reliever and sedative. In its purified form, it is a white, bitter-tasting crystalline powder.

Narcotic—A drug derived from opium or compounds similar to opium. Such drugs are potent pain relievers and can affect mood and behavior. Long-term use of narcotics can lead to dependence and tolerance. Also known as a narcotic analgesic.

Opium latex—The milky juice or sap of the opium poppy, used to produce morphine.

Palliative—Referring to a drug or a form of care that relieves pain without providing a cure. Persons in severe pain from terminal cancer are often prescribed narcotics as palliative care.

Stupor—A trance-like state that causes a person to appear numb to their environment.

Parents who suspect that their children are abusing opioids, either alone or in combination with other drugs, should get help as soon as possible.

Resources

BOOKS

"Opioid Dependence." Section 15, Chapter 195 in *The Merck Manual of Diagnosis and Therapy*, edited by Mark H. Beers, and Robert Berkow. Whitehouse Station, NJ: Merck Research Laboratories, 2002.

Pelletier, Kenneth R. *The Best Alternative Medicine*, Part II, "CAM Therapies for Specific Conditions: Pain." New York: Simon & Schuster, 2002.

PERIODICALS

Abebe, W. "Herbal Medication: Potential for Adverse Interactions with Analgesic Drugs." *Journal of Clinical Pharmacy and Therapeutics* 27 (December 2002): 391–401.

Cone, E. J., et al. "Oxycodone Involvement in Drug Abuse Deaths. II: Evidence for Toxic Multiple Drug-Drug Interactions." *Journal of Analytical Toxicology* 28 (May-June 2004): 217–25.

Elwood, W. N. "Sticky Business: Patterns of Procurement and Misuse of Prescription Cough Syrup in Houston." *Journal of Psychoactive Drugs* 33 (April-June 2001): 121–33.

Nevin, J. "Drug Update: Fentanyl Patch Abuse." *Emergency Medical Services* 33 (July 2004): 24–5.

Stern, J., and C. Ippoliti. "Management of Acute Cancer Treatment-Induced Diarrhea." *Seminars in Oncology Nursing* 19 (November 2003): 11–6.

Viscusi, E. R. "Emerging Techniques for Postoperative Analgesia in Orthopedic Surgery." *American Journal of Orthopedics* 33 (May 2004): 13–16.

ORGANIZATIONS

American Academy of Child and Adolescent Psychiatry. 3615 Wisconsin Avenue, NW, Washington, DC 20016–3007. Web site: <www.aacap.org.>.

National Institute on Drug Abuse (NIDA). 6001 Executive Boulevard, Room 5213, Bethesda, MD 20892–9561. Web site: <www.drugabuse.gov>.

United States Food and Drug Administration (FDA). 5600 Fishers Lane, Rockville, MD 20857–0001. Web site: <www.fda.gov>.

WEB SITES

Rehman, Ziaur, Suzan Khoromi, and James E. Douglas. "Opioid Abuse." *eMedicine*, August 15, 2004. Available online at <www.emedicine.com/med/topic1673.htm> (accessed November 30, 2004).

Stephens, Everett. "Toxicity, Narcotics." *eMedicine*, September 20, 2004. Available online at <www.emedicine.com/emerg/topic330.htm> (accessed November 30, 2004).

OTHER

American Academy of Child and Adolescent Psychiatry (AACAP). *Teens: Alcohol and Other Drugs.* AACAP Facts for Families #3. Washington, DC: AACAP, 2004.

National Institute on Drug Abuse (NIDA). *NIDA InfoFacts: Prescription Pain and Other Medications.* Bethesda, MD: NIAMS, 2004.

Rebecca Frey, PhD

Nasal trauma

Definition

Nasal trauma is defined as any injury to the nose or related structure that may result in bleeding, a physical deformity, a decreased ability to breathe normally because of obstruction, or an impaired sense of smell. The injury may be either internal or external.

Description

The human nose is composed of bone, soft tissue, and cartilage. It serves as a passageway for air to flow from the outside environment into the lower respiratory tract and lungs. At the same time the nasal passages warm and humidify the air that enters the body.

Internal injuries to the nose typically occur when a foreign object is placed in the nose or when a person takes in drugs of abuse (inhalants or cocaine) through the nose. External injuries to the nose are usually blunt force injuries related to **sports** participation, criminal violence, **child abuse**, or automobile or bicycle accidents. This type of injury may result in a nasal fracture. The nasal bones are the most frequently fractured facial bones due to their position on the face, and they are the third most common type of bone fracture in general after **fractures** of the wrist and collarbone. A force of only 30 g is required to break the nasal bones, compared to 70 g for the bones in the jaw and 200 g for the bony ridge above the eyes. The pattern of the fracture depends on the direction of the blow to the nose, whether coming from the front, the side, or above the nose. Although not usually life-threatening by itself, a fractured nose may lead to difficulties in breathing as well as facial disfigurement.

Fractures resulting from trauma to the nose may involve the bones of the septum (the partition of bone and cartilage dividing the two nostrils) as well as the bones surrounding the eyes. These bones include the nasal, maxilla, lacrimal, and frontal bones. Direct trauma to the bridge of the nose may also result in damage to a part of the base of the skull known as the cribriform plate. This injury in turn may allow cerebrospinal fluid to leak out of the skull and leave the body through the nose. Fractures may also damage the membranes that line the nasal passages, leading to possible formation of scar tissue, obstruction of the airway, and damage to the child's sense of smell.

In addition to fractures, external injuries of the nose include soft-tissue injuries resulting from **bites** (human and animal), insect **stings**, cuts, or scrapes. Penetrating injuries to the nasal area caused by air gun or BB pellets were as of 2004 also reported with increasing frequency in older children and adolescents. When fired at close range, these pellets can penetrate the skin and cheekbone and lodge in the nasal septum or the sinuses near the nose.

Lastly, nose **piercing** as a fashion trend is a type of intentional injury to the nose that has several possible complications, including infections of the cartilage and soft tissues in the nose; blockage of the airway due to a loosened stud or other nose ornament; and gastrointestinal emergencies caused by accidental swallowing of nose jewelry.

If a patient's nasal trauma leads doctors to suspect child abuse, the incident must be reported to the police.

Demographics

The demographics of nasal trauma vary according to the type of injury. Internal nasal injuries are unusual in infants but occur fairly frequently in toddlers and young children as a result of playfulness or curiosity. Children often insert small hard objects (buttons, coins, watch batteries, dried peas or beans, plastic parts from **toys**, etc.) in their nostrils. One Japanese study of children brought to the emergency room for removal of foreign bodies from the respiratory and digestive tracts found that the nose was the most common location (39.4% of patients) of these objects. Sixty-seven percent of the children treated were between one and four years of age, with two-year-olds the most common age group. Another common cause of injury to the nasal passages in children is scratching or picking the inside of the nose, often as a reaction to dry and **itching** nasal membranes during the heating season in colder climates.

In older children and adolescents, however, the single most common cause of internal nasal injuries is inhalant abuse or ingesting cocaine through the nose ("snorting"). Inhalants include such substances as toluene (paint thinner, nail polish remover, rubber cement, airplane glue), butane (lighter fluid, spray paint, room fresheners, hair spray), chlorinated hydrocarbons (dry cleaning fluid, spot removers, typewriter correction fluid), and acetone (rubber cement, permanent markers, nail polish remover). According to the American Academy of Family Practice (AAFP) and the U.S. Department of Health and Human Services, nearly 20 percent of children in the United States have used inhalants at least once by the time they are in eighth grade. The average age of children experimenting with inhalants is 13, with Hispanic and Caucasian youth more likely to abuse these substances than African Americans. With regard to cocaine, figures from the National Institute on Drug Abuse (NIDA) from the late 1990s indicate that that 3.2 percent of all eighth graders in the United States have used cocaine at least once, although young adults between the ages of 18 to 25 are the age group with the highest usage of the drug.

Nose piercing as a fashion statement is most common among adolescents and young adults. One study of undergraduates at a university in upstate New York found that 51 percent had body piercing, with the nose and ears the most common sites. Seventeen percent of these students reported medical complications from the piercing, ranging from skin or cartilage infections to periodic bleeding from the nose. A less common cause of internal injuries to the nose in older children and adolescents is the use of magnetized jewelry as a substitute for body piercing. The external piece of jewelry is held in place on the outside of the nostril by a small magnet placed inside the nose. Displacement of these magnets has been reported to cause bleeding and perforation of the nasal septum, while accidental swallowing of these magnets may require emergency surgery. One British hospital reported no fewer than 24 such cases over an eight-week period.

With regard to nasal fractures, one group of American researchers estimates that they account for about 24 percent of all facial fractures. The most common single cause is assault, accounting for 41 percent of nasal fractures. The second most common cause is automobile accidents (27%), followed by **sports injuries** (11%). Falls account for most other nasal fractures in children, although dog bites are reported with increasing frequency as a cause of nasal fractures in children below 16 years of age. Adolescents who have had plastic surgery on the nose (rhinoplasty) are at increased risk of nasal fractures in later life.

As many as 10 percent of nasal injuries in younger children, however, result from physical abuse. Doctors in the early 2000s are advised to consider abuse as a possible diagnosis when evaluating nasal fractures in children under six years of age. Suspected child abuse must be reported to police.

Causes and symptoms

Causes

External trauma to the nose may be accidental (transportation accidents, animal bites, air gun injuries, and sports injuries) or intentional (fights, criminal assault, domestic violence, nose piercing). Nasal injuries from athletic activities may result from contact with equipment (being hit in the face by a baseball, hockey ball, or other small ball hit at high speed, or by the bat or stick itself) or the bodies of other players (football, boxing, martial arts, rugby). Nasal injuries from piercing include bacterial infections of the skin and nasal cartilage, allergic reactions to the jewelry, tissue damage, and periodic bleeding. Direct trauma and/or delayed type hypersensitivity reaction to nickel may occur from nasal

rings and jewelry, facial adornments which as of 2004 are increasingly popular.

In a few cases, external trauma to the nose may also be iatrogenic, or caused by medical care. Most of these injuries result from medical examination of the nose—particularly in emergency circumstances—or as complications of plastic surgery.

Internal injuries to the nose may be either mechanical (caused by **foreign objects** in the nose or by picking or scratching the tissues lining the nose) or chemical (caused by environmental irritants or substance abuse).

Chemical injuries to the nose are caused by accidental or purposeful breathing or sniffing of irritating substances. These may include tobacco smoke; household cleaners (ammonia and chlorine bleach) and furniture polish; ozone and other air pollutants; cocaine; and glue, paint thinners, solvents, and similar household products that produce toxic vapors. An increasingly common form of chemical injury to the nasal membranes in toddlers is alkali **burns** caused by leakage from small batteries placed in the nose. While chemical damage to the nose is usually accidental in younger children, it is more often the result of substance abuse in adolescents. Taking cocaine through the nose ("snorting") or inhalant abuse ("sniffing" or "huffing") are the most common causes of chemical damage to the nose in older children or teenagers.

Symptoms

The symptoms of physical trauma to the nose may include the following:

- flattening or other deformation of the shape of the nose
- infections of the cartilage or soft tissue
- epistaxis, or bleeding from the nose
- crepitus, or the crackling or crunching sound heard when the ends of a fractured bone are rubbed together
- pain and tissue swelling
- airway blockage from bleeding, fluid discharge, or tissue swelling
- **rhinitis** or inflammation of the mucous membranes lining the nose (In the case of a fracture, rhinitis may lead to increased tear production in the eyes and a runny nose.)
- septal hematoma, a mass of blood from torn tissue that may collect within the cartilage that divides the two nostrils (It may become infected and form an abscess that eventually destroys the cartilage.)
- bruising or discoloration (ecchymosis) of the tissues around the eye

- leakage of cerebrospinal fluid through the nostrils

Chemical trauma to the nose may result in the following:

- runny nose and watering of the eyes
- pain
- loss of the sense of smell
- nasal congestion and sneezing
- reddening and swelling of the mucous membranes lining the nose
- eventual destruction of the cartilage in the nasal septum and the tissues lining the nose

When to call the doctor

Parents should call the doctor at once in the event of a nose injury when the following conditions are apparent:

- The child is bleeding profusely from the nose.
- The child is having difficulty breathing normally.
- The injury involves an air gun, BB gun, or animal or human bites.
- The child is seeing double, has other visual disturbances, or staggers when trying to walk.
- The child's nasal discharge is watery as well as bloody.
- The child is known to have inserted a battery into the nose or to have swallowed such a battery or piece of nose jewelry.
- The child's appearance or behavior suggests inhalant or cocaine abuse. Some danger signals are: a chemical odor on the child's breath; constant runny nose; unusual or excessive use of nose drops or **decongestants**; sores inside or around the mouth; stains on the fingernails; dazed appearance; **anxiety**, **sleep** disturbances, **nausea and vomiting**; slurred speech; visual disturbances; and loss of physical coordination.

Diagnosis

History and physical examination

In many cases the diagnosis of an injury to the child's nose is obvious to the doctor from taking a history, particularly if the parent witnessed the accident or saw the child putting something in his nose. The physical examination depends in part on the history. If the child's nose is bleeding without a history of a fall, blow to the face, or other obvious cause, the doctor gently examines inside the nose with a handheld speculum of the type used to examine the ears, in order to see where the nasal

bleeding originates. Bleeding from the lower part of the nose is more common and usually less serious. In most cases the doctor is able to tell whether there is a foreign object in the nose or whether the child has been scratching or picking at the nose. Bleeding from the upper part of the nose closer to the throat is more serious because it can block the airway and because it may indicate that the child has a bleeding disorder rather than a traumatic injury. The doctor may then examine the child's throat for signs of blood from the upper nose trickling down into the throat. He or she will remove any blood clots from the nose with suction.

In the case of a known accident, sports injury, or assault, the doctor begins with the ABCs, which means that he or she will check the child's *airway*, *breathing*, and *circulation*. The doctor will usually have the child sit upright or lie on one side, and will remove blood clots, broken teeth, or other foreign bodies from the nose or throat. He or she will then carry out a systematic examination of the child's face and head. The most common pattern of examination moves from the inside of the nose and mouth to the outside of the face and from the bottom of the face to the top.

The doctor looks for signs of bruising and tissue swelling as well as bleeding and gently palpates, or touches, the various facial bones for movement and stability. If the doctor suspects that the nose itself is fractured, he or she will listen for crepitus when the nose is gently moved and will look for evidence of a dislocated septum or a septal hematoma, which will appear as a bluish bulging mass within the nasal septum. The child's teeth will be examined for looseness, and the muscles and nerves of the face will be evaluated. If there is a discharge from the nose, the doctor will look at it to see whether it contains cerebrospinal fluid, which would indicate damage to the bones of the skull as well as the nasal bones. Lastly, the doctor examines the child's eyes to make sure that the pupils are responding normally to light and that the child is not seeing double or having other visual problems that might indicate nerve damage or damage to the eye itself.

In cases involving animal bites or other tearing or crushing injuries to the skin and external tissues of the nose, the doctor carefully cleanses the broken skin with soap and water or disinfectants such as benzalkonium chloride as well as checks for fractured facial bones.

Many of the early signs of inhalant or cocaine abuse are not specific to these disorders; however, a careful history-taking and examination of the child's eyes, nose, and throat may lead the doctor to ask the child or adolescent appropriate questions about his or her use of inhalants or cocaine.

Imaging studies and laboratory tests

Computed tomography (CT) scans are the type of imaging study most commonly done to evaluate suspected nasal fractures. X-ray studies may be ordered to identify the location of a foreign body if it is metal, such as a pellet from a BB gun or air gun, or to evaluate the nasal area for evidence of repeated fractures when abuse is suspected. A blood test will be performed prior to surgery in order to determine the child's blood type, clotting time, and complete blood count. In some cases the doctor may order a filter paper or glucose content test of nasal secretions to check for the presence of cerebrospinal fluid.

In some cases, the physician may ask the child's parents for photographs taken prior to the injury in order to determine the extent of deformity or other injuries to the nose. Photographs may also be taken for documentation if abuse is suspected and also for documentation of injuries for later plastic surgery.

Drug-specific blood or urine tests may be ordered for children or adolescents suspected of abusing inhalants or cocaine.

Treatment

Timing

Nasal injuries should be treated as promptly as possible to lower risk of infection. If the child has been bitten by an animal, the injury must be cleansed as soon as possible to lower the risk of **rabies**. Batteries placed in the nose should be removed as soon as possible, preferably within four hours to avoid serious burns from their contents. If a septal hematoma has developed, the doctor must remove it as quickly as possible to prevent infection or eventual death of the tissues in the nasal septum.

Treatment of nasal fractures is best performed during the first three hours after the injury. If this is impossible, management of a nasal fracture should be done within three to seven days. Timing is of utmost importance when treating nasal fractures because delays longer than seven to 10 days may allow the broken bones to set without proper alignment or lead to such complications as scar tissue formation and airway obstruction. Poorly set nasal fractures usually require surgical correction.

Specific procedures

Foreign objects in the nose can be removed by nasal suction in most cases. Most nosebleeds are treated by five to 30 minutes of direct pressure on the nostrils, with the child's head placed in an upright position. The doctor may also pack the child's nose with gauze coated with petroleum jelly. If the bleeding does not stop or if it appears to originate in the upper nose, the doctor will consult a head and neck surgeon or an otolaryngologist for specialized evaluation of the bleeding.

Air gun or BB pellets that have penetrated the nose or nearby sinuses are generally removed with the help of an endoscope, which is a slender tubular instrument that allows the doctor to examine the inside of a body cavity.

Treatment of nasal fractures depends on the extent of the injury; the most difficult fractures to treat are those that involve the nasal septum. The doctor will usually reduce the fracture, which means that he or she will restore the damaged bones to their proper position and alignment. Although local anesthesia is usually sufficient for treating nasal fractures in adults and older teenagers, general anesthesia is usually given when treating these injuries in younger children.

Reductions of nasal fractures may be either open or closed. A closed reduction involves manipulation of the bones without cutting into the overlying skin. This type of reduction is performed for fractures of the nasal bones that are limited in size and complexity. Open reductions are performed for more complex nasal fractures. In an open reduction, the nasal bones are moved back to their original location after the surgeon has made an incision in the overlying skin. This procedure is done for fractures involving dislocation of the septum as well as the nasal bones. In addition, an open reduction is necessary if the child has a septal hematoma or an open fracture in which the skin has been perforated. If a septal hematoma is present, the doctor will drain it and pack the nose to prevent subsequent accumulation of blood. The nasal bones are held in the proper position with external splints as well as the internal packing, and the splints are kept in place for seven to ten days. The child is given **antibiotics** to lower the risk of infection and may be referred to an otolaryngologist or plastic surgeon for further evaluation. Ice packs or cold compresses can be applied at home to reduce swelling and ease the child's discomfort.

In the case of animal bites, the child may be given passive or active immunization against rabies if there is a chance that the dog or other animal is rabid. This precaution is particularly important for animal bites on the nose or other parts of the face, as the incubation period of the rabies virus is much shorter for bites on the head and neck than for bites elsewhere on the body.

Prognosis

Most types of nasal trauma have a good prognosis. Nosebleeds or tissue damage caused by scratching or picking at the nose usually clear completely once the child stops these habits. Infections or allergic reactions caused by foreign objects in the nose or piercing usually clear up promptly once the object or piece of jewelry is removed. Nasal fractures that do not involve the nasal septum or other facial bones and receive prompt treatment generally heal without deformities of the nose, cartilage destruction, or other complications. More extensive facial fractures, however, may require a second operation to correct the positioning of the bones and restore the appearance of the nose.

The prognosis for soft-tissue injuries to the nose depends on the cause and extent of the injuries. Such tearing or crushing injuries as those caused by bites take longer to heal than simple cuts and may require plastic surgery at a later date to restore the appearance of the nose.

Damage to the tissues lining the nose caused by exposure to tobacco smoke or other irritants in the environment is usually reversible once the child is removed from contact with the irritating substance. Erosion or destruction of the nasal cartilage as a result of inhalant or cocaine abuse, however, usually requires surgical treatment.

Prevention

Preventive strategies for nasal trauma depend on the child's age group. For younger children, parents should take the following precautions:

- Keep such small objects as coins, disk batteries, and buttons in childproof drawers or cabinets and throw out broken toys or toy parts.
- Use a humidifier during heating season to prevent drying and itching of the nasal membranes and coat the inside of the child's nose with petroleum jelly.
- Quit **smoking** completely or stop smoking inside the house.
- Open windows or otherwise ventilate the room when using ammonia, chlorine bleach, oven cleaner, degreasers, spray paints, dry cleaning fluid, furniture polish, or other household products that give off strong vapors at room temperature. Keep all such products in a childproof cabinet or closet.
- Teach the child basic rules of **safety** in playing with household pets as well as in dealing with large dogs and other animals outside the house. Have pet dogs or cats immunized against rabies.
- Drive safely and make sure the child is using an age-appropriate protective seat or seat belt.

KEY TERMS

Crepitus—A crackling sound.

Dorsum—The medical term for the bridge of the nose.

Ecchymosis—The medical term for a bruise, or skin discoloration caused by blood seeping from broken capillaries under the skin.

Epistaxis—The medical term used to describe a bleeding from the nose.

Hematoma—A localized collection of blood, often clotted, in body tissue or an organ, usually due to a break or tear in the wall of blood vessel.

Iatrogenic—A condition that is caused by the diagnostic procedures or treatments administered by medical professionals. Iatrogenic conditions may be caused by any number of things including contaminated medical instruments or devices, contaminated blood or implants, or contaminated air within the medical facility.

Otolaryngologist—A doctor who is trained to treat injuries, defects, diseases, or conditions of the ear, nose, and throat. Also sometimes known as an otorhinolaryngologist.

Reduction—The restoration of a body part to its original position after displacement, such as the reduction of a fractured bone by bringing ends or fragments back into original alignment. The use of local or general anesthesia usually accompanies a fracture reduction. If performed by outside manipulation only, the reduction is described as closed; if surgery is necessary, it is described as open. Also describes a chemical reaction in which one or more electrons are added to an atom or molecule.

Rhinitis—Inflammation and swelling of the mucous membranes that line the nasal passages.

Rhinoplasty—Plastic surgery of the nose to repair it or change its shape.

Septum—A wall or partition. Often refers to the muscular wall dividing the left and right heart chambers or the partition in the nose that separates the two nostrils. Also refers to an abnormal fold of tissue down that center of the uterus that can cause infertility.

- Make sure that the child understands basic safety precautions and traffic laws before allowing him or her to ride a bicycle in the street.

• Check the home for safety hazards that might lead to falls (for example, loose carpeting, poorly lit stairwells, and toys allowed to lie on the floor after play).

• Teach the child to deal with quarrels with other children without physical fighting and set the child a good example in relationships with others.

For older children and adolescents, parents should take the following steps:

• Set a good example of safe driving and make sure that teenagers have a mature attitude toward driving before they acquire a driver's license.

• Inform themselves about such problems as drug abuse, bullying, or violence in dating relationships, and learn to identify the signs of these problems in their children.

• Make sure that their child's sports teams use the appropriate safety equipment, that the equipment is in good condition, and that the teams have appropriate adult supervision.

• Discourage the child from nose piercing and similar fads or at least make certain that he or she has the procedure done at a reputable business that follows Food and Drug Administration (FDA) guidelines for cleanliness and sterilization of equipment.

• Teach safe and responsible use of BB guns and air guns.

Parental concerns

Parental concerns regarding nasal trauma depend on the cause and severity of the injury. Minor nosebleeds and uncomplicated fractures of the nose caused by accidents generally heal without problems and are quickly absorbed into the family's routine. Complex fractures or other injuries requiring a second operation may require explanation or discussion with the child. Nasal injuries related to the neighborhood environment (street crime, chemical pollution), lifestyle choices (body piercing, smoking in the home), or family dysfunction (substance abuse, domestic violence), however, suggest the need for professional counseling and changes in the family's structure, geographical location, or increased level of functioning.

Resources

BOOKS

"Fractures of the Nose." Section 7, Chapter 86 in *The Merck Manual of Diagnosis and Therapy*, edited by Mark H. Beers and Robert Berkow. Whitehouse Station, NJ: Merck Research Laboratories, 2002.

PERIODICALS

Alvi, A., T. Doherty, and G. Lewen. "Facial Fractures and Concomitant Injuries in Trauma Patients." *Laryngoscope* 113 (January 2003): 102–6.

Anderson, Carrie E., and Glenn A. Loomis. "Recognition and Prevention of Inhalant Abuse." *American Family Physician* 68 (September 1, 2003): 869–76.

Brinson, G. M., B. A. Senior, and W. G. Yarbrough. "Endoscopic Management of Retained Airgun Projectiles in the Paranasal Sinuses." *Otolaryngology and Head and Neck Surgery* 130 (January 2004): 25–30.

Chhetri, Dinesh K., and N. L. Shapiro. "A Case of a BB-Gun Pellet Injury to the Ethmoid Sinus in a Child." *Ear, Nose, and Throat Journal* 83 (March 2004): 176–80.

Higo, R., et al. "Foreign Bodies in the Aerodigestive Tract in Pediatric Patients." *Auris, Nasus, Larynx* 30 (December 2003): 397–401.

Karkos, P. D., et al. "Magnetic Nasal Foreign Bodies: A Result of Fashion Mania." *International Journal of Pediatric Otorhinolaryngology* 67 (December 2003): 1343–45.

Mahajan, M., and N. Shah. "Accidental Lodgment of an Air Gun Pellet in the Maxillary Sinus of a 6-Year-Old Girl: A Case Report." *Dental Traumatology* 20 (June 2004): 178–80.

Mayers, L. B., et al. "Prevalence of Body Art (Body Piercing and Tattooing) in University Undergraduates and Incidence of Medical Complications." *Mayo Clinic Proceedings* 77 (January 2002): 29–34.

McCormick, S., et al. "Children and Mini-Magnets: An Almost Fatal Attraction." *Emergency Medical Journal* 19 (January 2002): 71–3.

Tu, A. H., et al. "Facial Fractures from Dog Bite Injuries." *Plastic and Reconstructive Surgery* 109 (April 1, 2002): 1259–65.

ORGANIZATIONS

American Academy of Family Physicians (AAFP). 11400 Tomahawk Creek Parkway, Leawood, KS 66211–2672. Web site: <www.aafp.org>.

American Academy of Otolaryngology—Head and Neck Surgery. One Prince Street, Alexandria, VA 22314–3357. Web site: <www.entnet.org>.

American College of Sports Medicine (ACSM). 401 West Michigan Street, Indianapolis, IN 46202–3233. Web site: <www.acsm.org>.

WEB SITES

Gluckman, William, Robert Baricella, and Huma Quraishi. "Epistaxis." *eMedicine*, January 23, 2004. Available online at <www.emedicine.com/ped/topic1618.htm> (accessed November 12, 2004).

Mayo Clinic Staff. "Tattoos and Piercings: What to Know before You Go under the Needle." *MayoClinic.com*, June 3, 2004. Available online at <www.mayoclinic.com/invoke.cfm?objectid=3DC17F76-13E3-499B-AE9111954BDFFCA5> (accessed November 12, 2004).

Ross, Adam T., and Daniel G. Becker. "Fractures, Nasal and Septal." *eMedicine*, July 13, 2004. Available online at <www.emedicine.com/ent/topic159.htm> (accessed November 12, 2004).

Rupp, Timothy J., Marian Bednar, and Stephen Karageanes. "Facial Fractures." *eMedicine*, August 29, 2004. Available online at <www.emedicine.com/sports/topic33.htm> (accessed November 12, 2004).

Rebecca Frey, PhD

Nausea and vomiting

Definition

Nausea is the sensation of being about to vomit. Vomiting, or emesis, is the expelling from the stomach of undigested food through the mouth.

Description

Nausea is a reaction to a number of causes that include overeating, infection, or irritation of the throat or stomach lining. Persistent or recurrent nausea and vomiting should be checked by a doctor.

A doctor should be called if nausea and vomiting occur in the following instances:

- after eating rich or spoiled food or taking a new medication
- repeatedly or for 48 hours or longer
- following intense dizziness

It is important to see a doctor if nausea and vomiting are accompanied by the following:

- yellowing of the skin and whites of the eyes
- **pain** in the chest or lower abdomen
- trouble with swallowing or urination
- **dehydration** or extreme thirst
- drowsiness or confusion
- constant, severe abdominal pain
- a fruity breath odor

Demographics

Nausea and vomiting are commonly experienced. There are no distinctive patterns of age, gender, or race.

Causes and symptoms

Persistent, unexplained, or recurring nausea and vomiting can be symptoms of a variety of serious illnesses. They can be caused by overeating or drinking too much alcohol. These symptoms can be due to stress, certain medications, or illness. For example, people who are given morphine or other opioid medications for pain relief after surgery sometimes feel nauseated by the drug. Such poisonous substances as arsenic and other heavy metals cause nausea and vomiting. Morning sickness is a consequence of pregnancy-related hormone changes. **Motion sickness** can be induced by traveling in a vehicle, plane, or on a boat. Many people experience nausea after eating spoiled food or foods to which they are allergic. Individuals who suffer migraine **headache** often experience nausea. **Cancer** patients receiving **chemotherapy** are often nauseated. Gallstones, **gastroenteritis**, and stomach ulcer may cause nausea and vomiting. These symptoms should be evaluated by a physician.

Nausea and vomiting may also be psychological in origin. Some people vomit under such conditions of emotional stress as **family** arguments, academic tests, airplane travel, losing a job, and similar high-stress situations. In addition, some eating disorders are characterized by self-induced vomiting.

When to call the doctor

A doctor should be notified if vomiting is heavy and/or bloody, if the vomitus looks like feces, or if the affected person has been unable to keep food down for 24 hours. Most vomiting episodes should stop in eight to 12 hours of onset. The pediatrician should be consulted if vomiting continues beyond that time, if the child shows signs of dehydration, seems extremely lethargic, or if the child is a very young infant.

An ambulance or emergency response number should be called immediately if the following occurs:

- The child's mouth and tongue are very dry.
- The child has very rapid heartbeat and breathing.
- The child cries but has no tears.
- The child has sunken eyes.
- Diabetic shock is suspected.
- Nausea and vomiting continue after other symptoms of viral infection have subsided.

- The person has a severe headache.
- The person is sweating and having chest pain and trouble breathing.
- The person is known or suspected to have swallowed a drug overdose or poisonous substance.
- The person has a high body temperature, **muscle cramps**, and other signs of heat exhaustion or heat stroke.
- Nausea, vomiting, and breathing problems occur after exposure to a known allergen.

Diagnosis

Diagnosis is based on the severity, frequency, and duration of symptoms, and other factors that could indicate the presence of a serious illness.

Diagnosis is based on a careful medical history that includes foods recently eaten, travel, and occupation. In some cases, the doctor may order laboratory tests or imaging studies to determine the presence of drugs or poisonous substances in the person's blood or urine, or evidence of head injuries or abnormalities in the digestive tract. If the nausea and vomiting appear to be related to **anxiety**, stress, or an eating disorder, the doctor may refer the person to a psychiatrist for further evaluation.

Treatment

Getting a breath of fresh air or getting away from whatever is causing the nausea can solve the problem. Eating olives or crackers or sucking on a lemon can calm the stomach by absorbing acid and excess fluid. Cola syrup is another proven remedy.

Vomiting relieves nausea quickly but can cause dehydration. Sipping clear juices, weak tea, and some sports drinks helps replace lost fluid and **minerals** without irritating the stomach. Infants and small children under age two do best with an oral rehydration solution like Pedialyte. The solution should be given a teaspoon at a time, at frequent intervals, starting 30–60 minutes after vomiting has ceased. Food should be reintroduced gradually, several hours after vomiting stops, beginning with small amounts of dry, bland food like crackers and toast.

Medications that are given to relieve nausea and vomiting are called antiemetics. Meclizine (Bonine), a medication for motion sickness, also diminishes the feeling of queasiness in the stomach. Dimenhydrinate (Dramamine), another motion-sickness drug, is not effective on other types of nausea and may cause drowsiness.

Other drugs that have been developed to treat postoperative or post-chemotherapy nausea and vomiting include ondansetron (Zofran) and granisetron (Kytril). Intravenous administration of supplemental fluid before the operation can lower the risk of nausea after surgery.

Alternative treatment

Advocates of alternative treatments suggest biofeedback, acupressure and the use of herbs to calm the stomach. Biofeedback uses **exercise** and deep relaxation to control nausea. Acupressure (applying pressure to specific areas of the body) can be applied by wearing a special wristband or by applying firm pressure to the following:

- the back of the jawbone
- the webbing between the thumb and index finger
- the top of the foot
- the inside of the wrist
- the base of the rib cage

Acupuncture is an alternative treatment found to be effective in relieving nausea. A few people, however, experience nausea as a side effect of acupuncture.

Chamomile (*Matricaria recutita*) or lemon balm (*Melissa officinalis*) tea may relieve symptoms. Ginger (*Zingiber officinale*), another natural remedy, can be ingested as tea or taken as candy, cookies, or powdered capsules.

Prognosis

Most instances of nausea and vomiting respond well to appropriate treatment, including removing any substance or condition that precipitates the nausea.

Prevention

Massage, meditation, **yoga**, and other relaxation techniques can help prevent stress-induced nausea. Antinausea medication taken before traveling can prevent motion sickness. Sitting in the front seat, focusing on the horizon, and traveling after dark can also minimize symptoms.

Food should be fresh, properly prepared, and eaten slowly. Overeating, tight-fitting clothes, and strenuous activity immediately after a meal should be avoided.

Vomiting related to emotional upsets may be avoided by forms of psychotherapy that teach people to manage stress in healthier ways.

KEY TERMS

Antiemetic drug—A medication that helps control nausea; also called an antinausea drug.

Dehydration—An excessive loss of water from the body. It may follow vomiting, prolonged diarrhea, or excessive sweating.

Diabetic coma—A life-threatening, reduced level of consciousness that occurs in persons with uncontrolled diabetes mellitus.

Emesis—An act or episode of vomiting.

Nutritional concerns

Prolonged vomiting can lead to fluid and electrolyte depletion. Nausea can curtail appetite. Over time, this can lead to nutritional problems.

Parental concerns

Parents should be especially concerned about prolonged vomiting in children younger than two years of age. This concern intensifies if the vomiting is accompanied by **diarrhea** that accelerates fluid and electrolyte depletion. Parents should consult a pediatrician for treatment options if an infant younger than six months of age vomits multiple times within several hours.

Resources

BOOKS

Diagnostic and Statistical Manual of Mental Disorders, 4th ed., text revision. Washington, DC: American Psychiatric Association, 2000.

"Functional Vomiting." Section 3, Chapter 21 in *The Merck Manual of Diagnosis and Therapy*. Edited by Mark H. Beers and Robert Berkow. Whitehouse Station, NJ: Merck Research Laboratories, 2002.

Hasler, Willliam L. "Nausea, Vomiting, and Indigestion." In *Harrison's Principles of Internal Medicine*, 15th ed. Edited by Eugene Braunwald, et al. New York: McGraw-Hill, 2001, pp. 236–40.

Pelletier, Kenneth R. *The Best Alternative Medicine, Part I: Western Herbal Medicine*. New York: Simon and Schuster, 2002.

PERIODICALS

Antonarakis, E. S., and R. D. Hain. "Nausea and vomiting associated with cancer chemotherapy: drug management in theory and in practice." *Archives of Disease in Childhood* 89, no. 9 (2004): 220–3.

Baggley A., et al. "Determinants of women's decision making on whether to treat nausea and vomiting of pregnancy pharmacologically." *Journal of Midwifery and Women's Health* 49, no. 4 (2004): 350–4.

Czeizel, A. E., et al. "Association between severe nausea and vomiting in pregnancy and lower rate of preterm births." *Pediatric and Perinatal Epidemiology* 18, no. 4 (2004): 253–9.

Donohew, B. E., and M. J. Griffin. "Motion sickness: effect of the frequency of lateral oscillation." *Aviation, Space, and Environmental Medicine* 75, no. 8 (2004): 649–56.

Einarson, A., et al. "The safety of ondansetron for nausea and vomiting of pregnancy: a prospective comparative study." *British Journal of Obstetrics and Gynecology* 111, no. 9 (2004): 940–3.

Hockenberry, M. "Symptom management research in children with cancer." *Journal of Pediatric Oncology Nursing* 21, no. 3 (2004): 132–6.

Shin, Y. H., et al. "Effect of acupressure on nausea and vomiting during chemotherapy cycle for Korean postoperative stomach cancer patients." *Cancer Nursing* 27, no. 4 (2004): 267–74.

ORGANIZATIONS

American Academy of Emergency Medicine. 611 East Wells Street, Milwaukee, WI 53202. Web site: <www.aaem.org/>.

American Academy of Family Physicians. 11400 Tomahawk Creek Parkway, Leawood, KS 66211–2672. Web site: <www.aafp.org/>.

American Academy of Pediatrics. 141 Northwest Point Boulevard, Elk Grove Village, IL 60007–1098. Web site: <www.aap.org/default.htm>.

American Academy of Physical Medicine and Rehabilitation. One IBM Plaza, Suite 2500, Chicago, IL 60611–3604. Web site: <www.aapmr.org/>.

American Association of Poison Control Centers. 3201 New Mexico Avenue NW, Washington, DC 20016. Web site: <www.aapcc.org/>.

American Board of Obstetrics and Gynecology. 2915 Vine Street Suite 300, Dallas TX. 75204. Web site: <www.abog.org/>.

American College of Gastroenterology. 4900 B South 31st Street, Arlington VA 22206. Web site: <www.acg.gi.org/>.

WEB SITES

"About Nausea and Vomiting." *Cleveland Clinic.* Available online at <www.clevelandclinic.org/health/health-info/docs/1800/1810.asp?index=8106> (accessed November 30, 2004).

"Nausea and Vomiting." *National Cancer Institute.* Available online at <http://cancer.gov/cancerinfo/pdq/supportivecare/nausea/patient/> (accessed November 30, 2004).

"Nausea and Vomiting." *National Library of Medicine.* Available online at <www.nlm.nih.gov/medlineplus/nauseaandvomiting.html> (accessed November 30, 2004).

"Nausea and Vomiting, Age 4 and Older." *Web MD.* Available online at <http://my.webmd.com/hw/parenting_and_pregnancy/hw96999.asp> (accessed November 30, 2004).

L. Fleming Fallon, Jr., MD, DrPH

Near-drowning

Definition

Near-drowning is the term for survival after suffocation caused by submersion in water or other fluid. Some experts exclude from this definition cases of temporary survival that end in death within 24 hours, which they prefer to classify as drownings.

Description

Drowning is always fatal, but near-drowning may result in survival with no long-lasting effects; survival with permanent damage, usually to the brain; or death after a 24-hour survival period. Near drowning sets into motion a collection of reactions in the body that ultimately can damage the lungs and lead to an absence of oxygen in tissues, even when individuals have been removed from the water and begun breathing either on their own or with mechanical help.

Near-drowning happens very quickly. Within three minutes of submersion, most people are unconscious, and within five minutes the brain begins to suffer from lack of oxygen. Abnormal heart rhythms (cardiac dysrhythmias) often occur in near-drowning cases, and the heart may stop pumping (cardiac arrest). The blood may increase in acidity (acidosis) and, under some circumstances, near drowning can cause a substantial increase or decrease in the volume of circulating blood. If not rapidly reversed, these events cause permanent damage to the brain.

Demographics

About 1,500 children drown every year in the United States. Drowning is the second leading cause of injury-related deaths in children ages one month to 14 years of age in the United States as a whole, and the first leading cause of injury-related deaths in California, Arizona, and Florida. The rate of near drowning is much higher, as not all near drownings are reported. It is estimated that for every drowning, there are four additional hospitalizations and 14 additional emergency room visits due to near drowning.

Children under age four and between 15 and 19 years of age are at highest risk of drowning or near drowning. Most young children drown in swimming pools and bathtubs, while teens drown in natural bodies of water. Teen drownings are often associated with boating accidents, alcohol consumption, and illicit drug use. Boys are 12 times more likely to drown than girls, especially during **adolescence**, when risk-taking behavior is more pronounced in males. However, even in younger age groups, except in bathtub drownings, substantially more boys drown than girls.

Causes and symptoms

The circumstances leading to near-drownings and drownings are varied. Rarely do they involve nonswimmers accidentally entering deep water. In older children and adults, near-drownings are often secondary to an event such as or a head or spinal injury or (in adults) a heart attack that causes unconsciousness and prevents a diver from resurfacing.

Near-drownings can occur in shallow as well as deep water. Small children have drowned or almost drowned in bathtubs, toilets, industrial-size cleaning buckets, and washing machines. Bathtubs are especially dangerous for infants six months to one year of age, who can sit up straight in a bathtub but may lack the ability to pull themselves out of the water if they slip under the surface. One 2004 study found that 88 percent of children who drowned were under the supervision of another person, usually a **family** member. Seventy-seven percent of these children were under age ten. The most common occurrence was that the supervising adult knew the child was in or near the water but was distracted long enough for the child to drown.

A reduced concentration of oxygen in the blood (hypoxemia) is common to all near-drownings. When drowning begins, the larynx (a part of the air passage) closes involuntarily, preventing both air and water from entering the lungs. In 10 to 20 percent of cases, hypoxemia results because the larynx spasms and stays closed.

This is called "dry drowning," and no water is breathed into the lungs. Hypoxemia also occurs in "wet drowning," when the larynx relaxes and water enters the lungs. Individuals who are close to drowning can also regurgitate their stomach contents and breathe these into the lungs.

The physiological mechanisms that produce hypoxemia in wet drowning are different for freshwater and saltwater, but only a small amount of either kind of water is needed to damage the lungs and interfere with lung's ability to remove oxygen from the air.

The signs and symptoms of near-drowning can differ from person to person depending in part on how long the individual has been submerged, the person's age, and the temperature of the water. Upon rescue, some victims are alert but agitated or disoriented, while others are comatose. Breathing and heartbeat may have stopped, or the victim may be gasping for breath. Bluish skin (cyanosis), coughing, **vomiting**, and frothy pink sputum (material expelled from the respiratory tract by coughing) are often observed. Rapid breathing (tachypnea) and a rapid heart rate (tachycardia) are common during the first few hours after rescue. The victim may experience hypothermia (drop in core body temperature).

When to call the doctor

Emergency medical aid should be sought with any near drowning incident. Even a child who appears to have recovered should be checked by a physician, since some internal reactions to near drowning can be delayed.

Diagnosis

Diagnosis relies on a physical examination of the victim, reports of observers, and a wide range of tests and other procedures. Blood is taken to measure oxygen levels and to determine electrolyte balances. Pulse oximetry, another way of assessing oxygen levels, involves attaching a device called a pulse oximeter to the patient's finger. An electrocardiograph is used to monitor heart activity. X rays can detect head and neck injuries and fluid in the lungs.

Treatment

Treatment begins with removing the victim from the water and performing **cardiopulmonary resuscitation** (CPR) as needed to restore heartbeat and provide oxygen until the individual is able to breath without assistance. When emergency medical help arrives, 100 percent oxygen is administered to the victim. If the victim's breathing has stopped or is otherwise impaired, a tube is inserted into the windpipe (trachea) to maintain the airway (endotracheal intubation). The victim is also checked for head, neck, and other injuries, and intravenously fluids may be started. Hypothermia from submersion in very cold water requires special handling to protect the heart.

On arriving at the emergency room, the individual continues receiving oxygen until blood tests show a return to normal. About one-third of near-drowning victims are intubated and initially need mechanical support to breathe. Treatment is administered as needed for cardiac arrest or cardiac dysrhythmias. Slow rewarming is undertaken when hypothermia is present. Individuals are observed for the development of acute **respiratory distress syndrome** (ARDS) or multi-organ failure, both of which can develop after near drowning. Lung problems can develop 12 or more hours after submersion.

Based on symptoms, individuals may be admitted to the hospital or discharged from the emergency department after four to six hours, if their blood oxygen level is normal and no signs or symptoms of near-drowning are present. Discharged individuals must understand that should complications arise, they must immediately seek additional medical care. Admission to a hospital for at least 24 hours for further observation and treatment is necessary for patients who do not appear to fully recover in the emergency department.

Prognosis

Recovery is directly related to the amount of time the body was without adequate oxygen (hypoxia). Brain damage is the major long-term concern in the treatment of near-drowning victims. Patients who arrive at an emergency department awake and alert usually survive with brain function intact, although they may initially have respiratory complications. **Pneumonia** is common following near drowning and often develops within the first 24 hours.

Death or permanent neurological damage is very likely when patients arrive at the emergency room comatose or without a heartbeat. Of these patients, 35 to 60 percent die in the emergency department, while almost all of those who survive have permanent disabilities. Early rescue of near-drowning victims (within five minutes of submersion) and prompt CPR (within less than ten minutes of submersion) seem to be the best guarantees of a complete recovery. However, in a phenomenon that is not well understood, extremely cold water (less than 41°F or 5°C) seems to protect individuals from some of the neurological damage that occurs with near drowning. Some hypothermic near-drowning victims

KEY TERMS

Cyanosis—A bluish tinge to the skin that can occur when the blood oxygen level drops too low.

Electrolytes—Salts and minerals that produce electrically charged particles (ions) in body fluids. Common human electrolytes are sodium chloride, potassium, calcium, and sodium bicarbonate. Electrolytes control the fluid balance of the body and are important in muscle contraction, energy generation, and almost all major biochemical reactions in the body.

Hypothermia—A serious condition in which body temperature falls below 95°F (35 °C). It is usually caused by prolonged exposure to the cold.

Hypoxemia—A condition characterized by an abnormally low amount of oxygen in the arterial blood. It is the major consequence of respiratory failure, when the lungs no longer are able to perform their chief function of gas exchange.

Hypoxia—A condition characterized by insufficient oxygen in the cells of the body

have been revived after they appeared dead and have experienced few permanent disabilities.

Prevention

Drowning and near drowning are almost always preventable. Prevention depends on educating adults and children about water **safety**. Children cannot be left in or near water without adult supervision even for a short time. Unsupervised young children are at risk around swimming pools, bathtubs, toilets, buckets, and natural bodies of water. Pools and spas need to be enclosed with a fence at least 5 ft (1.5 m) high and have a self-closing and self-locking gate. Adults and teens should consider learning CPR. No one should swim alone or **play** along flooded streams or streets. Teens and adults should be educated to understand that alcohol and illicit drug use substantially increase the chances of a drowning accident. Boat owners need to participate in boat safety classes, and children should wear approved life preservers when boating, water skiing, or riding on a jet ski.

Parental concerns

Parents should be aware that physicians are required to consider the possibility of **child abuse** in every

drowning or near drowning involving a child under the age of one year.

Resources

BOOKS

Kallas, Harry J. "Drowning and Near Drowning." In *Nelson Textbook of Pediatrics*,, 17th ed. Edited by Richard E. Behrman et al. Philadelphia: Saunders, 2004, pp 425–30.

Piantadosi, Claude A. "Physical, Chemical, and Aspiration Injuries of the Lung." In *Cecil Textbook of Medicine*, 21st ed. Edited by J. Claude Bennett and Fred Plum. Philadelphia: Saunders, 2000.

WEB SITES

Fiore, Michael, and Sabrina Heidemann. "Near Drowning." September 20, 2004. Available online at <www.emedicine.com/ped/topic2570.htm> (accessed January 14, 2005).

Plantz, Scott H., and Michael E. Zevitz. "Wilderness Near Drowning." December 14, 2004. Available online at <www.emedicine.com/wild/topic34.htm> (accessed January 14, 2005).

Shepherd, Suzanne, and James Martin. "Submersion Injury, Near Drowning." January 12, 2005. Available online at <www.emedicine.com/emerg/topic744.htm> (accessed January 14, 2005).

Tish Davidson, A.M.
Howard Baker

Nearsightedness *see* **Myopia**

Necrotizing enterocolitis

Definition

Necrotizing enterocolitis (NEC) is a serious bacterial infection in the intestine, primarily affecting sick or premature newborn infants. It can cause the death (necrosis) of intestinal tissue and progress to blood poisoning (septicemia).

Description

Necrotizing enterocolitis is a serious infection that can produce complications in the intestine itself such as ulcers, perforations or holes in the intestinal wall, and tissue necrosis. It can also progress to life-threatening septicemia. Necrotizing enterocolitis most commonly affects the ileum, the lower portion of the small intestine. It is less common in the colon and upper small bowel.

Demographics

It is estimated that narcotizing enterocolitis affects 2 percent of all newborns, but it is more frequently seen in very low birth weight infants, affecting as many as 13.3 percent of these babies. It has a high mortality rate, especially among very low birth weight babies. Some 20 to 40 percent of these infants die. It does not appear that male or females are more susceptible to this condition, and no one race or nationality has a higher incidence.

Causes and symptoms

The cause of necrotizing enterocolitis is not clear. It is believed that the infection usually develops after the bowel wall has already been weakened or damaged by a lack of oxygen, predisposing it to bacterial invasion. Bacteria grow rapidly in the bowel, causing a deep infection that can kill bowel tissue and spread to the bloodstream.

Necrotizing enterocolitis almost always occurs in the first month of life. Infants who require tube feedings may have an increased risk for the disorder. A number of other conditions also make newborns susceptible, including **respiratory distress syndrome**, congenital heart problems, and episodes of apnea (cessation of breathing). The primary risk factor, however, is **prematurity**. Not only is the immature digestive tract less able to protect itself, but premature infants are subjected to many stresses on the body in their attempt to survive.

Early symptoms of necrotizing enterocolitis include an intolerance to formula, distended and tender abdomen, **vomiting**, and blood (visible or not) in the stool. One of the earliest signs may also be the need for mechanical support of the infant's breathing. If the infection spreads to the bloodstream, infants may develop lethargy, fluctuations in body temperature, and may periodically stop breathing.

Diagnosis

The key to reducing the complications of this disease is early detection by the physician. A series of x rays of the bowel often reveals the progressive condition, and blood tests confirm infection.

Treatment

Over two-thirds of infants can be treated without surgery. Aggressive medical therapy with **antibiotics** is begun as soon as the condition is diagnosed or even suspected. Tube feedings into the gastrointestinal tract (enteral **nutrition**) are discontinued, and tube feedings into the veins (parenteral nutrition) are used instead until the condition has resolved. Intravenous fluids are given for several weeks while the bowel heals.

Some infants are placed on a ventilator to help them breathe, and some receive transfusions of platelets, which help the blood clot when there is internal bleeding. Antibiotics are usually given intravenously for at least 10 days. These infants require frequent evaluations by the physician, who may order multiple abdominal x rays and blood tests in order to monitor their condition during the illness.

Sometimes, necrotizing enterocolitis must be treated with surgery. This is often the case when an infant's condition does not improve with medical therapy or there are signs of worsening infection.

The surgical treatment depends on the individual patient's condition. Patients with infection that has caused serious damage to the bowel may have portions of the bowel removed. It is sometimes necessary to create a substitute bowel by making an opening (ostomy) into the abdomen through the skin, from which waste products are discharged temporarily. But many physicians avoid this and operate to remove diseased bowel and repair the defect at the same time.

Postoperative complications are common, including wound infections and lack of healing, persistent sepsis and bowel necrosis, and a serious internal bleeding disorder known as disseminated intravascular coagulation.

Prognosis

Necrotizing enterocolitis is the most common cause of death in newborns undergoing surgery. The average mortality is 30 to 40 percent, even higher in severe cases.

Early identification and treatment are critical to improving the outcome for these infants. Aggressive nonsurgical support and careful timing of surgical intervention have improved overall survival; however, this condition can be fatal in about one third of cases. With the resolution of the infection, the bowel may begin functioning within weeks or months. But infants need to be carefully monitored by a physician for years because of possible future complications.

About 10 to 35 percent of all survivors eventually develop a stricture, or narrowing, of the intestine that occurs with healing. This can create an intestinal obstruction that requires surgery. Infants may also be more susceptible to future bacterial infections in the gastrointestinal tract and to a delay in growth. Infants with severe cases may also suffer neurological impairment.

The most serious long-term gastrointestinal complication associated with necrotizing enterocolitis is short-bowel, or short-gut, syndrome. This refers to a condition that can develop when a large amount of bowel must be removed, making the intestines less able to absorb certain nutrients and enzymes. These infants gradually evolve from tube feedings to oral feedings, and medications are used to control the malabsorption, **diarrhea**, and other consequences of this condition.

Prevention

In very small or sick premature infants, the risk for necrotizing enterocolitis may be diminished by beginning parenteral nutrition and delaying enteral feedings for several days to weeks.

Breast-fed infants have a lower incidence of necrotizing enterocolitis than formula-fed infants; however, conclusive data showing that breast milk may be protective was as of 2004 not available. A large multicenter trial showed that steroid drugs given to women in preterm labor may protect their offspring from necrotizing enterocolitis.

Sometimes necrotizing enterocolitis occurs in clusters, or outbreaks, in hospital newborn (neonatal) units. Because there is an infectious element to the disorder, infants with necrotizing enterocolitis may be isolated to avoid infecting other infants. Persons caring for these infants must also employ strict measures to prevent spreading the infection.

Parental concerns

Approximately 75 percent of all babies with necrotizing enterocolitis survive. After discharge from the hospital, these infants return home still requiring special care. Many have an ostomy. This is an external opening for the intestinal contents to exit the body while the affected part of the intestine heals. Parents and caregivers need instruction on how to care for the ostomy. Many sources advise parents to room in with the baby prior to discharge from the hospital so that they can learn how to care for the special health needs of infants recovering from necrotizing enterocolitis. Additionally, many of these infants have a condition called short-gut syndrome, which results from the removal of a large part of the small intestine. The small bowel will grow in time, but for as long as two years in some cases, the child will require careful monitoring of his or her nutritional intake to insure that he is receiving adequate levels of **vitamins**, **minerals**, and calories. These children will require tube feedings, and parents will need proper instruction in this type of feeding.

Resources

BOOKS

Beers Mark H., and Robert Berkow, eds. *The Merck Manual*, 2nd home ed. West Point, PA: Merck & Co., 2004.

Moore, Keith L., et al. *Before We Are Born: Essentials of Embryology and Birth Defects*. Kent, UK: Elsevier—Health Sciences Division, 2002.

WEB SITES

Springer, Shelley C., and Annibale, David J. "Necrotizing Enterocolitis." *eMedicine*, November 25, 2002. Available online at <www.emedicine.com/ped/topic2601.htm> (accessed November 30, 2004).

Caroline A. Helwick
Deborah L. Nurmi, MS

Neisseria meningitidis disease *see* **Meningococcemia**

Neisseria meningitidis vaccine *see* **Meningococcal meningitis vaccine**

Neonatal jaundice

Definition

Neonatal **jaundice** is the term used when a newborn has an excessive amount of bilirubin in the blood. Bilirubin is a yellowish-red pigment that is formed and released into the bloodstream when red blood cells are broken down. Jaundice comes from the French word jaune, which means yellow; thus a jaundiced baby is one whose skin color appears yellow due to bilirubin.

Description

Normally, small amounts of bilirubin are found in everyone's blood. It is formed and released into the bloodstream when red blood cells are broken down. It is then carried to the liver where it is processed and eventually excreted from the body. When too much bilirubin is made, the excess is discarded into the bloodstream and deposited in tissues for temporary storage. In the neonate, however, there is more bilirubin than can be handled due to immature liver functioning and extra red blood cells that break down. Thus, the extra bilirubin remains in the tissues. Neonatal jaundice affects 60 percent of full-term infants and 80 percent of preterm infants in the first three days after birth.

Demographics

Infants of East Asian and Native American descent have higher levels of bilirubin than white infants, who in turn have higher bilirubin levels than infants of African descent. There is an enzyme, glucose-6-phosphate dehydrogenase (G6PD), deficiency that is more prevalent in infants of East Asian, Greek, and African descent which causes neonatal jaundice to appear at approximately the same time as physiological jaundice. **Sickle cell anemia** does not predispose newborn infants to jaundice.

Causes and symptoms

Typically, neonatal jaundice occurs in otherwise healthy infants for two reasons. First, infants have too many red blood cells and it is a natural process for the body to break down these excess red blood cells to form a large amount of bilirubin. It is this bilirubin that causes the skin to take on a yellowish color. Second, the newborn's liver is immature and cannot process bilirubin as quickly as the infant will be able to when older. This slow processing of bilirubin has nothing to do with liver disease. It merely means that the baby's liver is not as fully developed as it will be; thus, there is some delay in eliminating the bilirubin.

Breastfeeding is an important risk factor for hyperbilirubinemia in healthy infants and is related to inadequate maternal milk supply in the first few days, decreased caloric intake and delayed passage of meconium. Nonetheless, this is not a reason to give formula or stop breastfeeding. The breastfeeding mother just needs to nurse the baby more frequently and for longer periods of time to enhance the production of breastmilk. Other factors that cause neonatal jaundice are ABO incompatibility and Rh incompatibility. Both of these conditions result in a very fast breakdown of red blood cells. It is also possible for jaundice to appear in infants with physical defects in the organs that work to eliminate bilirubin from the body. An abnormal increase in red blood cells is frequently seen in infants who are large or small for their gestational age, as well as in trisomy syndromes, twin-to-twin transfusion syndrome, maternal-fetal transfusion, use of oxytocin in labor, Asian male babies, presence of bruising and cephalohematoma, and a **family** history of neonatal jaundice.

As the excess bilirubin builds up in the newborn, jaundice appears first in the face and upper body and progresses downward toward the toes. Most babies with jaundice have physiologic jaundice, which is the type caused by the natural process of breaking down red blood cells. If the baby's jaundice is caused by any other conditions, however, the healthcare giver will provide the parents with additional information for caring for the baby.

When to call the doctor

With short neonatal hospital stays, jaundice will not have peaked or become apparent at the time of hospital discharge. Therefore, infants at risk for severe hyperbilirubinemia should be identified so they can be observed closely both while in the hospital and after discharge. The parents need to be instructed on how to evaluate the infant for jaundice. They should look for it first in the face and upper body and if it progresses downward this means the concentration is getting too high and it is time to call the pediatrician. If there is an area of their living quarters that gets sunlight, it helps to let the baby lie there in only a diaper for a short period of time each day.

Diagnosis

Jaundice can be observed with the naked eye, but it is too difficult to estimate the variation in levels of bilirubin in that manner. Thus, if an infant begins to appear jaundiced, bilirubin levels will be ordered to determine the severity. Jaundice usually becomes apparent when total bilirubin levels exceed 5 mg/dL; however, the clinical significance of bilirubin levels depends on postnatal age in hours. A bilirubin level of 12 mg/dL may be pathologic in an infant younger than 48 hours but is benign in an infant older than 72 hours. In the determination of cause, it is suggested that laboratory testing be reserved for infants with nonphysiologic jaundice. In up to 50 percent of infants with severe jaundice, breastfeeding and lower gestational age were the only causes identified despite extensive workups.

Treatment

The mainstay in treatment of hyperbilirubinemia is phototherapy, which is safe and widely available. Its effectiveness was demonstrated in a study by the National Institute of Child Health and Human Development. Multiple factors can influence the effectiveness of phototherapy, including the type and intensity of the light and the extent of skin surface exposure. Special blue fluorescent light has been shown to be most effective, although many nurseries use a combination of daylight, white, and blue lamps. In the early 2000s, fiberoptic blankets have been developed that emit light in the blue-green spectrum, which is light at a wavelength of 425–475 nm. Light at this wavelength converts bilirubin to a water-soluble form that can be excreted in the bile or urine. The intensity of light delivered is inversely related to the distance between the light source and the skin surface. Since phototherapy acts by altering the bilirubin that is deposited in the tissue, the area of the skin exposed to phototherapy should be maximized. This has been made more practical with the development of fiberoptic phototherapy blankets that can be wrapped around an infant.

Home-based care for neonatal jaundice has become more prevalent than hospital care, and the availability of fiberoptic blankets has made it possible. Infants receiving home phototherapy need daily visits by a nurse, who performs a physical examination and measures the total serum bilirubin level. If bilirubin levels continue to rise, hospital readmission should be considered. Discontinuation of home phototherapy is safe once the total serum bilirubin level has decreased to less than 15 mg/dL in healthy full-term infants older than four days. Office evaluation within two to three days of discontinuing home phototherapy is recommended.

Potential side effects of phototherapy used for elevated bilirubin levels, include watery **diarrhea**, increased water loss, skin rash, and transient bronzing of the skin. Many infants who are readmitted to the hospital because of hyperbilirubinemia are mildly to moderately dehydrated. Breastfeeding should be increased to every two to two and a half hours. Increased feedings can increase peristalsis and meconium passage, decreasing bilirubin resorption into circulation.

Full-term infants rarely require an exchange transfusion if intense phototherapy is initiated in a timely manner. It should be considered if the total serum bilirubin level is approaching 20 mg/dL and continues to rise despite intense in-hospital phototherapy. Exchange transfusion corrects anemia associated with the destruc-

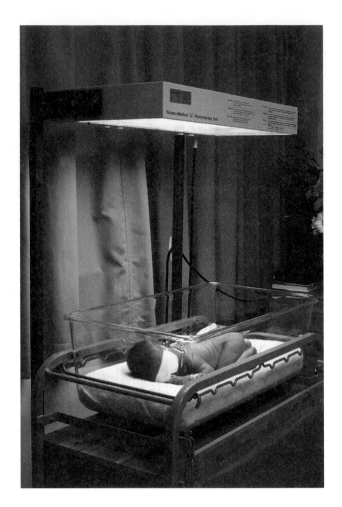

A **newborn baby undergoes phototherapy with visible blue light to treat his jaundice.** (Photograph by Ron Sutherland. Photo Researchers, Inc.)

tion of red blood cells and is effective in removing sensitized red blood cells before they are destroyed. It also removes about 60 percent of bilirubin from the plasma, resulting in a clearance of about 30 percent to 40 percent of the total bilirubin. If a transfusion is not performed and bilirubin levels get higher, the infant progresses through three phases. In the first two to three days the infant is lethargic, has muscle weakness, and sucks weakly. Progression is marked by a tensing of the muscles, arching, **fever**, seizures, and high-pitched crying. In the final phase, the patient is hypotonic for several years.

Prognosis

The prognosis for physiological neonatal jaundice is generally very good. Very few infants ever have bilirubin levels greater than 20 mg/dL, which is the level that is correlated with kernicterus (an abnormal accumulation

KEY TERMS

ABO incompatability—The reaction that occurs with blood groups that are of a different type.

Cephalohematoma—A benign swelling of the scalp in a newborn due to an effusion of blood beneath the connective tissue that surrounds the skull, often resulting from birth trauma.

Kernicterus—A potentially lethal disease of newborns caused by excessive accumulation of the bile pigment bilirubin in tissues of the central nervous system.

Meconium—A greenish fecal material that forms the first bowel movement of an infant.

Oxytocin—A hormone that stimulates the uterus to contract during child birth and the breasts to release milk.

Peristalsis—Slow, rhythmic contractions of the muscles in a tubular organ, such as the intestines, that move the contents along.

Rh incompatability—A factor of blood classified as negative or positive and related to the reaction that occurs between different types.

Trisomy—An abnormal condition where three copies of one chromosome are present in the cells of an individual's body instead of two, the normal number.

of bile pigment in the brain and other nerve tissue that causes yellow staining and tissue damage). It rarely occurs with bilirubin levels lower than 20 mg/dL but typically occurs when levels exceed 30 mg/dL. Levels between 20 and 30 mg/dL associated with **prematurity** and hemolytic disease may increase the risk of kernicterus. There are long-term neurological problems when this occurs. Affected children have marked developmental and motor delays in the form of **cerebral palsy** and **mental retardation** may also be present.

Prevention

Elevated bilirubin in the neonate is the most common reason for hospital readmission in the first two weeks of life. Kernicterus is still relatively uncommon but has been on the rise with the mandated early postnatal discharge policies. Bilirubin-induced complications can be prevented by introducing a neonatal jaundice protocol to identify infants at risk for significant bilirubin increases, by ensuring adequate parental education and providing for follow-up care.

Parental concerns

Parents of a newborn need to be vigilant in monitoring changes in their infant. If the mother is breastfeeding, she should nurse the baby at least once every three hours to ensure the onset of milk production and to maintain hydration, which can also be evaluated by the number of wet diapers. Many pediatricians recommend seeing the infant at two weeks but if the parents feel it should be sooner due to alterations in the newborn's physical status, they should take the infant in for a visit.

Resources

BOOKS

Klaus, M. H., and A. A. Fanaroff. *Care of the High-Risk Neonate*, 5th ed. Philadelphia, PA: Saunders Company, 2001.

Olds, Sally, et al. *Maternal-Newborn Nursing and Women's Health Care*, 7th ed. Saddle River, NJ: Prentice Hall, 2004.

Seidel, H. M., et al. *Primary Care of the Newborn*. St. Louis, MO: Mosby, 2001.

PERIODICALS

Morantz, C., and B. Torrey. "AHRQ report on neonatal jaundice: Agency for Healthcare Research and Quality." *American Family Physician* (June 1, 2003).

ORGANIZATIONS

Association of Women's Health, Obstetric and Neonatal Nursing. 2000 L Street, NW, Suite 740, Washington, DC 20036. Web site: <www.awhonn.org>.

American Academy of Pediatrics. 141 Northwest Point Blvd., Elk Grove Village, IL, 60007. Web site: <www.aap.org>.

American College of Obstetricians and Gynecologists. 409 12th Street, SW, PO Box 96920, Washington, DC 20090. Web site: <www.acog.org>.

Linda K. Bennington, MSN, CNS

▌Neonatal reflexes

Definition

Neonatal reflexes or primitive reflexes are the inborn behavioral patterns that develop during uterine life. They should be fully present at birth and are gradually inhibited by higher centers in the brain during the first three to 12 months of postnatal life. These reflexes, which are essential for a newborn's survival immediately after birth, include sucking, swallowing, blinking, urinating, hiccupping, and defecating. These typical reflexes are not learned; they are involuntary and necessary for survival.

Description

A normal birth is considered full term if the delivery occurs during the thirty-seventh to fortieth week after conception. Developmentally, the baby is considered a neonate for the first 28 days of life. At birth, the neonate must immediately make five major adjustments:

- Transition from an aquatic environment to a world of air. The first breath begins even before the umbilical cord is cut.

- Eat and digest his or her own food since the circulatory relationship between mother and baby stops with the severance of the umbilical cord.

- Excrete his or her own wastes.

- Maintain his or her own body temperature.

- Adjust to intermittent feeding since food is now only available at certain intervals.

Under normal developmental conditions, these neonatal reflexes represent important reactions of the nervous system and are only observable within a specific period of time over the first few months of life. The following reflexes are normally present from birth and are part of a normal newborn evaluation:

- The Moro reflex (or startle reflex) occurs when an infant is lying in a supine position and is stimulated by a sudden loud noise that causes rapid or sudden movement of the infant's head. This stimulus results in a symmetrical extension of the infant's extremities while forming a C shape with the thumb and forefinger. This is followed by a return to a flexed position with extremities against the body. Inhibition of this reflex occurs from the third to the sixth month. An asymmetrical response with this reflex may indicate a fractured clavicle or a birth injury to the nerves of the arm. Absence of this reflex in the neonate is an ominous implication of underlying neurological damage.

- Asymmetrical tonic neck reflex (sometimes called the tonic labyrinthine reflex) is activated as a result of turning the head to one side. As the head is turned, the arm and leg on the same side will extend while the opposite limbs bend, in a pose that mimics a fencer. The reflex should be inhibited by six months of age in the waking state. If this reflex is still present at eight to nine months of age, the baby will not be able to support its weight by straightening its arms and bringing its knees beneath its body.

- Symmetrical tonic neck reflex occurs with either the extension or flexion of the infant's head. Extension of the head results in extension of the arms and flexion of the legs, and a flexion of the head causes flexion of the arms and an extension of the legs. This reflex becomes inhibited by the sixth month to enable crawling.

- Grasping reflex occurs as the palmar reflex when a finger is placed in the neonate's palm and the neonate grasps the finger. The palmar reflex disappears around the sixth month. Similarly, the plantar reflex occurs by placing a finger against the base of the neonate's toes and the toes curl downward to grasp the finger. This reflex becomes inhibited around the ninth to tenth month.

- Rooting reflex is stimulated by touching a finger to the infant's cheek or the corner of the mouth. The neonate responds by turning the head toward the stimulus, opening the mouth and searching for the stimulus. This is a necessary reflex triggered by the mother's nipple during breastfeeding. It is usually inhibited by the third to fourth month.

- Sucking reflex is triggered by placing a finger or the mother's nipple in the infant's mouth. The neonate will suck on the finger or nipple forcefully and rhythmically and the sucking is coordinated with swallowing. Like the rooting reflex, it is inhibited by the third to fourth month.

- Babinski or plantar reflex is triggered by stroking one side of the infant's foot upward from the heel and across the ball of the foot. The infant responds by hyperextending the toes; the great toe flexes toward the top of the foot and the other toes fan outward. It generally becomes inhibited from the sixth to ninth month of post natal life.

- Blink reflex is stimulated by momentarily shining a bright light directly into the neonate's eyes causing him or her to blink. This reflex should not become inhibited.

- Pupillary reflex occurs with darkening the room and shining a penlight directly into the neonate's eye for several seconds. The pupils should both constrict equally; this reflex should not disappear.

- Galant reflex is stimulated by placing the infant on the stomach or lightly supporting him or her under the abdomen with a hand and, using a fingernail, gently stroking one side of the neonate's spinal column from the head to the buttocks. The response occurs with the neonate's trunk curving toward the stimulated side. This reflex can become inhibited at any time between the first and third month.

- Stepping reflex is observed by holding the infant in an upright position and touching one foot lightly to a flat

Neonatal reflexes

Reflex	Stimulation	Response	Duration
Babinski	Sole of foot stroked	Fans out toes and twists foot in	Disappears at nine months to a year
Blinking	Flash of light or puff of air	Closes eyes	Permanent
Grasping	Palms touched	Grasps tightly	Weakens at three months; disappears at a year
Moro	Sudden move; loud noise	Startles; throws out arms and legs and then pulls them toward body	Disappears at three to four months
Rooting	Cheek stroked or side of mouth touched	Turns toward source, opens mouth and sucks	Disappears at three to four months
Stepping	Infant held upright with feet touching ground	Moves feet as if to walk	Disappears at three to four months
Sucking	Mouth touched by object	Sucks on object	Disappears at three to four months
Swimming	Placed face down in water	Makes coordinated swimming movements	Disappears at six to seven months
Tonic neck	Placed on back	Makes fists and turns head to the right	Disappears at two months

SOURCE: Table after Child Development, 6th ed. Wm. C. Brown Communications, Inc., 1994.

(Table by GGS Information Services.)

surface, such as the bed. The infant responds by making walking motions with both feet. This reflex will disappear at approximately two months of age.

- Prone crawl reflex can be stimulated by placing the neonate prone (face down) on a flat surface. The neonate will attempt to crawl forward using the arms and legs. This reflex will be inhibited by three to four months of age.

- Doll's eye reflex can be noted with the infant supine (lying on the back) and slowly turning the head to either side. The infant's eyes will remain stationary. This reflex should disappear between three to four months of age.

Common problems

The presence and strength of a reflex is an important indication of neurological functioning. Within the first 24 hours after birth, a healthcare provider evaluates an infant's neurological functioning and development by testing and observing these reflexes. If a reflex is absent or abnormal in an infant, this may suggest significant neurological problems. In normal development, the primary reflex system is inhibited or transformed in the first year of life and a secondary or postural reflex system emerges. The secondary system forms the basis for later adult coordinated movement. Absence or presence of a reflex is a symptom, not a disorder.

Severe persistence of primary reflexes indicates predominantly persistent physical problems. Relatively milder persistence, however, is associated with less severe disorders that include specific reading difficulties.

The process of inhibition of these reflexes in the earliest months of life remains unknown but it has been assumed that this process cannot occur after early childhood because neonatal movement is largely stereotypical and follows the patterns of the primary reflex system. Thus, the early movements of the fetus and newborn were previously viewed as passive byproducts of the central nervous system. They are viewed as interactive and having a reciprocal effect on the underlying central nervous system structure and functioning. This implies that the actual rehearsal and repetition of primary reflex movements play a role in the inhibition process itself.

Parental concerns

An evaluation of neonatal reflexes is performed during well-baby examinations. The abnormal presence of infantile reflexes in an older child can be discovered during a neurological examination. **Assessment** of neonatal reflexes is a screening tool for at-risk children with neurological difficulties. Primary reflexes may persist for certain children beyond their normal time span causing a disruption in subsequent development. Children with neurological damage will have a common denomi-

KEY TERMS

Palmar—Referring to the palm of the hand.

Plantar—Relating to the sole of the foot.

Postural—Pertaining to the position of the head, neck, trunk and lower limbs in relation to the ground and the vertical.

Prone—Lying on the stomach with the face downward.

Supine—Lying on the back with the face upward.

Visuosensory—Pertaining to the perception of visual stimuli.

nator of prolonged neonatal reflexes. Since recent studies have demonstrated that repetition of these reflexes seems to eventually inhibit them, parents can work with the infant by assisting with the repetition of persistent reflexes.

When to call the doctor

Persistence of neonatal reflexes is not threatening to life and, therefore, can be discussed with the pediatrician during normal well-baby visits.

Resources

BOOKS

Blythe, Peter. *The Role of the Primitive Asymmetrical Tonic Neck Reflex (ATNR) in Balance, Co-ordination Problems and Specific Learning Difficulties, including Dyslexia.* Chester, UK: INPP, Monograph 2002.

Goddard, Sally. *Reflexes, Learning and Behavior.* Eugene, OR: Fern Ridge Press, 2002.

Seidel, Henry M., Rosenstein, et al. *Primary Care of the Newborn,* 3rd ed. St. Louis, MO: Mosby, 2001.

PERIODICALS

Bein-Wierzbinski, W. "Persistent Primitive Reflexes in Elementary School Children." *Presented at the 13th European Conference of Neuro-Developmental Delay in Children with Specific Learning Difficulties* Chester, UK (2001).

Blythe, Sally G. "Neurological Dysfunction, a Developmental Movement Programme used in Schools and the Effect upon Education." *The Bangor Dyslexia Conference, University of Bangor, North Wales* (July 2003).

ORGANIZATIONS

American Academy of Pediatrics. 141 Northwest Point Blvd., Elk Grove Village, IL 60007-1098. (847) 434-4000. Web site: <www.aap.org.>.

The International Dyslexia Association. Chester Building, Suite 382;8600 LaSalle Road; Baltimore, MD 21286-2044. (410) 296-0232 or (800) 222-3123. Web site: <www.interdys.org>.

WEB SITES

Primary Movement 2004. Available online at <www.primarymovement.org>.

Primitive and Postural Reflexes—The Theory. Available online at <www.inpp.org.uk/htm>.

Linda K. Bennington, MSN, CNS

Neonatal testing *see* **Apgar testing**

Nephroblastoma *see* **Wilms' tumor**

Neural tube defect *see* **Spina bifida**

Neurofibromatosis

Definition

Neurofibromatosis (NF) is a genetic disease in which multiple soft tumors (neurofibromas) develop under the skin and throughout the nervous system. Various sized tumors may grow on the nerves in or leading away from the brain and spinal cord (peripheral nerves) and in the vascular system (veins and arteries) and other organ systems. There are two types of NF: NF-1, also called vonRecklinghausen NF, and NF-2, also called acoustic NF (sometimes bilateral acoustic NF or BAN). NF-1 is more common, representing 90 percent of all cases, while NF-2 is diagnosed in 10 percent of NF cases.

Description

Neural crest cells are primitive cells that are present as part of the nervous system during fetal development. These cells eventually turn into the following:

- cells that form nerves throughout the brain, spinal cord, and body
- cells that serve as coverings around the nerves throughout the body
- pigment cells that provide color to body structures
- meninges, the thin, membranous coverings of the brain and spinal cord
- cells that ultimately develop into the bony structures of the head and neck

In both types of NF, a genetic defect causes these neural crest cells to develop abnormally, resulting in numerous tumors and malformations of the nerves, bones, and skin.

NF-1 affects nerves throughout the body, occurring as groups of soft, fibrous swellings that grow on nerves in the skin, brain, and spinal cord (central nervous system), muscles, and bone. Severe disfigurement can result from the development of these tumors as the disease progresses and bone deformities may occur as well.

NF-2 is a rare type of NF in which multiple tumors grow on the cranial (head) and spinal nerves and other growths can occur in the brain and spinal cord. Tumor growth (schwannoma) on the nerves to the ears (auditory nerves) is most characteristic of NF-2. Disfigurement does not occur although hearing and visual problems are typical.

Demographics

NF-1 is a common genetic disorder that occurs in about one of every 4,000 births worldwide. NF-2 is rare, occurring in one of every 40,000 births. Children with a **family** history of neurofibromatosis are at highest risk for having either form of the condition.

Causes and symptoms

Both forms of neurofibromatosis are caused by a defective gene. NF-1 is due to a defect on chromosome 17; NF-2 results from a defect on chromosome 22. Both of these disorders are inherited in a dominant fashion, which means that anyone who receives just one defective gene will have the disease. However, a family pattern of NF is only evident for about half of all cases of NF. The other cases of NF occur due to a spontaneous mutation (a permanent change in the structure of a specific gene). Once such a spontaneous mutation has been established in an individual, however, it can then be passed on to any offspring. The chance of a person with NF passing on the NF gene to a child is 50 percent.

NF-1 has a number of possible signs and can be diagnosed if any two of the following are present:

- The presence of coffee-colored spots. These are patches of tan or light brown skin, usually about 5 to 15 mm in diameter. Nearly all patients with NF-1 will display these spots.
- Multiple freckles in the armpit or groin area.
- Ninety percent of patients with NF-1 have tiny tumors called Lisch nodules in the iris (colored area) of the eye.

- Soft tumors (neurofibromas) are the hallmark of NF-1. They occur under the skin, often located along nerves or within the gastrointestinal tract. Neurofibromas are small and rubbery, and the skin overlying them may be somewhat purple in color.
- Skeletal deformities, such as a twisted spine (**scoliosis**), curved spine (humpback), or bowed legs.
- Tumors along the optic nerve, causing vision disturbances in about 20 percent of those affected.
- The presence of NF-1 in a child's parent or sibling.

Very high rates of speech impairment, learning disabilities, and attention deficit disorder occur in children with NF-1. Other complications include the development of a **seizure disorder** or the abnormal accumulation of fluid within the brain (**hydrocephalus**). A number of cancers are more common in individuals who have NF-1. These include various types of malignant brain tumors, as well as leukemia and cancerous tumors of certain muscles (rhabdomyosarcoma), the adrenal glands (pheochromocytoma), or the kidneys (**Wilms' tumor**).

Patients with NF-2 do not necessarily have the same characteristic skin symptoms that appear in NF-1. The characteristic symptoms of NF-2 are due to tumors along the acoustic nerve that result in nerve dysfunction and the loss of hearing. The tumor may also spread to neighboring nervous system structures, causing weakness of the muscles of the face, **headache**, **dizziness**, poor balance, and uncoordinated walking. Cloudy areas on the lens of the eye (cataracts) frequently develop at an unusually early age. As in NF-1, the chance of brain tumors developing is unusually high.

When to call the doctor

A history of either form of NF in the child's parent or sibling is reason to consult a physician. The presence of any of the symptoms associated with NF-1 or NF-2 should be investigated by a physician as well, particularly spots on the skin or small movable lumps under the skin and visual disturbances, memory loss, or difficulty maintaining balance. Hearing loss may be the first sign of NF-2 but can also be due to other unrelated conditions.

Diagnosis

Diagnosis is based on characteristic symptoms and physical examination. Diagnosis of NF-1 requires that at least two of the characteristic signs are present. Diagnosis of NF-2 requires the presence of either a nodule or mass (tumor) on the acoustic nerve or another distinctive nervous system tumor, which may only be identifiable through imaging studies. An important diagnostic clue for either NF-1 or NF-2 is the known presence of the disorder in a child's parent or sibling. Gene studies may be done to detect abnormalities on chromosomes 17 and 22.

Diagnosis of NF-1 will be confirmed by manipulation of the skin to reveal moveable, small, solid lumps (nodules) and the presence of coffee-colored spots on the skin of the trunk and pelvis. The spots may appear in childhood and typically become more noticeable in young adults. Two or more nodules and six or more discolored spots are usually definitive for a diagnosis of NF-1. Curvature of the spin (scoliosis) may be present, elevated blood pressure, and abnormalities in height, weight, and head size may also be noticed on physical examination.

Diagnosis of NF-2 also relies on manipulation of the skin to indicate the presence of nodules and evaluation of hearing and vision to determine any impairment.

X rays, CT scans, and MRI scans are performed to track the development/progression of tumors in the brain and along the nerves. Auditory evoked potential testing (the electric response evoked in the cerebral cortex by stimulation of the acoustic nerve) may be helpful to determine involvement of the acoustic nerve, and EEG (**electroencephalogram**, a record of electrical currents in the brain) may be needed for children who have possible seizures. As the disease progresses, hearing and vision are carefully monitored and imaging studies of the bones are frequently done to watch for the development of deformities.

Treatment

There is no standard treatment for either type of neurofibromatosis. To some extent, the symptoms of NF-1 and NF-2 can be treated individually. Skin tumors can be surgically removed. Some brain tumors and tumors along the nerves, can be surgically removed or treated with chemotherapeutic drugs or x-ray treatments (radiation therapy). Twisting or curving of the spine and bowed legs may be corrected to some degree by surgical treatment or the wearing of a special brace. Social adjustment problems are common among young children with physical deformities caused by the condition.

Prognosis

NF of either type is progressive, and the clinical outcome is not predictable. Prognosis varies depending on the types of tumors that develop. As tumors grow, they begin to destroy surrounding nerves and structures. Ultimately, this destruction can result in blindness,

KEY TERMS

Chromosome—A microscopic thread-like structure found within each cell of the human body and consisting of a complex of proteins and DNA. Humans have 46 chromosomes arranged into 23 pairs. Chromosomes contain the genetic information necessary to direct the development and functioning of all cells and systems in the body. They pass on hereditary traits from parents to child (like eye color) and determine whether the child will be male or female.

Mutation—A permanent change in the genetic material that may alter a trait or characteristic of an individual, or manifest as disease. This change can be transmitted to offspring.

Neurofibroma—A soft tumor usually located on a nerve.

Tumor—A growth of tissue resulting from the uncontrolled proliferation of cells.

deafness, increasingly poor balance, and increasing difficulty with the coordination necessary for walking. Deformities of the bones and spine can also interfere with walking and other kinds of movement. When cancers develop as a result of NF, prognosis worsens according to the specific type of **cancer**. Successful surgical removal of neurofibromas has a survival rate of 50 to 90 percent.

Prevention

There is no known way to prevent NF cases that occur as a result of spontaneous change in the genes (mutation). New cases of inherited NF can be prevented with careful genetic counseling. Parents with NF can be encouraged to understand that each of his or her offspring has a 50 percent chance of also having NF. When a parent has NF, and the specific genetic defect causing the parent's disease has been identified, tests can be performed on the fetus (developing baby) during pregnancy. Procedures such as **amniocentesis** or chorionic villus sampling allow small amounts of the baby's cells to be removed for examination. The tissue can then be examined for the presence of the parent's genetic defect. Some families choose to use this information in order to prepare for the arrival of a child with a serious medical problem. Other families may choose not to continue the pregnancy.

Parental concerns

Parents may worried about the development of deformities associated with NF-1. Social workers and psychologists can be consulted about possible counseling for children with the disease, helping them to cope with changes in their bodies that may be hard to accept. Hearing loss and visual disturbances associated with NF-2 are usually not reversible and specialists can be consulted about possible therapies to improve functioning in existing sight or hearing senses. Surgery to remove tumors may require the provision of educational information for both parents and children so that the procedure and possible complications are understood ahead of time.

Resources

ORGANIZATIONS

March of Dimes Birth Defects Foundation. Resource Center, 1275 Mamaroneck Ave., White Plains, NY 10605. Web site: <www.modimes.org>.

National Neurofibromatosis Foundation Inc. 95 Pine St., 16th Floor, New York, NY 10005. Web site: <nf.org>.

WEB SITES

"Neurofibromatosis." *MedlinePlus.* Available online at <www.nlm.nih.gov/medlineplus/neurofibromatosis.html> (accessed October 12, 2004).

"Neurofibromatosis." *Neurofibromatosis Inc.* Available online at <www.rfinc.org/> (accessed October 12, 2004).

L. Lee Culvert
Rosalyn Carson-DeWitt, MD

Neurologic exam

Definition

A neurological examination is an essential component of a comprehensive physical examination. It is a systematic examination that surveys the functioning of nerves delivering sensory information to the brain and carrying motor commands (peripheral nervous system) and impulses back to the brain for processing and coordinating (central nervous system).

Purpose

A careful neurological evaluation can help to determine the cause of impairment and help a clinician begin to localize the problem. Symptoms that occur unexpect-edly suggest a blood vessel or seizure problem. Those that are not so sudden suggest a possible tumor. Symptoms that have a waning course with recurrences and worsen over time suggest a disease that destroys nerve cells. Others that are chronic and progressive indicate a degenerative disorder. In cases of trauma, symptoms may be evident upon inspection and causes may be explained by third party witnesses. Some patients may require extensive neurological screening examination (NSE) and/or neurological examination (NE) to determine the cause. The NE will assist the clinician in diagnosing illnesses as diverse as seizure disorders, **narcolepsy**, migraine disorders, **dizziness**, and dementia.

Description

A neurological screening is an essential component of every comprehensive physical examination. In cases of neurological trauma, disease, or psychological disorders, patients are usually given an in-depth neurological examination. The examination is performed in a systematic manner, which means that there is a recommended order for procedures.

Neurological screening examination

The NSE is basic procedure, especially in patients who have a general neurological complaint or symptoms. The NSE consists of six areas of **assessment**:

- mental status: assessing normal orientation to time, place, space, and speech
- cranial nerves: checking the eyes with a special light source (ophthalmoscope) and also assessing facial muscles strength and functioning
- motor: checking for tone, drift, and heel and toe walking
- sensory: cold and vibration testing
- coordination: observing the patient walk and finger to nose testing
- reflexes: using a special instrument the clinician taps an area above a nerve to emit a reflex (usually movement of muscle groups)

Neurological examination

The NE should be performed on a patient suspected of having neurological trauma, or neurological or psychological diseases. The NE is performed in a systematic and comprehensive manner. It consists of several comprehensive and in-depth assessments of mental status, cranial nerves, motor abilities, reflexes, sensory acuity, and posture and walking (gait) abilities.

MENTAL STATUS EXAMINATION (MSE) There are two types of MSE, informal and formal. The informal MSE is usually done as clinicians are obtaining historical information from a patient. The formal MSE is performed for a patient suspected of a neurological problem. The patient is commonly asked his/her name, the location, the day, and date. Determining the number of digits that can be repeated in sequence can assess retentive memory capability and immediate recall. Recent memory is typically examined by testing recall potential of a series of objects after defined times, usually within five and 15 minutes. Asking the patient to review in a coherent and chronological fashion his or her illness or personal life events can provide the opportunity for assessment of remote memory. Patient recall of common historical or current events can be used to assess general knowledge. Brain processing capabilities can be assessed by spontaneous speech, repetition, reading, naming, writing, and comprehension. Modifications can be made based on the age and maturity of the child. The child may be asked to perform tasks such as identification of fingers, whistling, saluting, brushing teeth motions, combing hair, drawing, and tracing figures. These procedures allow for assessment of dominant (left-sided brain) functioning or higher cortical function.

The MSE is particularly important in psychotherapy. Psychotherapists recommend an in-depth MSE for all patients with possible organic (physiologica) or psychotic disorders. This examination is also performed in a systematic and orderly manner. It is divided into several categories:

- Appearance determines the child's presentation, i.e., how the child looks (clothes posture, grooming, and alertness).

- Behavior assesses the patient's motor activity (movements) such as walking, gestures, muscular twitching, and impulse control.

- Speech can be examined concerning volume, rate of speech, and coherence. Individuals who exhibit latent or delayed speech may be depressed, while those who have rapid or pressured speech may suffer from mania or **anxiety**.

- Mood and affect indicate attitude or feeling. Normal mood (euthymia) is healthy. Variations in mood include: flat, labile, blunted, constructed, or inappropriate mood. The child can also be euphoric (elevated) or dysphoric (on the down side).

- Thought processes and content is typically assessed by determining word usage (can indicate brain disease), thought stream (slow, restricted, blocked, or overabundant), continuity of thought (associations among ideas), and content of thought (delusional as opposed to reality-bound).

- Perception assessment examines the individual's sensory ability to hear, see, touch, taste, and smell. Certain psychological states may cause hearing and visual hallucinations. Impairments of smell and touch usually have medical (organic) causes or are side effects of certain medications.

- Attention and concentration assessment indicates the child's ability to focus on a specific task or activity. Abnormalities in attention and concentration can indicate problems related to anxiety or hallucinations.

- Orientation assessment determines if the child has a normal sense of time, place, and identification of self (can state his or her own name). Disturbances in orientation can be due to a medical condition (other than psychological), substance abuse, or to a side effect of certain medications such as those used to treat depression, anxiety, or psychosis, since these medications usually have a sedative affect.

- Memory assessment includes determining the child's remote, recent, and immediate memory capabilities. Remote and recent memory can be assessed by the patient's ability to recall historical and current events. Immediate memory can be tested by naming three objects and asking the child to repeat the named objects immediately, then after five and 15 minute intervals.

- Judgment assessment evaluates the individual's ability to exercise appropriate judgment. It also determines whether the individual has an understanding of consequences associated with their actions. This evaluation pertains primarily to older children.

- **Intelligence** and information measurement can be obtained by administering specialized intelligence tests, However, a preliminary assessment of intelligence can be made based on the child's fund of age-appropriate information, general knowledge, awareness of current events, and the ability for abstract thinking.

- Insight assessment pertains to determining the patient's awareness of their problem that prompted them to seek professional examination. Insight concerning the present illness can range from denial to fleeting admission of current illness.

CRANIAL NERVES (CN) Cranial nerves are nerves that originate in the brain and connect to specialized structures such as the nose, eyes, muscles in the face, scalp, ear, and tongue.

- CN I: This nerve checks for visual capabilities. Patients are usually given the Snellen Chart (a chart with rows of large and small letters). Patients read letters with one eye at a time.

- CN III, IV, and VI: These nerves examine the pupillary (the circular center structure of the eye that light rays enter) reaction. The pupils get smaller, normally when exposed to the light. The eyelids are also examined for drooping or retraction. The eyeball is also checked for abnormalities in movement.

- CN V: The clinician can assess the muscles on both sides of the scalp muscles (the temporalis muscle). Additionally the jaw can be tested for motion resistance, opening, protrusion, and side-to-side mobility. The cornea located is a transparent tissue covering the eyeball and can be tested for intactness by lightly brushing a wisp of cotton directly on the outside of the eye.

- CN VII: Examination of CN VII assesses asymmetry of the face at rest and during spontaneous movements. The patient is asked to raise eyebrows, wrinkle forehead, close eyes, frown, smile, puff cheeks, purse lips, whistle, and contract chin muscles. Taste for the front and middle portions of the tongue can also be examined.

- CN VIII: Testing for this CN deals with hearing. The clinician usually uses a special instrument called a tuning fork and tests for air conduction and structural problems which can occur inside the ear.

- CN IX and X: These tests evaluate certain structures in the mouth. The clinician will usually ask the patient to say "aah" and can detect abnormal positioning of certain structures such as the palatel-uvula. The examiner will also assess the sensation capabilities of the pharynx, by stimulating the area with a wooden tongue depressor, causing a gag reflex.

- CN XI: This nerve is usually examined by asking the patient to shrug shoulders (testing a muscle called the trapezius) and rotating the head to each side (testing a muscle called the sternocleidomastoid). These muscles are responsible for movement of the shoulders and neck. The test is usually done with resistance, meaning the examiner holds the area while the patient is asked to move. This is done to assess patient's strength in these areas.

- CN XII: This nerve tests the bulk and power of the tongue. The examiner looks for tongue protrusion and/or abnormal movements.

MOTOR EXAMINATION The motor examination assesses the patient's muscle strength, tone, and shape. Muscles could be larger than expected (hypertrophy) or smaller due to tissues destruction (atrophy). It is important to assess if there is evidence of twitching or abnor-

mal movements. Involuntary movements due to **tics** can be observed. Additionally, movements can be abnormal during maintained posture in some neurological disorders. Muscle tone is usually tested by applying resistance to passive motion of a relaxed limb. Power is assessed for movements at each joint. Decreases or increases in muscle tone can help the examiner localize the affected area.

REFLEXES The patient's reflexes are tested by using a special instrument that looks like a little hammer. The clinician taps the rubber triangular shaped end in several different areas in the arms, knee, and Achilles heel area. The clinician will ask the patient to relax and gently tap the area. If there is a difference in response from the left to right knee, then there may be an underlying problem that merits further evaluation. A difference in reflexes between the arms and legs usually indicates of a lesion involving the spinal cord. Depressed reflexes in only one limb, while the other limb demonstrates a normal response usually indicates a peripheral nerve lesion.

SENSORY EXAMINATION Although an essential component of the NE, the sensory examination is the least informative and least exacting since it requires patient concentration and cooperation. Five primary sensory categories are assessed: vibration (using a tuning fork), joint position (examiner moves the limb side-to-side and in a downward position), light touch, pinprick, and temperature. Patients who have sensory abnormalities may have a lesion above the thalamus. Spinal cord lesions or disease can possibly be detected by pinprick and temperature assessment.

COORDINATION The patient is asked to repetitively touch his nose using his index finger and then to touch the clinician's outstretched finger. Coordination can also be assessed by asking the patient to alternate tapping the palm then the back of one hand on the thigh. For coordination in the lower extremities (legs), the patient lies on his or her back and is asked to slide the heel of each foot from the knee down the shin of the opposite leg and to raise the leg and touch the examiner's index finger with the big toe.

WALKING (GAIT) Normal walking is a complex process and requires use of multiple systems such as power, coordination, and sensation, all working together in a coordinated fashion. The examination of gait can detect a variety of disease states. Decreased arm swinging on one side is indicative of corticospinal tract disease. A high-stepped, slapping gait may be the result of a peripheral nerve disease.

Precautions

A neurologic examination is not invasive and there are no risks or dangers associated with these tests. The results and validity of this exam may be affected by the child's age and ability to cooperate.

Preparation

The MSE is the first step in a continuous assessment to determine the diagnosis. A psychotherapist should take a detailed medical history in the process of ruling out a general medical condition. Little preparation is needed for this assessment, but parents should explain to young children what will happen in order to encourage their cooperation.

Aftercare

For suspected neurological diseases, the doctor uses information gained from the NE for ordering further tests. These tests may include a complete blood analysis, liver function tests, kidney function tests, hormone tests, and a lumbar puncture to determine abnormalities in cerebrospinal fluid. In trauma cases (e.g. car accident, **sports** injury), the NE is a quick and essential component of emergency assessment. Once a diagnosis is determined, emergency measures may include further tests and/or surgery.

In psychological cases the treatment may include therapy and/or medication. In cases of an acute insult such as trauma, the patient is usually admitted to the hospital for appropriate treatment. Some neurological diseases are chronic and require conservative medical treatment and frequent follow-up visits for monitoring and stability or progression of the disease.

Risks

The MSE and NE are good diagnostic tools. There are no risks associated with initial neurologic assessment.

Parental concerns

Parental concerns center on the cause of the medical disease or psychological disorder, rather than around the procedure, which is straightforward and non-threatening.

Resources

BOOKS

Haslam, Robert H. A. "The Nervous System." In *Nelson Textbook of Pediatrics*, 17th ed. Edited by Richard E. Behrman et al. Philadelphia: Saunders, 2004.

KEY TERMS

Corticospinal tract—A tract of nerve cells that carries motor commands from the brain to the spinal cord.

Gait—Walking motions.

Reflex—An involuntary response to a particular stimulus.

Thalamus—A pair of oval masses of gray matter within the brain that relay sensory impulses from the spinal cord to the cerebrum.

Jozefowicz, Ralph F. "The Neurologic History." In *Cecil's Textbook of Medicine*, 21st ed. Edited by Lee Goldman et al. Philadelphia: Saunders, 2000.

WEB SITES

Blumenthal, Hal. "An Interactive Online Guide to the Neurologic Examination." *neuroexam.com*, 2001. Available online at <www.neuroexam.com> (accessed January 16, 2005).

Tish Davidson, A.M.
Laith Farid Gulli, M.D.
Bilal Nasser, M.Sc.

Newborn life support *see* **Extracorporeal membrane oxygenation**

Nicotine *see* **Smoking**

Niemann-Pick disease *see* **Lipidoses**

Night terrors

Definition

Childhood night terrors are a parasomnia, or partial-sleep disorder, common in young children. They occur in the deepest stage of **sleep** and are characterized by an abrupt arousal, usually within the first hour of sleep. The child may sit bolt upright in acute terror, screaming inconsolably. Night terrors are a confusional arousal resulting from immature sleep patterns with an intense activation of the flight or fight emotion.

Description

Night terrors are not a dream or typical nightmare. They occur in non-REM, slow-wave sleep. The panicked screaming, kicking, thrashing, and flailing is alarming in its intensity. Sleepwalking, another parasomnia disorder, may also occur in as many as one third of children with night terrors. While experiencing the night terror the child is extremely disoriented and may stare straight ahead, eyes wide open, with the dark centers (pupils) enlarged. There is profuse sweating, the heartbeat is rapid, the breathing fast, and the blood pressure is elevated. As the child is not fully awake, she is unable to see or recognize her parent or caretaker and cannot be easily awakened. The night terror may last from one to 15 minutes or more and is usually followed by a return to deep sleep. Afterwards the child may have no memory of the experience.

Night terrors appear to run in families, though there is no scientific evidence of genetic factors. They are a developmental process and not typically a result of mental or physical illness.

Demographics

Childhood night terrors occur more frequently in boys. Children between the ages of three and five years of age are most likely to experience such nocturnal episodes. Such confusional arousals rarely persist beyond childhood, and they are significantly less frequent or cease entirely after age 12.

Causes and symptoms

Childhood night terrors appear to be a normal physiological process of the immature and developing nervous system. These confusional arousals can be triggered by stressful circumstances such as when a child is overly tired, when there is a loud noise or other unusual disruption, a change in the child's regular sleep-wake schedule, or even a full bladder. Night terrors occurring in **adolescence** and adult life may be more severe and are often linked with trauma and post-traumatic stress disorders.

When to call the doctor

Consult a pediatrician for night terrors if any of the following occur:

- Episodes occur more than once a week.
- Episodes persist after a schedule of preventive awakenings.
- Episodes last more than 45 minutes.

- The child exhibits drooling, jerking, and stiffening of the body.
- The child is physically endangered during an episode.
- Episodes occur later during the sleep cycle, more than two hours after going to sleep.
- The child has fears that persist throughout the day.

Diagnosis

Diagnosis is based on observation of the following characteristic symptoms:

- recurring episodes of abrupt and partial awakening from deep sleep with panicked screaming and disorientation
- increased heart rate, rapid breathing, and profuse sweating during an episode
- child is unresponsive to efforts to arouse or console during an episode
- child has little or no memory of the event after a full awakening

Treatment

Parents should not attempt to awaken a child experiencing a night terror. Efforts to console may be futile, though holding the child firmly and speaking with soothing words may facilitate the return to deep sleep. The primary effort should be to protect the child from possible harm to herself and others and ease them back to sleep.

In some severe cases, a pediatrician may prescribe a benzodiazepine tranquilizer, such as diazepam, known to suppress the stage four level of deep sleep. Though tranquilizers may be used for short-term control of night terrors, the result is uncertain and not generally advised.

Alternative treatment

Hypnosis, biofeedback, and various relaxation techniques have been used with some success to reduce or eliminate occurrence of childhood night terrors. Calming music or bedtime stories can help lull a child into deep sleep. Maintaining a quiet home without sudden disruptive noise will minimize some of the external stimuli that may trigger night terrors.

Nutritional concerns

Unusually heavy or spicy meals should be avoided before bedtime as indigestion might act as a trigger for night terror arousals.

Prognosis

Childhood night terrors are usually outgrown by the age of seven and rarely persist beyond adolescence.

Prevention

Some pediatricians suggest that parents maintain a sleep diary and observe the child throughout several night terror episodes, noting the amount of time following sleep when the night terror begins. After the sleep-wake pattern is determined, a series of 15–20 minutes prior to the usual occurrence of the night terror and keep the child awake and out of bed for a full five minutes. This may help to break the disruptive sleep pattern that has resulted in the night terrors.

Children often experience night terrors during the toilet-training years. The night terror might be triggered by a full bladder. Assisting the child to the toilet prior to bedtime and even during the course of a night-terror might be beneficial in reducing reoccurrence.

Parental concerns

Childhood night terrors are alarming to witness. Parents may find it particularly difficult when efforts to console the child fail and the child does not recognize them even though his or her eyes may be wide open. The screaming, flailing, and kicking that accompany a night terror may frighten parents who **fear** the child is having a

seizure. It is not a seizure unless the behavior includes eyes rolling back in the head, stiffening of the body, and drooling. Most childhood night terrors will last about 10 minutes.

Resources

BOOKS

Schroeder, Carolyn S., and Betty N. Gordon. *Assessment & Treatment of Childhood Problems*, 2nd ed. New York: Guilford Press, 2002.

ORGANIZATIONS

National Sleep Foundation. 1522 K Street, NW, Suite 500, Washington, DC 20005. Web site: <www.livingwithillness.com/id174.htm>.

WEB SITES

Driver, Helen. "Parasomnias." *Canadian Sleep Society.* Available online at <www.css.to/sleep/disorders/ parasomnia.htm> (accessed October 12, 2004).

Harvie, Jeni. "Disorders: A Wake-up Call for Parents." *Sydney Morning Herald*, January 29, 2004. Available online at <www.smh.com.au/articles/2004/01/29/ 10750881124899.html> (accessed October 7, 2004).

"Nightmares and Night Terrors." *Cincinnati Children's Hospital Medical Center.* Available online at <www.cincinnatichildrens.org/health/info/growth/ diagnose/nightmares.htm> (accessed October 12, 2004).

"Nightmares and Night Terrors in Children." *American Academy of Family Physicians.* Available online at <http:// familydoctor.org/566.xml> (accessed October 12, 2004).

Night Terror Resource Center. Available online at <www.nightterrors.org> (accessed October 12, 2004).

"Sleep Behavior Problems (Parasomnias)." *Kids Health for Parents.* Available online at <www.kidshealth.org/parent/ general/sleep/parasomnia.html> (accessed October 12, 2004).

"Sleep Problems in Children." *Sleep Matters*, March 31, 2004. Available online at <www.sleepfoundation.org/features/ children_sleep_problems.cfm#nightmares> (accessed October 12, 2004).

Clare Hanrahan

Nightmares

Definition

Nightmares are a type of **sleep** disruption, or parasomnia, characterized by frightening psychological content. Nightmares provoke a feeling of imminent physical danger with a sensation of being trapped or suffocated. These frightening dreams occur during rapid eye movement sleep (REM), or dream-time sleep, and trigger a partial or full awakening. Nightmares are a universal human experience occurring throughout the lifespan. They are especially common in early childhood and involve activation of the limbic brain, particularly the area that mediates negative emotion.

Description

Nightmares are greatly influenced by the particular stressors and anxieties present in the child's waking life. Typical childhood nightmares include dreams of **abandonment**; of being lost; of falling; or being chased, bitten, or eaten by a monster or hostile animal. Dream researchers have observed a developmental progression in the content and frequency of children's nightmares. A two-year-old dreamer may recall a fearful dream, but be unable to give form to the source of the threat. By the age of five, the frightened young dreamer may identify the attacker as a monster or wild animal. Older children who have developed more of an understanding of real-life dangers report dreams of pursuit by mean or bad people.

Children gradually develop the ability to understand the difference between dreams and reality. Very young children have great difficulty believing that the dream is not real. By three to four years of age, however, most children can distinguish between the nightmare content and their waking reality.

When a child is awakened by a nightmare she will soon become fully alert and able to remember the scary dream in elaborate detail, expressing emotions appropriate to the dream content. The frightened child will resist returning to bed and often seek the comfort and reassurance of a parent or caretaker. Nightmares are different than the non-dream sleep disturbance known as a night terror, which causes only a partial arousal from deep sleep and occurs during the first period of sleep known as slow-wave sleep (SWS). A child experiencing a night terror will be difficult to awaken or comfort, will not recognize her parent or caretaker, and will usually have no memory of the terrifying emotions that caused the sleep disturbance.

Demographics

Although infants spend most of their sleep time in the REM stage where dreams are known to occur, there is no reliable way to determine if dreaming actually takes place prior to the development of language and the reflective ability to think in images. Sleep researchers and developmental psychologists generally agree that nightmares first occur in children from 18 months to two years of age. By age three, more than half of all children will report having experienced a nightmare. The incidence of these frightening dreams increases considerably in elementary school children.

In a study of the dreams of four- to 12-year-old children published in the *Journal of Clinical Child Psychology* in 2000, researchers found that 67.7 percent of four to six year olds, 95.7 percent of seven to nine year olds, and 76.3 percent of ten to 12-year olds reported having had a nightmare experience. Nightmares are common throughout childhood, changing somewhat in content and frequency as children move through different developmental phases and acquire more skills to cope with the changing realities and stresses in their lives.

Causes and symptoms

Childhood nightmares are a normal maintenance function of the developing brain. They are a means of integrating recent and past learning and of establishing psychological equilibrium. Children who have not yet developed sufficient coping mechanisms to deal with many normal childhood fears and problems may feel overwhelmed and insecure. These distressing emotions provide the basis for nightmares. Common stressful events include moving to a different neighborhood or school, encountering a schoolyard bully, watching a horror movie or a violent television or video program, the birth of a sibling, ongoing conflict with siblings, parental marital problems, or any of numerous other stressful situations that may add to a child's sense of vulnerability or powerlessness.

Nightmares may increase and intensify following particularly traumatic events such as the death of a parent, a sibling, or other loved one; parental **divorce** or separation; an injury, illness, or other medical crises; or witnessing or being subjected to physical or verbal violence or sexual abuse. Children who have been traumatized may suffer ongoing post-traumatic stress and express it through recurring nightmares.

Certain medications used to treat **asthma**, **allergies**, and seizures can be a causal factor in the onset of sleep disturbances and nightmares. Abrupt withdrawal from drugs or medications, including barbiturates and benzodiazepines, can also induce these sleep disturbances. Illness with high **fever** may bring about delirium with frightening episodes of nighttime awakening. The following behaviors are usually present in a normal nightmare episode:

- Child awakens during the last third of her sleep period.
- Child is frightened and becomes fully alert.
- Child can describe the frightening dream in detail.
- Child seeks and responds to comfort and reassurance from a parent or caretaker.
- Child fears a recurrence of the frightful dream and may resist a return to bed.

When to call the doctor

If a child's nightmares increase in frequency and intensity, it is important to consult a physician or pediatrician to determine if the sleep disruption is due to any injury, illness, or infection, or if it might be caused by the use of or change in medications. Disturbed sleeping patterns in children are also present in some cases of juvenile rheumatoid arthritis, **autism**, and fibromyalgia.

Nightmares usually diminish in frequency and intensity over time. Recurring nightmares may indicate an ongoing problem that the child is having difficulty resolving. A child who is losing sleep and whose fears persist during day-time hours may benefit from the help of a pediatric psychotherapist in developing coping strategies for the stress and **anxiety** expressed through the dreams.

Diagnosis

Parental observation of the child's sleeping patterns and careful record-keeping of symptoms of any sleep disruption through use of a sleep journal will usually reveal any parasomnia patterns that may require professional **assessment**.

Treatment

Parents or caretakers should take into account the age and developmental maturity of their child when responding to the fears and anxieties that a nightmare brings to the surface. The child's ability to understand that the nightmare is not real and that it is an event happening only within their own mind increases with age. The nightmare reflects real fears and stressful circumstances present in the child's waking life. A parent's willingness to listen to and sympathize with a child's fears provides a necessary validation of the child's experience and helps to calm the child's anxiety. Very young children who lack the verbal skills to describe the frightening dream may require more reassurances that they are safe and more time in the comforting presence of a parent or caretaker before they are ready to return to bed.

Anne Sayre Wiseman, writing in her book *Nightmare Help: A Guide for Parents and Teachers*, suggests that parents approach the nightmare as a dream story with a problem to be solved. Parents who act as dream guides can help their children to find their own solution to the dream problem. The parents' goal, Wiseman counsels, is to "encourage autonomy so the child learns to empower themselves at whatever level they can handle."

Alan Siegel and Kelly Bulkeley, writing in their book, *Dreamcatching: Every Parent's Guide to Exploring and Understanding Children's Dreams and Nightmares*, suggest four beneficial remedies to help a child cope with disturbing nightmares. "The Four R's" of nightmare relief are:

- Reassurance: Provide physical and emotional reassurance and a listening ear so the frightened child will feel safe enough to share the dream images.
- Rescripting: Discuss the dream images with the child and work together with the frightened dreamer to imagine changes in the outcome. Encourage the child to express the images through artwork, fantasy, drama, and writing.
- Rehearsal: Encourage the child to imagine how the various alternative dream endings might change and assist the child in working through the different outcomes to find those that restore a sense of control and safety.
- Resolution: Work with the child to help her discover and acknowledge the life problems and stressful circumstances that may be reflected in the nightmare.

Nightmares are a common childhood parasomnia and medication is rarely indicated. Other parasomnias, such as **night terrors** and night walking, may call for medication if other interventions and treatments fail to relieve seriously disruptive symptoms.

Alternative treatment

Teaching the child simple relaxation skills through guided imagery will provide a valuable self-help resource that may minimize bed-time anxiety. Older children can be encouraged to connect with an "inner guide" as a source of strength when they are awakened by frightening dreams. Inner guides may take the form of a loving voice within that the child can listen for during times of **fear** or a beloved animal that they may call upon as a companionable inner helper when dealing with problems presented in scary dreams.

Nightmares

Preventing Nightmares

Have the child go to bed about the same time every day.
Avoid eating or exercising before bed.
Avoid scary books or movies before bed.
Put the child to sleep with a favorite stuffed toy or special blanket.
Keep a nightlight on in the child's room.
Keep the door to the child's room open.

(Table by GGS Information Services.)

Nutritional concerns

Nightmares are a sleep disturbance that is part of a normal adaptive mechanism of the developing child. They are usually not caused by a child's diet. However fatty foods or spicy meals that may bring about digestive distress at bedtime may trigger sleep disturbances and awaken a child out of an otherwise peaceful slumber.

Prognosis

Childhood nightmares are a normal process of coping with new challenges and integrating new life experiences into the child's understanding of the world. With guidance from a sensitive parent, a child's nightmares can provide an opportunity for parents and children to gain a deeper understanding of, and find solutions to childhood anxieties and insecurities.

Prevention

Nightmares are part of the normal developmental process that literally provide a "wake-up" call to both parent and child to pay attention to strong feelings and problems that may require some resolution. Nightmares diminish as children feel more confidence and control in their lives. If nightmares persist and intensify they may indicate a situation in the child's life that needs to be changed rather than worked through with dream problem-solving.

Establishing a regular bedtime schedule and routine, including a calming-down period prior to sleep, will help reduce the number of sleep disruptions. Eliminating the stimulation of television or **video games** at bedtime, particularly violent television shows, movies, and games may reduce the nightmares brought about by these unnecessary and sometimes disturbing stimulations.

Parental concerns

Sleep disruptions throughout childhood also cause disruptions for the entire **family**, particularly parents who must attend to the frightened child and soothe the child back to sleep. Childhood sleep disruptions that persist over time may interfere with the normal sleep-wake cycle of the caregivers. Loss of sleep has a cumulative impact on the well being of both children and adults. Parents may become anxious in sympathy with the child and lie awake in worry long after the frightened dreamer has returned to sleep. There are many good books available to help a parent understand the normal sleep-wake cycles of children and the common parasomnias that all children experience. This knowledge can bring much needed peace of mind and help the parent determine when professional assessment and assistance is appropriate.

Resources

BOOKS

Hobson, J. Allan. *Dreaming: An Introduction to the Science of Sleep.* Oxford: Oxford University Press, 2002.

Moorcroft, William H. *Understanding Sleep and Dreaming.* New York: Kluwer Academic/Plenum Publishers, 2003.

Schroeder, Carolyn S., and Betty N. Gordon. *Assessment and Treatment of Childhood Problems*, 2nd ed. New York: Guildford Press, 2002.

PERIODICALS

Muris, P., et al. "Fears, Worries, and Scary Dreams in 4 to 12 Year Old Children: Their Content, Developmental

Pattern, and Origins." *Journal of Clinical Child Psychology* 29, no. 1 (2000): 43–52. Available online at <www.leaonline.com/doi/abs/10.1207/S15374424jccp2901_5> (accessed August 2, 2004).

ORGANIZATIONS

National Sleep Foundation. 1522 K Street, NW, Suite 500, Washington, DC 20005. Web site: <www.livingwithillness.com/id174.htm>.

WEB SITES

Driver, Helen. "Parasomnias." *Canadian Sleep Society.* Available online at <www.css.to/sleep/disorders/parasomnia.htm> (accessed October 6, 2004).

Harvie, Jeni. "Disorders: A Wake-up Call for Parents." *Sydney Morning Herald*, January 29, 2004. Available online at <www.smh.com.au/articles/2004/01/29/10750881124899.html> (accessed October 7, 2004).

National Sleep Foundation. "Sleep Matters." *Sleep Problems in Children*, Winter 2004. Available online at <www.sleepfoundation.org/features/children_sleep_problems.cfm> (accessed October 6, 2004).

"Nightmares and Night Terrors." *Cincinnati Children's Hospital Medical Center.* Available online at <www.cincinnatichildrens.org/health/info/growth/diagnose/nightmares.htm> (accessed October 6, 2004).

"Nightmares and Night Terrors in Children." *American Academy of Family Physicians.* Available online at <www.aafp.org/afp/20000401/2044ph.html> (accessed October 7, 2004).

Siegel, Alan. *Nightmare Remedies: Helping Your Child Tame the Demons of the Night.* Available online at <www.dreamwisdom.info/library/nightmare_remedies_children_print.htm> (accessed October 6, 2004).

"Sleep Behavior Problems (Parasomnias)." *Kids Health for Parents.* Available online at <www.kidshealth.org/parent/general/sleep/parasomnia.html> (accessed October 6, 2004).

Clare Hanrahan

Nonsteroidal anti-inflammatory drugs

Definition

Nonsteroidal anti-inflammatory drugs are medicines that relieve **pain**, swelling, stiffness, and inflammation.

Description

Nonsteroidal anti-inflammatory drugs (NSAIDs) are prescribed for a variety of painful conditions, including arthritis, bursitis, tendonitis, gout, menstrual cramps, **sprains**, **strains**, and other injuries.

Although the NSAIDs are often discussed as a group, not all are approved for use in children. As of 2004, the following drugs are approved for pediatric use:

- Ibuprofen (Advil, Motrin, Nuprin).

- Indomethicin (Indocin), not recommended for children under the age of 14 except in circumstances that warrant the risk. Indomethicin has special application in some infants born with heart problems.

- Ketoprofen (Orudis, Oruvail), not given to children under the age of 16 unless directed by a physician.

- Ketorolac tromethamine (Toradol), not approved for use in children but has been reported safe by some pediatric authorities.

- Meclofenamate sodium, safety and efficacy in children under 14 years of age has not been established.

- Mefenamic acid (Ponstel), safety and efficacy in children under 14 years of age has not been established.

- Naproxen (Aleve, Anaprox, Naprosyn), safety and efficacy in children under two years of age has not been established.

- Tolmetin sodium (Tolectin), safety and efficacy in children under two years of age has not been established.

Other NSAIDs have been used in pediatric therapy, but should not be considered as first choice for treatment of children or adolescents.

A new class of NSAIDs, called COX-2 inhibitors, have a lower risk of causing ulcers than do the traditional NSAIDs. These drugs may be appropriate for use in older teenagers but have not been approved for use in younger children, and there is some evidence that they are inappropriate for infants.

General use

Nonsteroidal anti-inflammatory drugs relieve pain, stiffness, swelling, and inflammation, but they do not cure the diseases or injuries responsible for these problems. Two drugs in this category, ibuprofen and naproxen, also reduce **fever**. Some nonsteroidal anti-inflammatory drugs can be bought without a prescription; others are available only with a prescription from a physician or dentist.

Precautions

Children with certain medical conditions and those who are taking some other medicines can have problems if they take nonsteroidal anti-inflammatory drugs. Before giving children these drugs, parents need to let the physician know about any of the following conditions.

Allergies

The physician needs to know about any **allergies** to foods, dyes, preservatives, or other substances. For children who have had reactions to nonsteroidal anti-inflammatory drugs in the past, parents should check with a physician before having these drugs prescribed again.

Pregnancy

Teens and young women who are pregnant or who plan to become pregnant should check with their physicians before taking these medicines. Whether nonsteroidal anti-inflammatory drugs cause birth defects in people is unknown, but some do cause birth defects in laboratory animals. If taken late in pregnancy, these drugs may prolong pregnancy, lengthen labor time, cause problems during delivery, or affect the heart or blood flow of the fetus.

Breastfeeding

Some nonsteroidal anti-inflammatory drugs pass into breast milk. Women who are breastfeeding their babies should check with their physicians before taking these drugs.

Other medical conditions

A number of medical conditions may influence the effects of nonsteroidal anti-inflammatory drugs. Parents of children and teens who have any of the conditions listed below should tell their physician about the condition before having nonsteroidal anti-inflammatory drugs prescribed.

- stomach or intestinal problems, such as colitis or Crohn's disease
- liver disease
- current or past kidney disease or current or past kidney stones
- heart disease
- high blood pressure
- blood disorders, such as anemia, low **platelet count**, low white blood cell count
- bleeding problems
- diabetes mellitus
- hemorrhoids, rectal bleeding, or rectal irritation
- asthma
- epilepsy
- systemic lupus erythematosus
- diseases of the blood vessels, such as polymyalgia rheumatica and temporal arteritis
- fluid retention
- alcohol abuse
- mental illness

Side effects

The most common side effects are stomach pain or cramps, **nausea**, **vomiting**, indigestion, **diarrhea**, heartburn, **headache**, **dizziness** or lightheadedness, and drowsiness. As the patient's body adjusts to the medicine, these symptoms usually disappear. If they do not, the physician who prescribed the medicine should be contacted.

Serious side effects are rare, but do sometimes occur. If any of the following side effects occur, patients should stop taking the medicine and get emergency medical care immediately:

- swelling or puffiness of the face
- swelling of the hands, feet, or lower legs
- rapid weight gain
- fainting
- breathing problems
- fast or irregular heartbeat
- tightness in the chest

Other side effects do not require emergency medical care, but should have medical attention. If any of the following side effects occur, patients should stop taking the medicine and the physician who prescribed the medicine should be called as soon as possible:

- severe pain, cramps, or burning in the stomach or abdomen
- convulsions
- fever
- severe nausea, heartburn, or indigestion
- white spots or sores in the mouth or on the lips
- rashes or red spots on the skin
- any unusual bleeding, including nosebleeds and spitting up or vomiting blood or dark material
- black, tarry stool

• chest pain

• unusual bruising

• severe headaches

A number of less common, temporary side effects are also possible. They usually do not need medical attention and will disappear once the body adjusts to the medicine. If they continue or interfere with normal activity, the physician should be contacted. Among these side effects are:

• gas, bloating, or constipation

• bitter taste or other taste changes

• sweating

• restlessness, irritability, anxiety

• trembling or twitching

Interactions

Nonsteroidal anti-inflammatory drugs may interact with a variety of other medicines. When interaction occurs, the effects of the drugs may change, and the risk of side effects may be greater. Physicians prescribing this drug should know all other medicines the patient is already taking. Among the drugs that may interact with nonsteroidal anti-inflammatory drugs are:

• blood thinning drugs, such as warfarin (Coumadin)

• other nonsteroidal anti-inflammatory drugs

• heparin

• tetracyclines

• cyclosprorine

• digitalis drugs

• lithium

• phenytoin (Dilantin)

• zidovudine (AZT, Retrovir)

NSAIDs may also interact with certain herbal preparations sold as dietary supplements. Among the herbs known to interact with NSAIDs are bearberry (*Arctostaphylos uva-ursi*), feverfew (*Tanacetum parthenium*), evening primrose (*Oenothera biennis*), and gossypol, a pigment obtained from cottonseed oil and used as a male contraceptive. In most cases, the herb increases the tendency of NSAIDs to irritate the digestive tract. It is just as important for doctors to know which herbal remedies the patient is taking on a regular basis as it is for doctors to know the other prescription medications which are being taken.

KEY TERMS

Anemia—A lack of hemoglobin, the compound in blood that carries oxygen from the lungs throughout the body and brings waste carbon dioxide from the cells to the lungs, where it is released.

Bursitis—Inflammation of the tissue around a joint.

Colitis—Inflammation of the colon (large bowel).

COX-2 inhibitors—A class of newer NSAIDs that are less likely to cause side effects in the digestive tract. COX-2 inhibitors work by inhibiting the production of cyclooxygenase-2, an enzyme involved in inflammation.

Inflammation—Pain, redness, swelling, and heat that usually develop in response to injury or illness.

Salicylates—A group of drugs that includes aspirin and related compounds. Salicylates are used to relieve pain, reduce inflammation, and lower fever.

Tendonitis—Inflammation of a tendon, which is a tough band of tissue that connects muscle to bone.

Prevention

Many serious digestive system effects of NSAIDs can be prevented by taking mysoprostol (Cytotec), but this drug is only appropriate for patients with a high risk of ulcers. It is not called for when the NSAID is being used for a short period of time or in patients with other risk factors. Stomach upset can often be prevented by taking NSAIDs with food or milk.

Parental concerns

NSAIDs are very safe when used properly over a short period of time. They should not be used for longer periods or in larger doses than indicated on the label. If NSAIDs are to be used for prolonged periods, as in juvenile rheumatoid arthritis, there is a risk of potentially serious stomach and intestinal problems.

Resources

BOOKS

Pelletier, Kenneth R. *The Best Alternative Medicine, Part I: Western Herbal Medicine.* New York: Simon and Schuster, 2002.

PERIODICALS

Gordon, D. B. "Nonopioid and Adjuvant Analgesics in Chronic Pain Management: Strategies for Effective Use." *Nursing Clinics of North America* 38 (September 2003): 447–464.

Small, R. C., and A. Schuna. "Optimizing Outcomes in Rheumatoid Arthritis." *Journal of the American Pharmaceutical Association* 43, no. 5, suppl. 1 (September-October 2003): S16–S17.

Stempak, D., et al. "Single-dose and steady-state pharmacokinetics of celecoxib in children." *Clinical Pharmacological Therapy* 72, no. 5 (November 2002): 490–497.

ORGANIZATIONS

U. S. Food and Drug Administration (FDA). 5600 Fishers Lane, Rockville, MD 20857. Web site: <http://www.fda.gov>.

WEB SITES

Pediatric Rheumatology Online Journal. Available online at <www.pedrheumonlinejournal.org/> (accessed on September 29, 2004).

Nancy Ross-Flanigan
Rebecca J. Frey, PhD
Samuel Uretsky, PharmD

Nontropical sprue *see* **Celiac disease**

Nose injuries *see* **Nasal trauma**

Nosebleed

Definition

A nosebleed, also called epistaxis, is a loss of blood from any blood vessel in the nose. It usually appears in only one nostril.

Description

Although unexpected or persistent bleeding from anywhere is a warning sign of **cancer** and should be investigated, nosebleeds are rarely a sign of serious illness. They are usually the result of minor injury or irritation.

Nosebleeds most often come from the front of the septum, the cartilage that separates the nose into two nostrils. These anterior nosebleeds comprise 80 percent of all nosebleeds. A mass of blood vessels, called Kiesselbach's plexus, lie on either side of the septum. These blood vessels are easy to injure and bleeding can occur.

Posterior nosebleeds, which come from the back of the nose, are less common and much harder to manage. Bleeding usually begins in the upper part of the nose and flows toward the throat and mouth where it is swallowed. It is difficult to determine how much blood is lost in these nosebleeds.

Demographics

Though it is a common misconception that children are more susceptible to nosebleeds than adults, research has found that nosebleeds are more prevalent in older adults and more often are a sign of other health problems. Nosebleeds do, however, occur frequently in childhood. About 30 percent of children up to five years of age have had spontaneous nosebleeds that appeared without apparent injury to the nose. Of children six to ten years of age, 56 percent have had them and 64 percent of pre-adolescents and adolescents from 11 to 15 have as well. Moreover, over half of adults with recurring nosebleeds had them as children. Only about 10 percent of children with frequent nosebleeds have been found to have a previously undiagnosed bleeding disorder.

Rarely, menstruating women, even adolescents, who have endometriosis, a condition in which tissues resembling the lining of the uterus occur abnormally in other parts of the pelvic cavity and sometimes in other parts of the body, can have cyclical nosebleeds with their menstrual periods.

Causes and symptoms

Causes

The most common cause of nosebleeds is injury from picking or blowing the nose. People with respiratory **allergies**, hay fever, and sinus infections have swollen nasal membranes that are fragile and more likely to bleed. Physical injury to the nose from falls, **sports**, or fighting can also cause nosebleeds. Chemical irritants such as cleaning products, aerosols, and paint can irritate the nose, sometimes resulting in nosebleeds. In addition, some drugs, such as cocaine, inflame the nose, causing it to bleed. Children with deviated septums or crooked noses are also prone to nosebleeds.

Nosebleeds occur more frequently in the winter when the air is cold outside and homes are filled with dry air from furnaces and other heating sources. Changes from cold to warm air or dry to humid air stress the delicate membranes of the nose and make it vulnerable to injury and bleeding. Also, flu, colds, and other respiratory illnesses seem to occur more often in the winter. These also stress the nasal passages and make injury more likely. Bleeding from the nose, therefore, usually follows these seasonal stresses.

A nosebleed can also be an indication of illness. Certain blood disorders, such as **hemophilia**, can cause the nose to bleed. In this case, medical help should be sought immediately. Some head injuries produce nosebleeds. Uncontrolled high blood pressure, liver disease, leukemia, and tumors of the nasal passages and the brain can also cause the nose to bleed.

Even some medications can cause nosebleeds. Anticoagulants, medications used to thin the blood, including aspirin, can cause spontaneous bleeding from the nose. Overuse of nasal sprays can also produce nosebleeds. In addition, nosebleeds can be a side effect of alcohol abuse.

Nosebleeds in children can sometimes be caused by children putting objects into their noses. The object can tear the delicate membranes of the nose. Objects inserted into the nose can also cause obstruction of airflow and may need to be removed by a doctor.

Symptoms

Bleeding from one or both nostrils may be a trickle or a flood. Sometimes, it accompanies direct injury to the nose as in a sports injury or in picking the nose or too vigorous nose blowing. Children may experience frequent swallowing or a sensation of fluid in the back of the nose and throat.

When to call the doctor

If the bleeding does not stop after 20 minutes, it is necessary to seek medical help. Also, if there is a known or suspected **head injury** accompanying the nosebleed, there may be a skull fracture or brain disorder. In this case, the child should be taken to the emergency room immediately. In addition, if the nose is misshapen, especially after an accident, fall, or injury, it may be broken and will need to be evaluated by a doctor. Frequent nosebleeds, especially if they are occurring more often and are not due to colds, allergies, or trauma, will need to be seen by a doctor as well.

It may be a medical emergency if the bleeding is rapid or if there is a lot of blood. If the child feels faint or weak during a nosebleed, it may be do to blood loss and the child should see the doctor immediately.

Diagnosis

Bleeding from the nose is the obvious determinant of a nosebleed. The severity of it, however, may require blood work to look for bleeding disorders, diseases of the blood, or infections. X rays may be taken to determine if there has been a head injury or abnormalities within the structure of the nose. To further examine the nose, the doctor may perform a nasal endoscopy, a procedure that involves inserting a tiny camera into the nose to look at blood vessels and nasal structures.

Treatment

The first line of treatment is to gently pinch the nostrils together with the thumb and forefinger, while sitting upright and breathing through the mouth, for five to ten minutes. Leaning forward will prevent the child from swallowing blood. After at least five minutes, the parent or child can check to see if the bleeding has stopped. If it has not, then the pinching of the nose should be resumed and the child or parent should wait another five minutes. Most nosebleeds will stop within this time period, especially if the child is encouraged to remain calm. **Anxiety** or panic will cause blood to flow more rapidly and can hinder this self-healing process. It is very important for the child not to lie down while having a nosebleed.

Sometimes, a cold compress or crushed ice in a washcloth or plastic bag can be placed across the bridge of the nose and cheeks to encourage clotting. It is important not to pack the inside of the nose with gauze since this might further injure the nose.

In 2004, a new over-the-counter product was introduced for a quick home treatment for simple nosebleed. Called Nosebleed QR (Quick Relief), the product is composed of a hydrophilic polymer, a synthetic powder that absorbs blood, and potassium salt that aids in scab formation. The parent or child sprinkles the product onto a swab and coats the nostril then pinches the nose for 15 to 20 seconds. The product stops bleeding within one minute. However, it does sting and may not be a comfortable product to use with children.

Alternative treatment

Estrogen cream, the same preparation used to revitalize vaginal tissue, can toughen fragile blood vessels in the anterior septum and forestall the need for cauterization. Botanical medicines known as stiptics, which slow down and can stop bleeding, may be taken internally or applied topically. Some of the plants used are achillea (yarrow), trillium, geranium, and shepherd's purse (*Capsella bursa*).

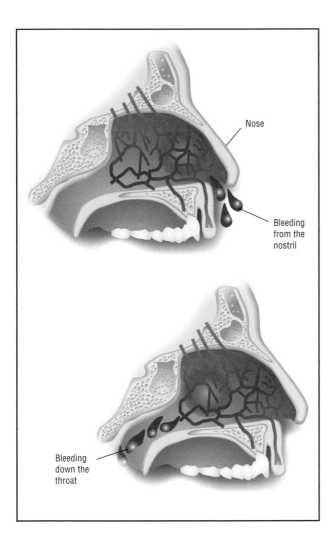

Anatomical sideview of a nosebleed. *(Illustration by GGS Information Services)*

KEY TERMS

Deviated septum—A shift in the position of the nasal septum, the partition that divides the two nasal cavities.

Endometriosis—A condition in which the tissue that normally lines the uterus (endometrium) grows in other areas of the body, causing pain, irregular bleeding, and frequently, infertility.

Hemophilia—Any of several hereditary blood coagulation disorders occurring almost exclusively in males. Because blood does not clot properly, even minor injuries can cause significant blood loss that may require a blood transfusion, with its associated minor risk of infection.

Kiesselbach's plexus—The mass of blood vessels on either side of the septum.

Nasal endoscopy—A procedure that involves inserting a tiny camera into the nose in order to look at blood vessels and nasal structures.

Otorhinolaryngologist—An ear, nose, and throat specialist.

Septum—A wall or partition. Often refers to the muscular wall dividing the left and right heart chambers or the partition in the nose that separates the two nostrils. Also refers to an abnormal fold of tissue down that center of the uterus that can cause infertility.

Homeopathic remedies can be one of the quickest and most effective treatments for nosebleeds. One well known remedy is phosphorus.

Another natural treatment includes swabbing the nose with vitamin E oil for three days. If nosebleeds recur within that time, it is recommended to take 500 mg of bioflavonoids twice a day. Bioflavonoids are antioxidants found in citrus fruits that help strengthen blood vessels.

Prognosis

Most common nosebleeds are easily managed and can be prevented. Children usually recover quickly. Serious nosebleeds need further investigation but are usually controlled by treating the underlying cause.

Prevention

Keeping the home cooler in winter and using a humidifier help keep the nasal passages moist and reduce the risk of nosebleeds due to dry air. Some doctors also recommend using a nasal saline spray to enhance moisture in the nose.

Also, before sending children out to **play** on cold, dry days, parents can put a bit of petroleum jelly on a cotton swab and wipe it just inside their children's nostrils. This keeps the nose from drying out and producing surface cracks which can damage blood vessels in the lining of the nose and cause bleeding. Some parents routinely apply a thin layer of A & D ointment, petroleum jelly, or a mentholated salve around their children's noses at night as well as when they go outside.

Gently blowing the nose and not picking it will also prevent nosebleeds. This is especially important for several hours after nasal bleeding has stopped. In some cases, strong sniffing is also discouraged to reduce further stress on the delicate tissues of the nose. Keeping the mouth open when sneezing can also reduce stress on the nose.

Treatment of hay fever and other respiratory allergies decreases sneezing and nasal inflammation. If a child is prone to sinus infections, some doctors may also use prophylactic or preventative treatment similar to allergy management.

Parental concerns

Nosebleeds can be frightening for children. Seeing any amount of blood may cause some children to panic or even faint. It is important to treat the nosebleed matter-of-factly as any parent would handle any other childhood scrape or wound. The parent's calm helps the child remain calm while waiting for the natural blood clotting mechanisms of the body to work. Parents should also be aware of any abnormal amount of blood during a nosebleed and make note of any recent falls or head injuries. These observations will inform parents about when to seek medical or emergency help.

Resources

PERIODICALS

"A Natural Solution for Nosebleeds: I Get Frequent Nosebleeds. Will Taking Bioflavonoids Help?" *Natural Health* 33 (April 2003).

"Dabbing That Bloody Nose." *Pediatrics for Parents* 19 (December 2001): 5.

"Nosebleeds Are Nothing to Sneeze At." *Nutrition Health Review* (Fall 2002): 6.

Pouliot, Janine S. "Nosing around for a Remedy." *Better Homes and Gardens* 82 (February 2004): 222.

"Quicker Relief for Nosebleeds." *Consumer Reports* 69 (February 2004): 45.

Janie Franz
J. Ricker Polsdorfer

NSAIDs *see* Nonsteroidal anti-inflammatory drugs

Numbness and tingling

Definition

Numbness and tingling are decreased or abnormal sensations caused by altered sensory nerve function.

Description

The feeling of having a foot "fall asleep" is a familiar one. This same combination of numbness and tingling can occur in any region of the body and may be caused by a wide variety of disorders. Sensations such as these, which occur without any associated stimulus, are called paresthesias. Other types of paresthesias include feelings of cold, warmth, burning, **itching**, and skin crawling.

Demographics

People of all ages experience episodes of numbness and tingling. These generally become more common as people age. Episodes of numbness and tingling are more common among people with diabetes, **hypothyroidism**, **alcoholism**, **malnutrition**, or who experience mechanical trauma, especially to their limbs, neck or spine.

Causes and symptoms

Causes

Sensation is carried to the brain by neurons (nerve cells) running from the outer parts of the body to the spinal cord in bundles called nerves. In the spinal cord, these neurons make connections with other neurons that run up to the brain. Paresthesias are caused by disturbances in the function of neurons in the sensory pathway. This disturbance can occur in the central nervous system (the brain and spinal cord), the nerve roots that are attached to the spinal cord, or the peripheral nervous system (nerves outside the brain and spinal cord).

Peripheral disturbances are the most common cause of paresthesias. "Falling asleep" occurs when the blood supply to a nerve is cut off—a condition called ischemia. Ischemia usually occurs when an artery is compressed as it passes through a tightly flexed joint. Sleeping with the arms above the head or sitting with the legs tightly crossed frequently cause numbness and tingling.

Direct compression of the nerve also causes paresthesias. Compression can be short-lived, as when a heavy backpack compresses the nerves passing across the shoulders. Compression may also be chronic. Chronic nerve compression occurs in entrapment syndromes. The most common example is carpal tunnel syndrome, which occurs when the median nerve is compressed as it passes through a narrow channel in the wrist. Repetitive motion or prolonged vibration can cause the lining of the channel to swell and press on the nerve. Chronic nerve root compression, or radiculopathy, can occur in disk disease or spinal arthritis.

Other causes of paresthesias related to disorders of the peripheral nerves include the following:

- metabolic or nutritional disturbances, including diabetes, hypothyroidism (a condition caused by too little activity of the thyroid gland), alcoholism, malnutrition, and vitamin B_{12} deficiency

- trauma, including injuries that crush, sever, or pull on nerves

- inflammation

- connective tissue disease, including arthritis, systemic lupus erythematosus (a chronic inflammatory disease that affects many systems of the body, including the nervous system), polyarteritis nodosa (a vascular disease that causes widespread inflammation and ischemia of small and medium-size arteries), and Sjögren's syndrome (a disorder marked by insufficient moisture in the tear ducts, salivary glands, and other glands)

- toxins, including heavy metals (metallic elements such as arsenic, lead, and mercury which can, in large amounts, cause **poisoning**), certain medications **antibiotics** and **chemotherapy** agents, solvents, and overdose of pyridoxine (vitamin B_6)

- malignancy

- infections, including **Lyme disease**, human **immunodeficiency** virus (HIV), and leprosy

- hereditary disease, including **Charcot-Marie-Tooth disease** (a disorder that causes wasting of the leg muscles, resulting in malformation of the foot), porphyria (a group of disorders in which there is abnormally increased production of substances called porphyrins), and Denny-Brown's syndrome (a disorder of the nerve root)

Paresthesias can also be caused by central nervous system disturbances, including **stroke**, transient ischemic attack (TIA), tumor, trauma, multiple sclerosis, or infection.

Symptoms

Sensory nerves supply or innervate particular regions of the body. Determining the distribution of symptoms is an important way to identify the nerves involved. For instance, the median nerve innervates the thumb, the first two fingers, half of the ring finger, and the part of the hand to which they connect. The ulnar nerve innervates the other half of the ring finger, the little finger, and the remainder of the hand. Distribution of symptoms may also aid diagnosis of the underlying disease. Diabetes usually causes a symmetrical glove-and-stocking distribution in the hands and feet. Multiple sclerosis may cause symptoms in several, widely separated areas.

Other symptoms may accompany paresthesias, depending on the type and severity of the nerve disturbance. For instance, weakness may accompany damage to nerves that carry both sensory and motor neurons. (Motor neurons are those that carry messages outward from the brain.)

When to call the doctor

A healthcare professional should be consulted when instances of numbness or tingling last for more than a few hours.

Diagnosis

A careful history of the affected individual is needed for a diagnosis of paresthesias. The medical history should focus on the onset, duration, and location of symptoms. The history may also reveal current related medical problems and recent or past exposure to drugs, toxins, infection, or trauma. The **family** medical history may suggest a familial disorder. A work history may reveal repetitive motion, chronic vibration, or industrial chemical exposure.

The physical and neurological examination tests for distribution of symptoms and alterations in reflexes, sensation, or strength. The distribution of symptoms may be mapped by successive stimulation over the affected area of the body.

Lab tests for paresthesia may include blood tests and urinalysis to detect metabolic or nutritional abnormalities. Other tests are used to look for specific suspected causes. Nerve conduction velocity tests, electromyography, and imaging studies of the affected area may be employed. Nerve biopsy may be indicated in selected cases.

Treatment

Treatment of paresthesias depends on the underlying cause. For limbs that have "fallen asleep," restoring circulation by stretching, exercising, or massaging the affected limb can quickly dissipate the numbness and tingling. Physical therapy can also be helpful. If the paresthesia is caused by a chronic disease such as diabetes or occurs as a complication of treatments such as chemotherapy, most treatments are aimed at relieving symptoms. Anti-inflammatory drugs such as aspirin or ibuprofen are recommended if symptoms are mild. In more difficult cases, antidepressant drugs such as amitriptyline (Elavil) are sometimes prescribed. These drugs are given at a much lower dosage for this purpose than for relief of depression. They are thought to help because they alter the body's perception of **pain**. In severe cases, opium derivatives such as codeine can be prescribed. In the early 2000s trials are being done to determine whether treatment with human nerve growth factor will be effective in regenerating the damaged nerves.

Several alternative treatments are available to help relieve symptoms of paresthesia. Nutritional therapy includes supplementation with B complex **vitamins**, especially vitamin B_{12} (intramuscular injection of vitamin B_{12} is most effective). Vitamin supplements should be used cautiously, however. Overdose of Vitamin B_6 is one of the causes of paresthesias. People experiencing paresthesia should also avoid alcohol. Acupuncture and massage are said to relieve symptoms. Self-massage with aromatic oils is sometimes helpful. The application of topical ointments containing capsaicin, the substance that makes hot peppers hot, provides relief for some. It may also be helpful to wear loosely fitting shoes and clothing. None of these alternatives should be used in place of traditional therapy for the underlying condition.

Prognosis

Treating the underlying disorder may reduce the occurrence of paresthesias. However, paresthesias resulting from damaged nerves may persist throughout or even beyond the recovery period. The overall prognosis depends on the cause.

Prevention

Preventing the underlying disorder may reduce the incidence of paresthesias. For those with frequent paresthesias caused by ischemia, changes in posture may help.

Nutritional concerns

Vitamin supplements should be used with caution as an overdose of vitamin B_6 is one of the causes of paresthesias. People experiencing paresthesia should avoid alcohol.

Parental concerns

Parents should monitor children who complain of numbness or tingling that lasts for more than a few minutes and fails to improve. They should recommend stretching and **exercise** and if relief does not come quickly, investigate other causes, such as clothing that is too tight.

KEY TERMS

Electrooculography (EOG)—A diagnostic test that records the electrical activity of the muscles that control eye movement.

Motor nerve—Motor or efferent nerve cells carry impulses from the brain to muscle or organ tissue.

Nerve condition velocity (NCV)—Technique for studying nerve or muscle disorders, measuring the speed at which nerves transmit signals.

Nerve growth factor—A protein resembling insulin that affects the growth and maintenance of nerve cells

Peripheral nervous system—The part of the nervous system that is outside the brain and spinal cord. Sensory, motor, and autonomic nerves are included.

Sensory nerves—Sensory or afferent nerves carry impulses of sensation from the periphery or outward parts of the body to the brain and spinal cord.

Resources

BOOKS

Asbury, Arthur K. "Approach to the patient with peripheral neuropathy." In *Harrison's Principles of Internal Medicine*, 15th ed. Edited by Eugene Braunwald, et al., New York: McGraw Hill, 2001, pp. 2498–2506.

Dyck, Patrick. *Peripheral Neuropathy*, 4th ed. New York: Elsevier, 2004.

Greenberg, David A., et al. *Clinical Neurology*, 5th ed. New York: McGraw Hill, 2002.

Griffin, John W. "Peripheral Neuropathies." In *Cecil Textbook of Medicine*, 22nd ed. Edited by Lee Goldman, et al. Philadelphia: Saunders, 2003, pp. 2379–86.

Nobak, C. R., et al. *Human Nervous System: Structure and Function*, 6th ed. Totawa, NJ: Humana Press, 2004.

PERIODICALS

Aldridge, T. "Diagnosing heel pain in adults." *American Family Physician* 70, no. 2 (2004): 332–8.

Carrero, G. "Paresthesia: what causes this sensory phenomenon?" *Regional Anesthesia and Pain Medicine* 29, no. 1 (2004): 69–70.

Hogan, Q. "Finding nerves is not simple." *Regional Anesthesia and Pain Medicine* 28, no. 5 (2004): 367–71.

Karaca, P., et al. "Painful paresthesiae are infrequent during brachial plexus localization using low-current peripheral nerve stimulation." *Regional Anesthesia and Pain Medicine* 28, no. 5 (2004): 380–3.

Nandi, D., and T. Z. Aziz. "Deep brain stimulation in the management of neuropathic pain and multiple sclerosis tremor." *Journal of Clinical Neurophysiology* 21, no. 1 (2004): 31–9.

Tuzun, E. H., et al. "A comparison study of quality of life in women with fibromyalgia and myofascial pain syndrome." *Disability Rehabilitation* 26, no. 4 (2004): 198–202.

ORGANIZATIONS

American Academy of Family Physicians. 11400 Tomahawk Creek Parkway, Leawood, KS 66211–2672. Web site: <www.aafp.org/>.

American Academy of Neurology. 1080 Montreal Avenue, St. Paul, Minnesota 55116. Web site: <www.aan.com/>.

American Academy of Pediatrics. 141 Northwest Point Boulevard, Elk Grove Village, IL 60007–1098. Web site: <www.aap.org/default.htm>.

American Academy of Physical Medicine and Rehabilitation. One IBM Plaza, Suite 2500, Chicago, IL 60611–3604. Web site: <www.aapmr.org/>.

American College of Occupational and Environmental Medicine. 55 West Seegers Road, Arlington Heights, IL 60005. Web site: <www.acoem.org/>.

American College of Physicians. 190 N Independence Mall West, Philadelphia, PA 19106–1572. Web site: <www.acponline.org/>.

American College of Sports Medicine. 401 W. Michigan St., Indianapolis, IN 46202–3233. Web site: <www.acsm.org/>.

WEB SITES

"Numbness and Tingling." *Medline Plus.* Available online at <www.nlm.nih.gov/medlineplus/ency/article/003206.htm> (accessed November 13, 2004).

"Numbness and Tingling." *University of Michigan Health System.* Available online at <www.med.umich.edu/obgyn/smartmoms/discomforts/numbness.htm> (accessed November 13, 2004).

"Paresthesia." *Family Practice Notebook.* Available online at <www.fpnotebook.com/NEU242.htm> (accessed November 13, 2004).

"Paresthesia Information Page." *National Institute of Neurological Disorders and Stroke.* Available online at <www.ninds.nih.gov/health_and_medical/disorders/paresthesia.htm> (accessed November 13, 2004).

L. Fleming Fallon, Jr., MD, DrPH

Nursemaid's elbow

Definition

Nursemaid's elbow is an injury to the ligament (strong band of tissue) that keeps the two bones of the forearm in the correct place.

Description

The two bones in the forearm are the radius and the ulna. The radius is on the thumb side of the forearm. The upper end of the radius is called the radius head. The radial head is held in place by a ligament called the annular ligament. When the annular ligament is torn, a part of it slides upward and becomes trapped in the elbow joint, which is very painful condition. The child holds the arm with the palm facing inward and the elbow bent. This injury is uncommon after the ages of three to four, due to stronger joints and ligaments. Also, youngsters are less likely to be in situations where this injury might occur.

Nursemaid's elbow is also called subluxation of the radial head, pulled elbow, slipped elbow, or toddler elbow.

Demographics

Nursemaid's elbow is a common occurrence in children from the ages of one to four or five. It is rarely seen after the age of six.

Causes and symptoms

Nursemaid's elbow is caused by a strong force on the elbow, such as a sudden pulling or yanking on the hand or forearm. This can occur when a child falls, when an adult pulls up a child's arm, to assist the child up a curb or step or to hurry the child along, or when a child falls away from an adult while being held by the arm. Swinging toddlers from the arms while playing can cause this injury. It can also occur when an infant rolls himself or herself over.

Symptoms of nursemaid's elbow include immediate **pain** in the injured arm, refusal or inability to move the injured arm, creating a condition called pseudo-paralysis, persistent crying, refusal to **play**, and **anxiety**. However each child may experience symptoms differently. These symptoms may also resemble other conditions or medical problems, so a physician should be consulted for a diagnosis.

Swinging a young child by the arms can cause nursemaid's elbow. *(© Raoul Minsart/Corbis.)*

When to call the doctor

The doctor should be called or the child should be taken to an emergency room when a child does not use the arm that has been injured, when the child seems to be in a lot of pain, or when there is a suspicion that someone has deliberately harmed the child.

After treatment for nursemaid's elbow, the doctor should be called if the child still refuses to use the arm six hours after it is put back into place; the child still has pain after 24 hours; the child's fingers get numb and tingly; or the child's elbow comes out of the socket again.

Diagnosis

The diagnosis of nursemaid's elbow is made through a physical examination by the child's physician. X rays of the elbow are usually not necessary.

Treatment

The child's arm should not be straightened or its position changed before the doctor examines it. An ice pack can be used, and the arm splinted in the position in which it is found. The area both above and below the elbow should be immobilized, including the shoulder and wrist if possible.

The physician or health care provider will move the bone and ligament back to their correct positions. This is an easy procedure that can be done in the office by supinating (externally rotating) the forearm (turning the thumb out with palm up), and then gently flexing the arm at the elbow (pushing the forearm up into the biceps). The ligament needs time to heal, so the child's arm should be treated gently after the procedure. The arm may be immobilized in a sling for one or two days, if desired.

Once the ligament and the radial head are returned to their proper position, the child can usually begin to use his or her arm again within a few minutes. Sometimes there is a short period of crying for a minute or two after the release. The earlier after the injury that the child is treated, the more rapid will be the recovery. Alternatively, if the problem has existed for some days, then relief from pain may not be so rapid. Bracing and **immo-**

KEY TERMS

Elbow—Hinged joint between the forearm and upper arm.

Ligament—A type of tough, fibrous tissue that connects bones or cartilage and provides support and strength to joints.

Nursemaid's elbow—An injury to the ligament (strong band of tissue) that keeps the two bones of the forearm in the correct place.

Radius—The bone of the forearm which joins the wrist on the same side as the thumb.

Ulna—One of the two bones of the forearm. Two pivot joints join it to the radius, one near the elbow, one near the wrist.

bilization is usually not required if this is the first occurrence of this condition. For repeat injuries, however, a posterior splint may be applied for several days. A few children may have swelling or pain in the joint. Regular doses of ibuprofen or other over-the-counter pain killers for a few days will help with the swelling and the pain.

If the child fails to use the arm after 15 minutes, the elbow should be x rayed to determine if it was fractured. If no fracture is found, the arm should be splinted and put into a sling, and the condition re-evaluated after 24 hours.

Prognosis

The child should be able to use the elbow after the injury has healed. However, once an elbow has been injured, it is more likely that it will happen again in the future if care is not taken to prevent further injury.

Prevention

A child should not be lifted or swung by the arms or hands nor should a child's arm be pulled hard. A small child should be lifted from under the arms.

Parental concerns

Parents should be aware of the damage to the ligament structures of the elbow and should not lift the child by the arm, as the pulled-elbow condition can reoccur up. Recurrence is especially likely for three to four weeks following the injury.

Unfortunately, nursemaid's elbow commonly occurs when an obstinate child is forcibly pulled along or lifted by the forearm by a parent or older sibling. For example, the injury might occur in a shopping center where a young child, typically two or three years old, is intent on pursuing a course or selecting an item somewhat different from the intentions of the parent. Another scenario that might result in nursemaid's elbow is when a parent or caregiver and a child are crossing the street where the parent or caregiver is forced to pull the child along quickly to avoid an approaching vehicle or to make it to the other curb before the traffic lights change. Care should also be taken to control anger or impatience to prevent re-injury in the future.

Resources

BOOKS

PM Medical Health News. *21st Century Complete Medical Guide to Elbow Injuries and Disorders: Authoritative Government Documents, Clinical References, and Practical Information for Patients and Physicians.* Washington, DC: Progressive Management, 2004.

WEB SITES

"Nursemaid's Elbow." National Institutes of Health. <http://www.nlm.nih.gov/medlineplus/ency/article/000983.htm>.

"Pediatrics, Nursemaid elbow." eMedicine.com, Inc. <http://www.emedicine.com/EMERG/topic392.htm>.

Judith Sims, MS

Nutrition

Definition

The process by which humans take in and use food in their bodies; also the study of diet as it relates to health.

Description

Good nutrition in childhood lays the foundation for good health throughout a person's lifetime. With the proliferation of fast food restaurants, the number of junk food commercials on television, and the increased trend toward eating out, it is more difficult than ever for parents to ensure that their children maintain a nutritious diet. Across the last decades of the twentieth century, increasing affluence and the widespread availability of vitamin-enriched foods have shifted the focus of nutritional concerns in the United States from obtaining minimum requirements to cutting down on harmful elements in one's diet. Parents need to be as concerned about high levels of fat, cholesterol, sugar, and salt, as well as adequate intake of **vitamins**, **minerals**, and other nutrients.

The American Academy of Pediatrics, the National Academy of Sciences, the American Heart Association, and other health-care organizations agree that fat should not account for more than 30 percent of the calorie intake of children over the age of two, and saturated fat should account for under 10 percent. The main dietary sources in children's diets of saturated fat are whole milk, cheese, hot dogs, and luncheon meats. Recommendations for dietary change include switching to 1 percent or skim milk, low-fat cheese, and meats from which the fat can be trimmed. Since fat is important for growth, experts also caution that fat intake should not be under 25 percent of daily calorie intake and that parents of children under age two should not restrict fat in their diets.

The amount of refined sugar in children's diets— typically accounting for 14 percent of calorie intake by adolescence—is another cause for concern. Although sugar is known to cause **tooth decay** and also may be associated with behavior problems, the greatest danger in consuming foods high in added sugar is that these "empty calories" may replace the more nutritious foods that children need in order to maintain good health. (Soft drinks, perhaps the single greatest source of refined sugar in the diet of children and teenagers, get virtually all their calories from sugar and offer no nutrients.) This high intake of fat can lead to excess weight and, potentially, **obesity**.

Another element that needs to be restricted in children's diets is the intake of sodium through salted foods. Sodium has been closely linked to **hypertension** (high blood pressure), which increases a person's risk of heart disease and **stroke**. It has been determined that 18-year-olds need only 500 milligrams of sodium daily. In addition to limiting the amounts of fat, cholesterol, salt, and sugar in their children's diets, health authorities also recommend that parents concerned about nutrition ensure that children obtain a generous supply of complex carbohydrates (found in such foods as beans, potatoes, whole-grain products, and pasta) and have at least five servings of fresh fruits and vegetables daily.

Infancy

The first nutritional decision that must be made for a child by a parent or primary caregiver is whether to breastfeed or bottle feed. Breast milk is generally considered the best food for an infant up to the age of six to nine months. It has virtually all the nutrients that babies need and in the right balance. In addition, it contains important antibodies that help protect infants from infection at a time when their own immune systems are not yet fully developed.

The composition of breast milk actually changes during the first two weeks after a baby is born. Initially, it consists largely of colostrum, a substance that has more protein than complete breast milk and lower amounts of fat and sugar. It is also rich in the antibody immunoglobin A, which helps protect against infections. By the tenth day after birth, the regular breast milk, containing more carbohydrates and fat and less protein, is produced. The amounts of carbohydrates and fat gradually continue to increase, as will the quantity of the milk itself, to match the needs of the growing baby. Although most full-term infants get all the necessary nutrients from breastfeeding, some may need supplements of vitamins D and K.

Women who are either unable to breastfeed or who choose not to do so usually feed their babies formula made from processed cow's milk, generally reconstituted skim milk with vegetable oils added to substitute for the missing butterfat, which is difficult for infants to digest. Lactose (milk sugar) is also added, and some formulas contain whey protein as well. For infants who demonstrate sensitivity to cow's milk, formulas based on soy protein are available.

Breast milk or formula provides all the nutrients an infant needs up to the age of four to six months. Contrary to past beliefs, it has been found that not only do babies not need solid foods before then, introducing solids too early may lead to **food allergies** or overfeeding. Regular grocery-store cow's milk, which cannot be adequately digested by infants and can cause gastrointestinal bleeding, should not be introduced until a child is a year old. As the first solid food, pediatricians often recommend cereal made from a grain other than wheat, such as rice. The first solid foods may be either commercial baby food or strained foods prepared at home. Once solid foods have been introduced, infants still need to receive most of their nourishment from either breast milk or formula during their first year.

Toddlerhood

During children's second year, their growth rate slows dramatically compared to the prior period. In the first year, their birth weight triples, their length increases by 50 percent, and the size of their brain doubles. After that first year, it takes several years for their weight to even double. They will grow in spurts, with each spurt followed by a period of weight gain. This decreased

A child should eat a variety of foods every day for good health and proper growth. (© *Brian Leng/Corbis.*)

growth leads to a decreased demand for food, often manifested in a newfound pickiness. As long as a child consumes an adequate, varied diet over a period of several days, parents are cautioned against becoming unduly concerned over a single day of unbalanced eating. Toddlers need to eat more than three times a day, either five or six small meals or three major ones with snacks in between.

Preschool

Preschoolers are still growing relatively slowly. Their weight increases about 12 percent between the ages of three and five, although their appearance changes considerably as they lose the baby fat of infancy and toddlerhood. They are still picky eaters, generally eating less—and less consistently—than their parents would like. Although their fat requirement is not as high as that of infants, preschoolers still require more fat and fewer

carbohydrates than adults. Fat is needed both for growth and for regulation of body temperature. Also, preschoolers need more than twice as much protein as adults. If the nutritional recommendations of the National Academy of Sciences are followed, a preschooler's diet will consist of 40 percent carbohydrates, 35 percent fats, 20 percent protein, and 5 percent fiber.

Between the ages of three and five, children's tastes expand considerably, and they are willing to consider foods they would have refused as toddlers. Four-year-olds can generally eat whatever foods the rest of the **family** is having. Preschoolers still cannot eat enough at three meals to meet their nutritional needs, and nutritious snacks are important. By this age, children's food choices can be strongly influenced by others. They will imitate good eating habits they see practiced by their parents, but they can also be easily swayed by television commercials for junk food.

School age

The diet of young school-age children, like that of preschoolers, should contain, in order of importance, carbohydrates, fat, and protein. A recommended proportion of these nutrients is 55 percent of the daily calorie intake from carbohydrates, 30 percent from fats, and 15 percent from protein. Once children begin spending a full day in school, a substantial, nutritious breakfast becomes more important than ever. Breakfast has been shown to affect the concentration and performance of elementary school children. Ideally, a balanced breakfast for a school-age child contains food high in protein as well as fruit and bread or another form of grain.

A major change affecting the nutrition of school-age children is the growth of opportunities to eat outside the home. The carefully packed homemade lunch may be traded for a salty snack or cupcake, and parts of it may be discarded. Vending machines and stores offer more temptations. In addition, school lunch programs differ widely in quality; even the nutritional value of a single food, such as a hamburger, can vary significantly depending on how it is prepared and what ingredients are used.

Adolescence brings its own set of nutritional needs and challenges. Beginning with the pre-teen years, children undergo their most intensive period of physical growth since infancy and need more food than at any other stage of life, particularly if they participate in **sports**. Teenagers, especially boys, are notorious for being able to empty the refrigerator of food, usually without gaining excess weight. Early adolescence in particular is a time of increased nutritional requirements for girls, who experience their greatest growth spurt at this time and also begin menstruating. It is difficult for weight-conscious teenage girls to eat enough to satisfy their minimum daily iron requirement of 18 milligrams, and they should try to eat either foods that are naturally rich in iron, such as turkey, beef, liver, and beans, or foods made from iron-enriched cereals. Adequate calcium intake is essential for the rapidly growing bones of teenagers, but milk has often been replaced by soft drinks as the beverage of choice among this age group. Parents should encourage adolescents, especially girls, to eat other foods rich in calcium, such as cheese, salmon, and broccoli.

As adolescents grow more independent, the number of meals and snacks eaten away from home increases as they spend more time with friends and take increased responsibility for arranging their own meals, with fast foods, soft drinks, and sweets often prominent on the menu. In addition to the natural appeal of these foods, **peer pressure** contributes to the choice of a diet soft drink over milk or juice, or pizza over broccoli. Although parents cannot control the eating habits of their teenagers, they can influence them by consistently making nutritious foods available at home and, at least in some cases, by discussing the benefits of good nutrition with them, especially if a relative or friend has had an illness, such as heart disease or colon **cancer**, that has known links to diet.

Common problems

A special problem that may affect childhood nutrition is the presence of food **allergies**, which are more common in children than in adults. They are most likely to begin when a child is very young and the immune system is still sensitive, usually in infancy. Food allergies also tend to run in families: if one parent has food allergies, a child has a 40 percent likelihood of developing one. This figure rises to 75 percent if both parents have food allergies. Common symptoms of food allergies include **hives** and **rashes**; swelling of the eyes, lips, and mouth; respiratory symptoms; and digestive problems. Foods that most often produce allergic reactions in infants are cow's milk, soy products, and citrus fruits. Other common childhood allergens include wheat, nuts, chocolate, strawberries, tomatoes, corn, and seafood. In time, childhood food allergies are often outgrown. Feeding a child with food allergies is a challenging but not impossible task for parents. A variety of foods can be substituted for those to which a child is allergic: soy products for milk and other dairy products; carob for chocolate; and, in the case of wheat allergies, products or flour made from grains such as rice or oats.

Parental concerns

Vegetarian kids

About 2 percent of Americans ages six to 17 (about 1 million) are vegetarian, the same percentage as among American adults, and 0.5 percent are vegan, according to a 2002 survey by the Vegetarian Resource Group (VRG). Six percent of six- to 17-year-olds do not eat meat but eat fish and/or poultry. Teens who follow a vegetarian diet are more likely to meet recommendations for total fat, saturated fat, and number of servings of fruits and vegetables as compared to non-vegetarians. They also have higher intakes of iron, vitamin A, fiber, and diet soda, and lower intakes of vitamin B12, cholesterol, and fast food. Most teens, whether they are vegetarian or not, do not meet recommendations for calcium, according to the VRG survey. The study concluded that rather than viewing adolescent **vegetarianism** as a phase or fad, the diet could be viewed as a healthy alternative

KEY TERMS

Colostrum—Milk secreted for a few days after birth and characterized by high protein and antibody content.

Essential fatty acid (EFA)—A fatty acid that the body requires but cannot make. It must be obtained from the diet. EFAs include omega-6 fatty acids found in primrose and safflower oils, and omega-3 fatty acids oils found in fatty fish and flax-seed, canola, soybean, and walnuts.

Immunoglobin A—A sugar protein with a high molecular weight that acts like an antibody and is produced by white blood cells during an immune response.

to the traditional American meat-based diet. The study also said that vegetarian diets in adolescence could lead to lifelong health-promoting dietary practices. The study was reported in the July-August 2002 issue of the VRG publication *Vegetarian Journal*.

Parents should closely monitor their vegetarian child's height, weight, and general health. A child who is not getting enough vitamins and nutrients may have symptoms such as skin rashes, fatigue, a painful and swollen tongue, irritability, pale skin, mental slowness, or difficulty breathing. The diets of vegetarian adolescents should be monitored closely to make sure they include a variety of foods, including fruits, vegetables, beans, whole grains, and non-meat protein sources. For vegetarians who do not eat fish, getting enough omega-3 essential fatty acids may be an issue, and supplements such as flaxseed oil should be considered, as well as walnuts and canola oil. Another essential fatty acid, omega-6, found in fish, can be obtained from borage oil or evening primrose oil supplements.

When to call the doctor

Parents should consult their child's pediatrician or physician if they are unsure the child's diet is nutritionally adequate. A doctor should also be consulted if a child's weight or height is not appropriate for their age.

Resources

BOOKS

Evers, Connie Liakos. *How to Teach Nutrition to Kids*. Portland, OR: 24 Carrot Press, 2003.

Salmon, Margaret Belais. *Food Facts for Teenagers: A Guide to Good Nutrition for Teens and Preteens*. Springfield, IL: Charles C. Thomas Publisher Ltd., 2002.

Schlosser, Eric. *Fast Food Nation: The Dark Side of the All-American Meal*. Wilmington, MA: Houghton Mifflin Company Trade & Reference Division, 2001.

Shield, Jodie, and Mary Catherine Mullen. *The American Dietetic Association Guide to Healthy Eating for Kids: How Your Children Can Eat Smart from Five to Twelve*. Hoboken, NJ: Wiley, 2002.

PERIODICALS

Feskanich, Diane, et al. "Modifying the Healthy Eating Index to Assess Diet Quality in Children and Adolescents" 104 *Journal of the American Dietetic Association* (September 2004): 1375–83.

Mangels, Reed. "Good News about Vegetarian Diets for Teens" *Vegetarian Journal* (July-August 2002): 20–1.

Nicklas, Theresa A., et al. "Children's Meal Patterns Have Changed Over 21-Year Period: The Bogalusa Heart Study" 104 *Journal of the American Dietetic Association* (May 2004): 753–61.

Nicklas, Theresa A., et al. "The Importance of Breakfast Consumption to Nutrition of Children, Adolescents, and Young Adults" *Nutrition Today* 39 (January-February 2004): 30–9.

Onderko, Patty. "The (Not So) Great American Baby Diet: A New Study Sheds Light on What Our Babies and Toddlers are Eating Today—And How You Can Improve Their Diet for Tomorrow" *Baby Talk* 69 (February 1, 2004): 45.

ORGANIZATIONS

American Dietetic Association. 120 South Riverside Plaza, Suite 2000, Chicago, IL 60606–6995. Web site: <www.eatright.org>.

International Food Information Council. 1100 Connecticut Ave. NW, Suite 430, Washington, DC 20036. Web site: <www.ific.org>.

WEB SITES

"Children's Nutrition Guide." Available online at <www.keepkidshealthy.com/nutrition> (accessed November 12, 2004).

"Kids Nutrition." *Baylor College of Medicine*. Available online at <www.kidsnutrition.org/> (accessed November 12, 2004).

Ken R. Wells

Nystagmus

Definition

Nystagmus is a condition in which there is involuntary and rhythmic movement or oscillation of the eye. It is often caused by an underlying ocular or neurological disorder.

Description

The eye movements associated with nystagmus are varied. They can be either pendular, in which the oscillations are equal in all directions and or jerk, in which the movements may be faster in one direction than another. The frequency of the oscillation or movement and the amplitude of the oscillation also vary. The movements themselves may be vertical, horizontal, circular, or oblique in direction. Nystagmus can be sensory and develop as a result of poor vision, or it can be motor and develop as a result of a neurological problem.

Nystagmus may be congenital, or it may be acquired. Congenital, or infantile, nystagmus appears within the first few months of life. Congenital nystagmus is usually binocular and affects both eyes, is horizontal in direction, and does not occur while the child is sleeping. It decreases when the child's eyes converge or move inward. Most of these cases of nystagmus develop because of poor vision and do not have an underlying neurological cause.

Children with congenital nystagmus usually have a point in their eye movement in which the intensity of the nystagmus is decreased. This is called the null point, and the child may adopt a head tilt or rotation to help maintain his or her eyes at this position. This point is usually not in straight ahead or in a primary gaze position. Children with nystagmus who have their the null point located at a position in which the eyes are positioned inward may develop an esotropia, a form of **strabismus** or eye turn.

One variant of congenital nystagmus is spasmus nutans, which appears as a triad with accompanying head nodding and torticollis (head turn or tilt), and is seen between four months and three-and-a-half years of age and usually resolves without treatment within one to two years of onset. Rarely does it persist past age five. Usually spasmus nutans appears bilaterally, and the nystagmus is in a horizontal direction. When the nystagmus of spasmus nutans is vertical or rotary, the child does not have a head tilt.

There are various types of nystagmus. Downbeat nystagmus is characterized by a nystagmus that is more pronounced when the child looks down, especially when looking to the side, or in lateral gaze. An accentuated oscillation when looking up is seen in upbeat nystagmus. Seesaw nystagmus is an unusual type of in which one eye moves in and down and the other out and up. A periodic alternating nystagmus (PAN) is observed in primary gaze when the patient is looking straight ahead and is characterized by eye movements that continuously change direction and speed. Peripheral vestibular nystagmus may be accompanied by vertigo, **nausea**, and tinnitus, or ringing in the ears. This type of nystagmus is not always apparent but can be seen by a doctor when he or she looks in the back of the eye with a direct ophthalmoscope.

Latent nystagmus appears only when one eye is covered. This is a congenital nystagmus caused by an ocular motor disturbance rather than visual deprivation. It is often accompanied by strabismus or an eye turn. A child with latent nystagmus will not see well when one eye is covered.

Gaze evoked nystagmus occurs only when one is looking to the side in extreme lateral gaze. This type of nystagmus can be caused by ethanol and recreational drug use, but is seen in myasthenia gravis and thyroid disease as well.

Some types of nystagmus are normal. If one looks at an object in extreme gaze for a long period of time, endpoint nystagmus may be noted. Optokinetic nystagmus (OKN) is a nystagmus that can be elicited involuntarily when a rapidly moving striped object is passed in front of an individual's eyes.

Transmission

Congenital nystagmus may be transmitted genetically, either as an autosomal recessive or dominant, or as an X-linked recessive trait. It can also be associated with other conditions that are genetically transmitted. For example, Leber's amaurosis is an autosomal dominant trait and **albinism** is X-linked.

Demographics

Congenital nystagmus occurs twice as frequently in males than in females. The prevalence of nystagmus in the pediatric population is .015 percent. Eighty percent of nystagmus is congenital, and the remaining 20 percent is acquired.

Causes and symptoms

The eyes of an individual with nystagmus cannot remain still and oscillate in some position of gaze. Those with nystagmus usually have decreased vision and poor depth perception, although those born with nystagmus, may not realize that their vision is poor. Those with acquired nystagmus may experience double vision or oscillopsia, or that objects in their visual space appear to move. An acquired nystagmus may be accompanied by other symptoms such as **dizziness**, difficulty with balance, hearing loss, poor coordination, and **numbness**. If an individual with nystagmus experiences oscillopsia, then the nystagmus is acquired.

The primary cause of congenital nystagmus is visual deprivation, and the causes of visual deprivation in an infant include cataracts, oculoalbinism, glaucoma, retinal detachments, Leber's amaurosis, developmental abnormalities of the optic nerve such as a coloboma, and achromatopsia, a condition in which the infant cannot see color.

Acquired nystagmus can be caused by demyelination of nerve fibers, such as occurs in multiple sclerosis, lesions or tumors of the vestibular or visual pathways, strokes of the central nervous system, and drug use, both recreational as well as a side effect of prescribed drugs, such as those used to treat seizures and depression. Other causes of acquired nystagmus are Arnold-Chiari malformations, vitamin deficiencies, syphilis, Wernicke's encephalopathy, Behcet's syndrome, and Meniere's disease.

When to call the doctor

Since nystagmus can be caused by tumors, **stroke**, and trauma or neurological disorder, any type of nystagmus must be evaluated by a qualified practitioner. The nystagmus can be a sign of a serious problem. For example, a type of tumor called chiasmal glioma has signs and symptoms similar to spasmus nutans.

Diagnosis

Diagnosis of nystagmus is made primarily by patient history as reported by a parent, the age of onset, and observation of any accompanying signs such as a head turn, tilt or tremor, or oscillopsia. If possible, the infant or child's best visual acuity is determined. If the onset is acute, then usually the nystagmus is acquired.

The type of nystagmus can accurately be determined by eye movement recordings, which map direction, frequency, null point, and amplitude of the nystagmus. For the infant with congenital nystagmus, evoked response potential (EVR) and electroretinogram (ERG) give the doctor objective information about visual potential, and **magnetic resonance imaging** (MRI) can determine if

and where a lesion is located. For the infant or young child, some of these tests may be done under anesthesia.

Treatment

The treatment for nystagmus, once the etiology is determined and treated, includes optical devices such as **contact lenses** and glasses, medication, and surgery.

For individuals with nystagmus correction of refractive error with glasses or contact lenses is the first step in treating the condition. For 85 percent of children with nystagmus, a spectacle prescription improves vision significantly. For those with congenital nystagmus, prism may be put in glasses to help position the eye at its null point or to help the eyes converge. For some people contact lenses are prescribed. Contact lenses slow down eye movements, and because the optical center of the prescription is always centered on the eye with the contact lens, vision improves. Low vision aids such as telescopes assist those whose vision cannot be fully corrected with spectacles and contact lenses alone. Tinting of the glasses or sunglasses may decrease the nystagmus of individuals with albinism. For the patient with oscillopsia, grinding prism into the spectacles may move the visual field to a point of decreased oscillopsia.

Congenital nystagmus, when due to a visual deprivation, is rarely improved by surgery. But when a head tilt or head turn accompanies nystagmus, surgery to correct a muscle imbalance may improve nystagmus and visual acuity. Surgery on the extraocular muscles of the eye may be helpful when the child's null point is in not in primary gaze but located at least 30 degrees from straight-ahead vision. When a tumor or stroke has caused an acquired nystagmus, then neurosurgery, if indicated for the underlying cause, may lead to resolution of the nystagmus. When surgery is considered, the risks of anesthesia must also be considered.

If oscillopsia is a co-existing symptom, then drugs can be given to reduce the ocular oscillations. Vestibular nystagmus can be treated by diazepam or scopolamine. Drugs called GABA agonists, such as baclofen and carbamazepine, are useful in treatment of seesaw nystagmus and PAN, if the nystagmus is acquired and not congenital. Baclofen cannot be given to children.

Botox (*Botulinum* toxin) injections can temporarily control the eye movements, but because of side effects such as double vision and ptosis or drooping of the eyelid, and because it is not a permanent solution, Botox is not used often.

KEY TERMS

Acupuncture—Based on the same traditional Chinese medical foundation as acupressure, acupuncture uses sterile needles inserted at specific points to treat certain conditions or relieve pain.

Albinism—An inherited condition that causes a lack of pigment. People with albinism typically have light skin, white or pale yellow hair, and light blue or gray eyes.

Autosomal—Relating to any chromosome besides the X and Y sex chromosomes. Human cells contain 22 pairs of autosomes and one pair of sex chromosomes.

Binocular—Affecting or having to do with both eyes.

Biofeedback—A training technique that enables an individual to gain some element of control over involuntary or automatic body functions.

Coloboma—A birth defect in which part of the eye does not form completely.

Lesion—A disruption of the normal structure and function of a tissue by an injury or disease process. Wounds, sores, rashes, and boils are all lesions.

Strabismus—A disorder in which the eyes do not point in the same direction. Also called squint.

X-linked—A gene carried on the X chromosome, one of the two sex chromosomes.

If the nystagmus is due to drug toxicity, then reducing or discontinuing the drug eventually resolves the problem.

Alternative treatment

Acupuncture and biofeedback and vision therapy have been successful for some patients.

Prognosis

Congenital nystagmus is usually a benign condition. It is not curable, but its symptoms can be diminished with spectacles or contact lenses. The best corrected vision for most individuals with congenital nystagmus is between 20/40 and 20/70, but correction to 20/20 is possible for some. Nystagmus associated with spasmus nutans resolves spontaneously before the child reaches school age.

The prognosis for an acquired nystagmus depends on its cause. If the condition is due to a side effect of a drug, then decreasing or changing the treatment drug eventually resolves the nystagmus.

Prevention

In general nystagmus cannot be prevented. Since the cause of acquired nystagmus can be due to a co-existing neurological condition, prompt attention to other neurological signs that may accompany nystagmus, such as dizziness, may prevent or decrease the severity of nystagmus itself. Careful monitor of dosage of those drugs with nystagmus as a side effect may prevent the condition.

Parental concerns

Because nystagmus can be associated with many medical problems, the child with this condition must undergo a complete ocular and neurological evaluation.

Children with nystagmus are not aware that they may have a visual deficiency and as they get older must be helped with the restrictions that nystagmus places on them. For instance, driving may be restricted or not permitted. Certain occupations for which good visual correction is a requirement may be not feasible. Every effort must be made to integrate the child with nystagmus into a normal school setting in order to prepare the child for adult life, even if cosmetic concerns may instinctively lead the parent to want to protect the child.

Support for families of those with nystagmus can be found through the American Nystagmus Network.

Resources

BOOKS

Halmagyi, G. Michael, and Phillip D. Cremer. "Central Eye Movements Disorders." Chapter 283 in *Principles and Practice of Ophthalmology* , 2nd ed. Philadelphia: Saunders, 2000.

Wheeler, David T. "Nystagmus." In *Current Ocular Therapy 5*. Philadelphia: Saunders, 2000, p. 407.

PERIODICALS

Hensil, Jennifer, and Andrew S. Gurwood. "Understanding Nystagmus." *Optometry* 71 (July 2000): 439–48.

Hertle, Richard W. "Examination of the Refractive Management of Patients with Nystagmus." *Survey of Ophthalmology* 45 (November-December 2000): 215–22.

Moster, Mark L. "Nystagmus." *Ophthalmology Clinics of North America* 14 (March 2001): 205–15.

WEB SITES

American Nystagmus Network. Available online at <www.nystagmus.org/entry.html> (accessed November 12, 2004).

Smith, Rodney J. "Solving the Diagnostic Puzzle of Congenital Nystagmus." *Review of Optometry*, June 1999 Case Report. Available online at <www.revoptom.com/archive/issue/ro06f9.htm> (accessed November 12, 2004).

Martha Reilly, OD

O

Obesity

Definition

Obesity is an abnormal accumulation of body fat, usually 20 percent or more over an individual's ideal body weight. Obesity is associated with increased risk of illness, disability, and death.

The branch of medicine that deals with the study and treatment of obesity is known as bariatrics. As obesity has become a major health problem in the United States, bariatrics has become a separate medical and surgical specialty.

Description

Childhood obesity is in the early 2000s a significant health problem in the United States. Obese children and adolescents are at increased risk for developing diabetes, **hypertension**, coronary artery disease, **sleep** apnea, orthopedic problems, and psychosocial disorders.

Obesity involves excessive weight gain and fat accumulation. For children and adolescents, obesity is defined in terms of body mass index (BMI) percentile. BMI is a formula that considers an individual's height and weight to determine body fat and health risk, and it is used differently for children and adolescents than it is for adults. In adults, BMI often misrepresents obesity because it does not consider healthy weight from muscle tissue; therefore, body fat percentage is considered a more accurate method for determining obesity in adults. In children and adolescents, because body fat changes as they mature, BMI is gender- and age-specific and plotted on gender-specific growth charts to determine BMI-for-age. Curved lines on the chart (percentiles) are used by healthcare professionals to identify children and adolescents at risk for overweight and obesity. Children and adolescents with a BMI-for-age in the 85th to 95th percentile are considered overweight and at risk for obesity, and those with a BMI-for-age greater than the 95th percentile are considered obese.

Demographics

According to the American Obesity Association and the Centers for Disease Control and Prevention, 30.3 percent of children aged six to 11 years are overweight and 15.3 percent are obese, and 30.4 percent of adolescents aged 12 to 19 years are overweight and 15.5 percent are obese. From 1980 to 2004, the prevalence of obesity among children quadrupled, and the prevalence of obesity in adolescents more than doubled. Overweight and obesity is more prevalent in boys (32.7%) than girls (27.8%). Obesity is more common in African American, Hispanic American, and Native American children and adolescents, than among Caucasians of the same ages.

Causes and symptoms

Although obesity can be a side effect of certain hormonal disorders or use of certain medications, the primary cause of obesity in children and adolescents is excess calorie consumption coupled with a sedentary lifestyle. Children and adolescents living in the twenty-first century are the most inactive generation ever. The majority of schools no longer offer daily physical education classes; and active leisure activities, such as bicycle riding, have been replaced by sedentary activities, such as television watching and playing computer games. Studies have documented dramatic changes in childhood food consumption from the 1970s to 2004. Fast foods and foods eaten at other restaurants have increased by 300 percent since 1977, and soft drink consumption has also increased significantly. In addition, standard meal portion sizes and snacking have increased.

Obesity is the result of a complex interaction of genetics and environmental factors. Genetics influence how the body regulates appetite and metabolism, while certain environmental factors encourage excess calorie

Obesity

consumption. The body requires a certain amount of energy for basic metabolism and to support additional physical activity. When calories consumed from food and beverages equal calories expended during physical activity, body weight is maintained. When calories consumed exceed calories expended, weight gain results. To gain one pound, 3,500 additional calories must be consumed. In American society, excess calories are easily consumed just by drinking soft drinks and eating "supersized" fast food meals. A sedentary lifestyle results in far fewer calories being burned daily.

The major symptoms of obesity are excessive weight gain and the presence of large amounts of fatty tissue. Obesity can cause a number of other conditions, including type 2 diabetes, hypertension, **high cholesterol**, joint **pain**, **asthma**, **hypothyroidism**, and gallstones. Type 2 diabetes, previously referred to as adult-onset diabetes, has increased dramatically in children, and this increase has been directly linked to obesity.

When to call the doctor

Overweight and obese children should be evaluated by a physician for diabetes, hypertension, high cholesterol, and other medical conditions that are influenced by excessive weight gain. Primary care physicians can be consulted for weight management counseling to help children lose weight.

Diagnosis

Obesity in children and adolescents is diagnosed using the BMI-for-age formula described above, which is used to define obesity. Comorbid conditions, such as diabetes and high cholesterol, are diagnosed using medical laboratory tests.

Treatment

As of 2004, no weight loss drugs were approved for use in children, although some drugs used to treat obesity are approved for use in adolescents age 16 years and older. A few drugs are under investigation for use in children. Although no drugs are specifically approved for pediatric weight loss, some physicians may prescribe them "off-label." Because the side effects of these medications in children are unknown, children should not use adult weight loss drugs.

For extremely obese adolescents, surgical procedures—called bariatric surgery—may be performed, but only rarely. These procedures involve significant surgical alteration of the digestive tract and require substantial modification of diet after the surgery to

much less than 1,000 calories per day. The long-term effects on growth and development from severe post-operative calorie restriction are not unknown, and weight loss surgery should only be performed on adolescents as a last resort.

The most effective treatment for obese children and adolescents is behavior and lifestyle modification under the guidance of a physician or weight management specialist experienced in dealing with children and adolescents. Behavior and lifestyle modification involves the following:

- **assessment** of child's and family's eating habits
- implementation of a regular, safe **exercise** program and increasing active leisure activities
- limiting television viewing and other sedentary activities
- setting reasonable goals and monitoring goal achievement using positive, non-food-related incentives
- counseling regarding how to keep a food/activity diary to track progress
- extensive support by involving entire **family** and/or joining a weight loss group of peers

Alternative treatment

Alternatives for weight loss involve the use of ephedra-containing drugs or herbal preparation or the use of diuretics and **laxatives**. Both of these practices are unsafe, especially for children and adolescents. Because ephedra can cause severe cardiac side effects, the Food and Drug Administration has issued warnings against its use. Diuretics and laxatives can result in severe **dehydration** and improper absorption of nutrients.

Acupressure and acupuncture can suppress food cravings. Visualization and meditation can create and reinforce a positive self-image that enhances the patient's determination to lose weight. By improving physical strength, mental concentration, and emotional serenity, **yoga** can provide the same benefits.

Given the drastic increase in childhood obesity, special summer programs and therapeutic schools have been formed to help children lose weight. Summer camp programs that focus on healthy eating and exercise habits are available for overweight and obese children. In addition, in early 2004, the first **alternative school** for overweight and obese children, which operates like other private and charter schools, but with a focus on healthy weight loss and maintenance, was established.

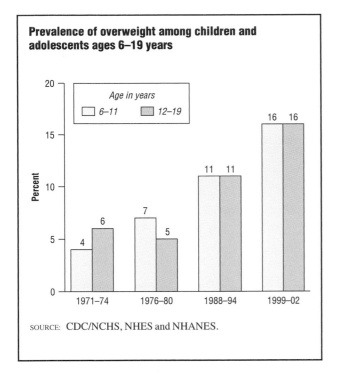

Prevalence of overweight among children and adolescents ages 6–19 years

SOURCE: CDC/NCHS, NHES and NHANES.

This graph shows the increasing numbers of overweight children in the United States. *(Illustration by GGS Information Services.)*

Prognosis

Obese and overweight children and adolescents are more likely to be obese or overweight as adults. According to the American Obesity Association, obese children aged 10 to 13 have a 70 percent chance of remaining obese for the rest of their lives. Obese individuals are at increased risk for many other diseases and early death. Behavior and lifestyle modification programs involving positive goal-setting, increased exercise, and group support can help children and adolescents successfully and safely lose weight.

Prevention

Obesity can be prevented by instilling healthy eating and regular exercise habits in children at an early age. Minimizing and structuring daily time for sedentary activities like television viewing and encouraging outdoor activities such as bicycle riding, walking, running, and active **play**, and active indoor activities such as dancing can help increase physical activity. Dietary modifications to help prevent obesity include limiting soft drink and fast food consumption, monitoring food portion sizes, and providing a well-balanced diet.

KEY TERMS

Adipose tissue—Fat tissue.

Bariatrics—The branch of medicine that deals with the prevention and treatment of obesity and related disorders.

Ghrelin—A peptide hormone secreted by cells in the lining of the stomach. Ghrelin is important in appetite regulation and maintaining the body's energy balance.

Hyperlipidemia—A condition characterized by abnormally high levels of lipids in blood plasma.

Hyperplastic obesity—Excessive weight gain in childhood, characterized by an increase in the number of new fat cells.

Hypertension—Abnormally high arterial blood pressure, which if left untreated can lead to heart disease and stroke.

Hypertrophic obesity—Excessive weight gain in adulthood, characterized by expansion of already existing fat cells.

Ideal weight—Weight corresponding to the lowest death rate for individuals of a specific height, gender, and age.

Leptin—A protein hormone that affects feeding behavior and hunger in humans. As of 2004 it is thought that obesity in humans may result in part from insensitivity to leptin.

Nutritional concerns

Nutrition is a primary factor for weight management of obese children and adolescents. Poor nutrition and dietary habits can lead to weight gain and obesity. Dietary modification is important for helping children lose weight and prevent obesity.

The following nutritional guidelines can help in the management of obesity:

- Limit soft drink consumption to one per day or less. One 12-ounce can of soda has 120 calories or more. Often, children and adolescents consume "super-size" sodas that may contain up to 1,000 calories.

- Limit fast food restaurant visits to one per week, and choose healthy options like grilled chicken and smaller sized portions of high-calorie items.

- Monitor food serving sizes.

- Increase consumption of fruits, vegetables, high-fiber foods, and whole-grain foods.

• Be aware that "low-fat" foods often substitute sugar for fat, and calories may actually be the same as the regular or high-fat version.

Parental concerns

Parents of obese children and adolescents should be concerned for their current and future health, since obesity can result in diabetes, hypertension, and coronary artery disease. Losing weight can be very difficult for obese children, and parental support is essential for success. Because children model behavior after their parents, obesity often affects both parents and children. Parents should strive to have healthy eating habits and exercise regularly to be effective role models for their children. Making healthy eating and exercise a family priority is better for everyone and helps reinforce positive changes in behavior for the obese child.

Obese children and adolescents are more susceptible to eating disorders, negative **self-esteem** and body image, and depression due to peer influences. Counseling, peer group therapy, and **family therapy** may be required to support lifestyle modifications for obese children and adolescents.

Resources

BOOKS

Burniat, Walter, et al. *Child and Adolescent Obesity: Causes and Consequences, Prevention and Management.* Cambridge, UK: Cambridge University Press, 2002.

Kiess, Wieland, et al. *Obesity in Childhood and Adolescence.* Basel, Switzerland: S. Karger AG, 2004.

PERIODICALS

Eissa, M. A. H., and K. B. Gunner. "Evaluation and Management of Obesity in Children and Adolescents." *Journal of Pediatric Health Care* 18(March 2004): 35–38.

Manson J. E., et al. "The Escalating Pandemics of Obesity and Sedentary Lifestyle." *Archives of Internal Medicine* 164(February 9, 2004): 249–258.

McWhorter, J. W., et al. "The Obese Child: Motivation as a Tool for Exercise." *Journal of Pediatric Health Care* 17(February 2003): 11–17.

Ritter, J. "Obese Teens Turn to Surgery of Last Resort." *Chicago Sun-Times*, March 29, 2004.

St-Onge M. P., et al. "Changes in Childhood Food Consumption Patterns: A Cause for Concern in Light of Increasing Body Weights." *American Journal of Clinical Nutrition* 78(December 2003): 1068–73.

ORGANIZATIONS

American Dietetic Association. Web site: <www.eatright.org>.

American Obesity Association (AOA). 1250 24th Street NW, Suite 300, Washington, DC 20037. Web site: <www.obesity.org>.

American Society of Bariatric Physicians. 5453 East Evans Place, Denver, CO 80222–5234. Web site: <www.asbp.org>.

American Society for Bariatric Surgery. 7328 West University Avenue, Suite F, Gainesville, FL 32607. Web site: <www.asbs.org>.

National Institute of Diabetes and Digestive and Kidney Diseases. 31 Center Drive, USC2560, Building 31, Room 9A-04, Bethesda, MD 20892–2560. Web site: <www.niddk.nih/gov>.

Shape Up America! Web site: <www.shapeup.org/>.

WEB SITES

"BMI for Children and Teens." *Centers for Disease Control and Prevention*, 2004. Available online at <www.cdc.gov/nccdphp/dnpa/bmi/bmi-for-age.htm> (accessed October 26, 2004).

"Fitness for Your Child." *IDEA Health and Fitness Association.* Available online at <www.ideafit.com/articles/fitness_child.asp> (accessed October 26, 2004).

"Obesity in Youth." *American Obesity Association.* Available online at <www.obesity.org/subs/fastfacts/obesity_youth.shtml> (accessed October 26, 2004)

OTHER

Childhood Assessment Calculator. Available online at <www.shapeup.org/oap/entry.php> (accessed October 26, 2004).

Jennifer E. Sisk, MA

Obsessive-compulsive disorder

Definition

Obsessive-compulsive disorder (OCD) is a type of **anxiety** disorder. Anxiety disorder is the experience of prolonged, excessive worry about circumstances in one's life. OCD is characterized by distressing repetitive thoughts, impulses, or images that are intense, frightening, absurd, or unusual. These thoughts are followed by ritualized actions that are usually bizarre and irrational. These ritual actions, known as compulsions, help reduce anxiety caused by the individual's obsessive thoughts. Often described as the "disease of doubt," the sufferer usually knows the obsessive thoughts and compulsions are irrational but, on another level, fears they may be true.

Description

Most people with obsessive-compulsive disorder have both obsessions and compulsions, but occasionally a person will have just one or the other. The degree to which this condition can interfere with daily living also varies. Some people are barely bothered, while others find the obsessions and compulsions to be profoundly traumatic and spend much time each day in compulsive actions. Because the symptoms are so distressing, sufferers often hide heir fears and rituals but cannot avoid acting on them. OCD sufferers are often unable to decide if their fears are realistic and need to be acted upon.

Obsessions are intrusive, irrational thoughts that keep popping up in a person's mind, such as the urgency to wash one's hands again. Typical obsessions include fears of dirt, germs, contamination, and violent or aggressive impulses. Other obsessions include feeling responsible or others' **safety** or an irrational **fear** of hitting a pedestrian with a car. Additional obsessions can involve excessive religious feelings or intrusive sexual thoughts. The patient may need to confess frequently to a religious counselor or may fear **acting out** the strong sexual thoughts in a hostile way. People with obsessive-compulsive disorder may have an intense preoccupation with order and symmetry or may be unable to throw anything out.

Compulsions usually involve repetitive rituals such as excessive washing (especially hand washing or bathing), cleaning, checking and touching, counting, arranging, and/or hoarding. As the person performs these acts, he may feel temporarily better, but there is no long-lasting sense of satisfaction or completion after the act is performed. Often, a person with obsessive-compulsive disorder believes that if the ritual is not performed, something dreadful will happen. While these compulsions may temporarily ease stress, short-term comfort is purchased at a heavy price—time spent repeating compulsive actions and a long-term interference with life.

The difference between OCD and other compulsive behavior is that while people who have problems with gambling, overeating, or with substance abuse may appear to be compulsive, these activities also provide pleasure to some degree. The compulsions of OCD, on the other hand, are never pleasurable.

OCD may be related to some other conditions, such as the continual urge to pull out body hair (**trichotillomania**); fear of having a serious disease (hypochondriasis); or preoccupation with imagined defects in personal appearance disorder (body dysmorphia). Some people with OCD also have **Tourette syndrome**, a condition featuring **tics** and unwanted vocalizations (such as swearing). OCD is often linked with depression and other anxiety disorders.

Demographics

Almost one out of every 40 people suffers from obsessive-compulsive disorder at some time in their lives. The condition is two to three times more common than either **schizophrenia** or manic depression and strikes men and women of every ethnic group, age, and social level.

If one person in a **family** has obsessive-compulsive disorder, there is a 25 percent chance that another immediate family member has the condition. It also appears that stress and psychological factors may worsen symptoms, which usually begin during **adolescence** or early adulthood.

Causes and symptoms

Research suggests that the tendency to develop obsessive-compulsive disorder is inherited. There are several theories behind the cause of OCD. OCD may be related to a chemical imbalance within the brain that causes a communication problem between the front part of the brain (frontal lobe) and deeper parts of the brain responsible for the repetitive behavior. The orbital cortex located on the underside of the brain's frontal lobe is overactive in OCD patients. This may be one reason for the feeling of alarm that pushes the patient into compulsive, repetitive actions. It is possible that people with OCD experience overactivity deep within the brain that causes the cells to get "stuck," much like a jammed transmission in a car damages the gears. This could lead to the development of rigid thinking and repetitive movements common to the disorder. The fact that drugs which boost the levels of serotonin, a brain messenger substance linked to emotion and many different anxiety disorders, in the brain can reduce OCD symptoms may indicate that to some degree OCD is related to levels of serotonin in the brain.

There may also be a link between childhood episodes of **strep throat** and the development of OCD. In some vulnerable children, strep antibodies attack a certain part of the brain. Antibodies are cells that the body produces to fight specific diseases. That attack results in

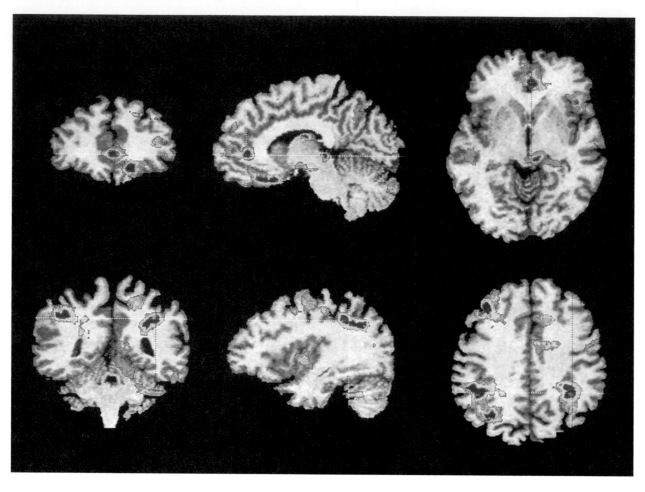

PET scans of a brain showing active areas in obsessive-compulsive disorder; positive correlations (activity increases as symptoms get stronger), top row; negative correlation (activity decreases as symptoms strengthen), bottom. *(Wellcome Department of Cognitive Neurology/SPL/Photo Researchers, Inc.)*

the development of excessive washing or germ **phobias**. A phobia is a strong but irrational fear. In this instance the phobia is fear of disease germs present on commonly handled objects. These symptoms would normally disappear over time, but some children who have repeated infections may develop full-blown OCD. Treatment with **antibiotics**, immunoglobulin, or blood cleansing procedures can decrease the circulating anti-strep antibodies in the blood, thus lessening the OCD symptoms in some of these children.

Diagnosis

People with obsessive-compulsive disorder feel ashamed of their problem and often try to hide their symptoms. They avoid seeking treatment. Because they can be very good at keeping their problem from friends and family, many sufferers do not get the help they need until the behaviors are deeply ingrained habits and hard to change. As a result, the condition is often misdiagnosed or underdiagnosed. All too often, it can take more than a decade between the onset of symptoms and proper diagnosis and treatment.

OCD appears to be related to a disruption in serotonin levels, there is no blood test for the condition. Instead, doctors diagnose OCD after evaluating a person's symptoms and history.

Treatment

Obsessive-compulsive disorder can be effectively treated by a combination of cognitive-behavioral therapy and medication that regulates the brain's serotonin levels. Drugs that are approved to treat obsessive-compulsive disorder include fluoxetine (Prozac), fluvoxamine (Luvox), paroxetine (Paxil), and sertraline (Zoloft), all selective serotonin reuptake inhibitors (SSRIs) that affect the level of serotonin in the brain. Older drugs include the antidepressant clomipramine (Anafranil), a widely studied drug in the treatment of OCD, but one that carries a greater risk of side effects. Drugs should be taken for at least 12 weeks before a person decides whether they are effective.

Cognitive-behavioral therapy (CBT) teaches patients how to confront their fears and obsessive thoughts by making the effort to endure or wait out the activities that usually cause anxiety without compulsively performing the calming rituals. Eventually their anxiety decreases. People who are able to alter their thought patterns in this way can lessen their preoccupation with the compulsive rituals. At the same time, the patient is encouraged to refocus attention elsewhere, such as on a hobby.

In a few very severe cases in which patients have not responded to medication or behavioral therapy, brain surgery may be tried as a way of relieving the unwanted symptoms. Surgery can help up to one third of patients with the most severe form of OCD. The most common operation involves removing a section of the brain called the cingulate cortex. The serious side effects of this surgery for some patients are seizures, personality changes, and less ability to plan.

Prognosis

Obsessive-compulsive disorder is a chronic disease that, if untreated, can last for decades, fluctuating from mild to severe and worsening with age. When treated by a combination of drugs and behavioral therapy, some patients go into complete remission. Unfortunately, not all patients have such a good response. About 20 percent of people cannot find relief with either drugs or behavioral therapy. **Hospitalization** may be required in some cases.

Despite the crippling nature of the symptoms, many successful doctors, lawyers, business people, performers, and entertainers function well in society despite their condition. Nevertheless, the emotional and financial cost of obsessive-compulsive disorder can be quite high.

Parental concerns

Some people have referred to obsessive-compulsive disorder as "the great pretender," because its symptoms can mimic a number of other disorders. Furthermore, children may become skilled at hiding the more embarrassing features of their condition. Because of these characteristics of the disorder, obsessive-compulsive disorder may go undiagnosed for some time.

KEY TERMS

Anxiety disorder—A mental disorder characterized by prolonged, excessive worry about circumstances in one's life. Anxiety disorders include agoraphobia and other phobias, obsessive-compulsive disorder, post-traumatic stress disorder, and panic disorder.

Cognitive-behavioral therapy—A type of psychotherapy in which people learn to recognize and change negative and self-defeating patterns of thinking and behavior.

Compulsion—A repetitive or ritualistic behavior that a person performs to reduce anxiety. Compulsions often develop as a way of controlling or "undoing" obsessive thoughts.

Obsession—A persistent image, idea, or desire that dominates a person's thoughts or feelings.

Selective serotonin reuptake inhibitors (SSRIs)—A class of antidepressants that work by blocking the reabsorption of serotonin in the brain, thus raising the levels of serotonin. SSRIs include fluoxetine (Prozac), sertraline (Zoloft), and paroxetine (Paxil).

Serotonin—A widely distributed neurotransmitter that is found in blood platelets, the lining of the digestive tract, and the brain, and that works in combination with norepinephrine. It causes very powerful contractions of smooth muscle and is associated with mood, attention, emotions, and sleep. Low levels of serotonin are associated with depression.

Resources

BOOKS

Herbert, Fredrick B. "Obsessive-Compulsive Disorder in Children and Adolescents." In *Psychiatric Secrets*. Edited by James L. Jacobson et al. Philadelphia: Hanley and Belfus, 2001.

Stafford, Brian, et al. "Anxiety Disorders." In *Nelson Textbook of Pediatrics*. Edited by Richard E. Behrman et al. Philadelphia: Saunders, 2004.

PERIODICALS

Barrett, P. "Cognitive-behavioral family treatment of childhood obsessive-compulsive disorder: a controlled trial." *Journal of the American Academy of Child and Adolescent Psychiatry* 43 (January 2004): 46–62.

Storch, E. A. "Behavioral treatment of a child with PANDAS." *Journal of the American Academy of Child and Adolescent Psychiatry* 86 (May 2004): 510–1.

ORGANIZATIONS

Anxiety Disorders Association of America. 11900 Park Lawn Drive, Suite 100, Rockville, MD 20852. Web site: <www.adaa.org>.

National Alliance for the Mentally Ill (NAMI). Colonial Place Three, 2107 Wilson Blvd., Suite 300, Arlington, VA 22201–3042. Web site: <www.nami.org>.

National Anxiety Foundation. 3135 Custer Dr., Lexington, KY 40517. Web site: <www.lexington-on-line.com/naf.html>.

Carol A. Turkington
Rosalyn Carson-DeWitt, MD

Oligomenorrhea

Definition

Medical dictionaries define oligomenorrhea as infrequent or very light **menstruation**. But physicians typically apply a narrower definition, restricting the diagnosis of oligomenorrhea to women whose periods were regularly established before they developed problems with infrequent flow. With oligomenorrhea, menstrual periods occur at intervals of greater than 35 days, with only four to nine periods in a year.

Description

True oligomenorrhea cannot occur until a young woman's menstrual periods have been established. In the United States, 97.5 percent of women have begun normal menstrual cycles by age 16. The complete absence of menstruation (menstrual periods never started or they stopped after having been established) is called **amenorrhea**. Oligomenorrhea can be redefined as amenorrhea if menstruation stops for six months or more; however, there is no universally agreed-upon cutoff point or timeline.

It is quite common for women at the beginning and end of their reproductive lives to miss periods or have them at irregular intervals. This variation is normal and is usually the result of imperfect coordination between the hypothalamus, the pituitary gland, and the ovaries. For no apparent reason, a few women menstruate (with ovulation occurring) on a regular schedule as infrequently as once every two months. For them that schedule is normal and not a cause for concern.

Women with polycystic ovary syndrome (PCOS) are also likely to suffer from oligomenorrhea. PCOS is a condition in which the ovaries become filled with small cysts. Women with PCOS show menstrual irregularities that range from oligomenorrhea and amenorrhea to very heavy and irregular periods. PCOS affects about 6 percent of premenopausal women and is related to excess androgen production.

Other physical and emotional factors also cause a woman to miss periods. These include the following:

- emotional stress
- chronic illness
- poor nutritional status
- such eating disorders as **anorexia nervosa**
- excessive **exercise**
- estrogen-secreting tumors
- abnormalities in the structure of the uterus or cervix that obstruct the outflow of menstrual fluid
- illicit use of anabolic steroid drugs to enhance athletic performance

Professional ballet dancers, gymnasts, and ice skaters are especially at risk for oligomenorrhea because they combine strenuous physical activity with a diet intended to keep their weight down. Menstrual irregularities are known to be one of the three disorders comprising the so-called "female athlete triad," the other disorders being disordered eating and osteoporosis. The triad was first formally named at the annual meeting of the American College of Sports Medicine in 1993, but doctors were aware of the combination of bone mineral loss, stress **fractures**, eating disorders, and participation in women's **sports** for several decades before the triad was named. Women's coaches have become increasingly aware of the problem since the early 1990s and are encouraging female athletes to seek medical advice.

Demographics

By definition, oligomenorrhea is a health concern only for women. It is estimated that about 5 percent of women in the United States in their childbearing years experience an episode of oligomenorrhea each year. This percentage appears to be constant across racial and ethnic groups.

Oligomenorrhea related to the female athlete triad is more common in this group of women than in the general female population. One study at the University of California at San Francisco found that 11 percent of female marathon runners had amenorrhea or oligomenorrhea. Although precise data are difficult to obtain because many athletes with the triad try to hide their symptoms from others, disordered eating and menstrual irregularities have been estimated to run as high as 62 percent of female athletes at the college level, with 4 percent to 39 percent meeting the criteria for anorexia nervosa or **bulimia nervosa** as defined by the fourth edition of the *Diagnostic and Statistical Manual of Mental Disorders*, or *DSM-IV*.

Causes and symptoms

Causes

Oligomenorrhea that occurs in adolescents is often caused by immaturity or lack of synchronization between the hypothalamus, pituitary gland, and ovaries. The hypothalamus is the part of the brain that controls body temperature, cellular metabolism, and such basic functions as appetite for food, the sleep/wake cycle, and reproduction. The hypothalamus also secretes hormones that regulate the pituitary gland.

The pituitary gland is then stimulated to produce hormones that affect growth and reproduction. At the beginning and end of a woman's reproductive life, some of these hormone messages may not be synchronized, resulting in menstrual irregularities.

Oligomenorrhea in PCOS is thought to be caused by inappropriate levels of both female and male hormones. Male hormones are produced in small quantities by all women, but in women with PCOS, levels of male hormone (androgens) are slightly higher than in other women. Some researchers hypothesize that the ovaries of women with PCOS are abnormal in other respects. In 2003, a group of researchers in London reported that there are fundamental differences between the development of egg follicles in normal ovaries and follicle development in the ovaries of women with PCOS.

In athletes, models, actresses, dancers, and women with anorexia nervosa, oligomenorrhea occurs because body fat drops too low compared to weight. Emotional stress related to performance anxiety may also be a factor in oligomenorrhea in these women.

Symptoms

Women with oligomenorrhea may have the following symptoms:

• menstrual periods at intervals of more than 35 days

• unusually light menstrual flow

• irregular menstrual periods with unpredictable flow

• difficulty conceiving

Young women whose oligomenorrhea is associated with the female athlete triad may have such other symptoms of the triad as frequent stress fractures, particularly in the bones of the hips, spine, or lower legs; abnormal eating patterns or extremely restrictive diets; and abnormal heart rhythms or low blood pressure.

When to call the doctor

A young woman should see her doctor as soon as she notices that a previously regular menstrual pattern has become irregular; it is not necessary to wait six months or longer to have oligomenorrhea investigated. A common rule is to consult the doctor after three missed periods.

Diagnosis

History and physical examination

Diagnosis of oligomenorrhea begins with the patient informing the doctor about infrequent periods. The doctor will ask for a detailed description of the problem and take a history of how long it has existed and any patterns the patient has observed. A woman can assist the doctor in diagnosing the cause of oligomenorrhea by keeping a record of the time, frequency, length, and quantity of bleeding. She should also tell the doctor about any recent illnesses, including longstanding conditions such as **diabetes mellitus**. The doctor may also inquire about the patient's diet, exercise patterns, sexual activity, contraceptive use, current medications, or past surgical procedures.

The doctor will then perform a physical examination to evaluate the patient's weight in proportion to her height, to check for signs of normal sexual development, to make sure the heart rhythm and other vital signs are normal, and to palpate (feel) the thyroid gland for evidence of swelling.

In the case of female athletes, the doctor may need to establish a relationship of trust with the patient before asking about such matters as diet, practice and workout schedules, and the use of such drugs as steroids or ephedrine. The presence of stress fractures in young women should be investigated. In some cases, the doctor may give the patients the Eating Disorder Inventory (EDI) or a similar screening questionnaire to help determine whether the patient is at risk for developing anorexia or bulimia.

Laboratory tests

After taking the young woman's history, the gynecologist or **family** practitioner does a pelvic examination and Pap smear. To rule out specific causes of oligomenorrhea, the doctor may also order a pregnancy test in sexually active women and blood tests to check the level of thyroid hormone. Based on the initial test results, the doctor may want to perform additional tests to determine the level of other hormones that play a role in reproduction.

As of 2003, more sensitive monoclonal assays had been developed for measuring hormone levels in the blood serum of women with PCOS, thus allowing earlier and more accurate diagnosis.

Imaging studies

In some cases the doctor may order an ultrasound study of the pelvic region to check for anatomical abnormalities or x rays or a bone scan to check for bone fractures. In a few cases the doctor may order an MRI to rule out tumors affecting the hypothalamus or pituitary gland.

Treatment

Treatment of oligomenorrhea depends on the cause. In adolescents and women near menopause, oligomenorrhea usually needs no treatment. For some athletes, changes in training routines and eating habits may be enough to return the woman to a regular menstrual cycle.

Most patients suffering from oligomenorrhea are treated with birth control pills. Other women, including those with PCOS, are treated with hormones. Prescribed hormones depend on which particular hormones are deficient or out of balance. When oligomenorrhea is associated with an eating disorder or the female athlete triad, the underlying condition must be treated. Consultation with a psychiatrist and nutritionist is usually necessary to manage an eating disorder. Female athletes may require physical therapy or rehabilitation as well.

Alternative treatment

As with conventional medical treatments, alternative treatments are based on the cause of the condition. If a hormonal imbalance is revealed by laboratory testing, hormone replacements that are more "natural" for the body (including tri-estrogen and natural progesterone) are recommended. Glandular therapy can assist in bringing about a balance in the glands involved in the reproductive cycle, including the hypothalamus, pituitary, thyroid, ovarian, and adrenal glands.

Since homeopathy and acupuncture work on deep, energetic levels to rebalance the body, these two forms of therapy may be helpful in treating oligomenorrhea. Western and Chinese herbal medicines also can be very effective. Herbs used to treat oligomenorrhea include dong quai (*Angelica sinensis*), black cohosh (*Cimicifuga racemosa*), and chaste tree (*Vitex agnus-castus*). Herbal preparations used to bring on the menstrual period are known as emmenagogues. For some women, meditation, guided imagery, and visualization can play a role in the treatment of oligomenorrhea by relieving emotional stress.

Nutritional concerns

Diet and adequate **nutrition**, including adequate protein, essential fatty acids, whole grains, and fresh fruits and vegetables are important for every woman, especially if deficiencies are present or if she regularly exercises very strenuously. Female athletes at the high school or college level should consult a nutritionist to make sure that they are eating a well-balanced diet that is adequate to maintain a healthy weight for their height. Girls participating in dance or in sports that emphasize weight control or a slender body type (gymnastics, track and field, swimming, and cheerleading) are at higher risk of developing eating disorders than those that are involved in such sports as softball, weight lifting, or basketball. In some cases the athlete may be given calcium or vitamin D supplements to lower the risk of osteoporosis.

Prognosis

Many women, including those with PCOS, are successfully treated with hormones for oligomenorrhea. They have more frequent periods and begin ovulating during their menstrual cycle, restoring their fertility.

For women who do not respond to hormones or who continue to have an underlying condition that causes oligomenorrhea, the outlook is less positive. Women who have oligomenorrhea as teenagers may have difficulty becoming pregnant and may receive fertility drugs. The absence of adequate estrogen increases the risk of osteoporosis, repeated bone fractures, and cardiovascular disease in later life. Female athletes who develop bone loss or osteoporosis in their late teens or early twenties are at increased risk of developing arthritis as they grow older. Women who do not have regular periods also are more likely to develop uterine **cancer**. Oligomenorrhea can become amenorrhea at any time, increasing the chance of having these complications.

KEY TERMS

Amenorrhea—The absence or abnormal stoppage of menstrual periods.

Anorexia nervosa—An eating disorder marked by an unrealistic fear of weight gain, self-starvation, and distortion of body image. It most commonly occurs in adolescent females.

Cyst—An abnormal sac or enclosed cavity in the body filled with liquid or partially solid material. Also refers to a protective, walled-off capsule in which an organism lies dormant.

Emmenagogue—A type of medication that brings on or increases a woman's menstrual flow.

Female athlete triad—A combination of disorders frequently found in female athletes that includes disordered eating, osteoporosis, and oligo- or amenorrhea. The triad was first officially named in 1993.

Osteoporosis—Literally meaning "porous bones," this condition occurs when bones lose an excessive amount of their protein and mineral content, particularly calcium. Over time, bone mass and strength are reduced leading to increased risk of fractures.

Prevention

Oligomenorrhea is preventable only in women whose low body fat to weight ratio is keeping them from maintaining a regular menstrual cycle. Adequate nutrition and less vigorous training schedules for female athletes will normally prevent oligomenorrhea. When oligomenorrhea is caused by hormonal factors, however, it is not preventable, but is usually treatable.

Parental concerns

Oligomenorrhea in teenagers who have only recently begun to menstruate is not usually a cause for parental concern, particularly if the girl's development during **puberty** has been otherwise normal or if there is a family history of oligomenorrhea. Oligomenorrhea in an adolescent should be investigated, however, if the girl is heavily involved in athletics or if she is otherwise at risk for developing an eating disorder. One way that parents can help college-age athletes is to be affectionate and emotionally supportive of their daughter, as girls who are away from home for the first time or who are "loners" are particularly at risk for developing the female athlete triad during their freshman year.

Resources

BOOKS

Diagnostic and Statistical Manual of Mental Disorders, 4th ed., Text Revision. Washington, DC: American Psychiatric Association, 2000.

"Menstrual Abnormalities and Abnormal Uterine Bleeding." Section 18, Chapter 235 in *The Merck Manual of Diagnosis and Therapy*, edited by Mark H. Beers and Robert Berkow. Whitehouse Station, NJ: Merck Research Laboratories, 2002.

Pelletier, Kenneth R. *The Best Alternative Medicine*, Part II, "CAM Therapies for Specific Conditions: Menstrual Symptoms, Menopause, and PMS." New York: Simon & Schuster, 2002.

PERIODICALS

Gourlay, M. L., and S. A. Brown. "Clinical Considerations in Premenopausal Osteoporosis." *Archives of Internal Medicine* 164 (March 22, 2004): 603–14.

Klentrou, P., and M. Plyley. "Onset of Puberty, Menstrual Frequency, and Body Fat in Elite Rhythmic Gymnasts Compared with Normal Controls." *British Journal of Sports Medicine* 37 (December 2003): 490–94.

Milsom, S. R., et al. "LH Levels in Women with Polycystic Ovarian Syndrome: Have Modern Assays Made Them Irrelevant?" *Blackwell Journal of Obstetrics and Gynaecology* 110 (August 2003): 760–64.

Suliman, A. M., et al. "Frequent Misdiagnosis and Mismanagement of Hyperprolactinemic Patients Before the Introduction of Macroprolactin Screening: Application of a New Strict Laboratory Definition of Macroprolactinemia." *Clinical Chemistry* 49 (September 2003): 1504–09.

Webber, L. J., et al. "Formation and Early Development of Follicles in the Polycystic Ovary." *Lancet* 362 (September 27, 2003): 1017–21.

ORGANIZATIONS

American Academy of Child and Adolescent Psychiatry. 3615 Wisconsin Avenue, NW, Washington, DC 20016–3007. Web site: <www.aacap.org>.

American College of Sports Medicine (ACSM). 401 West Michigan Street, Indianapolis, IN 46202–3233. Web site: <www.acsm.org>.

Polycystic Ovarian Syndrome Association. PO Box 80517, Portland, OR 7280. Web site: <www.pcosupport.org>.

WEB SITES

Barrow, Boone. "Female Athlete Triad." *eMedicine*, June 17, 2004. Available online at <www.emedicine.com/sports/topic163.htm> (accessed November 30, 2004).

Chandran, Latha. "Menstruation Disorders." *eMedicine*, August 9, 2004. Available online at

<www.emedicine.com/ped/topic2781.htm> (accessed November 30, 2004).

Nelson, Lawrence M., Vladimir Bakalov, and Carmen Pastor. "Amenorrhea." *eMedicine*, September 24, 2004. Available online at <www.emedicine.com/med/topic117.htm> (accessed November 30, 2004).

Tish Davidson AM

Omphalocele *see* **Abdominal wall defects**

Oppositional defiant disorder

Definition

Oppositional defiant disorder (ODD) is a childhood mental disorder characterized by a pattern of angry, antagonistic, hostile, negative, irritable, and/or vindictive behavior lasting at least six months and occurring more frequently than is typically observed for the child's age and developmental stage. Children diagnosed with ODD do not meet the clinical diagnostic criteria for **conduct disorder**.

Description

Oppositional defiant disorder (ODD), a relatively new clinical classification, involves an ongoing pattern of antagonistic, defiant, and hostile behavior toward parents and other authority figures. Children and adolescents with ODD often have frequent temper **tantrums**, blame others for their misbehavior, argue excessively with adults, actively refuse to comply with adult rules and requests, deliberately defy adults and attempt to annoy or upset them, and are easily annoyed by others.

Demographics

Before **puberty**, ODD is more common in boys than girls; however, after puberty ODD occurrence rates are about equal in boys and girls. The disorder typically begins by the age of eight. According to the American Academy of Child and Adolescent Psychiatry, approximately 5 to 15 percent of all school-aged children have ODD.

Causes and symptoms

Although the specific causes of ODD are unknown, genetics and environment are thought to play a role in its development. As of 2004 several theories about the causes of oppositional defiant disorder are being investigated. ODD may be related to the following:

- the child's **temperament** and the family's response to that temperament
- an inherited predisposition to the disorder in certain families
- a neurological cause, such as a head injury
- a chemical imbalance in the brain (especially with the brain chemical serotonin)

ODD appears to be more common in families in which at least one parent has a history of a mood disorder, conduct disorder, attention deficit hyperactivity disorder (ADHD), **antisocial personality disorder**, or a substance abuse-related disorder. Children with one parent who is alcoholic or who has been in trouble with the law are almost three times more likely to have ODD. Additionally, some studies suggest that mothers with a depressive disorder are more likely to have children that develop ODD. ODD can also occur in conjunction with other conditions such as ADHD, learning disabilities, **anxiety** disorders, and **mood disorders**. About 50 percent to 65 percent of children with ADHD also have ODD.

Symptoms of ODD include a pattern of negative, hostile, and defiant behavior lasting at least six months. During this time four or more of the following must be present for a child to be diagnosed with ODD:

- often loses his/her temper
- often argues with adults
- often actively defies or refuses to comply with adults' requests or rules
- often deliberately annoys people
- often blames others for his/her mistakes or misbehavior
- is often touchy or easily annoyed by others
- is often angry and resentful
- is often spiteful or vindictive
- misbehaves frequently
- swears or uses obscene language
- has a low opinion of him/herself

Additional problems may be present, including the following:

- learning problems
- a depressed mood
- hyperactivity (although ADHD must be ruled out)

- substance abuse or dependence
- dramatic and erratic behavior

When to call the doctor

Parents of children and adolescents who exhibit symptoms of ODD should see a physician as soon as possible. Usually, a referral to a psychologist, psychiatrist, or therapist will be given.

Diagnosis

ODD is diagnosed by psychological and psychiatric evaluations; interviews with **family** members, teachers, and caregivers; and observation and interviews with the child or adolescent. Diagnosis is based on clinical criteria defined in the American Psychiatric Association's *Diagnostic and Statistical Manual of Mental Disorders*, fourth edition, text revision C (DSM-IV-TR).

ODD often has characteristics in common with other psychological disorders and often occurs in conjunction with other conditions, such as ADHD or mood disorders. Therefore, diagnosis of ODD usually depends on exclusion of other disorders. A diagnosis of ODD is not made if the symptoms occur exclusively in psychotic or mood disorders, or if the child meets clinical criteria for conduct disorder, or, if the adolescent is 18 years old or older and meets clinical criteria for antisocial personality disorder. Children and adolescents with ODD do not exhibit the more serious aggressive behaviors or physical cruelty that is common in other disorders.

Treatment

Treatment of ODD usually involves medication, and group, individual, and/or **family therapy**. Of these, individual therapy is the most common. The goal of therapy is to help provide a consistent daily schedule, support, rules, **discipline**, and limits, as well as to help train patients to get along with others by modifying behaviors. Therapy can occur in residential or day treatment facilities, in a medical setting, or on an outpatient basis. Therapy can instruct patients on how to effectively deal with ODD and help them learn how to do the following:

- use self time-outs
- identify what increases anxiety
- talk about feelings instead of acting on them
- find and use ways to calm themselves
- frequently remind themselves of their goals
- get involved in tasks and physical activities that provide a healthy outlet for energy

- learn how to talk with others
- develop a predictable, consistent, daily schedule of activity
- develop ways to obtain pleasure and feel good
- learn how to get along with other people
- find ways to limit stimulation
- learn to admit mistakes in a matter-of-fact way

Therapy can also involve the parents. Parent management training focuses on teaching parents specific and more effective techniques for handling the child's opposition and defiance. Research has shown that parent management training is more effective than family therapy.

Stimulant medication is used only when ODD co-occurs with ADHD. Occasionally, children and adolescents with ODD may also have depression or anxiety disorders, and treatment with **antidepressants** and anti-anxiety medications can help alleviate some symptoms of ODD.

Prognosis

The prognosis for ODD varies. In some children, ODD evolves into a conduct disorder or a mood disorder. ODD, if left untreated, has approximately an 80 percent chance of turning into conduct disorder as a child ages. Later in life, ODD can develop into passive-aggressive personality disorder or antisocial personality disorder. ODD can cause significant social, academic, and/or occupational impairment. Generally, with treatment and long-term participation in therapy, adjustment in social settings and in the workplace can be made in adulthood.

Prevention

As of 2004, ODD could not be prevented.

Parental concerns

Children and adolescents with ODD usually have difficulties in school and at home. In some cases, ODD can result in expulsion from school. Parents should investigate **alternative school** settings that may be able to provide counseling and group therapy integrated with academics. Assistance is available through county social or mental health services, educational consultants, and local school counselors. Family therapy may help alleviate stressful family situations and help other family members understand the disorder.

KEY TERMS

Alternative school—An educational setting designed to accommodate educational, behavioral, and/or medical needs of children and adolescents that cannot be adequately addressed in a traditional school environment.

Antisocial personality disorder—A disorder characterized by a behavior pattern that disregards for the rights of others. People with this disorder often deceive and manipulate, or their behavior might include aggression to people or animals or property destruction, for example. This disorder has also been called sociopathy.

Attention deficit hyperactivity disorder (ADHD)—A condition in which a person (usually a child) has an unusually high activity level and a short attention span. People with the disorder may act impulsively and may have learning and behavioral problems.

Conduct disorder—A behavioral and emotional disorder of childhood and adolescence. Children with a conduct disorder act inappropriately, infringe on the rights of others, and violate societal norms.

Television viewing and video/computer games can contribute to ODD behaviors. For children with ADHD or ODD, the American Academy of Pediatrics recommends limiting use of television and video/computer games to no more than two hours per day, monitoring children's use of television and computers, and viewing family-oriented television programs with their children.

Parents may find it helpful to track their child's moods and behaviors and to help children learn to track their own moods and behaviors to help identify possible stresses and causative factors.

Parents should actively participate in their child's therapy and learn positive parenting techniques that can help ODD behaviors. When parents are too restrictive, children and adolescents with ODD can rebel, and power struggles can frequently occur. Therapists specializing in ODD can help families become more effective in handling ODD behaviors in order to avoid such rebellion. The American Academy of Child and Adolescent Psychiatry recommends the following for parents with children who have ODD:

- Choose battles by setting priorities regarding child's behavior.

- Set reasonable, age-appropriate limits with consistently enforceable consequences.

- Work with teachers, coaches, and other family members for support in dealing with the child with ODD.

- Use positive reinforcement praise when the child displays desired behaviors.

- Take time to manage stress by exercising and/or relaxing away from the child.

Resources

BOOKS

Sutton, James D. *What Parents Need to Know about ODD: Up-to-Date Insights and Ideas for Managing Oppositional Defiant Disorder and Other Defiant Behavior.* Pleasanton, TX: Friendly Oaks Publications, 2003.

PERIODICALS

Barrickman, L. "Disruptive Behavioral Disorders." *Pediatric Clinics of North America* 50 (2003):1005–17.

Greene R. W., et al. "Psychiatric Comorbidity, Family Dysfunction, and Social Impairment in Referred Youth with Oppositional Defiant Disorder." *American Journal of Psychiatry* 159 (July 2002): 1214–24.

ORGANIZATIONS

American Academy of Child and Adolescent Psychiatry. Web site: <www.aacap.org>.

American Psychiatric Association. 1000 Wilson Boulevard, Suite 1825, Arlington, VA 22209–3901. Web site: <www.psych.org/>.

WEB SITES

Tynan, W. Douglas. "Oppositional Defiant Disorder." *eMedicine,* November 2, 2003. Available online at <www.emedicine.com/ped/topic2791.htm> (accessed November 21, 2004).

Wood, D. "What is Oppositional Defiant Disorder (ODD)?" Available online at <www.mental-health-matters.com/disorders/dis_details.php?disID=67> (accessed November 21, 2004).

Jennifer E. Sisk, M.A.

Oral contraceptives

Definition

Oral contraceptives are medicines taken by mouth to help prevent pregnancy. They are also known as the pill, OCs, or birth control pills.

Description

Oral contraceptives, or birth control pills, contain synthetic forms of two hormones produced naturally in the body. These hormones, estrogen and progestin, regulate the female menstrual cycle. Some types of oral contraceptives use only progestational hormones, but most use a combination of estrogen and progestin. As of 2004, there were three types of oral contraceptives marketed:

• Monophasic use a fixed dose of both estrogen and progestin during the entire cycle.

• Biphasic oral contraceptives use a constant amount of estrogen during the full cycle, but the amount of progestin is lower during the first half of the cycle and increases in the second half. This shift in dosage is intended to mimic the natural ovarian cycle.

• Triphasic oral contraceptives may vary both the estrogen and progestin levels at different times during the cycle.

The goal of the biphasic and triphasic formulations is to achieve adequate control of the menstrual cycle while using lower doses of both estrogens and progestins, thereby reducing the risk of adverse effects. Reviews of controlled studies have not demonstrated a clear advantage of the newer formulations over the older monophasic drugs.

General use

When taken in the proper amounts, following a specific schedule, oral contraceptives are very effective in preventing pregnancy. Studies show that fewer than one of every 100 females who use oral contraceptives correctly becomes pregnant during the first year of use.

These pills have several effects that help prevent pregnancy. For pregnancy to occur, an egg must become mature inside a woman's ovary, be released, and travel to the fallopian tube. Sperm must travel through the reproductive track to fertilize the egg in the fallopian tube. Then the fertilized egg must travel to the woman's uterus (womb), where it lodges in the uterus lining and develops into a fetus.

The main way that oral contraceptives prevent pregnancy is by keeping an egg from ripening fully. Eggs that do not ripen fully cannot be fertilized. In addition, birth control pills thicken mucus in the woman's body through which the sperm has to swim. Thus it is more difficult for the sperm to reach the egg. Oral contraceptives also change the uterine lining so that a fertilized egg cannot lodge there to develop.

Although **contraception** is the primary use of these medications, they may also be used to treat adolescent and post-adolescent **acne** in girls. Some products have this as part of their official indications, but others may be used as well.

Precautions

No form of birth control (except abstinence from sexual intercourse) is 100 percent effective. However, oral contraceptives can be highly effective when used properly. Teens and young women who anticipate having sexual intercourse should discuss the options with a healthcare professional.

Oral contraceptives do not protect against **AIDS** or other **sexually transmitted diseases**. For some protection against such diseases, teenage males and young men need to use a latex **condom**. Also, oral contraceptives are not effective immediately after a young woman begins taking them. Physicians recommend using other forms of birth control for the first one to three weeks. Then users should follow the instructions of the physician who prescribed the medicine.

Smoking cigarettes while taking oral contraceptives greatly increases the risk of serious side effects. Females who take oral contraceptives should not smoke cigarettes.

Seeing a physician regularly while taking this medicine is very important. The physician will note unwanted side effects, and patients should follow his or her advice on how often they should be seen.

Young women who take oral contraceptives should be sure to tell the healthcare professional in charge before they undergo surgical or dental procedures, laboratory tests, or emergency treatment.

This medicine may increase sensitivity to sunlight. Females using oral contraceptives should avoid too much sun exposure and should not use tanning beds, tanning booths, or sunlamps until they know how the medicine affects them. Some females taking oral contraceptives may get brown splotches on exposed areas of their skin. These usually go away over time after the women stop taking birth control pills.

Oral contraceptives may cause the gums to become tender and swollen or to bleed. Careful brushing and flossing, gum massage, and regular cleaning may help prevent this problem. Users should check with a physician or dentist if gum problems develop.

Side effects

Serious side effects are rare in healthy females who do not smoke cigarettes. In women with certain health problems, however, oral contraceptives may cause problems such as liver **cancer**, noncancerous liver tumors, blood clots, or **stroke**. Healthcare professionals can help prospective users weigh the benefits of being protected against unwanted pregnancy against the risks of possible health problems.

The most common minor side effects are **nausea**, **vomiting**, abdominal cramping or bloating, breast **pain**, tenderness or swelling, swollen ankles or feet, tiredness, and acne. These problems usually go away as the body adjusts to the drug and do not need medical attention unless they continue or they interfere with normal activities. Other side effects should be brought to the attention of the physician who prescribed the medicine. Teens and young women should check with the physician as soon as possible if any of the following side effects occur:

- menstrual changes, such as lighter periods or missed periods, longer periods, or bleeding or spotting between periods

- headaches

- vaginal infection, **itching**, or irritation

- increased blood pressure

Women who have any of the following symptoms should get emergency help right away. These symptoms may be signs of blood clots:

- sudden changes in vision, speech, breathing, or coordination

- severe or sudden **headache**

- coughing up blood

- sudden, severe, or continuing pain in the abdomen or stomach

- pain in the chest, groin, or leg (especially in the calf)

- weakness, **numbness**, or pain in an arm or leg

The adverse effects of oral contraceptives can be impossible to predict. Other than avoiding smoking, there are no effective means of preventing side effects. All observed adverse effects should be reported to a physician promptly.

Oral contraceptives may continue to affect the menstrual cycle for some time after a young woman stops taking them. Women who miss periods for several months after stopping this medicine should check with their physicians. Other rare side effects may occur. Anyone who has unusual symptoms while taking oral contraceptives should get in touch with her physician.

A doctor explains to a teenage girl how to use birth control pills. *(© LWA-Stephen Welstead/Corbis.)*

Interactions

Oral contraceptives may interact with a number of other medicines. When interaction occurs, the effects of one or both of the drugs may change or the risk of side effects may be greater. Anyone who takes oral contraceptives should let the physician know all other medicines she is taking and should ask whether possible interactions can interfere with drug therapy.

These drugs may make oral contraceptives less effective in preventing pregnancy. Anyone who takes these drugs should use an additional birth control method for the entire cycle in which the medicine is used:

- ampicillin

- penicillin V

- rifampin (Rifadin)

- tetracyclines

- griseofulvin (Gris-PEG, Fulvicin)

KEY TERMS

Cyst—An abnormal sac or enclosed cavity in the body filled with liquid or partially solid material. Also refers to a protective, walled-off capsule in which an organism lies dormant.

Endometriosis—A condition in which the tissue that normally lines the uterus (endometrium) grows in other areas of the body, causing pain, irregular bleeding, and frequently, infertility.

Fallopian tubes—The pair of narrow tubes leading from a woman's ovaries to the uterus. After an egg is released from the ovary during ovulation, fertilization (the union of sperm and egg) normally occurs in the fallopian tubes.

Fetus—In humans, the developing organism from the end of the eighth week to the moment of birth. Until the end of the eighth week the developing organism is called an embryo.

Fibroid tumor—A non-cancerous tumor of connective tissue made of elongated, threadlike structures, or fibers, which usually grow slowly and are contained within an irregular shape. Fibroids are firm in consistency but may become painful if they start to break down or apply pressure to areas within the body. They frequently occur in the uterus and are generally left alone unless growing rapidly or causing other problems. Surgery is needed to remove fibroids.

Hormone—A chemical messenger secreted by a gland or organ and released into the bloodstream. It travels via the bloodstream to distant cells where it exerts an effect.

Jaundice—A condition in which the skin and whites of the eyes take on a yellowish color due to an increase of bilirubin (a compound produced by the liver) in the blood. Also called icterus.

Migraine—A throbbing headache that usually affects only one side of the head. Nausea, vomiting, increased sensitivity to light, and other symptoms often accompany a migraine.

Mucus—The thick fluid produced by the mucous membranes that line many body cavities and structures. It contains mucin, white blood cells, water, inorganic salts, and shed cells, and it serve to lubricate body parts and to trap particles of dirt or other contaminants.

Ovary—One of the two almond-shaped glands in the female reproductive system responsible for producing eggs and the sex hormones estrogen and progesterone.

Pelvic inflammatory disease (PID)—Any infection of the lower female reproductive tract (vagina and cervix) that spreads to the upper female reproductive tract (uterus, fallopian tubes and ovaries). Symptoms include severe abdominal pain, high fever, and vaginal discharge. PID is the most common and most serious consequence of infection with sexually transmitted diseases in women and is a leading cause of female fertility problems.

Uterus—The female reproductive organ that contains and nourishes a fetus from implantation until birth. Also called the womb.

- corticosteroids
- barbiturates
- carbamazepine (Tegretol)
- phenytoin (Dilantin)
- primidone (Mysoline)
- ritonavir (Norvir)

In addition, taking the following medicines with oral contraceptives may increase the risk of side effects or interfere with the medicine's effects:

- Theophylline: Effects of this medicine may increase, along with the chance of unwanted side effects.
- Cyclosporine: Effects of this medicine may increase, along with the chance of unwanted side effects.

- Troleandomycin (TAO): Chance of liver problems may increase. Effectiveness of oral contraceptive may also decrease, raising the risk of pregnancy.

The list above does not include every drug that may interact with oral contraceptives. Women should be sure to check with a physician or pharmacist before combining oral contraceptives with any other prescription or nonprescription (over-the-counter) medicine. As with any medication, the benefits and risks should be discussed with a physician.

Parental concerns

Parents become concerned that teens who use oral contraceptives are at risk of becoming sexually active. Although studies have been limited, they have failed to show that availability of oral contraceptives leads to an increase in sexual activity among adolescent girls.

Oral contraceptives do not protect against sexually transmitted diseases. When used for contraception, they should be limited to monogamous relationships.

Although the list of potential side effects and adverse effects is very long and contains some severe risks, the actual frequency of these risks is low. In most cases, oral contraceptives have a very high safety margin.

Resources

BOOKS

Mcevoy, Gerald K., et al. *AHFS Drug Information 2004.* Bethesda, MD: American Society of Healthsystems Pharmacists, 2004.

Siberry, George K., and Robert Iannone, eds. *The Harriet Lane Handbook*, 15th ed. Philadelphia: Mosby, 2000.

PERIODICALS

Kaunitz, Andrew M. "Enhancing oral contraceptive success: The potential of new formulations." *American Journal of Obstetrics & Gynecology* 190, no. 4, Suppl. (April 2004): S23–S29.

ORGANIZATIONS

American Academy of Dermatology. PO Box 4014, Schaumburg, IL 60168–4014. Web site: <www.aad.org>.

American Board of Obstetrics and Gynecology. 2915 Vine Street, Dallas, TX 75204. Web site: <www.abog.org>.

Planned Parenthood Federation of America. 434 West 33rd St., New York, NY 10001. Web site: <www.plannedparenthood.org>.

WEB SITES

"Update on Oral Contraceptives." *American Family Physician.* Available online at <www.aafp.org/afp/991101ap/html> (accessed September 28, 2004).

Deanna M. Swartout-Corbeil, R.N.
Samuel Uretsky, PharmD

Oral herpes *see* **Cold sore**

Oral hygiene

Definition

Oral hygiene is the practice of keeping the mouth clean and healthy by brushing and flossing to prevent **tooth decay** and gum disease.

Purpose

The purpose of oral hygiene is to prevent the build-up of plaque, the sticky film of bacteria and food that forms on the teeth. Plaque adheres to the crevices and fissures of the teeth and generates acids that, when not removed on a regular basis, slowly eat away, or decay, the protective enamel surface of the teeth, causing holes (cavities) to form. Plaque also irritates gums and can lead to gum disease, **periodontal disease**, and tooth loss. Brushing and flossing removes plaque from teeth, and antiseptic mouthwashes kill some of the bacteria that help form plaque. Fluoride, found in toothpaste, drinking water, or dental treatments, also helps to protect teeth by binding with enamel to make it stronger. In addition to such daily oral care, regular visits to the dentist promote oral health. Preventative services that the dentist can perform include fluoride treatments, sealant application, and scaling (scraping off the hardened plaque, called tartar). The dentist can also perform such diagnostic services as x-ray imaging and such treatments as filling cavities.

Description

The Centers for Disease Control and Prevention report that dental caries are perhaps the most prevalent of infectious diseases in children. More than 40 percent of all children have cavities by the time they reach kindergarten. It is, therefore, imperative that all parents learn the importance of early oral care and that they teach their children proper oral hygiene.

Good oral hygiene should start at the very beginning of a child's life. Even before his or her first teeth emerge, certain factors can affect their future appearance and health. Pregnant and nursing mothers should be careful about using medications, as some, like the antibiotic tetracycline, can cause tooth discoloration. Even before infants have teeth, they have special oral hygiene needs about which all parents should be aware. These include making certain the child receives adequate fluoride and guarding against baby bottle decay.

Fluoride in infancy

Fluoride is beneficial for babies even before their teeth erupt. It makes the tooth enamel stronger as the teeth are developing. In most municipal water supplies, the correct amount of fluoride is added for proper tooth development. If the water supply does not contain enough fluoride or if bottled water is used for drinking and cooking, the doctor or dentist should be informed. They may prescribe fluoride supplements for the baby.

Baby bottle decay

Baby bottle decay is caused by recurring exposure over time to sugary liquids. These include milk, formula, and fruit juices. These liquids pool for prolonged periods of time as the child sleeps. This exposure can lead to cavities forming, especially in the upper and lower front teeth. For this reason, children should not be allowed to fall asleep with a bottle of juice or milk in their mouths. An alternative is to give the child a bottle filled with water or a pacifier recommended by the dentist. Even breast-fed children are at risk. They should have their gums and teeth wiped with a clean, damp washcloth or gauze pad following each feeding.

Baby teeth, also known as primary teeth, are just as important as permanent teeth. They help the child to bite and chew food, help them speak correctly, save space for the child's permanent teeth, and help guide the permanent teeth into place. That is why it is so important to initiate a program of good oral hygiene for children early on.

Brushing

Once a baby has four teeth in a row, either on top or on the bottom, parents should begin using a toothbrush two times a day. When choosing a toothbrush, make sure the bristles are soft, polished, and made of nylon. Parents should administer only a pea-size amount of fluoride toothpaste that is made especially for children. Children tend to swallow, instead of spit out, toothpaste. If the child does not like the flavor of the toothpaste, using water alone is acceptable. Parents should also continue to wipe the toothless gum areas with a washcloth or gauze.

As the child gets older, parents should demonstrate proper brushing techniques. These include brushing the inside surface of each tooth first, where plaque tends to accumulate most. Then they should clean the outer surfaces of each tooth, angling the brush along the outer gum line. Next, they should brush the chewing surface of each tooth, then using the tip of the brush, clean behind each front tooth. They should use a gentle, back and forth motion when brushing and finish by brushing the tongue.

Children will, at some point, decide they would like to try brushing their teeth themselves. This is fine and should be encouraged, but parents should remain in charge of keeping children's teeth clean until they are between six to eight years old. Children do not have the dexterity or coordination to perform brushing well until this time. Even then, it is important that parents inspect their children's teeth each time they brush. They should

A boy flosses his teeth as part of a daily regimen for good oral hygiene. (© Joh Feingersh/Corbis.)

pay special attention to the molars, as these teeth have lots of tiny grooves and crevices where food particles can hide.

Good oral hygiene remains important as children grow into **adolescence**. In fact, adolescence can often be a time when cavities and periodontal disease happen more frequently. This higher rate is usually caused by an increased intake of junk food and sugary foods such as soft drinks, as well as inattention to oral hygiene procedures. Add to that the fact that many older children and teens wear braces, making the cleaning of teeth even more challenging. Parents should talk to their children about how important good oral hygiene is in preventing not only cavities, but teeth stains, bad breath, and an assortment of other dental problems.

Flossing

Flossing once a day helps to prevent gum disease by removing food particles and plaque at and below the gum line, as well as between teeth. Parents do not need to initiate flossing until the child has teeth that touch each other, which normally occurs in the molar areas first. Parents should continue to floss their child's teeth until they are six or seven years old. They should continue to monitor the child's techniques and consistency thereafter.

Proper flossing technique is essential in removing as much plaque as possible in a safe manner. The following procedure is recommended by dental hygienists. Wind 18 inches (45 cm) of dental floss around the middle fingers of each hand. Pinch the floss between the thumbs and index fingers, leaving about 1–2 inches (3–5 cm) length in between. Use the thumbs to direct the floss between the upper teeth. Try to keep the floss taut between the fingers. Use the index fingers to guide floss between lower teeth. Gently guide the floss between the teeth by using a zig-zag motion. Contour the floss around the side of each tooth. Slide the dental floss up and down against the tooth surface and under the gum line. Floss each tooth thoroughly with a clean section of floss.

Dental floss comes in many varieties (waxed, unwaxed, flavored, tape) and may be chosen based on personal preference. For those who have difficulty handling floss, floss holders and other types of interdental (between the teeth) cleaning aids are available. Some floss holders have animal and cartoon characters on them, which might make flossing more appealing to a child.

Precautions

It is important that younger children only use a very small amount of fluoridated toothpaste since using too much fluoride can be toxic to infants. Though brushing and flossing are important, neither should be performed too vigorously. The rough mechanical action may irritate or damage oral tissues. Parents should change their child's toothbrush three to four times a year and after every illness to avoid bacteria and germs.

Another factor that may affect a child's oral health is the increasingly popular practice among adolescents of oral piercings involving the tongue, lips, and cheeks. These piercings have been associated with infections, tooth fractures, periodontal disease, and nerve damage. Some life-threatening complications have occurred, including bleeding and airway obstruction. The American Academy of Pediatric Dentistry strongly opposes the practice of oral piercings.

Risks

The primary risks arise from a lack of proper oral hygiene practices. These major oral health problems are plaque, tartar, gingivitis, periodontitis, and tooth decay.

Parental concerns

Parents play an important role in both modeling and teaching good oral hygiene. Parents can make sure their child sees a dentist before the age of two. This can be a frightening experience for some children, but if parents exhibit a positive attitude, most children become comfortable with dentist visits. Children who learn proper oral care at a young age benefit from those good habits for the rest of their lives.

KEY TERMS

Calculus—Plural, calculi. Any type of hard concretion (stone) in the body, but usually found in the gallbladder, pancreas, and kidneys. They are formed by the accumulation of excess mineral salts and other organic material such as blood or mucous. Calculi (pl.) can cause problems by lodging in and obstructing the proper flow of fluids, such as bile to the intestines or urine to the bladder. In dentistry, calculus refers to a hardened yellow or brown mineral deposit from unremoved plaque, also called tartar.

Cavity—A hole or weak spot in the tooth surface caused by decay.

Gingivitis—Inflammation of the gums in which the margins of the gums near the teeth are red, puffy, and bleeding. It is most often due to poor dental hygiene.

Pediatric dentistry—The dental specialty concerned with the dental treatment of children and adolescents.

Plaque—A deposit, usually of fatty material, on the inside wall of a blood vessel. Also refers to a small, round demyelinated area that develops in the brain and spinal cord of an individual with multiple sclerosis.

Resources

BOOKS

Sutton, Amy. *Dental Care and Oral Health Sourcebook: Basic Consumer Health Information about Dental Care . . .* Detroit, MI: Omnigraphics, 2003.

Vogel, Elizabeth. *Brushing My Teeth.* New York: Rosen Publishing Group, 2001.

PERIODICALS

Garwood, Derrick. "Oral Hygiene." *The Pharmaceutical Journal* 270 (May 3, 2003): 619–21.

ORGANIZATIONS

American Academy of Pediatric Dentistry. 211 East Chicago Avenue, Suite 700, Chicago, IL 60611. Web site: <www.aapd.org>.

American Dental Hygienists' Association. 444 North Michigan Avenue, Suite 3400, Chicago, IL 60611. Web site: <www.adha.org>.

WEB SITES

"Oral Health Resources." *Centers for Disease Control and Prevention*. Available online at <www.cdc.gov/ OralHealth/index.htm> (accessed October 26, 2004).

Deanna M. Swartout-Corbeil, RN
Bethany Thivierge

Orthodontics

Definition

Orthodontics is a specialized branch of dentistry that diagnoses, prevents, and treats dental and facial irregularities called malocclusions. Orthodontics includes dentofacial orthopedics, which is used to correct problems involving the growth of the jaw.

Purpose

Humans have attempted to straighten teeth for thousands of years before orthodontics became a dental specialty in 1900. Although orthodontic treatment often improves facial appearance and occasionally is performed for solely cosmetic reasons, it is used primarily to correct health problems and to ensure the proper functioning of the mouth. Properly aligned teeth, which close together correctly, simplify **oral hygiene** and enable children to chew their food efficiently. Orthodontic treatment provides the following:

- straightens teeth that are rotated, tilted, or otherwise improperly aligned
- corrects crowded or unevenly spaced teeth
- corrects bite problems
- aligns the upper and lower jaws

Malocclusions

Few children have perfectly symmetrical teeth and a perfect bite. In an ideal bite, the following are characteristics:

- All of the teeth fit easily without crowding or spacing.
- The teeth are not rotated, twisted, or leaning forward or backward.
- The teeth of the upper jaw slightly overlap those of the lower jaw.
- The points of the molars fit into the grooves of the opposite molars.

Types of malocclusions include the following:

- crowded, crooked, or misaligned teeth
- extra or missing teeth
- bite problems
- jaws that are out of alignment

Causes of malocclusion

Most malocclusions are caused by hereditary factors that affect the contours of the face and the size of the teeth and jaw. The most common cause of **malocclusion** is a disproportion in size between the jaw and teeth or between the upper and lower jaws. A child who inherits a mother's small jaw and a father's large teeth may have teeth that are too big for the jaw, causing overcrowding. Specific inherited malocclusions include:

- overcrowded teeth
- too much space between teeth
- extra or missing teeth
- various irregularities in the teeth, jaw, or face

Malocclusions can be acquired through the following:

- accidents such as a jaw fracture that causes misalignment
- prolonged sucking on thumbs, fingers, or pacifiers, particularly after the age of four
- fingernail or lip biting
- a lost tooth that causes nearby teeth to move into the empty space, throwing them out of alignment
- airways that are obstructed by tonsils or adenoids
- dental disease
- tumors in the mouth or jaw
- improperly fitted fillings, crowns, or braces
- premature loss of baby teeth or permanent teeth
- late loss of baby teeth

Symptoms of malocclusion

Occasionally children have mild, temporary symptoms of malocclusion resulting from a growth spurt. However, symptoms of malocclusion usually develop gradually beginning at the age of six. Symptoms may include the following:

- crowded or misaligned teeth
- abnormal spacing between teeth, most often occurring because teeth are small or missing or the dental arch—

the arch-shaped jawbone that supports the teeth—is very wide

- incisors (front teeth) that do not meet
- an open bite, occurring when the upper and lower incisors do not touch each other during biting, thereby putting all of the chewing pressure on the back teeth and resulting in inefficient chewing and excessive tooth wear
- an overbite or overjet, in which the upper incisors protrude, often caused by a lower jaw that is significantly shorter than the upper jaw
- a deep or closed bite, an excessive overbite in which the lower incisors bite too closely to or into the gum tissue or palate behind the upper teeth
- a crossbite, in which a protruding lower jaw that is longer than the upper jaw causes the upper front or back teeth to bite inside the lower teeth

Early intervention

Although orthodontic treatment can be performed at any age, children are easier, faster, and less expensive to treat than adults. Most often orthodontic treatment is used on older children and adolescents whose teeth are still developing. However some types of problems are corrected more readily before all of the permanent teeth have erupted and facial growth is complete. If a child's permanent lower incisors erupt behind each other, braces may be required at a young age. Crossbites are usually treated early because they can interfere with biting and chewing. Early treatment also is used when thumb- or finger-sucking has affected teeth positioning.

Early orthodontic intervention can provide the following:

- straighten crooked teeth
- preserve or create space for incoming permanent teeth
- guide erupting permanent teeth into the correct positions
- prevent impacted permanent teeth, those that remain partially covered by gum tissue or partially or completely buried in the jawbone
- correct harmful habits such as thumb- or finger-sucking
- lower the risk of accidents to protruding upper incisors

Other advantages of early orthodontic treatment include the following:

- correction of bite problems by guiding jaw growth and controlling the width of the upper and lower dental arches

- reduction or elimination of abnormal swallowing or speech problems
- shortening and simplification of later orthodontic treatment
- prevention of later tooth extractions
- improvements in appearance and self-esteem

Untreated malocclusions

Minor misalignment or crowding may not require treatment. However untreated malocclusions can cause the following:

- teeth that are partially impacted or fail to erupt
- lips, tongue, or cheeks that contact biting surfaces due to poor tooth alignment
- inefficient or uncomfortable biting, chewing, and digestion
- speech impairments
- teeth that are hard to clean, leading to cavities and gum disease
- abnormal wear of tooth surfaces
- chipped teeth
- loosening or fracturing of a misaligned tooth that is overstrained
- injury to a protruding upper incisor
- thinning and receding of bone and gums covering the roots of very crowded teeth
- accelerated gum disease and bone loss
- temporomandibular joint (TMJ) misalignments at the point where the lower jaw attaches to the skull
- stress and trauma to the teeth, gum tissue, ligaments, muscles, jawbone, and jaw joints
- premature loss of teeth
- adverse effects on facial development and appearance
- the need for surgery

Untreated malocclusions often worsen with time. TMJ problems can cause chronic headaches or **pain** in the face and neck. A deep overbite can cause significant pain and bone damage and may contribute to excessive wear on the incisors.

Description

Orthodontics in young children

Alignment problems usually become apparent as the permanent teeth begin erupting at about age six. Dentists monitor the development of a child's permanent teeth and refer the child to an orthodontist if a problem is suspected. The American Association of Orthodontists recommends that all children be screened by an orthodontist by the age of seven.

Once a child's lower baby incisors have erupted, an orthodontist can measure the child's jaw and tooth size, project their growth rate, and possibly predict whether the child will have orthodontic problems with their permanent teeth. The orthodontist may be able to perform preventative or interceptive orthodontics that can reduce or eliminate the need for braces later.

In a procedure called selective serial extraction, the orthodontist removes one or more baby or permanent teeth. Doing so creates space for the permanent teeth, especially unerupted canine teeth that might become impacted or erupt in the wrong position. After the removal or loss of a tooth, braces or another orthodontic appliance may be used to prevent the remaining teeth from moving into the empty space. If a baby molar—that acts as a space-holder for later permanent teeth—is lost, a fixed orthodontic wire is inserted between the teeth to keep the space available.

Preparation

The orthodontist compiles pretreatment records that are used for diagnosis, determining the course of treatment, and measuring the progress of treatment. These records may include:

- a complete medical and dental history
- a clinical examination
- x rays revealing the positions of erupted and unerupted teeth, development of unerupted teeth, any missing or impacted teeth, shortened or damaged tooth roots, and the amount of bone supporting the teeth
- a facial-profile x ray or cephalometric film revealing the sizes, positions, and relationships of the teeth and jaw, as well as facial form, growth pattern, and the inclinations of tipped or tilted incisors
- plastic impressions of the bite and plaster models made from the impressions
- photographs and other measurements of the teeth and face

Based on the diagnosis the orthodontist develops a custom treatment plan and designs the appropriate corrective appliances that will gradually straighten or move the teeth. Severe overcrowding may necessitate the extraction of permanent teeth, usually the premolars, to create space prior to using braces to move teeth.

Braces and other orthodontic appliances

By applying constant gentle pressure in a specific direction, braces can slowly move teeth through the supporting bone to a new position. Springs and wires put pressure on teeth in order to straighten them. The pressure causes bone in the jaw to dissolve in front of the moving tooth as new bone grows behind the tooth. Braces and other appliances may be removable or fixed and are made of clear or colored metal, ceramic, or plastic. Removable appliances are often plastic plates that fit into the roof of the mouth and clip onto a tooth.

Fixed braces exert more pressure than removable braces and can achieve more complex movements. They consist of wires and springs that are held in place by small brackets glued to the outside surfaces of the incisors and sometimes the premolars. Lingual braces have brackets bonded to the back of the teeth. Bands encircling the molars also can be used for attachments. The wires, springs, and other devices attached to the brackets or bands put pressure on the teeth, gradually shifting them into new positions. The nickel-titanium wires are very light, and some are heat-activated. These are very flexible at room temperature and actively begin to move the teeth as they warm to body temperature. Elastic bands sometimes connect the upper and lower teeth to create tension.

Appliances used to direct jaw growth and development in growing children and adolescents include:

- Headgear attached to braces and usually worn for 10 to 12 hours at night puts pressure on the upper teeth and jaw and influences the direction and speed of upper jaw growth and upper teeth eruption.
- Herbst appliances attached to the upper and lower molars correct a severe overbite by holding the lower jaw forward, influencing jaw growth and tooth position; they force the jaw muscles to work in ways that promote forward development of the lower jaw; treatment with Herbst appliances must begin several years before the jaw stops growing and they must remain in place throughout the treatment.
- Palatal or upper jaw expansion devices can widen a narrow upper jaw and correct a crossbite within months.
- Removable bionators hold the lower jaw forward and guide tooth eruption while helping the upper and lower jaws to grow proportionately.

Headgear and Herbst appliances can significantly reduce protrusion of the four top incisors and enable the growing lower jaw to catch up with the upper jaw, eliminating swallowing problems.

Children with braces. *(Photograph by Robert J. Huffman/Field Mark Publications.)*

Duration of treatment

Orthodontic treatment usually continues until the desired outcome is reached. Active orthodontic treatment lasts an average of two years, with a range of one to three years. Some children respond to treatment faster than others and interceptive or early treatments may continue for only a few months. Appliances are adjusted periodically during treatment. Factors affecting the duration of treatment include:

- the growth of the mouth and face
- the severity of the problem
- the health of the teeth, gums, and supporting bones
- the child's level of cooperation

Precautions

Orthodontic appliances trap food, bacteria, and plaque, leading to **tooth decay**. Extra brushing with specially shaped and/or electric toothbrush and fluoride toothpaste is required around the areas where the braces or appliances attach to the teeth. Both the tops and bottoms of braces must be brushed and irrigated with a water jet directed from the top down and the bottom up. If possible, teeth should be flossed. A fluoride mouthwash may be recommended. Removable appliances should be brushed every time the teeth are brushed. Regular dental check-ups and cleanings must be continued.

Children with braces should eat raw fruits and vegetables and avoid soft, processed, and refined foods that attract bacteria, as well as hard or sticky foods, including gum, caramels, peanuts, ice chips, and popcorn. Chewing on hard items, such as fingernails or pencils, can damage braces. Children with braces should wear a protective mouth guard while playing contact **sports**.

Aftercare

After braces are removed the teeth must be stabilized in their new positions. This phase of treatment commonly takes two to three years. Occasionally it continues indefinitely. Types of retainers used for stabilization include:

KEY TERMS

Active treatment stage—The period during which orthodontic appliances or braces are used.

Bicuspid—Premolar; the two-cupped tooth between the first molar and the cuspid.

Canines—The two sharp teeth located next to the front incisor teeth in mammals that are used to grip and tear. Also called cuspids.

Crossbite—The condition in which the upper teeth bite inside the lower teeth.

Crown—The natural part of the tooth covered by enamel. A restorative crown is a protective shell that fits over a tooth.

Deep bite—A closed bite; a deep or excessive overbite in which the lower incisors bite too closely to or into the gum tissue or palate behind the upper teeth.

Eruption—The process of a tooth breaking through the gum tissue to grow into place in the mouth.

Impacted tooth—Any tooth that is prevented from reaching its normal position in the mouth by another tooth, bone, or soft tissue.

Incisors—The eight front teeth.

Interceptive orthodontics—Preventative orthodontics; early, simpler orthodontic treatment.

Malocclusion—The misalignment of opposing teeth in the upper and lower jaws.

Molars—The teeth behind the primary canines or the permanent premolars, with large crowns and broad chewing surfaces for grinding food.

Open bite—A malocclusion in which some teeth do not meet the opposing teeth.

Orthognatic surgery—Surgery to alter the relationships of the teeth and/or supporting bones, usually in conjunction with orthodontic treatment.

Overbite—Protrusion of the upper teeth over the lower teeth.

Plaque—A sticky film of saliva, food particles, and bacteria that attaches to the tooth surface and causes decay.

Retainer—An orthodontic appliance that is worn to stabilize teeth in a new position.

Retention treatment stage—The passive treatment period following orthodontic treatment, when retainers may be used to stabilize the teeth.

Temporomandibular joint (TMJ)—One of a pair of joints that attaches the mandible of the jaw to the temporal bone of the skull. It is a combination of a hinge and a gliding joint.

- positioners, rubber-like mouthpieces that are worn at night and bitten into for a few hours during the day

- removable retainers with a plastic plate that snaps onto the roof of the mouth and wires on the outside of the teeth

- removable, clear, plastic retainers that completely cover the sides and biting surfaces of the teeth

- semi-rigid wires that are bonded onto the inside of the incisors.

Risks

Braces may cause discomfort when they are first installed or adjusted during treatment. For the first three to five days teeth may hurt during biting. Lips, cheeks, and tongue may be irritated for one to two weeks before they toughen and adapt to the braces. Some appliances may interfere with speech for the first day or two. Damaged appliances can extend the length of treatment and negatively affect the outcome.

Food particles and plaque deposits around orthodontic appliances can cause demineralization of the tooth enamel, leading to cavities and permanent whitish scars on the teeth.

Normal results

Orthodontic treatment is usually very successful at correcting malocclusions. Even a significant size discrepancy between the upper and lower jaws often can be corrected. Sometimes, particularly in adults, corrective orthognathic surgery is required to shorten or lengthen a jawbone. The height of the lower face also can be shortened or lengthened. Sometimes surgery reduces the duration of the orthodontic treatment.

Maturational change can cause teeth to gradually shift with age—at least until one's early 20s—causing crowding. Nighttime retainers can prevent maturational movement.

Parental concerns

In general the earlier an orthodontic problem is detected, the easier and less expensive it is to correct. Parents can compare their child's **dental development** with standard charts and pictures.

When to call the doctor

Children with problems involving the width or length of the jaws should be evaluated no later than age 10 for girls and age 12 for boys. For children receiving orthodontic care, the orthodontist should be notified immediately if an appliance breaks. Indications that children may need an early orthodontic examination include:

- early or late loss of baby teeth
- crowded, misplaced, or blocked-out teeth
- upper and lower teeth that do not meet normally
- thumb- or finger-sucking
- biting of the cheek or roof of the mouth
- difficulty biting or chewing
- breathing through the mouth
- jaws that shift or make noise
- jaws and teeth that are out of proportion to the rest of the face

Resources

BOOKS

Ireland, Anthony J., and Fraser McDonald. *The Orthodontic Patient: Treatment and Biomechanics*. New York: Oxford University Press, 2003.

Sutton, Amy L., ed. *Dental Care and Oral Health Sourcebook: Basic Consumer Health Info*, 2nd ed. Detroit, MI: Omnigraphics, 2003.

Takada, K., and W. R. Proffit. *Orthodontics in the 21st Century: Where Are We Now? Where Are We Going?* Osaka, Japan: Osaka University Press, 2002.

van der Linden, Frans P. G. M. *Orthodontic Concepts and Strategies*. Chicago: Quintessence Publishing, 2004.

PERIODICALS

"Dental Health; New Orthodontic Appliance Designed to Straighten Teeth Without Braces." *Medical Devices & Surgical Technology Week* (May 16, 2004): 53.

Henrickson, T., and M. Nilner. "Temporomandibular Disorders, Occlusion and Orthodontic Treatment." *Journal of Orthodontics* 30 (2003): 129–37.

Joffe, L. "Current Products and Practice, Invisalign: Early Experiences." *Journal of Orthodontics* 30 (2003): 348–52.

ORGANIZATIONS

American Academy of Pediatric Dentistry. 211 East Chicago Avenue, Suite 700, Chicago, IL 60611–2663. Web site: <www.aapd.org>.

American Association of Orthodontists. 401 N. Lindbergh Blvd., St. Louis, MO 63141–7816. Web site: <www.braces.org>.

American Dental Association. 211 East Chicago Avenue, Chicago, IL 60611–2678. Web site: <www.ada.org>.

WEB SITES

"About Orthodontics." *American Association of Orthodontists*, 2004. Available online at <www.braces.org/braces/about/faq/faq_concerns.cfm> (accessed November 21, 2004).

"Early Orthodontic Care." *American Academy of Pediatric Dentistry*. Available online at <www.aapd.org/publications/brochures/content/earlyortho.html> (accessed November 21, 2004).

"Facts about Orthodontics." *American Association of Orthodontists*. Available online at <www.braces.org/about/faq/faq_background.cfm> (accessed November 21, 2004).

"Frequently Asked Questions: Braces and Orthodontics." *American Dental Association.*Available online at <www.ada.org/public/topics/braces_faq.asp> (accessed November 21, 2004).

Paladin, Pam. "Braced for a Century." *American Association of Orthodontists*. Available online at <www.braces.org/history/index.cfm> (accessed November 21, 2004).

"Problems to Watch for in Growing Children." *American Association of Orthodontists*. Available online at <www.braces.org/aaortho/braces/about/problems-to-watch-for.cfm> (accessed November 21, 2004).

Margaret Alic, PhD

Osgood-Schlatter disease *see* Osteochondroses

Osteochondroses

Definition

The term osteochondroses refers to a group of diseases of children and adolescents in which localized tissue death (necrosis) occurs, usually followed by full regeneration of healthy bone tissue. The singular term is osteochondrosis.

Description

During the years of rapid bone growth, blood supply to the growing ends of bones (epiphyses) may become insufficient resulting in necrotic bone, usually near joints. Since bone is normally undergoing a continuous rebuilding process, the necrotic areas are most often self-repaired over a period of weeks or months.

Osteochondrosis can affect different areas of the body and is often categorized by one of three locations: articular, non-articular, and physeal.

Physeal osteochondrosis is known as Scheuermann disease or juvenile kyphosis. It is a deformity of the thoracic spine (in the chest area, the vertebra to which ribs are attached) caused by abnormal centers of bone development at the intervertebral joints (physes). It is most common among children ages 13 to 16.

Articular disease occurs at the joints (articulations). One of the more common forms is Legg-Calvé-Perthes disease, which occurs at the hip joint. Other forms include Köhler disease (foot), Freiberg disease (second toe), and Panner disease (elbow). These diseases are most common during **adolescence**, although they have been found in individuals ranging in age from eight to 77.

Non-articular osteochondrosis occurs at any other skeletal location. For instance, Osgood-Schlatter disease of the tibia (the large inner bone of the leg between the knee and ankle) is relatively common. It is often the cause of knee and leg **pain** in active teens.

Osteochondritis dissecans (OCD) is a form of osteochondrosis in which loose bone fragments form in a joint. The knee is a common site for osteochondritis dissecans. The condition is found most often in people aged ten to 20, although it may occur at other ages. OCD is sometimes associated with some sort of past trauma to the joint. In about 30 to 40 percent of cases the same joint on both sides of the body is involved (e.g. both knees, both elbows).

Demographics

Osteochondroses are disorders of teens and young adults. Some are rare disorders, and in many cases, the number of individuals who have these disorders is not known, since cases many resolve on their own. Scheuermann disease is thought to occur in 0.4 to 8 percent of individuals. One Finnish study found that 13 percent of adolescents had Osgood-Schlatter disease. Freiberg disease is the one type of osteochondrosis that is more common in females than in males. OCD affects males about twice as often as females. All other osteochondrosis appear to affect the sexes equally.

Causes and symptoms

Many theories have been advanced to account for osteochondrosis, but none has proven fully satisfactory. Stress on the bone, ischemia (reduced blood supply), and trauma to the site are commonly mentioned factors. Athletic children are often affected when they overstress their developing limbs with a particular repetitive motion. Many cases are idiopathic, meaning that no specific cause is known.

The most common symptom for most types of osteochondrosis is pain, usually a dull, non-specific ache, at the affected joint. Pain is especially noticeable when pressure is applied. Locking of a joint or limited range of motion at a joint can also occur.

Scheuermann disease can (rarely) lead to serious kyphosis (hunchback condition) due to erosion of the vertebral bodies. Usually, however, the kyphosis is mild, causing no further symptoms and requiring no special treatment.

When to call the doctor

A doctor should be consulted whenever a child has a persistent joint pain that does not go away after resting the joint for a few days.

Diagnosis

Diagnosis is suspected based on history and symptoms. It can be confirmed by x-ray findings.

Treatment

Conservative treatment is usually attempted first. In many cases, resting the affected body part for a several days or weeks brings relief. A cast may be applied if needed to prevent movement of a joint.

Surgical intervention may be needed in some cases of osteochondritis dissecans to remove abnormal bone fragments in a joint. Rarely is spine curvature so pronounced in Scheuermann disease that the individual needs to wear a brace or have surgical intervention.

Prognosis

Accurate prediction of the outcome for individual adolescents is difficult with osteochondrosis. Some individuals heal spontaneously. Others heal with little treatment other than keeping weight or stress off the affected limb. The earlier the age of onset, the better the prospects for full recovery. Surgical intervention is often successful in osteochondritis dissecans.

Prevention

No preventive measures are known.

Parental concerns

Persistent pain in the joint may keep children temporarily from playing **sports**.

Resources

WEB SITES

Boyer, Matison, and James K. DeOrio. "Freiberg Infraction." *eMedicine.com*, April 21, 2004. Available online at <www.emedicine.com/orthoped/topic492.htm> (accessed January 16, 2005).

Ertl, James P., and Gyorgy Kovacs. "Knee Osteochondritis Dissecans." *eMedicine.com* 5 June 2002. Available online at <www.emedicine.com/sports/topic57.htm> (accessed January 16, 2005).

Joshi, Aparna. "Osgood-Schlatter Disease." *eMedicine.com*, July 2, 2004. Available online at <www.eMedicine.com/radio/topic491.htm> (accessed January 16, 2005).

Nowak, Jozef. "Scheuermann Disease." *eMedicine.com*, September 1, 2004. Available online at <www.emedicine.com/pmr/topic129.htm> (accessed January 16, 2005).

Tish Davidson, A.M.
Victor Leipzig, PhD

Osteogenesis imperfecta

Definition

Osteogenesis imperfecta (OI) is a group of genetic diseases in which the bones are formed improperly, making them fragile and prone to breaking.

Description

Collagen is a fibrous protein material that serves as the structural foundation of skin, bone, cartilage, and ligaments. In osteogenesis imperfecta, the collagen produced is abnormal and disorganized, which results in a number of abnormalities throughout the body, the most notable being fragile, easily broken bones.

There are four forms of OI, types I through IV. Of these, type II is the most severe and is usually fatal within a short time after birth. Types I, III, and IV have some overlapping and some distinctive symptoms, with the hallmark symptom being fragile bones.

OI is usually inherited as an autosomal dominant condition. In autosomal dominant inheritance, a single abnormal gene on one of the autosomal chromosomes (one of the first 22 non-sex chromosomes) from either parent can cause the disease. Only one parent needs to be a carrier in order for the child to inherit the disease. The parent affected by OI will have one abnormal gene and one normal gene. A child who has one parent with the disease therefore has a 50 percent chance of also inheriting the disease.

If both parents have OI caused by an autosomal dominant gene change, there is a 75 percent chance that the child will inherit one or both OI genes. In other words, there is a 25 percent chance of inheriting a faulty gene from the mother and a normal gene from the father, a 25 percent chance of inheriting a normal gene from the mother and a faulty gene from the father, a 25 percent chance of inheriting faulty genes from both parents, and a 25 percent chance of inheriting normal genes from both parents. It is difficult to predict the severity of OI in a child who has inherited two copies of the faulty gene because of its rarity.

There is no **family** history of OI in about 25 percent of children born with the disease. This occurs as a result of a spontaneous mutation of the gene in either the sperm or egg. The cause of such mutations is not known. Called new dominant mutation, the affected child subsequently has a 50 percent of passing the abnormal gene to his or her children. The risk of normal parents having a second child with OI, or of normal siblings going on to have affected children, does not appear to be greater than that of the general population.

In studies of families into which infants with OI type II were born, most of the babies had a new dominant mutation in a collagen gene. In some of these families, however, more than one infant was born with OI. Previously, researchers had seen this recurrence as evidence of recessive inheritance of OI type II. Subsequently, however, researchers concluded that the rare recurrence of OI to a couple with a child with autosomal dominant OI is more likely due to gonadal mosaicism. Instead of mutation occurring in an individual sperm or egg, it occurs in a percentage of the cells that give rise to a parent's multiple sperm or eggs. This mutation, present in a percentage of his or her reproductive cells, can result in more than one affected child without affecting the parent with the disorder. An estimated 2 percent to 4 percent of families into which an infant with OI type II is born are at risk of having another affected child because of gonadal mosaicism.

Demographics

OI affects equal numbers of males and females. It occurs in about one of every 20,000 births.

Causes and symptoms

Evidence suggests that OI results from abnormalities in the collagen gene COL1A1 or COL1A2 and possibly abnormalities in other genes. In OI, the genetic abnormality causes one of two things to occur. It may direct cells to make an altered collagen protein and the presence of this altered collagen causes OI type II, III, or IV. Alternately, the dominant altered gene may fail to direct cells to make any collagen protein. Although some collagen is produced by instructions from the normal gene, an overall decrease in the total amount of collagen produced results in OI type I.

Type I

OI type I is the most common and mildest type. Among the common features of type I are the following:

- Bones are predisposed to fracture, with most **fractures** occurring before **puberty**; people with OI type I typically have about 20 to 40 fractures before puberty.
- Stature is normal or near-normal.
- Joints are loose and muscle tone is low.
- Sclerae (whites of the eyes) have blue, purple, or gray tint.
- Face shape is triangular.
- Tendency toward **scoliosis** (a curvature of the spine) is present.
- Bone deformity is absent or minimal.
- Dentinogenesis imperfecta may occur, causing brittle teeth.
- Hearing loss is a possible symptom, often beginning in early 20s or 30s.

- Structure of collagen is normal but the amount is lower than normal.

Type II

Sometimes called the lethal form, type II is the most severe form of OI. Among the common features of type II are the following:

- Frequently, OI type II is lethal at or shortly after birth, often as a result of respiratory problems.
- Fractures are numerous and bone deformity is severe.
- Stature is small with underdeveloped lungs.
- Collagen is formed improperly.

Type III

Among the common features of type III are the following:

- Bones fracture easily (Fractures are often present at birth, and x rays may reveal healed fractures that occurred before birth; people with OI type III may have more than 100 fractures before puberty.)
- Stature is significantly shorter than normal.
- Sclerae have blue, purple, or gray tint.
- Joints are loose and muscle development is poor in arms and legs.
- Rib cage is barrel-shaped.
- Face shape is triangular.
- Scoliosis (a curvature of the spine) is present.
- Respiratory problems are possible.
- Bones are deformed and deformity is often severe.
- Dentinogenesis imperfecta may occur.
- Hearing loss is possible.
- Collagen is formed improperly.

Type IV

OI type IV falls between type I and type III in severity. Among the common features of type IV are the following:

- Bones fracture easily, with most fractures occurring before puberty.
- Stature is shorter than average.
- Sclerae are normal in color, appearing white or near-white.
- Bone deformity is mild to moderate.
- Scoliosis (curvature of the spine) is likely.

- Rib cage is barrel-shaped.
- Face is triangular.
- Dentinogenesis imperfecta may occur.
- Hearing loss is possible.
- Collagen is formed improperly.

When to call the doctor

Parents should contact a healthcare professional if their child exhibits any of the symptoms of OI, particularly a tendency to fracture bones easily.

Diagnosis

It is often possible to diagnose OI solely on clinical features and x-ray findings. Collagen or DNA tests may help confirm a diagnosis of OI; test results may take several weeks to confirm. Approximately 10 to 15 percent of individuals with mild OI who have collagen testing, and approximately 5 percent of those who have genetic testing, test negative for OI despite having the disorder.

Diagnosis is usually suspected when a baby has bone fractures after having suffered no apparent injury. Another indication is small, irregular, isolated bones in the sutures between the bones of the skull (wormian bones). Sometimes the bluish sclerae serve as a diagnostic clue. Unfortunately, because of the unusual nature of the fractures occurring in a baby who is not yet mobile, some parents have been accused of **child abuse** before the actual diagnosis of osteogenesis imperfecta was reached.

Prenatal diagnosis

Testing is available to assist in prenatal diagnosis. Women with OI who become pregnant or women who conceive a child with a man who has OI may wish to explore prenatal diagnosis. Because of the relatively small risk (2–4%) of recurrence of OI type II in a family, families may opt for ultrasound studies to determine if a developing fetus has the disorder.

Ultrasound is the least invasive procedure for prenatal diagnosis and carries the least risk. Using ultrasound, a doctor can examine the fetus's skeleton for bowing of the leg or arm bones, fractures, shortening, or other bone abnormalities that may indicate OI. Different forms of OI may be detected by ultrasound in the second trimester. When OI occurs as a new dominant mutation and is found inadvertently on ultrasound, it may be difficult to confirm the diagnosis until after delivery since other genetic conditions can cause bowing and/or fractures prenatally.

Chorionic villus sampling is a procedure that obtains a sampling of cells from the placenta for testing. Examination of fetal collagen proteins in the tissue can reveal information about the quantitative or qualitative collagen defects that leads to OI. When a parent has OI, it is necessary for the affected parent to have the results of his or her own collagen test available. Chorionic villus sampling can be performed at ten to 12 weeks of pregnancy.

Amniocentesis is a procedure that involves inserting a thin needle into the uterus, into the amniotic sac, and withdrawing a small amount of amniotic fluid. Genetic material can be extracted from the fetal cells contained in the amniotic fluid and tested for the specific mutation known to cause OI in that family. This technique is useful only when the mutation causing OI in a particular family has been identified through previous genetic testing of affected family members, including previous pregnancies involving a baby with OI. Amniocentesis is performed at 16 to 18 weeks of pregnancy.

Treatment

There are no treatments available to cure OI, nor to prevent most of its complications. Most treatments are aimed at treating the fractures and bone deformities caused by OI. Splints, casts, braces, and rods are all used. Rodding is a surgical procedure in which a metal rod is implanted within a bone (usually the long bones of the thigh and leg). This surgery is performed when bowing or repeated fractures of these bones has interfered with a child's ability to walk.

Other treatments include hearing aids and early capping of teeth. Patients may require the use of a walker or wheelchair. **Pain** may be treated with a variety of medications. **Exercise** is encouraged as a means to promote muscle and bone strength. Swimming is a form of exercise that puts a minimal amount of strain on muscles, joints, and bones. Walking is encouraged for those who are able.

Alternative treatment

Alternative treatment such as acupuncture, naturopathic therapies, hypnosis, relaxation training, visual imagery, and biofeedback have all been used to try to decrease the constant pain of fractures.

Nutritional concerns

Smoking, excessive alcohol and **caffeine** consumption, and steroid medications may deplete bone and exacerbate bone fragility.

KEY TERMS

Chromosome—A microscopic thread-like structure found within each cell of the human body and consisting of a complex of proteins and DNA. Humans have 46 chromosomes arranged into 23 pairs. Chromosomes contain the genetic information necessary to direct the development and functioning of all cells and systems in the body. They pass on hereditary traits from parents to child (like eye color) and determine whether the child will be male or female.

Collagen—The main supportive protein of cartilage, connective tissue, tendon, skin, and bone.

Ligament—A type of tough, fibrous tissue that connects bones or cartilage and provides support and strength to joints.

Mutation—A permanent change in the genetic material that may alter a trait or characteristic of an individual, or manifest as disease. This change can be transmitted to offspring.

Sclera—The tough, fibrous, white outer protective covering of the eyeball.

Scoliosis—An abnormal, side-to-side curvature of the spine.

Prognosis

The lifespan of people with OI types I, III, and IV is not generally shortened. The prognosis for people with these types of OI is quite variable, depending on the severity of the disorder and the number and severity of the fractures and bony deformities.

Fifty percent of all babies with OI type II are stillborn. The rest of these babies usually die within a very short time after birth. In the early 2000s, some people with type II have lived into young adulthood.

Prevention

As a congenital birth defect, OI cannot be prevented. Individuals at risk of having a child with OI should be encouraged to undergo genetic counseling to more accurately determine their chances of having a child with OI. The risk of fractures can be minimized with bone- and muscle-strengthening exercises, rehabilitative therapy, and use of leg braces.

Nutritional concerns

Because the symptoms of OI are caused by collagen abnormalities and not a calcium deficiency (such as in osteoporosis), supplementation of **vitamins** or **minerals** will not cure the disease. To prevent bone loss related to calcium deficiency, which could exacerbate the fragility of bones, it is important that children with OI consume an adequate amount of calcium (generally 500 mg for children ages one to three, 800 mg for children ages four to eight, and 1,300 mg a day for preteens and teenagers).

Parental concerns

In cases in which OI is not diagnosed at birth, a child may experience numerous fractures of seemingly unexplained cause, leading healthcare providers to suspect the child is being abused. Once a child has been diagnosed, it may be helpful for parents to carry with them a letter from the child's healthcare provider detailing the diagnosis in order to facilitate care in an emergency.

Resources

BOOKS

Marini, Joan C. "Osteogenesis Imperfecta." In *Nelson Textbook of Pediatrics*, 17th ed. Philadelphia: Saunders, 2004.

Pyeritz, Reed Edwin. "Osteogenesis Imperfecta Syndromes." In *Cecil Textbook of Medicine*, 21st ed. Edited by Lee Goldman et al. Philadelphia: Saunders, 2000.

Shapiro, Jay R. "Heritable Disorders of the Type I Collagen Family." In *Kelley's Textbook of Rheumatology*, 6th ed. Edited by Shaun Ruddy et al. Philadelphia: Saunders, 2001.

PERIODICALS

Kocher, M. S., and J. R. Kasser. "Orthopaedic aspects of child abuse." *Journal of the American Academy of Orthopedic Surgery* 8 (January-February 2000): 10+.

Niyibizi, C., et al. "Potential of gene therapy for treating osteogenesis imperfecta." *Clinical Orthopedics* 379 (October 2000): S126+.

Smith, R. "Severe osteogenesis imperfecta: new therapeutic options?" *British Medical Journal* 322 (January 13, 2001): 63+.

Wacaster, Priscilla. "Osteogenesis Imperfecta." *Exceptional Parent* 30 (April 2000): 94+.

ORGANIZATIONS

Children's Brittle Bone Foundation. 7701 95th St., Pleasant Prairie, WI 53158. Web site: <www.cbbf.org>.

Osteogenesis Imperfecta Foundation. 804 W. Diamond Ave.,
Suite 210, Gaithersburg, MD 20878. Web site:
<www.oif.org>.

WEB SITES

"Osteogenesis Imperfecta." *National Institutes of Health
Osteoporosis and Related Bone Diseases—National
Resource Center*, July 2004. Available online at
<www.osteo.org/oi.html> (accessed January 16, 2005).

Jennifer F. Wilson, MS
Stephanie Dionne Sherk

Osteopetroses

Definition

Osteopetrosis (plural osteopetroses) is a rare inherited disorder that makes bones increase in both size (mass) and fragility. It is a potentially fatal condition that can deform bone structure and distort the appearance. Osteopetrosis is also called chalk bones, ivory bones, or marble bones.

Description

In healthy individuals, bones are constantly being broken down (resorption) by cells called osteoclasts, and new bone material is constantly being formed by cells called osteoblasts. Osteopetrosis occurs when there is a failure in bone resorption. The mass of bone increases, but the new bone material that is added is porous, weak, and brittle.

There are three types of osteopetrosis. In some children with osteoporosis, bone mass begins to increase at birth, but symptoms may not become evident until adulthood. In mild cases, bone mass increases at gradual, irregular intervals until full adult height is attained. Some bones are not affected. Other forms of osteopetrosis progress at a more rapid pace and destroy bone structure, which can involve bones throughout the body, although the lower jaw is never affected.

Types of osteopetroses

Severe malignant infantile osteopetrosis (early-onset osteopetrosis) is the most severe form of osteopetrosis. It results from a child inheriting defective genes from both parents (autosomal recessive pattern of inheritance). It is most often discovered soon after birth. The ends of the long bones of the arms and legs appear widened and thickened (clubbed). Bone mass continues to increase rapidly, often filling in the hollow middle of the bone where the bone marrow, which produces red blood cells, is found. Early-onset osteopetrosis can be a fatal condition, with death occurring before the age of two. About one-third of all children with malignant infantile osteopetroses die before age ten. Although this form of osteopetrosis is called "malignant," it is not a type of **cancer**.

Intermediate osteopetrosis generally appears in children under age ten. This condition is usually less severe than early-onset or malignant infantile osteopetrosis and is not normally life-threatening.

Adult (delayed-onset) osteopetrosis may not become evident until after age 20. Albers-Schönberg disease is a mild form of this condition. People who have this disease are born with normal bone structure. Bone mass increases as they age but does not affect appearance, health, **intelligence**, or life span. Many people with adult osteopetrosis are diagnosed only when abnormalities are discovered on x rays taken for other purposes. There are two distinct types of adult osteopetrosis (types I and II). These types have different biochemical features. Individuals with type II disease have a higher risk of sustaining bone **fractures**.

Demographics

The incidence of osteopetroses is not known, although it is estimated that adult osteopetrosis occurs in about one of every 1,250 individuals. About 20,000 people in the United States have this form of the disease. Worldwide malignant infantile osteopetrosis occurs in about one in 100,000 to 500,000 births, making it exceedingly rare. Only eight to 40 children are born with this disease in the United States each year. Males and females appear to be equally affected.

Causes and symptoms

Osteopetrosis is the result of a genetic defect that causes the body to add new bone more rapidly than existing bone disintegrates. When fibrous or bony tissue invades bone marrow where red blood cells are made, the individual may develop anemia. Infection results when excess bone impairs the immune system, and hemorrhage can occur when platelet production is disrupted. When the skeleton grows so thick that nerves are unable to pass between bones, the individual may have a nerve damage, paralysis, or become blind or deaf.

Other symptoms associated with osteopetrosis include:

• bones that break easily and do not heal properly

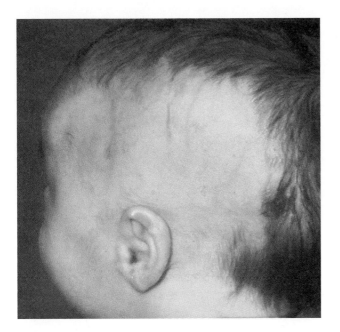

This infant has osteopetrosis, a condition which thickens and hardens the bone. Note the unusual shape of the skull. *(Custom Medical Stock Photo Inc.)*

- bruising
- bone **pain**
- carpal tunnel syndrome
- osteoarthritis
- convulsions
- enlargement of the liver, lymph glands, or spleen
- failure to thrive (delayed growth, weight gain, and development)
- hydrocephalus (fluid on the brain)
- macrocephaly (abnormal enlargement of the head)
- paralysis or loss of control of muscles in the face or eyes

When to call the doctor

A doctor should be consulted if the child has frequent broken bones, bone pain, or failure of normal growth and development.

Diagnosis

Osteopetrosis is usually diagnosed when x rays reveal abnormalities or increases in bone density. Bone biopsy can confirm the diagnosis. Additional tests may be done to look for associated problems in vision, hearing, blood composition, and so forth.

Treatment

Interferon gamma-1b (Actimmune) is the only drug approved by the United States Food and Drug Administration (FDA) to treat osteopetrosis. Injections delay the progress of severe osteopetrosis in both children and adults.

Bone marrow transplantation (BMT) is the only therapy that can completely cure severe malignant infantile osteopetrosis. It replaces the abnormal osteoclasts with normal cells. The survival rate for children with osteopetrosis who undergo BMT is 40 to 70 percent. Because of the high risk of death, this procedure is done only with the most severely affected children where a good bone marrow match can be found.

High doses of calcitriol, an active form of vitamin D, can stimulate osteoclasts responsible for disintegration of old bone and significantly alleviate symptoms of severe disease in some individuals.

When bone overgrowth deforms the shape of the skull, surgery may be required to relieve pressure on the brain. Orthodontic treatment is sometimes necessary to correct **malocclusion**, a condition that shifts the position of the teeth and makes closing the mouth impossible.

Physical and occupational therapy can help children reach their full potential and adults to retain function and independence. Speech therapy is often needed in young children, because the heavy skeleton can cause language delays even in children of normal intelligence. Professional counseling can help children and their families cope with the emotional aspects of deformed features.

Prognosis

The severity of anemia seems to determine the course of an individual's osteopetrosis. About two-thirds of children who have severe malignant infantile osteopetrosis die before age ten unless they have a successful bone marrow transplant. Individuals who develop the adult form of the disease have normal life spans, although they experience more bone fractures and complications related to compression of cranial nerves. Nerve compression can result in facial paralysis, deafness, or blindness.

Prevention

Osteopetrosis is an inherited disease that cannot be prevented.

Parental concerns

Parents with children who develop intermediate or adult forms of this disease as teens or young adults should be aware that their children are very susceptible to bone fractures and should avoid situations and **sports** where they are likely to be injured.

Resources

BOOKS

Berkow, Robert, ed. *The Merck Manual of Medical Information.* Whitehouse Station, NJ: Merck & Co., Inc, 2003.

ORGANIZATIONS

Osteoporosis and Related Bone Diseases—National Resource Center. 1150 17th S. NW, Ste. 500, Washington, DC 20036. Web site: <www.osteo.org>.

WEB SITES

Bhargava, Anuj. "Osteopetrosis." *eMedicine.com*, March 19, 2002. Available online at <www.emedicine.com/med/topic1692.htm> (accessed January 16, 2005).

"Information for Patients about Osteopetrosis." *National Institutes of Health Osteoporosis and Related Bone Diseases—National Resource Center*, August 2000. Available online at <www.osteo.org> (accessed January 16, 2005).

Tish Davidson, A.M.
Maureen Haggerty

Osteosarcoma *see* **Sarcomas**

Otitis externa

Definition

Otitis externa refers to an infection of the ear canal (outer ear), the tube leading from the outside opening of the ear in towards the ear drum. The infection usually develops in children and adolescents whose ears are exposed to persistent, excessive moisture.

Description

The external ear canal is a tube approximately 1 in (2.5 cm) in length that runs from the outside opening of the ear to the start of the middle ear, which is behind the tympanic membrane (ear drum). The canal is partly cartilage and partly bone. The lining of the ear canal is skin, which is attached directly to the covering of the bone. Glands within the skin of the canal produce a waxy substance called cerumen (popularly called earwax). Cerumen is designed to protect the ear canal, repel water, and keep the ear canal too acidic to allow bacteria to grow.

Continually exposing the ear canal to moisture may cause significant loss of cerumen. The delicate skin of the ear canal, unprotected by cerumen, retains moisture and becomes irritated. Without cerumen, the ear canal stops being appropriately acidic, which allows for the growth of microorganisms. Thus, the warm, moist, dark environment of the ear canal becomes a hospitable environment for development of an infection.

Otitis externa is commonly referred to as swimmer's ear.

Demographics

Although all age groups are affected by otitis externa, children, adolescents, and young adults whose ears are exposed to persistent, excessive moisture develop the infection most often. Otitis externa occurs most often in warm climates and during the summer months, when more people are participating in water activities. The ratio of occurrence in males is equal to that of females. People in some racial groups have a smaller size of the ear canal, which may predispose them to infection.

Causes and symptoms

Chidren and adolescents with otitis externa often have been diving or swimming for long periods of time, especially in polluted lakes, rivers, or ponds. Routine showering can also lead to otitis externa. Water in the ear canal can carry infectious microorganisms into the ear canal.

Bacteria, fungi, and viruses have all been implicated in causing otitis externa. However, most commonly otitis externa is caused by bacteria, especially *Pseudomonas aeruginosa*. Other bacteria that can cause otitis externa include *Enterobacter aerogenes*, *Proteus mirabilis*, *Klebsiella pneumoniae*, *Staphylococcus epidermidis*, and bacteria of the family called Streptococci. Occasionally, fungi may cause otitis externa. These include *Candida* and *Aspergillus*. Two types of viruses, called herpesvirus hominis and varicella-zoster virus, have also been identified as causing otitis externa.

Other conditions predisposing to otitis externa include the use of cotton swabs to clean the ear canals. This pushes cerumen and normal skin debris back into the ear canal, instead of allowing the ear canal's normal cleaning mechanism of the ear to work, which would ordinarily move accumulations of cerumen and debris out of the ear. Also, putting other items into the ear can scratch the canal, making it more susceptible to infection. For example, children may insert a foreign body in their ear canal and not mention it to their parents. Hair spray or hair coloring, which can irritate the ear canal, may also lead to otitis externa. A hearing aid can trap moisture in the ear canal and should be taken out as often as possible to allow the ear an opportunity to dry out.

The first symptom of otitis externa is often **itching** of the ear canal, followed by watery discharge from the ear. Eventually, the ear begins to feel extremely painful. Any touch, movement, or pressure on the outside structure of the ear may cause severe **pain**. If the canal is excessively swollen, hearing may become muffled. The canal may appear swollen and red, and there may be evidence of foul-smelling, greenish-yellow pus.

In severe cases, otitis externa may be accompanied by **fever**. Often, this indicates that the outside ear structure has become infected as well. It will become red and swollen, and there may be enlarged and tender lymph nodes in front of, or behind, the ear.

A serious and life-threatening type of otitis externa is called malignant otitis externa. This is an infection that most commonly affects persons who have diabetes or in persons with weakened immune systems. In malignant otitis externa, a patient has usually had minor symptoms of otitis externa for some months, with pain and drainage. The causative bacteria is usually *Pseudomonas aeruginosa*. This bacteria spreads from the external canal into all of the nearby tissues, including the bones of the skull. Swelling and destruction of these tissues may lead to damage of certain nerves, resulting in spasms of the jaw muscles or paralysis of the facial muscles. Other, more severe, complications of this destructive infection include **meningitis** (swelling and infection of the coverings of the spinal cord and brain), brain infection, or brain abscess (the development of a pocket of infection with pus).

When to call the doctor

The doctor should be called if any of the following symptoms are present:

- pain in an ear with or without fever
- persistent itching of the ear or in the ear canal
- loss of hearing or decreased hearing in one or both ears
- discharge from an ear, especially if it is thick, discolored, bloody, or foul-smelling

Diagnosis

Diagnosis of uncomplicated otitis externa is usually quite simple. The symptoms alone, of ear pain worsened by any touch to the outer ear, are characteristic of otitis externa. Examination of the ear canal will usually reveal redness and swelling. It may be impossible (due to pain and swelling) to see much of the ear canal, but this inability itself is diagnostic.

If there is a need to identify the types of organisms causing otitis externa, the canal can be gently swabbed to obtain a specimen. The organisms present in the specimen can then be cultured (allowed to multiply) in a laboratory, and then viewed under a microscope to allow identification of the causative organisms.

If the rare infection malignant otitis externa is suspected, **computed tomography** scan (CT scan) or **magnetic resonance imaging** (MRI) scans will be performed to determine how widely the infection has spread within bone and tissue. A swab of the external canal will not necessarily reveal the actual causative organism, so some other tissue sample (biopsy) will need to be obtained. The CT or MRI will help the doctor decide where the most severe focus of infection is located, in order to guide the choice of a biopsy site.

Treatment

Otitis externa us usually not a dangerous condition and often clears up by itself within a few days. To aid in the healing, the infected ear canal can be washed with an over-the-counter topical antiseptic. Pain can be relieved be placing a warm heating pad or compress on the infected ear as well as through the use of an over-the-counter pain reliever such as **acetaminophen** or aspirin. During the healing process, the infected ear canal must be kept dry, even while showering, through the use of ear plugs or a shower cap.

If the pain worsens or does not improve within 24 hours, or for the fastest way to relieve pain and to prevent the spread of infection, the doctor should be seen. The doctor will clean the ear with a suction-tipped probe or other type of suction device to relieve irritation and pain. **Antibiotics** will applied directly to the skin of the ear canal (**topical antibiotics**) to fight the infection. These antibiotics are often combined in a preparation that includes a steroid medication that reduces the itching, inflammation and swelling within the ear canal. For full treatment, eardrops are usually applied several times a day for seven to 10 days.

If the opening to the ear is narrowed by swelling, a cotton wick may be inserted into the ear canal to help carry the eardrops into the ear more effectively. The medications are applied directly to the wick, enough times per day to allow the wick to remain continuously saturated. After the wick is removed, usually after about 48 hours, the medications are then put directly into the ear canal three to four times each day.

For severe infection, oral antiobiotics may be prescribed. If the otitis externa infection is caused by the presence of a foreign body in the ear, the infection will not improve until the foreign body is removed.

In malignant otitis externa, antibiotics will almost always need to be given intravenously (IV). If the CT or MRI scan reveals that the infection has spread extensively, these IV antibiotics will need to be continued for six to eight weeks. If the infection is in an earlier stage, two weeks of IV antibiotics can be followed by six weeks of antibiotics by mouth.

Alternative treatment

Mullein (*Verbascum thapsus*) oil has anti-inflammatory properties and may be apppied to the infected ear canal (one to three drops every three hours) to help soothe and heal the ear. Garlic (*Allium sativum*) is a natural antibiotic. Garlic juice can be combined with equal parts of glycerin and a carrier oil such as olive or sweet olive and applied (one to three drops) to the infected ear every three hours.

Prognosis

The prognosis is excellent for otitis externa, for it is usually easily treated. Basic treatment measures will cure 90 percent of cases without complication. However, it may recur in certain susceptible individuals. Left untreated, malignant otitis externa may spread sufficiently to cause death.

KEY TERMS

Cerumen—The medical term for earwax.

Eardrum—A paper-thin covering stretching across the ear canal that separates the middle and outer ears.

Infectious disease—A disease caused by a virus or a bacterium. Examples of viruses causing an infectious disease are: HIV-1 virus, herpes simplex, cytomegalovirus, Epstein-Barr virus, leukemia virus. Examples of bacterial infectious diseases are: syphilis and tuberculosis.

Outer ear—Outer visible portion of the ear that collects and directs sound waves toward the tympanic membrane by way of a canal which extends inward through the temporal bone.

Prevention

Swimming in polluted water and in pools or hot tubs without good chlorine and pH control should be avoided.

Keeping the ear dry is an important aspect of prevention of otitis externa. Before swimming, a protective coating consisting of several drops of mineral oil, baby oil, or lanolin can be applied to the ear canal. After swimming, several drops of a mixture of isopropyl alcohol and white vinegar can be put into the ear canal to ensure that it dries adequately. The head should be tilted so that the solution reaches the bottom of the ear canal; then the liquid should be drained out.

Care should be taken when cleaning ears. The outer ear should be cleaned wiped with a clean washcloth. The use of pointed objects to dig into the ear canal, especially those that can scratch the skin, should be avoided.

The most serious complications of malignant otitis externa can be avoided by careful attention to early symptoms of ear pain and drainage from the ear canal. Children with conditions that put them at higher risk for this infection (diabetes or conditions that weaken the immune system) should always report new symptoms immediately to the doctor.

Parental concerns

Parents should teach their children how to clean their ears without using sharp objects and to dry their ears thoroughly after swimming, showering, or bathing.

Resources

BOOKS

"External Otitis." In *Nelson Textbook of Pediatrics*, ed. Richard E. Behrman. Philadelphia: W. B. Saunders Co., 1996.

Friedman, Ellen M. *My Ear Hurts!* Fireside, 2001.

PERIODICALS

"Keep Your Ears Dry." *Consumer Reports on Health*, 7, no. 7 (July 1995): 80+.

Moss, Richard. "Swimmers Ear." *Pediatrics for Parents* 17, no. 4 (Apr. 1996): 3+.

ORGANIZATIONS

American Academy of Otolaryngology-Head and Neck Surgery, Inc. One Prince St., Alexandria VA 22314-3357. (703) 836-4444. Web site:<http://www.entnet>.

WEB SITES

"Healthy Swimming." National Center for Infectious Diseases, Centers for Disease Control and Prevention. <cdc.gov/healthyswimming/swimmers_ear.htm>.

Judith Sims

Otitis media

Definition

Otitis media is an infection of the middle ear, which is located behind the eardrum. There are two main types of otitis media. In the first, called acute otitis media (AOM), parts of the ear are infected and swollen, and fluid and mucus are trapped inside the ear. AOM can be quite painful. In the second type, called otitis media with effusion (fluid), or OME, fluid and mucus remain trapped within the ear after the infection is over, making it more difficult for the ear to fight off new infections. This fluid may adversely affect a child's hearing.

Description

One of the most common childhood infections, Otitis media is the leading cause of visits to the doctor by children. It is also the most frequent reason children receive antibiotic prescriptions or undergo surgery.

In order to fully understand otitis media, it is helpful to have a basic knowledge of ear anatomy. Deep within the outer ear canal is the eardrum, which is a thin, transparent membrane that vibrates in response to sound. Behind the eardrum is the space called the middle ear.

When the eardrum vibrates, three tiny bones within the middle ear, called ossicles, transmit these sounds to the inner ear. Nerves are stimulated in the inner ear, which then relay the sound signals to the brain. The eustachian tube, which connects the middle ear to the nose, normally equalizes pressure in the middle ear, allowing the eardrum and ossicles to vibrate correctly, so that hearing is normal.

There are certain factors particular to children that make them more at risk for otitis media. In children, the eustachian tube is shorter and less slanted than in adults. Its size and position allow bacteria and viruses to travel to the middle ear more easily. Children also have clumps of infection fighting cells, commonly called adenoids, in the area of the eustachian tube. These adenoids may enlarge with repeated respiratory tract infections and ultimately block the eustachian tubes. When these tubes are blocked, the middle ear is more likely to fill with fluid, which in turn increases the risk for infection.

Demographics

Otitis media is common. Fifty percent of children have an episode before their first birthday, and 80 percent of children have an occurrence by their third birthday. It is estimated that $3 to $4 billion are spent per year on patients with a diagnosis of acute otitis media and related complications. Ear infections are found in all age groups, but they are considerably more common in children, especially those aged six months to three years. Boys are affected more commonly than girls. Other children at higher risk include those from poor families, Native Americans, children born with **cleft palate** or other defects of the facial structures, and children with **Down syndrome**. Exposure to cigarette smoke and early entrance into daycare also increase the risk. Otitis media occurs more frequently in winter and early spring. It is less common among children who are breastfeeding. Some studies show a genetic predisposition towards developing otitis media.

Causes and symptoms

The first precondition for the development of acute otitis media is exposure to an organism capable of causing the infection. Otitis media may be caused by either viruses or bacteria. Viral infections account for approximately 15 percent of cases. The majority of other cases are caused by a variety of bacteria. The three most common bacteria are *Streptococcus pneumoniae* (responsible for 25–50% of cases), *Haemophilus influenzae* (15–30%), and *Moraxella catarrhalis* (3–20%).

Acute otitis media often occurs as an aftereffect of upper respiratory infections, in which the eustachian tube and nasal membranes become swollen and congested. This condition can lead to an impaired clearance and pressure regulation in the middle ear, which, if sustained, may be followed by viruses and bacteria traveling from the nasopharynx to the middle ear.

Otitis media with effusion may develop within weeks of an acute episode of middle ear infection, but in many cases the cause is unknown. It is often associated with an abnormal or malfunctioning eustachian tube, which causes negative pressure in the middle ear and leaking of fluid from tiny blood vessels, or capillaries, into the middle ear.

Symptoms of acute otitis media (AOM)

The following are symptoms of acute otitis media:

- **fever**
- ear pulling
- complaints of ear **pain**, ear fullness, or hearing loss by older children
- fussiness, irritability, or difficulties in hearing, feeding, or sleeping in younger children
- bloody or greenish-yellow pus draining from the ear (This seepage is the sign of a perforated the eardrum. The pain leading up to such a perforation may be severe, but it is often relieved by the rupture.)

Otitis media with effusion (OME) is the presence of middle ear fluid for six weeks or longer after the initial episode of acute otitis media. The hallmark of OME is the lack of obvious symptoms in those who most commonly have the condition. Older children often complain of muffled hearing or a sense of fullness in the ear. Younger children may turn up the television volume. Most often OME is diagnosed when someone examines the ear for another reason, such as a well-child physical. For this reason, OME is often referred to as silent otitis media.

When to call the doctor

Unresolved episodes of otitis media may lead to a variety of complications, including hearing loss and **dizziness**. Any child who reports an earache or a sense of fullness in the ear, especially if combined with a prior upper respiratory tract infection, or fever, should be evaluated by a physician.

Diagnosis

The physician will visualize the ear canal and ear drum by using a special lighted instrument called an otoscope. Normally, the light from the otoscope reflects off the eardrum in a characteristic fashion called the "cone of light." In an infection, this reflection is often shifted or absent. If fluid or pus is draining from the ear, it can be collected and sent to a laboratory to determine if any specific infectious organisms are present. Additionally, a tympanometry test will be performed. Here, the doctor inserts a probe into the ear which emits a tone with a certain amount of sound energy. The probe measures how much sound energy bounces back off the eardrum, rather than being transmitted to the middle ear. The more energy that is returned to the probe, the more blocked the middle ear is.

A diagnosis of acute otitis media is based on the following:

- recent, usually abrupt, onset of signs and symptoms of middle ear inflammation and middle ear effusion
- the presence of middle ear effusion that is indicated by any of the following: bulging of the tympanic membrane; limited or absent movement of the tympanic membrane; or discharge from the external ear
- signs or symptoms of middle ear inflammation as indicated by either distinct redness of the eardrum or ear pain that results in an interference with **sleep** or other normal activities

Otitis media with effusion can be more difficult to detect, since it is not painful and the child usually does not appear ill. The physician may rely on one or several tests to determine the diagnosis.

- A physical examination may reveal fluid behind the eardrum and poor movement of the eardrum. The eardrum may look clear and have no signs of redness, but may not move in response to air, as a normal eardrum would.
- A tympanometry test may reveal an impairment of eardrum mobility.
- A hearing test often shows some degree of hearing loss.

Treatment

Acute otitis media (AOM)

Treatment of AOM is focused on relieving any pain that may be present and addressing the infection itself. Usually, **acetaminophen** or ibuprofen prove adequate in

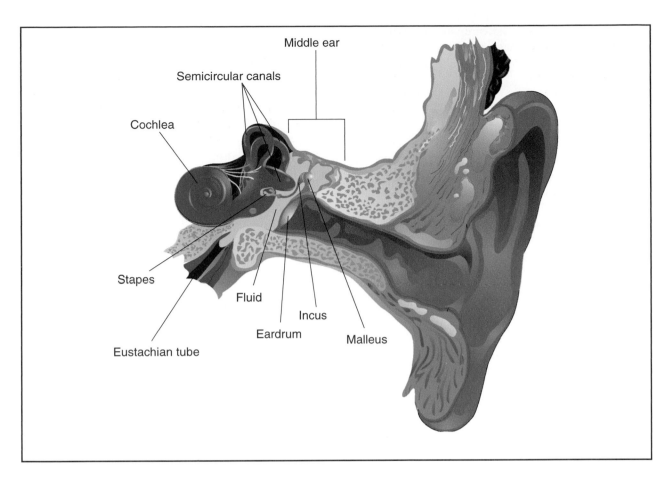

Middle ear

Semicircular canals

Cochlea

Stapes

Fluid

Incus

Eardrum

Malleus

Eustachian tube

Otitis media is an ear infection in which fluid accumulates within the middle ear. A common condition occurring in childhood, it is estimated that 85 percent of all American children will develop otitis media at least once. *(Illustration by Electronic Illustrators Group.)*

relieving the pain. In cases of severe pain, narcotics may occasionally be prescribed.

Occasionally, an "observation option" will be used in a child who has uncomplicated acute otitis media. This refers to delaying antibacterial treatment of certain children for 48 to 72 hours and limiting management to symptomatic relief. The decision to observe or treat is based on the child's age, the certainty of the diagnosis, and the severity of the illness. To observe a child without initial antibacterial therapy, it is important that the parent or caregiver has a ready means of communicating with the doctor. There also must be a system in place that permits a prompt reevaluation of the child if symptoms persist or worsen. If the decision is made to use an antibiotic, the usual recommendation is for amoxicillin, preferably at a dose of 80 to 90mg/kg/day. If the initial treatment plan fails to work within 48 to 72 hours, the

physician may reconsider the diagnosis of AOM. Further treatment may involve changing **antibiotics**.

Otitis media with effusion (OME)

For young children ages one to three years, most physicians prefer a conservative, or wait-and-see, approach, using antibiotics if the infection is persistent, the child is in pain, or there is evidence of hearing loss. Most cases of otitis media with effusion get better within three months without any treatment. If the child continues to have repeated episodes of OME, despite taking antibiotics, the physician may decide to try long-term, low-dose treatment with antibiotics, even after the condition has cleared. If OME persists for over three months, despite antibiotic treatment, the doctor may suggest a hearing test. If OME persists for more than four to six months, even if hearing tests are normal, the doctor may suggest surgery to drain the eardrum and implant **ear tubes** for continuous drainage.

Surgery

In some cases, a surgical perforation to drain pus from the middle ear may be performed. This procedure is called a **myringotomy**. The hole created by the myringotomy generally heals itself in about a week. In 2002 a new minimally invasive procedure was introduced that uses a laser to perform the myringotomy. It can be performed in the doctor's office and heals more rapidly than the standard myringotomy. In some cases, the physician may decide that the placement of tubes during the myringotomy is recommended. These small tubes are placed to aid in draining the fluid from the middle ear. They fall out on their own after a few months. The decision to place these tubes is based on the following criteria:

- presence of fluid in the ears for more than three or four months following an ear infection

- fluid in the ears and more than three months of hearing loss

- changes in the structure of the eardrum as a result of ear infections

- a delay in speaking

- repeated infections that do not improve with antibiotics over several months

Another type of surgery, called an adenoidectomy, removes the adenoids. Removing the adenoids has been shown to help some children with otitis media between the ages of four to eight. It is a procedure generally reserved for those children who have recurrent otitis media after myringotomy tubes are extruded.

Alternative treatment

Treatment guidelines from the American Academy of Pediatrics and the American Academy of Family Physicians in the early 2000s state that there is insufficient evidence to either support or discourage the use of alternative medicines for acute otitis media. Increasing numbers of parents and caregivers are using various forms of nonconventional treatment for their children. Treatments that have been used for AOM include homeopathy, acupuncture, herbal remedies, chiropractic treatments, and nutritional supplements. Although most treatments are harmless, some are not. Some can have a direct and dangerous effect, whereas others may interfere with the effects of conventional treatments. Parent should inform their doctor if they are using any alternative or unconventional methods to treat their child's otitis media.

KEY TERMS

Adenoids—Common name for the pharyngeal tonsils, which are lymph masses in the wall of the air passageway (pharynx) just behind the nose.

Effusion—The escape of fluid from blood vessels or the lymphatic system and its collection in a cavity.

Eustachian tube—A thin tube between the middle ear and the pharnyx. Its purpose is to equalize pressure on either side of the ear drum.

Myringotomy—A surgical procedure in which an incision is made in the ear drum to allow fluid or pus to escape from the middle ear.

Nasopharynx—One of the three regions of the pharynx, the nasopharynx is the region behind the nasal cavity.

Ossicles—The three small bones of the middle ear: the malleus (hammer), the incus (anvil) and the stapes (stirrup). These bones help carry sound from the eardrum to the inner ear.

Prognosis

The prognosis of acute otitis media is excellent. The duration is variable. There may be improvement within 48 hours even without any treatment. Treatment with antibiotics for a week to 10 days is usually effective.

Prevention

Breastfeeding helps to pass along immunities to a child that may prevent otitis media. The position the child is in while breastfeeding is better than the usual bottle-feeding position for optimal eustachian tube function. If a child must be bottle-fed, it is best to hold the infant rather than allow him or her to lie down with the bottle. Because multiple upper respiratory infections may increase the risk for acute otitis media, reducing the exposure to large groups of children, particularly in daycare centers, may reduce the incidence. Children should also be kept away from environmental irritants such as secondhand tobacco smoke.

Parental concerns

A common concern among parents has been whether recurring episodes of otitis media will cause impairments in their child's development. Research indicates that persistent otitis media in the first three years of life does not have an adverse effect on development.

Resources

BOOKS

Friedman, Ellen M., et al. *My Ear Hurts!: A Complete Guide to Understanding and Treating Your Child's Ear Infections.* Collingdale, PA: DIANE Publishing Co., 2004.

Schmidt, Michael. *A Parent's Guide to Childhood Ear Infection.* Berkeley, CA: North Atlantic Books, 2004.

PERIODICALS

Huffman, Grace Brooke. "Should Recurrent Otitis Media Be Treated Surgically?" *American Family Physician* (February 15, 2000): 1128.

Kaye, Donald. "Primary Care Groups Issue Management Guidelines for Otitis Media." *Clinical Infectious Diseases* 38 (May 1, 2004): iv.

Rovers, Maroeska M., et al. "Otitis Media." *The Lancet* 363 (February 7, 2004): 465.

Wellbery, Caroline. "Effect of Otitis Media and Tympanostomy Tubes." *American Family Physician* 69 (March 1, 2004): 1237.

ORGANIZATIONS

American Academy of Otolaryngology—Head and Neck Surgery. One Prince Street, Alexandria, VA 22314. Web site: <www.entnet.org>.

American Academy of Pediatrics. 141 Northwest Point Boulevard, Elk Grove Village, IL 60007–1098. <www.aap.org>.

WEB SITES

"Chronic Otitis Media (Middle Ear Infection) and Hearing Loss." *KidsENT.* Available online at <www.entnet.org/KidsENT/hearing_loss.cfm> (accessed October 27, 2004).

"Ear Infections (Otitis Media)." *Kidshealth.* Available online at <www.kidshealth.org/parent/infections/ear/otitis_media.html> (accessed October 27, 2004).

Henderson, Sean O. "Pediatrics, Otitis Media." *eMedicine.* Available online at <www.emedicine.com/emerg/topic393.htm> (October 27, 2004).

Deanna M. Swartout-Corbeil, RN
Rosalyn Carson-DeWitt, MD
Rebecca J. Frey, PhD

Otoscopic examination *see* **Ear exam with an otoscope**

Overhydration

Definition

Overhydration, also called water excess or water intoxication, is a condition in which the body contains too much water.

Description

Overhydration occurs when the body takes in more water than it excretes and its normal sodium level is diluted. This can result in digestive problems, behavioral changes, brain damage, seizures, or coma. An adult whose heart, kidneys, and pituitary gland are functioning properly would have to drink more than two gallons of water a day to develop water intoxication. This condition is most common in persons whose kidney function is impaired and may occur when doctors, nurses, or other healthcare professionals administer greater amounts of water-producing fluids and medications than the person's body can excrete.

Infants seem to be at greater risk for developing overhydration. The Centers for Disease Control and Prevention has declared that babies are especially susceptible to oral overhydration during the first month of life, when the kidneys' filtering mechanism is too immature to excrete fluid as rapidly as older infants do. Breast milk or formula provides all the fluids a healthy baby needs. Water should be given slowly, sparingly, and only during extremely hot weather. Overhydration, which has been cited as a hazard of infant swimming lessons, occurs whenever a baby drinks too much water, excretes too little fluid, or consumes and retains too much water.

Demographics

Overhydration is the most common electrolyte imbalance in hospitals, occurring in about 2 percent of all people.

Causes and symptoms

Drinking too much water rarely causes overhydration when the body's systems are working normally. People with heart, kidney, or liver disease are more likely to develop overhydration because their kidneys are unable to excrete water normally. It may be necessary for people with these disorders to restrict the amount of water they drink and/or adjust the amount of salt in their diets.

Since the brain is the organ most susceptible to overhydration, a change in behavior is usually the first symptom of water intoxication. The person may become confused, drowsy, or inattentive. Shouting and delirium are common. Symptoms of overhydration may include blurred vision, **muscle cramps** and twitching, paralysis on one side of the body, poor coordination, **nausea and vomiting**, rapid breathing, sudden weight gain, and weakness. The person's complexion is normal or flushed. Blood pressure is sometimes higher than normal, but elevations may not be noticed even when the degree of water intoxication is serious.

Overhydration can cause acidosis (a condition in which blood and body tissues have an abnormally high acid content), anemia, cyanosis (a condition that occurs when oxygen levels in the blood drop sharply), hemorrhage, and shock. The brain is the organ most vulnerable to the effects of overhydration. If excess fluid levels accumulate gradually, the brain may be able to adapt to them, and the person will have only a few symptoms. If the condition develops rapidly, confusion, seizures, and coma are likely to occur.

When to call the doctor

A doctor should be called when a person becomes confused, drowsy, or inattentive. Persons should also consider calling a doctor when a person experiences blurred vision, muscle cramps and twitching, paralysis on one side of the body, poor coordination, nausea and vomiting, rapid breathing, sudden weight gain, or weakness.

Diagnosis

Before treatment can begin, a doctor must determine whether an individual's symptoms are due to overhydration, in which excess water is found within and outside cells, or excess blood volume, in which high sodium levels prevent the body from storing excess water inside the cells. Overhydration is characterized by excess water both within and around the body's cells, while excess blood volume occurs when the body has too much sodium and cannot move water to reservoirs within the cells. In cases of overhydration, symptoms of fluid accumulation do not usually occur. On the other hand, in cases of excess blood volume, fluid tends to accumulate around cells in the lower legs, abdomen, and chest. Overhydration can occur alone or in conjunction with excess blood volume, and differentiating between these two conditions may be difficult.

KEY TERMS

Cyanosis—A bluish tinge to the skin that can occur when the blood oxygen level drops too low.

Electrolytes—Salts and minerals that produce electrically charged particles (ions) in body fluids. Common human electrolytes are sodium chloride, potassium, calcium, and sodium bicarbonate. Electrolytes control the fluid balance of the body and are important in muscle contraction, energy generation, and almost all major biochemical reactions in the body.

Shock—A medical emergency in which the organs and tissues of the body are not receiving an adequate flow of blood. This deprives the organs and tissues of oxygen and allows the build-up of waste products. Shock can be caused by certain diseases, serious injury, or blood loss.

Treatment

Mild overhydration can generally be corrected by following a doctor's instructions to limit fluid intake. In more serious cases, diuretics may be prescribed to increase urination, although these drugs tend to be most effective in the treatment of excess blood volume. Identifying and treating any underlying condition (such as impaired heart or kidney function) is a priority, and fluid restrictions are a critical component of every treatment plan.

In people with severe neurologic symptoms, fluid imbalances must be corrected without delay. A powerful diuretic and fluids to restore normal sodium concentrations are administered rapidly at first. When the person has absorbed 50 percent of the therapeutic substances, blood levels are measured. Therapy is continued at a more moderate pace in order to prevent brain damage as a result of sudden changes in blood chemistry.

Prognosis

Mild water intoxication is usually corrected by drinking less than a quart of water a day for several days. Untreated water intoxication can be fatal, but this outcome is quite rare.

Prevention

People should be careful not to drink excessive amounts of water. Persons with impaired kidney function must exert extra caution.

Parental concerns

Chronic illness, **malnutrition**, a tendency to retain water, and kidney diseases and disorders increase the likelihood of a person's becoming overhydrated. Infants and the elderly seem to be at increased risk for overhydration, as are people with certain mental disorders or **alcoholism**.

Resources

BOOKS

Greenbaum, Larry A. "Electrolytes and Acid-Base Disorders." In *Nelson Textbook of Pediatrics*, 17th ed. Edited by Richard E. Behrman et al. Philadelphia: Saunders, 2003, pp. 191–241.

Horne, Mima M. *Pocket Guide to Fluid, Electrolyte, and Acid-Base Balance*, 5th ed. Amsterdam: Elsevier Science, 2004.

Kokko, Juha P. "Fluids and Electrolytes." In *Cecil Textbook of Medicine*, 22nd ed. Edited by Lee Goldman et al. Philadelphia: Saunders, 2003, pp. 669–87.

Singer, Gary G., and Barry M. Brenner. "Fluid and Electrolyte Disturbances." In *Harrison's Principles of Internal Medicine*, 15th ed. Edited by Eugene Braunwald et al. New York: McGraw-Hill, 2001, pp. 271–82.

ORGANIZATIONS

American College of Sports Medicine. 401 W. Michigan St., Indianapolis, IN 46202–3233. Web site: <www.acsm.org/>.

WEB SITES

"Dehydration and fluid maintenance." *National Guideline Clearinghouse.* Available online at <www.guideline.gov/summary/summary.aspx?doc_id=3305> (accessed January 7, 2005).

"Overhydration." *Merck Manual.* Available online at <www.merck.com/mmhe/sec12/ch158/ch158c.html> (accessed January 7, 2005).

"Renal Subsystem." *Virtual Naval Hospital.* Available online at <www.vnh.org/EWSurg/ch10/10RenalSubsystem.html> (accessed January 7, 2005).

L. Fleming Fallon, Jr., MD, DrPH

Overweight *see* Obesity

Pacifier use

Definition

A pacifier is an artificial nipple designed for babies to suck on for comfort.

Purpose

Infants have an intense need to suck that is separate from their need to eat. Fetuses may suck their thumbs before they are born, and some newborns begin to suck immediately. Infants suck when they are tired, bored, or in need of comfort. Some babies have a stronger need to suck than others and—next to eating and being held—sucking may provide the most comfort to an infant. Babies who do not suck their thumbs or fingers often rely on pacifiers.

In Western societies 75 to 85 percent of children use pacifiers. Hospital nurseries commonly give them to newborns. Premature infants seem to grow better when they suck on pacifiers. Professionals refer to a pacifier as a transitional object that helps children adjust to new situations and relieves stress.

Most infants cry because they do not yet have methods for soothing themselves. Some newborns do not have the coordination to suck their fingers or thumb. Although breastfeeding is the most effective way to calm infants, and their hands or thumbs can be placed in their mouths, pacifiers can be very helpful for discontented babies who cannot or will not suck their thumbs or fingers.

Arguments for pacifier use

Pacifier use is controversial. Some physicians are completely opposed to pacifier use, whereas others view pacifiers as helpful if used in moderation. Pacifiers can be particularly useful for unhappy babies who are difficult to comfort. The child's energy goes into sucking on a pacifier rather than crying. Although pacifiers can give children a sense of calm and secur-

ity well into their toddler years, pacifier use may be most effective during the first few months of life when fussiness, **colic**, and the need to suck are at their peaks.

Pacifiers should only be used to satisfy the need to suck. They should never be used to delay or replace nurturing or feeding. As a child grows, a pacifier can be taken away, whereas it may be harder to discourage **thumb sucking**. For babies, pacifiers can be used for the following reasons:

- to sooth a baby to **sleep**
- to help a baby to stay asleep when disturbed
- to calm a frightened baby
- to keep the baby quiet

Arguments against pacifier use

The World Health Organization recommends against pacifier use. Disadvantages of pacifier use may include:

- They may get dirty and thus contribute to poor hygiene.
- If lost during sleep, the pacifier's absence may cause the baby to wake and cry.
- The pacifier may prevent babies from using their mouths to learn about **toys** and other objects.
- The pacifier may signal to a baby that crying is unacceptable even though crying is one of a baby's few means of communication.
- The pacifier is an easy fix that may cause parents not to seek to understand what is bothering the baby.
- Pacifiers may prevent children from learning how to comfort themselves.
- Older siblings may give the baby a pacifier to quiet a baby in situations where the parents would not use it.
- Many adults dislike the sight of babies with pacifiers.

The advantage of thumb sucking is that babies can adjust sucking to the feel of their skin. Some people believe that thumb sucking is an easier habit to break than pacifier use. Thumb sucking may be preferable to pacifier use because thumbs have the following benefits:

• Unlike pacifiers, the baby can find his thumb at night.

• Thumbs are more hygienic.

• Thumbs taste better.

Description

Types of pacifiers

Pacifiers consists of a latex or silicone nipple with a firm plastic shield and handle. Latex pacifiers are softer or more flexible but wear out faster than silicone. Silicone pacifiers are firmer, hold their shapes longer, and are easier to clean. The nipple should be knotted around the back of the handle and the shield and handle should be one piece. This prevents the nipple from falling off or the plastic from breaking in two and posing a **choking** hazard. The shield should be at least 1.5 inches (6 cm) across so that it will not fit in the baby's mouth. The shield should have air holes or vents to prevent saliva from collecting behind it and causing an irritation or rash. Large circular shields can obstruct an intensely sucking baby's nasal passages. Pacifiers should have easy-to-hold handles, be dishwasher-safe, and easy to clean.

Pacifiers come in several sizes designed for premature infants, newborns, babies younger than six months, and children older than six months. Pacifier nipples come in various shapes—long, short, flattened, or with a ball-shaped end. Some are shaped like bottle nipples and others resemble a breast nipple that is being sucked on. The latter may not always fit a baby's mouth. There is no evidence that one shape is preferable to another, although the baby may prefer a certain type. Some babies gag at the texture, taste, or smell of some pacifiers. A baby bottle nipple should never be used as a pacifier since the nipple could pop out of the ring and choke the baby.

Pacifier care

Infant pacifiers should be cleaned daily by boiling or washing in a dishwasher. Once a child is six months old, the pacifier can be washed daily with warm soapy water and rinsed with clean water. Children may be taught to wash their own pacifiers. Pacifiers should never be shared with playmates. They should never be stored in plastic bags where dampness can encourage fungal growth.

Pacifier nipples should be examined regularly for deterioration, including tears, frayed edges, holes, or a change in color. Emerging teeth can tear pacifiers. A worn or damaged pacifier should be replaced immediately. Since pacifiers are lost frequently, several should be kept on hand.

Precautions

Pacifiers are sometimes attached to a baby's clothing with a clip and a short cord or ribbon to prevent them from becoming lost or dirty. However a child can become entangled in even a short cord and should never be put to bed with a pacifier attached to a cord. A pacifier that is hung on a cord around the baby's neck, tied to the baby's hand, or attached to a crib can cause strangulation. Pacifiers should never be sweetened because sweetened pacifiers constitute a leading cause of **tooth decay** in babies under age three.

Pacifiers never should be used to replace a feeding, and children should never be given a pacifier if they are hungry. A hungry baby may become upset when there is no milk in the nipple and could develop feeding problems. Thus pacifiers should only be used between or after feedings.

Terminating pacifier use

Babies need their mouths for **play** and exploration. By the time a child is **crawling** and learning to walk, pacifiers are both unhygienic and limiting. Although many experts still recommend weaning a child from pacifier use at about age two, others suggest that six to ten months is the best time to end pacifier use. Before the age of two, children have short memories and may easily forget about a pacifier that has been lost for a few days. Pacifier use should not be terminated too soon or too abruptly since a baby may substitute thumb sucking or some other behavior such as hair pulling. A two-year-old is much less likely to revert to thumb sucking.

Sometimes severe stress or emotional upset causes a child to use a pacifier for a very long time. Even children who stop because of **peer pressure** at school may continue to use a pacifier to calm down at home or to go to sleep.

Risks

Breastfeeding

Pacifiers should never be given to a breastfeeding infant unless an efficient nursing routine is well-established. Pacifiers may cause nipple confusion. Newborns must learn to breastfeed effectively, and babies suck on breast nipples differently than on a pacifier. Pacifiers have a narrow base so that infants do not have to open their lips widely. Pacifier use may prevent infants from learning how to latch onto their mother's breast, resulting in poor feedings and sore nipples.

A number of studies have found that frequent pacifier use reduces the duration of breastfeeding and increases the likelihood that a baby will be weaned by six months. The earlier a pacifier is introduced the sooner breastfeeding ceases. The reasons for this include the following:

• Pacifier use causes babies to breastfeed less.

• Mothers may introduce a pacifier because they want to stop breastfeeding.

• Infants who are given a pacifier, with or without supplemental food, may lose interest in nursing.

• A reduction in breastfeeding decreases the mother's milk production.

• A reduction in nipple stimulation by a nursing infant decreases milk production.

Ear infections

Research has found that pacifier use increases a child's risk of ear infections—acute **otitis media**, the second most common childhood illness after colds. In one study pacifier use increased the frequency of ear infections by 50 percent. Another study found a 33 percent decrease in ear infections when pacifier use was limited to babies aged six to ten months and only used when they were falling asleep. It may be that pacifier use spreads infection or that intense sucking on pacifiers hinders proper functioning of the eustachian tube that normally keeps the middle ear open and clean. The studies suggest that pacifiers only be used with babies under ten months of age, when the need to suck is strongest and the incidence of ear infection is relatively low.

Dental development

Both dental cavities and misaligned teeth have long been associated with pacifier use. Neither pacifier use nor thumb sucking is likely to interfere with early **dental development**. However, if continued past about age three, either one can contribute to protruding front teeth and an overbite. Orthodontic pacifiers do not prevent dental abnormalities. Many dentists believe that neither pacifier use nor thumb sucking should continue once all of the baby teeth have erupted. A dentist may recommend devices that are designed to discourage pacifier use.

Other risks

Pacifiers can exacerbate any problems with developing speech and language. They have been shown to interfere with normal babbling and speech development in babies older than 12 months. A child learning to speak with a pacifier may have distorted speech. The child may replace "t" and "d" sounds—that require the front of the tongue to brush against the teeth—with "k" and "g" sounds that come from the back of the throat. Pacifiers also can interfere with children's willingness to talk and the development of their social skills.

Some research has suggested that babies exhibit fewer visually exploratory behaviors when using a pacifier; they look around less and can seem less alert. Some of these children receive less of the following:

• mental stimulation

• encouragement to explore and learn

• parental attention

Additional risks of pacifier use include the following:

• the transmission of thrush, a yeast infection, that can be difficult to eradicate in children with pacifiers

• product recall of pacifiers due to **safety** concerns

• children who are unable to give them up, even after years of use

Normal results

Many babies lose interest in their pacifiers at about four months of age, as the need to suck begins to subside. They suck on it less or spit it out. Failing to replace the pacifier after the baby cries or spits it out can be a good method for breaking the pacifier habit. It is easier to end pacifier use in a younger child. By the age of three most children have learned to communicate effectively and have other means of coping with stress. **Preschool** children may experience pressure from their peers to give up pacifiers. However, most children give up both pacifiers and thumb sucking long before they become social or dental concerns.

Parental concerns

There are numerous ways to console a crying baby other than using a pacifier. During at least the first six months of life, crying should always be responded to promptly. If infants have been well-fed within the past hour and do not need a diaper change, parents can comfort them by the following:

Toddler using a pacifier to comfort himself. *(© Lawrence Migdale/Photo Researchers, Inc.)*

- placing their face directly in front of the baby's face and talking to the child
- picking the baby up
- rocking the baby
- placing a gentle hand on the baby's stomach
- swaddling a baby in soft blankets

Parents who choose to give their baby a pacifier should take the following steps:

- not use it every time the baby's mouth is open
- try alternative methods of calming a crying baby
- encourage the child to sleep without it
- remove it as soon as the need for extra sucking is gone—usually between 12 and 15 months of age

It may take several weeks for children to give up their pacifiers. Parents can encourage their children to give them up gradually by trying the following:

- ignoring the behavior
- reassuring them with affection

KEY TERMS

Otitis media—Inflammation or infection of the middle ear space behind the eardrum. It commonly occurs in early childhood and is characterized by ear pain, fever, and hearing problems.

Overbite—Protrusion of the upper teeth over the lower teeth.

Thrush—An infection of the mouth, caused by the yeast *Candida albicans* and characterized by a whitish growth and ulcers.

Tooth eruption—The emergence of a tooth through the gum.

- limiting pacifier use to bedtime or stressful situations
- finding them a comforting alternative
- providing activities in situations where they are likely to be bored
- helping them to express their emotions in words
- gently reminding them to not to use their pacifiers
- praising them for not using a pacifier
- failing to take the pacifier to daycare or other activities
- using a calendar to mark down pacifier-free days
- rewarding pacifier-free days
- dipping the pacifier in pickle juice to make it is less appealing
- offering to trade in the pacifier for a "big kid's" toy
- not pressuring the child to give up their pacifiers
- not punishing or humiliating the child for pacifier use

See also Dental development; Orthodontics.

Resources

PERIODICALS

Howard, C. R., et al. "Randomized Clinical Trial of Pacifier Use and Bottle-Feeding or Cup-Feeding and Their Effect on Breastfeeding." *Pediatrics* 111, no. 3 (2003): 511–18.

Kramer, M. S., et al. "Pacifier Use, Early Weaning, and Cry/Fuss Behavior." *Journal of the American Medical Association* 286, no. 3 (2001): 322—6.

Meyerhoff, Michael K. "Pacifiers and Breast-Feeding." *Pediatrics for Parents* 20, no. 8 (2003): 9.

ORGANIZATIONS

American Academy of Pediatric Dentistry. 211 East Chicago Avenue, Suite 700, Chicago, IL 60611–2663. Web site: <www.aapd.org>.

American Academy of Pediatrics. 141 Northwest Point Boulevard, Elk Grove Village, IL 60007–1098. <www.aap.org>.

WEB SITES

Greene, Alan. "Pacifiers." Caring for the Next Generation, February 16, 2001. Available online at <www.drgreene.org/body.cfm?id=21&action=detail&ref=860> (accessed November 21, 2004).

Greene, Alan, and Khanh-Van Le-Bucklin. "Ear Infections and Pacifiers." Caring for the Next Generation, January 2002. Available online at <www.drgreene.org/body.cfm?id=21&action=detail&ref=303>(accessed November 21, 2004).

Hodne, Krista. "Pacifier Use Is Associated with Decreased Duration of Breastfeeding." University of Michigan Department of Pediatrics Evidence-Based Pediatrics Web Site, March 17, 2003. Available online at <www.med.umich.edu/pediatrics/ebm/cats/bfpaci.htm>(accessed November 21, 2004).

"Pacifier Use." BabyCenter. Available online at <www.babycenter.com/refcap/toddler/toddlerbeahvior/12254.html> (accessed November 21, 2004).

"Perils of the Pacifier." Available online at <www.kidsgrowth.com/resources/articledetail.cfm?id=94> (accessed November 21, 2004).

Margaret Alic, PhD

Pain

Definition

Pain is an unpleasant feeling that is conveyed to the brain by nerves in the body.

Description

Pain arises from any number of situations. Injury is a major cause, but pain may also arise from an illness. It may accompany a psychological condition, such as depression, or may even occur in the absence of a recognizable trigger. The discomfort signals actual or potential injury to the body. However, pain is more than a sensa-tion or the physical awareness of pain; it also includes perception, the subjective interpretation of the discomfort. Perception gives information on the pain's location, intensity, and something about its nature. The various conscious and unconscious responses to both sensation and perception, including the emotional response, add further definition to the overall concept of pain.

Acute pain

Acute pain often results from tissue damage, such as a skin burn or broken bone. Acute pain can also be asso-ciated with headaches or **muscle cramps**. This type of pain usually goes away as the injury heals or the cause of the pain (stimulus) is removed. To understand acute pain, it is necessary to understand the nerves that support it. Nerve cells, or neurons, perform many functions in the body. Although their general purpose, providing an interface between the brain and the body, remains con-stant, their capabilities vary widely. Certain types of neu-rons are capable of transmitting a pain signal to the brain. As a group, these pain-sensing neurons are called nociceptors, and virtually every surface and organ of the body is wired with them. The central part of these cells is located in the spine, and they send threadlike projections to every part of the body. Nociceptors are classified according to the stimulus that prompts them to transmit a pain signal. Thermoreceptive nociceptors are stimulated by temperatures that are potentially tissue damaging. Mechanoreceptive nociceptors respond to a pressure sti-mulus that may cause injury. Polymodal nociceptors are the most sensitive and can respond to temperature and pressure. Polymodal nociceptors also respond to chemi-cals released by the cells in the area from which the pain originates.

Nerve cell endings, or receptors, are responsible for pain sensation. A stimulus at this part of the nociceptor unleashes a cascade of neurotransmitters (chemicals that transmit information within the nervous system) in the spine. Each neurotransmitter has a purpose. For example, substance P relays the pain message to nerves leading to the spinal cord and brain. These neurotransmitters may also stimulate nerves leading back to the site of the injury. This response prompts cells in the injured area to release chemicals that not only trigger an immune response but also influence the intensity and duration of the pain.

Chronic and abnormal pain

Chronic pain refers to pain that persists after an injury heals, **cancer** pain, pain related to a persistent or degenerative disease, and long-term pain from an uni-dentifiable cause. It is estimated that one in three people in the United States experiences chronic pain at some point in their lives. Of these people, approximately 50 million are either partially or completely disabled. Chronic pain may be caused by the body's response to acute pain. In the presence of continued stimulation of nociceptors, changes occur within the nervous system. Changes at the molecular level are dramatic and may include alterations in genetic transcription of neurotransmitters and receptors. These changes may also occur in the absence of an identifiable cause; one of the frustrating aspects of chronic pain is that the stimulus may be unknown. For example, the stimulus cannot be medically identified in as many as 85 percent of individuals suffering from lower back pain.

Other types of abnormal pain include allodynia, hyperalgesia, and phantom limb pain. These types of pain often arise from some damage to the nervous system (neuropathic). Allodynia refers to a feeling of pain in response to a normally harmless stimulus. For example, some individuals who have suffered nerve damage as a result of viral infection experience unbearable pain from just the light weight of their clothing. Hyperalgesia is somewhat related to allodynia in that the response to a painful stimulus is extreme. In this case, a mild pain stimulus, such as a pinprick, causes a maximum pain response. Phantom limb pain occurs after a limb is amputated; although an individual may be missing the limb, the nervous system continues to perceive pain originating from the area.

Demographics

Pain is experienced by all age groups, both sexes, and all races and ethnic groups.

Causes and symptoms

Pain is the most common symptom of injury and disease, and descriptions can range in intensity from a mere ache to unbearable agony. Nociceptors have the ability to convey information to the brain that indicates the location, nature, and intensity of the pain. For example, stepping on a nail sends an information-packed message to the brain: the foot has experienced a puncture wound that hurts a lot. Pain perception also varies depending on the location of the pain. The kinds of stimuli that cause a pain response on the skin include pricking, cutting, crushing, burning, and freezing. These same stimuli would not generate much of a response in the intestine. Intestinal pain arises from stimuli such as swelling, inflammation, and distension.

When to call the doctor

Parents should notify their physician or pediatrician if any of the following occurs:

- The child is in severe pain.
- The child has pain that lasts for more than three days.
- Parents have questions or concerns about their child's treatment or condition.
- The child is in the hospital and the parent thinks he or she is in pain. The sooner the pain is treated, the easier it is to control.

Diagnosis

Pain is considered in view of other symptoms and individual experiences. An observable injury, such as a broken bone, may be a clear indicator of the type of pain a person is suffering. Determining the specific cause of internal pain is more difficult. Other symptoms, such as **fever** or **nausea**, help narrow the possibilities. In some cases, such as lower back pain, a specific physiological cause may not be identified. Diagnosis of the disease causing a specific pain is further complicated by the fact that pain can be referred to (felt at) a skin site that does not seem to be connected to the site of the pain's origin. For example, pain arising from fluid accumulating at the base of the lung may be referred to the shoulder.

Since pain is a subjective experience, it may be very difficult to communicate its exact quality and intensity to other people. There are no diagnostic tests that can determine the quality or intensity of an individual's pain. Therefore, a medical examination includes a lot of questions about where the pain is located, its intensity, and its nature. Questions are also directed at what kinds of things increase or relieve the pain, how long it has lasted, and whether there are any variations in it. An individual may be asked to use a pain scale to describe the pain. One such scale assigns a number to the pain intensity; for example, 0 may indicate no pain, and 10 may indicate the worst pain the person has ever experienced. Scales are modified for infants and children to accommodate their level of comprehension.

A subsequent method of evaluating pain in children up to age four years was as of 2004 set to be implemented in 60 hospitals in the Netherlands. The Pain Observation Scale for Young Children, called POCIS, measures pain levels according to children's behavior in seven categories: facial expressions, crying, breathing, torso movements, movements in the arms and fingers and in the legs and toes, and restlessness. Physicians and nurses observe the intensity of these behaviors and calculate a pain severity score ranging from 0 to 7. Researchers from the University of Amsterdam who developed the scale said that existing behavioral pain measures were created for premature neonates or infants and may not be appropriate for older children. Some of those measures are upsetting for children because they require restraint or physical contact by a healthcare professional.

Alternative treatment

Both physical and psychological aspects of pain can be dealt with through alternative treatment. Some of the most popular treatment options include acupressure and acupuncture, massage, chiropractic, and relaxation techniques, such as **yoga**, hypnosis, and meditation. Herbal therapies are increasingly recognized as viable options; for example, capsaicin, the component that makes cayenne peppers spicy, is used in ointments to relieve the joint pain associated with arthritis. Contrast hydrotherapy can also be very beneficial for pain relief. Lifestyles can be changed to incorporate a healthier diet and regular **exercise**. Regular exercise, aside from relieving stress, has been shown to increase endorphins, painkillers naturally produced in the body.

Prognosis

Successful pain treatment is highly dependent on successful resolution of the pain's cause. Acute pain will stop when an injury heals or when an underlying problem is treated successfully. Chronic pain and abnormal pain are more difficult to treat, and it may take longer to find a successful resolution. Some pain is intractable and requires extreme measures for relief.

Prevention

Pain is generally preventable only to the degree that the cause of the pain is preventable; diseases and injuries are often unavoidable. However, increased pain, pain from surgery and other medical procedures, and continuing pain are preventable through drug treatments and alternative therapies.

Parental concerns

If a child has a lot of pain, it is likely that more can be done to help. The first step is for parents to tell the child's doctor or nurse what their concerns are. They can ask what more can be done for the child to control pain. If parents are still concerned about their child's pain control, they can request a meeting with the doctor. Parents should list their concerns as clearly as possible. They should take a constructive approach and seek to form a partnership with the healthcare team in managing the child's pain. For parents who are still not satisfied with what is being done, some type of formal complaint to the

---

KEY TERMS

Acute pain—Pain in response to injury or another stimulus that resolves when the injury heals or the stimulus is removed.

Chronic pain—Pain that lasts over a prolonged period and threatens to disrupt daily life.

Neuron—The fundamental nerve cell of the nervous system.

Neurotransmitters—Chemicals in the brain that transmit nerve impulses.

Nociceptor—A nerve cell that is capable of sensing pain and transmitting a pain signal.

Referred pain—Pain that is experienced in one part of the body but originates in another organ or area. The pain is referred because the nerves that supply the damaged organ enter the spine in the same segment as the nerves that supply the area where the pain is felt.

Stimulus—Anything capable of eliciting a response in an organism or a part of that organism.

---

hospital may be unavoidable. **Pain management** is the right of every child. Parents working with health providers are the best advocates for this right. The U.S. Department of Health and Human Services Agency for Health Care Policy and Research has developed guidelines for pain management. These guidelines establish a standard of care that should be followed. Parents can get a copy from the hospital library or directly from the government.

Resources

BOOKS

Lehman, Thomas J. *It's Not Just Growing Pains: A Guide to Childhood Muscle, Bone, and Joint Pain, Rheumatic Diseases, and the Latest Treatments.* Oxford, UK: Oxford University Press, 2004.

McGrath, Patrick J., and Allen G. Finley. *Pediatric Pain: Biological and Social Context.* Seattle, WA: IASP Press, 2003.

Schechter, Neil L., et al. *Pain in Infants, Children, and Adolescents*, 2nd ed. New York: Lippincott Williams & Wilkins, 2002.

PERIODICALS

Leung, Alexander K. C., and David L. Sigalet. "Acute Abdominal Pain in Children." *American Family Physician* (June 1, 2003): 2321.

O'Rourke, Deborah. "The Measurement of Pain in Infants, Children, and Adolescents: From Policy to Practice." *Physical Therapy* (June 2004): 560–70.

Springen, Karen. "Small Patients, Big Pain: Ten Million American Children Suffer Chronic or Recurrent Pain. Treating Them Poses Special Challenges. Now Doctors and Researchers are Learning How to Help." *Newsweek* (May 19, 2003): 54.

Tanne, Janice Hopkins. "Children Are Often Undertreated for Pain." *British Medical Journal* (November 22, 2003): 1185.

Williams, Mathew E. "Trouble Underfoot: Heel Pain in Children: Practitioners Must Have a High Index of Suspicion and Conduct a Thorough Workup to Determine the True Cause of a Child's Symptoms." *Biomechanics* (July 1, 2004): 26.

ORGANIZATIONS

American Chronic Pain Association. PO Box 850, Rocklin, CA 95677. Web site: <www.theacpa.org>.

American Pain Society. 4700 W. Lake Ave., Glenview, IL 60025. Web site: <www.ampainsoc.org>.

WEB SITES

Rutherford, Kim. "The Truth about Pain." *KidsHealth*, August 2001. Available online at <www.kidshealth.org/parent/general/aches/pain.html> (accessed November 22, 2004).

Suresh, Santhanam. "Chronic Pain Management in Children and Adolescents." *The Child's Doctor*, 2004. Available online at <www.childsdoc.org/spring2002/chronicpain.asp> (accessed November 22, 2004).

OTHER

Carr, Daniel B., and Ada Jacox. "Acute Pain Management: Operative or Medical Procedures and Trauma; Clinical Practice Guideline." Available free by writing to AHCPR Publications Clearinghouse, PO Box 8547, Silver Spring, MD 20907. Available online at <www.ahrq.gov/clinic/medtep/acute.htm> (accessed November 22, 2004).

Julia Barrett
Ken R. Wells

Pain management

Definition

Pain management covers a number of methods to prevent, reduce, or stop pain sensations. These include the use of medications; physical methods such as ice and physical therapy; and psychological methods.

Purpose

Pain serves as an alert to potential or actual damage to the body. The definition for damage is quite broad; pain can arise from injury as well as disease. Pain that acts as a warning is called productive pain. After the message is received and interpreted, further pain offers no real benefit. Pain can have a negative impact on a person's quality of life and impede recovery from illness or injury. Unrelieved pain can become a syndrome in its own right and cause a downward spiral in a person's health and outlook. Managing pain properly facilitates recovery, prevents additional health complications, and improves a person's quality of life.

For many years it was believed that infants do not feel pain the way older children and adults do. As of the early 2000s, however, there has been a better understanding of the problems of pain, even in infancy.

Description

Before considering pain management, a review of pain definitions and mechanisms may be useful.

What is pain?

Pain is the means by which the peripheral nervous system (PNS) warns the central nervous system (CNS) of injury or potential injury to the body. The CNS comprises the brain and spinal cord, and the PNS is composed of the nerves that stem from and lead into the CNS. PNS includes all nerves throughout the body except the brain and spinal cord.

Once the brain has received and processed the pain message and coordinated an appropriate response, pain has served its purpose. The body uses natural pain killers, called endorphins, that are meant to derail further pain messages from the same source. However, these natural pain killers may not adequately dampen a continuing pain message. Pain is generally divided into two categories: acute and chronic.

Acute and chronic pain

Nociceptive pain, or the pain that is transmitted by nociceptors, is typically called acute pain. This kind of pain is associated with injury, headaches, disease, and many other conditions. It usually resolves once the condition that caused it is resolved. However, following some disorders, pain does not resolve. Even after healing or a cure has been achieved, the brain continues to perceive pain. In this situation, the pain may be considered chronic. The time limit used to define chronic pain typically ranges from three to six months, although some healthcare professionals prefer a more flexible definition and consider pain chronic when it endures beyond a normal healing time. The pain associated with **cancer**, persistent and degenerative conditions, and neuropathy, or nerve damage, is included in the chronic category. Also, constant pain that lacks an identifiable physical cause, such as the majority of cases of low back pain, may be considered chronic.

It has been hypothesized that uninterrupted and unrelenting pain can induce changes in the spinal cord. As of 2004 evidence was accumulating that unrelenting pain or the complete lack of nerve signals increases the number of pain receptors in the spinal cord. Nerve cells in the spinal cord may also begin secreting pain-amplifying neurotransmitters independent of actual pain signals from the body. Other studies indicate that even newborn and premature infants who have constant pain will reach adulthood with greater sensitivity to pain and lower tolerance of stress.

Managing pain

Considering the different causes and types of pain, as well as its nature and intensity, management can require an interdisciplinary approach. The elements of this approach include treating the underlying cause of pain, pharmacological and nonpharmacological therapies, and some invasive (surgical) procedures.

Treating the cause of pain underpins the idea of managing it. Injuries are repaired, diseases are diagnosed, and certain encounters with pain can be anticipated and prevented. However, there are no guarantees of immediate relief from pain. Recovery can be impeded by pain, and quality of life can be damaged.

Pharmacological options

Pain-relieving drugs, otherwise called **analgesics**, include **nonsteroidal anti-inflammatory drugs** (NSAIDs), **acetaminophen**, narcotics, **antidepressants**, anticonvulsants, and others. NSAIDs and acetaminophen are available as over-the-counter and prescription medications and are frequently the initial pharmacological treatment for pain. These drugs can also be used as adjuncts to other drug therapies, which might require a doctor's prescription.

NSAIDs include aspirin, ibuprofen (Motrin, Advil, Nuprin), naproxen sodium (Aleve), and ketoprofen (Orudis KT). These drugs are used to treat pain from inflammation and work by blocking production of pain-enhancing neurotransmitters, such as prostaglandins. Acetaminophen is also effective against pain, but it is not an anti-inflammatory drug.

NSAIDs and acetaminophen are effective for most forms of mild pain, but moderate and severe pain may require stronger medication. Narcotics handle intense pain effectively and are used for cancer pain and acute pain that does not respond to NSAIDs and acetaminophen.

Narcotics may be ineffective against some forms of chronic pain, especially since changes in the spinal cord may alter the usual pain signaling pathways. Furthermore, narcotics are usually not recommended for long-term use because the body develops a tolerance to narcotics, reducing their effectiveness over time. In such situations, pain can be managed with antidepressants and anticonvulsants, which are also only available with a doctor's prescription.

Although antidepressant drugs were developed to treat depression, it has been discovered that they are also effective in combating chronic headaches, cancer pain, and pain associated with nerve damage. Antidepressants that have been shown to have analgesic (pain reducing) properties include amitriptyline (Elavil), trazodone (Desyrel), and imipramine (Tofranil). Anticonvulsant drugs share a similar background with antidepressants. Developed to treat epilepsy, anticonvulsants were found to relieve pain as well. Drugs such as phenytoin (Dilantin) and carbamazepine (Tegretol) are prescribed to treat the pain associated with nerve damage.

Other prescription drugs are used to treat specific types of pain or specific pain syndromes. For example, corticosteroids are very effective against pain caused by inflammation and swelling, and sumatriptan (Imitrex) was developed to treat migraine headaches.

Drug administration depends on the drug type and the required dose. Some drugs are not absorbed very well from the stomach and must be injected or administered intravenously. Injections and intravenous administration may also be used when high doses are needed or if an individual is nauseous. Following surgery and other medical procedures, patients may have the option of controlling the pain medication themselves. By pressing a button, they can release a set dose of medication into an intravenous solution. This procedure has also been employed in other situations requiring pain management. Another mode of administration involves implanted catheters that deliver pain medication directly to the spinal cord. Delivering drugs in this way can reduce side effects and increase the effectiveness of the drug.

Nonpharmacological options

Pain treatment options that do not use drugs are often used as adjuncts to, rather than replacements for, drug therapy. One of the benefits of non-drug therapies is that an individual can take a more active stance against pain. Relaxation techniques, such as **yoga** and meditation, are used to decrease muscle tension and reduce stress. Tension and stress can also be reduced through biofeedback, in which an individual consciously attempts to modify skin temperature, muscle tension, blood pressure, and heart rate.

Participating in normal activities and exercising can also help control pain levels. Through physical therapy, an individual learns beneficial exercises for reducing stress, strengthening muscles, and staying fit. Regular **exercise** has been linked to production of endorphins, the body's natural pain killers.

Acupuncture involves the insertion of small needles into the skin at key points. Acupressure uses these same key points but involves applying pressure rather than inserting needles. Both of these methods may work by prompting the body to release endorphins. Applying heat or being massaged are very relaxing and help reduce stress. Transcutaneous electrical nerve stimulation (TENS) applies a small electric current to certain parts of nerves, potentially interrupt pain signals and induce the release of endorphins. To be effective, use of TENS should be medically supervised.

Invasive procedures

Three types of invasive procedures may be used to manage or treat pain: anatomic, augmentative, and ablative. These procedures involve surgery, and certain guidelines should be followed before carrying out a procedure with permanent effects. First, the cause of the pain must be clearly identified. Next, surgery should be done only if noninvasive procedures are ineffective. Third, any psychological issues should be addressed. Finally, there should be a reasonable expectation of success.

Anatomic procedures involve correcting the injury or removing the cause of pain. Relatively common anatomic procedures are decompression surgeries, such as repairing a herniated disk in the lower back or relieving the nerve compression related to carpal tunnel syndrome. Another anatomic procedure is neurolysis, also called a nerve block, which involves destroying a portion of a peripheral nerve.

Augmentative procedures include electrical stimulation or direct application of drugs to the nerves that are transmitting the pain signals. Electrical stimulation works on the same principle as TENS. In this procedure, instead of applying the current across the skin, electrodes

are implanted to stimulate peripheral nerves or nerves in the spinal cord.

Ablative procedures are characterized by severing a nerve and disconnecting it from the spinal cord.

Preparation

Prior to beginning management, pain is thoroughly evaluated. Pain scales or questionnaires are used to attach an objective measure to a subjective experience. Objective measurements allow healthcare workers a better understanding of the pain being experienced by the patient. Evaluation also includes physical examinations and diagnostic tests to determine underlying causes. Some evaluations require assessments from several viewpoints, including neurology, psychiatry, psychology, and physical therapy. If pain is due to a medical procedure, management consists of anticipating the type and intensity of associated pain and managing it preemptively.

Risks

Owing to toxicity over the long term, some drugs can only be used for acute pain or as adjuncts in chronic pain management. NSAIDs have the well-known side effect of causing gastrointestinal bleeding, and long-term use of acetaminophen has been linked to kidney and liver damage. Other drugs, especially narcotics, have serious side effects, such as **constipation**, drowsiness, and **nausea**. Serious side effects can also accompany pharmacological therapies; mood swings, confusion, bone thinning, cataract formation, increased blood pressure, and other problems may discourage or prevent use of some analgesics.

Nonpharmacological therapies carry little or no risk. However, it is advised that individuals recovering from serious illness or injury consult with their healthcare providers or physical therapists before making use of adjunct therapies. Invasive procedures carry risks similar to other surgical procedures, such as infection, reaction to anesthesia, iatrogenic (injury as a result of treatment) injury, and failure.

A traditional concern about narcotics use has been the risk of promoting **addiction**. As narcotic use continues over time, the body becomes accustomed to the drug and adjusts normal functions to accommodate to its presence. Therefore, to elicit the same level of action, it is necessary to increase dosage over time. As dosage increases, an individual may become physically dependent on **narcotic drugs**.

KEY TERMS

Acute—Refers to a disease or symptom that has a sudden onset and lasts a relatively short period of time.

Central nervous system—Part of the nervous system consisting of the brain, cranial nerves, and spinal cord. The brain is the center of higher processes, such as thought and emotion and is responsible for the coordination and control of bodily activities and the interpretation of information from the senses. The cranial nerves and spinal cord link the brain to the peripheral nervous system, that is the nerves present in the rest of body.

Chronic—Refers to a disease or condition that progresses slowly but persists or recurs over time.

Iatrogenic—A condition that is caused by the diagnostic procedures or treatments administered by medical professionals. Iatrogenic conditions may be caused by any number of things including contaminated medical instruments or devices, contaminated blood or implants, or contaminated air within the medical facility.

Neuropathy—A disease or abnormality of the peripheral nerves (the nerves outside the brain and spinal cord). Major symptoms include weakness, numbness, paralysis, or pain in the affected area.

Neurotransmitter—A chemical messenger that transmits an impulse from one nerve cell to the next.

Nociceptor—A nerve cell that is capable of sensing pain and transmitting a pain signal.

Nonpharmacological—Referring to therapy that does not involve drugs.

Peripheral nervous system (PNS)—The part of the nervous system that is outside the brain and spinal cord. Sensory, motor, and autonomic nerves are included. PNS nerves link the central nervous system with sensory organs, muscles, blood vessels, and glands.

Pharmacological—Referring to therapy that relies on drugs.

Stimulus—Anything capable of eliciting a response in an organism or a part of that organism.

However, physical dependence is different from psychological addiction. Physical dependence is characterized by discomfort if drug administration suddenly stops, while psychological addiction is characterized by an overpowering craving for the drug for reasons other than pain relief. Psychological addiction is a very real and necessary concern in some instances, but it should not interfere with a genuine need for narcotic pain relief. However, caution must be taken with people with a history of addictive behavior.

Parental concerns

Infants feel pain, but do not express it in the same manner as older children or young adults. Studies indicate that the majority of parents do not know how to recognize the signs of infant pain, and pediatricians fail to teach parents what to look for. Training of parents is essential in recognizing and dealing with pain in infants and young children.

In some cases, narcotic analgesics are essential for control of childhood pain. These drugs are safe when used properly and should not be withheld for fear of addiction.

Because exposure to chronic pain by children can lead to life-long changes in their pain response, parents must learn to recognize and treat pain promptly.

Over-the-counter pain relievers may be toxic. Parents must read the labeled directions carefully and follow them exactly. For liquids, it is essential to use the proper measuring devices, such as a measuring dropper or medicinal teaspoon. Household measures are not reliable.

See also Acetaminophen; Nonsteroidal anti-inflammatory drugs.

Resources

PERIODICALS

Byers, J. F., and K. Thornley. "Cueing into infant pain." *MCN American Journal of Maternal and Child Nursing* 29, no. 2 (March-April 2004): 84–89.

Stinshoff V. J., et al. "Effect of sex and gender on drug-seeking behavior during invasive medical procedures." *Academy of Radiology* 11, no. 4 (April 2004: 390–397.

ORGANIZATIONS

American Chronic Pain Association. PO Box 850, Rocklin, CA 95677–0850. Web site: <members.tripod.com/~widdy/ACPA.html>.

American Pain Society. 4700 West Lake Ave., Glenview, IL 60025. Web site: <www.ampainsoc.org>.

WEB SITES

"Instructions for the Infant Pain Scale." *Virtual Children's Hospital, Acute Pain Management for Pediatric Patients.* Available online at <www.vh.org/pediatric/provider/pediatrics/PediatricPainMgmt/infantpainscale.html> (accessed on September 28, 2004).

"Riley Infant Pain Scale Assessment Tool." *Cancer Pain Management in Children.* Available at <www.childcancerpain.org/content.cfm?content=assess09> (accessed September 28, 2004).

Julia Barrett
Samuel Uretsky, PharmD

Pain relievers *see* **Analgesics**

Parent-child relationships

Definition

The parent-child relationship consists of a combination of behaviors, feelings, and expectations that are unique to a particular parent and a particular child. The relationship involves the full extent of a child's development.

Description

Of the many different relationships people form over the course of the life span, the relationship between parent and child is among the most important. The quality of the parent-child relationship is affected by the parent's age, experience, and self-confidence; the stability of the parents' marriage; and the unique characteristics of the child compared with those of the parent.

Characteristics of the parent

Parental self-confidence is an important indicator of parental competence. Mothers who believe that they are effective parents are more competent than mothers who feel incompetent. Also, mothers who see themselves as effective also tend to believe their infants as less difficult to handle. Parental age and previous experience are also important. Older mothers tend to be more responsive to their infants than younger mothers. In addition, parents who have had previous experience with children, whether through younger siblings, career paths, or previous children, are often times better able to cope with parenthood.

Characteristics of the child

Characteristics that may affect the parent-child relationship in a **family** include the child's physical appearance, sex, and **temperament**. At birth, the infant's physical appearance may not meet the parent's expecta-

tions, or the infant may resemble a disliked relative. As a result, the parent may subconsciously reject the child. If the parents wanted a baby of a particular sex, they may be disappointed if the baby is the opposite sex. If parents do not have the opportunity to talk about this disappointment, they may reject the infant.

Children who are loved thrive better than those who are not. Either parent or a nonparent caregiver may serve as the primary caregiver or form the primary parent-child love relationship. Loss of love from a primary caregiver can occur with the death of a parent or interruption of parental contact through prolonged hospitalizations. **Divorce** can interfere with the child's need to eat, improve, and advance. Cultural norms within the family also affect a child's likelihood to achieve particular developmental milestones.

Cultural impact

In some countries, childrearing is considered protective nurturing. Children are not rushed into new experiences like **toilet training** or being in school. In other countries, children are commonly treated in a harsh, strict manner, using shame or corporal punishment for **discipline**. In Central American nations, toilet training may begin as early as when the child can sit upright.

Childhood in the United States stretches across many years. In other countries, children are expected to enter the adult world of work when they are still quite young: girls assume domestic responsibilities, and boys do outside farm work. In addition, in Asian cultures, parents understand an infant's personality in part in terms of the child's year and time of birth.

Impact of birth order

The position of a child in the family, whether a firstborn, a middle child, the youngest, an only child, or one within a large family, has some bearing on the child's growth and development. An only child or the oldest child in a family excels in **language development** because conversations are mainly with adults. Children learn by watching other children; however, a firstborn or an only child, who has no example to watch, may not excel in other skills, such as toilet training, at an early age.

Infancy

As babies are cared for by their parents, both parties develop understandings of the other. Gradually, babies begin to expect that their parent will care for them when they cry. Gradually, parents respond to and even anticipate their baby's needs. This exchange and familiarity create the basis for a developing relationship.

PARENT-INFANT ATTACHMENT One of the most important aspects of infant psychosocial development is the infant's attachment to parents. Attachment is a sense of belonging to or connection with a particular other. This significant bond between infant and parent is critical to the infant's survival and development. Started immediately after birth, attachment is strengthened by mutually satisfying interaction between the parents and the infant throughout the first months of life, called bonding. By the end of the first year, most infants have formed an attachment relationship, usually with the primary caretaker.

If parents can adapt to their babies, meet their needs, and provide nurturance, the attachment is secure. Psychosocial development can continue based on a strong foundation of attachment. On the other hand, if a parent's personality and ability to cope with the infant's needs for care are minimal, the relationship is at risk and so is the infant's development.

By six to seven months, strong feelings of attachment enable the infant to distinguish between caregivers and strangers. The infant displays an obvious preference for parents over other caregivers and other unfamiliar people. **Anxiety**, demonstrated by crying, clinging, and turning away from the stranger, is revealed when separation occurs. This behavior peaks between seven and nine months and again during toddlerhood, when separation may be difficult. Although possibly stressful for the parents, **stranger anxiety** is a normal sign of healthy child attachment and occurs because of **cognitive development**. Most children develop a secure attachment when reunited with their caregiver after a temporary absence. In contrast, some children with an insecure attachment want to be held, but they are not comfortable; they kick or push away. Others seem indifferent to the parent's return and ignore them when they return.

The quality of the infant's attachment predicts later development. Youngsters who emerge from infancy with a secure attachment stand a better chance of developing happy and healthy relationships with others. The attachment relationship not only forms the emotional basis for the continued development of the parent-child relationship, but can serve as a foundation for future social connections. Secure infants have parents who sensitively read their infant's cues and respond properly to their needs.

Toddlerhood

When children move from infancy into toddlerhood, the parent-child relationship begins to change. During infancy, the primary role of the parent-child relationship is nurturing and predictability, and much of the relationship revolves around the day-to-day demands of caregiving: feeding, toileting, bathing, and going to bed.

As youngsters begin to talk and become more mobile during the second and third years of life, however, parents usually try to shape their child's social behavior. In essence, parents become teachers as well as nurturers, providers of guidance as well as affection. Socialization (preparing the youngster to live as a member of a social group) implicit during most of the first two years of life, becomes clear as the child moves toward his or her third birthday.

Socialization is an important part of the parent-child relationship. It includes various child-rearing practices, for example weaning, toilet training, and discipline.

Dimensions of the parent-child relationship are linked to the child's psychological development, specifically how responsive the parents are, and how demanding they are. Responsive parents are warm and accepting toward their children, enjoying them and trying to see things from their perspective. In contrast, nonresponsive parents are aloof, rejecting, or critical. They show little pleasure in their children and are often insensitive to their emotional needs. Some parents are demanding, while others are too tolerant. Children's healthy psychological development is facilitated when the parents are both responsive and moderately demanding.

During toddlerhood, children often begin to assert their need for autonomy by challenging their parents. Sometimes, the child's newfound assertiveness during the so-called terrible twos can put a strain on the parent-child relationship. It is important that parents recognize that this behavior is normal for the toddler, and the healthy development of independence is promoted by a parent-child relationship that provides support for the child's developing sense of autonomy. In many regards, the security of the first attachment between infant and parent provides the child with the emotional base to begin exploring the world outside the parent-child relationship.

Preschool

Various parenting styles evolve during the **preschool** years. Preschoolers with authoritative parents are curious about new experiences, focused and skilled at **play**, self-reliant, self-controlled, and cheerful.

School age

During the elementary school years, the child becomes increasingly interested in peers, but this is not be a sign of disinterest in the parent-child relationship. Rather, with the natural broadening of psychosocial and cognitive abilities, the child's social world expands to include more people and settings beyond the home environment. The parent-child relationship remains the most important influence on the child's development. Children whose parents are both responsive and demanding continue to thrive psychologically and socially during the middle childhood years.

During the school years, the parent-child relationship continues to be influenced by the child and the parents. In most families, patterns of interaction between parent and child are well established in the elementary school years.

Adolescence

As the child enters **adolescence**, biological, cognitive, and emotional changes transform the parent-child relationship. The child's urges for independence may challenge parents' authority. Many parents find early adolescence a difficult period. Adolescents fare best and their parents are happiest when parents can be both encouraging and accepting of the child's needs for more psychological independence.

Although the value of peer relations grows during adolescence, the parent-child relationship remains crucial for the child's psychological development. Authoritative parenting that combines warmth and firmness has the most positive impact on the youngster's development. Adolescents who have been reared authoritatively continue to show more success in school, better psychological development, and fewer behavior problems.

Adolescence may be a time of heightened bickering and diminished closeness in the parent-child relationship, but most disagreements between parents and young teenagers are over less important matters, and most teenagers and parents agree on the essentials. By late adolescence most children report feeling as close to their parents as they did during elementary school.

Parenting styles

Parenting has four main styles: authoritarian, authoritative, permissive (indulgent), and detached. Although no parent is consistent in all situations, parents do follow some general tendencies in their approach to childrearing, and it is possible to describe a parent-child relationship by the prevailing style of parenting. These descriptions provide guidelines for both professionals and parents interested in understanding how variations in the parent-child relationship affect the child's development.

Parenting style is shaped by the parent's developmental history, education, and personality; the child's behavior; and the immediate and broader context of the parent's life. Also, the parent's behavior is influenced by the parent's work, the parents' marriage, family finances, and other conditions likely to affect the parent's behavior and psychological well-being. In addition, parents in different cultures, from different social classes, and from different ethnic groups rear their children differently. In any event, children's behavior and psychological development are linked to the parenting style with which they are raised.

Authoritarian parents

Authoritarian parents are rigid in their rules; they expect absolute obedience from the child without any questioning. They also expect the child to accept the family beliefs and principles without questions. Authoritarian parents are strict disciplinarians, often relying on physical punishment and the withdrawal of affection to shape their child's behavior.

Children raised with this parenting style are often moody, unhappy, fearful, and irritable. They tend to be shy, withdrawn, and lack self-confidence. If affection is withheld, the child commonly is rebellious and antisocial.

Authoritative parents

Authoritative parents show respect for the opinions of each of their children by allowing them to be different. Although there are rules in the household, the parents allow discussion if the children do not understand or agree with the rules. These parents make it clear to the children that although they (the parents) have final authority, some negotiation and compromise may take place. Authoritative parents are both responsive and demanding; they are firm, but they discipline with love and affection, rather than power, and they are likely to explain rules and expectations to their children instead of simply asserting them. This style of parenting often results in children who have high **self-esteem** and are independent, inquisitive, happy, assertive, and interactive.

Permissive parents

Permissive (indulgent) parents have little or no control over the behavior of their children. If any rules exist in the home, they are followed inconsistently. Underlying reasons for rules are given, but the children decide whether they will follow the rule and to what extent. They learn that they can get away with any behavior. Indulgent parents are responsive but not especially demanding. They have few expectations of their children and impose little or inconsistent discipline. There are empty threats of punishment without setting limits. Role reversal occurs; the children act more like the parents, and the parents behave like the children.

Children of permissive parents may be disrespectful, disobedient, aggressive, irresponsible, and defiant. They are insecure because they lack guidelines to direct their behavior. However, these children are frequently creative and spontaneous. Although low in both social responsibility and independence, they are usually more cheerful than the conflicted and irritable children of authoritarian parents.

Disengaged parents

Finally, disengaged (detached) parents are neither responsive nor demanding. They may be careless or unaware of the child's needs for affection and discipline. Children whose parents are detached have higher numbers of psychological difficulties and behavior problems than other youngsters.

Parental concerns

Child's development is affected by family conditions such as divorce, remarriage, and parental employment. The parent-child relationship has a more important influence on the child's psychological development than changes in the composition of the household. Parenting that is responsive and demanding is related to healthier child development regardless of the parent's marital or employment status. If changes in the parent's marital status or work life disrupt the parent-child relationship, short-term effects on the child's behavior may be noticeable. One goal of professionals who work with families under stress is to help them reestablish healthy patterns of parent-child interaction.

Discipline is also a concern of parents. Children's behavior offers challenges to even the most experienced and effective parents. The manner in which parents respond to a child's behavior has an effect on the child's self-esteem and future interactions with others. Children learn to view themselves in the same way the parent views them. Thus, if the parent views the child as wild, the child begins to view himself that way and soon his actions consistently reinforce his self image. This way, the child does not disappoint the parent. This pattern is a self-fulfilling prophecy. While discipline in necessary to

KEY TERMS

Adolescence—A period of life in which the biological and psychosocial transition from childhood to adulthood occurs.

Coping—In psychology, a term that refers to a person's patterns of response to stress.

Culture—A test in which a sample of body fluid is placed on materials specially formulated to grow microorganisms. A culture is used to learn what type of bacterium is causing infection.

Discipline—In health care, a specific area of preparation or training, i.e., social work, nursing, or nutrition.

Family—Two or more emotionally involved people living in close proximity and having reciprocal obligations with a sense of commonness, caring, and commitment.

teach a child how to live comfortably in society, it should not be confused with punishment.

Resources

BOOKS

Kohn, Alfie. *Unconditional Parenting: Moving from Rewards and Punishment to Reason and Love.* Riveside, NJ: Simon & Schuster, 2005.

Post, B. Bryan, et al. *For All Things a Season: An Essential Guide to a Peaceful Parent/Child Relationship.* Mountain View, OK: M. Brynn Publishing, 2003.

WEB SITES

"Parenting." *MedlinePlus.* Available online at <www.nlm.nih.gov/medlineplus/parenting.htm> (accessed December 18, 2004).

Aliene S. Linwood, RN, DPA, FACHE

Patau syndrome

Definition

Patau syndrome, also called trisomy 13, is a congenital (present at birth) disorder associated with the presence of an extra copy of chromosome 13. The extra chromosome 13 causes numerous physical and mental abnormalities, especially heart defects. Patau syndrome is named for Klaus Patau, who reported the syndrome and its association with trisomy in 1960.

Description

Children normally inherit 23 chromosomes from each parent, for a total of 46 chromosomes. A typical human being has 46 chromosomes: 22 pairs of non-sex linked chromosomes and one pair of sex-linked chromosomes that determine that person's sex. Sometimes a child may end up with more than 46 chromosomes because of problems with the father's sperm or the mother's egg or because of mutations that occurred after the sperm and the egg fused to form the embryo (conception).

Normally, there are two copies of each of the 23 chromosomes: one from each parent. A condition called trisomy occurs when three, instead of two, copies of a chromosome are present in a developing human embryo. An extra copy of a particular chromosome can come either from the egg or sperm or from mutations that occur after conception.

The most well-known trisomy-related disorder is **Down syndrome** (trisomy 21), in which the developing embryo has an extra copy of chromosome 21. Patau syndrome is trisomy 13, in which the developing embryo has three copies of chromosome 13.

An extra copy of chromosome 13 is not the only cause of Patau syndrome. Other changes in chromosome 13, such as mispositioning (translocation), can also result in the characteristics classified as Patau syndrome. In these cases, an error occurs that causes a portion of chromosome 13 to be exchanged for a portion of another chromosome. There is no production of extra chromosomes, but a portion of each affected chromosome is "misplaced" (translocated) to another chromosome.

Patau syndrome causes serious physical and mental abnormalities, including heart defects; incomplete brain development; unusual facial features such as a sloping forehead, a smaller than average head (microcephaly), small or missing eyes, low set ears, and **cleft palate** or hare lip; extra fingers and toes (**polydactyly**); abnormal genitalia; spinal defects; seizures; gastrointestinal hernias, particularly at the navel (omphalocele); and **mental retardation**. Due to the severity of these conditions, fewer than 20 percent of those affected with Patau syndrome survive beyond infancy.

Demographics

Patau syndrome occurs in approximately one in 10,000 live births. In many cases, spontaneous abortion (miscarriage) occurs, which means the fetus does not survive to term. In other cases, the affected individual is stillborn. As appears to be the case in all trisomies, the risks of Patau syndrome seem to increase with the mother's age, particularly if she is over 30 when pregnant. Male and female children are equally affected, and the syndrome occurs in all races.

Causes and symptoms

The severity and symptoms of Patau syndrome vary with the type of chromosomal anomaly, from extremely serious conditions to nearly normal appearance and functioning. Full trisomy 13, which is present in the majority of the cases, results in the most severe and numerous internal and external abnormalities. Commonly, the forebrain fails to divide into lobes or hemispheres (holoprosencephaly), and the entire head is unusually small (microcephaly). The spinal cord may protrude through a defect in the vertebrae of the spinal column (myelomeningocele). Children who survive infancy have profound mental retardation and may experience seizures.

Incomplete development of the optic (sight) and olfactory (smell) nerves often accompany the brain defects described above. The eyes may be unusually small (microphthalmia) or one eye may be absent (anophthalmia). The eyes are sometimes set close together (hypotelorism) or even fused into a single structure. Incomplete development of any structures in the eye (coloboma) or failure of the retina to develop properly (retinal dysplasia) produces vision problems. Patau syndrome affected individuals may be born either partially or totally deaf, and many are subject to recurring ear infections.

The facial features of many Patau syndrome affected individuals appear flattened. The ears are generally malformed and lowset. Frequently, a child with trisomy 13 has a **cleft lip**, a cleft palate, or both. Other physical characteristics include loose folds of skin at the back of the neck, extra fingers or toes (polydactyly), permanently flexed (closed) fingers (camptodactyly), noticeably prominent heels, "rocker-bottom foot," and missing ribs. Genital malformations are common in individuals affected with Patau syndrome and include undescended testicles (cryptorchidism), an abnormally developed scrotum, and ambiguous genitalia in males, or an abnormally formed uterus (bicornuate uterus) in females.

In nearly all cases, Patau syndrome affected infants have respiratory difficulties and heart defects, including atrial and ventricular septal defects (holes between chambers of the heart); malformed ducts that cause abnormal direction of blood flow (**patent ductus arteriosus**); holes in the valves of the lungs and the heart (pulmonary and aortic valves); and misplacement of the heart in the right, rather than the left, side of the chest (dextrocardia). The kidneys and gastrointestinal system may also be affected with cysts similar to those seen in polycystic kidney disease. These defects are frequently severe and life-threatening.

Partial trisomy of the distal segment of chromosome 13 results in generally less severe, but still serious, symptoms and a distinctive facial appearance including a short upturned nose, a longer than usual area between the nose and upper lip (philtrum), bushy eyebrows, and tumors made up of blood capillaries on the forehead (frontal capillary hemangiomata). Partial trisomy of the proximal segment of chromosome 13 is much less likely to be fatal and has been associated with a variety of facial features including a large nose, a short upper lip, and a receding jaw. Both forms of partial trisomy also result in severe mental retardation.

Beyond one month of age, other symptoms that are seen in individuals with Patau syndrome are: feeding difficulties and **constipation**, reflux disease, slow growth rates, curvature of the spine (**scoliosis**), irritability, sensitivity to sunlight, low muscle tone, high blood pressure, sinus infections, urinary tract infections, and ear and eye infections.

Diagnosis

Patau syndrome is detectable during pregnancy through the use of ultrasound imaging, **amniocentesis**, and chorionic villus sampling (CVS). At birth, the newborn's numerous malformations indicate a possible chromosomal abnormality. Trisomy 13 is confirmed by examining the infant's chromosomal pattern through karyotyping or another procedure. Karyotyping involves the separation and isolation of the chromosomes present in cells taken from an individual. These cells are generally extracted from cells found in a blood sample. The 22 non-sex linked chromosomes are identified by size, from largest to smallest, as chromosomes 1 through 22. The sex determining chromosomes are also identified. Patau syndrome is confirmed by the presence of three, rather than the normal two, copies of the thirteenth largest chromosome.

Treatment

Some infants born with Patau syndrome have severe and incurable birth defects. However, children with better prognoses require medical treatment to correct structural abnormalities and associated complications. For feeding problems, special formulas, positions, and techniques may be used. Tube feeding or the placement of a gastric tube (gastrostomy may be required. Structural abnormalities such as cleft lip and cleft palate can be corrected through surgery. Special diets, hearing aids, and vision aids can be used to mitigate some symptoms of Patau syndrome. Physical therapy, speech therapy, and other types of developmental therapy help the child reach his or her potential.

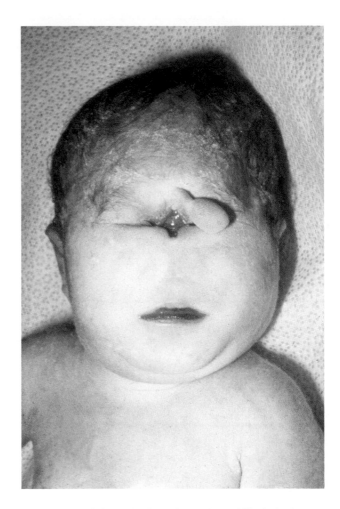

Stillborn term infant with Patau's syndrome. The baby has no eyes, no nose opening, and anelongated bulb hanging from forehead. (© Ralph C. Eagle, M.D./Photo Researchers, Inc.)

Since the translocation form of Patau syndrome is genetically transmitted, genetic counseling for the parents should be part of the management of the disease.

Prognosis

Approximately 45 percent of trisomy 13 babies die within their first month of life; up to 70 percent in the first six months; and over 70 percent by one year of age. Survival to adulthood is very rare. Only one adult is known to have survived to age 33.

KEY TERMS

Amniocentesis—A procedure performed at 16-18 weeks of pregnancy in which a needle is inserted through a woman's abdomen into her uterus to draw out a small sample of the amniotic fluid from around the baby for analysis. Either the fluid itself or cells from the fluid can be used for a variety of tests to obtain information about genetic disorders and other medical conditions in the fetus.

Chorionic villus sampling—A procedure used for prenatal diagnosis at 10–12 weeks gestation. Under ultrasound guidance a needle is inserted either through the mother's vagina or abdominal wall and a sample of the chorionic membrane. These cells are then tested for chromosome abnormalities or other genetic diseases.

Chromosome—A microscopic thread-like structure found within each cell of the human body and consisting of a complex of proteins and DNA. Humans have 46 chromosomes arranged into 23 pairs. Chromosomes contain the genetic information necessary to direct the development and functioning of all cells and systems in the body. They pass on hereditary traits from parents to child (like eye color) and determine whether the child will be male or female.

Karyotyping—A laboratory test used to study an individual's chromosome make-up. Chromosomes are separated from cells, stained, and arranged in order from largest to smallest so that their number and structure can be studied under a microscope.

Mosaicism—A genetic condition resulting from a mutation, crossing over, or nondisjunction of chromosomes during cell division, causing a variation in the number of chromosomes in the cells.

Translocation—The transfer of one part of a chromosome to another chromosome during cell division. A balanced translocation occurs when pieces from two different chromosomes exchange places without loss or gain of any chromosome material. An unbalanced translocation involves the unequal loss or gain of genetic information between two chromosomes.

Trisomy—An abnormal condition where three copies of one chromosome are present in the cells of an individual's body instead of two, the normal number.

Ultrasonography—A medical test in which sound waves are directed against internal structures in the body. As sound waves bounce off the internal structure, they create an image on a video screen. Ultrasonography is often used to diagnose fetal abnormalities, gallstones, heart defects, and tumors. Also called ultrasound imaging.

Most survivors have profound mental and physical disabilities; however, the capacity for learning in children with Patau syndrome varies from case to case. Older children may be able to walk with or without a walker. They may also be able to understand words and phrases, follow simple commands, use a few words or signs, and recognize and interact with others.

Prevention

There is no known way to prevent Patau syndrome though it can be diagnosed prenatally via amniocentesis.

Parental concerns

Parents of children born with Patau syndrome should prepare themselves for the possiblity of their child dying within days or weeks of birth, in addition to the poor survival rates past early childhood. Also, parents who have already had a child with the disease and want to have another child should discuss potential problems with their physician.

Resources

BOOKS

Berg, Bruce O. "Chromosomal Abnormalities and Neurocutaneous Disorders." In *Textbook of Clinical Neurology*. Edited by Christopher G. Goetz. Philadelphia: Saunders, 2003.

Hall, Judith G. "Chromosomal Clinical Abnormalities." In *Nelson Textbook of Pediatrics*. Edited by Richard E. Behrman et al. Philadelphia: Saunders, 2004.

ORGANIZATIONS

Support Organization for Trisomy 18, 13, and Related Disorders (SOFT). 2982 South Union St., Rochester, NY 14624. Web site: <www.trisomy.org>.

Paul A. Johnson, Ed.M.
Rosalyn Carson-DeWitt, MD

Patent ductus arteriosus

Definition

Patent ductus arteriosus (PDA) is a heart defect that occurs in infants when the ductus arteriosus (the temporary fetal blood vessel that connects the aorta and the pulmonary artery) does not close at birth.

Description

The ductus arteriosus is a temporary fetal blood vessel that connects the aorta and the pulmonary artery before birth. The ductus arteriosus should be present and open before birth while the fetus is developing in the uterus. Since oxygen and nutrients are received from the placenta and the umbilical cord instead of the lungs, the ductus arteriosus acts as a "short cut" that allows blood to bypass the deflated lungs and go straight out to the body. After birth, when the lungs are needed to add oxygen to the blood, the ductus arteriosus normally closes. The closure of the ductus arteriosus ensures that blood goes to the lungs to pick up oxygen before going out to the body. Closure of the ductus arteriosus usually occurs at birth as levels of certain chemicals, called prostagladins, change, and the lungs fill with air. If the ductus arteriosus closes correctly, the blood pumped from the heart goes to the lungs, back into the heart, and then out to the body through the aorta. The blood returning from the lungs and moving out of the aorta carries oxygen to the cells of the body. In some infants, the ductus arteriosus remains open (or patent), and the resulting heart defect is known as patent ductus arteriosus. In most cases, a small PDA does not result in physical symptoms. If the PDA is larger, health complications may occur.

In an average individual's body, the power of blood being pumped by the heart and other forces leads to a certain level of pressure between the heart and lungs. The pressure between the heart and lungs of an individual affected by PDA causes some of the oxygenated blood that should go out to the body (through the aorta) to return back through the PDA into the pulmonary artery. The pulmonary artery takes the blood immediately back to the lungs. The recycling of the already oxygenated blood forces the heart to work harder as it tries to supply enough oxygenated blood to the body. In this case, usually the left side of the heart grows larger as it works harder and must contain all of the extra blood moving back into the heart. This is known as a left-to-right or aortic-pulmonary shunt.

As noted, the size of the PDA determines how much harder the heart has to work and how much bigger the heart becomes. If the PDA is large, the bottom left side of the heart is forced to pump twice as much blood because it must supply enough blood to recycle back to the lungs and move out to the body. As the heart responds to the increased demands for more oxygenated blood by pumping harder, the pulmonary artery has to change in size and shape in order to adapt to the increased amount and force of the blood. In some cases, the increase in size and shape changes the pressure in the pulmonary artery and lungs. If the pressure in the lungs is higher than that of the heart and body, blood returning to the heart will take the short cut back into the aorta from the pulmonary artery through the PDA instead of going to the lungs. This backward flowing of blood does not carry much oxygen. If blood without much oxygen is being delivered to the body, the legs and toes will turn blue or cyanotic. This condition is called a shunt reversal.

When a PDA results in a large amount of blood being cycled in the wrong order, either through a left-to-right shunt or shunt reversal, the overworked, enlarged heart may stop working (congestive heart failure) and the lungs can become filled with too much fluid (pulmonary edema). At this time, there is also an increased risk for bacterial infection that can inflame the lining of the heart (endocarditis). These three complications are very serious.

Demographics

PDA is a very common heart defect, accounting for 5 to 10 percent of all types of **congenital heart disease**. Though an exact incidence of PDA is difficult to determine, researchers estimate that eight or nine in every 1,000 children are affected. PDA can occur in full-term infants, but it is seen most often in preterm infants, infants born at a high altitude, and babies whose mothers had a **rubella** infection during pregnancy. PDA occurs in individuals of every ethnic origin and does not occur more often in any one country or ethnic population; however, it is two to three times more common in females than males.

Causes and symptoms

PDA can be caused by environmental exposure before birth or the inheritance of a specific changed or mutated gene or genes. It can be a symptom of a genetic syndrome or may be caused by a combination of genetic and environmental factors (multifactorial).

Environmental exposures that can increase the chance for a baby to be affected by PDA include fetal exposure to rubella before birth, preterm delivery, and birth at a high altitude location.

PDA can be an inherited condition in families with isolated PDA or part of a genetic syndrome. In either case, there are specific gene changes or mutations which

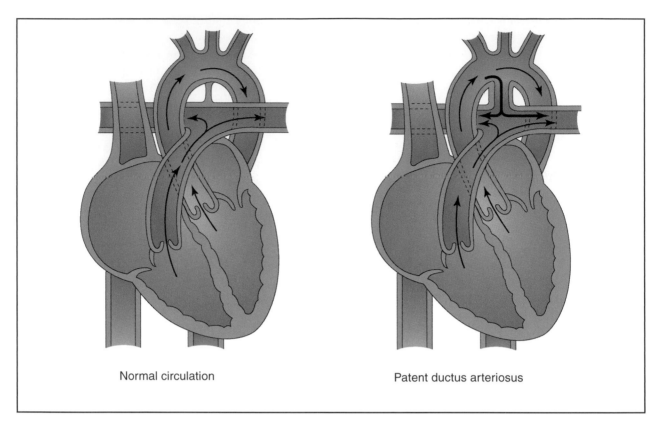

Normal circulation   Patent ductus arteriosus

Patent ductus arteriosus (PDA) is the failure of the ductus arteriosus to close after birth, allowing blood to inappropriately flow from the aorta into the pulmonary artery. *(Illustration by Electronic Illustrators Group.)*

lead to a defect in the elastic tissue forming the walls of the ductus arteriosus. As of 2004 the genes causing isolated PDA have not been identified, but it is known that PDA can be inherited through a **family** in an autosomal dominant pattern or an autosomal recessive pattern. Every person has approximately 30,000 genes, which tell the body how to grow and develop correctly. Each gene is present in pairs since one is inherited from the mother and one is inherited from the father. In an autosomal dominant condition, only one specific changed or mutated copy of the gene for PDA is necessary for a person to have PDA. If a parent has an autosomal dominant form of PDA, there is a 50 percent chance for each child to have the same or similar condition.

PDA can also be inherited in an autosomal recessive manner. A recessive condition occurs when a child receives two changed or mutated copies of the gene for a particular condition, such as PDA (one copy from each parent). Individuals with a single changed or mutated copy of a gene for a recessive condition are known as carriers and have no health problems related to the condition. However, when two people who each carry a changed or mutated copy of the same gene for a recessive condition have children, there is a chance with

each pregnancy for the child to inherit the two changed or mutated copies from each parent. In this case, the child would have PDA. For two known carriers, there is a 25 percent risk with each child to have a child with PDA, a 50 percent chance to have a child who is a carrier, and a 25 percent chance to have a child who is neither affected nor a carrier.

Most cases of PDA occur as the result of multifactorial inheritance which is caused by the combination of genetic factors and environmental factors. The combined factors lead to isolated defects in the elastic tissue forming the walls of the ductus arteriosus.

The main sign of PDA is a constant heart murmur that sounds like the hum of a refrigerator or other machinery. This murmur is usually heard by the doctor using a stethoscope.

Other signs and symptoms of PDA include:

• shortness of breath after exertion such as crying, eating, or activity

• labored or fast breathing at rest

- cyanosis, or blue lips or fingernails especially after eating, crying, or activity
- problems with feeding and poor weight gain
- frequent colds and problems with the lungs

Diagnosis

Diagnosis is most often made by detecting the characteristic "machinery" heart murmur heard by a doctor through a stethoscope. Tests such as a chest x ray, echocardiograph, and ECG are used to support the initial diagnosis and to determine the severity of the PDA.

Treatment

The treatment and management of PDA depends upon the size of the PDA, the presence of other heart defects, and the symptoms experienced by the affected individual. In some cases, the PDA will close spontaneously and no further treatment will be required. In individuals for whom the PDA remains open, there are three treatment options: medical management, device closure, and surgical repair.

Medical management with medications such as indomethocin is often the first course of treatment in premature infants with PDA. Indomethocin causes the muscles within the heart to tighten, closing the PDA. In infants for whom indomethocin does not close the PDA, full-term infants, and older children, device closure or surgery may be necessary.

Device closure of PDA is a medical procedure in which a device such as a coil, very small rings of wire, or an occluder, a tiny wire mesh patch, is placed over the PDA causing the blood to clot and thus closing the open ductus. The device is inserted into the heart in a process called cardiac catheterization. A small thin flexible tube is inserted into a blood vessel, usually in the groin area, and guided into the heart. The device is then passed through the catheter to the PDA. For most patients, this procedure is highly effective, and no further treatment is required. In children for whom this procedure is unsuccessful, children with very large PDA, or those with multiple heart defects, surgery may be necessary.

In surgical closure of PDA, called a ligation, the chest cavity is opened, the blood vessels are separated, and the PDA is sewn closed.

Prognosis

Individuals can survive with a small opening remaining in the ductus arteriosus. Treatment, including surgery, of a larger PDA is usually successful and fre-

KEY TERMS

Aorta—The main artery located above the heart that pumps oxygenated blood out into the body. The aorta is the largest artery in the body.

Cyanosis—A bluish tinge to the skin that can occur when the blood oxygen level drops too low.

Ductus arteriosus—The temporary channel or blood vessel between the aorta and pulmonary artery in the fetus.

Echocardiogram—A record of the internal structures of the heart obtained from beams of ultrasonic waves directed through the wall of the chest.

Electrocardiagram (ECG, EKG)—A record of the electrical activity of the heart, with each wave being labeled as P, Q, R, S, and T waves. It is often used in the diagnosis of cases of abnormal cardiac rhythm and myocardial damage.

Endocarditis—Inflammation of the inner membrane lining heart and/or of the heart valves caused by infection.

Oxygenated blood—Blood carrying oxygen through the body.

Pulmonary artery—An artery that carries blood from the heart to the lungs.

Pulmonary edema—An accumulation of fluid in the tissue of the lungs.

quently occurs without complications. Proper treatment allows children to lead normal lives.

Prevention

While there is no known prevention for PDA, appropriate prenatal care for expectant women is important and may prevent premature delivery, a major risk factor for PDA.

Parental concerns

Slow weight gain is common in children with congenital heart defects and may be alarming for parents. The pediatrician closely monitors the child's growth rate. There are many ways to increase the caloric intake of infants and children with PDA. A pediatrician, nurse, or dietitian can assist parents in ways to insure the child is getting proper **nutrition**. Infants with PDA may not be able to tolerate a large volume of breast milk or formula and therefore may need to be fed more frequently.

In addition to slow growth, children with PDA may be more susceptible to infections such as colds, pneumonia, and a rare but potentially life threatening infection of the heart called endocarditis. Children with PDA may need to receive preventative **antibiotics** prior to dental work. Annual flu vaccines are recommended, and parents should watch for signs of infection such as **fever**, **cough**, chills, and any difficulty breathing.

When to call the doctor

Parents of children with PDA should watch for the following symptoms and contact the doctor if any of these occurs:

- problems feeding or slow weight gain
- difficulty breathing
- shortness of breath after crying, eating, or activity
- blue color in the lips and fingernails with activity
- fever of 100.4°F (38°C) or higher
- chills, cough, or lethargy
- itchy rash or swollen skin

Resources

ORGANIZATIONS

Congenital Heart Anomalies Support, Education, and Resources (CHASER). 2112 North Wilkins Rd., Swanton, OH 43558. Web site: <www.csun.edu/~hfmth006/chaser>.

Kids with Heart. 1578 Careful Dr., Green Bay, WI 54304. Web site: <www.execpc.com/~kdswhrt>.

WEB SITES

"Patent Ductus Arteriosus: Signs, Symptoms, Diagnosis, Treatment, Benefit." *Heart Center Encyclopedia, Cincinnati Children's Hospital Medical Center*. Available online at <www.cincinnatichildrens.org/health/heart-encyclopedia/anomalies/pda.htm>.

Pflieger, Kurt. "Patent Ductus Arteriosus." *emedicine*, October 29, 2002. Available online at <www.emedicine.com/emerg/topic358.htm>.

Dawn A. Jacob
Deborah L. Nurmi, MS

Peer acceptance

Definition

Peer acceptance is the degree to which a child or adolescent is socially accepted by peers. It includes the level of peer popularity and the ease with which a child or adolescent can initiate and maintain satisfactory peer relationships.

Description

Peer acceptance and relationships are important to children's social and emotional development. Peer acceptance and friendship provide a wide range of learning and development opportunities for children. These include companionship, recreation, building social skills, participating in group problem solving, and managing competition and conflict. They also allow for self-exploration, emotional growth, and moral and ethical development. Parents, teachers, and other adults are a good source of social support for children, but it is among other children that kids learn how to interact with each other.

When examining peer acceptance among children, researchers usually look at two areas that are related to a child's psychological and social development. The first area is the child's social standing in the peer group as a whole and is indicated by the child's level of social acceptance by other members in the group, usually classmates. The second area is the child's individual friendships, characterized by both the quantity and quality of these friendships.

Although genes may be a factor in a child's **social competence** and level of peer acceptance, environmental factors are also extremely important. Some of the factors contributing to peer acceptance include:

- the quality of attachment between mother or primary caregiver and child during infancy
- during childhood, the quantity and quality of opportunities for interaction with different types of peers in different environments, such as in the **family**, at school, church, camp, activity centers, in **sports**, or in the neighborhood
- parenting style (A highly nurturing but moderately controlling authoritative parenting style is associated with the highest levels of social competence. By contrast, a low nurturing, highly controlling authoritarian parenting style is associated with children's aggressiveness, while the high nurturing but low-controlling permissive style is associated with failure to take responsibility for behavior.)

Regarding having friends, the academic benefits show up very early in a child's school career. Research suggests that those who start kindergarten from **preschool** with a friend in their class make a better adjustment to school than those who do not start with a friend. Furthermore, children who maintain their friendships as the school year progresses like school better, and children who make new friends make greater gains in school performance.

Infancy and toddlerhood

The first step in childhood affiliations is the categorization of people into groups. Although some researchers believe that the ability to categorize is an achievement of toddlerhood, others suggest it is present in infancy. In children, the top three categories of peer affiliation are age, sex, and race. Children do not appear to make racial distinctions before they are of preschool age but age and sex discriminations are made earlier. There is evidence that infants make categorical distinctions between males and females and between adults and children before they are a year old. Signs of a preferential attraction to others like the self also appear at an early age. Year-old infants are interested in and attracted to other infants—including those they have never met before—at an age when they are wary of strange adults. By the age of two, they begin to show a preference for children of their own sex. There is also research that suggests the quality of attachment between mothers or primary caregivers during infancy can contribute to peer acceptance later in childhood.

Customs of child rearing and patterns of parent-infant interaction vary widely from culture to culture, but the children's playgroup is universal. If the number of children in a given locality is small, the playgroup will consist of children of both sexes and a range of ages; if the number is larger, the children generally divide up into age- and sex-segregated groups. Girls' groups tend to be split up into subgroups. It is the social category, or psychological group that is important here. Children can categorize themselves as members of a social category even if it does not assemble in one place.

Preschool

It is important to recognize the role of the peer group in maintaining a preschool-age child's level of social acceptance. Once a child has established a reputation among peers either as someone with whom it is fun to **play** or as someone with whom joint play is unpleasant or dissatisfying, this reputation may influence the way other children perceive the child's later behavior. If a negative reputation is developed, helping the child become accepted may require more than a change in the child's behavior; it may also be necessary to point out to the other children when the child's behavior changes and to guide them to respond to the child in positive ways.

Research on imaginary companions suggests that young children who create them do so to compensate for poor social relationships, according to a study published in the May 2004 issue of the *International Journal of Behavioral Development*. As a result, there is less peer acceptance of children with imaginary companions. Several other studies have shown that fantasy play is also related to peer acceptance in children in preschool. Using a scoring system that included the reality and unfamiliarity levels of fantasy play, researchers found players who scored high had higher self-ratings of peer acceptance than did average scoring fantasy players. However, the high scoring fantasy players had lower teacher ratings of peer acceptance than the average scoring fantasy players. Researchers suggest the difference may occur because the high scoring fantasy players were unable to distinguish imagined popularity from actual peer acceptance.

School age

In school-aged children, factors such as physical attractiveness, cultural traits, and disabilities greatly affect the level of peer acceptance, with a child's degree of social competence being the best predictor of peer acceptance. The peer groups of **adolescence**, especially teens, are often based on athletic, social, or academic interests and abilities; on distinctions of race, ethnicity, and social class; and on proclivities such as drug use and delinquency. Children who are peer-accepted or popular have fewer problems in middle and high school, and teens who are peer-accepted have fewer emotional and social adjustment problems as adults. Peer-accepted children may be shy or assertive, but they often have well-developed **communication skills**.

Peer-accepted children tend to be able to function in the following ways:

- Correctly interpret other children's body language and tone of voice. Well-liked children can distinguish subtleties in emotions. For example, they can distinguish between anger directed toward them and anger directed toward a parent.

- Directly respond to the statements and gestures of other children. Well-liked children will say other children's names, establish eye contact, and use touch to get attention.

- Give reasons for their own statements, gestures, and actions. For example, well-liked children will explain why they want to do something the other child does not want to do.

- Cooperate with, show tact towards, and compromise with other children, demonstrating the willingness to subordinate the self by modifying behavior and opinions in the interests of others. For example, when joining a new group where a conversation is already in progress, well-liked children will listen first, establishing a tentative presence in the group before speaking, even if it is to change the subject.

Peer acceptance

These skills are crucial in initiating and maintaining relationships and in resolving conflicts. By contrast, rejected children tend either towards aggressive, **antisocial behavior** or withdrawn, depressive behavior. They also do not listen well, tend not to offer reasons for their behavior, do not positively reinforce their peers, and have trouble cooperating. Antisocial children interrupt people, dominate other children, and either verbally or physically attack them. Depressive or withdrawn children may be excessively reserved, submissive, anxious, and inhibited. Competitiveness or dominance by itself is not necessarily indicative of low peer acceptance. In fact, popular children tend to have characteristics associated with both competitiveness and friendliness.

The need to be "one of the gang" is stronger as children approach the teen years than at any other age. Children of all ages need to feel that they fit in—that they belong.

Common problems

Children learn to relate to peers by engaging in peer relationships. Some children have problems making friends or "fitting in." Often a vicious circle develops where a rejected child is given fewer and fewer opportunities by his peers to relate and thereby learn new skills. Lack of opportunity to participate normally in peer interaction is especially a problem for children who differ in some obvious way, either culturally, racially, or through some mental or physical disability. Parents and teachers should address issues of peer acceptance as early as possible in order to prevent loss of self-confidence and **self-esteem**.

In addition to providing direct social skills training or counseling for the child with peer acceptance problems, parents and teachers can create opportunities for non-threatening social interaction to occur. Though children should never be forced to play together since this can create the rejection it is intended to remedy, popular and less-popular preschoolers can be encouraged to interact with one another. For example, a less sociable child may be encouraged to answer and ask questions of others. Older children should be provided opportunities to interact in smaller groups and in one-on-one situations, where it may be easier to try out new behaviors and make up for social mistakes. Shy or withdrawn children can be encouraged to develop outside interests that will place them in structured contact with others. In school, peer helping programs and collaborative learning provide opportunities for popular and less-popular children to work together. Ideally, collaboration should highlight the less-popular students' strengths, such as special interests and talents, rather than weaknesses. At any age,

KEY TERMS

Fantasy play—Play activities in which children act out their fantasies.

Gene—A building block of inheritance, which contains the instructions for the production of a particular protein, and is made up of a molecular sequence found on a section of DNA. Each gene is found on a precise location on a chromosome.

Primary caregiver—A person who is responsible for the primary care and upbringing of a child.

the small, positive changes in behavior should be reinforced with attention and praise.

Parental concerns

Peer rejection in childhood often brings with it serious emotional difficulties. Rejected children are frequently discontent with themselves and with their relationships with other children. Many of these children experience strong feelings of loneliness and social dissatisfaction. Rejected children also report lower self-esteem and may be more depressed than other children. Peer rejection is also predictive of later life problems, such as dropping out of school, juvenile delinquency, and mental health problems. Dropping out of school seems to be a particularly frequent outcome. Results from research indicate that, on average, about 25 percent of low-accepted children drop out of school compared to 8 percent of other children, according to the National Network for Child Care at Iowa State University.

There are various reasons why children are disliked by their peers. When trying to find ways to help these children, it is easy to fall into the trap of thinking about what they do that bothers others. This focuses only on reducing these behavior problems but most rejected children also lack important social skills. They may not cooperate or be responsive to others, or they may not know how to respond in certain social situations. Teaching a child the missing skills is often more effective in improving peer relationships than working only on reducing negative behavior.

When to call the doctor

Parents may need to seek professional psychological help for children who suffer from peer rejection, especially when the child is depressed or shows overly **aggressive behavior**. Help may also be needed for adolescents whose acceptance by peers relates to common negative behaviors, such as gang affiliation, bullying, **smoking**, and drug and alcohol abuse.

Resources

BOOKS

Cuseo, Joseph B. *Igniting Student Involvement, Peer Interaction, and Teamwork*. Stillwater, OK: New Forums Press, 2002.

Giannetti, Charlene C., and Margaret Sagarese. *Cliques: 8 Steps to Help Your Child Survive the Social Jungle*. New York: Broadway Books, 2001.

Koubek, Christine Wickert. *Friends, Cliques, and Peer Pressure: Be True to Yourself*. Berkeley Heights, NJ: Enslow Publishers, 2002.

Schneider, Barry H. *Friends and Enemies: Peer Relations in Childhood*. Oxford, UK: Oxford University Press, 2001.

PERIODICALS

Brendgen, Mara, et al. "Assessing Aggressive and Depressed Children's Social Relations With Classmates and Friends: A Matter of Perspective." *Journal of Abnormal Child Psychology* (December 2002): 609–624.

Criss, Michael M., et al. "Family Adversity, Positive Peer Relationships, and Children's Externalizing Behavior: A Longitudinal Perspective on Risk and Resilience." *Child Development* (July-August 2002): 1220–37.

Gleason, T. "Imaginary Companions and Peer Acceptance." *International Journal of Behavioral Development* (May 2004): 204–09.

Martin, Joan M., et al. "Moderators of the Relation Between Popularity and Depressive Symptoms in Children: Processing Strength and Friendship Value." *Journal of Abnormal Child Psychology* (October 2003): 471–83.

Mostow, Allison J., et al. "Modeling Emotional, Cognitive, and Behavioral Predictors of Peer Acceptance." *Child Development* (November-December 2002): 1775–87.

Stiles, Anne Scott, and Thomas J. Raney. "Relationships Among Personal Space Boundaries, Peer Acceptance, and Peer Reputation in Adolescents." *Journal of Child and Adolescent Psychiatric Nursing* (January-March 2004): 29–40.

ORGANIZATIONS

National Academy of Child & Adolescent Psychiatry. 3615 Wisconsin Ave. NW, Washington, DC 20016. Web site: <www.aacap.org>.

National Network for Child Care. Iowa State University Extension, 1094 LeBaron Hall, Ames, IA 50001. Web site: <www.nncc.org>.

WEB SITES

"Peer Influence and Peer Relationships." *Focus Adolescent Services*, 2004. Available online at <www.focusas.com/Issues/PeerInfluence.html> (accessed October 12, 2004).

Rosenberg, Steven L., Loren M. McKean, and Thomas E. Dinero. "Positive Peer Solutions: One Answer for the Rejected Student." *Positive Peer Groups*, 2004. Available online at <www.pdkintl.org/kappan/kros9910.htm> (accessed October 12, 2004).

Ken R. Wells

Peer pressure

Definition

Peer pressure is the influence of a social group on an individual.

Description

Children and teenagers feel social pressure to conform to the group of peers with whom they socialize. This peer pressure can influence how children dress, what kind of music they listen to, and what types of behavior they engage in, including risky behaviors such as using drugs, cigarettes, and alcohol, and engaging in sex. The intensity of peer pressure differs from situation to situation.

Peer groups are usually cliques of friends who are about the same age. Peer pressure can begin in early childhood with children trying to get other kids to **play** the games they want. It generally increases through childhood and reaches its intensity in the preteen and teen years. Virtually all adolescents in middle and high school deal with peer pressure, often on a daily basis. It is how children and teens learn to get along with others of their own age group and eventually learn how to become independent. Depending on the group trying to apply the influence, peer pressure can be negative or positive.

Starting in middle school, children begin to spend more time with their friends and less time with their parents and **family**. Although some children remain loners and not part of any group, most preteens tend to be part of a small group of friends called a clique. In children ages eleven to fourteen, it is most common for members of these cliques to be of the same sex. Children will spend a lot of time with friends in their clique, interacting by going to the movies or the mall, talking on the telephone, or chatting online with instant messaging. They know which kids belong to particular cliques and who the loners are. Within the cliques, talk about the opposite sex is popular as is making arrangements for out of school activities.

Children also generally belong to a crowd, which is a larger group of kids from several cliques. While members of the cliques are close friends, members of the crowd outside a clique are casual acquaintances. Crowds are often large groups with common interests such as athletes (jocks), kids who like school (preppies), kids lacking good looks or social skills but who excel at particular intellectual interests (nerds), and drug users (druggies).

Some kids give in to peer pressure because they want to be liked, to fit in, or because they worry that other kids may make fun of them if they do not go along with the group. Others may go along because they are curious to try something new that others are doing. The idea that "everyone is doing it" may influence some kids to ignore their better judgment or their common sense. Peer pressure can be extremely strong and seductive. Experiments have shown how peer pressure can influence children to change their minds from what they know for sure is acceptable behavior to unacceptable behavior just because everyone else in their peer group is doing it. These studies have also shown that all it takes for individuals to stand their ground on what they know is right is for one other peer to join them. That principle holds true for youth of any age in peer pressure situations, according to the Online organization KidsHealth (<www.kidshealth.org>).

Children and adolescents cannot always avoid negative peer pressure. It may continue to be a fact of life through childhood, **adolescence**, and into adulthood. Quoted from an article in the September 2002 issue of *Current Health 2, A Weekly Reader Publication*, the following are strategies young people can use to deal with negative peer pressure effectively:

- Avoid putting yourself in situations that make you feel uncomfortable. For example, if you don't want to start **smoking**, stay away from areas where you know kids go to smoke.

- Choose your friends wisely. If you hang around with people who share your values, chances are you'll never be asked to do something you don't want to do.

- Think about the consequences whenever you are asked to do something you are not sure about. Stop for a moment and ask: Will this activity get me in trouble? Will it be harmful to my health?

- Be true to yourself. Think about the reasons why you are considering doing something you are uncomfortable with. Is it to gain popularity? Although there is nothing wrong with wanting to be popular, there are right ways and wrong ways to achieve it. If you change your behavior just to fit in with a particular group, you are not being true to yourself.

- Learn how to say no. This is perhaps the most difficult thing in the world for many people to do, but it is an essential skill if you are to successfully fend off negative peer pressure. There are many ways to say no, some of them subtle and some of them a little more "in your face." Several examples are: "You see it your way. I see it my way." "If you are really a friend, then back off." "You must think I'm pretty dumb to fall for that one."

Toddlerhood

Peer pressure can be found in groups as young as age two, when children will do things simply because other kids are doing it or tell them to. This can effect the child's behavior, social and emotional development, eating habits, play time, and sleeping patterns.

Preschool

Preschoolers will go out of their way to think and act like their friends, even though they know it may go against what they have been taught by their parents. At the ages of three and four, children start to see there are other values, opinions, and rules besides those set by their parents. They may demand to do things that their parents do not allow, such as watching television beyond a certain time or time limit, eating junk food, and playing with **toys** their parents do not deem appropriate, such as toy guns, simply because their friends do so.

At this age, it is normal for children to start challenging their parents, testing the limits and rules to see how far they can bend or break them. Many pediatricians suggest parents should remain firm, not overreact, and then move on. Peer pressure can have positive benefits for preschoolers, such as taking a nap or eating vegetables when they see their friends doing it.

School age

At ages five to eight, children make a concerted effort to please their friends, classmates, and playmates. Peer pressure can be a positive influence if friends encourage each other to strive to do better in school, **sports**, and creative activities. For example, a child may try harder at soccer if he or she has a friend who does well or may read more if that is what a friend does.

Peer pressure can also have a negative influence on children ages five to eight when a friend or friends encourage them to act in a way that is not natural for the child. Many pediatricians and child psychologists say it is best not to prohibit the child from hanging out with these friends but to make sure the child is aware of the consequences of unacceptable behavior. Focus on specific negative behaviors and explain why they are bad. Most children will not respond well if a parent or primary caregiver forbids them to associate with a friend or group of friends.

The effects of peer pressure usually begin to be seen heavily by middle school and through high school. As children turn into adolescents, involvement with their peers and the attraction of peer identification increases. Teens begin to experience rapid physical, emotional, and social changes, and they begin to question adult standards and the need for parental guidance. It is reassuring for teens to turn for advice to friends who understand and sympathize with them.

Adolescents expand their peer relationships to occupy a central role in their lives, often replacing their parents and family as their main source of advice, socializing, and entertainment activities. The peer group is a source of affection, sympathy, understanding, and experimentation. It is also a supportive setting for achieving the two primary developmental tasks of teens: finding answers to questions about their identity and discovering their autonomous self that is separate and independent from their parents.

At adolescence, peer relations expand to occupy a particularly central role in young people's lives. New types (opposite sex, romantic ties) and levels (crowds) of peer relationships emerge. Peers typically replace the family as the center of a young person's socializing and leisure activities. Teenagers have multiple peer relationships, and they confront multiple peer cultures that have remarkably different norms and value systems. The perception many adults have that peer pressure is one culture or a unified front of dangerous influence is inaccurate. More often than not, peers reinforce family values, but they have the potential to encourage problem behaviors as well. Although the negative peer influence is overemphasized, more can be done to help teenagers experience the family and the peer group as mutually constructive environments. The following are facts about parent, adolescent and peer relations.

- During adolescence, parents and adolescents become more physically and psychologically distant from each other. This normal distancing is seen in decreases in emotional closeness and warmth, increases in parent-adolescent conflict and disagreement, and an increase in time adolescents spend with peers. Unfortunately, this tendency sometimes is encouraged by parents who are emotionally unavailable to their teenaged children.

- Increases in family strains such as economic pressures or **divorce** may prompt teenagers to depend more on peers for emotional support. By the high school years, most teenagers report feeling closer to friends than parents. Stress caused by work, marital dissatisfaction, family break-up caused by divorce, entering a step-family relationship, lower family income or increasing expenses, all produce increased individual and family stress.

- In 10 to 20 percent of families, parents and adolescents are in distressed relationships characterized by emotional coldness and frequent outbursts of anger and conflict. Unresolved conflicts produce discouragement and withdrawal from family life. Adolescents in these families are at high risk for various psychological and behavioral problems.

- Youth **gangs**, commonly associated with inner-city neighborhoods, are a recognizable peer group among youth in smaller cities, suburbs, and even rural areas. Gangs are particularly visible in communities with a significant portion of economically disadvantaged families and when parents are conflicted, distant, or unavailable.

- Formal dating patterns of the 1980s have been replaced in the early 2000s with informal socializing patterns in mixed-sex groups. This may encourage casual sexual relationships that heighten the risk of exposure to human **immunodeficiency** virus (HIV) and other sexually transmitted diseases.

- There has been an increase in part-time employment among youth, but it has had little impact on peer relations. To find time for work, teenagers drop **extracurricular activities**, reduce time spent on homework, and withdraw from family interactions, but they protect time spent with friends.

Common problems

Negative peer pressure occurs when a child's or teen's friends or other people their age try to convince them to do something that is either harmful to their body or is against the law. Examples include drinking alcohol, taking drugs, smoking cigarettes, cutting classes, vandalizing, and **stealing**. Although teens usually know when something is bad for them, they often choose to do it because they want to be liked, to fit in, to be accepted, or because they're afraid they'll be looked down upon or made fun of.

KEY TERMS

Clique—A close group of friends having similar interests and goals and whom outsiders regard as excluding them.

Human immunodeficiency virus (HIV)—A transmissible retrovirus that causes AIDS in humans. Two forms of HIV are now recognized: HIV-1, which causes most cases of AIDS in Europe, North and South America, and most parts of Africa; and HIV-2, which is chiefly found in West African patients. HIV-2, discovered in 1986, appears to be less virulent than HIV-1 and may also have a longer latency period.

Primary caregiver—A person who is responsible for the primary care and upbringing of a child.

Bruce A. Epstein in "How to combat negative peer pressure," in the September 2002 issue of *Current Health 2, A Weekly Reader Publication*, is quoted as saying, The "desire to be accepted by their peers is perhaps the strongest motivating force during dolescence." Many studies reinforce his theory. One study showed, for example, that a student who knew the correct answer to a question gave the wrong answer just because everyone else in the class gave the wrong answer.

There are various reasons why children are disliked by their peers. When trying to find ways to help these children, it is easy to fall into the trap of thinking about what they do that bothers others. This focuses only on reducing these behavior problems but most rejected children also lack important social skills. They may not cooperate or be responsive to others, or they may not know how to respond in certain social situations. Teaching a child the missing skills is often more effective in improving peer relationships than working only on reducing negative behavior.

Parental concerns

Peer rejection in childhood often brings with it serious emotional difficulties. Rejected children are frequently discontent with themselves and with their relationships with other children. Many of these children experience strong feelings of loneliness and social dissatisfaction. Rejected children also report lower **self-esteem** and may be more depressed than other children. Peer rejection is also predictive of later life problems, such as dropping out of school, juvenile delinquency, and mental health problems. Dropping out of school

seems to be a particularly frequent outcome. Results from research indicate that, on average, about 25 percent of low-accepted children drop out of school compared to 8 percent of other children, according to the National Network for Child Care at Iowa State University.

When to call the doctor

Parents may need to seek professional psychological help for children suffering from peer rejection, especially when the child is depressed or shows overly **aggressive behavior**. Help may also be needed for adolescents whose acceptance by peers relates to common negative behaviors, such as criminal activities, gang affiliation, bullying, smoking, and drug and alcohol abuse. Professional psychological help may also be needed if the child is depressed. If the child talks about or threatens **suicide**, professional help should be sought immediately.

Resources

BOOKS

Auer, Jim, and R. W. Alley. *Standing Up to Peer Pressure: A Guide to Being True to You*. St. Louis, MO: Abbey Press, 2003.

Cherniss, Hilary, and Sara Jane Sluke. *The Complete Idiot's Guide to Surviving Peer Pressure for Teens*. New York: Alpha Books, 2001.

Koubek, Christine Wickert. *Friends, Cliques, and Peer Pressure: Be True to Yourself*. Berkeley Heights, NJ: Enslow Publishers, 2002.

Thompson, Michael, et al. *Best Friends, Worst Enemies: Understanding the Social Lives of Children*. New York: Ballantine, 2001.

PERIODICALS

Bednar, Dell Elaine, and Terri D. Fisher. "Peer Referencing in Adolescent Decision Making as a Function of Perceived Parenting Style." "*Adolescence* 38, no. 152 (Winter 2003): 607–21.

Frieden, Joyce. "Peer Pressure Likely to Prompt Tobacco Use: Behavior Predictors Studied." *Family Practice News* 34, no. 12 (June 15, 2004): 66.

MacReady, Norra. "Careful Questioning Can Uncover Drug Abuse (Peer Pressure is Powerful)." *Pediatric News* 36, no. 1(January 2002): 25.

Mostow, Allison J., et al. "Modeling Emotional, Cognitive, and Behavioral Predictors of Peer Acceptance." *Child Development* 73, no. 16 (November-December 2002): 1775–87.

Rafenstein, Mark. "How to Combat Negative Peer Pressure." *Current Health 2, a Weekly Reader Publication* 29, no. 1 (September 2002): 29–31.

Stone, Alan A. "Loss of Innocence: Sex, Drugs, and Peer Group Pressure in Middle School." *Psychiatric Times* (January 1, 2004): 28.

ORGANIZATIONS

National Academy of Child & Adolescent Psychiatry. 3615 Wisconsin Ave. NW, Washington, DC 20016. Web site: <www.aacap.org>.

National Network for Child Care. Iowa State University Extension, 1094 LeBaron Hall, Ames, IA 50001. Web site: <www.nncc.org>.

WEB SITES

"Dealing with Peer Pressure." *KidsHealth* March 2001. Available online at <http://kidshealth.org/kid/feeling/friend/peer_pressure.html> (accessed October 13, 2004).

"Peer Influence and Peer Relationships." *Focus Adolescent Services* 2004. Available online at <www.focusas.com/Issues/PeerInfluence.html> (accessed October 13, 2004).

Ken R. Wells

Penicillins

Definition

Penicillins are a group of closely related **antibiotics** that kill bacteria.

Description

There are several types of penicillins, each used to treat different kinds of infections, such as skin infections, dental infections, ear infections, respiratory tract infections, urinary tract infections, gonorrhea, and other infections caused by bacteria. These drugs will not work for olds, flu, and other infections caused by viruses.

Examples of penicillins are penicillin V (Beepen-VK, Pen-Vee K, V-cillin K, Veetids) and amoxicillin (Amoxil, Polymox, Trimox, Wymox). Penicillins are sometimes combined with other ingredients called beta-lactamase inhibitors, which protect the penicillin from bacterial enzymes that may destroy it before it can do its work. The drug Augmentin, for example, contains a combination of amoxicillin and a beta-lactamase inhibitor, clavulanic acid. Penicillins are available only with a prescription.

The original form of penicillin is called penicillin G. It is a narrow-spectrum antibiotic, which can be destroyed by stomach acid, but it is still useful against anaerobic bacteria (bacteria that can live in the absence of air). Newer penicillins are resistant to stomach acid, such as penicillin V, or have a broader spectrum, such as ampicillin and amoxicillin.

General use

Penicillins are useful against infections in many parts of the body, including the mouth and throat, skin and soft tissue, tonsils, heart, lungs, and ears. However, since many bacteria are resistant to penicillin, it is often wise to do a culture and sensitivity test before using penicillins. In some cases, there are only a few types of bacteria that are likely to be a problem, and so it is appropriate to use a penicillin without testing. For example, dentists often prescribe penicillin to prevent infections after dental surgery.

Precautions

Penicillins are usually very safe. The greatest risk is an allergic reaction, which can be severe. People who have been allergic to cephalosporins are likely to be allergic to penicillins. Moreover, people with certain medical conditions or who are taking certain other medicines can have problems if they take penicillins. Before taking these drugs, patients should be sure to let the physician know about any of the following conditions.

Low-sodium diet

Some penicillin medicines contain large enough amounts of sodium to cause problems for people on low-sodium diets. Parents of children on on such a diet should make sure that the physician treating the infection knows about the special diet.

Diabetes

Penicillins may cause false positive results on urine sugar tests for diabetes. People with diabetes should check with their physicians to see if they need to change their diet or the doses of their diabetes medicine.

Phenylketonuria

Some formulations of Augmentin contain phenylalanine. People with **phenylketonuria** (PKU) should consult a physician before taking this medicine.

Side effects

The most common side effect of penicillin is **diarrhea**. **Nausea**, **vomiting**, and upset stomach are also common. With some penicillins, particularly the broad spectrum products, there is a risk of increased growth of organisms that are not affected by penicillin. This situation can lead to candidal infections of the mouth and vagina.

Most side effects of penicillin cannot be prevented. Amoxicillin has a lower incidence of diarrhea than ampicillin and is the preferred drug in most cases.

Interactions

Birth control pills may not work properly when taken at the same time as penicillin. Penicillins may also interact with many other medicines. When this happens, the effects of one or both of the drugs may change or the risk of side effects may be greater. People who take penicillin should let their physician know all other medicines they are taking. Among the drugs that may interact with penicillins are the following:

- acetaminophen (Tylenol) and other medicines that relieve **pain** and inflammation
- medicine for overactive thyroid
- other antibiotics
- blood thinners
- antiseizure medicines such as Depakote and Depakene
- blood pressure drugs such as Capoten, Monopril, and Lotensin

The list above does not include every drug that may interact with penicillins. A physician or pharmacist should be consulted before a patient combines penicillins with any other prescription or nonprescription (over-the-counter) medicine.

Parental concerns

Parents should verify that their children have an infection requiring antibiotic therapy. Unnecessary use of antibiotics leads to development of bacterial resistance, while it subjects the child to some needless risk of adverse effects and wastes money.

Liquid forms of penicillin should be refrigerated after reconstitution. These preparations must be shaken well before use and measured with a medicinal teaspoon, not a household teaspoon.

Any adverse effects should be discussed with the prescriber. Penicillin should not be used in patients allergic to the drug; however, an incorrect report of an allergy to penicillin may cause prescribers to select a different drug which may cause even more severe side effects.

KEY TERMS

Anaerobic—An organism that grows and thrives in an oxygen-free environment.

Beta-lactamase—An enzyme produced by some bacteria that destroys penicillins.

Broad spectrum—A term applied to antibiotics to indicate that they are effective against many different types of bacteria.

Enzyme—A protein that catalyzes a biochemical reaction without changing its own structure or function.

Microorganism—An organism that is too small to be seen with the naked eye, such as a bacterium, virus, or fungus.

Mononucleosis—An infection, caused by the Epstein-Barr virus, that causes swelling of lymph nodes, spleen, and liver, usually accompanied by extremely sore throat, fever, headache, and intense long-lasting fatigue. Also called infectious mononucleosis.

Penicillins should be administered exactly as directed. Users should never give larger, smaller, more frequent, or less frequent doses. To make sure the infection clears up completely, patients should take the medicine for as long as it has been prescribed. They should not stop taking the drug just because symptoms begin to improve. This point is important with all types of infections, but it is especially important with strep infections, which can lead to serious heart problems if they are not cleared up completely.

This medicine should be used only for the infection for which it was prescribed. Different kinds of penicillins cannot be substituted for one another. Do not save some of the medicine to use on future infections. It may not be the right treatment for other kinds of infections, even if the symptoms are the same.

Resources

BOOKS

Beers, Mark. H., and Robert Berkow, eds. *The Merck Manual*, 2nd home ed. West Point, PA: Merck & Co., 2004.

Mcevoy, Gerald K., et al. *AHFS Drug Information 2004*. Bethesda, MD: American Society of Healthsystems Pharmacists, 2004.

Siberry, George K., and Robert Iannone, eds. *The Harriet Lane Handbook*, 15th ed. Philadelphia, PA: Mosby Publishing, 2000.

PERIODICALS

Apter Andrea J., et al. "Represcription of penicillin after allergic-like events." *Journal of Allergy and Clinical Immunology* 113, no. 4 (April 2004): 764–770.

ORGANIZATIONS

American Academy of Pediatrics. 141 Northwest Point Boulevard, Elk Grove Village, IL 60007–1098. Web site: <www.aap.org>.

Centers for Disease Control. 200 Independence Avenue, SW, Washington, DC, 20201. Web site: <www.cdc.gov>.

WEB SITES

"Penicillins (Systemic)." Available online at <www.nlm.nih.gov/medlineplus/druginfo/uspdi/202446.html> (accessed September 29, 2004).

"Treat Sore Throat without Penicillin." Available online at <www.medicinenet.com/script/main/art.asp?articlekey=25627> (accessed September 29, 2004).

Nancy Ross-Flanigan
Samuel Uretsky, PharmD

Perforated eardrum

Definition

A perforated eardrum (tympanum perforation) is an opening or rupture in the eardrum (tympanic membrane), the thin membrane that separates the outer ear canal from the middle ear. A perforated eardrum may be caused by infection, trauma, or negative pressure from underwater diving or an airplane flight. The hole or rupture can cause temporary hearing loss, **pain**, and occasional discharge.

Description

The eardrum (tympanic membrane) is a thin, semi-transparent membranous wall that stretches across the ear canal and separates the outer ear from the middle ear. The side that faces outward into the ear canal is covered with skin and the inside is covered with mucous membrane. The eardrum vibrates when sound waves travel into the ear canal and strike it. One of the bones of the middle ear (the malleus) attaches to the center of the membrane and receives vibrations, transmitting them to other bones (the incus and stapes) and the inner ear fluid, and finally to nerves in the brain where sound is perceived. The middle ear is connected to the nose by the eustachian tube, a narrow channel that runs from the ear drum to the back of the throat.

In addition to conducting sound, the eardrum also protects the middle ear from bacteria and possible infection. When perforation occurs, bacteria can pass more easily into the middle ear, potentially causing ear infections.

Perforation is most commonly caused by either chronic or acute infection of the middle ear, usually related to infection of the nose and throat (nasopharynx). It may also be the result of trauma from direct injury, pressure, or loud noise. In general, the larger the opening in the eardrum, the greater the potential for temporary hearing loss. The location of the perforation also affects the degree of hearing loss. Severe hearing loss may follow a skull fracture that disrupts the bones in the middle ear. Eardrum perforation caused by a loud noise may result in disturbing ear noise (tinnitus) as well as a temporary hearing loss. Tinnitus usually fades in a few days and, over time, hearing loss improves.

Demographics

Perforated eardrum occurs commonly in people of all ages; it is especially common in early childhood when children are exposed regularly to colds and upper respiratory infections in their contact with other children. Middle ear infection, the most frequent cause of perforated eardrum, is the most prevalent reported illness in children between six months and 20 months of age.

Causes and symptoms

Middle ear infection (**otitis media**) is the most common cause of perforation of the eardrum. Infection usually stems from an upper respiratory infection in which swelling (edema) in the eustachian tube causes fluid and mucous to gather behind the eardrum. Bacteria that find their way from the nasopharynx into the built up fluid may cause a middle ear infection. The resulting congestion builds up pressure behind the eardrum, causing severe pain and spontaneous rupture, which reduces the pain immediately. Infected or bloody mucus may then drain from the ear. In some cases, the doctor may decide to rupture the membrane on purpose, making an incision (**myringotomy**) that relives pressure, reduces pain, and allows the infection to drain. Chronic middle ear infections can also erode a hole in the eardrum, which can eventually destroy the tiny bones of the middle ear and increase the likelihood of infected material passing from the nasopharynx into the middle ear, causing more infections.

The eardrum can also become damaged by direct injury from a foreign object or sudden noise. It is possible to perforate the eardrum by injury from the following:

• cotton-tipped swabs

• trauma, such as a hard bang or hitting the ear with an open hand

• fracture of the skull

• a nearby explosion or other extremely loud noise

Other causes of tympanum perforation include pressure trauma (barotrauma) injury such as the following:

• sudden change of air pressure during diving into water

• sudden change of air pressure during air travel

• middle ear tumor, which puts pressure against the inner ear drum

Symptoms may include an earache or severe pain in the ear or a sudden decrease in ear pain followed by drainage of clear, bloody, or pus-filled fluid. Hearing loss may be the first symptom experienced, either immediate or delayed, but will usually be restored. Tinnitus may occur as buzzing, swishing, or ringing, which will typically subside after a few days. Rarely, a small hole may remain in the eardrum after a pressure-equalizing tube (tympanostomy tube) falls out or is removed by a doctor. Tympanostomy tube insertion can also cause perforation.

When to call the doctor

If a child with a cold or upper respiratory infection cries constantly or complains of pain in the ear, it is wise to have the ears checked by a physician. Likewise, if the child seems to have pain or difficulty hearing after any type of trauma to the ear (injury with a foreign object, a bang or slap to the head, exposure to extremely loud noise, or after recent air travel), the doctor should be consulted. Early treatment of ear infection may help avoid perforation or hearing loss.

Diagnosis

The doctor may examine the ear with an otoscope, a microscope-type device with a light source for direct inspection of the ear. This examination makes possible the diagnosis of eardrum perforation by allowing the doctor to see an opening in the eardrum or damage to bones in the middle ear. Hearing tests with an audiogram may be done to measure the extent of any hearing loss. If drainage from infection is present, the doctor may have the material cultured in the laboratory to identify the organism causing infection. The nose and throat may also be cultured to see

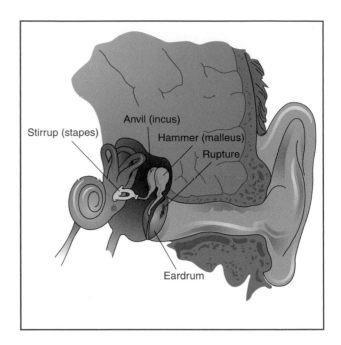

A perforated eardrum is a hole or rupture in the eardrum, the thin membrane that separates the outer ear canal from the middle ear. It may result in temporary hearing loss and occasional discharge. *(Illustration by Electronic Illustrators Group.)*

if the same organism is responsible for an upper respiratory infection. MRI or CT imaging studies may be done to rule out skull fracture, middle ear tumor, or acoustic neuroma, which may cause pain and hearing loss and be confused with a possible perforated eardrum.

Treatment

Treatment of a perforated eardrum is aimed at relieving pain or pressure behind the eardrum, treating any infection of the ear itself or of the upper respiratory tract, and restoring hearing. **Antibiotics** are usually the treatment of choice for existing ear infection or to prevent infection and reduce the likelihood of recurrence. Painkillers can relieve associated ear pain. Sometimes the doctor may lance a bulging eardrum and place a tympanostomy tube in it to relieve pain and pressure and allow the ear infection to drain before spontaneous rupture occurs.

A perforated eardrum usually heals by itself within two months. Sometimes, a paper patch is placed over the eardrum until the membrane heals. Three or four patches may be needed before the perforation closes completely. If the eardrum does not heal on its own, surgical repair (tympanoplasty) may be necessary to resolve the infection and restore hearing.

KEY TERMS

Edema—The presence of abnormally large amounts of fluid in the intercellular tissue spaces of the body.

Eustachian tube—A thin tube between the middle ear and the pharnyx. Its purpose is to equalize pressure on either side of the ear drum.

Otitis media—Inflammation or infection of the middle ear space behind the eardrum. It commonly occurs in early childhood and is characterized by ear pain, fever, and hearing problems.

Otoscope—A hand-held instrument with a tiny light and a funnel-shaped attachment called an ear speculum, which is used to examine the ear canal and eardrum.

Tinnitus—A noise, ranging from faint ringing or thumping to roaring, that originates in the ear not in the environment.

The ear should be kept clean and dry while the eardrum heals; it may help to insert ear plugs into the ears when showering or shampooing to block any water from getting in. (Cotton balls are not advised because they actually help moisture get into the ear through a wicking effect.) Pain in the ear may be eased by applying warm compresses.

Prognosis

While a perforated eardrum may be uncomfortable, it usually heals on its own within two months. Any hearing loss or ear noise that accompanies the perforation is usually temporary.

Prevention

A perforated eardrum can be prevented by avoiding insertion of any object into the ear to clean it or to remove ear wax (cerumen). Excess cerumen should only be removed by a doctor. If a foreign object becomes lodged in the ear, only a doctor should try to remove it.

Preventing ear infection is the primary way to prevent a perforated eardrum. Because infection-causing bacteria are found in the ears, nose, and throat in most cases (65-75%) of middle ear infection, avoiding contact as much as possible with children or adults who have colds or upper respiratory infections is one way to reduce the occurrence of infections in children that may lead to

middle ear infection. School-age children are especially susceptible to repeat infections. Promptly treating all nose and throat infections will help avoid ear infections. Early treatment of ear infection is another way to guard against a ruptured eardrum and associated hearing loss.

Parental concerns

Parents will likely be concerned about the possibility of ear infection, especially in children who have already had ear infections. It may help to be especially watchful for symptoms of colds, sinus infections, and upper respiratory symptoms that may lead to ear infection. Physicians may recommend immune system boosters to help prevent infection. Parents can also make sure the child is getting proper rest and **nutrition** to increase resistance to the **common cold** and infections present in other children with whom their child plays or attends school.

See also Otitis media (middle ear infection).

Resources

BOOKS

Gordon, Sharon. *Earaches.* Danbury, CT: Scholastic Library Publishing, 2003.

Lanksy, Vicki. *Koko Bear's Big Earache: Preparing Your Child for Ear Tube Surgery.* Minnetonka, MN: Book Peddlers, 2004.

Menner, Albert L. *A Pocket Guide to the Ear.* Temecula, CA: Textbook Publishers, 2003.

Royston, Angela. *Healthy Eyes and Ears.* Minneapolis, MN: Sagebrush Education Resources, 2003.

ORGANIZATIONS

American Academy of Otolaryngology—Head and Neck Surgery, Inc. One Prince St., Alexandria VA 22314-3357. Web site: <www.entnet.org>.

Better Hearing Institute. 515 King Street, Suite 420, Alexandria, VA 22314. Web site: <www.betterhearing.org/>.

WEB SITES

"Perforated Eardrum (Tympanic Membrane Perforation)." *Ear, Nose, & Throat Center.* Available online at <www.entcenter.net/I_a_eae.htm> (accessed October 13, 2004).

L. Lee Culvert
Carol A. Turkington

Perinatal infection

Definition

An infection caused by a bacteria or virus that can be passed from a mother to her baby during pregnancy or delivery is called a perinatal infection.

Description

Perinatal infections include bacterial or viral illnesses that can be passed from a mother to her baby either while the baby is still in the uterus or during the delivery process. Maternal infection can, in some cases, cause complications at birth. The mother may or may not experience active symptoms of the infection during the pregnancy. Some perinatal infections are sexually transmitted.

Transmission

Transmission of many perinatal infections occurs during **childbirth**, particularly in cases when invasive techniques such as episiotomy or artificial rupture of membranes are employed. In other cases, transmission may occur during pregnancy, if the infectious agent can cross the placental barrier, and it may occur during breastfeeding, if the infectious agent can be found in breast milk.

Demographics

The incidence of perinatal infection depends on the causative agent of infection. For example, perinatal transmission of cytomegalovirus occurs in two to 24 out of every 1,000 live births. The rate of transmission of genital herpes during pregnancy is one to two out of every 2,000 pregnancies; the rate of transmission during childbirth changes to one out of every 2,000 to 5,000 live births. Perinatal transmission of group beta streptococcus causes neonatal infection in one to five out of every 1,000 live births, and **rubella** (German **measles**), 0.02 out of every 1,000 live births. HIV is transmitted from untreated mother to child in 25 to 40 percent of cases, but in only 1 percent of cases if mother receives treatment and the infant receives prophylaxis.

Causes and symptoms

The following represent some of the more common infections that can be transmitted perinatally.

Chlamydia

The bacterium *Chlamydia trachomatis* is the cause of the most common bacterial sexually transmitted disease in the United States, causing more than 4 million infections each year. The majority of women with chlamydial infection experience no obvious symptoms. The infection affects the reproductive tract and causes pelvic inflammatory disease, infertility, and ectopic pregnancy (when the fertilized egg implants somewhere other than in the uterus). This infection can cause premature rupture of the membranes and early labor. It can be passed to the infant during delivery and can cause ophthalmia neonatorum (an eye infection) within the first month of life and **pneumonia** within one to three months of age. Symptoms of chlamydial pneumonia are a repetitive **cough** and rapid breathing. Wheezing is rare and the infant is usually without a **fever**.

Cytomegalovirus

Cytomegalovirus (CMV) is a common virus in the herpes virus family. It is found in saliva, urine, and other body fluids and can be spread through sexual contact or other more casual forms of physical contact such as kissing. In adults, CMV may cause mild symptoms of swollen lymph glands, fever, and fatigue. Many people who carry the virus experience no symptoms at all. Infants can become infected with CMV while still in the uterus if the mother becomes infected or develops a recurrence of the infection during pregnancy. Although most infants exposed to CMV before birth develop normally and do not show any symptoms, as many as 6,000 infants who were exposed to CMV before birth are born with serious complications each year. CMV interferes with normal fetal development and can cause **mental retardation**, blindness, deafness, or epilepsy in these infants.

Genital herpes

Genital herpes, which is usually caused by **herpes simplex** virus type 2 (HSV-2), is a sexually transmitted disease that causes painful sores on the genitals. Women who have their first outbreak of genital herpes during pregnancy are at high risk of miscarriage or delivering a low birth weight baby. The infection can be passed to the infant at the time of delivery if the mother has an active sore. The most serious risk to the infant is the possibility of developing HSV-2 **encephalitis**, an inflammation of the brain, with symptoms of irritability and poor feeding.

Hepatitis B

Hepatitis B is a contagious virus that causes liver damage and is a leading cause of chronic liver disease and cirrhosis. Approximately 20,000 infants are born each year to mothers who test positive for the hepatitis B virus. These infants are at high risk for developing hepatitis B infection through exposure to their mothers blood during delivery.

Human immunodeficiency virus (HIV)

Human **immunodeficiency** virus (HIV) is a serious, contagious virus that causes acquired immunodeficiency syndrome (**AIDS**). About 25 to 40 percent of untreated pregnant women pass the infection on to their newborn infants, while only 1 percent of treated pregnant women transmit the virus. There are often no symptoms of HIV in infants, but within a few months most infants who are infected show signs of opportunistic infections such as **failure to thrive**, chronic thrush, and persistent **diarrhea**.

Human papillomavirus

Human papillomavirus (HPV) is a sexually transmitted disease that causes genital **warts** and can increase the risk of developing some cancers. HPV appears to be transferred from the mother to the infant during the birth process and can cause tracheal narrowing due to lesions (warts) from the virus.

Rubella (German measles)

Rubella is a virus that causes German measles, an illness that includes rash, fever, and symptoms of an upper respiratory tract infection. Most people are exposed to rubella during childhood and develop antibodies to the virus so they never get it again. Rubella infection during early pregnancy can pass through the placenta to the developing infant and cause serious birth defects, including heart abnormalities, mental retardation, blindness, and deafness.

Group beta streptococcus

Group beta streptococcus (GBS) infection is the most common bacterial cause of infection and death in newborn infants. Although rates have declined in the United States since the introduction of **antibiotics** to at-risk women during labor in the 1980s, about 1,600 cases and 80 newborn deaths still occur each year. In women, GBS can cause vaginitis and urinary tract infections. Both infections can cause premature birth, and the bacteria can be transferred to the infant in the uterus or during delivery. GBS causes pneumonia, **meningitis**, and other serious infections in infants.

Syphilis

Syphilis is a sexually transmitted bacterial infection that can be transferred from a mother to an infant through the placenta before birth. Up to 50 percent of infants born to mothers with syphilis are premature or stillborn or die shortly after birth. Infected infants may have severe birth defects. Those infants who survive infancy may develop symptoms of syphilis up to two years later.

When to call the doctor

Pregnant women who exhibit symptoms of infection should contact their healthcare provider to determine if the infection can be passed vertically to the child during pregnancy, childbirth, and/or breastfeeding. In some cases, early detection and treatment of infection can minimize the risk of perinatal transmission.

Diagnosis

How a bacterial or viral infection is diagnosed depends on the causative agent. Examples include the following:

- Chlamydia can be diagnosed by taking a cotton swab sample of the cervix and vagina during the third trimester of the pregnancy. Chlamydial cell cultures take three to seven days to grow. DNA probes are available for more rapid diagnosis.

- Past or recent infection with cytomegalovirus (CMV) can be identified by antibody tests and CMV can be grown from body fluids.

- Genital herpes is suspected with the outbreak of a particular kind of genital sore. The sore can be cultured and tested to confirm that HSV-2 is present.

- Hepatitis B can be identified through a blood test for the hepatitis B surface antigen (HBsAg) in pregnant women. The test is part of prenatal health programs.

- Human immunodeficiency virus (HIV) can be detected using a blood test and is part of most prenatal screening programs.

- Human papillomavirus (HPV) causes the growth of warts in the genital area. The wart tissue can be removed with a scalpel and tested to determine what type of HPV virus caused the infection.

- Pregnant women are usually tested for antibodies to rubella, which would indicate that they have been previously exposed to the virus and, therefore, would not develop infection during pregnancy if exposed.

- Group beta streptococcus (GBS) can be detected by a vaginal or rectal swab culture and sometimes from a urine culture. Blood tests can be used to confirm GBS infection in infants who exhibit symptoms.

• Pregnant women are usually tested for syphilis as part of the prenatal screening, generally with a blood test.

Treatment

Methods of treating some of the more common causes of perinatal infection include:

• Chlamydia: Pregnant women can be treated during the third trimester with oral erythromycin, for seven to 14 days depending on the dose used. Newborn infants can be treated with erythromycin liquid for ten to 14 days at a dosage determined by their body weight.

• Cytomegalovirus (CMV): No drugs or vaccines were as of 2004 available for prevention or treatment of CMV except in immunocompromised persons.

• Genital herpes: The **antiviral drugs** acyclovir or famciclovir can be administered to the mother during pregnancy. Little is known about the risks of these drugs to the fetus; however, the risk of birth defects does not seem to be any higher than for women who do not take these medications. Infants with suspected HSV-2 can be treated with acyclovir. Delivery of the infant by **cesarean section** is recommended if the mother has an active case of genital herpes.

• Hepatitis B: Infants born to mothers who test positive to the HBsAg test should be treated with hepatitis B immune globulin at birth to give them immediate protection against developing hepatitis B. All infants should also receive a series of three **hepatitis B vaccine** injections as part of their routine immunizations.

• Human immunodeficiency virus (HIV): Recent studies have shown that prenatal care and HIV testing before delivery are major opportunities for preventing perinatal **HIV infection**. Pregnant women with HIV should be treated as early in the pregnancy as possible with zidovudine (AZT). Other newer drugs designed to treat HIV/AIDS also may be used during pregnancy with the knowledge that these drugs may have unknown effects on the infant. Infants born with HIV should receive aggressive drug treatment to prevent development of AIDS. Most of the drugs designed to treat HIV are routinely used during pregnancy because of the mother's health needs and because transmission rate is directly related to the mother's viral load. Teratogenicity is not fully established for some of the subsequent HIV medications.

• Human papillomavirus: Genital warts are very difficult to treat and frequently recur even after treatment. They can be removed by cryotherapy (freezing), laser or electrocauterization (burning), or surgical excision (cutting). Some medications (imiquimod 5% cream, podophyllin, trichloroacetic acid, or topical 5-fluorouracil) can be applied to help dissolve genital warts. Cesarean delivery rather than vaginal delivery reduces the risk of transmission of HPV from mothers to infants.

• Rubella (German measles): No treatment is available. Some healthcare providers may recommend giving the mother an injection of immune globulin (to boost the immune system to fight off the virus) if she is exposed to rubella early in the pregnancy. However, no evidence to support the use of these injections existed as of 2004. Exposure to rubella early in pregnancy poses a high risk that the infant will have serious birth defects. Termination of the pregnancy may be considered. Women who have not been previously exposed to rubella are usually vaccinated immediately after the first pregnancy to protect infants of future pregnancies.

• Group beta streptococcus (GBS): Pregnant women diagnosed with GBS late in the pregnancy should be treated with antibiotics injected intravenously to prevent premature labor. In 2003, the Centers for Disease Control and Prevention (CDC) issued revised guidelines for preventing perinatal GBS disease. They began recommending that women not only be tested as soon as they learn of their pregnancy, but again at 35 to 37 weeks of gestation. The CDC also recommended updated prophylaxis regimens for women with penicillin **allergies**, as well as other guidelines for patients with threatened preterm deliveries and other recommendations. If transmission of GBS to the newborn infant already is suspected or if the baby develops symptoms of infection, infants often are treated with antibiotics.

• Syphilis: Antibiotic therapy, usually penicillin, given early in the pregnancy can be used to treat the infection and may prevent transmission to the infant.

Prognosis

The prognosis of a neonate who has contracted an infection perinatally depends on the specific infection. Examples include the following:

• Chlamydia: Without treatment, the most serious consequences of chlamydial infection are related to complications of premature delivery. Treatment of the mother with antibiotics during the third trimester can prevent premature delivery and the transfer of the infection to the baby. Infants treated with antibiotics for eye infection or pneumonia generally recover.

• Cytomegalovirus: The chance for recovery after exposure to CMV is very good for both the mother and the infant. Exposure to CMV can be serious and even life threatening for mothers and infants whose immune systems are compromised, for example, those receiving **chemotherapy** or who have HIV/AIDS. Those infants who develop birth defects after CMV exposure may have serious, lifelong complications.

- Genital herpes: Once a woman or infant is infected, outbreaks of genital herpes sores can recur at any point during their lifetimes.

- Hepatitis B: Infants treated at birth with immune globulin and the series of vaccinations are protected from development of hepatitis B infection. Infants infected with hepatitis B develop a chronic, mild form of hepatitis and are at increased risk for developing liver disease.

- Human immunodeficiency virus (HIV): A combination of treatment with highly active antiretroviral therapy during pregnancy, zidovudine (AZT) during delivery, and AZT to the baby for six weeks after birth significantly reduces the chance that the infant will be infected with HIV from the mother.

- Human papillomavirus: Once infected with HPV, there is a lifelong risk of developing warts and an increased risk of some cancers.

- Rubella (German measles): Infants exposed to rubella virus in the uterus are at high risk for severe birth defects, including heart defects, blindness, and deafness.

- Streptococcus: Infection of the urinary tract or genital tract of pregnant women can cause premature birth. Infants infected with GBS can develop serious, life-threatening infections.

- Syphilis: Premature birth, birth defects, or the development of serious syphilis symptoms is likely to occur in untreated pregnant women.

Prevention

Use of a barrier method of contraceptive (e.g. **condom**) can prevent transmission of some sexually transmitted infections during intercourse. Intravenous drug use and sexual intercourse with infected partners increase the risks of exposure to most of these infections. Pregnant women can be tested for many of the bacterial or viral infections described; however, effective treatment may not be available to protect the infant.

In some cases, the method of childbirth may impact the chance of passing an infection from mother to child. For instance, research has shown that delivering a baby by caesarian section over vaginal delivery reduces the risk of transmitting HIV from mother to child.

KEY TERMS

Cesarean section—Delivery of a baby through an incision in the mother's abdomen instead of through the vagina; also called a c-section, cesarean birth, or cesarean delivery.

Ectopic pregnancy—A pregnancy that develops outside of the mother's uterus, such as in the fallopian tube. Ectopic pregnancies often cause severe pain in the lower abdomen and are potentially life-threatening because of the massive blood loss that may occur as the developing embryo/fetus ruptures and damages the tissues in which it has implanted.

Encephalitis—Inflammation of the brain, usually caused by a virus. The inflammation may interfere with normal brain function and may cause seizures, sleepiness, confusion, personality changes, weakness in one or more parts of the body, and even coma.

Episiotomy—An incision made in the perineum (the area between the vulva and the anus) during labor to assist in delivery and to avoid abnormal tearing of the perineum.

Perinatal—Referring to the period of time surrounding an infant's birth, from the last two months of pregnancy through the first 28 days of life.

Pneumonia—An infection in which the lungs become inflamed. It can be caused by nearly any class of organism known to cause human infections, including bacteria, viruses, fungi, and parasites.

Nutritional concerns

A woman's nutritional status may contribute to her ability to fight off infections, particularly in cases of **malnutrition**. A well-balanced diet rich in nutrients such as **folic acid**, calcium, iron, zinc, vitamin D, and the B **vitamins** is recommended for pregnant women. Mothers are recommended to eat approximately 300 additional calories day (above and beyond a normal non-pregnancy diet) to support the fetus's growth and development.

Parental concerns

Minimizing the risk of transmitting a maternal infection to a fetus is often a major concern for parents. The first step is identifying possible maternal infections. Proper prenatal care in many cases allows for early diagnosis and thus early treatment of certain infections, thus improving the newborn's prognosis.

Resources

BOOKS

Ford-Jones, E. Lee, and Greg Ryan. "Implications for the Fetus of Maternal Infections in Pregnancy." In *Infectious Diseases*, 2nd ed. Edited by Jonathan Cohen et all. New York: Mosby, 2004.

PERIODICALS

Cline, Matthew K., Chasse Bailey-Dorton, and Maria Cayelli. "Update in Maternity Care: Maternal Infections." *Clinics in Office Practice* 27, no. 1 (March 2000): 13–33.

Goldenberg, Robert L. "The Plausibility of Micronutrient Deficiency in Relationship to Perinatal Infection." *The Journal of Nutrition* (May 2003): 1645S.

Morantz, Carrie A. "CDC Updates Guidelines for Prevention of Perinatal Group B Streptococcal Disease." *American Family Physician* (March 1, 2003): 1121.

Peters, Vicki, et al. "Missed Opportunities for Perinatal HIV Prevention Among HIV-exposed Infants Born 1996–2000, Pediatric Spectrum of HIV Disease Cohort." *Pediatrics* (May 2003): S1186.

ORGANIZATIONS

American College of Obstetricians and Gynecologists. 409 12th St., SW, PO Box 96920, Washington, DC 20090–6920. Web site: <www.acog.com>.

March of Dimes Birth Defects Foundation. 1275 Mamaroneck Ave., White Plains, NY 10605. Web site: <www.marchofdimes.com>.

WEB SITES

Alter, Sherman. "Herpes Simplex Virus Infection." *eMedicine*, August 11, 2004. Available online at <www.emedicine.com/ped/topic995.htm> (accessed January 16, 2005).

Frye, Richard E., and Delia M. Rivera-Hernandez. "Human Immunodeficiency Virus Infection." *eMedicine*, December 14, 2004. Available online at <www.emedicine.com/ped/topic1027.htm>.

Kessler, Alexander T., and Athena P. Kourtis. "Hepatitis B." *eMedicine*, August 16, 2004. Available online at <www.emedicine.com/ped/topic978.htm> (accessed January 16, 2005).

Schleiss, Mark R. "Cytomegalovirus Infection." *eMedicine*, December 1, 2004. Available online at <www.emedicine.com/ped/topic544.htm> (accessed January 16, 2005).

Altha Roberts Edgren
Teresa G. Odle
Stephanie Dionne Sherk

Periodontal disease

Definition

Periodontal diseases are a group of diseases that affect the tissues that support and anchor the teeth. Left untreated, periodontal disease results in the destruction of the gums, alveolar bone (the part of the jaws where the teeth arise), and the outer layer of the tooth root.

Description

Periodontal (meaning "around the tooth") disease is usually seen as a chronic (long-term) inflammatory disease. An acute (sudden) infection of the tissue surrounding the teeth (periodontal tissue) may occur, but acute inflammation usually resolves on its own and is not treated by a dentist.

Periodontal diseases affect the gums, which consist of the gingiva, periodontal ligament, cementum, and alveolar bone. The gingiva is a pink-colored mucous membrane that covers part of the teeth and the alveolar bone. The periodontal ligament, also called the periodontal membrane, is the tough, fibrous tissue that holds the teeth in the gums. The cementum is a bony layer that covers the lower parts of the teeth. The alveolar bone is a set of ridges along the jaw bones (maxillary and mandible) from which the teeth arise.

Periodontal disease most often develops when a pocket or space is formed between the teeth and the gums. This pocket is called the gingival sulcus. A number of distinct forms of periodontal disease are known, including gingivitis, acute necrotizing ulcerative gingivitis, adult periodontitis, and localized juvenile periodontitis. Although many people have some form of periodontal disease, serious cases are not common.

Gingivitis is an inflammation of the outermost soft tissue of the gums. The gums become red and inflamed, lose their normal shape, and bleed easily. Gingivitis may remain a chronic disease for years without affecting other periodontal tissues. Chronic gingivitis may lead to a deepening of the pockets between the gum and tooth. In some children, gingivitis and bleeding gums are among the early signs of leukemia.

Acute necrotizing ulcerative gingivitis is seen mainly in young adults. This form of gingivitis is characterized by painful, bleeding gums, and death (necrosis) and erosion of gums between the teeth.

Localized juvenile periodontitis is a less common form of periodontal disease and is seen mainly in young people. Localized juvenile periodontitis usually affects the molars (back grinding teeth) and incisors. Among the distinctions that separate this form of periodontitis are the low incidence of bacteria in the periodontal pocket, minimal plaque formation, and mild inflammation.

Pericoronitis is a condition found in children whose molars are in the process of erupting through the gum. The disease is seen more frequently in the lower molar teeth. As the molar emerges, a flap of gum still covers the tooth. The flap of gum traps bacteria and food, leading to mild irritation. If the upper molar fully emerges before the lower one, it may bite down on the flap during chewing and increase the irritation of the flap, leading to infection. In severe cases, the infection can spread to the neck and cheeks.

Periodontitis, also called pyorrhea, is a condition in which gingivitis has extended down around the tooth and into the supporting bone structure. Plaque and tarter build-up lead to the formation of large pockets between the gums and teeth. When this happens, anaerobic bacteria (bacteria that do not need oxygen) grow in the pockets. The pockets eventually extend down around the roots of the teeth where the bacteria cause damage to the bone structure supporting the teeth.

Herpetic gingivostomatitis, which is relatively common in children, is an inflammation of the gums and mouth caused by the **herpes simplex** virus. This disease is contagious, but tends to heal without medical intervention in about two weeks.

Desquamative gingivitis occurs mainly in postmenopausal women and is not well understood.

Trench mouth, also called Vincent's disease, is a suddenly developing (acute) complication of gingivitis. It causes tissue death and open sores on the gums and is often accompanied by **fever**, fatigue, and painful bleeding gums. Trench mouth usually develops because of poor **oral hygiene**, stress, fatigue, and **smoking**. It requires immediate treatment by a dentist, since **pain** can increase to the point where eating and swallowing become difficult, and the inflammation can spread to nearby tissues of the face and neck.

Demographics

Periodontal disease is common. It is estimated that 9–17 percent of children between the ages of three and 11 years have gingivitis. The number increases sharply at **puberty**, with 70–90 percent of teens developing the disease. More boys than girls have gingivitis, probably because girls have better oral hygiene habits than boys, rather than because of any physiological differences.

Some medical conditions are associated with an increased likelihood of developing periodontitis. These diseases include diabetes, **Down syndrome**, **AIDS**, and any disease or condition that compromises the immune system and reduces the number of white blood cells in the body for extended periods.

Causes and symptoms

Bacteria present on the gingival tissues cause periodontal diseases. The mechanisms by which bacteria in the periodontal pocket cause tissue destruction in the surrounding region are not fully understood. However, removal of bacteria through good oral hygiene practices and regular dental care helps reduce or eliminate these diseases. There are indications that a tendency toward developing periodontal disease is genetic, with up to 30 percent of the population being highly susceptible despite aggressive oral hygiene habits.

Other factors that put individuals at higher risk for developing periodontal diseases include smoking, stress, poor diet, and taking certain medications such as antidepressants, some heart medicines, and **oral contraceptives**. Gingivitis can be aggravated by hormones and may temporarily worsen during puberty and pregnancy. Individuals with diabetes and diseases that depress the immune system are more likely to develop periodontal disease.

The main symptoms of periodontal disease include:

• bleeding gums

• red, sore, or swollen gums

• gums that have receded from the base of the teeth

• chronic bad breath

• loose permanent teeth

• open sores on the gums

When to call the dentist

Beginning as toddlers, all children need regular checks-up by a dentist. Children who have chronically bleeding gums, open sores on the gums, or who complain of gum or tooth pain, should see a dentist promptly. Those with bleeding gums should see their pediatrician urgently, as this is also a symptom of leukemia in some children.

Diagnosis

Diagnosis of periodontal disease is made by observation of infected gums. Usually a dentist diagnoses and characterizes the various types of periodontal disease.

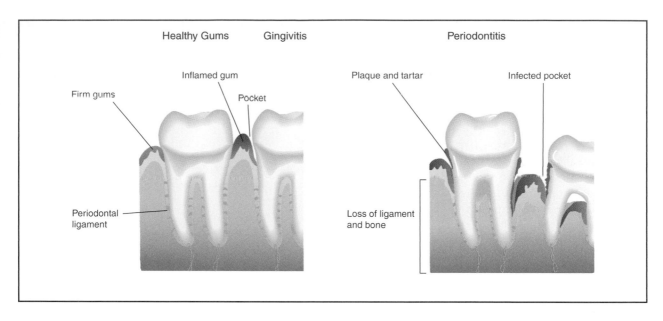

Diagram showing healthy gums (far left) with no pockets or redness; gingivitis (left) with inflamed gum and pocket; and periodontitis (right) with infected pockets, plaque, and tartar. *(Illustration by Argosy, Inc.)*

Many periodontal diseases are distinguished based on the severity of the infection and the number and type of tissues involved.

Diagnosis of periodontitis includes measuring the size of the pockets formed between the gums and teeth. Normal gingival pockets are shallow. If periodontal disease is severe, jawbone loss will be detected in **x rays** of the teeth. If too much bone is lost, the teeth become loose and can change position. This will also be seen in x-ray images.

Treatment

Tartar can be removed only by professional dental treatment. Following treatment, periodontal tissues usually heal quickly. Administering the needed **vitamins** and improving diet treats gingivitis caused by poor **nutrition** or vitamin deficiencies. Removing debris under the flap of gum covering the molar treats pericoronitis.

Treatment of periodontitis requires professional dental care. The pockets around the teeth are cleaned, and all tartar and plaque removed. In periodontitis, tartar and plaque can extend far down the tooth root. Normal dental hygiene, brushing and flossing, cannot reach deep enough to effectively treat periodontitis. In cases where pockets are very deep (more than 0.25 in, or 0.64 cm, deep), surgery is required to clean the pocket. This is performed in a dental office. Sections of gum that are not likely to reattach to the teeth may be removed to promote healing by healthy sections of gum. Abscesses are treated with a combination of **antibiotics** and surgery. If antibiotics are needed for gum disease, they are usually given orally. The antibiotics may be delivered directly to the infected gum and bone tissues to ensure that high concentrations reach the infected area. Abscess infections, especially of bone, are difficult to treat and require long term antibiotic therapy to prevent a reoccurrence of infection.

There are no useful drugs to treat herpetic gingivostomatitis, but acyclovir is used in high-risk patients or those with a compromised immune system. Herpes lesions heal by themselves without treatment. After the herpetic lesions have disappeared, the gums usually return to normal if good oral hygiene is resumed.

Prognosis

Most cases of periodontal disease are mild and can be cleared up with improved oral hygiene, as well as tooth and gum cleaning by a trained professional. Serious cases of periodontal disease may be persistent, but they can usually be controlled. Untreated periodontal disease may cause teeth to loosen and fall out, and infection may spread to surrounding tissues.

Prevention

Good oral hygiene, a well-balanced nutritious diet, and regular dental visits for tooth cleaning all help prevent periodontal disease. Prompt attention to gingivitis can prevent it from progressing to more serious periodontal diseases.

KEY TERMS

Alveolar bone—A set of ridges from the jawbones.

Cementum—A bony substance that covers the root of the tooth.

Gingiva—The gum tissue surrounding the teeth.

Gingival sulcus—The space between the tooth and the gum that often traps food and bacteria, leading to periodontal disease.

Periodontal ligament—Also called the periodontal membrane, this tough fibrous tissue holds the teeth in place in the gums.

Plaque—A deposit, usually of fatty material, on the inside wall of a blood vessel. Also refers to a small, round demyelinated area that develops in the brain and spinal cord of an individual with multiple sclerosis.

Tartar—A hardened yellow or brown mineral deposit from unremoved plaque. Also called calculus.

Parental concerns

Sometimes parents are less concerned about their child's first (baby) teeth than their permanent teeth. However, poor oral hygiene and lack of care of the first set of teeth are apt to be reflected in problems with the gums and the permanent teeth.

Resources

BOOKS

Berkow, Robert, ed. *Merck Manual of Medical Information.* Whitehouse Station, NJ: Merck Research Laboratories, 2003.

Gorbach, S. L., et al. *Infectious Diseases.* 2nd ed. Philadelphia: W. B. Saunders Co., 1998.

PERIODICALS

Academy of Periodontology. "Position Paper: Guidelines for Periodontal Therapy." *Journal of Periodontology* 72 (2001): 1624–28.

American Dental Association. "Preventing Periodontal Disease." *Journal of the American Dental Association* 132 (Sept. 2001): 1339.

American Dental Association. "Treating Periodontal Disease." *Journal of the American Dental Association* 134 (Feb. 2003): 259.

WEB SITES

"Periodontal (Gun) Diseases." *American Academy of Periodontology.* [cited June 11, 2004]. <www.perio.org>

Stephen, James. "Gingivitis." *eMedicine.com* [cited August 11, 2004]. <www.emedicine.com/emerg/topic217.htm>.

Tish Davidson, A.M.
John T. Lohr, Ph.D.

Peroneal muscular atrophy *see* **Charcot-Marie-Tooth disease**

Peroxisomal disorders

Definition

Peroxisomal disorders are a group of congenital diseases characterized by the absence of normal peroxisomes in the cells of the body.

Description

Peroxisomes are organelles within a cell that contain enzymes responsible for critical cellular processes. A cell can contain several hundred peroxisomes, round or oval bodies with diameters of about 0.5 micron that contain proteins that function as enzymes in metabolic processes. By definition, a peroxisome must contain catalase, which is an enzyme that breaks down hydrogen peroxide.

Peroxisomal disorders are subdivided into two major categories: those disorders resulting from a failure to form intact, normal peroxisomes, resulting in multiple metabolical abnormalities, which are referred to as peroxisome biogenesis disorders (PBD) or generalized peroxisomal disorders; and those disorders resulting from the deficiency of a single peroxisomal enzyme. There are about 25 known peroxisomal disorders, although the number of diseases that are considered to be separate, distinct peroxisomal disorders varies among researchers and healthcare practitioners.

Approximately 50 different biochemical reactions occur entirely or partially within a peroxisome. Some of the processes are anabolic (constructive), resulting in the synthesis of essential biochemical compounds, including bile acids, cholesterol, plasmalogens, and docosahexanoic acid (DHA), which is a long chain fatty acid that is a component of complex lipids, including the membranes of the central nervous system. Other reactions are catabolic (destructive) and lead to the destruction of some fatty acids, including very long chain fatty acids (VLCFAs, fatty acids with more than 22 carbon atoms in their chains), phytanic acid, pipecolic acid, and the prostoglandins. The peroxisome is involved in breaking down VLCFAs to lengths that the body can use or get rid of.

When VLCFAs accumulate due to abnormal functioning of the peroxisomes, they are disruptive to the structure and stability of certain cells, especially those associated with the central nervous system and the myelin sheath, which is the fatty covering of nerve fibers. The peroxisomal disorders that include effects on the growth of the myelin sheath are considered to be part of a group of genetic disorders referred to as leukodystrophies.

Peroxisomal disorders form a heterogeneous disease group, with different degrees of severity. The differences among these disorders are continuous, with overlap between abnormalities. Examples of peroxisomal disorders are:

- X-linked adrenoleukodystrophy (X-ALD), a sex-linked disorder characterized by progressive symptoms that begin as behavioral changes, muscle weakness, and speech difficulties.

- Zellweger syndrome (ZS), which is usually fatal within the first year of life.

- Neonatal adrenoleukodystrophy (NALD), which is usually fatal within the first ten years.

- Infantile Refsum disease (IRD), which is not as devastating as ZS and NALD, as the children with this disorder with time and patience can develop some degree of motor, cognitive, and **communication skills**, although death generally occurs during the second decade of life.

- Rhizomelic chondrodysplasia punctata (RCDP), which in its most severe form is fatal within the first year or two of life; however, survival into the teens has been known to occur. It is characterized by shortening of the proximal limbs (i.e., the legs from knee to foot and the arms from elbow to hand).

- Zellweger-like syndrome, which is fatal in infancy and known to be a defect of three particular enzymes.

Transmission

Most peroxisomal disorders are inherited autosomal recessive diseases. This means that both parents need to be carriers of the defective gene in order for a child to develop the disease. If both parents are carriers but do not show signs of disease, each child has a 25 percent chance of having the disease. If one parent has the dis-

ease and the other is a carrier, each child has a 50 percent chance of having the disease. As a sex-linked genetic disorder, the daughters of males affected with X-ALD become carriers and the sons are not affected. The children of female carriers have a 50 percent chance of having the genetic mutation, which means that sons who inherit the mutation have the disease, and daughters who inherit the mutation are carriers.

Demographics

Peroxisomal disorders occur in all countries, among all races and ethnic groups. They are extremely rare, with frequencies reported at one in 30,000 to one in 150,000, although these numbers are only estimates. X-ALD is the most common of the peroxisomal disorders, affecting about one in 20,000 males. It is estimated that there are about 1,400 people in the United States with the disorder. ZS is estimated to affect one in 50,000 to 100,000 live births.

Causes and symptoms

The range of disease abnormalities may be a result of a corresponding range of peroxisome failure. For example, in severe cases of ZS, the failure is nearly complete, while in IRD, there is some degree of peroxisome activity. In peroxisomal single-enzyme disorders, the peroxisome is intact and functioning, but there is a defect in only one enzymatic process, with only one corresponding biochemical abnormality. These disorders, however, can be as severe as those in which peroxisomal activity is nearly or completely absent.

In general, **developmental delay**, **mental retardation**, and vision and **hearing impairment** are common in those who have these disorders. Acquisition of speech appears to be especially difficult, and because of the reduced communication abilities, **autism** is common in those who live longer. Peroxisomal disorder patients have decreased muscle tone (**hypotonia**), which in the most severe cases is generalized, while in less severe cases, is usually restricted to the neck and trunk muscles. Sometimes this lack of control is only noticeable by a curved back in the sitting position. Head control and independent sitting is delayed, with most patients unable to walk independently.

Failure to thrive is a common characteristic of patients with peroxisomal disorder, along with an enlarged liver, abnormalities in liver enzyme function, and loss of fats in stools (steatorrhea). Peroxisomal disorders are also associated with facial abnormalities, including high forehead, frontal bossing (swelling), small face, low set ears, and slanted eyes. These characteristics may not be prominent in some children and are especially difficult to identify in an infant.

In X-ALD there is a deficiency in the enzyme that breaks down VLCFAs, which then accumulate in myelin and the adrenal glands. Onset of X-ALD-related neurological symptoms occurs at about five to 12 years of age, with death occurring within one to ten years after onset of symptoms. In addition to physical abnormalities seen in other types of peroxisomal disorders, common symptoms of X-ALD also include behavioral changes such as abnormal withdrawal or aggression, poor memory, dementia, and poor academic performance. Other symptoms are muscle weakness and difficulties with hearing, speech, and vision. As the disease progresses, muscle tone deteriorates, swallowing becomes difficult, and the patient becomes comatose. Unless treated with a diet that includes a mixture of oils called Lorenzo's oil, the disease will result in paralysis, hearing loss, blindness, vegetative state, and death. There are also milder forms of X-ALD, an adult onset ALD that typically begins between the ages of 21 and 35, and a form that is occasionally seen in women who are carriers of the disorder. In addition to X-ALD, there are at least ten other single-enzyme peroxisomal disorders, each with its own specific abnormalities.

When to call the doctor

A healthcare provider should be contacted if a child develops symptoms suggestive of peroxisomal disorder or if a child already diagnosed with a peroxisomal disorder shows signs of worsening disease.

Diagnosis

Since hearing and vision deficiencies may be difficult to identify in infants, peroxisomal disorders are usually detected by observations of failure to thrive, hypotonia, mental retardation, widely open fontanel, abnormalities in liver enzymes, and an enlarged liver. If peroxisomal disorders are suspected, blood plasma assays for VLCFAs, phytanic acid, and pipecolic acid are conducted. Additional tests include plasmalogen biosynthesis potential.

It is possible to diagnose peroxisomal disorders in utero. For example, for X-ALD, diagnosis can be made from cultured skin fibroblasts or amniotic fluid cells. This allows prenatal diagnosis and carrier identification in 90 percent of those affected. As of the early 2000s it has been shown that biochemical diagnosis can be performed through chorionic villus testing, a procedure performed very early in the first trimester of pregnancy.

Treatment

For many of the peroxisomal disorders, there is no standard course of treatment, with supportive treatment strategies focusing on alleviation of complications and symptoms. Bone marrow transplants may be effective for children with X-ALD if administered early in the course of the childhood form of the disease. Physical and psychological therapies are important for all types of peroxisomal disorders.

Alternative treatment

Patients with peroxisomal disorders, and particularly X-ALD, have been treated with a mixture of glycerol trioleate-glycerol trieucate (4:1 by volume), prepared from olive and rapeseed oils, and referred to as Lorenzo's oil (developed by the parents of a son, Lorenzo, who had X-ALD, whose story was documented in the 1992 movie, *Lorenzo's Oil*), to decrease the levels of VLCFA. Other diets that have been tried with varying success include dietary supplementation with plasmalogen precursors to increase plasmalogen levels and with cholic acid to normalize bile acids.

Nutritional concerns

In general, most treatments that are attempted for peroxisomal disorders are dietary, whereby attempts are made to artificially correct biochemical abnormalities associated with the disorders. Therapies include supplementation of the diet with antioxidant **vitamins** or limitation of intake of fatty acids, especially VLCFAs.

Another area of dietary therapy that is being investigated is the supplementation of the diet with pure DHA, given as early in life as possible, in conjunction with a normal well-balanced diet. Some results have indicated that if given soon enough during development, DHA therapy may prevent some of the devastating consequences of peroxisomal disorders, including the loss of vision and brain damage.

Other treatment strategies include addition of important missing chemicals. For example, in disorders where there is faulty adrenal function, replacement adrenal hormone therapy is used.

Any dietary changes should be monitored biochemically to determine if the supplements are having their desired effects and are not causing additional adverse effects.

Prognosis

Peroxisomal disorders range from life-threatening to cases in which people may function with some degree of mental and motor delays. As of 2004, there was not yet a cure for peroxisomal disorders. Enzyme replacement therapies, including enzyme infusion, transplantation, and gene therapy, may hold promise for future advances in the treatment of these disorders. As of the early 2000s research is conducted in order to increase scientific understanding of these disorders and find ways to prevent, treat, and cure them.

Prevention

It is not possible to prevent the transmission of an abnormal peroxisomal gene from parent to child or spontaneous mutations that may arise.

Parental concerns

Numerous professional and parent-led organizations exist to support parents as they first learn of a peroxisomal disorder diagnosis and as they provide care for their child. Genetic counseling is recommended for known or suspected carriers. As genes are identified that result in the disorders, genetic testing is being developed to identify carriers, who then can manage their reproduction to avoid the possibility of children being born with these deficiencies.

Resources

BOOKS

Moser, Hugo W. "Disorders of Very Long Chain Fatty Acids: Peroxisomal Disorders." In *Nelson Textbook of Pediatrics*, 17th ed. Edited by Richard E Behrman et al. Philadelphia: Saunders, 2004.

PERIODICALS

Martinez, Manuela. "The Fundamental and Practice of Docosahexanoic Acid Therapy in Peroxisomal Disorders." *Current Opinion in Clinical Nutrition and Metabolic Care* 3 (2000): 101–8.

Martinez, M., et al. "Therapeutic Effects of Docosahexanoic Acid in Patients with Generalized Peroxisomal Disorders." *American Journal of Clinical Nutrition* 71 (2000): 376–85.

Moser, Hugo W. "Molecular Genetics of Peroxisomal Disorders." *Frontiers in Bioscience* 5 (March 1, 2001): 298–306.

Senior, Kathryn. "Lorenzo's Oil May Help to Prevent ALD Symptoms." *The Lancet Neurology* 1, no. 8 (December 2002): 468.

ORGANIZATIONS

The Myelin Project. 2136 Gallows Rd., Suite E, Dunn Loring, VA 22027. Web site: <www.myelin.org>.

United Leukodystrophy Foundation. 2304 Highland Dr., Sycamore, IL 60178. Web site: <www.ulf.org>.

WEB SITES

Chedrawi, Aziza, and Gary Clark. "Peroxisomal Disorders." *eMedicine*, April 28, 2002. Available online at <www.emedicine.com/neuro/topic309.htm> (accessed January 16, 2005).

Judith Sims
Stephanie Dionne Sherk

Personality development

Definition

Personality development is the development of the organized pattern of behaviors and attitudes that makes a person distinctive. Personality development occurs by the ongoing interaction of **temperament**, character, and environment.

Description

Personality is what makes a person a unique person, and it is recognizable soon after birth. A child's personality has several components: temperament, environment, and character. Temperament is the set of genetically determined traits that determine the child's approach to the world and how the child learns about the world. There are no genes that specify personality traits, but some genes do control the development of the nervous system, which in turn controls behavior.

A second component of personality comes from adaptive patterns related to a child's specific environment. Most psychologists agree that these two factors—temperament and environment—influence the development of a person's personality the most. Temperament, with its dependence on genetic factors, is sometimes referred to as "nature," while the environmental factors are called "nurture."

While there is still controversy as to which factor ranks higher in affecting personality development, all experts agree that high-quality parenting plays a critical role in the development of a child's personality. When parents understand how their child responds to certain situations, they can anticipate issues that might be problematic for their child. They can prepare the child for the situation or in some cases they may avoid a potentially difficult situation altogether. Parents who know how to adapt their parenting approach to the particular temperament of their child can best provide guidance and ensure the successful development of their child's personality.

Finally, the third component of personality is character—the set of emotional, cognitive, and behavioral patterns learned from experience that determines how a person thinks, feels, and behaves. A person's character continues to evolve throughout life, although much depends on inborn traits and early experiences. Character is also dependent on a person's **moral development**.

In 1956, psychiatrist Erik Erikson provided an insightful description as to how personality develops based on his extensive experience in psychotherapy with children and adolescents from low, upper, and middle-class backgrounds. According to Erikson, the socialization process of an individual consists of eight phases, each one accompanied by a "psychosocial crisis" that must be solved if the person is to manage the next and subsequent phases satisfactorily. The stages significantly influence personality development, with five of them occurring during infancy, childhood, and **adolescence**.

Infancy

During the first two years of life, an infant goes through the first stage: *Learning Basic Trust or Mistrust (Hope)*. Well-nurtured and loved, the infant develops trust and security and a basic optimism. Badly handled, the infant becomes insecure and learns "basic mistrust."

Toddlerhood

The second stage occurs during early childhood, between about 18 months to two years and three to four years of age. It deals with *Learning Autonomy or Shame (Will)*. Well-parented, the child emerges from this stage with self-confidence, elated with his or her newly found control. The early part of this stage can also include stormy **tantrums**, stubbornness, and negativism, depending on the child's temperament.

Preschool

The third stage occurs during the "play age," or the later **preschool** years from about three to entry into formal school. The developing child goes through *Learning Initiative or Guilt (Purpose)*. The child learns to use imagination; to broaden skills through active **play** and fantasy; to cooperate with others; and to lead as well as to follow. If unsuccessful, the child becomes fearful, is unable to join groups, and harbors guilty feelings. The child depends excessively on adults and is restricted both in the development of play skills and in imagination.

School age

The fourth stage, *Learning Industry or Inferiority (Competence)*, occurs during school age, up to and possibly including junior high school. The child learns to master more formal skills:

- relating with peers according to rules
- progressing from free play to play that is structured by rules and requires teamwork (team sports)
- learning basic intellectual skills (reading, arithmetic)

At this stage, the need for self-discipline increases every year. The child who, because of his or her successful passage through earlier stages, is trusting, autonomous, and full of initiative, will quickly learn to be industrious. However, the mistrusting child will doubt the future and will feel inferior.

Adolescence

The fifth stage, *Learning Identity or Identity Diffusion (Fidelity)*, occurs during adolescence from age 13 or 14. Maturity starts developing during this time; the young person acquires self-certainty as opposed to self-doubt and experiments with different constructive roles rather than adopting a negative identity, such as delinquency. The well-adjusted adolescent actually looks forward to achievement, and, in later adolescence, clear sexual identity is established. The adolescent seeks leadership (someone to inspire him or her), and gradually develops a set of ideals to live by.

The Child Development Institute (CDI) rightfully points out that very little knowledge is available on the type of specific environment that will result, for example, in traits of trust being more developed in a person's personality. Helping the child through the various stages of emotional and personality development is a complex and difficult task. Searching for the best ways of accomplishing this task accounts for most of the research carried out in the field of child development today.

Renowned psychologist Carl Rogers emphasized how childhood experiences affect personality development. Many psychologists believe that there are certain critical periods in personality development—periods when the child will be more sensitive to certain environmental factors. Most experts believe that a child's experiences in the **family** are important for his or her personality development, although not exactly as described by Erikson's stages, but in good agreement with the importance of how a child's needs should to be met in the family environment. For example, children who are toilet trained too early or have their **toilet training** carried out too strictly may become rebellious. Another example is shown by children who learn appropriate behavior to their sex lives when there is a good relationship with their same-sex parent.

Another environmental factor of importance is culture. Researchers comparing cultural groups for specific personality types have found some important differences. For example, Northern European countries and the United States have individualistic cultures that put more emphasis on individual needs and accomplishments. In contrast, Asian, African, Central American, and South American countries are characterized more by community-centered cultures that focus on belonging to a larger group, such as a family, or nation. In these cultures, cooperation is considered a more important value than competitiveness, which will necessarily affect personality development.

Common problems

Infants who are just a few weeks old display differences between each other in how active they are, how responsive they are to change, and how irritable they are. Some infants cry constantly while others seem happy and stay fairly quiet. Child development research conducted by the CDI has identified nine temperamental traits that may contribute to a child's personality development being challenging or difficult:

- activity level (how active the child is generally)
- distractibility (degree of concentration and paying attention when the child is not particularly interested)
- intensity (how loud the child is)
- regularity (the predictability of biological functions like appetite and sleep)
- sensory threshold (how sensitive the child is to physical stimuli: touch, taste, smell, sound, light)
- approach/withdrawal (characteristic responses of a child to a new situation or to strangers)
- adaptability (how easily the child adapts to transitions and changes such as switching to a new activity)
- persistence (stubbornness, inability to give up)
- mood (tendency to react to the world primarily in a positive or negative way)

Temperamental traits are enduring personality characteristics that are neither "good" nor "bad." Early on, parents can work with the child's temperamental traits rather than oppose them. Later, as the child grows up, parents can help the child to adapt to his or her own world in spite of inborn temperament.

Parental concerns

Most children experience healthy personality development. However, some parents worry as to whether their infant, child, or teenager has a personality disorder. Parents are usually the first to recognize that their child has a problem with emotions or behaviors that may point to a personality disorder.

Children with **personality disorders** have great difficulty dealing with other people. They tend to be inflexible, rigid, and unable to respond to the changes and normal stresses of life and find it very difficult to participate in social activities. When these characteristics are present in a child to an extreme, when they are persistent and when they interfere with healthy development, a diagnostic evaluation with a licensed physician or mental health professional is recommended.

When to call the doctor

Parents who suspect that their child has a personality disorder should seek professional help. It is a very

KEY TERMS

Behavior—A stereotyped motor response to an internal or external stimulus.

Character—An individual's set of emotional, cognitive, and behavioral patterns learned and accumulated over time.

Cognition—The act or process of knowing or perceiving.

Cognitive—The ability (or lack of) to think, learn, and memorize.

Gene—A building block of inheritance, which contains the instructions for the production of a particular protein, and is made up of a molecular sequence found on a section of DNA. Each gene is found on a precise location on a chromosome.

Identity—The condition of being the same with, or possessing, a character that is well described, asserted, or defined.

Maturity—A state of full development or completed growth.

Personality—The organized pattern of behaviors and attitudes that makes a human being distinctive. Personality is formed by the ongoing interaction of temperament, character, and environment.

Socialization—The process by which new members of a social group are integrated in the group.

Temperament—A person's natural disposition or inborn combination of mental and emotional traits.

important first step in knowing for sure whether there is a disorder, and if so, what treatment can best help the child. Child and adolescent psychiatrists are trained to help parents sort out whether their child's personality development is normal.

See also Bonding; Cognitive development; Temperament.

Resources

BOOKS

AACAP and David Pruitt. *Your Child: Emotional, Behavioral, and Cognitive Development from Infancy through Pre-Adolescence.* New York: Harper Collins, 1998.

AACAP and David Pruitt. *Your Adolescent: Emotional, Behavioral, and Cognitive Development from Early Adolescence through the Teen Years.* New York: Harper Collins, 1999.

Allen, Bem P. *Personality Theories: Development, Growth, and Diversity.* Harlow, UK: Allyn & Bacon, 2002.

Berger, Elizabeth. *Raising Children With Character: Parents, Trust, and the Development of Personal Integrity.* Lanham, MD: Rowman & Littlefield Publishers, 1999.

Erikson, Erik. *Childhood and Society.* New York: W.W. Norton & Company, 1993.

Erikson, Erik. *The Erik Erikson Reader.* New York: W.W. Norton & Company, 2000.

Goleman, Daniel. *Working With Emotional Intelligence.* New York: Bantam, 1998.

Rogers, Carl. *On Becoming a Person.* Boston: Mariner Books, 1995.

Shaffer, David R. *Social and Personality Development.* Independence, KT: Wadsworth Publishing, 1999.

"Social, Emotional, and Personality Development." *Handbook of Child Psychology,* edited by William Damon and Nancy Eisenberg. 5th ed. New York: Wiley, 2000.

PERIODICALS

Biesanz, J. C. et al. "Personality over time: Methodological approaches to the study of short-term and long-term development and change." *Journal of Personality.* 71, no. 6 (December, 2003): 905–41.

Hart, D. et al. "Personality and development in childhood: a person-centered approach." *Monographs in Social Research on Child Development.* 68, no. 1 (2003): 1–119.

Jensen-Campbell, L. A. et al. "Interpersonal conflict, agreeableness, and personality development." *Journal of Personality.* 71, no. 6 (December, 2003): 1059–85.

Roberts, B. W. and R. W. Robins. "Person-Environment Fit and its implications for personality development: a longitudinal study." *Journal of Personality.* 72, no. 1 (February, 2004): 89–110.

Roberts, B. W. et al. "The kids are alright: growth and stability in personality development from adolescence to adulthood." *Journal of Personality & Social Psychology.* 81, no. 4 (October, 2001): 670–83.

Shiner, R, and A. Caspi. "Personality differences in childhood and adolescence: measurement, development, and consequences." *Journal of Child Psychology & Psychiatry.* 44, no. 1 (January, 2003): 2–32.

ORGANIZATIONS

American Academy of Child & Adolescent Psychiatry (AACAP). 3615 Wisconsin Ave., N.W., Washington, DC.

20016–3007. (202) 966–7300. Web site: <www.aacap.org>.

American Academy of Pediatrics (AAP). 141 Northwest Point Boulevard, Elk Grove Village, IL 60007–1098. (847) 434–4000. Web site: <www.aap.org>.

American Psychological Association (APA). 750 First Street, NE, Washington, DC 20002–4242. (800) 374–2721. Web site: <www.apa.org>.

Child Development Institute (CDI). 3528 E Ridgeway Road, Orange, California 92867. (714) 998–8617. Web site: <www.childdevelopmentinfo.com>.

WEB SITES

CDI. Child Development Basics. Available online at: <www.childdevelopmentinfo.com/development> (accessed March 5, 2005).

Great Ideas in Personality. Available online at: <www.personalityresearch.org/> (accessed March 5, 2005).

The Personality Project. Available online at: <www.personality-project.org/personality.html> (accessed March 5, 2005).

Monique Laberge, Ph.D.

Personality disorders

Definition

Personality disorders (PD) are a group of psychiatric conditions characterized by experience and behavior patterns that cause serious problems with respect to any two of the following: thinking, mood, personal relations, and the control of impulses.

Description

Most personality disorders are associated with problems in personal development and character which peak during **adolescence** and are then defined as personality disorders. Children and adolescents with a personality disorder have great difficulty dealing with others. They tend to be inflexible, rigid, with inadequate response to the changes and demands of life. They have a narrow view of the world and find it hard to participate in social activities. There are many formally identified personality disorders, each with its own types of associated behaviors. Most PDs, however, fall into three distinct categories or clusters, namely: cluster A, which includes disorders characterized by odd or eccentric behavior; cluster B, which includes disorders marked by dramatic, emotional or erratic behavior; and cluster C, which includes disorders accompanied by anxious and fearful behavior. The most common disorders in each cluster are given below.

Cluster A disorders

These disorders include the following:

• Schizoid personality disorder. Schizoid personalities are introverted, withdrawn, solitary, emotionally cold, and distant. Often absorbed with their own thoughts and feelings, they **fear** closeness and intimacy with others. People suffering from schizoid personality tend to be more daydreamers than practical action takers, often living "in a world of their own."

• Paranoid personality disorder. Paranoid personalities interpret the actions of others as deliberately threatening or demeaning. People with paranoid personality disorder are untrusting, unforgiving, and often resort to angry or aggressive outbursts without justification because they see others as unfaithful, disloyal, or dishonest. Paranoid personalities are often jealous, guarded, secretive, and scheming, and may appear to be emotionally "cold" or excessively serious.

• Schizotypal personality disorder. Schizotypal personalities tend to have odd or eccentric manners of speaking or dressing. They often have strange, outlandish, or paranoid beliefs and thoughts. People with schizotypal personality disorder have difficulties **bonding** with others and experience extreme **anxiety** in social situations. They tend to react inappropriately or not react at all during a conversation, or they may talk to themselves. They also have delusions characterized by "magical thinking," for example, by saying that they can foretell the future or read other people's minds.

Cluster B disorders

Cluster B disorders include the following:

• **Antisocial personality disorder**. Antisocial personalities typically ignore the normal rules of social behavior. These individuals are impulsive, irresponsible, and callous. They often have a history of violent and irresponsible behavior, aggressive and even violent relationships. They have no respect for other people and feel no remorse about the effects of their behavior on others. Antisocial personalities are at high risk for substance abuse, since it helps them to relieve tension, irritability, and boredom.

• Borderline personality disorder. Borderline personalities are unstable in interpersonal relationships, behavior, mood, and self-image. They are prone to sudden and extreme mood changes, stormy relationships, unpredictable and often self-destructive behavior. These personalities have great difficulty with their own sense of identity and often experience the world in extremes, viewing experiences and others as either "black" or "white." They often form intense personal attachments only to quickly dissolve them over a perceived offense. Fears of **abandonment** and rejection often lead to an excessive dependency on others. **Self-mutilation** or suicidal threats may be used to get attention or manipulate others. Impulsive actions, persistent feelings of boredom or emptiness, and intense anger outbursts are other traits of this disorder.

- Narcissistic personality disorder. Narcissistic personalities tend to have an exaggerated sense of self-importance, and are absorbed by fantasies of unlimited success. They also seek constant attention, and are oversensitive to failure, often complaining about multiple physical disorders. They also tend to be prone to extreme mood swings between self-admiration and insecurity, and tend to exploit interpersonal relationships.

Cluster C disorders

Cluster C disorders include the following:

- Avoidant personality disorder. Avoidant personalities are often fearful of rejection and unwilling to become involved with others. They are characterized by excessive social discomfort, **shyness**, fear of criticism, and avoidance of social activities that involve interpersonal contact. They are afraid of saying something considered foolish by others and are deeply hurt by any disapproval from others. They tend to have no close relationships outside the **family** circle and are upset at their inability to form meaningful relationships.

- **Dependent personality disorder**. As the name implies, dependent personalities exhibit a pattern of dependent and submissive behavior, relying on others to make decisions for them. They fear rejection, need constant reassurance and advice, and are oversensitive to criticism or disapproval. They feel uncomfortable and helpless if they are alone and can be devastated when a close relationship ends. Typically lacking in self-confidence, the dependent personality rarely initiates projects or does things independently.

- Compulsive personality disorder. Compulsive personalities are conscientious, reliable, dependable, orderly, and methodical, but with an inflexibility that often makes them incapable of adapting to changing circumstances. They have such high standards of achievement that they constantly strive for perfection. Never satisfied with their performance or with that of others, they take on more and more responsibilities. They also pay excessive attention to detail, which makes it very hard for them to make decisions and complete tasks. When their feelings are not under strict control, when events are unpredictable, or when they must rely on others, compulsive personalities often feel a sense of isolation and helplessness.

Demographics

In 2001 to 2002, fully 16.4 million Americans (7.9% of all adults) had obsessive-compulsive personality disorder; 9.2 million (4.4%) had paranoid personality disorder; 7.6 million (3.6%) had antisocial personality disorder; 6.5 million (3.1%) had schizoid personality disorder; 4.9 million (2.4%) had avoidant personality disorder; and 1.0 million (0.5%) had dependent personality disorder. According to the National Institutes of Health, nearly 31 million Americans meet criteria for at least one personality disorder. A 2004 survey showed that nearly 14.8 percent of adult Americans met diagnostic criteria for personality disorders as defined by the American Psychiatric Association's Diagnostic and Statistical Manual of Mental Disorders. The risk of having avoidant, dependent, and paranoid personality disorders is greater for females than males, whereas risk of having antisocial personality disorder is greater for males than females. There are no gender differences in the risk of having compulsive or schizoid personality disorders. In general, other risk factors contributing to the emergence of personality disorders include being Native American or African American; being a young adult; having a low socioeconomic status; and having any other status than married.

Causes and symptoms

The exact cause of personality disorders is unknown. However, evidence points to genetic and environmental factors such as a history of personality disorders in the family. Some experts believe that traumatic events occurring in early childhood exert a crucial influence upon behavior later in life. Others propose that people are genetically predisposed to personality disorders or that they have an underlying biological disturbance (anatomical, electrical, or neurochemical).

Symptoms vary widely depending on the specific type of PD, but according to the American Psychiatric Association, individuals with personality disorders have most of the following symptoms in common:

- self-centeredness that manifests itself through a "me-first," self-preoccupied attitude

- lack of individual accountability that results in a "victim mentality" and blaming others for their problems

- lack of empathy and caring

- manipulative and exploitative behavior

- unhappiness, suffering from depression, and other mood and anxiety disorders

- vulnerability to other mental disorders

- distorted or superficial understanding of self and others' perceptions that results in being unable to see how objectionable, unacceptable, and disagreeable their behavior is

- self-destructive behavior

- socially maladaptive, changing the "rules of the game," or otherwise influencing the external world to conform to their own needs

When to call the doctor

An appointment should be made with a healthcare provider or a mental health professional if a child has persistent symptoms of a personality disorder. Parents are often concerned about their child's emotional health or behavior, but they do not know where to start to get help. The mental health system can also be complicated and difficult for parents to understand. When worried about their child's behavior, parents can start by talking to the child's pediatrician or family physician about their concerns. Personality disorders require treatment and parents should try to find a mental health professional with advanced training and experience with children, adolescents, and families. Parents should always ask about the professional's training and experience. It is also very important to find a good match between child, family, and the mental health professional.

Diagnosis

The character of a person is shown through his or her personality, by the way the person thinks, feels, and behaves. When the behavior is inflexible, maladaptive, and antisocial, then that individual is diagnosed with a personality disorder. Personality disorders are diagnosed following a psychological evaluation that records the history and severity of the symptoms. A personality disorder must fulfill several criteria. A deeply ingrained, inflexible pattern of relating, perceiving, and thinking that is serious enough to cause distress or impaired functioning defines a personality disorder. Personality disorders are usually recognizable by adolescence or earlier, continue throughout adulthood, and become less obvious in middle age.

Treatment

There are many types of help available for the different personality disorders. Treatment may include individual, group, or family psychotherapy. Medications, prescribed by a patient's physician, may also be helpful in relieving some of the symptoms of personality disorders, such as problems with anxiety and delusions. Psychotherapy is a form of treatment designed to help children and families understand and resolve the problems due to PD and modify the inappropriate behavior. In some cases a combination of medication with psychotherapy may be more effective. PD psychotherapy focuses on helping patients see the unconscious conflicts that are causing their disorder. It also helps them become more flexible and is aimed at reducing the behavior patterns that interfere with everyday living. In psychotherapy, patients have the opportunity to learn to recognize the effects of their behavior on others. The different types of psychotherapies available to children and adolescents include the following:

- Cognitive behavior therapy (CBT). CBT is focused on improving a child's moods and behavior by examining confused or distorted patterns of thinking. With CBT, the child learns that thoughts cause feelings and moods that can influence behavior. For example, if a child has problematic behavior patterns, the therapist seeks to identify the underlying thinking that is causing them. The therapist then helps the child replace this thinking with thoughts that result in more appropriate feelings and behaviors.

- Dialectical behavior therapy (DBT). DBT is used to treat older adolescents with suicidal thoughts or who intentionally engage in self-destructive behavior or who have borderline personality disorder. DBT teaches how to take responsibility for one's problems and how to deal with conflict and negative feelings. DBT often involves a combination of group and individual sessions.

- **Family therapy**. This therapy approach is designed to help the family unit function in more positive and constructive ways by exploring patterns of communication and providing support and education. Family therapy sessions can include the child or adolescent along with parents and siblings.

- Group therapy (GT). GT uses group dynamics and peer interactions to increase understanding, communication, and improve social skills.

- **Play** therapy. This type of therapy is directed at helping younger children. It involves the use of **toys**, blocks, dolls, puppets, **drawings**, and games to help the child recognize, identify, and verbalize feelings. The psychotherapist observes how the child uses play materials and identifies themes or patterns to understand the child's problems. Through a combination of talk and play the child has an opportunity to better understand conflicts, feelings, and behavior.

Alternative treatment

Alternative treatments are available for personality disorders and most are complementary to conventional psychotherapy. They include the following:

- Coloring therapy. CT uses the activity of coloring as a self-help medium. While a person colors (with felt tipped markers, colored pens, pencils, etc.) a state of consciousness similar to meditation occurs. The approach is based on how people speak to themselves on the "inside." During a coloring session, people are asked to listen to the thoughts going on in their minds so as to become aware of where their thoughts, feelings, and opinions come from.

- Creative arts therapies. These therapies include art therapy, dance/movement therapy, drama therapy, music therapy, poetry therapy, and psychodrama. They use arts and creative processes to promote health, communication, and expression; they encourage the integration of physical, emotional, cognitive, and social functioning while enhancing self-awareness and facilitating change.

- Neurolinguistic programming. NLP is a method of examining the way a person thinks and acts through language and using this knowledge to effect change.

Nutritional concerns

The notion that foods and nutrients influence brain function and behavior generated in the early 2000s widespread interest in the general public and in the scientific community. However, the evaluation data are still ambiguous when it comes to establishing a direct link between personality disorders and diet, aside from recommending the avoidance of alcoholic and stimulant beverages.

Prognosis

The PD outlook varies. Some personality disorders diminish during middle age without any treatment, while others persist throughout life despite treatment.

Prevention

The prevention of personality disorders is an area surrounded with pessimism and controversy. Many mental health specialists believe that these disorders are untreatable, that individuals with personality disorder have little capacity for change; therefore not surprisingly, they remain skeptical about prevention prospects. However, even though the innate **temperament** of a person cannot be modified, understanding the factors that influence the development of personality disorders (such as genetic risks and environmental factors) may help prevention. Accordingly, some mental health professionals advocate primary prevention steps, which should include education of parents and primary healthcare workers, as well as early psychotherapy and protection of traumatized children, which can be carried out by child developing services. Some evidence suggests that traditional doctor-patient relationships are of much less value than programs which enable parents to see their own role as crucial and their own actions as able to bring changes for the better in their child's behavior. High quality parenting plays a critical role in child development and, thus, in the prevention of personality disorders.

Parental concerns

Understanding personality disorders can be challenging for parents as well as for children. During the last third of the twentieth century, great advances were made in the areas of diagnosis and treatment of personality disorders. Parents can help children understand that these are real illnesses that can be treated. In order for parents to talk with a child about a personality disorder, they must be knowledgeable of the subject. Parents may have to do some homework to become better informed. They should have a basic understanding and answers to questions such as what are personality disorders, who gets them, what causes them, how are diagnoses made, and what treatments are available. When explaining to a child about how personality disorders affect a person, it may be helpful to explain that feelings of anxiety, worry, and irritability are common for most people. However, when these feelings get very intense, last for a long period of time, and begin to interfere with school and relationships, it may be a sign of a personality disorder that can, however, be treated.

A child's personality disorder often causes disruption to both the parents' and the child's world. Parents may have difficulty being objective. They may blame themselves or worry that others such as teachers or family members will blame them. Recognizing these feelings and seeking the help of professional care providers and support groups is the best way to cope with this issue.

Medication can also be an effective part of the treatment for several personality disorders in childhood and adolescence. A doctor's recommendation to use

KEY TERMS

Anxiety—Worry or tension in response to real or imagined stress, danger, or dreaded situations. Physical reactions, such as fast pulse, sweating, trembling, fatigue, and weakness, may accompany anxiety.

Caring—The demonstration of an awareness of and a concern for the good of others.

Character—An individual's set of emotional, cognitive, and behavioral patterns learned and accumulated over time.

Delusion—A belief that is resistant to reason or contrary to actual fact. Common delusions include delusions of persecution, delusions about one's importance (sometimes called delusions of grandeur), or delusions of being controlled by others.

Eccentric—Deviating from the center; conduct and behavior departing from accepted norms and conventions.

Empathy—A quality of the client-centered therapist, characterized by the therapist s conveying appreciation and understanding of the client's point of view.

Erratic—Having no fixed course; behavior that deviates from common and accepted opinions.

Introversion—A personal preference for solitary, non-social activities and settings.

Maladaptive—Unsuitable or counterproductive; for example, maladaptive behavior is behavior that is inappropriate to a given situation.

Personality—The organized pattern of behaviors and attitudes that makes a human being distinctive. Personality is formed by the ongoing interaction of temperament, character, and environment.

Substance abuse—Maladaptive pattern of drug or alcohol use that may lead to social, occupational, psychological, or physical problems.

Temperament— A person's natural disposition or inborn combination of mental and emotional traits.

medication often raises many concerns and questions in both the parents and the child. The physician who recommends medication should be experienced in treating psychiatric illnesses in children and adolescents. He or she should fully explain the reasons for medication use, what benefits the medication should provide, as well as the possible negative side-effects or dangers and other treatment alternatives.

See also Antisocial behavior; Antisocial personality disorder; Anxiety.

Resources

BOOKS

Moskovitz, Richard, A. *Lost in the Mirror: An Inside Look at Borderline Personality Disorder*. Lanham, MD: Taylor Trade Publishing, 2001.

Kantor, Martin. *Distancing: Avoidant Personality Disorder*. Westport, CT: Praeger Publishers, 2003.

PERIODICALS

Chiesa, M. et al. "Residential versus community treatment of personality disorders: a comparative study of three treatment programs." *American Journal of Psychiatry* 161, no. 8 (August, 2004): 1463–70.

Gothelf, D., et al. "Life events and personality factors in children and adolescents with obsessive-compulsive disorder and other anxiety disorders." *Comprehensive Psychiatry* 45, no. 3 (May-June, 2004): 192–98.

Haugaard, J. J. "Recognizing and treating uncommon behavioral and emotional disorders in children and adolescents who have been severely maltreated: borderline personality disorder." *Child Maltreatment* 9, no. 2 (May, 2004): 139–45.

Krueger, R. F., and S. R. Carlson. "Personality disorders in children and adolescents." *Current Psychiatry Reports* 3, no. 1 (February, 2001): 46–51.

ORGANIZATIONS

American Academy of Child & Adolescent Psychiatry (AACAP). 3615 Wisconsin Ave., NW, Washington, DC 20016–3007. Web site: <www.aacap.org>.

American Psychiatric Association. 1000 Wilson Boulevard, Suite 1825, Arlington, Va. 22209–3901. Web site: <www.psych.org>.

Federation of Families for Children's Mental Health. 1101 King Street, Suite 420, Alexandria, VA 22314. Web site: <www.ffcmh.org>.

National Mental Health Association (NMHA). 2001 N. Beauregard Street, 12th Floor, Alexandria, VA 22311. Web site: <www.nmha.org>.

WEB SITES

Lebelle, Linda. "Personality Disorders." *Focus Adolescent Services*. Available online at <www.focusas.com/PersonalityDisorders.html> (accessed October 13, 2004).

Monique Laberge, Ph.D.

Pertussis *see* **Whooping cough**

Pervasive developmental disorders

Definition

Pervasive developmental disorders are a group of neurological disorders that include autistic disorder (**autism**), Asperger's syndrome, childhood disintegrative disorder, Rett's syndrome, and pervasive developmental disorder not otherwise specified (PDDNOS). These disorders are characterized by delayed development in functional, socialization, and **communication skills**.

Description

The term pervasive developmental disorders was first used in the 1980s to describe a class of neurological disorders that involved impaired social and communication skills and repetitive behaviors.

Due to difficulties in accurately describing these disorders using the term pervasive developmental disorders, some neurological and psychiatric specialists have proposed new terminology to describe this class of disorders, including autistic spectrum disorders and multi-system neurological disorders.

Asperger's syndrome

Asperger's syndrome is characterized by difficulties with social relationships and skills and with poor coordination and restricted range of interests. Children with Asperger's syndrome generally have a normal to above average **intelligence** level and adequate knowledge of vocabulary and grammar but poor concentration and ability to understand language subtleties, such as humor. Asperger's syndrome is often incorrectly referred to as "high-functioning autism."

Autistic disorder

Autistic disorder, also referred to as autism, is characterized by moderate to severe communication, socialization, and behavioral problems, and in some children, **mental retardation**.

Childhood disintegrative disorder

Childhood disintegrative disorder is extremely rare, relative to the other pervasive developmental disorders. Children with this disorder develop normally until at least two years of age, after which an obvious regression in multiple functional skills occurs, including bladder and bowel control, ability to move, and language skills.

Pervasive developmental disorder not otherwise specified (PDDNOS)

Children are diagnosed with PDDNOS if their symptoms do not fit any of the other four types and/or they do not have the degree of impairment of the other four types. PDDNOS involves developmental impairments, such as communication and social skills, and repetitive behaviors that cannot be attributed to a specific developmental disorder or personality disorder. Usually, children with PDDNOS do not exhibit symptoms until age three or four.

Rett's syndrome

Rett's syndrome occurs primarily in female children and is characterized by normal development for the first six to 18 months, followed by a noticeable change in behavior and loss of some abilities, especially motor skills. As the child ages, significant loss of speech, hand movement, and reasoning develops. Children with Rett's syndrome usually repeat certain movements and gestures, in particular, hand wringing or hand washing. Rett's syndrome is the rarest of the pervasive developmental disorders.

Demographics

About one in 1,000 children born in the United States is diagnosed with autistic disorder, and it is four to five times more common in boys. Rett's syndrome has been diagnosed primarily in girls. Although autism is the most well-known of these disorders, PDDNOS is at least twice as common in children.

Causes and symptoms

As of 2004, the causes of these disorders were unknown. While genetics is believed to play a primary role, some children in families with a history of pervasive developmental disorders do not have a disorder. Medical researchers believe that genetic susceptibility plus additional factors contribute to the development of one of these disorders. Factors under investigation as a cause of these disorders include immune system problems, **allergies**, drugs, environmental pollution, and infections. Autopsy studies of individuals with pervasive developmental disorders have shown that brain cell structure is different, particularly in the brain stem area. In addition, because many individuals with pervasive developmental disorders are also affected by seizures, "electrical miswiring" of the brain may also contribute to these disorders. Researchers have used **magnetic resonance imaging** (MRI) and positron emission tomography (PET) to find subtle differences in the brain structure and function of children with these disorders.

Symptoms of pervasive developmental disorders may be visible as early as infancy; however, the typical age of onset is age three. Although each of the five types has some distinctive symptoms, in general, early symptoms of a pervasive developmental disorder include the following:

• impaired language skills

• difficulties relating to people, objects, or activities

• unusual play

• repetitive body movements or behavior patterns

• difficulties handling changes in routine or surroundings

• unusual responses to sensory stimuli, like loud noises and lights

When to call the doctor

Parents should see a physician as soon as they notice developmental problems or delays in their infant or child.

Diagnosis

Pervasive developmental disorders are diagnosed using the *Diagnostic and Statistical Manual of Mental Disorders* (DSM), which provides criteria for physicians to diagnose the specific type. Diagnosis of a pervasive developmental disorder is difficult because there is no specific medical test, like a blood test or imaging test that can confirm the diagnosis. Some physicians may hesitate to diagnose very young children with a specific type of pervasive developmental disorder.

Diagnosis of these disorders usually requires consultation and **assessment** by a specialist in childhood developmental disorders, such as a child psychiatrist, pediatric neurologist, neuropsychologist, or developmental child psychologist. These specialists evaluate laboratory medical tests, neurological tests, and **psychological tests**; interview parents and children; and observe and assess behaviors. Educational skill testing, communication assessment, and motor skill assessment may also be conducted. Medical tests that may be performed to rule out other medical conditions include electroencephalography, MRI, and blood tests.

Once a pervasive developmental disorder is diagnosed, the diagnosis must be narrowed to one of the five types, which is achieved by using pre-established DSM criteria that outline the key differences among the types. For example, for childhood disintegrative disorder to be

diagnosed, symptoms must be preceded by at least two years of normal development and onset of decline and regression must occur prior to age 10 years.

Treatment

As of 2004, no cure existed for these disorders, and no specific therapy works for all individuals. Treatment depends on the severity of the disorder and consists of specialized therapy, **special education**, and medication to address specific behavioral problems. Medications that may be prescribed to treat specific symptoms include anti-depressants, anti-anxiety medications, anti-spasmodic and anti-seizure medications, and stimulants. Therapeutic interventions include applied behavior analysis (the Lovaas method), auditory integration training, behavior modification programs, play therapy, occupational and physical therapy, animal-assisted therapy, art/music/dance therapy, sensory integration, and speech therapy.

Alternative treatment

Alternative treatments for pervasive developmental disorders focus on **nutrition**. Some evidence has shown that vitamin therapy with vitamin B6 and magnesium supplementation can help children with autism and PDDNOS. Because some children with pervasive developmental disorders have **food sensitivities** or **food allergies**, allergy testing and subsequent dietary modification may help. In food-allergic children, certain foods have been shown to increase hyperactivity and autistic behavior. Anti-yeast therapy has also been proposed because children with autism and PDDNOS sometimes have higher yeast levels in their bodies. Administering anti-yeast medications has decreased negative behaviors in some children. Before parents turn to alternative therapy, they should consult a physician to make sure it does not interfere or interact with any other medications.

Prognosis

Pervasive developmental disorders are not life-threatening and do not affect normal life expectancy. Prognosis depends on the severity and type of disorder and the effectiveness of early interventions. Early intervention with specialized educational and behavioral support programs improves the quality of life and level of functioning of children with these disorders. However, because of their impaired communication and social skills, about 70 percent of individuals with a pervasive developmental disorder are never able to live on their own.

KEY TERMS

Electroencephalography—The recording of electrical impulses produced by the brain's activity via electrodes attached to a patient's scalp.

Magnetic resonance imaging (MRI)—An imaging technique that uses a large circular magnet and radio waves to generate signals from atoms in the body. These signals are used to construct detailed images of internal body structures and organs, including the brain.

Positron emission tomography (PET)—A computerized diagnostic technique that uses radioactive substances to examine structures of the body. When used to assess the brain, it produces a three-dimensional image that shows anatomy and function, including such information as blood flow, oxygen consumption, glucose metabolism, and concentrations of various molecules in brain tissue.

Prevention

Pervasive developmental disorders are caused by a complex interaction of genetics, neurological factors, and environmental factors. As of 2004, there was no genetic test to detect these disorders, and there is no way to prevent their development.

Parental concerns

The majority of children with a pervasive developmental disorder will require special education services. By law, public schools must evaluate children at no cost and provide special education services to eligible children with disabilities. Some private or alternative schools may be dedicated to serving children with such disorders and offer more comprehensive education and therapeutic options, but at an additional cost to parents.

Parenting children with pervasive developmental disorders is difficult and emotionally demanding. Parents and families can benefit from joining a support group. Benefits of parent support groups include information sharing, emotional support, and educational assistance.

Resources

BOOKS

Bashe, P. R., and B. L. Kirby. *The Oasis Guide to Asperger Syndrome.* Oakland, CA: PAR Bookworks, 2001.

Myles, B. S., and D. Adreon. *Asperger Syndrome and Adolescence: Practical Solutions for School Success.* Shawnee Mission, KS: Autism Asperger Publishing Company, 2001.

Stockman, Ida J. *Movement and Action in Learning and Development: Clinical Implications for Pervasive Developmental Disorders.* Kent, UK: Elsevier Science and Technology Books, 2004.

Volkmar, Fred R., et al. *Handbook of Autism and Pervasive Developmental Disorders.* New York: John Wiley & Sons, 2005.

PERIODICALS

Muhle, R., et al. "The Genetics of Autism." *Pediatrics* 113 (May 2004): 472–86.

Szatmari, P., et al. "Two-Year Outcome of Preschool Children with Autism or Asperger's Syndrome." *American Journal of Psychiatry* 157 (December 2000): 1980–87.

ORGANIZATIONS

Asperger Syndrome Education Network. Web site: <www.aspennj.org/>.

Developmental Delay Resources. Web site: <www.devdelay.org/>.

National Alliance for Autism Research. 99 Wall Street, Research Park, Princeton, NJ 08540. Web site: <www.naar.org/naar.asp>.

National Institute of Child Health and Human Development. Bldg 31, Room 2A32, MSC 2425, 31 Center Drive, Bethesda, MD 20892–2425. Web site: <www.nichd.nih.gov/default.htm>.

WEB SITES

"NINDS Pervasive Developmental Disorders Information Page." *National Institute of Neurological Disorders and Stroke,* July 2003. Available online at <www.ninds.nih.gov/health_and_medical/disorders/pdd.htm> (accessed October 27, 2004).

Sanders, Lisamarie. "Pervasive Developmental Disorders: What Parents Need to Know", 2004. Available online at <http://toddlerstoday.com/resources/articles/pdd.htm> (accessed October 27, 2004).

Jennifer E. Sisk, MA

Pharyngitis *see* **Sore throat**

Phenylketonuria

Definition

Phenylketonuria (PKU) is a rare metabolic disorder caused by a deficiency in the production of the hepatic (liver) enzyme phenylalanine hydroxylase (PAH).

Description

PKU is the most serious form of a class of diseases referred to as hyperphenylalaninemia, all of which involve above normal (elevated) levels of phenylalanine in the blood. The primary symptom of untreated PKU, **mental retardation**, is the result of consuming foods that contain the amino acid phenylalanine, which is toxic to brain tissue.

PKU is an inherited, autosomal recessive disorder. It is the most common genetic disease involving amino acid metabolism. As of 2004, PKU was incurable, but early, effective treatment can prevent the development of serious mental incapacity.

PKU is caused by the liver's inability to produce a particular type of PAH enzyme. This enzyme converts (metabolizes) the amino acid called phenylalanine into another amino acid, tyrosine. This is the only role of PAH in the body. A lack of PAH results in the buildup of abnormally high phenylalanine concentrations (or levels) in the blood and brain. Above normal levels of phenylalanine are toxic to the cells that make up the nervous system and cause irreversible abnormalities in brain structure and function in PKU patients. Phenylalanine is a type of teratogen (any substance or organism that can cause birth defects in a developing fetus).

The liver is the body's chief protein-processing center. Proteins are one of the major food nutrients. They are generally very large molecules composed of strings of smaller building blocks or molecules called amino acids. About twenty amino acids exist in nature. The body breaks down proteins from food into individual amino acids and then reassembles them into human proteins. Proteins are needed for growth and repair of cells and tissues and are the key components of enzymes, antibodies, and other essential substances.

PKU effects on the human nervous system

The extensive network of nerves in the brain and the rest of the nervous system are made up of nerve cells. Nerve cells have specialized extensions called dendrites and axons. Stimulating a nerve cell triggers nerve impulses (signals) that speed down the axon. These nerve impulses then stimulate the end of an axon to release chemicals called neurotransmitters that spread out and communicate with the dendrites of neighboring nerve cells.

Many nerve cells have long, wire-like axons that are covered by an insulating layer called the myelin sheath. This covering helps speed nerve impulses along the axon. In untreated PKU patients, abnormally high phenylalanine levels in the blood and brain can produce nerve cells with deformed axons and dendrites and cause imperfections in the myelin sheath referred to as hypomyelination and demylenation. This loss of myelin can short circuit nerve impulses (messages) and interrupt cell communication. A number of brain scan studies also indicate a degeneration of the white matter in the brains of older patients who have not maintained adequate dietary control.

PKU can also affect the production of one of the major neurotransmitters in the brain, called dopamine. The brain makes dopamine from the amino acid tyrosine. PKU patients who do not consume enough tyrosine in their diets cannot produce sufficient amounts of dopamine. Low dopamine levels in the brain disrupt normal communication between nerve cells, which results in impaired cognitive (mental) function.

Some research suggests that nerve cells of PKU patients also have difficulty absorbing tyrosine. This abnormality may explain why many PKU patients who receive sufficient dietary tyrosine still experience some form of learning disability.

Behavior and academic performance

IQ (**intelligence** quotient) tests provide a measure of cognitive function. The IQ of PKU patients is generally lower than the IQ of their healthy peers. Students with PKU often find academic tasks difficult and must struggle harder to succeed than their non-PKU peers. They may require special tutoring and need to repeat some of their courses. Even patients undergoing treatment programs may experience problems with typical academic tasks as math, reading, and spelling. Visual perception, visual-motor skills, and critical thinking skills can also be affected. Ten years of age seems to be an important milestone for PKU patients. After these individuals reach age 10, variations in their diets seem to have less influence on their IQ development.

People with PKU tend to avoid contact with others, appear anxious, and show signs of depression. However, some patients may be much more expressive and tend to have hyperactive, talkative, and impulsive personalities. It is also interesting to note that people with PKU are less likely to display such antisocial behaviors as **lying**, teasing, and active disobedience. It should be emphasized that, as of 2004, research findings were still quite preliminary and more extensive research is needed to clearly show how abnormal phenylalanine levels in the blood and brain might affect behavior and academic performance.

Demographics

One in 50 individuals in the United States has inherited a gene for PKU. About 5 million Americans are PKU carriers. About one in 15,000 babies tests positive for PKU in the United States. Studies indicate that the incidence of this disease in Caucasian and Native American populations is higher than in African-American, Hispanic, and Asian populations.

Causes and symptoms

PKU symptoms are caused by alterations or mutations in the genetic code for the PAH enzyme. Mutations in the PAH gene prevent the liver from producing adequate levels of the PAH enzyme needed to break down phenylalanine. The PAH gene and its PKU mutations are found on chromosome 12 in the human genome. In more detail, PKU mutations can involve many different types of changes, such as deletions and insertions, in the DNA of the gene that codes for the PAH enzyme.

PKU is described as an inherited, autosomal recessive disorder. The term autosomal means that the gene for PKU is not located on either the X or Y sex chromosome. The normal PAH gene is dominant to recessive PKU mutations. A recessive genetic trait, such as PKU, is one that is expressed—or shows up—only when two copies are inherited (one from each parent).

A person with one normal and one PKU gene is called a carrier. A carrier does not display any symptoms of the disease because the carrier's liver produces normal quantities of the PAH enzyme. However, PKU carriers can pass the PKU genetic mutation on to their children. Two carrier parents have a 25 percent chance of producing a baby with PKU symptoms, and a 50 percent chance having a baby that is a carrier for the disease. Although PKU conforms to these basic genetic patterns of inheritance, the actual expression, or phenotype, of the disease is not strictly an either/or situation. This is because there are at least 400 different types of PKU mutations. Although some PKU mutations cause rather mild forms of the disease, others can initiate much more severe symptoms in untreated individuals. The more severe the PKU mutation, the greater the effect on **cognitive development** and performance (mental ability).

Untreated PKU patients develop a broad range of symptoms related to severely impaired cognitive function, sometimes referred to as mental retardation. Other symptoms can include extreme patterns of behavior, delayed speech development, seizures, a characteristic body odor, and light body pigmentation. The light pigmentation is due to a lack of melanin, which normally colors the hair, skin, and eyes. Melanin is made from the amino acid tyrosine, which is lacking in untreated cases of PKU. Physiologically, PKU patients show high levels of phenylalanine and low levels of tyrosine in the blood. Babies do not show any visible symptoms of the disease for the first few months of life. However, typical PKU symptoms usually do show up by a baby's first birthday.

Diagnosis

The primary diagnostic test for PKU is the measurement of phenylalanine levels in a drop of blood taken from the heel of a newborn baby's foot. This screening procedure is referred to as the Guthrie test (Guthrie bacterial inhibition assay). In this test, PKU is confirmed by the appearance of bacteria growing around high concentrations of phenylalanine in the blood spot. PKU testing was introduced in the early 1960s and is the largest genetic screening program in the United States. It is required by law in all 50 states. Early diagnosis is critical. It ensures early the treatment PKU babies need to develop normally and avoid the ravages of PKU.

The American Academy of Pediatrics recommends that this test be performed on infants between 24 hours and seven days after birth. The preferred time for testing is after the baby's first feeding. If the initial PKU test produces a positive result, then follow-up tests are performed to confirm the diagnosis and to determine if the elevated phenylalanine levels may be caused by some medical condition other than PKU. Treatment for PKU is recommended for babies that show a blood phenylalanine level of 7 to 10 mg/dL or higher for more than a few consecutive days. Another, more accurate test procedure for PKU measures the ratio (comparison) of the amount of phenylalanine to the amount of tyrosine in the blood.

Subsequent diagnostic procedures (called mutation analysis and genotype determination) can actually identify the specific types of PAH gene mutations inherited by PKU infants. Large-scale studies have helped to clarify how various mutations affect the ability of patients to process phenylalanine. This information can help doctors develop more effective customized treatment plans for each of their PKU patients.

Treatment

The severity of the PKU symptoms experienced by people with this disease is determined by both lifestyle and genetic factors. In the early 1950s, researchers first demonstrated that phenylalanine-restricted diets could eliminate most of the typical PKU symptoms—except for mental retardation. As of 2004, dietary therapy (also called **nutrition** therapy) is the most common form of treatment for PKU patients. PKU patients who receive early and consistent dietary therapy can develop fairly normal mental capacity to within about five IQ points of their healthy peers. By comparison, untreated PKU patients generally have IQ scores below 50.

Infants with PKU should be put on a specialized diet as soon as they are diagnosed to avoid progressive brain damage and other problems caused by an accumulation of phenylalanine in the body. A PKU diet helps patients maintain very low blood levels of phenylalanine by restricting the intake of natural foods that contain this amino acid. Even breast milk is a problem for PKU babies. Special PKU dietary mixtures or formulas are usually obtained from medical clinics or pharmacies.

Phenylalanine is actually an essential amino acid. This means that it has to be obtained from food because the body cannot produce this substance on its own. Typical diets prescribed for PKU patients provide very small amounts of phenylalanine and higher quantities of other amino acids, including tyrosine. The amount of allowable phenylalanine can be increased slightly as a child grows older.

In addition, PKU diets include all the nutrients normally required for good health and normal growth, such as carbohydrates, fats, **vitamins**, and **minerals**. High protein foods such as meat, fish, chicken, eggs, nuts, beans, milk, and other dairy products are banned from PKU diets. Small amounts of moderate protein foods (such as grains and potatoes) and low protein foods (some fruits and vegetables and low protein breads and pastas) are allowed. Sugar-free foods, such as diet soda, which contain the artificial sweetener aspartame, are also prohibited foods for PKU patients because aspartame contains the amino acid phenylalanine.

Ideally, school-age children with PKU should be taught to assume responsibility for managing their diets, recording food intake, and for performing simple blood tests to monitor their phenylalanine levels. Blood tests should be done in the early morning when phenylalanine levels are highest. Infants and young children require more frequent blood tests than older children and adults. The amount of natural foods allowed in a diet can be adjusted to ensure that the level of phenylalanine in the

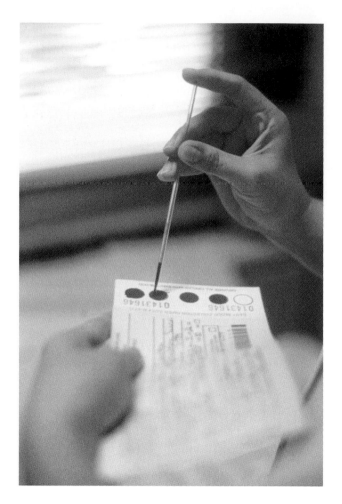

Blood taken from a newborn's heel is tested for phenylketornuia (PKU). (© Custom Medical Stock Photo, Inc.)

blood is kept within a safe range—2 to 6 mg/dL before 12 years of age and 2 to 15 mg/dL for PKU patients over 12 years old.

A specialized PKU diet can cause abnormal fluctuations in tyrosine levels throughout the day. Thus, some health professionals recommend adding time-released tyrosine that can provide a more constant supply of this amino acid to the body. It should be noted that some PKU patients show signs of learning disabilities even with a special diet containing extra tyrosine. Research studies suggests that these PKU patients may not be able to process tyrosine normally.

For PKU caregivers, providing a diet that is appealing as well as healthy and nutritious is a constant challenge. Many PKU patients, especially teenagers, find it difficult to stick to the relatively bland PKU diet for extended periods of time. Some older patients decide to go off their diet plan simply because they feel healthy. However, many patients who abandon careful nutritional

KEY TERMS

Amino acid—An organic compound composed of both an amino group and an acidic carboxyl group. Amino acids are the basic building blocks of proteins. There are 20 types of amino acids (eight are "essential amino acids" which the body cannot make and must therefore be obtained from food).

Axon—A long, threadlike projection that is part of a neuron (nerve cell).

Enzyme—A protein that catalyzes a biochemical reaction without changing its own structure or function.

Gene—A building block of inheritance, which contains the instructions for the production of a particular protein, and is made up of a molecular sequence found on a section of DNA. Each gene is found on a precise location on a chromosome.

Genetic disease—A disease that is (partly or completely) the result of the abnormal function or expression of a gene; a disease caused by the inheritance and expression of a genetic mutation.

Intelligence quotient (IQ)—A measure of somebody's intelligence, obtained through a series of aptitude tests concentrating on different aspects of intellectual functioning.

Metabolism—The sum of all chemical reactions that occur in the body resulting in growth, transformation of foodstuffs into energy, waste elimination, and other bodily functions. These include processes that break down substances to yield energy and pro-cesses that build up other substances necessary for life.

Mutation—A permanent change in the genetic material that may alter a trait or characteristic of an individual, or manifest as disease. This change can be transmitted to offspring.

Myelin—A fatty sheath surrounding nerves throughout the body that helps them conduct impulses more quickly.

Nervous system—The system that transmits information, in the form of electrochemical impulses, throughout the body for the purpose of activation, coordination, and control of bodily functions. It is comprised of the brain, spinal cord, and nerves.

Phenylalanine—An essential amino acid that must be obtained from food since the human body cannot manufacture it. It is necessary for normal growth and development and for normal protein metabolism.

Protein—An important building block of the body, a protein is a large, complex organic molecule composed of amino acids. It is involved in the formation of body structures and in controlling the basic functions of the human body.

Recessive—Refers to an inherited trait that is outwardly obvious only when two copies of the gene for that trait are present. An individual displaying a recessive trait must have inherited one copy of the defective gene from each parent.

management develop cognitive problems, such as difficulties remembering, maintaining focus, and paying attention. Many PKU health professionals contend that all PKU patients should adhere to a strictly controlled diet for life.

One promising line of PKU research involves the synthesis (manufacturing) of a new type of enzyme that can break down phenylalanine in food consumed by the patient. This medication would be taken orally and could prevent the absorption of digested phenylalanine into the patient's bloodstream.

In general, medical researchers express concern about the great variation in treatment programs available in the early 2000s to PKU patients around the world. They have highlighted the urgent need for consistent international standards for proper management of PKU patients, which should emphasize comprehensive psy-chological as well as physiological monitoring and **assessment**.

PKU and pregnancy

Women with PKU must be especially careful with their diets if they want to have children. They should ensure that phenylalanine blood levels are under control before conception and throughout pregnancy. Mothers with elevated (higher than normal) phenylalanine levels are high risk for having babies with significant birth defects, such as microencephaly (smaller than normal head size), **congenital heart disease** (abnormal heart structure and function), stunted growth, mental retardation, and psychomotor (coordination) difficulties. This condition is referred to as maternal PKU and can even affect babies who do not have the PKU disease.

Prognosis

Early newborn screening, careful monitoring, and life-long strict dietary management can help PKU patients to live normal, healthy, and long lives.

Parental concerns

Every state in the United States has mandatory newborn screening programs in place for phenylketonuria, as well as other diseases. Parents who suspect that other genetic diseases may run in their families should speak to their healthcare providers before their baby's birth to ascertain what other screening tests should be run.

BOOKS

Gascon, Generoso G., and Pinar T. Ozand. "Aminoacidopathies and Organic Acidopathies, Mitochondrial Enzyme Defects, and Other Metabolic Errors." In *Textbook of Clinical Neurology.* Edited by Christopher G. Goetz. Philadelphia: Saunders, 2003.

Rezvani, Iraj. "Defects in Metabolism of Amino Acids." In *Nelson Textbook of Pediatrics.* Edited by Richard E. Behrman et al. Philadelphia: Saunders, 2004.

PERIODICALS

Michals-Matalon, K. "Nutrient intake and congenital heart defects in maternal phenylketonuria." *American Journal of Obstetrics and Gynecology* 187 (August 2002): 441–4.

ORGANIZATIONS

Children's PKU Network. 1520 State St., Suite 111, San Diego, CA 92101–2930. Web site: <www.pkunetwork.org>.

March of Dimes Birth Defects Foundation. 1275 Mamaroneck Ave., White Plains, NY 10605. Web site: <www.modimes.org>.

National PKU News. 6869 Woodlawn Avenue, NE, #116, Seattle, WA 98115–5469. Web site: <www.pkunews.org>.

Marshall G. Letcher, MA
Rosalyn Carson-DeWitt, MD

Phenylpropanolamine *see* **Decongestants**

Phobias

Definition

A phobia is an intense and unrealistic **fear** brought on by an object, event, or situation, which can interfere with the ability to socialize, work, or go about everyday life.

Description

Almost all children develop specific fears at some age. Sometimes the fear is a result of a particular event, but some fears arise on their own. Many fears are associated with certain age groups. Very young children (through age two) tend to fear loud noises, strangers, large objects, and being away from their parents. Preschoolers often have imaginary fears, such as monsters who might eat them, strange noises, being alone in the dark, or thunder. School-age children have concrete fears, such being hurt, doing badly in school, dying, or natural disasters. When the child is afraid of something past the age at which it is normal, when the fear interferes with the child's ability to function normally, then the fear ranks as a phobia.

Phobias belong to a large group of mental problems known as **anxiety** disorders that include **obsessive-compulsive disorder** (OCD), panic disorder, and post-traumatic stress disorder. Phobias themselves can be divided into three specific types:

- specific phobias (formerly called simple phobias, most common in children)
- social phobia
- agoraphobia (not common in children)

Specific phobias

As its name suggests, a specific phobia is the fear of a particular situation or object, for example, flying on an airplane or going to the dentist. Found in one out of every 10 Americans, specific phobias seem to run in families and are roughly twice as likely to appear in women. If the person rarely encounters the feared object, the phobia does not cause much harm. However, if the feared object or situation is common, it can seriously disrupt the person's everyday life. Common examples of specific phobias, which can begin at any age, include fear of insects, snakes, and dogs; escalators, elevators, and bridges; high places; and open spaces. Children often have specific phobias that they outgrow over time, and they can learn specific fears from adults or other children around them, or even from television.

Social phobia

People with social phobia have deep fears of being watched or judged by others and being embarrassed in public. This may extend to a general fear of social situations. They may be more specific or circumscribed, such as a fear of giving speeches or of performing (stage fright). More rarely, people with social phobia may have trouble using a public restroom, eating in a restaurant, or signing their name in front of others. Young children often have a fear of strangers that is quite normal; social phobia is not usually diagnosed until a child reaches adolescence and has crippling fears that interfere with normal function.

Social phobia is not the same as **shyness**. Shy people may feel uncomfortable with others, but they do not experience severe anxiety, they do not worry excessively about social situations beforehand, and they do not avoid events that make them feel self-conscious. On the other hand, people with social phobia may not be shy; they may feel perfectly comfortable with people except in specific situations. Social phobias may be only mildly irritating, or they may significantly interfere with daily life. It is not unusual for people with social phobia to turn down job offers or avoid relationships because of their fears.

Agoraphobia

Agoraphobia is the intense fear of being trapped and having a panic attack in a public place. It usually begins between ages 15 and 35 and affects three times as many women as men or approximately 3 percent of the population.

An episode of spontaneous panic is usually the initial trigger for the development of agoraphobia. After an initial panic attack, the person becomes afraid of experiencing a second one. People are literally fearful of fear. They worry incessantly about when and where the next attack may occur. As they begin to avoid the places or situations in which the panic attack occurred, their fear generalizes. Eventually the person completely avoids public places. In severe cases, people with agoraphobia can no longer leave their homes for fear of experiencing a panic attack.

Demographics

Approximately one person in five (18 percent) of all Americans experience phobias that interfere with their daily lives. Almost all children experience some specific fears at some point, but not many rise to the level of phobia or require professional treatment.

Causes and symptoms

Experts do not really know why phobias develop, although research suggests the tendency to develop phobias may be a complex interaction between heredity and environment. Some hypersensitive people have unique chemical reactions in the brain that cause them to respond much more strongly to stress. These people also

may be especially sensitive to **caffeine**, which triggers certain brain chemical responses.

Advances in neuroimaging have also led researchers to identify certain parts of the brain and specific neural pathways that are associated with phobias. One part of the brain that was as of 2004 being studied is the amygdala, an almond-shaped body of nerve cells involved in normal fear conditioning. Another area of the brain that appears to be linked to phobias is the posterior cerebellum.

While experts believe the tendency to develop phobias runs in families and may be hereditary, a specific stressful event usually triggers the development of a specific phobia or agoraphobia. For example, someone predisposed to develop phobias who experiences severe turbulence during a flight might go on to develop a phobia about flying. What scientists do not understand is why some people who experience a frightening or stressful event develop a phobia and others do not.

Social phobia typically appears in childhood or **adolescence**, sometimes following an upsetting or humiliating experience. Certain vulnerable children who have had unpleasant social experiences (such as being rejected) or who have poor social skills may develop social phobias. The condition also may be related to low **self-esteem**, unassertive personality, and feelings of inferiority.

A person with agoraphobia may have a panic attack at any time, for no apparent reason. While the attack may last only a minute or so, the person remembers the feelings of panic so strongly that the possibility of another attack becomes terrifying. For this reason, people with agoraphobia avoid places where they might not be able to escape if a panic attack occurs. As the fear of an attack escalates, the person's world narrows.

While the specific trigger may differ, the symptoms of different phobias are remarkably similar: feelings of terror and impending doom, rapid heartbeat and breathing, sweaty palms, and other features of a panic attack. People may experience severe anxiety symptoms in anticipating a phobic trigger. For example, someone who is afraid to fly may begin having episodes of pounding heart and sweating palms at the mere thought of getting on a plane in two weeks.

When to call the doctor

A doctor, mental health professional, or counselor should be consulted when irrational fears interfere with a child's normal functioning.

Diagnosis

A mental health professional can diagnose phobias after a detailed interview and discussion of both mental and physical symptoms. Children are often less able to accurately describe their symptoms or discuss their fears, and so should be encouraged to talk about them with parents. Social phobia is often associated with other anxiety disorders, depression, or substance abuse.

Treatment

People who have a specific phobia that is easy to avoid (such as snakes) and that does not interfere with their lives may not need to get help. When phobias do interfere with a person's daily life, a combination of psychotherapy and medication can be quite effective. Medication is used less often in young children, but more frequently in older children or adolescents with severe phobias and associated depression. While most health insurance covers some form of mental health care, most do not cover outpatient care completely, and most have a yearly or lifetime maximum.

Medication can block the feelings of panic and, when combined with cognitive-behavioral therapy, can be quite effective in reducing specific phobias and agoraphobia.

Cognitive-behavioral therapy adds a cognitive approach to more traditional behavioral therapy. It teaches individuals how to change their thoughts, behaviors, and attitudes, while providing techniques to lessen anxiety, such as deep breathing, muscle relaxation, and refocusing.

One cognitive-behavioral therapy is desensitization (also known as exposure therapy), in which people are gradually exposed to the frightening object or event until they become used to it and their physical symptoms decrease. For example, someone who is afraid of snakes might first be shown a photo of a snake. Once the person can look at a photo without anxiety, he might then be shown a video of a snake. Each step is repeated until the symptoms of fear (such as pounding heart and sweating palms) disappear. Eventually, the person might reach the point where he can actually touch a live snake. Three-fourths of affected people are significantly improved with this type of treatment.

Another, more dramatic, cognitive-behavioral approach is called flooding. It exposes the person immediately to the feared object or situation. The person remains in the situation until the anxiety lessens.

Several drugs are used to treat specific phobias by controlling symptoms and helping to prevent panic attacks. These include anti-anxiety drugs (benzodiazepines) such as alprazolam (Xanax) or diazepam (Valium). Blood pressure medications called beta blockers, such as propranolol (Inderal) and atenolol (Tenormin), appear to work well in the treatment of circumscribed social phobia, when anxiety gets in the way of performance, such as public speaking. These drugs reduce over-stimulation, thereby controlling the physical symptoms of anxiety.

In addition, some **antidepressants** may be effective when used together with cognitive-behavioral therapy. These include the monoamine oxidase inhibitors (MAO inhibitors) phenelzine (Nardil) and tranylcypromine (Parnate), as well as selective serotonin reuptake inhibitors (SSRIs) like fluoxetine (Prozac), paroxetine (Paxil), sertraline (Zoloft) and fluvoxamine (Luvox).

In all types of phobias, symptoms may be eased by lifestyle changes, such as the following:

- eliminating caffeine
- cutting down on alcohol
- eating a good diet
- getting plenty of exercise
- reducing stress

Treating agoraphobia is more difficult than other phobias because there are often so many fears involved, such as fear of open spaces, traffic, elevators, and escalators. Treatment includes cognitive-behavioral therapy with antidepressants or anti-anxiety drugs. Paxil and Zoloft are used to treat panic disorders with or without agoraphobia.

Prognosis

Phobias are among the most treatable mental health problems; depending on the severity of the condition and the type of phobia, most properly treated people can go on to lead normal lives. Research suggests that once a person overcomes the phobia, the problem may not return for many years, if it returns at all. Children most often outgrow their specific phobias, with or without treatment.

Untreated phobias are another matter. In adults, only about 20 percent of specific phobias go away without treatment, and agoraphobia gets worse with time if untreated. Social phobias tend to be chronic and are not likely go away without treatment. Moreover, untreated phobias can lead to other problems, including depression, **alcoholism**, and feelings of shame and low self-esteem. Therefore, specific phobias that persist into adolescence should receive professional treatment.

KEY TERMS

Agoraphobia—Abnormal anxiety regarding public places or situations from which the person may wish to flee or in which he or she would be helpless in the event of a panic attack.

Benzodiazepine—One of a class of drugs that has hypnotic and sedative action, used mainly as tranquilizers to control symptoms of anxiety. Diazepam (Valium), alprazolam (Xanax), and chlordiazepoxide (Librium) are all benzodiazepines.

Beta blockers—The popular name for a group of drugs that are usually prescribed to treat heart conditions, but that also are used to reduce the physical symptoms of anxiety and phobias, such as sweating and palpitations. These drugs, including nadolol (Corgard) and digoxin (Lanoxin), block the action of beta receptors that control the speed and strength of heart muscle contractions and blood vessel dilation. Beta blockers are also called beta-adrenergic blocking agents and antiadrenergics.

Monoamine oxidase (MAO) inhibitors—A type of antidepressant that works by blocking the action of a chemical substance known as monoamine oxidase in the nervous system.

Neuroimaging—The use of x-ray studies and magnetic resonance imaging (MRI) to detect abnormalities or trace pathways of nerve activity in the central nervous system.

Selective serotonin reuptake inhibitors (SSRIs)—A class of antidepressants that works by blocking the reabsorption of serotonin in the brain, thus raising the levels of serotonin. SSRIs include fluoxetine (Prozac), sertraline (Zoloft), and paroxetine (Paxil).

Serotonin—A widely distributed neurotransmitter that is found in blood platelets, the lining of the digestive tract, and the brain, and that works in combination with norepinephrine. It causes very powerful contractions of smooth muscle and is associated with mood, attention, emotions, and sleep. Low levels of serotonin are associated with depression.

Social phobia—An anxiety disorder characterized by a strong and persistent fear of social or performance situations in which the individual might feel embarrassment or humiliation.

A group of researchers in Boston reported in 2003 that phobic anxiety appears to be a risk factor for Parkinson's disease (PD) in males, although as of 2004 it is not known whether phobias cause PD or simply share an underlying biological cause.

While most specific phobias appear in childhood and subsequently fade away, those that remain in adulthood often need to be treated. Unfortunately, most people never get the help they need; only about 25 percent of people with phobias ever seek help for their condition.

Prevention

There was, as of 2004, no known way to prevent the development of phobias. Medication and cognitive-behavioral therapy may help prevent the recurrence of symptoms once they have been diagnosed.

Nutritional concerns

Unless a phobia involves fear of eating a needed food, there are no nutritional concerns associated with phobias.

Parental concerns

Parents should be observant to ensure that unusual fears or phobias do not interfere in the lives of their children. Parents should recognize that a child's fears are real, and encourage the child to talk about his or her feelings, without trivializing the fear. Parents should be sympathetic, but not allow the child to avoid situations in which the child must encounter the feared object or events. If a school-age child has fears that interfere with the child's education, ability to make friends, or participate in other normal activities, a professional should be consulted.

Resources

BOOKS

Diagnostic and Statistical Manual of Mental Disorders, 4th edition. Washington, DC: American Psychiatric Association, 2000.

"Phobic Disorders." Section 15, chapter 187 in *The Merck Manual of Diagnosis and Therapy*. Edited by Mark H. Beers, and Robert Berkow. Whitehouse Station, NJ: Merck Research Laboratories, 2002.

Stafford, Brian, et al. "Anxiety Disorders." In *Nelson Textbook of Pediatrics*, 17th ed. Edited by Richard E. Behrman, et al. Philadelphia: Saunders, 2003, pp. 81–3.

PERIODICALS

Birk, L. "Pharmacotherapy for performance anxiety disorders: occasionally useful but typically contraindicated." *Journal of Clinical Psychology* 60, no. 8 (2004): 867–79.

Hofmann, S. G. "Cognitive mediation of treatment change in social phobia." *Journal of Consulting and Clinical Psychology* 72, no. 3 (2004): 393–9.

Ilomaki, R., et al. "Temporal relationship between the age of onset of phobic disorders and development of substance dependence in adolescent psychiatric patients." *Drug and Alcohol Dependence* 75, no. 3 (2004): 327–30.

Izquierdo, I., et al. "The inhibition of acquired fear." *Neurotoxicity Research* 6, no. 3 (2004): 175–88.

Krijn, M., et al. "Virtual reality exposure therapy of anxiety disorders: a review." *Clinical Psychology Review* 24, no. 3 (2004): 259–81.

ORGANIZATIONS

ABIL Incorporated. 400 West 32nd Street, Richmond, Virginia 23225. Web site: <www.anxietysupport.org/b001menu.htm>.

Agoraphobics in Motion. 1719 Crooks, Royal Oak, MI 48067. Web site: <www.aim-hq.org/>.

American Academy of Family Physicians. 11400 Tomahawk Creek Parkway, Leawood, KS 66211–2672. Web site: <www.aafp.org/>.

American Academy of Pediatrics. 141 Northwest Point Boulevard, Elk Grove Village, IL 60007–1098. Web site: <www.aap.org/>.

American Psychiatric Association. 1400 K Street NW, Washington, DC 20005. Web site: <www.psych.org/>.

American Psychological Association. 750 First Street NW, Washington, DC, 20002–4242. Web site: <www.apa.org/>.

Anxiety Disorders Association of America. 8730 Georgia Avenue, Suite 600, Silver Spring, MD 20910. Web site: <www.adaa.org/>.

National Anxiety Foundation. 3135 Custer Dr., Lexington, KY 40517. Web site: <www.lexington-on-line.com/naf.html>.

National Institute of Mental Health. 6001 Executive Boulevard, Rm. 8184, MSC 9663, Bethesda, MD 20892–9663. Web site: <www.nimh.nih.gov/home.cfm>.

WEB SITES

"Anxiety Disorders (Phobias)." *National Mental Health Association.* Available online at <www.nmha.org/infoctr/factsheets/35.cfm> (accessed November 2, 2004).

"Coping with Anxiety, Fears, and Phobias." *Kids Health for Parents.* Available online at <http://kidshealth.org/parent/emotions/feelings/anxiety.html> (accessed November 2, 2004).

"Phobias." *American Psychiatric Association.* Available online at <www.psych.org/public_info/phobias.cfm> (accessed November 2, 2004).

"Phobias." *National Library of Medicine.* Available online at <www.nlm.nih.gov/medlineplus/phobias.html> (accessed November 2, 2004).

L. Fleming Fallon, Jr., MD, DrPH

Pica

Definition

Pica is the persistent craving and compulsive eating of non-food substances.

Description

The puzzling phenomenon of pica has been recognized and described since ancient times. Pica has been observed in ethnic groups worldwide, in both primitive and modernized cultures, in both sexes, and in all age groups. The word pica comes from the Latin name for magpie, a bird known for its unusual and indiscriminate eating habits. In addition to humans, pica has been observed in other animals, including the chimpanzee.

Demographics

True pica affects people of all ages, although it is more common in children. There are some regional variations concerning specific substances. For example, eating clay is more prevalent among women in the American southeast than in other areas of the country. Adolescents may chew ice due to **peer pressure** or because they are deficient in iron. Without a blood test for serum iron, there is no way to differentiate these causes.

Causes and symptoms

Pica in humans has many different subgroups, defined by the substance that is ingested. Some of the most commonly described types of pica are eating earth, soil, or clay (geophagia); ice (pagophagia); and starch (amylophagia). However, pica involving dozens of other substances, including cigarette butts and ashes, hair, paint chips, and paper have also been reported.

Although pica can occur in individuals of any background, a higher incidence of pica is associated with:

- pregnancy
- developmental disabilities
- **mental retardation**
- psychiatric disease and autism
- early childhood (under age three)
- poor **nutrition** or low blood levels of iron and other **minerals**
- certain cultural or religious traditions

When to call the doctor

A health care professional should be consulted whenever a child over the age of three repeatedly ingests non-food substances for a period over one month. The behavior might be merely habitual, but it can become a compulsion that needs treatment.

Diagnosis

In order for the diagnosis of pica to be made, there must be a history of persistent consumption of a non-food substance continuing for a minimum period of one month. Infants and toddlers are typically excluded from this diagnosis since mouthing objects is a normal developmental behavior at that age. Individuals with mental retardation who function at or below an approximate cognitive level of 18 months may also be exempt from this diagnosis.

Pica is most often diagnosed when a report of such behaviors can be provided by an individual or documented by another person. In other cases, pica is diagnosed after studies have been performed to assess the presenting symptoms. For example, imaging studies ordered to assess severe gastrointestinal complaints may reveal intestinal blockage with an opaque substance; such a finding is suggestive of pica. Biopsy of intestinal contents can also reveal findings, such as parasitic infection, consistent with pica. Pica may also be suspected if abnormal levels of certain minerals or chemicals are detected in the blood.

Treatment

Treatment of pica will often depend on the cause and type of pica. Conventional medical treatment may be appropriate in certain situations. For example, supplementation with iron-containing **vitamins** has been shown to cause the unusual cravings to subside in some iron-deficient people.

Medical complications and health threats, including high lead levels, bowel perforation or intestinal obstruction, will require additional medical management, beyond addressing the underlying issue of pica.

Because most cases of pica do not have an obvious medical cause, treatment with counseling, education, and nutritional management is often more successful and more appropriate than treatment with medication. Some therapists specializing in eating disorders may have expertise in treating pica.

Prognosis

The prognosis for individuals with pica varies greatly, according to the type and amount of substance ingested, the extent of presenting side effects, and the success of treatment. Many of the side effects and complications of pica can be reversed once the behavior is stopped, while other complications, including infection and bowel perforation, pose significant health threats and if not successfully treated may result in death.

When seen in children, pica behavior tends to lessen with age. However, individuals with a history of pica are more likely to experience it again. Counseling and nutritional education can reduce the risk of recurrence.

Prevention

There are no known methods of preventing pica. However, once pica is known or suspected, measures can be taken to reduce further ingestion of non-food substances. Removing the particular substance from readily accessible areas can be helpful. Close observation of the individual with pica may limit inappropriate eating behaviors.

Nutritional concerns

Pica may be a symptom of an underlying nutritional deficiency. Correcting the deficiency usually stops the pica.

Parental concerns

Parents should monitor the food and other substances that their children eat. Repeated ingestion of non-food substances may be cause for concern. An evaluation by a pediatrician is recommended in such circumstances. Parents should be especially careful of children who eat paint chips, because this can cause lead poisoning if the paint is from an older home in which lead paint was used.

Resources

BOOKS

Heird, William C. "Food Insecurity, Hunger and Undernutrition." In *Nelson Textbook of Pediatrics.* 17th ed. Ed. by Richard E. Behrman, et al., Philadelphia: Saunders, 2003, 167-172.

Matthews, Dawn D. *Eating Disorders SourceBook* Detroit, MI: Omnigraphics, Incorporated, 2001.

Walsh, B. Timothy. "Eating Disorders." In *Harrison's Principles of Internal Medicine.* 15th ed. Ed. by Eugene Braunwald et al., New York, McGraw Hill, 2001, 486-90.

West, Delia S. "Eating Disorders." In *Cecil Textbook of Medicine.* 22nd ed. Ed. by Lee Goldman, et al. Philadelphia: Saunders, 2003, 1336–8.

PERIODICALS

Dreyer MJ, Chaushev PG, and Gledhill RF. "Biochemical investigations in geophagia." *Journal of the Royal Society of Medicine* 97, no. 1 (2004): 48-53.

Kuhn DE and Matson JL. "Assessment of feeding and mealtime behavior problems in persons with mental retardation." *Behavior Modification* 28, no. 5 (2004): 638–48.

Lavoie PM and Bailey B. "Lead poisoning from "lead-free" paint." *Canadian Medical Association Journal* 170, no. 6 (2004): 956–8.

Moya J, Bearer CF, and Etzel RA. "Children's behavior and physiology and how it affects exposure to environmental contaminants." *Pediatrics* 113, no. 4 Supplement (2004): 996–1006.

ORGANIZATIONS

National Eating Disorders Organization (NEDO). 6655 South Yale Ave, Tulsa, OK 74136. (918) 481-4044. Hotline: (800) 931.2237. Web site: <www.NationalEatingDisorders.org>.

OTHER

"Children and Eating Disorders." *Vanderbilt University.* Available online at <www.vanderbilt.edu/AnS/ psychology/health_psychology/childrenandED.html>.

"Eating Disorder: Pica." *eMedicine.* Available online at <www.emedicine.com/ped/topic1798.htm>.

"Eating Disorders." *Encyclopedia.Com.* Available online at <www.encyclopedia.com/html/e1/eatingdi.asp>.

"Pica." *Web MD Health.* Available online at <http:// my.webmd.com/hw/health_guide_atoz/nord214.asp>.

L. Fleming Fallon, Jr., MD, DrPH

Piercing and tattoos

Definition

Body piercing and tattoos are forms of body art that have been practiced throughout history by various cultures.

Purpose

Tattoos and body piercing are done as expressions of independence, for religious or cultural reasons, or to adorn one's body. Tattooing is accomplished by injecting pigment into the deeper layers of the skin, usually by way of needles or air pressure.

Piercing is performed quickly and without anesthesia by either a spring-loaded ear-piercing gun or piercing needles, with the needle diameter varying from six to 18 gauge. The skin is cleaned, and then the needle and jewelry are inserted through the tissue in one swift motion. Piercing is typically completed in tattoo or beauty parlors.

Description

Various cultures have embraced adorning the human body with piercings and tattoos throughout history. In 1992, the 4,000-year-old body of a tattooed man was discovered in a glacier on the Austrian border, and historical research has shown that Egyptians identified tattooing with fertility and nobility in the period from

Teenage girl with tattoos. *(© PictureNet/Corbis.)*

4000 to 2000 B.C. Similar to tattooing, body piercing also has a long history, which includes being used as a symbol of royalty and courage. In some hunting and gathering societies, body piercing and tattoos have long been used in initiation rites and as symbols of socialization and enculturation.

In industrialized cultures in the early 2000s, tattoos and piercing have become a popular art form enjoyed by people of all ages. They also are indicative of a psychology of **self-mutilation**, defiance, independence, and belonging, as for example in prison or gang cultures.

Popular piercing sites include the ear, nasal septum, eyebrow, tongue, cheek, nipple, navel, labia, and penis. Tattoos permanently mark various areas on the body.

Originating from the Tahitian word *tattau*, meaning "to mark," tattoos are relatively permanent marks or designs on the skin. An electric needle injects colored pigment into small, deep holes made in the skin to form the tattoo. Prison tattoo techniques are usually very crude, in marked contrast to the highly skilled art practiced in Japan and also performed in the United States and in Europe. In the early 2000s, the ancient art of

Mehndi, or temporary tattooing of the skin with a paste made of henna has become popular in the United States and around the world. Henna is a stain normally made for hair and, therefore, exempt from U.S. Food and Drug Administration regulation. Although seemingly safe because it does not pierce the skin, henna tattoos using black henna, a paste that contains parahenylenediamine, can actually be dangerous when absorbed into the skin of some people.

Risks

While piercing and tattooing are popular, both present distinct health risks. Tattoos can lead to the transmission of infectious diseases, such as **hepatitis B** and C and theoretically HIV, when proper sterilization and **safety** procedures are not followed. Black henna tattoos can cause significant **allergies** and **rashes**, leading to renal (kidney) failure and even death in those who are sensitive to their ingredients. These types of tattoos have appeared particularly dangerous to young children. Body piercing also presents the risk of chronic infection, scarring, hepatitis B and C, **tetanus**, and skin allergies to the jewelry that is used. One study reported that 17 percent of college students with piercings suffered a medical complication such as infection or tearing. Use of piercing guns and preferences for upper ear piercing have led to increased infections. The force of the gun's delivery further complicates matters around the delicate cartilage of the upper ear and some people require surgical intervention.

Body piercing and tattooing are unregulated in most parts of the United States, and illegal in some. The American Dental Association opposes oral (tongue, lip, or cheek) piercing, and the American Academy of Dermatology is against all forms of body piercing except ear lobe piercing.

Some of the signs of an infection from either piercing or tattoos are obvious, such as inflammation of the pierced or tattooed area, while the symptoms of hepatitis C, the most common blood-borne infection in the United States, may not be so obvious. Allergic responses to tattoos may occur due to the pigment compounds used, such as oxides of iron, mercury, chromium, cadmium, and cobalt and synthetic organic dyes. Symptoms of an allergic reaction include swelling, redness, and severe **itching**. The symptom of henna tattoo reaction is an eczema-like rash around the tattoo site. The patch should be tested for reaction severity before it proceeds to anaphylactic shock or severe allergic reaction.

Most infections from piercing are due to the use of non-sterile techniques. The skin pathogens streptococcus and staphylococcus are most frequently involved in skin infections from piercing. The fleshy tissue around the pierced area may weaken and tear, leading for example, to a badly disfigured earlobe. Other common complications include **contact dermatitis** and scars. Piercing can result in endocarditis (inflammation of the heart), urethral rupture (when the labia is pierced), and a serious infection of the penis foreskin (when the foreskin is pierced) leading to severe disability or even, on rare occasions, death.

Normal results

Though painful initially, many tattoos and piercings heal well, do not become infected, and are satisfying to the wearer. Those interested in getting a tattoo or piercing should look for an established business with clean facilities. Equipment should be sterilized between uses, and the person applying the tattoo or piercing should wear clean latex gloves. The skin should be cleaned and an antiseptic applied to minimize the risk of infection. Common problems are infection, which can range in

Common healing times for body piercings

Ear lobe: six to eight weeks

Ear cartilage: four months to one year

Eyebrow: six to eight weeks

Nostril: two to four months

Nasal septum: six to eight months

Nasal bridge: eight to ten weeks

Tongue: four weeks (Can cause partial paralysis if jewelry pierces a nerve.)

Lip: two to three months

Nipple: three to six months

Navel: four months to one year

Female genitalia: four to ten weeks

Male genitalia: four weeks to six months

SOURCE: Akron Children's Hospital, "Tips to Grow By," 2003.

(Table by GGS Information Services.)

severity from mild to severe, and deciding that a particular tattoo or piercing is unsatisfactory. Piercings can close on their own if allowed to heal naturally shortly after the piercing is done. If done too late, the hole may close incompletely or not at all. Tongue piercings are among the most likely to become infected and often cause tooth damage.

Treatment of a local infection from piercing includes warm compresses and antibacterial ointment for local infections to a five-day course of oral antibiotic therapy. If hepatitis B or C is confirmed, a series of diet and lifestyle changes, such as the elimination of alcohol, is recommended to control the disease.

There are five methods to remove tattoos when desired, including using a laser to break up tattoo pigments; surgical removal that involves cutting the tattoo away; sanding the skin with a wire brush to remove the epidermis and dermis layers in a process called dermabrasion; using a salt solution to soak the tattooed skin (salabrasion); and scarification, removing the tattoo with an acid solution to form a scar in its place. Topical steroids can often treat reactions to henna tattoos, but improvement may take several weeks.

Depending on the type of infection resulting from either piercing or tattoos, the treatment and prognosis vary. Minor infections respond well to antibiotic therapy, while blood-borne diseases such as hepatitis B and C cause life-altering results. Disfigurement may or may not be fully correctable by later plastic surgery. People particularly sensitive or allergic to the ingredients in

KEY TERMS

Endocarditis—Inflammation of the inner membrane lining of the heart and/or of the heart valves caused by infection.

Hepatitis—An inflammation of the liver, with accompanying liver cell damage or cell death, caused most frequently by viral infection, but also by certain drugs, chemicals, or poisons. May be either acute (of limited duration) or chronic (continuing). Symptoms include jaundice, nausea, vomiting, loss of appetite, tenderness in the right upper abdomen, aching muscles, and joint pain. In severe cases, liver failure may result.

Socialization—The process by which new members of a social group are integrated in the group.

black henna may suffer serious consequences, even death, if their reaction progresses. Others may be left with scarring or altered pigmentation along the tattoo design.

Parental concerns

Obviously, the best way to prevent infection from piercing or tattoos is not to get one in the first place. However, the risks can be minimized. Procedures should be performed in a sterile environment by an experienced professional. The person performing the procedure should remove a new needle from the plastic in front of the person to be tattooed and should put on a new pair of sterile gloves. Anyone considering a henna tattoo should require proof from the artist that he or she is using pure, safe brown henna, not the unsafe black henna.

Piercing should be completed with smoothly polished jewelry made of 14 or 18 carat gold, titanium, surgical steel, or niobium. An allergic reaction can result with the use of jewelry made of brass plate or containing a nickel alloy. Healing time from a piercing ranges from six months to two years. A piercing should be completed in a sterile environment that uses every precaution to reduce the risk of infection. Excessive force, such as exerting a strong pull, should never be applied to jewelry inserted into pierced body parts to avoid tearing and injuring tissues.

Resources

BOOKS

Mason, Paul. *Body Piercing and Tattooing.* London: Heinemann, 2003.

Whittington, Christine, and Kathlyn Gay. *Body Marks: Tattooing, Piercing, and Scarification.* Brookfield, CT: Millbrook Press, 2002.

Winkler, Kathleen. *Tattooing and Body Piercing: Understanding the Risks.* Berkeley Heights, NJ: Enslow Publishers, 2002.

PERIODICALS

Amatuzio, J. "The meaning of the mark: the fascinating forensic aspects of tattoos." *Minnesota Medicine* 87, no. 3 (2004): 22–5.

Armstrong, M. L., et al. "Contemporary college students and body piercing." *Journal of Adolescent Health* 35, no. 1 (2004): 58–61.

Dunn, W. J., and T. E. Reeves. "Tongue piercing: case report and ethical overview." *General Dentistry* 52, no. 3 (2004): 244–7.

Gunter, T. E., and B. M. McDowell. "Body piercing: issues in adolescent health." *Journal for Specialists in Pediatric Nursing* 9, no. 2 (2004): 67–9.

ORGANIZATIONS

American Academy of Dermatology. 930 N. Meacham Road, PO Box 4014, Schaumburg, IL 60168–4014. Web site: <www.aad.org/>.

American Academy of Family Physicians. 11400 Tomahawk Creek Parkway, Leawood, KS 66211–2672. Web site: <www.aafp.org/>.

American Academy of Pediatrics. 141 Northwest Point Boulevard, Elk Grove Village, IL 60007–1098. Web site: <www.aap.org/default.htm>.

American College of Physicians. 190 N Independence Mall West, Philadelphia, PA 19106–1572. Web site: <www.acponline.org/>.

WEB SITES

"How Tattoos Work." *How Stuff Works.* Available online at <http://science.howstuffworks.com/tattoo.htm> (accessed November 2, 2004).

"Tattoos and Permanent Makeup." *U.S. Food and Drug Administration.* Available online at <http://vm.cfsan.fda.gov/dms/cos-204.html> (accessed November 2, 2004).

"Tattoos, Piercings, and Body Markings." *National Geographic.* Available online at <www.nationalgeographic.com/tattoos/> (accessed November 2, 2004).

L. Fleming Fallon, Jr., MD, DrPH

Pimples *see* **Acne**

Pinkeye *see* **Conjuctivitis**

Pinta

Definition

Pinta is a bacterial infection of the skin that causes lesions, red to bluish-black colored spots and splotches, and discoloration of the skin.

Description

Pinta is a skin infection caused by the bacterium *Treponema carateum*, a relative of the bacterium that causes syphilis. The word "pinta" comes from Spanish and means "painted." Pinta is also known as "azula" (blue), and "mal de pinto" (pinto sickness). It is one of several infections caused by different *Treponema* bacteria, which are called "endemic" or "non-venereal" treponematoses.

Transmission

Pinta is spread from one person to another by direct skin-to-skin contact. The bacteria enter the skin through a small cut, scratch, or other skin damage. Once inside the body, warmth and moisture allow the bacteria to multiply. The bacterial infection causes red, scaly lesions on the skin.

Demographics

Pinta is primarily found in rural, poverty-stricken areas of northern South America, Mexico, and the Caribbean. The disease is usually acquired during late childhood and **adolescence**. It is very rare in the United States. In the 1950s, it is estimated that there were about one million cases of Pinta in South and Central America. That number has been reduced drastically, and recently there are believed to be only a few hundred cases a year in those areas.

Causes and symptoms

Pinta is caused by an infection with the bacterium *Treponema carateum*. Symptoms occur two to four weeks after exposure to the bacteria. The first sign of infection is a red, scaly, slowly enlarging bump on the skin. This is called the primary lesion. The primary lesion usually appears at the site where the bacteria entered the skin, most often on the arms, legs, or face. Smaller lesions then form around the primary lesion. These are called satellite lesions. Lymph nodes located near the infected area may become enlarged, but are painless.

The second stage of pinta occurs between one and 12 months after the primary lesion stage. Many flat, red, scaly, itchy lesions called pintids occur either near the primary lesion, or scattered around the body. Pintid lesions progress through a range of color changes, from red to bluish-black. The skin of older lesions will become depigmented (lose normal color).

When to call the doctor

If the parent notices red scaly lumps, strange patterns of discoloration, or lesions on a child's skin the doctor should be contacted.

Diagnosis

Pinta can be diagnosed by dermatologists (doctors who specialize in skin diseases) and infectious disease specialists. The appearance of the lesions helps in the diagnosis. A blood sample will be taken from the patient's arm to test for antibodies to *Treponema carateum*. A scraping of a lesion will be examined under the microscope to look for *Treponema* bacteria.

Treatment

Pinta is usually treated with a single injection of benzathine penicillin G (Bicillin). This is very effective and is the treatment of choice. However if the child is allergic to penicillin, alternate **antibiotics** can be prescribed.

Prognosis

Approximately 24 hours after the treatment the skin lesions are no longer infectious and the child can no longer transmit the disease to others. Treatment results in a complete cure, but will not undo any skin damage caused by the late stages of disease. The lesions heal slowly over many months. If pinta spreads to the eyes, irreversible eyelid deformities may persist.

Prevention

Good personal hygiene may help prevent pinta. In general, children should avoid physical contact with persons who have skin lesions.

Parental concerns

Pinta only affects the skin and does not affect life expectancy, even if not treated, and it can usually be cured completely. The most significant concern is that if pinta is not diagnosed and treated promptly, the pigmentation changes in the skin may be permanent. This can cause the child to have a negative self-image and possibly lead to rejection by other children.

Resources

BOOKS

Desowitz, Robert S. *Who Gave Pinta to the Santa Maria?: Torrid Diseases in a Temperate World* San Diego: Harcourt Brace, 1998

Weinberg, Samuel, Neil S. Prose and Leonard Kristal *Color Atlas of Pediatric Dermatology* New York: McGraw-Hill Health Professions Division, 1998.

ORGANIZATIONS

National Organization for Rare Disorders, Inc. 55 Kenosia Ave, PO Box 1968, Danbury, CT 06813-1968. (203) 744-0100. <www.rarediseases.org>

Tish Davidson, A.M.
Belinda Rowland, PhD

Pinworms

Definition

Pinworms, *Enterobius vermicularis*, are small, white worms that can live in the intestines, are common in young children, and are easily treated.

Description

Adult pinworms live in the large intestines. Males and females are about 5 mm and 10 mm long, respectively, with the diameter of a strand of thread. After copulation, the males die. When the female is ready to lay eggs, she crawls out of the anus, and violently expels the eggs on the skin around the anus. Some of the eggs become airborne and land elsewhere, but the majority stay on the skin of the buttocks. A single female can produce more than 10,000 eggs. After laying her eggs, the female also dies. At body temperature, the eggs develop quickly and are infective in about six hours. When ingested by another person, the eggs hatch in the small intestine. Juvenile worms grow into adult, sexually mature worms in about a month. These tiny worms are quite complex in that they have mouths, throats, gastrointestinal tracts, and a nervous system. The males and females have a complex reproductive tract and reproduce sexually. There is evidence that a protozoan parasite (*Dientamoeba fragilis*) is transmitted among humans in the eggs of pinworms. Thus, they may occur simultaneously.

Transmission

Pinworms are extremely contagious, and the eggs are infective within a few hours of being laid. They are usually spread from child to child by contaminated fingers. When children scratch their itchy bottoms, the tiny eggs get under their fingernails. As they move around the house or classroom, the eggs can be spread. Eggs can stay on a child's skin for several hours. They can survive for two weeks on clothes, bedding, and **toys**. Children who touch the contaminated materials and then place their fingers in their mouths have provided a route for the tiny eggs to enter their bodies. The eggs stay in the upper part of the intestine until they hatch, then move down the length of the intestine and out the anus to lay eggs, and the cycle continues. The entire life cycle lasts four to six weeks. Sometimes adults breathe in the eggs when the bed covers are shaken; however, this is very uncommon. Transmission easily occurs by children not washing their hands thoroughly and spreading the infection to others. It is for this reason that if one member of a **family** is infected with pinworms, the whole family is treated.

Demographics

The pinworm *Enterobius vermicularis* is one of the most common nematode parasitic infections of humans in North America and Europe. It is estimated that pinworms infect more than 400,000,000 people throughout the world or approximately 10 percent of humans. There are no differences in pinworm infections on the basis of race or socioeconomic class. Neither is pinworm infection an indication of poor hygiene. This is a very easily transmissible infection that is quite widespread in children. Since the majority of children experience no ill effects whatsoever, extreme measures to treat pinworms are not indicated.

Causes and symptoms

Pinworm infections can be asymptomatic or result in mild gastrointestinal upsets. A common symptom associated with pinworm infections is perianal (around the anus) **itching**. Scratching of the perianal skin to relieve the itching can lead to bacterial infections that result in more itching, etc. Eventually, this cycle produces a great deal of discomfort. Children who are infected with pinworms often show symptoms that include restlessness, irritability, and insomnia. In females, the adult pinworms can enter the vagina and cause additional irritation. Since the pinworm almost always stays in the gastrointestinal tract or vagina, there is usually no systemic illness. A few children do develop intense nighttime itching of the skin around the anus. Girls who develop vaginal pinworm may experience vaginal itching or a vaginal discharge.

When to call the doctor

If the child seems restless at night and complains of itching in the morning, parents should call their health-care provider to obtain a pinworm lab kit. The kit consists of a tongue depressor with a piece of clear tape on the end. To use the kit, a parent should press the end of the tongue depressor, with the tape on it, against the child's anal skin. The tape is then placed, sticky-side down on a glass slide. The health-care provider will be able to see the eggs with a microscope, and the parent may even see them around the anus during the tape test.

Diagnosis

Stool and blood tests are not helpful in diagnosing pinworms. Seeing a worm is what determines the diagnosis. The parent must check the child's skin with a flashlight during the night and the first thing in the morning and look for white, wiggling threads. Occasionally a wiggling worm may be seen on the surface of a stool. Since pinworms are so common, children with nighttime anal itching are often treated without any lab test. The classic diagnostic tool is to apply a piece of transparent tape to the skin near the anus first thing in the morning. The health-care provider can attach it to a glass slide and then examine it under a microscope for the presence of eggs. A pinworm lab kit can usually be supplied by a provider's office if necessary.

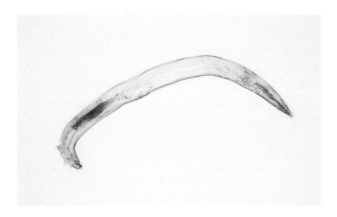

Pinworm (*Enterobius vermicularis*) is a common parasite acquired through fecal-oral transmission. *(© J. Seibert/Custom Medical Stock Photo, Inc.)*

Treatment

Treatment is with a single dose of an anti-pinworm drug such as albendazole (Albenza) or mebendazole (Vermox). Vermox comes as a chewable tablet and most children, as well as adults, experience no side effects with the medication. Allergic reactions have been rarely reported, and very rare cases of convulsions have occurred. The medication kills the worms about 95 percent of the time, but it does not kill the eggs. Therefore, retreatment in two weeks is recommended. Girls with vaginal itching alone do not necessarily need treatment, since the problem will often disappear on its own. Many healthcare providers disagree as to whether to treat the whole family, while others believe it is essential to treat the entire household. It is possible that a girl may be an asymptomatic carrier, which results in numerous reinfections. If everyone is treated, however, this problem will be alleviated. If the child is over two years of age, Pin-X (pyrantel pamoate) is an over-the-counter alternative to Vermox that is available as a liquid.

Prognosis

Treatment is usually very successful if followed with the prevention guidelines to prevent reinfection and doing a retreatment within two weeks after the first.

Prevention

Pinworm infections and reinfections can be diminished by the following:

• Make certain children wash their hands before meals and after using the restroom.

- Keep children's fingernails trimmed.

- Discourage nail-biting and scratching the anal area.

- Have children change into a clean pair of underwear each day.

- Have children bathe in the morning to reduce egg contamination.

- Open bedroom blinds and curtains during the day as eggs are sensitive to sunlight.

- After each treatment, change night clothes, underwear, and bedding and wash them.

Parental concerns

Since pinworms are so common and usually occur in children age 12 and under, there is no reason for concern unless the infection keeps reoccurring. In that case, meticulous cleaning and treatment with retreatment needs to be enforced.

Resources

ORGANIZATIONS

American Academy of Pediatrics. 141 Northwest Point Blvd., Elk Grove Village, IL 60007-1098. (847) 434-4000. Web site: <www.aap.org>.

WEB SITES

Center of Disease Control and Prevention. *Fact Sheet: Pinworms* [cited March 6, 2005]. Available online at: </www.cdc.gov/ncidod/dpd/parasites/pinworm/factsht_pinworm.htm>.

iVillage. *Pinworms: Why do they keep coming back?* [cited March 6, 2005]. Available online at: <www.parentsplace.com/toddlers/health/qas/0,,239278_101260,00.html>.

Ohio State University. *Pinworms.* [cited March 6, 2005]. Available online at: <www.biosci.ohio-state.edu/~parasite/enterobius.html>.

Linda K. Bennington, MSN, CNS

Pituitary dwarfism

Definition

Dwarfism is a condition in which the growth of the individual is very slow or delayed, resulting in less than normal adult stature. The word pituitary refers to the pituitary gland, which regulates the production of certain chemicals called hormones. Therefore, pituitary dwarfism is decreased bodily growth due primarily to hormonal problems. The end result is a proportionate little person, because the height and the growth of all other structures of the individual are decreased.

Description

Pituitary dwarfism is caused by problems arising from the pituitary gland. The pituitary gland, also called the hypophysis, is a gland at the base of the brain that produces many different hormones. This gland is divided into the anterior (front) and posterior (back) halves. The anterior pituitary produces six hormones: growth hormone, adrenocorticotropin (corticotropin), thyroid stimulating hormone (thyrotropin), prolactin, follicle stimulating hormone, and lutenizing hormone. The posterior pituitary gland only produces two hormones: antidiuretic hormone (vasopressin) and oxytocin.

The growth process begins in the lower part of the forebrain in a small organ called the hypothalamus. The hypothalamus releases hormones that regulate the production of other hormones. When the hypothalamus releases growth hormone-releasing hormone (GHRH), the anterior pituitary is stimulated to release growth hormone (GH). Growth hormone then acts on the liver and other tissues and stimulates them to secrete insulin-like growth factor-1 (IGF-1). IGF-1 directly promotes the development of bone and muscle, causing bones to grow in length, and muscles to increase protein synthesis (make more protein).

Since growth is a complex phenomenon, it may be slowed down or stopped by abnormalities arising at any point in the process. Thus, dwarfism can result if there is a deficiency in any of these hormones, if there is a failure in the receptor cells receiving the hormonal stimuli, or if the target cells are unable to respond.

At its most basic, pituitary dwarfism results from decreased production of hormones by the anterior pituitary. When none of the hormones of the anterior pituitary are adequately produced, this is called panhypopituitarism. A common form of pituitary dwarfism is due to deficiencies in the production of growth hormone (GH). When less GH than normal is produced during childhood, an individual's arms, legs, and other structures continue to develop in normal proportions, but at a decreased rate.

Demographics

It is estimated that between one in 14,000 and one in 27,000 babies born each year have some form of dwarfism. In 2004, more than 20,000 children in United States were receiving supplemental GH therapy. It is estimated that about one quarter of them had organic causes of GH deficiencies. There appears to be no racial or ethnic component to pituitary dwarfism, but males seem to be afflicted more than females.

Causes and symptoms

Investigations are underway to determine the specific genetic mutations that can cause dwarfism. Pituitary dwarfism can be caused by:

- genetics
- accident-related trauma to the pituitary gland
- surgical injury of the pituitary
- central nervous system tumor
- central nervous system trauma
- central nervous system radiation
- leukemia

In most cases, the cause of dwarfism is not known (idiopathic).

A child with a growth hormone deficiency is often small with an immature face and chubby body build. The child's growth does not follow the normal growth curve patterns. In cases of tumor, most commonly craniopharyngioma (a tumor near the pituitary gland), children and adolescents may have neurological symptoms such as headaches, **vomiting**, and problems with vision. The child may also have symptoms of double vision. The symptom, however, that all children with pituitary dwarfism share is that they do not grow at the same rate as their peers.

When to call the doctor

If a child appears to be smaller than children two or more years younger than he or she is, the doctor should be consulted.

Diagnosis

Growth hormone deficiency is present at birth, but since the primary symptoms of pituitary dwarfism are height and growth at a reduced rate, the condition is not diagnosed until later in childhood. Charting a child's growth in comparison to age norms will help lead to a diagnosis. Another diagnostic technique uses an x ray of the child's hand to determine the child's bone age by comparing this to the child's actual chronological age. The bone age in affected children is usually two or more years behind the chronological age. This means that if a child is 10 years old, his or her bones will look like they are those of an eight-year-old. The levels of growth hormone and IGF-1 may also be measured with blood tests.

The doctor will do a complete examination to make sure that delayed growth is not caused by other underlying problems, such as tumor. **X rays** of the area where the pituitary gland is located, or more advanced imaging such as **magnetic resonance imaging** (MRI) or **computed tomography** (CT), may help the doctor make a diagnosis and may show whether there have been any changes to the pituitary gland itself.

Treatment

Growth hormone replacement therapy can be administered if the child is lacking growth hormone. A pediatric endocrinologist, a doctor specializing in the hormones of children, administers this type of therapy before a child's bone growth plates have fused or joined. Once the growth plates have fused, GH replacement therapy is rarely effective.

Until 1985, growth hormone was obtained from the pituitary glands of human cadavers. However, some disease complications resulted, and the United States Food and Drug Administration (FDA) banned this source of GH. In 1985, recombinant DNA techniques produced a safe and unlimited supply of GH in the lab. Now, the only growth hormone used for treatment is that which is made in a laboratory.

If growth hormone is not the only hormone deficiency, the doctor must prescribe ways to raise the levels of the other deficient hormones, if these options are available. A careful balancing of all of the hormones produced by the pituitary gland is necessary for patients with panhypopituitarism, making this form of dwarfism complex and difficult to manage.

Prognosis

The prognosis depends on the cause of the dwarfism. A panhypopituitarism dwarf does not pass through the initial onset of adult sexual development (**puberty**) and never produces enough gonadotropic (sex) hormones to develop adult sexual function. These individuals also have other medical conditions that may prove fatal.

KEY TERMS

Adrenocorticotropic hormone (ACTH)—Also called adrenocorticotropin or corticotropin, this hormone is produced by the pituitary gland to stimulate the adrenal cortex to release various corticosteroid hormones.

Antidiuretic hormone (ADH)—Also called vasopressin, a hormone that acts on the kidneys to regulate water balance.

Craniopharyngioma—A tumor near the pituitary gland in the craniopharyngeal canal that often results in intracranial pressure.

Deprivational dwarfism—A condition where emotional disturbances are associated with growth failure and abnormalities of pituitary function.

Follicle-stimulating hormone (FSH)—A pituitary hormone that in females stimulates the ovary to mature egg capsules (follicles) and in males stimulates sperm production.

Growth hormone—A hormone that eventually stimulates growth. Also called somatotropin.

Hormone—A chemical messenger secreted by a gland or organ and released into the bloodstream. It travels via the bloodstream to distant cells where it exerts an effect.

Luteinizing hormone—A hormone secreted by the pituitary gland that regulates the menstrual cycle and triggers ovulation in females. In males it stimulates the testes to produce testosterone.

Oxytocin—A hormone that stimulates the uterus to contract during child birth and the breasts to release milk.

Panhypopituitarism—Generalized decrease of all of the anterior pituitary hormones.

Prolactin—A hormone that helps the breast prepare for milk production during pregnancy.

Puberty—The point in development when the ability to reproduce begins. The gonads begin to function and secondary sexual characteristics begin to appear.

Thyroid-stimulating hormone (TSH)—A hormone produce by the pituitary gland that stimulates the thyroid gland to produce the hormones that regulate metabolism. Also called thyrotropin.

Dwarfism due only to growth hormone deficiency has a much better prognosis if treated early with replacement GH. These individuals do pass through puberty and mature sexually; however, without treatment, they remain proportionately small in stature.

The success of treatment with GH varies. An increase in height of 4–6 in. (10–15 cm) can occur in the first year of treatment. Following this first year, the response to the hormone replacement therapy is less pronounced. Even after this first year, however, the child usually continues to grow at a faster rate than he or she would without GH therapy. Long-term use is considered successful if the individual grows at least 0.75 in. (2 cm) per year more than he or she would without the hormone. However, if GH therapy is not given before the growth plates of the long bones—such as the legs and arms—fuse, the individual will not grow. Prognosis is generally better the earlier a child starts GH replacement therapy.

Improvement for individuals with other causes of dwarfism, such as a tumor, varies greatly. The prognosis usually depends on successful resolution of the underlying problem, whether there is any permanent damage, and the age of the child.

Prevention

There is no known way to prevent pituitary dwarfism, although in some cases it may be caused by traumatic injury to the pituitary gland. Engaging in safe behaviors may reduce the risk of injury-induced pituitary deficiencies.

Parental concerns

Children with pituitary dwarfism are smaller than other children, but they are just as smart and can lead long, healthy lives. It is important for parents not to expect less of their child with pituitary dwarfism simply because the child looks younger than he or she actually is. Chores and conversations should be appropriate to the actual age of the child. Children with pituitary dwarfism may face thoughtless comments from others on occasion, and the parents' reaction to such comments can strongly determine how the child feels about himself or herself.

Resources

BOOKS

Ghigo, C. et al, eds. *Growth Hormone Secretagogues.* New York: Elsevier, 1999.

Melmed, Shlomo, ed. *The Pituitary.* Malden, MA: Blackwell Pub., 2002.

PERIODICALS

Klotter, Jule. "Growth Hormone Replacement Therapy." *Townsend Letter for Doctors and Patients* 251 (June 2004): 28.

"Message to Parents: Hold Off on Growth Hormone for Short Kids." *Life Science Weekly* (Sept. 14, 2004): 1172.

Sandberg, David E. et al. "Height and Social Adjustment: are Extremes a Cause for Concern and Action?" *Pediatrics* 114, no. 3 (Sept. 2004): 744–51.

ORGANIZATIONS

Human Growth Foundation. 997 Glen Cove Avenue, Suite 5 Glen Head, NY 11545. (800) 451-6434 Fax: (516) 671-4055 <www.hgfound.org>

Little People of America, Inc. 5289 NE Elam Young Parkway, Suite F-700 Hillsboro, OR 97124. (888) LPA-2001 or (530) 846-1562 Fax: (503) 846-1590. <www.plaonline.org.org>

Tish Davidson, A.M.
Jason S. Schliesser, D.C.

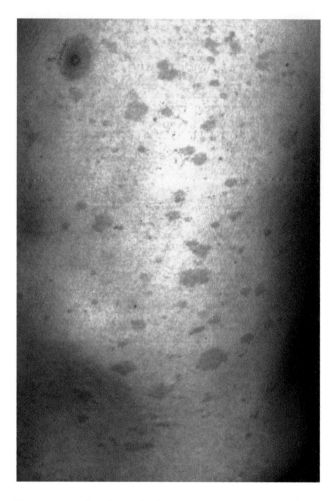

Torso covered with pityriasis rosea. It often appears on the torso and upper parts of the limbs of young people and may be contagious. *(Photograph by Dr. P. Marazzi. Photo Researchers, Inc.)*

Pityriasis rosea

Definition

Pityriasis rosea is a mild skin disorder common among children and young adults, manifesting initially as a single round spot on the body and followed later by a rash of colored spots on the body and upper arms.

Demographics

Pityriasis rosea is most common in young adults and appears up to 50 percent more often in women. The condition occurs most often in spring and fall and can occur in epidemics within dormitories, army barracks, or other locations where young people live in close proximity to each other.

Causes and symptoms

It is unclear whether pityriasis rosea is contagious. Although some experts suspect the rash may be triggered by a virus, no infectious agent had, as of 2004, been found. Some scientists believe that the rash is an immune response to some type of infection in the body.

Sometimes, before the symptoms appear, people experience preliminary symptoms, including **fever**, malaise, **sore throat**, or **headache**. Symptoms begin with a single, large round spot called a herald patch on the body, followed days or weeks later by slightly raised, scaly-edged round or oval pink-copper colored spots on the trunk and upper arms. The distribution of the spots, which have a wrinkled center and a sharp border, sometimes resemble a Christmas tree. They may be mild to severely itchy, and they can spread to other parts of the body.

Diagnosis

Although the diagnosis is usually obvious, if there is any confusion, other conditions (such as a fungal condition or syphilis) can be ruled out through examination of skin scrapings or blood tests.

KEY TERMS

Antihistamine—A drug used to treat allergic conditions that blocks the effects of histamine, a substance in the body that causes itching, vascular changes, and mucus secretion when released by cells.

Steroids—Hormones, including aldosterone, cortisol, and androgens, that are derived from cholesterol and that share a four-ring structural characteristic.

Treatment

The rash usually clears up on its own, over the course of about 12 weeks. During that time, external and internal medications may be given for **itching** and inflammation. Mild inflammation and itching can be relieved with antihistamine drugs or calamine lotion, zinc oxide, or other mild lubricants or anti-itching creams. Gentle, soothing strokes should be used to apply the ointments, since vigorous rubbing may cause the lesions to spread. More severe itching and inflammation is treated with topical steroids. Moderate exposure to sun or ultraviolet light may help heal the lesions, but patients should avoid being sunburned.

Soap makes the rash more uncomfortable; patients should bathe or shower with plain lukewarm water and apply a thin coating of bath oil to freshly-dried skin afterwards.

Prognosis

These spots, which may be itchy, last for three to 12 weeks. Symptoms rarely recur.

Parental concerns

After the rash has cleared up, parents often notice that areas where there were spots may appear lighter (hypopigmented) or darker (hyperpigmented) in color than the surrounding skin. Hypopigmentation can be particularly obvious in darker skinned patients. These skin changes will resolve within weeks to months after the rash has cleared.

Resources

BOOKS

"Disease of the Epidermis." In *Nelson Textbook of Pediatrics.* Edited by Richard E. Behrman et al. Philadelphia: Saunders, 2004.

"Psoriasis and Other Papulosquamous Diseases." In *Clinical Dermatology*, 4th ed. Edited by Thomas B. Habif. St. Louis, MO: Mosby, 2004.

ORGANIZATIONS

American Academy of Dermatology. 930 N. Meacham Road, PO Box 4014, Schaumburg, IL 60168–4014. Web site: <www.aad.org>.

Carol A. Turkington
Rosalyn Carson-DeWitt, MD

PKU *see* **Phenylketonuria**

Platelet count

Definition

A platelet count is a diagnostic test that determines the number of platelets in the patient's blood. Platelets, which are also called thrombocytes, are small disk-shaped blood cells produced in the bone marrow and involved in the process of blood clotting. There are normally between 150,000–450,000 platelets in each microliter of blood. Low platelet counts or abnormally shaped platelets are associated with bleeding disorders. High platelet counts or low platelet counts sometimes indicate disorders of the bone marrow.

Purpose

The primary functions of a platelet count are to assist in the diagnosis of bleeding disorders and to monitor patients who are being treated for any disease involving bone marrow failure. Patients who have leukemia, polycythemia vera, or aplastic anemia are given periodic platelet count tests to monitor their health.

Description

Blood collection and storage

Platelet counts use a freshly collected blood specimen to which a chemical called EDTA has been added to prevent clotting before the test begins. About 5 mL of blood are drawn from a vein in the patient's inner elbow region, or other area. Blood drawn from a vein helps to produce a more accurate count than blood drawn from a fingertip. Collection of the sample takes only a few minutes. After collection, the mean platelet volume of EDTA-blood will increase over time. This increase is

Platelet count

caused by a change in the shape of the platelets after removal from the body. The changing volume is relatively stable for a period of one to three hours after collection. This period is the best time to count the sample when using electronic instruments, because the platelets will be within a standard size range.

Counting methods

Platelets can be observed in a direct blood smear for approximate quantity and shape. A direct smear is made by placing a drop of blood onto a microscope slide and spreading it into a thin layer. After staining to make the various blood cells easier to see and distinguish, a laboratory technician views the smear through a light microscope. Accurate assessment of the number of platelets requires other methods of counting. There are three methods used to count platelets: hemacytometer, voltage-pulse counting, and electro-optical counting.

Hemacytometer counting: The microscopic method uses a phase contrast microscope to view blood on a hemacytometer slide. A sample of the diluted blood mixture is placed in a hemacytometer, which is an instrument with a grid etched into its surface to guide the counting. For a proper count, the platelets should be evenly distributed in the hemacytometer. Errors in platelet counting are more common when blood is collected from capillaries than from veins.

Electronic counting: Electronic counting of platelets is the most common method. There are two types of electronic counting, voltage-pulse and electro-optical counting systems. In both systems, the collected blood is diluted and counted by passing the blood through an electronic counter. For these instruments to work properly, the sample must not contain other material that might mistakenly be counted as platelets. Electronic counting instruments sometimes produce artificially low platelet counts. If a platelet and another blood cell pass through the counter at the same time, the instrument will not count the larger cell, which will cause the instrument to accidentally miss the platelet. Clumps of platelets will also not be counted. In addition, if the patient has a high white blood cell count, electronic counting may yield an unusually low platelet count because white blood cells may filter out some of the platelets before the sample is counted. On the other hand, if the red blood cells in the sample have burst, their fragments will be falsely counted as platelets.

Aftercare

Because platelet counts are sometimes ordered to diagnose or monitor bleeding disorders, patients with

KEY TERMS

Capillaries—The tiniest blood vessels with the smallest diameter. These vessels receive blood from the arterioles and deliver blood to the venules. In the lungs, capillaries are located next to the alveoli so that they can pick up oxygen from inhaled air.

EDTA—A colorless compound used to keep blood samples from clotting before tests are run.

Hemocytometer—An instrument used to count platelets or other blood cells.

Leukemia—A cancer of the blood-forming organs (bone marrow and lymph system) characterized by an abnormal increase in the number of white blood cells in the tissues. There are many types of leukemias and they are classified according to the type of white blood cell involved.

Phase contrast microscope—A light microscope in which light is focused on the sample at an angle to produce a clearer image.

Thrombocyte—Another name for platelet.

Thrombocytopenia—A persistent decrease in the number of blood platelets usually associated with hemorrhaging.

Thrombocytosis—An abnormally high platelet count. It occurs in polycythemia vera and other disorders in which the bone marrow produces too many platelets.

these disorders should be cautioned to watch the puncture site for signs of additional bleeding.

Risks

Risks for a platelet count test are minimal in normal individuals. Children with bleeding disorders, however, may have prolonged bleeding from the puncture wound or the formation of a bruise (hematoma) under the skin where the blood was withdrawn. Rarely an infection may occur at the needle puncture site.

Normal results

The normal range for a platelet count is 150,000–450,000 platelets per microliter of blood.

Abnormal results

An abnormally low platelet level (thrombocytopenia) is a condition that may result from increased destruction of platelets, decreased production, or increased usage of platelets. In **idiopathic thrombocytopenic purpura** (ITP), platelets are destroyed at abnormally high rates. Another cause of a low platelet count is an enlarged spleen. Hypersplenism is characterized by the collection (sequestration) of platelets in the spleen. Disseminated intravascular coagulation (DIC) is a condition in which blood clots occur within blood vessels in a number of tissues. Leukemia and aplastic anemia can result in a low platelet count because of decreased production of platelets in the bone marrow. All of these diseases produce reduced platelet counts. Abnormally high platelet levels (thrombocytosis) may indicate either a benign reaction to an infection, surgery, or certain medications; or a disease like polycythemia vera, in which the bone marrow produces too many platelets too quickly.

Parental concerns

The **pain** from the needle puncture only lasts a moment. The parent should comfort a child as needed. Older children can be prepared for the test ahead of time, and the reason why the test is being given should also be explained if the child is old enough to understand.

When to call a doctor

If the bleeding does not stop at the needle puncture site, or hours to days later, there are signs of infection (redness and swelling), then parents should contact a doctor.

Resources

BOOKS

Henry, John B. *Clinical Diagnosis and Management by Laboratory Methods, 20th Ed.* Philadelphia: W. B. Saunders Co., 2001.

Wallach, Jacques. *Interpretation of Diagnostic Tests, 7th Ed.* Philadelphia: Lippincott, Williams, and Wilkins, 2000.

Mark A. Best

Play

Definition

Play is the work of children. It consists of those activities performed for self-amusement that have behavioral, social, and psychomotor rewards. It is child-directed, and the rewards come from within the individual child; it is enjoyable and spontaneous.

Description

Play is an important part of the childhood development. Through play children learn about shapes, colors, cause and effect, and themselves. Besides cognitive thinking, play helps the child learn social and psychomotor skills. It is a way of communicating joy, **fear**, sorrow, and **anxiety**.

In the early 2000s, children of all ages and from every socioeconomic background often prefer television, computers, and battery-operated **toys** to self-directed, imaginative, and creative play. This tendency leaves children developmentally deprived, because imaginative and fantasy play allows children to explore their world and express their innermost thoughts and feelings, hopes and fears, likes and dislikes. Through play, decisions are made without penalty or fear of failure. Play allows children to gain control of their thoughts, feelings, actions, and helps them achieve self-confidence.

Play takes different forms for different children, and its definition entails many aspects. Play is the direct opposite of work; it is frivolous. It provides freedom and invites the impulse to engage in foolishness. Yet it provides a means for ego development and a process by which social skills and physical skills develop as well.

Play with imagination and fantasy is the child's natural medium of self-expression and one that gives cues about the child's conscious and unconscious states. In play therapy, clinicians employ various techniques designed to reveal the child's psychological and social development. Clinician-directed play therapy is, therefore, not naturally self-directed play, but play designed by a professional to facilitate understanding of the child and the child's healing process.

Categories of play

Categories of play are not mutually exclusive; different forms or categories of play may overlap. Having choices is important since an action that appeals to one child may be of no interest to another, and the child's interest is likely to change throughout the play period. An understanding of play in many forms can help parents understand its importance for children of all ages. Some specific categories of play are as follows.

• Physical play. When children run, jump, and play games such as chase, hide-and-seek, and tag, they engage in physical play. This play has a social nature because it involves other children. It also provides **exercise**, which is essential for normal development.

- Expressive play. Certain forms of play give children opportunities to express feelings by engaging with materials. Materials used in expressive play include tempera paints, fingerpaints, watercolors, crayons, colored pencils and markers, and drawing paper; clay, water, and sponges; beanbags, pounding benches, punching bags, and rhythm instruments; and shaving cream, pudding, and gelatin. Parents can take an active role in expressive play by using the materials alongside the child.

- Manipulative play. Children control or master their environment through manipulative play. They manipulate the environment and other people as much as possible. Manipulative play starts in infancy. Infants play with their parents; for example, they drop a toy, wait for the parent to pick it up, clean it, and return it, and then they drop it again. This interaction brings the infant and parent together in a game. Children move objects such as puzzle pieces and gadgets to better understand how they work.

- Symbolic play. Certain games can symbolically express a child's problems. Because there are no rules in symbolic play, the child can use this play to reinforce, learn about, and imaginatively alter painful experiences. The child who is in an abusive **family** may pretend to be a mother who loves and cuddles her child rather than one who verbally or physically abuses her child. Or in play this same child might act out abusive experience by hitting or screaming at a doll that symbolizes the child. Parents can be surprised by their child's perception of family issues. Children mimic their parents in certain play; in other games they may pretend they are the heroes they read about in books or see on television. At certain developmental stages children believe they can fly or disappear. Symbolic play may be used by children to cope with fear of separation when they go to school or to the hospital.

- Dramatic play. Children act out situations they suspect may happen to them, that they are fearful will happen, or that they have witnessed. Dramatic play can be either spontaneous or guided and may be therapeutic for children in the hospital.

- Familiarization play. Children handle materials and explore experiences in reassuring, enjoyable ways. Familiarization prepares children for potentially fearful and painful experiences, such as surgery or parental separation.

- Games. Some video and card games are played by one child alone. Games with rules are rarely played by children younger than four years of age. Board games, card games, and **sports** are enjoyed typically by school-age children. In these games children learn to play by the rules and to take turns. Older children enjoy games with specific rules; however, younger children tend to like games that allow them to change the rules.

- Surrogate play. For children who are too ill or incapacitated to play, another child or a parent may serve as surrogate. Watching the surrogate who plays on behalf of the sick child is stimulating to the sick child. When parents engage in expressive art by painting or redecorating a room while the physically challenged child watches, they stimulate the child.

Functions of play

Play reinforces the child's growth and development. Some of the more common functions of play are to facilitate physical, emotional, cognitive, social, and **moral development**.

PHYSICAL DEVELOPMENT Play aids in developing both fine and **gross motor skills**. Children repeat certain body movements purely for pleasure, and these movements develop body control. For example, an infant will first hit at a toy, then will try to grasp it, and eventually will be able to pick it up. Next, the infant will shake the rattle or perhaps bring it to the mouth. In these ways, the infant moves from simple to more complex gestures.

EMOTIONAL DEVELOPMENT Children who are anxious may be helped by role playing. Role playing is a way of coping with emotional conflict. Children may escape through play into a fantasy world in order to make sense out of the real one. Also, a child's self-awareness deepens as he explores an event through role-playing or symbolic play.

When a parent or sibling plays a board game with a child, shares a bike ride, plays baseball, or reads a story, the child learns self-importance. The child's **self-esteem** gets a boost. Parents send positive messages to their child when they communicate pleasure in providing him or her with daily care. From these early interactions, children develop a vision of the world and gain a sense of their place in it.

COGNITIVE DEVELOPMENT Children gain knowledge through their play. They exercise their abilities to think, remember, and solve problems. They develop cognitively as they have a chance to test their beliefs about the world.

Children increase their problem-solving abilities through games and puzzles. Children involved in make-believe play can stimulate several types of learning. Language is strengthened as the children model others and organize their thoughts to communicate. Children playing house create elaborate narratives concerning their roles and the nature of daily living.

Children also increase their understanding of size, shape, and texture through play. They begin to understand relationships as they try to put a square object in a round opening or a large object in a small space. Books, videos, and educational toys that show pictures and matching words also increase a child's vocabulary while increasing the child's concept of the world.

SOCIAL DEVELOPMENT A newborn cannot distinguish itself from others and is completely self-absorbed. As the infant begins to play with others and with objects, a realization of self as separate from others begins to develop. The infant begins to experience joy from contact with others and engages in behavior that involves others. The infant discovers that when he coos or laughs, mother coos back. The child soon expects this response and repeats it for fun, playing with his mother.

As children grow, they enjoy playful interaction with other children. Children learn about boundaries, taking turns, teamwork, and competition. Children also learn to negotiate with different personalities and the feelings associated with winning and losing. They learn to share, wait, and be patient.

MORAL DEVELOPMENT When children engage in play with their peers and families, they begin to learn some behaviors are acceptable while others are unacceptable. Parents start these lessons early in the child's life by teaching the child to control **aggressive behavior**. Parents can develop morals while reading to children by stressing the moral implications in stories. Children can identify with the moral fictional characters without assuming their roles. With peers they quickly learn that taking turns is rewarding and cheating is not. Group play helps the child appreciate teamwork and share and respect others' feelings. The child learns how to be kind and charitable to others.

Age-related play

As children develop, their play evolves, too. Certain types of play are associated with, but not restricted to, specific age groups.

- Solitary play is independent. The child plays alone with toys that are different from those chosen by other children in the area. Solitary play begins in infancy and is common in toddlers because of their limited social, cognitive, and physical skills. However, it is important for all age groups to have some time to play by themselves.

- Parallel play is usually associated with toddlers, although it happens in any age group. Children play side by side with similar toys, but there is a lack of group involvement.

- Associative play involves a group of children who have similar goals. Children in associate play do not set rules, and although they all want to be playing with the same types of toys and may even trade toys, there is no formal organization. Associative play begins during toddlerhood and extends though **preschool** age.

- Cooperative play begins in the late preschool period. The play is organized by group goals. There is at least one leader, and children are definitely in or out of the group.

- Onlooker play is present when the child watches others playing. Although the child may ask questions of the players, there is no effort to join the play. This type of play usually starts during toddler years but can take place at any age.

Common problems

Promoting play for a sick child is a challenge when the child cannot voluntarily engage in play. Parents need to realize the importance of play to the well being of a sick child. Children can bring favorite books, games, and stuffed animals to the hospital. In hospitals young children need toys that they can manipulate independently, so that parents are free sometimes to focus on medical issues and the healthcare team.

Play activities vary depending on cultural and socioeconomic circumstances. When children do not speak the group's language, games such as stacking blocks or building with tinker toys are appealing. Playing tapes of well-loved children's songs can be effective too. The child does not need to be able to understand the words to enjoy the music or clap with the rhythm.

Assessing child health through play

Acutely ill children do not have the strength, the attention span, or the interest in play. They may enjoy being read to and the comfort of holding a favorite stuffed animal. Once the acute phase of an illness is over, the child's interest in playing returns. Spontaneous interest in play is a good index of health. The toys selected for play are good indicators of the child's recovery progress.

Play in a medical setting

When a child goes to see the doctor, the waiting room is likely to have other children in it. The arriving child may hear other children cry as they leave the examining room. The child may dread the examination.

Parents should pack a favorite toy or book with which to distract the child. Having a parent sit with them is comforting, and they may venture a few feet away to examine toys in the toy box. Older children who go with the parent and the sick sibling to see the doctor should have toys and games for their entertainment, too, so the parent can focus on the sick child.

Hospitalized children can release fear, anger, or tension through effective play. Children in the hospital for a week or longer may enjoy playing school or socializing in the playroom with other children of their age. However, physical play for sick children must be supervised by a parent or healthcare provider.

Therapeutic play

When a child is ill or traumatized the care plan may include therapeutic play. Unlike normal play in design and intent, therapeutic play is guided by the health professional to meet the physical and psychological needs of the child. Because play is the language of children, children who have difficulty putting their thoughts in words can often speak clearly through play therapy. There are three divisions of therapeutic play, including:

- Energy release. Children release anxiety by pounding, hitting, running, punching, or shouting. Toddlers pound pegs with a plastic hammer or pretend to cut wood with a toy saw. An anxious preschooler pounds a ball of modeling clay flat; a relaxed child may build the clay into shapes. Balloons tied over the bed of a school-age child or adolescent can be punched.

- Dramatic play. Children act out or dramatize real-life situations. They act out anxiety and emotional stress from abuse, neglect, **abandonment**, and various painful physical experiences. Imaginative preschool children enjoy dramatic play. An abused or wounded child might not communicate the experience verbally but may be able to use an anatomically correct doll to show what happened. Therapeutic play can teach children about medical procedures or help them work through their feelings about what has happened to them in the medical setting.

- Creative play. Some children are too angry or fearful to act out their feelings through dramatic play. However, they may be able to draw a picture that expresses their emotions or communicates what they know. To encourage this expression children can be given blank paper and crayons or markers and asked to draw a picture about how they feel. Some children are so concerned about a particular body part that instead of drawing a self portrait, they will draw only the body part that worries them.

Many children draw pictures that reflect punitive images to explain unhappy experiences. They need reassurance that they are not being punished. Health-care providers need to make sure that these children are not being abused. Other children may draw pictures that are symbolic of death (an airplane crashing, boats sinking, burning buildings, or children in graves). These children need assurances that they are not going to die. Some **drawings** express the child's fear of abandonment and loss of independence. Pictures may suggest the parent cannot find the little child who is in the hospital. The child needs to be reassured that their parents know where they are. They need to know when the parents will visit and the parents should appear when they say they will be there.

Older school-age children and adolescents may not be interested in drawing, but they can make a list of experiences they like and dislike.

Parental concerns

Parents express interest in age-related play that prepares children for group exercises in preschool. They want to know the right kind of play for an only child or sick child who may not be able to play with other children in their age group. The following age-related play and toys serve as a guide to parents with these concerns.

- Infant. The infant enjoys watching other members of the family; the infant enjoys rocking, strolling, time spent in a swing, supervised time on a blanket on the floor, **crawling**, walking with help, and being sung and read to. Play is self-absorbed; it is difficult, if not impossible to direct play. Infants are engaged in the vigorous process of self-discovery, learning their world by looking, listening, chewing, smelling, and grasping. Most of their learning comes through play. They need safe toys that appeal to all of their senses and stimulate their interest and curiosity. Infants need toys and play that include oral movements. They like peek-a-boo; playing with the parent's fingers, hair, face, and the infant's own body parts; playing in water. Soft stuffed animals, crib mobiles, squeeze toys rattles, busy boxes, mirrors, and musical toys. Parents can give them water toys for the bath, safe kitchen utensils, and push toys (after they begin to walk), and large print books.

- Toddler. Toddlers fill and empty containers and begin dramatic play. As they increase their motor skills, they enjoy feeling different textures, exploring the home environment, and mimicking others. They like to be read to and to look at books and television. Toddlers enjoy manipulating small objects such as toy people, cars, and animals. Favorite toys are mechanical; objects of different textures such as clay, sand, finger paints, and bubbles; push-pull toys; large balls; sand and water play; blocks; painting or coloring with large crayons; nesting toys; large puzzles; and trucks and dolls. Toddlers explore their bodies and those of others. Therapeutic play can begin at this age.

- Preschooler. Dramatic play is prominent. This age group likes to run, jump, hop, and in general increase motor skills. The children like to build and create whether it is sand castles or mud pies. Play is simple and imaginative. Simple collections begin. Preschoolers enjoy riding toys, building materials such as sand and blocks, dolls, drawing materials, cars, puzzles, books, appropriate television and videos, nonsense rhymes, and singing games. Preschoolers love pretending to be something or somebody and playing dress up They enjoy finger paints, clay, cutting, pasting, and simple board and card games.

- School-age child. Play becomes organized and has a direction. The early school-age child continues dramatic play with increased **creativity** but loses some spontaneity. The child gains awareness of rules when playing games and begins to compete in sports. Children in this age group enjoy collections (comic books, baseball cards, and stamps), dolls, pets, guessing games, board games, riddles, physical games, competitive play, reading, bike riding, hobbies, sewing, listening to the radio, television, and videos, and cooking.

- Adolescent. Athletic sports are the most common form of play. Strict rules are in place, and competition is important. Adolescents also enjoy movies; telephone conversations and parties; listening to music; and experimenting with makeup, hairstyles, and fashion. They also begin developing an interest in peers of the opposite sex.

Play for the sick child

Children who are confined to a bed need to have play periods built into their day. The length of play and the toys will depend the individual child's age and physical and emotional states. Short-term school projects appeal to school-age children because these activities help the children feel industrious and think about their future wellness. Parents can help children with their baths; encourage them to drink enough fluids; and prompt them to do deep breathing and muscle strengthening exercises.

Safety issues

Toys and games should be screened for **safety**, especially those used by a sick child. The toys should be washable with no sharp edges and no small parts that

Toddler playing by himself with toys. (© Villareal/Photo Researchers, Inc.)

could be swallowed or aspirated. Cylinder-shaped toys of 1-inch (2.5-cm) diameter (the size of a regular hot dog) are the most dangerous size because they can occlude the trachea (windpipe) if they are aspirated. As a rule, if a toy can fit through the center of a toilet tissue tube, it is too small.

Parents should be certain that toys do not lead children into danger. Tossing a ball to a toddler on bed rest may be safe, but if a child in a cast leans to catch the ball, he may fall. Chasing a ball may lead to falls and collisions. If children are bored with a toy because it is not stimulating enough or they have played with it too long, they may begin to use the toy in an unsafe way. For example, the child may throw blocks across the room for fun instead of stacking them.

Indoor toys

For home care of the sick child, parents may need to buy new toys suitable for indoor use. The ill child may need soft toys for bed play and sit-down toys such as magic markers, puzzles, books, or board games, for quiet out-of-bed play.

When to call the doctor

Parents and teachers who spend time observing and understanding childhood behaviors may want to report to the child's therapist what they see the child do.

Skin care is essential for children who are bedridden or in a cast or restraints. Children lose interest in playing if they are uncomfortable or in **pain**. Parents should look for pressure over the buttocks, elbows, heels, and other parts of the child's body. The skin should be inspected often and massaged with a moisturizing lotion to increase circulation. Redness, irritation, and sores should be reported immediately to the healthcare provider.

When children are ill, the rate of bladder and bowel elimination may slow down because of reduced physical action. School-age children and adolescents may hesitate to drink or eat a normal diet because toileting is uncomfortable or performed without privacy. Parents may need to seek medical advice about digestive and elimination aids and about adjusting the child's diet and fluid intake to promote normal elimination.

Resources

BOOKS

Barbour, Ann, et al. *Prop Box Play: 50 Themes to Inspire Dramatic Play*. Beltsville, MD: Gryphon House Inc., 2002.

Cassou, Michelle. *Kids' Play—Igniting Children's Creative Passion*. East Rutherford, NJ: Penguin Group, 2004.

Drake, Jane. *Organizing Play in the Early Years: Practical Ideas for Teachers and Assistants*. Philadelphia: Taylor & Francis Inc., 2003.

Humphrey, James Harry. *Learning the 3 Rs through Active Play*. Hauppauge, NY: Nova Science Publishers Inc., 2001.

Scarlett, W. George. *Children's Play*. Thousand Oaks, CA: Sage Publications, 2004.

PERIODICALS

Schulman, Lisa. "Good guys, bad guys: Pretend play." *Parents Magazine*. (June 2003): 169–70.

WEB SITES

Games Kids Play. Available online at <www.gameskidsplay.net> (accessed October 13, 2004).

Aliene S. Linwood, RN, DPA, FACHE

PMS *see* **Premenstrual syndrome**

Pneumonia

Definition

Pneumonia is an infection of the lungs that can be caused by nearly any class of organism known to cause human infections, including bacteria, viruses, fungi, and parasites. It results in an inflammatory response within the small air spaces of the lung (alveoli).

Description

Pneumonia can develop gradually in children after exposure to the causative organism, or it can develop quickly after another illness, reducing the lungs' ability to receive and distribute oxygen. It can be mild and easily cured with **antibiotics** and rest, or it can be severe and require **hospitalization**. The onset, duration, and severity of pneumonia depend upon the type of infective organism invading the body and the response of the child's immune system in fighting the infection. Respiratory distress represents 20 percent of all admissions of children to hospitals, and pneumonia is the underlying cause of most of these admissions.

To understand pneumonia, it is important to understand the basic anatomic features of the respiratory system. The human respiratory system begins at the nose and mouth, where air is breathed in (inspired) and out (expired). The nasopharynx is the air tube extending from the nose that directs air into the lungs. Air breathed in through the mouth travels through the oropharynx, which also carries swallowed food, water, and salivary secretions through the food tube (esophagus) and then into the stomach. The nasopharynx and oropharynx merge into the larynx, which is protected by a trap door called the epiglottis. The epiglottis normally prevents substances that have been swallowed, as well as substances that have been regurgitated (vomited), from heading down through the larynx into the lungs.

The larynx flows into the trachea, which is the broadest part of the respiratory tract. The trachea divides into the right and left bronchi, each branching off into multiple smaller bronchi that course throughout the lung tissue. Each bronchus divides into tubes of smaller and smaller diameter, finally ending in the terminal bronchioles. The alveoli, in which oxygen and carbon dioxide are exchanged, are clustered at the ends of the bronchioles. Lung stroma, the tissue of the lung, serves a supportive role for the bronchi, bronchioles, and alveoli.

The main function of the respiratory system is to help distribute oxygen, the most important energy source for the body's cells. Oxygen enters the body as inspired air and travels through the respiratory system to the alveoli. The oxygen is then picked up by hemoglobin, the oxygen-carrying protein in red blood cells, and delivered throughout the body through the circulatory system. Oxygen in the inspired air is exchanged within the alveoli of the lungs for carbon dioxide, a waste product of human metabolism. Carbon dioxide leaves the lungs during expiration.

The healthy human lung is sterile, with no normally resident bacteria or viruses, unlike the upper respiratory system and parts of the gastrointestinal system, where bacteria dwell even in a healthy state. Multiple safeguards along the path of the respiratory system are designed to keep invading organisms from causing infection. The first line of defense includes tiny hairs in the nostrils that filter out large particles. The epiglottis helps prevent food and other swallowed substances from entering the larynx and the trachea. Sneezing and coughing, both provoked by the presence of irritants within the respiratory system, help to clear such irritants from the respiratory tract. Mucus produced through the respiratory system also serves to trap dust and infectious organisms. Tiny hair like projections (cilia) from cells lining the respiratory tract beat constantly to move debris trapped by mucus upwards and out of the respiratory tract. This mechanism of protection is referred to as the mucociliary escalator. Finally, cells lining the respiratory tract produce several types of immune substances that protect against various organisms. Other cells (macrophages) along the respiratory tract surround and kill invading organisms.

Organisms that cause pneumonia, then, are usually prevented from entering the lungs by virtue of these host defenses. However, when a large number of organisms are encountered at once or when the immune system is weakened, the usual defenses may be overwhelmed and infection may occur. This can happen either by inhaling contaminated air droplets or by the aspiration of organisms inhabiting the upper airways. Aspiration pneumonia is a type of pneumonia in which something is aspirated from the upper airway into the lungs. This can be food from the mouth, a foreign object or substance that has entered the mouth, or regurgitated stomach contents (vomitus) aspirated into the lungs as it travels to the mouth.

The invading organism causing pneumonia provokes an immune response in the lungs that causes inflammation of the lung tissue (pneumonitis), a condition that actually makes the lung environment more ideal for infection. Small blood vessels in the lungs (capillaries) begin to empty protein-rich fluid into the alveoli, a condition that results in a less functional area for oxygen-carbon dioxide exchange. The individual becomes relatively oxygen deprived, while retaining potentially damaging carbon dioxide. This results in rapid respiration (tachypnea or faster and faster breathing) in an effort to bring in more oxygen and blow off more carbon dioxide.

Consolidation, a feature of bacterial pneumonia, occurs when the alveoli, which are normally hollow air spaces within the lung, instead become solid due to quantities of fluid and debris. Viral pneumonias and mycoplasma pneumonias do not result in consolidation. These types of pneumonia primarily infect the walls of the alveoli and the stroma of the lung. Bacterial and viral pneumonia occur mostly in winter months, while mycoplasma pneumonia is more common in summer and fall.

Bacterial pneumonia develops after the child inhales or aspirates pathogens. Viral pneumonia stems primarily from inhaling infected droplets from the upper airway into the lungs. In neonates, pneumonia may result from colonization of the infant's nasopharynx by organisms that were in the birth canal at the time of delivery.

In addition to exposure to sufficient quantities of causative organisms, certain other conditions can increase the risk of pneumonia. These include the following:

- abnormal anatomical structure, particularly of the chest or lungs
- cigarette smoke, inhaled directly by a smoker or second-hand
- immune system deficiencies (**common variable immunodeficiency**, **immunoglobulin deficiency syndromes**, **HIV infection**, and others)
- swallowing difficulties as a result of **stroke** or seizures
- intoxication by alcohol and drugs that may interfere with normal **cough** reflex and decrease the chance of clearing unwanted debris from the respiratory tract
- viruses that may interfere with ciliary function, allowing themselves or other invading microorganisms such as bacteria access to the lower respiratory tract
- various chronic conditions such as **asthma**, **cystic fibrosis**, diabetes, emphysema, and neuromuscular diseases that may interfere with the seal of the epiglottis
- advanced age and associated immune system weakness
- esophageal disorders that may result in stomach contents passing upwards
- genetic factors and associated changes in DNA
- post-operative complications including the use of certain therapeutic drugs, suppressed cough reflex, breathing difficulties, and **pain** at the surgical site that affects breathing
- malnutrition
- radiation treatment for breast **cancer**, which may weaken lung tissue

The epidemic of immmunodeficiency virus (HIV), the virus that causes acquired **immunodeficiency** syndrome (**AIDS**), has resulted in a huge increase in the incidence of pneumonia. Because AIDS results in immune system suppression, individuals with AIDS are highly susceptible to all kinds of pneumonia, including some previously rare parasitic types that would not cause illness in someone with a normal immune system.

Pneumonia is also the most common fatal infection acquired by already hospitalized patients. Even in nonfatal cases, pneumonia is a significant economic burden on the healthcare system. One study estimates that U.S. workers who develop pneumonia cost employers five times as much in health care as the average worker.

Transmission

Pneumonia is not usually passed from one person to another. The bacterial and viral organisms that cause pneumonia, however, can be transmitted through airborne or direct contact.

Demographics

Every year in the United States, two million people of all ages develop pneumonia, including 4 percent of all the children in the country. It is the sixth most common disease leading to death and the fourth leading cause of death in the elderly; 40,000 to 70,000 people die from pneumonia each year. The incidence of pneumonia in children younger than one year of age is 35 to 40 per 1,000; 30 to 35 per 1,000 children ages two to four; and 15 per 1,000 children between ages five and nine. Fewer than 10 children in 1,000 over age nine are reported to develop pneumonia. The Centers for Disease Control and Prevention (CDC) reports that the number of deaths from pneumonia in the United States declined between 2001 and 2004.

Causes and symptoms

The list of organisms that can cause pneumonia is lengthy and includes nearly every class of infecting organism: viruses, bacteria, bacteria-like organisms, fungi, and parasites (including certain worms). Different organisms are more frequently encountered by different age groups, and other individual characteristics may increase risk for infection by particular types of organisms:

- Viruses cause the majority of pneumonias in young children, especially respiratory syncytial virus, parainfluenza and **influenza** viruses, and adenovirus.
- Adults are more frequently infected with bacteria such as *Streptococcus pneumoniae*, *Haemophilus influenzae*, and *Staphylococcus aureus*.
- Pneumonia in older children and young adults is often caused by the bacteria-like *Mycoplasma pneumoniae*, the cause of pneumonia that is often called "walking" pneumonia.
- *Pneumocystis carinii* causes pneumonia in immunosuppressed individuals such as patients being treated with **chemotherapy** or people with AIDS. Classically

considered a parasite, it appears to be more related to fungi.

- *Chlamydia psittaci* can be infective in some individuals, such as poultry farm workers, who have direct contact with bird droppings.

Pneumonia is suspected in a child who has symptoms such as **fever**, cough, chest pain, difficulty breathing (shortness of breath or dyspnea), and an increased number of breaths per minute (respiration). Fever with a shaking chill is even more suspicious. Mucus production is typically increased and leaky capillaries in the lungs may tinge the mucus with blood. The alveoli fill further with fluid and debris from the large number of white blood cells being produced to fight the infection. Children may cough up clumps of sputum or phlegm, secretions produced in the alveoli during the infection or inflammatory condition. These clumps may appear streaked with pus or blood. In severe pneumonia, mucus plugs and the accumulation of fluid together decrease the efficiency of gas exchange in the lung, resulting in signs of oxygen deprivation. Reduced oxygen levels in the blood may produce a blue appearance of the nail beds or lips (cyanosis).

Diagnosis

Diagnosis is based on the parents' report of the onset of illness and the symptoms that have developed, combined with examination of the chest. Physical examination may indicate labored breathing. Listening with a stethoscope may reveal abnormal crackling sounds (rales), and tapping on the back, which normally yields a resonant sound due to air filling the alveoli, may yield a dull thump if the alveoli are filled with fluid and debris.

Laboratory diagnostic tests may include staining sputum samples on a glass slide and looking at the stained specimen under a microscope to determine if white cells, red cells, or bacteria are present. Identification of the specific type of bacteria may require culturing the sputum, a microbiological technique that identifies disease-causing bacterial organisms in infected material. A small sample of sputum will be streaked on a special plate filled with medium that allows the specific organism to be grown in the laboratory under certain conditions. The bacteria can then be identified and, by performing antibiotic sensitivity tests on the bacteria, appropriate treatment can usually be prescribed. In addition, oxygen and carbon dioxide levels may be measured (blood gases) and the exchange evaluated (oximetry).

If pneumonia is present, a rapid rate of respiration may be noted; tachypnea is defined as a respiratory rate over 50 respirations per minute in infants younger than

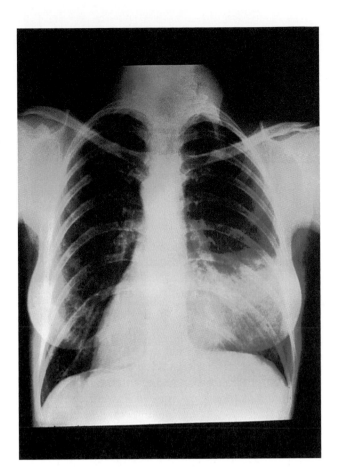

A chest x ray showing pneumonia in the lower lobe of a patient's right lung. The alveoli (air sacs) of the lung become blocked with pus, which forces air out and causes the lung to become solidified. *(National Audubon Society Collection/Photo Researchers, Inc.)*

one year. Older children will have tachypnea if the respiratory rate is greater than 40 per minute.

X-ray examination of the chest may reveal certain abnormal changes associated with pneumonia. Localized shadows obscuring areas of the lung may indicate a bacterial pneumonia, while streaky or patchy changes in the x-ray film may indicate viral or mycoplasma pneumonia. These changes on x ray, however, are known to lag in time behind actual symptoms.

Treatment

Prior to the discovery of penicillin and other antibiotics, bacterial pneumonia was almost always fatal. In the early 2000s, especially given early in the course of the disease, antibiotics are very effective against bacterial causes of pneumonia. Penicillin was, as of 2004, still the first choice for treating children with pneumonia unless the child is known to be penicillin-resistant. Oral

KEY TERMS

Alveoli—The tiny air sacs clustered at the ends of the bronchioles in the lungs in which oxygen-carbon dioxide exchange takes place.

Aspiration—The process of removing fluids or gases from the body by suction. Also refers to the inhalation of food or liquids into the lungs.

Cilia—Tiny hairlike projections on certain cells within the body. Cilia produce lashing or whipping movements to direct or cause motion of substances or fluids within the body. Within the respiratory tract, the cilia act to move mucus along, in an effort to continually flush out and clean the respiratory tract.

Consolidation—A condition in which lung tissue becomes firm and solid rather than elastic and air-filled, arising because of accumulated fluids and tissue debris.

Culture—A test in which a sample of body fluid is placed on materials specially formulated to grow microorganisms. A culture is used to learn what type of bacterium is causing infection.

Cyanosis—A bluish tinge to the skin that can occur when the blood oxygen level drops too low.

Pneumocystis carinii—An organism that causes pneumonia in immunodeficient individuals, such as people with AIDS.

Respiratory system—The organs that are involved in breathing: the nose, the throat, the larynx, the trachea, the bronchi and the lungs. Also called the respiratory tract.

Sputum—The substance that is coughed up from the lungs and spit out through the mouth. It is usually a mixture of saliva and mucus, but may contain blood or pus in patients with lung abscess or other diseases of the lungs.

Stroma—A term used to describe the supportive tissue surrounding a particular structure. An example is the tissue that surrounds and supports the actually functional lung tissue.

Tachypnea—Rapid breathing.

amoxicillin or cephalosporins are often administered first in treating milder cases of pneumococcal pneumonia in children younger than age five, though they are not used in newborns. Erythromycin and tetracycline are broad-spectrum antibiotics that are known to improve recovery time for symptoms of mycoplasma pneumonia.

They do not, however, eradicate the organisms. If the results of culture and sensitivity positively identify the causative bacteria, an antibiotic is prescribed for that demonstrated sensitivity. Viruses do not usually respond to antibiotics. Amantadine and acyclovir may be helpful against certain viral pneumonias.

Linezolid (Zyvox), the first of a new line of antibiotics known as oxazolidinones, is used to treat penicillin-resistant organisms that cause pneumonia. Another newer drug known as ertapenem (Invanz) is reported to be effective in treating bacterial pneumonia.

The child is also be given fluids and possibly drug therapy to thin mucus secretions (mucolytic agents) or medication to open the airways of the lung (brochodilators). **Cough suppressants** may be given as well as pain medication and fever-reducing medication. Hospitalized children may receive extra oxygen, respiratory therapy, and intravenous antibiotics and fluids.

Alternative treatment

Vitamin C is known to improve immune response and to help reduce inflammation. Grape seed extract enhances immune system functioning and helps protect lung tissue. These are adjunctive measures that do not destroy the causative organism as antibiotics do. Although garlic and certain herbs such as yerba mansa may have antibiotic properties, they cannot replace specific antibiotics used to treat pneumonia.

Prognosis

Prognosis varies according to the type of organism causing the infection, the status of the immune system, and the overall health of the affected child. Generally, there are lower mortality rates from pneumonia in the United States than elsewhere in the world. *Streptococcus pneumoniae*, the most common organism causing pneumonia, has a significantly lower death rate of about 5 percent. More complications occur in the very young or very old with multiple areas of the lung infected simultaneously. The presence of chronic illnesses such as diabetes, cirrhosis, and congestive heart failure may increase the chance of complications. Individuals with immunodeficiency disorders, various types of cancer, or AIDS are also more prone to complications. In children, cystic fibrosis, aspiration problems, immunodeficiencies, and congenital or acquired lung malformation may increase the risk of pneumonia from *S. pneumoniae*.

Recovery following pneumonia with *Mycoplasma pneumoniae* is nearly 100 percent. However, in the very young or very old or immunodeficient, *Staphylococcus aureus* has a death rate of 30 to 40 percent. Similarly, infections with a number of gram negative bacteria (such as those in the gastrointestinal tract that can cause infection following aspiration) have a death rate of 25 to 50 percent.

Prevention

Because many bacterial pneumonias occur in people who were first infected with the influenza virus (the flu), yearly flu vaccinations can decrease the risk of pneumonia for the elderly and children or adults with chronic diseases such as asthma, cystic fibrosis, other lung or heart diseases, **sickle cell anemia**, diabetes, kidney disease, and cancer.

A specific vaccine against *Streptococcus pneumoniae* can be protective for people with chronic illnesses.

Immunodeficient individuals are at higher risk for infection with *Pneumocystis carinii* and are frequently put on a regular preventive drug regimen of trimethoprim sulfa and/or inhaled pentamidine to avoid pneumocystis pneumonia.

Parental concerns

Pneumonia in a child can produce severe symptoms that can be frightening to both the child and parents, particularly when breathing is compromised or cyanosis is noted. When symptoms seem to suggest pneumonia, immediate attention allows early treatment so that breathing difficulties can be corrected quickly and drug therapy begun in order to destroy the causative organism. Parents can try to reassure young children and keep them as calm as possible, knowing that **anxiety** also increases breathing difficulties.

See also Common variable immunodeficiency.

Resources

BOOKS

"Pneumonia." Section 6, Chapter 73 in *The Merck Manual of Diagnosis and Therapy*, edited by Mark H. Beers and Robert Berkow. Whitehouse Station, NJ: Merck Research Laboratories, 2003.

ORGANIZATIONS

American Lung Association. 1740 Broadway, New York, NY 10019. Web site: <www.lungusa.org>.

Centers for Disease Control and Prevention. 1600 Clifton Rd., NE, Atlanta, GA 30333. Web site: <www.cdc.gov>.

WEB SITES

Cantu, Santos, Jr. "Pneumonia, Mycoplasma." *eMedicine*, July 13, 2001. Available online at <www.emedicine.com/EMERG/topic467.htm> (accessed November 22, 2004).

National Heart Lung and Blood Institute (NHLBI), Available online at <www.nhlbi.nih.gov> (accessed November 22, 2004).

L. Lee Culvert
Rosalyn Carson-DeWitt, MD
Rebecca J. Frey, PhD

Poison ivy, oak, and sumac

Definition

Poison ivy, oak, and sumac are allergic skin **rashes** (or *Rhus dermatitis*) caused by the plants of the same name. All three plants secrete a potent, irritating oil known as urushiol that causes blistering and intense **itching** once it penetrates the skin.

Description

The allergic rash of poison ivy, oak, and sumac is characterized by red, weeping blisters and severe itching. The rash usually appears within one to two days of initial contact with the plant oil, although it may take longer to appear in areas where the skin is thicker, and lasts from one to three weeks (longer in severe cases). It starts as itchy, inflamed red patches or streaks, and as the oil penetrates into the skin, blisters and small papules form.

Poison plant rash cannot be spread from person to person by contact with the rash itself or fluid from the blisters, and scratching does not spread the rash (although it can cause scarring and potential infection). Only urushiol oil can cause the rash.

Transmission

Urushiol oil or resin is found in the leaves, roots, and woody parts (i.e., vines and stems) of the poison ivy, oak, and sumac plants. It is a clear substance that is released by the plant when it is cut or bruised. Leaves are bruised easily, especially in the spring, so even a gentle brush against a plant can cause the urushiol to seep out and onto the skin.

Urushiol can remain active for years. For that reason, even dead poison ivy, oak, or sumac plants must be handled with care. Plants should never be burned or shredded, as airborne particles can spread the oil to sensitive areas like the face and eyes and may potentially cause damage to lungs.

The three main sources of poison plant rash—poison ivy, poison oak, and poison sumac—are members of the *Anacardiaceae*, or cashew, family. While they are usually concentrated most heavily in a few specific regions of the country, all three have been found in locations throughout the United States. Identifying the plant, particularly if people live in a wooded area or have a lot of vegetation in their yards or neighborhood, is essential to preventing the rash.

Poison ivy, known as *Rhus radicans* or *Toxicondendron radicans*, is found throughout the United States. The plant grows in vines (typical in the Midwest, East coast, and South) or small bushes (in the North, West, and Great Lakes region), and has clusters of three leaves. (Hence the popular saying: "Leaves of three, let them be.") The leaves are red in the spring; green throughout the summer; and yellow, red, and orange in the fall when they also produce white berries.

Poison oak is a small shrub. The plant, which is also known as *Rhus diversiloba* or *Toxicondendron diversilobum*, is found in the western United States. Like poison ivy, poison oak leaves change color with the seasons. The plant also produces white berries in the fall.

The small, woody shrubs that are poison sumac are most common in the Eastern United States. Also known as *Rhus vernix* or *Toxicondendron vernix*, poison sumac differs in appearance from the three-leaf clusters of poison ivy and oak. It is feather-like in appearance, with two rows of leaves arranged on either side of a long stem, topped off by a long leaf at the tip. It can be distinguished from regular, non-poisonous sumac by its berries, which are green to white as opposed to the bright red berries of regular sumac.

Demographics

According to the American Academy of Dermatology, an estimated 85 percent of the population is allergic to the urushiol oil found in poison ivy, oak, and sumac. Every year up to 50 million Americans develop a poison ivy, oak, or sumac rash. The chance of developing an allergic sensitivity to these poison plants decreases with age, and adults who have never been exposed to urushiol only have a 50 percent chance of developing **contact dermatitis** when exposed to poison ivy, oak, or sumac.

In addition, allergic sensitivity to poison plants tends to lessen with age. It is possible for children who are highly reactive to urushiol to grow into adults who are barely sensitive to poison ivy, oak, or sumac, regardless of how many times they have been exposed to the plant oil.

Causes and symptoms

While direct skin-to-plant contact with poison ivy, oak, or sumac is probably the most frequent cause of the rash, the irritants from the plants can also be passed on indirectly. Urushiol oil can be transmitted on clothing, pets, garden tools, shoes, or virtually anything that touches a plant.

Most children will not get a rash the very first time they are exposed to poison ivy, oak, or sumac, although this is when the sensitivity, or immune response, to urushiol develops. Not everyone acquires an allergic sensitivity to urushiol, but in those that do, the next time they are exposed to the plant and urushiol penetrates the skin, a rash is inevitable.

The first and most annoying symptom of a poisonous plant rash is severe itching. This may precede the rash or start at the same time as the rash appears. The rash, which is red and inflamed, usually begins to appear within two days after the initial exposure and is usually in a pattern of streaks or patches that approximates where the plant made contact with the skin. Blisters and/or red papules may form soon after the rash appears.

When to call the doctor

Mild cases of poison plant rash can usually be treated at home with over-the-counter creams and itch-relief measures, such as ice packs. A child who is not getting adequate relief from these treatments should see a doctor. Prescription cortisone cream or prednisone treatment may be necessary to relieve the itching.

Anyone who is experiencing symptoms of anaphylactic shock (such as difficulty breathing, **dizziness**, **nausea**, rash, swelling, itchy eyes, loss of consciousness) after exposure to poison ivy, oak, or sumac should be taken to the nearest hospital or emergency care facility for immediate treatment. Poison plant rashes that spread to the eyes and affect vision should also be treated by a doctor as soon as possible. If rash blisters are broken while scratching and begin to show signs of infection (for example, **pain**, swelling, puss, systemic **fever**), a doctor should examine them as soon as possible in case **antibiotics** are necessary.

Diagnosis

Poison plant rashes are diagnosed through an examination of the rash. A physician can distinguish poison ivy, oak, or sumac from other allergic contact **dermatitis** through a brief patient interview. If the contact with the plant was direct, the diagnosis may be obvious. If it was indirect (for example, from dog fur or garden tools), the doctor may need to rule out other **allergies**, especially if there were other new potential allergens in the child's environment (for example, a new pet, food, soap, or medication).

Treatment

Treatments for the itching of poison ivy, oak, or sumac rashes range from calamine lotion and oatmeal baths to over-the-counter **antihistamines** and topical creams. Mild rashes may be relieved with a tub soak in baking soda solution, an oatmeal bath, or aluminum acetate (Domeboro solution). Calamine lotion and menthol ointments lessen the itching and dry out weeping blisters. Over-the-counter hydrocortisone creams and ointments and numbing sprays and lotions containing benzocaine and other anesthetic agents can relieve itching as well.

Benadryl and other oral antihistamines are also effective in soothing the discomfort and itch of poison plant rashes, but they can also cause drowsiness and are best used before bedtime.

In severe cases of poison plant rash, a prescription-strength cortisone cream or corticosteroid treatment (either oral or injections) may be required to relieve swelling and itching. These medications should be taken under a doctor's supervision according to the directions for use only for the period of time prescribed, as overuse of corticosteroid creams has the potential of interfering with a child's normal growth and development. Corticosteroid treatment may not be a preferred treatment in children with diabetes, as the drug has the potential of increasing blood glucose levels.

There are several lotions and creams on the market that remove urushiol oil from the skin and can prevent further spreading of the rash if oil remains, or even prevent the rash entirely if applied early enough following exposure. Rubbing (isopropyl) alcohol can also remove urushiol on both skin and household objects.

Alternative treatment

The sap of the jewelweed plant (*Impatiens capensis*) is thought to be helpful in binding to and removing urushiol from skin. Either the plant itself (which grows wild in the Eastern United States, particularly in damp environments) can be rubbed on exposed skin, or a soap product made from Jewelweed (e.g., Burt's Bees Poison Ivy Soap) can be used to wash away urushiol. The plant must be used shortly after exposure to poison ivy, oak, or sumac to work.

A soak in tea tree oil (*Melaleuca alternaifolia*) or the application of gel from the aloe vera plant can also be

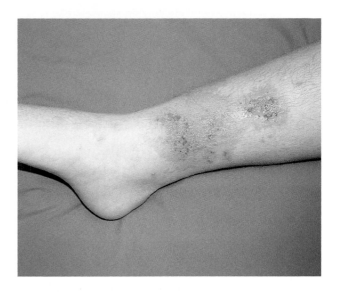

Poison ivy rash. (© *Scott Camazine/Photo Researchers, Inc.*)

useful in alleviating itching and in drying the blisters of poison plant rash. Tea tree oil also has antiseptic properties and may be useful in warding off infection when poison plant rash blisters break. Jewelweed, tea tree oil, and aloe vera are not recognized by the U.S. Food and Drug Administration as treatments for poison plant rash.

Prognosis

The rash of poison ivy, oak, or sumac may last anywhere from a week to three weeks. In severe cases, it may linger up to a month. Usually there is no long-term effects or skin damage, but scratching that breaks the skin could potentially lead to permanent scarring. Infections can occur if blisters break and bacteria enters the open wound. Keeping the rash clean and any open blisters bandaged can lessen the chance of infection.

If urushiol enters the respiratory tract, which typically happens when the plant is burned and the smoke is breathed in, it can be life threatening. Anyone who encounters this type of exposure to poison ivy, oak, or sumac should seek emergency medical care immediately.

Prevention

Children should be advised to stay out of areas where poison ivy, oak, or sumac is known to grow. When people are hiking or camping, exposed skin should be covered with long sleeves and pants. There are several topical skin creams on the market that contain bentoquatum, which forms a protective barrier designed to repel urushiol oil (e.g., Ivy Block, Stokoguard). These may be a useful preventative tool against poison plant rash as well.

If exposure does occur, washing with soap and cool water within the first 30 minutes of contact can sometimes prevent a rash. If soap is not available, rinse with water alone. A full body shower is best to eliminate all traces of the urushiol and prevent re-exposure from undetected oil remaining on other parts of the body. Again, water should be cool, as warm water will open pores and allow urushiol to penetrate the skin more quickly.

Other over-the-counter skin cleansers formulated to remove urushiol oil (e.g. Tecnu, IvyStat, IvyCleanse) can also stop or lessen the severity of a rash if they are applied early enough following exposure (i.e., before the urushiol begins penetrating the skin). These products can also be used to decontaminate garden tools and other items that have come in contact with the plant oil. Rubbing alcohol (isopropyl alcohol) is also helpful in decontaminating objects and skin.

Any clothing that has been exposed to poisonous plants should be handled carefully and laundered immediately. The same goes for shoes and garden gloves, which are common culprits of harboring urushiol oil. If possible, use latex or other disposable gloves to handle contaminated items and throw them away immediately afterwards.

Pet fur can also carry urushiol oil into the home. People should make sure outdoor pet areas are free of poisonous plants and never let a dog run unleashed in the woods or other areas with dense vegetation. Pets are typically not sensitive to urushiol, but a dog or cat that seems to be experiencing symptoms of poison plant rash following exposure should be taken to the veterinarian for **assessment**.

Eliminating known poison ivy, oak, or sumac growth in the yard or garden is also an important preventative step, but eradicating the weeds can be difficult. Glyphosate-based herbicides like Roundup and triclopyr-based herbicides like Ortho Brush-B-Gon will kill poison plants, but they can also take out any other surrounding foliage they come into contact with. If herbicides are used they should be applied carefully and may have to be rubbed directly on to the leaves and stems to avoid damaging other plantings.

Another option for eliminating poison plants is to pull them by hand. Proper protection of all exposed skin is important to prevent a reaction. The entire plant, including the root system, must be pulled. As an alternative, landscaping fabric or another barrier can be placed over poison ivy, oak, or sumac to kill the plants and pre-

vent future growth. Dead plants still contain urushiol and must be handled carefully during removal. All plants should be disposed of according to local waste regulations. Never compost or burn poison plants because of the potential of spreading the oil through the garden or air. Mowing over the vines or plants can also send urushiol into the air and has the potential to cause a serious allergic reaction.

Parental concerns

The itching and discomfort of poison ivy, oak, and sumac rashes can disrupt **sleep**, make a child irritable and anxious, and pose a major distraction to schoolwork and other tasks that require concentration.

Soothing the itching is the best way to help a child get through the misery of a poisonous plant rash. Covering the affected areas with bandages may be useful in curtailing scratching and preventing potential scarring. A child's fingernails should be kept clean and trimmed short to lessen the chance of bursting and infecting blisters if scratching does occur.

Resources

BOOKS

Hauser, Susan Carol. *Outwitting Poison Ivy*. Guilford, CT: The Lyons Press, 2001.

Ratner-Connolly, Heidi, and Randy Connolly. *Poison Ivy, Pets, & People*. Brookings, OR: 2Lakes Press, 2003.

PERIODICALS

Allen, Patricia L. Jackson. "Leaves of three, let them be: if it were only that easy!" *Pediatric Nursing* 30 (March- April 2004): 129–35.

Krautwurst, Terry. "The ITCH and You." *Mother Earth News* (June 2001): 24–26, 86.

> ## KEY TERMS
>
> **Corticosteroids**—A group of hormones produced naturally by the adrenal gland or manufactured synthetically. They are often used to treat inflammation. Examples include cortisone and prednisone.
>
> **Papule**—A solid, raised bump on the skin.
>
> **Urushiol**—The oil from poison ivy, oak, and sumac that causes severe itching, blistering, and rash.

Sadovsky, Richard. "Poison Ivy, Oak, and Sumac Contact Dermatitis." *American Family Physician* 61 (June 1, 2000): 3408.

Thornton, Jim. "An itch for all seasons." *National Geographic Adventure* 4 (November 2002): 36.

ORGANIZATIONS

Find a Dermatologist. American Academy of Dermatology, PO Box 4014, Schaumburg, IL 60168–4014. Web site: <www.aad.org/>.

WEB SITES

Beaulieu, David. "Get Rid of Poison Ivy." *About Landscaping.* Available online at <www.landscaping.about.com/cs/weedsdiseases/a/poison_ivy_3.htm> (accessed November 30, 2004).

Sachs, John. "What Poison Ivy Looks Like." Available online at <www.poison-ivy.org/> (accessed November 30, 2004).

Paula Ford-Martin

Poisoning

Definition

Poisoning occurs when any substance interferes with normal body functions after it is swallowed, inhaled, injected, or absorbed. The branch of medicine that deals with the detection and treatment of poisons is known as toxicology.

Description

Children are the most common victims of poisoning in the United States. Curiosity, inability to read warning labels, a desire to imitate adults, and inadequate supervision lead to most childhood poisonings.

The elderly are the second most likely group to be poisoned. Mental confusion, poor eyesight, and the use of multiple drugs are the leading reasons this group has a high rate of accidental poisoning. A substantial number of poisonings also occur as **suicide** attempts or drug overdoses.

Poisons are common in the home and workplace, yet there are basically two major types. One group consists of products that were never meant to be ingested or inhaled, such as shampoo, paint thinner, pesticides, houseplant leaves, and carbon monoxide. The other group contains products that can be ingested in small quantities, but which are harmful if taken in large amounts, such as pharmaceuticals, medicinal herbs, or alcohol. Other types of poisons include the bacterial toxins that cause **food poisoning**, such as *Escherichia coli*; heavy metals, such as the lead found in the paint on older houses; and the venom found in the **bites and stings** of some animals and insects. The staff at a poison control center and emergency room doctors have the most experience diagnosing and treating poisoning cases.

Demographics

Poisonings are a common occurrence. About 10 million cases of poisoning occur in the United States each year. In 80 percent of the cases, the victim is a child under the age of five. About 50 children die each year from poisonings.

Causes and symptoms

The effects of poisons are as varied as the poisons themselves; however, the exact mechanisms of only a few are understood. Some poisons interfere with the metabolism. Others destroy the liver or kidneys, such as heavy metals and some **pain** relief medications, including **acetaminophen** and **nonsteroidal anti-inflammatory drugs** (ibuprofen). A poison may severely depress the central nervous system, leading to coma and eventual respiratory and circulatory failure. Potential poisons in this category include anesthetics (e.g. ether and chloroform), opiates (e.g., morphine and codeine), and barbiturates. Some poisons directly affect the respiratory and circulatory system. Carbon monoxide causes death by binding with hemoglobin that would normally transport oxygen throughout the body. Certain corrosive vapors trigger the body to flood the lungs with fluids, effectively drowning the person. Cyanide interferes with respiration at the cellular level. Another group of poisons interferes with the electrochemical impulses that travel between neurons in the nervous system. Yet another group, including cocaine, ergot, strychnine, and some snake venoms, causes potentially fatal seizures.

Severity of symptoms can range from **headache** and **nausea** to convulsions and death. The type of poison, the amount and time of exposure, and the age, size, and health of the victim are all factors which taken together determine the severity of symptoms and the chances for recovery.

Plant poisoning

There are more than 700 species of poisonous plants in the United States. Plants are second only to medicines in causing serious poisoning in children under age five. There is no way to tell by looking at a plant if it is poisonous. Some plants, such as the yew shrub, are almost entirely toxic: needles, bark, seeds, and berries. In other plants, only certain parts are poisonous. The bulb of the hyacinth and daffodil are toxic, but the flowers are not; while the flowers of the jasmine plant are the poisonous part. Moreover, some plants are confusing because portions of them are eaten as food while other parts are poisonous. For example, the fleshy stem (tuber) of the potato plant is nutritious, however, its roots, sprouts, and vines are poisonous. The leaves of tomatoes are poisonous, while the fruit is not. Rhubarb stalks are good to eat, but the leaves are poisonous. Apricots, cherries, peaches, and apples all produce healthful fruit, but their seeds contain a form of cyanide that can kill a child if chewed in sufficient quantities. One hundred milligrams (mg) of moist, crushed apricot seeds can produce 217 mg of cyanide.

Common houseplants that contain some poisonous parts include the following:

- aloe
- amaryllis
- cyclamen
- dumb cane (also called Dieffenbachia)
- philodendron

Common outdoor plants that contain some poisonous part include the following:

- bird of paradise flower
- buttercup
- castor bean
- chinaberry tree
- daffodil
- English ivy
- eucalyptus
- foxglove
- holly
- horse chestnut
- iris
- jack-in-the-pulpit
- jimsonweed (also called thornapple)
- larkspur
- lily-of-the-valley
- morning glory
- nightshade (several varieties)

- oleander
- potato
- rhododendron
- rhubarb
- sweet pea
- tomato
- wisteria
- yew

Symptoms of plant poisoning range from irritation of the skin or mucous membranes of the mouth and throat to nausea, **vomiting**, convulsions, irregular heartbeat, and even death. It is often difficult to tell if a person has eaten a poisonous plant because there are no tell-tale empty containers and no unusual lesions or odors around the mouth.

Many cases of plant poisoning involve plants that contain hallucinogens, such as peyote cactus buttons, certain types of mushrooms, and marijuana. Poisoning has occurred with *Datura*, or moonflower, a plant that has become popular with young people trying to imitate Native American **puberty** rites.

Other cases of plant poisoning result from the use of herbal dietary supplements that have been contaminated by toxic substances. The Food and Drug Administration (FDA) has the authority to monitor herbal products on the market and issue warnings about accidental poisoning or other adverse affects associated with these products. For example, in 2002 a manufacturer of nettle capsules found to contain lead recalled the product following a warning from the FDA. Other dietary supplements have been found to contain small quantities of prescription medications or even toxic plants.

Household chemicals

Many products used daily in the home are poisonous if swallowed. These products often contain strong acids or strong bases (alkalis). Toxic household cleaning products include the following:

- ammonia
- bleach
- dishwashing liquids
- drain openers
- floor waxes and furniture polishes
- laundry detergents, spot cleaners, and fabric softeners
- mildew removers
- oven cleaners

- toilet bowl cleaners

Personal care products found in the home can also be poisonous. These include:

- deodorant
- hairspray
- hair straighteners
- nail polish and polish remover
- perfume
- shampoo

Signs that a person has swallowed one of these substances include evidence of an empty container nearby, nausea or vomiting, and **burns** on the lips and skin around the mouth if the substance is a strong acid or alkali. The chemicals in some of these products may leave a distinctive odor on the breath.

Pharmaceuticals

Both over-the-counter and prescription medicines can help the body heal if taken as directed. However, when taken in large quantities, or with other drugs with which there may be an adverse interaction, they can act as poisons. Drug overdoses, both accidental and intentional, are the leading cause of poisoning in adults. Medicinal herbs should be treated like pharmaceuticals and taken only in designated quantities under the supervision of a knowledgeable person. Herbs that have healing qualities when taken in small doses can be toxic in larger doses or may interact with prescription medications in unpredictable ways.

Drug overdoses cause a range of symptoms, including excitability, sleepiness, confusion, unconsciousness, rapid heartbeat, convulsions, nausea, and changes in blood pressure. The best initial evidence of a drug overdose is the presence of an empty container near the victim.

Other causes of poisonings

People can be poisoned by fumes they inhale. Carbon monoxide is the most common form of inhaled poison. Other toxic substances that can be inhaled include:

- farm and garden insecticides and herbicides
- gasoline fumes
- insect repellent
- paint thinner fumes

When to call the doctor

A doctor or poison control center should be called if any form of poisoning is suspected or if children or other persons behave in an odd manner.

Diagnosis

Initially, poisoning is suspected if the victim shows changes in behavior and signs or symptoms previously described. Hallucinations or other psychiatric symptoms may indicate poisoning by a hallucinogenic plant. Evidence of an empty container or information from the victim is helpful in determining exactly what substance has caused the poisoning. Some acids and alkalis leave burns on the mouth. Petroleum products, such as lighter fluid or kerosene, leave a distinctive odor on the breath. The vomit may be tested to determine the exact composition of the poison. Once hospitalized, the person may be given blood and urine tests to determine his or her metabolic condition.

Treatment

Treatment for poisoning depends on the poison swallowed or inhaled. Contacting the poison control center or hospital emergency room is the first step in getting proper treatment. The poison control center's telephone number is often listed with emergency numbers on the inside cover of the telephone book, or it can be reached by dialing the operator. The poison control center will ask for specific information about the victim and the poison then give appropriate first aid instructions. If the person is to be taken to a hospital, a sample of vomit and the poison container should be taken along, if they are available.

For acid, alkali, or petroleum product poisonings, the person should not vomit. Acids and alkalis can burn the esophagus if they are vomited, and petroleum products can be inhaled into the lungs during vomiting, resulting in **pneumonia**.

Once the victim is under medical care, doctors have the option of treating the person with a specific remedy to counteract the poison (antidote) or with activated charcoal to absorb the substance inside the individual's digestive system. In some instances, pumping the stomach may be required. This technique, which is known as gastric lavage, involves introducing 20 to 30 mL of tap water or 9 percent saline solution into the person's digestive tract and removing the stomach contents with a siphon or syringe. The process is repeated until the washings are free of poison. Medical personnel will also provide supportive care as needed, such as intravenous fluids or mechanical ventilation.

If the doctor suspects that the poisoning was not accidental, he or she is required to notify law enforcement authorities. Most cases of malicious poisoning concern **family** members or acquaintances of the victim, but the number of intentional random poisonings of the general public has increased in the late 1990s and early 2000s. A case reported in 2003 involved the use of nicotine to poison 1,700 pounds of ground beef in a Michigan supermarket. Over 100 persons fell ill after eating the poisoned beef.

Prognosis

The outcome of poisoning varies from complete recovery to death and depends on the type and amount of the poison, the health of the victim, and the speed with which medical care is obtained.

Prevention

Most accidental poisonings are preventable. The number of deaths of children from poisoning has declined from about 450 per year in the 1960s to about 50 each year in the 1990s. This decline has occurred mainly because of better packaging of toxic materials and better public education.

Actions to prevent poisonings include:

- removing plants that are poisonous
- keeping medicines and household chemicals locked and in a place inaccessible to children
- keeping medications in child-resistant containers
- never referring to medicine as candy
- keeping cleaners and other poisons in their original containers
- disposing of outdated prescription medicines
- not purchasing over-the-counter medications with damaged protective seals or packaging
- avoiding the use of herbal preparations not made by a reputable manufacturer

Parental concerns

Parents should monitor the activities and substances to which their children are exposed. The number of the nearest Poison Control Center should be posted next to every telephone in the house. The number can be found on the first page of any telephone book.

KEY TERMS

Antidote—A remedy to counteract a poison or injury. Also refers to a substance which cancels the effect of homeopathic remedies

Emetic—A medication intended to cause vomiting. Emetics are sometimes used in aversion therapy in place of electric shock. Their most common use in mainstream medicine is in treating accidental poisoning.

Gastric lavage—Also called a stomach pump. For this procedure, a flexible tube is inserted through the nose, down the throat, and into the stomach and the contents of the stomach are suctioned out. The inside of the stomach is rinsed with a saline (salt water) solution.

Toxicology—The branch of medical pharmacology dealing with the detection, effects, and antidotes of poisons.

Resources

BOOKS

Hu, Howard. "Heavy Metal Poisoning." In *Harrison's Principles of Internal Medicine*, 15th ed. Edited by Eugene Braunwald et al. New York: McGraw-Hill, 2001, pp. 2590–4.

Klaasen, Curtis D. *Casarett and Doull's Toxicology: The Basic Science of Poisons*, 6th ed. New York: McGraw-Hill, 2001.

Linden, Christopher H., and Michael J. Burns. "Poisoning and Drug Overdosage." In *Harrison's Principles of Internal Medicine*, 15th ed. Edited by Eugene Braunwald et al. New York: McGraw-Hill, 2001, pp. 2595–615.

Robertson, William O. "Chronic Poisoning: Trace Metals and Others." In *Cecil Textbook of Medicine*, 22nd ed. Edited by Lee Goldman et al. Philadelphia: Saunders, 2003, 91–9.

Rodgers, George C., and Nancy J. Matyunas. "Poisonings: Drugs, Chemicals and Plants." In *Nelson Textbook of Pediatrics*, 17th ed. Edited by Richard E. Behrman et al. Philadelphia: Saunders, 2003, pp. 2362–74.

Salerno, Denise A., and Stephen C. Aronoff. "Non-bacterial Food Poisoning." In *Nelson Textbook of Pediatrics*, 17th ed. Edited by Richard E. Behrman et al. Philadelphia: Saunders, 2003, pp. 2375–7.

PERIODICALS

Dahlgren, J. G., et al. "Health effects of diazinon on a family." *Journal of Toxicology. Clinical Toxicology* 42, no. 5 (2004): 579–91.

Munidasa, U. A., et al. "Survival pattern in patients with acute organophosphate poisoning receiving intensive care." *Journal of Toxicology. Clinical Toxicology* 42, no. 4 (2004): 343–7.

Richardson, W. H., et al. "A case of type F botulism in southern California." *Journal of Toxicology. Clinical Toxicology* 42, no. 4 (2004): 383–7.

Vanarsdale, J. L., et al. "Lead Poisoning from a Toy Necklace." *Pediatrics* 114, no. 4 (2004): 1096–9.

ORGANIZATIONS

American Academy of Clinical Toxicology. 777 East Park Dr., PO Box 8820, Harrisburg, PA 17105–8820. Web site: <www.clintox.org/index.html>.

American Academy of Emergency Medicine. 611 East Wells St., Milwaukee, WI 53202. Web site: <www.aaem.org/>.

American Academy of Family Physicians. 11400 Tomahawk Creek Parkway, Leawood, KS 66211–2672. Web site: <www.aafp.org/>.

American Academy of Pediatrics. 141 Northwest Point Blvd., Elk Grove Village, IL 60007–1098. Web site: <www.aap.org/default.htm>.

American Association of Poison Control Centers. 3201 New Mexico Ave., NW, Washington, DC 20016. Web site: <www.aapcc.org/>.

American College of Emergency Physicians. PO Box 619911, Dallas, TX 75261–9911. Web site: <www.acep.org/>.

American College of Occupational and Environmental Medicine. 55 West Seegers Rd., Arlington Heights, IL 60005. Web site: <www.acoem.org/>.

American College of Osteopathic Emergency Physicians. 142 E. Ontario St., Suite 550, Chicago, IL 60611. Web site: <www.acoep.org/>.

WEB SITES

"About Food Poisoning." *Virginia Department of Agriculture & Consumer Services.* Available online at <www.vdacs.virginia.gov/foodsafety/poisoning.html> (accessed December 22, 2004).

"Childhood Lead Poisoning Prevention Program." *Centers for Disease Control and Prevention.* Available online at <www.cdc.gov/nceh/lead/lead.htm>(accessed December 22, 2004).

"Diseases and Disorders: Links Pertaining to Poisoning." *Karolinska Institute.* Available online at <www.mic.ki.se/Diseases/C21.613.html> (accessed December 22, 2004).

"Mushroom Poisoning in Children." *American Academy of Family Practice.* Available online at <http://familydoctor.org/129.xml> (accessed December 22, 2004).

"Poisoning." *MedlinePlus.* Available online at <www.nlm.nih.gov/medlineplus/poisoning.html> (accessed December 22, 2004).

"Poisoning." *The Merck Manual.* Available online at <www.merck.com/mrkshared/mmanual/section23/chapter307/307a.jsp> (accessed December 22, 2004).

"Signs and Symptoms of Pesticide Poisoning." *University of Nebraska Cooperative Extension.* Available online at <http://ianrpubs.unl.edu/Pesticides/ec2505.htm> (accessed December 22, 2004).

L. Fleming Fallon, Jr., MD, DrPH

Polio

Definition

Poliomyelitis, also called polio or infantile paralysis, is a highly infectious viral disease that may attack the central nervous system and is characterized by symptoms that range from a mild nonparalytic infection to total paralysis in a matter of hours.

Description

There are three known types of polioviruses (called 1, 2, and 3), each causing a different strain of the disease and all being members of the viral family of enteroviruses (viruses that infect the gastrointestinal tract). Type 1 is the cause of epidemics, and many cases of paralysis, which is the most severe manifestation of the infection. The virus is usually a harmless parasite of human beings. Some statistics quote one in 200 infections as leading to paralysis, while others state that one in 1,000 cases reach the central nervous system (CNS). When it does reach the CNS, inflammation and destruction of the spinal cord motor cells (anterior horn cells) occurs, which prevents them from sending out impulses to muscles. This causes the muscles to become limp or soft, and they cannot contract, a condition called flaccid paralysis and is the type found in polio. The extent of the paralysis depends on where the virus strikes and the number of cells that it destroys. Usually, some of the limb muscles are paralyzed; the abdominal muscles or muscles of the back may be paralyzed, affecting posture. The neck muscles may become too weak for the head to be lifted. Paralysis of the face muscles may cause the mouth to twist or the eyelids to droop. Life may be threatened if paralysis of the throat or of the breathing muscles occurs.

Humans are the only natural host for polioviruses, and it most commonly infects younger children, although older children and adults can be infected. Crowded living conditions and poor hygiene encourage the spread of poliovirus. Risk factors for this paralytic illness include older age, pregnancy, abnormalities of the immune system, and a recent episode of excessively strenuous **exercise** concurrent with the onset of the CNS phase. As of 2004, the last naturally occurring polio case in the United States was diagnosed in 1979.

Causes and symptoms

Poliovirus can be spread by direct exposure to an infected individual, and more rarely, by eating foods contaminated with waste products from the intestines (feces) and/or droplets of moisture (saliva) from an infected person. Thus, the major route of transmission is fecal-oral, which occurs primarily with poor sanitary conditions. The virus is believed to enter the body through the mouth with primary multiplication occurring in the lymphoid tissues in the throat, where it can persist for about one week. During this time, it is absorbed into the blood and lymphatics from the gastrointestinal tract where it can reside and multiply, sometimes for as long as 17 weeks. Once absorbed, it is widely distributed throughout the body until it ultimately reaches the CNS (the brain and spinal cord). The infection is passed on to others when poor hand washing allows the virus to remain on the hands after eating or using the bathroom. Transmission remains possible while the virus is being excreted and it can be transmitted for as long as the virus remains in the throat or feces. The incubation period ranges from three to 21 days, but cases are most infectious from seven to ten days before and after the onset of symptoms.

There are two basic patterns to the virus: the minor illness (abortive type) and the major illness (which may be paralytic or nonparalytic). The minor illness accounts for 80 to 90 percent of clinical infections and is found mostly in young children. It is mild and does not involve the CNS. Symptoms include a slight **fever**, fatigue, **headache**, **sore throat**, and **vomiting**, which generally develop three to five days after exposure. Recovery from the minor illness occurs within 24 to 72 hours. Symptoms of the major illness usually appear without a previous minor illness and generally affect older children and adults.

About 10 percent of people infected with poliovirus develop severe headache and **pain** and stiffness of the neck and back. This is due to an inflammation of the meninges (tissues which cover the spinal cord and brain). This syndrome is called aseptic **meningitis**. The term aseptic is used to differentiate this type of meningitis from those caused by bacteria. The patient usually recovers completely from this illness within several days.

About 1 percent of people infected with poliovirus develop the most severe form. Some of these patients may have two to three symptom-free days between the minor illness and the major illness, but the symptoms often appear without any previous minor illness. Symptoms again include headache and back and neck pain. The major symptoms, however, are due to invasion of the motor nerves, which are responsible for movement of the muscles. This viral invasion causes inflammation and then destruction of these nerves. The muscles, therefore, no longer receive any messages from the brain or spinal cord. The muscles become weak, floppy, and then totally paralyzed. All muscle tone is lost in the affected limb and the muscle becomes soft (flaccid). Within a few days, the muscle begins to decrease in size (atrophy). The affected muscles may be on both sides of the body (symmetric paralysis) but are often on unbalanced parts of the body (asymmetric paralysis). Sensation or the ability to feel is not affected in these paralyzed limbs.

When poliovirus invades the brainstem (the stalk of brain which connects the two cerebral hemispheres with the spinal cord, called bulbar polio), a person may begin to have trouble breathing and swallowing. If the brainstem is severely affected, the brain's control of such vital functions as heart rate and blood pressure may be disturbed, a condition that can lead to death.

The maximum state of paralysis is usually reached within just a few days. The remaining, unaffected nerves then begin the process of attempting to grow branches, which can compensate for the destroyed nerves. Fortunately, the nerve cells are not always completely destroyed. By the end of a month, the nerve impulses start to return to the apparently paralyzed muscle and by the end of six months, recovery is almost complete. If the nerve cells are completely destroyed; however, paralysis is permanent.

Diagnosis

Fever and asymmetric flaccid paralysis without sensory loss in a child or young adult almost always indicate poliomyelitis. Using a long, thin needle inserted into the lower back to withdraw spinal fluid (lumbar puncture) will reveal increased white blood cells and no bacteria (aseptic meningitis). Nonparalytic poliomyelitis cannot be distinguished clinically from aseptic meningitis due to other agents. Virus isolated from a throat swab and/or feces or blood tests demonstrating the rise in a specific antibody is required to confirm the diagnosis.

Treatment

There is no specific treatment for polio except symptomatic. Therapy is designed to make the patient more comfortable (pain medications and hot packs to soothe the muscles), and intervention if the muscles responsible for breathing fail (for instance, a ventilator to take over the work of breathing). During active infection, rest on a firm bed is indicated. Physical therapy is the most important part of management of paralytic polio during recovery.

Prognosis

When poliovirus causes only the minor illness or simple aseptic meningitis, the patient can be expected to recover completely. Among patients with the major illness, about 50 percent recover completely. About 25 percent of such patients have slight disability, and about 25 percent have permanent and serious disability. Approximately 1 percent of all patients with major illness die. The greatest return of muscle function occurs in the first six months, but improvements may continue for two years.

Post-polio syndrome (PPS) is a condition that can strike polio survivors anywhere from 10 to 40 years after their recovery from polio. It is caused by the death of individual nerve terminals in the motor units that remain after the initial polio attack. Symptoms include fatigue, slowly progressive muscle weakness, muscle and joint pain, and muscular atrophy. The severity of PPS depends upon how seriously the survivors were affected by the first polio attack.

Prevention

There are two types of polio immunizations available in the United States, but since the year 2000, one is rarely used. A vaccine takes advantage of the fact that infection with polio leads to an immune reaction, which will give the person permanent, lifelong immunity from reinfection with the form of poliovirus for which the person was vaccinated.

The Salk vaccine (also called the killed **polio vaccine** or inactivated polio vaccine, IPV) consists of a ser-

---

KEY TERMS

Aseptic—Sterile; containing no microorganisms, especially no bacteria.

Asymmetric—Not occurring equally on both sides of the body.

Atrophy—The progressive wasting and loss of function of any part of the body.

Brainstem—The stalk of the brain which connects the two cerebral hemispheres with the spinal cord. It is involved in controlling vital functions, movement, sensation, and nerves supplying the head and neck.

Epidemic—Refers to a situation in which a particular disease rapidly spreads among many people in the same geographical region in a relatively short period of time.

Flaccid—Flabby, limp, weak, or floppy.

Gastrointestinal—Pertaining to the digestive organs and structures, including the stomach and intestines.

Lymph—Clear, slightly yellow fluid carried by a network of thin tubes to every part of the body. Cells that fight infection are carried in the lymph.

Paralysis—Loss of the ability to move one or more parts of the body voluntarily due to muscle or nerve damage.

Symmetric—Occurring on both sides of the body, in a mirror-image fashion.

---

ies of three shots that are given just under the skin to children at the ages of two months, four months, and any time between six and 18 months. A fourth injection is given between the ages of four to six years as a booster. This immunization contains no live virus, just the components of the virus that provoke the recipient's immune system to react as if the recipient were actually infected with the poliovirus. The recipient thus becomes immune to infection with the poliovirus.

Since the year 2000, the Sabin vaccine (also called the oral polio vaccine or OPV) has been discontinued in the United States, although it is still being used in other countries. It contains the live, but weakened, poliovirus and because OPV uses the live virus, it has the potential to cause infection in individuals with weak immune defenses (both in the person who receives the vaccine and in close contacts). Approximately nine cases a year of vaccine related polio was associated with OPV in the United States. Although this is a rare complication, occurring in only one in 6.8 million doses administered and one in every 6.4 million doses from having close contact with someone who received the vaccine, the risk of having polio from OPV was greater than it was of naturally acquiring it.

Following the launching of the Global Polio Eradication Initiative, the number of cases fell 99 percent from an estimated 350,000 cases to less than 3,500 cases worldwide in 2000. At the end of 2000, the number of polio-infected countries was approximately 20, down from 125. The goal of the World Health Organization (WHO) is to have polio eliminated from the planet by the year 2005. The virus has still been identified in Africa and parts of Asia, so travelers to those areas may want to check with their physicians concerning booster vaccinations.

Resources

BOOKS

Oshinsky, David. *Polio: An American Story.* Oxford, UK: Oxford University Press, 2004.

PERIODICALS

Alexander, L. N., et al. "Vaccine Policy Changes and Epidemiology of Poliomyelitis in the United States" *Journal of the American Medical Association* 292 (2004): 1696–1701.

ORGANIZATION

International Polio Network. 4207 Lindell Blvd., Suite 110, St. Louis, MO 63108–2915. Web site: <www.post-polio.org>.

March of Dimes Birth Defects Foundation. National Office, 1275 Mamaroneck Avenue, White Plains, NY 10605. Web site: <www.modimes.org/>.

WEB SITES

World Health Organization. *Global Polio Eradication Progress 2004.* Available online at <www.polioeradication.org/>.

Linda K. Bennington, MSN,CNS

Polio vaccine

Definition

The poliomyelitis (**polio**) vaccine protects against poliovirus infections. The vaccine helps the body produce antibodies (protective substances) that will prevent an individual from contracting polio. There are two

forms of the vaccine that can be given; the one preferred is the inactivated poliovirus vaccine (IPV). IPV is preferred because it contains the inactivated or dead virus, which is considered safer for administration. The Sabin oral polio vaccine was made with a live but weakened virus, which gives the advantage of passive immunity for large groups (i.e. because it is easily passed on through the oral fecal route in households, schoolrooms, etc., even if only a portion of the community is immunized, everyone eventually develops immunity). The Sabin oral polio vaccine has the disadvantage of causing polio-like symptoms in some immune compromised hosts. Since 2000, the live virus vaccine is rarely used in the United States, but it is still being used in other countries.

Description

The purpose of any vaccine is to prevent disease. Mass immunizations in the United States have served to eradicate polio in the Americas. In 1988, the World Health Organization embarked upon a mission to eradicate polio by the year 2000. The intent was to immunize the world's children by methodically establishing sites where the masses could be reached. The mandate was to eradicate the virus by 2005. Most of the remaining virus can be found on the Indian subcontinent and Nigeria. Attempts to immunize children in Indian have met with good results, but Nigeria halted their immunization sites due to rumors that Western donors had tampered with the vaccine to spread HIV and cause sterility in Muslim males. Following a ban on the vaccine that lasted nearly one year, the virus spread across Nigeria to 10 African countries that were previously polio-free. The Muslim leaders in Nigeria lifted the ban in summer 2004. Immunization from the IPV triggers an excellent immune response and long-lasting immunity to all three poliovirus types.

General use

The inactivated poliovirus vaccine is injected into a muscle or under the skin and is usually given by a health care professional in a hospital, clinic, or provider's office. The use of this vaccine must be officially recorded. Federal law requires that the vaccine manufacturer's name, the lot number of the vaccine, the name, address, and phone number of the person giving the vaccine, and the date of vaccine administration be recorded in a permanent medical record. For children, the vaccine is usually started at two months of age and given again at four months of age. The next dose should be given between six and 18 months of age with a final booster dose at age four to six years, for a total of four doses. Serious reactions to the inactivated poliovirus vaccine are rare in small children. It is necessary to receive all doses of the vaccine and there is no generic vaccine available.

Precautions

Individuals with an immune deficiency disease need to be counseled before taking the vaccine, and anyone with allergic reactions to prior vaccines and preservatives should be cautious. A provider may want to delay giving a child a dose of IPV or may not give it at all if the child has a known severe allergy to the **antibiotics** neomycin, streptomycin, or polymyxin B. A child who had a life-threatening reaction to a previous IPV should not receive another one.

There is no preparation necessary for the vaccine; however, if an individual is ill on the scheduled date, it is essential to make arrangements for a follow-up appointment as no dose can be missed.

Side effects

Children receiving the inactivated poliovirus vaccine should be carefully observed for 24–72 hours after receiving the injection. If any serious side effects occur, the healthcare provider or an emergency service provider should be called immediately. For problems that may occur following the vaccine, parents are asked to call the vaccine adverse event reporting system toll-free at (800) 822–7967 to report them. The health care professional may administer a dose of a non-aspirin pain/fever reliever at the time of the vaccine and advise giving the medicine every four to six hours for 24 hours after the vaccine. This may serve to reduce **pain** and **fever** associated with the vaccine.

Side effects that usually do not require immediate medical attention, unless they persist and are bothersome, include:

• fussiness

• decreased appetite

• low-grade fever (102°F [39° C] or less)

• pain, tenderness, redness, swelling, or a "knot" at the injection site

• fatigue

• vomiting

Side effects that should be reported as soon as possible are:

• limp, pale, or less alert child

• difficulty breathing, shortness of breath, or wheezing

• difficulty swallowing

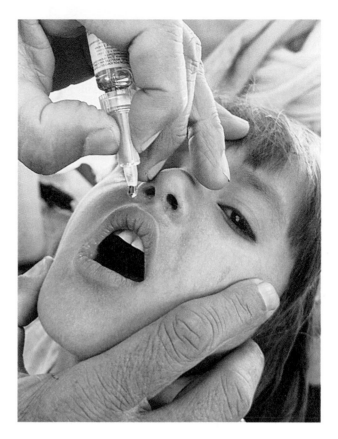

Oral polio vaccines are no longer recommended for use in the United States, but are still used in many parts of the world. (© Reuters/Corbis)

• high fever (103°F [39.4°C] or more)

• inconsolable crying for three hours or more

• seizures (convulsions)

• severe skin rash, **hives**, or itching

• swelling of eyes or face

• unusual sleepiness

Interactions

Before administering the vaccine, the healthcare provider should be informed as to whether the recipient has any of the following conditions:

• an immune deficiency (natural or due to **cancer chemotherapy** radiation, steroid therapy, or HIV infection)

• fever or infection

• an unusual reaction to this poliovirus vaccine, oral poliovirus vaccine, other medicines, foods, dyes, or preservatives

- pregnant or trying to get pregnant
- breastfeeding

Prevention

While it is important to mention these items to the physician, they are not necessarily contraindications for the vaccine. The provider also needs to know what medicines an individual is taking, including non-prescription medicines, nutritional supplements, herbal products, tobacco, and whether or not he or she is a user of illegal drugs or a frequent user of drinks with **caffeine** or alcohol. Any of these may affect the way the vaccine works.

Risks

There have been no adverse effects from IPV reported to date. However, IPV induces only little immunity in the intestinal tract. If an individual is infected with the wild-type poliovirus, the virus can multiply in the intestines and be shed in stools, ultimately heightening the risk of viral circulation within the community. This scenario is unlikely in the United States.

Parental concerns

Parents need to be aware of any existing **allergies** in their families that might cause a reaction from vaccines and their preservatives, and they need to be observant of a child for the first 24–72 hours after receiving the vaccine. Traveling to other parts of the world may necessitate a booster vaccine if the polio virus is known to be present in that vicinity.

See also Polio.

Resources

BOOKS

*2004 Childhood and Adolescent Immunization Schedule.*Atlanta: GA, Centers for Disease Control and Prevention, 2004. <www.cdc.gov/nip/recs/child-schedule.htm#Printable>

PERIODICALS

Osterrieth, Paul. "Oral polio vaccine: fact vs. fiction." *Vaccine* 22 (2004): 1831–35. <www.elsevier.com/locate/vaccine>

ORGANIZATIONS

March of Dimes Birth Defects Foundation. National Office, 1275 Mamaroneck Avenue, White Plains, NY 10605.

WEB SITES

"Polio Vaccine." <familydoctor.org/x1998.xml>.

World Health Organization. Global Polio Eradication Progress 2000.

Linda K. Bennington, MSN, CNS

Polydactyly and syndactyly

Definition

Polydactyly and syndactyly are congenital malformations of the fingers and/or toes. Polydactyly is the presence of extra fingers or toes, and syndactyly is the fusing together or webbing of two or more fingers or toes.

Description

Polydactyly and syndactyly can vary in the degree of severity. Polydactyly may range from small skin tags on the side of the hands to fully formed extra fingers with bone, blood vessels, and muscle tissue. Polydactyly is classified as postaxial if the extra digit is located beside the little finger or preaxial if the extra digit is located near the thumb. Syndactyly may be either a complete fusion of fingers or toes or a looser webbing of skin between them. Syndactyly and polydactyly may occur simultaneously when extra digits are fused in a condition known as polysyndactyly. Polydactyly and syndactyly are usually isolated conditions, meaning the child will have no other birth defects; however, both are also found in many complex and sometimes lethal groups of anomalies or syndromes.

Demographics

Syndactyly of the fingers is the most common malformation affecting the hand. It occurs in approximately one in 2,000 live births. Postaxial polydactyly, or an extra pinky finger, is the second most common malformation of the hand, occurring in approximately one in 3,000 births. Polydactyly of the toes, especially of the little toe, is also a common malformation, occurring in approximately two in 1,000 births. Thirty percent of all children with polydactyly have **family** members with some type of polydactyly, and it is more common in African Americans. Syndactyly is an equally common malformation and runs in families as well.

Causes and symptoms

Polydactyly and syndactyly are conditions that occur in the developing fetus. Most often these conditions are caused by genetic factors. Both polydactyly and syndactyly can be caused by the presence of an autosomal dominant trait. An autosomal dominant trait is a gene that is not related to the chromosome that determines gender; therefore, it affects boys and girls equally. Because the gene is dominant, when one parent has the gene, each of his or her children has a 50 percent chance of having polydactyly or syndactyly.

The primary symptom of polydactyly is the presence of extra digits on the hands or feet. Polydactyly rarely causes any difficulties for the child. The extra fingers and/or toes are usually removed for cosmetic reasons. In children with syndactyly of the hand, finger function may be impaired and, in cases where fingers of different lengths are connected by tissue, finger growth may be limited unless surgery to separate the fingers is performed.

Diagnosis

Diagnosis is made during the initial physical examination at birth. Some children with polydactyly will need radiographs or x rays to determine if there is bone present in the extra digit. This will indicate what type of surgery is necessary to remove the extra finger or toe. When polydactyly is more severe and involves digits with bone, a pediatric orthopedic surgeon will perform the repair. In children with syndactyly, the surgeon must determine if the fusion involves muscle tissue and blood vessels, and in children with severe polydactyly of the fingers, a surgeon specializing in hands may evaluate the child as well. Some children with syndactyly may also have cardiac or heart problems; therefore, an electrocardiogram (EKG) may be ordered to evaluate heart function.

Treatment

For children with minor cases of polydactyly, the extra finger or toe may be tied at its base to restrict blood

Polydactyly is the occurrence of extra or partial fingers or toes. (Photograph by Joseph R. Siebert. Custom Medical Stock Photo, Inc.)

flow into it. Eventually the extra digit will fall off. In more significant cases, a pediatric orthopedic surgeon will remove the extra finger or toe and reconstruct the part of the hand or foot that was affected. The surgeon will save the digit that best fits with the others. This surgery usually occurs when the child is between one and two years old.

Prognosis

For children with isolated polydactyly and syndactyly, the prognosis is excellent. After surgery most children will have full use of their fingers and toes. In children with syndromes and additional birth defects, the prognosis may be poor; however, the problems these children may experience will not be related to polydactyly or syndactyly, but rather to the sometimes lethal conditions that accompany the other defects present.

Prevention

There is no known prevention for polydactyly and syndactyly.

Parental concerns

Parents may be concerned about their child's ability to use his hands and feet. For most children, surgery corrects the condition and allows normal use of the hands and feet. Parents may also be concerned about the appearance of the hands and feet. In most cases, following surgery, they will have a normal appearance.

Children with more severe polydactyly and syndactyly will have surgery to correct the malformation. These children will need to be prepared for the experience.

KEY TERMS

Autosomal dominant trait—One of the non-X or non-Y chromosomes that will always express itself when present.

Congenital—Present at birth.

Electrocardiagram (ECG, EKG)—A record of the electrical activity of the heart, with each wave being labeled as P, Q, R, S, and T waves. It is often used in the diagnosis of cases of abnormal cardiac rhythm and myocardial damage.

Gene—A building block of inheritance, which contains the instructions for the production of a particular protein, and is made up of a molecular sequence found on a section of DNA. Each gene is found on a precise location on a chromosome.

Malformation—An irregular or abnormal formation or structure.

Postaxial—Situated behind or away from the axis or midline of the body.

Preaxial—Situated in front of the axis or midline of the body.

Radiograph—The actual picture or film produced by an x-ray study.

Syndrome—A group of signs and symptoms that collectively characterize a disease or disorder.

Webbing—A tissue or membrane that connects two digits at their base or for the greater part of their length.

- Unexpected bleeding from the wound
- An oral temperature of over 101 degrees
- **Pain** that is nor relieved by pain medication
- A persistent dry cough
- Nausea or **vomiting** that does not improve
- Redness or swelling around the incision site

Resources

BOOKS

Behrman, Richard E., Robert M. Kliegman, and Hal B. Jenson, editors. *Nelson Textbook of Pediatrics.*16th ed. Philadelphia: W.B. Saunders Company, 2000.

Friedman, William F., and John S. Child. "Congenital Heart Disease in the Adult." In *Harrison's Principles of Internal Medicine,* edited by Anthony S. Fauci, et al. New York: McGraw-Hill, 1997.

Rudolph, Colin D., and Abraham M. Rudolph, editors. *Rudolph's Pediatrics.* 21st ed. New York: McGraw-Hill, 2003.

WEB SITES

Somerset Medical Center, "Pediatric Same Day Surgery," Somerset Medical Center, Somerville, NJ, <www.somersetmedicalcenter.com/body.cfm?id=380> (accessed August 11, 2004).

Deborah L. Nurmi,, MS

Polydactyly and syndactyly correction surgery is usually performed when the child is between the ages of one and two years. When talking to children of this age, tone of voice is as important as the words used. Using a calm and comforting voice and simple language, parents can tell the child what will happen. Young children should be told the day before surgery that they will be going to the hospital. Parents may want to use dolls or stuffed animals to show their child where the doctor will work. If a child must spend the night, it is helpful to bring a toy or familiar object to make the child feel more comfortable in the hospital. Afterwards, the child may reenact the experience during **play** or in **drawings**. Parents should be prepared to talk and play with their child in this way.

When to call the doctor

Following surgery, parents should call the doctor if any of these symptoms occur:

Porphyrias

Definition

The porphyrias are disorders in which the body produces too much porphyrin and insufficient heme (an iron-containing nonprotein portion of the hemoglobin molecule). Porphyrin is a foundation structure for heme and certain enzymes. Excess porphyrins are excreted as waste in urine and stool. Overproduction and overexcretion of porphyrins causes low, unhealthy levels of heme and certain important enzymes, creating various physical symptoms.

Description

Biosynthesis of heme is a multistep process that begins with simple molecules and ends with a large, complex heme molecule. Each step of the chemical pathway is directed by its own task-specific protein, called an enzyme. As a heme precursor molecule moves through each step, an enzyme modifies the precursor in some way. If a precursor molecule is not modified, it cannot proceed to the next step, causing a buildup of that specific precursor.

This situation is the main characteristic of the porphyrias. Owing to a defect in one of the enzymes of the heme biosynthesis pathway, protoporphyrins or porphyrins (heme precursors) are prevented from proceeding further along the pathway. These precursors accumulate at the stage of the enzyme defect, causing an array of physical symptoms in an affected child. Specific symptoms depend on the point at which heme biosynthesis is blocked and which precursors accumulate. In general, the porphyrias primarily affect the skin and the nervous system. Symptoms can be debilitating or life threatening in some cases. Porphyria is most commonly an inherited condition. It can also, however, be acquired after exposure to poisonous substances.

Heme

Heme is produced in several tissues in the body, but its primary biosynthesis sites are the liver and the bone marrow. Heme synthesis for immature red blood cells, namely the erythroblasts and the reticulocytes, occurs in the bone marrow.

Although production is concentrated in the liver and bone marrow, heme is utilized in various capacities in virtually every tissue in the body. In most cells, heme is a key building block in the construction of factors that oversee metabolism and transport of oxygen and energy. In the liver, heme is a component of several vital enzymes, particularly cytochrome P450. Cytochrome P450 is involved in the metabolism of chemicals, **vitamins**, fatty acids, and hormones; it is very important in transforming toxic substances into easily excretable materials. In immature red blood cells, heme is the featured component of hemoglobin. Hemoglobin is the red pigment that gives red blood cells their characteristic color and their essential ability to transport oxygen.

Heme biosynthesis

The heme molecule is composed of porphyrin and an iron atom. Much of the heme biosynthesis pathway is dedicated to constructing the porphyrin molecule. Porphyrin is a large molecule shaped like a four-leaf clover. An iron atom is placed at its center point in the last step of heme biosynthesis.

The production of heme may be compared to a factory assembly line. At the start of the line, raw materials are fed into the process. At specific points along the line, an addition or adjustment is made to further development. Once additions and adjustments are complete, the final product rolls off the end of the line.

The heme "assembly line" is an eight-step process, requiring eight different and properly functioning enzymes:

1. delta-aminolevulinic acid synthase
2. delta-aminolevulinic acid dehydratase
3. porphobilogen deaminase
4. uroporphyrinogen III cosynthase
5. uroporphyrinogen decarboxylase
6. coproporphyrinogen oxidase
7. protoporphyrinogen oxidase
8. ferrochelatase

The control of heme biosynthesis is complex. Various chemical signals can trigger increased or decreased production. These signals can affect the enzymes themselves or the production of these enzymes, starting at the genetic level. For example, one point at which heme biosynthesis may be controlled is at the first step. When heme levels are low, greater quantities of delta-aminolevulinic acid (ALA) synthase are produced. As a result, larger quantities of heme precursors are fed into the biosynthesis pathway to step up heme production.

Porphyrias

Under normal circumstances, when heme concentrations are at an appropriate level, precursor production decreases. However, a glitch in the biosynthesis pathway—represented by a defective enzyme—means that heme biosynthesis does not reach completion. Because heme levels remain low, the synthesis pathway continues to churn out precursor molecules in an attempt to correct the heme deficit.

The net effect of this continued production is an abnormal accumulation of precursor molecules and development of some type of porphyria. Each type of porphyria corresponds with a specific enzyme defect and an accumulation of the associated precursor. Although there are eight steps in heme biosynthesis, there are only seven types of porphyrias; a defect in ALA synthase activity does not have a corresponding porphyria.

Enzymes involved in heme biosynthesis display subtle, tissue-specific variations; therefore, heme biosynthesis may be impeded in the liver, but normal in the immature red blood cells, or vice versa. Incidence of porphyria varies widely between types and occasionally by geographic location. Although certain porphyrias are more common than others, their greater frequency is only relative to other types. All porphyrias are considered to be rare disorders.

In the past, the porphyrias were divided into two general categories based on the location of the porphyrin production. Porphyrias affecting heme biosynthesis in the liver were referred to as hepatic porphyrias. Porphyrias that affect heme biosynthesis in immature red blood cells were referred to as erythropoietic porphyries. (Erythropoiesis is the process through which red blood cells are produced.) As of 2001, porphyrias are usually grouped into acute and non-acute types. Acute porphyrias produce severe attacks of **pain** and neurological effects. Non-acute porphyrias present as chronic diseases.

The acute porphyrias, and the heme biosynthesis steps at which enzyme defects occur, are:

- ALA dehydratase deficiency porphyria (step 2). This porphyria type is very rare. The inheritance pattern appears to be autosomal recessive. In autosomal recessively inherited disorders, a child must inherit two defective genes, one from each parent. A parent with only one gene for an autosomal recessive disorder does not display symptoms of the disease.

- Acute intermittent porphyria (step 3). Acute intermittent porphyria (AIP) is also known as Swedish porphyria, pyrroloporphyria, and intermittent acute porphyria. AIP is inherited as an autosomal dominant trait, which means that only one copy of the defective gene needs to be present for the disorder to occur. Simply inheriting this gene, however, does not necessarily mean that a child will develop the disease. Approximately five to 10 per 100,000 children in the United States carry a gene for AIP, but only 10 percent of these people, mostly teenage or older, ever develop symptoms of the disease.

- Hereditary coproporphyria (step 6). Hereditary coproporphyria (HCP) is inherited in an autosomal dominant manner. As with all porphyrias, it is an uncommon ailment. By 1977, only 111 cases of HCP were recorded; in Denmark, the estimated incidence is two in one million people.

- Variegate porphyria (step 7). Variegate porphyria (VP) is also known as porphyria variegata, protocoproporphyria, South African genetic porphyria, and Royal malady (supposedly King George III of England and Mary, Queen of Scots, suffered from VP). VP is inherited in an autosomal dominant manner and is especially prominent in South Africans of Dutch

descent. Among that population, the incidence is approximately three in 1,000 persons. It is estimated that there are 10,000 cases of VP in South Africa. Interestingly, it appears that the affected South Africans are descendants of two Dutch settlers who came to South Africa in 1680. Among other populations, the incidence of VP is estimated to be one to two cases per 100,000 persons.

The non-acute porphyrias, and the steps of heme biosynthesis at which they occur, are:

- Congenital erythropoietic porphyria (step 4). Congenital erythropoietic porphyria (CEP) is also called Gunther's disease, erythropoietic porphyria, congenital porphyria, congenital hematoporphyria, and erythropoietic uroporphyria. CEP is inherited in an autosomal recessive manner. It is a rare disease, estimated to affect fewer than one in one million people. Onset of dramatic symptoms usually occurs in infancy, but may hold off until adulthood.

- Porphyria cutanea tarda (step 5). Porphyria cutanea tarda (PCT) is also called symptomatic porphyria, porphyria cutanea symptomatica, and idiosyncratic porphyria. PCT may be acquired, typically as a result of disease (especially hepatitis C), drug or alcohol use, or exposure to certain poisons. PCT may also be inherited as an autosomal dominant disorder, however most people remain latent—that is, symptoms never develop. PCT is the most common of the porphyrias, but the incidence of PCT is not well defined. However, PCT does not typically develop in children.

- Hepatoerythopoietic porphyria (step 5). Hepatoerythopoietic porphyria (HEP) affects heme biosynthesis in both the liver and the bone marrow. HEP results from a defect in uroporphyrinogen decarboxylase activity (step 5), and is caused by defects in the same gene as PCT. Disease symptoms, however, strongly resemble congenital erythropoietic porphyria. HEP seems to be inherited in an autosomal recessive manner.

- Erythropoietic protoporphyria (step 8). Also known as protoporphyria and erythrohepatic protoporphyria, erythropoietic protoporphyria (EPP) is more common than CEP; more than 300 cases have been reported. In these cases, onset of symptoms typically occurred in childhood.

Causes and symptoms

General characteristics

The underlying cause of all porphyrias is a defective enzyme important to the heme biosynthesis pathway.

Porphyrias are inheritable conditions. In virtually all cases of porphyria, an inherited factor causes the enzyme's defect. An environmental trigger—such as diet, drugs, or sun exposure—may be necessary before any symptoms develop. In many cases, symptoms do not develop. These asymptomatic individuals may be completely unaware that they have a gene for porphyria.

All of the hepatic porphyrias—except porphyria cutanea tarda—follow a pattern of acute attacks separated by periods during which no symptoms are present. For this reason, this group is often referred to as the acute porphyrias. The erythropoietic porphyrias and porphyria cutanea tarda do not follow this pattern and are considered to be chronic conditions.

The specific symptoms of each porphyria vary based on which enzyme is affected and whether that enzyme occurs in the liver or in the bone marrow. The severity of symptoms can vary widely, even within the same type of porphyria. If the porphyria becomes symptomatic, the common factor between all types is an abnormal accumulation of protoporphyrins or porphyrin.

ALA dehydratase porphyria (ADP)

ADP is characterized by a deficiency of ALA dehydratase. ADP is caused by mutations in the delta-aminolevulinate dehydratase gene (ALAD) at 9q34. Being located at 9q34 means that it is on the long arm (q) of chromosome 9 in the 34 region. Of the few cases on record, the prominent symptoms are **vomiting**, pain in the abdomen, arms, and legs, and neuropathy. (Neuropathy refers to nerve damage that can cause pain, **numbness**, or paralysis.) The nerve damage associated with ADP could cause breathing impairment or lead to weakness or paralysis of the arms and legs.

Acute intermittent porphyria (AIP)

AIP is caused by a deficiency of porphobilinogen deaminase, which occurs due to mutations in the hydroxymethylbilane synthase gene (HMBS) located at 11q23.3. Symptoms of AIP usually do not occur unless a person with the deficiency encounters a trigger substance. Trigger substances can include hormones (for example **oral contraceptives**, **menstruation**, pregnancy), drugs, and dietary factors. Most people with this deficiency never develop symptoms.

Attacks occur after **puberty** and commonly feature severe abdominal pain, **nausea**, vomiting, and **constipation**. Muscle weakness and pain in the back, arms, and legs are also typical symptoms. During an attack, the urine is a deep reddish color. The central nervous system may also be involved. Possible psychological symptoms include hallucinations, confusion, seizures, and mood changes.

Congenital erythropoietic porphyria (CEP)

CEP is caused by a deficiency of uroporphyrinogen III cosynthase due to mutations in the uroporphyrinogen III cosynthase gene (UROS) located at 10q25.2-q26.3. Symptoms are often apparent in infancy and include reddish urine and possibly an enlarged spleen. The skin is unusually sensitive to light and blisters easily if exposed to sunlight. (Sunlight induces protoporphyrin changes in the plasma and skin. These altered protoporphyrin molecules can cause skin damage.) Increased hair growth is common. Damage from recurrent blistering and associated skin infections can be severe. In some cases facial features and fingers may be lost to recurrent damage and infection. Deposits of protoporphyrins can sometimes lead to red staining of the teeth and bones.

Porphyria cutanea tarda (PCT)

PCT is caused by deficient uroporphyrinogen decarboxylase. PCT is caused by mutations in the uroporphyrinogen decarboxylase gene (UROD) located at 1p34. PCT may occur as an acquired or an inherited condition. The acquired form usually does not appear until adulthood. The inherited form may appear in childhood, but often demonstrates no symptoms. Early symptoms include blistering on the hands, face, and arms following minor injuries or exposure to sunlight. Lightening or darkening of the skin may occur along with increased hair growth or loss of hair. Liver function is abnormal but the signs are mild.

Hepatoerythopoietic porphyria (HEP)

HEP is linked to a deficiency of uroporphyrinogen decarboxylase in both the liver and the bone marrow. HEP is an autosomal recessive disease caused by mutations in the gene responsible for PCT, the uroporphyrinogen decarboxylase gene (UROD), located at 1p34. The gene is shared, but the mutations, inheritance, and specific symptoms of these two diseases are different. The symptoms of HEP resemble those of CEP.

Hereditary coproporphyria (HCP)

HCP is similar to AIP, but the symptoms are typically milder. HCP is caused by a deficiency of coproporphyrinogen oxidase due to mutations in a gene by the same name at 3q12. The greatest difference between HCP and AIP is that people with HCP may have some skin sensitivity to sunlight. However, extensive damage to the skin is rarely seen.

Variegate porphyria (VP)

VP is caused by a deficiency of protoporphyrinogen oxidase. There is scientific evidence that VP is caused by mutation in the gene for protoporphyrinogen oxidase located at 1q22. Like AIP, symptoms of VP occur only during attacks. Major symptoms of this type of porphyria include neurological problems and sensitivity to light. Areas of the skin that are exposed to sunlight are susceptible to burning, blistering, and scarring.

Erythropoietic protoporphyria (EPP)

Owing to deficient ferrochelatase, the last step in the heme biosynthesis pathway—the insertion of an iron atom into a porphyrin molecule—cannot be completed. This enzyme deficiency is caused by mutations in the ferrochelatase gene (FECH) located at 18q21.3. The major symptoms of this disorder are related to sensitivity to light—including both artificial and natural light sources. Following exposure to light, a child with EPP experiences burning, **itching**, swelling, and reddening of the skin. Blistering and scarring may occur but are neither common nor severe. EPP is associated with increased risks for gallstones and liver complications. Symptoms can appear in childhood and tend to be more severe during the summer when exposure to sunlight is more likely.

Diagnosis

Depending on the array of symptoms a child may exhibit, the possibility of porphyria may not immediately come to a physician's mind. In the absence of a **family** history of porphyria, non-specific symptoms, such as abdominal pain and vomiting, may be attributed to other disorders. Neurological symptoms, including confusion and hallucinations, can lead to an initial suspicion of psychiatric disease. Diagnosis is more easily accomplished in cases in which non-specific symptoms appear in combination with symptoms more specific to porphyria, like neuropathy, sensitivity to sunlight, or certain other manifestations. Certain symptoms, such as urine the color of port wine, are hallmark signs very specific to porphyria. DNA analysis is not yet of routine diagnostic value.

A common initial test measures protoporphyrins in the urine. However, if skin sensitivity to light is a symptom, a blood plasma test is indicated. If these tests reveal abnormal levels of protoporphyrins, further tests are done to measure heme precursor levels in red blood cells and the stool. The presence and estimated quantity of porphyrin and protoporphyrins in biological samples are easily detected using spectrofluorometric testing. Spectrofluorometric testing uses a spectrofluorometer that directs light of a specific strength at a fluid sample. The porphyrins and protoporphyrins in the sample absorb the light energy and fluoresce, or glow. The spectrofluorometer detects and measures fluorescence, which indicates the amount of porphyrins and protoporphyrins in the sample.

Whether heme precursors occur in the blood, urine, or stool gives some indication of the type of porphyria, but more detailed biochemical testing is required to determine their exact identity. Making this determination yields a strong indicator of which enzyme in the heme biosynthesis pathway is defective; which, in turn, allows a diagnosis of the particular type of porphyria.

Biochemical tests rely on the color, chemical properties, and other unique features of each heme precursor. For example, a screening test for acute intermittent porphyria (AIP) is the Watson-Schwartz test. In this test, a special dye is added to a urine sample. If one of two heme precursors—porphobilinogen or urobilinogen—is present, the sample turns pink or red. Further testing is necessary to determine whether the precursor present is porphobilinogen or urobilinogen—only porphobilinogen is indicative of AIP.

Other biochemical tests rely on the fact that heme precursors become less soluble in water (able to be dissolved in water) as they progress further through the heme biosynthesis pathway. For example, to determine whether the Watson-Schwartz urine test is positive for porphobilinogen or urobilinogen, chloroform is added to the test tube. Chloroform is a water-insoluble substance. Even after vigorous mixing, the water and chloroform separate into two distinct layers. Urobilinogen is slightly insoluble in water, while porphobilinogen tends to be water-soluble. The porphobilinogen mixes more readily in water than chloroform, so if the water layer is pink (from the dye added to the urine sample), that indicates the presence of porphobilinogen, and a diagnosis of AIP is probable.

As a final test, measuring specific enzymes and their activities may be done for some types of porphyrias; however, such tests are not done as a screening method. Certain enzymes, such as porphobilinogen deaminase (the defective enzyme in AIP), can be easily extracted from red blood cells; other enzymes, however, are less readily collected or tested. Basically, an enzyme test involves adding a certain amount of the enzyme to a test tube that contains the precursor it is supposed to modify. Both the production of modified precursor and the rate at which it appears can be measured using laboratory equipment. If a modified precursor is produced, the test indicates that the enzyme is doing its job. The rate at which the modified precursor is produced can be compared to a standard to measure the efficiency of the enzyme.

Treatment

Treatment for porphyria revolves around avoiding acute attacks, limiting potential effects, and treating symptoms. Treatment options vary depending on the specific type of porphyria diagnosed. Gene therapy has been successful for both CEP and EPP. In the future, scientists expect development of gene therapy for the remaining porphyrias. Given the rarity of ALA dehydratase porphyria, definitive treatment guidelines for this rare type have not been developed.

Acute intermittent porphyria, hereditary coproporphyria, and variegate porphyria

Treatment for acute intermittent porphyria, hereditary coproporphyria, and variegate porphyria follows the same basic regime. A child who has been diagnosed with one of these porphyrias can prevent most attacks by avoiding precipitating factors, such as certain drugs that have been identified as triggers for acute porphyria attacks. Individuals must maintain adequate **nutrition**, particularly with respect to carbohydrates. In some cases, an attack can be stopped by increasing carbohydrate consumption or by receiving carbohydrates intravenously.

When attacks occur prompt medical attention is necessary. Pain is usually severe, and narcotic **analgesics** are the best option for relief. Phenothiazines can be used to counter nausea, vomiting, and **anxiety**, and chloral hydrate or diazepam is useful for sedation or to induce **sleep**. Hematin, a drug administered intravenously, may be used to halt an attack. Hematin seems to work by signaling the pathway of heme biosynthesis to slow production of precursors. Older girls, who tend to develop symptoms more frequently than boys owing to hormonal fluctuations, may find ovulation-inhibiting hormone therapy to be helpful.

Gene therapy is a possible future treatment for these porphyrias. An experimental animal model of AIP has been developed and research is in progress.

Congenital erythropoietic porphyria

The key points of congenital erythropoietic porphyria treatment are avoiding exposure to sunlight and prevention of skin trauma or skin infection. Liberal use of **sunscreens** and consumption of beta-carotene supplements can provide some protection from sun-induced damage. Medical treatments such as removing the spleen or administering transfusions of red blood cells can cre-

ate short-term benefits, but these treatments do not offer a cure. Remission can sometimes be achieved after treatment with oral doses of activated charcoal. Severely affected patients may be offered bone marrow transplantation which appears to confer long-term benefit.

Porphyria cutanea tarda

As with other porphyrias, the first line of defense is avoidance of factors, especially alcohol, that could bring about symptoms. Regular blood withdrawal is a proven therapy for pushing symptoms into remission. If an individual is anemic or cannot have blood drawn for other reasons, chloroquine therapy may be used.

Erythropoietic protoporphyria

Avoiding sunlight, using sunscreens, and taking beta-carotene supplements are typical treatment options for erythropoietic protoporphyria. The drug cholestyramine may reduce the skin's sensitivity to sunlight as well as the accumulated heme precursors in the liver. Liver transplantation has been used in cases of liver failure, but it has not effected a long-term cure of the porphyria.

Alternative treatment

Acute porphyria attacks can be life-threatening events, so attempts at self-treatment can be dangerous. Alternative treatments can be useful adjuncts to conventional therapy. For example, some people may find relief for the pain associated with acute intermittent porphyria, hereditary coproporphyria, or variegate porphyria through acupuncture or hypnosis. Relaxation techniques, such as **yoga** or meditation, may also prove helpful in **pain management**.

Prognosis

Even when porphyria is inherited, symptom development depends on a variety of factors. In the majority of cases, a person remains asymptomatic throughout life. About 1 percent of acute attacks can be fatal. Other symptoms may be associated with temporarily debilitating or permanently disfiguring consequences. Measures to avoid these consequences are not always successful, regardless of how diligently they are pursued. Although pregnancy has been known to trigger porphyria attacks, dangers associated with pregnancy as not as great as was once thought.

Prevention

For the most part, the porphyrias are attributable to inherited genes; such inheritance cannot be prevented.

KEY TERMS

Autosomal dominant—A pattern of inheritance in which only one of the two copies of an autosomal gene must be abnormal for a genetic condition or disease to occur. An autosomal gene is a gene that is located on one of the autosomes or non-sex chromosomes. A person with an autosomal dominant disorder has a 50 percent chance of passing it to each of their offspring.

Autosomal recessive—A pattern of inheritance in which both copies of an autosomal gene must be abnormal for a genetic condition or disease to occur. An autosomal gene is a gene that is located on one of the autosomes or non-sex chromosomes. When both parents have one abnormal copy of the same gene, they have a 25 percent chance with each pregnancy that their offspring will have the disorder.

Biosynthesis—The manufacture of materials in a biological system.

Bone marrow—The spongy tissue inside the large bones in the body that is responsible for making the red blood cells, most white blood cells, and platelets.

Chromosome—A microscopic thread-like structure found within each cell of the human body and consisting of a complex of proteins and DNA. Humans have 46 chromosomes arranged into 23 pairs. Chromosomes contain the genetic information necessary to direct the development and functioning of all cells and systems in the body. They pass on hereditary traits from parents to child (like eye color) and determine whether the child will be male or female.

Enzyme—A protein that catalyzes a biochemical reaction without changing its own structure or function.

Erythropoiesis—The process through which new red blood cells are created; it begins in the bone marrow.

Erythropoietic—Referring to the creation of new red blood cells.

Gene—A building block of inheritance, which contains the instructions for the production of a particular protein, and is made up of a molecular sequence found on a section of DNA. Each gene is found on a precise location on a chromosome.

Hematin—A drug administered intravenously to halt an acute porphyria attack. It causes heme biosynthesis to decrease, preventing the further accumulation of heme precursors.

Heme—The iron-containing molecule in hemoglobin that serves as the site for oxygen binding.

Hemoglobin—An iron-containing pigment of red blood cells composed of four amino acid chains (alpha, beta, gamma, delta) that delivers oxygen from the lungs to the cells of the body and carries carbon dioxide from the cells to the lungs.

Hepatic—Refers to the liver.

Neuropathy—A disease or abnormality of the peripheral nerves (the nerves outside the brain and spinal cord). Major symptoms include weakness, numbness, paralysis, or pain in the affected area.

Porphyrin—An organic compound found in living things that founds the foundation structure for hemoglobin, chlorophyll, and other respiratory pigments. In humans, porphyrins combine with iron to form hemes.

Protoporphyrin—A kind of porphyrin that links with iron to form the heme of hemoglobin.

However, symptoms can be limited or prevented by avoiding factors that trigger symptom development.

Children with a family history of an acute porphyria should be screened for the disease. Even if symptoms are absent, it is useful to know about the presence of the gene to assess the risks of developing the associated porphyria. This knowledge also reveals whether a person's offspring may be at risk. Prenatal testing for certain porphyrias is possible. Prenatal diagnosis of congenital erythropoietic porphyria has been successfully accomplished. Any prenatal tests, however, would not indicate whether a child would develop porphyria symptoms; only that the potential is there.

Parental concerns

Many children with porphyria do not have symptoms. Many acute attacks can be prevented by knowing what causes the attacks, and avoiding those things in the diet or environment that result in acute attacks.

When to call a doctor

Notify a doctor if the child appears to have an acute attack. Some signs and symptoms of an acute attack are: pain, red, burning or blistering skin, red urine, neurological changes, or psychological changes.

Resources

BOOKS

Deats-O'Reilly, Diana. *Porphyria: The Unknown Disease.* Grand Forks, N.D.: Porphyrin Publications Press/ Educational Services, 1999.

PERIODICALS

Gordon, Neal. "The Acute Porphyrias." *Brain & Development* 21 (September 1999): 373–77.

Thadani, Helen et al. "Diagnosis and Management of Porphyria." *British Medical Journal* 320 (June 2000): 1647–51.

ORGANIZATIONS

American Porphyria Foundation. PO Box 22712, Houston, TX 77227. (713) 266-9617. <www.porphyriafoundation. com/>.

OTHER

Gene Clinics. Available online at <www.geneclinics.org>.

National Institute of Diabetes & Digestive & Kidney Diseases. Available online at <www.niddk.nih.gov>.

Online Mendelian Inheritance in Man (OMIM). Available online at <www3.ncbi.nlm.nih.gov/Omim>.

Mark A. Best
Julia Barrett
Judy C. Hawkins, MS

Port-wine stain *see* **Birthmarks**

Post-concussion syndrome

Definition

Post-concussion syndrome (PCS) is a common but controversial disorder with a variety of symptoms including, but not limited to, **headache**, **dizziness**, fatigue, and personality changes.

Description

Post-concussion syndrome occurs in some patients after a **concussion**. A concussion is a form of mild traumatic **head injury**. Often a concussion involves loss of consciousness for a brief period, but it is possible to have a concussion without ever losing consciousness. There are many different ways of defining PCS, but it is usually considered present if three or more symptoms (such as insomnia, headache, and dizziness) are present for at least three months. PCS is a controversial syndrome, because multiple studies have resulted in conflicting findings. Also, some experts believe that many of the symptoms are largely psychological, because usually no neurological causes for the symptoms can be found. Other experts, however, maintain that just because no one has been able to pinpoint neurological causes does not mean they do not exist.

Demographics

PCS occurs in approximately 23–93 percent of individuals with mild to severe head injuries. It is estimated that a neurologist (a physician who specializes in nerve and brain disorders) sees five patients with PCS per month. There is no accurate correlation between the severity of injury and the development of PCS symptoms, since signs of the disorder can occur in someone who was just dazed by an injury. Some studies suggest that PCS symptoms occur at a higher rate in individuals who were unconscious after trauma. Females may be more likely to develop PCS than males.

Causes and symptoms

PCS is most commonly caused by a minor head injury called a concussion. Many patients who have experienced minor head injury develop PCS with distinct symptoms. They may report problems with concentration, short and medium term memory, and abstract thinking. Additionally, patients may develop dizziness, irritability, fatigue, and personality changes. It is not known what causes these symptoms. No studies have been able to deduce definitively any kind of neurological basis for the syndrome.

When to call the doctor

If a child is displaying the signs and symptoms of post-concussion syndrome, especially if known to have recently experienced a head injury, a doctor should be consulted.

Diagnosis

There are no specific or reliable tests to diagnose PCS. A doctor will do a physical examination. A neuropsychologist can perform an in-depth neuropsychologic **assessment** that can determine presence or absence and extent of impairment. Sometimes tests used to measure memory or cognitive capacity will be performed. Doctors may recommend seeing a psychologist to determine if depression or **anxiety** is present. **Magnetic resonance imaging** (MRI) or **computed tomography** (CT) scans may be done to ensure that a lesion or bleeding is not responsible for the symptoms.

Treatment

Treatment for PCS can be extensive. Medications for headache and **pain** may be indicated (**analgesics** and muscle relaxants). **Antidepressants** may be given to improve insomnia, irritability, anxiety, or depression. Pain control could be achieved with acupuncture, nerve blocks, or transcutaneous electrical nerve stimulation (TENS, electrical stimulation of muscle groups). It is important for clinicians to educate caretakers and to provide referrals for **family therapy** and cognitive rehabilitation for the affected child. The overall aim of treatment for PCS is to allow the child to return to school and to the activities that he or she participated in before the traumatic incident.

Prognosis

The overall outcome is difficult to assess. Most individuals who have PCS recover fully, although if recovery has not occurred in one year it is less likely that it will ever occur. Patient recovery is determined by cognitive function changes, subjective symptoms, and return to school or work. Cases of PCS can be a strain and threaten **family** stability. There may be compensation and litigation claims, which are often stressful and aggravate symptoms.

Prevention

The only way to prevent post-concussion syndrome is to prevent the original concussion. Wearing a helmet while riding a bike, rollerblading, or skateboarding can reduce the risk of head injury. Putting children in age-appropriate **safety** seats in the car can also help to prevent head trauma in the event of an automobile accident.

Parental concerns

Post-concussion syndrome can be very frustrating, because the symptoms are persistent and can affect the child's ability to perform in school or other activities.

Counseling is thought to help the patient and family deal with the incapacitation and develop coping strategies. The best way to prevent PCS is to make sure that children avoid situations where they are likely to injure themselves.

See also Concussion.

Resources

BOOKS

Mark R. Lovell et al, eds. *Traumatic Brain Injury in Sports.* Exton, PA: Swets and Zeitlinger, 2004.

Rizzo, Matthew and Daniel Tranel, eds. *Head Injury and Postconcussive Syndrome.* New York: Churchill Livingstone, 1996.

PERIODICALS

Mangan, Doreen. "This Syndrome Can Occur in Kids with Concussions." *RN* v66 i6 (June 2003): 77.

Piland, SG et al. "Comparison of Recovery Curves Using Post Concussive Symptomology." *Journal of Athletic Training.* v36 i2 (April-June 2001): 50-59.

Taylor, Sherrod, J. "Recognizing Post-Concussion Syndrome Cases." *Claims.* V48 i4 (April 2000): 32-33.

ORGANIZATIONS

Brain Injury of America 8201 Greensboro Drive, Suite 611, McLean, VA 22102. Telephone: (703) 761-0750. Family Helpline: 1-800-444-6443. familyhelpline@biausa.org. <www.biausa.org>

Tish Davidson, A.M.
Laith Farid Gulli, M.D.

Postural drainage *see* **Chest physical therapy**

Potty training *see* **Toilet training**

Prader-Willi syndrome

Definition

Prader-Willi syndrome (PWS) is a genetic condition caused by the absence of chromosomal material from chromosome 15. Characteristics of the syndrome include developmental delays, poor muscle tone, short stature, small hands and feet, incomplete sexual development, and unique facial features. Insatiable appetite is a classic feature of PWS. This uncontrollable appetite can lead to morbid **obesity** and behavior disturbances.

Description

The first patients with features of PWS were described by Dr. Prader, Dr. Willi, and Dr. Lambert in 1956. Since that time, the complex genetic basis of PWS has begun to be understood. Initially, scientists found that individuals with PWS have a portion of genetic material deleted (erased) from chromosome 15. In order to have PWS, the genetic material must be deleted from the chromosome 15 received from one's father. If the deletion is on the chromosome 15 inherited from one's mother, a different syndrome develops. This was an important discovery, for it demonstrated for the first time that the genes inherited from one's mother can be expressed differently than the genes inherited from one's father.

Over time, scientists realized that some individuals with PWS do not have genetic material deleted from chromosome 15. Further studies found that these patients inherit both copies of chromosome 15 from their mother, which is not typical. Normally, an individual receives one chromosome 15 from his or her father and one chromosome 15 from his or her mother. When a person receives both chromosomes from the same parent it is called "uniparental disomy." When a person receives both chromosomes from his or her mother, it is called "maternal uniparental disomy."

Scientists are still discovering other causes of PWS. A small number of patients with PWS have a change (mutation) in the genetic material on the chromosome 15 inherited from their father. This mutation prevents certain genes on chromosome 15 from working properly. PWS develops when these genes do not work normally.

Newborns with PWS generally have poor muscle tone, (**hypotonia**) and do not feed well. This can lead to poor weight gain and **failure to thrive**. Genitalia can be smaller than normal, and a male with PWS may have undescended testicles. Hands and feet are also typically smaller than normal. Some patients with PWS have unique and subtle facial characteristics that are detectable only by physicians.

As children with PWS age, development is typically slower than normal. Developmental milestones, such as **crawling**, walking and talking occur later than usual. **Developmental delay** continues into adulthood for approximately 50 percent of individuals with PWS. At about one to two years of age, children with PWS develop an uncontrollable, insatiable appetite. These children, if not controlled, will eat until they suffer from life-threatening obesity, including respiratory failure with hypoxia (low blood oxygen levels), cor pulmonale

(right-sided heart failure), and death. The desire to eat can also lead to significant behavior problems.

The symptoms and features of PWS require life-long support and care. If food intake is strictly monitored and various therapies provided, individuals with PWS have a normal life expectancy.

Prader-Willi syndrome is also referred to as crypto-chidism-dwarfism-subnormal mentality syndrome, Willi-Prader syndrome, Labhart-Willi syndrome, Prader-Labhart-Will Fancone syndrome, and hypotonia-hypomentia-hypogonadism-obesity syndrome.

Demographics

PWS affects approximately one in 12,000 to 15,000 live births. It is the most common genetic cause of life-threatening obesity. It affects both males and females and can be seen in all races and ethnic groups.

Causes and symptoms

Human beings have 46 chromosomes in the cells of their body. Chromosomes contain genes that regulate the function and development of the body. An individual's chromosomes are inherited from his or her parents. Each parent normally gives a child 23 chromosomes. A child receives 23 chromosomes from the egg and 23 chromosomes from the sperm.

The 46 chromosomes in the human body are divided into pairs based on their physical characteristics. Each pair is assigned a number or a letter. When viewed under a microscope, chromosomes within the same pair appear identical because they contain the same genes.

Most chromosomes have a constriction near the center called the centromere. The centromere separates the chromosome into long and short arms. The short arm of a chromosome is called the p arm; the long arm and is called the q arm.

Chromosomes in the same pair contain the same genes. However, some genes work differently depending on if they were inherited from the egg or the sperm. Sometimes, genes are silenced when inherited from the mother. Other times, genes are silenced when inherited from the father. When genes in a certain region on a chromosome are silenced, they are said to be imprinted. Imprinting is a normal process that does not typically cause disease. However, if normal imprinting is disrupted, a genetic disease can develop.

Individuals have two complete copies of chromosome 15. One chromosome 15 is inherited from the mother, or is maternal in origin. The other chromosome 15 is inherited from the father, or is paternal in origin.

Chromosome 15 contains many different genes. There are several genes found on the q arm of chromosome 15 that are imprinted. A gene called SNPRN is an example of one of these genes. It is normally imprinted, or silenced, if inherited from the mother. The imprinting of this group of maternal genes does not typically cause disease. The genes in this region should not be imprinted if paternal in origin. Normal development depends on these paternal genes being present and active. If these genes are deleted, not inherited, or incorrectly imprinted, PWS develops.

Deletion in the paternally contributed chromosome 15

Seventy percent of the cases of PWS are caused when a piece of material is deleted, or erased, from the paternal chromosome 15. This deletion occurs in a specific region on the q arm of chromosome 15. The piece of chromosomal material that is deleted contains genes that must be present for normal development. These paternal genes must be working normally, because the same genes on the chromosome 15 inherited from the mother are imprinted. When these paternal genes are missing, the brain and other parts of the body do not develop as expected. This is what causes the symptoms associated with PWS.

In 99 percent of the cases of PWS, the deletion is sporadic. This means that it happens randomly, there is not an apparent cause, and the condition is not inherited. If a child has PWS due to a sporadic deletion in the paternal chromosome 15, the chance the parents could have another child with PWS is less than 1 percent. In fewer than 1 percent of the cases of PWS there is a chromosomal rearrangement in the **family** that causes the deletion. This chromosomal rearrangement is called translocation. If a parent has a translocation the risk of having a child with PWS is higher than 1 percent.

Maternal uniparental disomy

PWS can also develop if a child receives both chromosome 15s from his or her mother. This is seen in approximately 25 percent of the cases of PWS. Maternal uniparental disomy for chromosome 15 leads to PWS because the genes on chromosome 15 that should have been inherited from the father are missing, and the genes on both the chromosome 15s inherited from the mother are imprinted.

PWS caused by maternal uniparental is sporadic. This means that it occurs randomly and there is not an apparent cause. If a child has PWS due to maternal uniparental disomy, the chance the parents could have another child with PWS is less than 1 percent.

Error in imprinting process than renders paternal contribution non-functional

Approximately 2–5 percent of patients with PWS have a change (mutation) in a gene located on the q arm of chromosome 15. This mutation leads to incorrect imprinting. This mutation causes genes inherited from the father to be imprinted or silenced, which should not normally be imprinted. If a child has PWS due to a mutation that changes imprinting, the chance the parents could have another child with PWS is approximately 5 percent.

Signs of PWS can be seen at birth. Infants with PWS have weak muscle tone (hypotonia). This hypotonia causes problems with sucking and eating so that infants with PWS may initially have problems gaining weight. Consequently, some infants with PWS may be diagnosed with failure to thrive due to slow growth and development. Hypotonia may also During infancy, babies with PWS may also **sleep** more than normal and have problems controlling their temperature.

Some of the unique physical features associated with PWS can be seen during infancy. Genitalia (**hypogonadism**) that is smaller than normal is common. This may be more evident in males with PWS. Hands and feet may also be smaller than average. The unique facial features seen in some patients with PWS may be difficult to detect in infancy. These facial features are very mild and do not cause physical problems.

As early as six months, but more commonly at one to two years, a compulsive desire to eat develops. This uncontrollable appetite is a classic feature of PWS. Individuals with PWS lack the ability to feel full or satiated because of a flaw in the hypothalamus part of their brain, which normally registers feelings of hunger and satiety. Over-eating (hyperpahgia), a lack of a desire to **exercise**, and decreased calorie utilization (typically 1,000–1,200 calories per day for adults, due to low muscle mass and inactivity) places individuals with PWS at high risk for severe obesity. Obesity-related problems include hypoventilation, hyertension, right-sided heart failure, cellulitis, and skin problems with fat folds. Some individuals with PWS may also have a reduced ability to vomit.

Behavior problems are a common feature of PWS. Although infants and young children are typically happy and loving and exhibit few behavior problems, most older children and adults do have difficulties with behavior regulation, such as difficulties with transistions and unanticipated changes. Onset of behavioral problems usually coincides with the onset of the compulsive eating. Difficulties peak in **adolescence** or early adulthood. Reported problems include obsessive/compulsive behaviors, depression, temper **tantrums** and violent outbursts, and tendencies to be argumentative, oppositional, rigid, manipulative, possessive, and stubborn. Individuals with PWS may also pick their own skin (skin picking). This unusual behavior may be due to a reduced **pain** threshold.

IQs range from 40 to 105, with an average of 70. Those with normal IQs typically have learning disabilities. Problem areas may include attention, short-term auditory memory, and abstract thinking. Common strengths include long-term memory, reading ability, and receptive language.

Puberty may occur early or late, but it is usually incomplete. In addition to the effects on sexual development and fertility, individuals do not undergo the normal adolescent growth spurt and may be short as adults. Muscles often remain underdeveloped and body fat is increased.

When to call the doctor

Parents should call a doctor if they notice symptoms that are characteristic of PWS.

Diagnosis

During infancy the diagnosis of PWS may be suspected if poor muscle tone, feeding problems, small genitalia, or the unique facial features are present. If an infant has these features, testing for PWS should be performed. This testing should also be offered to children and adults who display features commonly seen in PWS (developmental delays, uncontrollable appetite, small genitalia, etc.). There are several different genetic tests that can detect PWS. All of these tests can be performed usnig a blood sample.

Methylation testing detects 99 percent of the cases of PWS. Methylation testing can detect the absence of the paternal genes that should be normally active on chromosome 15. Although methylation testing can accurately diagnose PWS, it can not determine if the PWS is caused by a deletion, maternal uniparental disomy, or a mutation that disrupts imprinting. This information is important for genetic counseling. Therefore, additional testing should be performed.

Chromosome analysis can determine if the PWS is the result of a deletion in the q arm of chromosome 15. Chromosome analysis, also called karyotyping, involves staining the chromosomes and examining them under a microscope. In some cases the deletion of material from chromosome 15 can be easily seen. In other cases, further testing must be performed. FISH (fluorescence in-situ hybridization) is a special technique that detects small deletions that cause PWS.

More specialized DNA testing is required to detect maternal uniparental disomy or a mutation that disrupts imprinting. This DNA testing identifies unique DNA patterns in the mother and father. The unique DNA patterns are then compared with the DNA from the child with PWS.

PWS can be detected before birth if the mother undergoes amniocentesis testing or chorionic villus sampling (CVS). This testing is only recommended if the mother or father is known to have a chromosome rearrangement, or if they already have a child with PWS syndrome.

Treatment

There is currently not a cure for PWS. Treatment during infancy includes therapies to improve muscle tone. Some infants with PWS also require special nipples or tube feeding to improve weight gain.

Growth hormone therapy has been shown to improve the poor muscle tone and reduced height typically associated with PWS. Hypogonadism may be corrected at puberty with hormone replacement. Skin picking is best managed by ignoring the behavior, treating and bandaging sores, and providing substitute activities for the hands. Other behavioral problems can be managed through daily routines and structure, firm rules and limits, "time outs," positive rewards, and the use of psychotropic drugs.

Special education may be helpful in treating developmental delays and behavior problems. Individuals with PWS typically excel in highly structured environments. Physical and occupational therapies promote skill development and proper function. Exercise and sport activities should be encouraged, with adaptations made as necessary. Proficiency with jigsaw puzzles have been frequently reported, reflecting strong visual-perceptual skills. The need for speech therapy, due to speech difficulties caused by hypotonia, should be assessed. Sign language and picture communication boards can be used to reduce frustration and to aid communication. Products to increase saliva may help articulation problems. Social skills training can improve pragmatic language use. Verbal ability often becomes an area of strength for children with PWS.

KEY TERMS

Centromere—The constricted region of a chromosome. It performs certain functions during cell division.

Deletion—The absence of genetic material that is normally found in a chromosome. Often, the genetic material is missing due to an error in replication of an egg or sperm cell.

DNA—Deoxyribonucleic acid; the genetic material in cells that holds the inherited instructions for growth, development, and cellular functioning.

Fluorescence in situ hybridization (FISH)—A technique for diagnosing genetic disorders before birth by analyzing cells obtained by amniocentesis with DNA probes.

Gene—A building block of inheritance, which contains the instructions for the production of a particular protein, and is made up of a molecular sequence found on a section of DNA. Each gene is found on a precise location on a chromosome.

Hyperphagia—Over-eating.

Hypotonia—Having reduced or diminished muscle tone or strength.

Imprinting—A process that silences a gene or group of genes. The genes are silenced depending on whether they are inherited through the egg or the sperm.

Maternal uniparental disomy—A chromosome abnormality in which both chromosomes in a pair are inherited from one's mother.

Methylation testing—DNA testing that detects if a gene is active or if it is imprinted.

Mutation—A permanent change in the genetic material that may alter a trait or characteristic of an individual, or manifest as disease. This change can be transmitted to offspring.

Translocation—The transfer of one part of a chromosome to another chromosome during cell division. A balanced translocation occurs when pieces from two different chromosomes exchange places without loss or gain of any chromosome material. An unbalanced translocation involves the unequal loss or gain of genetic information between two chromosomes.

Uniparental disomy—Chromosome abnormality in which both chromosomes in a pair are inherited from the same parent.

Nutritional concerns

Treatment and management of PWS during childhood, adolescence, and adulthood is typically focused on weight control. Strict control of food intake is vital to prevent severe obesity. In many cases food must be made inaccessible. This may involve unconventional measures such as locking the refrigerator or kitchen cabinets. A lifelong balanced restricted-calorie diet with vitamin and calcium supplementation and a regular exercise program (at least 30 minutes per day) are also suggested. The best meal and snack plan is one that the family or caregiver is able to aply routinely and consistently. Unfortunately, diet medications nor surgery have not been shown to significantly prevent obesity in PWS or eliminate the need for strict dieting and supervision around food.

Prognosis

With help, people with PWS can expect to accomplish many of the things their "normal" peers do: complete school, achieve in their outside areas of interest, be successfully employed, and even move away from their family home. They do, however, need a significant amount of support from their families and from school, work, and residential service providers to both achieve these goals and to avoid obesity and the serious health consequences that accompany it. Even those with IQs in the normal range need lifelong diet supervision and protection from food availability.

Although in the past many people with PWS died in adolescence or young adulthood, prevention of obesity can enable those with the syndrome to live a normal lifespan. New medications, including psychotropic drugs and synthetic growth hormone, are already improving the quality of life for some people with PWS. Ongoing research offers the hope of new discoveries that will enable people affected by this unusual condition to live more independent lives.

Prevention

PWS currently cannot be prevented. Genetic counseling is recommended for parents who may be at risk for having a child with PWS.

Parental concerns

While there is no medical prevention or cure, early diagnosis of Prader-Willi syndrome gives parents time to learn about and prepare for the challenges that lie ahead and to establish family routines that will support their child's diet and behavior needs. The constant need for food restriction and behavior management may be stressful for family members. It is also important for the parents to provide basic sex education to promote good health and to protect against abuse. Knowing the cause of their child's developmental delays can facilitate a family's access to important early intervention services and may help program staff identify areas of specific need or risk. Additionally, a diagnosis of PWS opens the doors to a network of information and support from professionals and other families who are dealing with the syndrome. Adolescents and adults with PWS can function well in group and supported living programs, if the necessary diet control and structured environment are provided. Employment in sheltered workshops and other highly structured and supervised settings is successful for many. However, residential and vocational providers must be fully informed regarding management of PWS.

Resources

BOOKS

Couch, Cheryl. *My Rag Doll.* Couch Publishing, October 2000.

Icon Health Publications. *Prader-Willi Syndrome: A Medical Dictionary, Bibliography, and Annotated Research Guide to Internet References.* San Diego, CA: Icon Health Publications, 2004.

Jones, Kenneth Lyons. "Prader-Willi Syndrome." In *Smith's Recognizable Patterns of Human Malformation. 5th edition* Philadelphia: W.B. Saunders, 1997.

PM Medical Health News. *21st Century Complete Medical Guide to Prader-Willi Syndrome: Authoritative Government Documents, Clinical References, and Practical Information for Patients and Physicians. CD-ROM.* Washington, DC: Progressive Management, 2004.

PERIODICALS

Butler, Merlin G. and Travis Thompson. "Prader-Willi Syndrome: Clinical and Genetic Findings." *The Endocrinologist* 10 (2000): 3S–16S.

State, Matthew W. and Elisabeth Dykens. "Genetics of Childhood Disorders: XV. Prader-Willi Syndrome: Genes, Brain and Behavior." *J. Am. Acad. Child. Adolesc. Psychiatry* 39, no. 6 (June 2000): 797–800.

ORGANIZATIONS

Alliance of Genetic Support Groups. 4301 Connecticut Ave. NW, Suite 404, Washington DC 20008. (202) 966-5557. Fax: (202) 966-8553. <www.geneticalliance.org>.

International Prader-Willi Syndrome Organization. <www.ipwso.org>.

National Organization for Rare Disorders, Inc. P.O. Box 8923, New Fairfield, CT 06812. (800) 999-6673. <www.rarediseases.org>.

Prader-Willi Foundation. 223 Main Street, Port Washington, NY 11050. (800)253- 7993. <www.prader-willi.org>.

Prader-Willi Syndrome Association (USA). 5700 Midnight Pass Rd., Sarasota, FL 34242. (800) 926-4797. <www.pwsausa.org>.

WEB SITES

Prader-Willi Syndrome. National Institutes of Health. <www.nlm.nih.gov/medlineplus/ praderwillisyndrome.html>.

Judith Sims, MS
Holly Ann Ishmael, MS

Precocious puberty

Definition

Precocious puberty is sexual development before the age of eight in girls, and age 10 in boys.

Description

Precocious **puberty** often begins before age eight in girls, triggering the development of breasts and hair under the arms and in the genital region. The onset of ovulation and **menstruation** also may occur. In boys, the condition triggers the development of a large penis and testicles, with spontaneous erections and the production of sperm. Hair grows on the face, under arms and in the pubic area, and **acne** may become a problem.

While the early onset of puberty may seem fairly benign, in fact it can cause problems when hormones trigger changes in the growth pattern, essentially halting growth before the child has reached normal adult height. Girls may never grow above 5 ft (152 cm) and boys often stop growing by about 5 ft 2 in (157 cm).

The abnormal growth patterns are not the only problem, however. Children with this condition look noticeably different than their peers, and may feel rejected by their friends and socially isolated. Adults may expect these children to act more maturely simply because they look so much older. As a result, many of these children, especially boys, are much more aggressive than others their own age, leading to behavior problems both at home and at school.

Demographics

Not every child reaches puberty at the same time, but in most cases it is safe to predict that sexual development will begin at about age 11 in girls and 12 or 13 in boys. However, occasionally a child begins to develop sexually much earlier. Between four to eight times more common in girls than boys, precocious puberty occurs in one out of every 5,000–10,000 U.S. children.

Causes and symptoms

Puberty begins when the brain secretes a hormone that triggers the pituitary gland to release gonadotropins, which in turn stimulate the ovaries or testes to produce sex hormones. These sex hormones (especially estrogen in girls and testosterone in boys) are what causes the onset of sexual maturity.

The hormonal changes of precious puberty are normal—it is just that the whole process begins a few years too soon. Especially in girls, there is not usually any underlying problem that causes the process to begin too soon. However, some boys do inherit the condition; the responsible gene may be passed directly from father to son, or inherited indirectly from the maternal grandfather through the mother, who does not begin early puberty herself. This genetic condition in girls can be traced in only about one percent of cases.

In about 15 percent of cases, there is an underlying cause for the precocious puberty, and it is important to search for these causes. The condition may result from a benign tumor in the part of the brain that releases hormones. Less commonly, it may be caused by other types of brain tumors, central nervous system disorders, or adrenal gland problems.

When to call the doctor

A pediatrician should be consulted when girls under age eight start to show signs breast development and menstruation, or if boys under age 10 show enlarged genitals and body hair.

Diagnosis

Physical exams can reveal the development of sexual characteristics in a young child. Bone **x rays** can reveal bone age, and pelvic ultrasound may show an enlarged uterus and rule out ovarian or adrenal tumors.

Blood tests can highlight higher-than normal levels of hormones. MRI or CAT scans should be considered to rule out intracranial tumors.

Treatment

Treatment aims to halt or reverse sexual development so as to stop the accompanying rapid growth that will limit a child's height. There are two possible approaches: either treat the underlying condition (such as an ovarian or intracranial tumor) or change the hormonal balance to stop sexual development. It may not be possible to treat the underlying condition; for this reason, treatment is usually aimed at adjusting hormone levels.

There are several drugs that have been developed to do this:

- histrelin (Supprelin)
- nafarelin (Synarel)
- synthetic gonadotropin-releasing hormone agonist
- deslorelin
- ethylamide
- triptorelin
- leuprolide

Prognosis

Drug treatments can slow growth to 2–3 in (5–7.5 cm) a year, allowing these children to reach normal adult height, although the long-term effects are not known.

Prevention

There is no way to prevent precocious puberty.

Parental concerns

Support and appropriate treatment of any underlying medical disorders are appropriate for parents. The vast majority of children experiencing precocious puberty become lost in the crowd of their peers when their age peers enter puberty. Counseling may be useful for both parents and affected child.

Resources

BOOKS

Garibaldi, Luuigi. "Disorders of Pubertal Development." In *Nelson Textbook of Pediatrics.* 17th ed. Ed. by Richard E. Behrman, et al., Philadelphia: Saunders, 2003, 1863-9.

New, Maria and Josso, Nathalie. "Disorders of Sexual Diferentiation." In *Cecil Textbook of Medicine.* 22nd ed. Ed. by Lee Goldman, et al. Philadelphia: Saunders, 2003, 1163-71.

PERIODICALS

Carel, J.C., et al. "Precocious puberty and statural growth." *Human Reproduction Update* 10, no. 2 (2004): 135-47.

Grosso, S., et al. "Central precocious puberty and abnormal chromosomal patterns." *Endocrine Pathology* 11, no. 1 (2004): 69-76.

Kaplowitz, P. "Clinical characteristics of 104 children referred for evaluation of precocious puberty." *Journal of Clinical Endocrinology and Metabolism* 89, no. 8 (2004): 3644-50.

Lanes, R., Soros, A., and Jakubowicz, S. "Accelerated versus slowly progressive forms of puberty in girls with precocious and early puberty." *Journal of Pediatric Endocrinology and Metabolism* 17, no. 5 (2004): 759-66.

L. Fleming Fallon, Jr., MD, DrPH

Prematurity

Definition

The average length of a normal pregnancy is 40 weeks (280 days) from the date of conception. Infants born before 37 weeks gestation are considered premature and may be at risk for complications.

Description

More than one out of every ten infants born in the United States is born prematurely. Advances in medical technology have made it possible for infants born as young as 23 weeks gestational age (17 weeks premature) to survive. These premature infants, however, are at higher risk for death or serious complications, which include heart defects, respiratory problems, blindness, and brain damage.

Demographics

According to the March of Dimes Foundation, there were 480,812 births in the United States in 2002 that occurred before 37 weeks gestation. This number represents 12.1 percent of live births that year. In an average week, approximately 9,200 infants are born prematurely, and approximately 1,500 are born before 32 weeks gestation. Black infants have the highest prematurity rate with 17.6 percent of live births; Native American (12.9%); Hispanic infants (11.4%); white infants (10.7%); and Asian infants (10.2%). Mothers younger than 20 years of age or older than 35 years of age have higher rates of preterm delivery.

Causes and symptoms

The birth of a premature baby can be brought on by several different factors, including the following:

- premature labor
- placental abruption, in which the placenta detaches from the uterus
- placenta previa, in which the placenta grows too low in the uterus
- premature rupture of membranes, in which the amniotic sac is torn, causing the amniotic fluid to leak out
- incompetent cervix, in which the cervix opens too soon
- maternal toxemia or preeclampsia

Prematurity is much more common in pregnancy of multiples and for mothers who have a history of miscarriages or prior premature birth. Another identifiable cause of prematurity is drug abuse (e.g. cocaine) by the mother.

Infants born prematurely may experience major complications due to their low birth weight and the immaturity of their organ systems. Some of the common problems among premature infants are **jaundice** (yellow discoloration of the skin and whites of the eyes), apnea (a long pause in breathing), and inability to breast or bottle feed. Body temperature, blood pressure, and heart rate may be difficult to regulate in premature infants. The lungs, digestive system, and nervous system (including the brain) are underdeveloped in premature babies and are particularly vulnerable to complications.

Complications

Respiratory distress syndrome (RDS) is the most common problem in premature infants. Babies born too soon have immature lungs that have not developed surfactant, a protective film that helps air sacs in the lungs to stay open. With RDS, breathing is rapid and the center of the chest and rib cage pull inward with each breath. Extra oxygen can be supplied to the infant through tubes that fit into the nostrils of the nose or by placing the baby under an oxygen hood. In more serious cases, the baby may have to have a breathing tube inserted and receive air from a respirator or ventilator. A surfactant drug can be given in some cases. Extra oxygen may be needed for a few days or weeks. Bronchopulmonary dysplasia is the development of scar tissue in the lungs and can occur in severe cases of RDS.

Necrotizing enterocolitis (NEC) is another complication of prematurity. In this condition, part of the baby's intestine is destroyed as a result of bacterial infection. In cases where only the innermost lining of the bowel dies, the infant's body can regenerate it over time; however, if the full thickness of a portion dies, it must be removed surgically and an opening (ostomy) must be made for the passage of wastes until the infant is healthy enough for the remaining ends to be sewn together. Because NEC is potentially fatal, doctors are quick to respond to its symptoms, which include lethargy, **vomiting**, a swollen and/or red abdomen, **fever**, and blood in the stool. Measures include taking the infant off mouth feedings and feeding him or her intravenously, administering **antibiotics**, and removing air and fluids from the digestive tract via a nasal tube. Approximately 70 percent of NEC cases can be successfully treated without surgery.

Intraventricular hemorrhage (IVH) is another serious complication of prematurity. It is a condition in which immature and fragile blood vessels within the brain burst and bleed into the hollow chambers (ventricles) normally reserved for cerebrospinal fluid and into the tissue surrounding them. Physicians grade the severity of IVH according to a scale of I through IV, with I being bleeding confined to a small area around the burst vessels and IV being an extensive collection of blood in the ventricles and in the brain tissue itself. Grades I and II are not uncommon, and the baby's body usually reabsorbs the blood with no ill effects. However, more severe IVH can result in **hydrocephalus**, a potentially fatal condition in which too much fluid collects in the ventricles, exerting increased pressure on the brain and causing the baby's head to expand abnormally. To drain fluid and relieve pressure on the brain, doctors either perform lumbar punctures, a procedure in which a needle is inserted into the spinal canal to drain fluid; install a reservoir, a tube that drains fluid from a ventricle and into an artificial chamber under or on top of the scalp; or install a ventricular shunt, a tube that drains fluid from the ventricles and into the abdomen, where it is reabsorbed by the body. Infants who are at high risk for IVH

usually have an ultrasound taken of their brain in the first week after birth, followed by others if bleeding is detected. IVH cannot be prevented; however, close monitoring can ensure that procedures to reduce fluid in the brain are implemented quickly to minimize possible damage.

Apnea of prematurity is a condition in which the infant stops breathing for periods lasting up to 20 seconds. It is often associated with a slowing of the heart rate. The baby may become pale, or the skin color may change to a blue or purplish hue. Apnea occurs most commonly when the infant is asleep. Infants with serious apnea may need medications to stimulate breathing or oxygen through a tube inserted in the nose. Some infants may be placed on a ventilator or respirator with a breathing tube inserted into the airway. As the baby gets older, and the lungs and brain tissues mature, the breathing usually becomes more regular. A group of researchers in Cleveland reported in 2003, however, that children who were born prematurely are three to five times more likely to develop sleep-disordered breathing by age 10 than children who were full-term babies.

As the fetus develops, it receives the oxygen it needs from the mother's blood system. Most of the blood in the infant's system bypasses the lungs. Once the baby is born, its own blood must start pumping through the lungs to get oxygen. Normally, this bypass duct closes within the first few hours or days after birth. If it does not close, the baby may have trouble getting enough oxygen on its own. **Patent ductus arteriosus** is a condition in which the duct that channels blood between two main arteries does not close after the baby is born. In some cases, a drug called indomethacin can be given to close the duct. Surgery may be required if the duct does not close on its own as the baby develops.

Retinopathy of prematurity is a condition in which the blood vessels in the baby's eyes do not develop normally, and can, in some cases, result in blindness. Premature infants are also more susceptible to infections. They are born with fewer antibodies, which are necessary to fight off infections.

When to call the doctor

In some cases, healthcare professionals are able to stop or delay premature labor if treated early enough. A pregnant woman should contact her healthcare provider if she observes any of the signs of premature labor, including the following:

- contractions closer than 10 minutes apart
- leaking fluid or bleeding from the vagina
- menstrual-like cramps

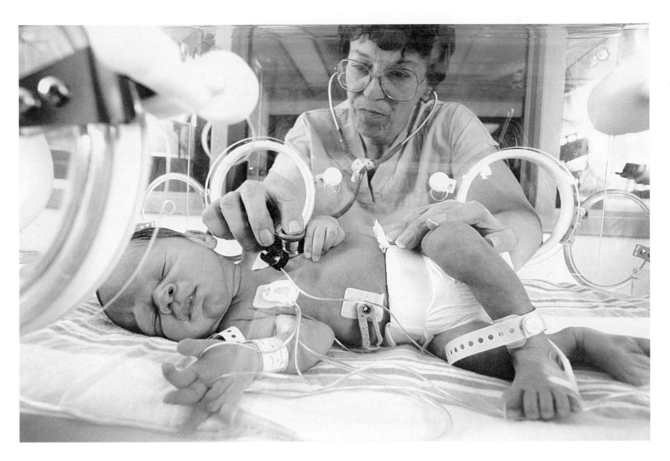

Premature infant in an incubator. *(© Royalty-Free/Corbis.)*

- abdominal cramps, with or without diarrhea
- low, dull backache
- pelvic pressure

Diagnosis

Many of the problems associated with prematurity depend on how early the baby is born and how much it weighs at birth. The most accurate way of determining the gestational age of an infant in utero is calculating from a known date of conception or using ultrasound imaging to observe development. When a baby is born, doctors can use the Dubowitz exam to estimate gestational age. This standardized test scores responses to 33 specific neurological stimuli to estimate the infant's neural development. Once the baby's gestational age and weight are determined, further tests and **electronic fetal monitoring** may need to be used to diagnose problems or to track the baby's condition. A blood pressure monitor may be wrapped around the arm or leg. Several types of monitors can be taped to the skin. A heart monitor or cardiorespiratory monitor may be attached to the baby's chest, abdomen, arms, or legs with adhesive patches to monitor breathing and heart rate. A thermometer probe may be taped on the skin to monitor body temperature. Blood samples may be taken from a vein or artery. X-ray or ultrasound imaging may be used to examine the heart, lungs, and other internal organs.

Treatment

Treatment depends on the types of complications that are present. It is not unusual for premature infants to be placed in heat-controlled units (incubators) to maintain their temperature. Infants who are having trouble breathing on their own may need oxygen either pumped into the incubator, administered through small tubes placed in their nostrils, or through a respirator or ventilator, which pumps air into a breathing tube inserted into the airway. They may require fluids and nutrients to be administered through an intravenous line, in which a small needle is inserted into a vein in the hand, foot, arm, leg, or scalp. If the baby needs drugs or medications, these may also be administered through the intravenous line. Another type of line may be inserted into the baby's umbilical cord. This can be used to draw blood samples or to administer medications or nutrients. If heart rate is irregular, the baby may have heart monitor leads taped to the chest. Many premature infants require time and support with breathing and feeding until they mature enough to breathe and eat unassisted. Depending on the complications, the baby may require drugs or surgery.

Alternative treatment

Research has shown that the risks of massaging preterm infants are minimal and that infants benefit from improved developmental scores, more rapid weight gain, and earlier discharge from the hospital. An additional benefit of **massage therapy** is closer **bonding** between the parents and their newborn child. Another method, called kangaroo care, entails placing a medically stable, diaper-clad premature infant on a parent's chest for periods of time so that the parent and child are touching skin-to-skin. A 2002 study published in *Pediatrics* found that both the parent and infant benefited from the practice: mothers reported lower rates of depression and more sensitivity to the infant's needs, and the infants showed improved cognitive and motor development.

Nutritional concerns

If a premature infant is unable to nurse at the breast or drink from a bottle, fluids and nutrients may be administered intravenously or with a tube in the nose or mouth that empties into the stomach (called gavage feeding). Even if a baby is unable to feed at the breast, a mother may pump her breast milk to be given to the infant via gavage feeding. Once the infant learns to suck and swallow effectively, breast or bottle feedings can commence.

Prognosis

Advances in medical care have made it possible for many premature infants to survive and develop normally. Whether a premature infant survives, however, is still intimately tied to his or her gestational age:

- 21 weeks or less: 0 percent survival rate
- 22 weeks: 0 to 10 percent survival rate
- 23 weeks: 10 to 35 percent survival rate
- 24 weeks: 40 to 70 percent survival rate
- 25 weeks: 50 to 80 percent survival rate
- 26 weeks: 80 to 90 percent survival rate
- 27 weeks: greater than 90 percent survival rate

Physicians cannot predict long-term complications of prematurity; some consequences may not become evi-

dent until the child is school age. Minor disabilities like learning problems, poor coordination, or short attention span may be the result of premature birth but can be overcome with early intervention. The risks of serious long-term complications depend on many factors, including how premature the infant was at birth, the weight at birth, and the presence or absence of breathing problems. Gender is an associated factor: a Swedish study published in 2003 found that boys are at greater risk of death or serious long-term consequences of prematurity than girls. For example, 60 percent of boys born at 24 weeks' gestation die compared to 38 percent mortality for girls. The development of infection or the presence of a birth defect can also affect long-term prognosis. Infants who have infections in prematurity and very low birth weight are at risk for later disorders of the nervous system; a study done at Johns Hopkins reported that 77 out of a group of 213 premature infants developed neurologic disorders. Severe disabilities such as brain damage, blindness, and chronic lung problems are possible and may require ongoing care.

Prevention

Some of the risks and complications of premature delivery can be reduced if the mother receives good prenatal care, follows a healthy diet, avoids alcohol or drug consumption, and refrains from cigarette **smoking**. In some cases of premature labor, the mother may be placed on bed rest or given drugs that can stop labor contractions for days or weeks, giving the developing infant more time to develop before delivery. The physician may prescribe a steroid medication to be given to the mother before the delivery to help speed up the baby's lung development. The availability of a neonatal intensive care unit (NICU), a special hospital unit equipped and trained to deal with premature infants, can also increase an infant's chances of survival.

A new medication may help to prevent spontaneous premature births. Researchers at Wake Forest University reported in June 2003 that a drug known as 17 alpha-hydroxyprogesterone caproate reduced the number of premature births in a group of women who received weekly injections of the drug compared to a placebo group and lowered the rates of necrotizing enterocolitis, intraventricular hemorrhage, and need for supplemental oxygen in their infants.

Nutritional concerns

Poor **nutrition** during pregnancy may lead to an increased risk of premature delivery. Research supported by the U.S. Public Health Service during the 1990s found that an inadequate diet during pregnancy was asso-

KEY TERMS

Apnea—The temporary absence of breathing. Sleep apnea consists of repeated episodes of temporary suspension of breathing during sleep.

Dubowitz exam—Standardized test that scores responses to 33 specific neurological stimuli to estimate an infant's neural development and, hence, gestational age.

Intraventricular hemorrhage (IVH)—A condition in which fragile blood vessels within the brain burst and bleed into the hollow chambers (ventricles) of the brain and into the tissue surrounding them.

Jaundice—A condition in which the skin and whites of the eyes take on a yellowish color due to an increase of bilirubin (a compound produced by the liver) in the blood. Also called icterus.

Necrotizing enterocolitis—A serious bacterial infection of the intestine that occurs primarily in sick or premature newborn infants. It can cause death of intestinal tissue (necrosis) and may progress to blood poisoning (septicemia).

Respiratory distress syndrome (RDS)—Also known as hyaline membrane disease, this is a condition of premature infants in which the lungs are imperfectly expanded due to a lack of a substance (surfactant) on the lungs that reduces tension.

Retinopathy of prematurity—A condition in which the blood vessels in a premature infant's eyes do not develop normally. It can, in some cases, result in blindness.

Surfactant—A protective film secreted by the alveoli in the lungs that reduces the surface tension of lung fluids, allowing gas exchange and helping maintain the elasticity of lung tissue. Surfactant is normally produced in the fetal lungs in the last months of pregnancy, which helps the air sacs to open up at the time of birth so that the newborn infant can breathe freely. Premature infants may lack surfactant and are more susceptible to respiratory problems without it.

ciated with premature rupture of amniotic sac membranes and premature birth. A well-balanced diet rich in nutrients such as **folic acid**, calcium, iron, zinc, vitamin D, and the B **vitamins** is recommended for pregnant women. Mothers are recommended to eat approximately 300 additional calories a day (above and beyond a normal non-pregnancy diet) to support the fetus's growth and development.

Parental concerns

Parents are often overwhelmed at the prospect of caring for a premature baby. Parents of infants being cared for in the NICU are often recommended to feed, change, and hold their child as long as he or she is medically stable. After the infant leaves the hospital, the parents can seek support from many professional and parent-to-parent resources, including books, web sites, support groups, and national organizations.

Resources

BOOKS

"Premature Infant." Section 19, chapter 260 in *The Merck Manual of Diagnosis and Therapy*, edited by Mark H. Beers and Robert Berkow. Whitehouse Station, NJ: Merck Research Laboratories, 2002.

PERIODICALS

Beachy, J. M. "Premature Infant Massage in the NICU." *Neonatal Network* 22 (May-June 2003): 39–45.

Feldman, Ruth, et al. "Comparison of Skin-to-Skin (Kangaroo) and Traditional Care: Parenting Outcomes and Preterm Infant Development." *Pediatrics* 110, no. 1 (July 2002): 16–26.

Holcroft, C. J., et al. "Association of Prematurity and Neonatal Infection with Neurologic Morbidity in Very Low Birth Weight Infants." *Obstetrics and Gynecology* 101 (June 2003): 1249–53.

Ingemarsson, I. "Gender Aspects of Preterm Birth." *British Journal of Obstetrics and Gynecology* 110 (April 2003): Supplement 20, 34–38.

Meis, P. J., et al. "Prevention of Recurrent Preterm Delivery by 17 Alpha-Hydroxyprogesterone Caproate." *New England Journal of Medicine* 348 (June 12, 2003): 2379–85.

Rosen, C. L., et al. "Prevalence and Risk Factors for Sleep-Disordered Breathing in 8- to 11-Year-Old Children: Association with Race and Prematurity." *Journal of Pediatrics* 142 (April 2003): 383–89.

Ward, R. M., and J. C. Beachy. "Neonatal Complications Following Preterm Birth." *British Journal of Obstetrics and Gynecology* 110 (April 2003): supplement 20, 8–16.

ORGANIZATIONS

American Academy of Pediatrics (AAP). 141 Northwest Point Boulevard, Elk Grove Village, IL 60007. Web site: <www.aap.org>.

National Institute of Child Health and Human Development (NICHD) Information Resource Center (IRC). PO Box 3006, Rockville, MD 20847. Web site: <www.nichd.nih.gov>.

WEB SITES

"Born Too Soon and Too Small in the United States." *March of Dimes Foundation*, 2003. Available online at <www.marchofdimes.com/peristats> (accessed November 2, 2004).

"Prematurity." *March of Dimes Foundation*, 2004. Available online at <www.marchofdimes.com/prematurity/prematurity.asp>.

Altha Roberts Edgren
Rebecca J. Frey, PhD
Stephanie Dionne Sherk

Premenstrual syndrome

Definition

Premenstrual syndrome (PMS) refers to symptoms that occur between ovulation and the onset of **menstruation**. The symptoms include both physical symptoms, such as breast tenderness, back **pain**, abdominal cramps, **headache**, and changes in appetite, and psychological symptoms of **anxiety**, depression, and unrest. Severe forms of this syndrome are referred to as premenstrual dysphoric disorder (PMDD). These symptoms may be related to hormones and emotional disorders.

Description

Approximately 75 percent of all menstruating women experience some symptoms that occur before or during menstruation. PMS encompasses symptoms severe enough to interfere with daily life. About 3 to 7 percent of women experience the more severe PMDD. These symptoms can last four to ten days and can have a substantial impact on a woman's life. The reason some women get severe PMS while others have none was as of 2004, not understood.

Demographics

Not really a characteristic of adolescent girls, PMS symptoms usually begin between ages 20 and 30 years. The disease may run in families and is also more prone to occur in women with a history of psychological problems. Overall however, it is difficult to predict who is most at risk for PMS.

Causes and symptoms

Because PMS is restricted to the second half of a woman's menstrual cycle, after ovulation, it is thought that hormones play a role. During a woman's monthly menstrual cycle, which lasts 24 to 35 days, hormone levels change. The hormone estrogen gradually rises during the first half of a woman's cycle, the preovulatory phase, and falls dramatically at ovulation. After ovulation, the postovulatory phase, progesterone levels gradually increase until menstruation occurs. Both estrogen and progesterone are secreted by the ovaries, which are responsible for producing the eggs. The main role of these hormones is to cause thickening of the lining of the uterus (endometrium). However, estrogen and progesterone also affect other parts of the body, including the brain. In the brain and nervous system, estrogen can affect the levels of neurotransmitters, such as serotonin. Serotonin has long been known to have an effect on emotions, as well as eating behavior. It is thought that when estrogen levels go down during the postovulatory phase of the menstrual cycle, decreases in serotonin levels follow. Whether these changes in estrogen, progesterone, and serotonin are responsible for the emotional aspects of PMS was not, as of 2004, known with certainty. However, most researchers agree that the chemical transmission of signals in the brain and nervous system are in some way related to PMS. This belief is supported by the fact that the times following **childbirth** and menopause are also associated with both depression and low estrogen levels.

Symptoms for PMS are varied and many, including both physical and emotional aspects that range from mild to severe. The physical symptoms include: bloating, headaches, food cravings, abdominal cramps, headaches, tension, and breast tenderness. Emotional aspects include mood swings, irritability, and depression.

When to call the doctor

A physician or other healthcare provider should be called whenever a woman experiences symptoms of PMS that exceed her ability to cope.

Diagnosis

The best way to diagnose PMS is to review a detailed diary of a woman's symptoms for several months. PMS is diagnosed by the presence of physical, psychological, and behavioral symptoms that are cyclic and occur in association with the premenstrual period of time. PMDD, which is far less common, was officially recognized as a disease in 1987. Its diagnosis depends on the presence of at least five symptoms related to mood that disappear within a few days of menstruation. These symptoms must interfere with normal functions and activities of the individual. The diagnosis of PMDD has caused controversy connected to the concern that it may be used against women, labeling them as being impaired by their menstrual cycles.

Treatment

There are many treatments for PMS and PMDD depending on the symptoms and their severity. For mild cases, treatment includes **vitamins**, diuretics, and pain relievers. Vitamins E and B6 may decrease breast tenderness and help with fatigue and mood swings in some women. Diuretics work for some women. For more severe cases and for PMDD, treatments available include antidepressant drugs, hormone treatment, or (only in extreme cases) surgery to remove the ovaries. Hormone treatment usually involves **oral contraceptives**. This treatment, as well as removal of the ovaries, is used to prevent ovulation and the changes in hormones that accompany ovulation. Some studies in the early 2000s, however, indicate that hormone treatment has little effect over placebo.

Antidepressants

The most progress in the treatment of PMS and PMDD has been through the use of antidepressant drugs. The most effective of these are sertraline (Zoloft), fluoxetine (Prozac), and paroxetine (Paxil). They are termed selective serotonin reuptake inhibitors (SSRIs) and act by indirectly increasing the brain serotonin levels, thus stabilizing emotions. Some doctors prescribe antidepressant treatment for PMS throughout the cycle, while others direct women to take the drug only during the latter half of the cycle. **Antidepressants** should be avoided by women who want to become pregnant. Sertraline appears to significantly improve productivity, social activities, and relationships compared. Side effects of sertraline were found to include **nausea**, **diarrhea**, and decreased libido.

There are alternative treatments that can both affect serotonin and hormone responses, as well as affect some of the physical symptoms of PMS.

Vitamins and minerals

Some women find relief with the use of vitamin and mineral supplements. Magnesium can reduce the fluid retention that causes bloating, while calcium may decrease both irritability and bloating. Magnesium and calcium also help relax smooth muscles, and this may reduce cramping. Vitamin E may reduce breast tenderness, nervous tension, fatigue, and insomnia. Vitamin B6 may decrease fluid retention, fatigue, irritability, and mood swings. Vitamin B5 supports the adrenal glands and may help reduce fatigue.

Phytoestrogens and natural progesterone

The Mexican wild yam (*Dioscorea villosa*) contains a substance that may be converted to progesterone in the body. Because this substance is readily absorbed through the skin, it can be found as an ingredient in many skin creams. (Some products also have natural progesterone added to them.) Some herbalists believe that these products can have a progesterone-like effect on the body and decrease some of the symptoms of PMS.

The most important way to alter hormone levels may be by eating more phytoestrogens. These plant-derived compounds have an effect similar to estrogen in the body. One of the richest sources of phytoestrogens is soy products, such as tofu. Additionally, many supplements can be found that contain black cohosh (*Cimicifugaracemosa*) or dong quai (*Angelica sinensis*), which are herbs high in phytoestrogens. Red clover (*Trifolium pratense*), alfalfa (*Medicago sativa*), licorice (*Glycyrrhiza glabra*), hops (*Humulus lupulus*), and legumes are also high in phytoestrogens. Increasing the consumption of phytoestrogens is also associated with decreased risks of osteoporosis, **cancer**, and heart disease.

Antidepressant alternatives

Many antidepressants act by increasing serotonin levels. An alternative means of achieving this result is to eat more carbohydrates. For instance, two cups of cereal or a cup of pasta have enough carbohydrates to effectively increase serotonin levels. An herb known as St. John's wort (*Hypericum perforatum*) has stood up to scientific trials as an effective antidepressant. As with the standard antidepressants, however, it must be taken continuously and does not show an effect until used for four to six weeks. There are also herbs, such as skullcap (*Scutellaria lateriflora*) and kava (*Piper methysticum*), that can relieve the anxiety and irritability that often accompany depression. An advantage of these herbs is that they can be taken when symptoms occur rather than continually. Chaste tree (*Vitex agnus-castus*) in addition to helping rebalance estrogen and progesterone in the body, also may relieve the anxiety and depression associated with PMS.

KEY TERMS

Antidepressant drug—A medication prescribed to relieve major depression. Classes of antidepressants include selective serotonin reuptake inhibitors (fluoxetine/Prozac, sertraline/Zoloft), tricyclics (amitriptyline/Elavil), MAOIs (phenelzine/Nardil), and heterocyclics (bupropion/Wellbutrin, trazodone/Desyrel).

Estrogen—Female hormone produced mainly by the ovaries and released by the follicles as they mature. Responsible for female sexual characteristics, estrogen stimulates and triggers a response from at least 300 tissues. After menopause, the production of the hormone gradually stops.

Neurotransmitter—A chemical messenger that transmits an impulse from one nerve cell to the next.

Phytoestrogens—Compounds found in plants that can mimic the effects of estrogen in the body.

Progesterone—The hormone produced by the ovary after ovulation that prepares the uterine lining for a fertilized egg.

Serotonin—A widely distributed neurotransmitter that is found in blood platelets, the lining of the digestive tract, and the brain, and that works in combination with norepinephrine. It causes very powerful contractions of smooth muscle and is associated with mood, attention, emotions, and sleep. Low levels of serotonin are associated with depression.

Prognosis

The prognosis for women with both PMS and PMDD is good. Most women who are treated for these disorders do well.

Prevention

Maintaining a good diet, one low in sugars and fats and high in phytoestrogens and complex carbohydrates, may prevent some of the symptoms of PMS. Women should try to **exercise** three times a week and keep in generally good health. Because PMS is often associated with stress, avoidance of stress or developing better means to deal with stress can be important.

Nutritional concerns

Consuming foods, such as soy products, that are good sources of phytoestrogens may provide relief of PMS symptoms. In general, eating a balanced diet is beneficial.

Parental concerns

Parents should be aware of the symptoms of PMS in their adolescent daughters. The condition is uncommon but can occur in women under the age of 20.

Resources

BOOKS

Carr, Bruce R., and Karen D. Bradshaw. "Disturbances of Menstruation and Other Common Gynecologic Complaints in Women." In *Harrison's Principles of Internal Medicine*, 15th ed. Edited by Eugene Braunwald et al. New York: McGraw-Hill, 2001, pp. 295–6.

Jenkins, Renee R. "Menstrual Problems." In *Nelson Textbook of Pediatrics*, 17th ed. Edited by Richard E. Behrman et al. Philadelphia: Saunders, 2003, pp. 667–70.

Moe, Barbara. *PMS (Premenstrual Syndrome)*. New York: Rosen Publishing Group, 2002.

Premenstrual Syndrome: A Medical Dictionary, Bibliography, and Annotated Research Guide to Internet References. San Diego, CA: Icon Group International, 2004.

Rebar, Robert W., and Gregory E. Erickson. "Menstrual Cycle and Fertility." In *Cecil Textbook of Medicine*, 22nd ed. Edited by Lee Goldman et al. Philadelphia: Saunders, 2003, pp. 1513–20.

PERIODICALS

Dell, D. L. "Premenstrual Syndrome, Premenstrual Dysphoric Disorder, and Premenstrual Exacerbation of Another Disorder." *Clinical Obstetrics and Gynecology* 47, no. 3 (2004): 568–75.

Derman, O., et al. "Premenstrual syndrome and associated symptoms in adolescent girls." *European Journal of Obstetrics, Gynecology and Reproductive Biology* 116, no. 2 (2004): 201–6.

Johnson, S. R., et al. "Premenstrual syndrome, premenstrual dysphoric disorder, and beyond: a clinical primer for practitioners." *Obstetrics and Gynecology* 104, no. 4 (2004): 845–59.

ORGANIZATIONS

American Society for Reproductive Medicine. 1209 Montgomery Highway, Birmingham, AL 35216–2809. Web site: <www.asrm.com>.

WEB SITES

"Menstruation." *National Library of Medicine.* Available online at <www.nlm.nih.gov/medlineplus/menstruation.html> (accessed January 8, 2005).

"PMS: What You Can Do to Ease Your Symptoms." *American Academy of Family Physicians.* Available online at <http://familydoctor.org/x5126.xml> (accessed January 8, 2005).

"Premenstrual Syndrome." *Mayo Clinic.* Available online at <www.mayoclinic.com/invoke.cfm?id=DS00134> (accessed January 8, 2005).

"Premenstrual Syndrome." *The National Women's Health Information Center.* Available online at <www.4woman.gov/faq/pms.htm> (accessed January 8, 2005).

"Premenstrual Syndrome." *University of Pennsylvania Health System.* Available online at <www.obgyn.upenn.edu/pms/pms.html> (accessed January 8, 2005).

L. Fleming Fallon, Jr., MD, DrPH

Prenatal development

Definition

Prenatal development refers to the process in which a baby develops from a single cell after conception into an embryo and later a fetus.

Description

The average length of time for prenatal development to complete is 38 weeks from the date of conception. During this time, a single-celled zygote develops in a series of stages into a full-term baby. The three primary stages of prenatal development are the germinal stage, the embryonic stage, and the fetal stage.

Germinal stage

Conception occurs when the female egg (ovum) is fertilized by a the male sperm. Under normal circumstances, one egg is released approximately once a month from a woman's ovary during a process called ovulation. The egg makes its way into a fallopian tube, a structure that guides the egg away from the ovary toward the uterus. For fertilization to occur, sperm ejaculated during sexual intercourse (or introduced during artificial insemination) in a substance called semen must have made their way from the vagina into the uterus and subsequently into the fallopian tube where the ovum has been released. This process can take up to ten hours after ejaculation. For fertilization to occur, a sperm must penetrate the tough outer membrane of the egg called the zona pellucida. When one sperm successfully binds with the zona pellucida, a series of chemical reactions occurs to allow only that sperm to penetrate. Fertilization occurs when the sperm successfully enters the ovum's membrane. The genetic material of the sperm and egg then combine to form a single cell called a zygote and the germinal stage of prenatal development commences.

The zygote soon begins to divide rapidly in a process called cleavage, first into two identical cells called blastomeres, which further divide to four cells, then into eight, and so on. The group of diving cells begins to move along the fallopian tube toward the uterus. About sixty hours after fertilization, approximately sixteen cells have formed to what is called a morula, still enclosed by the zona pellucida; three days after fertilization, the morula enters the uterus. As cell division continues, a fluid-filled cavity called a blastocoele forms in the center of the group of cells, with the outer shell of cells called trophoblasts and an inner mass of cells called embryoblasts. The zona pellucida disappears and the morula becomes a blastocyst. At this stage the blastocyst consists of 200 to 300 cells and is ready for implantation.

Implantation, the process in which the blastocyst implants into the uterine wall, occurs approximately six days after conception. Hormones secreted from the mother's ovaries and a chemical secreted by the trophoblasts begin to prepare the uterine wall. The blastocyst first adheres to the wall then moves into the uterine tissue. Implantation marks the end of the germinal stage and the beginning of the embryonic stage.

Embryonic stage

The embryonic stage begins after implantation and lasts until eight weeks after conception. Soon after implantation, the cells continue to rapidly divide and clusters of cells begin to take on different functions (called differentiation). A process (gastrulation) leads to the formation of three distinct layers called germ layers: the ectoderm (outer layer), the mesoderm (middle layer), and the endoderm (inner layer). As the embryo develops, each germ layer differentiates into different tissues and structures. For example, the ectoderm eventually forms skin, nails, hair, brain, nervous tissue and cells, nose, sinuses, mouth, anus, tooth enamel, and other tissues. The mesoderm develops into muscles, bones, heart tissue, lungs, reproductive organs, lymphatic tissue, and other tissues. The endoderm forms the lining of lungs, bladder, digestive tract, tongue, tonsils, and other organs.

The process of differentiation takes place over a period of weeks with different structures forming simultaneously. Some of the major events that occur during the embryonic stage are as follows:

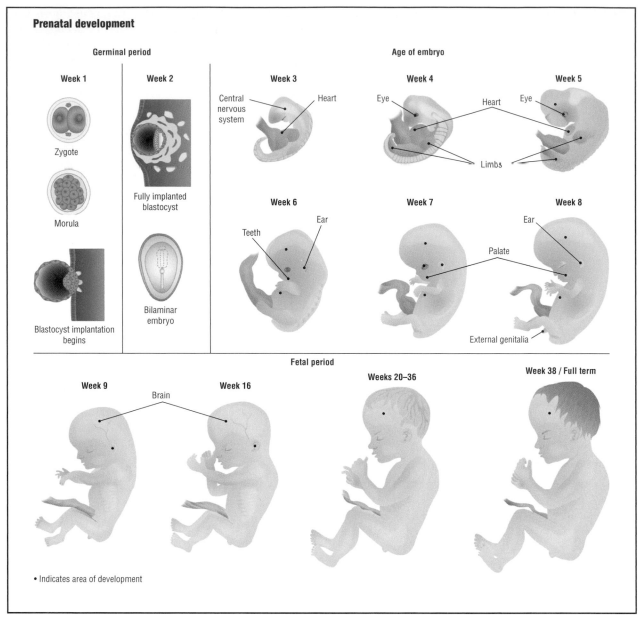

Prenatal development

Germinal period

Week 1

Zygote

Morula

Blastocyst implantation begins

Week 2

Fully implanted blastocyst

Bilaminar embryo

Age of embryo

Week 3
Central nervous system — Heart

Week 4
Eye — Heart — Limbs

Week 5
Eye

Week 6
Teeth — Ear

Week 7

Week 8
Ear — Palate — External genitalia

Fetal period

Week 9
Brain

Week 16

Weeks 20–36

Week 38 / Full term

• Indicates area of development

Illustration of prenatal development, from the two-cell, or zygote, stage through the embryonic stage, in which the major body systems develop, to the fetal stage, during which the baby's brain develops and the body adds size and weight. *(Illustration by GGS Information Services.)*

• Week 3: Beginning development of the brain, heart, blood cells, circulatory system, spinal cord, and digestive system.

• Week 4: Beginning development of bones, facial structures, and limbs (presence of arm and leg buds); continuing development of the heart (which begins to beat), brain, and nervous tissue.

• Week 5: Beginning development of eyes, nose, kidneys, lungs; continuing development of the heart (formation of valves), brain, nervous tissue, and digestive tract.

• Week 6: Beginning development of hands, feet, and digits; continuing development of brain, heart, and circulation system.

- Week 7: Beginning development of hair follicles, nipples, eyelids, and sex organs (testes or ovaries); first formation of urine in the kidneys and first evidence of brain waves.
- Week 8: Facial features more distinct, internal organs well developed, the brain can signal for muscles to move, heart development ends, external sex organs begin to form.

By the end of the embryonic stage, all essential external and internal structures have been formed. The embryo is now referred to as a fetus.

Fetal stage

Prenatal development is most dramatic during the fetal stage. When an embryo becomes a fetus at eight weeks, it is approximately 3 centimeters (1.2 inches) in length from crown to rump and weighs about 3 grams (0.1 ounce). By the time the fetus is considered full-term at 38 weeks gestation, he or she may be 50 centimeters (20 inches) or 3.3 kilograms (7.3 pounds). Although all of the organ systems were formed during embryonic development, they continue to develop and grow during the fetal stage. Examples of some of the major features of fetal development by week are as follows:

- Weeks 9–12: The fetus reaches approximately 8 cm. (3.2 in.) in length; the head is approximately half the size of the fetus. External features such as the face, neck, eyelids, limbs, digits, and genitals are well formed. The beginnings of teeth appear, and red blood cells begin to be produced in the liver. The fetus is able to make a fist.
- Weeks 13–15: The fetus reaches approximately 15 cm. (6 in.) in length. Fine hair called lanugo first develops on the head; structures such as the lungs, sweat glands, muscles, and bones continue to develop. The fetus is able to swallow and make sucking motions.
- Weeks 16–20: The fetus reaches approximately 20 cm. (8 in.) in length. Lanugo begins to cover all skin surfaces, and fat begins to develop under the skin. Features such as finger and toenails, eyebrows, and eyelashes appear. The fetus becomes more active, and the mother can sometimes begin to feel fetal movements at this stage.
- Weeks 21–24: The fetus reaches approximately 28.5 cm. (11.2 in.) in length and weighs approximately 0.7 kg (1 lb. 10 oz.). Hair grows longer on the head, and the eyebrows and eye lashes finish forming. The lungs continue to develop with the formation of air sac (alveoli); the eyes finish developing. A startle reflex develops at this time.

- Weeks 25–28: The fetus reaches approximately 38 cm. (15 in.) in length and weighs approximately 1.2 kg (2 lb. 11 oz.). The next few weeks mark a period of rapid brain and nervous system development. The fetus gains greater control over movements such as opening and closing eyelids and certain body functions. The lungs have developed sufficiently that air breathing is possible.
- Weeks 29–32: The fetus reaches approximately 38–43 cm. (15–17 in.) in length and weighs approximately 2 kg (4 lb. 6 oz.). Fat deposits become more pronounced under the skin. The lungs remain immature but breathing movements begin. The fetus's bones are developed but not yet hardened.
- Weeks 33–36: The fetus reaches approximately 41–48 cm. (16–19 in.) in length and weighs 2.6–3.0 kg (5 lb. 12 oz. to 6 lb. 12 oz.). Body fat continues to increase, lanugo begins to disappear, and fingernails are fully grown. The fetus has gained a high degree of control over body functions.
- Weeks 36–38: The fetus reaches 48–53 cm. (19–21 in.) in length is considered to be full-term by the end of this period. Lanugo has mostly disappeared and is replaced with thicker hair on the head. Fingernails have grown past the tips of the fingers. In a healthy fetus, all organ systems are functioning.

Common problems

Although 90 percent of babies born in the United States are considered healthy, abnormalities may arise during prenatal development that are considered congenital (inherited or due to a genetic abnormality) or environmental (such as material derived abnormalities). In other cases, problems may arise when a fetus is born prematurely.

Congenital abnormalities

In some cases abnormalities may arise during prenatal development that cause physical malformations or developmental delays or affect various parts of the body after the child is born. The cause may be a small mutation in or damage to the genetic material of cells, or a major chromosomal abnormality (each normal cell has two copies each of 23 strands [called chromosomes] of genetic material, and abnormalities can arise if there are three copies of a strand or only one). Sometimes the abnormality is inherited from one or both parents; in other cases, the defect occurs because of an error in prenatal development.

Some abnormalities are minor and do not affect the long-term prognosis once the child is born. At the other end of the spectrum, abnormalities may be so severe that fetal demise is inevitable. Approximately 10 to 15 percent of pregnancies end before the twentieth week, a process called miscarriage or spontaneous abortion; congenital abnormalities account for a significant proportion of miscarriages. Genetic abnormalities account for approximately 5 percent of miscarriages.

Maternal derived abnormalities

The age, health status, nutritional status, and environment of the mother are all closely tied to the health of a growing embryo or fetus. Some examples of environmental factors that may lead to developmental abnormalities include:

- Age: As of 2004, research showed that babies born to mothers between the ages of seventeen and thirty-five tend to be healthier. One reason is that the risk of certain congenital abnormalities such as **Down syndrome** increases with mother's age (particularly mothers over forty). Another reason is that the risk of having pregnancy or birth complications is greater with women over the age of thirty-five.

- Health status: In some cases a mother may pass a viral or bacterial infection to the fetus, such as in human **immunodeficiency** virus (HIV). In other cases, a mother's illness may cause congenital malformations; an example is **rubella**, which can cause heart defects, deafness, developmental delays, and other problems in a fetus if the mother contracts it during pregnancy.

- Nutritional status: A well-balanced diet rich in nutrients such as **folic acid**, calcium, iron, zinc, vitamin D, and the B **vitamins** is recommended for pregnant women. Certain vitamin and mineral deficiencies can interfere with normal prenatal development. For example, a deficiency in folic acid during the early stages of pregnancy may lead to neural tube defects such as **spina bifida**. Mothers are recommended to eat approximately 300 additional calories a day (above and beyond a normal non-pregnancy diet) to support the fetus's growth and development.

- Other environmental factors: Exposure to certain substances called teratogens (agents that may interfere with prenatal development) during pregnancy may cause embryonic or fetal malformations. Examples of teratogens include alcohol, thalidomide, cocaine, certain seizure medications, diethylstilbestrol (DES), and the anti-acne drug Accutane.

Prematurity

Advances in medical care have made it possible for many infants born prematurely to survive and develop

KEY TERMS

Miscarriage—Loss of the embryo or fetus and other products of pregnancy before the twentieth week. Often, early in a pregnancy, if the condition of the baby and/or the mother's uterus are not compatible with sustaining life, the pregnancy stops, and the contents of the uterus are expelled. For this reason, miscarriage is also referred to as spontaneous abortion.

Ovary—One of the two almond-shaped glands in the female reproductive system responsible for producing eggs and the sex hormones estrogen and progesterone.

Teratogen—Any drug, chemical, maternal disease, or exposure that can cause physical or functional defects in an exposed embryo or fetus.

Uterus—The female reproductive organ that contains and nourishes a fetus from implantation until birth. Also called the womb.

normally. The earlier the gestational age, the greater the chance of death or significant medical problems. Whether or not a premature infant will survive is intimately tied to his or her gestational age:

- 21 weeks or less: 0 percent survival rate
- 22 weeks: 0–10 percent survival rate
- 23 weeks: 10–35 percent survival rate
- 24 weeks: 40–70 percent survival rate
- 25 weeks: 50–80 percent survival rate
- 26 weeks: 80–90 percent survival rate
- 27 weeks: greater than 90 percent survival rate

Parental concerns

Many parents have questions or concerns about the prenatal development of an existing or anticipated child and what steps they should take to ensure their child's health. During prenatal visits to an obstetrician, a pregnant mother should be educated in proper **nutrition** and prenatal care; often, prenatal vitamins are prescribed to avoid nutritional deficiencies. Prenatal testing is often recommended to parents-to-be as a means of assessing the fetus's health and the risk of developing certain conditions. Some common prenatal tests that relate to prenatal development are as follows:

- blood tests to check for diseases that could affect the fetus, such as HIV, **hepatitis B**, or other sexually transmitted diseases

- blood tests to check if the mother carries a protein called Rh factor on her red blood cells; if she does not and her baby does (determined by whether the father is Rh-positive or not), she will require treatment to prevent a potentially damaging reaction to the baby

- chorionic villus sampling, a prenatal test that takes a tiny sample of the placenta with a needle to test for chromosomal abnormalities

- nuchal fold or nuchal translucency screening test, which measures a small space at the back of the fetus's neck using ultrasound; fetuses with larger nuchal folds have a greater risk of having a chromosomal abnormality

- amniocentesis, a test that takes a sample of the fluid that surrounds the fetus in the uterus to identify certain genetic disorders, congenital malformations, or the maturity of the fetus's lungs

Resources

BOOKS

Gilbert, Scott F. *Developmental Biology*, 6th ed. Sunderland, MA: Sinauer Associates, Inc., 2000.

PERIODICALS

Miller, Sharon M., and Jeanne M. Isabel. "Prenatal Screening Tests Facilitate Risk Assessment." *Medical Laboratory Observer* 34, no. 2 (February 2002): 8–21.

ORGANIZATIONS

March of Dimes Birth Defects Foundation. 1275 Mamaroneck Ave., White Plains, NY 10605. Web site: <www.marchofdimes.com>.

National Institute of Child Health and Human Development (NICHD) Information Resource Center (IRC). PO Box 3006, Rockville, MD 20847. Web site: <www.nichd.nih.gov>.

WEB SITES

Hill, Mark. *UNSW Embryology*, 2004. Available online at <http://embryology.med.unsw.edu.au> (accessed December 11, 2004).

McPherson, Katrina. "Fetal Development." *MedlinePlus*, May 8, 2004. Available online at <www.nlm.nih.gov/medlineplus/ency/article/002398.htm> (accessed December 11, 2004).

Stephanie Dionne Sherk

Prenatal surgery

Definition

Prenatal surgery is a surgical procedure performed on a fetus prior to birth.

Purpose

Prenatal surgery, also called fetal surgery, antenatal surgery, or maternal-fetal surgery, usually is performed under circumstances in which the fetus is not expected to survive delivery or to live long after birth without prenatal intervention. The most common prenatal surgeries are for conditions in which the child will not be able to breathe on its own after birth. There are only about 600 candidates for prenatal surgery in the United States each year and far fewer prenatal surgeries are performed. Most of these procedures are high-risk and may be considered experimental.

More common prenatal surgeries

Urinary tract obstructions in male fetuses are usually caused by a narrowing of the urinary tract. This can cause the urine, which normally flows out into the amniotic fluid surrounding the fetus, to back up and injure the kidneys. If only one kidney is affected and there is a normal amount of amniotic fluid, prenatal intervention is not required. However, in addition to kidney damage, urinary tract obstructions can lead to multiple abnormalities and depleted amniotic fluid, which endangers the fetus and prevents the lungs from growing. About 10 percent of fetuses with urinary tract obstructions may require prenatal surgery in which a device is placed in the fetus's bladder to drain the urine into the amniotic sac.

Congenital diaphragmatic **hernia** (CDH) occurs when the diaphragm does not form completely at about eight weeks of gestation, leaving a hole in this muscle that separates the chest and the abdomen. The stomach, intestines, liver, spleen, and kidneys can move into the chest cavity through this hole, which is most often on the left side. Most babies with CDH are treated after birth. However, about 50 percent of fetuses with CDH do not survive after birth because their lungs are too small (pulmonary hypoplasia). A fetus whose liver has moved into its chest, seriously restricting lung development, whose lung-to-head ratio is less than one in four, and whose chance of survival through delivery is less than 50 percent may be a candidate for surgery. CDH fetuses whose livers have not moved into the chest have a survival rate of about 90 percent without prenatal intervention.

Congenital cystic adenomatoid malformation (CCAM) occurs when one or more lobes of the lungs develop into fluid-filled sacs called cysts rather than into normal lung tissue. Most CCAMs disappear on their own or are small enough to not cause problems. Large CCAMs can limit lung development, causing pulmonary hypoplasia. About 10 percent of fetuses with CCAMs are at risk of heart failure because the cysts push into the heart. CCAMs also can push on the trachea and the esophagus where they prevent the fetus from ingesting amniotic fluid. Prenatal surgery to drain or remove the cyst is performed only on severely affected fetuses.

Sometimes prenatal surgery is performed to remove a tumor. Sacrococcygeal teratoma (SCT) is the most common tumor in newborns, occurring in one out of every 35,000 to 40,000 births. It is more common in girls than in boys. These tumors at the base of the tailbone can grow very large. With early diagnosis, most SCT babies are delivered normally and the tumor is removed after birth. However, a small percentage of these tumors are large, hard, and full of blood vessels and may stress the fetal heart. These may be treated with a surgical procedure that destroys the blood vessels leading to the tumor, thereby preventing its growth.

Up to 15 percent of **twins** who share a placenta (monochorionic twins) have twin-twin transfusion syndrome (TTTS). Because of abnormal blood vessel connections in the placenta, one twin pumps the circulating blood for both twins. As a result the pumping twin has reduced volumes of blood and amniotic fluid and the recipient twin as increased volumes, leading to a variety of problems, including the risk of heart failure in both fetuses. TTTS may be treated by removing fluid from the overfilled recipient amniotic sac and placing it into the depleted sac of the pumping twin. If this fails, prenatal surgery may be used to destroy the abnormal blood vessel connections in the placenta.

Twin-twin reverse arterial perfusion (TRAP) sequence occurs in about 1 percent of monochorionic twins. In a TRAP sequence one twin develops normally and the other lacks a heart. The normal twin pumps all the blood for both twins and is at risk for heart failure. If left untreated 50 to 75 percent of these normal twins die. In prenatal surgery for TRAP sequence, the connections between the twins are severed.

Other prenatal surgeries

Other conditions that may be treated by prenatal surgery include:

- various congenital defects that block air passages and will prevent the newborn from breathing on its own

- various lung malformations

- omphalocele, a birth defect in which an opening in the fetus's abdominal wall enables portions of the stomach, liver, and intestines to protrude

- fetal gastroschisis, a birth defect in which the abdominal wall muscles do not form correctly and the stomach and intestines protrude and float in the amniotic fluid, a condition that occurs primarily in fetuses of mothers in their late teens or early 20s

- bowel obstructions, usually caused by a narrowing in the small intestine

- experimental hematopoietic stem cell transplants for X-linked **severe combined immunodeficiency** syndrome

Hypoplastic left heart syndrome, in which the blood flow through the left side of the heart is obstructed, is the most common congenital heart defect that is a candidate for prenatal surgery. In this condition, which is often fatal, the left side of the heart is very small and stops working.

Spina bifida

Until the late 1990s, prenatal surgery was almost exclusively limited to life-threatening conditions. However in 1994 the first prenatal surgery to treat **spina bifida** (myelomeningocele) was performed. This is the second most common birth defect in the United States, affecting one out of every 2,000 newborns. It is not considered to be life-threatening.

Spina bifida occurs during the first month of fetal development when a small bit of bone and skin fails to fully enclose the nerves of the spinal cord, leaving a hole or lesion. Depending on the location of the lesion, spina bifida may not require treatment; the higher up the opening in the spinal cord, the more severe the condition, and myelomeningocele can cause severe deformities, paralysis, and **mental retardation**. The damage appears to be caused by leakage of fluid from the spinal cord and exposure of the cord to amniotic fluid. The risk of infant death is about 10 percent and after the age of one, about 1 percent of affected children die each year.

Surgery for spina bifida requires closing the opening in the cord. Since the damage from spina bifida occurs during fetal development, prenatal surgery may reduce the damage. However, prenatal surgery for spina bifida has become enmeshed in the politics of reproductive rights and fetal rights. As of 2004, prenatal surgery for spina bifida was available only as part of a prospective randomized clinical trial.

Description

The decision to have prenatal surgery is made on the basis of detailed ultrasound imaging of the fetus, including an echocardiogram that uses ultrasound to obtain images of the fetal heart, as well as other diagnostic tools. Consultations include a perinatologist, a neonatologist, a pediatric surgeon, a clinical nurse specialist, and a social worker. Usually only fetuses with a very poor prognosis are candidates for maternal-fetal surgery. Only about 10 percent of those referred for evaluation actually undergo the surgery. Since additional congenital defects preclude prenatal surgery, **amniocentesis** or chorionic villi sampling (CVS) are used to check for chromosomal abnormalities in the fetus. Prenatal surgeries usually are performed between 18 and 26 weeks of gestation.

Prenatal surgery usually requires a general anesthetic. The fetus receives the anesthetic via the mother's blood. During the operation the anesthesiologist controls the mother's breathing through a tube into her throat and airway. The anesthesiologist and a perinatologist monitor the heart rates of the mother and fetus. For some procedures an epidural anesthetic that numbs the abdominal region may be used instead of general anesthesia.

Open surgeries

Open prenatal surgery requires a procedure similar to a **cesarean section** (C-section) for delivering a baby through the mother's abdomen. Incisions are made through the mother's abdominal wall. In some procedures the fetus is partially removed from the uterus. In other procedures the entire uterus is removed from the mother's body cavity through her abdomen.

Using ultrasound as a guide, the surgeon feels for the affected fetal part. The fetus must be moved away from the placenta, the disk-shaped organ within the uterus that provides the blood supply to the fetus. The surgeon may knead and push on the uterus to move or flip the fetus. A narrow tube in placed through a tiny hole in the uterine wall, through which the amniotic fluid is drained and collected in syringes. Opening the uterus is the riskiest component of prenatal surgery. The first incision is made at a point away from the placenta to prevent damaging it. A special device simultaneously makes the incision and clamps the edges to prevent bleeding. Following the procedure the fetus is replaced in the uterus and the incision is stitched. Prior to the final stitch the amniotic fluid is re-injected into the uterus. The uterus is repositioned in the mother's body cavity and her abdominal wall is closed.

The first successful open fetal surgery was performed in 1981 for a urinary tract obstruction. A tiny hole was made in the bladder of the fetus and a catheter (a long, thin tube) was inserted to drain the urine directly into the amniotic fluid. The first successful open fetal surgery for CDH was performed in 1989.

Prenatal open surgery for CCAM requires opening the fetal chest. If a large cyst does not have a hard component, procedures called thoracoamniotic shunting or catheter decompression may be used to drain the cyst. Otherwise the surgeon must remove all or a portion of the mass. The first successful resection (removal) of a CCAM from a fetal lung was performed in 1990. The first resectioning of a fetal SCT was performed in 1992.

Between 1997 and 2004, more than 200 open surgeries were performed for myelomeningocele. An incision the size of a small fist is made in the uterus. The surgeon loosens and lifts the tissues of the spinal canal lesion and stitches them closed. The entire procedure takes about one hour.

Less invasive procedures

For urinary tract obstructions a needle may be used to insert a catheter through the mother's abdomen and uterus and into the fetal bladder where it drains the urine into the amniotic fluid. The catheter may have an expandable wire mesh that expands in the bladder to prevent the catheter from plugging up or dislodging.

The first successful fetoscopic temporary tracheal occlusion for CDH was performed in 1996. Small surgical openings are made in the uterus, and a tiny fiber optic fetoscope is inserted to guide the operation. A needle-like instrument enters the uterus through a small incision in the mother's abdomen. A balloon placed in the fetus's trachea prevents lung fluid from escaping through the mouth, enabling the lungs to expand, grow, and push the abdominal organs out of the chest and back into the abdomen. The balloon is removed at birth. In a successful procedure the lungs are developed enough that the baby will breathe on its own at birth.

Hypoplastic left heart syndrome is treated by passing a needle, guided by ultrasound, through the mother's abdominal wall, into the uterus and the fetal heart. A catheter is passed through the needle across the fetus's aortic valve. A balloon is inflated, opening the valve and allowing blood to flow through the left side of the heart.

Radiofrequency ablation

Radiofrequency ablation (RFA) sometimes can be used for SCT. Guided by ultrasound a needle is inserted through the mother's abdomen and uterus and into the tumor. Radiofrequency waves sent through the needle destroy the blood supply to the tumor with heat. This slows the tumor's growth and may enable the fetus to survive until delivery. The first RFA of a SCT was performed in 1998.

A TRAP sequence also may be treated by RFA. A 3-mm needle targets the exact point where the blood enters the twin without a heart. Using an echocardiogram device, RFA is applied until the blood vessels and surrounding tissue are destroyed and the blood flow is halted. This procedure has eliminated the need for open surgery or larger fetoscopes to treat a TRAP sequence.

Laser treatment

TTTS is a progressive disorder and early intervention may prevent later complications. The most common treatment for TTTS is amnioreduction in which a syringe through the mother's abdomen is used to remove amniotic fluid from the overfilled sac and place it in the sac of the other twin. This procedure may need to be repeated during the course of the pregnancy. If TTTS does not respond to amnioreduction, laser treatment may be attempted to stop the abnormal blood circulation. Following detailed ultrasound, a thin fetoscope is inserted through the mother's abdominal and uterine walls and into the amniotic cavity of the recipient twin to examine the surface placental vessels. The abnormal blood vessel connections are located and eliminated with a laser beam. The first successful fetoscopic laser treatment for TTTS was performed in 1999.

EXIT

Ex utero intrapartum treatment (EXIT) is a surgery performed for a congenital defect that blocks the fetus's airway. The fetus is removed from the womb by cesarean section but the umbilical cord is left intact so that the mother's placenta continues to sustain the fetus. After the air passage is cleared, the umbilical cord is cut and the newborn can breathe on its own. The EXIT procedure is used for various types of airway obstruction including CCAM.

Precautions

The decision to undergo prenatal surgery is a difficult one. Considerations must include the following:

- serious risks for the mother and fetus
- time commitment for the surgery
- extended postoperative bed rest, perhaps until delivery
- travel to a hospital that performs the procedure
- possible need to stay near the hospital until delivery

- significant commitment of financial resources; some surgeries may not be covered by insurance
- arrangements for care of other children

Preparation

Prior to surgery the mother will need to do the following:

- arrange for help and support following the surgery since she will be on bed rest to prevent preterm labor
- prepare for the possibility of having to remain near the hospital until delivery
- possibly make arrangements for a blood donor in the unlikely event that she needs a blood transfusion
- take betamethasone, a steroid, in two intramuscular injections 12–24 hours apart to accelerate lung maturity in the fetus; if delivery occurs earlier than 34 weeks, the mother may have to take it again closer to the delivery date
- wear a fetal/uterine monitor after hospital admission
- have urine and blood samples taken
- have her blood typed and cross-matched in case of the need for a transfusion
- have an intravenous (IV) infusion of fluid and electrolytes
- take a sleeping medication
- sign a surgical consent
- wear thick elastic stockings
- take a medication for decreasing stomach acids

The mother usually is given medications called tocolytics to prevent contractions and labor during and after surgery. Tocolytics include:

- indocin suppositories before surgery and up to 48 hours after surgery
- magnesium sulfate for one to two days after surgery with careful monitoring
- nifedipine, a pill given every four to six hours as the indocin is being decreased; usually nifedipine is continued until 37 weeks of gestation or delivery
- terbutalin in pill form

Aftercare

Following the surgery the mother lies in bed on her side to provide the best circulation to the fetus and to help prevent contractions. The mother will have:

- an oxygen mask to provide post-anesthetic supplemental oxygen

- an IV catheter to supply fluids and **antibiotics** for at least 48 hours after surgery

- a urinary catheter to collect urine from the bladder for 48–72 hours

- an epidural catheter to supply constant **pain** medication, usually morphine, for several days after surgery, followed by oral pain medications

- a sequential compression device to improve blood circulation in the legs during bed rest

- a continuous electronic fetal/uterine monitor to check the fetal heart and the uterine response to the tocolytics and to check for signs of preterm labor

- a transparent dressing over the abdominal incision so that the fetus can be monitored and the incision site observed without removing the dressing

Fluids and food are not taken by mouth until the mother's digestive function returns. She usually remains in the hospital for four to seven days following surgery.

To prevent or treat postoperative lung or circulatory problems, the mother should:

- practice deep breathing to keep all airways clear

- perform incentive spirometer exercises, using a small simple device to assist deep breathing and opening of the lungs, five times during each waking hour

- be turned from side to side at least every two hours to increase circulation and relieve areas of pressure

- practice foot flexion exercises to improve circulation and help prevent blood clots

After discharge from the hospital the mother will be on modified bed rest, lying on her side until 37 weeks of gestation. This increases blood flow to the fetus and reduces pressure on the cervix to help prevent uterine contractions. She will be given bed rest exercises and prescribed a special diet. She will see a perinatologist once a week and have at least one ultrasound per week.

Risks

A major risk of prenatal surgery is nicking the placenta, causing blood hemorrhaging, uterine contractions, and birth of a premature infant who may not survive. Preterm labor is the most common complication of prenatal surgery. Fetoscopic surgeries are less dangerous and traumatic than open fetal surgery and reduce the risk of premature labor. Subsequent children of a mother who has undergone fetal surgery usually are delivered by cesarean section because of scarring of the uterus.

Other risks to the mother include:

- extensive blood loss

- complications from general anesthesia

- side effects, potentially fatal, from medications to control premature labor

- rupturing of the uterine incision

- infection of the wound or uterus

- psychological stress

- inability to have additional children

- death

All fetuses that undergo surgery are born prematurely. Infants born even six weeks early are at risk for delays in walking and talking and for learning problems. Infants born at 30 weeks of gestation or less are at risk for blindness, **cerebral palsy**, and brain hemorrhages.

About 25 percent of women undergoing prenatal surgery lose some amniotic fluid, often because of leakage at the uterine incision. Amniotic fluid is essential for lung development and protects the fetus from injury and infection. If all of the amniotic fluid is lost, the fetal lungs may not develop properly. Without the cushion that enables the fetus to float, the fetus may compress the umbilical cord causing death.

Other risks to the fetus include:

- birth during surgery

- membrane separation between the tissues surrounding the amniotic fluid sac and the uterus, causing early delivery or interference with blood flow to some fetal body part such as an arm or leg

- further damage to the spinal cord and nerves during prenatal surgery for spina bifida

- intrauterine infection requiring immediate birth of the fetus

- brain damage

- physical deformities

- death

Normal results

Although fetal surgeries heal without scarring, they are rare and risky, and it is difficult to predict the outcome. In general, the following usually occurs:

- Fetal surgery for CDH lessens the severity of the condition so that the fetus usually survives delivery and lives long enough to undergo corrective surgery.

- Thoracoamniotic shunting for CCAM usually results in survival.

Amniocentesis—A procedure performed at 16-18 weeks of pregnancy in which a needle is inserted through a woman's abdomen into her uterus to draw out a small sample of the amniotic fluid from around the baby for analysis. Either the fluid itself or cells from the fluid can be used for a variety of tests to obtain information about genetic disorders and other medical conditions in the fetus.

Amniotic fluid—The liquid in the amniotic sac that cushions the fetus and regulates temperature in the placental environment. Amniotic fluid also contains fetal cells.

Cesarean section—Delivery of a baby through an incision in the mother's abdomen instead of through the vagina; also called a C-section, Cesarean birth, or Cesarean delivery.

Chorion—The outer membrane of the amniotic sac. Chorionic villi develop from its outer surface early in pregnancy. The villi establish a physical connection with the wall of the uterus and eventually develop into the placenta.

Chorionic villus sampling—A procedure used for prenatal diagnosis at 10-12 weeks gestation. Under ultrasound guidance a needle is inserted either through the mother's vagina or abdominal wall and a sample of the chorionic membrane. These cells are then tested for chromosome abnormalities or other genetic diseases.

Congenital cystic adenomatoid malformation (CCAM)—A condition in which one or more lobes of the fetal lungs develop into fluid-filled sacs called cysts.

Congenital diaphragmatic hernia (CDH)—A condition in which the fetal diaphragm (the muscle dividing the chest and abdominal cavity) does not close completely.

Echocardiography—A non-invasive technique, using ultrasound waves, used to look at the various structures and functions of the heart.

Ex utero intrapartum treatment (EXIT)—A cesarean section in which the infant is removed from the uterus but the umbilical cord is not cut until after surgery for a congenital defect that blocks the air passage.

Fetoscope—A fiber optic instrument for viewing the fetus inside the uterus.

Monochorionic twins—Twins that share a single placenta.

Omphalocele—A birth defect where the bowel and sometimes the liver, protrudes through an opening in the baby's abdomen near the umbilical cord.

Placenta—The organ that provides oxygen and nutrition from the mother to the unborn baby during pregnancy. The placenta is attached to the wall of the uterus and leads to the unborn baby via the umbilical cord.

Pulmonary hypoplasia—Incomplete or defective development of the lungs.

Radiofrequency ablation (RFA)—A procedure in which radiofrequency waves are used to destroy blood vessels and tissues.

Sacrococcygeal teratoma (SCT)—A tumor occurring at the base of the tailbone in a fetus.

Spina bifida—A birth defect (a congenital malformation) in which part of the vertebrae fail to develop completely so that a portion of the spinal cord, which is normally protected within the vertebral column, is exposed. People with spina bifida can suffer from bladder and bowel incontinence, cognitive (learning) problems, and limited mobility.

Tocolytic drug—A compound given to women to stop the progression of labor.

Twin-twin transfusion syndrome (TTTS)—A condition in identical monochorionic twins in which there is a connection between the two circulatory systems so that the donor twin pumps the blood to the recipient twin without a return of blood to the donor.

Twin:twin reverse arterial perfusion (TRAP) sequence—A condition in which one fetus lacks a heart and the other fetus pumps the blood for both.

Ultrasonography—A medical test in which sound waves are directed against internal structures in the body. As sound waves bounce off the internal structure, they create an image on a video screen. Ultrasonography is often used to diagnose fetal abnormalities, gallstones, heart defects, and tumors. Also called ultrasound imaging.

- Removal of solid CCAM cysts has a survival rate of about 50 percent.
- RFA to slow the growth of a tumor usually enables the fetus to survive delivery, after which the tumor can be removed.
- Survival rates for prenatal treatment of TTTS are about 70 percent.

Prenatal surgery for spina bifida does not cure the condition. However, babies who survive the surgery appear to be 33 to 50 percent less likely to have **hydrocephalus**, a condition that requires surgically implanted tubes or shunts to remove fluid from the ventricles (cavities of the brain). The surgery also appears to reverse hindbrain herniation, in which the back of the brain slips down into the spinal canal. This condition can cause difficulties in breathing and swallowing and leads to death in 15 percent of children with spina bifida. In addition, children who have prenatal surgery for spina bifida appear to have better brain function than children who do not have surgery. However prenatal surgery does not prevent two of the most serious conditions associated with spina bifida: leg movement and bladder and bowel control. As of 2004, the long-term prognosis for these children was not known.

When to call the doctor

The doctor should be called if any of the following occurs:

- The abdominal incision become red, warm, tender to the touch, or is draining fluid.
- The mother's body temperature rises above 101°F (38.5°C).
- Fluid is leaking from the vagina.
- Vaginal bleeding occurs.
- The baby does not move daily.
- Persistent back pain, cramping, abdominal tightening, or pelvic pressure occurs.
- Chest pain or difficulty breathing develops.

Signs of preterm labor include:

- gas pain
- abdominal tightening
- cramping
- backache
- pelvic pressure
- change in vaginal discharge
- leakage of vaginal fluid
- bleeding

Resources

BOOKS

Bianchi, Diana W., et al. *Fetology: Diagnosis and Management of the Fetal Patient.* New York: McGraw-Hill, 2005.

PERIODICALS

Hedrick, Holly L., et al. "History of Fetal Diagnosis and Therapy: Children's Hospital of Philadelphia Experience." *Fetal Diagnosis and Therapy* 18, no. 2 (March-April 2003): 65–82.

Jones, Maggie. "A Miracle, and Yet." *New York Times Magazine* (July 15, 2001): 38–43.

Kalb, Claudia. "Treating the Tiniest Patients." *Newsweek,* June 9, 2003.

Paek, Bettina W., et al. "Advances in Fetal Surgery." *Female Patient* 25, no. 6 (June 2000): 15–18.

ORGANIZATIONS

Fetal Treatment Center. University of California at San Francisco (UCSF) Children's Hospital. 505 Parnassus Ave., San Francisco, CA 94143. Web site: <www.ucsfhealth.org/childrens/medical_services/surgical/fetal>.

Management of Myelomeningocele Study (MOMS). The George Washington University Biostatistics Center, 6110 Executive Blvd., Suite 750, Rockville, MD 20852. Web site: <www.spinabifidamoms.com>.

WEB SITES

Bunch, Kathy. "Giving Baby a Chance, Before Birth." *WebMDHealth,* 2001. Available online at <http://my.webmd.com/content/article/14/3606_466.htm?lastselectedguid={5FE84E90-BC77-4056-A91C-9531713CA348> (accessed January 17, 2005).

"Fetal Treatment." *UCSF Children's Hospital,* April 2002. Available online at <www.ucsfhealth.org/childrens/medical_services/surgical/fetal> (accessed January 17, 2005).

"Fetal Treatment: Patient Education." *UCSF Children's Hospital,* March 2003. Available online at <www.ucsfhealth.org/childrens/medical_services/surgical/fetal/moreinfo/patient_education.html> (accessed January 17, 2005).

Mayo Clinic Staff. "Spina Bifida: Treatment." *Mayo Foundation for Medical Education and Research,* December 8, 2003. Available online at <www.mayoclinic.com/invoke.cfm?objectid=CB5F085A-6152-42FC-8CFC55380EF705A2&dsection=8> (accessed January 17, 2005).

Margaret Alic, Ph.D.

Preschool

Definition

Preschool is an early childhood program in which children combine learning with **play** in a program run by professionally trained adults. Children are most commonly enrolled in preschool between the ages of three and five, though those as young as two can attend some schools. Preschools are different from traditional **day care** in that their emphasis is learning and development rather than enabling parents to work or pursue other activities.

Description

Before 1960, the education of young children was primarily regarded as the responsibility of families within the home. As of 2004, most young children in the United States spend some portion of their days apart from their parents. Most attend some sort of center-based program prior to kindergarten. In 2001, 52 percent of three- and four-year-olds were in a nursery school or preschool program. The enrollment rate for four-year-olds in 2001 was nearly the same as the enrollment rate for five-year-olds in 1970. There are several factors influencing this dramatic change, including a rise in the numbers of mothers working outside the home, a decline in the size of families (leading more parents to turn to preschools as a social outlet for their children), and a growing desire to give children a head start academically. The higher the income and educational level of the parents, the more likely it is that a child will attend preschool. This correlation remains true in spite of increasing governmental support for programs targeting children in low-income households.

In addition to being called preschool, these programs are known by other names, including child care, day care, and nursery school. They vary widely in their setting, format, and educational philosophy. Preschools may meet all-day or half-day, either every day or just a few days per week. They may be sponsored by a church, operate as an independent non-profit, or run for profit. They may be part of the public school system or part of the Federal Head Start program.

Types of preschool programs

PRIVATE PRESCHOOLS Private preschools operate as for-profits, independent nonprofits, and programs sponsored by religious organizations. Most are part-day programs. Some so-called lower schools are affiliated with private schools and maintain an educational philosophy in accord with the parent institution. Though the margin is small, private preschools still claimed the majority of total preschool enrollment in 2001. The educational quality of private preschools varies from program to program. Regulation is primarily by state child care agencies, but the arrangement varies from state to state.

HEAD START Since 1965, the federal Head Start program has provided free education for young children in many low-income families across the United States. In 2000, Head Start served 11 percent of all three- and four-year olds in the United States. In 2001, Head Start reported enrollment of over 900,000 children, at a cost of roughly $7,000 per child. **Head Start programs** are available in all 50 states and are offered in a variety of formats, including both all-day and half-day programs. Some of them are held at the public school the child will eventually attend.

Since its inception, there has been debate about Head Start's effectiveness. Research has shown that children enrolled in Head Start enjoy immediate, measurable gains in cognitive test scores; however, researchers disagree as to the long-term impact. Some research has shown that Head Start has long-term effects on academic ability and success that do not fade over time. These effects include: persistent gains in achievement test scores, fewer occurrences of grade retention, and less placement in **special education** programs. Other long-term benefits include higher high school graduation rates and decreased crime and delinquency rates. As adults, Head Start graduates are more likely to get better jobs and earn more money. On the other hand, some experts believe the research shows that disadvantaged children in Head Start start off a step behind and never catch up. One of the primary concerns about the program is with its teachers, who only subsequently were required to have a two-year degree and who made less than half the average salary of a public school teacher. To help determine Head Start's effectiveness, a research project called The National Head Start Impact Study was underway as of 2004. It intends to follow between 5,000 to 6,000 preschool aged children through 2006 to determine if Head Start is effective and how Head Start works best for children.

PUBLIC PRESCHOOLS A growing number of states have started to fund preschool programs offered at public schools, called pre-kindergarten (or pre-K) programs. They may be administered by the local school board or by an independent contractor paid by the state. Like private preschools, they may operate for a full day or just half a day.

Preschool class. *(© Ariel Skelley/Corbis.)*

Most state-run preschool programs began like Head Start and focused their services on children with the greatest needs, either children with disabilities or children from low-income families. Most states in the early 2000s choose to have their prekindergarten programs serve children in low-income families or children who have other risk factors that place them at greater risk of school failure or educational difficulties. These risk factors may include having a disability, being a child of teen parents, or having limited proficiency in the English language. Georgia was the first state to have a universally available pre-K program, which was started in 1995. It is still the only state to make preschool available to all students. Other states, including West Virginia and Florida, are making long-term plans to move toward universal prekindergarten.

Research tends to find that public preschool programs (public schools and Head Start) exhibit a greater effect on children than do private preschools. One of the reasons is public school programs provide the same quality of services whether children are rich or poor, while private provider quality is lower for children from lower-income families. It may be an issue of getting what a

parent can pay for. Most of the long-term research on the effects of preschool focuses on low-income children. There is very little data on any long-term benefits for middle-class children.

Qualities of a good preschool

According to the National Institute for Early Education Research, the types of teaching activities and classroom emphases that contribute to a high-quality early education for children include the following:

- opportunities to learn persistence when working at tasks, direction following, and good listening skills

- focus on language and literacy skills, as well as interactive book reading

- emphasis on teaching children problem-solving skills

- helping children expand their knowledge and increase their vocabulary

- opportunities to learn beginning skills involving the alphabet, numbers, and spatial awareness

- focus on scientific thinking skills as well as information about the everyday environment, the world, and how things work

- emphasis on teaching early literacy and mathematics through a variety of activities and projects

- opportunity for preschoolers to engage in music, art, and dramatic play

- educational program in which parents are involved and have opportunities to watch and take part in classroom activities

Advantages of preschool

Many children who attend high-quality preschool programs have their lives changed for the better. In the first five years of life, children acquire the basic capabilities that prepare them for later success in school and life. Many studies show that high-quality preschools improve achievement, behavior, and school readiness for economically disadvantaged children. Follow-up research with these same children shows that they earn more money, experience more stable home lives, and become more responsible citizens than they would have if they had not attended preschool. Children who attend preschool are better prepared to enter kindergarten, both academically and socially. Whatever their format, preschools offer parents and children typical benefits. A good program can help children develop their gross and **fine motor skills**, improve their language and communication abilities, and exercise their **creativity**.

Disadvantages of preschool

The greatest academic and social progress seen in preschools is in children from deprived backgrounds. However, few programs have the quality necessary to bring about the benefits promised. The costs of a high-quality program can be far greater than the costs of education at some public universities. Most children in preschool, however, are not disadvantaged, and some researchers believe the same gains can be had at home by providing educational **toys**, games and books for the child. In some preschools, the emphasis on groups might mean that children will not receive the individual attention they require. This is a particular risk if the preschool does not follow the National Association for the Education of Young Children's recommended teacher-to-child ratio of no more than ten preschoolers per staff member. One-on-one instruction is an advantage parents will not likely find in any preschool. Opportunities for playing with other children exist in churches, clubs, and other outlets, where the child can learn social skills. Some believe that what children need most is lots of play and free time and close interaction with their parents, some-

thing that may be compromised if the child is away from home for long periods of time. Another disadvantage is that some children experience acute **separation anxiety**, indicating that they are not yet ready to make the transition to the preschool environment. Many programs also expect the child to be toilet-trained, a milestone that not all children have achieved at the preschool age.

Common problems

When selecting a preschool for their child, parents should be aware of certain problems or warning signs that might make them decide to look at a different preschool provider. These problems or warning signs may include:

- negative reactions from other parents

- inattention to established rules and regulations (Schools should have clearly established written guidelines for everything from operating hours to managing emergencies.)

- lack of a sick-child policy (The preschool should require both staff and children to have current immunizations and regular checkups.)

- indicating they are hiding something, schools that balk at parents dropping by unannounced

- schools that either have no structure whatsoever or a structure that is inflexible

- lack of age-appropriate activities and toys

- an underqualified staff

- large class sizes

- dirty, unsafe facilities

- an expired license

- schools that promise to put a child on an academic fast track (These highly structured, intensive preschool academic programs create inappropriate expectations from children and may cause emotional stress.)

Parental concerns

Parents considering sending their child to preschool should investigate several different ones and consider many factors before choosing one. However, parents should realize that in spite of the potential advantages, preschool may not be for every child. Parents can be assured that there are alternative ways of introducing their child to early academic skills and social activities.

Resources

PERIODICALS

Barnett, W. Steven, and Jason T. Hustedt. "Preschool: The Most Important Grade." *The First Years of School* 60 (April 2003): 54–57.

"Early Assessments Show Children Make Head Start Gains at Age 4." *Report on Preschool Programs* 36 (July 14, 2004): 107.

ORGANIZATIONS

National Institute for Early Education Research. Rutgers, The State University of New Jersey, 120 Albany Street, Suite 500, New Brunswick, NJ 08901. Web site: <www.nieer.org>.

WEB SITES

Barnett, W. Steven, et al. "The State of Preschool: 2003 State Preschool Yearbook." *National Institute for Early Education Research,*2004. Available online at <http://nieer.org/yearbook> (accessed December 11, 2004).

Kafer, Krista. "A Head Start for Poor Children?" *The Heritage Foundation*, May 4, 2004. Available online at <www.heritage.org/Research/Education/bg1755.cfm> (accessed December 11, 2004).

Moffatt, Gregory K. "Child's Play." *The Citizen*, July 2002. Available online at <www.mpsconsultations.com/702.htm> (accessed December 11, 20040).

"Signs of a Bad Preschool." *Babycenter.com* Available online at <http://parentcenter.babycenter.com/refcap/bigkid/gpreschool/64639.html> (accessed December 11, 2004).

Deanna M. Swartout-Corbeil, RN

Prickly heat

Definition

Prickly heat is also known as sweat retention syndrome or miliaria rubra. It is a common disorder of the sweat glands.

Description

The skin contains two types of glands. One type produces oil and the other produces sweat. Sweat glands are coil-shaped and extend deep into the skin. They are capable of plugging up at several different depths, producing four distinct skin **rashes**.

- Miliaria crystallina is the most superficial of the occlusions. At this level, only the thin upper layer of skin is affected. Little blisters of sweat that cannot escape to the surface form. A bad **sunburn** as it just starts to blister can look exactly like this condition.

- Deeper plugging causes miliaria rubra as the sweat seeps into the living layers of skin, where it irritates and itches.

- Miliaria pustulosis (a complication of miliaria rubra) occurs when the sweat is infected with pyogenic bacteria and turns to pus.

- Deeper still is miliaria profunda. The skin is dry and goose bumps may or may not appear.

There are two requirements for each of these phases of sweat retention: hot enough weather to induce sweating, and failure of the sweat to reach the surface.

Demographics

Infants are more likely to get miliaria rubra than adults. All the sweat retention rashes are also more likely to occur in hot, humid weather.

Causes and symptoms

As of 2004, the best evidence suggested that bacteria form the plugs in the sweat glands. These bacteria are probably normal inhabitants of the skin, and why they suddenly interfere with sweat flow is still not known.

Besides **itching**, these conditions prevent sweat from cooling the body, which it is supposed to do by evaporating from the skin surface. Sweating is the most important cooling mechanism available in hot environments. If it does not work effectively, the body can rapidly become too hot.

When to call the doctor

A doctor should be called when an infant's temperature rises above 100°F (37.8°C) and cannot be brought down within a few minutes. Infants whose temperatures exceed 102°F (38.9°:C) should be immersed in tepid or lukewarm water to reduce body temperature slowly.

A physician should be notified if a baby becomes dehydrated. Signs of **dehydration** include lethargy, poor skin tone, generalized weakness, and reduced urination.

Diagnosis

Rash and dry skin in hot weather are usually sufficient to diagnose these conditions.

Treatment

The rash itself may be treated with topical antipruritics (itch relievers). Preparations containing aloe, menthol, camphor, eucalyptus oil, and similar ingredients are available commercially. Even more effective, particularly for widespread itching in hot weather, are tepid baths with corn starch and/or oatmeal (about 0.5 lb [224 g] of each per bathtub-full).

Dermatologists can peel off the upper layers of skin using a special ultraviolet light. This procedure removes the plugs and restores sweating but is not necessary in most cases.

Much more important, however, is to realize that the body cannot cool itself adequately without sweating. Careful monitoring for symptoms of heat disease is important. If they appear, some decrease in the ambient temperature must be achieved by moving to the shade, taking a tepid bath or shower, or turning up the air conditioner.

Prognosis

The rash disappears in a day with cooler temperatures, but the skin may not recover its ability to sweat for two weeks—the time needed to replace the top layers of skin with new growth from below.

Prevention

Experimental application of topical antiseptics such as hexachlorophene almost completely prevent the rashes of prickly heat. Parents should consult their doctors before applying such antiseptics to their child's skin.

Nutritional concerns

Babies should receive adequate water and other liquids during periods of high heat. They should consume adequate amounts of electrolytes such as sodium, chloride, potassium, phosphate and bicarbonate during hot weather.

KEY TERMS

Ambient—Surrounding.

Pyogenic—Capable of generating pus. *Streptococcus, Staphococcoccus,* and bowel bacteria are the primary pyogenic organisms.

Syndrome—A group of signs and symptoms that collectively characterize a disease or disorder.

A physician should be notified if a baby becomes dehydrated. Signs of dehydration include lethargy, poor skin tone, and generalized weakness. If oral replacement of fluid and electrolytes is suggested, then commercial or homemade preparations can be used. Commercial preparations such as Pedialyte are available. The World Health Organization has provided the following recipe for home preparation, which can be administered in small, frequent sips:

- table salt, 3/4 tsp
- baking powder, 1 tsp
- orange juice, 1 cup
- water, 1 quart

Parental concerns

Parents should carefully monitor their young children for symptoms of heat disease. Babies should be carefully bathed to maintain normal sweating, especially during periods of hot weather.

Resources

BOOKS

Candlish, Louise. *Prickly Heat.* London: Random House, 2004.

Nee, Tekla S. *Everything Baby's First Year Book: Complete, Practical Advice to Get You and Baby through the First 12 Months.* Avon, MA: Adams Media Corporation, 2002.

Shu, Jennifer. *American Academy of Pediatrics: Baby and Child Health.* New York: DK Publishing, 2004.

Thompson, June. *Spots, Birthmarks, and Rashes: The Complete Guide to Caring for Your Child's Skin.* Tonawanda, NY: Firefly Books, 2003.

PERIODICALS

Atherton, D. J. "A review of the pathophysiology, prevention and treatment of irritant diaper dermatitis." *Current Medical Research and Opinion* 20, no. 5 (2004): 645–9.

Hedberg, C. L., et al. "An infant with generalized rash and abnormal hair." *Annals of Allergy, Asthma, and Immunology* 92, no. 2 (2004): 210–6.

Sanfilippo, A. M., et al. "Common pediatric and adolescent skin conditions." *Journal of Pediatric and Adolescent Gynecology* 16, no. 5 (2003): 269–83.

ORGANIZATIONS

American Academy of Dermatology. 930 N. Meacham Road, PO Box 4014, Schaumburg, IL 60168–4014. Web site: <www.aad.org/>.

American Academy of Pediatrics. 141 Northwest Point Boulevard, Elk Grove Village, IL 60007–1098. Web site: <www.aap.org/>.

WEB SITES

"Prickly Heat." *The Merck Manual.* Available online at <www.merck.com/mmhe/sec18/ch206/ch206b.html> (accessed January 17, 2005).

"Prickly Heat." *National Health Service (UK)*, August 4, 2003. Available online at <www.nhsdirect.nhs.uk/en.asp?TopicID=370> (accessed January 17, 2005).

L. Fleming Fallon, Jr., MD, DrPH

Protein-energy malnutrition

Definition

Protein-energy **malnutrition** (PEM) is a potentially fatal body-depletion disorder. It is the leading cause of death in children in developing countries.

Description

PEM is also referred to as protein-calorie malnutrition. It develops in children whose consumption of protein and energy (measured by calories) is insufficient to satisfy their nutritional needs. While pure protein deficiency can occur when a person's diet provides enough energy but lacks an adequate amount of protein, in most cases deficiency will exist in both total calorie and protein intake. PEM may also occur in children with illnesses that leave them unable to absorb vital nutrients or convert them to the energy essential for healthy tissue formation and organ function.

Types of PEM

Primary PEM results from a diet that lacks sufficient sources of protein. Secondary PEM is more common in the United States, where it usually occurs as a complication of **AIDS**, **cancer**, chronic kidney failure, inflammatory bowel disease, and other illnesses that impair the body's ability to absorb or use nutrients or to compensate for nutrient losses. PEM can develop gradually in a child who has a chronic illness or experiences chronic semi-starvation. It may appear suddenly in a patient who has an acute illness.

Kwashiorkor, also called wet protein-energy malnutrition, is a form of PEM characterized primarily by protein deficiency. This condition usually appears at about the age of 12 months when breastfeeding is discontinued, but it can develop at any time during a child's formative years. It causes fluid retention (edema); dry, peeling skin; and hair discoloration.

Marasmus, a PEM disorder, is caused by total calorie/energy depletion rather than primarily protein calorie/energy depletion. Marasmus is characterized by stunted growth and wasting of muscle and tissue. Marasmus usually develops between the ages of six months and one year in children who have been weaned from breast milk or who suffer from weakening conditions such as chronic **diarrhea**.

Demographics

It is not entirely clear how common PEM is in the United States. Primary PEM is common in impoverished areas of developing countries. In the United States, secondary PEM is more common. Children at particular risk for secondary PEM are those who have diseases that involve diarrhea or that otherwise interfere with nutrient absorption. Children with chronic illnesses that require frequent **hospitalization** are more likely to develop PEM.

Causes and symptoms

Secondary PEM symptoms range from mild to severe, and can alter the form or function of almost every organ in the body. The type and intensity of symptoms depend on the patient's prior nutritional status, the nature of the underlying disease, and the speed at which the PEM is progressing.

Mild, moderate, and severe classifications for PEM have not been precisely defined, but patients who lose 10–20 percent of their body weight without trying may have moderate PEM. Some of the cause is replacement dependent (i.e. patients do not take in adequate protein during recovery from illness). This level of PEM is characterized by a weakened grip and inability to perform high-energy tasks.

Losing 20 percent of body weight or more is generally classified as severe PEM. Children with this condition cannot eat normal-sized meals. They have slow heart rates and low blood pressure and body temperatures. Other symptoms of severe secondary PEM include baggy, wrinkled skin; **constipation**; dry, thin, or brittle hair; lethargy; pressure sores, and other skin lesions.

Children suffering from kwashiorkor often have extremely thin arms and legs, but liver enlargement and ascites (abnormal accumulation of fluid) can distend the abdomen and disguise weight loss. Hair may turn red or yellow. Anemia, diarrhea, and fluid and electrolyte disorders are common. The body's immune system is often weakened, behavioral development is slow, and **mental retardation** may occur. Children may grow to normal height but are abnormally thin.

Kwashiorkor-like secondary PEM usually develops in children who have been severely burned, suffered trauma, or had sepsis (massive tissue-destroying infection) or another life-threatening illness. The condition's onset is so sudden that body fat and muscle mass of normal-weight people may not change. Some patients even gain weight because of fluid retention.

Profound weakness accompanies severe marasmus. Since the body breaks down its own tissue to use for energy, children with this condition lose all their body fat and muscle strength, and acquire a skeletal appearance most noticeable in the hands and in the temporal muscle in front of and above each ear. Children with marasmus are small for their age. Since their immune systems are weakened, they suffer from frequent infections. Other symptoms include loss of appetite, diarrhea, skin that is dry and baggy, sparse hair that is dull brown or reddish yellow, mental retardation, behavioral retardation, low body temperature (hypothermia), and slow pulse and breathing rates.

The absence of edema (fluid retention) distinguishes marasmus-like secondary PEM, a gradual wasting process that begins with weight loss and progresses to mild, moderate, or severe malnutrition (cachexia). It is usually associated with cancer, chronic obstructive pulmonary disease (COPD), or another chronic disease that progresses very slowly.

Difficulty chewing, swallowing, and digesting food, **pain**, **nausea**, and lack of appetite are among the most common reasons that many hospital patients do not consume enough nutrients. Nutrient loss can be accelerated by bleeding, diarrhea, abnormally high blood sugar levels (glycosuria), kidney disease, malabsorption disorders, and other factors. **Fever**, infection, surgery, and benign or malignant tumors increase the amount of nutrients that hospitalized patients need. Trauma, **burns**, and some medications also increase caloric requirements.

When to call the doctor

The doctor should be consulted if a child has lost a significant amount of weight without trying, has persistent diarrhea, or has any other signs of PEM.

Diagnosis

When the physician suspects PEM, A thorough physical examination is performed, and these areas assessed:

- eating habits and weight changes
- body-fat composition and muscle strength
- gastrointestinal symptoms
- presence of underlying illness
- developmental delays and loss of acquired milestones in children
- nutritional status

Doctors further quantify a patient's nutritional status by:

- comparing height and weight to standardized norms
- calculating body mass index (BMI)
- measuring skinfold thickness or the circumference of the upper arm

Treatment

Treatment is designed to provide adequate **nutrition**, restore normal body composition, and cure the condition that caused the deficiency. Tube feeding or intravenous feeding is used to supply nutrients to patients who cannot or will not eat protein-rich foods.

In patients with severe PEM, the first stage of treatment consists of correcting fluid and electrolyte imbalances, treating infection with **antibiotics** that do not affect protein synthesis, and addressing related medical problems. The second phase involves replenishing essential nutrients slowly to prevent taxing the patient's weakened system with more food than it can handle. Physical therapy may benefit patients whose muscles have deteriorated significantly.

Prognosis

Most children can lose some of their body weight without side effects, but losing more than 40 percent is usually fatal. Death usually results from heart failure, an

KEY TERMS

Electrolytes—Salts and minerals that produce electrically charged particles (ions) in body fluids. Common human electrolytes are sodium chloride, potassium, calcium, and sodium bicarbonate. Electrolytes control the fluid balance of the body and are important in muscle contraction, energy generation, and almost all major biochemical reactions in the body.

electrolyte imbalance, or low body temperature. Patients with certain symptoms, including semi- consciousness, persistent diarrhea, **jaundice**, and low blood sodium levels, have a poorer prognosis than other patients. Recovery from marasmus usually takes longer than recovery from kwashiorkor. The long-term effects of childhood malnutrition are uncertain. Some children recover completely, while others may have a variety of lifelong impairments, including an inability to properly absorb nutrients in the intestines, as well as mental retardation. The outcome appears to be related to the length and severity of the malnutrition, as well as to the age of the child when the malnutrition occurred.

Prevention

Breastfeeding a baby for at least six months is considered the best way to prevent early-childhood malnutrition. Talking to a doctor before putting a child on any kind of diet, such as vegan, vegetarian, or low-carbohydrate, can help assure that the child gets the full supply of nutrients that he or she needs.

Every child being admitted to a hospital should be screened for the presence of illnesses and conditions that could lead to PEM. The nutritional status of patients at higher-than-average risk should be more thoroughly assessed and periodically reevaluated during extended hospital stays.

Parental concerns

Protein-energy malnutrition is fairly easily treated. If, however, it occurs for a prolonged period, it can have very serious and permanent health consequences. It is important to ensure that children are getting a healthy and balanced diet. Children should not be put on weight loss or other special diets without first consulting a pediatrician.

Resources

BOOKS

Kessler, Daniel B. and Peter Dawson, eds. *Failure to Thrive and Pediatric Undernutrition: a Transdisciplinary Approach.* Baltimore: P.H. Brookes, 1999.

PERIODICALS

Gonzalez-Barranco, et al. "Early Malnutrition and Metabolic Abnormalities Later in Life." *Nutrition Reviews* 62, no.7 (July 2004): 134–40.

Hamer, C. et al. "Detection of Severe Protein-Energy Malnutrition by Nurses in the Gambia." *Archives of Disease in Childhood* (Feb. 2004): 181–5.

ORGANIZATIONS

American Academy of Pediatrics. 141 Northwest Point Boulevard, Elk Grove Village, IL 60007-1098. (847) 434-4000 Fax: (847) 434-8000. <www.aap.org>

American Dietetic Association. 120 South Riverside Plaza, Suite 2000 Chicago, IL 60606-6995. (800) 877-1600. <www.eatright.org>

Tish Davidson, A.M.
Maureen Haggerty

Prozac *see* **Antidepressants**

Pseudoephedrine *see* **Decongestants**

Psoriasis

Definition

Named for the Greek word *psōra* meaning itch, psoriasis is a chronic, non-contagious disease characterized by inflamed lesions covered with silvery-white scabs of dead skin.

Description

Normal skin cells mature and replace dead skin every 28 to 30 days. In psoriasis, the immune system triggers the immune system to make T cells, a type of white blood cell, that cause skin cells to mature in two to three days. Because the body cannot shed old skin as rapidly as the new cells appear, raised patches of dead skin form on the body.

Psoriasis is considered mild if it affects less than 5 percent of the surface of the body; moderate, if 5 to 30 percent of the skin is involved, and severe, if the disease affects more than 30 percent of the body surface.

There is no cure for psoriasis. The disease is managed through treatment. Psoriasis can seriously impact children's lives when the hands and feet are affected so the children cannot take notes or walk or **play**, or when the disease becomes so widespread that the immune system becomes compromised. Children also experience low **self-esteem** and depression because of the disfiguring aspects of the disease.

Types of psoriasis

Dermatologists distinguish different forms of psoriasis according to what part of the body is affected, how severe symptoms are, how long they last, and the pattern formed by the scales. Though children usually have only one form of the disease, some do experience two more types of psoriasis throughout their lifetimes.

PLAQUE PSORIASIS Plaque psoriasis (psoriasis vulgaris), the most common form of the disease, is characterized by small, red bumps that enlarge, become inflamed, and form scales. The top scales flake off easily and often, but those beneath the surface of the skin clump together. Removing these scales exposes tender skin, which bleeds and causes the plaques (inflamed patches of skin) to grow.

Plaque psoriasis can develop on any part of the body, but most often occurs on the elbows, knees, scalp, and trunk. Patches of psoriasis are found in the scalp for nearly half of all psoriasis sufferers.

GUTTATE PSORIASIS Named for the Latin word *gutta*, which means "a drop," guttate psoriasis is characterized by small, red, drop-like dots that enlarge rapidly and may be somewhat scaly. Often found on the arms, legs, trunk, scalp, and sometimes in the diaper area, guttate psoriasis can clear up without treatment or disappear and resurface in the form of plaque psoriasis.

Guttate psoriasis is the most common form of psoriasis in children. It usually first appears in children around four or five years old after a streptococcal infection.

PUSTULAR PSORIASIS Pustular psoriasis usually occurs in adults but can occur in children and adolescents. It is characterized by blister-like lesions filled with non-infectious pus and surrounded by reddened skin. Pustular psoriasis, which can be limited to one part of the body or can be widespread, may be the first symptom of psoriasis or develop in a patient with chronic plaque psoriasis.

Generalized pustular psoriasis is also known as Von Zumbusch pustular psoriasis. Widespread, acutely painful patches of inflamed skin develop suddenly. Pustules appear within a few hours, then dry, and peel within two days. It can make life-threatening demands on the heart and kidneys.

Palomar-plantar pustulosis (PPP) generally appears between the ages of 20 and 60.

INVERSE PSORIASIS Inverse psoriasis occurs in the armpits and groin, under the breasts, and in other areas where skin flexes or folds. This disease is characterized by smooth, inflamed lesions and can be debilitating.

ERYTHRODERMIC PSORIASIS Characterized by severe scaling, **itching**, and **pain** that affects most of the body, erythrodermic psoriasis disrupts the body's chemical balance and can cause severe illness or even death when the body's immune system becomes compromised. Erythrodermic psoriasis interferes with the body's ability to control temperature and prevent infections. This particularly inflammatory form of psoriasis can be the first sign of the disease but often develops in patients with a history of plaque psoriasis.

PSORIATIC ARTHRITIS About 10 percent of patients with psoriasis develop a complication called psoriatic arthritis. This type of arthritis can be slow to develop and mild, or it can develop rapidly. Symptoms of psoriatic arthritis include:

- joint discomfort, swelling, stiffness, or throbbing
- swelling in the toes and ankles
- pain in the digits, lower back, wrists, knees, and ankles
- eye inflammation or pink eye (conjunctivitis)

Children who have psoriatic arthritis also have nail deformations, usually pitting of the fingernails or toenails. Size, shape, and depth of the marks vary, and affected nails may thicken, yellow, or crumble. The skin around an affected nail is sometimes inflamed, and the nail may peel away from the nail bed.

Demographics

Psoriasis affects 4.5 million Americans and is slightly more common in women than in men. Although the disease can develop at any time, a third of all cases occur in childhood with 10 to 15 percent of them being diagnosed in children under ten. It appears between the ages of 15 and 35. It is rare in infants but does occur. Nearly 20,000 U.S. children are diagnosed with psoriasis every year. Psoriasis affects people of all ethnicities, but fair-skinned individuals have a slightly higher incidence.

About 1.5 million Americans have moderate to severe psoriasis. Of them, 75 percent report that their disease has a serious impact on their daily lives. One-third report sleeping problems, disruptions with their normal routine, and negative self-image because of the disease.

In adults, psoriasis can be serious enough that four hundred people are granted disability by the Social Security Administration each year, and having psoriasis disqualifies individuals from serving in the military. Annually, three hundred and fifty people die annually from psoriasis or complications of treatment.

Nearly one million people in the United States have psoriatic arthritis. Though psoriatic arthritis usually develops between the age of 30 and 50, it does occur in children. About 10 to 30 percent of psoriasis patients have psoriatic arthritis, but the condition can occur before the characteristic scaly lesions occur.

Having one parent with psoriasis increases a child's risk of developing the disease to 20 to 25 percent. If both parents have psoriasis, the risk is doubled.

Patients with psoriasis make 2.4 million visits to dermatologists each year, with costs exceeding $3 million annually.

Causes and symptoms

Causes

The cause of psoriasis is, as of 2004, unknown, but research suggests that it is genetic and is related to the immune-system. Having both parents with the disease increases a child's risk by 50 percent.

Psoriasis is usually cyclical, with episodes flaring up for weeks or months throughout the child's life and then receding. Certain factors, however, do seem to trigger bouts of the disease. Injury to the skin seems to precipitate many episodes of plaque psoriasis, usually within seven to ten days. This is called the Koebner reaction. **Streptococcal infections** are associated with guttate psoriasis and some plaque psoriasis cases. Both trauma and certain bacteria may also trigger psoriatic arthritis.

Environmental factors are also implicated in reoccurrence of psoriasis. Exposure to cold temperatures can trigger episodes of the disease. Though sunlight is usually beneficial to most patients, for a few children, too much sun can cause a flare up or worsen the condition.

Some drugs have been found to aggravate psoriasis. Antimalarial drugs, beta-blockers used to treat high blood pressure, and lithium, a drug used to treat depression and bi-polar disorder, can make episodes worse in some individuals. Non-steroid anti-inflammatory (NSAID) drugs, such as ibuprofen or naproxen used to

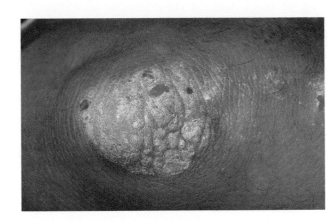

Psoriasis, a chronic skin disorder, may appear on any area of the body, including the elbow, as shown above. *(Photograph by Scott Camazine. Photo Researchers, Inc.)*

manage pain and inflammation can also aggravate psoriasis.

During **puberty**, adolescents report more frequent flare ups and more severe ones. The hormonal changes within their bodies seem to trigger the immune system.

Stress is also a factor in increased frequency of psoriatic episodes. Because stress pumps large amounts of adrenalin, a hormone, into the body, the immune system is overstimulated and reacts by triggering flare ups of the disease.

Symptoms

The most common symptoms of psoriasis are skin **rashes** or red patches covered with white scales that may itch or burn. In plaque psoriasis, the skin may crack and bleed and is susceptible to infection. When the scales are removed, the skin underneath is deep red and shiny and may bleed. Psoriasis on the scalp is distinguished from **seborrheic dermatitis**, or dandruff, because the scales of psoriasis are dry, not greasy. There may be a red drop-like rash (guttate psoriasis) or patches of scaly skin that crack and ooze pus (pustular psoriasis).

In young children, the scaly patches in plaque psoriasis do not appear as thick or as scaly as those of adults. Psoriasis appears often in the diaper area and affects the face more in children than adolescents or adults.

When to call the doctor

Many children routinely see their doctors to supervise their regime of treatment for psoriasis flare ups. Others only see their doctors at the first sign of a recurrence of the disease. There are circumstances, however, when the doctor should be notified. If a treatment does not seem to be working, episodes worsen with treatment, or the child experiences a serious side effect to medications give, the doctor should be consulted to discuss alternative treatment. If there are signs of infections, such as red streaks on the skin or pus, or if there is **fever** or increased pain, the doctor should be called immediately.

Diagnosis

A complete medical history and examination of the skin, nails, and scalp are the basis for a diagnosis of psoriasis. In some cases, a microscopic examination of skin cells is also performed.

Blood tests can distinguish psoriatic arthritis from other types of arthritis. Rheumatoid arthritis, in particular, is diagnosed by the presence of a particular antibody present in the blood. That antibody is not present in the blood of patients with psoriatic arthritis.

Treatment

Age, general health, lifestyle, and the severity and location of symptoms influence the type of treatment used to reduce inflammation and decrease the rate at which new skin cells are produced. Because the course of this disease varies with each individual, doctors must experiment with or combine different treatments to find the most effective therapy for a particular patient.

Treating children with this disease with drugs is problematic. Though treatment regimes have been developed that are effective on adults, research has not been conducted sufficiently on children, except in the area of psoriatic arthritis. Treatment in children is usually not aggressive because of their small, developing bodies. Long-term use can produce toxicity so potent drugs, such as methotrexate (MTX) and cyclosporine, are not used with children. Although MTX is sometimes used in extreme cases for brief amounts of time. Topical steriods are also not used on children because their bodies can absorb the steriods in the medication.

Mild psoriasis

Typically, steroid creams and ointments are commonly used to treat mild or moderate psoriasis in adults. These topical ointments are not generally used with children for mild psoriasis. However, new creams that are used in treating eczema appear to be effective in treating psoriasis as well and do not appear to have long-term problems. In addition, tazarotene (Tazorac), a drug approved by the United States Food and Drug Administration (FDA) in 1997, is proving to be effective for mild-to-moderate plaque psoriasis. This water-based gel has chemical properties similar to vitamin A.

A more subdued approach is undertaken with children who have less severe psoriasis. Brief daily doses of natural sunlight can significantly relieve most symptoms. **Sunburn**, however, has the opposite effect.

Moisturizers and bath oils are used to loosen scales, soften skin, and eliminate the itch. Adding a cup of oatmeal to a tub of bath water is also helpful. Salicylic acid (an ingredient in aspirin) can be used to remove dead skin or increase the effectiveness of other therapies.

Moderate psoriasis

Administered under medical supervision, ultraviolet light B (UVB) is used to control psoriasis that covers many areas of the body or that has not responded to topical preparations. Doctors combine UVB treatments with topical medications to treat some patients and sometimes prescribe home phototherapy, in which the parent administers the UVB treatments.

Tanning beds use ultraviolet A and produce a more intense experience. Adolescents should avoid tanning salons and should sunbathe but without tanning. Any sun exposure or UVB treatment should be coordinated with a dermatologist.

Severe psoriasis

Methotrexate (MTX), given as a pill or as an injection, is sometimes used in extreme cases to alleviate symptoms of severe psoriasis or psoriatic arthritis. Patients who take MTX must be carefully monitored to prevent liver damage.

Enbrel is another drug dermatologists prescribe for children. It appears to be very safe when used for long periods of time.

A new self-injected medication called efalizumab (Raptiva) has the potential to be effective for severe cases of psoriasis. Since it is suppresses the immune system, its use with children or over the long-term is cautioned because it can increase the risk of infection.

Psoriatic arthritis can also be treated with NSAIDs, such as **acetaminophen** (Tylenol) or aspirin. Hot compresses and warm water soaks may also provide some relief for painful joints.

Photochemotherapy (PUVA) is a medically supervised procedure that combines medication with exposure to ultraviolet light (UVA) to treat localized or widespread psoriasis. An individual with widespread psoriasis that has not responded to treatment may enroll in one of the day treatment programs conducted at special facilities throughout the United States. Psoriasis patients who participate in these intensive sessions are exposed to UVA and given other treatments for six to eight hours a day for two to four weeks.

Alternative treatment

Non-traditional psoriasis treatments include:

- soaking in warm water and German chamomile (*Matricaria recutita*) or bathing in warm salt water

- drinking as many as three cups a day of hot tea made with one or a combination of the following herbs: burdock (*Arctium lappa*) root, dandelion (*Taraxacum mongolicum*) root, Oregon grape (*Mahonia aquifolium*), sarsaparilla (*Smilax officinalis*), and balsam pear (*Momardica charantia*)

- taking two 500-mg capsules of evening primrose (*Oenothera biennis*) oil a day (Pregnant women should not use evening primrose oil, and patients with liver disease or **high cholesterol** should use it only under a doctors supervision.)

- eating a diet that includes plenty of fish, turkey, celery (for cleansing the kidneys), parsley, lettuce, lemons (for cleansing the liver), limes, fiber, and fruit and vegetable juices

- eating a diet that eliminates animal products high in saturated fats, since they promote inflammation

- drinking plenty of water (at least eight glasses) each day

- taking nutritional supplements including **folic acid**, lecithin, vitamin A, vitamin E, selenium, and zinc

- regularly imagining clear, healthy skin

Other helpful alternative approaches include identifying and eliminating food allergens from the diet, enhancing the function of the liver, augmenting the hydrochloric acid in the stomach, and completing a detoxification program. Constitutional homeopathic treatment, if properly prescribed, can also help resolve psoriasis.

Prognosis

Most cases of psoriasis can be controlled, and most people who have psoriasis can live normal lives. However, some people who have psoriasis are so self-conscious and embarrassed about their appearance that they become depressed and withdrawn. Others may become disabled because of psoriatic arthritis or because their psoriasis affects their hands and feet so that they cannot walk or handle objects.

Prevention

Psoriasis cannot be prevented. However, recurrences can be avoided or minimized by maintaining a healthy lifestyle by getting plenty of **sleep**, eating a balanced diet, participating in regular **exercise**, and minimizing stress. Avoiding overexposure to cold temperatures, sunburn, and skin irritants, such as drying soaps and lotions, can also minimize flare-ups. Not **smoking** or drinking alcohol can also prevent or minimize some episodes.

Parental concerns

Children living with psoriasis often find the disease overwhelming. It is an emotionally charged disease that can have a child feeling anger one minute and deep depression the next. Because the disfigurement of their skin, though often temporary, is sometimes quite pronounced, children will turn inward, avoiding contact with friends or relatives. School can be particularly traumatizing due to teasing by other children. Teenagers, who already feel awkward and ugly, may feel worse during flare-ups of the disease. Complicating this already emotional situation is the discouragement of treatments that do not work as expected and the uncertainty of finding something that will work.

Parents can help their children by providing education about the psoriasis. This is the first step in managing the disease and feeling some control in their lives. Sometimes this education includes discussing the disease with the childs teachers or the parents of their friends so that these adults will understand more about the emotional state of the child.

Parents can listen to their children when they are able to talk about their feelings about the disease. Emphasizing their childrens strengths, especially when these children appear sad or depressed, and encouraging them to stay active and see their friends can help a child cope with the disease.

Sometimes, participating in a childrens psoriasis support group may be helpful. In addition, sending the child to a special camp for school age children with childhood skin diseases can help them learn tools for coping with the disease as well as establish a support system.

Children can often feel shame as well as guilt, thinking that they have somehow brought on the disease. Coupled with anger and resentment, these powerful emotions can contribute to stress, which can trigger the recurrence of the disease. Stress reduction techniques, such as exercise, **yoga**, and meditation, are also helpful.

KEY TERMS

Adrenaline—Another name for epinephrine, the hormone released by the adrenal glands in response to stress. It is the principal blood-pressure raising hormone and a bronchial and intestinal smooth muscles relaxant.

Arthritis—A painful condition that involves inflammation of one or more joints.

Plaque—Inflamed patches of skin present in some forms of psoriasis.

T cell—A type of white blood cell that is produced in the bone marrow and matured in the thymus gland. It helps to regulate the immune system's response to infections or malignancy.

Parents should be available to their child and offer as much tangible and emotional support they can. However, they should not encourage the child to become too dependent on the parent or others. Parents can also help children find creative solutions to deal with teasing, camouflage their lesions, and educate their peers about the disease. One of the most important lessons parents can teach their child, who is living with psoriasis, is not to be embarrassed because of the disease. Psoriasis can be treated matter-of-factly as people do diabetes, another chronic disorder.

See also Depressive disorders; Itching; Self-esteem.

Resources

BOOKS

Cram, David L. *Coping with Psoriasis: A Patients Guide to Treatment.* Omaha, NB: Addicus Books, 2000.

Scott, Jerry G. *Psoriasis: The Real Way Out: A Self-Education Guide to Complete Natural Healing.* Kenora, Ont.: Psoriasis Connection International, 2003.

PERIODICALS

"Generic Name: Efalizumab Injection." *Drug Topics* 148 (January 26, 2004): HSE21.

Harrar, Sari. "New, Inject-it-yourself." *Prevention* 56 (2004): 48.

ORGANIZATIONS

American Academy of Dermatology. 930 N. Meacham Road, PO Box 4014, Schaumburg, IL 601684014. Web site: <www.aad.org>.

American Skin Association Inc. 150 E. 58th St., 3rd floor, New York, NY 101550002. Web site: <www.americanskin.org>.

National Psoriasis Foundation. 6600 SW 92nd Ave., Suite 300, Portland, OR 97223. Web site: <www.psoriasis.org>.

WEB SITES

"Juvenile Psoriatic Arthritis." *Arthritis Foundation*, 2004. Available online at <www.arthritis.org/conditions/diseasecenter/juvenilepsoriaticarthritis.asp>(accessed December 11, 2004).

Janie Franz
Maureen Haggerty

Psychological tests

Definition

Psychological tests are written, visual, or verbal evaluations administered to assess the cognitive and emotional functioning of children and adults.

Purpose

Psychological tests are used to assess a variety of mental abilities and attributes, including achievement and ability, personality, and neurological functioning.

For children, academic achievement, ability, and **intelligence** tests may be used as tools in school placement, in determining the presence of a learning disability or a **developmental delay**, in identifying giftedness, or in tracking intellectual development. Intelligence testing may also be used with teens and young adults to determine vocational ability (e.g., in career counseling).

Personality tests are administered for a wide variety of reasons, from diagnosing psychopathology (e.g., personality disorder, depressive disorder) to screening job candidates. They may be used in an educational setting to determine personality strengths and weaknesses.

Description

Psychological tests are formalized measures of mental functioning. Most are objective and quantifiable; however, certain projective tests may involve some level of subjective interpretation. Also known as inventories, measurements, questionnaires, and scales, psychological tests are administered in a variety of settings, including preschools, primary and secondary schools, colleges and universities, hospitals, outpatient healthcare settings, and social agencies. They come in a variety of formats, including written, verbal, and computer administered.

Achievement and ability tests

Achievement and ability tests are designed to measure the level of a child's intellectual functioning and cognitive ability. Most achievement and ability tests are standardized, meaning that norms were established during the design phase of the test by administering the test to a large representative sample of the test population. Achievement and ability tests follow a uniform testing protocol, or procedure (i.e., test instructions, test conditions, and scoring procedures) and their scores can be interpreted in relation to established norms. Common achievement and ability tests include the Wechsler intelligence scale for children (WISC-III) and the **Stanford-Binet intelligence scales**.

Personality tests

Personality tests and inventories evaluate the thoughts, emotions, attitudes, and behavioral traits that comprise personality. The results of these tests can help determine a child's personality strengths and weaknesses, and may identify certain disturbances in personality, or psychopathology. Tests such as the **Minnesota Multiphasic Personality Inventory** for Adolescents (MMPI-A) and the Millon Pre-Adolescent Clinical Inventory III (M-PACI), are used to screen children for specific psychopathologies or emotional problems.

Another type of personality test is the projective personality **assessment**. A projective test asks a child to interpret some ambiguous stimuli, such as a series of inkblots. The child's responses provide insight into his or her thought processes and personality traits. For example, the Holtzman Ink blot Test (HIT) uses a series of inkblots that the test subject is asked to identify. Another projective assessment, the **Thematic Apperception Test** (TAT), asks the child to tell a story about a series of pictures. Some consider projective tests to be less reliable than objective personality tests. If the examiner is not well-trained in psychometric evaluation, subjective interpretations may affect the evaluation of these tests.

Neuropsychological tests

Children and adolescents who have experienced a traumatic brain injury, brain damage, or other organic neurological problems, are administered neuropsychological tests to assess their level of functioning and identify areas of mental impairment. Neuropsychological tests may also be used to evaluate the progress of a patient who has undergone treatment or rehabilitation for a neu-rological injury or illness. In addition, certain neuropsychological measures may be used to screen children for developmental delays and/or learning disabilities.

Precautions

Psychological testing requires a clinically trained examiner. All psychological tests should be administered, scored, and interpreted by a trained professional, preferably a psychologist or psychiatrist with expertise in the appropriate area.

Psychological tests are only one element of a psychological assessment. They should never be used as the sole basis for a diagnosis. A detailed clinical and personal history of the child and a review of psychological, medical, educational, or other relevant records are required to lay the groundwork for interpreting the results of any psychological measurement.

Cultural and language differences among children may affect test performance and may result in inaccurate test results. The test administrator should be informed before psychological testing begins if the test taker is not fluent in English and/or belongs to a minority culture. In addition, the child's level of motivation may also affect test results.

Preparation

Prior to the administration of any psychological test, the administrator should provide the child and the child's parent with information on the nature of the test and its intended use, complete standardized instructions for taking the test (including any time limits and penalties for incorrect responses), and information on the confidentiality of the results. After these disclosures are made, informed consent should be obtained from the child (as appropriate) and the child's parent before testing begins.

Normal results

All psychological and neuropsychological assessments should be administered, scored, and interpreted by a trained professional. When interpreting test results, the test administrator will review with parents what the test evaluates, its precision in evaluation, any margins of error involved in scoring, and what the individual scores mean in the context of overall test norms and the specific background of the individual child.

Risks

There are no significant risks involved in psychological testing.

KEY TERMS

Norms—A fixed or ideal standard; a normative or mean score for a particular age group.

Psychopathology—The study of mental disorders or illnesses, such as schizophrenia, personality disorder, or major depressive disorder.

Quantifiable—A result or measurement that can be expressed as a number. The results of quantifiable psychological tests can be translated into numerical values, or scores.

Representative sample—A random sample of people that adequately represents the test-taking population in age, gender, race, and socioeconomic standing.

Standardization—The process of determining established norms and procedures for a test to act as a standard reference point for future test results.

Parental concerns

Test anxiety can have an impact on a child's performance, so parents should not place undue emphasis on the importance of any psychological testing. They should speak with their child before any scheduled tests and reassure them that their best effort is all that is required. Parents can also ensure that their children are well-rested on the testing day and have a nutritious meal beforehand.

Resources

BOOKS

The American Psychological Association. *Standards for Educational and Psychological Testing.* Washington, DC: APA Press, 1999.

Braaten, Ellen and Gretchen Felopulos. *Straight Talk About Psychological Testing for Kids.* New York: Guilford Press, 2003.

The Buros Institute of Mental Measurements at the University of Nebraska-Lincoln. *The Fifteenth Mental Measurements Yearbook* ed. Barbara S. Plake and James C. Impara. Lincoln, NE: University of Nebraska Press, 2003.

ORGANIZATIONS

American Psychological Association. Testing and Assessment Office of the Science Directorate. 750 First St., N.E., Washington, D.C. 20002–4242. (202)336–6000. Web site: <www.apa.org/science/testing.html>.

National Association of School Psychologists. 4340 East West Highway, Suite 402, Bethesda, MD 20814. (301) 657–0270.

WEB SITES

Buros Institute Test Reviews Online. <www.buros.unl.edu/buros/jsp/search.jsp> (accessed September 1, 2004).

Paula Ford-Martin

Psychosocial personality disorders

Definition

A psychosocial disorder is a mental illness caused or influenced by life experiences, as well as maladjusted cognitive and behavioral processes.

Description

The term psychosocial refers to the psychological and social factors that influence mental health. Social influences such as **peer pressure**, parental support, cultural and religious background, socioeconomic status, and interpersonal relationships all help to shape personality and influence psychological makeup. Children and adolescents with psychosocial disorders frequently have difficulty functioning in social situations and may have problems effectively communicating with others.

In the *Diagnostic and Statistical Manual of Mental Disorders 4th edition, text revision (DSM-IV-TR)* , the American Psychiatric Association distinguishes 16 different subtypes (or categories) of mental illness. Although psychosocial variables arguably have some degree of influence on all subtypes of mental illness, the major categories of mental disorders thought to involve significant psychosocial factors include:

- Substance-related disorders. Disorders related to alcohol and drug use, abuse, dependence, and withdrawal.

- **Schizophrenia** and other psychotic disorders. These include the schizoid disorders (schizophrenia, schizophreniform, and schizoaffective disorder), delusional disorder, and psychotic disorders.

- Mood disorders. Affective disorders such as depression (major, dysthymic) and bipolar disorders.

- **Anxiety** disorders. Disorders in which a certain situation or place triggers excessive **fear** and/or anxiety symptoms (i.e., **dizziness**, racing heart), such as panic disorder, agoraphobia, social phobia, **obsessive-compulsive disorder**, post-traumatic stress disorder, and generalized anxiety disorders. **Separation anxiety** disorder is one permutation of anxiety disorders that is common in children.

- Somatoform disorders. Somatoform disorders involve clinically significant physical symptoms that cannot be explained by a medical condition (e.g., somatization disorder, conversion disorder, **pain** disorder, hypochondriasis, and body dysmorphic disorder).

- Factitious disorders. Disorders in which an individual creates and complains of symptoms of a non-existent illness in order to assume the role of a patient (or sick role).

- Sexual and **gender identity** disorders. Disorders of sexual desire, arousal, and performance. It should be noted that the categorization of gender identity disorder as a mental illness has been a point of some contention among mental health professionals.

- Eating disorders. Anorexia and bulimia nervosa.

- **Adjustment disorders**. Adjustment disorders involve an excessive emotional or behavioral reaction to a stressful event.

- Personality disorders. Maladjustments of personality, including conduct, paranoid, narcissistic, avoidant, dependent, and obsessive-compulsive personality disorder (not to be confused with the anxiety disorder OCD).

- Disorders usually first diagnosed in infancy, childhood, or **adolescence**. Some learning and developmental disorders (i.e., ADHD) may be partially psychosocial in nature.

Demographics

According to the National Institute of Mental Health, an estimated one in 10 children and adolescents in the United States suffers from mental illness severe enough to cause significant impairment in their day-to-day living. The MECA Study (Methodology for Epidemiology of Mental Disorders in Children and Adolescents) put the number even higher, estimating that nearly 21 percent of U.S. children between the ages of nine and 17 had a diagnosable mental disorder associated with at least minimum impairment.

Causes and symptoms

It is important to note that the causes of mental illness are diverse and not completely understood. The majority of psychological disorders are thought to be caused by a complex combination of biological, genetic (hereditary), familial, and social factors or biopsychosocial influences. In addition, the role that each of these plays can differ from person to person, so that a disorder such as depression that is caused by genetic factors in one person may be caused by a traumatic life event in another.

The symptoms of psychosocial disorders vary depending on the diagnosis in question. In addition to disorder-specific symptoms, children with psychosocial dysfunction usually have difficulty functioning normally in social situations and may have trouble forming and maintaining close interpersonal relationships.

When to call the doctor

Any child or adolescent that exhibits symptoms of psychosocial personality disorder should be taken to his or her health care provider as soon as possible for evaluation and possible referral to a mental health care professional. If a child or teen reveals at any time that he or she has had recent thoughts of self-injury or **suicide**, or if he or she demonstrates behavior that compromises personal **safety** or the safety of others, professional assistance from a mental health care provider or care facility should be sought immediately.

Diagnosis

Children with symptoms of psychosocial disorders or other mental illness should undergo a thorough physical examination and patient history to rule out an organic cause for the illness (such as a neurological disorder). If no organic cause is suspected, a psychologist or other mental healthcare professional will meet with the child and her parents or guardians to conduct an interview and take a detailed social and medical history. Interviews with caretakers and teachers may also be part of the diagnostic process.

The child and/or the child's parents may be asked to complete one or more psychological questionnaires or tests (also called clinical inventories, scales, or assessments). These may include the Children's Depression Inventory (CDI), the Diagnostic Interview Schedule for Children (DISC), Youth Self-Report, the School Social Behavior Scales (SSBS), the Overt Aggression Scale (OAS), Behavioral Assessment System for Children (BASC), Child Behavior Checklist (CBCL), the Nisonger Child Behavior Rating Form (N-CBRF), Clinical Global Impressions scale (CGI), the Minnesota Multiphasic Personality Inventory-2 (MMPI-2), and the Millon Adolescent Personality Inventory (MAPI).

Treatment

Counseling is typically a front-line treatment for psychosocial disorders. A number of counseling or talk therapy approaches exist, including psychotherapy, cognitive therapy, behavioral therapy, and group therapy. **Family therapy** may be recommended to help parents and siblings understand and cope with a child's mental illness. Therapy or counseling may be administered by social workers, nurses, licensed counselors and therapists, psychologists, or psychiatrists.

Psychotropic medication may also be prescribed for symptom relief in patients with mental disorders considered psychosocial in nature. For disorders such as major depression or **bipolar disorder**, which may have psychosocial aspects but also have known organic causes, drug therapy is a primary treatment approach. In cases such as personality disorder that are thought to not have biological roots, psychoactive medications are usually considered a secondary, or companion treatment to psychotherapy. It is important to note that there is limited data on the long-term repercussions of the use of most psychotropic medications in children and teens; the prescribing physician should present parents with an analysis of the risks and benefits of drug therapy before a course of treatment begins.

In some cases, treating mental illness requires **hospitalization**. This hospitalization, also known as inpatient treatment, is usually employed in situations where a controlled therapeutic environment is critical for the patient's recovery (e.g., rehabilitation treatment for **alcoholism** or other drug addictions), or when there is a risk that the patient may harm himself (suicide) or others. It may also be necessary when the patient's physical health has deteriorated to a point where life-sustaining treatment is necessary, such as with severe **malnutrition** associated with **anorexia nervosa**.

Adolescents may be successful in treating psychosocial disorders through regular attendance in self-help groups or 12-step programs such as Alcoholics Anonymous. This approach, which allows them to seek advice and counsel from others in similar circumstances, can be extremely effective.

Alternative treatment

Therapeutic approaches, such as art therapy, which encourages self-discovery and empowerment, may be useful in treating psychosocial disorders. Art therapy, the use of the creative process to express and understand emotion, encompasses a broad range of humanistic disciplines, including visual arts, dance, drama, music, film, writing, literature, and other artistic genres. This use of

KEY TERMS

Affective disorder—An emotional disorder involving abnormal highs and/or lows in mood. Now termed mood disorder.

Bipolar disorder—A severe mental illness, also known as manic depression, in which a person has extreme mood swings, ranging from a highly excited state, sometimes with a false sense of well being, to depression.

Bulimia nervosa—An eating disorder characterized by binge eating and inappropriate compensatory behavior, such as vomiting, misusing laxatives, or excessive exercise.

Cognitive processes—Thought processes (i.e., reasoning, perception, judgment, memory).

Learning disorders—Academic difficulties experienced by children and adults of average to above-average intelligence that involve reading, writing, and/or mathematics, and which significantly interfere with academic achievement or daily living.

Schizophrenia—A severe mental illness in which a person has difficulty distinguishing what is real from what is not real. It is often characterized by hallucinations, delusions, and withdrawal from people and social activities.

the creative process is believed to provide the patient/artist with a means to gain insight to emotions and thoughts they might otherwise have difficulty expressing. After the artwork is created, the patient/artist continues the therapeutic journey by interpreting its meaning under the guidance of a trained therapist.

Prognosis

According to the National Institute of Mental Health, fewer than one in five of those children suffering from mental illness receive treatment for the problem. Because of the diversity of types of mental disorders influenced by psychosocial factors, and the complexity of diagnosis and treatment, the prognosis for psychosocial disorders is highly variable. In some cases, they can be effectively managed with therapy and/or medication. In others, mental illness can cause long-term disability.

The U.S. Centers for Disease Control reports that suicide is the third leading cause of death among children and youth between the ages of 10 and 24. Because more than 90 percent of those who commit suicide have a diagnosable mental disorder, seeking swift and appropriate treatment as soon as symptoms appear is critical

Prevention

Patient education (i.e., therapy or self-help groups) can encourage patients to take an active part in their treatment program and to recognize symptoms of a relapse of their condition. In addition, educating friends and **family** members on the nature of the psychosocial disorder can assist them in knowing how and when to provide support to the patient.

Parental concerns

While seeking help for their child, parents must remain sensitive to the emotional needs and physical well being of their other children. This may mean adjusting regular routines to avoid leaving siblings alone together, getting assistance with childcare, or even seeking residential or hospital treatment for the child if the safety of other family members is in question. Parents should also maintain an open dialog with their child's teachers to ensure that their child receives appropriate educational assistance.

See also Anorexia nervosa; Bipolar disorder; Depressive disorders.

Resources

BOOKS

Diagnostic and Statistical Manual of Mental Disorders. 4th edition, text revision (DSM-IV-TR). Washington, DC: American Psychiatric Press, Inc., 2000.

PERIODICALS

Satcher, David. *Mental Health: A Report of the Surgeon General.* Washington, DC: Government Printing Office, 1999.

Sullivan, Michele G. "Look for risk factors, protective factors in suicide attempters: psychiatric illness is strong risk factor." *Family Practice News.* 34, no. 4 (Feb 14, 2004): 62.

ORGANIZATIONS

The American Academy of Child and Adolescent Psychiatry. 3615 Wisconsin Ave., N.W., Washington, D.C. 20016–3007. (202) 966–7300. Web site: <www.aacap.org>.

National Institute of Mental Health. 6001 Executive Boulevard, Rm. 8184, MSC 9663, Bethesda, MD 20892–9663. (301) 443–4513.

WEB SITES

The National Mental Health Association. <www.nmha.org/>.

NYU Child Study Center. *Changing the Face of Child Mental Health* <www.aboutourkids.org/>.

Paula Ford-Martin

Puberty

Definition

Puberty is the period of human development during which physical growth and sexual maturity occurs.

Description

The word puberty is derived from the Latin *pubertas*, which means adulthood. Puberty is initiated by hormonal changes triggered by a part of the brain called the hypothalamus, which stimulates the pituitary gland, which in turn activates other glands as well. These changes begin about a year before any of their results are visible. Both the male reproductive hormone testosterone and female hormone estrogen are present in children of both sexes. However, their balance changes at puberty, with girls producing relatively more estrogen and boys producing more testosterone.

Beginning as early as age eight in girls—and two years later, on average, in boys—the hypothalamus signals hormonal change that stimulates the pituitary. In turn, the pituitary releases its own hormones called gonadotrophins that stimulate the gonads and adrenals. From these glands come a flood of sex hormones—androgen and testosterone in the male, estrogen and progestin in the female—that regulate the growth and function of the sex organs. It is interesting to note that the gonadotrophins are the same for males and females, but the sex hormones they induce are different.

The experience of puberty is new and unusual for both boys and girls. It is not something that happens overnight, but rather it is a process that occurs in stages and at different ages for different people. It is perfectly normal, for example, for one person to have already started developing while one's best friend of the same age has not. The age at which puberty begins can vary widely between individuals. Timing of onset is affected by genetic factors, body mass, nutritional state, and general health.

School age

The average age for first signs of **breast development** in girls is about 10.5 years, with **menstruation** and fertility following about two years later. Average age for first signs of testicle enlargement in boys is 11.5 years. Puberty may not begin until age 16 in boys and continue in a random fashion beyond age 20. In contrast to puberty, **adolescence** is more a social/cultural term that refers to the interval between childhood and adulthood. The duration of puberty, from time of onset to completion, varies less between children than does the age of onset. Duration of puberty in girls from onset of breast development to cessation of growth is roughly five years. Duration of puberty in boys from first testicle enlargement to cessation of growth is about six years.

Puberty has been divided into five Sexual Maturity Rating (SMR) stages by two doctors, W. Marshall and J. M. Tanner. These ratings are often referred to as Tanner Stages one through five. Staging is based on pubic hair growth, on genital development, and female breast development. Staging helps determine whether development is normal for a given age. Both sexes also grow armpit hair and develop pimples. Males develop muscle mass, a deeper voice, and facial hair. Females redistribute body fat. Along with the maturing of the sex organs, there is a pronounced growth spurt averaging three to four inches (8–10 centimeters) and culminating in full adult stature. Puberty can be early or delayed.

PUBERTY STAGES IN GIRLS

- Stage One (approximately between the ages of eight and eleven): The ovaries enlarge and hormone production starts, but external development is not yet visible.

- Stage Two (approximately between the ages of eight and fourteen): The first external sign of puberty is usually breast development. At first breast buds develop. The nipples will be tender and elevated. The area around the nipple (the aureole) will increase in size. The first stage of pubic hair may also be present at this time. It may be coarse and curly or fine and straight. Height and weight increase at this time. The body gets rounder and curvier.

- Stage Three (approximately between the ages of nine and 15): Breast growth continues and pubic hair gets coarser and darker. During this stage, whitish discharge from the vagina may be present. For some girls, this is the time that the first menstrual period begins.

- Stage Four (approximately from ages 10 to 16): Some girls notice that their aureoles get even darker and separate into a little mound rising above the rest of the breast. Pubic hair may begin to have a more adult triangular pattern of growth. If it did not happen in Stage Three,

menarche (first menstruation) should start now. Ovulation may start now, too. But it will not necessarily occur on a regular basis. (It is possible to have regular periods even if ovulation does not occur every month.)

- Stage Five (approximately between ages 12 and 19): This is the final stage of development. Full height is reached, and young women are ovulating regularly. Pubic hair is filled in, and the breasts are developed fully for the body.

PUBERTY STAGES IN BOYS

- Stage One (approximately between ages nine and 12): No visible signs of development occur, but, internally, male hormones become a lot more active. Sometimes a growth spurt begins at this time.

- Stage Two (approximately between ages nine to 15): Height increases and the shape of the body changes. Muscle tissue and fat develop at this time. The aureole, the dark skin around the nipple, darkens and increases in size. The testicles and scrotum grow, but the penis probably does not. A little bit of pubic hair begins to grow at the base of the penis.

- Stage Three (approximately between ages 11 and 16): The penis starts to grow during this stage. It tends to grow in length rather than width. Pubic hair is getting darker and coarser and spreading to where the legs meet the torso. Also, boys continue to grow in height, and even their faces begin to appear more mature. The shoulders broaden, making the hips look smaller. Muscle tissue increases and the voice starts to change and deepen. Finally, facial hair begins to develop on the upper lip.

- Stage Four (approximately 11 to 17): At this time, the penis starts to grow in width, too. The testicles and scrotum also continue to grow. Hair may begin to grow on the anus. The texture of the penis becomes more adult-looking. Underarm and facial hair increases as well. Skin gets oilier, and the voice continues to deepen.

- Stage Five (approximately 14 to 18): Boys reach their full adult height. Pubic hair and the genitals look like an adult man's do. At this point, too, shaving is a necessity. Some young men continue to grow past this point, even into their twenties.

Common problems

When puberty occurs outside the age limits considered normal parents may be prompted to search for the cause. As health and **nutrition** have improved over the past few generations, there has been a gradual decrease

Puberty: Male genital development

Stage 1   Stage 2   Stage 3

Stage 4   Stage 5

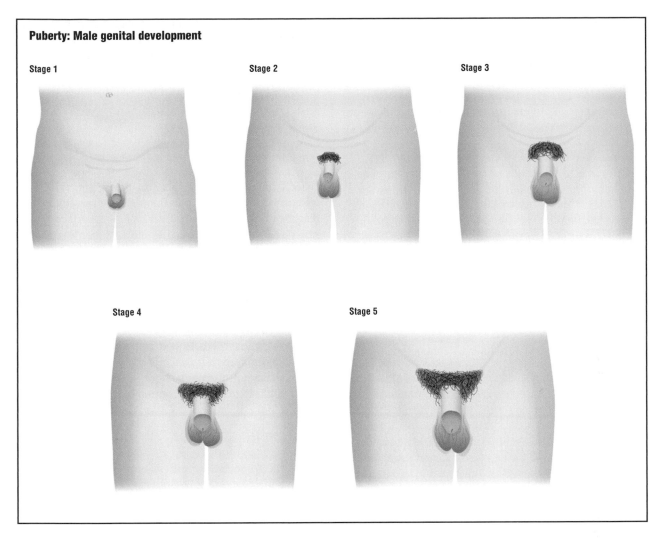

The five stages of male genital development. Stage 1 shows the undeveloped genitals of childhood. In Stage 2, pubic hair growth begins and the testicles begin to enlarge. By Stage 3, the penis grows longer and wider. The testicles continue to enlarge. In Stage 4, the penis and testicles continue to enlarge while the head of the penis becomes more developed. In Stage 5, the genitals have become their adult size, and pubic hair covers the region. *(Illustration by GGS Information Services.)*

in the average age for the onset of puberty. These causes of early or late puberty may include the following:

- Excess hormone stimulation is the cause for early puberty. It can come from the brain in the form of gonadotrophins or from the gonads and adrenals. Functioning tumors may cause overproduction of sex hormones. Brain overproduction of factors promoting sex hormone production can also be the result of brain infections or injury.

- Likewise, delayed puberty is due to insufficient hormone. If the pituitary output is inadequate, so will be the output from the gonads and adrenals. By contrast, a normal pituitary overproduces if it senses there are not enough hormones in the circulation.

- There are several congenital disorders called polyglandular deficiency syndromes that include failure of

hormone output. Children with these syndromes do not experience normal puberty, but it may be induced by giving them hormones at the proper time.

- Finally, there are in females abnormalities in hormone production that produce male characteristics, so called virilizing syndromes. Should one of these appear during adolescence, it will disturb the normal progress of puberty. Notice that virilizing requires abnormal hormones in the female, while feminizing results from absent hormones in the male. Each embryo starts out life as female. Male hormones transform it if they are present.

Delayed or early puberty requires measurement of the several hormones involved to determine which are lacking or which are in excess. There are blood tests for each one. If a tumor is suspected, imaging of the suspect organ needs to be done with x rays, **computed tomography** scans (CT scans), or **magnetic resonance imaging** (MRI).

Puberty is a period of great stress, both physically and emotionally. The psychological changes and challenges of puberty are made infinitely greater if its timing is off.

In early puberty, the offending gland or tumor may require surgical attention, although there are several drugs as of 2004 that counteract hormone effects. If delayed, puberty can be stimulated with the correct hormones. Treatment should not be delayed because necessary bone growth is also affected.

Early puberty often begins before age eight in girls, triggering the development of breasts and hair under the arms and in the genital region. The onset of ovulation and menstruation also may occur. In boys, the condition triggers the development of a large penis and testicles, with spontaneous erections and the production of sperm. Hair grows on the face, under arms, and in the pubic area, and **acne** may become a problem.

Several studies indicate an increase in incidences of early puberty and other forms of early sexual development in the United States. Sexual development in children seven years of age and younger should be evaluated by a physician. In some cases, early sexual development can be caused by a tumor or other pathological conditions. Properly administered hormones can restore the normal growth pattern.

Parental concerns

Most experts suggest that parents begin short and casual discussions about the body changes that occur in puberty with their children by the age of seven or eight. Offering the child reading materials about puberty can impart information to the young person without the awkwardness that may characterize the parent-child conversations. Parents can then offer their children opportunities to ask questions or to discuss any aspects of puberty and sexuality that may arise from their reading.

It is also a good idea for parents to talk to their children about proper hygiene at the onset and during puberty. While good hygiene is important for everyone at any age, it can require greater care at the onset of puberty. Hormones produced by the maturing body bring about physical changes that require greater attention when it comes to hygiene. For a young girl or boy, this means taking more time to clean the body, especially the sexual organs, to treat acne, use mouthwash for bad breath, and deodorant for stronger body odor.

Puberty

	Boys	Girls
Stage one	Prepubertal: no sexual development	Prepubertal: no sexual development
Stage two	Testes enlarge Body odor	Breast budding First pubic hair Body odor Height spurt
Stage three	Penis enlarges Pubic hair starts growing Ejaculation (wet dreams)	Breasts enlarge Pubic hair darkens, becomes curlier Vaginal discharge
Stage four	Continued enlargement of testes and penis Penis and scrotal sac deepen in color Pubic hair curlier and coarser Height spurt Male breast development	Onset of menstruation Nipple is distinct from areola
Stage five	Fully mature male Pubic hair extends to inner thighs Increases in height slow, then stop	Fully mature female Pubic hair extends to inner thighs Increases in height slow, then stop

SOURCE: Child Development Institute. http://www.childdevelopmentinfo.com. 2005.

(Table by GGS Information Services.)

When a boy or girl begins to go through puberty, the body produces more perspiration because sweat glands, some of which are located near the underarms, become more active. More perspiration means a different type of body odor, one that is stronger and similar to an adult's. Daily bathing and showering are enough to control body odor, along with deodorants and antiperspirants.

Boys should be instructed to wash their genitals every day. This includes washing the penis, the scrotum that holds the testicles, the anus, and pubic hair with water and mild soap. Uncircumcised boys need to be instructed that the foreskin should be pulled down daily to expose the tip of the penis, which should then be washed with mild soap and water.

In girls, it is perfectly natural to have a slight sweet smell from the vagina that is inoffensive. A strong, foul odor indicates a possible infection. With treatment, the infection goes away and so does the strong odor. Vaginal discharge is a necessary part of the body's regular functioning. Normal discharge, usually clear to white, is part of the body's self-cleaning process. As discharge leaves the body, it takes bacteria with it, which helps prevent vaginal infections. Parents should stress that girls clean the vaginal area with a mild soap and water

KEY TERMS

Adrenal gland—A small gland located above the kidney (one on each side) that secretes various hormones.

Circumcision—A surgical procedure, usually with religious or cultural significance, where the prepuce or skin covering the tip of the penis on a boy, or the clitoris on a girl, is cut away.

Estrogen—Female hormone produced mainly by the ovaries and released by the follicles as they mature. Responsible for female sexual characteristics, estrogen stimulates and triggers a response from at least 300 tissues. After menopause, the production of the hormone gradually stops.

Estrus—A regular period of sexual excitement in females.

Gonadotrophin—Hormones that stimulate the ovary and testicles.

Gonads—Organs that produce gametes (eggs or sperm), i.e., the ovaries and testes.

Hypothalamus—A part of the forebrain that controls heartbeat, body temperature, thirst, hunger, body temperature and pressure, blood sugar levels, and other functions.

Menstruation—The periodic discharge from the vagina of blood and tissues from a nonpregnant uterus.

Pituitary gland—The most important of the endocrine glands (glands that release hormones directly into the bloodstream), the pituitary is located at the base of the brain. Sometimes referred to as the "master gland," it regulates and controls the activities of other endocrine glands and many body processes including growth and reproductive function. Also called the hypophysis.

Testosterone—Male hormone produced by the testes and (in small amounts) in the ovaries. Testosterone is responsible for some masculine secondary sex characteristics such as growth of body hair and deepening voice. It also is sometimes given as part of hormone replacement therapy to women whose ovaries have been removed.

Virilizing syndromes—Abnormalities in female hormone production that produce male characteristics.

on a regular basis to help control bacteria growth and limit infections.

When to call the doctor

Parents should consult a pediatrician or physician when their child shows signs of either early or delayed puberty.

Resources

BOOKS

Bailey, Jacqui, and Jan McCafferty. *Sex, Puberty, and All that Stuff.* Hauppauge, NY: Barrons Educational Series, 2004.

Madaras, Lynda, et al. *What's Happening to My Body? Book for Boys.* New York: Newmarket Press, 2000.

———. *What's Happening to My Body? Book for Girls.* New York: Newmarket Press, 2000.

McCave, Marta. *Puberty's Wild Ride.* Philadelphia: Family Planning Council, 2004.

PERIODICALS

Brunk, Doug, "Navigating Tx [Treatment] of Boys on the Brink of Puberty." *Pediatric News* (October 2001): 31.

Herman-Giddens, Marcia E., et al. "Navigating the Recent Articles on Girls' Puberty in Pediatrics: What Do We Know and Where Do We Go from Here?" *Pediatrics* (April 2004): 911–17.

"New Study Identifies Gene Signaling Puberty." *Genomics & Genetics Weekly* (November 14, 2003): 33.

Ramsayer, K. "Pesticide May Hinder Development in Boys." *Science News* (December 13, 2003): 372–73.

Wang, Youfa. "Is Obesity Associated with Early Sexual Maturation? A Comparison of the Association in American Boys Versus Girls." *Pediatrics* (November 2002): 903–10.

Wellbery, Caroline. "Cut-Off Age for Precocious Puberty Is Too Young." *American Family Physician* (May 1, 2003): 2001.

ORGANIZATIONS

American Academy of Pediatrics. 141 Northwest Point Blvd., Elk Grove Village, IL 60007. Web site: <www.aao.org>.

Precocious Puberty Support Network. c/o MAGIC Foundation, 6645 W. North Ave., Oak Park, IL 60302. Web site: <www.magicfoundation.org>.

WEB SITES

"Female Puberty." Available online at <www.teenpuberty.com/index.php?section=female> (accessed October 29, 2004).

"Male Puberty." Available online at <www.teenpuberty.com/index.php?section=male> (accessed October 29, 2004).

"Puberty and Adolescence." *National Institutes of Health.* Available online at <www.nlm.nih.gov/medlineplus/ency/article/001950.htm> (accessed October 29, 2004).

J. Ricker Polsdorfer, MD
Ken R. Wells

Pulled elbow *see* **Nursemaid's elbow**

Pulmonary function tests

Definition

Pulmonary function tests are a group of procedures that measure how well the lungs are functioning.

Purpose

Pulmonary function tests help a doctor to diagnose respiratory diseases and disorders such as **asthma**, chronic obstructive pulmonary disease (COPD), and emphysema, and mechanical injury by measuring the degree of lung impairment. These tests are also done before major lung surgery to make sure the patient will not be disabled by having a reduced lung capacity. When performed over time, these tests are helpful in evaluating how a lung disease is progressing, and how serious the lung disease has become. They are also be used to assess how a patient is responding to different treatments.

Description

There are many types of pulmonary function tests. The most common are:

- peak expiratory flow rate (PEFR) measures airflow during forced expirations
- forced vital capacity (FVC) measures the maximum amount of air exhaled after taking a deep breath
- forced expiratory volume in one second (FEV1) measures the amount of air that can be exhaled in one second
- maximum voluntary volume (MVV) measures the amount of air a person can breathe in and out in one minute
- total lung capacity (TLC) is the measure of the amount of air the lungs can hold
- residual volume (RV) is the amount of air left in the lungs after forced expiration

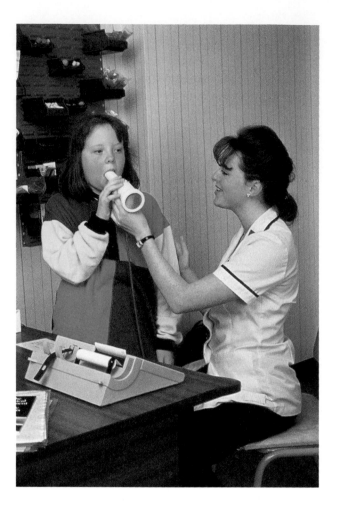

A cystic fibrosis patient receives a pulmonary function test. *(Custom Medical Stock Photo Inc.)*

- arterial blood gas (ABG) measures the amount of oxygen and carbon dioxide in the blood and gives a picture of how efficiently the lungs are functioning
- pulse oximetry measures the percentage of oxygen in the blood

With the exception of arterial blood gas, pulse oximetry, and total lung capacity, pulmonary function tests are performed using spirometry (from the Greco-Latin term meaning "to measure breathing"). Spirometry tests can be done a hospital or doctor's office. The patient places a clip over the nose and breathes through the mouth into a tube connected to a machine called a spirometer. The patient breathes in deeply, and then exhales as quickly and forcefully as possible into the tube. The machine records the volume of air that moves through the tube. The exhalation must last at least six seconds for the machine to work properly. Usually the patient repeats this test three times, and the best of the three results is considered the measure of the lung function. A similar machine called a peak flow meter may be used to measure PERF. Sometimes when airways are obstructed, the patient is given a bronchodilator, and the test is performed again.

Total lung capacity is measured by body plethysmography. The patient sits in a sealed box that resembles a telephone booth and breathes against a mouthpiece. A device measures the changes in air pressure in the box during inhalation and exhalation. From these air pressure measurements, the total capacity of the lungs can be calculated.

Arterial blood gases are measured on a blood sample that is taken from an artery. Pulse oximetry uses a sensor placed on the earlobe or fingertip to measure the amount of oxygen in the blood.

Taken together, pulmonary function tests give a good picture of how much air is moving in and out of the lungs and how efficiently oxygen is moved into the blood and carbon dioxide is moved out. Some of these tests are performed as part of a routine health screening, while others are used most often to evaluate the condition of diseased or damaged lungs.

Precautions

Except for the arterial blood gas tests and pulse oximetry, pulmonary function tests should not be given to patients who have had a recent heart attack, or who have certain other types of heart disease. Conditions that cause **pain** on breathing, such as broken ribs, may interfere with the performance of the tests and produce inac-

curate results. Children must be old enough to follow directions and inhale and exhale as instructed.

Preparation

The patient should not eat a heavy meal before the test, nor smoke for four to six hours beforehand. The doctor will give specific instructions about whether or not to use medications before the test.

Aftercare

No special aftercare is needed following these tests.

Risks

Risks with these tests are minimal. However, some people become lightheaded or faint. The tests may also trigger an asthma attack in individuals with asthma.

Parental concerns

Normal results are based on a person's age, height, and gender. Normal results are expressed as a percentage of the predicted lung capacity. Results of 80 percent or less suggest some sort of lung impairment.

Resources

BOOKS

Pulmonary Function Testing and Cardiopulmonary Stress Testing. Delmar Publishing, 1997.

Ruppel, Gregg L. *Manual of Pulmonary Function Testing.* St. Louis: Mosby, 1997.

WEB SITES

Blaivas, Allen J." Pulmonary Function Tests." *MedlinePlus Encyclopedia.* 27 January 2004. <www.nim.nih.gov/medlineplus/ency/article/003853.htm>.

HealthGuide A-Z "Lung Function Tests" *WebMD.com* 5 May 2003. <my.webmd.com/hw/health_guide_atoz/hw5022.asp?lastselectedguid+{5FE84E90-BC77-4056-A91C-9}>.

Tish Davidson, A.M.
Carol A. Turkington

Punishment *see* **Discipline**

Purging *see* **Bulimia nervosa**

Rabies

Definition

Rabies is an acute viral disease of the central nervous system that is transmitted through saliva from the bite of an infected animal.

Description

Rabies affects humans and other mammals but is most common in carnivores (flesh eaters). It is sometimes referred to as a zoonosis, or disease of animals that can be communicated to humans. Rabies is almost exclusively transmitted through saliva from the bite of an infected animal. Another name for the disease is hydrophobia, which literally means **fear** of water, a symptom shared by half of all people infected with rabies. Other symptoms include **fever**, depression, confusion, painful **muscle spasms**, sensitivity to touch, loud noise, and light, extreme thirst, painful swallowing, excessive salivation, and loss of muscle tone. If rabies is not prevented by immunization, it is almost always fatal.

In late 2002, rabies re-emerged as an important public health issue. Charles E. Rupprecht, director of the World Health Organization (WHO) Collaborating Center for Rabies Reference and Research, listed several factors responsible for the increase in the number of rabies cases worldwide:

- Rapid evolution of the rabies virus. Bats in the United States have developed a particularly infectious form of the virus.
- Increased diversity of animal hosts for the disease.
- Changes in the environment that are bringing people and domestic pets into closer contact with infected wildlife.
- Increased movement of people and animals across international borders. In one case, a man who had contracted rabies in the Philippines was not diagnosed until he began to feel ill in the United Kingdom.
- Lack of advocacy about rabies.

Demographics

Cases of rabies in humans are very infrequent in the United States, averaging one or two a year (down from over 100 cases annually in 1900), but the worldwide incidence is estimated to be between 30,000 and 50,000 cases each year. These figures are based on data collected by the World Health Organization (WHO) in 1997 and updated in 2002. Rabies is most common in developing countries in Africa, Latin America, and Asia, particularly India. Dog **bites** are the major origin of infection for humans in developing countries, but other important host animals are the wolf, mongoose, and bat. Worldwide, the highest risk groups for contracting rabies are boys under the age of fifteen. Most deaths from rabies in the United States result from bat bites.

People whose work frequently brings them in contact with animals are also considered to be at higher risk than the general population. This group includes those in the fields of veterinary medicine, animal control, wildlife work, and laboratory work involving live rabies virus. People in these occupations and residents of or travelers to areas where rabies is a widespread problem should consider being immunized.

Causes and symptoms

Rabies is caused by a rod- or bullet-shaped virus that belongs to the family Rhabdoviridae. The virus is usually transmitted via an animal bite; however, cases have also been reported in which the virus penetrated the body through infected saliva, moist tissues such as the eyes or lips, a scratch on the skin, or the transplantation of infected tissues. Inhalation of the virus from the air, as might occur in a highly populated bat cave, is also thought to occur.

From the bite or other area of penetration, the virus multiplies as it spreads along nerves that travel away from the spinal cord and brain (efferent nerves) and into the salivary glands. The rabies virus may lie dormant in the body for several weeks or months, but rarely much longer, before symptoms appear. Initially, the area around the bite may burn and be painful. Early symptoms may also include a **sore throat**, low-grade fever, headaches, loss of appetite, **nausea and vomiting**, and **diarrhea**. Painful spasms develop in the muscles that control breathing and swallowing. The individual may begin to drool thick saliva and may have dilated or irregular pupils, increased tears and perspiration, and low blood pressure.

As the disease progresses, the patient becomes agitated and combative and may exhibit increased mental confusion. The affected person usually becomes sensitive to touch, loud noises, and bright lights. The victim also becomes extremely thirsty but is unable to drink because swallowing is painful. Some patients begin to dread water because of the painful spasms that occur. Other severe symptoms during the later stage of the disease are excessive salivation, **dehydration**, and loss of muscle tone. Death usually occurs three to 20 days after symptoms have developed. Recovery is very rare.

Diagnosis

After the onset of symptoms, blood tests and **cerebrospinal fluid (CSF) analysis** tests will be conducted. **CSF** will be collected during a procedure called a lumbar puncture in which a needle is used to withdraw a sample of CSF from the area around the spinal cord. The CSF tests do not confirm diagnosis but are useful in ruling out other potential causes for the patient's altered mental state.

The two most common diagnostic tests are the fluorescent antibody test and isolation of the rabies virus from an individual's saliva or **throat culture**. The fluorescent antibody test involves taking a small sample of skin (biopsy) from the back of the neck of the patient. If specific proteins, called antibodies, that are produced only in response to the rabies virus are present, they will bind with the fluorescent dye and become visible. Another diagnostic procedure involves taking a corneal impression in which a swab or slide is pressed lightly against the cornea of the eye to determine whether viral material is present.

Treatment

Because of the extremely serious nature of a rabies infection, the need for rabies immunizations should be carefully considered for anyone who has been bitten by an animal, based on a personal history and results of diagnostic tests.

If necessary, treatment includes the following:

- The wound is washed thoroughly with medicinal soap and water. Deep puncture **wounds** should be flushed

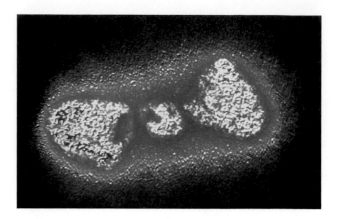

Rabies virus shown in yellow. *(Custom Medical Stock Photo Inc.)*

with a catheter and soapy water. Unless absolutely necessary, a wound should not be sutured.

- Tetanus toxoid and **antibiotics** will usually be administered.

- Rabies **vaccination** may or not be given, based on the available information. If the individual was bitten by a domestic animal and the animal was captured, the animal will be placed under observation in quarantine for ten days. If the animal does not develop rabies within four to seven days, then no immunizations are required. If the animal is suspected of being rabid, it is killed, and the brain is examined for evidence of rabies infection. In cases involving bites from domestic animals in which the animal is not available for examination, the decision for vaccination is made based on the prevalence of rabies within the region where the bite occurred. If the bite was from a wild animal and the animal was captured, it is generally killed because the incubation period of rabies is unknown in most wild animals.

- If necessary, the patient is vaccinated immediately, generally through the administration of human rabies immune globulin (HRIG) for passive immunization, followed by human diploid cell vaccine (HDCV) or **rabies vaccine** adsorbed (RVA) for active immunization. Passive immunization is designed to provide the individual with antibodies from an already immunized individual, while active immunization involves stimulating the individual's own immune system to produce antibodies against the rabies virus. These rabies vaccines are equally effective and carry a lower risk of side effects than some earlier treatments. Unfortunately, however, in underdeveloped countries, these vaccines are usually not available. Antibodies are administered to the patient in a process called passive immunization. To do so, the HRIG vaccine is administered once, at the beginning of treatment. Half of the dose is given around the bite area, and the rest is given in the muscle. Inactivated viral material (antigenic) is then given to stimulate the patient's own immune system to produce antibodies against rabies. For active immunization, either the HDCV or RVA vaccine is given in a series of five injections. Immunizations are typically given on days 1, 3, 7, 14, and 28.

In those rare instances in which rabies has progressed beyond the point where immunization would be effective, the patient is given medication to prevent seizures, relieve some of the **anxiety**, and relieve painful muscle spasms. **Pain** relievers are also given. In the later stages, aggressive supportive care will be provided to maintain breathing and heart function. Survival is rare but can occur.

Prognosis

If preventative treatment is sought promptly, rabies need not be fatal. Immunization is almost always effective if started within two days of the bite. Chance of effectiveness declines, however, the longer vaccination is put off. It is, however, important to start immunizations, even if it has been weeks or months following a suspected rabid animal bite, because the vaccine can be effective even in these cases. If immunizations do not prove effective or are not received, rabies is nearly always fatal within a few days of the onset of symptoms.

Prevention

The following precautions should be observed in environments where humans and animals are likely to come into contact:

• Domesticated animals, including household pets, should be vaccinated against rabies. If a pet is bitten by an animal suspected to have rabies, its owner should contact a veterinarian immediately and notify the local animal control authorities. Domestic pets with current vaccinations should be revaccinated immediately; unvaccinated dogs, cats, or ferrets are usually euthanized (killed).

• Wild animals should not be touched or petted, no matter how friendly they may appear. It is also important not to touch an animal that appears ill or passive or whose behavior seems odd, such as failing to show the normal fear of humans. These are all possible signs of rabies. Many animals, such as raccoons and skunks, are nocturnal and their activity during the day should be regarded as suspicious.

• People should not interfere in fights between animals.

KEY TERMS

Active immunization—Treatment that provides immunity by challenging an individual's own immune system to produce antibody against a particular organism.

Antibody—A special protein made by the body's immune system as a defense against foreign material (bacteria, viruses, etc.) that enters the body. It is uniquely designed to attack and neutralize the specific antigen that triggered the immune response.

Biopsy—The surgical removal and microscopic examination of living tissue for diagnostic purposes or to follow the course of a disease. Most commonly the term refers to the collection and analysis of tissue from a suspected tumor to establish malignancy.

Efferent nerves—Peripheral nerves that carry signals away from the brain and spinal cord.

Fluorescent antibody test—A test in which a fluorescent dye is linked to an antibody for diagnostic purposes.

Lumbar puncture—A procedure in which the doctor inserts a small needle into the spinal cavity in the lower back to withdraw spinal fluid for testing. Also known as a spinal tap.

Passive immunization—Treatment that provides immunity through the transfer of antibodies obtained from an immune individual.

Rhabdovirus—A family of viruses named for their rod- or bullet-like shapes. The rabies virus is a rhabdovirus.

Vector—A carrier organism (such as a fly or mosquito) which serves to deliver a virus (or other agent of infection) to a host. Also refers to a retrovirus that had been modified and is used to introduce specific genes into the genome of an organism.

Zoonosis—Any disease of animals that can be transmitted to humans. Rabies is an example of a zoonosis.

• Because rabies is transmitted through saliva, a person should wear rubber gloves when handling a pet that has had an encounter with a wild animal.

• Garbage or pet food should not be left outside the house or camp site because it may attract wild or stray animals.

- Windows and doors should be screened. Some victims of rabies have been attacked by infected animals, particularly bats, that entered through unprotected openings.

- State or county health departments should be consulted for information about the prevalence of rabies in an area. Some areas, such as New York City, have been rabies-free, only to have the disease reintroduced at a later time.

- Preventative vaccination against rabies should be considered if one's occupation involves frequent contact with wild animals or non-immunized domestic animals.

- Bites from mice, rats, or squirrels rarely require rabies prevention because these rodents are typically killed by any encounter with a larger, rabid animal, and would, therefore, not be carriers.

- Travelers should ask about the prevalence of the disease in countries they plan to visit.

Parental concerns

Parents should speak with their children about the importance of avoiding contact with wild animals and reporting strange behavior in any animal, even a pet.

Resources

BOOKS

Adams, William G. "Rabies." In *Nelson Textbook of Pediatrics*. Edited by Richard E. Behrman et al. Philadelphia: Saunders, 2004.

Plotkin, Stanley A. "Rabies Virus." In *Principles and Practice of Pediatric Infectious Diseases*, 2nd ed. Edited by Sarah S. Long et al. St. Louis, MO: Elsevier, 2003.

PERIODICALS

Fooks, A. R., et al. "Risk Factors Associated with Travel to Rabies Endemic Countries." *Journal of Applied Microbiology* 94 Suppl. (2003): 31S–6S.

"Human Rabies—Iowa, 2002." *Morbidity and Mortality Weekly Report* 52 (January 24, 2003): 47–8.

Messenger, S. L., et al. "Emerging Pattern of Rabies Deaths and Increased Viral Infectivity." *Emerging Infectious Diseases* 9 (February 2003): 151–4.

National Association of State Public Health Veterinarians Inc. "Compendium of Animal Rabies Prevention and Control, 2003." *Morbidity and Mortality Weekly Report Recommendations and Reports* 52 (March 21, 2003): 1–6.

Smith, J., et al. "Case Report: Rapid Ante-Mortem Diagnosis of a Human Case of Rabies Imported into the UK from the Philippines." *Journal of Medical Virology* 69 (January 2003): 150–5.

Stringer, C. "Post-Exposure Rabies Vaccination." *Nursing Standard* 17 (February 5–11, 2003): 41–2.

Weiss, R. A. "Cross-Species Infections." *Current Topics in Microbiology and Immunology* 278 (2003): 47–71.

ORGANIZATIONS

American Veterinary Medical Association (AVMA). 1931 North Meacham Road, Suite 100, Schaumburg, IL 60173–4360. Web site: <www.avma.org>.

Centers for Disease Control and Prevention. 1600 Clifton Rd., NE, Atlanta, GA 30333. Web site: <www.cdc.gov>.

WEB SITES

"Epidemiology [of rabies]." *National Center for Infectious Diseases*. Available online at <www.cdc.gov/ncidod/dvrd/rabies/Epidemiology/Epidemiology.htm> (accessed January 9, 2005).

Janet Byron Anderson
Rebecca J. Frey, PhD
Rosalyn Carson-DeWitt, MD

Rabies vaccine

Definition

Rabies vaccine is an injection that provides protection against the rabies virus that can be transmitted to humans via the saliva of an infected animal. Rabies is fatal in humans unless it is prevented with a vaccine.

Description

Rabies are caused by viruses of the genus *Lyssavirus* in the family Rhabdoviridae. Although all mammals are thought to be susceptible to rabies infection, the primary hosts are carnivores and bats. Most human exposure to rabies occurs via an animal bite in which the skin is broken and the virus is transmitted from the infected animal's saliva to the blood and tissues of the victim. The rabies virus infects the human nervous system causing acute encephalomyelitis, an inflammation of the brain and spinal cord. Death, usually by respiratory failure, occurs within seven to 10 days after appearance of the first symptoms. The average incubation period before symptoms of the disease appear is three to seven weeks, with a range of 10 days to seven years.

Prevalence of rabies

UNITED STATES Cases of human rabies are very rare in the United States due to the routine **vaccination** of domestic animals. In the past most human rabies resulted from **bites** by infected dogs. However as the incidence of rabies in dogs has decreased dramatically, rabies among wildlife has increased across the continental United States. Bat bites are now the most common source of human rabies infection. Hawaii remains rabies-free.

Between 1990 and 2003, there were 39 diagnosed cases of rabies among Americans. Every year an estimated 18,000 Americans receive rabies pre-exposure prophylaxis and an additional 16,000-39,000 receive post-exposure prophylaxis as a result of animal bites.

WORLDWIDE Rabies is common in some parts of the world, particularly in the developing countries of Africa, Asia, and Latin America. Rabies has been eradicated in the United Kingdom. Rabies is considered to be a reemerging viral disease because it is poorly controlled in many developing countries despite widely available human and animal vaccines. WHO estimates that every year about 10–12 million people worldwide receive post-exposure prophylaxis and that about 35,000 people—primarily children—die of rabies every year. However the incidence of rabies in the developing world is believed to be severely underreported. Most rabies exposures are from bites by unvaccinated dogs.

Vaccine development

The French scientist Louis Pasteur developed the first vaccine against rabies. In 1885, he injected his attenuated (weakened) virus into a nine-year-old boy who had been bitten by a rabid dog. The child's life was saved. Over the following century several generations of rabies vaccines were developed.

Although there is no cure for rabies once symptoms of the disease have appeared, in the 1980s scientists developed a highly effective vaccine that provides protection from the virus both before exposure—pre-exposure prophylaxis—or after exposure—post-exposure prophylaxis. The vaccine consists of killed rabies virus that, when injected, induces the child's immune system to produce antibodies that bind to and destroy the virus. The antibody response develops within seven to 10 days of vaccination and provides protection for up to two years. A second type of rabies vaccine, rabies immune globulin (RIG), provides immediate, short-term protection after exposure to the virus.

Pre-exposure prophylaxis

Routine rabies vaccination and booster immunizations are necessary only for those in high-risk professions such as veterinarian medicine and laboratory workers. However pre-exposure prophylaxis of children who are at risk of being exposed to rabid animals eliminates the need for RIG and decreases the number of required vaccinations after exposure. Pre-exposure prophylaxis is particularly important for children who may be exposed to rabies in places where vaccines, if available, may cause adverse reactions. Pre-exposure prophylaxis also may be helpful for children who are exposed unknowingly or do not report the exposure.

Children traveling internationally are at particular risk for rabies exposure because they may not exhibit caution in approaching animals. Such children may be considered for pre-exposure prophylaxis if they will be:

* in an area where rabies is prevalent or endemic
* camping in rural areas
* in an area where appropriate rabies vaccines and RIG may not be available

Post-exposure prophylaxis

After exposure to a potentially rabid animal, a child's risk of contracting rabies is assessed based on:

* the rabies vaccination status of the animal
* the type of animal
* whether the animal can be captured and tested for rabies
* the geographical location of the exposure
* whether the contact was provoked or unprovoked Unprovoked attacks are more likely to come from a rabid animal. Provoked attacks can include bites received while feeding or handling an animal.

Post-exposure prophylaxis usually is recommended when a child has been:

* bitten by any animal, including a pet dog or cat, that has not been vaccinated against rabies
* scratched or bitten by a wild animal, particularly a bat, raccoon, skunk, fox, or coyote (Some animals, particularly bats, may not leave obvious bite marks.)

When a child is bitten by a healthy domestic dog, cat, or ferret, the animal is usually confined for 10 days and observed for signs of rabies prior to initiating post-exposure prophylaxis. The rabies status of an animal also can be determined by testing for antibodies against rabies in its blood or by killing the animal and testing its brain tissue.

Post-exposure prophylaxis should be considered following any contact between a child and a bat, even if there is no evidence of a bite or scratch, since the child may be unaware of the contact and marks may not be apparent. For example, post-exposure prophylaxis should be considered if an unattended child is found in a room with a bat and the bat cannot be tested for rabies.

Vaccine types

Four formulations of three inactivated rabies virus vaccines are licensed for use by the U.S. Food and Drug Administration (FDA). Two RIG formulations are also FDA-licensed.

HUMAN DIPLOID CELL VACCINE (HDCV) Human diploid cell vaccines (HDCVs) use inactivated rabies viruses. HDCV comes in two formulations: one for intramuscular (IM) injection and one for intradermal (ID) injection into a deep layer of skin.

PURIFIED CHICK EMBRYO CELL VACCINE (PCEC) Purified chick embryo cell (PCEC) vaccine became available in the United States in 1997. PCEC is made from rabies virus grown in cultures of chicken embryos and then inactivated. The drug is formulated for IM administration only.

RABIES VACCINE ADSORBED (RVA) Rabies vaccine adsorbed (RVA) is manufactured from virus grown in cell cultures of fetal rhesus monkey lung cells and then inactivated.

RABIES IMMUNE GLOBULIN (RIG) Human rabies immune globulin (RIG, HRIG) is a vaccine made from human serum that contains high levels of antibodies against rabies. It is used in conjunction with an inactivated-rabies vaccine for post-exposure prophylaxis. RIG provides immediate but short-lived protection against rabies. Approximately one-half of the antibodies are lost within 21 days after administration.

RIG is separated from the blood plasma of hyperimmunized human donors. Numerous procedures are used to clear the serum of rabies virus.

OTHER VACCINES Although the four types of inactivated-rabies vaccines and the two RIGs are the only rabies vaccines available in the United States, various other rabies vaccines are produced throughout the world. Although inactivated-rabies vaccines from diploid cell cultures are safe and effective, they are expensive. In developing countries, rabies vaccines often contain nerve tissue which can cause adverse effects. Various less expensive but safe and effective vaccines are under development.

General use

Inactivated-rabies vaccines are injected, either before or after exposure to the virus, in 1.0-ml. doses containing at least 2.5 IU/ml. of rabies virus antigen.

This is the recommended standard of the World Health Organization (WHO). The size and number of vaccine doses are the same for children and adults. Although the same rabies vaccine usually is used throughout an immunization series, there is no evidence of adverse reactions or loss of effectiveness when two different vaccines are used in the same series. Modern rabies vaccines are relatively painless.

Pre-exposure prophylaxis

For preventative rabies immunization in an unexposed child, an inactivated-rabies vaccine is administered in three 1.0-ml. doses, with the second dose seven days after the first, and the third dose 21 or 28 days after the first. The vaccine is injected into the upper arm. Studies have found that this regimen produces adequate antibodies against rabies in the blood serum of all subjects.

Post-exposure prophylaxis

Following an animal bite or contact between a child's mucous membranes and an animal's saliva, an attempt is usually made to determine whether the animal has rabies. If there is a threat of rabies, an unvaccinated child receives RIG and a series of five rabies vaccinations over a 28-day period. Ideally, treatment should begin within two days of exposure, however it may be started at any time thereafter.

The wound is cleaned thoroughly and, if possible, RIG is injected into the wound and the surrounding tissues to block the virus's entry into the central nervous system. The recommended dose is 20 IU/kg (1 kg = 2.2 lb) of body weight. This is equivalent to 22 mg of the antibody immunoglobulin G (IgG) per kilogram of body weight. Any remaining RIG is injected intramuscularly at a site removed from the vaccination site. RIG also may be injected into the buttocks. RIG is never injected with the same syringe or at the same site as the vaccine. RIG is used only once to provide antibodies until the child's immune system begins producing its own antibodies in response to the vaccine. RIG is administered concurrently with the first dose of inactivated-rabies vaccine or up to seven days thereafter. Additional treatment with RIG may interfere with antibody production in response to the inactivated-rabies vaccine.

Inactivated-rabies vaccine is administered in 1.0-ml. doses, at three, seven, 14, and 28 days after the first vaccination. It is injected intramuscularly in the upper arm or the upper thigh. If an animal is found to be rabies-free after the vaccination series has been initiated, the series can be discontinued.

Exposure following vaccination

Children exposed to rabies following vaccination receive a 1.0-ml. dose of vaccine immediately and a second dose three days later. These children do not receive RIG because it will diminish the rapid antibody response resulting from the previous vaccination.

Precautions

Precautions should be taken before vaccinating a child who has:

- a weakened immune system due to HIV/AIDS or other disease or condition
- **cancer**
- had a life-threatening reaction to a previous rabies vaccine or to any component of the vaccine

Children with suppressed immune systems should not receive pre-exposure prophylaxis against rabies. Medical conditions and medications that suppress the immune system can interfere with antibody production in response to a rabies vaccine. If a child has exhibited a serious hypersensitivity to a previous rabies vaccine, **antihistamines** may be used concurrently. Children who are allergic to eggs should not be give vaccines cultured in chicken embryos.

A minor illness, such as a cold, does not preclude rabies vaccination. However pre-exposure vaccination should be postponed if the child has a moderate or severe illness. Post-exposure prophylaxis should be administered regardless of any other illness or condition. Children should not be vaccinated against **measles** or **chickenpox** (varicella) for four months after being treated with RIG. Children receiving post-exposure prophylaxis outside of the United States should have their antibody levels against rabies measured after their return.

Side effects

Side effects from the rabies vaccines currently used in the United States are much less common and less severe than the side effects of earlier rabies vaccines. However side effects may vary with the brand of vaccine and adverse reactions to rabies vaccines used in some other countries are quite common. The risk of side effects also increases with the number of vaccine doses. However a vaccination series should not be interrupted because of localized or mild side effects.

Mild side effects from rabies vaccines include:

- soreness, redness, swelling, **itching**, or **pain** at the site of the injection in 30–74 percent of recipients
- headache, **nausea**, abdominal pain, muscle aches, or **dizziness** in 5–40 percent of recipients

More serious side effects of rabies vaccines include:

- hives, joint pain, or **fever** in about 6 percent of those receiving a booster vaccination
- very rarely, an illness resembling Guillain-Barré syndrome, a disorder of the motor nerves that can result in temporary paralysis, lasting no longer than 12 weeks and resulting in complete recovery Other nervous system disorders occur so rarely following rabies vaccination that they may not be related to the vaccine. However, a physician should be consulted if a high fever or behavioral changes occur following rabies vaccination.

Reported side effects of RIG include:

- local pain
- low-grade fever

Although any vaccine is capable of inducing an allergic reaction, serious reactions to rabies vaccine are very rare. Signs of an allergic reaction include:

- paleness
- weakness
- dizziness
- hoarseness or wheezing
- difficulty breathing
- a fast heartbeat

In case of a serious reaction to a rabies vaccine:

- A doctor should be consulted immediately.
- The date, time, and type of reaction should be recorded.
- Medical personnel or the local health department should file a Vaccine Adverse Event Report.

Interactions

Immune system-suppressing treatments, including cancer drugs and radiation and steroids, can interfere with the antibody response to rabies vaccination. If possible, immunosuppressive medications should be suspended during the vaccination series, and the vaccine injections should be intramuscularly. Alternatively, the child's serum can be checked for antibody production to determine if the vaccination was successful.

Chloroquine phosphate or similar anti-malarial drugs such as mefloquine may interfere with the response to HDCV. Children who will be taking anti-malarial drugs while traveling in areas with endemic rabies should begin the three-dose regimen of ID vaccine one month prior to travel, before they begin taking drugs to prevent malaria. However, a three-dose, pre-exposure regimen of IM vaccine provides an adequate response even in the presence of anti-malarial drugs.

Parental concerns

Preparing a child for an injection

Most children are afraid of injections; however there are simple methods for easing a child's **fear**. Prior to the vaccination parents should:

- Tell children that they will be getting a shot.
- Explain to children that the shot will prevent them from becoming sick.
- Have older siblings comfort and reassure a younger child.
- Bring along the child's favorite toy or blanket.
- Never threaten children by telling them they will get a shot.
- Read the vaccination information statement (VIS) and ask questions of the medical practitioner.

During the vaccination parents should:

- Hold the child.
- Make eye contact with the child and smile.
- Talk softly and comfort the child.
- Distract the child by using a hand puppet or pointing out pictures or objects.
- Sing or tell the child a story.
- Have the child tell a story.
- Teach the child to focus on something other than the shot.
- Help the child take deep breaths.
- Allow the child to cry.
- Stay calm.

After the injection

Following an injection parents should:

- Hold and caress a child or breastfeed an infant.
- Talk soothingly and reassuringly.
- Hug and praise the child for doing well.
- Use a cool, wet cloth to reduce soreness or swelling at the injection site.

KEY TERMS

Antibody—A special protein made by the body's immune system as a defense against foreign material (bacteria, viruses, etc.) that enters the body. It is uniquely designed to attack and neutralize the specific antigen that triggered the immune response.

Antigen—A substance (usually a protein) identified as foreign by the body's immune system, triggering the release of antibodies as part of the body's immune response.

Booster immunization—An additional dose of a vaccine to maintain immunity to the disease.

Encephalomyelitis—Encephalitis or another acute inflammation of the brain and spinal cord that can be caused by the rabies virus.

Human diploid cell vaccine (HDCV)—A rabies vaccine in which the virus is grown in cultures of human cells, concentrated, and inactivated for IM or ID injection.

Intracutaneous—Into the skin, in this case directly under the top layer of skin.

Intramuscular(IM)—An injection into a muscle.

Prophylaxis—Protection against or prevention of a disease. Antibiotic prophylaxis is the use of antibiotics to prevent a possible infection.

Purified chicken embryo cell vaccine (PCEC)—A rabies vaccine in which the virus is grown in cultures of chicken embryo cells, inactivated, and purified for IM injection.

Rabies immune globulin (RIG or HRIG)—A human serum preparation containing high levels of antibodies against the rabies virus; used for post-exposure prophylaxis.

Rabies virus adsorbed (RVA)—A rabies vaccine in which the virus is grown in cultures of lung cells from rhesus monkeys, inactivated, and adsorbed to aluminum phosphate.

Parents should also be aware that:

- The child may eat less during the first 24 hours following a vaccination.
- The child should drink plenty of fluids.
- The medical practitioner may suggest a non-aspirin-containing pain reliever for the child.

Resources

BOOKS

Jackson, Alan C., and William H. Wunner, eds. *Rabies.* Boston: Academic Press, 2002.

PERIODICALS

Kammer, A. R., and H. C. Ertl. "Rabies Vaccines: From the Past to the 21st Century." *Hybrid Hybridomics* 21, no. 2 (April 2002): 123-7.

ORGANIZATIONS

Centers for Disease Control and Prevention. 1600 Clifton Rd. NE, Atlanta, GA 30333. (800) 311-3435. Web site: <www.cdc.gov>.

Immunization Action Coalition. 1573 Selby Ave., St. Paul, MN 55104. (651) 647-9009. Web site: <www.immunize.org>.

WEB SITES

"About RabAvert." *RabAvert Rabies Vaccine.* Chiron Corporation. 2001 [cited August 10, 2004]. Available online at: <www.rabavert.com/about.html>.

CDC's Rabies Web Page That's Just for Kids! Centers for Disease Control and Prevention. February 6, 2002 [cited July 27, 2004]. Available online at: <www.cdc.gov/ncidod/dvrd/kidsrabies/Vaccination/Vaccination.htm>.

"First Rabies Cases from Organ Transplant Reported." *Reuters Health.* July 1, 2004 [cited July 27, 2004]. Available online at: <www.nlm.nih.gov/medlineplus/news/fullstory_18699.html>.

"Human Rabies Prevention—United States, 1999 Recommendations of the Advisory Committee on Immunization Practices (ACIP)." *Morbidity and Mortality Weekly Report.* Centers for Disease Control and Prevention. January 8, 1999 [cited August 9, 2004]. Available online at: <www.cdc.gov/epo/mmwr/preview/mmwrhtml/00056176.htm>.

Rabies. Centers for Disease Control and Prevention. July 9, 2004 [cited July 27, 2004]. Available online at: <www.cdc.gov/ncidod/dvrd/rabies>.

"Rabies." *Travelers' Health.* Centers for Disease Control and Prevention. April 12, 2004 [cited July 27, 2004]. Available online at: <www.cdc.gov/travel/diseases/rabies.htm>.

Rabies Prevention and Control. National Center for Infectious Diseases. December 1, 2003 [cited July 27, 2004]. Available online at: <www.cdc.gov/ncidod/dvrd/rabies>.

Rabies Vaccine: What You Need to Know. National Immunization Program. November 4, 2003 [cited August 5, 2004]. Available online at: <www.cdc.gov/nip/publications/VIS/vis-rabies.pdf>.

Sherman, Max. "Rabies: A History and Update on Prophylaxis Regimens in the U.S." *U.S. Pharmacist.* [cited August 10, 2004]. Available online at: <www.uspharmacist.com/oldformat.asp?url=newlook/files/Feat/aug00rabies.cfm&pub_id=8&article_id=563>.

Margaret Alic, Ph.D.

Rape and sexual assault

Definition

Rape and sexual assault are crimes that involve the use of threats, **fear** tactics, and/or physical violence to force a child or adolescent to submit to sexual intercourse or to engage in other sexual activity (e.g., oral sex, anal sex).

Description

Rape and sexual assault are violent crimes, and children and adolescents constitute a large number of the victims of these crimes. Rape and sexual assault are defined according to the degree of sexual interaction. Rape and sexual assault can involve contact between the penis and vagina or penis and anus that involves penetration; contact between the mouth and genitals or anus; penetration of the vagina or anus with an object; or direct touching (not through clothing). Sexual assault is defined as intentional touching of the genitals, breasts, buttocks, anus, inner thigh, or groin with no sexual penetration that is forced upon the victim. Rape and sexual assault that recurs is considered sexual abuse. When the perpetrator is a **family** member, these crimes are also referred to as incest.

Rape and sexual assault are especially traumatic for children and adolescents, who often do not fully understand normal sexual activity. Studies and statistics have shown that **adolescence** is the riskiest life stage for sexual assault, and the time when the most psychological trauma can result.

Demographics

The 2000 Victim, Incident, and Offender Characteristics, published by the National Center for Juvenile Justice (NCJJ), analyzed sexual assault data collected by law enforcement agencies over a five-year span. The following characteristics were found to be significant among victims of sexual assault:

- Age: Over two-thirds of reported victims of sexual assault were juveniles under the age of 18. Adolescents aged 12 to 18 years represented the largest group of victims at 33 percent; 20 percent were between the ages of six and 11; children younger than five years old and adults between 18 and 24 years of age each constituted 14 percent of victims. One out of every seven victims surveyed in the study was under the age of six.

- Gender: Females were more than six times more likely to be a victim of sexual assault than males; more than 86 percent of victims were females. The great majority (99%) of the victims of forcible rapes were women, while men constituted the majority (54%) of the victims of forcible sodomy (oral or anal intercourse). Females are most likely to be the victim of sexual assault at age 14, while males are at most risk at age four.

- Location: The residence of the victim was the most commonly noted location of sexual assault (70%). Other common locations included schools, hotels/motels, fields, woods, parking lots, roadways, and commercial/office buildings.

Similar statistics were gathered by the NCJJ regarding the perpetrators of rape and sexual assault. These characteristics included the following:

- Age: Over 23 percent of offenders were under the age of 18; juveniles were more likely to be perpetrators of forcible sodomy and fondling. The remaining 77 percent of offenders were adults and were responsible for 67 percent of juvenile victims. For younger juvenile victims (under the age of 12), juvenile offenders were responsible for approximately 40 percent of assaults.

- Gender: The great majority of all reported offenders were male (96%). The number of female offenders rose for victims under the age of six (12%), in contrast to 6 percent for victims aged six through 12, 3 percent for victims aged 12 through 17, and 1 percent for adult victims.

- Relationship with offender: Approximately 59 percent of offenders were acquaintances of their victims, compared to family members (27%) or strangers (14%). Family members were more likely to be perpetrators against juveniles (34%) than against adults (12%). In contrast, strangers accounted for 27 percent of adult victims and 7 percent of juveniles.

- Past offenses: In 19 percent of juvenile cases, the victim was not the only individual to be assaulted by the offender, compared to only 4 percent of adult cases.

Of particular importance are the number of rapes and sexual assaults that go unreported, especially in adolescents. Although one in five sexual assault reports occurs for adolescents between 12 and 17 years of age, and adolescents between ages 16 and 19 years have the highest rate of reported sexual assault, anonymous school surveys have revealed that only 5 percent of sexually assaulted adolescents actually report the crime to law enforcement.

When to call the doctor

Many children and adolescents are reluctant to report rape and sexual assault for a number of reasons. Often the victim fears retaliation from the offender. He or she may be afraid that family, friends, the community, or the media may learn about the offense. There may be a concern about being judged or blamed by others. The victim may think that no one will believe the assault occurred or that they were somehow at fault. Unreported rape and sexual assault are especially common when the offender is known to the victim, such as a family member or respected member of the community (e.g., clergy, teacher).

Parents who suspect that their child or adolescent has been raped or sexually assaulted should take the child to see a doctor and psychologist or psychiatrist. Signs that a child or adolescent may have been raped or sexually assaulted include shying away from physical affection, unexplained bleeding from the rectum and/or vagina, bruising around the breasts and genitals, and hiding or throwing away undergarments. Any child or adolescent who is raped or sexually assaulted should be taken to an emergency room immediately so that evidence against the perpetrator can be gathered, and medical treatment can be given.

Diagnosis

Rape and sexual assault are diagnosed by interviewing the patient and parents, physical and gynecological examination, and laboratory tests for the presence of seminal fluid. In many cases, children or adolescents do not report the rape or sexual assault, but they do show obvious signs of physical violence. When rape is suspected, diagnosis may be made by a psychiatrist or psychologist based on sessions with the victim. In cases where obvious signs of the crime are not visible, and immediate treatment is not received, the victim may develop post-traumatic stress disorder (PTSD), also known as rape trauma syndrome, which is a mental health disorder that describes a range of symptoms often experienced by someone who has undergone a severely traumatic event. In such cases, diagnosis of rape or sexual assault is revealed through therapy sessions for PTSD.

Approximately 31 percent of rape victims develop PTSD as a result of their assault. The symptoms of PTSD include:

- recurrent memories or flashbacks of the incident
- nightmares
- insomnia
- mood swings
- difficulty concentrating
- panic attacks
- emotional numbness
- depression
- **anxiety**

Treatment

Once a victim of rape or sexual assault reports the crime to local authorities, calls a rape crisis hotline, or arrives at the emergency room to be treated for injuries, a multidisciplinary team is often formed to address his or her physical, psychological, and judicial needs. This team usually includes law enforcement officers, physicians, nurses, mental health professionals, victim advocates, and/or prosecutors.

The victim may continue to feel fear and anxiety for some time after the incident, and in some instances this may significantly impact his or her personal and academic life. Follow-up counseling should, therefore, be provided for the victim, particularly if symptoms of PTSD become evident.

Forensic medical examination

Because rape is a crime, there are certain requirements for medical evaluation of the patient and for record keeping. The forensic medical examination is an invaluable tool for collecting evidence against a perpetrator that may be admissible in court. Since the great majority of victims know their assailant, the purpose of the medical examination is often not to establish identity but to establish nonconsensual sexual contact. The Sexual Assault Nurse Examiner program is an effective model that is used in many U.S. hospitals and clinics to collect and document evidence, evaluate and treat for **sexually transmitted diseases** (STDs) and pregnancy, and refer victims to follow-up medical care and counseling. Many nurse examiners are specially trained to handle cases that involve children and adolescents. The "Sexual Assault Nurse Examiner Development and Operation Guide," prepared by the Sexual Assault Resource Service, describes the ideal protocol for collecting evidence from a sexual assault victim. This protocol includes the following:

- performing the medical examination within 72 hours of the assault
- taking a history of the assault
- documenting the general health of the victim, including menstrual cycle, potential **allergies**, and pregnancy status
- assessing for trauma and taking photographic evidence of injuries
- taking fingernail clippings or scrapings
- taking samples for sperm or seminal fluid
- combing head/pubic hair for foreign hairs, fibers, and other substances
- collecting bloody, torn, or stained clothing
- taking samples for blood typing and DNA screening

After evidence is collected, rape victims are treated with appropriate medical care for their injuries. In female children and adolescents, vaginal tears and injuries may require suturing; in male children and adolescents, anal tears and injuries are common and may require suturing and other treatment.

Prognosis

Children and adolescents who have been raped or sexually assaulted are three times more likely to experience another rape in adulthood. Victims of rape and sexual assault who report their attack greater than one month afterwards are more likely to suffer from PTSD, mood swings, and major depression than victims who report their attack immediately, most likely because victims who report their attacks immediately receive appropriate interventional care, particularly mental health support and counseling. For adolescents, untreated rape and sexual assault can result in serious long-term psychological effects. One in 10 sexually assaulted adolescents attempt **suicide**, and about 50 percent are diagnosed with **phobias**, depression, substance abuse, and other psychological disorders. Compared to those who have never been victimized, rape victims are three times more likely to have a major depressive episode, four times more likely to have contemplated suicide, 13 times more likely to develop alcohol dependency problems, and 26 times more likely to develop substance abuse problems. In addition, school performance in many sexually assaulted adolescents declines, and many eventually fail academically. Even when treated, rape and sexual assault can cause poor **self-esteem**, sexual dysfunction and impaired sexual and personal relations, insomnia, anxiety, eating disorders, and other psychological symptoms that last into adulthood.

Lasting psychological trauma is especially serious in male children and adolescents who are raped or sexually assaulted. Young boys may be more reluctant to discuss their attack and may harbor feelings of resentment and anxiety over potential **homosexuality**. Assaulted young boys may, in turn, commit sexual assault themselves in the future. Appropriate psychological therapy is necessary for improved long-term outcomes.

Prevention

Usually, rape and sexual assault cannot be prevented, and it is important that children and adolescents, who often think they are at fault after an attack, be told that there was nothing they could have done to prevent the attack. However, measures to reduce the likelihood of a rape or sexual assault and to increase the chances of an assailant being caught can be taken:

- Children and adolescents can be instructed on **safety** and strangers and inappropriate touching, and the importance of telling parents about any uncomfortable situation.

- Parents can monitor social activities, particularly for older adolescents, who may attend events (e.g., parties with no adult supervision) without their parents' knowledge.

- Adolescents can be educated about "date-rape" drugs and methods to prevent their consumption (e.g., never leaving drinks unattended at a party). And they can be informed about the dangers of alcohol consumption.

- Parents can encourage open communication regarding normal sexual development and activity and emphasize the importance of saying no in compromising or uncomfortable situations.

Sexually transmitted disease (STD) prevention

STDs are a source of concern for many victims of sexual assault. The most commonly transmitted diseases are gonorrhea, chlamydia, genital **warts**, and acquired **immunodeficiency** syndrome (AIDS)/human immunodeficiency virus (HIV). STDs are transmitted in up to 30 percent of rapes. Treatment involves **antibiotics** and antiviral medications, depending on the STD. In some instances, cultures may be taken during the medical examination and at time point afterward to test for gonorrhea or chlamydia. It is important that the victim receive information regarding the symptoms of STDs and be counseled to return for further examination if any of these symptoms occur.

KEY TERMS

Aggravated sexual abuse—When an individual is forced to submit to sexual acts by use of physical force; threats of death, injury, or kidnapping; or substances that render that individual unconscious or impaired.

Forcible sodomy—Forced oral or anal intercourse.

Forensic—Pertaining to courtroom procedure or evidence used in courts of law.

Incest—Unlawful sexual contact between persons who are biologically related. Many therapists, however, use the term to refer to inappropriate sexual contact between any members of a family, including stepparents and stepsiblings.

Post-traumatic stress disorder (PTSD)—A disorder that occurs among survivors of extremely stressful or traumatic events, such as a natural disaster, an airplane crash, rape, or military combat. Symptoms include anxiety, insomnia, flashbacks, and nightmares. Patients with PTSD are unnecessarily vigilant; they may experience survivor guilt, and they sometimes cannot concentrate or experience joy.

Sexual abuse—Forced sexual contact through the use of threats or other fear tactics, or instances in which an individual is physically unable to decline sexual activity.

Sexual assault nurse examiner—A registered nurse who is trained to collect and document evidence from a sexual assault victim, evaluate and treat for STDs and pregnancy, and refer victims to follow-up medical care and counseling.

Pregnancy prevention

Female adolescents at risk of becoming pregnant after an assault should be counseled on the availability of emergency **contraception**. According to the Food and Drug Administration (FDA), emergency contraception (in the form of a course of pills) is not effective if there is a pregnancy but works to prevent pregnancy from occurring by delaying or preventing ovulation, by affecting the transport of sperm, and/or by thinning the inner layer of the uterus (endometrium) so that implantation is prevented.

Parental concerns

Parents of children and adolescents who are raped or sexually assaulted are understandably upset, angry, and even violent toward perpetrators. For the best mental health of the victim, parents should strive to listen to their children, use healthy coping strategies, and reassure the victim that he/she was not at fault. Parents should resist letting anger toward the assailant take precedence over attention to their child or adolescent.

Because rape and sexual assault cause long-term psychological trauma, parents should be aware of symptoms of PTSD, depression, substance abuse, high-risk behaviors, and anxiety in their children. Long-term therapy with a counselor experienced in rape and sexual assault trauma can benefit both the victim and parents.

Parents should also be aware that PTSD and other psychological effects of rape can manifest as poor school performance. Impaired concentration, **acting out** in school, diminished energy, embarrassment, and frustration may all occur in traumatized children and adolescents. School officials and counselors should be contacted to help students with academic problems; temporary homebound instruction or day therapy programs may be necessary.

Resources

BOOKS

Matsakis, Aphrodite. *The Rape Recovery Handbook: Step-by-Step Help for Survivors of Sexual Assault.* Oakland, CA: New Harbinger Publications, 2003.

PERIODICALS

Kawsar, M., et al. "Prevalence of Sexually Transmitted Infections and Mental Health Needs of Female Child and Adolescent Survivors of Rape and Sexual Assault Attending a Specialist Clinic." *Sexually Transmitted Infections* 80 (April 2004): 138–141.

Pharris, Margaret D., and Sarah S. Nafstad. "Nursing Care of Adolescents Who Have Been Sexually Assaulted." *Nursing Clinics of North America* 37 (2002): 475–97.

Ruggiero, Kenneth J., et al. "Is Disclosure of Childhood Rape Associated with Mental Health Outcome? Results from the National Women's Study." *Child Maltreatment* 9 (February 2004): 62–77.

ORGANIZATIONS

American College of Obstetricians and Gynecologists. 409 12th St., SW, PO Box 96920, Washington, DC 20090–6920. Web site: <www.acog.org/>.

Rape, Abuse, and Incest National Network (RAINN). 635-B Pennsylvania Ave. SE, Washington, DC 20003. National Sexual Assault Hotline: 1–800–656-HOPE. Web site: <www.rainn.org/>.

WEB SITES

"Adolescent Update: Drugs and Date Rape." *American College of Emergency Physicians.* Available online at <www.acep.org/1%2C2830%2C0.html> (accessed November 3, 2004).

Jennifer E. Sisk, M.A.

Rashes

Definition

The popular term for a group of spots or red, inflamed skin that is usually a symptom of an underlying condition or disorder. Often temporary, a rash is only rarely a sign of a serious problem.

Description

A rash may occur on only one area of the skin, or it may cover almost all of the body. Also, a rash may or may not be itchy. Depending on how it looks, a rash may be described as having the following characteristics:

- blistering (raised oval or round collections of fluid within or beneath the outer layer of skin)
- macular (flat spots)
- nodular (small, firm, knotty rounded mass)
- papular (small solid slightly raised areas)
- pustular (pus-containing skin blister)

Demographics

Most persons experience rashes at many times in their lives. Rashes are not reportable events. As such, their prevalence is not precisely known. Rashes are common among infants, and most are harmless.

Causes and symptoms

There are many theories about the development of skin rashes, but experts are not completely sure what causes some of them. Generally a skin rash is an intermittent symptom, fading and reappearing. Rashes may accompany a range of disorders and conditions, such as the following:

- Infectious illness: A rash is a symptom of many different kinds of childhood infectious illnesses, including **chickenpox** and **scarlet fever**. It may be triggered by other infections, such as **Rocky Mountain spotted fever** or ringworm.

- Allergic reactions: One of the most common symptoms of an allergic reaction is an itchy rash. **Contact dermatitis** is a rash that appears after the skin is exposed to an allergen, such as metal, rubber, some cosmetics or lotions, or some types of plants (e.g. **poison ivy**). Drug reactions are another common allergic cause of rash; in this case, a rash is only one of a variety of possible symptoms, including **fever**, seizures, **nausea and vomiting**, **diarrhea**, heartbeat irregularities, and breathing problems. This rash usually appears soon after the first dose of the course of medicine is taken.

- Autoimmune disorders: Conditions in which the immune system turns on the body itself, such as systemic lupus erythematosus or purpura, often have a characteristic rash.

- Nutritional disorders: For example, scurvy, a disease caused by a lack of vitamin C, has a rash as one of its symptoms.

- **Cancer**: A few types of cancer, such as chronic lymphocytic leukemia, can be the underlying cause of a rash.

Rashes in infancy

Rashes are extremely common in infancy. They are usually not serious at all and can be treated at home.

Diaper rash is caused by prolonged skin contact with bacteria and the baby's waste products in a damp diaper. This rash has red, spotty sores, and there may be an ammonia smell. In most cases the rash will respond within three days to drying efforts. A diaper rash that does not improve in this time may be a yeast infection requiring prescription medication. A doctor should be consulted if the rash is solid, bright red, causes fever, or the skin develops blisters, boils, or pus.

Infants also can get a rash on cheeks and chin caused by contact with food and stomach contents. This rash will come and go, but usually responds to a good cleaning after meals. About one-third of all infants develop **acne** usually after the third week of life in response to their mothers' hormones before birth. This rash can last a few weeks to a few months. Heat rash is a mass of tiny pink bumps on the back of the neck and upper back caused by blocked sweat glands. The rash usually appears during hot, humid weather, although a baby with a fever can also develop the rash.

A baby should be seen by a doctor immediately if the rash appears suddenly and looks purple or blood-colored, looks like a burn, or appears while the infant seems to be sick.

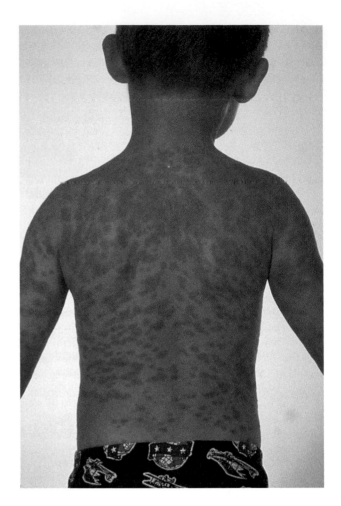

An unidentified rash on young boy's back. (*Custom Medical Stock Photo Inc.*)

When to call the doctor

A doctor or other healthcare provider should be called when a rash that cannot accurately be identified appears or when an identified rash does not disappear in two to three days.

Diagnosis

A physician can make a diagnosis based on the medical history and the appearance of the rash, where it appears, and any other accompanying symptoms.

Treatment

Treatment of rashes focuses on resolving the underlying disorder and providing relief of the **itching** that often accompanies them. Soothing lotions or oral **antihistamines** can provide some relief, and **topical antibiotics** may be administered if the person, particularly a

KEY TERMS

Purpura—A group of disorders characterized by purplish or reddish brown areas of discoloration visible through the skin. These areas of discoloration are caused by bleeding from broken capillaries.

Scurvy—A nutritional disorder caused by vitamin C deficiency that is characterized by tiredness, muscle weakness, joint and muscle aches, a rash on the legs, bleeding gums, and skin bruising.

child, has caused a secondary infection by scratching. The rash triggered by **allergies** should disappear as soon as the allergen is removed; drug rashes will fade when the person stops taking the drug causing the allergy. For the treatment of diaper rash, the infant's skin should be exposed to the air as much as possible; ointments are not needed unless the skin is dry and cracked. Experts also recommend switching to cloth diapers and cleaning affected skin with plain water.

Prognosis

Most rashes that have an acute cause, such as an infection or an allergic reaction, will disappear as soon as the infection or irritant is removed from the body's system. Rashes that are caused by chronic conditions, such as autoimmune disorders, may remain indefinitely or fade and return periodically.

Prevention

Some rashes can be prevented, depending on the triggering factor. A person known to be allergic to certain drugs or substances should avoid those things in order to prevent a rash. Diaper rash can be prevented by using cloth diapers, keeping the diaper area very clean, changing diapers often, and by breastfeeding.

Nutritional concerns

Foods that are known to trigger rashes in persons should be avoided.

Parental concerns

Parents should monitor the foods that their children eat so that they will be able to identify foods that cause

rashes and avoid their consumption. In addition, children who are prone to skin allergies should avoid contact with strong, perfumed soaps; nickel-based jewelry; and irritating fabrics (such as wool).

Resources

BOOKS

Bolognia, Jean L., and Irwin M. Braverman. "Skin Manifestations of Internal Disease." In *Harrison's Principles of Internal Medicine*, 15th ed. Edited by Eugene Braunwald et al. New York: McGraw-Hill, 2001, pp. 315–30.

Darmstadt, Gary L., and Robert Sidbury. "Eczematous Disorders." In *Nelson Textbook of Pediatrics*, 17th ed. Edited by Richard E. Behrman et al. Philadelphia: Saunders, 2003, pp. 2188–90.

———. "Nutritional Dermatoses." In *Nelson Textbook of Pediatrics*, 17th ed. Edited by Richard E. Behrman et al. Philadelphia: Saunders, 2003, pp. 2248–50.

Lim, Henry M. "Eczemas, Photodermatoses, Papulosquamous (Including Fungal) Diseases, and Figurate Erythemas." In *Cecil Textbook of Medicine*, 22nd ed. Edited by Lee Goldman et al. Philadelphia: Saunders, 2003, pp. 2458–65.

Swerlick, Robert A., and Thomas J. Lawley. "Eczema, Psoriasis, Cutaneous Infections, Acne, and Other Common Skin Disorders." In *Harrison's Principles of Internal Medicine*, 15th ed. Edited by Eugene Braunwald et al. New York: McGraw-Hill, 2001, pp. 309–14.

PERIODICALS

Ahmed, M., et al. "A peculiar rash and red eye." *Postgraduate Medical Journal* 80, no. 944 (2004): 370–1.

Blackwood, C. L. "Rash and fever in an ill-appearing child." *American Family Physician* 70, no. 2 (2004): 361–3.

Buccolo, L. S. "Severe rash after dermatitis." *Journal of Family Practice* 53, no. 8 (2004): 613–5.

Healy, C. P., and D. E. Thomas. "Leg rash." *American Family Physician* 69, no. 10 (2004): 2429–31.

Hedberg, C. L., et al. "An infant with generalized rash and abnormal hair." *Annals of Allergy, Asthma, and Immunology* 92, no. 2 (2004): 210–6.

Langran, M., and C. Laird. "Management of allergy, rashes, and itching." *Emergency Medicine Journal* 21, no. 6 (2004): 728–41.

ORGANIZATIONS

American Academy of Dermatology. 930 N. Meacham Road, PO Box 4014, Schaumburg, IL 60168–4014. Web site: <www.aad.org/>.

American Academy of Family Physicians. 11400 Tomahawk
    Creek Parkway, Leawood, KS 66211–2672. Web site:
    .

American Academy of Pediatrics. 141 Northwest Point Blvd.,
    Elk Grove Village, IL 60007–1098. Web site:
    .

American College of Occupational and Environmental
    Medicine. 55 West Seegers Rd., Arlington Heights, IL
    60005. Web site: .

American College of Physicians. 190 N Independence Mall
    West, Philadelphia, PA 19106–1572. Web site:
    .

WEB SITES

"Drug Rashes." The Merck Manual. Available online at
    <www.merck.com/mmhe/sec18/ch203/ch203d.html>
    (accessed December 22, 2004).

"Rashes." MedlinePlus. Available online at
    <www.nlm.nih.gov/medlineplus/ency/article/
    003220.htm> (accessed December 22, 2004).

"Rashes and Skin Allergies." American Academy of Family
    Physicians Foundation. Available online at <http://
    quickcare.org/skin/rashes.html> (accessed December 22,
    2004).

"Skin Rashes and Other Changes." American Academy of
    Family Physicians. Available online at <http://
    familydoctor.org/545.xml> (accessed December 22, 2004).

L. Fleming Fallon, Jr., MD, DrPH

RAST test see **Allergy tests**

Rat-bite fever

Definition

Rat-bite fever refers to an infection which develops
in a person after being bitten or scratched by an infected
animal.

Description

Rat-bite fever occurs most often among laboratory
workers who handle lab rats in their jobs, and among
people who live in poor conditions, with rodent infestation. Children are particularly likely to be bitten by
rodents infesting their home and are, therefore, most
likely to contract rat-bite fever. Other animals that can
carry the types of bacteria responsible for this illness
are mice, squirrels, weasels, dogs, and cats. One kind of

bacteria can cause the same illness if it is ingested in
unpasteurized milk or in water that has been contaminated with rat waste.

Demographics

About half of all cases of rat-bite fever occur in
children.

Causes and symptoms

There are two variations of rat-bite fever, caused by
two different organisms. In the United States, the bacteria Streptobacillus moniliformis is the most common
cause (causing streptobacillary rat-bite fever). In other
countries, especially Africa, Spirillum minus causes a
different form of the infection (called spirillary rat-bite
fever).

Streptobacillary rat-bite fever occurs up to 22 days
after the initial bite or scratch. The patient becomes ill
with fever, chills, **nausea and vomiting**, **headache**, and
pain in the back and joints. A rash made up of tiny pink
bumps develops, covering the palms of the hands and the
soles of the feet. Without treatment, the patient is at risk
of developing serious infections of the lining of the heart
(endocarditis), the sac containing the heart (pericarditis),
the coverings of the brain and spinal cord (**meningitis**),
or lungs (**pneumonia**). Any tissue or organ throughout
the body may develop a pocket of infection and pus,
called an abscess.

Spirillary rat-bite fever occurs some time after the
initial injury has already healed, up to about 28 days
after the bite or scratch. Although the wound had
appeared completely healed, it suddenly grows red and
swollen again. Lymph nodes in the area become swollen
and tender, and the patient develops fever, chills, and
headache. The skin in the area of the original wound
sloughs off. Although rash is less common than with
streptobacillary rat-bite fever, there may be a lightly
rosy, itchy rash all over the body. Joint and muscle pain
rarely occur. If left untreated, the fever usually subsides,
only to return again in repeated two- to four-day cycles.
Though these cycles can last for a year, the illness
usually resolves without treatment in four to eight
weeks. This can go on for up to a year although, even
without treatment, the illness usually resolves within
four to eight weeks.

Diagnosis

In streptobacillary rat-bite fever diagnosis can be
made by taking a sample of blood or fluid from a painful

joint, which can be cultured to allow the growth of organisms. Examination under a microscope will then allow identification of the bacteria *Streptobacillus moniliformis*.

In spirillary rat-bite fever, diagnosis can be made by examining blood or a sample of tissue from the wound for evidence of *Spirillum minus*.

Treatment

Either injections of procaine penicillin G or penicillin V by mouth are effective against both streptobacillary and spirillary rat-bite fever. When a patient is allergic to the **penicillins**, either erythromycin may be given by mouth for streptobacillary infection or tetracycline by mouth for spirillary infection.

Prognosis

With treatment, prognosis is excellent for both types of rat-bite fever. Without treatment, the spirillary form usually resolves on its own, although it may take up to a year to do so.

The streptobacillary form, found in the United States, however, can progress to cause extremely serious, potentially fatal complications. In fact, before **antibiotics** were available to treat the infection, streptobacillary rat-bite fever frequently resulted in death.

Prevention

Prevention involves avoiding contact with those animals capable of passing on the causative organisms. This can be a difficult task for people whose economic situations do not allow them to move out of rat-infested buildings. Because streptobacillary rat-bite fever can occur after drinking contaminated milk or water, only pasteurized milk, and water from safe sources, should be ingested.

Parental concerns

The parents of children living in rodent-infested conditions, or who have pet rodents (mice, rats, gerbils) should be vigilant to illness in their children.

Resources

BOOKS

Barnett, S. Anthony. *The Story of Rats: Their Impact on Us and Our Impact on Them.* Crows Nest, New South Wales, Australia: Allen & Unwin, Pty., Limited, 2002.

Conniff, Richard. *Rats: The Good, the Bad, and the Ugly.* New York: Random House Children's Books, 2002.

Sullivan, Robert. *Rats: Observation on the History and Habitat of the City's Most Unwanted Inhabitant.* London: Bloomsbury Publishing, 2005.

ORGANIZATIONS

Centers for Disease Control and Prevention. 1600 Clifton Rd., NE, Atlanta, GA 30333. Web site: <www.cdc.gov>.

WEB SITES

"Rat-bite fever." *MedlinePlus.* Available online at <www.nlm.nih.gov/medlineplus/ency/article/001348.htm> (accessed December 29, 2004).

Rosalyn Carson-DeWitt, MD

Red blood cell indices

Definition

Red blood cell (RBC) indices are calculations derived from the complete blood count that aid in the diagnosis and classification of anemia. Measurements needed to calculate indices are the red blood cell count, hemoglobin, and hematocrit. The hematocrit is the percentage of blood by volume that is occupied by the red cells. The three RBC indices are:

- Mean corpuscular volume (MCV). The average size of the red blood cells expressed in femtoliters. MCV is calculated by dividing the hematocrit (as percent) by the RBC count in millions per microliter of blood, then multiplying by 10.

- Mean corpuscular hemoglobin (MCH). The average amount of hemoglobin inside an RBC expressed in picograms. The MCH is calculated by dividing the hemoglobin concentration in grams per deciliter by the RBC count in millions per microliter, then multiplying by 10.

- Mean corpuscular hemoglobin concentration (MCHC). The average concentration of hemoglobin in the RBCs expressed as a percent. It is calculated by dividing the hemoglobin in grams per deciliter by the hematocrit, then multiplying by 100.

Purpose

Red blood cell indices help classify types of anemia, a decrease in the oxygen carrying capacity of the blood. Healthy people have an adequate number of correctly sized red blood cells containing enough hemoglobin to carry sufficient oxygen to all the body's tissues. Anemia is diagnosed when either the hemoglobin or hematocrit of a blood sample is too low.

The mechanisms by which anemia occurs will alter the RBC indices in a predictable manner. Therefore, the RBC indices permit the physician to narrow down the possible causes of an anemia. The MCV is an index of the size of the RBCs. When the MCV is below normal, the RBCs will be smaller than normal and are described as microcytic. When the MCV is elevated, the RBCs will be larger than normal and are termed macrocytic. RBCs of normal size are termed normocytic. Failure to produce hemoglobin results in smaller than normal cells. This occurs in many diseases, including **iron deficiency anemia**, **thalassemia** (an inherited disease in which globin chain production is deficient), and **anemias** associated with chronic infection or disease. Macrocytic cells occur when division of RBC precursor cells in the bone marrow is impaired. The most common causes of macrocytic anemia are vitamin B_{12} deficiency, folate deficiency, and liver disease. Normocytic anemia may be caused by decreased production (e.g. malignancy and other causes of bone marrow failure), increased destruction (hemolytic anemia), or blood loss. The RBC count is low, but the size and amount of hemoglobin in the cells are normal.

A low MCH indicates that cells have too little hemoglobin. This is caused by deficient hemoglobin production. Such cells will be pale when examined under the microscope and are termed hypochromic. Iron deficiency is the most common cause of a hypochromic anemia.

The MCH is usually elevated in macrocytic anemias associated with vitamin B_{12} and folate deficiency.

The MCHC is the ratio of hemoglobin mass in the RBC to cell volume. Cells with too little hemoglobin are lighter in color and have a low MCHC. The MCHC is low in microcytic, hypochromic anemias such as iron deficiency, but is usually normal in macrocytic anemias. The MCHC is elevated in hereditary spherocytosis, a condition with decreased RBC survival caused by a structural protein defect in the RBC membrane.

Description

Cell indices are usually calculated from tests performed on an automated electronic cell counter. However, these counters measure the MCV, which is directly proportional to the voltage pulse produced as each cell passes through the counting aperture. Electronic cell counters calculate the MCH, MCHC, hematocrit, and an additional parameter called the red cell distribution width (RDW). The RDW is a measure of the variance in red blood cell size. It is calculated by dividing the standard deviation of RBC volume by the MCV and multiplying by 100. A large RDW indicates abnormal variation in cell size, termed anisocytosis. The RDW aids in differentiating anemias that have similar indices. For example, thalassemia minor and iron deficiency anemia are both microcytic and hypochromic anemias, and overlap in MCV and MCH. However, iron deficiency anemia has an abnormally wide RDW, but thalassemia minor does not.

Precautions

Certain prescription medications may affect the test results. These drugs include zidovudine (Retrovir), phenytoin (Dilantin), and azathioprine (Imuran). When the hematocrit is determined by centrifugation, the MCV and MCHC may differ from those derived by an electronic cell counter, especially in anemia. Plasma trapped between the RBCs tends to cause an increase in the hematocrit, giving rise to a somewhat higher MCV and lower MCHC.

RBC indices require 3–5 mL of blood collected by venipuncture. A nurse or phlebotomist usually collects the sample following standard precautions for the prevention of transmission of bloodborne pathogens.

Aftercare

Discomfort or bruising may occur at the puncture site. Pressure to the puncture site until the bleeding stops reduces bruising; warm packs relieve discomfort. Some people feel dizzy or faint after blood has been drawn and should be treated accordingly.

KEY TERMS

Anemia—A condition in which there is an abnormally low number of red blood cells in the bloodstream. It may be due to loss of blood, an increase in red blood cell destruction, or a decrease in red blood cell production. Major symptoms are paleness, shortness of breath, unusually fast or strong heart beats, and tiredness.

Hypochromic—A descriptive term applied to a red blood cell with a decreased concentration of hemoglobin.

Macrocytic—A descriptive term applied to a larger than normal red blood cell.

Mean corpuscular hemoglobin concentration (MCHC)—A measurement of the average concentration of hemoglobin in a red blood cell.

Mean corpuscular hemoglobin (MCH)—A measurement of the average weight of hemoglobin in a red blood cell.

Mean corpuscular volume (MCV)—A measurement of the average volume of a red blood cell.

Microcytic—A descriptive term applied to a smaller than normal red blood cell.

Normochromic—A descriptive term applied to a red blood cell with a normal concentration of hemoglobin.

Normocytic—A descriptive term applied to a red blood cell of normal size.

Red blood cell indices—Measurements that describe the size and hemoglobin content of red blood cells. The indices are used to help in the differential diagnosis of anemia. Also called red cell absolute values or erythrocyte indices.

Red cell distribution width (RDW)—A measure of the variation in size of red blood cells.

Risks

The risks are potential bruising at the puncture site, and mild **dizziness**. Rarely excess bleeding, or infection of the puncture site occurs.

Normal results

Normal results for red blood cell indices are as follows:

- MCV: 78–102 fl (femtoliters) for ages 12–18 years, 77–95 fl for ages six to 12 years, 75–87 fl for ages two

to six years, 70–86 fl for ages six months to two years, 85–123 fl for age one month

- MCH: 25–35 pg (picograms) for ages 12–18 years, 25–33 pg for ages six to 12 years, 24–30 pg for ages two to six years, 23–31 pg for ages six months to two years, 28–40 pg for age one month

- MCHC: 31–37 g/dL for ages two to 18 years, 30–36 g/dL for ages six months to two years, 29–37 pg for age one month

- RDW: 12–15 percent

Parental concerns

The **pain** from the needle puncture only lasts a moment. The parent should comfort a child as needed. Older children can be prepared for the test ahead of time, and the reason why the test is being given should also be explained if the child is old enough to understand.

When to call a doctor

If the bleeding does not stop at the needle puncture site, or if hours to days later, there appears to be infection (redness and swelling), then parents should contact a doctor.

Resources

BOOKS

Chernecky, Cynthia C., and Barbara J. Berger. *Laboratory Tests and Diagnostic Procedures,* 3rd ed. Philadelphia, PA: W. B. Saunders Company, 2001.

Kee, Joyce LeFever. *Handbook of Laboratory and Diagnostic Tests,* 4th ed. Upper Saddle River, NJ: Prentice Hall, 2001.

Kjeldsberg, Carl, et al. *Practical Diagnosis of Hematologic Disorders, 3rd Ed.* Chicago: ASCP Press, 2000.

Mark A. Best

Reflex tests

Definition

Reflex tests are simple physical tests of nervous system function.

Purpose

A reflex is a simple nerve circuit. A stimulus, such as a light tap with a rubber hammer, causes sensory

Doctor performing a reflex test on a young girl's elbow.
(Photo Researchers, Inc.)

neurons (nerve cells) to send signals to the spinal cord. Here, the signals are conveyed both to the brain and to nerves that control muscles affected by the stimulus. Without any brain intervention, these muscles may respond to an appropriate stimulus by contracting. Newborn babies have a particular set of reflexes not present in older babies, children, and adults.

Reflex tests measure the presence and strength of a number of reflexes. In so doing, they help to assess the integrity of the nerve circuits involved. Reflex tests are performed as part of a neurological exam, either a mini-exam done to quickly confirm integrity of the spinal cord or a more complete exam performed to diagnose the presence and location of **spinal cord injury** or neuromuscular disease.

Deep tendon reflexes are responses to muscle stretch. The familiar knee-jerk reflex is an example; this reflex tests the integrity of the spinal cord in the lower back region. The usual set of deep tendon reflexes tested,

involving increasingly higher regions of the spinal cord, are:

- ankle
- knee
- abdomen
- forearm
- biceps
- triceps

Another type of reflex test is called the Babinski test, which involves gently stroking the sole of the foot to assess proper development of the spine and cerebral cortex.

Description

The examiner places the person in a comfortable position, usually seated on the examination table with legs hanging free. The examiner uses a rubber mallet to strike different points on the individual's body and observes the response. The examiner may position, or hold, one of the limbs during testing, and may require exposure of the ankles, knees, abdomen, and arms. Reflexes can be difficult to elicit if the person is paying too much attention to the stimulus. To compensate for this, the person may be asked to perform some muscle contraction, such as clenching teeth or grasping and pulling the two hands apart. When performing the Babinski reflex test, the doctor will gently stroke the outer soles of the person's feet with the mallet while checking to see whether the big toe extends out as a result.

Risks

Reflex tests are entirely safe, and no special precautions are needed.

Normal results

The strength of the response depends partly on the strength of the stimulus. For this reason, the examiner will attempt to elicit the response with the smallest stimulus possible. Learning the range of normal responses requires some clinical training. Responses should be the same for both sides of the body. A normal response to the Babinski reflex test depends upon the age of the person being examined. In children under the age of one-and-a-half years, the big toe will extend out with or without the other toes. This is due to the fact that the fibers in the spinal cord and cerebral cortex have not been completely covered in myelin, the protein and lipid sheath that aids in processing neural signals. In adults and children over

KEY TERMS

Babinski sign—Dorsiflexion (curling) of the big toe on stimulating the sole of the foot.

Neuron—The fundamental nerve cell of the nervous system.

the age of one-and-a-half years, the myelin sheath should be completely formed, and, as a result, all the toes will curl under (planter flexion reflex).

Parental concerns

Parents should expect reflex tests to be included in every examination given to their children by a doctor or other healthcare provider. Reflex tests present no risks. Parents should only be concerned when they are told of abnormal reflex test results.

See also Neonatal reflexes.

Resources

BOOKS

Bickley, Lynn S., and Peter G. Szilagyi. *Bates' Guide to Physical Examination and History Taking*, 6th ed. Philadelphia: Lippincott Williams & Wilkins, 2004.

Jarvis, Carolyn. *Physical Examination and Health Assessment*, 4th ed. Amsterdam, Netherlands: Elsevier, 2003.

LeBlond, Richard F., and Donald D. Brown. *DeGowin's Diagnostic Examination*, 8th ed. New York: McGraw-Hill, 2004.

Simel, David L. "Approach to the Patient: History and Physical Examination." In *Cecil Textbook of Medicine*, 22nd ed. Edited by Lee Goldman et al. Philadelphia: Saunders, 2003, pp. 18–22.

PERIODICALS

Berilgen, M. S., et al. "Effects of epilepsy on autonomic nervous system and respiratory function tests." *Epilepsy and Behavior* 5, no. 4 (2004): 513–6.

Calancie B., et al. "Tendon reflexes for predicting movement recovery after acute spinal cord injury in humans." *Clinical Neurophysiology* 115, no. 10 (2004): 2350–63.

Lefaucheur, J. P., and A. Creange. "Neurophysiological testing correlates with clinical examination according to fiber type involvement and severity in sensory neuropathy." *Journal of Neurology, Neurosurgery, and Psychiatry* 75, no. 3 (2004): 417–22.

Mold, J. W., et al. "The prevalence, predictors, and consequences of peripheral sensory neuropathy in older

patients." *Journal of the American Board of Family Practice* 17, no. 5 (2004): 309–18.

Nadler, M. A., et al. "Cutaneomuscular reflexes following stroke: a 2-year longitudinal study." *Journal of the Neurological Sciences* 217, no. 2 (2004): 195–203.

ORGANIZATIONS

American Academy of Family Physicians. 11400 Tomahawk Creek Parkway, Leawood, KS 66211–2672. Web site: <www.aafp.org/>.

American Academy of Neurology. 1080 Montreal Avenue, St. Paul, MN 55116. Web site: <www.aan.com/>.

American Academy of Pediatrics. 141 Northwest Point Blvd., Elk Grove Village, IL 60007–1098. Web site: <www.aap.org/default.htm>.

American Academy of Physical Medicine and Rehabilitation. One IBM Plaza, Suite 2500, Chicago, IL 60611–3604. Web site: <www.aapmr.org/>.

American College of Emergency Physicians. PO Box 619911, Dallas, TX 75261–9911. Web site: <www.acep.org/>.

American College of Physicians. 190 N Independence Mall West, Philadelphia, PA 19106–1572. Web site: <www.acponline.org/>.

American College of Sports Medicine. 401 W. Michigan St., Indianapolis, IN 46202–3233. Web site: <www.acsm.org/>.

International Brain Injury Association. 1150 South Washington St., Suite 210, Alexandria, VA 22314. Web site: <www.internationalbrain.org/>.

WEB SITES

"Moro reflex." *MedlinePlus.* Available online at <www.nlm.nih.gov/medlineplus/ency/article/003293.htm> (accessed December 22, 2004).

"Neuro-Ophthalmologic Disorders." *The Merck Manual.* Available online at <www.merck.com/mrkshared/mmanual/section14/chapter178/178b.jsp> (accessed December 22, 2004).

L. Fleming Fallon, Jr., MD, DrPH

Reflexes, neonatal *see* **Neonatal reflexes**

Refsum disease *see* **Peroxisomal disorders**

Rehydration therapy *see* **Intravenous rehydration**

Remarriage *see* **Stepfamilies**

Renal vein thrombosis

Definition

Renal vein thrombosis develops when a blood clot forms in the renal vein, which is the blood vessel that carries blood from the kidneys back to the heart. The disorder is not common.

Description

Normally, kidneys rid the body of wastes by filtering the wastes into the bladder where they exit the body through the urine. When one or more blood vessels in the kidneys become narrowed (renal artery stenosis) because of debris and plaque build-up, or blocked because of a blood clot (renal vein thrombosis), the kidneys are unable to function properly. There is usually a rise in blood pressure, and kidney failure can occur without prompt treatment.

The onset of renal vein thrombosis can be rapid (acute) or gradual.

Blood clots in the renal arteries are uncommon, but when they do occur, there is a risk of pulmonary embolism, a dangerous condition that occurs when the clot or a portion of the clot dislodges and travels to the lungs. There is also an increased risk of congestive heart failure, a condition in which the heart's pumping power is weaker than normal.

Demographics

Renal vein thrombosis occurs in both infants and adults. The number of people who suffer from renal vein thrombosis is difficult to determine, as many do not show symptoms, and the disorder is diagnosed only by specific tests. Ninety percent of pediatric cases of renal vein thrombi occur in infants less than one year old; 75 percent occur in infants under one month of age.

Causes and symptoms

Causes

In children, most cases of renal vein thrombosis are thought to be caused by an episode of severe **dehydration**. Severe dehydration decreases blood volume and causes the blood to clot more readily. Symptoms occur rapidly.

In adults, renal vein thrombosis can be caused by injury to the abdomen or back, malignant kidney tumors growing into the renal vein, scar formation (stricture) and other blockages in the vein, or kidney diseases that cause degenerative changes in the cells of the renal tubules (nephrotic syndrome).

Renal vein thrombosis is more common in patients with nephrotic syndrome, although studies have shown high variability among these patients, with rates of 5 to 62 percent reported. Nephrotic syndrome is marked by abnormally low levels of albumin (hypoalbuminemia), abnormally high levels of cholesterol in the blood (hypercholesterolemia), and fluid retention (edema). Minimal change disease is a form of nephrotic syndrome seen in children, characterized by swelling and weight (from fluid retention), foamy urine, and loss of appetite.

Symptoms

Acute onset of renal vein thrombosis at any age causes **pain** in the lower back and sides of the abdomen, **fever**, bloody urine, decreased urine output, and sometimes kidney failure.

Other symptoms include high blood pressure or a "whooshing" sound heard by the physician when he or she places a stethoscope on the abdomen. This sound is the result of blood attempting to pass through the blocked vessel. The doctor may also feel an enlarged kidney during a physical exam. Some patients have no symptoms.

When to call the doctor

If the child has any of these symptoms, the parent should seek emergency medical care:

- a high fever of 102° F, or 38.9°C, or above
- sudden onset of lower back pain
- sudden, severe leg swelling
- difficulty breathing
- blood in the urine
- decreased urination

If the child has any of these symptoms of dehydration, the parent should give the child clear fluids and an oral rehydrating solution, such as Pedialyte, and contact the child's pediatrician:

- dry mouth
- increased or excessive thirst
- few or no tears when crying
- dark yellow urine
- irritability
- low energy or severe weakness
- lightheadedness or fainting
- sunken abdomen, eyes, and cheeks

Diagnosis

A physician makes the diagnosis of renal vein thrombosis based on the presence of symptoms and the results of a medical examination and diagnostic tests. When examining the child, the doctor will palpate (feel) the child's abdomen to detect kidney enlargement. The doctor will listen to the child's heartbeat with a stethoscope. He or she will also place the stethoscope over the child's abdomen; when renal vein thrombosis is present, the doctor may hear an abnormal "whooshing" as blood tries to flow through the blocked vessel.

Urine tests and blood tests are usually performed. If nephrotic syndrome is present, the urine test may indicate an abnormally large quantity of protein, and the blood test may show abnormally high levels of cholesterol.

Vascular ultrasound is a non-invasive ultrasound method used to examine blood circulation and detect the presence of blood clots. During a vascular ultrasound, an ultrasound transducer (small hand-held device) is placed over the area being examined. The transducer generates high-frequency sound waves through the tissues. These sound waves reflect off blood cells moving within the blood vessels, allowing the radiologist to calculate their speed. The sound waves are measured, recorded, and displayed on a computer screen.

Other tests that may be used to detect a blood clot include **computed tomography** scans (CT scans) and **magnetic resonance imaging** (MRI).

A less common test used to diagnose renal vein thrombosis is renal venography, also called renal angiography, an x-ray examination of the renal veins after a contrast material (dye) has been injected. This test may be performed to locate the narrowing or blockage in the renal vein. During this test, a catheter (long, thin tube) is inserted into the vein in the groin area (femoral vein) and threaded first into the right kidney and then into the vein of the other kidney. Blood samples may be taken from each kidney for further testing. The contrast material is injected through the catheter into each vein and **x rays** are taken. This test is not common, since other less invasive imaging tests, including MRI and CT scans, are available to aid the physician in making an accurate diagnosis.

Treatment

One of the major goals of treatment is to prevent the blood clot in the renal vein from detaching and moving into the lungs (pulmonary embolism), where it can cause serious complications.

Clot-busting medications, such as tissue plasminogen activator (t-PA, also called streptokinase enzymes or thrombolytic drugs), may be given to help dissolve the renal clot. Clot busters must be administered quickly and properly through several specifically timed intravenous infusions according to a rigid protocol established for each drug and the body weight of each patient. Research has shown that these medications are most effective when given within two hours of the onset of symptoms.

Anticoagulant medications, including heparin or warfarin and low-dose aspirin, may be prescribed to prevent existing blood clots from enlarging and to prevent the formation of new clots. The use of these medications in children remains controversial because of the risk of **Reye's syndrome**. Sometimes the potential benefits of these medications outweigh the risk of side effects. Researchers agree that more studies are needed to determine the proper dosage and effectiveness of aspirin and other anticoagulant medications in children.

Bedrest or limited activity may be recommended for a brief period.

Severe dehydration requires medical treatment with intravenous (IV) fluids and may require **hospitalization**. IV therapy can be followed with oral rehydration as the child's condition improves.

If the renal artery is partially or completely blocked, an interventional catheter-based procedure may be performed. During the catheterization, a long, slender tube called a catheter is inserted into a vein or artery and slowly directed to the blocked blood vessel, using x-ray guidance (angiography). A specialized balloon tip or other device at the end of the catheter can be used to open the blocked or narrowed vessel. The balloon is rapidly inflated and deflated to open or widen the area. In some patients, a stent (metal mesh tube) can be placed to act as a scaffold and hold the area open.

Intra-arterial thrombolysis involves threading a catheter with clot-busting medication through a large blood vessel in the groin to the site of the clot. Using renal angiography, doctors pinpoint the precise location of the blockage and deliver the medication to that spot.

Endarterectomy and surgical bypass are two surgical treatment options, but they are not common in children. In a renal endarterectomy, a vascular surgeon removes the blockage from the inner lining of the renal artery. Bypass surgery reroutes the blood flow around the narrowed or blocked sections of the renal artery. Rarely, when there is a complete blockage of the renal vein in infants, the kidney must be surgically removed.

KEY TERMS

Albumin—A blood protein that is made in the liver and helps to regulate water movement in the body.

Anticoagulant drug—A drug used to prevent clot formation or to prevent a clot that has formed from enlarging. Anticoagulant drugs inhibit clot formation by blocking the action of clotting factors or platelets. They fall into three groups: inhibitors of clotting factor synthesis, inhibitors of thrombin, and antiplatelet drugs.

Antiplatelet drug—Drugs that inhibit platelets from aggregating to form a plug. They are used to prevent clotting and alter the natural course of atherosclerosis.

Arteriosclerosis—A chronic condition characterized by thickening, loss of leasticity, and hardening of the arteries and the build-up of plaque on the arterial walls. Arteriosclerosis can slow or impair blood circulation. It includes atherosclerosis, but the two terms are often used synonymously.

Artery—A blood vessel that carries blood away from the heart to the cells, tissues, and organs of the body.

Blood clotting—Also called coagulation. A natural process in which blood cells and fibrin strands clump together to stop bleeding after a blood vessel has been injured.

Clot—A soft, semi-solid mass that forms when blood coagulates.

Clot busters—Also called thrombolytics. Medications used to break up a blood clot.

Clotting factors—Substances in the blood, also known as coagulation factors, that act in sequence to stop bleeding by triggering the formation of a clot. Each clotting factor is designated with a Roman numeral I through XIII.

Coagulate—To clot or cause hemostasis; in electrosurgery, to cause tissue dehydration without cutting.

Computed tomography (CT)—An imaging technique in which cross-sectional x rays of the body are compiled to create a three-dimensional image of the body's internal structures; also called computed axial tomography.

Dehydration—An excessive loss of water from the body. It may follow vomiting, prolonged diarrhea, or excessive sweating.

Embolism—A blood clot, air bubble, or mass of foreign material that travels and blocks the flow of blood in an artery. When blood supply to a tissue or organ is blocked by an embolism, infarction, or death of the tissue the artery feeds, occurs. Without immediate and appropriate treatment, an embolism can be fatal.

Embolus—Plural, emboli. An embolus is something that blocks the blood flow in a blood vessel. It may be a gas bubble, a blood clot, a fat globule, a mass of bacteria, or other foreign body that forms somewhere else and travels through the circulatory system until it gets stuck.

Hypercoagulable state—(Also called thromboembolic state or thrombophilia.) A condition characterized by excess blood clotting.

Hypertension—Abnormally high arterial blood pressure, which if left untreated can lead to heart disease and stroke.

Intravenous (IV) therapy—Administration of fluids or medications through a vein, usually in the hand or arm.

Magnetic resonance imaging (MRI)—An imaging technique that uses a large circular magnet and radio waves to generate signals from atoms in the body. These signals are used to construct detailed images of internal body structures and organs, including the brain.

Nephrologist—A physician who specializes in treating diseases of the kidney.

Platelet—A cell-like particle in the blood that plays an important role in blood clotting. Platelets are activated when an injury causes a blood vessel to break. They change shape from round to spiny, "sticking" to the broken vessel wall and to each other to begin the clotting process. In addition to physically plugging breaks in blood vessel walls, platelets also release chemicals that promote clotting.

Stenosis—A condition in which an opening or passageway in the body is narrowed or constricted.

Thrombolysis—The process of dissolving a blood clot.

Thrombolytics—Drugs that dissolve blood clots. Thrombolytics are used to treat embolisms.

Thrombus—A blood clot that forms within a blood vessel or the heart.

KEY TERMS (contd.)

Ultrasonography—A medical test in which sound waves are directed against internal structures in the body. As sound waves bounce off the internal structure, they create an image on a video screen. Ultrasonography is often used to diagnose fetal abnormalities, gallstones, heart defects, and tumors. Also called ultrasound imaging.

Urologist—A physician who specializes in the anatomy, physiology, diseases, and care of the urinary tract (in men and women) and male reproductive tract.

Blood pressure medications may be prescribed to treat high blood pressure, and other medications may include diuretics, beta blockers, ACE inhibitors, and calcium channel blockers. Some of these drugs have not been extensively studied in children, and a specific pediatric dose has not been established.

Nutritional concerns

Impaired kidneys cause an increased level of phosphorus in the blood, which interferes with calcium absorption. In addition, damaged kidneys cannot activate vitamin D, which is needed to absorb calcium. Dietary changes may include limiting foods high in phosphorus, such as dairy products, meat, and poultry. A phosphate binder may be recommended to keep phosphorus in the bowel (so it does not interfere with calcium absorption) where it is excreted during a bowel movement. Calcium or vitamin D supplements also may be recommended. To maintain adequate **nutrition**, a registered dietitian can help parents and children implement specific dietary changes.

Prognosis

Most cases of renal vein thrombosis resolve over time, without permanent injury to the kidneys. Acute renal failure can occur with severe dehydration. Death from renal vein thrombosis is rare, and is often caused by the blood clot detaching and lodging in the heart or lungs.

Prevention

Renal vein thrombosis cannot be prevented. Preventing dehydration by maintaining fluids in the body may help reduce the risk of renal vein thrombosis.

Parental concerns

Most cases of renal vein thrombosis resolve without complication. When a child has been diagnosed with renal vein thrombosis, it is important to follow the doctor's recommendations for follow-up checkups to closely monitor his or her condition. If an anticoagulant medication has been prescribed, it is important to keep all scheduled laboratory appointments so the effectiveness of the medication can be evaluated.

If the child has developed any new symptoms, the parents should call the child's doctor.

Resources

BOOKS

"Vascular Diseases of Acute Onset: Renal Vein Thrombosis." In *The Merck Manual of Diagnosis and Therapy.* 17th ed. Eds. Mark H. Beers and Robert Berkow. Indianapolis, IN: John Wiley and Sons, Inc., 1999.

ORGANIZATIONS

American Kidney Fund. 6110 Executive Blvd., Suite 1010, Rockville, MD 20852. (800) 638-8299. <www.akfinc.org>

National Institute of Diabetes and Digestive and Kidney Diseases (NIDDK). 2 Information Way, Bethesda, MD 20892-3570. (800) 891- 5389. nddic@info.niddk.nih.gov. <www.niddk.nih.gov>

National Kidney and Urologic Diseases Information Clearinghouse. 3 Information Way, Bethesda, MD 20892-3580. (800) 891-5390. nkudic@info.niddk.nih.gov. <http://kidney.niddk.nih.gov>

National Kidney Foundation. 30 East 33rd St., New York, NY 10016. (800) 622-9010 or (212) 889-2210. info@kidney.org. <www.kidney.org>

WEB SITES

VascularWeb. Provided by the Society for Vascular Surgery. <www.vascularweb.org>

Angela M. Costello

Rendu-Osler-Weber disease *see* **Hereditary hemorrhagic telangiectasia**

Respiratory distress syndrome

Definition

Respiratory distress syndrome (RDS) of the newborn, also known as infant RDS, is an acute lung disease present at birth, which usually affects premature babies. Layers of tissue called hyaline membranes keep the oxygen that is breathed in from passing into the blood. The lungs are said to be airless. Without treatment, the infant will die within a few days after birth, but if oxygen can be provided, and the infant receives modern treatment in a neonatal intensive care unit, complete recovery with no after-effects can be expected.

Description

If a newborn infant is to breathe properly, the small air sacs (alveoli) at the ends of the breathing tubes must remain open so that oxygen in the air can get into the tiny blood vessels that surround the alveoli. Normally, in the last months of pregnancy, cells in the alveoli produce a substance called surfactant, which keep the surface tension inside the alveoli low so that the sacs can expand at the moment of birth, and the infant can breathe normally. Surfactant is produced starting at about 34 weeks of pregnancy and, by the time the fetal lungs mature at 37 weeks, a normal amount is present.

If an infant is born prematurely, enough surfactant might not have formed in the alveoli causing the lungs to collapse and making it very difficult for the baby to get enough air (and the oxygen it contains). Sometimes a layer of fibrous tissue called a hyaline membrane forms in the air sacs, making it even harder for oxygen to get through to the blood vessels. RDS in newborn infants used to be called hyaline membrane disease.

Demographics

According to the National Heart, Lung, and Blood Institute, in 2003, approximately 40,000 infants and 150,000 adults were reported to have RDS. Translated, these figures means RDS affected about one person in 6,800.

Causes and symptoms

RDS nearly always occurs in premature infants, and the more premature the birth, the greater is the chance that RDS will develop. RDS also is seen in some infants whose mothers are diabetic. Paradoxically, RDS is less likely in the presence of certain states or conditions which themselves are harmful: abnormally slow growth of the fetus; high blood pressure, a condition called preeclampsia in the mother; and early rupture of the birth membranes.

Labored breathing (the respiratory distress of RDS) may begin as soon as the infant is born, or within a few hours. Breathing becomes very rapid, the nostrils flare,

and the infant grunts with each breath. The ribs, which are very flexible in young infants, move inwards each time a breath is taken. Before long the muscles that move the ribs and diaphragm, so that air is drawn into the lungs, become fatigued. When the oxygen level in the blood drops severely the infant's skin turns bluish in color. Tiny, very premature infants may not even have signs of trouble breathing. Their lungs may be so stiff that they cannot even start breathing when born.

There are two major complications of RDS. One is called pneumothorax, which means "air in the chest." When the infant itself or a breathing machine applies pressure on the lungs in an attempt to expand them, a lung may rupture, causing air to leak into the chest cavity. This air causes the lung to collapse further, making breathing even harder and interfering with blood flow in the lung arteries. The blood pressure can drop suddenly, cutting the blood supply to the brain. The other complication is called intraventricular hemorrhage; this is bleeding into the cavities (ventricles) of the brain, which may be fatal.

When to call the doctor

A doctor attending a birth should recognize respiratory distress and immediately begin appropriate treatment. A doctor should be called if a baby delivered outside of a hospital setting is observed to have any difficulty in breathing or whose skin becomes blue in color (cyanotic).

Diagnosis

When a premature infant has obvious trouble breathing at birth or within a few hours of birth, RDS is an obvious possibility. If premature birth is expected, or there is some condition that calls for delivery as soon as possible, the amount of surfactant in the amniotic fluid will indicate how well the lungs have matured. If little surfactant is found in an amniotic fluid sample taken by placing a needle in the uterus (**amniocentesis**), there is a definite risk of RDS. Often this test is done at regular intervals so that the infant can be delivered as soon as the lungs are mature. If the membranes have ruptured, surfactant can easily be measured in a sample of vaginal fluid.

The other major diagnostic test is a chest x ray. Collapsed lung tissue has a typical appearance, and the more lung tissue is collapsed, the more severe the RDS. An x ray also can demonstrate pneumothorax, if this complication has occurred. The level of oxygen in the blood can be measured by taking a blood sample from an artery, or, more easily, using a device called an oximeter, which is clipped to an earlobe. Pneumothorax may have occurred if the infant suddenly becomes worse while on ventilation; x rays can help make the diagnosis.

Treatment

If only a mild degree of RDS is present at birth, placing the infant in an oxygen hood may be enough. It is important to guard against too much oxygen, as this may damage the retina and cause loss of vision. Using an oximeter to keep track of the blood oxygen level, repeated artery punctures or heel sticks can be avoided. In more severe cases a drug very like natural surfactant (Exosurf Neonatal or Survanta) can be dripped into the lungs through a fine tube (endotracheal tube) placed in the infant's windpipe (trachea). Typically, the infant will be able to breathe more easily within a few days at the most, and complications such as lung rupture are less likely to occur. The drug is continued until the infant starts producing its own surfactant. There is a risk of bleeding into the lungs from surfactant treatment; about 10 percent of the smallest infants are affected.

Infants with severe RDS may require treatment with a ventilator, a machine that takes over the work of the lungs and delivers air under pressure. In tiny infants who do not breathe when born, ventilation through a tracheal tube is an emergency procedure. Assisted ventilation must be closely supervised, as too much pressure can cause further lung damage. A gentler way of assisting breathing, continuous positive airway pressure (CPAP), delivers an oxygen mixture through nasal prongs or a tube placed through the nose rather than an endotracheal tube. CPAP may be tried before resorting to a ventilator or after an infant placed on a ventilator begins to improve. Drugs that stimulate breathing may speed the recovery process.

Pneumothorax is an emergency condition that must be treated right away. Air may be removed from the chest using a needle and syringe. A tube then is inserted into the lung cavity, and suction applied.

Prognosis

If an infant born with RDS is not promptly treated, lack of an adequate oxygen supply will damage the body's organs and eventually cause them to stop functioning altogether. Death is the result. The central nervous system in particular—made up of the brain and spinal cord—is very dependent on a steady oxygen supply and is one of the first organ systems to feel the effects of RDS. By contrast, if the infant's breathing is supported until the lungs mature and make their own surfactant, complete recovery within three to five days is the pattern.

KEY TERMS

Alveoli—The tiny air sacs clustered at the ends of the bronchioles in the lungs in which oxygen-carbon dioxide exchange takes place.

Amniotic fluid—The liquid in the amniotic sac that cushions the fetus and regulates temperature in the placental environment. Amniotic fluid also contains fetal cells.

Endotracheal tube—A hollow tube that is inserted into the trachea (windpipe) through the nose or mouth. It is used to administer anesthesia, to deliver oxygen under pressure, or to deliver medications (e.g. surfactants).

Hyaline membrane—A fibrous layer that settles in the alveoli in respiratory distress syndrome and prevents oxygen from escaping from inhaled air to the bloodstream.

Pneumothorax—A collection of air or gas in the chest or pleural cavity that causes part or all of a lung to collapse.

Preeclampsia—A condition that develops after the twentieth week of pregnancy and results in high blood pressure, fluid retention that doesn't go away, and large amounts of protein in the urine. Without treatment, it can progress to a dangerous condition called eclampsia, in which a woman goes into convulsions.

Steroid—A class of drugs resembling normal body substances that often help control inflammation in the body tissues.

Surfactant—A protective film secreted by the alveoli in the lungs that reduces the surface tension of lung fluids, allowing gas exchange and helping maintain the elasticity of lung tissue. Surfactant is normally produced in the fetal lungs in the last months of pregnancy, which helps the air sacs to open up at the time of birth so that the newborn infant can breathe freely. Premature infants may lack surfactant and are more susceptible to respiratory problems without it.

Ventilator—A mechanical device that can take over the work of breathing for a patient whose lungs are injured or are starting to heal. Sometimes called a respirator.

If an air leak causes pneumothorax, immediate removal of air from the chest allows the lungs to re-expand. Bleeding into the brain is a very serious condition that worsens the outlook for an infant with RDS.

Prevention

The best way of preventing RDS is to delay delivery until the fetal lungs have matured and are producing enough surfactant, generally at about 37 weeks of pregnancy. If delivery cannot be delayed, the mother may be given a steroid hormone, similar to a natural substance produced in the body, which crosses the barrier of the placenta and helps the fetal lungs to produce surfactant. The steroid should be given at least 24 hours before the expected time of delivery. If the infant does develop RDS, the risk of bleeding into the brain will be much less if the mother has been given a dose of steroid.

If a very premature infant is born without symptoms of RDS, it may be wise to deliver surfactant to its lungs. This may prevent RDS or make it less severe if it does develop. An alternative is to wait until the first symptoms of RDS appear and then immediately give surfactant. Pneumothorax may be prevented by frequently checking the blood oxygen content and limiting oxygen treatment under pressure to the minimum needed.

Parental concerns

Parents should monitor their newborn infant's breathing status closely for the first week of life. Premature infants are of particular concern, although many may be hospitalized through the neonatal period. While a newborn is hospitalized, parents should try to maintain as much physical contact with the infant as is allowed by the hospital, and let the infant frequently hear the familiar voices of the parents, especially the mother, when physical contact is not recommended.

Resources

BOOKS

Beamis, John F., et al. *Interventional Pulmonary Medicine.* New York: Marcel Dekker, 2003.

Frankel, Larry R. "Respiratory Distress and Failure." In *Nelson Textbook of Pediatrics*, 17th ed. Edited by Richard E. Behrman et al. Philadelphia: Saunders, 2003, pp. 301–2.

Hanley, Michael E., and Carolyn H. Welsh. *Current Diagnosis & Treatment in Pulmonary Medicine.* New York: McGraw-Hill, 2003.

PERIODICALS

Bandi, V. D., et al. "Acute lung injury and acute respiratory distress syndrome in pregnancy." *Critical Care Clinics* 20, no. 4 (2004): 577–607.

Dicker, R. A., et al. "Acute respiratory distress syndrome criteria in trauma patients: why the definitions do not work." *Journal of Trauma* 57, no. 3 (2004): 522–6.

Louis, J. M., et al. "Perinatal intervention and neonatal outcomes near the limit of viability." *American Journal of Obstetrics and Gynecology* 191, no. 4 (2004): 1398–402.

Verger, J. T., et al. "The pragmatics of feeding the pediatric patient with acute respiratory distress syndrome." *Critical Care Nursing Clinics of North America* 16, no. 3 (2004): 431–43.

ORGANIZATIONS

American Academy of Emergency Medicine. 611 East Wells St., Milwaukee, WI 53202. Web site: <www.aaem.org/>.

American Academy of Family Physicians. 11400 Tomahawk Creek Parkway, Leawood, KS 66211–2672. Web site: <www.aafp.org/>.

American Academy of Pediatrics. 141 Northwest Point Boulevard, Elk Grove Village, IL 60007–1098. Web site: <www.aap.org/default.htm>.

American College of Emergency Physicians. PO Box 619911, Dallas, TX 75261–9911. Web site: <www.acep.org/>.

American Lung Association. 1740 Broadway, New York, NY 10019. Web site: <www.lungusa.org/diseases/lungtb.html>.

American Thoracic Society. 1740 Broadway, New York, NY 10019. Web site: <www.thoracic.org/>.

Canadian Cystic Fibrosis Foundation. 2221 Yonge St., Suite 601, Toronto, Ontario, M4S 2B4, Canada. Web site: <www.ccff.ca/home.cfm>.

Cystic Fibrosis Foundation. 6931 Arlington Road, Bethesda, MD 0814. Web site: <www.cff.org/>.

WEB SITES

"Infant Respiratory Distress Syndrome." *Penn State Children's Hospital.* Available online at <www.hmc.psu.edu/childrens/healthinfo/r/respiratorydistress.htm> (accessed December 23, 2004).

"Respiratory distress syndrome (RDS) in infants." *National Library of Medicine.* Available online at <www.nlm.nih.gov/medlineplus/ency/article/001563.htm> (accessed December 23, 2004).

Rothenhaus, Todd. "Acute Respiratory Distress Syndrome." *eMedicine*, May 16, 2003. Available online at <www.emedicine.com/EMERG/topic15.htm> (accessed December 23, 2004).

Udobi, Kahdi, and Ed Childs. "Acute Respiratory Distress Syndrome." *American College of Family Physicians.* Available online at <www.aafp.org/afp/20030115/315.html> (accessed December 23, 2004).

L. Fleming Fallon, Jr., MD, DrPH

Respiratory syncytial virus infection

Definition

Respiratory syncytial virus (RSV) is a virus that can cause severe lower respiratory infections in children younger than two years of age and milder upper respiratory infections in older children and adults. RSV infection in young children is also called **bronchiolitis**, because it is marked by inflammation of the bronchioles, the narrow airways that lead from the large airways (bronchi) to the tiny air sacs (alveoli) in the lungs. The symptoms include wheezing, difficulty breathing, and sometimes respiratory failure.

Description

RSV infection is caused by a group of viruses found worldwide. There are two different subtypes of the virus with numerous different strains. Taken together, these viruses account for a significant number of deaths in infants.

RSV infection shows distinctly different symptoms, depending on the age of the infected person. In young children, the virus causes a serious lower respiratory infection in the lungs. In older children and healthy adults, it causes a mild upper respiratory infection often mistaken for the **common cold**.

Although anyone can get this disease, infants suffer the most serious symptoms and complications. Breast-feeding seems to provide partial protection from the virus. Conditions in infants that increase their risk of infection include:

- premature birth
- lower socio-economic environment
- congenital heart disease
- chronic lung diseases, such as cystic fibrosis
- immune system deficiencies, including HIV infection
- immunosuppressive therapy, such as that given to organ transplant or **cancer** patients

Many older children and adults get RSV infection, but the symptoms are so similar to the common cold that the true cause is undiagnosed. People of any age with compromised immune systems, either from such diseases as **AIDS** or leukemia, or as the result of **chemotherapy** or corticosteroid medications, and patients with chronic lung disease are more at risk for serious RSV infections.

Demographics

RSV infection is primarily a disease of winter or early spring, with waves of illness sweeping through a community. The rate of RSV infection is estimated to be 11.4 cases for every 100 children during their first year of life. In the United States, RSV infection occurs most frequently in infants between the ages of two months and six months.

Respiratory syncytial virus is spread through close contact with an infected person. It has been shown that if a person with RSV infection sneezes, the virus can be carried to others within a radius of 6 feet (1.8 m). This group of viruses can live on the hands for up to half an hour and on **toys** or other inanimate objects for several hours.

Scientists had, as of 2004, not understood why RSV viruses attack the lower respiratory system in infants and the upper respiratory system in adults. In infants, RSV begins with such cold symptoms as a low **fever**, runny nose, and **sore throat**. Soon, other symptoms appear that suggest an infection that involves the lower airways. Some of these symptoms resemble those of **asthma**. RSV infection is suggested by the following characteristics:

- wheezing and high-pitched, whistling breathing
- rapid breathing (more than 40 breaths per minute)
- shortness of breath
- labored breathing out (exhalations)
- bluish tinge to the skin (cyanosis)
- croupy, seal-like, barking **cough**
- high fever

Breathing problems occur in RSV infections because the bronchioles swell, making it difficult for air to get in and out of the lungs. If the child is having trouble breathing, immediate medical care is needed. Breathing problems are most common in infants under one year of age; they can develop rapidly.

Diagnosis

Physical examination and imaging studies

RSV infection is usually diagnosed during a physical examination by the pediatrician or primary care doctor. The doctor listens with a stethoscope for wheezing and other abnormal lung sounds in the patient's chest. The doctor will also take into consideration whether there is a known outbreak of RSV infection in the area. Chest x rays give some indication of whether the lungs are hyperinflated from an effort to move air in and out.

X rays may also show the presence of a secondary bacterial infection, such as **pneumonia**.

Laboratory tests

A nasal swab can be obtained to isolate the virus or antibodies to the virus in secretions. If infants are hospitalized, other tests such as an arterial blood gas analysis are done to determine if the child is receiving enough oxygen.

Treatment

Home care

Home treatment for RSV infection is primarily supportive. It involves taking steps to ease the child's breathing. **Dehydration** can be a problem, so children should be encouraged to drink plenty of fluids. **Antibiotics** have no effect on viral illnesses. In time, the body will make antibodies to fight the infection and return itself to health.

Home care for keeping a child with RSV comfortable and breathing more easily includes:

- use of a cool mist room humidifier to ease congestion and sore throat
- elevation of that baby's head by putting books under the head end of the crib
- acetaminophen (Tylenol, Pandol, Tempra) for fever (Aspirin should not be given to children because of its association with **Reye's syndrome**, a serious disease.)
- For babies too young to blow their noses, suctioning mucus with an infant nasal aspirator

Hospital treatment

In the United States, RSV infections are responsible for 90,000 hospitalizations and 4,500 deaths each year. Children who are hospitalized receive oxygen and humidity through a mist tent or vaporizer. They also are given intravenous fluids to prevent dehydration. Mechanical ventilation may be necessary. Blood gases are monitored to assure that the child is receiving enough oxygen.

Medications

Bronchiodilators, such as albuterol (Proventil, Ventilin), may be used to keep the airways open. Ribavirin (Virazole) is used for desperately ill children to stop the growth of the virus. Ribavirin is both expensive and has toxic side effects, so its use is restricted to the most severe cases.

KEY TERMS

Alveoli—The tiny air sacs clustered at the ends of the bronchioles in the lungs in which oxygen-carbon dioxide exchange takes place.

Antibody—A special protein made by the body's immune system as a defense against foreign material (bacteria, viruses, etc.) that enters the body. It is uniquely designed to attack and neutralize the specific antigen that triggered the immune response.

Reye's syndrome—A serious, life-threatening illness in children, usually developing after a bout of flu or chickenpox, and often associated with the use of aspirin. Symptoms include uncontrollable vomiting, often with lethargy, memory loss, disorientation, or delirium. Swelling of the brain may cause seizures, coma, and in severe cases, death.

Prognosis

RSV infection usually runs its course in seven to 14 days. The cough may linger for weeks. There are no medications that can speed the body's production of antibodies against the virus. Opportunistic bacterial infections that take advantage of a weakened respiratory system may cause ear, sinus, and throat infections or pneumonia.

Hospitalization and death are much more likely to occur in children whose immune systems are weakened or who have underlying diseases of the lungs and heart. People do not gain permanent immunity to respiratory syncytial virus and can be infected many times. Children who suffer repeated infections seem to be more likely to develop asthma in later life.

Prevention

As of 2004, there were no vaccines against RSV. Respiratory syncytial virus infection is so common that prevention is impossible. However, steps can be taken to reduce a child's contact with the disease. People with RSV symptoms should stay at least six feet away from young children. Frequent hand washing, especially after contact with respiratory secretions, and the correct disposal of used tissues help keep the disease from spreading. Parents should try to keep their children under 18 month of age away from crowded environments where they are likely to come in contact with older people who have only mild symptoms of the disease. Childcare centers should regularly disinfect surfaces that children touch.

Parental concerns

Because symptoms of severe respiratory distress may be subtle in very young babies, parents need to keep a high level of suspicion when young babies contract a respiratory illness, particularly young babies with a history of **prematurity** or other risk factor for severe RSV infection.

Resources

BOOKS

McIntosh, Kenneth. "Respiratory Syncytial Virus." In *Nelson Textbook of Pediatrics*. Edited by Richard E. Behrman et al. Philadelphia: Saunders, 2004.

Tristram, Debra A., and Robert C. Welliver. "Respiratory Syncytial Virus." In *Principles and Practice of Pediatric Infectious Diseases*, 2nd ed. Edited by Sarah S. Long et al. St. Louis, MO: Elsevier, 2003.

Tish Davidson, A.M.
Rosalyn Carson-DeWitt, MD

Retention in school

Definition

The term "retention" in regards to school means repeating an academic year of school. Retention in school is also called grade retention, being held back, or repeating a grade. Grade retention is the opposite of social promotion, in which children continue with their age peers regardless of academic performance.

Description

According to the National Association of School Psychologists, in 2003 as many as 15 percent or more than 2.4 million American students are held back and repeat a grade each year. Other studies have found that between 30 percent and 50 percent of all students are retained at least once by the time they are freshmen in high school (about age 14). In most cases, teachers recommend retention for one of three reasons: developmental immaturity that has resulted in learning difficulties; emotional immaturity that has resulted in severely disruptive behavior; or failure to pass standardized proficiency or achievement tests at the end of specific years. Another less common reason for retention is poor attendance due either to **truancy** or medical absences. Grade retention has become increasingly controversial as early 2000s education initiatives such as No Child Left Behind

have pressed schools to meet certain standards defined by scores on standardized tests.

Students at highest risk of being retained share certain characteristics:

- They tend to be boys.
- They tend to be African American or Hispanic.
- They are young or immature for their grade.
- They show developmental delays.
- They show attention, behavioral, or emotional problems.
- They are not proficient in English (English language learners).
- They have problems reading.
- They have changed schools often.
- They live in families with incomes below the poverty level.
- They live in single-parent families.
- They live with adults who are uninvolved in their education.

Preschool

Sometimes **preschool** teachers will recommend that a child attend an extra year of preschool before enrolling in kindergarten. This practice is more common in suburban school districts than in urban ones. The theory behind this practice is to allow children, especially those who would be young compared to their peers in kindergarten (birthdays falling near the cutoff date for school entry), to gain maturity and a greater likelihood of success in kindergarten. One 1984 study found that more than 11 percent of six year olds were enrolled in kindergarten or pre-first classes rather than in first grade.

In some athletically competitive families, children are held back and start school one year later because parents believe this will give them an edge in high school **sports** that require strength and size. Studies have found that as a group students who begin kindergarten a year late do no better or worse academically than their younger classmates.

Elementary school

Retention is most likely to be recommended by teachers in grades one through three. The most common reason for retention is poor reading skills. As a group, students who are retained in these grades show initial improvement in academics. However, this improvement disappears after two to three years, after which retained students do no better or even slightly worse than similarly achieving students who were promoted. Studies also show that most elementary school teachers overestimate the academic benefits of retention. It has been suggested that this occurs because lower grade teachers see only the initial gains made by the student in the first few years after retention but do not follow the student's progress through middle and high school.

Retention in early elementary school does not appear to have an immediate effect on **self-esteem** or adjustment to school. However, by junior and senior high school, retained students tend to have more behavior problems, more difficulties with peer relationships, lower self-esteem, and poorer attendance.

Middle school

Retention can be emotionally traumatic for middle school students. A 1990 study found that being held back a grade was the third most stressful life event for sixth grade students topped only by the death of a parent or going blind. When this study was repeated in 2001, sixth grade students ranked flunking a grade as first in stress among these three events.

Middle school students who have been retained have more negative behaviors than their peers in academic ability who were not retained. These behaviors include **smoking** cigarettes, alcohol use, early sexual activity, and aggressive or violent behaviors. The retained group also had worse academic performance than similar students who were not retained.

In some school districts red shirting of student athletes is tacitly endorsed. This practice occurs when students are retained to improve performance in a nonacademic area, namely sports. Regardless of academic performance, a student is retained, usually in junior high school, to increase his or her likelihood of winning a college athletic scholarship. In addition, retention of strong athletes allows the school to build teams of older, bigger athletes. In these cases, retention is usually carried out with the knowledge and support of the student and his **family** and is not likely to carry a social stigma, as would be the case if the retention were for academic reasons.

High school

Grade retention is an excellent predictor of who will drop out of high school. Studies spanning several decades suggest that being retained one grade increases the risk of dropping out by 40 to 50 percent. Being retained twice or more almost guarantees the student will drop out. High school students who have been retained, even in earlier years, have the same unhealthful behaviors as retained middle-school students as well as more

incidents of driving while using alcohol, marijuana use, suicidal behaviors, and high-risk sexual behavior. Individuals who have repeated a grade are more likely as adults to be unemployed, live on welfare, or be in prison than adults who did not repeat a grade.

Alternatives to retention

Given research finding that retention does not help learning difficulties, the question remains regarding what to do with a child who is, for whatever reason, unprepared to move to the next grade. Schools feel pressure to adhere to academic standards, while at the same time being fully aware of studies that show retention is counter-productive. However, the social promotion policies common in the 1970s, where students were kept with their age peers regardless of readiness for the next grade, does not produce academic success for at-risk students either.

Strong evidence indicates that at-risk students need remedial intervention, not simply more time or the repetition of material that retention provides. Potential remediations that can serve as alternatives to retention include:

- mixed-age classes where students advance at their own rate without grade-level labeling
- individual instruction and/or tutoring
- smaller classes for students who are struggling academically
- intensive early reading programs in lower grades for students who fail to achieve reading fluency
- early evaluation for learning disorders/deficits and emotional disorders followed by appropriate modifications in instruction
- extended day and summer school programs
- transfer to an alternative school
- programs to educate and involve parents in their child's academic program

Common problems

It is difficult to separate the effects of retention and the influence of other socioeconomic and family factors that affect children. Research suggests that social promotion and grade retention are not educationally effective policies. As of 2004, some people in the educational field believed that better educational gains may be made by linking the community organizations that deliver social services (health, mental health, family support services) with the school system in order to serve the child and family as a unit.

Parental concerns

Research evaluates outcomes for groups, not individual students. Parents may have valid reasons for believing that their child may benefit or suffer from retention. Most experts support the idea that parents should be involved in the decision to promote or retain their child and should make their concerns known to the teacher and school. Parents need to understand their school district's policy on retention and request evidence supporting a retention decision, including details of their child's academic performance, standardized test results, or other pertinent factors, such as the student's emotional maturity and behavior in class. Parents also need to advocate for early evaluation of learning disabilities if their child is falling behind.

Resources

BOOKS

Alexander, Karl L., et al. *On the Success of Failure: A Reassessment of the Effects of Retention in the Primary School Grades.* Cambridge, UK: Cambridge University Press, 2002.

McKay, Elizabeth, ed. *Moving Beyond Retention and Social Promotion.* Bloomington, IN: Phi Delta Kappa International, 2001.

ORGANIZATIONS

National Association of School Psychologists. 4340 East West Highway, Suite 402, Bethesda, MD 20814. Web site: <www.nasponline.org>.

WEB SITES

"Position Paper on Student Grade Retention and Social Promotion." *National Association of School Psychologists*, April 12, 2003. Available online at <www.nasponline.org/information/pospaper_graderetent.html> (accessed December 11, 2004).

Robertson, Anne. "Retention in School." *People with Attention and Developmental Disabilities Association (PADDA) News.* Available online at <www.padda.org/newsletter.shtml> (accessed December 11, 2004).

Tish Davidson, A.M.

Retin-A *see* **Antiacne drugs**

Retinoblastoma

Definition

Retinoblastoma is a malignant tumor of the retina that occurs predominantly in young children.

Description

The eye has three layers, the sclera, the choroid, and the retina. The sclera is the outer protective white coating of the eye. The choroid is the middle layer and contains blood vessels that nourish the eye. The front portion of the choroid is colored and is called the iris. The opening in the iris is called the pupil. The pupil is responsible for allowing light into the eye and usually appears black. When the pupil is exposed to bright light it contracts (closes), and when it is exposed to low light conditions it dilates (opens) so that the appropriate amount of light enters the eye. Light that enters through the pupil hits the lens of the eye. The lens then focuses the light onto the retina, the innermost of the three layers. The job of the retina is to transform the light into information that can be transmitted to the optic nerve, which will transmit this information to the brain. It is through this process that people are able to see the world around them.

Occasionally a tumor, called a retinoblastoma, develops in the retina of the eye. Usually this tumor forms in young children, but it can occasionally occur in adults. Most people with retinoblastoma develop only one tumor (unifocal) in only one eye (unilateral). Some, however, develop multiple tumors (multifocal) in one or both eyes. When retinoblastoma occurs independently in both eyes, it is then called bilateral retinoblastoma.

Occasionally, children with retinoblastoma develop trilateral retinoblastoma, which results from the development of an independent brain tumor that forms in a part of the brain called the pineal gland. In order for retinoblastoma to be classified as trilateral retinoblastoma, the tumor must have developed independently and not as the result of the spread of the retinal **cancer**. The prognosis for trilateral retinoblastoma is quite poor.

The retinal tumor which characterizes retinoblastoma is malignant, meaning that it can metastasize (spread) to other parts of the eye and eventually other parts of the body. In most cases, however, retinoblastoma is diagnosed before it spreads past the eye to other parts of the body (intraocular) and the prognosis is quite good. The prognosis is poorer if the cancer has spread beyond the eye (extraocular).

Retinoblastoma can be inherited or can arise spontaneously. Approximately 40 percent of people with retinoblastoma have an inherited form of the condition and approximately 60 percent have a sporadic (not inherited) form. Individuals with multiple independent tumors, bilateral retinoblastoma, or trilateral retinoblastoma are more likely to be affected with the inherited form of retinoblastoma.

Demographics

Approximately one in 15,000 to one in 30,000 infants are born with retinoblastoma, making it the most common childhood eye cancer. It is, however, a relatively rare childhood cancer and accounts for approximately 3 percent of childhood cancers. Retinoblastoma is found mainly in children under the age of five but can occasionally be seen in older children and adults. Retinoblastoma is found in individuals of all ethnic backgrounds and is found equally frequently in males and females.

Causes and symptoms

Causes

Retinoblastoma is caused by changes in or absence of a gene called RB1. RB1 is located on chromosome 13. Cells of the body, with the exception of the egg and sperm cells, contain 23 pairs of chromosomes. All of the cells of the body excluding the egg and the sperm cells are called the somatic cells. The somatic cells contain two of each chromosome 13 and, therefore, two copies of the RB1 gene. Each egg and sperm cell contains only one copy of chromosome and, therefore, only one copy of the RB1 gene.

RB1 produces a tumor suppressor protein that normally helps to regulate the cell cycle of cells such as those of the retina. A normal cell of the retina goes through a growth cycle during which it produces new cells. Genes such as tumor suppressor genes tightly regulate this growth cycle.

Cells that lose control of their cell cycle and replicate out of control are called cancer cells. These undergo many cell divisions, often at a quicker rate than normal cells and do not have a limited lifespan. A group of adjacent cancer cells can form a mass called a tumor. Malignant (cancerous) tumors can spread to other parts of the body. A malignant tumor of the retina (retinoblastoma) can result when just one retinal cell loses control of it cell cycle and replicates out of control.

Normally, the tumor suppressor protein produced by RB1 prevents a retinal cell from becoming cancerous. Each RB1 gene produces tumor suppressor protein. Only one functioning RB1 gene in a retinal cell is necessary to prevent the cell from becoming cancerous. If both RB1 genes in a retinal cell become non-functional, then a retinal cell can become cancerous and retinoblastoma can result. An RB1 gene is non-functional when it is changed or missing (deleted) and no longer produces normal tumor suppressor protein.

Approximately 40 percent of people with retinoblastoma have inherited a non-functional or deleted RB1 gene from either their mother or father. Therefore, they have a changed/deleted RB1 gene in every somatic cell. A person with an inherited missing or non-functional RB1 gene will develop a retinal tumor if the remaining RB1 gene becomes changed or deleted in a retinal cell. The remaining RB1 gene can become non-functional when exposed to environmental triggers such as chemicals and radiation. In most cases, however, the triggers are unknown. Approximately 90 percent of people who inherit a changed or missing RB1 gene develop retinoblastoma.

People with an inherited form of retinoblastoma are more likely to have a tumor in both eyes (bilateral) and are more likely to have more than one independent tumor (multifocal) in one or both eyes. The average age of onset for the inherited form of retinoblastoma is one year, which is earlier than the sporadic form of retinoblastoma. Although most people with the inherited form of retinoblastoma develop bilateral tumors, approximately 15 percent of people with a tumor in only one eye (unilateral) are affected with an inherited form of retinoblastoma.

A person with an inherited missing or non-functional RB1 gene has a 50 percent chance of passing on this abnormal gene to his or her offspring. The chance that the children will inherit the changed/deleted gene and actually develop retinoblastoma is approximately 45 percent.

Some people with retinoblastoma have inherited a non-functioning or missing RB1 gene from either their mother or father even though their parents have never developed retinoblastoma. It is possible that one parent has a changed or missing RB1 gene in every somatic cell but has not developed retinoblastoma because his or her remaining RB1 gene has remained functional. It is also possible that the parent had developed a retinal tumor that was destroyed by the body. In other cases, one parent has two normal RB1 genes in every somatic cell, but some egg or sperm cells contain a changed or missing RB1 gene. This is called gonadal mosaicism.

Retinoblastoma can also result when both RB1 genes become spontaneously changed or deleted in a retinal cell but the RB1 genes are normal in all the other cells of the body. Approximately 60 percent of people with retinoblastoma have this type of disease, called sporadic retinoblastoma. A person with sporadic retinoblastoma does not have a higher chance of having children with the disease. His or her relatives do not have a higher risk of developing retinoblastoma or having children who develop retinoblastoma. Sporadic retinoblastoma is usually unifocal and has an average age of onset of approximately two years.

Symptoms

The most common symptom of retinoblastoma is leukocoria. Leukocoria results when the pupil reflects a white color rather than the normal black or red color that is seen on a flash photograph. It is often most obvious in flash photographs; since the pupil is exposed to a lot of light and the duration of the exposure is so short, the pupil does not have time to constrict. Children with retinoblastoma can also have problems seeing and this can cause them to appear cross-eyed (**strabismus**). People with retinoblastoma may also experience red, painful, and irritated eyes, inflamed tissue around the eye, enlarged pupils, and possibly different-colored eyes.

Diagnosis

Children who have symptoms of retinoblastoma are usually first evaluated by their pediatrician. The pediatrician will often perform a red reflex test to diagnose or confirm leukocoria. Prior to this test the doctor inserts medicated eye drops into the child's eyes so that the pupils remain dilated and not contract when exposed to bright light. The doctor then examines the eyes with an ophthalmoscope, which shines a bright light into the eyes and allows the doctor to check for leukocoria. Leukocoria can also be diagnosed by taking a flash Polaroid photograph of a patient who has been in a dark room for three to five minutes.

If the pediatrician suspects retinoblastoma on the basis of these evaluations, he or she will most likely refer the patient to an ophthalmologist (eye doctor) who has experience with retinoblastoma. The ophthalmologist will examine the eye using an indirect ophthalmoscope. The opthalmoscope shines a bright light into the eye, which helps the doctor to visualize the retina. This evaluation is usually done under general anesthetic, although some very young or older patients may not require it. Prior to the examination, medicated drops are put into the eyes to dilate the pupils, and anesthetic drops may also be used. A metal clip is used to keep the eyes open during the evaluation. During the examination, a cotton swab or a metal instrument with a flattened tip is used to press on the outer lens of the eye so that a better view of the front areas of the retina can be obtained. Sketches or photographs of the tumor as seen through the ophthalmoscope are taken during the procedure.

An ultrasound evaluation is used to confirm the presence of the tumor and to evaluate its size. Computed axial tomography (CT scan) is used to determine whether the tumor has spread outside of the eye and to the brain. Sometimes **magnetic resonance imaging** (MRI) is also used to look at the eyes, eye sockets, and the brain to see if the cancer has spread.

In most cases, the cancer has not spread beyond the eye, and other evaluations are unnecessary. If the cancer appears to have spread beyond the eye, then other assessments such as a blood test, spinal tap (lumbar puncture), and/or bone marrow biopsy may be recommended. During a spinal tap, a needle is inserted between the vertebrae of the spinal column and a small sample of the fluid surrounding the spinal cord is obtained. In a bone marrow biopsy, a small amount of tissue (bone marrow) is taken from inside the hip or breast bone for examination.

Genetic testing

Establishing whether someone is affected with an inherited or non-inherited form of retinoblastoma can help to determine whether other **family** members such as siblings, cousins, and offspring are at increased risk for developing retinoblastoma. It can also sometimes help guide treatment choices, since patients with an inherited form of retinoblastoma may be at increased risk for developing recurrent tumors or other types of cancers, particularly when treated with radiation. It is helpful for the families of a child diagnosed with retinoblastoma to meet with a genetic specialist such as a genetic counselor and/or geneticist. These specialists can help to ascertain the chances that the retinoblastoma is inherited and facilitate genetic testing if desired.

If a patient with unilateral or bilateral retinoblastoma has a relative or relatives with retinoblastoma, it can be assumed that they have an inherited form of retinoblastoma. However, it cannot be assumed that a patient without a family history of the disease has a sporadic form.

Even when there is no family history, most cases of bilateral and trilateral retinoblastoma are inherited, as are most cases of unilateral, multifocal retinoblastoma. However, only 15 percent of unilateral, unifocal retinoblastoma cases are inherited.

The only way to establish whether someone has an inherited form of retinoblastoma is to see if the retinoblastoma gene is changed or deleted in the blood cells obtained from a blood sample. Approximately 5 to 8 percent of individuals with retinoblastoma possess a chromosomal abnormality involving the RB1 gene that can be detected by looking at their chromosomes under the microscope. The chromosomes can be seen by obtaining a blood sample. If this type of chromosomal abnormality is detected in a child, then analysis of the parents' chromosomes should be performed. If one of the parents possesses a chromosomal abnormality, then they are at higher risk for having other offspring with retinoblastoma. Chromosome testing would be recommended for the blood relatives of the parent with the abnormality.

Usually, however, a chromosomal abnormality is not detected in a child with retinoblastoma. In this case, specialized DNA tests that look for small RB1 gene changes need to be performed on the blood cells. DNA testing can be difficult, time consuming, and expensive, since there are many possible RB1 gene changes that can cause the gene to become nonfunctional.

If a sample of tumor is available, then it is recommended that DNA testing be performed on the tumor cells prior to DNA testing of the blood cells. This testing can usually identify the gene changes/deletions in the RB1 genes that caused the tumor to develop. In some cases, RB1 gene changes/deletions are not found in the tumor cells (approximately 20% of RB1 gene changes or deletions are not detectable). In these cases, DNA testing of the blood cells will not be able to ascertain whether someone is affected with an inherited or non-inherited form of retinoblastoma.

If the changes in both RB1 genes are detected in the tumor cell, then these same changes can be looked for in the blood cells. If an RB1 gene is deleted or changed in all of the blood cells tested, the patient can be assumed to have been born with a changed/deleted RB1 gene in all of his or her cells. This person has a 50 percent chance of passing the RB1 gene change/deletion on to his or her children. Most of the time, this change/deletion has been inherited from a parent. Occasionally the gene change/deletion occurred spontaneously in the original cell that was formed when the egg and sperm came together at conception (de novo).

If an RB1 gene change/deletion is found in all of the blood cells tested, both parents should undergo blood testing to check for the same RB1 gene change/deletion. If the RB1 gene change/deletion is identified in one of the parents, it can be assumed that the retinoblastoma was inherited and that siblings have a 50 percent chance of inheriting the altered gene. More distant blood relatives of the parent with the identified RB1 gene change/deletion may also be at risk for developing retinoblastoma. Siblings and other relatives could undergo DNA testing to see if they have inherited the RB1 gene change/deletion.

If the RB1 gene change/deletion is not identified in either parent, then the results can be more difficult to interpret. In this case, there is a 90 to 94 percent chance that the retinoblastoma was not inherited.

In some cases, a person with retinoblastoma will have an RB1 gene change/deletion detected in some of their blood cells and not others. It can be assumed that this person did not inherit the retinoblastoma from either parent. Siblings and other relatives would, therefore, not be at increased risk for developing retinoblastoma. Offspring would be at increased risk since some of the egg or sperm cells could have the changed/deleted RB1 gene. The risks to offspring would probably be less than 50 percent.

In families where there are multiple family members affected with retinoblastoma, blood samples from multiple family members are often analyzed and compared through DNA testing. Ninety-five percent of the time, this type of analysis is able to detect patterns in the DNA that are associated with a changed RB1 gene in that particular family. When a pattern is detected, at-risk relatives can be tested to establish whether they have inherited an RB1 gene change/deletion.

PRENATAL TESTING If chromosome or DNA testing identifies an RB1 gene/deletion in someone's blood cells, then prenatal testing can be performed on this person's offspring. An **amniocentesis** or chorionic villus sampling can be used to obtain fetal cells which can be analyzed for the RB1 gene change/deletion or chromosomal abnormality.

Treatment

A number of different classification (staging) systems are used to establish the severity of retinoblastoma and aid in choosing an appropriate treatment plan. The most widely used staging system is the Reese-Ellsworth system. This system is used to classify intraocular tumors and predict which tumors are favorable enough that sight can be maintained. The Reese-Ellsworth classification system is divided into several groups:

- Group I (very favorable for maintenance of sight): small solitary or multiple tumors, less than 6.4 mm in size (1 inch equals 25.4 mm), located at or below the equator of the eye.

- Group II (favorable for maintenance of sight): solitary or multiple tumors, 6.4 to 16 mm in size, located at or behind the equator of the eye.

- Group III (possible for maintenance of sight): any tumor located in front of the equator of the eye, or a solitary tumor larger than 16 mm in size and located behind the equator of the eye.

- Group IV (unfavorable for maintenance of sight): multiple tumors, some larger than 16 mm in size, or any tumor extending in front of the outer rim of the retina (ora serrata).

- Group V (very unfavorable for maintenance of sight): large tumors involving more than half of the retina, or vitreous seeding, in which small pieces of tumor are broken off and floating around the inside of the eye.

When choosing a treatment plan, the first criterion is to determine whether the cancer is localized within the eye (intralocular) or has spread to other parts of the body (extralocular). An intraocular retinoblastoma may only involve the retina or could involve other parts of the eye. An extraocular retinoblastoma could involve only the tissues around the eye or could result from the spread of cancer to the brain or other parts of the body.

It is also important to establish whether the cancer is unilateral (one eye) or bilateral (both eyes), multifocal or unifocal. In order for the tumors to be considered multifocal, they must have arisen independently and not as the result of the spread of cancer cells. It is also important to check for trilateral retinoblastoma.

The treatment chosen depends on the size and number of tumors, whether the cancer is unilateral or bilateral, and whether the cancer has spread to other parts of the body. The goal of treatment is to cure the cancer and prevent as much loss of vision as possible.

TREATMENT OF INTRAOCULAR TUMORS Surgical removal of the affected eye (enucleation) is performed when the tumor(s) are so large and extensive that preservation of sight is not possible. This surgery is performed under general anesthetic and usually takes less than an hour. Most children who have undergone this surgery can leave the hospital on the same day. A temporary ball is placed in the eye socket after the surgery. Approximately three weeks after the operation, a plastic artificial eye (prosthesis) that looks like the normal eye is inserted into the eye socket.

Radiation therapy is often used for treatment of large tumors when preservation of sight is possible. External beam radiation therapy involves focusing a beam of radiation on the eye. If the tumor has not spread extensively, the radiation beam can be focused on the cancerous retinal cells. If the cancer is extensive, radiation treatment of the entire eye may be necessary. External beam radiation is performed on an outpatient basis and usually occurs over a period of three to four weeks.

Some children may need sedatives prior to the treatment. This type of therapy can result in a temporary loss of a patch of hair on the back of the head and a small area of "sun-burned" skin. Long-term side effects of radiation treatment can include cataracts, vision problems, bleeding from the retina, and decreased growth of the bones on the side of the head. People with an inherited form of retinoblastoma have an increased risk of developing other cancers as a result of this therapy. Some consideration should, therefore, be given to alternative treatment therapies for those with an inherited form of retinoblastoma.

Photocoagulation therapy is often used in conjunction with radiation therapy but may be used alone to treat small tumors that are located on the back of the eye. Photocoagulation involves using a laser to destroy the cancer cells. This type of treatment is performed under local or general anesthesia and is usually not associated with post-procedural **pain**.

Thermotherapy is also often used in conjunction with radiation therapy or drug therapy (**chemotherapy**). Thermotherapy involves the use of heat to help shrink tumor cells. The heat is either used on the whole eye or localized to the tumor area. It is performed under local or general anesthesia and is usually not painful.

Cryotherapy is a treatment often used in conjunction with radiation therapy but can also be used alone on small tumors located on the front part of the retina. Cryotherapy involves the use of intense cold to destroy cancer cells and can result in harmless, temporary swelling of the external eye and eyelids that can last for up to five days. Eye drops or ointment are sometimes provided to reduce the swelling.

Brachytherapy involves the application of radioactive material to the outer surface of the eye at the base of the tumor. It is generally used for tumors of medium size. A patient undergoing this type of procedure is usually hospitalized for three to seven days. During that time, he or she undergoes one surgery to attach the radioactive material and one surgery to remove it. Eye drops are often administered for three to four weeks following the operation to prevent inflammation and infection. The long-term side effects of this treatment can include cataracts and damage to the retina, which can lead to impaired vision.

Intravenous treatment with one or more drugs (chemotherapy) is often used for treatment of both large and small tumors. Chemotherapy is sometimes used to shrink tumors prior to other treatments such as radiation therapy or brachytherapy. Occasionally, it is also used alone to treat very small tumors.

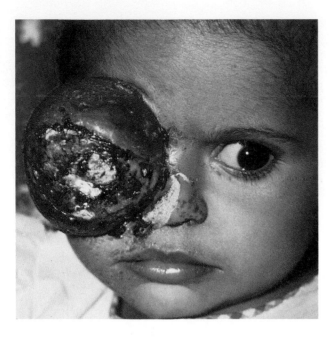

Child's right eye completely covered with a tumor associated with retinoblastoma. *(Custom Medical Stock Photo Inc.)*

TREATMENT OF INTRAOCULAR AND UNILATERAL RETINOBLASTOMA Often, by the time that unilateral retinoblastoma is diagnosed, the tumor is so large that useful vision cannot be preserved. In these cases removal of the eye (enucleation) is the treatment of choice. Other therapies are unnecessary if enucleation is used to treat intraocular unilateral retinoblastoma. If the tumor is small enough, other therapies such as external beam radiation therapy, photocoagulation, cryotherapy, thermotherapy, chemotherapy, and brachytherapy may be considered.

TREATMENT OF INTRAOCULAR AND BILATERAL RETINOBLASTOMA If vision can be preserved in both eyes, radiation therapy of both eyes may be recommended. Smaller, more localized tumors can sometimes be treated by local therapies such as cryotherapy, photocoagulation therapy, thermotherapy or brachytherapy. Some centers may use chemotherapy in place of radiation therapy when the tumors are too large to be treated by local therapies or are found over the optic nerve of the eye. As of the early 2000s, many centers are moving away from radiation treatment and toward chemotherapy because it is less likely to induce future tumors. Enucleation is performed on the more severely affected eye if sight cannot be preserved in both.

EXTRAOCULAR RETINOBLASTOMA There is no proven effective therapy for the treatment of extraocular retinoblastomas. Commonly, radiation treatment of the eyes and chemotherapy is provided.

Alternative treatment

As of 2004 there are no alternative or complementary therapies specific to the treatment of retinoblastoma. Since most people diagnosed with retinoblastoma are small children, most drug-based alternative therapies designed to treat general cancer would not be recommended. Many specialists would, however, stress the importance of establishing a well-balanced diet, including certain fruits, vegetables, and vitamin supplements, to ensure that the body is strengthened in its fight against cancer. Some advocate the use of visualization strategies, in which patients are encouraged to visualize the immune cells of their body attacking and destroying the cancer cells.

Prognosis

Individuals with intraocular retinoblastoma who do not have trilateral retinoblastoma usually have a good survival rate with a 90 percent chance of disease-free survival for five years. Those with extraocular retinoblastoma have less than a 10 percent chance of disease-free survival for the same amount of time. Trilateral retinoblastoma generally has a very poor prognosis. Patients with trilateral retinoblastoma who receive treatment have an average survival rate of approximately eight months, while those who remain untreated have an average survival rate of approximately one month. Patients with trilateral retinoblastoma who are asymptomatic at the time of diagnosis may have a better prognosis then those who experience symptoms.

Patients with an inherited form of unilateral retinoblastoma have a 70 percent chance of developing retinoblastoma in the other eye. Retinoblastoma reoccurs in the other eye in approximately 5 percent of people with a non-inherited form of retinoblastoma, so it is advisable for even these patients to be closely monitored. People with an inherited form of retinoblastoma who have not undergone radiation treatment have approximately a 26 percent chance of developing cancer in another part of the body within 50 years of the initial diagnosis. Those with an inherited form who have undergone radiation treatment have a 58 percent chance of developing a secondary cancer within 50 years after the initial diagnosis. Most of the secondary cancers are skin cancers, bone tumors (osteosarcomas), and soft-tissue **sarcomas**. Soft-tissue sarcomas are malignant tumors of the muscle, nerves, joints, blood vessels, deep skin tissues, or fat.

Prevention

Although retinoblastoma cannot be prevented, appropriate screening and surveillance should be applied to

KEY TERMS

Amniocentesis—A procedure performed at 16–18 weeks of pregnancy in which a needle is inserted through a woman's abdomen into her uterus to draw out a small sample of the amniotic fluid from around the baby for analysis. Either the fluid itself or cells from the fluid can be used for a variety of tests to obtain information about genetic disorders and other medical conditions in the fetus.

Benign tumor—An abnormal proliferation of cells that does not spread to other parts of the body.

Bilateral—Occurring on two sides. For example, a patient with bilateral retinoblastoma has this retinal tumor in both eyes.

Brachytherapy—A method of treating cancers, such as prostate cancer, involving the implantation near the tumor of radioactive seeds.

Chorionic villus sampling—A procedure used for prenatal diagnosis at 10–12 weeks gestation. Under ultrasound guidance a needle is inserted either through the mother's vagina or abdominal wall and a sample of the chorionic membrane. These cells are then tested for chromosome abnormalities or other genetic diseases.

Chromosome—A microscopic thread-like structure found within each cell of the human body and consisting of a complex of proteins and DNA. Humans have 46 chromosomes arranged into 23 pairs. Chromosomes contain the genetic information necessary to direct the development and functioning of all cells and systems in the body. They pass on hereditary traits from parents to child (like eye color) and determine whether the child will be male or female.

Cryotherapy—The use of a very low-temperature probe to freeze and thereby destroy tissue. Cryotherapy is used in the treatment skin lesions, Parkinson's disease, some cancers, retinal detachment, and cataracts. Also called cryosurgery.

DNA—Deoxyribonucleic acid; the genetic material in cells that holds the inherited instructions for growth, development, and cellular functioning.

DNA testing—Analysis of DNA (the genetic component of cells) in order to determine changes in genes that may indicate a specific disorder.

Enucleation—Surgical removal of the eyeball.

Equator—Imaginary line encircling the eyeball and dividing the eye into a front and back half.

Extraocular retinoblastoma—Cancer that has spread from the eye to other parts of the body.

Gene—A building block of inheritance, which contains the instructions for the production of a particu-lar protein, and is made up of a molecular sequence found on a section of DNA. Each gene is found on a precise location on a chromosome.

Intraocular retinoblastoma—Cancer of the retina that is limited to the eye and has not spread to other parts of the body.

Malignant tumor—An abnormal proliferation of cells that can spread to other sites.

Multifocal—Having many focal points. When referring to a disease, it means that damage caused by the disease occurs at multiple sites. When referring to a cancer, it means that more than one tumor is present.

Oncologist—A physician specializing in the diagnosis and treatment of cancer

Ophthalmologist—A physician who specializes in the anatomy and physiology of the eyes and in the diagnosis and treatment of eye diseases and disorders.

Optic nerve—A bundle of nerve fibers that carries visual messages from the retina in the form of electrical signals to the brain.

Photocoagulation—A type of cancer treatment in which cancer cells are destroyed by an intense beam of laser light.

Prenatal testing—Testing for a disease, such as a genetic condition, in an unborn baby.

Protein—An important building blocks of the body, a protein is a large, complex organic molecule composed of amino acids. It is involved in the formation of body structures and in controlling the basic functions of the human body.

Retina—The inner, light-sensitive layer of the eye containing rods and cones. The retina transforms the image it receives into electrical signals that are sent to the brain via the optic nerve.

Somatic cells—All the cells of the body with the exception of the egg and sperm cells.

Tumor—A growth of tissue resulting from the uncontrolled proliferation of cells.

Tumor-suppressor gene—A gene involved in controlling normal cell growth and preventing cancer.

Unifocal—Only one tumor present in one eye.

Unilateral—Refers to one side of the body or only one organ in a pair.

Vitreous—The transparent gel that fills the back part of the eye.

Vitreous seeding—Small pieces of tumor have broken off and are floating around the vitreous.

all at-risk individuals to ensure that the tumor(s) are diagnosed at an early stage. The earlier the diagnosis, the more likely that an eye can be salvaged and vision maintained.

Screening of people diagnosed with retinoblastoma

Children who have been diagnosed with retinoblastoma should receive periodic dilated retinal examinations until the age of five. Young children will need to undergo these evaluations under anesthetic. After five years of age, periodic eye examinations are recommended. It may be advisable for patients with bilateral retinoblastoma or an inherited form of retinoblastoma to undergo periodic screening for the brain tumors found in trilateral retinoblastoma. There are no specific screening protocols designed to detect non-ocular tumors. All lumps and complaints of bone pain, however, should be thoroughly evaluated.

Screening of relatives

When a child is diagnosed with retinoblastoma, it is recommended that parents and siblings receive a dilated retinal examination by an ophthalmologist who is experienced in the diagnosis and treatment of the disease. It is also recommended that siblings continue to undergo periodic retinal examinations under anesthetic until they are three years of age. For children three to seven years of age, periodic eye examinations are recommended. The retinal examinations can be avoided if DNA testing indicates that the patient has a non-inherited form of retinoblastoma or if the sibling has not inherited the RB1 gene change/deletion. Any relatives who are found through DNA testing to have inherited an RB1 gene change/deletion should undergo the same surveillance procedures as siblings.

The children of someone diagnosed with retinoblastoma should also undergo periodic retinal examinations under anesthetic. Retinal surveillance should be performed unless DNA testing proves that their child does not possess the RB1 gene change/deletion. If desired, prenatal detection of tumors using ultrasound may also be performed. During the ultrasound procedure, a hand-held instrument is placed on the maternal abdomen or inserted vaginally. The ultrasound produces sound waves that are reflected back from the body structures of the fetus, producing a picture that can be seen on a video screen. If a tumor is detected through this evaluation, the affected baby may be delivered a couple of weeks earlier. This can allow for earlier intervention and treatment.

Parental concerns

Careful attention to a child's diet can be very helpful for patients with cancer. This can be difficult when the cancer and/or the treatments are affecting the appetite, however. Whole foods, including grains, beans, fresh fruits and vegetables, and high quality fats, should be emphasized in the diet, while processed foods should be avoided. Increased consumption of fish, especially cold-water fish like salmon, mackerel, halibut, and tuna, provides a good source of omega-3 fatty acids. Nutritional supplements can build strength and help maintain it during and following chemotherapy, radiation, or surgery.

Guided imagery and relaxation techniques can be helpful for children undergoing difficult treatments. Support groups for the child and the family can be very helpful and can provide an important emotional outlet for the child, the parents, and the siblings.

Resources

BOOKS

Elner, Victor M. et al. "Eye, Orbit, and Adnexal Structures." In *Clinical Oncology*. Edited by Martin D. Abeloff. London: Churchill Livingstone, 2000.

Herzog, Cynthia E. "Retinoblastoma." In *Nelson Textbook of Pediatrics*. Edited by Richard E. Behrman et al. Philadelphia: Saunders, 2004.

PERIODICALS

Castillo, B. V. "Pediatric tumors of the eye and orbit." *Pediatric Clinics of North America* 50 (February 2003): 149–72.

Pakakasama, S. "Genetic predisposition and screening in pediatric cancer." *Pediatric Clinics of North America* 49 (December 2002): 1393–413.

Pratt, C. B. "Successful treatment of intraocular retinoblastoma with chemotherapy." *Journal of Pediatrics* 140 (May 2002): 635.

ORGANIZATIONS

Institute for Families with Blind Children. PO Box 54700, Mail Stop 111, Los Angeles, CA 90054–0700. Web site: <www.instituteforfamilies.org>.

Retinoblastoma International. 4650 Sunset Blvd., Mail Stop #88, Los Angeles, CA 90027. Web site: <www.retinoblastoma.net>.

WEB SITES

"Retinoblastoma." *CancerNet*. Available online at <cancernet.nci.nih.gov/cancertopics/types/retinoblastoma> (accessed December 30, 2004).

Lisa Andres, MS, CGC
Rosalyn Carson-DeWitt, MD

Reye's syndrome

Definition

Reye's syndrome is a disorder principally affecting the liver and brain, marked by rapid development of life-threatening neurological symptoms.

Description

Reye's syndrome is an emergency illness chiefly affecting children and teenagers. It almost always follows a viral illness such as a cold, the flu, or **chickenpox**. Reye's syndrome may affect all the organs of the body, but it most seriously affects the brain and liver. Brain swelling and massive accumulations of fat in the liver and other organs lead to the rapid development of severe neurological symptoms, including lethargy, confusion, seizures, and coma. Reye's syndrome is a life-threatening emergency, with a fatality rate of about 30 to 50 percent.

Demographics

Reye's syndrome is a rare illness, even rarer in the early 2000s than when it was first described in the early 1970s. The incidence of the disorder peaked in 1980, with 555 cases reported. The number of cases declined rapidly thereafter once researchers made the association between aspirin use and the development of Reye's syndrome. Cases dropped precipitously when parents and healthcare providers were clearly warned against using any aspirin-containing products in children. As of 2004, fewer than 20 cases of Reye's syndrome are reported annually. Because of the rarity of Reye's syndrome, it is often misdiagnosed as **encephalitis**, **meningitis**, diabetes, or **poisoning**, and the true incidence may be higher than the number of reported cases indicates.

Causes and symptoms

Reye's syndrome causes fatty accumulation in the organs of the body, especially the liver. In the brain, it causes fluid accumulation (edema), which leads to a rise in pressure in the brain (intracranial pressure). This pressure compresses blood vessels, preventing blood from entering the brain. Untreated, this pressure increase leads to brain damage and death.

Although as of 2004 the cause remains unknown, Reye's syndrome appears to be linked to an abnormality in the energy-converting structures (mitochondria) within the body's cells.

Reye's syndrome usually occurs after a viral illness with **fever**, most often an upper respiratory tract infection. It is most often associated with use of aspirin during the fever, and for this reason aspirin and aspirin-containing products are not recommended for people under the age of 19 during fever. Although rare, Reye's syndrome may occur without aspirin use and in adults.

After the beginning of recovery from the viral illness, the affected person suddenly becomes more ill again, with the development of persistent **vomiting**. This may be followed rapidly by quietness, lethargy, agitation or combativeness, seizures, and coma. In infants, **diarrhea** may be more common than vomiting. Fever is usually absent at this point.

Diagnosis

Reye's syndrome may be suspected in a child who begins vomiting three to six days after a viral illness, followed by an alteration in consciousness. Diagnosis involves blood tests to determine the levels of certain liver enzymes, which are highly elevated in Reye's syndrome. Other blood changes may occur as well, including an increase in the level of ammonia and amino acids, a drop in blood sugar, and an increase in clotting time. A liver biopsy may also be done after clotting abnormalities are corrected with vitamin K or blood products. A lumbar puncture (spinal tap) may be needed to rule out other possible causes, including meningitis or encephalitis.

Treatment

Reye's syndrome is a life-threatening emergency that requires intensive management. The likelihood of recovery is greatest if it is recognized early and treated promptly. Children with Reye's syndrome should be managed in an intensive-care unit.

Treatment in the early stages includes intravenous sugar to return blood sugar levels to normal and plasma transfusion to restore normal clotting time in the blood. Intracranial pressure is monitored and, if elevated, is treated with drugs such as mannitol and barbiturates placing the patient on a ventilator so that hyperventilation can be used.

Prognosis

The mortality rate for Reye's syndrome is between 30 and 50 percent. The likelihood of recovery is increased to 90 percent by early diagnosis and treatment. Almost all children who survive Reye's syndrome

KEY TERMS

Acetylsalicylic acid—Aspirin; an analgesic, antipyretic, and antirheumatic drug prescribed to reduce fever and to relieve pain and inflammation.

Edema—The presence of abnormally large amounts of fluid in the intercellular tissue spaces of the body.

Mitochondria—Spherical or rod-shaped structures of the cell. Mitochondria contain genetic material (DNA and RNA) and are responsible for converting food to energy.

recover fully, although recovery may be slow. In some patients, permanent neurologic damage may remain, requiring physical or educational special services and equipment.

Prevention

Because Reye's syndrome is so highly correlated with use of aspirin for fever in young people, avoidance of aspirin use by children is strongly recommended. Aspirin is in many over-the-counter and prescription drugs, including drugs for **headache**, fever, menstrual cramps, muscle **pain**, **nausea**, upset stomach, and arthritis. It may be used in drugs taken orally or by suppository.

Any of the following ingredients indicates that aspirin is present:

- aspirin
- acetylsalicylate
- acetylsalicylic acid
- salicylic acid
- salicylate

Teenagers who take their own medications without parental consultation should be warned not to take aspirin-containing drugs.

Resources

BOOKS

Michaels, Marian G. "Reye Syndrome." In *Principles and Practice of Pediatric Infectious Diseases*, 2nd ed. Edited by Sarah S. Long et al. St. Louis, MO: Elsevier, 2003.

Rudolph, Jeffrey A., and William F. Balistreri. "Reye's Syndrome and the Mitochondrial Hepatophathies." In

Nelson Textbook of Pediatrics. Edited by Richard E. Behrman et al. Philadelphia: Saunders, 2004.

ORGANIZATIONS

National Reye's Syndrome Foundation. PO Box 829, Bryan, OH 43506-0829. Web site: <www.reyessyndrome.org>.

Richard Robinson
Rosalyn Carson-DeWitt, MD

Rh disease *see* **Erythroblastosis fetalis**

Rheumatic fever

Definition

Rheumatic fever (RF) is an illness that arises as a complication of untreated or inadequately treated **strep throat** infection. Rheumatic fever can seriously damage the valves of the heart.

Description

Throat infection with a member of the Group A streptococcus (strep) bacteria is a common problem among school-aged children. It is easily treated with a 10-day course of **antibiotics** by mouth. However, when such a throat infection occurs without symptoms, or when a course of medication is not taken for the full ten days, there is a 3 percent chance the person will develop rheumatic fever. Other types of strep infections (such as of the skin) do not put the patient at risk for RF.

Demographics

Children between the ages of five and 15 are most susceptible to strep throat, and therefore most susceptible to rheumatic fever. Other risk factors include poverty, overcrowding (as in military camps), and lack of access to good medical care. Just as strep throat occurs most frequently in fall, winter, and early spring, so does rheumatic fever. Rheumatic fever used to be a leading cause of death and disability in children. Since 1960, it has become much less common in the United States, partially because of increasingly accurate and swift diagnosis of strep throat. It is still a large problem in many developing countries. Moreover, children who have **family** members who have had rheumatic fever are more likely to get rheumatic fever themselves.

Causes and symptoms

Two different theories exist about how a bacterial throat infection can develop into rheumatic fever. One theory suggests that the bacteria produce some kind of poisonous chemical (toxin). This toxin is sent into circulation throughout the bloodstream, thus affecting other systems of the body.

Research seems to point to a different theory, however. The second theory suggests that the disease is caused by the body's immune system acting inappropriately. The body produces immune cells (called antibodies), that are specifically designed to recognize and destroy invading agent—in this case, streptococcal bacteria. The antibodies are able to recognize the bacteria because the bacteria contain special markers called antigens. Due to a resemblance between Group A streptococcus bacteria's antigens and antigens present on the body's own cells, the antibodies may mistakenly attack the body itself.

It is interesting to note that members of certain families seem to have a greater tendency to develop rheumatic fever than do others. This statistical fact could be related to the above theory, in that these families may have cell antigens that more closely resemble streptococcal antigens than do members of other families.

In addition to fever, in about 75 percent of all cases of RF one of the first symptoms is arthritis. The joints (especially those of the ankles, knees, elbows, and wrists) become red, hot, swollen, shiny, and extraordinarily painful. Unlike many other forms of arthritis, this arthritis may not occur symmetrically (affecting a particular joint on both the right and left sides, simultaneously). The arthritis of RF rarely strikes the fingers, toes, or spine. The joints become so tender that even the touch of bed sheets or clothing is terribly painful.

A particular type of involuntary movement, coupled with emotional instability, occurs in about 10 percent of all RF patients. The patient begins experiencing a change in coordination, often first noted by changes in handwriting. The arms or legs may flail or jerk uncontrollably. The patient seems to develop a low threshold for anger and sadness. This feature of RF is called Sydenham's chorea or St. Vitus' dance.

A number of skin changes are common to RF. A rash called erythema marginatum often develops (especially in those patients who will develop heart problems from their illness), composed of pink splotches that may eventually spread into each other. The rash does not itch. Bumps the size of peas may occur under the skin. These are called subcutaneous nodules. They are hard to the touch, but not painful. These nodules most commonly occur over the knee and elbow joint, as well as over the spine.

The most serious problem occurring in RF is called pancarditis ("pan" means total; "carditis" refers to inflammation of the heart). Pancarditis is an inflammation that affects all aspects of the heart, including the lining of the heart (endocardium), the sac containing the heart (pericardium), and the heart muscle itself (myocardium). About 40 to 80 percent of all RF patients develop pancarditis. This RF complication has the most serious, long-term effects. The valves within the heart (structures that allow the blood to flow only in the correct direction and only at the correct time in the heart's pumping cycle) are frequently damaged during the course of pancarditis. This effect may result in blood that either leaks back in the wrong direction or has a difficult time passing a stiff, poorly moving valve. Either way, damage to a valve can result in the heart having to work very hard in order to move the blood properly. The heart may not be able to "work around" the damaged valve, which may result in a consistently inadequate amount of blood entering the circulation.

When to call the doctor

The doctor should be contacted if the child is displaying any of the signs or symptoms of rheumatic fever. If they are not indications of rheumatic fever, they could be indicative of another disease or disorder. The doctor should also be contacted if the child has had a **sore throat** and fever for more than 24 hours. The doctor will do a strep test, and if the child does have strep throat the doctor can administer antibiotics that will help prevent rheumatic fever.

Diagnosis

There are no laboratory tests that can determine with complete certainty if a child has rheumatic fever. Some laboratory tests may be used in conjunction with careful examination of the patient to determine if the child has RF. A list of diagnostic criteria has been created. These "Jones Criteria" are divided into major and minor criteria. A patient can be diagnosed with RF if he or she has either two major criteria (conditions) or one major and two minor criteria. In either case, it must also be proved that the individual has had a previous infection with streptococcus.

The major criteria include:

- carditis
- arthritis
- chorea
- subcutaneous nodules
- erythema marginatum

The minor criteria include:

- fever
- joint **pain** (without actual arthritis)
- evidence of electrical changes in the heart (determined by measuring electrical characteristics of the heart's functioning during a test called an electrocardiogram, or EKG)
- evidence (through a blood test) of the presence in the blood of certain proteins that are produced early in an inflammatory/infectious disease

Tests are also performed to provide evidence of recent infection with group A streptococcal bacteria. A swab of the throat can be taken and smeared on a gel-like substance in a petri dish to see if bacteria will multiply and grow over 24 to 72 hours. These bacteria can then be specially processed and examined under a microscope to identify streptococcal bacteria. Other tests can be performed to see if the patient is producing specific antibodies that are only made in response to a recent strep infection.

Treatment

A 10-day course of penicillin by mouth or a single injection of penicillin G is usually the first line of treatment for RF. If the child does not tolerate or is allergic to penicillin, other antibiotics can be used effectively. These antibiotics are given to help cure a strep infection, if the child still has one. Patients will need to remain on some regular dose of antibiotic to prevent recurrence of RF. This can mean a small daily dose of antibiotic by mouth or an injection every three to four weeks. Some practitioners keep patients on this regimen for five years or until they reach 18 years of age whichever comes first. Other practitioners prefer to continue treating those patients who will be regularly exposed to streptococcal bacteria (teachers, medical workers), as well as those patients with known RF heart disease.

Arthritis quickly improves when the patient is given a preparation containing aspirin or some other anti-inflammatory agent (e.g. ibuprofen). Mild carditis also improves with such anti-inflammatory agents, although more severe cases of carditis require steroid medications. A number of medications are available to treat the involuntary movements of chorea, including diazepam for mild cases and haloperidol for more severe cases.

Prognosis

The long-term prognosis of an RF patient depends primarily on whether he or she develops carditis. This manifestation of RF is the only one that can have perma-

nent effects. Those patients with no or mild carditis have an excellent prognosis. Those with more severe carditis have a risk of heart failure, as well as a risk of future heart problems that may lead to the need for valve replacement surgery. Patients who have had rheumatic fever are at an increased risk of getting it again.

Prevention

Prevention of the development of RF involves proper diagnosis of initial strep throat infections and adequate treatment within 10 days with an appropriate anti-

KEY TERMS

Antibody—A special protein made by the body's immune system as a defense against foreign material (bacteria, viruses, etc.) that enters the body. It is uniquely designed to attack and neutralize the specific antigen that triggered the immune response.

Antigen—A substance (usually a protein) identified as foreign by the body's immune system, triggering the release of antibodies as part of the body's immune response.

Arthritis—A painful condition that involves inflammation of one or more joints.

Autoimmune disorder—One of a group of disorders, like rheumatoid arthritis and systemic lupus erythematosus, in which the immune system is overactive and has lost the ability to distinguish between self and non-self. The body's immune cells turn on the body, attacking various tissues and organs.

Chorea—Involuntary movements in which the arms or legs may jerk or flail uncontrollably.

Immune system—The system of specialized organs, lymph nodes, and blood cells throughout the body that work together to defend the body against foreign invaders (bacteria, viruses, fungi, etc.).

Inflammation—Pain, redness, swelling, and heat that develop in response to tissue irritation or injury. It usually is caused by the immune system's response to the body's contact with a foreign substance, such as an allergen or pathogen.

Pancarditis—Inflammation of the lining of the heart, the sac around the heart, and the muscle of the heart.

biotic. Prevention of RF recurrence requires continued antibiotic treatment, perhaps for life. Prevention of complications of already-existing RF heart disease requires that the patient always take a special course of antibiotics when he or she undergoes any kind of procedure (even dental cleanings) that might allow bacteria to gain access to the bloodstream.

Parental concerns

Rheumatic fever can be life-threatening if not treated. It can also lead to lifelong heart problems. The best way for parents to prevent rheumatic fever is to take seriously sore throats that are accompanied with fever and to take the child to a doctor to test for strep throat. Children who have had rheumatic fever need to take extra precautions to ensure they do not have repeat attacks triggered by strep infections.

See also Strep throat.

Resources

BOOKS

Margulies, Phillip. *Everything You Need to Know about Rheumatic Fever.* New York: Rosen Publishing Group, 2004.

PERIODICALS

Mercadante, Marcos T., et al. "The Psychiatric Symptoms of Rheumatic Fever." *American Journal of Psychiatry* 157, i.12 (December 2000): 2036.

Steeg, Carl N., et al. "Rheumatic Fever: No Cause for Complacence." *Patient Care* 34, i.14 (July 30, 2000): 40.

Stollerman, Gene H. "Rheumatic Fever in the 21st Century." *Clinical Infectious Diseases* 33, no. 16 (September 15, 2001): 806.

ORGANIZATIONS

American Heart Association. 7272 Greenville Ave., Dallas, TX 75231. Web site: <www.americanheart.org>.

Tish Davidson, A.M.
Rosalyn Carson-DeWitt, MD

Rhinitis

Definition

Rhinitis is inflammation of the mucous lining of the nosc.

Description

Rhinitis is a nonspecific term that covers infections, **allergies**, and other disorders whose common feature is the location of their symptoms. In rhinitis, the mucous membranes become infected or irritated, producing a discharge, congestion, and swelling of the tissues. The most widespread form of infectious rhinitis is the **common cold**. Doctors sometimes designate two different forms of rhinitis. These are **allergic rhinitis** and nonallergic rhinitis. Allergic rhinitis is cause by allergies, and nonallergic rhinitis is caused by other conditions such as the common cold.

Transmission

Nonallergic rhinitis is generally transmitted in the same ways as the common cold. It is transmitted from person to person. The sick person touches his or her nose and then another person's hands. If that person then touches his nose, mouth, or eyes, the infection is transmitted. Infection can also be transmitted through sharing of cups, silverware, or eating utensils, or by coughing or sneezing. Allergic rhinitis cannot be transmitted from person to person.

Demographics

The most frequent cause of nonallergic rhinitis is the common cold. The common cold is the most frequent viral infection in the general population, causing more absenteeism from school or work than any other illness. Colds are self-limited, lasting about three to 10 days, although they are sometimes followed by a bacterial infection. Children are more susceptible than adults; teenage boys more susceptible than teenage girls; and adult women more susceptible than adult men. In the United States, colds are most frequent during the late fall and winter. Allergic rhinitis is less common that nonallergic rhinitis. Allergic rhinitis affects between 20 and 40 million people in the United States. Children are more at risk for allergic rhinitis if one or both parents has allergies.

Causes and symptoms

The onset of a cold is usually sudden. The virus causes the lining of the nose to become inflamed and produce large quantities of thin, watery mucus. Children sometimes develop a **fever** with a cold. The inflammation spreads from the nasal passages to the throat and upper airway, producing a dry **cough**, **headache**, and watery eyes. Some people develop muscle or joint aches and feel generally tired or weak. After several days, the nose becomes less inflamed and a thick, sticky mucus replaces the watery discharge. This change in the appearance of the nasal discharge helps to distinguish rhinitis caused by a viral infection from rhinitis caused by an allergy.

Allergic rhinitis is caused by allergens such as pollen, animal dander, dust mites, or grass. The symptoms of allergic rhinitis are similar to those of nonallergic rhinitis, except that they are usually much longer lasting and are rarely accompanied by a fever. These symptoms often occur at specific times of year if they are not constant.

When to call the doctor

If the symptoms of rhinitis persist for more than a week, or it they frequently occur in specific situations or during specific times of year, a doctor should be consulted. The doctor can then do tests to determine if the rhinitis is viral, bacterial, or caused by allergies and treat it accordingly.

Diagnosis

There is no specific test for viral rhinitis. The diagnosis is based on the symptoms. In children, the doctor will examine the child's throat and glands to rule out other childhood illnesses that have similar early symptoms. If the symptoms last for more than a week, the child may be tested further to rule out bacterial infections or allergies. Allergies can be evaluated by blood tests, skin testing for specific substances, or nasal smears.

Treatment

There is no cure for viral nonallergic rhinitis; treatment is given for symptom relief. Medications include aspirin or **nonsteroidal anti-inflammatory drugs** (NSAIDs) for headache and muscle **pain**, and **decongestants** to relieve stuffiness or runny nose. Patients should be warned against overusing decongestants, because they can cause a rebound effect. Over-the-counter (OTC) **antihistamines** are also available; however, most antihistamines carry warnings of drowsiness and the inability to do some tasks while medicated. Claritin is a prescription-strength OTC non-drowsy antihistamine that helps relieve symptoms of rhinitis. **Antibiotics** are not given for viral nonallergic rhinitis because they do not kill viruses. Supportive care includes bed rest and drinking plenty of fluid. Treatments under investigation, as of 2004, included the use of ultraviolet light and injections of interferon. If the nonallergic rhinitis has a bacterial cause at its root, antibiotics can be given; however, bacterial causes of rhinitis are not very common.

Allergic rhinitis is treated in a number of ways, including seasonal allergy medication, nasal sprays, and decongestants. If the cause of the allergies is determined to be an indoor allergen such as dust mites or pet dander, steps can be taken to rid the home of some of the allergens. Injections, or **allergy shots**, are also sometimes used to treat allergic rhinitis. A small amount of the allergen is injected at first, with tolerance built up over weeks or months. The shots are given frequently at first, but when a maintenance level of the allergen is reached, they are given less frequently. After a few years, they are no longer given at all. These shots have been found to be very effective in some cases, but there are often problems with compliance. Children may also find the experience of regular injections over such a long period to be distressing.

Alternative treatment

Homeopaths might prescribe any of 10 different remedies, depending on the appearance of the nasal discharge, the patients emotional state, and the stage of infection. Naturopaths may recommend vitamin A and zinc supplements, together with botanical preparations made from echinacea (Echinacea spp.), goldenseal (*Hydrastis canadensis*), licorice (*Glycyrrhiza glabra*), or astragalus (*Astragalus membraneceus*) root.

Prognosis

Most rhinitis caused by a cold resolves completely in about a week. Complications are unusual but may include **sinusitis** (inflammation of the nasal sinuses), bacterial infections, or infections of the middle ear. Allergic rhinitis can usually be treated very effectively. Bacterial causes of rhinitis can usually be resolved fairly quickly with the use of antibiotics.

Prevention

There is no known way to successfully prevent allergic rhinitis. The only way to prevent viral and bacterial nonallergic rhinitis is to take the steps which prevent transmission of the common cold. These include:

- washing hands often, especially before touching the face
- minimizing contact with people already infected
- not sharing hand towels, eating utensils, or water glasses

Parental concerns

Rhinitis causes symptoms such as runny nose, **itching**, and sneezing that may be uncomfortable for the child. Nonallergic rhinitis is not thought to have any significant long-term consequences. Children who have allergic rhinitis may be at increased risk for developing **asthma**.

See also Allergic rhinitis; Allergies; Common cold.

Resources

BOOKS

Busse, William W., and Holgate, Stephan T. eds. *Asthma and Rhinitis.* Malden, MA: Blackwell Science, 2000.

Long, Aidan, et al. *Management of Allergic and Nonallergic Rhinitis.* Rockville, MD: U.S. Dept. of Health and Human Services, Public Health Service, Agency for Healthcare Research and Quality, 2002.

PERIODICALS

Hopkinson, Kate, and Pauline Powell. "Management of Allergic Rhinitis." *Primary Health Care* 14, n0. 4 (May 2004): 43.

Wachter, Kerri. "Allergy Is Not Always Behind Rhinitis Symptoms: Separating Allergic from Nonallergic." *Family Practice News* 33, i.23 (December 1, 2003): 20.

ORGANIZATIONS

American Academy of Allergy, Asthma, Immunology. 555 East Wells Street, Suite 1100, Milwaukee, WI 53202-3823. Web site: <www.aaaai.org>.

Tish Davidson, A.M.
Rebecca J. Frey, PhD

Rickets *see* **Vitamin D deficiency**

Rickettsia infection *see* **Rocky Mountain spotted fever**

Ringworm

Definition

Ringworm is a common fungal infection of the skin. The name is a misnomer because the disease is not caused by a worm.

Description

Ringworm is characterized by patches of rough, reddened skin. Raised eruptions usually form the circular pattern that gives the condition its name. As lesions grow, the centers start to heal. The inflamed borders expand and spread the infection. Ringworm may also be referred to as dermatophyte infection. It is more common in males than females, and is most common among children ages three to nine years.

Types of ringworm

Ringworm is a term that is commonly used to encompass several types of fungal infection. Sometimes, however, only body ringworm is classified as true ringworm.

Body ringworm (tinea corporis) can affect any part of the body except the scalp, feet, and facial area where a man's beard grows. The well-defined, flaky sores can be dry and scaly or moist and crusty.

Scalp ringworm (tinea capitis) is most common in children. It causes scaly, swollen blisters or a rash that looks like black dots. Sometimes inflamed and filled with pus, scalp ringworm lesions can cause crusting, flaking, and round bald patches. Most common in black children, scalp ringworm can cause scarring and permanent hair loss.

Ringworm of the groin (tinea cruris or jock itch) produces raised red sores with well-marked edges. It can spread to the buttocks, inner thighs, and external genitals.

Ringworm of the nails (tinea unguium) generally starts at the tip of one or more toenails, which gradually thicken and discolor. The nail may deteriorate or pull away from the nail bed. Fingernail infection is far less common.

Demographics

Ringworm can affect people at any age. It is more common among children, athletes, and people with poor hygiene habits.

Causes and symptoms

Ringworm can be transmitted by infected people or pets or by towels, hairbrushes, or other objects contaminated by them. Symptoms include inflammation, scaling, and sometimes, **itching**.

Diabetes mellitus increases susceptibility to ringworm. Dampness, humidity, and dirty, crowded living areas also increase susceptibility. Braiding hair tightly and using hair gel also raise the risk.

When to call the doctor

A health professional should be consulted when signs of ringworm appear or if exposure to someone with ringworm is suspected.

Diagnosis

Diagnosis is based on microscopic examination of scrapings taken from lesions. A dermatologist may also study the scalp of a person with suspected tinea capitis under ultraviolet light.

Treatment

Some infections disappear without treatment. Others respond to such topical antifungal medications as naftifine (Caldesene Medicated Powder) or tinactin (Desenex) or to griseofulvin (Fulvicin), which is taken by mouth. Medications should be continued for two weeks after lesions disappear.

A person with body ringworm should wear loose clothing and check daily for raw, open sores. Wet dressings applied to moist sores two or three times a day can lessen inflammation and loosen scales. The doctor may suggest placing special pads between folds of infected skin, and anything the person has touched or worn should be sterilized in boiling water.

Infected nails should be cut short and straight and carefully cleared of dead cells with an emery board.

People with jock itch should:

- wear cotton underwear and change it more than once a day
- keep the infected area dry
- apply antifungal ointment over a thin film of antifungal powder

Shampoo containing selenium sulfide can help prevent spread of scalp ringworm, but prescription shampoo or oral medication is usually needed to cure the infection.

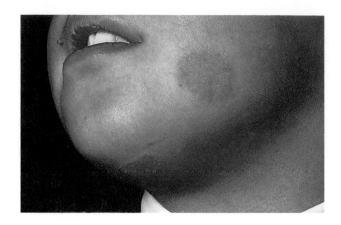

Child with a patch of rough, reddened skin in a circular pattern on his jaw caused by ringworm. *(© NMSB/Custom Medical Stock Photo, Inc.)*

Alternative treatment

The fungal infection ringworm can be treated with homeopathic remedies. Among the homeopathic remedies recommended are:

- sepia for brown, scaly patches
- tellurium for prominent, well-defined, reddish sores
- graphites for thick scales or heavy discharge
- sulfur for excessive itching

Topical applications of antifungal herbs and essential oils also can help resolve ringworm. Tea tree oil (*Melaleuca* spp.), thuja (*Thuja occidentalis*), and lavender (*Lavandula officinalis*) are the most common. Two drops of essential oil in 0.25 oz (7 ml) of carrier oil is the dose recommended for topical application. Essential oils should not be applied to the skin undiluted. Botanical medicine can be taken internally to enhance the body's immune response. A person must be susceptible to exhibit this overgrowth of fungus on the skin. Echinacea (*Echinacea* spp.) and astragalus (*Astragalus membranaceus*) are the two most common immune-enhancing herbs. A well-balanced diet, including protein, complex carbohydrates, fresh fruits and vegetables, and good quality fats, is also important in maintaining optimal immune function.

Prognosis

Ringworm can usually be cured, but recurrence is common. Chronic infection develops in one person in five.

It can take six to 12 months for new hair to cover bald patches, and three to 12 months to cure infected fingernails. Toenail infections do not always respond to treatment.

Prevention

Likelihood of infection can be lessened by avoiding contact with infected people or pets or contaminated objects and staying away from hot, damp places.

Parental concerns

Parents should monitor the children with whom their own children interact or **play**. Children should not be allowed to play with other children who have open skin sores or scratch excessively.

Resources

BOOKS

Bennett, John C. "Diagnosis and Treatment of Fungal Infections." In *Harrison's Principles of Internal Medicine*. 15th ed. Ed. by Eugene Braunwald et al., New York, McGraw Hill, 2001, 1168–70.

Darmstadt, Gary L and Sidbury, Robert. "Diseases of the Epidermis." In *Nelson Textbook of Pediatrics*. 17th ed. Ed. by Richard E. Behrman, et al., Philadelphia: Saunders, 2003, 2195–9.

PERIODICALS

Gupta, A.K., et al. "Optimal management of fungal infections of the skin, hair, and nails." *American Journal of Clinical Dermatology* 5, no. 4 (2004): 225-37.

McLeod, R.P. "Lumps, bumps, and things that go itch in your office!" *Journal of School Nursing* 20, no. 2 (2004): 115-6.

Sladden, M.J. and G.A. Johnston. "Common skin infections in children." *British Medical Journal* 329, no. 7457 (2004): 95-9.

ORGANIZATIONS

American Academy of Dermatology, 930 N. Meacham Road, PO Box 4014, Schaumburg, IL 60168-4014.

(847) 330-0230. Fax: (847) 330-0050. Web site: <www.aad.org>.

WEB SITES

"Ringworm on Scalp." *eMedicine*. Available online at: <www.emedicinehealth.com/articles/15983-1.asp>.

"Ringworm." *Directors of Health Promotion and Education*. Available online at: <www.astdhpphe.org/infect/ringworm.html>.

"Tinea." *Kid's Health*. Available online at: <kidshealth.org/parent/infections/fungal/ringworm.html>.

L. Fleming Fallon, Jr., MD, DrPH

Ritalin *see* **Methlphenidate**

Rocky Mountain spotted fever

Definition

Rocky Mountain spotted fever (RMSF) is a tick-borne illness caused by a bacteria, resulting in a high fever and a characteristic rash.

Description

The bacteria causing RMSF is passed to humans through the bite of an infected tick. The illness begins within about two weeks of such a bite. RMSF is the most widespread tick-borne illness in the United States, occurring in every state except Alaska and Hawaii. The states in the south-Atlantic region, (Delaware, Maryland, Washington DC, Virginia, West Virginia, North Carolina, South Carolina, Georgia, and Florida) have a great deal of tick activity during the spring and summer months, and the largest number of RMSF cases come from those states. About 5 percent of all ticks carry the causative bacteria.

Demographics

About 90 percent of all cases of RMSF occur between the months of April and September. Children under the age of 15 years have the majority of RMSF infections (about 66% of all infections). The peak incidence of RMSF occurs in five to nine year old children, with boys more likely to be infected than girls. A higher risk of infection seems to occur in individuals who spend time with dogs or who live near wooded or grassy areas.

Causes and symptoms

The bacterial culprit in RMSF is *Rickettsia rickett-sii*. It causes no illness in the tick carrying it and can be passed on to the tick's offspring. When a tick attaches to a human, the bacteria are passed. The tick must be attached to the human for about six hours for this passage to occur. Although prompt tick removal will cut down on the chance of contracting RMSF, removal requires great care. If the tick's head and body are squashed during the course of removal, the bacteria can be inadvertently rubbed into the tiny bite wound.

Symptoms of RMSF begin within two weeks of the bite of the infected tick. Symptoms usually begin suddenly, with high fever, chills, **headache**, severe weakness, and muscle **pain**. Pain in the large muscle of the calf is very common, and may be particularly severe. The patient may be somewhat confused and delirious. Without treatment, these symptoms may last two weeks or more.

The rash of RMSF is quite characteristic. It usually begins on the fourth day of the illness and occurs in at least 90 percent of all patients with RMSF. It starts around the wrists and ankles, as flat pink marks (called macules). The rash spreads up the arms and legs, toward the chest, abdomen, and back. Unlike **rashes** that accompany various viral infections, the rash of RMSF does spread to the palms of the hands and the soles of the feet. Over a couple of days, the macules turn a reddish-purple color. In this new stage they are called petechiae, which are tiny areas of bleeding under the skin (pinpoint hemorrhages). Over the next several days, the individual petechiae may spread into each other, resulting in larger patches of hemorrhage.

The most severe effects of RMSF occur due to damage to the blood vessels, which become leaky. This action accounts for the production of petechiae. As blood and fluid leak out of the injured blood vessels, other tissues and organs may swell and become damaged. Other symptoms that may occur are as follows:

- breathing difficulties as the lungs are affected
- heart rhythms abnormal
- kidney failure in very ill patients
- liver function decrease
- nausea, **vomiting**, abdominal pain, and diarrhea
- brain inflammation (**encephalitis**) in about 25 percent of RMSF patients (Brain injury can result in seizures, changes in consciousness, actual coma, loss of coordination, imbalance on walking, **muscle spasms**, loss of bladder control, and various degrees of paralysis.)

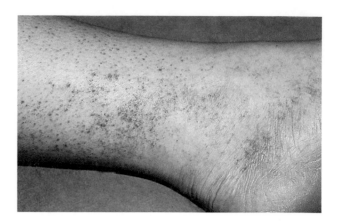

Rash caused by Rocky Mountain spotted fever. *(Photograph by Ken E. Greer. Visuals Unlimited.)*

- the clotting system impaired and blood evident in the stools or vomit

Diagnosis

Diagnosis of RMSF is almost always made on the basis of the characteristic symptoms, coupled with either a known tick bite (noted by about 60 to 70 percent of patients) or exposure to an area known to harbor ticks. Complex tests exist to determine conclusively the diagnosis of RMSF, but these are performed in only a few laboratories. The results of these tests take so long to obtain that they are seldom used; delaying treatment is the main cause of death in patients with RMSF.

Treatment

It is essential to begin treatment absolutely as soon as RMSF is seriously suspected. Delaying treatment can result in death.

Antibiotics are used to treat RMSF. The first choice is doxycycline; the second choice is chloramphenicol. If the patient is well enough, treatment by oral intake of medicine is perfectly effective. Sicker patients may need to be given the medication through a needle in the vein (intravenously). Penicillin and sulfa drugs are not suitable for treatment of RMSF, and their use may increase the death rate by delaying the use of truly effective medications.

Very ill patients need to be hospitalized in an intensive care unit. Depending on the types of complications a particular patient experiences, a variety of treatments may be necessary, including intravenous fluids, blood transfusions, anti-seizure medications, kidney dialysis, and mechanical ventilation (a breathing machine).

Prognosis

Prior to the regular use of antibiotics to treat RMSF, the death rate was about 25 percent. Although the death rate from RMSF has improved greatly with an understanding of the importance of early use of antibiotics, there is still a 5 percent death rate. This rate is believed to be due to delays in the administration of appropriate medications.

Certain risk factors suggest a worse outcome in RMSF. Death rates are higher in males and increase as people age. It is considered a bad prognostic sign to develop symptoms of RMSF within only two to five days of a tick bite.

Prevention

The mainstay of prevention involves avoiding areas known to harbor ticks. However, because many people enjoy recreational activities in just such areas, the following preventative steps can be taken:

- wearing light colored clothing (so that attached ticks are more easily noticed)
- wearing long sleeved shirts and long pants and tucking pant legs into socks
- spraying clothing with appropriate tick repellents
- examining oneself (Anybody who has been outside for any amount of time in an area known to have a population of ticks should examine his or her body carefully for ticks. Parents should examine their children at the end of the day.)
- removing any ticks using tweezers, so that infection does not occur due to handling the tick. (Parents should grasp the tick's head with the tweezers and pull gently but firmly so that the head and body are entirely removed.)

- keeping areas around homes clear of brush, which may serve to harbor ticks

Parental concerns

When children have been playing outside, it is important to carefully examine them for ticks when they come indoors. Rapidly yet carefully removing any ticks may help prevent or decrease the injection of infection-causing material. Dogs that are kept as **family** pets should also be examined for the presence of ticks and treated regularly with tick-killing products.

Resources

BOOKS

Dumler, J. Stephen. "Spotted Fever Group Rickettsioses." In *Nelson Textbook of Pediatrics.* Edited by Richard E. Behrman et al. Philadelphia: Saunders, 2004.

Paddock, Christopher D., and James E. Childs. "Rickettsia rickettsii (Rocky Mountain Spotted Fever)." In *Principles and Practice of Pediatric Infectious Diseases*, 2nd ed. Edited by Sarah S. Long et al. St. Louis, MO: Elsevier, 2003.

ORGANIZATIONS

Centers for Disease Control and Prevention. 1600 Clifton Rd., NE, Atlanta, GA 30333. Web site: <www.cdc.gov>.

Rosalyn Carson-DeWitt, MD

Roseola

Definition

Roseola is a common disease of babies or young children, in which several days of very high **fever** are followed by a characteristic rash.

Demographics

Roseola is an extraordinarily common infection, caused by a virus. About 90 percent of all children have been exposed to the virus, with about 33 percent actually demonstrating the syndrome of fever followed by rash.

The most common age for a child to contract roseola is between six and twelve months. Roseola infection strikes boys and girls equally. The infection may occur at any time of year, although late spring and early summer seem to be peak times for it.

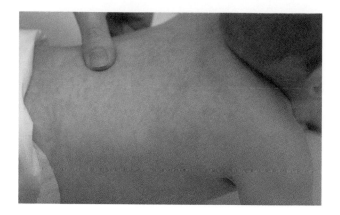

Roseola rash on infant's back and shoulders. *(Photograph by Keith. Custom Medical Stock Photo, Inc.)*

Causes and symptoms

About 85 percent of the time, roseola is caused by a virus called human herpesvirus 6 (HHV-6). Although the virus is related to those herpesviruses known to cause sores on the lips or genitalia, HHV-6 causes a very different type of infection. HHV-6 is believed to be passed between people via infected saliva. A few other viruses (called enteroviruses) can produce a similar fever-then-rash illness, which is usually also called roseola.

Researchers believe that it takes about five to 15 days to develop illness after having been infected by HHV-6. Roseola strikes suddenly, when a previously well child spikes an impressively high fever. The temperature may reach 106°F (41°C) . As is always the case with sudden fever spikes, the extreme change in temperature may cause certain children to have seizures. About 5 to 35 percent of all children with roseola have **febrile seizures**.

The most notable thing about this early phase of roseola is the absence of symptoms, other than the high fever. Although some children have a slightly reddened throat or a slightly runny nose, most children have no symptoms whatsoever, other than the sudden development of high fever. This fever lasts for between three and five days.

Somewhere around the fifth day, a rash begins on the body. The rash is usually composed of flat pink patches or spots, although there may be some raised patches as well. The rash usually starts on the chest, back, and abdomen then spreads out to the arms and neck. It may or may not reach the legs and face. The rash lasts for about three days then fades.

Very rarely, roseola causes more serious disease. Patients so afflicted experience significant swelling of the lymph nodes, the liver, and the spleen. The liver may become sufficiently inflamed to interfere with its functioning, resulting in a yellowish color to the whites of the eyes and the skin (**jaundice**). This syndrome (called a mononucleosis-like syndrome, after the disease mononucleosis that causes many of the same symptoms) has occurred in both infants and adults.

Diagnosis

The diagnosis of roseola is often made by carefully examining the feverish child to make sure that other illnesses are not causing the temperature spike. Once it is clear that no **pneumonia**, ear infection, **strep throat**, or other common childhood illness is present, the practitioner usually feels comfortable waiting to see if the characteristic rash of roseola begins.

Treatment

As of 2004, there were no treatments available to stop the course of roseola. **Acetaminophen** or ibuprofen is usually given to try to lower the fever. Children who are susceptible to seizures may be given a sedative medication when the fever first spikes in an attempt to prevent such a seizure.

Prognosis

Children recover quickly and completely from roseola. The only complications are those associated with seizures or the rare mononucleosis-like syndrome.

Prevention

Other than the usual good hygiene practices always recommended to decrease the spread of viral illness, no methods as of 2004 are available to specifically prevent roseola.

Parental concerns

Roseola is usually a benign illness, from which the child recovers uneventfully. One of the more major potential complications is the development of febrile seizures secondary to the rapid, high rise in fever. Rare cases of **encephalitis** or meningoencephalitis have also been reported.

Resources

BOOKS

Hall, Caroline Breese. "Human Herpesviruses 6 and 7 (Roseola, Exanthem Subitum)." In *Principles and Practice of Pediatric Infectious Diseases*, 2nd ed. Edited by Sarah S. Long et al. St. Louis, MO: Elsevier, 2003.

Leach, Charles T. "Roseola (Human Herpesviruses 6 and 7)." In *Nelson Textbook of Pediatrics*. Edited by Richard E. Behrman et al. Philadelphia: Saunders, 2004.

Rosalyn Carson-DeWitt, MD

Rotavirus infections

Definition

Rotavirus is the major cause of **diarrhea** and **vomiting** in young children worldwide. The infection is highly contagious and may lead to severe **dehydration** (loss of body fluids) and even death.

Description

Gastroenteritis (inflammation of the stomach and the intestine) is the second most common illness in the United States, after the **common cold**. More than one-third of such cases are caused by viruses. Many different viruses can cause gastroenteritis, but the most common ones are the rotavirus and the Norwalk virus.

The name rotavirus comes from the Latin word "rota" for wheel and is given because the viruses have a distinct wheel-like shape. Rotavirus infection is also known as infantile diarrhea or winter diarrhea, because it mainly targets infants and young children. The outbreaks are usually in the cooler months of winter.

The virus is classified into different groups (Group A through group G), depending on the type of protein marker (antigen) that is present on its surface. The diarrheal infection of children is caused by the group A rotaviruses. Group B rotaviruses have caused major epidemics of adult diarrhea in China. Group C rotavirus has been associated with rare cases of diarrheal outbreaks in Japan and England. Groups D through G have not been detected in humans.

Demographics

In the United States, more than 50,000 children are hospitalized and up to 125 die each year as a result of rotavirus infection. Moreover, worldwide, rotavirus is thought to be responsible for more than 5 to 10 million deaths in children every year. Children in developing countries are particularly hard-hit by this infection, which is thought to be the leading cause of childhood death globally.

Causes and symptoms

The main symptoms of the rotavirus infection are **fever**, stomach cramps, vomiting, and diarrhea (which can lead to severe dehydration). The symptoms last from four to six days. Symptoms of dry lips and tongue, dry skin, sunken eyes, and fewer than six diapers wet per day indicate dehydration, and a physician needs to be notified. Because of excellent U.S. healthcare, rotavirus is rarely fatal to American children. In developing countries, however, with insufficient means to rehydrate children, rotavirus is oftentimes fatal.

The virus is usually spread by the fecal-oral route. In other words, a child can catch a rotavirus infection if she puts her finger in her mouth after touching **toys** or things that have been contaminated by the stool of another infected child. This usually happens when children do not wash their hands after using the toilet or before eating food.

The viruses can also spread by way of contaminated food and drinking water. Infected food handlers who prepare salads, sandwiches, and other foods that require no cooking can spread the disease. Generally, symptoms appear within four to 48 hours after exposure to the contaminated food or water.

Children between the ages of six months and two years, especially in a daycare setting, are the most susceptible to this infection. Breastfed babies may be less likely to become infected, because breast milk contains antibodies (proteins produced by the white blood cells of the immune system) that fight the illness. Nearly every child by the age of four has been infected by this virus and has rotavirus antibodies in their body. The disease also targets the elderly and people who have weak immune systems.

Children who have been infected once can be infected again. However, second infections are less severe than the first infections. By the time a child has had two infections, the chance of subsequent severe infection is remote.

Diagnosis

The rotavirus infection is diagnosed by identifying the virus in the patient's stool. This is done using electron microscopy. Immunological tests such as Enzyme-linked immunosorbent assay (ELISA) are also widely used for diagnosis, and several commercial kits are available.

Treatment

Oral rehydration therapy (drinking enough fluids to replace those lost through bowel movements and vomiting) is the primary aim of the treatment. Electrolyte and fluid replacement solutions are available over the counter in food and drug stores. Dehydration is one of the greatest dangers for infants and young children. If the diarrhea becomes severe, it may be necessary to hospitalize the patient so that fluids can be administered intravenously.

Anti-diarrheal medication should not be given to children unless the parent or caregiver is directed to do so by the physician. Antibiotic therapy is not useful in viral illness. Specific drugs for the virus were, as of 2004, not available.

Prognosis

Most of the infections resolve spontaneously. Dehydration due to severe diarrhea is one of the major complications.

Prevention

The best way to prevent the disease is by proper food handling and thorough hand washing, after using the toilet and whenever hands are soiled. In childcare centers and hospital settings, the staff should be educated about personal and environmental hygiene. All dirty diapers should be regarded as infectious and disposed of in a sanitary manner.

Parental concerns

As with any illness that may cause dehydration, the primary parental concern is using an appropriate rehy-

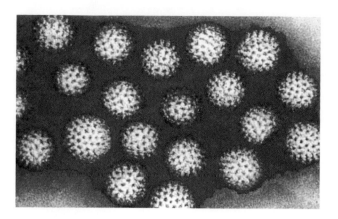

Rotaviruses are probably the most common viruses to infect humans and animals. These viruses are associated with gastroenteritis and diarrhea in humans and other animals. (Photograph by Dr. Linda Stannard. Photo Researchers, Inc.)

dration solution. Several balanced electrolyte rehydration solutions are available. Some healthcare providers also give their patients a homemade recipe for such a solution. It is crucial that parents and children use excellent hand-washing technique after toileting and diaper changes to prevent further spread of rotavirus diarrhea throughout the **family**. The healthcare provider should also give guidance concerning how long a child with rotavirus diarrhea should be kept home from daycare or school.

Resources

BOOKS

Bass, Dorsey. "Rotavirus and other agents of viral gastroenteritis." In *Nelson Textbook of Pediatrics.* Edited by Richard E. Behrman et al. Philadelphia: Saunders, 2004.

Mattson, David O. "Rotaviruses." In *Principles and Practice of Pediatric Infectious Diseases*, 2nd ed. Edited by Sarah S. Long et al. St. Louis, MO: Elsevier, 2003.

Lata Cherath, PhD
Rosalyn Carson-DeWitt, MD

RSV infection *see* **Respiratory syncytial virus infection**

Rubella

Definition

Rubella, also called German **measles** or three-day measles, is a highly contagious viral disease that in most children and adults causes mild symptoms of low **fever**, swollen glands, joint **pain**, and a fine red rash. Although rubella causes only mild symptoms in child and adult sufferers, the infection can have severe complications for the fetus of a woman who becomes infected with the virus during the first trimester of pregnancy. These complications include severe birth defects or death of the fetus.

Description

Rubella is spread through contact with fluid droplets expelled from the nose or throat of an infected person. A person infected with the rubella virus is contagious for about seven days before any symptoms appear and continues to be able to spread the disease for about four days after the appearance of symptoms. Rubella has an incubation period of 12 to 23 days.

Although rubella is generally considered a childhood illness, people of any age who have not been vaccinated or previously caught the disease can become infected. Having rubella once or being immunized against rubella normally gives lifetime immunity. For this reason **vaccination** is highly effective in reducing the number of rubella cases.

Women of childbearing age who do not have immunity against rubella should be particularly concerned about getting the disease. Rubella infection during the first three months of pregnancy can cause a woman to miscarry or cause her baby to be born with birth defects. Although it has been practically eradicated in the United States, rubella is still common in less developed countries because of poor immunization penetration, creating a risk to susceptible travelers. Some countries have chosen to target rubella vaccination to females only and outbreaks in foreign-born males have occurred on cruise ships and at U.S. summer camps.

Demographics

Although rubella was once a common childhood illness, its occurrence has been drastically reduced since vaccine against it became available in 1969. According to statistics for 1964–1965, prior to routine rubella immunization in the United States, there were 2,100 newborn deaths and 11,250 miscarriages attributed to rubella infection of pregnant women. In addition, about 20,000 infants were born with birth defects attributable to rubella infection in utero. Of these babies, 11,600 were born deaf; 3,580 were born blind; and 1,800 suffered severe **developmental delay**. In the 20 years following the introduction of the vaccine, reported rubella cases dropped 99.6 percent. In 2000, there were only 152 reported cases of rubella infection and seven reported cases of congenital rubella.

Causes and symptoms

Rubella is caused by the rubella virus (*Rubivirus*). Symptoms are generally mild, and complications are rare in anyone who is not pregnant.

The first visible sign of rubella is a fine red rash that begins on the face and rapidly moves downward to cover the whole body within 24 hours. The rash lasts about three days, which is why rubella is sometimes called the three-day measles. A low fever and swollen glands, especially in the head (around the ears) and neck, often accompany the rash. Joint pain and sometimes joint swelling can occur, more often in women. It is quite common to get rubella and not show any symptoms (subclinical infection).

Symptoms disappear within three to four days, except for joint pain, which may linger for a week or two. Most people recover fully with no complications. However, severe complications may arise in the unborn children of women who get rubella during the first three months of their pregnancy. These babies may be miscarried or stillborn. A high percentage is born with birth defects. Birth defects are reported to occur in 50 percent of women who contract the disease during the first month of pregnancy, 20 percent of those who contract it in the second month, and 10 percent of those who contract it in the third month.

The most common birth defects resulting from congenital rubella infection are eye defects such as cataracts, glaucoma, and blindness; deafness; congenital heart defects; and **mental retardation**. Taken together, these conditions are called congenital rubella syndrome (CRS). The risk of birth defects drops after the first trimester, and by the twentieth week, there are rarely any complications.

Diagnosis

The rash caused by the rubella virus and the accompanying symptoms are so similar to other viral infections that it is impossible for a physician to make a confirmed diagnosis on visual examination alone. The only sure way to confirm a case of rubella is by isolating the virus with a blood test or in a laboratory culture.

A blood test is done to check for rubella antibodies. When the body is infected with the rubella virus, it produces both immunoglobulin G (IgG) and immunoglobulin M (IgM) antibodies to fight the infection. Once IgG exists, it persists for a lifetime, but the special IgM

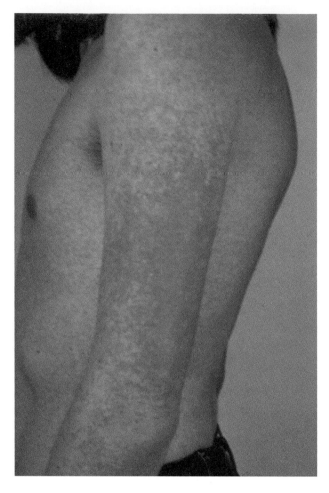

A red rash is one characteristic of rubella, or German measles, as seen on this teenager's arm. *(Custom Medical Stock Photo, Inc.)*

antibody usually wanes over six months. A blood test can be used either to confirm a recent infection (IgG and IgM) or determine whether a person has immunity to rubella (IgG only). The lack of antibodies indicates that a person is susceptible to rubella.

All pregnant women should be tested for rubella early in pregnancy, whether they have a history of vaccination. If the woman lacks immunity, she is counseled to avoid anyone with the disease and to be vaccinated after giving birth.

Treatment

There is no drug treatment for rubella. Bed rest, fluids, and **acetaminophen** for pain and temperatures over 102°F (38.9°C) are usually all that is necessary.

Babies born with suspected CRS are isolated and cared for only by people who are sure they are immune

to rubella. Congenital heart defects are treated with surgery.

Prognosis

Complications from rubella infection are rare in children, pregnant women past the twentieth week of pregnancy, and other adults. For women in the first trimester of pregnancy, there is a high likelihood of the child being born with one or more birth defect. Unborn children exposed to rubella early in pregnancy are also more likely to be miscarried, stillborn, or have a low birth weight. Although the symptoms of rubella pass quickly for the mother, the consequences to the unborn child can last a lifetime.

Prevention

Vaccination is the best way to prevent rubella and is normally required by law for children entering school. Rubella vaccine is usually given in conjunction with measles and **mumps** vaccines in a shot referred to as MMR (mumps, measles, and rubella). Children receive one dose of **MMR vaccine** at 12 to 15 months and another dose at four to six years.

Pregnant women should not be vaccinated, and women who are not pregnant should avoid conceiving for at least three months following vaccination. As of 2004, however, accidental rubella vaccinations during pregnancy had not clearly been associated with the same risk as the natural infection itself. Women may be vaccinated while they are breastfeeding. People whose immune systems are compromised, either by the use of drugs such as steroids or by disease, should discuss possible complications with their doctor before being vaccinated.

Parental concerns

While rubella infection in an older child or adult is rarely complicated, the risks of not immunizing a child against rubella are highest in the unborn. Congenital rubella is a serious, life-changing condition, and adherence to immunization recommendations is crucial to the public health.

Resources

BOOKS

Maldonado, Yvonne A. "Rubella Virus." In *Principles and Practice of Pediatric Infectious Diseases*, 2nd ed. Edited by Sarah S. Long et al. St. Louis, MO: Elsevier, 2003.

Thompson, George H. "The Neck." In *Nelson Textbook of Pediatrics*. Edited by Richard E. Behrman et al. Philadelphia: Saunders, 2004.

ORGANIZATIONS

March of Dimes Birth Defects Foundation. 1275 Mamaroneck Ave., White Plains, NY 10605. Web site: <www.modimes.org>.

National Organization for Rare Disorders. PO Box 8923, New Fairfield, CT 06812-8923. Web site: <www.rarediseases.org>.

Tish Davidson, A.M.
Rosalyn Carson-DeWitt, MD

Rubeola *see* **Measles**

Running away

Definition

Running away involves being voluntarily absent from home at least overnight without permission from a parent or caretaker.

Description

Every year about 800,000 children in the United States are reported missing and another estimated 500,000 go missing without being reported. Not all of these children are runaways. This number also includes children abducted by **family** members, usually in custody disputes, and a very small number of stranger abductions. In addition, when children run away, each time it is reported as a separate event. Some children are repeat runaways, so it is difficult to know the exact number of runaway children. What is clear is that the number is large. Runaways include "throwaways," who leave with the overt or tacit approval of parents or caretakers, and "push-outs," who are turned out by parents who do not want them, as well as teens who leave because they are dissatisfied with their home life.

The 2002 White House Conference on Missing, Exploited, and Runaway Children estimated that there were about 1.3 million American children living on the streets each day and that one in seven children between the ages of 10 and 18 will run away. Most runaways return voluntarily within a few days. Many go to homes of friends or relatives who encourage them to return. Some are aided by police and social agencies and eventually return home or are placed in alternative stable environments. Children who remain on the street are exposed to sexual exploitation, drug **addiction**, violent crime, and the other harmful mental and physical effects of homelessness.

Why children run away

Rather than seeking adventures, most runaways in the early 2000s are running from intolerable domestic situations. It has been estimated that at least 60 to 70 percent of these young people are fleeing from families in which they have been mentally, physically, or sexually abused. Historically, attention to the role played by a child's family environment in the treatment of a runaway is relatively new. In past eras, runaways themselves were uniformly blamed for their situation and seen as hostile and destructive lawbreakers who needed to be reformed. In the nineteenth century, they were generally sent to reform schools that were similar to prisons. Even after the establishment of the juvenile justice system toward the end of the nineteenth century, most runaways were regarded as delinquents, and the home situations from which they had fled received little scrutiny. In the early and mid-twentieth century, the prevailing view of runaways underwent a partial shift in emphasis from crime to pathology. Early versions of the American Psychiatric Association's *Diagnostic and Statistical Manual* included "runaway reaction" as a mental disorder.

As of 2004, researchers had identified several common characteristics of the abusive family environments that prompt young people to run away. These include financial troubles, sexual abuse, alcohol and drug abuse, physical and verbal abuse, and intolerance of deviant behavior. Besides outright physical or sexual abuse, runaways may be reacting to persistent tension between family members, including parental fighting or competition among siblings (especially step-siblings), feelings of rejection by their families, or authoritarian parenting that allows too little room for normal self-expression or social life.

Other events may also prompt children to run away. They may have done something to get into trouble (for example, become pregnant or been arrested) and feel unable to face their families. Still other children flee out of romantic notions of being with a girlfriend or boyfriend. Cyber predators who meet young people in Internet chat rooms and convince them to leave home to meet or live with them constitutes a relatively new, but growing, problem. Some children leave with friends for adventure. These children are usually ones who have had difficulties with parents, school, and authority figures in the past. Running away is one component of **conduct disorder**, a diagnosis recognized by the American Psychiatric Association.

Legislation affecting the treatment of runaways

In the 1960s, with the growth of the hippie counterculture and the associated "youth rebellion," the number of teen runaways increased dramatically, drawing attention to the risks these youths faced on the streets. Growing public concern over their fate was reflected in the 1974 passage of the Runaway Youth Act, which funded a program to establish a network of centers for runaways. Increased attention to the plight of these young people revealed the dangers of child prostitution and pornography, which they faced on the streets. It also began to change the public image of runaways from that of thrill-seekers to that of young people from families in crisis fleeing intolerable conditions with no place else to go. This perception of runaways has become influential in both public opinion and government policy.

The 1982 Missing Children's Act enabled the entry of missing child information into the FBI's national crime computer (NCIC). The 1984 Missing Children's Assistance Act mandated a national resource center to address child abduction and exploitation. The private, nonprofit National Center for Missing and Exploited Children (NCMEC) was established in cooperation with the United States Department of Justice, to find missing children and prevent child victimization. It created a 24-hour hotline (1–800–THE-LOST). In 1990, the National Child Search Assistance Act eliminated the waiting time for law enforcement action on missing children, mandating an immediate police report and NCIC entry for missing children cases.

Common problems

What happens to runaway children?

Young people who run away and do not return home may remain on the street, go to a shelter, or be placed in foster homes by welfare agencies. Some eventually join the armed services or take jobs that keep them on the road, such as carnival or sales work. Others end up in jails

or mental institutions. Those who remain on the streets have few options that would provide them with decent living conditions. Their age, lack of work experience, and uncompleted education make it difficult for them to find a job, especially one that pays more than minimum wage. It is common for both male and female runaways living on the streets to steal, panhandle, deal and abuse drugs, engage in prostitution, and pose for pornographic pictures. For shelter they may stay with strangers, spend nights in bus stations, all-night coffee shops, and other public places, or stow away in empty or abandoned buildings or even in stairwells. Many never get off the streets, becoming part of the adult homeless population.

There are an estimated 750 runaway shelters and youth crisis centers in the United States. These offer safe shelter, food, counseling, and advocacy services to help young people deal with parents, police, and the courts. Many also provide educational and vocational assistance. However, shelters do set certain conditions for accepting runaways, the most common being parental notification. This is an obstacle for some young people who do not want their parents contacted, even though the shelter does not press them to return home. One problem that has occurred at some shelters is sexual molestation by other runaways and staff members. Nevertheless, many young people have had positive experiences at shelters, which they either find on their own or are sent to by the legal or welfare systems.

Since the 1970s, hotlines have been available to help runaways and their families. The Runaway Hotline and the National Runaway Switchboard (1–800–621–4000) have become widely used 24-hour help lines that offer crisis counseling and referrals to service agencies that can provide food, shelter, medical aid, and other types of help. The National Runaway Switchboard will put runaways and their parents in touch without revealing the location from which the teenager is calling.

Parental concerns

Parents are often emotionally devastated when their child runs away. Their fluctuating emotions may include anger, grief, guilt, and **fear**. Sometimes they are not sure if their child has run away or been abducted. A parent's first concern is to find his or her child and/or make sure he or she is in a safe environment. To help achieve this, the National Center for Missing and Exploited Children recommends these steps for parents.

• They should check with friends and relatives to try to locate the child and enlist their help in thinking about where the child might be.

- They should check diaries and e-mails for clues about the child's plans. They can ask the child's friends if they know the child's online passwords.

- They should report to local law enforcement immediately that the child has run away or is missing. There is no waiting period to report a missing or runaway minor or to enter their information into the FBI NCIC database.

- They should provide a description and photograph of the child to law officers.

- They should check local places where the child may be hanging out.

- They should check again with the child's friends. They may know something but initially be reluctant to tell the parents.

- They should call the National Runaway Switchboard (1–800–621–4000) and see if the child has left a message for them. They can leave a message for the child here in case the child calls the hotline.

If the child contacts the parents and refuses to return home, the parents should encourage him or her to contact the National Runaway Switchboard and ask for assistance or encourage the child to go to a friend or relative. Parents can ask their child to stay in touch and make a plan about when the child will call again. If the child returns home, parents need to try to respond with concern and love, rather than anger. Children who have been away for more than a few days should have a complete medical examination. They also can benefit from seeing a mental health practitioner for help dealing with the distress that drove them away from home. **Family therapy** to help resolve whatever family problems may have driven the child away from home initially can also be beneficial in preventing a repeat running away incident.

Resources

BOOKS

Cooper, Edith Fairman. *Missing and Exploited Children: Overview and Policy Concerns.* Hauppauge, NY: Nova Science Publishing, 2004.

Raphael, Maryanne, et al. *Runaways: America's Lost Youth.* Lincoln, NE: iUniverse, 2000.

Starks, Mary. *Missing Children: Never Give Up Hope until You Know the Truth.* Pittsburgh, PA: Dorrance Publishing Co., 2004.

Vaughan, Brian K., et al. *Teenage Wasteland.* New York: Marvel Enterprise, 2004.

Veladota, Christine. *Teen Runaways.* Farmington Hills, MI: Gale, 2004.

ORGANIZATIONS

Covenant House. Telephone: toll-free 800/999–9999 (Referrals and counseling for youth in need); Web site: <www.covenanthouse.org>.

National Center for Missing and Exploited Children (NCMEC). Charles B. Wang International Children's Building, 699 Prince St., Alexandria, VA 22314–2175. Telephone: 24-hour toll-free hotline 800/THE-LOST [800/843–5678]; Web site: <www.missingkids.com>.

National Runaway Switchboard. Telephone: toll-free hotline 800/621–4000; Web site: <www.nrscrisisline.org>.

The Runaway Hotline. PO Box 12428, Austin, TX 78711. Telephone: toll-free hotline 800/231–6946; Web site: <www.nrscrisisline.org>.

Tish Davidson, A.M.